Almanac of the Christian Faith

*A Prologue of Notable Lives,
Insights and Achievements Among
God's People Through the Ages*

COMPILED BY
William D. Blake

YAV PUBLICATIONS
ASHEVILLE, NORTH CAROLINA

Copyright ©1987, 2008, 2011, 2020 by William D. Blake

All rights reserved. No part of this book shall be reproduced or transmitted in any form or by any means, electronic, mechanical, magnetic, photographic including photo-copying, recording, or by any information storage and retrieval system, without prior written permission of the publisher. No patent liability is assumed with respect to the use of the information contained herein. Although every precaution has been taken in the preparation of this book, the publisher and author assume no responsibility for errors or omissions. Neither is any liability assumed for damages resulting from the use of the information contained herein.

First Edition

ISBN: 978-1-937449-47-6

Published by:

YAV PUBLICATIONS
ASHEVILLE, NORTH CAROLINA

YAV books may be purchased in bulk for educational, business, fund-raising, or sales promotional use. For information, contact Books@yav.com or phone toll-free 888-693-9365. Visit our website: www.InterestingWriting.com

3 5 7 9 10 8 6 4 2

Cover Design: F. Clay Martin

Assembled in the United States of America
Published January 2020

Dedicated to our family:

Cyndi, Andrew
Erin & Brian, Avery & Natalie
Adam & Olivia, Emilia

You all have taught me
that God is the Giver
of many good gifts.

FOREWORD

As the life and growth of the Church proceed, her corporate consciousness, enriched by all the discoveries of the saints, grows richer: so that she has more and more to give to each of her sons.
—Evelyn Underhill

IT'S EASY TO BE A CHRISTIAN. It's hard to be a good Christian. Some say it takes a village to raise a believer to the place of deeply trusting God. Not many in today's generation appear to be given this luxury — at least, not like the West once seemed to provide. Even experts in theology often pass over religious questions raised by a grass roots seeker after God, debating traditions instead that cease to motivate the individual today.

If we read the Bible carefully, we soon learn the outline of Judeo-Christian beliefs of three millennia ago. But what of those men and women of God who cultivated a serious faith in the two millennia since? Did the Voice of God stop speaking to God's world, beyond the pages (and era!) of Scripture?

In spite of "the Preacher's" conclusion in Ecclesiastes 1:9, there have been a number of issues cultivated by the godly since New Testament times: questions regarding human rights, gender equality, marital and domestic relationships, ecclesiastical polity. There have also been new developments in education, science and technology, business, career planning, mental health, medicine, warfare, humanitarianism, use of leisure time, economy and politics — all of which invite theological discussion. Yet many of these topics are addressed in little more than embryonic form within the canonical limits of Scripture.

Fortunately, men and women of faith from the post-biblical centuries have relied on the strength and vitality of their communion with God to hammer out insights, more mature confessions and increasingly sacralized responses to the urgencies of their generation — and to some issues beyond their time.

These resulting words and deeds — both timely and timeless — are present within all the major and minor denominations of the historical Church. Their insights bear reporting, apart from the credal confines of any one tradition. What follows, therefore, is a portion of that report.

—*William D. Blake*

The Jewish Calendar

The Creation of the world, as reckoned by Judaism, took place 3,760 years and 3 months before the start of the Christian Era. To determine the number of a modern Hebrew year, therefore, one should begin in the autumn of a given Christian (A.D. or C.E.) year, and add 3761 to its number. (Thus, for example, September 2000 began the Jewish year 5761.)

The Hebrew word for month means "moon" or "new moon." And so, each of the twelve Jewish months begins when the first sliver of moon becomes visible after the dark of the moon. The average lunation of a Jewish month is 29 days, 12 hours, 44 min., and 30 sec.

A purely lunar year, unfortunately, falls short of a full solar year by about 11 days. To correct for this, Judaism periodically appends another month — "We-Adar" (Second Adar) — after the twelfth lunar month of Adar. In a Jewish liturgical cycle of nineteen years, this 13th month is added during the 3rd, 6th, 8th, 11th, 14th, 17th and 19th years — called "leap-years" — making the typical length of these years 384 days (instead of 354 purely "lunar" days).

Seven of the twelve Jewish months (as listed below) are named in the Hebrew Bible:

1. Nisan (Neh. 2:1; Esth. 3:7)
2. Iyyar (not named in Scripture)
3. Sivan (Esth. 8:9; Baruch 1:8)
4. Tammuz (Cf. KJV Ezek. 8:14)
5. Av (not named in Scripture)
6. Elul (Nehem. 6:15; I Mach. 14:27)
7. Tishri (not named in Scripture)
8. Heshvan (not named in Scripture)
9. Kislev (Zach. 7:1; Neh. 1:1)
10. Tevet (Esth. 2:16)
11. Shevat (Zach. 1:7, I Macc. 16:14)
12. Adar (I Esdras 6:15; Esth. 3:7, 8:12)

Each month of the Christian (AD or CE) year typically begins somewhere in the middle of one Jewish month and ends at nearly the same point of the following Jewish month. The approximate correlation between these two calendars (as noted at the top of the following pages) is thus:

Month	Begins in	Ends in
JANUARY	Tevet טבת	Shevat שבט
FEBRUARY	Shevat שבט	Adar אדר
MARCH	Adar אדר	Nisan ניסן
APRIL	Nisan ניסן	Iyyar אייר
MAY	Iyyar אייר	Sivan סיון
JUNE	Sivan סיון	Tammuz תמוז
JULY	Tammuz תמוז	Av אב
AUGUST	Av אב	Elul אלול
SEPTEMBER	Elul אלול	Tishri תשרי
OCTOBER	Tishri תשרי	Heshvan חשון
NOVEMBER	Heshvan חשון	Kislev כסלו
DECEMBER	Kislev כסלו	Tevet טבת

שבט SHEVAT ALMANAC OF THE CHRISTIAN FAITH טבת TEVET

~ January 1 ~

Highlights in History

439 The Theodosian Code went into effect in the Eastern Church. It was originally commissioned by Roman Emperor Theodosius II (401-50) as an attempt to codify all general constitutions enacted in the Catholic Church since Emperor Constantine I (d. 337).

1622 The Roman Catholic church first adopted January 1st as the beginning of the calendar year, rather than March 25th.

1779 The Universalist Church of America was organized in Gloucester, MA, at a meeting led by the Reverend John Murray, who was appointed the first minister. A church built in Gloucester, was dedicated the following year.

1832 In Lexington, Kentucky, 12,000 followers of Alexander Campbell merged with the 10,000 followers of Barton W. Stone to form the denomination known today as the Disciples of Christ (Christian) Church.

1901 Historians trace the beginning of modern Pentecostalism to Bethel Bible School in Topeka, Kansas where, at about 7 p.m. on this first day of the 20th century, Miss Agnes Ozman, one of the students, began speaking in tongues. The school was operated by former Methodist preacher Charles F. Parham (1873-1929).

Notable Birthdays

1431 Birth of Rodrigo Borgia who, as Alexander VI (1492-1503), is considered by some scholars to have been "the worst pope" in history. The execution of Savonarola took place by his order in 1498. [d. 8/18/1503]

1484 Birth of Swiss Reformer Ulrich Zwingli. His sermons criticizing the Catholic Mass started the Reformation in Switzerland. Zwingli began preaching the "true divine Scriptures" in 1520, and helped stir revolts against fasting and clerical celibacy. Like Luther, he accepted the supreme authority of Scripture but applied this belief more comprehensively. [d. 10/11/1531]

The Last Passage

1730 Death of Samuel Sewall, 77, the American colonial judge who presided over the Salem witch trials (1692), sentencing 19 people to death. He publicly confessed his error in 1697. In 1700 he published *The Selling of Joseph*, the first antislavery tract published in America. (b. 3/28/1652)

1888 Death of Eliza Emily Chappell Porter, 81, American educator. She opened schools for Indians, blacks, and other needy children in New York, Michigan, Illinois, Wisconsin, Tennessee, Kentucky and Texas. (b. 1/5/1807)

1937 Death of J[ohn] Gresham Machen, 55, American Presbyterian apologist. Defrocked by the PCUSA in 1935, he afterward became a leading organizer of the Orthodox Presbyterian Church (1936), and was later called "Fundamentalism's most gifted theologian." (b. 7/28/1881)

Words for the Soul

1517 Reformer Martin Luther, in a sermon on the commandment against stealing, concluded: *'Gambling is always contrary to love and is motivated by greed, because a man seeks, to the harm of another, what does not belong to him.'*

1637 Exiled Scottish clergyman Samuel Rutherford testified in a letter: *'[Christ] hath in patience waited on, while I come to myself, and hath not taken advantage of my weak apprehensions of his goodness. Great and holy is his name. He looketh to what I desire to be, and not to what I am.'*

1780 English-born pioneer American Methodist bishop and circuit rider Francis Asbury gave voice to this prayer in his journal: *'My God, keep me through the water and fire, and let me rather die than live to sin against thee!'*

1833 Scottish clergyman and biographer Andrew Bonar wrote in his diary: *'I began last year the custom of private fasts, and never have I found more answers to direct petitions than since then.'*

IN GOD'S WORD... OT: Genesis 1:1–2:25 ~ NT: Matthew 1:1–2:12 ~ Psalms 1:1-6 ~ Proverbs 1:1-6

שבט ALMANAC OF THE CHRISTIAN FAITH טבת
SHEVAT   TEVET

~ January 2 ~

Highlights in History

1887 The Jewish Theological Seminary of America was founded in New York City by Alexander Kohut and Sabato Morais. Established by moderate traditionalists, the seminary became an institution of higher learning within Conservative Judaism.

1909 Future Foursquare Gospel evangelist Aimee [née Kennedy] Semple [later McPherson] and her husband Robert Semple were ordained to the ministry in Chicago by evangelist William H. Durham. Aimee, who married Harold McPherson after Robert died, afterward became founder of the International Church of the Foursquare Gospel, and one of America's most popular preachers of the twentieth century.

1921 The first religious program in U.S. broadcast history was heard on radio when the Calvary Episcopal Church of Pittsburgh aired its worship service over local Pittsburgh radio station KDKA. The preacher was the Reverend Edwin Jan Van Etten.

1964 Pope Paul VI began a three-day visit to the Holy Land – the first papal visit there since New Testament times.

Notable Birthdays

1532 Birth of William Allen, English Catholic cardinal and scholar. In 1568 he founded the English College at Douai, France, from which flowed publications in English in defense of Catholicism. The first English Catholic translation of the N.T. (published in 1582 at Rheims, to which the college was transferred after anti-English riots in 1578), and of the O.T. (1609) also originated there. [d. 10/16/1594]

1828 Birth of Jeremiah E. Rankin, American Congregational clergyman, educator, and hymn author. He served as president of Howard University (1889-1903), and penned the hymn, "God Be With You Till We Meet Again." [d. 11/28/1904]

1873 Birth of French Carmelite nun, Thérèse of Lisieux. Known as the "Little Flower of Jesus," Thérèse died of tuberculosis at age 24. She was canonized in 1925, and remains one of the most popular of the Catholic saints. [d. 9/30/1897]

The Last Passage

1777 John Rosbrugh of Allen Township, Pennsylvania, was killed in the battle of Assunpink, during the Second Battle of Trenton. Serving as chaplain of Northampton County during the American Revolution, Rosbrugh became the first American Army chaplain to be killed in action.

1878 Death of Edward Caswall, 63, an Anglican who turned Catholic under the influence of John Henry Newman. Caswall translated over 200 hymns from the Latin to English, including: "Jesus, The Very Thought of Thee" and "When Morning Gilds the Skies." (b. 7/15/1814)

1924 Death of Sabine Baring-Gould, 89, Anglican rector, scholar, author and hymnwriter. In addition to compiling a 15-volume *Lives of the Saints* and authoring other theological works, he also wrote the hymns, "Onward, Christian Soldiers" and "Now the Day is Over." (b. 1/28/1834)

Words for the Soul

1848 Scottish clergyman and biographer Andrew Bonar wrote: *'I sin against the Lord by labouring more than I pray. Is this not "serving tables"?'*

1868 Scottish clergyman and biographer Andrew Bonar wrote in his diary: *'Lord, this year may the Spirit fill my soul, revealing the fulness of Christ to me from day to day.'*

1966 French-born American Trappist monk Thomas Merton wrote in a letter: *'There is in my heart this great thirst to recognize totally the nothingness of all that is not God.... It is not 'thinking about' anything, but a direct seeking of the Face of the Invisible, which cannot be found unless we become lost in Him who is Invisible.'*

IN GOD'S WORD...   OT: Genesis 3:1–4:26 ~ NT: Matthew 2:13–3:6 ~ Psalms 2:1-12 ~ Proverbs 1:7-9

שבט — ALMANAC OF THE CHRISTIAN FAITH — טבת

SHEVAT   TEVET

~ January 3 ~

Highlights in History

1521 Leo X issued "Decet romanum pontificem," the papal notice formally excommunicating Martin Luther from the Catholic Church. Leo's earlier encyclical, "Exsurge, Domine," issued six months earlier, condemned the German Reformer as a heretic, and gave him 60 days to recant his heresies and burn all his writings. Instead, Luther burned the earlier papal bull on Dec 10, 1520, which soon led to this final and official severing action by Leo.

1934 A two-day synod opened at Barmen-Gemarke, in Germany, at which 320 pastors of the German Confessing Church gathered to formulate a theological opposition to the tenets of the newly-appointed Nazi German Nationalist Church. Led by Karl Barth and Martin Niemöller, the gathering led to the Barmen Declaration on May 29th — a document which afterward became the theological rallying point of the German Confessing Church.

1956 The Colored Methodist Episcopal Church officially changed its name to the Christian Methodist Episcopal Church. The denomination originated in 1870, when the Methodist Episcopal Church, South, approved the request of its black membership for the formation of a separate ecclesiastical body. Headquartered today in Memphis, TN, membership in the C.M.E. Church is 500,000 in strength.

Notable Birthdays

1793 Birth of Lucretia C. Mott, American Quaker minister, reformer, and abolitionist. She was a co-founder of the women's rights movement in the U.S., and was active in anti-slavery movement with husband, James. [d. 11/11/1880]

1816 Birth of Ann Ayres, American Episcopal religious. Influenced by the preaching of Dr. William A. Mühlenberg, she was converted and began a social work in 1845. In 1852 she founded the Sisterhood of the Holy Communion – the first U.S. Episcopal sisterhood. Ayres was thus the first woman in the United States to become a Protestant sister. [d. 2/9/1896]

1830 Birth of Alexander Ewing, Scottish musician, soldier and hymnwriter. A skilled linguist who also studied law, Ewing is best remembered today for composing the hymn tune EWING ("Jerusalem the Golden"). [d. 7/11/1895]

1840 Birth of missionary priest Joseph (Father Damien) de Veuster, in Belgium. After joining the Picpus Fathers, he volunteered in 1873 to work with the lepers on Molokai Island, Hawaii. Father Damien contracted the disease in 1883, and died six years later. [d. 4/15/1889]

1892 Birth of J[ohn] R[onald] R[euel] Tolkien, English philologist and fantasy novelist. A devout Catholic, he wrote *The Hobbit* (1938) and *The Lord of the Rings* (1954-56), and became a strong spiritual influence in the life of fellow academic C. S. Lewis. [d. 9/2/1973]

The Last Passage

1918 Death of Annie Sherwood Hawks, 82, American Baptist hymnwriter. She composed over 400 hymns in her lifetime, including two which still endure: "I Need Thee Every Hour" and "Thine, Most Gracious Lord." (b. 5/28/1835)

1970 Death of Gladys May Aylward, 67, English missionary to China. Her fictionalized biography (*The Small Woman*) became the popular 1958 film, "The Inn of the Sixth Happiness" — based on her life in China between the years 1932-48. (b. 2/24/1902)

Words for the Soul

1764 Anglican clergyman and hymnwriter John Newton wrote in a letter: *'Oh, the name of Jesus, when we can speak of him as our's; ...it is as ointment poured forth, diffusing a fragrance through the whole soul, and driving away the hurtful fumes and fogs of distrust and discontent!'*

IN GOD'S WORD...   OT: Genesis 5:1–7:24 ~ NT: Matthew 3:7–4:11 ~ Psalms 3:1-8 ~ Proverbs 1:10-19

שבט SHEVAT ALMANAC OF THE CHRISTIAN FAITH טבת TEVET

~ January 4 ~

Highlights in History

1915 Moses Alexander was sworn in as governor of Idaho, serving until January 1919. He was the first Jewish governor elected for a full term in one of the American states.

1840 A group of Yale Congregational students opened Illinois College at Jacksonville, IL. It was the first denominational seminary established in that state, and inspired a subsequent and rapid spread of Congregationalism in Illinois.

Notable Birthdays

1581 Birth of James Ussher, Anglican prelate. In 1625 he was made the Archbishop of Armagh (primacy of Ireland). A scholar as well as a tolerant church leader, Ussher also distinguished the seven genuine letters of Ignatius, created a history of the Latin Church, and published a Biblical chronology which dated the Creation at 4004 B.C. [d. 3/21/1656]

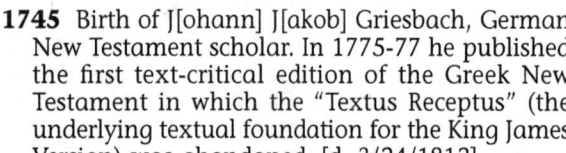

1745 Birth of J[ohann] J[akob] Griesbach, German New Testament scholar. In 1775-77 he published the first text-critical edition of the Greek New Testament in which the "Textus Receptus" (the underlying textual foundation for the King James Version) was abandoned. [d. 3/24/1812]

1804 Birth of Samuel M. Isaacs, American Orthodox rabbi, in Leeuwarden, Netherlands. He served as rabbi in New York (1838-79). He was also the founder and editor of the "Jewish Messenger" (1857-78), a founder of Mt. Sinai Hospital, the Hebrew Free School Association, and the United Hebrew Charities. [d. 5/19/1878]

The Last Passage

1821 Death of Elizabeth Ann (née Bayley) Seton, 46, American Catholic educator. The mother of five children, she founded the Society for the Relief of Poor Widows with Small Children in 1797, and is known today as the mother of the American parochial school system. She was also founder of the American Sisters of Charity (1809) — the first U.S. Catholic order. She was canonized in 1975 — the first American-born Catholic to become a saint. (b. 8/28/1774)

1854 Death of Thomas Campbell, 90, founder (with his son Alexander and with Barton W. Stone) of the Baptist sect which later became the Disciples of Christ Church. (b. 2/1/1763)

1965 Death of T[homas] S[tearns] Eliot, 76, American-born English dramatist, critic and poet. Raised Unitarian, he later became a High Church Anglican. The most influential English writer in the twentieth century, Eliot was a devout Christian who openly wove his religious convictions into his work. (b. 9/26/1888)

Words for the Soul

1540 German Reformer Martin Luther declared in a sermon: *'Faith is the "yes" of the heart, a conviction on which one stakes one's life.'*

1780 English-born pioneer American Methodist bishop and circuit rider Francis Asbury drew this analogy in his journal: *'How much skill is required to be a doctor! What diseases the human body is subject to! What regimen and care are necessary! How many diseases hath the soul! What skill ought a preacher to have to know the causes and cures! – it will require all his time and study: the consequences of miscarriages are greater in the soul than the body.'*

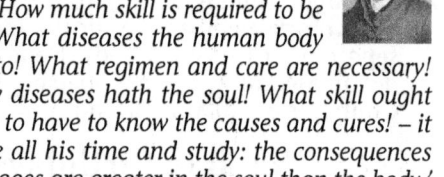

1891 Scottish clergyman and children's novelist George MacDonald wrote in a letter to his daughter: *'I take small satisfaction in looking on my past, but I do live expecting great things in the life that is ripening for me and all mine – when we shall all have the universe for our own, and be good merry helpful children in the great house of our father. I think then we shall be able to pass into and through each other's very souls as we please, knowing each other's thought and being, along with our own, and so being like God.'*

IN GOD'S WORD... OT: Genesis 8:1–10:32 ~ NT: Matthew 4:12-25 ~ Psalms 4:1-8 ~ Proverbs 1:20-23

שבט — ALMANAC OF THE CHRISTIAN FAITH — טבת

SHEVAT   TEVET

~ January 5 ~

Highlights in History

1371 Pierre Roger de Beaufort (1329-78) was crowned Pope Gregory XI, the last of the Avignon (French) popes. Upon his death in 1378, the attempt to elect his successor resulted in the Western Schism. It was also Gregory who, in 1377, condemned the doctrines of Wycliffe.

1800 The first worship service was held at the New Church Temple, in Baltimore, MD. The brick structure was the first Swedenborgian temple to be built in the United States.

1922 Following her sensational divorce, popular American evangelist Aimee Semple McPherson resigned her denominational ordination and returned her fellowship papers to the General Council of the Assemblies of God.

1964 Pope Paul VI and Athenagoras I, ecumenical patriarch of Constantinople, met in Jerusalem – the first meeting between Roman Catholic and Greek Orthodox church prelates since 1439.

Notable Birthdays

1548 Birth of Francisco de Suárez, Spanish Jesuit leader, philosopher and theologian, in Granada, Spain. Suárez is considered the greatest of the Jesuit theologians. [d. 9/25/1617]

1811 Birth of Cyrus Hamlin, American Congregational missionary to Turkey and mission educator, in Waterford, Maine. Hamlin founded and headed Robert College, in Turkey (1863-77). He was also president of Middlebury (Vermont) College, in Vermont (1881-87). [d. 8/8/1900]

1906 Birth of British archaeologist Kathleen Kenyon, who supervised major excavations in Palestine. Associated with the University of London Institute of Archaeology (1935-62), she led researches in Jordan (1952-58) on the site of Old Testament Jericho. Kenyon was the first archaeologist to use radioactive carbon dating. [d. 8/24/1978]

The Last Passage

1066 Death of Edward the Confessor, 63, son of Aethelred II. As king of England (1042-66), he framed a code believed to be the origin of the common law of England. He also restored to Malcolm the throne of Scotland, which had been usurped by Macbeth. The founder of Westminster Abbey, Edward was the only English king canonized by the Roman Catholic church. (b. 1003)

1527 Martyrdom of Felix Manz, 29, Swiss Anabaptist Reformer. A close associate of reformer Conrad Grebel, Manz was drowned in punishment for preaching adult baptism – thus gaining the distinction of becoming the first Protestant martyred by other Protestants. (b. ca. 1498)

1840 Scottish Presbyterian poet Mary Lundie Duncan died of pneumonia at age 35. She was the wife of Rev. William Wallace Duncan, founder of the Scottish Free Church. During her short life, Mary penned 23 hymns for children, of which the most enduring has been "Jesus, Tender Shepherd, Hear Me." (b. 4/26/1814)

Words for the Soul

1839 Scottish pastor Robert Murray McCheyne concluded in a letter: 'There is nothing like a calm look into the eternal world to teach us the emptiness of human praise, the sinfulness of self-seeking and vain glory — to teach us the previousness of Christ.'

1889 Scottish clergyman and biographer Andrew Bonar, 78, chided himself in his diary: 'Busy with too many meetings at this season, leaving me too little time for prayer.'

1949 U.S. Senate chaplain Peter Marshall, only days before his early death at 47, prayed: 'Our Father in heaven, give us the long view of our work and our world. Help us to see that it is better to fail in a cause that will ultimately succeed than to succeed in a cause that will ultimately fail.'

IN GOD'S WORD... OT: Genesis 11:1–13:4 ~ NT: Matthew 5:1-26 ~ Psalms 5:1-12 ~ Proverbs 1:24-28

שבט ALMANAC OF THE CHRISTIAN FAITH טבת
SHEVAT   TEVET

~ January 6 ~

Highlights in History

548 This was the last year the Church of Jerusalem celebrated the nativity of Jesus on this date. (Although the Philocalian Calendar of A.D. 336 is the earliest extant document to mention the observance of Christ's birth on December 25th, the general change-of-date for the celebration didn't begin until the later 4th century in the Western Church.)

1494 The first mass in America was celebrated in the Roman Catholic church on Isabella Island in Haiti. This was the first church established in the New World — founded by Christopher Columbus himself.

1540 England's King Henry VIII married Anne of Cleves (1515-1557), the fourth of his six successive wives. Anne was selected by Thomas Cromwell in order to ally Henry with German Protestants against the Holy Roman Emperor. However, at Henry's request, the marriage was annulled a few months later by Parliament.

1924 In England, the first worship service broadcast over radio from a church was aired by the British Broadcasting Company. The service was conducted by H. R. L. Sheppard in St. Martin-in-the-Fields Church.

Notable Birthdays

1740 Birth of John Fawcett, English Baptist preacher and poet. Like Isaac Watts, he often wrote verse as an extension of his sermons. Over 160 of Fawcett's hymns were published during his lifetime, including "Blest Be the Tie That Binds" and "Lord, Dismiss Us With Thy Blessing." [d. 7/25/1817]

1887 Birth of Virgil P. Brock, American Quaker gospel singer and songwriter. He married Blanche Kerr in 1914, and as the Singing Brocks, Virgil co-authored a number of gospel songs, including "He's a Wonderful Savior to Me" and "Beyond the Sunset." [d. 3/12/1978]

The Last Passage

1800 Death of William Jones (of Nayland), 73, Anglican divine. Perpetual curate at Nayland, England (1777-1800), he spent his life seeking evidences, both from Scripture and in nature, which supported the doctrine of the Trinity. His best-known work was *The Catholic Doctrine of the Trinity* (1756). (b. 7/30/1726)

1884 Death of Gregor Mendel, 61, Austrian Augustinian monk and botanist. His experimental breeding of garden peas in the monastery gardens, beginning in 1856, formed the basis of the modern laws of genetics. Mendel's work, virtually ignored at first, was rediscovered in 1900. (b. 7/22/1822)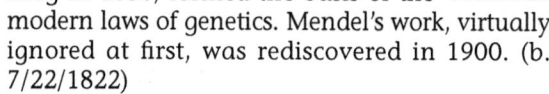

Words for the Soul

1538 In an Epiphany sermon on the virgin birth, German Reformer Martin Luther explained: 'Though Mary had been conceived in sin, the Holy Spirit takes her flesh and blood and purifies them; and thence He creates the body of the Son of God... Thus He assumed a genuine body from His mother Mary, but this body was cleansed from sin by the Holy Spirit. If this were not the case, we could not be saved.'

1637 Exiled Scottish clergyman Samuel Rutherford testified in a letter: 'I shall think it mercy to my soul, if my faith shall out-watch all this winter-night, and not nod or slumber, till my Lord's summer-day dawn upon me.'

1850 Young Charles Spurgeon, 16, who became one of the greatest preachers of the 19th century, was first converted to Christianity after receiving a vision — 'not a vision to my eyes, but to my heart. I saw what a Saviour Christ was.... I can never tell you how it was, but I no sooner saw Whom I was to believe than I also understood what it was to believe, and I did believe in one moment.'

IN GOD'S WORD... OT: Genesis 13:5–15:21 ~ NT: Matthew 5:27-48 ~ Psalms 6:1-10 ~ Proverbs 1:29-33

שבט ALMANAC OF THE CHRISTIAN FAITH טבת

SHEVAT

TEVET

~ January 7 ~

Highlights in History

367 Early Church Father Athanasius, famous for his battles against the Arian heresy, wrote a letter containing a list of what he regarded as authoritative books of Scripture. Over time, his list was adopted by the Church at large as comprising the canon of the New Testament.

1451 In Scotland, the University of Glasgow was founded, making it the second oldest university in Scotland and the fourth oldest in Britain.

Notable Birthdays

1722 Birth of Peter Williams, Welsh preacher and hymn translator. Converted under George Whitefield, Williams became one of the most prominent leaders of the Methodist revival in Wales. He also translated the Welsh hymn, "Guide Me, O Thou Great Jehovah," into English. [d. 8/8/1796]

1805 Birth of David Whitmer, early Mormon leader. He brought Joseph Smith to his father's farm near Palmyra, New York, where the golden plates which Smith had uncovered were translated into the *Book of Mormon* (1830). Whitmer was privileged to examine the plates. (Later the two men disagreed and Whitmer was excommunicated in 1838). [d. 1/25/1888]

1829 Birth of Frederick Whitfield, English clergyman and writer. The author of 30 books, Whitfield's *Sacred Poems and Prose* (1864) included a hymn lyric which is still sung today: "There is a Name I Love to Hear." [d. 9/13/1904]

1844 Birth of Bernadette Soubirous, French Roman Catholic visionary. At the age of 14, in 1858, she experienced 18 visions of the Virgin Mary in a grotto at Lourdes. Canonized in 1933, she was made subject of the 1943 Oscar-winning film, "Song of Bernadette." [d. 4/16/1879]

1858 Birth of Henry Weston Frost, American Presbyterian mission society director. He established the American branch of the China Inland Mission, known today as Overseas Missionary Fellowship (OMF). [d. 1/8/1945]

The Last Passage

1868 Death of William B. Bradbury, 51, American music teacher, publisher and hymnwriter. He edited several music collections, and composed the hymn tunes JUST AS I AM; SWEET HOUR [of Prayer]; ['Tis Midnight, and On] OLIVE'S BROW; CHINA ["Jesus Loves Me, This I Know"]; THE SOLID ROCK; BRADBURY ["Savior, Like a Shepherd Lead Us"]; and YARBROUGH ["Take My Life, and Let It Be"]. (b. 10/6/1816)

1887 Death of John Jacob Glossbrenner, 73, American Moravian bishop. In May 1849 he became the first elected bishop of the United Brethren in Christ. (b. 7/24/1813)

1918 Death of Julius Wellhausen, 73, German Orientalist, theologian and biblical critic. His part in the "Graf-Wellhausen Hypothesis" produced a revolution in understanding the written text of the Old Testament. (b. 5/17/1844)

1921 Death of Edgar P. Stites, 84, American Mayflower descendant, American Civil War veteran, Methodist lay preacher and hymn author: "Simply Trusting Every Day." (b. 3/22/1836)

1940 Death of Carl Gustaf Boberg, 80, Swedish lay preacher and hymnwriter. He authored "O Store Gud," the original Swedish version of Russell K. Hine's English-translated hymn, "How Great Thou Art." (b. 8/16/1859)

Words for the Soul

1792 Anglican Evangelical Henry Venn wrote in a letter: 'May peace national, peace domestic, peace internal, and peace everlasting, be with you, and all our fellow citizens!'

1843 Scottish clergyman and biographer Andrew Bonar wrote in his diary: 'We should pray with the belief of receiving something as good as we seek always, if not the very thing. We thus cannot pray without being the better of it.'

IN GOD'S WORD... OT: Genesis 16:1–18:19 ~ NT: Matthew 6:1–24 ~ Psalms 7:1–17 ~ Proverbs 2:1–5

שבט ALMANAC OF THE CHRISTIAN FAITH טבת
SHEVAT   TEVET

～ January 8 ～

Highlights in History

1198 Italian cardinal Lotario de Conti de Segni was elected Innocent III. His reign (-1216) marked the climax of medieval Catholicism. His was the most powerful papacy in the Middle Ages, and Innocent was the first to adopt the title "Vicar of Christ." The Fourth Lateran Council, which he convened in 1215, adopted many of his ideas. He also urged the Fourth Crusade, which resulted in the capture of Constantinople and the establishment of the Latin Empire.

Notable Birthdays

1583 Birth of Simon Episcopius (Simon Bisschop), the Dutch Protestant theologian who systematized the tenets of Arminianism. As one of the greatest theologians of his age, Episcopius maintained that theology is ultimately without value if its application fails in one's spiritual and moral life. He was among those condemned and expelled by the Synod of Dort (1619). [d. 4/4/1643]

1735 Birth of John Carroll, first Catholic bishop in America and the main figure in establishing Catholicism in the United States. Carroll became a bishop in 1790, an in 1808 was elevated to Archbishop of Baltimore, serving until his death (1815). He also founded Georgetown University in 1789. [d. 12/3/1815]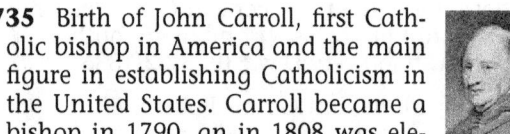

1792 Birth of Lowell Mason, American educator, and hymnwriter. He established the first public school music program in 1838, and also composed such enduring hymns as BETHANY ("Nearer, My God, To Thee"); AZMON ("O For a Thousand Tongues to Sing") (arr.); HAMBURG ("When I Survey the Wondrous Cross"); OLIVET ("My Faith Looks Up to Thee"); MISSIONARY HYMN ("From Greenland's Icy Mountains"); and BOYLSTON ("A Charge to Keep I Have"). [d. 8/11/1872]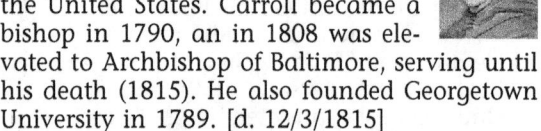

The Last Passage

1941 Death of Baron Robert Smyth Baden-Powell, 85, English military leader. He founded the Boy Scouts in 1907, the Girl Scouts (with his sister Agnes) in 1910, and the Cub Scouts in 1916. Baden-Powell had conceived his original idea after he had taken some boys camping. (b. 2/22/1857)

1942 Death of "Judge" Joseph F. Rutherford, 72, successor to Charles Taze Russell as head of the "Russellites," 1916-42. As founding president (1925), Rutherford took the loosely organized Watch Tower Bible and Tract Society and welded it into the Jehovah's Witnesses. (b. 11/8/1869)

1956 Death of Jim Elliot, 28, American Plymouth Brethren missionary. He was one of five martyrs (also including Nate Saint, Roger Youderian, Ed McCully and Pete Fleming) who were killed by the Auca Indians of Ecuador, whom they were attempting to evangelize. The story of the missionaries, and their deaths, was popularized by Jim Elliot's widow Elizabeth in her book, *Through Gates of Splendor*, published the following year. (b. 10/8/1927)

Words for the Soul

1837 Scottish clergyman and biographer Andrew Bonar wrote in his diary: *'I desire now just to enjoy Christ as my Lord and my Friend, and let Him send me among men, or keep me unknown and unoccupied, as He pleases.'*

1866 Founder of the Lutheran Church, Missouri Synod, C. F. W. Walther observed in a letter: *'The joy of the world is like drinking salt water – the more you drink, the thirstier you get.'*

1979 American Presbyterian missionary and Christian apologist, Francis Schaeffer wrote in a letter: *'A Christian is a person who has the possibility of innumerable new starts.'*

IN GOD'S WORD... OT: Genesis 18:20–19:38 ~ NT: Matthew 6:25–7:14 ~ Psalms 8:1-9 ~ Proverbs 2:6-15

שבט ALMANAC OF THE CHRISTIAN FAITH טבת
SHEVAT   TEVET

January 9

Highlights in History

1532 In Switzerland, the Synod of Bern convened. It was the first Reformed synod held in the city since it had embraced the Reformation in 1528. At this six-day convocation, a pastor's manual was created, noteworthy for its warmth, simplicity, sincerity and practical wisdom.

1836 The first Roman Catholic college to be founded in the deep South, Spring Hill College was established in Spring Hill, Alabama.

1873 Henry Ward Beecher, the most popular clergyman of his time, was charged with adultery by Theodore Tilton, who alleged the alienation of his wife's affection. Beecher was acquitted.

1943 The popular World War II song, "Praise The Lord And Pass The Ammunition!" reached #1 on the popular music charts. Performed by Kay Kyser, the title of the song was inspired by the Pearl Harbor events of Dec. 7, 1941.

Notable Birthdays

1554 Birth of Italian cardinal Alessandro Ludovisi who served as Pope Gregory XV (1621-23). As history's first Jesuit-trained pontiff, Gregory was one of the most likable of the popes. He established the Sacred Congregation for the Propagation of the Faith (1622), and also canonized such immortals as Ignatius Loyola, Philip Neri, Teresa of Avila and Francis Xavier. [d. 7/8/1623]

1626 Birth of Armand-Jean Le Bouthillier de Rancé, French monk, and reformer of La Trappe. He founded the Trappist branch of the Cistercian Order in 1664, and served as abbot of LaTrappe monastery 1664-95. [d. 10/12/1700]

1724 Birth of Isaac Backus, American Baptist minister, historian and champion of religious liberty. He pastored First Baptist Church in Middleborough, MA for 50 years (1756-1806), and was associated with the New Light (Separatist Congregationalist) movement. [d. 11/20/1806]

The Last Passage

1889 Death of Alessandro Gavazzi, 79, Italian religious reformer. He organized Italian Protestants in London (1850-60), helped set up the Free Church of Italy (1870), and established a theological school in Rome (1875). (b. 3/21/1809)

1924 Death of Frederick C. Conybeare, 68, After seven years at Oxford University (1881-87), he resigned his chair to devote himself to research in the Armenian language. Conybeare later became interested in church history and in textual criticism, and how they both related to the Septuagint (the Greek Old Testament) and the New Testament. (b. 1856)

1924 Death of Henry Wace, 87, Anglican churchman. As Dean of Canterbury (1903-24), he was a staunch Evangelical and equally opposed to "higher criticism" of the Bible and to the High Church attempts to revise the *Book of Common Prayer*. Wace was editor, with William Smith, of the *Dictionary of Christian Biography* (4 vols., 1880-86), and with Philip Schaff of the Second Series of the *Nicene and Post-Nicene Fathers* (14 vols., 1890-1900). (b. 12/10/1836)

1957 Death of Joseph M. M. Gray, 79, American Methodist clergyman, educator and author: *The Contemporary Christ* (1921); *An Adventur in Orthodoxy* (1923); *Concerning the Faith* (1928); *Prophets of the Soul* (1936). Gray served as President of American University in Washington, DC (1933-40). (b. 8/31/1877)

Words for the Soul

1777 Circuit-rider and Methodist bishop, Francis Asbury confided in his journal: *'My soul lives constantly as in the presence of God, and enjoys much of His divine favor. His love is better than life!'*

1795 In a letter to William Smith, British statesman Edmund Burke penned the now-famous warning: *'All that is necessary for evil to triumph is for good men to do nothing.'*

IN GOD'S WORD...   OT: Genesis 20:1–22:24 ~ NT: Matthew 7:15-29 ~ Psalms 9:1-12 ~ Proverbs 2:16-22

שבט ALMANAC OF THE CHRISTIAN FAITH טבת
SHEVAT   TEVET

January 10

Highlights in History

236 St. Fabian was elected pope, serving until 250, when he became the first martyr victim under Roman Emperor Decius.

1514 The first of six volumes of the world's first multilingual Bible – the *Complutensian Polyglot* – were published in Alcala, Spain.

1984 The U.S. and the Vatican re-established full diplomatic relations more than 100 years after severing them in 1867.

Notable Birthdays

1479 Birth of Johannes Cochlaeus (Wendelstinus Dobneck), Catholic controversialist. He was a prominent opponent of Martin Luther. [d. 1/10/1552]

1607 Birth of Isaac Jogues, French Jesuit missionary and Indian martyr. He joined the Jesuits in 1624, became a missionary to Canada and worked among the Huron Indians. In 1646 he sought to negotiate a treaty with the Iroquois but was taken captive, blamed for a pestilence that had struck the tribe, and was tomahawked to death. [d. 10/18/1646]

1800 Birth of Heinrich August Wilhelm Meyer, German Protestant clergyman and New Testament commentator. Known for his careful philological-historical method, Meyer is chiefly remembered for the New Testament commentary he initiated, and which is named after him today. [d. 6/21/1873]

1822 Birth of Theodore Ledyard Cuyler, American clergyman and author. From 1860-90 he pastored the Lafayette Avenue Presbyterian Church in Brooklyn, during which time he became one of New York City's most popular preachers. Cuyler's sermons were forceful and evangelical in tone, and he wrote incessantly for the religious press, contributing 22 books and over 4,000 articles in all. [d. 2/26/1909]

The Last Passage

1569 St. Philip of Moscow, primate of the Russian Orthodox Church, was murdered by Czar Ivan IV ("Ivan the Terrible"). (b. 2/11/1507)

1645 Death of William Laud, 71, controversial English Archbishop of Canterbury (1633-40). An enemy and persecutor of the Puritans and a staunch defender of the Divine Right of Kings, Laud found himself on the wrong side of history when the Puritan revolution began in the 1640s. He was ultimately impeached for high treason, and beheaded. (b. 10/7/1573)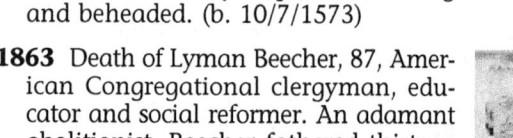

1863 Death of Lyman Beecher, 87, American Congregational clergyman, educator and social reformer. An adamant abolitionist, Beecher fathered thirteen children (including Henry Ward Beecher and Harriet Beecher Stowe). All nine of his sons became ministers after him. (b. 10/12/1775)

1888 Death of Peter Parker, 83, first American medical missionary to China. A skilled surgeon and ophthalmologist, he first sailed in 1834, sent by the ABCFM. Parker returned to China a married man in 1842, and his bride, Harriet Webster, became the first Western woman permitted residence in China. (b. 6/18/1804)

Words for the Soul

1538 In a Table Talk, German reformer Martin Luther testified: *'God has placed two ways before us in His Word: salvation by faith, damnation by unbelief (Mark 16:16). He does not mention purgatory at all. Nor is purgatory to be admitted, for it obscures the benefits and grace of Christ.'*

1781 Anglican clergyman and hymnwriter John Newton wrote in a letter: *'Whatever we do for those we love, we do with pleasure.'*

1947 U.S. Senate Chaplain Peter Marshall prayed: *'May we resolve, God helping us, to be part of the answer and not part of the problem.'*

IN GOD'S WORD... OT: Genesis 23:1–24:51 ~ NT: Matthew 8:1-17 ~ Psalms 9:13-20 ~ Proverbs 3:1-6

שבט SHEVAT — ALMANAC OF THE CHRISTIAN FAITH — טבת TEVET

~ January 11 ~

Highlights in History

1759 The first American life insurance company was incorporated in Philadelphia: the Corporation of Poor and Distressed Presbyterian Ministers and of the Poor and Distressed Widows and Children of Presbyterian Ministers.

1791 The First Day (or Sunday School) Society was organized in Philadelphia by members of several churches, thereby making it the first interdenominational Sunday School organization in America. Other S.S. unions were soon organized in nearby cities. In 1824, this group and others merged with the American Sunday School Union.

1869 Rev. Kelly Lowe organized the first Black Sunday School in the United States in the Springfield Baptist Church in Augusta, Georgia.

Notable Birthdays

1799 Birth of Charles Henry Purday, English hymn composer: SANDON ("God of Our Life, Through All the Circling Years"). [d. 4/23/1885]

1892 Birth of Francis Xavier Ford, American Catholic bishop and martyr. During a 200-mile trip to Canton, he was arrested by the Chinese Communists, and for 14 months was tortured and vilified at a series of public trials. Ford was reported to have died in a prison in Canton as a result of the tortures. [d. 2/21/1952]

The Last Passage

1791 Death of William Williams, 73, Welsh Calvinistic Methodist evangelist and hymnwriter. Known as the "Sweet Singer of Wales," he authored 900 hymns, including "Guide Me, O Thou Great Jehovah." (b. 2/11/1717)

1817 Death of Timothy Dwight, 64, American Congregational clergyman, theologian, educator and hymnwriter. The grandson of Jonathan Edwards, Dwight served as eighth president of Yale College from 1795 until his death. He published *Theology Explained and Defended* (5 vols., 1818-19), and wrote 33 hymns, including "I Love Thy Kingdom, Lord." Though little-known, Dwight suffered from migraine headaches most of his life, and could never read for longer than 15 minutes a day. (b. 5/14/1752)

1843 Death of Francis Scott Key, 63, Maryland-born lawyer and poet. Popularly remembered as author of America's National Anthem, Key was also a devoted member of the Episcopal Church, and taught Bible classes for many years. He was among the organizers of the Domestic and Foreign Missionary Society, founded in 1820. (b. 8/9/1779)

1877 Death of Charles W. Everest, 62, American Catholic priest and hymnwriter. He was Rector of Hamden, CT from 1842-73. Today, Everest is remembered as author of the hymn of invitation, "Take Up Thy Cross." (b. 5/27/1814)

1950 Death of Walter A. Maier, 56, American Lutheran scholar and pioneer radio preacher (1930-50). His messages were both Christocentric and strongly evangelical. (b. 10/4/1893)

Words for the Soul

1523 German reformer Martin Luther admonished in a letter: *'It is unchristian, even unnatural, to derive benefit and protection from the community and not also to share in the common burden and expense; to let other people work but to harvest the fruit of their labors.'*

1777 Anglican hymnwriter John Newton encouraged in a letter: *'A soul may be in as thriving a state... when fighting in the valley as when singing upon the mount. Dark seasons afford the surest and strongest manifestations of the power of faith.'*

1853 Scottish clergy biographer Andrew Bonar wrote in his diary: *'I need not change of place nor people, but of heart, in order to be more useful.'*

IN GOD'S WORD... OT: Genesis 24:52–26:16 ~ NT: Mark 8:18-34 ~ Psalms 10:1-15 ~ Proverbs 3:7-8

שבט ALMANAC OF THE CHRISTIAN FAITH טבת
SHEVAT   TEVET

~ January 12 ~

Highlights in History

1953 Pope Pius XII elevated to the cardinalate Paul L. Leger, Archbishop of Montreal, and James Francis McIntyre, Archbishop of Los Angeles. With his elevation and appointment, Father McIntyre became the first Catholic cardinal whose see was located west of the U.S. Rockies.

1972 The South Dakota Episcopal Diocese consecrated Rev. Harold S. Jones a suffragan bishop. As a Sioux, he became the first Native American bishop in the Episcopal Church.

1974 Bishop Seraphim was chosen Archbishop of the Greek Orthodox Church. He was enthroned four days later in the Athens Cathedral.

Notable Birthdays

1825 Birth of B[rooke] F[oss] Westcott, British New Testament scholar. Regius Professor of Divinity at Cambridge from 1870, in 1881 he and Fenton J. A. Hort (1828-1892) completed a 30-year writing project by publishing the first modern critical text of the Greek New Testament. "Westcott-Hort" has since become the prime textual basis for the majority of the modern critical editions and updated translations of the Greek New Testament. [d. 7/27/1901]

The Last Passage

689 Death of Benedict Biscop, 42, Northumbrian (English) Benedictine abbot and founder of the monasteries of Wearmouth and Jarrow. He introduced the stone-built church and the art of glassmaking into England, and was the teacher of the Venerable Bede. (b. ca. 628)

1167 Death of Aelred [Ethelred], 58, Anglo-Saxon Catholic cleric and mystic. A contemporary of St. Bernard of Clairvaux, Aelred was one of the Middle Ages' best-known devotional writers and penned several treatises on the Christian faith from a mystical viewpoint. (b. 1109)

1730 Death of Johann Christoph Schwedler, 57, Silesian clergyman. He wrote over 500 hymns during his lifetime, but is principally remembered today for one: "Ask Ye What Great Thing I Know." (b.12/21/1672)

1871 Death of Henry Alford, 70, theologian, scholar, poet, writer, artist and musician. He published *The Expositor's Greek Testament* (4 vols., 1849-61). A lifelong wish to visit the Holy Land was never realized, but it was remembered by those who inscribed on his tombstone: *"The inn of a pilgrim traveling to Jerusalem."* Today, Alford is remembered for authoring the hymn: "Come, Ye Thankful People, Come." (b. 10/7/1810)

1960 Death of African-American evangelist Charles Emmanuel Grace, 78. Known as "Sweet Daddy Grace," he set up a black Pentecostal holiness sect in 1926, with its first "House of Prayer for All People" in Charlotte, NC. (b. 1/25/1881)

Words for the Soul

1837 Scottish clergyman and biographer Andrew Bonar wrote in his diary: *'Our place in Christ's kingdom will be determined by our progress in holiness personally, as much as by the efforts we have used for converting men to Jesus.'*

1839 Scottish pastor Robert Murray McCheyne observed in a letter to another pastor: *'It is not the tempest, nor the earthquake, nor the fire, but the still small voice of the Spirit that carries on the glorious work of saving souls.'*

1886 In a letter consoling a young girl who had lost her mother, Scottish clergyman and novelist George MacDonald wrote: *'God knows and cares.... It is not needful that we understand the motive power in the processes that go on within us. It is enough to him who believes it that the Lord did rise again, although after that he was hidden from their sight. Yes, I will believe that I shall hold my own in my arms again, their hearts nearer to mine than ever before.'*

IN GOD'S WORD...   OT: Genesis 26:17–27:46 ~ NT: Matthew 9:1-17 ~ Psalms 10:16-18 ~ Proverbs 3:9-10

שבט ALMANAC OF THE CHRISTIAN FAITH טבת
SHEVAT   TEVET

~ January 13 ~

Highlights in History

1501 Christianity's first vernacular hymnal was printed in Prague, Czechoslovakia. It contained 89 hymns in the Czech language.

1547 The Council of Trent issued its Decree on Justification, which recognized "merit" as a supernatural value assigned by God to a believer's good act. The reward for merit can be an increase in God's grace on earth and/or an increase of glory in heaven. The Protestant Reformers later rejected any notion of saving merit by declaring that human justification with God is based on the merits of Christ alone.

1987 Geneticists claimed to have traced the human lineage back to one common ancestor who lived approximately 200,000 years ago in Africa. Their evidence was derived from a single gene that they determined had evolved at a regular rate through time.

Notable Birthdays

1731 Birth of John Darwall, Anglican vicar and sacred composer. He composed two volumes of piano sonatas and hymn tunes for all 150 psalms, including the enduring melody for Psalm 148: DARWALL ("Rejoice, The Lord is King"). [d. 12/18/1789]

1817 Birth of John H. A. Bomberger, American German Reformed clergyman, educator and theologian. He was founder and first president of Ursinus College in Pennsylvania. (1869-90). Some of his best writings were penned in opposition to the Mercersburg Theology of John W. Nevin and Philip Schaff. [d. 8/19/1890]

1836 Birth of Alexander Whyte, Scottish clergyman. Known as the "last of the Puritans," he taught New Testament at New College, Edinburgh (1909-18), but was at heart a pastor, and authored a number of devotional books. In a nation of preachers, Whyte's impact and appeal were unparalleled. [d. 1/7/1921]

The Last Passage

1691 Death of George Fox, 67, English religious leader, mystic and itinerant preacher. Fox left the Anglican church in 1647 to rely on the "inner light of the living Christ." A magnetic personality of great spiritual power, selfless devotion, and patience, Fox formed the "Friends of the Truth" (ca. 1650). Frequently persecuted, the Friends (called Quakers by their enemies) taught that the truth could be found through the inner voice of God speaking to the soul. (b. 7/1624)

1855 Death of John Scudder, 61, Dutch Reformed physician and the first American foreign medical missionary. He and his wife traveled to Ceylon under the ABCFM in 1819. In 1835 he relocated to India, establishing one of the first medical missions in that country. (b. 9/3/1793)

1909 Death of Josiah Kelley Alwood, 80, American United Brethren clergyman and hymnwriter. He wrote and composed "The Unclouded Day" (1890). (b. 7/15/1828)

1935 Death of Eleanor Henrietta Hull, 75, English writer. She was founder and secretary of the Irish Text Society, and authored several volumes on Irish literature and history. She also versified the hymn, "Be Thou My Vision." (b. 1/15/1860)

1962 Death of Edgar J. Goodspeed, 90, American Baptist Greek scholar and educator. As a Bible translator, he published *New Testament: An American Translation* (1923). Goodspeed taught in the Dept. of Bible Literature at the University of Chicago from 1898-1937, and co-authored *The Complete Bible: An American Translation* (with J. M. Powis Smith, 1939). (b. 10/23/1871)

Words for the Soul

1691 These were the last words of George Fox, 67, English religious reformer and founder of the Society of Friends: *'All is well, and the Seed of God reigns over all, and over death itself.'*

IN GOD'S WORD...   OT: Genesis 28:1–29:35 ~ NT: Matthew 9:18-38 ~ Psalms 11:1-7 ~ Proverbs 3:11-12

January 14

Highlights in History

1505 Pope Julius II issued the constitution, "De fratrum nostrorum," which declared that any pontifical election procured by simony was null and void.

1529 Spanish diplomat and writer Juan de Valdes published his *Dialogue on Christian Doctrine*, which paved the way for Protestant ideas in Spain, even though the writing itself was cleared of doctrinal error by the Spanish Inquisition.

1604 In England, the Hampton Court Conference began, wherein Puritan representatives met with their new king, James I, to discuss proposed changes in the Church of England.

1615 John Biddle, father of English Unitarianism, was baptized. He wrote *Twelve Arguments*, which denied the Trinity. Biddle was imprisoned, and later banished (1655) by Oliver Cromwell to the Scilly Islands, to save his life. He returned, however, and died in a London prison (1662).

Notable Birthdays

1484 Birth of Georg Spalatin, German Reformer. He was Martin Luther's close friend (Luther wrote him some 400 letters) and go-between with Frederick the Wise. Spalatin translated many of the Latin writings of Luther, Philipp Melanchthon, and Erasmus, and also supervised the publication of Luther's works. [d. 1/16/1545]

1811 Birth of Roland H. Prichard, Welsh choralist and hymnwriter. In 1844 he published *The Singer's Friend*. It contained many of his original hymn tunes, including one melody he composed at about age 20: HYFRYDOL ("Come, Thou Long-Expected Jesus"). [d. 1/25/1887]

1875 Birth of Albert Schweitzer, French (Alsatian) theologian, music scholar, physician and medical missionary. His *Quest of the Historical Jesus* (1906) is considered a foundational work in that subject. In 1913, he founded Lambarene Hospital in French Equatorial Africa. Schweitzer was known for his humanitarianism and "reverence of life" philosophy, and was awarded the 1952 Nobel Peace Prize. [d. 9/4/1965]

1892 Birth of Martin Niemöller, German Lutheran pastor and theologian. He helped found Germany's Confessing Church, which afterward led to his arrest (1938-45) for opposing Hitler. After the war years, Niemöller later served as president of the World Council of Churches (1961-68). [d. 3/6/1984]

The Last Passage

1841 Death of John Leland, 86, pioneer Baptist preacher and religious libertarian. He wrote against privileges of the Anglican clergy in Virginia, and authored *Short Essays on Government*, which advocated a separation of church and state. (b. 5/14/1754)

1983 Death of Lillian Dickson, 83, Minnesota-born Canadian Presbyterian missionary to Taiwan (Formosa), (1927-40, 1946-64). Her desire for providing local church buildings, adequate child care, orphan protection and vocational training led Lillian to found The Mustard Seed Mission, an evangelical and interdenominational missions agency. (b. 1/29/1901)

Words for the Soul

1960 Romanian-born comparative religions scholar Mircea Eliade noted in his journal:  *'Symbols bring into the reality of experience transpersonal values and events that the individual was not capable of apprehending consciously and voluntarily. Thanks to symbols, psychic life is neither insipid, mediocre, nor sterile.'*

1966 French-born American Trappist monk Thomas Merton advised in a letter: *'The best way to solve the problem of rendering to Caesar what is Caesar's is to have nothing that is Caesar's.'*

IN GOD'S WORD... OT: Genesis 30:1–31:16 ~ NT: Matthew 10:1-23 ~ Psalms 12:1-8 ~ Proverbs 3:13-15

שבט ALMANAC OF THE CHRISTIAN FAITH טבת

SHEVAT   TEVET

~ January 15 ~

Highlights in History

1535 The Act of Supremacy was passed, in which King Henry VIII declared himself "Protector and Only Supreme Head of the Church and Clergy of England." (Henry broke with the Church of Rome after Clement VII voided the annulment of his marriage to Catherine of Aragón and excommunicated him.)

1697 Five years after the event, the citizens of Massachusetts spent a day of fasting and repentance for their roles in the 1692 Salem Witch Trials. Judge Samuel Sewall, who had presided over many of the 20 capital judgments, submitted a written confession, acknowledging his own "blame and shame" regarding those who were hanged, as well as the 150 other victims who had been imprisoned.

Notable Birthdays

1809 Birth of Cornelia A.P. Connelly, American Episcopalian-turned-Catholic. She established the Society of the Holy Child Jesus (an order of teaching nuns) among English Catholics and Irish immigrants in England, of which she was made first superior (1847-79). [d. 4/18/1879]

1832 Birth of Susannah (née Thompson), wife of Charles Spurgeon. Aged 24 when she and Charles married (1856), Susannah soon after began a ministry enabling students of her husband's newly established Pastors' College to buy their needed textbooks. Susannah was an invalid her last 35 years, although she outlived her husband by 11 years. [d. 10/22/1903]

1841 Birth of Charles A. Briggs, American Presbyterian (later Episcopal) clergyman, biblical theologian, educator and author. With Francis Brown and Samuel R. Driver he compiled the *New Hebrew Lexicon*. A vigorous exponent of "higher criticism," Briggs was defrocked (1893) by the Presbyterian General Assembly, following a heresy trial for inadequate belief in the doctrine of Scriptural inerrancy. Briggs was later ordained by Episcopal Church (1900). [d. 6/8/1913]

1860 Birth of Eleanor Henrietta Hull, 75, English writer. She was founder and secretary of the Irish Text Society, and authored several volumes on Irish literature and history. She also versified the hymn, "Be Thou My Vision." [d. 1/13/1935]

1898 Birth of Frank Spencer Mead, American church historian. He is best remembered for his *Handbook of Denominations in the United States* (1951) – now in its 11th edition! [d. 6/16/1982]

The Last Passage

1951 Death of Harry A. Ironside, 74, American clergyman. Associated at different periods in his life with the Salvation Army and the Plymouth Brethren, Ironside pastored at Chicago's Moody Memorial Church from 1930-48 (his only pastorate), and authored over 60 books, many of which were commentaries on books of the Bible. (b. 10/14/1876)

Words for the Soul

1629 In a letter comforting a woman who had lost her daughter to illness, Scottish clergyman Samuel Rutherford wrote: *'She is not lost to you who is found to Christ; ...you see her not, yet she doth shine in another country. If her glass was but a short hour, what she wanteth of time, that she hath gotten of eternity; and you have to rejoice that you have now some treasure laid up in heaven.'*

1770 English founder of Methodism John Wesley wrote in a letter: *'The same Spirit worketh in every one; and yet worketh several ways, according to his own will. It concerns us to follow our own light, seeing we are not to be judged by another's conscience.'*

1910 British Roman Catholic novelist and literary critic G.K. Chesterton wrote: *'The most orthodox doctors have always maintained that faith is something superior to reason but not contrary to it.'*

IN GOD'S WORD... OT: Genesis 31:17–32:12 ~ NT: Matthew 10:24–11:6 ~ Psalms 13:1-6 ~ Proverbs 3:16-18

שבט   ALMANAC OF THE CHRISTIAN FAITH   טבת
SHEVAT   TEVET

January 16

Highlights in History

1604 In London, at the Hampton Court Conference, John Rainolds (representing a delegation of Puritans) suggested to King James I *'...that there might bee a newe translation of the Bible, as consonant as can be to the original Hebrew and Greek.'* James granted his approval, and the ensuing project led to the 1611 publication of the "Authorized" (King James) Version of the Bible.

1756 American champion of religious liberty, Isaac Backus founded a Baptist church in Middleborough, Rhode Island. He then served as its pastor for the next 50 years.

1786 Virginia's legislature adopted Thomas Jefferson's *Ordinance of Religious Freedom*. It later became the model for the First Amendment.

1882 The first Knights of Columbus meeting convened at St. Mary's Catholic Church in New Haven, CT. The organization was founded as a fraternal benefit association for Roman Catholic men by the Reverend Michael Joseph McGivney and nine parishioners.

1953 Pope Pius XII issued the apostolic constitution, "Christus dominus," which standardized the relaxations in the Eucharistic Fast introduced during World War II.

Notable Birthdays

1813 Birth of Georges Darboy, third Archbishop of Paris (1863-71), who consecrated the newly-restored Cathedral of Notre Dame. His Gallicanism made him unduly subservient to the emperor. Darboy was seized by the Communists and shot to death as a prisoner during Franco-Prussian War in 1871. He died blessing his executioners. [d. 5/24/1871]

1819 Birth of Johannes Rebmann, German missionary/explorer to East Africa. He translated the Gospel of Luke into one of the native languages and helped prepare dictionaries for three African tongues. [d. 10/4/1876]

1895 Birth of J[ames] O. Buswell, Jr., American Presbyterian fundamentalist educator and organizational leader. He served as president of Wheaton College, 1926-40. [d. 2/2/1977]

The Last Passage

1545 Death of Georg Spalatin, 61, German reformer. A close friend and associate of Martin Luther (who wrote him 400 letters), Spalatin helped advance the Protestant Reformation, and translated the writings of Luther, Melanchthon, and Erasmus. (b. 1/14/1484)

1866 Death of Phineas P. Quimby, 63, American mentalist. Originally a clockmaker in Maine, he became the founder of mental healing in America. Today, Quimby's philosophy forms the basis of the Unity Church and other New Thought movements. (b. 2/16/1802)

1876 Death of Edmund H. Sears, 65, American Unitarian clergyman. His pastorates were in Massachusetts, and he once wrote to Bishop Bickersteth, *'Though I was educated in the Unitarian denomination, I believe and preach the divinity of Christ.'* Sears wrote a number of hymns, including the popular Christmas carol, "It Came Upon the Midnight Clear." (b. 4/6/1810)

Words for the Soul

1740 English revivalist George Whitefield testified in a letter: *'If I see a man who loves the Lord Jesus in sincerity, I am not very solicitous to what cultural communion he belongs. The Kingdom of God, I think, does not consist in any such thing.'*

1867 Founder of the Lutheran Church, Missouri Synod, C. F. W. Walther observed in a letter: *'He shapes our poor lives so that when they are past, they are not like flowers that wither, the places of which no one recognizes, but they leave behind in the future of the Kingdom of God signs of powerful results which reach into eternity.'*

IN GOD'S WORD...   OT: Genesis 32:13–34:31 ~ NT: Matthew 11:7-30 ~ Psalms 14:1-7 ~ Proverbs 3:19-20

ALMANAC OF THE CHRISTIAN FAITH

SHEVAT · TEVET

January 17

Highlights in History

395 Emperor Theodosius I (the Great) died, making this the last day that the Roman Empire (now Christianized) was controlled by a single leader. In his wisdom, Theodosius had divided his empire into both the western and eastern portions.

1377 Gregory XI (1370-78), the last French pope, entered Rome, signalling the end of the 72-year Avignonese papacy. When Gregory died the next year, the Great Schism began. (N.B. The break between the Eastern and Western Church in 1054 is also called "The Great Schism.")

1562 The Edict of St. Germain, issued by queen mother Catherine de Médici, formally recognized French Protestantism. The edict created a violent reaction among French Catholics, however, and, prompted by the massacre of Huguenots at Vassy in March, led to the First French civil war.

1970 John M. Burgess was installed as bishop of the Protestant Episcopal diocese of Massachusetts, making him the first African-American bishop to head an Episcopal diocese in America.

1997 A court in Ireland granted the first divorce in that Roman Catholic country's modern history.

Notable Birthdays

1463 Birth of Frederick III, the Wise, Elector of Saxony (1486-25). He founded the University of Wittenberg in 1502 and, because of his increasing sympathy for the Protestant Reformation, became the protector of German Reformer Martin Luther. [d. 5/5/1525]

1504 Birth of Italian Cardinal Michele Ghislieri, who was elected Pius V (1566-72). Like his predecessor, Pius furthered the work of the Council of Trent, reformed the Roman Breviary and Missal, and actively sought to stop the spread of Protestantism. [d. 5/1/1572]

1829 Birth of Catherine [née Mumford] Booth, English reformer. The wife of founder William Booth, she was called the "mother of the Salvation Army." Catherine designed the denominational flag and its famous poke bonnet. She was also instrumental in introducing the Salvation Army into the U.S., Australia, Europe, India and Japan. [d. 10/4/1890]

1927 Birth of Thomas A. Dooley, American physician and medical missionary. He established medical facilities in war-torn East Asia and, before his early death from cancer, authored *Deliver Us From Evil* (1956) and *The Night They Burned the Mountain* (1960). [d. 1/18/1961]

The Last Passage

356 St. Anthony of Egypt ("Anthony the Abbot") died at age 105. An early desert monk, Anthony is regarded as the founder of Christian monasticism (ca. 305). (b. ca. 251)

1932 Death of Charles Gore, 78, controversial Anglican Bishop of Oxford. Though a High Churchman, Gore reflected the liberalism of the Anglo-Catholic movement. His numerous books included *The Ministry of the Christian Church* (1880) and *Lux Mundi* (1889). (b. 1/22/1853)

Words for the Soul

1745 Colonial American missionary to the Indians, David Brainerd recorded in his journal: *'Oh, how comfortable and sweet it is, to feel the assistance of divine grace in the performance of the duties which God has enjoined on us!'*

1778 Anglican Evangelical Henry Venn wrote in a letter to his son: *'What an animating thought, to look up to so many of my intimates, now amongst the spirits of the just made perfect! It familiarizes the thought of my own departure, as a translation to the society of those who were so dear to me when in the body, and I to them, through the love of our common Saviour.'*

IN GOD'S WORD... OT: Genesis 35:1–36:43 ~ NT: Matthew 12:1-21 ~ Psalms 15:1-5 ~ Proverbs 3:21-26

January 18

ALMANAC OF THE CHRISTIAN FAITH

שבט SHEVAT · טבת TEVET

Highlights in History

1460 In his concern over the decline in papal authority, Pius II issued the bull, "Execrabilis," which banned any appeal of a papal action to an ecumenical council. It was a complete reversal of Pius's own earlier views.

1836 Union Theological Seminary was founded in New York City by a group of New School Presbyterians. It first opened for instruction on December 5, 1836, and became a fully non-denominational seminary in 1904. Among Union's most notable professors have been Edward Robinson, Harry E. Fosdick, Reinhold Niebuhr, Paul Tillich and Raymond E. Brown.

1891 The first Armenian Church in the United States was consecrated in Worcester, MA. New churches were later consecrated in Fresno, CA (1900); in West Hoboken, NJ (1907); and in Fowler, CA (1910). (In 1898, an encyclical of Catholicos Mugurditch I formally established the Diocese of the Armenian Church of America, and by the beginning of the 20th century, the Armenian community in the U.S. numbered over 15,000.)

1936 The American Bishops Committee on the Confraternity of Christian Doctrine (CCD), convened a meeting of Catholic biblical scholars in Washington, D.C. The meeting yielded two proposals: (1) that a new English translation of the Bible be made; and (2) that a permanent society of Catholic biblical scholars be formed. From these proposals, the Catholic Biblical Association of America (CBA) was formed in 1937; and the *New American Bible* translation was published in 1970.

Notable Birthdays

1778 Birth of Joseph Tuckerman, Massachusetts-born Unitarian clergyman. He founded (1812) Boston Society for the Religious and Moral Improvement of Seamen – the first sailor's aid society in the United States. [d. 4/20/1840]

1815 Birth of German theologian and textual scholar L. F. Konstantin von Tischendorf. He is remembered in biblical circles for discovering and deciphering the Codex Sinaiticus, an important fifth century Greek manuscript of the Pauline epistles. [d. 12/7/1874]

1886 Birth of Tertius Van Dyke, American Presbyterian clergyman, educator, and author: *Songs of Seeking and Finding* (1920); *Light My Candle* (with Henry Van Dyke, 1926); *Henry van Dyke* (1935). The son of Henry Van Dyke, Tertius served as headmaster of Gunnery School, Washington, CT (1936-42), and Dean of Hartford Theological Seminary (1943-54). [d. 2/28/1958]

The Last Passage

1806 Death of William Shrubsole, 46, hymn composer: MILES LANE ("All Hail the Power of Jesus' Name"). (baptized 1/13/1760)

1875 Death of Joseph P. Webster, 55, hymn composer: SWEET BY AND BY ("There's a Land That is Fairer Than Day"). (b. 3/22/1819)

1917 Death of Andrew Murray, 88, South African Dutch Reformed missionary and devotional writer. Influenced by the writings of William Law, Murray was mystically inclined, and wrote much for the holiness movement. His most popular book was *Abide in Christ* (1864). (b. 5/9/1828)

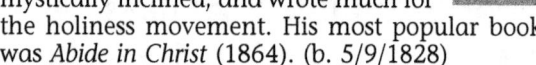

1951 Death of Amy Carmichael, 83, English missionary to India. Sent in 1895, she remained at the work for the rest of her life. (b. 12/16/1867)

Words for the Soul

1839 Scottish pastor Robert Murray McCheyne confided in a letter: *'Often God does not bless us when we are in the midst of our labours, lest we should say, "My hand and my eloquence have done it." He removes us into silence, and then pours down a blessing so that there is no room to receive it; so that all that see it cry out, "It is the Lord!"'*

IN GOD'S WORD...   OT: Genesis 37:1–38:30 ~ NT: Matthew 12:22-45 ~ Psalms 16:1-11 ~ Proverbs 3:27-32

ALMANAC OF THE CHRISTIAN FAITH

שׁבט SHEVAT

טבת TEVET

~ January 19 ~

Highlights in History

1563 The Heidelberg Catechism was published in the Palatinate (located in SW Germany where the Holy Roman Emperor resided). Composed by Peter Ursinus and Caspar Olevianus, it comprised a statement of Calvinist tradition designed to unify conflicting Protestant ideologies. Accepted by nearly all of the Reformed churches in Europe, it was the most ecumenical of Protestant catechisms and is still in use in some Dutch and German Reformed churches.

1961 In England, Rev. Arthur Michael Ramsey (1904-88), Archbishop of York, was appointed to succeed retiring Archbishop of Canterbury Geoffrey F. Fisher. Lord Ramsey served as the 100th prelate over the Anglican Church (–1974). During this time he also served as president of the World Council of Churches (1961-68).

Notable Birthdays

1798 Birth of Samuel Austin Worcester, American Congregational missionary among the Cherokee Indians in Georgia and Arkansas. He published newspapers and other documents in the Cherokee language. Imprisoned for two years by the state, Worcester then moved his operation to an Oklahoma mission. [d. 1859]

1836 Birth of Henry Lake Gilmour, Irish-born Methodist church leader and hymnwriter. For decades he directed large choruses at New England Methodist camp meetings. He is best remembered today as author of the hymn, "My Soul in Sad Exile Was Out on Life's Sea." [d. 5/20/1920]

1847 Birth of Josiah Strong, American Congregational clergyman and social gospel leader. A conspicuous figure in Protestant missions, reform and unitive movements, Strong published two popular tracts – *Our Country*, which emphasized evils and dangers in social and economic life, and *The New Era*, which defined the functions of the Church on earth. [d. 4/28/1916]

The Last Passage

1900 Death of Henry Twells, 76, Anglican clergyman, educator and hymnwriter. He was called "a powerful preacher, a beloved teacher, an unostentatious and peace-loving man." Today, Twells is best known as author of the old classic English hymn: "At Even, Ere the Sun Did Set." (b. 3/13/1823)

1931 Death of Mary Elizabeth Byrne, 50, Irish Catholic Gaelic scholar. She contributed much research to the *Old and Mid-Irish Dictionary*, and in 1905 rendered an ancient Irish text into the English hymn, "Be Thou My Vision." (b. 7/1/1880)

1949 Death of Charles P. Jones, 83, black American holiness pioneer. While pastoring a Baptist church in Selma, Alabama, Jones encountered the Holiness movement. He underwent personal sanctification in 1894, and in 1909 established the Church of Christ (Holiness). (b. 12/9/1865)

Words for the Soul

1773 Anglican clergyman and hymnwriter John Newton wrote in a letter: *'I find that many of my complaints arise more from the spirit of self, than I was formerly aware of. Self, as well as Satan, can transform itself into an angel of light.'*

1804 Anglican missionary Henry Martyn confided in his journal: *'To be made fit for the work of a missionary I resigned the comforts of a married life when they were dear to me, and that was a severe struggle. Now again will I put forth the hand of faith, though the struggle will be far more severe.'*

1868 Scottish clergyman and biographer Andrew Bonar acknowledged in his diary: *'I praise too little, and let thanks too often die away.'*

1882 American Quaker holiness author Hannah Whitall Smith wrote in a letter: *'Only characters that are like each other can "see" each other in the true sense of seeing. And as you become Christlike, you will "see" Christ.'*

IN GOD'S WORD... OT: Genesis 39:1–41:16 ~ NT: Matthew 12:46–13:23 ~ Psalms 17:1-15 ~ Proverbs 3:33-35

שבט ALMANAC OF THE CHRISTIAN FAITH טבת
SHEVAT TEVET

January 20

Highlights in History

1561 Princes and representatives of German Protestant leaders convened at Naumburg, Germany, for the purpose of securing doctrinal unity, especially in the matter of the Eucharist. The proposed agreement was based on the Augsburg Confession. The Naumburg Convention met through Feb. 8th, but failed in its intended purpose, because Calvinists stood by the "variata" edition of 1540, and Lutherans by the "invariata" of 1531.

1891 Dr. Charles A. Briggs delivered an address at Union Theological Seminary in New York City on "The Authority of the Scriptures," which led to an ensuing heresy trial. The New York Presbytery dismissed the charge of heresy (Nov. 4) but referred the matter to the denomination's General Assembly, which eventually found Briggs guilty and defrocked him.

1942 Nazi officials held the notorious Wannsee Conference in Berlin, at which they decided on their "final solution," which called for a total extermination of Europe's Jews.

Notable Birthdays

1669 Birth of Susannah (née Annesley) Wesley, reformers' mother. The youngest of 25 children, she married at age 20 and bore her clergyman husband Samuel nineteen children, of whom the 15th and 18th were John and Charles Wesley. Susannah's discipline undoubtedly influenced the two brothers, who themselves built a highly systematic order into the character of Methodism. [d. 7/23/1742]

1874 Birth of Karl Heim, German Lutheran systematic theologian. Influenced by the Swabian pietism of J. A. Bengel, he presented the Gospel on a scientific-philosophical level, stressing the contrast between faith and reason and emphasizing the transcendence of faith. Heim's major work was the six-volume *Evangelical Faith and the Thought of the Present*. [d. 8/30/1958]

The Last Passage

1569 Death of Miles Coverdale, 81, English clergyman, and the first scholar to translate the entire Bible into English (1539). Coverdale had earlier completed William Tyndale's translation of the Old Testament. He also edited the second Great Bible (called Cranmer's Bible), in 1540. Parts of Coverdale's Bible were revisions of Tyndale's, but unlike his predecessor, it included no contentious notes, and there was an obsequious dedication to the king. (b. 1488)

1825 Death of John Henry Livingston, 78, Dutch Reformed clergyman and educator. He was the last American to go to Holland for theological training and ordination. Livingston helped reunite the Dutch Reformed Church in the U.S., and also served as president at Queens (later Rutgers) College (1810-1825). (b. 5/30/1746)

Words for the Soul

1758 English founder of Methodism, John Wesley confessed in a letter: *'I cannot think of you, without thinking of God. Others often lead me to Him, as it were, going round about. You bring me straight into His presence.'*

1775 Anglican clergyman John Newton pondered in a letter: *'Why should any, that have tasted that the Lord is gracious, wish to live another day, but that they may have the honour to be fellow-workers with him, instrumental in promoting his designs, and of laying themselves out to the utmost of their abilities and influence in his service?'*

1792 Anglican Evangelical Henry Venn wrote in a letter to his son: *'Usefulness is all, in Christians.'*

1860 American Quaker holiness author Hannah Whitall Smith wrote in a letter: *'Once I knew what it was to rest upon the rock of God's promises, and it was indeed a precious resting place, but now I rest in His grace, He is teaching me that the bosom of His love is a far sweeter resting-place than even the rock of His promises.'*

IN GOD'S WORD... OT: Genesis 41:17–42:17 ~ NT: Matthew 13:24-46 ~ Psalms 18:1-15 ~ Proverbs 4:1-6

שבט ALMANAC OF THE CHRISTIAN FAITH טבת
SHEVAT   TEVET

January 21

Highlights in History

1276 Pierre de Champagni was elected Innocent V, the first Dominican pope. During his brief 6-month reign, he brought peace to the warring cities of Italy.

1525 At a secret (and illegal) gathering of six men in Zurich, Conrad Grebel (Ulrich Zwingli's former protege) rebaptized George Blaurock, a former monk. This meeting is now considered the birth of the German Anabaptist movement.

1549 The first of four British "Acts of Uniformity" were passed. This first Act imposed the exclusive use of the *First Book of Common Prayer of Edward VI* in all public services of the Anglican Church. (The three other Acts of Uniformity were passed in 1552, in 1559 and in 1662.)

1986 Charismatic Bible Ministries was founded in Oklahoma. A fraternal fellowship of charismatic organizations, CBM's stated purpose is to create an organization "far bigger than any denomination." It held its first major conference in June 1986, in Tulsa.

Notable Birthdays

1797 Birth of Edward Mote, hymn author: "The Solid Rock" (a.k.a. "My Hope is Built on Nothing Less"). [d. 11/13/1874]

1849 Birth of Julia Harriette Johnston, American Presbyterian author of S.S. literature and hymnwriter. She created 500 hymn poems, of which the most memorable was: "Grace Greater Than Our Sin" (a.k.a. "Marvelous Grace of our Loving Lord"). [d. 3/6/1919]

1887 Birth of Alfred Henry Ackley, American Presbyterian cello virtuoso and hymnwriter. He composed over 1,500 sacred and secular songs, and helped compile hymnals for the Rodeheaver Publishing Company. But he is best remembered as author/composer of the hymn, "He Lives." [d. 7/3/1960]

The Last Passage

1609 Death of Joseph Justus Scaliger, 68, French Huguenot scholar. He laid the basis for modern textual criticism. (b. 8/5/1540)

1815 Death of Matthias Claudius, 74, German poet. Though he wrote no specific hymns for the church, he did author a great volume of sacred verse, including the stanzas which became the hymn, "We Plough the Fields and Scatter." (b. 8/15/1740)

1886 Death of Laura Maria Sheldon Wright, 76, American missionary to the Seneca Indians in western New York state. She later influenced the establishment of the Thomas Asylum for Orphan and Destitute Indian Children (later the Thomas Indian School). (b. 7/10/1809)

1896 Death of Thomas Armitage, 76, American Baptist clergyman. Born in England, he came to America in 1838 and became a Methodist minister. In 1848 he converted to the Baptist faith and soon established himself as a leading writer and preacher for that denomination. In 1850 he became one of the founders (later president) of the American Bible Union. (b. 8/2/1819)

Words for the Soul

1531 German Reformer Martin Luther, in a sermon, drove home the meaning of John 6:39-40: *'Then, when devil and death come near, no one can help except this Person who says: "I am He who will not lose you; this is the will of the Father." Then one learns what faith really is.'*

1974 Russian Orthodox liturgical scholar Alexander Schmemann noted in his journal: *'I am really not interested at all in any of the Eastern religions provoking such interest in [Mircea] Eliade and others around him.... I am certain that the meeting of East and West is necessary (Eliade's dream), and what he writes about it is quite noteworthy, but ... I feel stifled by these eerie and scary worlds, in spite of their liberating and cosmic character.'*

IN GOD'S WORD... OT: Genesis 42:18–43:34 ~ NT: Matthew 13:47–14:12 ~ Psalms 18:16-36 ~ Proverbs 4:7-10

ALMANAC OF THE CHRISTIAN FAITH

שבט SHEVAT   טבת TEVET

~ January 22 ~

Highlights in History

1899 Pope Leo XIII published the apostolic letter "Testem benevolentiae." Addressed to James Gibbons, Cardinal Archbishop of Baltimore, the letter is remembered primarily as communicating the Vatican's condemnation of "Americanism" — the adaptation of Roman Catholic doctrine to the more independent ideologies of modern civilization, represented primarily by American character. Cardinal Gibbons, in a reply which was not published until 1944, claimed that no Catholic leader in the U.S. had ever held such opinions. Scholars have continued to debate this question ever since.

1978 A special study group of the 2,600,000 member United Presbyterian Church in the U.S.A. recommended the church adopt a policy permitting the ordination of practicing homosexuals who otherwise met the requirements for the clergy. The recommendation was disapproved by the General Assembly in May.

Notable Birthdays

1588 [OS=1/12] Birth of John Winthrop, English-born lawyer. He served twelve terms (1629-48) as first governor of Massachusetts Bay Colony, during which he helped banish Ann Hutchinson. Profoundly religious, Winthrop, who left England because of its persecution of Puritans, believed New England to be "a citty upon a hill" for the world to see and emulate. [d. 4/5/1649]

1838 Birth of George Frederick Wright, American Congregational clergyman, theologian and geologist. He served as editor of "Bibliotheca Sacra" (1884-1921). [d. 4/20/1921]

1843 Birth of Friedrich W. Blass, German biblical philologist. His wide researches produced a New Testament Greek grammar (in German), of which the English translation of the 10th edition has come to be known affectionately as *Blass, Debrunner, Funk*. [d. 3/5/1907]

1855 Birth of Carrie Ellis Breck, hymnwriter: "Face to Face with Christ My Savior." [d. 3/27/1934]

The Last Passage

1876 Death of John Bacchus Dykes, 52, Anglican clergyman and composer. Among his 300 hymn tunes, Dykes is best remembered for DOMINUS REGIT ME ("The King of Love My Shepherd Is"); LUX BENIGNA ("Lead, Kindly Light"); MELITA ("Eternal Father, Strong to Save") and VOX DILECTI ("I Heard the Voice of Jesus Say"). (b. 3/10/1823)

1913 Death of John Julian, 73, English musicologist extraordinaire. He devoted his life to sacred music research, represented in his monumental *Dictionary of Hymnology* (1892), which was updated and reissued (1957). (b. 1/27/1839)

1922 Death of Giacomodella Chiesa, 67, Italian cardinal. He was elected Pope Benedict XV in 1914, following the death of Pius X. Called "the Pope of the Missions," his pontificate main tained neutrality, urged peace and spurred missionary activity. (b. 11/21/1854)

Words for the Soul

1522 German Reformer Martin Luther declared in a letter to George Spalatin: *'Love cares for the problems of others as if they were one's own.'*

1947 U.S. Senate Chaplain Peter Marshall prayed: *'Deliver us, O Lord, from the foolishness of impatience. Let us not be in such a hurry as to run on without Thee. We know that it takes a lifetime to make a tree; we know that fruit does not ripen in an afternoon; and Thou Thyself didst take a week to make the universe.'*

1963 Swiss Reformed theologian Karl Barth asserted in a letter: *'In Jesus Christ, God and man... are already at peace — not as enemies but as true companions. In Him salvation is already present and at work.'*

IN GOD'S WORD...   OT: Genesis 44:1–45:28 ~ NT: Matthew 14:13-36 ~ Psalms 18:37-50 ~ Proverbs 4:11-13

ALMANAC OF THE CHRISTIAN FAITH

שבט SHEVAT

טבת TEVET

~ January 23 ~

Highlights in History

1356 Holy Roman Emperor Charles IV (1355-78) enacted the 31-chapter constitution known as the "Golden Bull." The document mandated the selection of German kings by seven electors: archbishops of Mainz, Trier, Cologne; the king of Bohemia, duke of Saxony, margrave of Brandenburg, and the count of the Palatinate. The document received its name from the seal (bulla), which was affixed in gold rather than the more customary wax or lead. Although the "Golden Bull" was theoretically in force until 1806, it ceased to be effective after 1648.

1552 The *Second Prayer Book of Edward VI* (also called the *Second Book of Common Prayer*) became mandatory in England. Among its changes was the exclusion of prayers for the dead and the omission of all references to "Mass" and "Altar."

1789 In Georgetown, Maryland, Father John Carroll, superior of the United States Catholic Mission, founded the Academy of Georgetown — forerunner of Georgetown University, and the first Roman Catholic college established in the United States. Authority to grant degrees was authorized by Congress in 1815.

1950 Israel's parliament named Jerusalem to be the capital of their recently-reclaimed nation, to which the Israeli government afterward transferred all its activities.

1955 The United Presbyterian Church U.S.A. formally approved the ordination of women as clergy, making it the first mainline Protestant denomination to do so.

Notable Birthdays

1635 Birth of Philipp Jakob Spener, German founder of Pietism. His emphasis on spiritual conversion and holy living revitalized German Lutheranism. Spener published his famous tract, *Pia Desideria* (*Pious Desires*) in 1675. [d. 2/5/1705]

1837 Birth of Amanda Berry Smith, an African-American Methodist who rose from slavery and poverty to become a world-famous evangelist and missionary. [d. 2/24/1915]

The Last Passage

1893 Death of Phillips Brooks, 55, American Episcopal bishop. Considered one of the greatest preachers of his generation, Brooks delivered the funeral sermon for Abraham Lincoln, and in 1868 penned the Christmas hymn, "O Little Town of Bethlehem." (b. 12/13/1835)

1915 Death of Anna B. Warner (pen name Amy Lathrop), 87, prolific American author of children's fiction. She never married, but lived with her sister Susan in New York state. In 1860, a novel they co-authored contained a poem which became one of the most beloved of all children's hymns: "Jesus Loves Me, This I Know." (b. 8/31/1827)

1941 Death of John Oxenham (born William A. Dunkerley), 88, English novelist and poet. Among his several writings, Oxenham is most remembered for the hymn, "In Christ There Is No East or West." (b. 11/12/1852)

Words for the Soul

1771 During his first year as missionary in America, English-born Methodist bishop and circuit rider Francis Asbury drew this observation in his journal: *'Though a stranger in a strange land, God has taken care of me.'*

1777 Anglican Evangelical Henry Venn wrote in a letter to his son: *'A family fearing God, working righteousness, obtaining promises, living in peace and love, is a picture of Heaven in miniature.'*

1935 British Bible expositor Arthur W. Pink commented in a letter: *'Growth in grace is like the growth of a cow's tail – the more it truly grows, the closer to the ground it is brought.'*

IN GOD'S WORD... OT: Genesis 46:1–47:31 ~ NT: Matthew 15:1-28 ~ Psalms 19:1-14 ~ Proverbs 4:14-19

January 24

Highlights in History

1722 In Cambridge, MA, Edward Wigglesworth was named to fill the Thomas Hollis chair at Harvard College, thereby becoming the first divinity professor in the American colonies. He served until his death on January 16, 1765.

1989 Rev. Barbara C. Harris, 55, of Boston, was confirmed as the first female bishop in the history of the Church of England. (Her ordination ceremony took place on February 11, 1989.)

Notable Birthdays

1573 Birth of John Donne, renowned English metaphysical poet and dean of St. Paul's Church, London (1621-24). His preaching was unexcelled in the 17th century, and he is known for such memorable lines as: "Death be not proud"; "No man is an island"; and "Ask not for whom the bell tolls? It tolls for thee." [d. 3/31/1631]

1818 Birth of John Mason Neale, Anglican clergyman and hymnwriter. Ordained in 1842, he became a champion of social welfare. Neale also translated many Eastern Christian liturgical writings into English, including the hymns, "All Glory, Laud and Honor," "Good Christian Men, Rejoice," "Jerusalem the Golden," "O Come, O Come, Emmanuel" and "The Day of Resurrection." [d. 8/6/1866]

1902 Birth of Ephraim A. Speiser, American Jewish Semitics scholar (Univ. of PA 1931-65). His researches showed that archaeological records support the historical background of the Old Testament. Speiser authored the "Genesis" volume of the *Anchor Bible Commentary*. [d. 6/15/1965]

1918 Birth of Oral Roberts, American charismatic faith healer and evangelist. He built up his Pentecostal Church to millions of members through personal and media evangelism. He was also founder and first president of Oral Roberts University, in Tulsa, OK (1963–).

The Last Passage

1737 Death of William Wake, 80, Archbishop of Canterbury from 1716-37. Between 1717-20 he negotiated with French Jansenists on a proposed union with the Anglican Church. A man of liberal views, Wake was in sympathy with the English Nonconformists. (b. 1/26/1657)

1986 Death of L. Ron Hubbard, 74, American sectarian religious leader. Born in Tilden, Nebraska, he founded Church of Scientology (1954), based on his book *Dianetics: The Modern Science of Mental Health*. (b. 3/13/1911)

1978 Death of William Barclay, 70, Scottish clergyman and theologian. He taught New Testament at the University of Glasgow (1947-74). Rudolf Bultmann called him the most evangelical preacher he had ever heard, because all his writings aimed at confronting the individual with Christ. Of his literary output, which was immense, Barclay's most influential writing was his *Daily Study Bible* series. (b. 12/5/1907)

Words for the Soul

1738 Four months before his life-changing conversion at Aldersgate Church in London, English missionary John Wesley, 34, penned in his journal: 'I went to America to convert the Indians. But oh! who shall convert me? I have a fair summer religion; I can talk well; nay, and believe myself, while no danger is near. But let death look me in the face, and my spirit is troubled. Nor can I say, "To die is gain!"'

1760 English founder of Methodism John Wesley wrote in a letter: 'Even the rich _may_ enter the kindgom: For with God all things are possible.'

1986 Dutch Catholic diarist Henri J. M. Nouwen, on his 54th birthday, reflected in his *Road to Daybreak* journal: 'I am still the restless, nervous, intense, distracted, and impulse-driven person I was when I set out on this spiritual journey. At times this obvious lack of inner maturation depresses me as I enter into the "mature" years.'

IN GOD'S WORD... OT: Genesis 48:1–49:33 ~ NT: Matthew 15:29–16:12 ~ Psalms 20:1-9 ~ Proverbs 4:20-27

שבט | ALMANAC OF THE CHRISTIAN FAITH | טבת
SHEVAT | | TEVET

~ January 25 ~

Highlights in History

1077 In Canossa, Italy, Holy Roman emperor Henry IV (1050-1106) began a penance in submission to Pope Gregory VII. The king is said to have stood in the snow outside the pope's lodging three days before Gregory absolved Henry from his excommunication of him.

1841 In England, at the height of the Oxford Movement, John Henry Newman's famous *Tract 90* appeared, comprised of a Catholic interpretation of Anglicanism's "Thirty-nine Articles." An ensuing storm of controversy brought the series (begun in 1833) to an end. Newman, then Bishop of Oxford, was forced to resign his parish. (In 1845 he converted to Catholicism.)

1944 In the Anglican Diocese of Hong Kong and South China, Bishop R. O. Hall ordained Florence Tim-Oi Lee of Macao a priest at Shie Hing in Kwangtung Province, China. It was an emergency wartime measure, owing to the lack of male priests in Macao. In 1946 the Diocesan Synod of Hong Kong and South China endorsed the action, thereby making Florence Tim-Oi Lee the first-ever female Anglican clergyperson.

Notable Birthdays

1825 Birth of Edward Henry Bickersteth, English clergyman and hymnwriter. He served as Bishop of Exeter (1885-1900), and authored 12 books, including *Psalms and Hymns* (1858). Hymnnologist John Julian suggests that Bickersteth's best works were hymns he penned for private devotions, including one enduring favorite: "Peace, Perfect Peace." [d. 5/16/1906]

1863 Birth of Rufus M. Jones, American Quaker scholar, educator, humanitarian and mystic. He was a founder of the American Friends Service Committee (1917), and professor of philosophy at Haverford College (1904-34). He also shared the 1947 Nobel Peace Prize. [d. 6/16/1948]

The Last Passage

1887 Death of Roland Hugh Prichard, 76, Welsh hymn composer: HYFRYDOL ("Come, Thou Long-Expected Jesus"). (b. 1/14/1811)

1949 Death of Peter Marshall, 46, Scottish-born American Presbyterian minister. He emigrated to the U.S. in 1927, and pastored New York Avenue Presbyterian Church in Washington, D.C. (1937-49). Serving as U.S. Senate chaplain, 1947-49, he died suddenly, and was later immortalized in the book by his widow, Catherine Marshall: *A Man Called Peter* (1951). (b. 5/27/1902)

1972 Death of Frank Houghton, 78, Anglican clergyman and hymnwriter. Consecrated Bishop of East Szechwan in 1937, Houghton served from 1940-1951 as General Director of the China Inland Mission. Today he is better remembered for authoring the hymn, "Thou Who Wast Rich Beyond All Splendour." (b. 1894)

Words for the Soul

1534 In the words of a sermon, German Reformer Martin Luther offered a definition of spiritual conversion: 'To be converted to God means to believe in Christ, to believe that He is our Mediator and that we have eternal life through Him.'

1771 English founder of Methodism John Wesley assured in a letter: 'All the knowledge you want is comprised in one book – the Bible. When you understand this, you will know enough.'

1786 Anglican Evangelical Henry Venn wrote in a letter: 'Too many parents greatly err, in expecting the religion of a child should be nearly the same as their own.'

1984 In his Second Inaugural Address, President Ronald Reagan clarified: 'America was founded by people who believed that God was their rock of safety. I recognize we must be cautious in claiming that God is on our side, but I think it's all right to keep asking if we're on His side.'

IN GOD'S WORD... OT: Genesis 50:1–Exodus 2:10 ~ NT: Matthew 16:13–17:9 ~ Psalms 21:1-13 ~ Proverbs 5:1-6

ALMANAC OF THE CHRISTIAN FAITH

שבט SHEVAT | טבת TEVET

~ January 26 ~

Highlights in History

1776 Rev. Louis Eustace Lotbinière was made the first chaplain of the American army. He was appointed by General Benedict Arnold to act as chaplain to the regiment of Colonel James Livingston in the Continental Army.

1951 The Temple Beth Israel of Meridian, MS appointed Paula Ackerman to serve in the place of her late husband as rabbi. It was the first Jewish congregation to allow women to perform the functions of a rabbi. (The first woman to receive ordination as a Reform rabbi was Sally Jane Priesand, who was ordained June 3, 1972, at the Isaac M. Wise Temple in Cincinnati, OH. The Conservative movement ordained its first female rabbi, Amy Eilberg, May 12, 1985, at the Jewish Theological Seminary in New York City.)

Notable Birthdays

1657 Birth of English prelate William Wake, Archbishop of Canterbury from 1716-1737. Wake authored *Principles of the Christian Religion* (1700), a popular commentary on the Catechism of the Anglican Church. [d. 1/24/1737]

1799 Birth of Samuel Gobat, Swiss-born Lutheran prelate and missionary to Abyssinia and Malta. In 1845 he was appointed the second Anglican Bishop of Jerusalem. During his administration (1854-79), Gobat supervised a translation of the Bible into Arabic. [d. 5/11/1879]

1842 Birth of colonial Anglican prelate, Enos Nuttall. He was appointed to St. George's Church in Kingston, Jamaica in 1866, and in 1880 was consecrated the first Anglican archbishop of the West Indies. [d. 5/31/1916]

1905 Birth of Maria Augusta von Trapp, Austrian-American musician. She fled Nazi-occupied Austria in the 1930s and formed the world-famous Trapp Family Singers. Her story became the subject of both the 1959 musical and the 1965 award-winning film, "The Sound of Music." [d. 3/28/1987]

The Last Passage

1902 Death of A. B. Davidson, 70, Scottish biblical scholar. He spent a lifetime on language research and historical interpretation of the Old Testament. Davidson's commentary on Job (1862) became the first scientific treatment of the Old Testament in English. (b. 12/1831)

1962 Death of George Jeffreys, 72, Welsh Pentecostal evangelist. The founder of the Elim Foursquare Gospel Alliance, Jeffreys is claimed by Pentecostals to be "England's greatest evangelist since Wesley and Whitefield." (b. 2/28/1889)

1973 Death of E[li] Stanley Jones, 89, American evangelical Methodist missionary to India (from 1907). He was a close friend of Gandhi, and sought to present the gospel, disentangled from western cultural systems and their sometimes non-Christian expressions. (b. 1/3/1884)

Words for the Soul

1779 English-born pioneer American Methodist bishop and circuit rider Francis Asbury advised in his journal: *'We should so work as if we were to be saved by the proper merit of our works; and so rely on Jesus Christ... as if we did no works.'*

1852 Scottish clergyman and biographer Andrew Bonar noted in his diary: *'I am persuaded that the other world is in a measure felt when a soul is truly in the act of communion with the Lord.'*

1930 American Congregational missionary to the Philippines, Frank C. Laubach confessed in a letter: *'I am disgusted with the pettiness and futility of my unled self. If the way out is not more perfect slavery to God, then what is the way out?'*

1948 U.S. Senate Chaplain Peter Marshall prayed: *'We need Thy help to do something about the world's true problems — the problem of greed, which is often called profit; the problem of license, disguising itself as liberty; the problem of materialism, the hook of which is baited with security.'*

IN GOD'S WORD... OT: Exodus 2:11–3:22 ~ NT: Matthew 17:10-27 ~ Psalms 22:1-18 ~ Proverbs 5:7-14

ALMANAC OF THE CHRISTIAN FAITH

שבט SHEVAT   טבת TEVET

~ January 27 ~

Highlights in History

417 Pelagius, a British monk whose teachings were declared heretical, was excommunicated by Pope Innocent I. Pelagius's doctrine denied original sin and taught that one could become righteous by the exercise of their own free will.

1302 Italian writer Dante Alighieri (1265-1321) was condemned on false charges of religious corruption, and exiled, on pain of death, from Florence. Dante soon began writing *The Divine Comedy*, an epic poem in which he traverses through hell, purgatory, and finally heaven.

1343 Pope Clement VI published the bull "Unigenitus," which gave official papal recognition of the efficacy of indulgences. (In 1518, 175 years later, Cardinal Thomas de Vio Cajetan accused Martin Luther of contravening this point in Clement's papal document.)

1521 The Diet of Worms convened – a 4-month-long series of Imperial meetings held at Worms (to May 25), at which Martin Luther defended his "reforming" doctrines before the Emperor Charles V. On April 18, during this convocation, Luther gave a final refusal to recant his doctrines with his famous statement: *'Hier stehe ich. Ich kann nicht anders. Gott mir helffen. Amen.'*

Notable Birthdays

1662 Birth of Richard Bentley, English divine, classical scholar and Christian apologist against the Deists. He was the first to use philology as a test of literary authenticity, and delivered the 1692 Boyle Lectures in London on the *Evidences of Natural and Revealed Religion*. [d. 7/14/1742]

1825 Birth of William H. Green, American Presbyterian clergyman, Hebrew scholar and American leader of the ultraconservative school of biblical criticism. Green served as chairman of the Anglo-American Bible Revision Committee that produced the *American Standard Version* (ASV) (1901, 1905). [d. 2/10/1900]

1852 Birth of James Rendel Harris, English-born Quaker biblical scholar. In 1889 he discovered the Syriac text of the *Apology of Aristides* (a 2nd century Christian apologist) at the St. Catherine's monastery on Mt. Sinai. [d. 3/1/1941]

The Last Passage

1540 Death of St. Angela Merici, 65, Italian foundress. In 1533 she trained 12 young women to assist her in teaching girls. By 1535 the group had become the Company of St. Ursula. It was formally recognized by Pope Paul III in 1544. Her company has been called 'the oldest and most considerable teaching order of women in the Roman Catholic church.' (b. 3/21/1474)

1683 Death of Roger Williams, 79, English-born American clergyman, founder of Rhode Island Colony and champion of religious toleration. He was the first to advocate complete religious tolerance, and so became founder of the first Baptist church in America. (b. 12/21/1603)

1863 Death of Edward Robinson, 68, American scholar. Considered the father of biblical geography, he traveled through Palestine 1837-40, identifying more biblical archaeological sites than had been discovered since the time of Eusebius of Caesarea. Robinson also edited both "Bibliotheca Sacra" (1843-63), and also Gesenius' *Hebrew-English Lexicon of the Old Testament*. (b. 4/10/1794)

Words for the Soul

1774 Methodist bishop and circuit rider Francis Asbury observed in his journal: *'If my labours should be in vain for the people, the Lord gives me a gracious reward in my own soul.'*

1842 Scottish pastor Robert Murray McCheyne exhorted in a letter: *'Call upon the name of the Lord. Your time may be short, God only knows. The longest lifetime is short enough. It is all that is given you to be converted in. They are the happiest who are brought soonest to the bosom of Jesus.'*

IN GOD'S WORD...   OT: Exodus 4:1–5:21 ~ NT: Matthew 18:1-22 ~ Psalms 22:19-31 ~ Proverbs 5:15-21

שבט SHEVAT — ALMANAC OF THE CHRISTIAN FAITH — טבת TEVET

January 28

Highlights in History

1916 In Washington, D.C., Louis Brandeis was appointed to the United States Supreme Court. He was the first Jewish associate justice.

1977 An 18-page declaration prepared by the Sacred Congregation for the Doctrine of Faith, and personally approved by Pope Paul VI, flatly ruled out the admission of women to the priesthood of the Catholic Church, because women lacked a "natural resemblance which must exist between Christ and his ministers."

Notable Birthdays

1805 Birth of Patrick Fairbairn, Scottish Presbyterian clergyman and theologian. In his *Typology of Scripture* (2 vols., 1845-47), he argued there were many more Old Testament types than those mentioned in the New Testament. Fairbairn also served on the committee for the 1885 *English Revised Version* [ERV] of the Old Testament. [d. 8/6/1874]

1822 Birth of William D. Longstaff, English philanthropist and hymnwriter. He was a close friend of Dwight L. Moody, Ira Sankey and William Booth, and also authored the hymn: "Take Time to Be Holy." [d. 4/2/1894]

1834 Birth of Sabine Baring-Gould, English clergyman, author and hymnwriter. In addition to editing a 15-volume *Lives of the Saints* and various other theological works, he also penned the hymns "Onward, Christian Soldiers" and "Now the Day is Over." [d. 1/2/1924]

1856 Birth of R[euben] A. Torrey, American Congregational clergyman. As successor to Dwight L. Moody, Torrey served as superintendent of the Moody Bible Institute (1889-1908). Later, he became dean of the Bible Institute of Los Angeles (1912-24) and pastor of the Church of the Open Door in Los Angeles (1915-24). [d. 10/26/1928]

The Last Passage

1547 Death of Henry VIII, 55, most renowned of the English kings. Notorious for his conflicts with the Rome over his divorces, he married six times in an attempt to father a male heir to the throne. Henry founded the Anglican Church in 1534, which afterward severed all financial, judicial and administrative links with Roman Catholicism. (b. 6/28/1491)

1613 Death of Sir Thomas Bodley, 68, English diplomat and scholar. He organized Oxford University's famed Bodley Library, which first opened in 1602. (b. 3/2/1545)

1860 Death of Joseph Addison Alexander, 50, American Presbyterian biblical scholar, linguist, educator and author. The son of Archibald Alexander, Joseph was a remarkable linguist who helped prepare the first American edition of *Donnegan's Greek Lexicon*. He also did much to introduce German theological literature in the United States. (b. 4/24/1809)

1896 Death of Joseph Barnby, 57, English organist, choral conductor and composer. He penned 250 hymn tunes, including JUST AS I AM ("Just As I Am, Thine Own to Be"); LAUDES DOMINI ("When Morning Gilds the Skies"); MERRIAL ("Now the Day is Over"); and SANDRINGHAM ("O Perfect Love, All Human Thought Transcending"). (b. 8/12/1838)

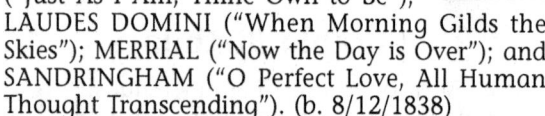

1987 Death of Valerian Trifa, 72, American Romanian Orthodox archbishop. In 1970 he became a founding father of the Orthodox Church in America. (b. 6/28/1914)

Words for the Soul

1860 Scottish clergyman and biographer Andrew Bonar reflected in his diary: *'I have been led to see that family worship is my opportunity of daily ... directly speaking to my ... children for instruction in righteousness, and for quickening for that day. It is not merely a worship together.'*

IN GOD'S WORD... OT: Exodus 5:22–7:24 ~ NT: Matthew 18:23–19:12 ~ Psalms 23:1-6 ~ Proverbs 5:22-23

שבט ALMANAC OF THE CHRISTIAN FAITH טבת
SHEVAT   TEVET

~ January 29 ~

Highlights in History

993 Ulrich (c. 890-973), bishop of Augsburg from 923, was officially declared a saint by Pope John XV at the Lateran Synod held on this date. It was the first recorded canonization by a pope.

1523 At a public disputation with papal representative Johann Faber in Zurich, reformer Ulrich Zwingli successfully defended 67 theses opposing Catholicism before an audience of 600. Following the debate, the Zurich city council gave Zwingli their full support and the city declared itself independent from Roman episcopal control. The Swiss Reformation had begun.

1972 The historic separation of white and black Methodist conferences in South Carolina ended when the two bodies met together for the first time, voting to accept a plan of union.

Notable Birthdays

1499 Birth of Katherine von Bora, the former German nun who married Martin Luther. Born into a noble family, Katherine became a Cistercian nun in 1515, but ran away from the convent in 1523. When she and Luther married in 1525, she was 26 and he was 41. All biographers agree their marriage was a happy one, and produced six children. Katy survived her husband by only six years. [d. 12/20/1552]

1688 Birth of Emmanuel Swedenborg, Swedish scientist, mystic, and theologian. Known for his voluminous works on interpretations of the Bible, he inspired the founding, after his death, of the Church of the New Jerusalem (Swedenborgian Church). Two famous Swedenborgians in American history were Johnny Appleseed and Helen Keller. [d. 3/29/1772]

1850 Birth of Rufus H. McDaniel, American Disciples of Christ clergyman and author of over 100 hymns, including: "Since Jesus Came Into My Heart." [d. 2/13/1940]

The Last Passage

1855 Death of William Capers, 65, American Methodist missionary and prelate. He ministered to the Creek Indians, and to African-Americans on hundreds of plantations. Capers later served as a bishop of the Methodist Episcopal Church, South (1846-55). (b. 1/26/1790)

1918 Death of George Thomas Caldbeck, 66, Irish-born schoolmaster, and independent itinerant preacher. He had wanted to be a missionary, but ill health prevented his acceptance. Today, Caldbeck is remembered as a hymnwriter: PAX TECUM ("Peace, Perfect Peace"). (b. 1852)

1929 Death of Charles Fox Parham, 55, American evangelist and founder of the modern Pentecostal movement. Influenced by the Holiness movement, he founded and directed Bethel College in Topeka, KS where, on January 1, 1901, student Agnes Ozman became the first person in modern times to speak in tongues. (b. 6/4/1873)

Words for the Soul

1780 English-born pioneer American Methodist bishop and circuit rider Francis Asbury noted a personal secret for Christian victory in his journal: *'My soul is more at rest from the tempter when I am busily employed.'*

1930 American Congregational missionary to the Philippines Frank C. Laubach wrote in a letter: *'I feel simply carried along each hour, doing my part in a plan which is far beyond myself. This sense of cooperation with God in little things is what so astonishes me; God takes care of all the rest.'*

1973 Russian Orthodox liturgical scholar Father Alexander Schmemann reflected in his journal: *'Twenty-five years ago, ... it seemed to me that, either today or maybe tomorrow, I would sit down, think a little, and sort it all out. I thought I just had to find some leisure. But after twenty-five years, when without any doubt the greater part of my life is over, there is less clarity than ever.'*

IN GOD'S WORD... OT: Exodus 7:25-9:35 ~ NT: Matthew 19:13-30 ~ Psalms 24:1-10 ~ Proverbs 6:1-5

שבט ALMANAC OF THE CHRISTIAN FAITH טבת
SHEVAT   TEVET

~ January 30 ~

Highlights in History

1536 Parish priest Menno Simons left the Catholic church over his doubts about transubstantiation. He converted to the Anabaptist faith, and led a group of followers who eventually would come to be called "Mennonites."

1592 Clement VIII was elected pope, served until 1605. He ordered revisions in the Vulgate, breviary, and liturgical books. The revised Vulgate (known as the Clementine) was issued in 1592, and served as the standard Bible text of the Catholic Church for more than 300 years.

1750 In Colonial America, the Rev. Jonathan Mayhew of Boston delivered a sermon entitled, "Discourse Concerning Unlimited Submission." The sermon attacked both the divine right of kings and ecclesiastical absolutism.

Notable Birthdays

1517 Birth of Johannes Aurifaber (of Breslau), German reformer and church administrator. He formed a close, lifelong friendship with Philipp Melanchthon, and in 1551-52 took a leading part in the drafting and promulgation of the Mecklenburg church order. [d. 10/19/1568]

1801 Birth of Pierre Jean De Smet, the Belgian-born Jesuit missionary who labored 30 years among the American Indians of the Pacific Northwest. Also, as an intermediary between the Indians and the U.S. government, De Smet was once the only white man who could safely enter the camp of Sitting Bull. [d. 5/23/1873]

1813 Birth of Samuel P. Tregelles, English Presbyterian Biblical scholar. Having learned Greek, Hebrew and Aramaic while still a boy, in 1838 he conceived of a new critical text of the N.T. which should replace the "Textus Receptus." He spent the rest of his life traveling and collating Greek texts. The result of his research was published as *An Account of the Printed Text of the Greek New Testament* (1870). [d. 4/24/1875]

The Last Passage

1644 William Chillingworth, 42, Anglican clergyman and theologian, died in captivity during the English Civil War. His book, *The Religion of Protestants a Safe Way to Salvation* (1638), was a defense of the sole authority of the Bible in matters of salvation and of the individual's right to interpret it. Chillingworth was best known for his statement 'The Bible, the Bible alone ... is the religion of Protestants.' (b. 10/12/1602)

1869 Death of Charlotte A. Barnard, 38, English pastor's wife. She was one of the most prolific ballad writers of the 19th century, and authored the hymn, "Jesus, Tender Shepherd." She also composed the hymn tune BARNARD ("Give of Your Best to the Master"). (b. 12/23/1830)

1896 Death of William H. Furness, 93, American Unitarian clergyman and writer. He served First Unitarian Congregational Church in Philadelphia (1825-75), and was a pioneer in pointing out the distinction between the Jesus of history and the Christ of theology. Furness authored *Remarks on the Four Gospels* (1836) and *A History of Jesus* (1850). (b. 4/20/1802)

Words for the Soul

1788 English-born pioneer American Methodist bishop and circuit rider Francis Asbury set down this personal observation in his journal: *'Alas for the rich! They are so soon offended.'*

1839 Scottish preacher Robert Murray McCheyne, recovering from an illness some distance away from his congregation, encouraged them in a letter: *'God feeds the wild flowers on the lonely mountain side, without the help of man.... So God can feed his own planted ones without the help of man, by the sweetly falling dew of his Spirit.'*

1857 Scottish clergyman and biographer Andrew Bonar declared in his diary: *'In hour by hour living in fellowship I greatly fail, and yet I prize it above all things.'*

IN GOD'S WORD... OT: Exodus 10:1–12:13 ~ NT: Matthew 20:1-28 ~ Psalms 25:1-15 ~ Proverbs 6:6-11

שבט ALMANAC OF THE CHRISTIAN FAITH טבת

SHEVAT · TEVET

~ January 31 ~

Highlights in History

314 Sylvester I was elected 33rd pope of the Catholic Church. During his long pontificate (–335), Sunday was first decreed as a state holiday; the Arian dispute (denying the eternal divinity of Christ) arose; and the first Nicene Council was held, resulting in the Nicene Creed which declared God the Son was "homoousios" (of the same eternal substance) with God the Father.

1911 In North Carolina, the Fire-Baptized Holiness Church (FBHC) and the Pentecostal Holiness Church (PHC) officially merged. Four years later, in 1915, the Tabernacle Pentecostal Church (TPC) also joined the merger. In 1975, the name of this united body officially became the International Pentecostal Holiness Church (IPHC).

Notable Birthdays

1640 Birth of Samuel Willard, New England theologian and president of Harvard College. His monthly lectures delivered on the Westminster Assembly's Shorter Catechism were published posthumously (1726) in the first major folio-size book published in America. [d. 9/12/1707]

1714 Birth of Howell Harris, Welsh lay evangelist. He was a founder of Welsh Calvinistic Methodism and the first lay preacher in the movement. As "the Welsh Boanerges," Harris underwent an evangelical conversion in 1735, and founded the religious community at his hometown of Trevecca in 1752. [d. 7/21/1773]

1915 Birth of Thomas Merton (as Tom Feverel), French-American Catholic Trappist monk, mystic, poet and author. More than anyone else in the 20th century, Merton succeeded in interpreting to the Western mind the meaning of contemplation and the role of the monk. He published his autobiography, *The Seven Storey Mountain*, in 1948. [d. 12/10/1968]

The Last Passage

1561 Death of Menno Simons, 65 or 69, Dutch Anabaptist leader. Emerging out of obscurity in 1524, Menno's leadership gave a united direction to the Anabaptists of Holland and Northern Germany. From him the Mennonite Church of today takes its name. (b. 1492 or 1496)

1892 Death of English Baptist clergyman Charles H. Spurgeon, 57. A powerful orator, and the most popular preacher of his day, Spurgeon's London congregation grew to 6,000. He was a prolific writer as well: his sermons alone fill over 50 large volumes. (b. 6/19/1834)

1955 Death of John R. Mott, 89, American Methodist YMCA and missions leader. A pioneer of the ecumenical movement, he led in founding the World Council of Churches. (b. 5/25/1865)

Words for the Soul

1843 Two months before his premature death at age 39, Scottish clergyman Robert Murray McCheyne wrote in a letter: *'Is not a Christian's darkest hour calmer than the world's brightest?'*

1908 Three years before her death at 79, American Quaker holiness author Hannah Whitall Smith wrote in a letter to her daughter: *'To grow old... in this life only means a day by day nearer approach to the entrance upon another life far higher and grander than this life is or ever could be; and naturally I am in a hurry to get there.'*

1949 American missionary and Auca Indian martyr Jim Elliot concluded in his journal: *'One does not surrender a life in an instant – that which is lifelong can only be surrendered in a lifetime.'*

1952 British Christian literary scholar C.S. Lewis wrote in a letter: *'That suffering is not always sent as a punishment is clearly established for believers by the book of Job and by John 9:1-4. That it sometimes is, is suggested by parts of the Old Testament and Revelation. It would certainly be most dangerous to assume that any given pain was penal.'*

IN GOD'S WORD... OT: Exodus 12:14–13:16 ~ NT: Matthew 20:29–21:22 ~ Psalms 25:16-22 ~ Proverbs 6:12-15

JANUARY INDEX

A

ABCFM 1/10, 1/13
Abolition 1/3, 1/10
Ackerman, Paula 1/26
Ackley, Alfred Henry
  b. 1/21/1887 [d. 7/3/1960]
Act of Supremacy 1/15
Acts of Uniformity, British 1/21
Aelred [Ethelred]
  (b. 1109) d. 1/12/1167
Aethelred II, English King
  (978-1016) 1/5
AFRICAN-AMERICANS
  Burgess, John M. 1/17
  Christian Methodist Episcopal Church 1/3
  Colored Methodist Episcopal Church 1/3
  First black S.S. in the U.S. 1/11
  Grace, Charles Emmanuel 1/12
  Harris, Barbara C. 1/24
  House of Prayer for All People 1/12
  Jones, Charles P. 1/19
  Lowe, Kelly 1/11
  Smith, Amanda Berry 1/23
  South Carolina Methodism 1/29
Alexander, Archibald 1/28
Alexander, Joseph Addison
  (b. 4/24/1809) d. 1/28/1860
Alexander, Moses 1/4
Alexander VI, Pope (1492-1503)
  b. 1/1/1431 [d. 8/18/1503]
Alford, Henry
  (b. 10/7/1810) d. 1/12/1871
Allen, William
  b. 1/2/1532 [d. 10/16/1594]
Alwood, Josiah Kelley
  b. 1/13/1909 [d. 7/15/1828]
American Bishops Committee 1/18
American Friends Service Committee 1/25
American Sunday School Union 1/11
Americanism 1/22
Anglo-American Bible Revision Committee 1/27
Anglo-Catholic movement 1/17
Anne of Cleves 1/6
Anthony of Egypt, St.
  (b. ca. 251) d. 1/17/356
Anthony the Abbot
  (b. ca. 251) d. 1/17/356
Archbishop of Armagh 1/4
Arianism 1/7
Armitage, Thomas
  (b. 7/10/1809) d. 1/21/1896
Arnold, Benedict 1/26
Athanasius 1/7
Athenagoras I, Ecumenical Patriarch 1/5
Augsburg Confession 1/20
Aurifaber (of Breslau), Johannes
  b. 1/30/1517 [d. 10/19/1568]
Avignon Papacy 1/5, 1/17
Aylward, Gladys May
  (b. 2/24/1902) d. 1/3/1970
Ayres, Ann
  b. 1/3/1816 [d. 2/9/1896]

B

Backus, Isaac 1/16
  b. 1/9/1724 [d. 11/20/1806]
Baden-Powell, Robert Smyth
  (b. 2/22/1857) d. 1/8/1941
Barclay, William
  (b. 12/5/1907) d. 1/24/1978
Baring-Gould, Sabine
  b. 1/28/1834 d. 1/2/1924
Barnard, Charlotte A.
  (b. 12/23/1830) d. 1/30/1869
Barnby, Joseph
  (b. 8/12/1838) d. 1/28/1896
BATTLES
  Assunpink, Battle of 1/2
  Trenton, Second Battle of 1/2
  Vassy, Massacre at 1/17
Beaufort, Pierre Roger de 1/5. See Gregory XI, Pope (1371-78)
Bede the Venerable 1/12
Beecher, Henry Ward 1/9, 1/10
Beecher, Lyman
  (b. 10/12/1775) d. 1/10/1863
Benedict XV, Pope (1914-22) 1/22
Bengel, J. A. 1/20
Bentley, Richard
  b. 1/27/1662 [d. 7/14/1742]
Bernard of Clairvaux, St. 1/12
BIBLE VERSIONS
  American Standard Version (1905) 1/27
  An American Translation (1923, 1939) 1/13
  Arabic Version 1/26
  Authorized Version (1611) 1/16
  Complutensian Polyglot (1514) 1/10
  Coverdale's Bible 1/20
  Cranmer's Bible (1540) 1/20
  English Revised Version [ERV] 1/28
  Great Bible (1540) 1/20
  King James (1611) 1/4, 1/16
  New American Bible (1970) 1/18
  Septuagint (Greek O.T.) 1/9
Biblical chronology 1/4
BIBLICAL MANUSCRIPTS
  Codex Sinaiticus 1/18
  Textus Receptus 1/30
Bickersteth, Edward Henry 1/16
  b. 1/25/1825 [d. 5/16/1906]
Biddle, John 1/14
Biscop, Benedict
  (b. ca. 628) d. 1/12/689
Blass, Friedrich W.
  b. 1/22/1843 [d. 3/5/1907]
Blaurock, George 1/21
Boberg, Carl Gustaf
  (b. 8/16/1859) d. 1/7/1940
Bodley Library 1/28
Bodley, Thomas
  (b. 1545) d. 1/28/1613
Bomberger, John H. A.
  b. 1/13/1817 [d. 8/19/1890]
Booth, Catherine [née Mumford]
  b. 1/17/1829 [d. 10/4/1890]
Booth, William 1/17, 1/28
Bora, Katherine von
  b. 1/29/1499 [d. 12/20/1552]
Borgia, Rodrigo 1/1
Boston Society for Religious and Moral Improvement 1/18
Boy Scouts 1/8
Bradbury, William B.
  (b. 10/6/1816) d. 1/7/1868
Brandeis, Louis 1/28
Breck, Carrie Ellis
  b. 1/22/1855 [d. 3/27/1934]
Briggs, Charles A. 1/20
  b. 1/15/1841 [d. 6/8/1913]
British Broadcasting Company 1/6
Brock, Blanche (née Kerr) 1/6
Brock, Virgil P.
  b. 1/6/1887 [d. 1978]
Brooks, Phillips
  (b. 12/13/1835) d. 1/23/1893
Brown, Francis 1/15
Brown, Raymond E. 1/18
Bultmann, Rudolf 1/24
Burgess, John M. 1/17
Buswell, J[ames] O., Jr.
  b. 1/16/1895 [d. 1977]
Byrne, Mary Elizabeth
  (b. 7/1/1880) d. 1/19/1931

C

Cajetan, Thomas de Vio 1/27
Caldbeck, George Thomas
  (b. 1852) d. 1/29/1918
Campbell, Alexander 1/1, 1/4
Campbell, Thomas
  (b. 2/1/1763) d. 1/4/1854
CANTERBURY ARCHBISHOPS
  Fisher, Geoffrey F. (1945-61) 1/19
  Laud, William (1633-40) 1/10
  Ramsey, Arthur Michael (1961-74) 1/19
  Wake, William (1716-37) 1/24, 1/26
Capers, William
  (b. 1/26/1790) d. 1/29/1855
Carbon dating 1/5
Carmichael, Amy Wilson
  (b. 12/16/1867) d. 1/18/1951
Carroll, John 1/23
  b. 1/8/1735 [d. 12/3/1815]
Caswall, Edward
  (b. 7/15/1814) d. 1/2/1878
Catherine de Médicis 1/17
Catherine of Aragón 1/15
Catholic Biblical Association of America (CBA) 1/18
Champagni, Pierre de 1/21
Charismatic Bible Ministries 1/21
Charles IV, Holy Roman Emperor (1355-78) 1/23
Charles V, Holy Roman Emperor (1520-56) 1/27
Chiesa, Giacomo della
  (b. 11/21/1854) d. 1/22/1922
Chillingworth, William
  (b. 1602) d. 1/30/1644
Claudius, Matthias
  (b. 8/15/1740) d. 1/21/1815
Clement VI, Pope (1342-52) 1/27
Clement VII, Pope (1523-34) 1/15
Clement VIII, Pope (1592-1605) 1/30
Cochlaeus, Johannes
  b. 1/10/1479 [d. 1/10/1552]
Codex Sinaiticus 1/18
Columbus, Christopher 1/6
Communism, Chinese 1/11
Confraternity of Christian Doctrine 1/18
Congregation for the Propagation of the Faith 1/9
Connelly, Cornelia A. P.
  b. 1/15/1809 [d. 4/18/1879]

JANUARY INDEX

Constantine I, Roman Emperor (312-37) 1/1
Continental Army, American 1/26
Conybeare, Frederick C.
  (b. 1856) d. 1/9/1924
Corporation of Poor and Distressed Presbyterian Ministers 1/11
COUNCILS, CHURCH
  Council of Trent (1545-63) 1/13, 1/17
  Fourth Lateran Council (1215) 1/8
  Lateran Synod (993) 1/29
  Nicene Council (325) 1/31
  Synod of Bern (1532) 1/9
  Synod of Dort (1619) 1/8
Coverdale, Miles
  b. 1488 [d. 1/20/1569]
CREEDS, CONFESSIONS
  "Thirty-Nine Articles" 1/25
  Westminster Assembly's Shorter Catechism 1/31
Cromwell, Oliver 1/14
Cromwell, Thomas 1/6
CRUSADES
  Fourth Crusade 1/8
Cub Scouts 1/8
CULTS & SECTS, CHRISTIAN
  Church of the New Jerusalem 1/29
  Mental Healing 1/16
  New Thought 1/16
  Swedenborgian Church 1/29
Cuyler, Theodore Ledyard
  b. 1/10/1822 [d. 2/26/1909]

D

Damien, Father
  b. 1/3/1840 [d. 4/15/1889]
Dante Alighieri 1/27
Darboy, Georges
  b. 1/16/1813 [d. 5/24/1871]
Darwall, John
  b. 1/13/1731 [d. 12/18/1789]
Davidson, A. B.
  (b. 12/1831) d. 1/26/1902
De Smet, Pierre Jean
  b. 1/30/1801 [d. 5/23/1873]
de Veuster, Joseph
  b. 1/3/1840 [d. 4/15/1889]
Dickson, Lillian
  (b. 1901) [d. 1/14/1983]
Diet of Worms (1521) 1/27
Diocese of the Armenian Church of America 1/18
Divine Right of Kings 1/10
Dobneck, Wendelstinus
  b. 1/10/1479 [d. 1/10/1552]
Donne, John
  b. 1/24/1573 [d. 3/31/1631]

Dooley, Thomas A.
  b. 1/17/1927 [d. 1/18/1961]
Driver, Samuel R. 1/15
Duncan, Mary Lundie
  (b. 4/26/1814) d. 1/5/1840)
Duncan, William Wallace 1/5
Dunkerley, William A.. See Oxenham, John
  (b. 11/12/1852) d. 1/23/1941]
Durham, William H. 1/2
Dwight, Timothy
  (b. 5/14/1752) d. 1/11/1817
Dykes, John Bacchus
  (b. 3/10/1823) d. 1/22/1876

E

Edward the Confessor, English King (1042-66)
  (b. 1003) d. 1/5/1066
Edward VI, English King (1547-53) 1/21, 1/23
Edwards, Jonathan 1/11
Eilberg, Amy 1/26
Eliade, Mircea 1/21. See also QUOTATIONS
Elim Foursquare Gospel Alliance 1/26
Eliot, T[homas] S[tearns]
  (b. 9/26/1888) d. 1/4/1965
Elliot, Elizabeth 1/8
Elliot, Jim. See also QUOTATIONS
  (b. 10/8/1927) d. 1/8/1956
Episcopius (Bisschop), Simon
  b. 1/8/1583 [d. 4/4/1643]
Erasmus, Desiderius 1/14, 1/16
Eucharistic Fast 1/16
Eusebius of Caesarea 1/27
Everest, Charles W.
  (b. 5/27/1814) d. 1/11/1877
Ewing, Alexander
  b. 1/3/1830 [d. 7/11/1895]

F

Faber, Johann 1/29
Fabian, Pope St. (236-250) 1/10
Fairbairn, Patrick 1/28
Father Damien. See de Veuster, Joseph
Fawcett, John
  b. 1/6/1740 [d. 7/25/1817]
Feverel, Tom. See also Merton, Thomas
  b. 1/31/1915 [d. 12/10/1968]
"Final Solution" 1/20. See also JUDAISM
First Amendment to the U.S. Constitution 1/16

First Day Society 1/11
Fleming, Pete 1/8
Ford, Francis Xavier
  b. 1/11/1892 [d. 2/21/1952]
Fosdick, Harry E. 1/18
Fox, George. See also QUOTATIONS
  (b. 7/1624) d. 1/13/1691
Frederick III, the Wise (1486-1525) 1/14, 1/17
Friends of the Truth (Quakers) 1/13
Frost, Henry Weston
  b. 1/7/1858 [d. 1/8/1945]
Furness, William H.
  (b. 4/20/1802) d. 1/30/1896

G

Gavazzi, Alessandro
  (b. 3/21/1809) d. 1/9/1889
Genetics, Laws of 1/6
Ghislieri, Michele Cardinal
  b. 1/17/1504 [d. 5/1/1572]
Gibbons, James Cardinal 1/22
Gilmour, Henry Lake
  b. 1/19/1836 [d. 5/20/1920]
Girl Scouts 1/8
Glossbrenner, John Jacob
  (b. 7/24/1813) d. 1/7/1887
Gobat, Samuel
  b. 1/26/1799 [d. 5/11/1879]
Golden Bull, The 1/23
Goodspeed, Edgar J.
  (b. 10/23/1871) d. 1/13/1962
Gore, Charles
  (b. 1/22/1853) d. 1/17/1932
Grace, Charles Emmanuel
  (b. 1/25/1881) d. 1/12/1960
"Graf-Wellhausen Hypothesis" 1/7
Great Schism 1/17
Grebel, Conrad 1/5, 1/21
Green, William H.
  b. 1/27/1825 [d. 2/10/1900]
Gregory VII, Pope (1073-85) 1/25
Gregory XI, Pope (1370-78) 1/5, 1/17
Gregory XV, Pope (1621-23)
  b. 1/9/1554 [d. 7/8/1623]
Griesbach, J. J.
  b. 1/4/1745 [d. 3/24/1812]

H

Hall, R. O. 1/25
Hamlin, Cyrus 1/5
Hampton Court Conference 1/14, 1/16

Harris, Barbara C. 1/24
Harris, Howell
  b. 1/31/1714 [d. 7/21/1773]
Harris, James Rendel 1/28
  b. 1/27/1852 [d. 3/1/1941]
Hawks, Annie Sherwood
  (b. 5/28/1835) d. 1/3/1918
Heidelberg Catechism 1/19
Heim, Karl
  b. 1/20/1874 [d. 8/30/1958]
Henry IV, Holy Roman Emperor (1050-1106) 1/25
Henry VIII, English King (1509-47) 1/6, 1/15
  (b. 6/28/1491) d. 1/28/1547
HERESIES, CHRISTIAN
  Arianism 1/7, 1/31
HERETICS, CHRISTIAN
  Pelagius 1/27
Higher Criticism 1/9
Hine, Russell K. 1/7
Hitler, Adolf 1/14
"Homoousios" 1/31
Homosexuals, Ordination of 1/22
Hort, F. J. A. 1/12
Houghton, Frank
  (b. 1894) d. 1/25/1972
House of Prayer for All People 1/12
Hubbard, L. Ron
  (b. 3/13/1911) d. 1/24/1986
Hull, Eleanor Henrietta
  b. 1/15/1860 d. 1/13/1935
Hutchinson, Ann 1/22
HYMNS
  "A Charge to Keep I Have" 1/8
  "All Glory, Laud and Honor" 1/24
  "All Hail the Power of Jesus' Name" 1/18
  "Ask Ye What Great Thing I Know" 1/12
  "At Even, Ere the Sun Did Set" 1/19
  "Be Thou My Vision" 1/13, 1/15, 1/19
  "Beyond the Sunset" 1/6
  "Blest Be the Tie That Binds" 1/6
  "Come, Thou Long-Expected Jesus" 1/14, 1/25
  "Come, Ye Thankful People, Come" 1/12
  "Eternal Father, Strong to Save" 1/22
  "Face to Face with Christ My Savior" 1/22
  "From Greenland's Icy Mountains" 1/8
  "Give of Your Best to the Master" 1/30
  "God Be With You Till We Meet Again" 1/2
  "God of Our Life, Through All the Circling Years" 1/11
  "Good Christian Men, Rejoice" 1/24

"Grace Greater Than Our Sin" 1/21
"Guide Me, O Thou Great Jehovah" 1/7, 1/11
"He Lives" 1/21
"He's a Wonderful Savior to Me" 1/6
"How Great Thou Art" 1/7
"I Heard the Voice of Jesus Say" 1/22
"I Love Thy Kingdom, Lord" 1/11
"I Need Thee Every Hour" 1/3
"In Christ There Is No East or West" 1/23
"It Came Upon the Midnight Clear" 1/16
"Jerusalem the Golden" 1/3, 1/24
"Jesus Loves Me, This I Know" 1/7, 1/23
"Jesus, Tender Shepherd, Hear Me" 1/5, 1/30
"Jesus, The Very Thought of Thee" 1/2
"Just As I Am, Thine Own to Be" 1/28
"Lead, Kindly Light" 1/22
"Lord, Dismiss Us With Thy Blessing" 1/6
"Marvelous Grace of our Loving Lord" 1/21
"My Faith Looks Up to Thee" 1/8
"My Hope is Built on Nothing Less" 1/21
"My Soul in Sad Exile Was Out on Life's Sea" 1/19
"Nearer, My God, To Thee" 1/8
"Now the Day is Over" 1/2, 1/28
"O Come, O Come, Emmanuel" 1/24
"O For a Thousand Tongues to Sing" 1/8
"O Little Town of Bethlehem" 1/23
"O Perfect Love, All Human Thought Transcending" 1/28
"O Store Gud" 1/7
"Onward, Christian Soldiers" 1/2
"Peace, Perfect Peace" 1/25, 1/29
"Rejoice, The Lord is King" 1/13
"Savior, Like a Shepherd Lead Us" 1/7
"Simply Trusting Every Day" 1/7
"Since Jesus Came Into My Heart" 1/29
"Sweet Hour of Prayer" 1/7
"Take My Life, and Let It Be" 1/7
"Take Time to Be Holy" 1/28
"The Day of Resurrection" 1/24
"The King of Love My Shepherd Is" 1/22
"The Solid Rock" 1/21
"The Unclouded Day" 1/13
"There is a Name I Love to Hear" 1/7
"There's a Land That is Fairer Than Day" 1/18
"Thine, Most Gracious Lord" 1/3
"Thou Who Wast Rich Beyond All Splendour" 1/25
"'Tis Midnight, and On Olive's Brow" 1/7
"When I Survey the Wondrous Cross" 1/8
"When Morning Gilds the Skies" 1/2, 1/28

I

INDIANS, AMERICAN 1/24
  Cherokee Indians 1/19
  First Native American Episcopal bishop 1/12
  Huron Indians 1/10
  Iroquois Indians 1/10
  Pacific Northwest Indians 1/30
  Seneca Indians 1/21
  Sitting Bull 1/30
Indulgences 1/27
Innocent I, Pope (401-17) 1/27
Innocent V, Pope (1276) 1/21
Irish Text Society 1/13, 1/15
Ironside, Harry A.
  (b. 10/14/1876) d. 1/15/1951
Isaacs, Samuel M.
  b. 1/4/1804 [d. 5/19/1878]

J

James I, English King (1603-25) 1/14, 1/16
Jan Van Etten, Edwin 1/2
Jarrow Monastery 1/12
Jefferson, Thomas 1/16
Jeffreys, George
  (b. 2/28/1889) d. 1/26/1962
Jericho, Old Testament 1/5
Jogues, St. Isaac
  b. 1/10/1607 d. 10/18/1646]
John XV, Pope (985-96) 1/29
Johnny Appleseed 1/29
Johnston, Julia Harriette
  b. 1/21/1849 [d. 3/6/1919]
Jones, Charles P.
  (b. 12/9/1865) d. 1/19/1949
Jones, E[li] Stanley
  (b. 1/3/1884) d. 1/26/1973
Jones, Harold S. 1/12
Jones, Rufus M.
  b. 1/25/1863 [d. 6/16/1948]
Jones, William (of Nayland)
  (b. 7/30/1726) d. 1/6/1800
JUDAISM
  Conservative Judaism 1/2
  First female Reform rabbi 1/26
  First Jewish associate justice 1/28
  First Jewish U.S. governor 1/4
  Hebrew Free School Association 1/4
  Jerusalem the modern capital 1/23
  Orthodox, American 1/4
  United Hebrew Charities 1/4
Julian, John 1/25
  (b. 1/27/1839) d. 1/22/1913
Julius II, Pope (1503-13) 1/14

K

Keller, Helen 1/29
Kenyon, Kathleen
  b. 1/5/1906 [d. 8/24/1978]
Key, Francis Scott
  (b. 8/9/1779) d. 1/11/1843
Knights of Columbus 1/16
Kohut, Alexander 1/2
Kyser, Kay 1/9

L

Lambarene Hospital 1/14
Lathrop, Amy 1/23. See also Warner, Anna B.
Latin Empire 1/8
LaTrappe monastery 1/9
Laud, William
  (b. 10/7/1573) d. 1/10/1645
LECTURES / ADDRESSES
  "Authority of the Scriptures" 1/20
Lee, Florence Tim-Oi 1/25
Leger, Paul L. 1/12
LEGISLATION
  Act of Supremacy 1/15
  "Acts of Uniformity," British 1/21
  Edict of St. Germain 1/17
  Theodosian Code 1/1
LEGISLATION, AMERICAN
  Ordinance of Religious Freedom (1786) 1/16
Leland, John
  (b. 5/14/1754) d. 1/14/1841
Leo X, Pope (1513-21) 1/3
Leo XIII, Pope (1878-1903) 1/22
Lewis, C. S. 1/3. See also QUOTATIONS
Lincoln, Abraham 1/23
Livingston, James 1/26
Livingston, John Henry
  (b. 5/30/1746) d. 1/20/1825
Longstaff, William D.
  b. 1/27/1822 [d. 4/2/1894]
Lotbinière, Louis Eustace 1/26
Lowe, Kelly 1/11
Loyola, Ignatius 1/9. See also RELIGIOUS ORDERS, CATHOLIC
Ludovisi, Alessandro
  b. 1/9/1554 [d. 7/8/1623]
Luther, Martin 1/1, 1/3, 1/9, 1/10, 1/14, 1/16, 1/17, 1/27, 1/29. See also QUOTATIONS

M

Macbeth, Scottish King (1040-57) 1/5
Machen, J[ohn] Gresham
  (b. 7/28/1881) d. 1/1/1937
Maier, Walter A.
  (b. 10/4/1893) d. 1/11/1950
Malcolm III MacDuncan, Scottish King (1058-93) 1/5
Manz, Felix
  (b. ca. 1498) d. 1/5/1527
Marshall, Catherine 1/25
Marshall, Peter. See also QUOTATIONS
  (b. 5/27/1902) d. 1/25/1949
MARTYRS
  Elliot, Jim 1/8, 1/31
  Fabian, Pope St. 1/10
  Fleming, Pete 1/8
  Ford, Francis Xavier 1/11
  Jogues, St. Isaac 1/10
  Laud, William 1/10
  Manz, Felix
  McCully, Ed 1/8
  Saint, Nate 1/8
  Savonarola, Girolamo 1/1
  Youderian, Roger 1/8
Mason, Lowell
  b. 1/8/1792 [d. 8/11/1872[
Massachusetts Bay Colony 1/22
Mayflower descendants 1/7
Mayhew, Jonathan 1/30
McCully, Ed 1/8
McDaniel, Rufus H.
  b. 1/29/1850 [d. 2/13/1940]
McGivney, Michael Joseph 1/16
McIntyre, James Francis 1/12
McPherson, Aimee Semple 1/2, 1/5
McPherson, Harold 1/2
Mead, Frank Spencer
  b. 1/15/1898 [d. 6/16/1982]
Mecklenburg church order 1/30
Melanchthon, Philipp 1/14, 1/16, 1/30
Mendel, Gregor
  (b. 7/22/1822) d. 1/6/1884
Mercersburg Theology 1/13
Merici, St. Angela
  (b. 3/21/1474) d. 1/27/1540
Merton, Thomas
  b. 1/31/1915 [d. 12/10/1968]
Meyer, Heinrich August Wilhelm
  b. 1/10/1800 [d. 6/21/1873]
Middle Ages 1/8
MISSION AGENCIES
  ABCFM 1/13
  American Bible Union 1/21
  China Inland Mission 1/7, 1/25
  Domestic and Foreign Missionary Society 1/11

Mustard Seed Mission 1/14
Overseas Missionary Fellowship (OMF) 1/7
YMCA 1/31
MISSIONARIES
Aylward, Gladys May 1/3
Brainerd, David 1/17
Capers, William 1/29
Carmichael, Amy Wilson
De Smet, Pierre Jean 1/30
Dickson, Lillian 1/14
Dooley, Thomas A. 1/17
Elliot, Jim 1/8
Father Damien 1/3
Fleming, Pete 1/8
Gobat, Samuel
Hamlin, Cyrus 1/5
Jogues, St. Isaac 1/10
Jones, E[li] Stanley 1/26
Laubach, Frank C. 1/26
Loyola, Ignatius 1/9
McCully, Ed 1/8
Murray, Andrew 1/18
Saint, Nate 1/8
Schaeffer, Francis 1/8
Schweitzer, Albert 1/14
Smith, Amanda Berry 1/23
Veuster, Joseph de 1/3
Wright, Laura Maria Sheldon 1/21
Xavier, Francis 1/9
Youderian, Roger 1/8
MONASTERIES
Jarrow (England) 1/12
LaTrappe (France) 1/9
St. Catherine's (Mt. Sinai) 1/27
Wearmouth (England) 1/12
Moody, Dwight L. 1/28
Morais, Sabato 1/2
Mote, Edward
b. 1/21/1849 [d. 11/13/1874]
Mott, James 1/3
Mott, John R.
(b. 5/25/1865) d. 1/31/1955
Mott, Lucretia C.
b. 1/3/1793 [d. 11/11/1880]
MOVEMENTS, CHRISTIAN
American Evangelicalism 1/23
French Protestantism 1/17
Great Schism 1/17
Medieval Catholicism 1/8
Mercersburg Theology 1/13
Protestant Reformation 1/16, 1/17
Swiss Reformation 1/1, 1/29
MOVIES / FILMS
"Song of Bernadette" (1943) 1/7
"The Inn of the Sixth Happiness" (1958) 1/3
"The Sound of Music" (1965) 1/26
Mugurditch I, Armenian Catholicos 1/18
Mühlenberg, William A. 1/3
Murray, Andrew
(b. 5/9/1828) d. 1/18/1917

Murray, John 1/1
MUSICAL GROUPS
Singing Brocks, The 1/6
Trapp Family Singers, The 1/26

N

National Anthem, American 1/11
Naumburg Convention 1/20
Naziism, German 1/20, 1/26
Neale, John Mason
b. 1/24/1818 [d. 8/6/1866]
Neri, Philip 1/9
Nevin, John W. 1/13
Newman, John Henry 1/2, 1/25
Nicene Creed 1/31
Niebuhr, Reinhold 1/18
Niemöller, Martin
b. 1/14/1892 [d. 3/6/1984]
Nobel Peace Prize 1/14, 1/25
Nuttall, Enos
b. 1/26/1842 [d. 1916]

O

Olevianus, Caspar 1/19
Oxenham, John
(b. 11/12/1852) d. 1/23/1941
Ozman, Agnes 1/1, 1/29

P

PAPAL DECREES
"Christus dominus" (1953) 1/16
"De fratrum nostrorum" 1/14
"Decet romanum pontificem" 1/3
"Execrabilis" (1460) 1/18
"Exsurge, Domine" 1/3
"Testem benevolentiae" 1/22
"Unigenitus" 1/27
Parham, Charles Fox 1/1
(b. 6/4/1873) d. 1/29/1929
Parker, Peter
(b. 6/18/1804) d. 1/10/1888
Paul III, Pope (1534-49) 1/27
Paul VI, Pope (1963-78) 1/2, 1/5, 1/28
Pearl Harbor 1/9
Pelagius 1/27
Philocalian Calendar (A.D. 336) 1/6
Pius II, Pope (1558-64) 1/18
Pius V, Pope (1566-72) 1/17
Pius X, Pope (1903-14) 1/22
Pius XII, Pope (1939-58) 1/12, 1/16

POPES
Alexander VI (1492-1503) 1/1
Benedict XV (1914-22) 1/22
Clement VI (1342-52) 1/27
Clement VII (1523-34) 1/15
Clement VIII (1592-1605) 1/30
Fabian, St. (236-250) 1/10
Gregory XI (1370-78) 1/17
Gregory XI (1371-78) 1/5
Gregory XV (1621-23) 1/9
Innocent I (401-17) 1/27
Innocent III (1198-1216) 1/8
Innocent V (1276) 1/21
John XV (985-96) 1/29
Julius II (1503-13) 1/14
Leo X (1513-21) 1/3
Leo XIII (1878-1903) 1/22
Paul III (1534-49) 1/27
Paul VI (1963-78) 1/2, 1/5, 1/28
Pius II (1558-64) 1/18
Pius V (1566-72) 1/17
Pius X (1903-14) 1/22
Pius XII (1939-58) 1/12, 1/16
Sylvester I (314-35) 1/31
Porter, Eliza Emily Chappell
(b. 1/5/1807) d. 1/1/1888
Prichard, Roland Hugh
b. 1/14/1811 d. 1/25/1887
Priesand, Sally Jane 1/26
Protestant Reformation 1/16, 1/17
PUBLICATIONS
"Bibliotheca Sacra" 1/22
"Jewish Messenger" 1/4
Our Country 1/19
The New Era 1/19
PUBLICATIONS / PERIODICALS
"Bibliotheca Sacra" 1/27
Purday, Charles Henry
b. 1/11/1799 [d. 4/23/1885]
Purgatory 1/10

Q

Quimby, Phineas P.
(b. 2/16/1802) d. 1/16/1866
QUOTATIONS
Asbury, Francis 1/1, 1/4, 1/9, 1/23, 1/26, 1/27, 1/30
Barth, Karl 1/22, 1/26
Bonar, Andrew 1/1, 1/2, 1/5, 1/7, 1/8, 1/11, 1/12, 1/19, 1/26, 1/28, 1/30
Brainerd, David 1/17
Burke, Edmund 1/9
Chesterton, G. K. 1/15
Eliade, Mircea 1/14
Elliot, Jim 1/31
Fox, George 1/13
Laubach, Frank C. 1/26, 1/29
Lewis, C. S. 1/31
Luther, Martin 1/1, 1/4, 1/6, 1/10, 1/11, 1/21, 1/22, 1/25, 1/27

MacDonald, George 1/4, 1/12
Marshall, Peter 1/5, 1/10, 1/22, 1/26
Martyn, Henry 1/19
McCheyne, Robert Murray 1/5, 1/12, 1/18, 1/27, 1/30, 1/31
Merton, Thomas 1/2, 1/14
Newton, John 1/3, 1/10, 1/11, 1/19, 1/20
Nouwen, Henri J. M. 1/24
Pink, Arthur W. 1/23
Reagan, Ronald 1/25
Rutherford, Samuel 1/1, 1/6, 1/15
Schaeffer, Francis 1/8
Schmemann, Alexander 1/21, 1/29
Smith, Hannah Whitall 1/19, 1/20, 1/31
Spurgeon, Charles 1/6
Venn, Henry 1/7, 1/17, 1/20, 1/23, 1/25
Walther, C. F. W. 1/8, 1/16
Wesley, John 1/15, 1/20, 1/24
Whitefield, George 1/16

R

RADIO BROADCASTING
KDKA (Pittsburgh) 1/2
Rancé, Armand-Jean Le Bouthillier de
b. 1/9/1626 [d. 10/12/1700]
Rankin, Jeremiah E.
b. 1/2/1828 [d. 11/28/1904]
Rebmann, Johannes
b. 1/16/1819 [d. 10/4/1876]
Reformation, The 1/9
RELIGIOUS ORDERS, CATHOLIC
American Sisters of Charity 1/4
Augustinians 1/6
Benedictines 1/12
Carmelite Nuns 1/2
Cistercian Nuns 1/29
Cistercians 1/9
Company of St. Ursula (1535) 1/27
Jesuits 1/5, 1/10
Picpus Fathers 1/3
Sisterhood of the Holy Communion 1/3
Society for the Relief of Poor Widows with Small Children 1/4
Society of the Holy Child Jesus 1/15
Trappists 1/9, 1/31
Rhode Island Colony 1/27
Roberts, Oral
b/ 1/24/1918
Robinson, Edward 1/18
(b. 4/10/1794) d. 1/27/1863
Rodeheaver Publishing Co. 1/21
Roman Empire 1/17
Rosbrugh, John 1/2

Russell, Charles Taze 1/8
Rutherford, Joseph F.
  (b. 11/8/1869) d. 1/8/1942

S

Sacred Congregation for the Doctrine of Faith 1/28
Saint, Nate 1/8
Salem Witch Trials (1692) 1/1, 1/15
Sanctification, Personal 1/19
Sankey, Ira 1/28
Savonarola, Girolamo 1/1
Scaliger, Joseph Justus
  (b. 8/5/1540) d. 1/21/1609
Schaff, Philip 1/9, 1/13
Schwedler, Johann Christoph
  (b. 12/21/1672) d. 1/12/1730
Schweitzer, Albert
  b. 1/14/1875 [d. 9/4/1965]
Scriptural Inerrancy 1/15
Scudder, John
  (b. 9/3/1793) d. 1/13/1855
Sears, Edmund H.
  (b. 4/6/1810) d. 1/16/1876
SECTS, CHRISTIAN
  Church of Scientology 1/24
  Jehovah's Witnesses 1/8
  Mormonism 1/7
  Russellites 1/8
  Watch Tower Bible and Tract Society 1/8
Segni, Lotario de Conti de 1/8. See also Innocent III, Pope (1198-1216)
SEMINARIES / BIBLE COLLEGES
  Bethel Bible School (Topeka, KS) 1/1
  Bible Institute of Los Angeles 1/28
  Hartford Theological Seminary (CT) 1/18
  Jewish Theological Seminary (NY) 1/2, 1/26
  Lane Seminary 1/10
  Moody Bible Institute 1/28
  Thomas Indian School 1/21
  Union Theological Seminary (NY) 1/18, 1/20
Semple, Robert 1/2
Septuagint (Greek O.T.) 1/9
Seraphim 1/12
SERMONS
  "Discourse Concerning Unlimited Submission" 1/30
Seton, Elizabeth Ann (née Bayley)
  (b. 8/28/1774) d. 1/4/1821
Sewall, Samuel 1/15
  (b. 3/28/1652) d. 1/1/1730
Sheppard, H. R. L. 1/6

Shrubsole, William
  (bapt. 1/13/1760) d. 1/18/1806
Simons, Menno 1/30
  (b. 1496) d. 1/31/1561
Singing Brocks 1/6
Sitting Bull 1/30
Smith, Amanda Berry
  b. 1/23/1837 [d. 2/24/1915]
Smith, J. M. Powis 1/13
Smith, Joseph 1/7
Smith, Sir William 1/9
SONGS, POPULAR
  "Praise The Lord And Pass The Ammunition!" 1/9
Soubirous, Bernadette
  b. 1/7/1844 [d. 4/16/1879]
Spalatin, Georg
  b. 1/14/1484 d. 1/16/1545
Spanish Inquisition 1/14
Speiser, Ephraim A.
  b. 1/24/1902 [d. 1965]
Spener, Philipp Jakob
  b. 1/23/1635 [d. 2/5/1705]
Spurgeon, Charles H. 1/15
  (b. 6/19/1834) d. 1/31/1892
Spurgeon, Susannah (née Thompson)
  b. 1/15/1832 [d. 10/22/1903]
St. Catherine's monastery (Mt. Sinai) 1/27
Stites, Edgar P.
  (b. 3/22/1836) d. 1/7/1921
Stone, Barton W. 1/1, 1/4
Stowe, Harriet Beecher 1/10
Strong, Josiah
  b. 1/19/1847 [d. 4/28/1916]
Suárez, Francisco de
  b. 1/5/1548 d. 9/25/1617
Swedenborg, Emmanuel 1/29
Swiss Reformation 1/1, 1/29
Sylvester I, Pope (314-35) 1/31

T

Teresa of Avila 1/9
Textual criticism 1/21
Textus Receptus 1/4, 1/30
Theodosius I, Roman Emperor (379-95) 1/17
Theodosius II (401-50), E. Roman Emperor 1/1
Therese of Lisieux, St.
  b. 1/2/1873 [d. 9/30/1897]
"Thirty-nine Articles" of Anglicanism 1/25
Tillich, Paul 1/18
Tilton, Theodore 1/9
Tischendorf, L. F. Konstantin von

  b. 1/18/1815 [d. 12/7/1874]
Tolkien, J. R. R.
  b. 1/3/1892 [d. 9/2/1973]
Torrey, R[euben] A.
  b. 1/28/1856 [d. 10/26/1928]
Tract 90 (Oxford Movement) 1/25
Trapp Family Singers 1/26
Trapp, Maria Augusta von 1/26/1905 [d. 3/28/1987]
Tregelles, Samuel P.
  b. 1/30/1813 [d. 4/24/1875]
Trifa, Valerian
  (b. 6/28/1914) d. 1/28/1987
Tuckerman, Joseph
  b. 1/18/1778 [d. 4/20/1840]
Twells, Henry
  (b. 3/13/1823) d. 1/19/1900
Tyndale, William 1/20

U

Ulrich 1/29
United States Catholic Mission 1/23
Ursinus, Peter 1/19
Ussher, James
  b. 1/4/1581 [d. 3/21/1656]

V

Valdes, Juan de 1/14
Van Dyke, Henry 1/18
Van Dyke, Tertius
  b. 1/18/1886 [d. 2/28/1958]
Vassy, Massacre at 1/17
Vatican 1/10
Virgin Mary 1/7

W

Wace, Henry
  (b. 12/10/1836) d. 1/9/1924
Wake, William
  b. 1/26/1657 d. 1/24/1737
Wannsee Conference 1/20
Warner, Anna B.
  (b. 8/31/1827) d. 1/23/1915
Warner, Susan 1/23
WARS
  American Civil War (1861-65) 1/7
  American Revolution 1/2
  English Civil War 1/30
  First French civil war 1/17
  Franco-Prussian War 1/16
  World War II 1/9, 1/14, 1/16
Watts, Isaac 1/6
Wearmouth Monastery 1/12
Webster, Harriet 1/10
Webster, Joseph P.

  (b. 3/22/1819) d. 1/18/1875
Wellhausen, Julius
  (b. 5/17/1844) d/ 1/7/1918
Wesley, Charles 1/20
Wesley, John 1/20. See also QUOTATIONS
Wesley, Susannah (née Annesley)
  b. 1/20 1669 [d. 7/23/1742]
Westcott, B[rooke] F[oss]
  b. 1/12/1825 [d. 7/27/1901]
Western Schism 1/5
Westminster Assembly's Shorter Catechism 1/31
Whitefield, George 1/7. See also QUOTATIONS
Whitfield, Frederick
  b. 1/7/1829 [d. 9/13/1904]
Whitmer, David
  b. 1/7/1805 [d. 1/25/1888]
Whyte, Alexander
  b. 1/13/1836 [d. 1/7/1921]
Wigglesworth, Edward 1/24
Willard, Samuel
  b. 1/31/1640 [d. 9/12/1707]
Williams, Peter
  b. 1/7/1722 [d. 8/8/1796]
Williams, Roger
  (b. 12/21/1603) d. 1/27/1683
Williams, William
  b. 2/11/1717 [d. 1/11/1791]
Winthrop, John
  b. 1/22/1588 [d. 4/5/1649]
Worcester, Samuel Austin
  b. 1/19/1798 [d. 1859]
World Council of Churches 1/14, 1/19, 1/31
World War II 1/9
Wright, George Frederick
  b. 1/22/1838 [d. 4/20/1921]
Wright, Laura Maria Sheldon
  (b. 7/10/1809) d. 1/21/1886
Wycliffe, John 1/5

X

Xavier, Francis 1/9

Y

Youderian, Roger 1/8
Young Men's Christian Association (YMCA) 1/31

Z

Zwingli, Ulrich 1/21, 1/29
  b. 1/1/1484 [d. 10/11/1531]

אדר ADAR

ALMANAC OF THE CHRISTIAN FAITH

שבט SHEVAT

~ February 1 ~

Highlights in History

1750 Anglican clergyman and hymnwriter John Newton (author of "Amazing Grace"), 24, wedded Mary Catlett. Their marriage lasted 40 years, before Mary's death in 1790. John survived another 17 years, dying in 1807.

1901 Pioneer American missionaries Charles (age 37) and Lettie (age 31) Cowman set sail for Japan. Later in the year they founded the Oriental Missionary Society. The Cowmans labored in the foreign field until Charles' declining health forced them to retire in 1917.

Notable Birthdays

1763 Birth of Thomas Campbell, Irish-born Scottish Presbyterian church leader. He immigrated to America, and in 1809 became a founder (along with his son Alexander and with Barton W. Stone) of the Disciples of Christ Restoration Movement, for the purpose of promoting biblical Christianity and Christian union. Campbell's reform eventually grew to become the Disciples of Christ (Christian) Church. [d. 1/4/1854]

1801 Birth of Titus Coan, American Presbyterian missionary to Hawaii. Commissioned by ABCFM, he arrived in Honolulu in 1835, and worked at Hilo and Puna, Hawaii most of the rest of his life. The religious awakening that began in 1837 was attributed to Coan's preaching. [d. 12/1/1882]

1834 Birth of Henry McNeal Turner, American Methodist bishop. Made a chaplain by Abraham Lincoln in 1863, Turner became the first African-American so commissioned. Later, Turner was forced to resign his commission (1865), when he began advocating the return of blacks to Africa. [d. 5/8/1915]

1909 Birth of George Beverly Shea, Canadian-born music evangelist. He sang at many of the Billy Graham Crusades during the 1950s-1970s.

The Last Passage

523 Death of Bridget (Brigid) of Kildare, 70, the Irish religious figure who inspired the convent system. The patron saint of Ireland, she founded the first religious community for women in that country, and is revered only less than St. Patrick. (b. ca. 453)

1828 Death of Salmon Giddings, 45, American Presbyterian clergyman. In 1815 he was appointed a missionary to "the West." His assembling of several congregations in Missouri in 1816 established Giddings as the first missionary of the Presbyterian Church to the land west of the Mississippi. Today, the Giddings-Lovejoy Presbytery (a denominational district which centers around St. Louis) is named (in part) after him. (b. 3/2/1782)

1891 Death of Edward H. Plumptre, 69, Anglican clergyman, theologian, poet and hymnwriter. He taught pastoral theology (1853-63) and New Testament exegesis (1864-81) at King's College in London, and was a member of the Old Testament Committee for the 1885 *English Revised Version* (ERV) of the Bible. Plumptre also published several volumes of verse, but is best remembered today as author of the hymn "Rejoice, Ye Pure in Heart." (b. 8/6/1821)

Words for the Soul

1630 Scottish clergyman Samuel Rutherford wrote in a letter: *'Think it not hard if you get not your will, nor your delights in this life; God will have you to rejoice in nothing but himself.'*

1791 English founder of Methodism John Wesley wrote in a letter: *'Probably I should not be able to do so much did not many of you assist me by your prayers.'*

1803 Anglican missionary to Persia, Henry Martyn wrote in his journal: *'Oh, that I may learn my utter helplessness without Thee, and so by deep humiliation be qualified for greater usefulness.'*

IN GOD'S WORD... OT: Exodus 13:17–15:18 ~ NT: Matthew 21:23-46 ~ Psalms 26:1-12 ~ Proverbs 6:16-19

ALMANAC OF THE CHRISTIAN FAITH

ADAR · SHEVAT

~ February 2 ~

Highlights in History

522 Pope Leo X bestowed the title "Fidei Defensor" ("Defender of the Faith") on England's Henry VIII, in recognition of *Assertio Septem Sacramentorum*, a writing by Henry defending the seven Catholic sacraments. In 1544 Parliament made "Defender of the Faith" an official title of the English monarch, and it has since remained the title of all British sovereigns.

1881 The first formal church youth organization was established in the Williston Congregational Church in Portland, Maine, by the Rev. Francis E. Clark, 29. Originally called "Christian Endeavor," it became the forerunner of the denominational "youth fellowships" in modern churches.

1891 The Bethel Moravian Church was formally organized in Leonard, North Dakota. It is one of only four congregations of the Moravian Church in America established in this state. The other three congregations are located in Davenport, Durbin and Fargo.

Notable Birthdays

1745 Birth of Hannah More, English philanthropist and Christian writer. A popular poet and dramatist, she renounced society and concentrated on religious efforts through her writings and by setting up Sunday schools. She also authored *Sacred Dramas, Religion of the Fashionable World* and *Practical Piety*. [d. 9/7/1833]

1892 Birth of Wendell P. Loveless, American hymnwriter. He directed the radio department at Moody Bible Institute (1926-47), and later entered the pastorate. He also composed many gospel songs and choruses, including LOVELESS ("Trust in the Lord With All Your Heart"). [d. 10/3/1987]

1924 Birth of Jack McAlister, American missions pioneer. In 1946 he became founder and first president of World Literature Crusade, a worldwide Bible distributing and church planting organization. [d. 1/12/2006]

The Last Passage

1784 Death of Henry Alline, 35, leader of the Great Awakening in Nova Scotia. During the American Revolution, his emotional and highly speculative preaching stimulated the growth of New Light Congregational and Baptist churches in the Maritime Provinces. (b. 6/14/1748)

1834 Death of Lorenzo Dow, 55, itinerant Methodist evangelist. He inspired the Primitive Methodist movement in England. (b. 10/16/1777)

1895 Death of A[doniram] J[udson] Gordon, 58, American Baptist clergyman and educator. He composed the hymn tunes GORDON ("My Jesus, I Love Thee") and CLARENDON ("In Tenderness He Sought Me"). (b. 4/19/1836)

Words for the Soul

1779 Pioneer American Methodist bishop Francis Asbury reflected in his journal: '*God is gracious beyond the power of language to describe.*'

1881 American Quaker holiness author Hannah Whitall Smith wrote in a letter: '*Slowness of movement is no disadvantage in the more advanced stages of spiritual growth.... God is always slow when He is doing a deep and lasting work.*'

1907 In a letter to American statesman William Jennings Bryan, Russian spiritual novelist Leo Tolstoy counseled: '*The most important thing is to know the will of God concerning one's life, i.e., to know what he wishes us to do and fulfill it.*'

1955 English apologist C.S. Lewis wrote in a letter: '*We should be much concerned about the salvation of those we love. But we must be careful not to... demand that their salvation should conform to some ready-made pattern of our own.*'

IN GOD'S WORD... OT: Exodus 15:19–17:7 ~ NT: Matthew 22:1-33 ~ Psalms 27:1-6 ~ Proverbs 6:20-26

אדר ALMANAC OF THE CHRISTIAN FAITH שבט
ADAR   SHEVAT

~ February 3 ~

Highlights in History

1864 In Columbus, Ohio, a fellowship of independent Methodist, Presbyterian, Congregational and United Brethren churches organized itself into a separate Protestant denomination known as the Christian Union.

1943 During World War II, the Allied troopship S.S. Dorchester was torpedoed by a German U-boat and sank with a loss of 600 lives. As it went down, four chaplains gave  their life jackets to shipmates, and so perished in the icy waters. The bravery of Rev. Clark Poling (Dutch Reformed), Rev. George L. Fox (Methodist), Catholic priest Father John Washington and Jewish rabbi Alexander D. Goode led Congress afterward to mark February 3rd as "Four Chaplains Day."

1985 In South Africa, Desmond Tutu, 53, became Johannesburg's first black Anglican bishop. A trained ecumenist, Tutu went on to become Archbishop of Cape Town and Anglican primate of South Africa.

1988 In Washington, DC, the National Religious Broadcasters, representing most television and radio evangelists, voted 324 to 6 requiring its members soliciting tax-exempt donations to meet the standards of its Ethics and Financial Accountability Commission (EFAC).

Notable Birthdays

540 Birth of St. Gregory I (the Great). Pope from 590, he was a reformer of the clerical discipline and was responsible for the Gregorian Chant. He also sent St. Augustine [of Canterbury] to convert the Anglo-Saxons. [d. 3/12/604]

1816 Birth of Frederick W. Robertson, Evangelical Anglican clergyman. He gained renown while preaching at Holy Trinity Church in Brighton, England. Robertson possessed a rare gift  of empathy and understanding, especially for the unchurched working class of Brighton. [d. 8/15/1853]

1832 Birth of William H. Doane, American Baptist hymnwriter. He edited *Sabbath School Gems* (1862) and *The Baptist Hymnal* (1886). He also composed the hymns TO GOD BE THE GLORY; PRECIOUS NAME ("Take the Name of Jesus With You"); I AM THINE ("I am Thine, O Lord"); MORE LOVE TO THEE ("More Love to Thee, O Christ"); NEAR THE CROSS ("Jesus, Keep Me Near the Cross"); and RESCUE ("Rescue the Perishing"). [d. 12/24/1915]

The Last Passage

619 Martyrdom of St. Lawrence of Canterbury. He accompanied St. Augustine to England in 597, and became Archbishop of Canterbury in 608.

1468 Death of Johannes Gutenberg (Gensfleisch), 67, German printer. The inventor (ca. 1449) of movable type printing in Europe, Gutenberg published the Mazarin Bible (completed  1456) — the first full-length book to be produced by this method. In spite of his fame, Gutenberg died blind and destitute. (b. 2/23/1400)

Words for the Soul

1744 Colonial missionary to the American Indians David Brainerd explained in a tract: *'God designs that those whom He sanctifies... shall tarry awhile in this present evil world, that their own experience of temptations may teach them how great the deliverance is, which God has wrought for them.'*

1839 Scottish clergyman and biographer Andrew Bonar wrote in his diary: *'I met in the evening this remark in [Jonathan] Edwards: "It is God's way to let ministers try all their strength first, and then He Himself comes and subdues the hearts they cannot." Perhaps God is trying me thus. I am using all means, and all my power, and it avails nothing.'*

IN GOD'S WORD...   OT: Exodus 17:8–19:15 ~ NT: Matthew 22:34–23:12 ~ Psalms 27:7-14 ~ Proverbs 6:27-35

אדר ADAR

ALMANAC OF THE CHRISTIAN FAITH

שבט SHEVAT

~ February 4 ~

Highlights in History

1441 Pope Eugenius IV published the encyclical "Cantante domino." It asserted that the biblical canon of the Roman Catholic Church contains the 66 protocanonical books (i.e., the complete Protestant Bible) and 12 deuterocanonical (a.k.a. "apocryphal") books – 78 writings in all.

1874 English poet and devotional writer Frances Ridley Havergal, 37, penned the words to the popular hymn of commitment, "Take My Life and Let It Be [Consecrated, Lord, to Thee]."

Notable Birthdays

1802 Birth of Mark Hopkins, American educator and moral philosopher. In 1871, future President James Garfield made a speech at Delmonico's in NY, in which he said: *'A pine bench, with Mark Hopkins at one end of it and me at the other, is a good enough college for me!'* [d. 6/17/1887]

1850 Birth of David L. Anderson, American Methodist missionary to China. He became the founder and first president of Soochow University (1901-11). [d. 2/16/1911]

1856 Birth of Ernest DeWitt Burton, American Baptist biblical scholar, theologian and educator. Associated with the University of Chicago from 1892 until his death, he served as chairman of the New Testament and Early Christian Literature Dept. (1892-1923), and afterward as president (1923-25). [d. 5/26/1925]

1873 Birth of George Bennard, American evangelist and hymnwriter. Converted at age 16, he was a worker in the Salvation Army. Later, he became a Methodist evangelist, preaching mostly in the north-central part of the United States and in Canada. Bennard penned over 300 gospel songs, but is perhaps best remembered as author of "The Old Rugged Cross" (which for years was regarded as America's favorite gospel song). [d. 10/10/1958]

1906 Birth of Dietrich Bonhoeffer, German Lutheran pastor and theologian. A secret member of the Nazi resistance movement, Bonhoeffer was arrested by the Gestapo in April 1943.   He remained a prisoner through the remainder of World War II, and was hanged at the Flossenburg concentration camp. Bonhoeffer's best-known writings were: *The Cost of Discipleship* (1948), *Ethics* (1950) and *Letters and Papers from Prison* (1953). [d. 4/9/1945]

The Last Passage

1856 Death of Rabanus Maurus, about 80, Archbishop of Mainz. A student of Alcuin, he was called "the first teacher of Germany." Today he is remembered as author of the hymn, "Come, Holy Ghost, Our Souls Inspire." (b. ca. 776)

1555 Death of John Rogers, English reformer and theologian. He published a complete Bible (1537) under the pseudonym of Thomas Matthew, and continued Tyndale's version of the Old Testament. Burned at the stake as a heretic, Rogers became the first Protestant martyr under the reign of Mary I. (b. ca. 1505)

1944 Death of Cleland B. McAfee, 77, American Presbyterian clergyman, educator and hymnwriter. He taught theology at McCormick Theological Seminary, Chicago (1912-30), and authored *Mosaic Law in Modern Life* (1906) and *The Uncut Nerve of Missions* (1932). McAfee also wrote and composed the hymn, "There Is a Place of Quiet Rest" (& McAFEE). (b. 9/25/1866)

Words for the Soul

1950 American missionary and martyr Jim Elliot resolved in his journal: *'I may no longer depend on pleasant impulses to bring me before the Lord. I must rather respond to principles I know to be right, whether I feel them to be enjoyable or not.'*

IN GOD'S WORD... OT: Exodus 19:16–21:21 ~ NT: Matthew 23:13-39 ~ Psalms 28:1-9 ~ Proverbs 7:1-5

אדר ALMANAC OF THE CHRISTIAN FAITH שבט
ADAR   SHEVAT

~ February 5 ~

Highlights in History

1631 English-born clergyman Roger Williams, 28, first arrived in America. He soon began questioning Massachusetts' religious policies which fused church and state matters. Williams was banished to Rhode Island five years later, where at Providence he established the first Baptist church in America.

1736 The English Wesley brothers – John (age 32) and Charles (age 28) – first arrived in America at Savannah. They had been invited by Georgia colonial governor James Oglethorpe to be missionaries to the American Indians.

1812 American missionary Adoniram Judson, 23, married schoolteacher Ann Hasseltine, 22. Two weeks later the couple set sail for India under sponsorship of the American [Congregational] Board of Commissioners for Foreign Missions.

1887 The Chicago Evangelization Society was organized by evangelist Dwight L. Moody, 50. Two years later, the Society established the Bible Institute for Home and Foreign Missions. Moody died in 1899, and in 1900 the Chicago school was renamed Moody Bible Institute.

Notable Birthdays

1703 Birth of Gilbert Tennent, Irish-born American Presbyterian minister and revivalist. He became chief spokesman for supporters of the Great Awakening. His 1740 sermon, "The Dangers of Unconverted Ministry," attacked ministers who resisted the Awakening, and helped create a division within Presbyterianism. [d. 7/23/1764]

1723 [OS] Birth of John Witherspoon, Scottish-American Presbyterian clergyman, educator, and author. He was a member of the Continental Congress (1776-82); a signer of the Declaration of Independence; president of College of New Jersey (later Princeton University) (1768-94); and an organizer of the Presbyterian Church in the United States (1789). [d. 11/15/1794]

1837 Birth of Dwight L. Moody, foremost American evangelist of the latter 19th century. His message blended simple American optimism and evangelical Arminianism. A founder of religious conferences and institutes, he helped organize the Northfield Seminary for Girls and the Chicago (now Moody) Bible Institute. [d. 12/22/1899]

The Last Passage

1705 Death of Philipp Jakob Spener, 70, German Lutheran churchman and founder of Pietism. At Frankfort he introduced reforms in church discipline, use of the catechism and training of youth, his methods becoming the foundation of confirmation. Spener's *Pia Desideria* (1675) encouraged private devotions among serious Christian believers. (b. 1/23/1635)

1888 Death of George Bowen, 71, American missionary. Sent by the American Board of Commissioners for Foreign Missions (ABCFM) to India in 1847, Bowen became known as the "White Saint of India." (b. 4/30/1816)

1898 Death of William F. Moulton, 62, English Wesleyan Methodist clergyman and biblical scholar. He translated Winer's *Grammar of New Testament Greek*, authored *History of the English Bible*, and was an editor of the ERV/EV New Testament (1870-81). (b. 3/14/1835)

Words for the Soul

1742 English revivalist George Whitefield wrote in a letter: *'Fear not the smallness of your beginning. What is begun in the fear of God, he will prosper.'*

1944 German theologian and Nazi martyr Dietrich Bonhoeffer wrote in a letter from prison: *'Much that worries us beforehand can afterwards, quite unexpectedly, have a happy and simple solution.... Things really are in a better hand than ours.'*

IN GOD'S WORD...   OT: Exodus 21:22–23:13 ~ NT: Matthew 24:1-28 ~ Psalms 29:1-11 ~ Proverbs 7:6-23

ADAR — ALMANAC OF THE CHRISTIAN FAITH — SHEVAT

February 6

Highlights in History

1902 The first Young Women's Hebrew Association was organized in New York City. Mrs. Bella Unterberg was the founder and the first president. The first building used by the organization was at 1584 Lexington Avenue, New York City.

1924 Station KFSG (Kall Four Square Gospel) went on the air. One of the earliest radio stations licensed, it broadcast the services of Angelus Temple, the flagship congregation of the International Foursquare Gospel Church, founded in 1923 by Aimee Semple McPherson.

Notable Birthdays

1754 Birth of Andrew Fuller, English Baptist clergyman, missionary and theologian. He was the first secretary (1792) of the Baptist Missionary Society. [d. 5/7/1815]

1834 Birth of Ludwig I. Nommensen, Rhenish (Dutch German) pioneer (first) missionary to Sumatra (Indonesia). Called the "Apostle of the Bataks," he first arrived in the region of Lake Toba in 1864, and established a theological training school there in 1877. In 1878 he completed a translation of the New Testament into the Batak language. [d. 5/23/1918]

1874 Birth of David Evans, Welsh Presbyterian musical scholar. He is remembered today for creating arrangements of the hymn tunes MADRID ("Come, Christians, Join to Sing"); NYLAND ("In Heavenly Love Abiding"); BUNESSAN ("Morning Has Broken"); and SLANE ("Be Thou My Vision"). [d. 5/17/1948]

1908 Birth of Robert Gordis, American Conservative Jewish rabbi and scholar. He taught Scripture at the Jewish Theological Seminary in New York City, and was co-founder (later editor) of the journal "Judaism." Gordis authored over 20 volumes, many in the area of O.T. wisdom, including *The Biblical Text in the Making* (1937) and *The Song of Songs* (1954). [d. 1/3/1982]

The Last Passage

891 Death of St. Photius, 71, Patriarch of Constantinople (858-867). Excommunicated by Pope Nicholas I (863), Photius issued an encyclical (867) against the West, which ultimately caused the Great Schism. Restored in 877, he was again excommunicated in 882 and banished to an Armenian cloister (886). (b. ca. 820)

1804 Death of Joseph Priestley, 70, the English Nonconformist Unitarian clergyman famous for his scientific work in the chemistry of gases. His researches resulted in the discovery of oxygen, ammonia, sulfur dioxide, hydrogen chloride. Altogether, Priestley published in the areas of philosophy, religion, education and political theory. (b. 3/13/1733)

1910 Death of Harriett Eugenia Peck Buell, 75, an American Methodist poet who in 1877 became author of the hymn: "My Father is Rich in Houses and Lands." (b. 11/2/1834)

Words for the Soul

1839 Scottish evangelistic clergyman Robert Murray McCheyne wrote in a letter: 'Even in the wildest storms the sky is not all dark; and so in the darkest dealings of God with His children, there are always some bright tokens for good.'

1868 American Quaker and holiness writer Hannah Whitall Smith penned in her journal: 'Isn't this the true secret of the guidance of the Spirit? Is it not God taking possession of our wills, and through them carrying out His own will?'

1931 American missionary and literacy pioneer Frank Laubach wrote in a letter: 'There is a deep peace that grows out of... loneliness and a sense of failure. God cannot get close when everything is delightful. He seems to need these darker hours, these empty-hearted hours, to mean the most to people.'

IN GOD'S WORD... OT: Exodus 23:14–25:40 ~ NT: Matthew 24:29-51 ~ Psalms 30:1-12 ~ Proverbs 7:24-27

February 7

Highlights in History

1528 Bern, the strongest canton (territory) in southern Switzerland in its day, officially embraced the Protestant faith of Swiss reformers Ulrich Zwingli and John Oecolampadius.

1550 Italian cardinal Giammaria Ciocchi del Monte was elected Pope Julius III. During his five-year reign, the Jesuit religious order was confirmed, and Francis Xavier was encouraged to evangelize Japan. Also, England briefly returned to Roman obedience with the accession of Mary to the throne.

Notable Birthdays

1478 Birth of Sir Thomas More, English Catholic author and statesman. The first layman to hold the office of lord chancellor (1529), More refused to accept Henry VIII's Act of Supremacy (nor sanction his marriage to Anne Boleyn).  Defending Roman Catholicism in the climate of an emerging Anglicanism, More was martyred for his religious beliefs. [d. 7/6/1535]

1710 Birth of William Boyce, 69, English chorister, organist and composer. His compilations (of more than two centuries of English church music) kept alive the sacred music from the  Tudor period on. Boyce suffered from increasing deafness later in life. [d. 2/16/1779]

1832 Birth of Hannah Whitall Smith, American Quaker evangelist, reformer, holiness evangelist and speaker. Married to holiness speaker Robert Pearsall Smith in 1851, Hannah's most influential publication was *The Christian's Secret of a Happy Life* (1875). It remains a popular devotional guide to this day. [d. 5/1/1911]

1872 Birth of H. Wheeler Robinson, English Baptist theologian and Biblical scholar. His most important work was in Hebrew psychology and O.T. theology. Robinson authored *The Religious Ideas of the Old Testament* (1913). [d. 5/12/1945]

The Last Passage

1877 Death of Henry Boynton Smith, 61, American Presbyterian theologian, educator, and author. He taught church history and theology at Union Theological Seminary in NY (1850-74). Among his publications were: *Textbook of Church History* (5 vols, 1855-79) and *Apologetics* (1882). Smith was also editor of "The American Theological Review" (1859-74). (b. 11/21/1815)

1878 Death of Pius IX, 85, Italian pope, 1846-78. Born Giovanni Maria Mastai-Ferretti, his was the longest pontificate in history and among the more controversial. Also known as "Pio Nono," he defined the dogma of the Immaculate Conception (1854), and convened the First Vatican Council (1869-70), during which he established the Dogma of Papal Infallibility. (b. 5/13/1792)

Words for the Soul

1738 English founder of Methodism John Wesley, 34, recorded in his journal: '(A day much to be remembered.) At the house of... a Dutch merchant, I met Peter Böhler... just then landed from Germany.' [Moravian missionary Peter Böhler, 26, met Wesley on the first day of Bohler's arrival in London. Their subsequent friendship later influenced Wesley's theology of holiness.]

1947 U.S. Presbyterian clergyman and Senate Chaplain Peter Marshall prayed: 'We want to do right, and to be right; so start us in the right way, for Thou knowest that we are very hard to turn.'

1982 Dutch Catholic theologian and spiritual writer Henri J. M. Nouwen recorded in his *¡Gracias!* journal: 'In times of depression, one of the few things to hold onto is a schedule. When  there is little inner vitality, the outer order of the day allows me to function somewhat coherently. It is like a scaffolding put around a building that needs restoration.'

IN GOD'S WORD... OT: Exodus 26:1–27:21 ~ NT: Matthew 25:1-30 ~ Psalms 31:1-8 ~ Proverbs 8:1-11

February 8

ADAR / **SHEVAT**

ALMANAC OF THE CHRISTIAN FAITH

Highlights in History

1693 The College of William and Mary was founded in Williamsburg, Virginia for the purpose of educating Anglican clergymen. After Harvard, it is the second oldest institution of higher learning in America.

1966 In Rome, the Vatican announced that the office charged with the censure of books had been abolished in a reorganization of the Sacred Congregation for the Doctrine of Faith.

Notable Birthdays

1718 Birth of Jean Joseph Amiot, French Jesuit missionary to China for about 50 years. His writings on Chinese music, geography and history greatly aided the European understanding of Eastern Asia. [d. 10/9/1793]

1801 Birth of George Dana Boardman, Sr., American Baptist missionary. He founded mission stations in Burma at Moulmein (1827) and at Tavoy (1828). (Following Boardman's early death, in 1834 his widow Sarah married fellow-missionary Adoniram Judson.) [d. 2/11/1831]

1865 Birth of Lewis E. Jones, American YMCA director and hymnwriter: "Would You Be Free From Your Burden of Sin?" (& POWER IN THE BLOOD)." [d. 9/1/1936]

1878 Birth of Martin Buber, Austrian-born Jewish religious philosopher. Buber was a Hasidic scholar who worked for the recognition of the cultural significance of Judaism. As professor at Hebrew University in Jerusalem (1938-65), his philosophy of religious existentialism is best described in his enduring book, *I and Thou* (1922). [d. 6/13/1965]

The Last Passage

1851 Death of James Alexander Haldane, 82, a Scottish evangelist whose theological ideas were similar to those of the Plymouth Brethren. He founded the Society for the Propagation of the Gospel at Home in 1797. (b. 7/14/1768)

1874 Death of David Friedrich Strauss, 66, controversial German Lutheran philosopher and theological writer. He described the Gospels as "historical myth," and his 1835 *Leben Jesu* was a turning point in the scholarly search for the "historical Jesus." (b. 1/27/1808)

1895 Death of William M. Taylor, 65, Scottish-born American Congregational clergyman, educator and writer. He authored *Moses, the Lawgiver* (1879); *John Knox* (1885); *Contrary Winds, and Other Sermons* (1899). (b. 10/23/1829)

1920 Death of James M. Buckley, 83, American Methodist clergyman, editor and author. Buckley was editor of "The Christian Advocate" (1880-1912), and also authored *A History of Methodism in the United States*, (1897). (b. 12/16/1836)

1936 Death of James Henry Fillmore, 86, Ohio-born clergyman, singing school teacher and sacred music publisher. He wrote and published many cantatas, anthems and hymn tunes, including RESOLUTION ("I Am Resolved No Longer to Linger") and HANNAH ("I Know That My Redeemer Liveth"). (b. 6/1/1849)

Words for the Soul

1744 Colonial American missionary to the New England Indians, David Brainerd wrote in his journal: *'I find that both mind and body are quickly tired with intenseness and fervor in the things of God. Oh that I could be as incessant as angels in devotion and spiritual fervor.'*

1950 American missionary Jim Elliot wrote in his journal: *'Sin in a Christian makes God seem distant, deaf. In the body, sin saps animation, as cancer. In the soul, sin stifles the affections; as corrosion in the spirit, sin solidifies the attitudes, as a callous.'*

IN GOD'S WORD... OT: Exodus 28:1-43 ~ NT: Matthew 25:31–26:13 ~ Psalms 31:9-18 ~ Proverbs 8:12-13

אדר ADAR

ALMANAC OF THE CHRISTIAN FAITH

שבט SHEVAT

~ February 9 ~

Highlights in History

1812 Pioneer missionary Samuel Newell married fellow Congregationalist Harriet Atwood. They afterward sailed for India with Adoniram and Ann (Hasseltine) Judson. (Harriet Newell and Ann Judson became the first American women commissioned for missionary work abroad.)

1918 The Army Chaplain School was first organized at Fort Monroe, in Hampton, Virginia. It was the first school for chaplains established by U.S. armed services, and instruction was offered in military science and international law.

Notable Birthdays

1819 Birth of William True Sleeper, New England Congregational clergyman and author of the hymns, "Jesus, I Come" and "Ye Must Be Born Again." [d. 9/24/1904]

1914 Birth of Bruce Manning Metzger, American Presbyterian New Testament scholar. Metzger taught at Princeton University from 1938-1984, and was a member of the RSV Bible translation committee. [d. 2/13/2007]

The Last Passage

1555 Death of John Hooper, about 60, Anglican bishop and Protestant martyr. He was one of the chief exponents of Continental Protestantism, and influenced the Puritans through his writings. Often called the "first Puritan," Hooper was burned at the stake — the first prominent victim of ("Bloody") Queen Mary Tudor's counter-reformation. (b. ca. 1495)

1896 Death of Ann Ayres, 80, American Episcopal religious. The first woman consecrated an Episcopal sister, Ayres was converted under the preaching of William A. Muhlenberg. She afterward began a social work, and in 1852 formally organized the Sisterhood of the Holy Communion in New York City. It was the first U.S. Episcopal sisterhood. Following Ayres' death, the organization survived to 1940. (b. 1/3/1816)

1912 Death of Andrew Martin Fairbairn, 73, Scottish-born Congregationalist clergyman, theologian, lecturer and writer. His most notable publications include *Studies in the Life of Christ* (1880) and *Philosophy of the Christian Religion* (1902). (b. 11/4/1838)

1965 Death of Harry Dixon Loes, 72, American Baptist evangelist, teacher and hymnwriter. Loes taught music at Moody Bible Institute during the 1940s. During his lifetime he wrote some 1500 hymn texts and composed 3000 hymn tunes, including "Up Calvary's Mountain, One Dreadful Morn." (b. 10/20/1892)

Words for the Soul

1555 Anglican bishop John Hooper, on his way to martyrdom at the stake, was quoted as saying: *'Death is bitter, and life is sweet, but alas! consider that death to come is more bitter, and life to come is more sweet.'*

1637 Exiled Scottish clergyman Samuel Rutherford wrote in a letter: *'Alas, we but chase feathers flying in the air, and tire our own spirits, for the froth and over-gilded clay of a dying life. One sight of what my Lord hath let me see within this short time, is worth a world of worlds.'*

1839 Scottish clergyman Robert Murray McCheyne wrote in a letter: *'In spiritual things, this world is all wintertime so long as the Saviour is away.'*

1866 In a letter to the widow of a dear friend, Scottish clergyman George MacDonald remarked in consolation: *'Life is not very long in this place.... All we have to mind is to do our work, while the chariot of God's hours is bearing us to the higher life beyond.'*

1948 U.S. Senate chaplain Peter Marshall prayed: *'We are tempted to despair of our world. Remind us, O Lord, that Thou hast been facing the same thing in all the world since time began.'*

IN GOD'S WORD... OT: Exodus 29:1–30:10 ~ NT: Matthew 26:14-46 ~ Psalms 31:19-24 ~ Proverbs 8:14-26

February 10

Highlights in History

1495 King's College was founded under Roman Catholic sponsorship in Aberdeen, Scotland. In 1860 it merged with the Protestant Marischal College (established in 1593) to become the University of Aberdeen.

1899 The Church of England first authorized use of the 1885 *English Revised Version* (RV or ERV) of the Bible in Anglican liturgy and worship.

1929 In London, renowned Baptist clergyman and devotional author F. B. Meyer, 81, preached his last sermon. He afterward entered a nursing home where his health soon failed. He died March 28.

Notable Birthdays

1791 Birth of Henry Hart Milman, Anglican historian and clergyman. He was dean of St. Paul's 1849-68, and authored the hymn, "Ride On, Ride On in Majesty." [d. 9/24/1868]

1819 Birth of Richard Storrs Willis, American sacred music editor and hymn composer. He edited numerous hymn collections, and composed the hymn tunes CAROL ("It Came Upon the Midnight Clear") and CRUSADER'S HYMN ("Fairest Lord Jesus"). [d. 5/7/1900]

1824 Birth of Thomas Beecher, American Congregational clergyman. The sixth son of Lyman Beecher, he pastored the Independent Congregational Church of Elmira, New York (1854-1900). Thomas was a pioneer in the "institutional church" movement. [d. 3/14/1900]

1859 Birth of Jonathan Goforth, Canadian Presbyterian missionary to Honan and Changte, China. He was noted for training native evangelists and preachers. [d. 10/8/1936]

The Last Passage

1543 Death of Johann Maier von Eck, 56, German Catholic theologian, scholar and orator. He was originally on good terms with Martin Luther, but he opposed him in public debate at Leipzig in 1519, and was afterward largely responsible for securing Luther's excommunication. Eck thus became the first to force Luther into public opposition to Catholicism. (b. 11/13/1486)

1787 Death of Charles Chauncy, 82, American "Old Light" Congregational leader. A leading liberal of his era, Chauncy was the chief antagonist of Jonathan Edwards and George Whitefield, and opposed the religious excitement of "the Great Awakening." Chauncy's writings regarded revivalism as merely a manifestation of abnormal psychology. (b. 1/1/1705)

1912 Death of Tullius C. O'Kane, 81, Ohio-born educator, piano salesman, author and hymn composer. Of his many tunes, two which endure today are O'KANE ("On Jordan's Stormy Banks I Stand"), and "[Oh Think of the] HOME OVER THERE." (b. 3/10/1830)

1939 Death of Pius XI, pope from 1922-39. He is best remembered for negotiating the Lateran Treaty (1929), which established the Vatican's independence from Italy. Pius was also a tireless worker for world peace. (b. 5/31/1857)

Words for the Soul

1546 In one of the German reformer's last letters, Martin Luther wrote to his wife Katie: *'Pray, and let God worry.'*

1846 Scottish author George MacDonald, 22, remarked in a letter to his father: *'I think God is leading me slowly on to know more of him. What I most need is a deep sense of sinfulness, and the evil of it. I think the want [i.e., lack] of this must be very much the reason why so many Christians are careless and lukewarm.'*

1947 U.S. Senate Chaplain Peter Marshall prayed: *'Save Thy servants from the tyranny of the nonessential. Give them the courage to say "No" to everything that makes it more difficult to say "Yes" to Thee.'*

IN GOD'S WORD... OT: Exodus 30:11-31:18 ~ NT: Matthew 26:47-68 ~ Psalms 32:1-11 ~ Proverbs 8:27-32

ALMANAC OF THE CHRISTIAN FAITH

אדר ADAR — שבט SHEVAT

~ February 11 ~

Highlights in History

1790 The Society of Friends (Quakers) presented a petition to the American Congress calling for the abolition of slavery.

1858 In Lourdes, France, 14-year-old French peasant Bernadette Soubirous experienced her first vision of the Virgin Mary. By July 16th, she had had 18 such visions. A number of miraculous healings occurred at the site shortly afterward, and Lourdes soon became a major attraction for Catholic pilgrimages.

1989 In Boston, Rev. Barbara C. Harris, 58, was consecrated the first female bishop in the Anglican Church. (In 1988 the Church of England had passed the first legislation which opened the Anglican priesthood to women.)

Notable Birthdays

1717 Birth of William Williams ("of Pantycelyn"), Welsh clergyman and hymn author. Converted under the preaching of Howell Harris, he afterward became an evangelist of the Welsh Calvinistic Methodist Church. Williams penned 800 hymns in Welsh, and another 100 in English, including "Guide Me, O Thou Great Jehovah." [d. 1/11/1791]

1826 Birth of Alexander Maclaren, Scottish-born English clergyman. He pastored Union Chapel in London 1858-1903, achieving a world reputation for his expository sermons. In 1905 Maclaren presided at the first Convention of the Baptist World Alliance. [d. 5/5/1910]

1836 Birth of (Solomon) Washington Gladden, American Congregational clergyman, theologian and exponent of the social gospel. Widely known in his time as a preacher and lecturer, Gladden is chiefly remembered today as the author of the hymn, "O Master, Let Me Walk With Thee." [d. 7/2/1918]

The Last Passage

731 Death of St. Gregory II, 62, pope from 715-31. In 719 he sent St. Boniface to evangelize the German tribes. During Gregory's reign, in 726 Byzantine Emperor Leo III, the Isaurian (or Syrian), initiated the Iconoclastic controversy. (b. ca. 669)

1729 Death of Solomon Stoddard, 85, American Colonial Congregational clergyman. The maternal grandfather of Jonathan Edwards, Stoddard pastored the church at Northampton, Massachusetts for over 50 years. (b. 9/27/1643)

1831 Death of George Dana Boardman, Sr., 30, American Baptist missionary to Burma. Sent in 1825, he baptized the first convert among the Karen people. Following Boardman's early death, his widow Sarah stayed on in Burma, and in 1834 married fellow-missionary Adoniram Judson. (b. 2/8/1801)

1888 Death of James Grindlay Small, 71, Scottish Free Church clergyman, poet and hymn author. He published two volumes of poems, including the words to the popular hymn, "I've Found a Friend, Oh, Such a Friend." (b. 1817)

Words for the Soul

1779 English founder of Methodism John Wesley reminded in a letter: *'Chance has no share in the government of the world. The Lord reigns, and disposes all things, strongly and sweetly, for the good of them that love him.'*

1860 Scottish clergyman and biographer Andrew Bonar wrote in his diary: *'Felt to-day that what I must be is simply this, a channel down which the water is to run. The Lord may send it by me, making my words a channel, or making my books a channel, or making my class a channel. But all is no more than this, He makes me a channel.'*

1948 U.S. Senate Chaplain Peter Marshall prayed: *'We ask Thee not for tasks more suited to our strength, but for strength more suited to our tasks.'*

IN GOD'S WORD... OT: Exodus 32:1–33:23 ~ NT: Matthew 26:69–27:14 ~ Psalms 33:1-11 ~ Proverbs 8:33-36

אדר
ADAR

ALMANAC OF THE CHRISTIAN FAITH

שבט
SHEVAT

~ February 12 ~

Highlights in History

1948 The Pentecostal awakening known as the "Latter Rain Movement" traces its origin to this date, when students at the Sharon Orphanage and Schools in North Battleford, Saskatchewan, Canada began experiencing a mass spiritual awakening.

1952 The Roman Catholic TV program "Life is Worth Living" debuted. Hosted by Bishop Fulton J. Sheen, the half-hour program aired on Tuesday nights. It was the longest-running religious series of its day, and ran through April 1957.

Notable Birthdays

1644 Birth of Jacob Ammann, Mennonite minister from Alsace/Switzerland. He was the founder of Amish Mennonites. [d. ca. 1711]

1663 Birth of Cotton Mather, colonial American clergyman. The most famous of the Puritan clerics, Mather was a leader in conducting the Salem "witch trials," which he later believed to have been unfair. A founder of Yale University (1703), he also authored over 450 writings on theology and science. [d. 2/13/1728]

1816 Birth of Charles Henry Appleton Dall, American Unitarian clergyman. In 1855 he became the first foreign missionary of the Unitarian Church in America, and the first Unitarian missionary to India. [d. 7/18/1886]

The Last Passage

1737 Death of Benjamin Schmolck, 64, Lutheran clergyman and hymnwriter. Regarded as the most popular German hymnwriter of his day, Schmolck penned over 900 hymns, including "My Jesus, As Thou Wilt." (b. 12/21/1672)

1877 Death of Henry Williams Baker, 55, English clergyman and musical compiler. He served nearly 20 years as chairman of the historic Anglican publication, *Hymns Ancient and Modern* (1861). Baker also authored the hymn, "The King of Love My Shepherd Is." (b. 5/27/1821)

1878 Death of Alexander Duff, 71, first missionary of the Church of Scotland to be sent to India. His English school in Calcutta grew to become a missionary college. (b. 4/26/1806)

1915 Death of Fanny [Frances Jane] Crosby, 94, American Methodist gospel songwriter. Though blind from the age of six weeks, Fanny penned 8,000 hymns — beginning in her 40s! — including "He Hideth My Soul"; "All the Way My Savior Leads Me"; "Jesus, Keep Me Near the Cross"; and "Rescue the Perishing." (b. 3/24/1820)

1971 Death of Nelson Glueck, 70, American Jewish archaeologist, educator and author. He discovered King Solomon's copper mines, and over 1,000 artifacts in the Trans-Jordan area, the Negev, using the Bible as a guide. (b. 6/4/1900)

1984 Death of Roland H. Bainton, 89, American Congregational clergyman and ecclesiastical historian. As professor of church history at Yale Divinity School (1920-62), he was a leading authority on the history of the Reformation, and published 32 books, including *Here I Stand* (1950), a life of Martin Luther. (b. 3/30/1894)

Words for the Soul

1807 Anglican missionary to Persia Henry Martyn reflected in his journal: 'Amazing patience, He bears with this faithless foolish heart and suffers me to come, laden with sins, to receive new pardon, new grace, every day! Why does not such love make me hate sin that grieves Him and hides me from His sight?'

1932 As a corrective to Revelation 3:15f, English scholar and mystic Evelyn Underhill advised in a letter: 'The normal movement of the soul to a much quieter, deeper and less emotional type of realization is an advance and not a loss.'

IN GOD'S WORD... OT: Exodus 34:1–35:9 ~ NT: Matthew 27:15-31 ~ Psalms 33:12-22 ~ Proverbs 9:1-6

February 13

Highlights in History

1826 The American Temperance Society (later renamed the American Temperance Union) was organized in Boston. It quickly grew into a national crusade, and within a decade over 8,000 similar groups had been formed.

1849 Otterbein College was chartered in Westerville, Ohio, under sponsorship of the United Brethren Church.

1936 The Lutheran Army and Navy Commission was organized by the Lutheran Church Missouri Synod for the purpose of commissioning chaplains for military service overseas. In 1947 the organization changed its name to the Armed Services Commission.

Notable Birthdays

1800 Birth of Orange Scott, American Methodist minister, abolitionist and a co-founder of the Wesleyan Methodist Church. [d. 7/31/1847]

1881 Birth of Eleanor Farjeon, English author and hymnwriter. An Anglican who converted to Roman Catholicism at age 70, Farjeon authored 80 works, including novels, plays, poems and music. Her most famous hymn was "Morning Has Broken." [d. 6/5/1965]

1919 Birth of Ernest Jennings Ford, Christian country entertainer. "Tennessee Ernie," as he was affectionately called, hosted his own television program between 1955-1965, but is better remembered for the many sacred musical recordings he made during his career. [d. 10/17/1991]

The Last Passage

1602 Death of Alexander Nowell, about 95, English clergyman. While dean of St. Paul's Cathedral in London (1560-1602), he wrote a catechism which was later incorporated into the 1604 Anglican *Book of Common Prayer*. (b. ca. 1507)

1728 Death of Cotton Mather, 65, colonial clergyman and writer. The son of Increase and grandson of Richard Mather, Cotton became the most famous of the early American Puritan clerics. (b. 2/12/1663)

1798 Death of Christian Friedrich Schwartz, 71, German-born Anglican missionary to India for 50 years. He became known as "the Apostle of India." (b. 10/26/1726)

1882 Death of Henry Highland Garnet, 66, American Presbyterian preacher, orator and abolitionist. Garnet helped enlist the first black troops (1863), and became the first African-American to deliver a sermon in the House of Representatives (1865). He later served as minister to Liberia (1879-82). (b. 12/23/1815)

1951 Death of Lloyd C. Douglas, 73, American Congregational clergyman and novelist. He published his first religious novel, *Magnificent Obsession*, in 1929, followed by *The Robe* (1942) and *The Big Fisherman* (1948). (b. 8/27/1877)

1975 Death of Henry Pitney Van Dusen, 77, American Presbyterian clergyman and ecumenical leader. In 1941 Van Dusen co-founded along with Reinhold Niebuhr the journal "Christianity and Crisis," and also helped found the World Council of Churches in 1948. (b. 12/11/1897)

Words for the Soul

1640 Scottish clergyman Samuel Rutherford encouraged in a letter: *'To believe Christ's cross to be a friend, as he himself is a friend, is also a special act of faith.'*

1839 Scottish evangelical clergyman Robert Murray McCheyne wrote in his "Third Pastoral Letter": *'There will be an end of your affliction. Christians must have great tribulation, but... shall we come out the same as we went in? Ah! no, we shall "come out like gold" [Job 23:10]. It is this that sweetens the bitterest cup.... Affliction will certainly purify a believer.'*

IN GOD'S WORD... OT: Exodus 35:10–36:38 ~ NT: Matthew 27:32-66 ~ Psalms 34:1-10 ~ Proverbs 9:7-8

אדר ADAR ALMANAC OF THE CHRISTIAN FAITH שבט SHEVAT

~ February 14 ~

Highlights in History

1805 Colonial American theologian Henry Ware, 41, was confirmed as the first Unitarian professor to teach at Harvard University. Soon after, the Trinitarian teachers began withdrawing from this Congregationalist school, and in 1808 established Andover Theological Seminary.

1949 Russian-born English chemist and Zionist leader Chaim Weizmann, 74, was elected first president of the newly restored State of Israel.

1985 The U.S. Rabbinical Assembly of Conservative Judaism announced its decision to begin accepting women as rabbis. (Orthodox Judaism has yet to officially accept women in its rabbinate, although a few Orthodox women have been ordained in some seminaries.)

Notable Birthdays

1760 Richard Allen, the first African-American ordained in the Methodist Episcopal Church (1799), and founder of the African Methodist Episcopal (AME) Church in 1816, was born in slavery in Philadelphia. [d. 3/26/1831]

1515 Birth of Frederick III, The Pious: Elector of the Palatinate 1557-1576. Raised a Catholic, he embraced Lutheranism in 1549, and later converted to Calvinism in 1561. [d. 10/26/1576]

1792 Birth of William Goodell, pioneer American Congregational missionary to the Near East. He authored *Forty Years in the Turkish Empire* (1876), and also translated the Bible into Armeno-Turkish. [d. 2/18/1867]

1843 Birth of Jesse L. Hurlbut, American Methodist clergyman and Sunday School promoter. He was active in the work at Chautauqua, and was one of the founders of the Epworth League (forerunner of the modern UMY). Hurlbut's most enduring title was for children: *Story of the Bible Told for Young and Old* (1904). [d. 8/2/1930]

1847 Birth of Anna Howard Shaw, English-born American Methodist clergywoman, physician, reformer and suffrage leader. After being denied ordination by the Methodist Episcopal Church, in 1880 she became the first woman to be ordained a minister in the Methodist Protestant Church. [d. 7/2/1919]

1884 Birth of Luther Burgess Bridges, American Methodist clergyman, evangelist and hymnwriter. He lost his wife and three sons in a fire in 1910, and later wrote and composed the hymn, SWEETEST NAME ("There's Within My Heart a Melody"). [d. 5/27/1948]

1914 Birth of Ira F. Stanphill, American Assemblies of God clergyman and song evangelist. He is best known today for his hymn, "Room at the Cross," also for the gospel song "Mansion Over the Hilltop" and the hymn tune HAPPINESS IS THE LORD. [d. 12/30/1993]

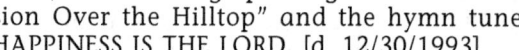

The Last Passage

869 Death of St. Cyril, 43, Apostle (with St. Methodius his brother) to the Southern Slavs. The two Greek brothers devised the Glagolithic alphabet, which gave the Slavs their first written language. John Paul II in 1980 proclaimed both as patron saints of Europe. (b. 826)

1953 Death of Arthur Cyril Barham-Gould, 62, Anglican clergyman and hymn composer: ST. LEONARDS ("May the Mind of Christ My Savior"). (b. 1891)

Words for the Soul

1883 American Quaker and holiness author Hannah Whitall Smith, 51, wrote in a letter to her grown daughter: *'Not that I do not expect you to grow better and better in every way. But... for now I am content with your present stage at your present age. God is making you, and His making is often slow, but it is always sure and I am content to leave it with Him.'*

IN GOD'S WORD... OT: Exodus 37:1–38:31 ~ NT: Matthew 28:1-20 ~ Psalms 34:11-22 ~ Proverbs 9:9-10

ALMANAC OF THE CHRISTIAN FAITH

ADAR — SHEVAT

~ February 15 ~

Highlights in History

1386 King Jagiello of Lithuania was baptized into the Christian faith. Lithuania being the last heathen nation in Europe, Jagiello's conversion became the final fulfillment of the Macedonian Vision in Acts 16:9, which led St. Paul to begin taking the Gospel to Europe.

1860 Wheaton College (located 20 miles west of Chicago) was chartered in Illinois under Methodist sponsorship. The following year the school passed into Congregational control. Today, Wheaton is non-denominational, and hosts a student body which hovers around 3,000.

Notable Birthdays

1571 Birth of Michael Praetorius, German Lutheran musician. As the author of over 20 titles, he became one of the leading and most innovative musicologists in history – all before dying on his 50th birthday! [d. 2/15/1621]

1782 Birth of William Miller, American Baptist lay religious leader. He predicted the second coming of Christ in 1843, then in 1844. His followers were called "Millerites," then "Adventists." The Seventh Day Adventist Church was later founded in the 1860s, based on Miller's teachings. [d. 12/20/1849]

1843 Birth of Russell H. Conwell, American Baptist clergyman, educator, lecturer and author. He was the most noted lecturer on the Chautauqua circuit. Though he published over 30 books, he is best remembered for *Acres of Diamonds* (1888), a lecture he delivered over 6,000 times nationwide. [d. 12/6/1925]

1932 Birth of W. Elmo Mercer, American composer and popular arranger of contemporary Christian music. Among his most popular sacred compositions are "Each Step I Take" and "The Way That He Loves."

The Last Passage

1730 Death of Thomas Bray, 74, Anglican clergyman and missions promoter. In 1698 he founded the Society for Promoting Christian Knowledge (SPCK). Bray was also a co-founder in 1701 of the Society for the Propagation of the Gospel in Foreign Parts. (b. 1656)

1865 Death of Nicholas Patrick Stephen Wiseman, 62, English Catholic cardinal. He was the first Archbishop of Westminster, 1850, and became chiefly responsible for the re-establishment by Pius IX of the Catholic hierarchy in England. (b. 8/2/1802)

1895 Death of John H. Oberholtzer, 86, Pennsylvania-born Mennonite clergyman and founder of the General Conference Mennonite Church. (b. 1/10/1809)

1905 Death of Lew[is] Wallace, 77, American Civil War soldier, lawyer and religious novelist. He penned *Ben Hur: A Tale of the Christ* (1880); *The Boyhood of Christ* (1888); and *Lew Wallace: An Autobiography* (1906). (b. 4/10/1827)

1930 Death of Franklin L. Sheppard, 78. He served on the editorial committee of the 1911 edition of the *Presbyterian Hymnal*, but is better remembered for composing the hymn tune TERRA BEATA, to which "This Is My Father's World" is most commonly sung. (b. 8/7/1852)

Words for the Soul

1762 Anglican hymnwriter John Newton wrote in a letter: *'We serve a gracious Master who knows how to overrule even our mistakes to His glory and our own advantage.'*

1868 Scottish clergyman and biographer Andrew Bonar, 57, observed in his diary: *'I learned one thing over again, that while the Lord seems to use evangelists to awaken souls, He keeps a place for older labourers, in the instruction and leading of the saved. We must all know our own place, and be satisfied.'*

IN GOD'S WORD... OT: Exodus 39:1–40:38 ~ NT: Mark 1:1-28 ~ Psalms 35:1-16 ~ Proverbs 9:11-12

February 16

Highlights in History

1801 In Baltimore, the African Methodist Episcopal Zion (AMEZ) Church officially separated from its parent, the Methodist Episcopal Church. The denomination later became part of the AME Church, reconstituted in 1816 under Richard Allen. It held its first national conference in 1821.

1865 English clergyman Sabine Baring-Gould, 31, first published "Now the Day is Over." This hymn of repose was based on the text of Proverbs 3:24: *'When thou liest down, thou shalt not be afraid... and thy sleep shall be sweet.'*

1911 William P. Merrill, 44, first published his hymn, "Rise Up, O Men of God," in the Presbyterian periodical, "The Continent."

Notable Birthdays

1497 Birth of Philip Melanchthon (Philipp Schwarzerd), German Protestant reformer, theologian and associate of Martin Luther. He penned the first systematic theology of the Protestant Reformation and for the emerging Lutheran Church, instituted the Protestant public school system and created the basic Protestant creed. [d. 4/19/1560]

1790 Birth of Chrétien Urhan, French hymn composer: RUTHERFORD ("The Sands of Time Are Sinking"). [d. 11/2/1845]

1802 Birth of Phineas P. Quimby, American mentalist. Originally a clockmaker in Maine, he later became the founder of mental healing in America. His philosophy lies at the basis of the Unity movement; his teachings are the source for the New Thought movement. [d. 1/16/1866]

1810 Birth of Cushing Eells, American Congregational missionary to the Oregon Territory. He labored for 55 years (1838-93), and at least two of the schools he taught in grew to become institutions of higher learning. [d. 2/17/1893]

1852 Birth of Charles Taze Russell, American sectarian religious leader. Russell established the International Bible Students Association (1878), which later became the Jehovah's Witnesses (1931). He also founded the Watch Tower Bible and Tract Society (1879). [d. 10/31/1916]

The Last Passage

1872 Death of Henry F. Chorley, 63, English Quaker writer and musical editor. He produced many literary works, and is remembered today as the author of the hymn, "God the Omnipotent." (b. 12/15/1808)

1928 Death of William Boyd, 80, Jamaica-born Anglican clergyman and hymnwriter. A student of another hymnwriter, Sabine Baring-Gould, Boyd's own name endures as author of the hymn, "Fight the Good Fight With All Thy Might." (b. 1847)

1953 Death of Francis Hodur, 86, Polish-born American religious leader. Ordained a Catholic priest in 1893, Hodur later became a leader of disaffected Polish Catholic immigrants to the U.S., and in 1907 became the founder and prime bishop (1907-53) of the Polish National Catholic Church of America. (b. 4/2/1866)

Words for the Soul

1741 English revivalist George Whitefield advised in a letter: *'Use the world, but let it be as though you used it not.'*

1809 Former U.S. President John Adams wrote in a letter to Judge F. A. Van der Kemp: *'The Hebrews have done more to civilize men than any other nation.... [God] ordered the Jews to preserve and propagate to all mankind the doctrine of a supreme, intelligent, wise, almighty sovereign of the universe... the great essential principle of morality, and consequently all civilization.'*

IN GOD'S WORD... OT: Leviticus 1:1–3:17 ~ NT: Mark 1:29–2:12 ~ Psalms 35:17-28 ~ Proverbs 9:13-18

February 17

Highlights in History

1815 In deciding the legal case "Terrett v. Taylor," the U.S. Supreme Court declared unconstitutional an act of the Virginia Legislature which denied property rights to Protestant Episcopal churches in the state. The Court ruled that religious corporations, like other corporations, have rights to their property.

1889 Billy Sunday, 27, baseball player-turned-preacher, made his first appearance as an evangelist in Chicago. Sunday preached Fundamentalism, supported temperance and opposed scientific evolution. Over 100 million are said to have heard him preach before his death in 1935.

Notable Birthdays

1816 Birth of Edward Hopper, American Presbyterian clergyman. He pastored several churches in New York state, but is better remembered today for authoring the hymn, "Jesus, Savior, Pilot Me." [d. 4/23/1888]

1888 Birth of Ronald A. Knox, English Catholic scholar and writer. He served as the Catholic chaplain of Oxford University, 1926-39, and also published an English translation of the Bible based on the Vulgate's Latin text. [d. 8/24/1957]

1952 Birth of William Patrick (Pat) Terry, contemporary American Christian music artist and songwriter: "Home Where I Belong."

The Last Passage

1647 Death of Johann Heermann, 61, Silesian clergyman and hymnwriter. He is regarded as the greatest hymnwriter between Martin Luther and Paul Gerhardt. Sixteen of Heermann's lyrics have been translated into English, including "Ah, Holy Jesus, How Hast Thou Offended." (b. 10/11/1585)

1688 Death of James Renwick, 26, Scottish Covenanter. A field preacher for the Cameronians (who had declared Charles II a tyrant and usurper), Renwick was captured and executed, the last of the Scottish Covenanter martyrs. (b. 2/15/1662)

1708 Death of William Rittenhouse, 64, Mennonite clergyman and industrialist. Emigrating from Amsterdam in 1687, he built the first paper mill in America (1690). Rittenhouse was also the first Mennonite clergyman in PA, and in 1703 was elected the first American Mennonite bishop (1703). (b. 1644)

1818 Death of Henry Obookiah (Opukahaia), ca. 26, a Hawaiian Christian convert who came to New England in 1809 to be educated. Obookiah's early death from a fatal fever sparked American missionary interest in the Sandwich (Hawaiian) Islands. (b. ca. 1792)

1903 Death of Joseph Parry, 61, Welsh sacred music scholar. He taught music in Danville, PA, and in the Welsh universities at Aberystwyth and Cardiff. Parry composed "Blodwen," the first Welsh opera, as well as 400 hymn tunes, including ABERYSTWYTH ("Jesus, Lover of My Soul"). (b. 5/21/1841)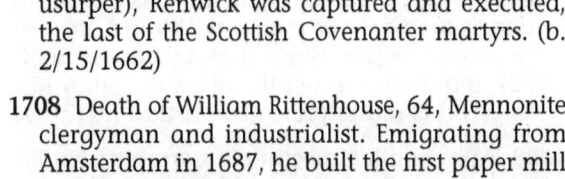

1921 Death of B[enjamin] B. Warfield, 69, American Presbyterian scholar. Teaching at Princeton Seminary from 1887 until his death, Warfield helped shape the Fundamentalist Christian doctrine of Scriptural inerrancy. (b. 11/5/1851)

Words for the Soul

1741 English revivalist George Whitefield advised in a letter: *'Be content with no degree of sanctification. Be always crying out, "Lord, let me know more of myself and of thee."'*

1878 Scottish clergyman and novelist George MacDonald remarked in a letter: *'I want to be God's man, not the man of my own idea.'*

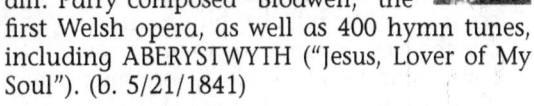

IN GOD'S WORD... OT: Leviticus 4:1–5:19 ~ NT: Mark 2:13–3:6 ~ Psalms 36:1-12 ~ Proverbs 10:1-2

February 18

Highlights in History

1678 John Bunyan's *Pilgrim's Progress* was first published, in England. Bunyan was frequently imprisoned for preaching without a license. During these sequestered times (between 1660-72), Bunyan collected the ideas enabling him to pen this masterpiece of Christian literature.

1688 At a monthly meeting in Germantown, PA, a group of Quakers and Mennonites became the first white body in English America to register a formal abolitionist protest. The historic "Germantown Protest" denounced both slavery and the slave trade.

1867 The Augusta Institute was founded in Georgia. It was established as an institution of higher learning for black students. Augusta moved to Atlanta in 1879, and in 1913 the school changed its name to Morehouse College.

Notable Birthdays

1781 Birth of Henry Martyn, Anglican missionary to India and Persia. Martyn first sailed for the East in 1805. His great linguistic gifts led him to translate the New Testament both into Urdu (Hindustani) and Arabic, before his premature death at age 31. [d. 10/16/1812]

1877 Birth of Douglas Clyde Macintosh, Canadian Baptist clergyman, liberal theologian and educator. Macintosh taught theology at Yale University (1916-38), and authored *The Reaction Against Metaphysics in Theology* (1911); *The Problem of Knowledge* (1915); *The Reasonableness of Christianity* (1925); and *Personal Religion* (1942). [d. 7/6/1948]

1888 Birth of Bernard James Sheil, American Catholic leader. He served as a chaplain during World War I. Later, as auxiliary bishop of Chicago (1928-69), Sheil founded and directed the Catholic Youth Organization (CYO) from 1930-1954. [d. 9/13/1969]

1915 Birth of Matthias Defregger, Auxiliary Catholic bishop of Munich, Germany. During WWII he became a center of controversy over his Army service when Italian villagers were killed on Nazi orders. Defregger refused to carry out the order.

The Last Passage

1546 Death of Martin Luther, 62, German Augustinian priest and Reformer. In 1517, he symbolically inaugurated the Protestant Reformation, and remained its leader until his death. Luther also translated the Bible into German, and penned the hymn, "A Mighty Fortress" (& EIN FESTE BURG). (b. 11/10/1483)

1564 Death of Michelangelo Buonarroti, 88, Italian artist extraordinaire (painter, sculptor, architect, poet). He was a leader of the High Renaissance, and his works include the marble sculpture "David" (1504) and the paintings in the Sistine Chapel (1508-12). (b. 3/6/1475)

1874 Death of William Sandys, 81, English lawyer. It was Sandys who composed the Christmas carol, THE FIRST NOEL. (b. 10/29/1792)

Words for the Soul

1811 Anglican missionary to Persia Henry Martyn, on his 30th birthday (and a year before his death), observed in his journal: *'This day I finished the thirtieth year of my unprofitable life; the age at which David Brainerd finished his course. I am now at the age at which the Saviour of men began his ministry, and at which John the Baptist called a nation to repentance.... Hitherto I have made my youth and insignificance an excuse for sloth,... now let me have a character, and act boldly for God.'*

1901 American Quaker and holiness writer Hannah Whitall Smith, 69, contemplated in a letter: *'How restful it is now, in our old age, to have folded our wings in the blessed haven of absolute certainty that God is enough!'*

IN GOD'S WORD... OT: Leviticus 6:1–7:27 ~ NT: Mark 3:7-30 ~ Psalms 37:1-11 ~ Proverbs 10:3-4

February 19

Highlights in History

842 The Medieval Iconoclastic Controversy ended when a Council in Constantinople, led by Empress Theodora, formally reinstated the veneration of icons (images) in the churches. (This debate over icons is considered the last event which led to the Great Schism between the Eastern and Western Churches in 1054.)

1812 Congregational missionaries Adoniram Judson, 23, and his wife Ann, 22, first sailed from New England to Calcutta, India. From there, they went on to concentrate their labors in Burma, and became two of the most famous American missionaries of their day.

1960 The Christian-based comic strip "Family Circus" appeared for the first time. It was created by American cartoonist Bil Keane (b. 10/5/1922). Today, The "Family Circus" is the most widely syndicated comic panel in the world, appearing in 1,500 newspapers.

Notable Birthdays

1473 Birth of Nicolas Copernicus [Niklas Kopernik], the Polish astronomer who, in 1543, first proposed the heliocentric theory – that the sun is the center of the universe, around which our planets revolve. [d. 5/24/1543]

1802 Birth of Leonard W. Bacon, American Congregational clergyman, educator and editor. He pastored First Congregational Church in New Haven, CT for 56 years (1825-81), and was a leader in the antislavery and temperance movements. He also authored the hymn, "O God, Beneath Thy Guiding Hand." [d. 12/24/1881]

1821 Birth of James George Walton, English composer. He edited *Plain Song Music for the Holy Communion Office* (1874), which contained his adaptation of the hymn tune ST. CATHERINE ("Faith of Our Fathers"). [d. 9/1/1905]

1822 Birth of William Burt Pope, Nova Scotia-born English Methodist theologian. He was sympathetic to the Wesleyan doctrine of Christian perfection, and in 1875-76 produced his greatest work: *A Compendium of Christian Theology* (3 vols.). [d. 7/5/1903]

The Last Passage

1568 Death of Miles Coverdale, 80, a leader of the English Puritan movement, and translator and publisher of the first complete Bible to be printed in English (1535). Coverdale was also editor of the *Great Bible* of 1539. (b. 1488)

1869 Death of Elizabeth Clephane, 39, an orphaned Scottish poet who left the Church with two hauntingly beautiful hymns: "Beneath the Cross of Jesus" and "The Ninety and Nine." (The entire sum of Clephane's poetry was published posthumously.) (b. 6/18/1830)

1849 Death of Bernard Barton, 65, remembered as England's "Quaker poet." Though a bank clerk for 40 years, he enjoyed the friendship of such famous authors as Charles Lamb, Lord Byron, Sir Walter Scott and Robert Southey. Barton is also credited with 20 hymns, which came from his several volumes of poetry. (b. 1/31/1784)

Words for the Soul

1701 French clergyman François Fénelon encouraged in a letter: 'People who love themselves rightly... deal with self as they would deal with someone else they wished to bring to God. They set to work patiently,... not being disheartened, because perfection is not attainable in a day.... They do not heed the peevishness... which so often... discourages a man, makes him self-absorbed, repels him from God's service,... fills him with disgust and despair of ever reaching his end.... The only thing to be done is to let such [peevishness] pass away, like a headache or a feverish attack.'

IN GOD'S WORD... OT: Leviticus 7:28–9:6 ~ NT: Mark 3:31–4:25 ~ Psalms 37:12-29 ~ Proverbs 10:5

אדר ALMANAC OF THE CHRISTIAN FAITH שבט
ADAR   SHEVAT

~ February 20 ~

Highlights in History

1878 Following the death of Pius IX, Italian cardinal Gioacchino Pecci, 67, was elected Pope Leo XIII. His papacy, possibly the century's most productive, was best known for his teaching encyclicals and for establishing in 1902 the Pontifical Biblical Commission.

Notable Birthdays

1464/69 Birth of Jacopo Tommaso de Vio Cajetan, Italian cardinal, theologian, and general of the Dominican order (1508-18). Leo X sent him to Germany to unite the princes against the Turks. While there Cajetan tried unsuccessfully to get Martin Luther to recant and win him back to the Church. Cajetan was also one of the 19 cardinals who met with Clement VII and rejected the request of Henry VIII for a divorce from Catherine of Aragon. [d. 8/10/1534]

1803 Birth of John W. Nevin, American German Reformed theologian and educator. His teachings were basic to the "Mercersburg Theology," of which he was spokesman. He served as professor at Mercersburg (PA) Seminary (1840-53), president of Franklin and Marshall College (1866-76), and as editor of the "Mercersburg Review." [d. 6/6/1886]

1833 Birth of Charles Nelson Crittenton, American businessman, evangelist and philanthropist. In 1884 he opened a home for unwed mothers in New York City that became the beginning of the Florence Crittenton Mission (named after his 4-year-old daughter whose death had precipitated his conversion). The number of "Florence Homes" totaled more than 70 by the time of Crittenton's death. [d. 11/16/1909]

1872 Birth of Charles G. Trumbull, American evangelical journalist and author. He was a leader of the American holiness movement, having gained widespread acceptance for Keswick Holiness teachings among American and Canadian evangelicals. He authored several books, and was editor of "The Sunday School Times" (1893-1941). [d. 1/13/1941]

The Last Passage

1715 Death of Charles Calvert, 78, the English third Lord Baltimore, and last Catholic proprietor of Maryland. He governed the colony from 1661-1684. (b. 8/27/1637)

1860 Death of Henry Drummond, 73, English-born writer and one of the founders of the Catholic Apostolic Church. (b. 12/5/1786)

1960 Death of English archaeologist Sir Charles Leonard Woolley, 80. He spent over 40 years in the field, and is remembered for excavating Ur of the Chaldees, and for discovering the ancient Sumerian civilization. (b. 4/17/1880)

1976 Death of Kathryn Kuhlman, 69, popular American radio and TV evangelist. A member of the American Baptist Convention, Kuhlman's preaching emphasized the healing power of the Holy Spirit. (b. 5/9/1907)

Words for the Soul

1637 While in exile from his parishioners, Scottish clergyman Samuel Rutherford wrote in a letter: *'See that you buy the field where the Pearl is; sell all, and make a purchase of salvation. Think it not easy: for it is a steep ascent to eternal glory: many are lying dead by the way, slain with security.'*

1743 Colonial missionary to the American Indians David Brainerd wrote in his journal: *'Selfish religion loves Christ for his benefits, but not for himself.'*

1950 American missionary and Auca Indian martyr Jim Elliot recorded in his journal: *'One may know God's work for his soul without understanding it all.... Let the heart be warm, at all costs to the head, in the getting of Christianity.'*

IN GOD'S WORD...   OT: Leviticus 9:7–10:20 ~ NT: Mark 4:26–5:20 ~ Psalms 37:30-40 ~ Proverbs 10:6-7

ADAR — ALMANAC OF THE CHRISTIAN FAITH — **SHEVAT**

February 21

Highlights in History

1529 The first Diet of Speyer convened, in Germany. Summoned by Charles V, the Roman Catholic majority passed legislation ending all toleration of Lutherans in Catholic districts. During this proceedings, six Lutherans princes and fourteen cities made a formal "protest," defending freedom of conscience. From this date on, the Reformers were known as "Protestants."

1795 Freedom of worship was established in France under the constitution that came out of the French Revolution of 1789.

1864 In Baltimore, MD, the first Catholic parish church established for African-Americans, St. Francis Xavier's Church – purchased on Oct. 10, 1863 – was dedicated.

Notable Birthdays

1801 Birth of John Henry Cardinal Newman, English clergyman, theologian and author. He helped found the Oxford Movement, which sought to return the Church of England to the high ideals of the latter 17th century. Ultimately, Newman converted to Catholicism (1845), explaining why in his autobiographical *Apologia Pro Vita Sua* (1864). He also authored the hymn, "Lead, Kindly Light." [d. 8/11/1890]

1808 Birth of Johannes K. W. Loehe, German clergyman, philanthropist and missions pioneer. Working with groups of immigrants to America, Loehe helped lay the foundations of the Lutheran Church Missouri Synod, although he never left Germany. [d. 10/2/1872]

The Last Passage

1513 Death of Julius II, 69, Italian-born pope from 1503-13. Julius was the greatest art patron of all the popes. He laid the cornerstone of St. Peter's Basilica and commissioned Michelangelo's Sistine Chapel frescoes. It was also, however, the issuance of Julius' indulgence for the rebuilding of St. Peter's that occasioned Martin Luther to post his "Ninety-Five Theses." (b. 12/5/1443)

1876 Death of Henry John Gauntlett, 70, English sacred organist and hymnwriter. One of Britain's leading musicians in the mid-19th century, Gauntlett composed as many as 10,000 hymn tunes, including IRBY ("Once in Royal David's City"). (b. 7/9/1805)

1945 Death of Eric Liddell, 43, Scottish Olympic champion runner. Liddell – who became a missionary to China after finishing his college education – was captured by the Japanese during WWII, and died of a brain tumor while still imprisoned. (His college running days were portrayed in the 1981 British film, "Chariots of Fire.") (b. 1/16/1902)

Words for the Soul

1756 English founder of Methodism John Wesley wrote in a letter: *'The longer I live, the larger allowances I make for human infirmities.'*

1836 Scottish evangelist and clergyman Robert Murray McCheyne reflected in his journal: *'In the morning was more engaged in preparing the head than the heart. This has been frequently my error, and I have always felt the evil of it, especially in prayer.'*

1930 English scholar and mystic Evelyn Underhill advised in a letter: *'It is quite impossible for any of us to measure ourselves and estimate our progress. Our job, having found the path we honestly believe God wishes us to follow, is to go quietly on with it and leave the results to Him!'*

1974 Russian Orthodox liturgical scholar Alexander Schmemann reflected in his journal: *'The meaning of religion consists only in filling life with light, in referring it to God, transforming it into a relationship with God.'*

IN GOD'S WORD... OT: Leviticus 11:1–12:8 ~ NT: Mark 5:21-43 ~ Psalms 38:1-22 ~ Proverbs 10:8-9

February 22

Highlights in History

1281 Italian cardinal Simon de Brie was elected Pope Martin IV, serving until 1285. During his pontificate, he excommunicated Greek Emperor Michael Paleologus (1281), thus destroying the union between the Eastern and Western Churches which had been strengthened at the 1274 Council of Lyons.

1354 Pope Innocent VI declared that, in England, the Archbishop of York should be called "the Primate of England," and the Archbishop of Canterbury "the Primate of All England." Thus was settled the ancient dispute regarding the privileges and veneration order of these two prestigious Catholic diocesan appointments.

1819 The American Catholic parochial school system was begun by Mother Elizabeth Ann Seton in Emmittsburg, MD.

1906 Louisiana-born Baptist evangelist William J. Seymour, 35, first arrived in Los Angeles and began holding evangelistic meetings. The "Azusa Street Revival" soon broke out under Seymour's leadership, in the Apostolic Faith Mission located at 312 Azusa Street in L.A. It became one of the landmark events in the history of 20th century American Pentecostalism.

Notable Birthdays

1805 Birth of English Unitarian poet and hymnwriter, Sarah Flower Adams. She published much of her verse in "The Repository," a periodical edited by her minister, William Johnson Fox. The best-known of her hymns is "Nearer, My God, To Thee," to which her sister Eliza Flower wrote the music. [d. 8/14/1848]

1838 Birth of Margaret E. M. Sangster, American Presbyterian author and editor. Her essays, published in dozens of periodicals, reflected Sangster's belief that she had a "mission to girlhood" to be a Christian leader. [d. 6/3/1912]

1906 Birth of Betty (née Scott) Stam, American Presbyterian missionary and martyr. She met her husband John at Moody Bible Institute, afterward going to China in 1931 together as missionaries of the China Inland Mission. While there, both were martyred – beheaded by Communists who invaded their station at Tsingteh, Anhui. [d. 12/7/1934]

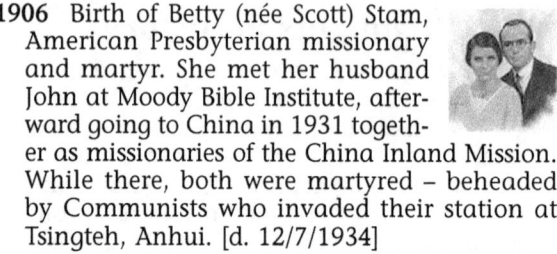

The Last Passage

1846 Death of Martin Stephan, 68, Lutheran clergyman. He led 612 Saxon Lutheran immigrants to America in 1839 (the nucleus of what later became the Lutheran Church Missouri Synod). Shortly after their arrival in Missouri, Stephan was expelled from the group on charges of sexual immorality. He afterward moved to Illinois, where he served another congregation until his death. (b. 8/13/1777)

1985 Death of Alexander Scourby, 71, American film actor. His most memorable screen role was in "Giant" (1956). Known best for a resonant bass elocution, Scourby lent his voice to reading the King James Version on early audio cassette tapes of the Bible. (b. 11/13/1913)

Words for the Soul

1980 American Presbyterian apologist Francis Schaeffer wrote in a letter: *'None of us are normal, even after we are Christians – if we mean by that being perfect. What is possible, however, is for us to live in the fullness of life in the circle of who we are, constantly pressing on the border lines to try to take further steps.'*

1996 Dutch Catholic spiritual writer Henri J. M. Nouwen reflected in his **Sabbatical Journey** diary: *'It is sad that the [Matt 16:17-19] dialogue between Jesus and Peter has, in my church, been almost exclusively used to explain the role of the papacy. By doing so, it seems to me that we miss seeing that this exchange is for all of us. We all have to confess our need for salvation.'*

IN GOD'S WORD... OT: Leviticus 13:1-59 ~ NT: Mark 6:1-29 ~ Psalms 39:1-13 ~ Proverbs 10:10

אדר ALMANAC OF THE CHRISTIAN FAITH שבט

ADAR · SHEVAT

~ February 23 ~

Highlights in History

1970 For the first time in a Roman Catholic service, the Holy Eucharist was distributed by women.

1982 The U.S. Supreme Court ruled that members of the Old Order Amish Church who operate businesses must pay Social Security and unemployment taxes, despite their religious belief that paying taxes is sin.

Notable Birthdays

1400 Birth of Johannes Gutenberg, German printer. Regarded as the inventor (ca.1449) of movable type printing in Europe, Gutenberg published the Mazarin Bible in 1456, the first full-length book ever thus printed. [d. 2/3/1468]

1685 Birth of Georg Frideric Handel, German-born English composer. Of his religious compositions, the most famous of his oratorios, "Messiah," was first performed in 1742. He also composed the hymn tunes CHRISTMAS ("While Shepherds Watched Their Flocks By Night"); ANTIOCH ("Joy to the World! The Lord is Come") and MACCABEUS ("Thine Be the Glory, Risen, Conquering Son"). [d. 4/20/1759]

1798 Birth of Thomas Evans, American Quaker clergyman. He made extensive compilations of Quaker history and doctrine. [d. 1868]

1816 Birth of John Ernest Bode, English clergyman and poet. He served as rector, both in Oxfordshire (1847-60) and in Cambridgeshire (1860-74). Today, Bode is remembered as author of the hymn, "O Jesus, I Have Promised." [d. 10/6/1874]

1832 Birth of John H. Vincent, American Methodist bishop (1888-1904) and a promoter of the Sunday School. As general agent of the Methodist Sunday School Union (1866-86), he co-founded the world-famous Chautauqua conferences (for training Methodist S.S. teachers) in western New York state (1874). [d. 5/9/1920]

The Last Passage

156 Martyrdom of Polycarp, 86, Bishop of Smyrna, under Roman Emperor Marcus Aurelius. According to legend, Polycarp was to be burned at the stake, but the flames would not touch him, and when pierced with a sword, his blood quenched the flames. (b. ca. 70)

1072 Death of St. Peter Damian, 65, Italian monk and hermit. A leader of the 11th century reform movement, he was famous as an uncompromising preacher against worldliness and against simony among the clergy. A trusted advisor to several popes, he served as a papal legate to Germany in 1069. (b. 1007)

1447 Pope Eugenius IV (born Gabriele Condulmaro) died at 64. Under his pontificate (1431-1447) Joan of Arc was burned at the stake (1431), and the Greek and Roman Churches underwent their last and permanent division. (b. 1383)

1662 Death of German hymnwriter Johann Crüger, 63. He penned the hymn tunes NUN DANKET ALLE GOTT ("Now Thank We All Our God"); HERZLIEBSTER JESU ("Ah, Holy Jesus, How Hast Thou Offended"); and ZUVERSICHT ("Jesus Lives, and So Shall I"). (b. 4/9/1598)

Words for the Soul

1690 French mystical theologian François Fénelon advised in a letter: 'It is only in beholding and loving God that we can... measure duly the nothingness of that which has dazzled us, and accustom ourselves thankfully to "decrease" beneath that great majesty that absorbs all things.'

1785 Anglican "Methodist" vicar John Fletcher detailed in a letter: 'A lesson I learn daily is to see things and persons in their invisible root and in their eternal principle, where they are not subject to change, decay, and death.... By this means I learn to walk by faith and not by sight.... "Lord, let me see all things more clearly, that I may never mistake a shadow for the substance."'

IN GOD'S WORD...   OT: Leviticus 14:1-57 ~ NT: Mark 6:30-56 ~ Psalms 40:1-10 ~ Proverbs 10:11-12

ALMANAC OF THE CHRISTIAN FAITH

ADAR / SHEVAT

~ February 24 ~

Highlights in History

303 The first official Roman edict for the persecution of Christians was issued by Roman Emperor Galerius Valerius Maximianus.

1208 St. Francis of Assisi, 26, received his vocation in the Italian village of Portiuncula. He founded the Franciscans the following year, and is regarded by some Catholics as the greatest of all Christian saints.

Notable Birthdays

1463 Birth of Giovanni Pico Della Mirandola, Italian Renaissance theologian and philosopher who stressed free will. Knowing Hebrew, Aramaic and Arabic, he was the first to seek in the Cabbala (Kabbalah) a clue to the Christian mysteries. [d. 11/17/1494]

1500 Birth of Holy Roman Emperor Charles V. Reigning 1519-56, it was Charles who officially pronounced Martin Luther an outlaw and a heretic. [d. 9/21/1558]

1536 Birth of Clement VIII (Ippolito Aldobranini), pope from 1592-1605. Clement, beloved by the poor in Rome, also revised the *Latin Vulgate* translation of the Bible. [d. 3/5/1605]

1811 Birth of Daniel Alexander Payne, African Methodist Episcopal bishop, educator and church historian. [d. 11/29/1893]

1887 Birth of Mary Ellen Chase, Maine-born American educator and author. She taught English literature at Smith College (1929-55), and authored *The Bible and the Common Reader* (1944) and *Life and Language in the Old Testament* (1955). [d. 7/28/1973]

1902 Birth of English missionary Gladys Aylward. The award-winning 1958 Ingrid Bergman film, "Inn of the Sixth Happiness," was based on her life and work among the Chinese between 1932-1948. [d. 1/3/1970]

The Last Passage

1816 Death of Charles Inglis, 82, first Anglican bishop in colonial North America. He served in the mid-Atlantic colonies, and in 1787 was consecrated Bishop of Nova Scotia. (b. 1734)

1863 Death of Anton Günther, 79, German religious philosopher. He held that human reason could scientifically prove the mysteries of the Trinity and Incarnation, and that there was no cleavage between natural and supernatural truth. (b. 11/17/1783)

1915 Death of Amanda Berry Smith, 78, African-American Methodist evangelist and missionary to India and Africa. (b. 1/23/1837)

1946 Death of Charles M. Sheldon, 89, American Congregational clergyman, reformer, and devotional writer. He is best remembered for authoring the spiritual novel *In His Steps* (1897), which first introduced the recently popularized question: "What Would Jesus Do?" (b. 2/26/1857)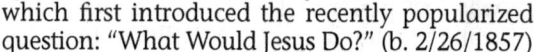

Words for the Soul

1782 Pioneer American Methodist bishop Francis Asbury wrote in his journal: *'It is my constitutional weakness to be gloomy and dejected; the work of God puts life into me.'*

1867 American Quaker holiness author Hannah Whitall Smith, 35, penned in her journal: *'I find that I have been looking for an experience, instead of Jesus. My soul has been drawn out after the gifts of my Beloved, instead of after my Beloved himself. But I trusted Him to teach me, and He has taught me that He himself is enough to satisfy my utmost need, and my soul rests in Him.'*

1967 Swiss Reformed theologian Karl Barth wrote in a letter: *'The statement that God is dead comes from Nietzsche and has recently been trumpeted abroad by some German and American theologians. But the good Lord has not died of this; He who dwells in the heaven laughs at them.'*

IN GOD'S WORD... OT: Leviticus 15:1–16:28 ~ NT: Mark 7:1-23 ~ Psalms 40:11-17 ~ Proverbs 10:13-14

February 25

Highlights in History

1570 Elizabeth I of England was excommunicated by Pope Pius V for her persecution of Roman Catholics. (It was the last such judgment made against a reigning monarch by any pope.)

1913 Pioneer missionary Eduard L. Arndt first arrived in Shanghai, China, 10 months after having founded the Evangelical Lutheran Missions for China. He went on to establish mission schools in the Hankow territory, and translated hymns and sermons into Chinese. (In 1917 the LCMS took over the ELMC mission.)

Notable Birthdays

1803 Birth of Heinrich Ernst Ferdinand Guericke, German theologian and author. Among his best-known writings were: *Handbook of Church History*; *Christian Symbolism*; and *Manual of Christian Archaeology*. [d. 2/4/1878]

1902 Birth of Oscar Cullmann, German New Testament scholar. Best known for pioneering a "salvation history" view of the New Testament, Cullmann's two best-known publications were *Christ and Time* (1946) and *Christology of the New Testament* (1959). [d. 1/19/1999]

1927 Birth of Bruce Ritter, American Franciscan priest who founded Covenant House (1972), an international child care agency that operates short-term crisis centers. [d. 10/7/1999]

The Last Passage

779 Death of St. Walburga, English missionary to Germany. The sister of Sts. Willibald and Winnibald, she is said to have aided St. Boniface in converting the Germans. (b. ca. 710)

1536 Death of Berthold Haller, 44, Swiss Protestant Reformer. As a fellow-student with Philipp Melanchthon, Haller came to Bern, Switzerland in 1521, and allied himself with Zwingli. The Reformation leader in Bern after Zwingli's death in 1531, Haller spent his last years in disputes with the Anabaptists. (b. 1492)

1723 Death of Christopher Wren, 90, English architect and astronomer. He proposed a plan for rebuilding London after the Great Fire of 1666. Wren designed over 50 churches in London, including St. Paul's Cathedral. (b. 10/20/1632)

1796 Death of Samuel Seabury, 66, American Episcopal theologian and pamphleteer. A loyalist during the American revolution, he later became the first American-born Protestant Episcopal bishop in America. (b. 11/30/1729)

1940 Death of Mary Mills Patrick, 89, American educator and missionary. She was sent to Turkey in 1871 by the American Board of Commissioners for Foreign Missions. In 1890 she founded the American College for Girls at Constantinople. Her autobiography, *Under Five Sultans*, was published in 1929. (b. 3/10/1850)

1957 Death of William Frederick Arndt, 76, American Lutheran New Testament scholar. He co-edited (with F. Wilbur Gingrich) *A Greek-English Lexicon of the New Testament and Other Early Christian Literature* (1957, 1971). (b. 12/1/1880)

1984 Death of Jessamyn West, 81, an American author whose stories were based on the lives of her Quaker ancestors. Her first collection, *The Friendly Persuasion*, published in 1945, was later made into a 1956 film. (b. 7/18/1902)

Words for the Soul

1738 English revivalist George Whitefield wrote in a letter: *'God, I find, has a people everywhere; Christ has a flock, though but a little flock, in all places.'*

1865 Scottish clergyman Andrew Bonar reasoned in his diary: *'Shall I ever have a hard thought of such a Lord as mine? His afflictions are sent in deep love, and then followed up by new mercies, as if He were hastening to soften the stroke.'*

IN GOD'S WORD... OT: Leviticus 16:29–18:30 ~ NT: Mark 7:24–8:10 ~ Psalms 41:1-13 ~ Proverbs 10:15-16

February 26

Highlights in History

1732 In Philadelphia, Mass was celebrated for the first time at St. Joseph's Church — the first and only Roman Catholic church built and maintained in the American colonies before the American Revolutionary War. The service was led by Rev. Joseph Greaton.

1963 The Lutheran World Federation's missionary radio station at Addis Ababa, in Ethiopia, was dedicated. (Founded in 1947 in Lund, Sweden, the LWF is a voluntary association of Lutheran churches throughout the world.)

Notable Birthdays

1807 Birth of Johann K. F. Keil, German biblical scholar. An orthodox conservative of the E.W. Hengstenberg school, he regarded "scientific theology" as a passing fad. Keil's Old Testament commentary (1861) was written in collaboration with Franz J. Delitzsch. It is affectionately known today as *Keil & Delitzsch*. [d. 5/5/1888]

1846 Birth of George C. Stebbins, American Baptist music evangelist. He composed over 1,500 songs, but is remembered today primarily for the melodies to the hymns: "I've Found a Friend," "Take Time to Be Holy," "Have Thine Own Way, Lord" and "Jesus is Tenderly Calling Thee Home." [d. 10/6/1945]

1857 Birth of Charles M. Sheldon, American Congregational clergyman, social reformer, and devotional writer. His religious novel *In His Steps* (1897) was a bestseller and eventually sold 23 million copies. It was this book, and this author, who first asked the W.W.J.D. question: "What Would Jesus Do?" [d. 2/24/1946]

The Last Passage

1536 Death of Austrian Anabaptist pastor Jakob Hutter, 36. He first appeared among the Swiss (Anabaptist) Brethren in Austerlitz, Moravia and organized the group (later called Hutterites) into a communal form of life. In the end, Hutter died a martyr: burned at the stake in Innsbruck. (b. 1500)

1927 Death of Henry Preserved Smith, 79, American Presbyterian clergyman and O.T. scholar. He authored *A Critical and Exegetical Commentary on the Books of Samuel* (1899). (b. 10/23/1847)

1954 Death of William Ralph Inge, 93, Anglican clergyman, theologian and author. Referred to as "the Gloomy Dean" because of his pessimism, he was Divinity professor at Oxford (1907-11); Dean of St. Paul's in London (1911-34). Though not a mystic, he was interested in advanced spiritual experience as the foundation for one's faith. Inge's career flourished between the two World Wars, and he urged readers to take refuge in the assurance of direct spiritual intuition at a time when morals were in chaos, and scientists held no hope for a paradise on earth. (b. 6/6/1860)

Words for the Soul

1776 Founder of Methodism John Wesley advised in a letter: 'Visit the poor, the widow, the sick, the fatherless, in their affliction.... It is true, this is not pleasing to flesh and blood.... But yet the blessing which follows this labour of love will more than balance the cross.'

1840 Scottish evangelistic clergyman Robert Murray McCheyne wrote in a letter: 'Our soul should be a mirror of Christ; we should reflect every feature: for every grace in Christ there should be a counterpart in us.'

1891 American Quaker holiness author Hannah Whitall Smith, 59, wrote in a letter: 'It is a delightful feeling to find one's self gradually getting done with this world. It seems such an assurance or prophecy of the better country.... Not that I have any immediate prospect of getting there, but I do like to feel that I have begun to pack up to go.' [N.B: Smith died 20 years later, in 1911, at age 79.]

IN GOD'S WORD... OT: Leviticus 19:1–20:21 ~ NT: Mark 8:11-38 ~ Psalms 42:1-11 ~ Proverbs 10:17

ADAR — ALMANAC OF THE CHRISTIAN FAITH — SHEVAT

February 27

Highlights in History

380 Emperor Theodosius issued an edict suppressing Arianism and making Christianity the official faith of the Roman Empire. (Although the emperor Constantine legitimized the Christian faith after his conversion in A.D. 312, it was the Theodosian Codes and Edicts which first attempted to codify Christianity within the wider culture of the Roman Empire.)

1847 Rev. John L Lenhart was commissioned a chaplain of the Navy. In 1862, off Hampton Roads, Virginia, when the Confederate ironclad *Merrimac* drove her iron prow into the Union frigate *Cumberland*, Chaplain Lenhart died with his sinking ship, thereby making him the first U.S. Navy chaplain to be killed in action.

Notable Birthdays

280 Birth of Constantine the Great, the Roman emperor who, in A.D. 312, was first converted to the Christian faith. [d. 3/22/337]

1717 Birth of Johann D. Michaelis, German Protestant biblical scholar. He pioneered in the historical critical study of Scripture, and also did important work in Arabic studies and on early versions of the Bible. [d. 8/22/1791]

1746 Birth of Samuel Spring, American Congregational clergyman. He served the church in Newburyport, MA for 42 years (1777-1819). An extreme Calvinist in theology, Spring was instrumental in founding Andover Seminary and also the American Board of Commissioners for Foreign Missions. [d. 3/4/1819]

1838 Birth of William J. Kirkpatrick, American Methodist sacred composer. He edited his first collection of hymns at age 21, and is remembered today for composing the melodies to such sacred favorites as "He Hideth My Soul," "'Tis So Sweet to Trust in Jesus," "Redeemed, How I Love to Proclaim It" and "Lord, I'm Coming Home." [d. 9/20/1921]

1843 Birth of Joseph Y. Peek, American Methodist hymnwriter. He was a farmer, a drug store clerk, a Civil War soldier, a florist, also a violin, piano and banjo player. Peek then entered the Methodist ministry, but was fully ordained only two months before his death. Today, he is remembered as the composer of the hymn tune PEEK ("I Would Be True"). [d. 3/17/1911]

1871 Birth of Lewis Sperry Chafer, American Presbyterian clergyman and educator. He was founder, president and professor of systematics at Dallas Theological Seminary. [d. 8/22/1952]

The Last Passage

1659 Death of Henry Dunster, 49, Congregational minister and educator. He was the first president of Harvard College. (b. 11/26/1609)

1830 Death of Elias Hicks, 81, noted American Quaker preacher and abolitionist. In 1827-28 he organized a "liberal" faction of the Society of Friends, afterward known as Hicksites. He also authored *Observations on the Slavery of the Africans* (1811); *The Quaker* (4 vols., 1827-28); and *Journal* (1832). (b. 3/19/1748)

1893 Death of Benjamin Titus Roberts, 69, American Methodist clergyman, and an organizer of the Free Methodist Church. (b. 7/25/1823)

Words for the Soul

1742 English revivalist George Whitefield predicted in a letter: *'The greater advances you make in the divine life, the more you will see what a dream you and the polite world have been in.'*

1769 Founder of Methodism John Wesley, while in London, wrote in his journal: *'I had one more agreeable conversation with my old friend and fellow laborer, George Whitefield. His soul appeared to be vigorous still, but his body was sinking apace; unless God interposes, he must soon finish his labors.'* [N.B. Whitefield died the following Sept. 30, 1770, at the relatively young age of 56.]

IN GOD'S WORD... OT: Leviticus 20:22–22:16 ~ NT: Mark 9:1-29 ~ Psalms 43:1-5 ~ Proverbs 10:18

February 28

Highlights in History

870 The Fourth Constantinople Council closed, under Pope Adrian II in the West and Emperor Basil I in the East. The council had condemned iconoclasm, and became the last ecumenical council held in the Eastern Mediterranean area.

1759 Pope Clement XIII granted permission for the Bible to be translated into the languages of the Roman Catholic states.

1784 English churchman John Wesley, 80, formally chartered the movement within Anglicanism which afterward came to be known as (in England: Wesleyan) Methodism.

Notable Birthdays

1764 Birth of Robert Haldane, Scottish evangelist, writer and philanthropist. He was the elder brother of another evangelist, James Haldane (1768-1851). Along with his brother Robert founded The Society for Propagating the Gospel at Home, which influenced the development of the Congregational Churches. [d. 12/12/1842]

1797 Birth of Mary Lyon, American Christian educator. She was founding president of Mt. Holyoke College (originally Female Seminary) in Mass., 1837-49 – the first women's college in the U.S. [d. 3/5/1849]

1799 Birth of Johann Joseph Ignaz von Döllinger, German Catholic church historian and theologian. He was professor of church history at Munich for 47 years (1826-73). A leading German Catholic, Döllinger refused to accept the decree of papal infallibility, and was excommunicated in 1871. [d. 1/10/1890]

1815 Birth of German Protestant Orientalist Karl Heinrich Graf. He lent his name to the Graf-Welhausen (a.k.a. Documentary) Hypothesis, which postulated four earlier (oral or written) sources to the final text of the Pentateuch: a J[ahwist], an E[lohist], a D[euteronomist] and a P[riestly editor]. [d. 5/16/1869]

1823 Birth of Joseph E. Renan, French humanist, historian of religions and philologist. He wrote *Life of Jesus* (1863), the first biography to treat Jesus as a historical figure. [d. 10/2/1892]

1865 Birth of Sir Wilfred T. Grenfell, English-born medical missionary to Labrador, Newfoundland. He built hospitals and schools, supporting his missionary labors with his writings. Grenfell fitted out the first hospital ship to serve fishermen in the North Sea. [d. 10/9/1940]

1889 Birth of George Jeffreys, Welsh Pentecostal evangelist. The founder and leader of the Elim Foursquare Gospel Alliance, Jeffreys is claimed by Pentecostals as "England's greatest evangelist since Wesley and Whitefield." [d. 1/26/1962]

The Last Passage

1551 Death of Martin Bucer (Butzer), 59, German Protestant reformer. He sought to unite the followers of Zwingli and Luther, and became leader of the Reformed churches after Zwingli's death. (b. 11/11/1491)

1953 Death of Eliezer L. Sukenik, 64, Israeli archaeologist. The father of archaeologist Yigael Yadin, Sukenik was the first scholar to identify the newly discovered Dead Sea Scrolls (1947). He was also the first to suggest that the Scrolls were Essene in origin. (b. 8/12/1889)

Words for the Soul

1783 Anglican Evangelical Henry Venn testified in a letter: *'He who knoweth all hearts, knoweth I long to be doing something for Him!'*

1846 Scottish clergyman and biographer Andrew Bonar prayed in his diary: *'The Lord make me as humble as if I had been deserted, and yet as thankful as if it had been twice as good a day.'*

1947 U.S. Senate Chaplain Peter Marshall prayed: *'Let not the past ever be so dear to us as to set a limit to the future. Give us the courage to change our minds when that is needed.'*

IN GOD'S WORD... OT: Leviticus 22:17-33 ~ NT: Mark 9:30-50 ~ Psalms 44:1-3 ~ Proverbs 10:19

February 29

Highlights in History

1692 The Salem Witch Trials began when Tituba, female West Indies servant of the Rev. Samuel Parris of Salem, Massachusetts, and one Sarah Goode were arrested and accused of witchcraft. During the next two years, 150 individuals were imprisoned, and 20 were executed — many on the testimony of 12-year-old Anne Putnam. Under the influence of Increase Mather, the mania was eventually brought to an end.

1880 American New England evangelist Frank Sandford, 18, was converted to a believing Christian faith. As a Bible school founder and utopian visionary, Sandford founded the Shiloh movement in the 1890s, and went on to become an instrumental figure in Holiness and Pentecostal history, influencing many Holiness people who ultimately became Pentecostals.

Notable Birthdays

1468 Birth of Paul III (Alessandro Farnese), Italian Catholic leader. His pontificate (1534-49) marked the first stages of Counter-Reformation. It was Paul who called the Council of Trent, 1545; established the Inquisition; approved the Society of Jesus (Jesuits), 1540; and excommunicated England's Henry VIII. [d. 11/10/1549]

1692 Birth of John Byrom, English poet and hymnologist. Byrom was originator of the phrase "tweedledum and tweedledee." Among his best-known hymns is "Christians, Awake, Salute the Happy Morn." [d. 9/26/1763]

1736 Birth of Ann Lee, English-born religious leader. She founded the United Society of Believers in Christ's Second Appearing — more popularly known as the Shaking Quakers, or Shakers. "Mother Ann" also established the first Shaker colony in America at Watervliet, NY in 1776, becoming leader of American history's first conscientious objectors. [d. 9/8/1784]

The Last Passage

468 Death of Pope St. Hilary (Hilarius), 46th Bishop of Rome. During his seven-year pontificate, he reaffirmed the earlier Church Councils of Nicea (325), Ephesus (431) and Chalcedon (451), through which the major creeds of the Early Church were hammered out.

1528 Martyrdom of Scottish reformer Patrick Hamilton, 24. After spending time with Martin Luther and William Tyndale, Hamilton began promoting the Reformation in Scotland. He was eventually arrested and burned at the stake — one of the first martyrs of the Scottish Reformation. (b. 1504)

1604 Death of John Whitgift, about 74, Archbishop of Canterbury from 1583-1604. He was a stern disciplinarian, and strove to strengthen and unify the Church of England, opposing both papal and Puritan influences. Whitgift helped draft the 1595 Lambeth Articles, nine Calvinist propositions which lent their support to double predestination. (b. ca. 1530)

1960 Death of Thomas O. Chisholm, 93, American poet and hymnwriter. He penned over 1200 poems, 800 of which were published. Many of these were later set to music, giving us the hymns: "Great Is Thy Faithfulness"; "Oh to be Like Thee"; "Living for Jesus a Life That is True." (b. 7/29/1866)

Words for the Soul

1740 English revivalist George Whitefield confessed in a letter: *'To the best of my knowledge, I preach the truth as it is in Jesus, and simply aim at bringing souls to him. Blessed be his free grace for the success he hath been pleased to give me.'*

1948 American missionary and Auca Indian martyr Jim Elliot wrote in his journal: *'Redemption marks the new beginning of life. Men and women do not live at all until they have life eternal.'*

IN GOD'S WORD... OT: Leviticus 23:1-44 ~ NT: Mark 10:1-12 ~ Psalms 44:4-8 ~ Proverbs 10:20

FEBRUARY INDEX

A

Abbott, Lyman
b. 12/18/1835 [d. 10/22/1922]
Act for Separation of Church and State (1905) 12/9
Adoptionist Heresy 12/25
Adrian I, Pope (772-95)
(b. unknown) d. 12/25/795
Adrian IV, Pope (1154-59) 12/4
Alcoholics Anonymous 12/27
Allen, George Nelson
(b. 9/7/1812) d. 12/9/1877
Alvarez de Toledo
(b. 10/29/1507) d. 12/12/1582
Amana Society 12/30
American Civil War 12/19
American Friends Service Committee 12/1
Amsdorf, Nicholas von
b. 12/3/1483 [d. 5/14/1565]
Anselm of Canterbury, St. 12/4
Apocrypha 12/20
Aquinas, Thomas 12/6
Arianism 12/9, 12/11
Aristotelian philosophy 12/13
Arndt, Ernst Moritz
b. 12/26/1769 [d. 1/29/1860]
Asbury, Francis 12/6
Association of Evangelical Lutheran Churches 12/3
Athenagoras I, Patriarch 12/7
Aurora Commune (WA) 12/30
AWANA (Approved Workmen Are Not Ashamed) 12/15

B

Bacon, Leonard
(b. 2/19/1802) d. 12/24/1881
Baptism, Infant 12/20
Barclay, Robert
b. 12/23/1648 [d. 10/3/1690]
Barclay, William
b. 12/5/1905 [d. 1/24/1978]
Barnard, Charlotte A.
b. 12/23/1830 [d. 1/30/1869]
Barnes, Albert
b. 12/1/1798 d. 12/24/1870
Barraclough, Henry
b. 12/14/1891 [d. 8/1983]
Barth, Karl
(b. 5/10/1886) d. 12/9/1968
Barton, Clar[iss]a
b. 12/25/1821 [d. 4/12/1912]
Battle of Assunpink 12/26
Battle of Dreux 12/19
Battle of Frankenhausen 12/20
Battle of Trenton, Second 12/26

Baur, Ferdinand Christian
(b. 6/21/1792) d. 12/2/1860
Baxter, Richard
(b. 11/12/1615) d. 12/8/1691
Becket, Thomas à
(b. 12/21/1117) d. 12/29/1170
Beecher, Henry Ward 12/18
Beethoven, Ludwig von
b. 12/16/1770 [d. 3/26/1827]
Bell, Eudorus N. 12/20
Benedict XIV, Pope (1740-58) 12/3
Beran, Josef 12/29
Bethel Commune (MO) 12/30
BIBLE VERSIONS
 Bay Psalm Book (1640) 12/22
 English Revised Version (1881, 1885) 12/11
 Fijian New Testament 12/22
 Latin Vulgate 12/11, 12/13
 Leeser's English Hebrew Bible (1845) 12/12
 Mandarin Chinese 12/14
 Polyglot Bible 12/6
 Revised Standard Version (1946, 1952) 12/1, 12/8
 Torah 12/6
Bingham, Rowland 12/4
Black, James M.
(b. 8/19/1856) d. 12/21/1938
Blanchard, Jonathan 12/14
Bliss, Philip Paul
(b. 7/9/1838) d. 12/29/1876
Bohler, Peter
b. 12/31/1712 [d. 4/27/1775]
Bolshevik Revolution 12/28
Bonar, Andrew
(b. 5/29/1810) d. 12/31/1892
Bonar, Horatius
b. 12/19/1808 [d. 7/31/1889]
Bonar, Marjory 12/31
Boniface V, Pope (619-25) 12/23
BOOKS
 Apology for the True Christian's Divinity (1675) 12/23
 Apostolici 12/30
 Barnes Notes on the N.T. (1832-53) 12/1
 Bay Psalm Book (1640) 12/22 12/23
 Beginnings of Christianity (1919-32) 12/1
 Bible: Notes, Explanatory and Practical, The 12/24
 Bonar's Diary and Letters 12/31
 Book of Common Prayer (BCP) 12/14
 Book of Mormon 12/23
 Christian Tradition (1971-89) 12/17
 Dark Night of the Soul 12/14
 Discourses on Government (1698) 12/7
 Faith Seeking Understanding 12/4
 Greek New Testament (UBS) 12/3
 Guide of the Perplexed (1190) 12/13
 Handbook of Old Testament Hebrew (1901) 12/20
 Handbook to the Grammar of the Greek New Testament 12/20
 Histoire ecclésiastique (1691-1720) 12/6
 History of Primitive Christianity 12/13
 History of the Expansion of Christianity 12/26
 Honest to God (1963) 12/5
 Hymns Ancient and Modern 12/16
 Hymns of Faith and Hope 12/19
 Jewish Encyclopedia, The 12/7
 Latin American Journal 12/2
 Luther's Works (Univ. of Jena) 12/3
 Memoir of Robert Murray McCheyne (1844) 12/23, 12/31
 New Testament in Modern Speech (1903) 12/27
 Olney Hymnbook (1779) 12/21
 Outline of Christian Theology (1898) 12/2
 Paradise Lost (1667) 12/9
 Paradise Regained (1671) 12/9
 Peloubet's Notes on the Int'l. S.S. Lessons (1832-53) 12/23
 Poems (1893) 12/18
 Primitive Christianity Reviewed (1711) 12/9
 Saints' Everlasting Rest, (1650) 12/8
 Serious Call to a Devout and Holy Life 12/13
 Seven Storey Mountain, The (1948) 12/10
 Style and Literary Method of Luke (1919-20) 12/1
 Systematic Theology 12/28
Booth, Charles B.
b. 12/26/1887 [d. 4/14/1975]
Booth, Evangeline
b. 12/25/1865 [d. 7/17/1950]
Booth, William 12/25, 12/26
Bora, Katherine von 12/17
(b. 1/29/1499) d. 12/20/1552
Borden, William 12/17
Borthwick, Jane 12/25
Bosio, Antonio 12/10
Boys Town 12/1
Breakspear, Nicholas (Pope Adrian IV) 12/4
Bresee, Phineas F.
b. 12/31/1838 [d. 11/13/1915]
Brooks, Phillips
b. 12/13/1835 [d. 1/23/1893]
Brown, William A.
b. 12/29/1865 [d. 12/15/1943]
Bullinger, Heinrich 12/23
Bultmann, Rudolf 12/5

C

Cabrini, Frances Xavier
(b. 7/15/1850) d. 12/22/1917

Cadbury, Henry Joel
b. 12/1/1883 [d. 10/7/1974]
Calixtus, George
b. 12/14/1586 [d. 3/19/1656]
Calvert, Cecelius 12/27
Calvin, John 12/28
Campbell, Alexander 12/24
Campion, Edmund
(b. 1/25/1540) d. 12/1/1581
CANTERBURY ARCHBISHOPS
 Anselm, St. (1093-1109) 12/4
 Becket, Thomas à (1162-1170) 12/29
 Fisher, Geoffrey (1945-1961) 12/2
 Temple, Frederick (1896-1902) 12/23
 Tenison, Thomas (1695-1715) 12/14
Carmichael, Amy
b. 12/16/1867 [d. 1/18/1951]
Carroll, John
(b. 1/8/1735) d. 12/3/1815
Cave, William
b. 12/30/1678 [d. 8/4/1713]
Caven, William
b. 12/26/1830 [d. 12/1/1904]
Celibacy, Clerical 12/22
Cennick, John
b. 12/12/1718 [d. 7/4/1755]
Cerularius, Michael 12/7
Chabanel, Noël
(b. 2/17/1613) d. 12/8/1649
Champollion, Jean F.
b. 12/23/1790 [d. 3/4/1832]
CHAPLAINS
 Forgy, Howell M. 12/7
 McCabe, Charles C. 12/19
 Rosbrugh, John 12/26
 Wycliffe, John 12/31
Chapman, J. Wilbur
(b. 6/17/1859) d. 12/25/1918
Charlemagne 12/25
Charles II, English King (1660-85) 12/7
Charles V, Holy Roman Emperor (1519-56) 12/31
Cheney, Charles E. 12/2
Christmas Day Celebration 12/24
Christmas Seals 12/8
Clarke, William Newton
b. 12/2/1841 [d. 1/14/1912]
Clement III, Pope (1187-91) 12/19
Clement of Alexandria 12/21
Cleveland, James
b. 12/5/1932 [d. 2/9/1991]
Clovis, French King (482-511) 12/25
Coan, Titus
(b. 2/1/1801) d. 12/1/1882
Codex Sinaiticus 12/7
Coke, Thomas 12/6

FEBRUARY INDEX

COLLEGES / UNIVERSITIES
  Aberdeen (Scotland) 12/11
  Cambridge University (England) 12/7, 12/9
  Cokesbury College (MD) 12/6
  Emory College (GA) 12/18
  Emory University (GA) 12/18
  Georgetown University (MD) 12/3
  Harvard (MA) 12/4
  Helmstadt (Germany) 12/14
  Illinois Institute (Wheaton College) 12/14
  Knox College (Toronto, Ont.) 12/26
  Maimonides College (PA) 12/12
  Moody Bible Institute (IL) 12/15
  Newberry College (SC) 12/20
  Nyack College (NY) 12/15
  Oxford University (England) 12/31
  Stanford University (CA) 12/12
  Temple University (PA) 12/6
  Wheaton College (IL) 12/14
  Yale College (CT) 12/15
  Yale University (CT) 12/17, 12/20
  Yale University (xx) 12/17
Columba, St.
  b. 12/7/521 [d. 6/9/597]
Community of True Inspiration 12/30
Conwell, Russell
  (b. 2/15/1842) d. 12/6/1925
Cotton, John
  (b. 12/4/1585) d. 12/23/1652
COUNCILS, CHURCH
  Council of Trent (1545-63) 12/13
  Vatican I (1869-70) 12/8
  Vatican II (1962-65) 12/2, 12/8
Counter-Reformation 12/28
Cousin, Anne Ross
  (b. 4/27/1824) d. 12/6/1906
Cowper, William 12/21
Croft, William
  b. 12/30/1678 [d. 8/14/1727]
CRUSADES 12/9, 12/22
  First Crusade (1096-99) 12/17
  Third Crusade (1189-91) 12/12, 12/19
Cummins, George David 12/2
  b. 12/11/1822 [d. 6/25/1876]
Cuneiform Alphabet 12/15
Cushing, William Orcutt
  b. 12/31/1832 [d. 10/19/1902]
Cutler, Henry Stephen 12/28
  (b. 10/13/1824) d. 12/5/1902
Cyril of Alexandria 12/7

D

Darwall, John
  (b. 1/13/1731) d. 12/18/1789
Davies, David 12/25
Daye, Stephen
  (b. 1594) d. 12/22/1668
DENOMINATIONS
  African Methodist Episcopal Church 12/25
  AME Zion Church 12/25
  Anabaptists 12/15, 12/20

Anglicanism 12/1, 12/2, 12/5, 12/13, 12/14, 12/16, 12/26, 12/27
Apostolic Faith Movement 12/20
Assemblies of God 12/20
Association of Evangelical Lutheran Churches 12/3
Baptists 12/2, 12/6, 12/12, 12/15, 12/17, 12/24, 12/29
Christian and Missionary Alliance 12/15
Christian Church 12/24
Christian Methodist Episcopal Church 12/15
Church of God 12/4
Church of God (Anderson, IN) 12/12
Church of God in Christ Holiness, U.S.A. 12/9
Church of the Nazarene 12/31
Colored Methodist Episcopal Church 12/15, 12/25
Congregationalism 12/2, 12/9, 12/14, 12/15, 12/18, 12/24
Disciples of Christ 12/16, 12/24
Dutch Reformed Church 12/15
Eastern Church 12/25
Episcopalianism 12/13, 12/28
Fundamentalism, American 12/11, 12/29
German Reformed Church 12/12
Holiness 12/16
Huguenots, French 12/19
International Church of the Foursquare Gospel 12/30
Lollards, English 12/14
Lutheranism 12/18
Lutheranism, American 12/1
Lutheranism, German 12/1, 12/31
Lutheran Church in America 12/20
Lutheran Church Missouri Synod 12/3
Methodism 12/5, 12/18, 12/19, 12/21, 12/22
Methodism, American 12/24, 12/27
Methodism, English 12/31
Moravian Church 12/12, 12/31
Mormon Church 12/5, 12/23
Nonconformity 12/13
Orthodoxy, Greek 12/13
Orthodoxy, Russian 12/1, 12/2, 12/6, 12/7, 12/11, 12/16, 12/19, 12/20, 12/31
Pentecostalism 12/9, 12/20
Pentecostal Church of the Nazarene 12/31
Pietism 12/30
Pillar of Fire 12/29
Plymouth Brethren 12/13, 12/28
Presbyterianism 12/1, 12/13, 12/14, 12/15, 12/24
Presbyterianism, American 12/19, 12/28, 12/29
Presbyterianism, Canadian 12/26
Presbyterian Church in the Confederate States of America 12/4
Presbyterian Church U.S. 12/4
Puritanism 12/21
Puritanism, American 12/23
Puritanism, English 12/9, 12/15
Quakerism 12/1, 12/12, 12/17, 12/24
Reformed Episcopal Church 12/11

Renewed Unitas Fratrum 12/27
Roman Catholicism 12/2, 12/4
Salvation Army 12/25, 12/26
Scottish Free Church 12/31
Seventh Day Adventist 12/20
Shakers, The 12/20
Southern Baptist Church 12/24
Unitarianism 12/4, 12/12
Volunteers of America 12/26
Winebrennerian (German Reformed) 12/12
Dexter, Henry Martyn 12/21
Doane, William H.
  (b. 2/3/1832) d. 12/24/1915
DOCUMENTS
  "Root and Branch" Petition 12/11
  "Twelve Steps" of A.A. 12/27
  "Universal Declaration of Human Rights" 12/10
  Edict of Nantes (1598) 12/21
  Gospels of Henry the Lion 12/6
  Great Law of the Colony of Pennsylvania 12/12
  Luther's "95 Theses" 12/5
  Root and Branch Bill 12/11
  U. S. Bill of Rights 12/15
Dohnavur Fellowship 12/16
DRAMA / DRAMATIC ARTS
  "Murder in the Cathedral" (1935) 12/29

E

Eastern Church 12/7, 12/22, 12/25
Ecstatic Doctor (Jan Van Ruysbroek) 12/2
Eddy, Mary Morse Baker
  (b. 7/16/1821) d. 12/3/1910
Eliot, T. S. 12/29
Ellerton, John 12/16
Elvey, George J.
  b. 3/27/1816 [d. 12/9/1893]
Evans, Christmas
  b. 12/24/1766 [d. 7/19/1838]
Evans, Robert P.
  b. 12/21/1818

F

Fénelon, François 12/6
FILMS / MOVIES
  "The Song of Bernadette" 12/27
Findlater, Sarah L. Borthwick
  (b. 11/26/1823) d. 12/25/1907
Finney, Charles G. 12/30
First Covenant, Scottish 12/3
First Day Society 12/19, 12/26
Fisher, Geoffrey 12/2
Fleury, Claude
  b. 12/6/1640 [d. 7/14/1723]
Flint, Annie Johnson 12/24
Form Criticism 12/1
Francis, Samuel T.
  (b. 11/19/1834) d. 12/28/1925
Fuchida, Mitsuo
  b. 12/3/1902 [d. 5/30/1976]

G

Gallitzin, Demetrius A.
  b. 12/22/1770 [d. 5/6/1840]
Gellert, Christian F.
  (b. 7/4/1715) d. 12/13/1769
Goss, Howard 12/20
Goss, John
  b. 12/27/1800 [d. 5/10/1880]
Gowans, Walter 12/4
Gray, Thomas
  b. 12/26/1716 [d. 7/30/1771]
Greater Europe Mission 12/21
Green, Harold
  (b. 10/23/1871) d. 12/20/1930
Green, Samuel G.
  b. 12/20/1822 [d. 9/15/1905]
Greenwell, Dora
  b. 12/6/1821 [d. 3/29/1882]
Gregory VIII, Pope (1187)
  (b. unk.) d. 12/17/1187
Grotefend, Georg Friedrich
  (b. 6/9/1775) d. 12/15/1853
Gruber, Franz 12/11, 12/24

H

Harding, Warren G. 12/25
Havergal, Frances Ridley
  b. 12/14/1836 [d. 6/3/1879]
Hayes, Rutherford B. 12/30
Hearn, Marianne
  b. 12/17/1834 [d. 3/16/1909]
Hecker, Isaac Thomas
  b. 12/18/1819 d. 12/22/1888
Henkel, Paul
  b. 12/15/1754 [d. 11/27/1825]
Henry II, English King (1154-89) 12/29
Henry IV, French King (1589-1610) 12/21
Herder, Johann Gottfried von
  (b. 8/25/1744) d. 12/18/1803
HERESIES
  Adoptionism 12/25
  Arianism 12/11
  Nestorianism 12/7
Heschel, Abraham J.
  (b. 1907) d. 12/23/1972
Hodge, Charles
  (b. 6/19/1878) d. 12/28/1797
Honorius III, Pope (1216-27) 12/22
How, William Walsham
  b. 12/13/1823 [d. 8/10/1897]
Humbert of Silva Candida 12/7
Hunt, Hanna 12/22
Hunt, John 12/22
Hus, Jan 12/25, 12/28
Hutchinson, Anne 12/23
HYMNS
  "'Man of Sorrows,' What a Name" 12/29
  "All Glory, Laud, and Honor" 12/1
  "All Hail the Power of Jesus' Name" 12/17

ALMANAC OF THE CHRISTIAN FAITH

ALMANAC OF THE CHRISTIAN FAITH — FEBRUARY INDEX

"Amazing Grace" 12/21
"America The Beautiful" 12/28
"And Can It Be That I Should Gain" 12/18
"Ask Ye What Great Thing I Know" 12/21
"A Mighty Fortress" 12/3
"Be Present At Our Table, Lord" 12/12
"Be Still, My Soul" 12/8
"Blest Be the Tie That Binds" 12/26
"Come, Ye Thankful People, Come" 12/9
"Crown Him With Many Crowns" 12/9
"Day by Day" 12/17
"Dear Lord and Father of Mankind" 12/17
"Father in Heaven, Who Lovest All" 12/30
"For All the Saints Who From Their Labors Rest" 12/13
"For the Beauty of the Earth" 12/16
"Give of Your Best to the Master" 12/23
"Glorious Things of Thee Are Spoken" 12/21
"God of Our Fathers, Known of Old" 12/30
"God the Omnipotent" 12/16, 12/28
"God Will Take Care of You" 12/16
"Hark! The Herald Angels Sing" 12/18
"Have Thine Own Way Lord" 12/20
"Here, O My Lord, I See Thee Face to Face" 12/19
"He Giveth More Grace" 12/24
"Hiding in Thee" 12/31
"How Firm a Foundation" 12/17
"How Sweet the Name of Jesus Sounds" 12/21
"Ivory Palaces" 12/14
"I Am Not Skilled to Understand" 12/6
"I Heard the Voice of Jesus Say" 12/19
"I Will Sing of My Redeemer" 12/29
"Jesus! What a Friend for Sinners" 12/25
"Jesus, Lover of My Soul" 12/18
"Jesus Only" 12/15
"Jesus Saves" 12/5
"Joyful, Joyful, We Adore Thee" 12/16
"Just As I Am, Thine Own to Be" 12/17
"Lift High the Cross" 12/7
"Lord, Speak to Me That I May Speak" 12/14
"Love Came Down at Christmas" 12/5
"Love Divine, All Loves Excelling" 12/18
"Make Me a Captive, Lord" 12/9
"More About Jesus" 12/31
"Must Jesus Bear the Cross Alone?" 12/9
"My Jesus, As Thou Wilt" 12/21
"One Day When Heaven Was Filled With His Praises" 12/25

"O God, Beneath Thy Guiding Hand" 12/24
"O God, Our Help in Ages Past" 12/30
"O Happy Home, Where Thou Art Loved" 12/25
"O Jesus, Thou Art Standing" 12/13
"O Little Town of Bethlehem" 12/13
"O Safe to the Rock that is Higher Than I" 12/31
"O the Deep, Deep Love of Jesus" 12/28
"O Word of God Incarnate" 12/13
"Peace Be Still" 12/5
"Rejoice, The Lord is King" 12/18
"Savior, Again to Thy Dear Name We Raise" 12/16
"Shepherd of Tender Youth" 12/21
"Silent Night" 12/4, 12/11, 12/24
"Soldiers of Christ, Arise" 12/9
"Speak, Lord, in the Stillness" 12/20
"Stille Nacht" 12/4, 12/11, 12/24
"Take My Life and Let It Be" 12/14
"Tell Me the Stories of Jesus" 12/2
"Tell Me the Story of Jesus" 12/31
"There is Sunshine in My Soul Today" 12/31
"The Light of the World is Jesus" 12/29
"The Sands of Time are Sinking" 12/6
"The Son of God Goes Forth to War" 12/5
"The Strife Is O'er, The Battle Done" 12/29
"The Strife Is O'er, The Battle Done" 12/27
"Under His Wings I Am Safely Abiding" 12/31
"Welcome, Happy Morning" 12/16
"We Give Thee But Thine Own" 12/13
"We Have an Anchor" 12/5
"What Will You Do With Jesus?" 12/15
"When the Roll is Called Up Yonder" 12/21
"Where Cross the Crowded Ways of Life" 12/3
"Who Is On the Lord's Side?" 12/14, 12/27
"Wonderful Words of Life" 12/29
"Would You Live For Jesus, and Be Always Pure and" 12/27
"Yesterday, Today, Forever" 12/15
HYMN TUNES
ALL SAINTS NEW 12/5
ARMAGEDDON 12/27
BARNARD 12/23
DARWALL'S 148th 12/18
DIADEMATA 12/9
DIX 12/16
FINLANDIA 12/8
GOD CARES 12/16
MAITLAND 12/9
MATERNA 12/28
MONTREAT 12/14
MORE LOVE TO THEE 12/24
NEAR THE CROSS 12/24
ODE TO JOY 12/16

QUIETUDE 12/20
RUSSIAN HYMN 12/28
ST. ANNE 12/30
ST. GEORGE'S, WINDSOR 12/9
ST. THEODULPH 12/1
STORY OF JESUS 12/31
SUNSHINE 12/31
SWENEY 12/31
VICTORY 12/27

I

Ignatius of Loyola
  b. 12/24/1491 [d. 7/31/1556]
Immaculate Conception 12/8
Innocent VIII, Pope (1484-92) 12/5
Inquisition, German 12/5
Inquisition, The 12/22
Isidore of Seville 12/5
Israel, Modern 12/14

J

Jackson, John Frederick Foakes-
  (b. 8/10/1855) d. 12/1/1941
Jerome, St. 12/11
JEWS
  Sephardic Jews 12/2
  Spanish Conversion of Jews 12/5
John, Griffith
  b. 12/14/1831 [d. 7/25/1912]
Johnson, Samuel
  (b. 9/18/1709) d. 12/13/1784
John of the Cross, St.
  (b. 6/24/1542) d. 12/14/1591
John XII, Pope (955-64) 12/16
John XXIII, Pope (1958-63) 12/2
Jones, Charles Price
  b. 12/9/1865 [d. 1/19/1949]
Jones, Clarence W.
  12/15/1900 [d. 4/29/1986]
Josephus 12/9
JUDAISM
  Conservative Judaism 12/7
  Jewish Encyclopedia, The 12/7
  Maimonides College 12/12
  Medieval Judaism 12/13
  Sephardic Jews 12/2
Judson, Adoniram 12/22
Judson, Ann Hasseltine
  b. 12/22/1789 [d. 10/24/1826]
Julius II, Pope (1503-13)
  b. 12/5/1443 [d. 2/21/1513]

K

Keil, William
  (b. 3/6/1812) d. 12/30/1877
Kent, Thomas 12/4
Keswick Movement 12/16
Kipling, Rudyard 12/30
Kitchin, George William
  b. 12/7/1827 [d. 10/13/1912]
Knox, John 12/3

Kocher, Conrad
  b. 12/16/1786 [d. 3/12/1872]
Kunheim, George von 12/17

L

Latourette, Kenneth Scott
  (b. 8/9/1884) d. 12/26/1968
Law, William 12/13
LECTURES
  "Acres of Diamonds" 12/6
Lee, Mother Ann 12/20
Leeser, Isaac
  b. 12/12/1806 [d. 2/1/1868]
Lenin, Nikolai 12/28
Leonty, Metropolitan of the U.S. 12/6
Leo X, Pope (1513-21) 12/10
  b. 12/11/1475 [d. 12/1/1521]
Lewis, C. S. 12/10
Lightfoot, John
  (b. 3/29/1602) d. 12/6/1675
Lightfoot, Joseph B.
  (b. 4/13/1828) d. 12/21/1889
Lincoln, Abraham 12/13
Livingstone, David 12/21
London's Religious Tract Society 12/20
London Missionary Society 12/14
Lorenzo the Magnificent 12/11
Luther, Margaret 12/17
Luther, Martin 12/5, 12/10, 12/17, 12/20, 12/28, 12/29
Lutheran Church Missouri Synod 12/3
Lvov, Alexis F.
  (b. 6/6/1799) d. 12/28/1870

M

MacDonald, George 12/28
  b. 12/10/1824 [d. 9/18/1905]
Maimonides, Moses
  (b. 3/30/1135) d. 12/13/1204
Makarios III, Orthodox Archbishop 12/13
Margaret of Navarre
  (b. 4/11/1492) d. 12/21/1549
Marsden, Samuel 12/27
Martin, Walter S.
  (b. 3/8/1862) d. 12/16/1935
MARTYRS
  Campion, Edmund 12/1
  Chabanel, Noël 12/8
  Elliot, Jim 12/1, 12/5, 12/13
  Oldcastle, Sir John 12/14
  Sidney, Algernon 12/7
  Stam, John and Betty 12/8
Massachusetts Bay Colony 12/23
Mayflower, The 12/21
Mayo, J. A. 12/22
McCabe, Charles C.
  (b. 10/11/1836) d. 12/19/1906

FEBRUARY INDEX

McPherson, Aimee Semple 12/30
Meacham, Joseph 12/20
Merton, Thomas
   (b. 1/31/1915) d. 12/10/1968
Methodist Board of Foreign
   Missions 12/3
Metz, Christian
   b. 12/30/1794 [d. 7/27/1867]
Michelangelo Buonarroti 12/5
Miles, W. H. 12/15
Miller, William
   (b. 2/15/1782) d. 12/20/1849
Milligan, William
   (b. 3/15/1821) d. 12/11/1893
Milton, John
   b. 12/9/1608 [d. 11/8/1674]
MISSIONARIES
   Bingham, Rowland 12/4
   Borden, William 12/17
   Carmichael, Amy 12/16
   Coan, Titus 12/1
   Columba, St. 12/7
   Gowans, Walter 12/4
   Green, Harold 12/20
   Hecker, Isaac T. 12/22
   Hunt, John and Hanna 12/22
   Judson, Adoniram 12/22
   Judson, Ann Hasseltine 12/22
   Kent, Thomas 12/4
   Marsden, Samuel 12/27
   McCabe, Charles C. 12/19
   Moffat, Robert and Mary 12/27
   Moody, Dwight L. 12/17
   Moon, Lottie 12/12, 12/24
   Newell, Harriet 12/22
   Reed, Mary 12/4
   Scott, Peter Cameron 12/4
   Van Der Kemp, Johannes Theodorus
     12/15
   Wesley, Charles 12/22
   Wesley, John 12/22
   White, Andrew 12/27
   Xavier, Francis 12/3
MISSION AGENCIES
   Africa Inland Mission 12/4
   China Inland Mission 12/5
   Greater Europe Mission 12/21
   Latin America Evangelization
     Campaign 12/6
   Latin America Mission 12/6
   London Missionary Society 12/14,
     12/21
   Methodist Board of Foreign Missions 12/3
   Pocket Testament League 12/3
   Rhenish Mission 12/26
   Society for the Propagation of the
     Gospel 12/14
   Southern Baptist Mission Board
     12/12
   Student Volunteer Movement 12/5
   Sudan Interior Mission 12/4
   Worldwide Evangelization Crusade
     12/5
   Zenana Missionary Society 12/16
Moffat, Robert 12/27
   b. 12/21/1795 [d. 8/9/1883]
Mohr, Joseph 12/24
   b. 12/11/1792 d. 12/4/1848

Moody, Dwight L. 12/17
   (b. 2/5/1837) d. 12/22/1899
Moon, Lottie (Charlotte Diggs)
   b. 12/12/1840 d. 12/24/1912
Morgan, G. Campbell
   b. 12/9/1863 [d. 5/16/1945]
Mueller, George 12/9, 12/18
Muhlenberg, Henry Melchior 12/1
Münzer, Thomas
   b. 12/20/ 1490 [d. 5/27/1525]
Murray, John
   b. 12/10/1741 [d. 9/3/1815]
MUSIC
   "Symphony of Psalms" 12/13
   Hymns Ancient and Modern 12/16
   Hymns of Faith and Hope 12/19
   Olney Hymnbook 12/21
Mysticism, German 12/2

N

Nägeli, Johann (Hans) Georg
   (b. 5/26/1768/73) d. 12/26/1836
Naismith, James 12/1
Napoleon's Concordat (1801-02)
   12/9
National Council of the Churches of
   Christ in the 12/2
Nestorius 12/7
Newell, Harriet 12/22
Newton, John
   (b. 7/24/1725) d. 12/21/1807
Nicholas II, Russian Czar (1894-
   1917) 12/30
NICKNAMES / TITLES
   "Apostle of Maryland" 12/27
   "Apostle to Scotland" 12/7
   "Borden of Yale" 12/17
   "Boy Pope" 12/16
   "Bunyan of Wales" 12/25
   "Columbus of the Catacombs" 12/10
   "Congregational Pope" 12/24
   "Ecstatic Doctor" 12/2
   "Father of German Rationalism,"
     12/18
   "Father of Modern Catholic Missions" 12/3
   "Father of Scholasticism" 12/4
   "Father of Universalism in America"
     12/10
   "Grandfather of Methodism" 12/16
   "Lamplighter, The" 12/8
   "Lemonade Lucy" 12/30
   "Morning Star of the Reformation"
     12/28
   "Mother Cabrini" 12/22
   "Patriarch of New England" 12/23
   "People's Priest" 12/11
   "Poet of Methodism" 12/18
   "Scottish Christina Rossetti" 12/6
   "Greatest Hymnwriter Among the
     Scots" 12/19
   "Patron Saint of Southern Baptist
     Missions" 12/12
Nitschmann, David 12/27
North, Frank Mason
   b. 12/3/1850 [d. 12/17/1935]

Nusbaum, Cyrus S.
   (b. 7/27/1861) d. 12/27/1937

O

Oberlin Conservatory of Music
   12/9
Oglethorpe, James E.
   b. 12/22/1696 [d. 6/30/1785]
Oldcastle, Sir John
   (b. ca. 1378) d. 12/14/1417
Ottoman Empire 12/9
Owens, Priscilla Jane
   (b. 7/21/1829) d. 12/5/1907

P

Palestrina, Giovanni
   b. 12/27/1525 [d. 2/2/1594]
PAPAL DECREES
   "Decet Romanum Pontificem" 12/10
   "Exsurge, Domine" 12/10
   "Ineffabilis Deus" (1854) 12/8
   "Summis desiderantes" 12/5
   "Ubi arcano" (1922) 12/23
   "Ubi primum" 12/3
Parker, William Henry
   (b. 3/4/1845) d. 12/2/1929
Parliament, British 12/24
Parrish, Anne
   (b. 10/17/1760) d. 12/26/1800
Paulists 12/18, 12/22
Paul III, Pope (1534-49) 12/13
Paul VI, Pope (1963-78) 12/7
Payne, Robert 12/15
Peabody, Francis G.
   b. 12/4/1847 [d. 12/28/1936]
Peasants War 12/20
Pelikan, Jaroslav
   b. 12/17/1923 [d. 5/13/2006]
Peloubet, Francis Nathan
   b. 12/2/1831 [d. 3/27/1920]
Penn, William 12/12
Pennsylvania Bible Society 12/12
Philaret, Metropolitan of Moscow
   (b. 12/26/1782) d. 12/1/1867
Philocalian Calendar (A.D. 354)
   12/25
Picts, The 12/7
Pilgrims, Mayflower 12/21
Pius IX, Pope (1846-78) 12/8
Pius XI, Pope (1922-39) 12/23
Pocket Testament League 12/3
POETRY
   "Elegy Written in a Country Churchyard" (1751) 12/26
   "Hands and Feet of Him" 12/24
   "Ichabod" 12/17
   "The Hound of Heaven" 12/18
Pollard, Adelaide A.
   (b. 11/27/1862) d. 12/20/1934
POPES
   Adrian I (772-95) 12/25
   Adrian IV (1154-59) 12/4
   Benedict XIV (1740-58) 12/3

   Boniface V (619-25) 12/23
   Clement III (1187-91) 12/19
   Gregory VIII (1187) 12/11, 12/17
   Honorius III (1216-27) 12/22
   John XII (955-64) 12/16
   John XXIII (1958-63) 12/2
   Julius II (1503-13) 12/5
   Leo X (1513-21) 12/10, 12/11
   Paul III (1534-49) 12/13
   Paul VI (1963-78) 12/7
   Pius IX (1846-78) 12/8
   Pius XI (1922-39) 12/23
Possehl, Floyd F. 12/5
Pott, Francis
   (b. 12/29/1832) d. 10/26/1909
Presbyterian Church in the
   Confederate States of A 12/4
Presbyterian Church U.S. 12/4
PRESIDENTS, U.S.
   Adams, John Quincy 12/31
   Harding, Warren G. 12/25
   Hayes, Rutherford B. 12/30
   Lincoln, Abraham 12/13
   Roosevelt, Theodore 12/17
Primate of Czechoslovakia 12/29
Pseudepigrapha 12/20
PUBLICATIONS
   Daily Study Bible 12/5
   "The Sword of the Lord" 12/11

Q

QUOTATIONS
   Adams, John Quincy 12/31
   Aquinas, Thomas 12/6
   Barth, Karl 12/4, 12/20
   Bonar, Andrew 12/18, 12/23, 12/29,
     12/30
   Bonhoeffer, Dietrich 12/17, 12/24
   Cowper, William 12/4, 12/7
   Darby, John Nelson 12/13
   Elliot, Jim 12/1, 12/5, 12/13
   Henry, Matthew 12/31
   Hus, Jan 12/25
   Laubach, Frank C. 12/6
   Lee, Robert E. 12/27
   Lewis, C. S. 12/6, 12/7, 12/10,
     12/15, 12/21, 12/26, 12/29
   Luther, Martin 12/11, 12/12, 12/16,
     12/19, 12/21, 12/25, 12/28
   MacDonald, George 12/11, 12/19,
     12/20
   McCheyne, Robert Murray 12/8
   Newton, John 12/21
   Nouwen, Henri J. M. 12/2, 12/3,
     12/4, 12/8, 12/9, 12/13, 12/19,
     12/22, 12/24, 12/26, 12/30
   Schaeffer, Francis 12/26
   Schmemann, Alexander 12/2, 12/6,
     12/7, 12/11, 12/16, 12/20, 12/31
   Simons, Menno 12/15
   Smith, Hannah Whitall 12/4, 12/14,
     12/17
   Venn, Henry 12/7
   Wesley, John 12/22, 12/27
   Whitefield, George 12/1, 12/9,
     12/10, 12/12, 12/15, 12/18,
     12/19, 12/30

QUOTATIONS, NOTABLE
"Jesus loves me this I know, for the Bible tells me so" 12/9
"No Reserve! No Retreat! No Regrets!" 12/17
"God helps those who help themselves" 12/7
"Praise the Lord and pass the ammunition!" 12/7

R

RABBIS, JEWISH
   Leeser, Isaac 12/12
   Maimonides, Moses 12/13
   Schechter, Solomon 12/7
   Tarshish, Jacob 12/8
Radical Biblical Criticism, German 12/2
RADIO PROGRAMS
   "Catholic Hour" 12/10
   "Voice of Revival" 12/11
RADIO STATIONS
   WPIX-TV (NY City) 12/5
Rasputin, Grigorii
   (b. 1/10/1869) d. 12/30/1916
Reed, Mary
   b. 12/4/1854 [d. 4/8/1943]
Reformed (Calvinistic) Orthodoxy 12/28
Reformed Episcopal Church 12/2
RELIGIOUS ORDERS, CATHOLIC
   Cistercians 12/20
   Dominicans (Order of Preachers) 12/22
   Missionary Sisters of the Sacred Heart 12/22
   Missionary Society of St. Paul the Apostle (Paulists) 12/18, 12/22
   Society of Jesus (Jesuits) 12/1, 12/24, 12/27
Rice, John R.
   b. 12/11/1895 d. 12/29/1980
Richard I, English King (1189-99) 12/12
Rippon, John 12/17
Robinson, John A. T.
   (b. 6/15/1919) d. 12/5/1983
Roosevelt, Theodore 12/17
Rosbrugh, John 12/26
Rosetta Stone 12/23
Rossetti, Christina G. 12/6
   b. 12/5/1830 [d. 12/29/1894]
Rossi, G. B. de 12/10
Russian Imperial Chapel 12/28
Ruysbroek, Jan Van
   (b. unk.) d. 12/2/1381

S

Saladin, Turkish Conqueror 12/17
Sales, St. Francis of
   (b. 8/21/1567) d. 12/28/1622
Sanctification, Crisis 12/29
Sandell, Lina 12/17
Schechter, Solomon
   b. 12/7/1847 [d. 11/19/1915]
Schleiermacher, F. D. E. 12/18
Schmalkald League 12/31
Schmolck, Benjamin
   b. 12/21/1672 [d. 2/12/1737]
Schwedler, Johann Christoph
   b. 12/21/1672 [d. 1/12/1730]
Schwenkfeld, Kaspar
   (b. 1489) d. 12/10/1561
Scott, Peter Cameron
   (b. 3/7/1867) d. 12/4/1896
SEMINARIES / BIBLE INSTITUTES
   Bible Institute for Home and Foreign Missions (IL) 12/17
   Colgate Seminary (NY) 12/2
   Earlham School of Religion (IN) 12/12
   European Bible Institute 12/21
   Jewish Theological Seminary (NY) 12/7
   Princeton Seminary (NJ) 12/28
   Union Seminary (NY) 12/29
   Union Theological Seminary (VA) 12/1, 12/23
Semler, Johann S.
   b. 12/18/1725 [d. 3/14/1791]
SERMONS
   "The Way in Salvation" 12/1, 12/24
Sheen, Fulton J.
   (b. 5/8/1895) d. 12/10/1979
Shoemaker, Samuel M.
   b. 10/27/1893 [d. 10/31/1963]
Sibelius, Jean
   b. 12/8/1865 [d. 9/20/1957]
Sidney, Algernon
   (b. 1/1623) d. 12/7/1683
Simpson, Albert B.
   12/15/1843 [d. 10/29/1919]
Singh, Sundar 12/18
Six-Day War (1967) 12/14
Skoog, Andrew L.
   b. 12/17/1856 [d. 10/30/1934]
Smith, Joseph 12/5
   b. 12/23/1805 [d. 6/27/1844]
Society for the Propagation of the Gospel 12/12
Soubirous, Bernadette 12/27
Southern Baptist Mission Board 12/12
Spurgeon, Charles H. 12/19
Stam, Betty (Scott)
   (b. 2/22/1906) d. 12/8/1934
Stam, John
   (b. 1/18/1907) d. 12/8/1934
Stiles, Ezra
   b. 12/15/1727 [d. 5/12/1795]
Stone, Barton W.
   b. 12/24/1772 [d. 11/9/1844]
Strachan, Harry 12/6
Strachan, Kenneth 12/6
Strachan, Susan
   (b. 4/28/1874) d. 12/6/1950
Straus, Oscar Solomon 12/17
Stravinsky, Igor 12/13
Studd, C[harles] T[homas]
   b. 12/5/1862 [d. 7/16/1931]
Sudan Interior Mission 12/4
Sweney, John R.
   b. 12/31/1837 [d. 4/10/1899]

T

"Twelve Steps" of A.A. 12/27
Tanner, Benjamin T.
   b. 12/25/1835 [d. 1/15/1923]
Tarshish, Jacob
   12/8/1892 [d. 1960]
TELEVISION PROGRAMS
   "Life is Worth Living" 12/10
Temple, Frederick
   (b. 11/30/1821) d. 12/23/1902
Tenison, Thomas
   (b. 9/29/1636) d. 12/14/1715
Teschner, Melchior
   (b. 4/29/1584) d. 12/1/1635
Textual Criticism 12/18
Thomas, Norman Matoon
   (b. 11/20/1884) d. 12/19/1968
Thompson, Francis
   b. 12/18/1859 [d. 11/13/1907]
Tikhon (Vasili Belavin), Patriarch of Moscow
   b. 12/19/1866 [d. 4/7/1925]
Tischendorf, L. F. K. von
   (b. 1/18/1815) d. 12/7/1874
Toledo, Alvarez de
   (b. 10/29/1507) d. 12/12/1582
Tomlinson, Homer A.
   (b. 10/25/1892) d. 12/4/1968
Torrey, Charles C.
   b. 12/20/1863 [d. 11/2/1956]
Touro Synagogue 12/2
Transcendentalism 12/18
Trinity, Doctrine of the 12/11
Trueblood, David Elton
   b. 12/12/1900 [d. 12/20/1994]
Tübingen School 12/2
Tyndale, William 12/31

U

U.S. Catholic Bishops Conference 12/2
United Bible Society 12/3
United Nations 12/10

V

Vanderhorst, R. H. 12/15
Van Der Kemp, Johannes Theodorus
   (b. 1747) d. 12/15/1811
Vasey, Thomas
   (b. ca. 1746) d. 12/27/1826
Victoria, (English) Queen 12/9

W

Walton, Brian 12/6
Ward, Samuel A.
   b. 12/28/1847 [d. 9/28/1903]
Warneck, Gustav
   (b. 3/6/1834) d. 12/26/1910
Warner, Daniel Sidney
   (b. 6/25/1842) d. 12/12/1895
Weiss, Johannes
   b. 12/13/1863 [d. 8/24/1914]
Wells, Amos R.
   b. 12/23/1862 [d. 3/6/1933]
Wesley, Charles 12/16, 12/18, 12/22, 12/27, 12/31
Wesley, John 12/12, 12/16, 12/18, 12/22, 12/27, 12/31
Wesley, Samuel, Sr. 12/18
   b. 12/16/1662 [d. 4/25/1735]
Wesley, Samuel S. 12/27
Wesley, Susanna 12/18
Western Church 12/7, 12/22
Weymouth, Richard F.
   (b. 10/26/1822) d. 12/27/1902
Whiston, William
   12/9/1667 [d. 8/22/1752]
White, Alma 12/29
White, Andrew
   (b. 1579) d. 12/27/1656
White, William 12/12
Whitefield, George 12/12, 12/28
   b. 12/16/1714 [d. 9/30/1770]
Whittaker, Joseph 12/20
Whittier, John Greenleaf
   12/17/1807 [d. 9/7/1892]
Widney, Joseph P. 12/31
Wikgren, Allen P.
   b. 12/3/1906 [d. 5/7/1998]
Williams, George 12/29
Williams, Roger 12/8, 12/23
   b. 12/21/1603 [d. 1/27/1683]
Witches 12/5
Woolman, John 12/6
World War II 12/3
Wycliffe, John 12/14, 12/28
   (b. 12/31/1320) d. 12/31/1384

X

Xavier, Francis
   (b. 4/7/1506) d. 12/3/1552

Y

Young, Brigham 12/5
Young Men's Christian Association (YMCA) 12/29

Z

Zenana Missionary Society 12/16
Zwingli, Ulrich 12/11, 12/23

ALMANAC OF THE CHRISTIAN FAITH

נִיסָן NISAN | אֲדָר ADAR

~ March 1 ~

Highlights in History

1562 Armed Catholics massacred a congregation of French Protestants (Huguenots) in Vassy, setting off a series of eight religious civil wars in France that lasted 36 years.

1692 In colonial Massachusetts, the Salem Witch Trials began with the conviction of West Indian slave, Tituba, for witchcraft.

1810 Georgetown College was chartered in Washington, D.C. Opening in 1791, it was the first Roman Catholic college established in the U.S.

1854 Pioneer American missionary Hudson Taylor first arrived in Shanghai, China. He founded the China Inland Mission in 1865, and popularized the idea that missionaries should live the culture and dress like the people they sought to evangelize.

1941 Rabbi David Goldberg of Corsicana, Texas retired from the U.S. Navy chaplaincy. He was appointed in 1917, the first Jewish chaplain to serve in this branch of the U.S. Armed Forces.

Notable Birthdays

1820 Birth of Richard Redhead, English sacred composer, chorister and organist. He co-edited the first Gregorian psalter (*Laudes Diurnae*) used in the Anglican Church. Today, Redhead is remembered for composing the hymn tune REDHEAD / GETHSEMANE ("Go To Dark Gethsemane"). [d. 4/27/1901]

1861 Birth of Carrie E. Rounsefell, hymn composer: MANCHESTER ("It May Not Be on the Mountain's Height"). [d. 9/18/1930]

The Last Passage

589 St. David of Wales died at age 94. He was a bishop and founded 12 monasteries, his ascetic path of restraint earned him the love of the Welsh people and he is now regarded the patron saint of that country. (b. 495)

1546 Scottish reformer George Wishart, about 33, was burned at the stake as a heretic. His crime was his attempt to bring the Reformation to Scotland. Wishart had been influenced by Hugh Latimer at Cambridge. Back in his native Scotland, Wishart's spiritual witness influenced John Knox. (b. ca. 1513)

1633 Beloved English clergyman and poet, George Herbert, died of tuberculosis at age 39. He gained fame for his writings (many of which were published posthumously), but is now remembered as author of the hymn, "The God of Love My Shepherd Is." (b. 4/3/1593)

1889 Death of William H. Monk, 65, English musician and sacred composer. He served as organist at several high churches, edited hymn collections for the Church of Scotland and composed numerous hymns, including EVENTIDE ("Abide With Me") and VICTORY ("The Strife is O'er, The Battle Done"). (b. 3/16/1823)

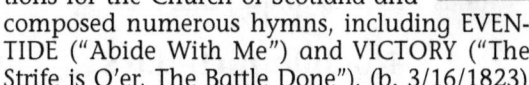

1969 Death of Helen C. A. Dixon, 92, English-born musician and hymnwriter. She was married to song evangelist C. M. Alexander (1904) and, after Alexander's death, to A. C. Dixon (1924). She traveled with revivalists Reuben A. Torrey and J. Wilbur Chapman, and is remembered today for writing the hymn, "Anywhere with Jesus I Can Safely Go." (b. 1877)

Words for the Soul

1856 Scottish clergyman and biographer Andrew Bonar reflected in his diary: *'I scarcely ever have set apart special times for prayer and waiting upon the Lord without getting some token of acceptance soon. O the folly of not praying more!'*

1966 Swiss Reformed theologian Karl Barth explained in a letter: *'In the Bible the world is all humanity. If Jesus is and does what we read in 1 John 2:2, then He prays for all men: for those who already pray and for those who do not yet pray.'*

IN GOD'S WORD... OT: Leviticus 24:1–25:46 ~ NT: Mark 10:13-31 ~ Psalms 44:9-26 ~ Proverbs 10:20-21

נִיסָן NISAN — ALMANAC OF THE CHRISTIAN FAITH — אֲדָר ADAR

March 2

Highlights in History

1855 Italy's King Victor Immanuel (reigned 1849-78) installed "The Cloister Act," under which all religious orders in Italy were abolished and all their property not devoted to philanthropy was confiscated by the state.

1930 American missionary to Eastern Europe Gustav Herbert Schmidt (1891-1958) opened the Danzig Instytut Biblijny in the Free City of Danzig. It was the first Pentecostal Bible institute to be established in Eastern Europe.

1979 More than 1,100 Christian organizations, with $1 billion in combined income, formed the Evangelical Council for Financial Accountability (ECFA). The purpose of this fund-raising oversight agency is to show the public that religious groups are accountable for the funds they raise and spend.

Notable Birthdays

1725 Birth of Henry Venn, Anglican clergyman. He was one of the first evangelical divines to hold a parish, and was a warm friend of George Whitefield. One of the founders of the Clapham Group, Venn authored the popular book, *The Complete Duty of Man* (1736). [d. 6/24/1797]

1880 Birth of Robert Harkness, Australian-born American song evangelist. He accompanied R. A. Torrey in round-the-world revival tours. Harkness composed hundreds of gospel songs, but is most popularly remembered today for creating an enduring harmony to R. H. Pritchard's Welsh hymn tune HYFRYDOL ("Jesus, What a Friend of Sinners" and also "Come, Thou Long Expected Jesus"). [d. 5/8/1961]

1911 Birth of John S. B. Monsell, Irish Anglican clergyman. He penned 300 hymns during his life, including "Fight the Good Fight with All Thy Might" and "Worship the Lord in the Beauty of Holiness." [d. 4/9/1875]

1934 Birth of Dottie Rambo, contemporary American gospel songwriter and musical artist. She is known for such gospel songs as: "Build My Mansion Next Door to Jesus" and "I Just Came to Talk with You, Lord."

The Last Passage

672 Death of St. Chad (Ceadda), English prelate. He was bishop of the East Saxons (664) in Litchfield, York, and became one of the most popular of the English saints.

1791 Death of John Wesley, 87, a leader of the Great Awakening in 18th century England. Accompanied by the music of his brother Charles, John founded a renewal movement within Anglicanism which ultimately grew worldwide to become the United Methodist Church. (b. 6/28/1703)

1909 Death of Daniel March, 92, American Presbyterian clergyman and writer. He traveled widely in support of missionary endeavors around the world. March also published several written works, but is primarily remembered today for authoring a single hymn: "Hark, the Voice of Jesus Calling." (b. 7/21/1816)

Words for the Soul

1768 Anglican clergyman and hymnwriter Augustus M. Toplady recorded in his diary: 'Lord, pardon my unworthiness.... Thou art faithful, who hast promised; nor is my interest in thee the less secure because I have not always eyes to see it clearly.'

1948 U.S. Senate chaplain Peter Marshall prayed: 'Forgive the poverty and pettiness of our prayers. Listen not to our words but to the yearnings of our hearts. Hear beneath our petitions the crying of our need.'

1959 American Presbyterian missionary and apologist Francis A. Schaeffer observed in a letter: 'Christianity is the greatest intellectual system the mind of man has ever touched.'

IN GOD'S WORD... OT: Leviticus 25:47–27:13 ~ NT: Mark 10:32-52 ~ Psalms 45:1-17 ~ Proverbs 10:22

ALMANAC OF THE CHRISTIAN FAITH

נִיסָן NISAN

אֲדָר ADAR

March 3

Highlights in History

1547 At the Seventh Session of the Council of Trent, the Catholic Church officially detailed the seven sacraments which it believes are necessary for salvation – Baptism, Confirmation, the Eucharist, Penance, Extreme Unction, [Holy] Orders and Matrimony.

1638 In New Towne, MA, the seminary founded by the Great and General Court of Massachusetts changed its name to Harvard — named after English-born American clergyman John Harvard, who bequeathed his library (400 books) and half his estate (£800) to the school. (Because John Harvard was a graduate of Cambridge University in England, New Towne later also changed its name to Cambridge.)

1865 Congress approved U.S. Treasury Secretary Salmon P. Chase's mandate to the U.S. mint to prepare a "device" with which to inscribe the motto "In God We Trust" on U.S. coins.

1943 In California, founder Dawson Trotman (1905-56) formally incorporated the Navigators, a youth discipleship organization which stresses Scripture memorization. Today, this non-denominational agency works in over 90 countries.

Notable Birthdays

1877 Birth of William M. Strong, American missions pioneer. He founded the Gospel Mission of South America in Chile in 1923. Today, it is headquartered in Ft. Lauderdale, FL. [d. 2/20/1960]

The Last Passage

1263 Death of Hugh of St. Cher, 64, French cardinal and Dominican scholar. Remembered for correcting and indexing the Latin Vulgate, Hugh became the first compiler of a concordance to the Bible. (b. ca. 1199)

1706 Death of Johann Pachelbel, 52, German organist and composer. Pachelbel composed the "Hexachordum Apollinis." (b. 9/1/1653)

1921 Death of Jessie Brown Pounds, 59, Ohio-born Christian pastor's wife, poet and composer. Though in poor health as a child, Ms. Pounds authored 50 librettos for cantatas and operettas, 9 books, and (in collaboration with James Fillmore) more than 400 gospel song texts, including "Anywhere With Jesus"; "Beautiful Isle of Somewhere"; "I Know That My Redeemer Liveth"; "The Way of the Cross Leads Home" and "The Touch of His Hand on Mine." (b. 8/31/1861)

1955 Death of [Mary] Katharine Drexel, 96, American Catholic religious. She worked with the Pueblo and Navajo Indians in the West, and in 1891 founded the Sisters of the Blessed Sacrament for Indians and Colored People. In 1915 her religious order founded Xavier University in New Orleans, LA. It was the only Catholic university for African-American students in the U.S. at that time. (b. 11/26/1858)

Words for the Soul

1744 Colonial missionary to the American Indians David Brainerd recorded in his journal: 'In the morning, spent an hour in prayer. Prayer was so sweet an exercise to me that I knew not how to cease, lest I lose the spirit of prayer.'

1787 English founder of Methodism John Wesley wrote in a letter: 'If God sends you, He will make a way for you. The hearts of all men are in His hands.'

1950 Trappist monk Thomas Merton remarked: 'The Christian life... is a continual discovery of Christ in new and unexpected places. And these discoveries are sometimes most profitable when you find Him in something you had tended to overlook or even despise.'

1982 In his Latin American Journal ¡Gracias! Catholic diarist Henri J. M. Nouwen wrote: 'In a world of poverty, the lines between darkness and light, good and evil, destructiveness and creativity, are much more distinct than in a world of wealth.'

IN GOD'S WORD... OT: Leviticus 24:14–Numbers 1:54 ~ NT: Mark 11:1-26 ~ Psalms 46:1-11 ~ Proverbs 10:23

נִיסָן NISAN ALMANAC OF THE CHRISTIAN FAITH אדר ADAR

~ March 4 ~

Highlights in History

1791 Rev. John Hurt was appointed the first chaplain in the history of the U.S. Army. (Hurt had earlier served as chaplain of the Sixth Virginia Infantry, from 1776 until the close of the American Revolution.)

1838 On her 57th birthday, American Jewish humanitarian Rebecca Gratz organized the first Jewish Sunday School in America in Philadelphia. She had previously helped organize the Female Association for the Relief of Women and Children in Reduced Circumstance (1801), and the Philadelphia Orphan Asylum (1815).

1966 "The Evening Standard," a London newspaper, published an interview with Beatle John Lennon, in which he remarked: *'Christianity will go. It will vanish and shrink.... We're more popular than Jesus Christ right now.'* The quote touched off a storm of international protest, resulting in a world-wide series of Beatles record-burnings, and even a decline in the group's own popularity within the music world.

Notable Birthdays

1845 Birth of William H. Parker, English Baptist machinest and hymnwriter. Most of Parker's hymns were written for Sunday School events, including one which has become timeless: "Tell Me the Stories of Jesus." [d. 12/2/1929]

1942 Birthday of Gloria Gaither, contemporary Christian singer and songwriter. The wife of fellow songwriter Bill Gaither, Gloria co-wrote the lyrics to "Because He Lives," "Something Beautiful" and "The King is Coming."

The Last Passage

1866 Death of Alexander Campbell, 77, Scottish clergyman and reformer. By 1827 he and his father Thomas Campbell had developed a "Restoration Movement" among the Baptists which later became the denomination known as the Disciples of Christ. (b. 9/12/1788)

1870 Death of John McClintock, 55, American Methodist clergyman and scholar. Associated with Drew Theological Seminary, McClintock's most important literary work was the 12-volume *Cyclopaedia of Biblical, Theological, and Ecclesiastical Literature*, which he co-edited with James Strong (1867-87). (b. 10/27/1814)

1875 Death of John Edgar Gould, 53, New England music store owner. A business partner with fellow-hymnwriter William G. Fischer, Gould himself composed the hymn tune PILOT ("Jesus, Savior, Pilot Me"). (b. 1822)

1890 Death of Franz J. Delitzsch, 77, German Lutheran biblical scholar. From 1846 until his death, Delitzsch co-authored (with J. F. K. Keil after 1861) his greatest contribution to O.T. scholarship – the *Keil & Delitzsch Old Testament Commentary*. (b. 2/23/1813)

1901 Death of Daniel W. Whittle, 60, American Civil War veteran and revivalist. Associated with several popular song evangelists (P. P. Bliss, James McGranahan, George C. Stebbins), Whittle authored several hymns which remain popular today: "Showers of Blessing," "I Know Whom I Have Believed" and "Moment by Moment." (b. 11/22/1840)

Words for the Soul

1738 Moravian missionary Peter Böhler chiastically advised John Wesley (who later founded Methodism): *'Preach faith until you have it; and then, because you have it, you will preach faith.'*

1968 American Presbyterian missionary Francis A. Schaeffer testified in a letter: *'My joy is in seeing many who have such little hope come to the place not only of being saved for eternity, but of being more human in the present life.'*

1986 Catholic mystic Henri J. M. Nouwen wrote in his journal: *'Life is humbling, very humbling. I have to let it be that way. Someone said today, "We need a lot of humiliation for a little bit of humility."'*

IN GOD'S WORD... OT: Numbers 2:1–3:51 ~ NT: Mark 11:27–12:17 ~ Psalms 47:1-9 ~ Proverbs 10:24-25

נִיסָן NISAN

ALMANAC OF THE CHRISTIAN FAITH

אֲדָר ADAR

March 5

Highlights in History

1179 The Third Lateran Council opened, named because it was held at the Church of St. John Lateran in Rome. During its two weeks of sessions, measures were enacted against the Waldenses and Albigensians. The council also gave the College of Cardinals exclusive right to elect the pope.

1743 In the midst of the Great Awakening, clergyman Thomas Prince, an avid collector of colonial historical records, published "The Christian History," America's first religious magazine.

1984 In the case of Lynch v. Donnelly, the U.S. Supreme Court ruled 5-4 that public financing of a Nativity scene did not of itself violate the doctrine of separation of church and state.

Notable Birthdays

1820 Birth of Robert L. Dabney, Virginia-born theologian and educator. Associated with Union Seminary (VA) for 30 years (1853-83), Dabney is today regarded as the second greatest theologian (after Charles Hodge) of the Southern Presbyterian Church. [d. 1/3/1898]

1850 Birth of Daniel Brink Towner, American Methodist music educator and hymn composer. He was associated with Moody Bible Institute (1893-1919), and composed over 2,000 gospel songs during his life, including MOODY ("Marvelous Grace of Our Loving Lord"); CALVARY ("Years I Spent in Vanity and Pride"); and TRUST AND OBEY ("When We Walk with the Lord"); [d. 10/3/1919]

1895 Birth of Moshe Feinstein, Russian-born religious leader. He was a widely respected Jewish Orthodox rabbi who helped make New York's Mesivta Tiferet Jerusalem one of the leading American yeshivas. Feinstein's ideas also solved contemporary problems for Orthodox Jews throughout the world. [d. 3/23/1986]

The Last Passage

1605 Death of Clement VIII, 71, pope from 1592. He revised Jerome's Latin Vulgate, which then served as the standard Bible text of the Catholic Church for the next 300 years. (b. 2/24/1536)

1778 Death of Thomas A. Arne, 67, English composer of the British patriotic song, "Rule, Britannia!" He was among the first to introduce women's voices into choral writing. Arne is also remembered for the hymn tune ARLINGTON ("O For a Faith That Will Not Shrink" and "Am I a Soldier of the Cross?"). (b. 3/12/1710)

1835 Death of William McKendree, 77, the first American-born bishop of the early Methodist Episcopal Church. His field of labor extended from Maine to Missouri! (b. 7/6/1757)

1907 Death of Friedrich W. Blass, 64, German Lutheran classical philologist. His best-known work was an N.T. Greek grammar (1896), affectionately known in its English translation today as *Blass-Debrunner-Funk*. (b. 1/22/1843)

Words for the Soul

1555 French-born Swiss reformer John Calvin encouraged his friend Philip Melanchthon in a letter: *'It behooves us to accomplish what God requires of us, even when we are in the greatest despair respecting the results.'*

1767 Founder of Methodism John Wesley wrote in response to a newspaper criticism: *'I have told all the world I am not perfect.... I tell you flatly, I have not attained the character I draw.'*

1982 In his Latin American Journal ¡Gracias! Dutch Catholic mystic Henri J. M. Nouwen wrote: *'We come in touch with our hidden drives only after long and hard work in the field. Preparatory formation and training cannot do everything. The issue is not to have perfectly motivated missioners [missionaries], but missioners who are willing to be purified again and again as they struggle to find their true vocation in life.'*

IN GOD'S WORD... OT: Numbers 4:1–5:31 ~ NT: Mark 12:18-37 ~ Psalms 48:1-14 ~ Proverbs 10:26

נִיסָן NISAN — ALMANAC OF THE CHRISTIAN FAITH — אדר ADAR

March 6

Highlights in History

1447 Italian cardinal Tommaso Parentucelli was elected Pope Nicholas V, serving until 1455. He was probably the best of the Renaissance popes. A patron of the arts and literature, Nicholas restored many ruined churches and founded the Vatican Library. He also sought to reconcile religion with the new learning, and so led a blameless personal life. Nicholas brought about the submission of the last antipope, Felix V.

1521 German reformer Martin Luther was summoned to the Diet (Council) of Worms, to give an account of his theological views. (It was at this assembly Luther would declare: *"Here I stand, I can do no other. God help me. Amen."*)

1642 Urban VIII forbad the reading of Cornelius Otto Jansen's "Augustinus" because it attacked the ethics of the Jesuits. Jansen, a Dutch theologian, had inspired a reform in the Catholic Church. The Jansenists stressed the primacy of grace in human redemption.

1858 American Catholic reformer Isaac Hecker and his companions founded the Missionary Society of St. Paul (Paulists), whose purpose was to convert Americans to Roman Catholicism.

Notable Birthdays

1475 Birth of Michelangelo Buonarroti, Italian artist extraordinaire. The giant of the High Renaissance, his works included the sculptures "Pieta" (1498) and "David" (1504), the architectural plans for rebuilding St. Peter's Cathedral, and the paintings on the 5,808-square-foot ceiling of the Sistine Chapel (1508-12). [d. 2/18/1564]

1811 Birth of Edward H. Browne, Anglican prelate and writer. As Bishop of Winchester, 1873-90, he was on the translation committee for the *English Revised Version* of the Bible (1881-85), and prepared the volume on Genesis for *The Speaker's Commentary*. Browne's *Exposition of the 39 Articles* (1850-53), his best-known work, was long a standard authority on the subject. [d. 12/18/1891]

The Last Passage

1893 Death of Frederick W. Evans, 84, English-born Shaker leader and writer. He authored *Ann Lee* [founder of the Shakers]: *A Biography* (1858) and *Autobiography of a Shaker* (1869). (b. 6/9/1808)

1919 Death of Julia H. Johnston, 70, an American Presbyterian Sunday School leader. She authored over 500 hymns, including "Marvelous Grace of Our Loving Lord" (a.k.a. "Grace Greater Than Our Sin"). (b. 1/21/1849)

1933 Death of Amos. R. Wells, 70, American Sunday School educator. He was associated with the newly-established United Society of Christian Endeavor (forerunner of the church youth fellowships), and from 1901 until his death he authored *Peloubet's Notes on the (International) Sunday School Lessons*. (b. 12/23/1862)

1984 Death of Martin Niemöller, 92, German Lutheran pastor and theologian of Germany's Confessing Church which resisted Nazi control of the German Evangelical Church. Imprisoned by Adolf Hitler (1938-45) for his outspoken opposition, Niemöller became a prominent pacifist, and later served as president of the World Council of Churches (1961-68). (b. 1/14/1892)

Words for the Soul

1735 English revivalist George Whitefield wrote in a letter: *'The renewal of our natures is a work of great importance. It is not to be done in a day. We have not only a new house to build up, but an old one to pull down.'*

1902 American Quaker holiness author Hannah Whitall Smith wrote in a letter to her daughter Mary: *'There are dreadful possibilities all around us, but generally I think life goes on pretty quietly, and especially if we learn how to take it quietly. Somehow even tragedies seem less tragical, when you are the actors in them, than they look to outsiders.'*

IN GOD'S WORD... OT: Numbers 6:1–7:89 ~ NT: Mark 12:38–13:13 ~ Psalms 49:1-20 ~ Proverbs 10:27-28

ניסן NISAN — ALMANAC OF THE CHRISTIAN FAITH — אדר ADAR

March 7

Highlights in History

321 As the first Christian emperor of the Roman Empire, Constantine I issued the first civil law requiring observance of a Sunday sabbath.

1526 The city council of Zurich, Switzerland mandated death by drowning for all who embraced the doctrine of the Anabaptists.

1804 The non-sectarian British and Foreign Bible Society (BFBS) was founded in London. Its purpose was *'to promote the circulation of the Holy Scriptures, without note or comment, both at home and in foreign lands.'* BFBS funds and publications aided such missionary pioneers as William Carey, Robert Morrison and Henry Martyn.

1964 At a parish church in Rome, Pope Paul VI celebrated a mass in Italian instead of Latin, thereby implementing one of the most significant changes to come out of the Second Vatican Council – worship in the vernacular (i.e., the spoken language of the local congregation).

Notable Birthdays

1825 Birth of Alfred Edersheim, Jewish-born popular Anglican Bible scholar, theologian and writer. His most widely read title, *The Life and Times of Jesus the Messiah* (2 vols., 1883), was a work of great learning. Written in an easy style, the title is still in print! [d. 3/16/1889]

1836 Birth of James Mills Thoburn, American Methodist missionary. He served in India for 27 years (1859-86). In 1888 he was elected a missionary bishop of his church, afterward residing in Calcutta and Bombay. Thoburn became the first Methodist Episcopal missionary to serve in Asia (1888-1908). [d. 11/28/1922]

1867 Birth of Peter Cameron Scott, American missionary pioneer. He founded the Africa Inland Mission in 1895, but died at 29 while leading the first party of missionaries in their mission trek in East Africa. [d. 12/4/1896]

The Last Passage

1274 Death of Thomas Aquinas, 49, considered the greatest philosopher and theologian of the medieval Catholic Church. He adapted Aristotle's writings to Christianity, and systematized Latin theology in his *Summa Theologica*. Aquinas distinguished between reason and revelation, but taught these did not contradict each other, and that each may be regarded as legitimate fountains of knowledge, because each comes from God. (b. 1225)

1755 Death of Thomas Wilson, 91, Anglican prelate and writer. He was appointed bishop of the Isle of Man in 1697. Wilson showed interest both in the missionary work of James Oglethorpe in Georgia, and in the Unitas Fratrum (Moravian Brethren) churches. In 1707 Bishop Wilson published *Principles and Duties of Christianity*, the first book ever printed in the Manx language. (b. 12/20/1663)

Words for the Soul

1646 In a letter to Sir Thomas Fairfax, Oliver Cromwell wrote: *'It's a blessed thing to die daily. For what is there in this world to be accounted of! The best men according to the flesh, and things, are lighter than vanity. I find this only good, to love the Lord and his poor despised people, to do for them and to be ready to suffer with them....'*

1736 English founder of Methodism John Wesley, 33, while beginning his work as an Anglican missionary in the American colony of Georgia, wrote in his journal: *'I entered upon my ministry at Savannah by preaching on the epistle for the day, being the thirteenth of First Corinthians.... All who love not the light must hate Him who is continually laboring to pour it in upon them.'*

1881 American holiness author Hannah Whitall Smith wrote in a letter: *'True humility consists in a deep view of our utter unworthiness, and in an absolute abandonment to God, without the slightest doubt that He will do the greatest things in us.'*

IN GOD'S WORD... OT: Numbers 8:1–9:23 ~ NT: Mark 13:14-37 ~ Psalms 50:1-23 ~ Proverbs 10:29-30

נִיסָן NISAN — ALMANAC OF THE CHRISTIAN FAITH — אֲדָר ADAR

March 8

Highlights in History

1698 British missioner Thomas Bray and four laymen founded the Society for Promoting Christian Knowledge (SPCK). The purpose of this pioneering mission agency was *'to advance the honor of God and the good of mankind by promoting Christian knowledge both at home and in the other parts of the world by the best methods that should offer.'*

1740 In Nottingham, PA, colonial American Presbyterian revivalist Gilbert Tennent preached his famous sermon, "The Danger of An Unconverted Ministry." Reaction by opponents of the Great Awakening produced the first split in the Presbyterian Church into the Old Side and New Side factions. (The two sides reunited in 1758.)

1782 Ninety-six Christian Native Americans who were living peacefully in the Moravian Brethren town of Gnadenhutten (now New Philadelphia, Ohio) were massacred by militiamen, in retaliation for Indian raids made elsewhere in the Ohio Territory.

1948 The U.S. Supreme Court ruled (in McCollum v. Board of Education) that religious education in the public schools was a violation of the First Constitutional Amendment.

Notable Birthdays

1607 Birth of Johann Rist, German Lutheran pastor and hymnwriter. He was crowned poet laureate in 1644. Rist penned over 650 hymns, many to comfort his people and himself, including "Break Forth, O Beauteous Heavenly Light." [d. 8/31/1667]

1875 Birth of Richard B. Hoyle, English Baptist clergyman, scholar and hymn translator. He moved to America in 1934 to teach at Western Theological Seminary. Hoyle gave us the English rendering of the hymn, "Thine Be the Glory, Risen, Conquering Son." [d. 12/14/1939]

The Last Passage

1862 Navy chaplain John L. Lenhart was among the casualties when his Union frigate "Cumberland" was crushed by the Confederate ironclad "Merrimac" and sank off Hampton Roads, VA. Commissioned in 1847, Lenhart, who died with his sinking ship, became the first U.S. Navy chaplain to be killed in action.

1887 Death of Henry Ward Beecher, 73, American Congregational clergyman, abolitionist, orator and writer. The brother of Harriet Beecher Stowe, his dramatic flair made him a leading spokesman for tough social issues of his day. As a writer, he imparted life to the dullest subjects. (b. 6/24/1813)

1982 Death of Mitchell Dahood, 60, American Jesuit biblical scholar. He was a world-recognized authority on ancient Ugaritic. In addition to publishing hundreds of articles, Dahood authored *Ugaritic Hebrew Philology* (1965), and also the three-volume translation and commentary on Psalms in the *Anchor Bible Commentary* Series. (b. 2/2/1922)

Words for the Soul

1522 German reformer Martin Luther explained in a letter: *'Human authority is not always to be obeyed, namely, when it undertakes something against the commandments of God; yet it should never be despised but always honored. Christ did not justify Pilate's verdict; but He did not depose him or the emperor, nor did He show any contempt for him.'*

1871 American holiness writer Hannah Whitall Smith reasoned in a letter: *'I don't see how anyone who is not a Christian can be happy for a single minute. Children of God, who know their sins forgiven and who cast all their cares upon the One who cares for them, certainly have a right to be joyful and lighthearted. As to being so sober and solemn, it is all wrong. The merriest people I know are the most devoted Christians.'*

IN GOD'S WORD... OT: Numbers 10:1–11:23 ~ NT: Mark 14:1-21 ~ Psalms 51:1-19 ~ Proverbs 10:31-32

נִיסָן
NISAN

ALMANAC OF THE CHRISTIAN FAITH

אדר
ADAR

~ March 9 ~

Highlights in History

1074 After this date, all married priests were excommunicated from the Roman Catholic Church. (Up to this time, celibacy of the clergy was not always strictly enforced.)

1552 In England, the Second Act of Uniformity was passed, requiring churches to implement the revised *Book of Common Prayer*. Absence from church on Sundays and Holy Days was punishable by ecclesiastical censure. Attendance at any other form of worship service was punishable by imprisonment.

1931 World Radio Missionary Fellowship was incorporated by Clarence W. Jones and Reuben Larson in Lima, Ohio. It became one of the widest-reaching radio ministries, broadcasting the gospel in many countries.

Notable Birthdays

1568 Birth of St. Aloysius Gonzaga, Italian Jesuit and patron saint of youth. He died while ministering to those stricken by famine and pestilence in Rome, and was canonized in 1726. [d. 1591]

1836 Birth of Martin F. Shaw, English church organist and hymnwriter. He edited the *Oxford Book of Carols* (1928), and also composed the hymn tune GENTLE JESUS ("Gentle Jesus, Meek and Mild"). [d. 10/24/1958]

1839 Birth of Phoebe Palmer Knapp, American Methodist humanitarian. She was a close friend of Fanny Crosby, and published over 500 gospel songs during her life, including the hymn tune ASSURANCE ("Blessed Assurance, Jesus is Mine"). [d. 7/10/1908]

1907 Birth of Mircea Eliade, Romanian-born American historian of religions. He taught at the University of Chicago (1964-1986) and was noted for his research into the symbolic language used in comparative religions. [d. 4/22/1986]

The Last Passage

1661 Death of Jules Mazarin, 58, French Catholic statesman. He succeeded Richelieu (1643-61) as the prime minister of France. Mazarin greatly increased his country's influence as a European power, and also laid the foundations for the monarchy of Louis XIV. (b. 7/14/1602)

1825 Death of Anna L. A. Barbauld, 82, English Presbyterian writer. She did not have the benefit of a formal education. However, influenced by Joseph Priestley, she launched out on a literary career which produced eleven books and 21 hymns, including "Praise to God, Immortal Praise." (b. 6/20/1743)

1907 Death of John A. Dowie, 59, Scottish-born faith healer and flamboyant founder of the Christian Catholic Apostolic Church. He established Zion City, north of Chicago, as the home for his sect. He later proclaimed himself Elijah the Restorer, and was eventually deposed in a revolt by his followers. (b. 5/25/1847)

Words for the Soul

1843 Scottish clergyman Robert Murray McCheyne encouraged in a letter: 'You will never find Jesus so precious as when the world is one vast howling wilderness. Then He is like a rose blooming in the midst of the desolation, a rock rising above the storm.'

1883 Scottish clergyman and biographer Andrew Bonar, 73, reflected in his diary: 'A new providence. My daughter Isabella is engaged.... My ship now sails into a new region. New experiences will be given me, new anxieties, sorrow, joy. Job i.5 comes up.'

1930 Linguistics education pioneer and Congregational missionary Frank C. Laubach surmised in a letter: 'It seems to me now that the very Bible cannot be read as a substitute for meeting God soul to soul and face to face.'

IN GOD'S WORD... OT: Numbers 11:24–13:33 ~ NT: Mark 14:22-52 ~ Psalms 52:1-9 ~ Proverbs 11:1-3

נִיסָן NISAN

ALMANAC OF THE CHRISTIAN FAITH

אדר ADAR

~ March 10 ~

Highlights in History

1681 England's King Charles II made Quaker William Penn sole proprietor of the American colonial territory known today as Pennsylvania. Penn was generous in offering religious freedom to persecuted Christian groups.

1748 OS [NS=3/21] During a storm at sea, slave ship captain John Newton was converted to a saving Christian faith. Some years later, Newton studied for the Anglican ministry and also wrote the hymn, "Amazing Grace." [N.B. The Gregorian or "New Style" Calendar, which dropped 11 days when first implemented in 1582, was adopted by England in 1751. Near dates, like this one, were sometimes "reconfigured" by later English historians.]

1880 English evangelist, writer and missionary George Scott Railton (1849-1913), along with seven women, landed in New York City from London, and inaugurated the first mission of the Salvation Army in the United States.

Notable Birthdays

1452 Birth of Ferdinand II (V) of Aragon. The 1469 marriage between him and his cousin, Isabella of Castile, made him Ferdinand V of Castile and unified the Spanish crown. It was Ferdinand who supported the American discovery voyages of Christopher Columbus. [d. 1/23/1516]

1823 Birth of John B. Dykes, English clergyman and sacred composer. His many enduring hymn tunes include NICAEA ("Holy, Holy, Holy! Lord God Almighty"); MELITA ("Almighty Father, Strong to Save"); DOMINUS REGIT ME ("The King of Love My Shepherd Is"); ST. AGNES ("Jesus, The Very Thought of Thee"); VOX DILECTI ("I Heard the Voice of Jesus Say"); BEATITUDO ("O For a Closer Walk with God"); LUX BENIGNA ("Lead, Kindly Light"); ALFORD ("Ten Thousand Times Ten Thousand"); and ST. BEES ("Take My Life and Let It Be"). [d. 1/22/1876]

1830 Birth of Tullius C. O'Kane, American educator and hymnwriter. He was the first musical instructor at Ohio Wesleyan Female College. Today, he is remembered for the hymn tune O'KANE ("On Jordan's Stormy Banks I Stand"). [d. 2/10/1912]

The Last Passage

1528 Martyrdom of Balthasar Hübmaier, 48, a German Anabaptist who converted from Catholicism in 1525. Regarded now as the most well known and respected Anabaptist theologian of the Reformation, Hübmaier was burned for heresy in Vienna. (Three days after his execution, his wife, with a stone tied around her neck, was drowned in the River Danube.) (b. ca. 1480)

1898 Death of George Müller, 92, English pastor, evangelist, philanthropist and leader in the Christian Brethren movement. An advocate of believing prayer, Müller thus provided care for over 10,000 orphans during his life, all without public advertisement. (b. 9/27/1805)

1946 C. Austin Miles, 78, Pennsylvania pharmacist and hymnwriter. Associated with Hall-Mack and Rodeheaver Publishing Companies, Miles composed cantatas and anthems, but is best remembered for creating the hymn, "I Come to the Garden Alone" (& GARDEN). (b. 1/7/1868)

Words for the Soul

1880 American holiness author Hannah Whitall Smith wrote in a letter: *'I know that God's choice for each one of us is always a perfect choice.'*

1937 British historian Arnold J. Toynbee observed: *'In this really very brief period of less than 2,000 years Christianity has in fact produced greater spiritual effects in the world than have been produced in a comparable space of time by any other spiritual movement that we know of in history.'*

IN GOD'S WORD... OT: Numbers 14:1–15:16 ~ NT: Mark 14:53-72 ~ Psalms 53:1-6 ~ Proverbs 11:4

נִיסָן NISAN — ALMANAC OF THE CHRISTIAN FAITH — אֲדָר ADAR

March 11

Highlights in History

843 Ending an 89-year controversy, a Greek Orthodox synod repealed the Iconoclastic decrees of the 754 Council of Constantinople. Use of icons in Christian worship was again restored within the Eastern churches. Advocates of iconoclasm stressed the difference between the "reverence of worship" and the "reverence of respect" that attended these visible symbols of an invisible God.

1513 Giovanni de' Medici was elected Pope Leo X, serving to 1521. His pontificate was notorious for its moral laxity, and for permitting the emergence of the Protestant movement. Leo is largely remembered for his 1520 excommunication of Martin Luther, and for terminating the Fifth Lateran Council in order to prevent schism.

1829 Felix Mendelssohn conducted Johann Sebastian Bach's "St. Matthew Passion" (its first performance in one hundred years). It revived scholarly interest in a composer whose works had been initially ignored after his death. Today, many music scholars consider Bach the greatest composer who ever lived.

Notable Birthdays

1742 Birth of Samuel Provoost, American Episcopal bishop. Born into a Dutch Reformed Church family, Provoost supported the American colonies during the American Revolution. In 1786 he was elected the first Episcopal bishop of the Diocese of New York (serving until 1801), and later served as chaplain to the United States Senate (1789-1801). [d. 9/6/1815]

1860 Birth of Hannah Frances Davidson, American missionary. She was the first woman in the Brethren in Christ Church to earn an M.A. degree (1892). In 1897 Hannah became one of her denomination's first missionaries to the African continent (remaining until 1923). She afterward taught at Messiah College (PA) until 1932. [d. 12/1935]

The Last Passage

1847 Death of Jonathan Chapman, 72, the American pioneer and horticultural evangelist better known as "Johnny Appleseed." Chapman's "nature theology" derived from his Swedenborgian beliefs, and he traveled throughout the Midwest, preaching and distributing apple seeds. Chapman's life was immortalized in a poem by Vachel Lindsay. (b. 9/26/1774)

1897 Death of Henry Drummond, 45, Scottish evangelical writer and lecturer. He sought to reconcile Christianity with evolution, but is better remembered for his famous 1887 address on 1 Corinthians 13, entitled "The Greatest Thing in the World." (b. 8/17/1851)

1923 Death of Mary Ann Thomson, 88, English-born American Episcopal poet. She published numerous poems, among which one became the popular hymn: "O Zion, Haste, Thy Mission High Fulfilling." (b. 12/5/1834)

1932 Death of Hermann Gunkel, 69, German Protestant Old Testament scholar. A pioneer investigator into literary styles, Gunkel became one of the first to develop the method of biblical analysis now known as form criticism. (b. 5/23/1862)

Words for the Soul

1738 English revivalist George Whitefield noted in his journal: *'Suffering times are a Christian's best improving times; for they break the will, wean us from the creature, prove the heart.'*

1883 In his famous "Incense and Light" sermon, English Baptist preacher Charles Spurgeon recalled: *'Dr. Adam Clarke used to say to young ministers, "Study yourselves dead and then pray yourselves alive again," and that is an excellent rule. Work in your study as if it all depended upon you and then go forth and speak, trusting in God because all depends upon Him!'*

IN GOD'S WORD... OT: Numbers 15:17–16:40 ~ NT: Mark 15:1-47 ~ Psalms 54:1-7 ~ Proverbs 11:5-6

נִיסָן NISAN | ALMANAC OF THE CHRISTIAN FAITH | אֲדָר ADAR

~ March 12 ~

Highlights in History

1088 French monk Urban II was elected pope, serving until 1099. He issued the 1095 summons that led to the First Crusade against the Muslims (1097-99), declaring, *"God wills it."*

1621 Having arrived in New England four months earlier, the Pilgrims finally left the ship Mayflower to live ashore.

1622 Gregory XV published the decretal, "Decet Romanum Pontificem," which instituted the process of secret ballot, to be used whenever the conclave of cardinals elects a new pope.

1904 Syrian-born Raphael Hawaweeny was consecrated Orthodox bishop of Brooklyn, New York by Russian Patriarch, Archbishop Tikhon. It made Hawaweeny the first Eastern Orthodox bishop to be ordained in America.

Notable Birthdays

1607 Birth of Paul Gerhardt, one of the best-loved of the German hymnwriters. His life was marked with tragedy. Four of Gerhardt's children died in infancy, and he lost his wife after only 13 years.  Yet his Passion hymn, "O Sacred Head, Now Wounded," influenced by Catholic mysticism, reflects a strong spiritual serenity. [d. 5/27/1676]

1710 Birth of Thomas A. Arne, English sacred composer. He created the sacred tune ARLINGTON, to which two hymns are still sung today: "Am I a Soldier of the Cross?" and "O For a Faith That Will Not Shrink." [d. 3/5/1778]

1826 Birth of Robert Lowry, American Baptist clergyman and orator. He is also remembered for the gospel songs he penned: CHRIST AROSE (& "Low In the Grave He Lay"); MARCHING  TO ZION ("Come, We That Love the Lord"); NEED ("I Need Thee Every Hour"); ALL THE WAY ("...My Savior Leads Me"). [d. 11/25/1899]

The Last Passage

604 Gregory I (the Great) died at 64. As pope (590-604), he was an exemplary reformer of clerical discipline. In addition to sending St. Augustine (of Canterbury) to convert the Anglo-Saxons, Gregory also collected and codified the melodies of the Church of his day into what came to be known as Gregorian chant. (b. 2/3/540)

1022 Death of San Simeon the New Theologian, Byzantine mystic and writer. As abbot of the monastery at St. Mamas (in Constantinople), 981-1005, he was known as the greatest of the Byzantine mystical writers. His theology combined a strong Christocentrism with an emphasis on the vision of the "Divine Light."

1963 Death of G[arfield] Bromley Oxnam, 71, American Methodist bishop and ecumenical leader. He traveled widely in support of missions, and published over 20 books on faith and social issues.  Bromley was a founding officer of the National Council of Churches, and a president of the World Council of Churches (1948-54). (b. 8/14/1891)

Words for the Soul

1522 German reformer Martin Luther emphasized in a sermon: *'Wine and women bring many a man to misery and make a fool of him. Shall we, therefore, kill all the women and pour out all the wine? Likewise, gold and silver cause much evil. Shall we, therefore, condemn them? Nay, if we wanted to drive away our worst enemy, who does us the most harm, we should have to kill ourselves; for we have no more injurious enemy than our own heart.'*

1867 American Quaker and holiness author Hannah Whitall Smith, 35, wrote in her journal: *'I only want to be like clay in His hands, to be used by Him or laid aside, just as He pleases.... How marvelously He has been working in me to will and to do of His good pleasure. When I look back at my experience and at all the darkness of my former life, I am lost in wonder at His marvelous working.'*

IN GOD'S WORD... OT: Numbers 16:41–18:32 ~ NT: Mark 16:1-20 ~ Psalms 55:1-23 ~ Proverbs 11:7

March 13

Highlights in History

483 St. Felix III was named pope, and served until 492. He began a schism between the Roman Catholic and the Greek Orthodox churches, which lasted 34 years.

1456 German printer Johann Gutenberg completed publication of the Bible on his printing press. It was the first copy of the Scriptures produced with movable type.

1687 Father Eusebio Kino (1645-1711), an Italian-born Jesuit, began his missionary work in the American Southwest. As an explorer in the service of Spain, Father Kino established 25 Indian missions in the area now divided between northern Mexico (Sonora), Arizona and southern California.

1904 The "Christ of the Andes" was dedicated — a 26-foot-tall bronze statue of Christ located on the Argentina-Chile border. It symbolized a peace treaty averting a war between the two nations which would have drawn the entire South American continent into its wake. Old cannons were melted down to make the casting, and a plaque at its base reads: *'He is our peace who hath made us one.'*

Notable Birthdays

1804 Birth of James W. Alexander, preacher, math teacher and poet. The son of Archibald Alexander, James translated Paul Gerhardt's German verses into the English hymn, "O Sacred Head, Now Wounded." [d. 7/31/1859]

1823 Birth of Henry Twells, English clergyman, educator and hymnwriter. He was of frail health, but a generous supporter of missionary projects and a defender of the rural clergy. He was also a member of the committee which published *Hymns Ancient and Modern* (1861), but today Twells is better remembered for authoring the hymn, "At Even E'er the Sun Was Set." [d. 1/19/1900]

1868 Birth of Charles E. Cowman, American missionary to the Orient. In 1901 he sailed with his wife Lettie (who later authored the devotional *Streams in the Desert*) to Japan, where in 1910 they founded the Oriental Missionary Society. Charles' health broke in 1917, and the Cowmans returned to America. [d. 9/25/1924]

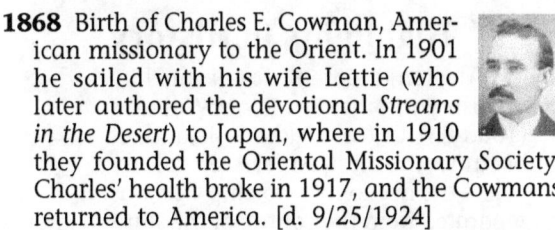

The Last Passage

1569 Death of Louis de Bourbon, 38, Prince of Condé. He was the first great Huguenot leader. His military expertise helped French Calvinism to become a political power. (b. 5/7/1530)

1965 Founder and bishop of the Albanian Orthodox Church in America, Rev. Fan Stylian Noli, died at 83. Ordained at age 26 by the Russian Orthodox bishop in New York City, Noli helped organize Albanian worshipers into an independent diocese in 1919, and later into autocephalous body in 1922. (b. 1882)

Words for the Soul

1533 During one of his "Table Talks," German reformer Martin Luther testified: *'For a number of years now I have annually read through the Bible twice. If the Bible were a large, mighty tree and all its words were little branches, I have tapped at all the branches, eager to know what was there and what it had to offer.'*

1637 Exiled Scottish clergyman Samuel Rutherford testified in a letter: *'His love hath neither brim nor bottom; his love is like himself, it passeth all natural understanding.'*

1982 In his Latin American Journal *¡Gracias!* Catholic diarist Henri J. M. Nouwen wrote: *'Two Churches are gradually developing in Peru.... On the one side is the Church that speaks primarily about God, with little reference to the daily reality in which the people live; on the other side is the Church that speaks primarily about the struggle of the people for freedom, with little reference to the Divine mysteries to which this struggle points.'*

IN GOD'S WORD... OT: Numbers 19:1–20:29 ~ NT: Luke 1:1-25 ~ Psalms 56:1-13 ~ Proverbs 11:8

ALMANAC OF THE CHRISTIAN FAITH

נִיסָן NISAN   אֲדָר ADAR

~ March 14 ~

Highlights in History

1644 A colonial patent was granted by English Parliament to Roger Williams (1603-83) to found Rhode Island. It became the first American colony where the freedom to worship God was separated from the control of the state. Williams had earlier established the first Baptist church in America (1639) in Providence, RI.

1873 In Japan, a long-standing edict against Christianity was reversed. The gospel had been brought to Japan as early as 1549 but, especially after 1868, persecution of Christians became severe enough to drive both native believers and foreign missionaries into exile.

1897 The Polish National Catholic Church of America was organized in Scranton, PA.

1949 Dr. Robert P. Evans chartered the European Bible Institute in Chicago. Its name was later changed to the Greater Europe Mission, and the headquarters today are in Monument, CO.

Notable Birthdays

1808 Birth of Narcissa Prentiss Whitman, pioneer American Presbyterian ABCFM missionary. She was one of the first white female missionaries to reach the Pacific Northwest. Narcissa and her husband Dr. Marcus Whitman set up a mission in the Oregon Territory in 1836, but in superstitious retaliation for a measles epidemic, they and 12 others were attacked by Cayuse Indians and murdered. [d. 11/29/1847]

1826 Birth of William F. Sherwin, American Baptist vocal instructor and sacred chorister. He directed the music at the Methodists' Chautauqua Assembly in New York, and left the Church two enduring hymn tunes: BREAD OF LIFE ("Break Thou The...") and CHAUTAUQUA ("Day is Dying in the West"). [d. 4/14/1888]

1835 Birth of Henry Barclay Swete, Anglican biblical and patristics scholar. He taught at Cambridge University (1890-1915) and published numerous scholarly works on the ancient biblical text, including *The Old Testament in Greek According to the Septuagint* (3 vols., 1887-91). [d. 5/10/1917]

The Last Passage

1361 Icelandic monk Eysteinn Ásgrímsson, 51, died in Norway. He authored *Lilja* (1870 Eng. trans.: "The Lily"), a survey of Christian history from the Creation to the Last Judgment, considered to be the finest recorded example of pre-Reformation Icelandic poetry. (b. ca. 1310)

1791 Death of Johann S. Semler, 65, German Lutheran theologian and biblical scholar. Called the "father of German rationalism," Semler developed the first principles of textual criticism (i.e., textual analysis of the early manuscripts) for the Bible. (b. 12/18/1725)

1912 Death of Albert L. Peace, 68, English sacred organist. He edited a number of hymn collections for the Church of Scotland, and composed the haunting tune ST. MARGARET ("O Love That Wilt Not Let Me Go"). (b. 1/26/1844)

Words for the Soul

1871 American holiness author Hannah Whitall Smith wrote in a letter: 'It is a mistake to think we must feel good before we pray; we need to pray most of all when we feel poor, and empty, and weak.'

1937 Pope Pius XI declared in his encyclical against the Nazi "cult": 'Race, nation, state... all have an essential and honorable place within the secular order.... To abstract them, however, from the earthly scale of values and make them the supreme norm of all values, including religious ones, and divinize them with an idolatrous cult, is to be guilty of perverting and falsifying the order of things created and commanded by God.'

IN GOD'S WORD... OT: Numbers 21:1–22:20 ~ NT: Luke 1:26-56 ~ Psalms 57:1-11 ~ Proverbs 11:9-11

March 15

Highlights in History

1517 Needing money to rebuild St. Peter's Basilica, Pope Leo X announced the sale of indulgences. Proclamations by Johann Tetzel, Leo's Dominican agent in Germany, angered Augustinian monk Martin Luther. In opposition to indulgences, he posted "95 Theses" on Oct. 31st.

1729 In a ceremony of profession at the Ursuline convent in New Orleans, Sister Stanislaus Hachard took her vows, making her the first Catholic nun to be professed in America.

1804 New York City-born Elizabeth Bayley Seton (1774-1821) converted to Roman Catholicism, 14 months after her husband's death from tuberculosis. Mrs. Seton later founded one of America's first religious communities, the Sisters of Charity of St. Joseph. In 1975 she was canonized the first American-born Catholic saint.

1856 Haverford College was chartered in Haverford, PA (just west of Philadelphia). Founded in 1833, it was the first Quaker college to be established in the United States.

1988 Bishop Eugene Antonio Marino was elevated to Archbishop of Atlanta by Pope John Paul II. It made him the first African-American Catholic archbishop to serve in the U.S.

Notable Birthdays

1708 Birth of John Hulse, English clergyman and philanthropist. He bequeathed most of his inherited property to Cambridge University for the advancement of religious learning. [d. 12/14/1790]

1859 Birth of American Methodist clergyman Henry J. Zelley. He served 19 charges in New Jersey before retiring in 1929. Zelley also penned more than 1500 poems, hymns and gospel songs during his lifetime, including "Heavenly Sunlight." [d. 3/16/1942]

1935 Birth of Jimmy Lee Swaggart, American Pentecostal televangelist and vocal artist. Involved in a sex scandal in 1988, Swaggart's spiritual influence fell, and he was subsequently defrocked by his Assemblies of God denomination.

The Last Passage

752 Death of Pope Zacharias, who served from 741. He was the last of the Greek popes.

1587 Death of Kaspar Olevianus, 50, early German theologian and reformer. He introduced the Calvinist Reformation into parts of Germany, and was a founder of the German Reformed Church. (b. 8/19/1536)

1862 Death of Mother Benedicta Riepp, 36, Bavarian-born Catholic religious. She sailed to America with two companions in 1852, and helped establish the first Benedictine convent in America, in Elk County, PA. (b. 6/28/1825)

Words for the Soul

1839 Scottish clergyman Robert Murray McCheyne maintained in a letter: *'All my ideas of peace and joy are linked in with my Bible; and I would not give the hours of secret converse with it for all the other hours I spend in this world.'*

1934 English Bible expositor Arthur W. Pink advised in a letter: *'It is the tendency of youth to be speculative, and to accept what others say without much examination. But as one grows older, one becomes more cautious, and slower to accept man's interpretations.'*

1950 American Auca Indian missionary and martyr Jim Elliot lamented in his journal: *'The believer is a displaced person. He loses the controlling features of both environment and heredity.'*

1986 In his *Road to Daybreak* journal, Catholic diarist Henri J. M. Nouwen wrote: *'I love Jesus but want to hold on to my own independence even when that independence brings me no real freedom.'*

IN GOD'S WORD... OT: Numbers 22:21–23:30 ~ NT: Luke 1:57-80 ~ Psalms 58:1-11 ~ Proverbs 11:12-13

March 16

Highlights in History

597 [BC] According to the calculations of some archaeologists, King Nebuchadnezzar of Babylon completed the first of his two conquests of Jerusalem on this date. (The biblical account is found in 2 Kings 24:1ff and in 2 Chronicles 36:5-8, as well as being implied in the written prophecies of Jeremiah and Ezekiel.)

1517 Leo X closed the Fifth Lateran Council (which had opened in May 1512). Among other business, the Council prohibited the printing of books without ecclesiastical authority.

1952 The first religious program on TV, "This Week in Religion" debuted on the Dumont Television Network. It was the only ecumenical program of the early religious offerings on TV and aired Sunday nights for over two years.

1970 The complete text of the *New English Bible* was simultaneously published by the Oxford and Cambridge presses. (The NEB New Testament was first published in 1961.)

Notable Birthdays

1621 Birth of Georg Neumark, German court poet, librarian and hymnwriter. Blind during his last year of life, Neumark produced 34 hymns in all, many written in times of struggle, including: "If Thou But Suffer God to Guide Thee" (& NEUMARK). [d. 7/18/1681]

1823 Birth of William Henry Monk, English sacred organist. He served in a number of London churches, and was organist of St. Mathias' Church, Stoke Newington, from 1852 until his death. In addition, he taught music in several schools. Monk gave his time as editor, and also contributed 50 original tunes, to the historic Anglican hymnal, *Hymns Ancient and Modern*. His hymn tunes include DIX ("For the Beauty of the Earth"); EVENTIDE ("Abide with Me"); and VICTORY ("The Strife is O'er, The Battle Done"). [d. 3/1/1889]

1870 Birth of Ernst William Olson, Swedish-born American Lutheran publishing associate and author. He translated 28 hymns, including Carolina Sandell Berg's Swedish lyrics to "Children of the Heavenly Father." [d. 10/6/1958]

The Last Passage

1649 French Jesuit missionary to the North American Indians (1625-49), Jean de Brébeuf, 55, was tortured and murdered by the Iroquois Indians at St. Ignace, Canada. In 1930, Brébeuf was canonized along with six other North American martyrs. (b. 3/25/1593)

1889 Death of Alfred Edersheim, 64, Anglican biblical scholar and theologian. His *Life and Times of Jesus the Messiah* (1883) is still popular today. (b. 3/7/1825)

1909 Death of Marianne Hearn, 74, English poet. Prominent in British Baptist circles, she produced a vast literary output (often under the name Marianne Farningham). Her writings were later published in 20 volumes. Hearn is remembered today for authoring the hymn, "Just As I Am, Thine Own to Be." (b. 12/17/1834)

Words for the Soul

1538 German reformer Martin Luther declared in a sermon: *'A man may be a pious and God-fearing person and yet be in error.'*

1894 American Quaker and holiness author Hannah Whitall Smith revealed in a letter: *'The coming generation are not going to see things as we have seen them, that is very clear; and the food that has satisfied us will not satisfy them. But this does not trouble me. We did not see things as the generation before us did.'*

1976 In an interview with Robert L. Turner, future president Jimmy Carter explained: *'We believe that the first time we're born, as children, it's human life given to us; and when we accept Jesus as our Savior, it's a new life. That's what "born again" means.'*

IN GOD'S WORD... OT: Numbers 24:1–25:18 ~ NT: Luke 2:1-35 ~ Psalms 59:1-17 ~ Proverbs 11:14

ALMANAC OF THE CHRISTIAN FAITH

NISAN | ADAR

~ March 17 ~

Highlights in History

752 In the briefest pontificate in history, an elderly presbyter (of whose previous career nothing is known) was elected Pope Stephen I. He died of a stroke four days later, before his official consecration. Later popes named Stephen (who followed this election) are usually designated by a dual numbering. Thus, the next pope, who reigned from 752-757, is called Stephen II (III).

1856 Ex-slave Amanda Smith was converted. She had gone to the cellar and prayed, saying she would either be saved or die. She afterward dedicated her life to God's service at the Green Street Methodist Episcopal Church in New York. Amanda went on to become a world-renowned evangelist and missionary, and traveled to England, Scotland, Liberia and India.

1897 Emilie Grace Briggs became the first woman in America to graduate from a Presbyterian theological seminary, when she received her Bachelor of Divinity degree from Union Theological Seminary in New York City.

Notable Birthdays

1780 Birth of Thomas Chalmers, Scottish Presbyterian clergyman and reformer. In 1843 he led the withdrawal of 470 ministers (one-third of the clergy) from the Church of Scotland's General Assembly to form the Free Church of Scotland. Chalmers' chief pastoral concern was evangelization of the urban poor. [d. 5/20/1847]

1841 Birth of James R. Murray, American sacred music editor. A Union veteran of the American Civil War, Murray afterward edited sacred music periodicals. Today he is probably best remembered for composing the hymn tune MUELLER, to which is sung the Christmas carol, "Away in a Manger." [d. 3/10/1905]

1874 Birth of Stephen S. Wise, Hungarian-born American Jewish Reformed rabbi and Zionist. He worked to establish Palestine as a national home for the Jews, and also helped create both the American and the World Jewish Congresses. [d. 4/19/1949]

The Last Passage

1649 French Jesuit missionary to Native Americans, Gabriel Lalemant, 48, died as the sun rose, after a night of torture. He was killed by the same Iroquois Indians who had murdered his superior, Jean de Brébeuf, the previous day. (b. 10/10/1610)

1858 Death of Laban Ainsworth, 100, American clergyman. Ordained pastor of the Congregational Church at Jaffrey, NH, in 1782, Ainsworth remained at this pulpit for 76 years, making his the longest known pastorate to be held in America. (b. 7/19/1757)

1902 Death of George W. Warren, 73, American Episcopal church organist and hymn composer. Though largely self-taught, he became an accomplished sacred musician, and served Episcopal churches in Albany, Brooklyn and New York City. He composed anthems and hymn tunes, including NATIONAL HYMN ("God of Our Fathers"). (b. 8/17/1828)

1911 Death of Joseph Y. Peek, 68, an American Civil War veteran who afterward became a Methodist lay preacher. He became fully ordained less than two months before his death, yet Peek still ministers to the Church today through his hymn tune PEEK ("I Would Be True"). (b. 2/27/1843)

Words for the Soul

1539 German reformer Martin Luther, in a "Table Talk" recorded on this date, coined the familiar aphorism: *'A penny saved is better than a penny earned. Thus thrift is the best income.'*

1951 American Plymouth Brethren missionary to Ecuador and Auca Indian martyr Jim Elliot wrote in his journal: *'There are answers not yet discovered for which I must wait.'*

IN GOD'S WORD... OT: Numbers 26:1-51 ~ NT: Luke 2:36-52 ~ Psalms 60:1-12 ~ Proverbs 11:15

March 18

Highlights in History

1314 Under false charges, thirty-nine Knights Templars were burned at the stake in Paris. (The Templars were a military religious order, created to protect pilgrims going to the Holy Land. But they had become wealthy after the Crusades and aroused the jealousy of the French monarchy.)

1795 Demetrius A. Gallitzin (1770-1840), the first Catholic priest to receive full theological training in the United States, was ordained by Bishop John Carroll in Baltimore — also making Gallitzin the first Catholic priest ordained in the U.S.

Notable Birthdays

1789 Birth of Charlotte Elliott, one of the outstanding female British hymnists. She was closely associated with Swiss evangelist H. A. César Malan, and devoted her life to religious and humanitarian writing. Though an invalid during her last 50 years, Elliott penned 150 hymns, of which the best-known is "Just As I Am." [d. 9/22/1871]

1823 Birth of Joseph Augustus Seiss, a popular Philadelphia Lutheran clergyman. A student of liturgy and hymnody, he authored over 100 books (including *Lectures on the Gospels*) and penned the 4th stanza of the hymn, "Fairest Lord Jesus." [d. 6/20/1904]

1856 Birth of John L. Zimmerman, a prominent American Lutheran layman who authored the merger resolution that led to the formation of the United Lutheran Church in America (ULCA) in 1918. [d. 9/17/1941]

The Last Passage

1227 Death of Honorius III, pope from 1216. He was loved for his gentle spirit, and for fostering learning. Honorius also approved the Dominican (1216) and Franciscan (1223) and Carmelite religious orders. (b. unk.)

1612 Death of Bartholomew Legate, 37, the last heretic burned in London. (b. ca. 1575)

1819 Death of John Bakewell, 98, ardent English Wesleyan revivalist and hymnwriter. Bakewell penned for the Church the beloved hymn: "Hail, Thou Once Despised Jesus." (b. 1721)

1983 Death of Catherine Marshall, 68, American Presbyterian inspirational author. The widow of U.S. Senate chaplain Peter Marshall, she published his biography, *A Man Called Peter* (1951), following his premature death. She also wrote the bestseller *Christy* (1967), a semi-biographical work based on her mother's early years as a home missionary, on which a television series was based. (b. 9/27/1914)

Words for the Soul

1525 German reformer Martin Luther declared in a sermon: *'The Law has been set up, not for the righteous but for the wicked. One of the uses and purposes of the Law is... to repress wickedness and check it outwardly... making it possible for people to have peace and keeping everyone from following the whims of his wantonness. In this manner the Law is properly preached and used.'*

1767 Anglican clergyman and hymnwriter John Newton wrote in a letter: *'The more you know Him, the better you will trust Him; the more you trust Him, the better you will love Him; the more you love Him, the better you will serve Him.'*

1867 American Quaker Holiness author Hannah Whitall Smith wrote in a letter to her mother: *'Jesus is just as much my Saviour from the daily power of sin, as He was long ago from its guilt.'*

1952 British literary scholar and Christian apologist C. S. Lewis, in a letter, set down the following prayer: *'Almighty God, who art the father of lights and who hast promised by thy dear Son that all who do thy will shall know thy doctrine: give me grace so to live that by daily obedience I daily increase in faith and in the understanding of thy Holy Word, through Jesus Christ our Lord. Amen.'*

IN GOD'S WORD... OT: Numbers 26:52–28:15 ~ NT: Luke 3:1-22 ~ Psalms 61:1-8 ~ Proverbs 11:16-17

נִיסָן NISAN — ALMANAC OF THE CHRISTIAN FAITH — אֲדָר ADAR

March 19

Highlights in History

416 Pope St. Innocent I wrote a letter to Decentius, Bishop of Eugubium (near Florence, Italy). The letter became important for its early mention of the rites of unction and penance.

1227 Urgolino, Count of Segni, was elected to the papacy as Gregory IX. During his pontificate he sought to reunite with Eastern Orthodoxy, collected decretals of the earlier popes and developed the Holy Office of the Inquisition.

1904 Pius X issued a *motu proprio* calling for a complete overhauling of the codification of canon law in the Catholic Church. It resulted in the *Codex Iuris Canonici*, published in 1917.

1953 Emmanuel Holiness Church was organized in Whiteville, NC. Its founding members withdrew from the Fire-Baptized Holiness Church because they believed the parent denomination had become lax in its Holiness standards.

Notable Birthdays

1657 Birth of Jean LeClerc, French Arminian theologian and biblical scholar. He edited three influential encyclopedias and, as a critic of religious dogmatism, defended the rights of reason in the practice of one's faith. [d. 1/8/1736]

1748 Birth of Elias Hicks, noted American Quaker missionary and leader. He opposed the influence of Methodism on his denomination, and was subsequently blamed for a schism in 1827-28, when he led a conservative faction of Friends afterward known as Hicksites. [d. 2/27/1830]

1813 Birth of David Livingstone, British missionary-explorer. He married Mary Moffat, daughter of a fellow missionary, in 1845, discovered Victoria Falls in 1855, and was "found" by Henry Stanley in 1871. During his explorations, Livingstone declared the gospel as he penetrated the heart of the African continent. [d. 5/1/1873]

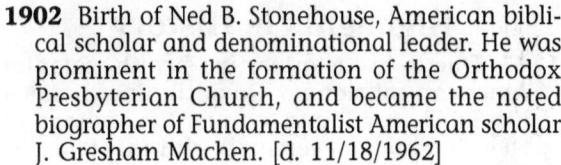

1902 Birth of Ned B. Stonehouse, American biblical scholar and denominational leader. He was prominent in the formation of the Orthodox Presbyterian Church, and became the noted biographer of Fundamentalist American scholar J. Gresham Machen. [d. 11/18/1962]

1928 Birth of Hans Küng, Swiss-German Catholic priest and theologian. Along with Joseph Ratzinger (who is now Pope Benedict XVI), Küng was named an official theological advisor at the Vatican II Ecumenical Council (1962).

The Last Passage

1710 Death of Thomas Ken, 72, Anglican clergyman and poet. He authored four volumes of verse, but is most remembered for authoring a hymn sung today as a doxology: "Praise God From Whom All Blessings Flow." (b. 7/1637)

1721 Death of Clement XI, 71, pope from 1700. During his pontificate, he condemned Jansenism in his famous "Unigenitus Dei Filius" decree (1713). Clement also promoted Christian missions, but ruled against the Jesuits in their use of the so-called Chinese Rites. (b. 7/23/1649)

1825 Death of John J. Husband, about 65, an English-born Episcopal churchman who came to America in 1809. He became a successful singing school master and a composer of anthems and hymns, including REVIVE US AGAIN ("We Praise Thee, O God!"). (b. 1760)

Words for the Soul

1944 German Lutheran theologian and Nazi martyr Dietrich Bonhoeffer wrote in a letter from prison: *'We can have abundant life, even though many wishes remain unfulfilled.'*

1947 English Catholic psychiatrist Caryll Houselander advised in a letter: *'Every time you hesitate, feel anxious, feel guilty, turn to God, say: "I'm doing my best as far as I see it. I put it into your hand to complete."'*

IN GOD'S WORD...   OT: Numbers 28:16–29:40 ~ NT: Luke 3:23-38 ~ Psalms 62:1-12 ~ Proverbs 11:18-19

March 20

Highlights in History

1747 Due to his deteriorating health, colonial American missionary David Brainerd ended his 2-1/2-year labors among the Indians of New England. (Severely ill with tuberculosis, Brainerd died seven months later.)

1931 The practice of birth control was defended by the Federal Council of Churches of Christ in America. (Contraception was a topic of heated debate in the churches at this time, and Pius XI, at the end of this year, issued his encyclical "Casti connubii" which opposed all forms of "artificial fertility regulation" with the exception of the "rhythm method.")

1987 The American Lutheran Church (ALC) voted to merge with the Lutheran Church in America (LCA) and the Association of Evangelical Lutheran Churches (AELC). The full merger of the three groups created the 5.3-million-member Evangelical Lutheran Church in America (ELCA), and became effective January 1, 1988.

Notable Birthdays

1544 Birth of Cuthbert Mayne, English martyr. He was the first seminary priest in England executed for his Catholic faith under Elizabeth I. His name was included among the "Forty Martyrs," canonized in 1970. [d. 11/30/1577]

1819 Birth of Isaac Mayer Wise, the Bohemian-born American Jewish rabbi who advocated modifying Orthodox tradition to meet the needs of contemporary life. In 1873, Wise became the key figure in the formation of American Reform Judaism. [d. 3/26/1900]

1870 Birth of May Whittle Moody, sacred vocal artist. The daughter of song evangelist Daniel W. Whittle, she married William Moody, the son of Dwight L. Moody. In 1893 May composed the hymn tune, WHITTLE, which was set to the words of her father's hymn, "Dying With Jesus, By Death Reckoned Mine." [d. 8/20/1963]

1928 Birth of Fred M. Rogers, American Presbyterian clergyman, educator and TV personality. He produced and hosted "Mr. Rogers' Neighborhood" (1965-75). [d. 2/27/2003]

The Last Passage

687 Death of St. Cuthbert, 53, English monk and bishop of Lindisfarne. He was vocal in supporting Celtic forms of Christian worship over Roman forms. After his death, the Lindisfarne Gospels were created in his honor. (b. ca. 634)

1826 American Congregational pioneer missionary Gordon Hall, 41, died of cholera. His enthusiasm for missions while attending Andover Seminary led to the formation in 1810 of the American Board of Commissioners for Foreign Missions (ABCFM). Hall later became the first American missionary to reach Bombay, India, where he spent the next 13 years. (b. 4/8/1784)

1889 Death of Albrecht Ritschl, 66, German Protestant theologian and historian. He founded a school of "theology of moral value," in which he sought to eliminate all mystical and philosophical elements from Christian theology. Ritschl insisted that faith should rest on moral values. (b. 3/25/1822)

Words for the Soul

1739 Founder of Methodism John Wesley wrote in a letter: *'I look upon all the world as my parish.'*

1780 Future first lady Abigail Adams wrote in a letter to her 13-year-old son John Quincy: *'Let this important truth be engraven upon your heart.... Justice, humanity and benevolence are the duties you owe to society in general. To your Country the same duties are incumbent upon you with the additional obligation of sacrificing ease, pleasure, wealth and life itself for its defense and security.'*

1840 Scottish clergyman Robert Murray McCheyne wrote: *'The more God opens your eyes, the more you will feel that you are lost in yourself.'*

IN GOD'S WORD... OT: Numbers 30:1–31:54 ~ NT: Luke 4:1-30 ~ Psalms 63:1-11 ~ Proverbs 11:20-21

March 21

NISAN — ALMANAC OF THE CHRISTIAN FAITH — **ADAR**

Highlights in History

1098 Benedictine monk Robert of Molesme established a monastery at Citeaux in France, hoping to create a stricter form of his Catholic religious order. Robert's efforts led to the founding of the Cistercians.

1146 Urged by Bernard of Clairvaux, France's King Louis VII announced he would lead the Second Crusade. When the cause was lost two years later, Christians were devastated that such an undertaking, preached by a moral exemplar and led by royalty, could fail.

1292 Franciscan John of Peckham was elevated by Pope Nicholas IV to England's archbishopric of Canterbury. John's interest in the newly translated Arabic mathematical writings popularized science as a legitimate Christian vocation.

1843 American Baptist lay preacher William Miller (1782-1849) predicted the Second Coming of Christ would occur on this date, but the day passed without event. Miller adjusted his prediction of Christ's return to occur on this same date of the following year. (He was wrong again.)

1900 In Chicago, following the death of founder Dwight L. Moody, the Bible Institute for Home and Foreign Missions changed its name to Moody Bible Institute. The school afterward became a bulwark of Christian Fundamentalism.

Notable Birthdays

1474 Birth of St. Angela Merici, Italian religious leader and founder (in 1535) of the Ursuline nuns. Her congregation has been called "the oldest and most considerable order of women in the Roman Catholic Church." [d. 1/27/1540]

1685 Birth of Johann Sebastian Bach, German Lutheran composer and musical genius. Today considered one of history's greatest musical masters, he was also a devout Christian. Nearly 3/4 of his 1,000 compositions were written for use in Christian worship! [d. 7/28/1750]

1917 Birth of Yigael Yadin, Israeli archaeologist. He published many scholarly works, and organized digs both at Masada and at the Dead Sea caves. [d. 6/28/1984]

The Last Passage

547 Death of St. Benedict of Nursia, about 67, Italian-born "patriarch of western monks." He founded Catholic monasticism in the 530s, and the Benedictine Rule (based on obedience, charity and voluntary poverty) established the model for monastic life throughout the Middle Ages. (b. ca. 480)

1556 Archbishop Thomas Cranmer, 66, who supported Henry VIII, was burned at the stake as a heretic by Queen Mary (Tudor) for refusing to recant his Protestantism. (b. 7/2/1489)

1656 Death of James Ussher, 75, Anglican Archbishop of Armagh and Primate of Ireland (1625-40). He is remembered today for publishing a timeline of biblical chronology which dated the creation at 4004 B.C. (b. 1/4/1581)

1885 Death of Christopher Wordsworth, 77, Anglican clergyman and Greek scholar. He wrote a commentary on the entire Bible. Wordsworth was also a prolific hymnwriter, and penned for the Church, "O Day of Rest and Gladness." (b. 10/30/1807)

Words for the Soul

1847 Scottish clergyman Andrew Bonar, 36, reflected in his diary: *'There is an intense joy in God which I have not yet drawn out of Him.'*

1871 American Quaker and holiness author Hannah Whitall Smith advised in a letter: *'There is no peace and no joy in a half-hearted religion. There is such a thing as having just enough religion to make one miserable.... Oh, do let Jesus have all of your heart! He will give you such a fullness of joy in Himself that will far more than repay you for any earthly pleasure you may think you may miss because of it.'*

IN GOD'S WORD... OT: Numbers 32:1–33:39 ~ NT: Luke 4:31–5:11 ~ Psalms 64:1-10 ~ Proverbs 11:22

נִיסָן NISAN — ALMANAC OF THE CHRISTIAN FAITH — אֲדָר ADAR

March 22

Highlights in History

33 The Council of Nicea (325) decided that Easter (the celebration of the resurrection of Jesus Christ) would be observed on the first Sunday following the first full moon after the spring equinox (March 21). This reckoning means that Easter, on any given year, will not occur earlier than on this date, and no later than April 25.

1638 American colonial religious dissident Anne Hutchinson was expelled from the Massachusetts Bay Colony. She was charged with promoting women teachers and other religious ideas that offended the leading pastors of the colony.

1874 The first Young Men's Hebrew Association (YMHA) was established in N.Y. City. (A second club was founded in Philadelphia in 1875.)

1882 Congress passed a federal law forbidding the practice of polygamy in the United States. It was the government's way of dealing with utopian and millennial cults that had sprung up during the second half of the 19th century (chief among which were the Mormons). The new law prevented polygamists from voting or from holding public office.

Notable Birthdays

1836 Birth of Edgar Page Stites, a New Jersey descendant of the Mayflower pilgrims. During his life Stites was a Civil War veteran, a riverboat pilot, a Methodist local preacher and a home missionary. He also authored the hymn, "Simply Trusting Every Day." [d. 1/7/1921]

1861 Birth of Nona L. Brooks, Kentucky-born sectarian. She was founder of the Divine Science Church (1899), and a leading figure in the New Thought Movement. [d. 3/14/1945]

1930 Birthday of Marion G. "Pat" Robertson, pioneer religious television broadcaster. In 1960 he founded the Christian Broadcasting Network (CBN) – the first Christian television network established in the United States.

The Last Passage

1758 Death of early American theologian Jonathan Edwards, 54. During his 24-year pastorate at Northampton, MA (1726-50), he became acquainted with both George Whitefield and David Brainerd. Following a brief tenure as a missionary to the American Indians, Edwards was made president of the College of New Jersey (aka Princeton). Two months into his administration, however, "the greatest philosopher-theologian yet to grace the American scene" died from a smallpox vaccination gone awry. (b. 10/5/1703)

1832 Death of Johann W. Goethe, 82, German poet, novelist, dramatist and scientist. The author of *Faust* (1770, 1831), Goethe was essentially a rationalist who believed in self-redemption through striving to comprehend the secrets of nature. (b. 8/28/1749)

1884 Death of Ezra Abbot, 64, American Unitarian biblical scholar. Associated with Harvard Divinity School (1872-84), Abbot was also a member of the N.T. committee for both the *English Revised* (1881-85) and *American Standard* (1901-05) versions of the Bible. (b. 4/28/1819)

1903 Death of Frederick W. Farrar, 71, Anglican clergyman, educator and theological writer. Described as a "Broad Church Evangelical," Farrar was also a temperance advocate and wrote a number of books for youth. (b. 8/7/1831)

Words for the Soul

1986 In his *Road to Daybreak* journal, Dutch Catholic mystic Henri J. M. Nouwen wrote: *'Wherever I turn I am confronted with my deep-seated resistance against following Jesus on his way to the cross and my countless ways of avoiding poverty, whether material, intellectual, or emotional. Only Jesus, in whom the fullness of God dwells, could freely and fully choose to be completely poor.'*

IN GOD'S WORD... OT: Numbers 33:40–35:34 ~ NT: Luke 5:12-28 ~ Psalms 65:1-13 ~ Proverbs 11:23

נִיסָן NISAN — ALMANAC OF THE CHRISTIAN FAITH — אדר ADAR

March 23

Highlights in History

1540 Waltham Abbey in Essex became the last monastery in England to transfer its allegiance from the Roman Catholic Church to the newly established Church of England.

1729 Johann Sebastian Bach's "St. Matthew Passion" was first performed in Leipzig, Germany. Today the oratorio is considered one of the most sublime masterpieces in Western music. From its score comes the haunting Good Friday hymn, "O Sacred Head, Now Wounded."

1743 George Frideric Handel's "Messiah" was performed for the first time in London. The oratorio was quite controversial, because it used the words of God in the theater.

1858 Following his studies in divinity and medicine, John G. Paton, 34, was ordained for overseas service by the Reformed Presbyterian Church in Scotland.  He soon sailed to the South Seas, where he began missionary work among the cannibals of the New Hebrides. Paton faced incredible dangers and disease, and lost both his wife and infant son within the first year. (Paton remarried in 1864, and three successive generations of his descendants have served at his mission in Vanuatu.)

1899 At the site of the ancient city of Babylon, German archaeologist Robert Koldeway uncovered a basket filled with 300 cuneiform tablets. The ancient texts verified the historical existence of King Jehoiachin of Judah.

1966 Archbishop of Canterbury Arthur Michael Ramsey, while visiting Rome, exchanged public greetings with Pope Paul VI. It was the first official meeting between heads of the Anglican and Catholic Churches in over 400 years.

Notable Birthdays

1812 Birth of Stephen R. Riggs, American ABCFM missionary to the Dakota Indians (1837-83). He reduced the Indian tongue to writing, prepared a Dakota dictionary and translated most of the Bible into the Dakota language. [d. 8/24/1883]

The Last Passage

332 Death of Gregory the Illuminator, about 92. Even before Roman emperor Constantine I was converted, Gregory established the Christian faith in his homeland, represented his national churches at the Council of Nicea, and is regarded today as "the Apostle of Armenia." (b. ca. 240)

1877 Mormon bishop John D. Lee was executed by a firing squad for taking leadership, 20 years earlier, in the 1857 Mountain Meadows Massacre of 120 emigrants from the Eastern U.S. who were bound by wagon train for California.

Words for the Soul

1538 German reformer Martin Luther declared in a sermon: *'Two facts can stand side by side: that men are believers and that, in spite of this, one cannot trust them. For men can err and sin; they have not yet put off their old skin. For although we believe and are spiritual, nevertheless we are not yet as clean as we should be.'*

1738 English revivalist George Whitefield recorded in his journal: *'Was fervent in intercession for absent friends and all mankind. Oh, intercession is a most delightful exercise! How it does sweeten and purify the heart!'*

1775 American patriot Patrick Henry delivered the historic ultimatum: *'Give me liberty or give me death!'* (Henry was a devout Christian, and defended persecuted Baptists at his own expense.)

1801 Newly-elected U.S. president Thomas Jefferson wrote in a letter: *'The Christian Religion, when divested of the rags in which they [the clergy] have enveloped it, and brought to the original purity and simplicity of its benevolent institutor, is a religion of all others most friendly to liberty, science, and the freest expansion of the human mind.'*

IN GOD'S WORD... OT: Numbers 36:1—Deuteronomy 1:46 ~ NT: Luke 5:29–6:11 ~ Psalms 66:1-20 ~ Proverbs 11:24-26

נִיסָן
NISAN

ALMANAC OF THE CHRISTIAN FAITH

אֲדָר
ADAR

~ March 24 ~

Highlights in History

1644 [NS] A royal charter was granted to Roger Williams (1603-83) for establishing the American Colony of Rhode Island. (Following his expulsion from the Massachusetts Bay Colony, Williams founded Providence, RI in 1636, adopting the governing principle that "God requireth not an uniformity of religion.") In 1639 he formed the first Baptist church on American soil, but withdrew from it a few months later and, for the rest of his life, remained a religious loner — an independent evangelical Christian without a denomination.

1816 English-born "missionary bishop" Francis Asbury, aged 70, preached his last sermon at Richmond, VA. (He died seven days later.) As a circuit riding superintendent, Asbury was instrumental in organizing the Methodist Church in the U.S. during its formative years.

1940 The first religious program broadcast over television. An Easter service officiated by Samuel Cavert of the Federal Council of the Churches of Christ in America was carried by New York City's W2XBS, an NBC affiliate station.

Notable Birthdays

1820 Birth of Frances Jane (née Crosby) Van Alstyne, American blind Methodist gospel songwriter. Better known as "Fanny Crosby," she began composing sacred verse in her mid-40s, and penned over 8,000 hymn texts before her death at 95. Fanny Crosby's most enduring hymns include: "Rescue the Perishing"; "Blessed Assurance"; "Jesus is Tenderly Calling"; "Pass Me Not, O Gentle Savior"; "Sweet Hour of Prayer" and "I am Thine, O Lord." [d. 2/12/1915]

1890 Birth of Harold H. Rowley, English Baptist missionary to China and Semitics scholar. Rowley taught Hebrew at Manchester University (1945-59), and left behind a number of scholarly works on biblical linguistics, including *The Aramaic of the Old Testament* (1929) and *The Relevance of Apocalyptic* (1944). [d. 10/4/1969]

The Last Passage

1396 Death of Walter Hilton, 56, English mystic and devotional writer. His most famous English work, *The Scale of Perfection*, describes how the reforming of the defaced image of God within the human soul occurs in two stages, separated by a mystical "dark night" in which the soul, detaching itself from earthly things, is directed to the things of the Spirit. (b. ca. 1340)

1980 El Salvadoran Catholic archbishop and human rights activist Oscar A. Romero, 62, was shot and killed while saying Mass at a hospital chapel in San Salvador. Because of his conservative allegiance to Rome, Romero's criticism of government repression made him a modern-day martyr of his faith. (b. 8/15/1917)

Words for the Soul

1525 German reformer Martin Luther declared in a sermon: 'The greatest necessity in the world is a strict temporal power. The world cannot be ruled according to the Gospel, for the sphere of influence which the Word has is too small and limited.'

1774 Anglican clergyman and hymnwriter John Newton concluded in a letter: 'What a mercy it is to be separated in spirit, conversation, and interest from the world that knows not God.'

1818 In a speech given in the House of Representatives, American statesman Henry Clay declared: 'All religions united with government are more or less inimical to liberty. All separated from government, are compatible with liberty.'

1982 In his Latin American Journal ¡Gracias! Catholic mystic Henri J. M. Nouwen wrote: 'Because God is the God of life, a life stronger than death and destruction... there is always reason to hope, even when our eyes are filled with tears.'

IN GOD'S WORD... OT: Deuteronomy 2:1–3:29 ~ NT: Luke 6:12-38 ~ Psalms 67:1-7 ~ Proverbs 11:27

נִיסָן NISAN

ALMANAC OF THE CHRISTIAN FAITH

אדר ADAR

~ March 25 ~

Highlights in History

0 In his chronological history of the Christian Church, Russian-born monk Dionysius Exiguus (d. 544) began from this date as the time of the Annunciation. March 25th was afterward considered the first day of the year, until the Gregorian Calendar of 1582 restored New Year's Day to January 1st.

1634 The Catholic Church gained a permanent foothold in the American colonies when 128 Catholic immigrants arrived on the Potomac River from England. They settled in the colony of Maryland, which was founded by Cecilius Calvert, Lord Baltimore.

1740 In the American colony of Georgia, construction began on the Bethesda Orphanage. It had been founded by English evangelist George Whitefield. (The care of the orphanage afterward plagued Whitefield financially, and when the main building of the institution burned in 1773, it was never rebuilt.)

1891 Father Alexis Georgievich Toth (1853-1909) and his entire St. Mary's parish of Wilkes-Barre, PA, became the first Greek Catholics in America to convert to Russian Orthodoxy. Their decision followed the refusal of Americanist archbishop John Ireland of St.-Paul-Minneapolis to recognize Toth's catholicity.

Notable Birthdays

1347 Birth of Catherine of Siena, greatest of the 14th Century Italian mystics. She influenced Pope Gregory XI to return the papal seat (1376) from Avignon, France back to Rome. Catherine died prematurely, at age 33. [d. 4/29/1380]

1783 Birth of Luther Rice, American Baptist missionary and philanthropist. He set sail for India, in 1812, along with Adoniram Judson. Rice left no published works, but exerted a lasting influence for missions within Baptist circles. He was also instrumental in founding the Baptist General Tract Society. [d. 9/25/1836]

1823 Birth of Godfrey Thring, Anglican clergyman, hymnbook publisher and hymn author: "Crown Him With Many Crowns." [d. 9/13/1903]

1906 Birth of Dawson Trotman, American Baptist youth ministry pioneer. He founded the Navigators, a youth-centered discipling ministry, in 1933. (Trotman died of a heart attack while rescuing a swimmer during a summer Navigator conference in the Adirondacks.) [d. 6/18/1956]

The Last Passage

1843 Death of Robert Murray McCheyne, 29, Church of Scotland clergyman. Considered one of the most saintly and popular among the young ministers in his day, McCheyne suffered from a delicate constitution, further weakened by an ardent devotion to the pastoral ministry. (b. 5/21/1813)

1877 Death of John H. Stockton, 63, American Methodist clergyman, sacred choral author and composer. Among the hymns he published: "Come, Every Soul By Sin Oppressed" (& STOCKTON or MINERVA); GREAT PHYSICIAN ("The Great Physician Now is Near"); and GLORY TO HIS NAME ("Down at the Cross Where My Savior Died"). (b. 4/19/1813)

Words for the Soul

1864 Scottish clergyman and biographer Andrew Bonar, 53, reflected in his diary: *'Today... remembered the anniversary of the death of my father and also of Robert McCheyne. Do those in glory above think of such times and seasons? Do they think of the time when they left us?'*

1883 American Quaker Holiness author Hannah Whitall Smith, 51, wrote: *'I think I have learned more about the character of God from remembering what my own father and mother were to me than in almost any other way. And I do long to be to my children a little faint picture of what God is.'*

IN GOD'S WORD... OT: Deuteronomy 4:1-49 ~ NT: Luke 6:39–7:10 ~ Psalms 68:1-18 ~ Proverbs 11:28

נִיסָן NISAN — ALMANAC OF THE CHRISTIAN FAITH — אדר ADAR

March 26

Highlights in History

655 Saxon-born Deusdedit was consecrated Archbishop of Canterbury, following the death of Honorius. Deusdedit was the sixth individual to hold this historic office, and the first of English origin. He served until 664.

1775 American-born evangelist, mystic and hymnwriter Henry Alline, 27, underwent a profound spiritual conversion. He later became a leader of the "New Light" movement in the Presbyterian Church, and went on to evangelize the people of Nova Scotia.

1830 Religious founder Joseph Smith, 25, first published *The Book of Mormon*. Its text, he claimed, was originally inscribed on golden plates, which Smith had himself discovered near his family's property in upstate New York.

Notable Birthdays

1780 Birth of Moses Stuart, American Congregational theologian, Hebraist and educator. Associated with Andover Theological Seminary, he translated many German scholarly works, including a Hebrew and Greek grammar of the New Testament. Stuart sought to show the importance of German scholarship on biblical criticism. [d. 1/4/1852]

1833 [OS] Birth of Greek ecclesiastic and scholar Philotheos Bryennios. He was metropolitan of Nicomedia (1877ff), but his fame rests upon his 1873 discovery of an early manuscript of the *Didache* (a second century manual of Christian discipline, now numbered among the writings of the *Apostolic Fathers*). [d. 1914]

The Last Passage

1827 Death of Ludwig van Beethoven, 56, German composer, the "Michelangelo of Music." From age 28 he began suffering from a deafness which was total by age 45. Beethoven composed three outstanding sacred works: "Christ on the Mount of Olives" (ca. 1803), "Mass in C" (1807), and "Missa Solemnis" (1818-23). He also created the popular HYMN TO JOY ("Joyful, Joyful, We Adore Thee"). (b. 12/16/1770)

1831 Death of Richard Allen, 71, U.S. denominational pioneer. Born of a slave family, he converted to Methodism at 17, and began preaching at 22. Allen was ordained in 1799, and later became the founder and first bishop (1816-31) of the AME (African Methodist Episcopal) Church. (b. 2/14/1760)

1934 Death of Carrie E. Breck, 79, an Oregon Presbyterian housewife who wrote more than 2000 poems. She claimed "she could not carry a tune... but loved music." One of her poems, indeed, became the beloved hymn, "Face to Face with Christ My Savior." (b. 1/22/1855)

Words for the Soul

1862 After preaching on Psalm 23 at Philadelphia's First Baptist Church, 28-year-old pastor Joseph H. Gilmore penned the words to the hymn, "He Leadeth Me!":

> He leadeth me! O blessed thought!
>   Oh words with heavenly comfort fraught!
> Whate'er I do, where'er I be,
>   Still 'tis God's hand that leadeth me.
>
> Lord, I would clasp thy hand in mine,
>   Nor ever murmur nor repine,
> Content, whatever lot I see,
>   Since 'tis thy hand that leadeth me!
>
> (Verses 1 & 3)

1986 In his *Road to Daybreak* journal, Dutch Catholic mystic Henri J. M. Nouwen wrote: 'It is not easy to let the voice of God's mercy speak to us because it is a voice asking for an always open relationship, one in which sins are acknowledged, forgiveness received, and love renewed. It does not offer us a solution, but a friendship. It does not take away our problems, but... assures us that we will never be alone.'

IN GOD'S WORD... OT: Deuteronomy 5:1–6:25 ~ NT: Luke 7:11-35 ~ Psalms 68:19-35 ~ Proverbs 11:29-31

נִיסָן ALMANAC OF THE CHRISTIAN FAITH אֲדָר
NISAN   ADAR

March 27

Highlights in History

1536 A document was signed representing a provisional definition of the Swiss Protestant faith. As an important writing of the Reformation, the First Helvetic Confession became the first uniform statement of faith for all German-speaking Switzerland.

1667 English Puritan poet John Milton (1608-74) published *Paradise Lost*, an epic-length poem about humanity's creation and fall. (Milton had been totally blind since 1651.)

1836 The first Mormon temple, built in Kirtland, Ohio by founder Joseph Smith, was dedicated. (Smith had moved to Ohio from New York state with about 50 families, sometime after founding the Mormon religion in the 1830s.)

1955 The first mobile Jewish synagogue, the "Circuit Riding Rabbi Bus," was dedicated at the Amity Country Club in Charlotte, NC. The vehicle was equipped with desks, blackboards, maps, a projector, a record player and a library.

Notable Birthdays

1816 Birth of George J. Elvey, English sacred organist. He served Queen Victoria 50 years as organist at St. George's Chapel, Windsor. Among his compositions are the two hymn tunes: ST. GEORGE'S, WINDSOR ("Come, Ye Thankful People, Come") and DIADEMATA, to which three hymns are sung: "Crown Him With Many Crowns"; "Make Me a Captive, Lord"; "Soldiers of Christ, Arise." [d. 12/9/1893]

1842 Birth of George Matheson, Scottish Free Church clergyman. He was almost blind from the age of 18, yet excelled in school and in the pulpit. In addition to writing many theological and devotional volumes, Matheson also penned two enduring hymns: "O Love That Wilt Not Let Me Go" and "Make Me a Captive, Lord." [d. 8/28/1906]

The Last Passage

1191 Death of Clement III, pope from 1187. He organized the Third Crusade (1189-91), which sought to recapture Jerusalem after its loss to the Muslim armies in 1187. The use of bells during the celebration of Mass was also instituted during Clement's pontificate. (b. unk.)

1699 Death of Edward Stillingfleet, 63, Anglican prelate and theologian. As Dean of St. Paul's (1678-89) and Bishop of Worcester (1689-99), he sought a middle ground between the Presbyterian and Episcopal systems of church government, and defended the Church of England against the charge of schism. (b. 4/17/1635)

1929 Death of Charles H. Brent, 66, Canadian Episcopal prelate and ecumenical leader. In 1901 he was consecrated the first Protestant Episcopal bishop of the Philippine Islands. Brent was a principal force in motivating his denomination to sponsor the Faith and Order World Conference in Lausanne, Switzerland in 1927. (b. 4/9/1862)

Words for the Soul

1637 Exiled Scottish clergyman Samuel Rutherford testified in a letter: *'All that conscience saith is not scripture.... Because many have pardon with God, that have not peace with themselves, you are to stand or fall by Christ's esteem and verdict of you, and not by that which your heart saith.'*

1751 Founder of Methodism John Wesley argued in his Journal: *'I cannot understand how a Methodist preacher can answer it to God to preach one sermon or travel one day less in a married than in a single state. In this respect sure, "it remaineth that they who have wives be as though they had none."'* [N.B. Wesley was newly married at this time, but in 1776 he and his wife Molly separated.]

1840 Scottish clergyman Robert Murray McCheyne challenged in a letter: *'No person can be a child of God without living in secret prayer; and no community of Christians can be in a lively condition without unity in prayer.'*

IN GOD'S WORD... OT: Deuteronomy 7:1–8:20 ~ NT: Luke 7:36–8:3 ~ Psalms 69:1-18 ~ Proverbs 12:1

נִיסָן NISAN — ALMANAC OF THE CHRISTIAN FAITH — אֲדָר ADAR

March 28

Highlights in History

1638 Following her banishment from Massachusetts for teaching antinomianism, religious dissident Anne Hutchinson moved with her family to Rhode Island. Relocating later in the New York colony, in August 1643 Anne and most of her family and servants were killed during an Indian raid on their settlement.

1646 Baptists in Boston held their first recorded meeting. Baptists were long rejected in the American colonies, but eventually grew to become a major denominational group in the U.S.

1661 Scottish Parliament passed the Rescissory Act, which repealed all church-state legislation created since 1633 (during Charles I's reign). In effect, the Act restored the Anglican episcopacy to Scotland, and overthrew Presbyterianism, the national church since 1638. (In 1690, Parliament again established the Church of Scotland as Presbyterian.)

1982 In England, two fires damaged the altar of Salisbury Cathedral, where the original copy of the Magna Carta is housed. (The document itself was not damaged.)

Notable Birthdays

1515 Birth of Teresa of Avila, Spanish Carmelite nun, mystic and writer. During her life she was admired for her administrative skills, but her legacy derives from her mysticism, as evidenced in her writings: *Way of Perfection*, *Book of Foundations*, and *Interior Castle*. [d. 10/4/1582]

1592 Birth of Johannes A. Comenius, Bohemian Brethren (Moravian) clergyman and educator. He was widely traveled, and his groundbreaking educational ideals and writings were deeply influenced by his personal religious experience. Comenius's ideas had considerable influence on the educational philosophies of later centuries, and today he is known as the "Father of Modern Education." [d. 11/15/1670]

1652 Birth of Samuel Sewall, colonial American judge. He presided over the Salem Witch Trials (1692), which sentenced 19 people to death. In 1697, he publicly confessed his judgments had been in error. In 1700 he wrote *The Selling of Joseph*, the first anti-slavery tract published in America. [d. 1/1/1730]

1811 Birth of John Nepomucene Neumann, Czech-born U.S. Catholic prelate. Appointed fourth bishop of Philadelphia, he organized the first Catholic diocesan school system in America. In 1963 Neumann became the first American male to be proclaimed a saint in the Catholic Church. [d. 1/5/1860]

The Last Passage

1929 Death of Katharine L. Bates, 69, American educator and poet. She published both textbooks and several volumes of verse, but is better remembered today as the author of the patriotic hymn, "America the Beautiful" (1911). (b. 8/12/1859)

Words for the Soul

1525 In one of his "Table Talks," German reformer Martin Luther declared: *'Music is a very fine art. The notes can make the words come alive. It puts to flight every spirit of sadness.'*

1740 English revivalist George Whitefield advised in a letter: *'Our extremity is God's opportunity.'*

1982 In his Latin American journal ¡Gracias! Dutch Catholic mystic Henri J. M. Nouwen wrote: *'Jesus learned obedience from what he suffered. This means that the pains and struggles of which Jesus became part made him listen more perfectly to God. In and through his sufferings, he came to know God and could respond to his call.... Suffering accepted and shared in love breaks down our selfish defenses and sets us free to accept God's guidance.'*

IN GOD'S WORD... OT: Deuteronomy 9:1–10:22 ~ NT: Luke 8:4-21 ~ Psalms 69:19-36 ~ Proverbs 12:2-3

March 29

Highlights in History

537 Vigilius was consecrated pope, serving until 555. He was condemned by the Council of Constantinople for seeking to annul the decrees of the Council of Chalcedon. Kept out of Rome for seven years, Vigilius died on his return.

1139 Innocent II made the Templars an independent order within the Catholic Church. The Knights Templars were originally created to protect pilgrims from bandits in the Holy Land. Over the years, however, this military order increased in influence and wealth and, in the end, drew its members into persecution.

1882 In Connecticut, founder Father Michael J. McGivney chartered the Knights of Columbus, a fraternal benefit society for Roman Catholic men. Today, 1.6 million members of the K of C are active in community programs, and its publication "Columbia" has the greatest circulation of any Catholic monthly in North America.

Notable Birthdays

1847 Birth of Winfield S. Weeden, Ohio-born public school teacher, evangelist, hotel owner and hymnwriter. An able singer and song leader as well, Weeden is remembered today for composing the hymn tune SURRENDER ("All to Jesus I Surrender"). [d. 7/31/1908]

1906 Birth of Rulon Clark Allred, American sectarian leader. He was a founder of the Apostolic United Brethren, a fundamentalist Mormon sect which practices polygamy. [d. 5/10/1977]

The Last Passage

1661 Death of Samuel Rutherford, 61, Scottish pastor and theologian. His best work, *Lex Rex* ("A Dispute for the Just Prerogatives of King and People"), was published in 1644. But Rutherford is better known today for 365 spiritual "Letters" he wrote while living in exile in Aberdeen for his Nonconformity (1636-38). (b. ca. 1600)

1788 Death of Charles Wesley, 80, co-founder (with his brother John) of Methodism. Called the "Sweet Singer of Methodism," Charles was also a poet and penned over 8,000 hymns, including: "O for a Thousand Tongues to Sing"; "Love Divine, All Loves Excelling"; "Come, Thou Long Expected Jesus"; "Hark! The Herald Angels Sing"; "Christ the Lord is Risen Today"; "Jesus, Lover of My Soul"; "And Can It Be That I Should Gain"; and "A Charge to Keep I Have." (b. 12/18/1707)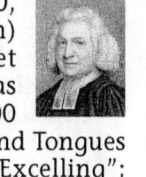

1866 Death of John Keble, 73, Anglican high churchman and poet. It was his sermon, "National Apostasy" (1833), that set the Oxford Movement in motion. Keble was a brilliant scholar, but self-effacing. It was his poetic mind that created the hymn, "Sun of My Soul, Thou Savior Dear." (b. 4/25/1792)

1882 Death of Dora Greenwell, 60, English humanitarian and devotional writer. Though of fragile health, she published many volumes of verse and devotional writings. Her style has been compared to that of Thomas à Kempis, Fénelon and Woolman. She is most recognized today as author of the hymn, "I Am Not Skilled to Understand." (b. 12/6/1821)

1887 Death of Ray Palmer, 78, American Congregational clergyman and hymnwriter. He created a number of original hymns, and also created translations from the Latin. Palmer's two best-known hymns today are: "My Faith Looks Up to Thee," "Jesus, Thou Joy of Loving Hearts." (b. 11/12/1808)

Words for the Soul

1884 Scottish clergyman and biographer Andrew Bonar penned in his diary: *'Much struck with the remark of Flavel: "The devil is aware that one hour of close fellowship, hearty converse with God in prayer, is able to pull down what he hath been contriving and building many a year."'*

IN GOD'S WORD... OT: Deuteronomy 11:1–12:32 ~ NT: Luke 8:22-39 ~ Psalms 70:1-5 ~ Proverbs 12:4

נִיסָן
NISAN

ALMANAC OF THE CHRISTIAN FAITH

אדר
ADAR

March 30

Highlights in History

1492 Ferdinand II (Ferdinand V of Aragon) and Isabella (of Castile) issued a joint royal edict expelling all Jews from Spanish soil, except those willing to convert to Christianity. The legislation was inspired by their confessor and advisor, Tomás Torquemada, who had previously become the first Grand Inquisitor of Spain. In all, 160,000 Jews fled the country.

1533 Thomas Cranmer was consecrated Archbishop of Canterbury, England's highest ecclesiastical post. Serving until his martyrdom in 1556, he supported Henry VIII's marriage annulment, and later became chief architect of the English Reformation. Cranmer also created the first *Book of Common Prayer*.

1871 The Boston University School of Theology was formed by a merger of the Boston Theological Seminary and Boston University. It was the first theological school to admit women as students. (The first B. Div. degree awarded to a woman was granted to Anna Oliver in 1876.)

1917 All imperial lands and lands belonging to monasteries were confiscated by the Russian provisional government.

Notable Birthdays

1135 Birth of Moses Maimonides, Spanish rabbi, scholar and physician. A leading Jewish philosopher of his time, he believed in freedom of the will and condemned asceticism. Maimonides sought to reconcile Judaism with Aristotelian philosophy. His *Guide of the Perplexed* (1190) exerted strong influence on Christian thought throughout the Middle Ages. [d. 12/13/1204]

1799 Birth of Friedrich A. G. Tholuck, mediating German Lutheran clergyman and theologian. Earlier inner and outward afflictions had driven him nearly suicidal. But his strong personal faith later enabled him to help others in their own spiritual struggles. Theologically, Tholuck was an outspoken critic of the common rationalism of his day. [d. 6/10/1877]

1894 Birth of Roland H. Bainton, American Congregational clergyman and ecclesiastical historian. Associated with Yale Divinity School for over 40 years, Bainton was a leading authority on the history of the Reformation. His 32 books included *Here I Stand* (1950), a popular biography of Martin Luther. [d. 2/12/1984]

The Last Passage

1876 Death of James L. Breck, 57, American Episcopal missionary to the Wisconsin Territory. He worked with the Chippewa Indians, established a school for Indian children,  and in 1855 founded the Seabury Divinity School. Breck exhibited special concern for the training of indigenous clergy. (b. 6/27/1818)

1942 Death of Anne S. Murphy, American potter's wife, humanitarian and hymnwriter. During the Depression, Anne lost her husband and her wealth, but discovered an inner strength and serenity which became the message of her music: "There's a Peace in My Heart" (& CONSTANTLY ABIDING). (b. unk.)

Words for the Soul

1810 Anglican missionary to Persia Henry Martyn prayed in a letter: 'May the world always appear as vain as it does now, and my own continuance in it as short and uncertain. . . . I would  rather never have been born, than be born and died, were it not for Jesus, the Prince of Life, the resurrection and the life. How inexpressibly precious is this Saviour, when eternity seems near!'

1986 In his *Road to Daybreak* journal, Dutch Catholic diarist Henri J. M. Nouwen wrote: 'It is such a comfort to know that Jesus' wounds remain visible in his risen body. Our wounds are not taken away, but become sources of hope to others.'

IN GOD'S WORD... OT: Deuteronomy 13:1–15:23 ~ NT: Luke 8:40–9:6 ~ Psalms 71:1–24 ~ Proverbs 12:5-7

נִיסָן
NISAN

ALMANAC OF THE CHRISTIAN FAITH

אֲדָר
ADAR

~ March 31 ~

Highlights in History

1534 A convocation of the lower house of Parliament voted that the Roman Catholic bishop had no more authority than any other bishop over England. This was an important step in the separation of England from papal authority.

1820 The first group of American Protestant missionaries arrived in Hawaii (then called the Sandwich Islands). The party included Hiram Bingham, Asa Thursday, Dr. Thomas Holman, Samuel Whitney and Samuel Ruggles.

Notable Birthdays

1499 Birth of Giovanni Angelo de' Medici, who served as Pope Pius IV (1559-65). During his papacy, he brought the Council of Trent (1545-63) to a successful conclusion, although the council was unable to restore unity of belief within the Catholic territories. [d. 12/9/1555]

1732 Birth of Franz Joseph Haydn, Austrian composer. He composed no specific hymn tunes, but adaptations from his larger works have yielded the two sacred melodies AUSTRIAN HYMN ("Glorious Things of Thee Are Spoken") and CREATION ("The Spacious Firmament on High"). [d. 5/31/1809]

1770 Birth of John Wyeth, American Unitarian hymnbook publisher. Wyeth's works give us the earliest source of hymn tunes DAVIS ("O Thou, In Whose Presence") and NETTLETON ("Come, Thou Fount of Every Blessing"). [d. 1/23/1858]

1860 Birth of Rodney "Gipsy" Smith, itinerant English evangelist. Born of gypsy parentage, Smith was converted in his mid-teens. During his crusades, he visited America several times. [d. 8/4/1947]

The Last Passage

1631 Death of John Donne, 59, Anglican clergyman and poet. He was noted for his secular poetry ("Come live with me, and be my love...."), most of which was written before his ordination in 1615. But Donne was also famous for his sermons and religious writings ("No man is an island...."), which rank among the best of the 17th century. (b. 1/24 [or 6/19] /1572)

1816 Death of Francis Asbury, 70, English-born leader of American Methodism. Sent by John Wesley (1771) to superintend the emerging American Methodist societies, Asbury averaged 5,000 miles a year on horseback during his 45-year ministry. Preaching an estimated 17,000 sermons, his work enabled Methodism to become a leading denomination in the United States. (b. 8/20/1745)

1901 Death of John Stainer, 60, a leading British church musician of the late 19th century. He was organist at St. Paul's Cathedral (1872-88), and was knighted by Queen Victoria in 1888. Stainer's musical accomplishments include a number of anthems, cantatas, oratorios and 150 hymn tunes, including THE FIRST NOEL. (b. 6/6/1840)

Words for the Soul

1868 Scottish clergyman and biographer Andrew A. Bonar penned in his diary: *'The Lord has enabled me to acquiesce in whatever may be His manner of working.'*

1958 British literary scholar and Christian apologist C. S. Lewis confessed in a letter: *'What most often interrupts my own prayers is not great distractions but tiny ones – things one will have to do or avoid in the course of the next hour.'*

1976 American Presbyterian missionary and apologist Francis A. Schaeffer encouraged in a letter: *'You must not lose confidence in God because you lost confidence in your pastor. If our confidence in God had to depend upon our confidence in any human person, we would be on shifting sand.'*

IN GOD'S WORD... OT: Deuteronomy 16:1–17:20 ~ NT: Luke 9:7-27 ~ Psalms 72:1-20 ~ Proverbs 12:8-9

ALMANAC OF THE CHRISTIAN FAITH

MARCH INDEX

A

Abbot, Ezra 3/22
ABCFM (American Board of Commissioners for Foreign Missions) 3/14, 3/20, 3/23
Adams, Abigail
    See QUOTATIONS
Adams, John Quincy 3/20
Africa Inland Mission 3/7
Ainsworth, Laban
    (b. 7/19/1757) d. 3/17/1858
Albanian Orthodox Church in America 3/13
Albigensians 3/5
Alexander, Archibald 3/13
Alexander, C. M. 3/1
Alexander, James W.
    b. 3/13/1804 [d. 7/31/1859]
Allen, Richard
    (b. 2/14/1760) d. 3/26/1831
Alline, Henry 3/26
Allred, Rulon Clark
    b. 3/29/1906 [d. 5/10/1977]
American Board of Commissioners for Foreign Missions (ABCFM) 3/14, 3/20, 3/23
AMERICANS, NATIVE
    American Indians 3/22
    Cayuse Indians 3/14
    Chippewa Indians 3/30
    Dakota Indians 3/23
    Indians of New England 3/20
    Iroquois Indians 3/16, 3/17
    Navajo Indians 3/3
    North American (Canadian) Indians 3/16
    Ohio Moravian Brethren Indians 3/8
    Pueblo Indians 3/3
American Jewish Congress 3/17
American Lutheran Church (ALC) 3/20
American Revolutionary War 3/4, 3/11
American Standard Version Bible 3/22
Anabaptists 3/7
Andover Theological Seminary 3/26
Angelo de' Medici, Giovanni 3/31
Apostolic Fathers 3/26
Aquinas, Thomas
    (b. 1225) d. 3/7/1274
Aristotelian Philosophy 3/30
Aristotle 3/7
Arne, Thomas A.
    b. 3/12/1710 d. 3/5/1778

Asbury, Francis 3/24
    (b. 8/20/1745) d. 3/31/1816
Ásgrímsson, Eysteinn 3/14
Assemblies of God 3/15
Association of Evangelical Lutheran Churches (AELC) 3/20
Augustine (of Canterbury), St. 3/12
Avignon Papacy 3/25

B

Babylon, Ancient 3/23
Bach, Johann Sebastian 3/11, 3/23
    b. 3/21/1685 [d. 7/28/1750]
Bainton, Roland H.
    b. 3/30/1894 [d. 2/12/1984]
Bakewell, John
    (b. 1721) d. 3/18/1819
Baptist General Tract Society 3/25
Barbauld, Anna L. A.
    (b. 6/20/1743) d. 3/9/1825
Barth, Karl
    See QUOTATIONS
Bates, Katharine L.
    (b. 8/12/1859) d. 3/28/1929 3/28
Beatles, The 3/4
Beecher, Henry Ward
    (b. 6/24/1813) d. 3/8/1887
Beethoven, Ludwig van
    (b. 12/16/1770) d. 3/26/1827
Benedictine Rule, The 3/21
Benedict of Nursia, St.
    (b. 480) d. 3/21/547
Berg, Carolina Sandell 3/16
Bernard of Clairvaux 3/21
Bethesda Orphanage 3/25
BIBLE TRANSLATIONS
    American Standard (1901-05) 3/22
    English Revised (1881-85) 3/6, 3/22
    Latin Vulgate, Jerome's 3/3, 3/5
    New English Bible (1961-70) 3/16
Biblical Chronology, Ussher's 3/21
Bingham, Hiram 3/31
Blass, Friedrich W.
    (b. 1/22/1843) d. 3/5/1907
Bliss, Philip P. 3/4
Böhler, Peter
    See QUOTATIONS
Bonar, Andrew
    See QUOTATIONS
Bonhoeffer, Dietrich
    See QUOTATIONS
BOOKS
    Augustinus 3/6
    Anchor Bible Commentary Series 3/8

Ann Lee: A Biography 3/6
Aramaic of the Old Testament, The (1929) 3/24
Autobiography of a Shaker (1869) 3/6
A Man Called Peter (1951) 3/18
Blass-Debrunner-Funk 3/5
Book of Foundations 3/28
Book of Mormon 3/26
Christy (by Catherine Marshall) 3/18
Cyclopaedia of Biblical, Theological, and Ecclesiastical Literature 3/4
Didache, The 3/26
Exposition of the 39 Articles (1850-53) 3/6
Faust (Goethe's) 3/22
Guide of the Perplexed (1190) 3/30
Here I Stand (1950) 3/30
Hymns Ancient and Modern (1861) 3/13, 3/16
Interior Castle 3/28
Keil & Delitzsch Old Testament Commentary 3/4
Lectures on the Gospels (Seiss) 3/18
Letters, Rutherford's 3/29
Lex Rex 3/29
Life and Times of Jesus the Messiah (1883) 3/7
Old Testament in Greek According to the Septuagint 3/14
Oxford Book of Carols (1928) 3/9
Paradise Lost 3/27
Peloubet's Notes on the (International) Sunday Sch 3/6
Principles and Duties of Christianity (1707) 3/7
Relevance of Apocalyptic, The (1944) 3/24
Scale of Perfection, The 3/24
Selling of Joseph, The 3/28
Streams in the Desert 3/13
Summa Theologica (Aquinas) 3/7
Ugaritic Hebrew Philology (1965) 3/8
Way of Perfection, The 3/28
Book of Common Prayer 3/9, 3/30
Book of Mormon 3/26
Bourbon, Louis de, Prince of Condé
    (b. 5/7/1530) d. 3/13/1569
Brainerd, David 3/20, 3/22
    See QUOTATIONS
Bray, Thomas 3/8
Brébeuf, Jean de 3/17
    (b. 3/25/1593) d. 3/16/1649

Breck, Carrie E.
    (b. 1/22/1855) d. 3/26/1934
Breck, James L.
    (b. 6/27/1818) d. 3/30/1876
Brent, Charles H.
    (b. 4/9/1862) d. 3/27/1929
Briggs, Emilie Grace 3/17
British and Foreign Bible Society (BFBS) 3/7
Brooks, Nona L.
    3/22/1861 [d. 3/14/1945]
Browne, Edward H.
    3/6/1811 [d. 12/18/1891]
Bryennios, Philotheos
    b. 3/26/1833 [OS] [d. 1914]
Buonarroti, Michelangelo
    b. 3/6/1475 [d. 2/18/1564]

C

Calendar, Gregorian 3/10
Calvert, Cecilius 3/25
Calvin, John
    See QUOTATIONS
Calvinist Reformation 3/15
Campbell, Alexander
    (b. 9/12/1788) d. 3/4/1866
Campbell, Thomas 3/4
CANTERBURY ARCHBISHOPS
    Cranmer, Thomas (1533-56) 3/30
    Deusdedit (655-64) 3/26
    Honorius (631-53) 3/26
    Ramsey, Michael (1961-74) 3/23
Carey, William 3/7
Carroll, John 3/18
Carter, (President) Jimmy
    See QUOTATIONS
"Casti connubii" (papal encyclical) 3/20
Catherine of Siena 3/25
Cavert, Samuel 3/24
Celibacy of Catholic Clergy 3/9
Celtic Christian Worship 3/20
Chad (Ceadda), St.
    (b. unk.) d. 3/2/672
Chalcedon, Council of (451) 3/29
Chalmers, Thomas
    b. 3/17/1841 [d. 5/20/1847]
Chapman, J. Wilbur 3/1
Chapman, Jonathan
    (b. 9/26/1774) d. 3/11/1847
Charles I, (English) King 3/28
Charles II, (English) King 3/10
Chase, Salmon P. 3/3
Chautauqua Assembly 3/14
China Inland Mission 3/1

Chinese Rites of the Jesuits 3/19
Christian Brethren 3/10
Christian Broadcasting Network (CBN) 3/22
Christocentrism 3/12
CHURCHES
  Philadelphia's First Baptist Church 3/26
  Salisbury Cathedral 3/28
  Sistine Chapel (Rome) 3/6
  St. George's Chapel, Windsor 3/27
  St. John Lateran 3/5
  St. Paul's Cathedral 3/31
  St. Peter's Basilica 3/15
  St. Peter's Cathedral (Rome) 3/6
Church of Scotland 3/1, 3/14, 3/17
Ciocchi del Monte, Giammaria.
  See Julius III, Pope (1550-1555)
Civil War, American 3/8, 3/17, 3/22
Clapham Group, The 3/2
Clay, Henry
  See QUOTATIONS
Clement III, Pope (1187-1191) 3/27
Clement VIII, Pope (1592-1605)
  (b. 2/24/1536) d. 3/5/1605
Clement XI, Pope (1700-21)
  (b. 7/23/1649) d. 3/19/1721
Codex Iuris Canonici 3/19
COLLEGES AND UNIVERSITIES
  Boston University 3/30
  Cambridge University 3/14, 3/15
  College of New Jersey (aka Princeton) 3/22
  Danzig Instytut Biblijny 3/2
  European Bible Institute 3/14
  Haverford College (PA) 3/15
  Manchester University 3/24
  Messiah College (PA) 3/11
  Moody Bible Institute 3/5, 3/21
  Ohio Wesleyan Female College 3/10
  University of Chicago 3/9
  Xavier University (LA) 3/3
College of Cardinals 3/5
Columbus, Christopher 3/10
Comenius, Johannes A.
  b. 3/28/1592 [d. 11/15/1670]
Constantine I, (Roman) Emperor (312-37) 3/7, 3/23
Constantinople, Council of (553) 3/29
COUNCILS, CHURCH
  Chalcedon (451) 3/29
  Constantinople (553) 3/29
  Constantinople (754) 3/11
  Lateran, Fifth (1512-17) 3/11
  Lateran, Third (1179) 3/5
  Nicea (325) 3/22
  Trent (1545-63) 3/3, 3/31
Council of Nicea (325) 3/22

Cowman, Charles E.
  b. 3/13/1868 [d. 9/25/1924]
Cowman, Lettie 3/13
Cranmer, Thomas 3/30
  (b. 7/2/1489) d. 3/21/1556
Cromwell, Oliver
  See QUOTATIONS
Crosby, Fanny 3/9
CRUSADES, THE
  First Crusade (1097-99) 3/12
  Second Crusade (1147) 3/21
  Third Crusade (1189-92) 3/27
Crusades, The 3/18
Cuthbert, St.
  (b. ca. 634) d. 3/20/687

D

Dabney, Robert L.
  b. 3/5/1820 [d. 1/3/1898]
Dahood, Mitchell
  (b. 2/2/1922) d. 3/8/1982
Dark Night of the Soul 3/24
Davidson, Hannah Frances
  b. 3/11/1860 [d. 12/1935]
David of Wales, St.
  (b. 495) d. 3/1/589
Dead Sea Caves, The 3/21
Delitzsch, Franz J.
  (b. 2/23/1813) d. 3/4/1890
DENOMINATIONS
  African Methodist Episcopal (AME) Church 3/26
  American Lutheran Church (ALC) 3/20
  Anabaptists 3/10
  Anglicanism 3/23, 3/31
  Apostolic United Brethren 3/29
  Association of Evangelical Lutheran Churches (AELC) 3/20
  Baptists 3/28
  Bohemian Brethren 3/28
  Christian Brethren 3/10
  Christian Catholic Apostolic Church 3/9
  Church of England 3/27
  Church of Scotland 3/25
  Church of Scotland (Anglican) 3/28
  Church of Scotland (Presbyterian) 3/28
  Congregationalism 3/26, 3/29
  Disciples of Christ 3/4
  Divine Science Church 3/22
  Dutch Reformed Church 3/11
  Eastern Orthodoxy 3/19
  Emmanuel Holiness Church 3/19
  Evangelical Lutheran Church in America (ELCA) 3/20
  Fire-Baptized Holiness Church 3/19
  Free Church of Scotland 3/27

  German Reformed Church 3/15
  Greek Orthodoxy 3/25
  Hicksite Quakers 3/19
  Huguenots French Protestants) 3/1
  Lutheran Church 3/18
  Lutheran Church in America (LCA) 3/20
  Methodist Episcopal Church 3/5, 3/17
  Moravian Brethren 3/7, 3/28
  Mormonism 3/27, 3/29
  Nonconformity, English 3/29
  Orthodox Presbyterian Church 3/19
  Plymouth Brethren 3/17
  Quakerism (Society of Friends) 3/15, 3/19
  Reformed Presbyterian Church in Scotland 3/23
  Russian Orthodoxy 3/12, 3/25
  Salvation Army 3/10
  Southern Presbyterian Church 3/5
  Swedenborgianism 3/11
  Swiss Protestantism 3/27
  Unitarianism 3/22, 3/31
  United Lutheran Church in America 3/18
  Wesleyan Church (English) 3/18
Deusdedit, Archbishop of Canterbury 3/26
Didache, The 3/26
Diet (Council) of Worms (1521) 3/6
Dionysius Exiguus (d. 544) 3/25
Divine Science Church (1899) 3/22
Dixon, A. C. 3/1
Dixon, Helen C. A.
  (b. 1877) d. 3/1/1969
Donne, John
  (b. 1/24 (or 6/19) / 1572) d. 3/31/1631
Dowie, John A.
  (b. 5/25/1847) d. 3/9/1907
Drexel, [Mary] Katharine
  (b. 11/26/1858) d. 3/3/1955
Drummond, Henry
  (b. 8/17/1851) d. 3/11/1897
Dumont Television Network 3/16
Dykes, John B.
  b. 3/10/1823 [d. 1/22/1876]

E

Easter, Date of 3/22
Edersheim, Alfred
  b. 3/7/1825 d. 3/16/1889
Edwards, Jonathan
  (b. 10/5/1703) d. 3/22/1758
Eliade, Mircea
  3/9/1907 [d. 4/22/1986]
Elijah the Restorer (John A. Dowie) 3/9

Elizabeth I, (English) Queen 3/20
Elliot, Jim
  See QUOTATIONS
Elliott, Charlotte
  b. 3/18/1789 [d. 9/22/1871]
Elvey, George J.
  b. 3/27/1816 [d. 12/9/1893]
Emmanuel Holiness Church 3/19
English Reformation 3/30
Evangelical Council for Financial Accountability (ECFA) 3/2
Evangelical Lutheran Church in America (ELCA) 3/20
Evans, Frederick W.
  (b. 6/9/1808) d. 3/6/1893
Evans, Robert P. 3/14
Exiguus, Dionysius (d. 544) 3/25

F

Fairfax, Sir Thomas 3/7
Faith and Order World Conference 3/27
Farrar, Frederick W.
  (b. 8/7/1831) d. 3/22/1903
Father of German Rationalism 3/14
Federal Council of Churches of Christ in America 3/20, 3/24
Feinstein, Moshe
  3/5/1895 [d. 3/23/1986]
Felix III, St., Pope (483-92) 3/13
Felix V (Antipope) 3/6
Fénelon, François 3/29
Ferdinand II (V) of Aragon
  b. 3/10/1452 [d. 1/23/1516]
Fire-Baptized Holiness Church 3/19
FIRSTS
  African-American Catholic Archbishop in the U.S. 3/15
  American-born Bishop of the Early Methodist Episco 3/5
  American-Born Catholic Saint 3/15
  American Male Proclaimed a Catholic Saint 3/28
  American Missionary to Bombay, India 3/20
  American Protestant Missionaries to Hawaii 3/31
  Bachelor of Divinity Degree Awarded to a Woman 3/30
  Baptist Church Established on American Soil 3/24
  Baptist church in America 3/14
  Benedictine Convent in America 3/15
  Bishop of the African Methodist Episcopal Church 3/26
  Book of Common Prayer 3/30
  Catholic Diocesan School System in America 3/28
  Catholic Nun Professed in America 3/15

ALMANAC OF THE CHRISTIAN FAITH

MARCH INDEX

Catholic Priest Ordained in the U.S. 3/18
Catholic Priest to Receive Full Theological Training in the U.S. 3/18
Chaplain of the U.S. Army 3/4
Christian TV Network in the U.S. 3/22
Civil Law Requiring Sunday Sabbath Observance 3/7
Episcopal Bishop of New York 3/11
Gregorian Psalter in the Anglican Church 3/1
Jewish Chaplain of the U.S. Navy 3/1
Jewish Sunday School in America 3/4
Methodist Episcopal Missionary to Asia 3/7
Mobile Jewish Synagogue 3/27
Mormon Temple 3/27
Orthodox Bishop Ordained in America 3/12
Pentecostal Bible institute in Europe 3/2
Protestant Episcopal Bishop of Philippines 3/27
Quaker College Established in the U.S. 3/15
Recorded Meeting of Baptists 3/28
Religious Magazine Published in America 3/5
Roman Catholic college established in the U.S. 3/1
Salvation Army Mission in the U.S. 3/10
Scriptures Produced with Movable Type 3/13
Seminary Priest in England Executed for His Cathol 3/20
Statement of Faith for German-Speaking Switzerland 3/27
Theological School to Admit Women 3/30
U.S. America to Graduate from a Presbyterian Semin 3/17
U.S. Navy Chaplain Killed in Action 3/8
Woman in the Brethren in Christ Church to earn an 3/11
First Crusade (1097-99) 3/12
First Helvetic Confession 3/27
Fischer, William G. 3/4
Flavel, John (1628-91) 3/29
Form Criticism 3/11
Forty Martyrs 3/20
Franciscans 3/21
Free Church of Scotland 3/17
French Civil Wars 3/1
Fundamentalism, Christian 3/21

G

Gaither, Gloria
   b. 3/4/1942
Gallitzin, Demetrius A. 3/18
General Court of Massachusetts 3/3
Georgetown College 3/1
Georg Neumark
   b. 3/16/1621 [d. 7/18/1681]
Gerhardt, Paul
   b. 3/12/1607 [d. 5/27/1676]
German Reformed Church 3/15
Gilmore, Joseph H.
   See QUOTATIONS
Goethe, Johann W.
   (b. 8/28/1749) d. 3/22/1832
Goldberg, (Rabbi) David 3/1
Gonzaga, St. Aloysius
   b. 3/9/1568 [d. 1591]
Gould, John Edgar
   (b. 1822) d. 3/4/1875
Gratz, Rebecca 3/4
Greater Europe Mission 3/14
Great Awakening, The 3/2, 3/5, 3/8
Greek Orthodoxy 3/11, 3/13
Greenwell, Dora
   (b. 12/6/1821) d. 3/29/1882
Gregorian Calendar 3/25
Gregorian Chant 3/12
Gregory IX, Pope (1227-41) 3/19
Gregory I (the Great), Pope (590-604)
   (b. 2/3/540) d. 3/12/604
Gregory the Illuminator 3/23
Gregory XI, Pope (1370-78) 3/25
Gregory XV, Pope (1621-23) 3/12
Gunkel, Hermann
   (b. 5/23/1862) d. 3/11/1932
Gutenberg, Johann 3/13

H

Hachard, Stanislaus 3/15
Hall, Gordon
   (b. 4/8/1784) d. 3/20/1826
Hall-Mack Publishing Co. 3/10
Handel, George F. 3/23
Harkness, Robert
   b. 3/2/1880 [d. 5/8/1961]
Harvard, John 3/3
Harvard Divinity School 3/22
Harvard Seminary 3/3
Hawaiian Islands 3/31
Hawaweeny, Raphael 3/12
Haydn, Franz Joseph
   b. 3/31/1732 [d. 5/31/1809]
Hearn, Marianne
   (b. 12/17/1834) d. 3/16/1909
Hecker, Isaac 3/6
Henry, Patrick
   See QUOTATIONS
Henry VIII, (English) King (1509-47) 3/21, 3/30
Herbert, George
   (b. 4/3/1593) d. 3/1/1633
Hicks, Elias
   b. 3/19/1748 [d. 2/27/1830]
Hicksites (Quakers) 3/19
Hilton, Walter
   (b. ca. 1340) d. 3/24/1396
Hitler, Adolf 3/6
Hodge, Charles 3/5
Holman, Thomas 3/31
Honorius, Archbishop of Canterbury (631-53) 3/26
Honorius III, Pope (1216-27) 3/18
Hoyle, Richard B.
   b. 3/8/1875 [d. 12/14/1939]
Hübmaier, Balthasar
   (b. ca. 1480) d. 3/10/1528
Hugh of St. Cher
   (b. ca. 1199) d. 3/3/1263
Huguenots 3/1
Hulse, John
   b. 3/15/1708 [d. 12/14/1790]
Hurt, John 3/4
Husband, John J.
   (b. 1760) d. 3/19/1721
Hutchinson, Anne 3/22, 3/28
HYMNS
   "Abide With Me" 3/1, 3/16
   "All the Way My Savior Leads Me" 3/12
   "All to Jesus I Surrender" 3/29
   "Almighty Father, Strong to Save" 3/10
   "Amazing Grace" 3/10
   "America the Beautiful" 3/28
   "Am I a Soldier of the Cross?" 3/5, 3/12
   "And Can It Be That I Should Gain" 3/29
   "Anywhere With Jesus" 3/3
   "Anywhere with Jesus" 3/1
   "At Even E'er the Sun Was Set" 3/13
   "Away in a Manger" 3/17
   "A Charge to Keep I Have" 3/29
   "Beautiful Isle of Somewhere" 3/3
   "Because He Lives" 3/4
   "Blessed Assurance" 3/9, 3/24
   "Break Forth, O Beauteous Heavenly Light" 3/8
   "Break Thou The Bread of Life" 3/14
   "Build My Mansion Next Door to Jesus" 3/2
   "Children of the Heavenly Father" 3/16
   "Christ the Lord is Risen Today" 3/29
   "Come, Every Soul By Sin Oppressed" 3/25
   "Come, Thou Fount of Every Blessing" 3/31
   "Come, Thou Long Expected Jesus" 3/2, 3/29
   "Come, We That Love the Lord" 3/12
   "Come, Ye Thankful People, Come" 3/27
   "Crown Him With Many Crowns" 3/25, 3/27
   "Day is Dying in the West" 3/14
   "Down at the Cross Where My Savior Died" 3/25
   "Dying With Jesus, By Death Reckoned Mine" 3/20
   "Face to Face with Christ My Savior" 3/26
   "Fairest Lord Jesus" 3/18
   "Fight the Good Fight with All Thy Might" 3/2
   "For the Beauty of the Earth" 3/16
   "Gentle Jesus, Meek and Mild" 3/9
   "Glorious Things of Thee Are Spoken" 3/31
   "God of Our Fathers" 3/17
   "Go To Dark Gethsemane" 3/1
   "Grace Greater Than Our Sin" 3/6
   "Hail, Thou Once Despised Jesus" 3/18
   "Hark! The Herald Angels Sing" 3/29
   "Hark, the Voice of Jesus Calling" 3/2
   "Heavenly Sunlight" 3/15
   "Holy, Holy, Holy! Lord God Almighty" 3/10
   "If Thou But Suffer God to Guide Thee" 3/16
   "It May Not Be on the Mountain's Height" 3/1
   "I Am Not Skilled to Understand" 3/29
   "I am Thine, O Lord" 3/24
   "I Come to the Garden Alone" 3/10
   "I Heard the Voice of Jesus Say" 3/10
   "I Just Came to Talk with You, Lord" 3/2
   "I Know That My Redeemer Liveth" 3/3
   "I Know Whom I Have Believed" 3/4
   "I Need Thee Every Hour" 3/12
   "I Would Be True" 3/17
   "Jesus, Lover of My Soul" 3/29
   "Jesus, Savior, Pilot Me" 3/4
   "Jesus, The Very Thought of Thee" 3/10
   "Jesus, Thou Joy of Loving Hearts" 3/29
   "Jesus, What a Friend of Sinners" 3/2

"Jesus is Tenderly Calling" 3/24
"Joyful, Joyful, We Adore Thee" 3/26
"Just As I Am, Thine Own to Be" 3/16
"Just As I Am" 3/18
"Lead, Kindly Light" 3/10
"Love Divine, All Loves Excelling" 3/29
"Low In the Grave He Lay" 3/12
"Make Me a Captive, Lord" 3/27
"Marvelous Grace of Our Loving Lord" 3/5, 3/6
"Moment by Moment" 3/4
"My Faith Looks Up to Thee" 3/29
"On Jordan's Stormy Banks I Stand" 3/10
"O Day of Rest and Gladness" 3/21
"O For a Closer Walk with God" 3/10
"O For a Faith That Will Not Shrink" 3/5, 3/12
"O For a Thousand Tongues to Sing" 3/29
"O Love That Wilt Not Let Me Go" 3/14, 3/27
"O Sacred Head, Now Wounded" 3/12, 3/13, 3/23
"O Thou, In Whose Presence" 3/31
"O Zion, Haste, Thy Mission High Fulfilling" 3/11
"Pass Me Not, O Gentle Savior" 3/24
"Praise God From Whom All Blessings Flow" 3/19
"Praise to God, Immortal Praise" 3/9
"Rescue the Perishing" 3/24
"Showers of Blessing" 3/4
"Simply Trusting Every Day" 3/22
"Soldiers of Christ, Arise" 3/27
"Something Beautiful" 3/4
"Sun of My Soul, Thou Savior Dear" 3/29
"Sweet Hour of Prayer" 3/24
"Take My Life and Let It Be" 3/10
"Tell Me the Stories of Jesus" 3/4
"Ten Thousand Times Ten Thousand" 3/10
"There's a Peace in My Heart" 3/30
"The God of Love My Shepherd Is" 3/1
"The Great Physician Now is Near" 3/25
"The King is Coming" 3/4
"The King of Love My Shepherd Is" 3/10
"The Spacious Firmament on High" 3/31
"The Strife is O'er, The Battle Done" 3/1, 3/16
"The Touch of His Hand on Mine" 3/3
"The Way of the Cross Leads Home" 3/3
"Thine is the Glory, Risen, Conquering Son" 3/8
"We Praise Thee, O God!" 3/19
"When We Walk with the Lord" 3/5
"Worship the Lord in the Beauty of Holiness" 3/2
"Years I Spent in Vanity and Pride" 3/5
Hymns Ancient and Modern 3/13, 3/16

I

"In God We Trust" 3/3
Icelandic Poetry 3/14
Iconoclasm Controversy 3/11
Innocent I, Pope St. (401-17) 3/19
Innocent II, Pope (1130-43) 3/29
Inquisition, Holy Office of the 3/19
Isabella (of Castile), (Spanish) Queen 3/10, 3/30

J

Jansen, Cornelius Otto 3/6
Jansenists 3/6
Jefferson, (President) Thomas
    See QUOTATIONS
Jehoiachin of Judah, King 3/23
Johnston, Julia H.
    (b. 1/21/1849) d. 3/6/1919
John of Peckham 3/21
John Paul II, Pope (1978-) 3/15
Jones, Clarence W. 3/9
JUDAISM
    American Reform Judaism 3/20
    Orthodox Judaism 3/5, 3/20
    Reform Judaism 3/20
Judson, Adoniram 3/25

K

Keble, John
    (b. 4/25/1792) d. 3/29/1866
Keil, J. F. K. 3/4
Kempis, Thomas à 3/29
Ken, Thomas
    (b. 7/1637) d. 3/19/1710
Kino, Eusebio 3/13
Knapp, Phoebe Palmer
    b. 3/9/1839 [d. 7/10/1908]
Knights of Columbus 3/29
Knights Templars 3/18, 3/29
Knox, John 3/1
Koldeway, Robert 3/23
Küng, Hans
    b. 3/19/1928

L

Lalemant, Gabriel
    (b. 10/10/1610) d. 3/17/1649
Larson, Reuben 3/9
Lateran Council, Fifth (1512-17) 3/11
Latimer, Hugh 3/1
Laubach, Frank C.
    See QUOTATIONS
Leclerc, Jean
    b. 3/19/1657 [d. 1/8/1736]
LECTURES
    "The Greatest Thing in the World" (1887) 3/11
Lee, John D.
    (b. unk.) d. 3/23/1877
Legate, Bartholomew 3/18
Lenhart, John L.
    (b. unk.) d. 3/8/1862
Lennon, John 3/4
Leo X, Pope (1513-21) 3/11, 3/15, 3/16
Lewis, C. S.
    See QUOTATIONS
Lindisfarne Gospels 3/20
Lindsay, Vachel 3/11
Livingstone, David
    b. 3/19/1813 [d. 5/1/1873]
Louis VII, (French) King (1137-80) 3/21
Louis XIV, (French) King (1643-1715) 3/9
Lowry, Robert
    b. 3/12/1826 [d. 11/25/1899]
Luther, Martin 3/6, 3/11, 3/15, 3/30
    See QUOTATIONS
Lutheran Church in America (LCA) 3/20

M

"Messiah," Handel's 3/23
Machen, J. Gresham 3/19
Magna Carta, The 3/28
Maimonides, Moses 3/30
Malan, H. A. César 3/18
March, Daniel
    (b. 7/21/1816) d. 3/2/1909
Marino, Eugene Antonio 3/15
Marshall, Catherine
    (b. 9/27/1914) d. 3/18/1983
Marshall, Peter 3/18
    See QUOTATIONS
Martyn, Henry 3/7
    See QUOTATIONS
MARTYRS
    Anabaptists 3/7
    Brébeuf, Jean de 3/16, 3/17
    Cranmer, Thomas 3/21, 3/30
    Elliot, Jim 3/15, 3/17
    Forty Martyrs 3/20
    Gnadenhutten Indians 3/8
    Gonzaga, St. Aloysius 3/9
    Hübmaier, Balthasar 3/10
    Hutchinson, Anne 3/28
    Knights Templars 3/18, 3/29
    Lalemant, Gabriel 3/17
    Latimer, Hugh 3/1
    Legate, Bartholomew 3/18
    Mayne, Cuthbert 3/20
    Romero, Oscar A. 3/24
    Smith, Joseph 3/26, 3/27
    Whitman, Narcissa Prentiss 3/14
    Wishart, George 3/1
Mary (Tudor), (English) Queen (1553-58) 3/21
Masada 3/21
Massachusetts Bay Colony 3/22, 3/24
Mastai-Ferretti, Giovanni Maria.
    See Pius IX, Pope (1846-1878)
Matheson, George
    b. 3/27/1842 [d. 8/28/1906]
Mayflower Pilgrims 3/22
Mayne, Cuthbert
    b. 3/20/1544 [d. 11/30/1577]
Mazarin, Jules
    (b. 7/14/1602) d. 3/9/1661
McCheyne, Robert Murray
    (b. 5/21/1813) d. 3/25/1843
    See also QUOTATIONS
McClintock, John
    (b. 10/27/1814) d. 3/4/1870
McCollum v. Board of Education 3/8
McGivney, Father Michael J. 3/29
McGranahan, James 3/4
McKendree, William
    (b. 7/6/1757) d. 3/5/1835
Medici, Giovanni de' 3/11
Mendelssohn, Felix 3/11
Merici, Angela, St.
    b. 3/21/1474 [d. 1/27/1540]
Merton, Thomas
    See QUOTATIONS
Michelangelo Buonarroti
    b. 3/6/1475 [d. 2/18/1564]
Middle Ages 3/21
Miles, C. Austin
    (b. 1/7/1868) d. 3/10/1946
Miller, William 3/21
Milton, John 3/27
MISSION AGENCIES
    Africa Inland Mission 3/7
    China Inland Mission 3/1
    Greater Europe Mission 3/14
    World Radio Missionary Fellowship 3/9
Moffat, Mary 3/19
MONASTERIES
    Citeaux (France) 3/21
    St. Mamas (Constantinople) 3/12

ALMANAC OF THE CHRISTIAN FAITH — MARCH INDEX

Monasticism, Religious 3/21
Monk, William Henry
  (b. 3/16/1823) d. 3/1/1889
  b. 3/16/1823 [d. 3/1/1889]
Monsell, John S. B.
  b. 3/2/1911 [d. 4/9/1875]
Moody, Dwight L. 3/20, 3/21
Moody, May Whittle
  b. 3/20/1870 [d. 8/20/1963]
Moody, William 3/20
Moravian Brethren 3/7, 3/8
Morrison, Robert 3/7
Mountain Meadows Massacre 3/23
Müller, George
  (b. 9/27/1805) d. 3/10/1898
Murphy, Anne S.
  (b. unk.) d. 3/30/1942
Murray, James R.
  b. 3/17/1841 [d. 3/10/1905]
MUSIC
  "Christ on the Mount of Olives" 3/26
  "Hexachordum Apollinnis" 3/3
  "Mass in C" 3/26
  "Messiah" (oratorio) 3/23
  "Missa Solemnis" 3/26
  "Rule, Brittania!" 3/5
  "St. Matthew Passion" (J.S. Bach) 3/11, 3/23

N

National Council of Churches 3/12
Navigators, The 3/3, 3/25
Nebuchadnezzar of Babylon 3/16
Neumann, John Nepomucene
  b. 3/28/1811 [d. 1/5/1860]
Neumark, Georg 3/16
Newton, John 3/10
  See QUOTATIONS
New English Bible 3/16
New Light Presbyterians 3/26
New Style Calendar 3/10
New Thought Movement 3/22
Nicholas IV, Pope (1288-92) 3/21
Nicholas V, Pope (1447-1455) 3/6
NICKNAMES/TITLES
  Father of German Rationalism 3/14
  Patriarch of Western Monks 3/21
  Sweet Singer of Methodism 3/29
Niemöller, Martin
  (b. 1/14/1892) d. 3/6/1984
Noli, Fan Stylian
  (b. 1882) d. 3/13/1965
Nouwen, Henri J. M.
  See QUOTATIONS
NS (New Style) Calendar 3/10, 3/24

O

O'Kane, Tullius C.
  b. 3/10/1830 [d. 2/10/1912]
Oglethorpe, James 3/7
Olevianus, Kaspar
  (b. 8/19/1536) d. 3/15/1587
Oliver, Anna 3/30
Olson, Ernst William
  b. 3/16/1870 [d. 10/6/1958]
Oregon Territory 3/14
Oriental Missionary Society 3/13
Orthodox Presbyterian Church 3/19
OS (Old Style) Calendar 3/10, 3/26
Oxford Movement 3/29
Oxnam, G. Bromley
  (b. 8/14/1891) d. 3/12/1963

P

Pachelbel, Johann
  (b. 9/1/1653) d. 3/3/1706
Palmer, Ray
  (b. 11/12/1808) d. 3/29/1887
PAPAL DECREES
  Decet Romanum Pontificem (1622) 3/12
  Unigenitus Dei Filius (1713) 3/19
Parentucelli, Tommaso (Pope Nicholas V) 3/6
Parker, William H.
  b. 3/4/1845 [d. 12/2/1929]
Paton, John G. 3/23
Paul VI, Pope (1963-78) 3/7, 3/23
Peace, Albert L.
  (b. 1/26/1844) d. 3/14/1912
Peek, Joseph Y.
  (b. 2/27/1843) d. 3/17/1911
Penn, William 3/5
Pentecostalism, American 3/15
PERIODICALS
  "Columbia" (Knights of Columbus) 3/29
  "The Christian History" 3/5
Pilgrims, The Mayflower 3/12
Pink, Arthur W.
  See QUOTATIONS
Pius IV, Pope (1559-65) 3/31
Pius X, Pope (1903-14) 3/19
Pius XI, Pope (1922-39) 3/14, 3/20
Plymouth Brethren 3/17
Polish National Catholic Church of America 3/14
Polygamy 3/22
POPES
  Clement III (1187-91) 3/27
  Clement XI (1700-21) 3/19
  Felix III, St. (483-92) 3/13
  Gregory IX (1227-41) 3/19
  Gregory I (the Great) (590-604) 3/12
  Gregory XI (1370-78) 3/25
  Gregory XV (1621-23) 3/12
  Honorius III (1216-27) 3/18
  Innocent I, St. (401-17) 3/19
  Innocent II (1130-43) 3/29
  John Paul II (1978 -) 3/15
  Leo X (1513-21) 3/11, 3/15, 3/16
  Nicholas IV (1288-92) 3/21
  Paul VI (1963-78) 3/23
  Pius IV (1559-65) 3/31
  Pius XI (1922-39) 3/14, 3/20
  Pius X (1903-14) 3/19
  Stephen II (III) (752-57) 3/17
  Stephen I (752) 3/17
  Urban II (1088-99) 3/12
  Vigilius (537-55) 3/29
Pounds, Jessie Brown
  (b. 11/26/1858) d. 3/3/1921
Presbyterians, New Side 3/8
Presbyterians, Old Side 3/8
PRESIDENTS, U.S.
  Adams, John Quincy (1825-1829) 3/20
  Carter, Jimmy (1977-1981) 3/16
  Jefferson, Thomas (1801-1809) 3/23
Priestley, Joseph 3/9
Prince, Thomas 3/5
Pritchard, R. H. 3/2
Provoost, Samuel
  b. 3/11/1742 [d. 9/6/1815]

Q

QUOTATIONS
  Adams, Abigail 3/20
  Barth, Karl 3/1
  Böhler, Peter 3/4
  Bonar, Andrew 3/1, 3/9, 3/25, 3/29, 3/31
  Bonhoeffer, Dietrich 3/19
  Brainerd, David 3/3
  Calvin, John 3/5
  Carter, (President) Jimmy 3/16
  Clay, Henry 3/24
  Cromwell, Oliver 3/7
  Elliot, Jim 3/15, 3/17
  Gilmore, Joseph H. 3/26
  Henry, Patrick 3/23
  Jefferson, (President) Thomas 3/23
  Laubach, Frank C. 3/9
  Lewis, C. S. 3/18, 3/31
  Luther, Martin 3/8, 3/12, 3/13, 3/16, 3/17, 3/18, 3/23, 3/24, 3/28
  Marshall, Peter 3/2
  Martyn, Henry 3/30
  McCheyne, Robert Murray 3/9, 3/15, 3/20, 3/27
  Merton, Thomas 3/3
  Newton, John 3/18, 3/24
  Nouwen, Henri J. M. 3/3, 3/4, 3/5, 3/13, 3/15, 3/22, 3/24, 3/26, 3/28, 3/30
  Pink, Arthur W. 3/15
  Rutherford, Samuel 3/13, 3/27
  Schaeffer, Francis A. 3/2, 3/4, 3/31
  Smith, Hannah Whitall 3/6, 3/7, 3/8, 3/10, 3/12, 3/14, 3/16, 3/18, 3/21, 3/25
  Toynbee, Arnold J. 3/10
  Wesley, John 3/3, 3/5, 3/7, 3/20, 3/27
  Whitefield, George 3/6, 3/23, 3/28

R

Railton, George Scott 3/10
Rambo, Dottie
  b. 3/2/1934
Ramsey, Michael 3/23
Redhead, Richard
  b. 3/1/1820 [d. 4/27/1901]
Reformation, The 3/27
RELIGIOUS ORDERS, CATHOLIC
  Benedictines 3/21
  Carmelite Nuns 3/18, 3/28
  Cistercians 3/21
  Dominicans 3/18
  Franciscans 3/18, 3/21
  Missionary Society of St. Paul (the Paulists) 3/6
  Sisters of Charity of St. Joseph 3/15
  Ursuline Nuns 3/15, 3/21
Religious Programs on TV, 3/16
Renaissance, High 3/6
Renaissance Popes 3/6
Rescissory Act 3/28
Rice, Luther
  b. 3/25/1783 [d. 9/25/1836]
Richelieu, Armand-Jean 3/9
Riepp, Mother Benedicta 3/15
Riggs, Stephen R.
  b. 3/23/1812 [d. 8/24/1883]
Rist, Johann
  b. 3/8/1607 [d. 8/31/1667]
Ritschl, Albrecht
  (b. 3/25/1822) d. 3/20/1889
Robertson, Marion G. "Pat"
  b. 3/22/1930
Robert of Molesme 3/21
Rodeheaver Publishing Co. 3/10
Rogers, Fred M.
  b. 3/20/1928 [d. 2/27/2003]
Romero, Oscar A.
  (b. 8/15/1917) d. 3/24/1980
Rounsefell, Carrie E.
  b. 3/1/1861 [d. 9/18/1930]
Rowley, Harold H.
  b. 3/24/1890 [d. 10/4/1969]

Ruggles, Samuel 3/31
Russian Orthodoxy 3/25
Rutherford, Samuel
  (b. ca. 1600) d. 3/29/1661
  See also QUOTATIONS

S

Sacraments, Catholic 3/3
Salem Witch Trials (1692) 3/1, 3/28
Salvation Army 3/10
Sandwich Islands 3/31
Schaeffer, Francis A.
  See QUOTATIONS
Schmidt, Gustav Herbert 3/2
Schwarzerd, Philipp. See
  also Melanchthon, Philipp
Scott, Peter Cameron
  b. 3/7/1867 [d. 12/4/1896]
Scottish Reformation 3/1
SCULPTURES
  "Pieta" (1498) 3/6
Second Act of Uniformity (England) 3/9
Second Crusade (1147) 3/21
Second Vatican Council 3/7
SECTS, CHRISTIAN
  Divine Science Church 3/22
Seiss, Joseph Augustus
  b. 3/18/1823 [d. 6/20/1904]
SEMINARIES
  Andover Theological Seminary 3/20, 3/26
  Boston Theological Seminary 3/30
  Drew Theological Seminary 3/4
  Harvard Divinity School 3/22
  Union Theological Seminary (NYC) 3/17
  Union Theological Seminary (VA) 3/5
  Western Theological Seminary 3/8
  Yale Divinity School 3/30
Semler, Johann S.
  (b. 12/18/1725) d. 3/14/1791
SERMONS
  "National Apostasy" (1833) 3/29
  "No man is an island...." 3/31
  "The Danger of An Unconverted Ministry" 3/8
Seton, Elizabeth Bayley 3/15
Sewall, Samuel
  b. 3/28/1652 [d. 1/1/1730]
Shaw, Martin F.
  b. 3/9/1836 [d. 10/24/1958]
Sherwin, William F.
  b. 3/14/1826 [d. 4/14/1888]
Simeon the New Theologian, San
  (b. unk.) d. 3/12/1022
Sisters of the Blessed Sacrament for Indians and Colored People 3/3

Smith, Amanda 3/17
Smith, Hannah Whitall
  See QUOTATIONS
Smith, Joseph 3/26, 3/27
Smith, Rodney "Gipsy"
  b. 3/31/1860 [d. 8/4/1947]
Society for Promoting Christian Knowledge (SPCK) 3/8
Southern Presbyterian Church 3/5
Stainer, John
  (b. 6/6/1840) d. 3/31/1901
Stanley, Henry 3/19
STATUES
  "Christ of the Andes" (1904) 3/13
Stebbins, George C. 3/4
Stephen I, Pope (752) 3/17
Stephen II (III), Pope (752-57) 3/17
Stillingfleet, Edward
  (b. 4/17/1635) d. 3/27/1699
Stites, Edgar Page
  b. 3/22/1836 [d. 1/7/1921]
Stockton, John H.
  (b. 4/19/1813) d. 3/25/1877
Stonehouse, Ned B.
  b. 3/19/1902 [d. 11/18/1962]
Stowe, Harriet Beecher 3/8
Strong, James 3/4
Strong, William M.
  b. 3/3/1877 [d. 2/20/1960]
Stuart, Moses
  b. 3/26/1780 [d. 1/4/1852]
Supreme Court, U. S. 3/5
Swaggart, Jimmy (Lee)
  b. 3/15/1935
Swedenborgianism 3/11
Sweet Singer of Methodism 3/29
Swete, Henry Barclay
  b. 3/14/1835 [d. 5/10/1917]

T

Taylor, Hudson 3/1
TELEVISION PROGRAMS
  "Mr. Rogers' Neighborhood" 3/20
  "This Week in Religion" 3/16
Tennent, Gilbert 3/8
Teresa of Avila
  b. 3/28/1515 [d. 10/4/1582]
Tetzel, Johann 3/15
Textual Criticism 3/14
Third Crusade (1189-92) 3/27
Third Lateran Council (1179) 3/5
Thoburn, James Mills
  b. 3/7/1836 [d. 11/28/1922]
Tholuck, Friedrich A. G.
  b. 3/30/1799 [d. 6/10/1877]
Thomas Aquinas
  (b. 1225) d. 3/7/1247

Thomson, Mary Ann
  (b. 12/5/1834) d. 3/11/1923
Thring, Godfrey
  b. 3/25/1823 [d. 9/13/1903]
Thursday, Asa 3/31
Tikhon, Russian Orthodox Archbishop 3/12
Tituba 3/1
Torquemada, Tomás 3/30
Torrey, Reuben A. 3/1, 3/2
Toth, Alexis Georgievich 3/25
Towner, Daniel Brink
  b. 3/5/1850 [d. 10/3/1919]
Toynbee, Arnold J.
  See QUOTATIONS
Trent, Council of (1545-63) 3/3, 3/31
Trotman, Dawson 3/3
  b. 3/25/1906 [d. 6/18/1956]
Turner, Robert L. 3/16
Twells, Henry
  b. 3/13/1823 [d. 1/19/1900]

U

U. S. Navy Chaplaincy 3/1
Unitarianism 3/22
Unitas Fratrum (Moravian Brethren) 3/7
United Society of Christian Endeavor 3/6
Urban II, Pope (1088-99) 3/12
Urban VIII, Pope (1623-44) 3/6
Urgolino, Count of Segni 3/19
Ussher, James
  (b. 1/4/1581) d. 3/21/1656

V

Van Alstyne, Frances Jane
  b. 3/24/1820 [d. 2/12/1915]
Vassy, Massacre of 3/1
Vatican II Ecumenical Council (1962-65) 3/19
Vatican Library 3/6
Venn, Henry
  b. 3/2/1725 [d. 6/24/1797]
Victoria, (English) Queen 3/27, 3/31
Victor Immanuel, (Italian) King 3/2
Vigilius, Pope (537-555) 3/29

W

Waldenses 3/5
Waltham Abbey 3/23
Warren, George W.
  (b. 8/17/1828) d. 3/17/1902
Weeden, Winfield S.
  b. 3/29/1847 [d. 7/31/1908]
Wells, Amos. R.
  (b. 12/23/1862) d. 3/6/1933

Wesley, Charles 3/2
  (b. 12/18/1707) d. 3/29/1788
Wesley, John 3/4, 3/29, 3/31
  (b. 6/28/1703) d. 3/2/1791
  See also QUOTATIONS
Whitefield, George 3/2, 3/11, 3/22, 3/25
  See QUOTATIONS
Whitman, Marcus 3/14
Whitman, Narcissa Prentiss
  b. 3/14/1808 [d. 11/29/1847]
Whitney, Samuel 3/31
Whittle, Daniel W. 3/20
  (b. 11/22/1840) d. 3/4/1901
Williams, Roger 3/14, 3/24
Wilson, Thomas
  (b. 12/20/1663) d. 3/7/1755
Wise, Isaac Mayer
  b. 3/20/1819 [d. 3/26/1900]
Wise, Stephen S.
  b. 3/17/1874 [d. 4/19/1949]
Wishart, George
  (b. ca. 1513) d. 3/1/1546
Woolman, John 3/29
Wordsworth, Christopher
  (b. 10/30/1807) d. 3/21/1885
World Council of Churches 3/6, 3/12
World Jewish Congress 3/17
Wyeth, John
  b. 3/31/1770 [d. 1/23/1858]

Y

Yadin, Yigael
  3/21/1917 [d. 6/28/1984]
Young Men's Hebrew Association (YMHA) 3/22

Z

Zacharias, Pope (741-52)
  (b. unk.) d. 3/15/752
Zelley, Henry J.
  b. 3/15/1859 [d. 3/16/1942]
Zimmerman, John L.
  b. 3/18/1856 [d. 9/17/1941]

IYYAR — ALMANAC OF THE CHRISTIAN FAITH — NISAN

~ April 1 ~

Highlights in History

1548 Parliament ordered publication of the first official liturgy to be printed in the English language: "The Book of Common Prayer." Though Thomas Cranmer is rightly credited with the final form of the first BCP, he worked with a committee of scholars, including Reformer Martin Bucer, to shape his famous liturgy. This masterwork was first introduced in English worship the following year, on Whitsunday (which in 1549 fell on June 9th).

1745 David Brainerd began missionary work among the Native Americans of New Jersey, having previously labored in Massachusetts and Pennsylvania. His New Jersey period was his most fruitful, but he died of tuberculosis only two years into his work there. Nevertheless, his diary (afterward published by Jonathan Edwards) became a major force in promoting missions, inspiring missionaries like William Carey, Henry Martyn, and Thomas Coke.

1925 British statesman Arthur J. (Lord) Balfour dedicated Hebrew University at Jerusalem.

1933 An official Anti-Semitic Day was held in Germany as systematic persecution of the Jews began. (Before Hitler's rise to power, it is estimated Germany contained 503,000 Jews – comprising less than 1% of the total population.)

1959 Archbishop Iakovos was enthroned as head of the Greek Archdiocese of North and South America at the Cathedral of the Holy Trinity in New York City. He served until retiring in 1996.

Notable Birthdays

1764 Birth of Henry Ware, Sr., American Unitarian clergyman and theologian. He was Hollis professor of divinity, Harvard University (1805-40). His courses helped lead to the formation (in 1816) of the Harvard Divinity School. Ware is considered one of the founders of American Unitarianism. [d. 7/12/1845]

1827 Birth of John Coleridge Patteson, the first Anglican missionary bishop of Melanesia (1861). He left England for the South Seas in 1855. Landing alone on the island of Nukapu, he was murdered in revenge for an earlier kidnapping of some of the inhabitants by white men. Patteson's death stirred an interest in England in missionary work. [d. 9/20/1871]

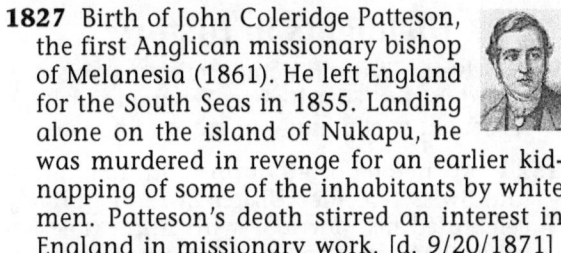

1854 Birth of Augustine Tolton, American Catholic leader. In 1886, at age 32, Tolton became the first black American to be ordained a Roman Catholic priest. [d. 7/9/1897]

The Last Passage

1849 Death of Ludovic Pavonia, 65, founder in 1847 of the Congregation of Sons of Mary Immaculate (Claretian Missionaries). (b. 1784)

1956 Death of William Reed Newell, 82, Plymouth Brethren Bible teacher and hymn writer. He authored the still-popular hymn, "Years I Spent in Vanity and Pride." (b. 5/22/1868)

1973 Death of Gordon Lindsay, 66, American mission strategist and leader (along with his wife Freda) in the charismatic healing movement. (b. 6/18/1906)

Words for the Soul

1633 To a woman grieving the recent loss of her child, Scottish clergyman Samuel Rutherford encouraged in a letter: *'Our kind Lord, who hath wounded you, will not be so cruel as not to allay the pain of your green wound; and therefore claim Christ still as you own, and own him as your One thing.'*

1877 Scottish clergyman and children's novelist George MacDonald wrote in a letter: *'Sometimes I do not know how to thank God for a special gift, because from him it is all and equally gift. But I can thank him for making me the surer that he is and that he does care for the sparrows.'*

IN GOD'S WORD... OT: Deuteronomy 18:1–20:20 ~ NT: Luke 9:28-50 ~ Psalms 73:1-28 ~ Proverbs 12:10

April 2

Highlights in History

999 Sylvester II (birth name Gerbert) was consecrated the first French pope. Serving until 1003, he sought to eliminate simony and nepotism.

1524 At the age of 40, former Catholic priest and Swiss reformer Ulrich Zwingli publicly celebrated his marriage with Anna (née Reinhard) Meyer in the Zürich Cathedral. Their union lasted seven years, until his death in the Battle of Kappel in 1531.

1914 The Assemblies of God church traces its beginnings back to this date, when 300 Pentecostals met at the Grand Opera House in Hot Spring, Arkansas, to hold a ten-day constitutional convention. They formed what has since become Pentecostalism's largest denomination, with more than 1 million members.

Notable Birthdays

742 Charlemagne (Charles the Great) was born. When Pope Leo III crowned him "Emperor of the Romans" on Christmas Day, 800, Charlemagne announced: *"Our [secular] task is... to defend with our arms the holy Church of Christ against attacks by the heathen... and... to strengthen the Church."* During his reign, Charlemagne was, in fact, more influential in church affairs than the pope. [d. 1/28/814]

1827 Birth of [William] Holman Hunt, English painter of religious subjects. A founder of the pre-Raphaelite Brotherhood (1848), he aimed at detail and truth to nature. Hunt's most famous work, "The Light of the World" (1854), represents Christ knocking at the door of the soul. [d. 9/7/1910]

1877 Birth of Mordecai F[owler] Ham, Kentucky-born Fundamentalist Baptist itinerant evangelist. Among the one million converts he reached was Billy Graham, who made a declaration of faith at a 1934 Ham meeting in Charlotte, North Carolina. [d. 11/1/1961]

The Last Passage

1657 Death of Jean-Jacques Olier de Verneuil, 48, founder of the Society of Priests at St.-Sulpice. He had lost his sight, but during a pilgrimage to Loreto he was cured, and afterward converted to a life of active Christian faith. (b. 9/20/1608)

1872 Death of Thomas Cogswell Upham, 73, American Congregational clergyman and writer. He taught mental and moral philosophy at Bowdoin College (1825-67) in Maine, and was an early advocate of international peace by tribunals. Upham also authored the *Life of Madame Guyon* (1847). (b. 1/30/1799)

1908 Death of Frederic Mayer Bird, 69, Philadelphia-born Episcopal clergyman, hymnologist, novelist and editor. He compiled (with B. M. Schmucker) *Hymns For Use of the Evangelical Lutheran Church* (1865). During his lifetime, Bird's library of hymns was said to be the largest in the United States. (b. 6/28/1838)

Words for the Soul

1526 German reformer Martin Luther declared in a sermon: *'Psalm 51:5 says: "Behold... in sin did my mother conceive me," and Ephesians 2:3: "We were by nature the children of wrath." This means that by nature, as we are conceived and born, we bring sin with us into the world, and through sin come God's wrath and death so that we are all lost and damned. And this hereditary sin is the true fountainhead whence spring and issue all the actual sins of men.'*

1955 British literary scholar and Christian apologist C. S. Lewis wrote in one of his **Letters to An American Lady**: *'Fear is horrid, but there's no reason to be ashamed of it. Our Lord was afraid (dreadfully so) in Gethsemane. I always cling to that as a very comforting fact.'*

1976 Russian Orthodox liturgical scholar Alexander Schmemann concluded in his journal: *'Religion and ideology make slaves; only faith is liberating.... Faith speaks of obedience, but only in faith is there... freedom in this world.'*

April 3

Highlights in History

1058 Benedict X, born Johannes Mincius, was named pope by the nobles who dominated the papacy of his day. He served only until 1059, then lived 20 years longer as a prisoner in the monastery of St. Agnes, before he died.

1189 The Peace of Strasbourg was signed, effecting a reconciliation between Emperor Frederick Barbarossa of Germany and Pope Clement III.

1851 Irish-born John J. Hughes, Catholic Bishop of New York, became its first archbishop, serving until his death in 1864. It was Hughes' influence that led to the parochial school system established within each modern Catholic parish.

Notable Birthdays

1593 Birth of George Herbert, English poet. Not known as a hymnwriter during his lifetime (the psalms were sung in worship), a century after Herbert's death, 40 of his poems were included by the Wesleys in their *Hymns and Sacred Poetry* (1739). [d. 2/1632]

1772 Birth of Hugh Bourne, English clergyman and a founder of the Primitive Methodist Church (ca. 1810). Influenced by New England revivalist Lorenzo Dow, Bourne later expanded the denomination across the Atlantic, into Canada and the United States. [d. 10/11/1852]

1822 Birth of Edward Everett Hale, American Unitarian clergyman and author. A co-founder of the National Conference of Unitarian Churches (1865), Hale later served as chaplain of U.S. Senate (1903-09). He is best-remembered today, however, as author of the 1863 short story, "The Man Without a Country." [d. 6/10/1909]

1935 Birth of Harold Samuel Kushner, American Jewish rabbi and popular author. His 1981 bestseller, *When Bad Things Happen to Good People*, was published after the death of his young son from progeria.

The Last Passage

1769 Death of Gerhard Tersteegen, 71, German Reformed mystic and hymnwriter. He translated hymns from the French and Latin, authoring at least two that are still in use today: "God Calling Yet! Shall I Not Hear" and "God Himself is With Us." (b. 11/25/1697)

1897 Death of German composer Johannes Brahms, 63. Though he was not employed in an official ecclesiastical position, the devout Lutheran wrote many compositions extensively for the church. His "German Requiem" (1868) is considered by some to be the greatest major sacred choral work of his century. (b. 5/7/1833)

1929 Death of Gerald Birney Smith, 60, American Baptist linguistic scholar and theologian. He edited (with Shailer Mathews) *A Dictionary of Religion and Ethics* (1921). (b. 5/3/1868)

1950 Death of Ira B. Wilson, 69, American hymnwriter. He wrote several sacred cantatas and anthems, as well as authoring the hymn, "Make Me a Blessing" (a.k.a. "Out in the Highways and Byways of Life"). (b. 9/6/1880)

Words for the Soul

1759 Anglican clergyman and hymnwriter John Newton commented in a letter: *'I believe that love to God, and to man for God's sake, is the essence of religion and the fulfilling of the law.'*

1883 Scottish clergyman and children's novelist George MacDonald wrote in a letter: *'When we cannot climb the ladder of prayer, surely God comes down to the foot of it where we lie.... We are his and he is of our kind – only all that is infinitely better.'*

1968 The evening before his assassination, while giving an address in Birmingham, American civil rights leader Martin Luther King, Jr. declared: *'I just want to do God's will. And He's allowed me to go to the mountain. And I've looked over, and I've seen the promised land.'*

IN GOD'S WORD... OT: Deuteronomy 23:1–25:19 ~ NT: Luke 10:13-37 ~ Psalms 75:1-10 ~ Proverbs 12:12-14

April 4

Highlights in History

1139 The Second Lateran Council was called by Pope Innocent II primarily to condemn the followers of Arnold of Brescia (ca.1090-1155) and to end the schism caused by the election of the antipope Anacletus II.

1507 Martin Luther, 24, was ordained a priest in Erfurt, Germany, one year after he had been consecrated a monk within the Augustinian Order. (Ten years later. Luther would nail his "95 Theses" to the Wittenberg Castle church door, and set off the Protestant Reformation.)

1541 Spanish theologian and mystic Ignatius Loyola was elected the first General of the Jesuit Order. Founded in 1534, the Society of Jesus was formally approved in 1540. It was Ignatius' supreme desire to reform the Catholic Church from within. He was canonized in 1622.

Notable Birthdays

1748 Birth of William White, organizer and patriarch of the Protestant Episcopal Church. Born in Philadelphia, he led the move to create the Protestant Episcopal Church of America, thereby "Americanizing" the Anglican Church. He served as presiding bishop (1795-1836) of the new denomination, and introduced the principle that laity should share with clergy in church government. White drafted the original constitution of the church and collaborated with William Smith in preparing an American revision of *The Book of Common Prayer*. [d. 7/17/1836]

1810 Birth of James Freeman Clarke, American Unitarian clergyman and abolitionist. Many of Clarke's writings also sought to establish a system of faith larger than that espoused by American frontier "hard-shell" Calvinists. His *Orthodoxy: Its Truths and Errors* (1866) has been read by more orthodox Christians than by Unitarians. Clarke's later writings include: *Every-Day Religion* (1886) and *Sermons on the Lord's Prayer* (1888). [d. 6/8/1888]

1862 Birth of Ernest W. Shurtleff, American Congregational clergyman, poet and hymn author. Born in Boston, Shurtleff organized the American (Congregational) Church in Frankfurt, Germany (1905-1906), but is better remembered today as author of the hymn, "Lead on, O King Eternal." [d. 8/29/1917]

The Last Passage

397 Death of St. Ambrose, 57, one of the four traditional Doctors of the Early Church. As Bishop of Milan (374-397), Ambrose brought Roman Emperor Theodosius I to his knees (marking the first time the state submitted to the Church). Ambrose was also the father of hymnology in the Western Church, writing such hymns as "Deus creator omnium" and "Veni redemptor gentium." He is also known as the teacher of his most famous convert, St. Augustine of Hippo. (b. ca. 340)

1743 Death of Daniel Neal, 64, English Independent clergyman and a historian of the Puritans. His most lasting work was *History of the Puritans, or Protestant Nonconformists, from the Reformation in 1517, till the Revolution in 1688* (4 vols., 1732-38). (b. 12/14/1678)

Words for the Soul

1857 Scottish clergyman and biographer Andrew Bonar concluded in his journal: *'For nearly ten days past have been much hindered in prayer, and feel my strength weakened thereby. I must at once return through the Lord's strength to not less than three hours a day spent in prayer and meditation upon the Word.'*

1944 Dutch diarist and Jewish Holocaust victim Anne Frank wrote: *'I want to go on living even after my death! And therefore I am grateful to God for giving me this gift... of expressing all that is in me.'*

IN GOD'S WORD... OT: Deuteronomy 26:1–27:26 ~ NT: Luke 10:38–11:13 ~ Psalms 76:1–12 ~ Proverbs 12:15-17

אייר
IYYAR

ALMANAC OF THE CHRISTIAN FAITH

ניסן
NISAN

~ April 5 ~

Highlights in History

1953 In Washington, D.C., Dwight D. Eisenhower inaugurated the National Prayer Breakfast (first called the Presidential Prayer Breakfast). President Eisenhower frequently spoke about religious values, and attempted to make the National Day of Prayer a major ceremony. Also, in 1956, he signed an act making "In God We Trust" the national motto. Altogether, the presidency brought with it not only a rebirth of Eisenhower's own personal faith, but also a renewal of America's civil religion as well.

Notable Birthdays

1617 Birth of Seth Ward, Anglican bishop, a determined opponent of dissenters, and a vigorous supporter of the Conventicle (1664) and Five Mile (1665) Acts. [d. 1/6/1689]

1809 Birth of George Augustus Selwyn, English missionary and Anglican prelate. He became the first Anglican bishop of New Zealand (1841-68), and did much to lay the foundations of the Church throughout the islands of Polynesia and Melanesia. [d. 4/11/1878]

1882 Birth of William L. Sperry, American Congregational theologian. Born in Peabody, MA, he served as professor of practical theology with Andover Theological Seminary (1917-25), and also with Harvard Divinity School (1908-53) (dean, 1922-53). [d. 5/15/1954]

The Last Passage

1649 Death of John Winthrop, 61, first governor of the Puritans in Massachusetts. Winthrop, who left England because of its persecution of Puritans, believed New England to be "a city upon a hill" for the world to see and emulate. Between 1629-1648, he served 12 times as governor of Massachusetts Bay Colony, and helped banish Anne Hutchinson. (b. 1/22/1588)

1811 Robert Raikes, English newspaper editor and philanthropist, died at age 75. In 1780 Raikes set up an experimental "Sabbath School" for the neglected children of his native Gloucester. The idea caught on, and similar schools were soon opened on both sides of the Atlantic, leading to the establishment in 1803 of the first Sunday School Union. (b. 9/14/1735)

1896 Death of Harriet Starr Cannon, 72, American Anglican religious. Born in Charleston, SC in 1865 she became a founding member and was elected first mother superior of the (Episcopal) Community of St Mary – the first woman superior of a women's monastic order constituted by an Anglican bishop. (b. 5/7/1823)

1922 Death of Pandita Sarasvati Ramabai, 64, Indian Christian educator and reformer. During a severe famine in 1896, she established an orphanage for over 300 women and children, called Mukti Sadan ("House of Salvation"). She also supervised a Marathi translation of the Bible free from Sanscrit. (b. 1858)

Words for the Soul

1538 German reformer Martin Luther once remarked: *'Our Lord God fills His high office in an odd manner. He entrusts it to preachers, poor sinners, who tell and teach the message and yet live according to it only in weakness. Thus God's power always goes forward amid extreme weakness.'*

1538 German reformer Martin Luther once remarked: *'Music is an outstanding gift of God and next to theology. I would not want to give up my slight knowledge of music for a great consideration.'*

1802 English-born pioneer Methodist bishop and American circuit rider Francis Asbury reflected in his journal: *'I am often drawn out in thankfulness to God, who hath saved a mother of mine, and, I trust, a father also, who are already in glory, where I hope to meet them both, after time, and cares, and sorrows shall have ceased with me.'*

IN GOD'S WORD... OT: Deuteronomy 28:1-68 ~ NT: Luke 11:14-36 ~ Psalms 77:1-20 ~ Proverbs 12:18

אייר IYYAR — ALMANAC OF THE CHRISTIAN FAITH — ניסן NISAN

~ April 6 ~

Highlights in History

1249 King Louis IX of France, was taken prisoner by Moslems during the Seventh Crusade. (After showing bravery in the face of torture, he was allowed to buy his freedom for a huge sum in gold — and the city of Damietta.)

1415 At the Fifth Session of Council of Constance, the assembly laid down the decree "Haec sancta," proclaiming the principle that its authority is from Christ and that even the pope had to submit to its decrees.

1735 The first Moravians from Europe arrived in Georgia. Invited by GA governor James Oglethorpe, ten males of the Unitas Fratrum (as they called themselves), under leadership of Augustus G. Spangenberg, John Toltschig and Anton Siefert, landed in Savannah, after sailing from England in February.

1789 The first Catholic diocese in the U.S. was established at Baltimore. Later, in 1808, it was raised to the first archdiocese in the United States. By a decree of the Sacred Congregation of the Propaganda, approved by Pius IX on July 5, 1858, prerogative of place was conferred on the archdiocese of Baltimore, and it is known today as the Premier See of this country.

Notable Birthdays

1810 Birth of Edmund Hamilton Sears, American Unitarian clergyman. He penned a number of hymns, including the Christmas carol, "It Came Upon the Midnight Clear." (d. 1/14/1876)

The Last Passage

1199 Death of Richard I, "the Lionhearted" (Coeur-de-Lion), 41, King of England from 1189. He was one of the three leaders of the Third Crusade, 1189-92, and negotiated Christian access to Jerusalem. Kidnapped by Austrians in 1191, he was ransomed and returned to England in 1194, and became the subject of numerous legends. (b. 9/8/1157)

1528 Death of Albrecht Dürer, 56, German artist. One of the geniuses of the Renaissance in Germany, he excelled in engraving as well as in painting, and is noted for his religious scenes. There is some evidence that he was so influenced by Martin Luther (whom he called "the great Christian man who has helped me out of great anxieties") that he converted to Protestantism. (b. 5/21/1471)

1877 Death of Alexander R. Reinagle, 77, distinguished British sacred organist and hymnwriter. He served 31 years as organist of St. Peter's-in-the-Fields at Oxford (1822-53), and composed much sacred music, including the hymn-tune ST. PETER ("In Christ There Is No East Or West"). (b. 8/21/1799)

1966 Death of Heinrich Emil Brunner, 76, prominent 20th century Swiss theologian. Along with Karl Barth, Brunner is commonly associated with the neo-orthodox (or dialectical) theology movement of the 1930s-1950s. His most enduring titles include *The Mediator* (1927) and *The Divine Imperative* (1932). Beginning in 1955, Brunner suffered a series of strokes, effectively ending his academic career. (b. 12/23/1889)

Words for the Soul

1781 Devoted Anglican-Methodist pastor John Fletcher reminded in a letter: *'Jesus... has all power to deliver us, and He may do it by ways we little think of. "As Thou wilt, when Thou wilt, and where Thou wilt," said [Richard] Baxter.'*

1952 American missionary to Ecuador and Auca Indian martyr Jim Elliot maintained in his journal: *'Faith makes life so even, gives one such confidence, that the words of men are as wind.'*

1955 In a letter to Sheldon Vanauken, British literary scholar and Christian apologist C. S. Lewis explained: *'There is great good in bearing sorrow patiently: I don't know that there is any virtue in sorrow just as such. It is a Christian duty, as you know, for everyone to be as happy as he can.'*

IN GOD'S WORD... OT: Deuteronomy 29:1–30:20 ~ NT: Luke 11:37–12:7 ~ Psalms 78:1-31 ~ Proverbs 12:19-20

April 7

Highlights in History

1449 Felix V, who served as the last antipope, voluntarily resigned the pontificate and urged his followers to acknowledge Nicholas II as rightful pontiff.

1541 On his 35th birthday, Francis Xavier, Spanish co-founder of the Society of Jesus (Jesuits), set sail from Lisbon, Portugal, to evangelize the East Indies. In May 1542 he landed at Goa, India, which he afterward made his headquarters. (He later traveled to Japan, Sri Lanka, and other areas of Asia.) One of the greatest of the Catholic missionaries, Francis Xavier is known today as "the Apostle of the Indies" and "of Japan." It is hard to say how many people he converted, but modern scholars estimate around 30,000, while the Jesuits claim 700,000.

1628 Jonas Michaelius (b. 1577) arrived in New Amsterdam (New York City), the first minister of the Dutch Reformed Church to come to America. Michaelius is best remembered for a rather mournful letter he sent later this year (8/11/1628) to Adrian Smoutius in Amsterdam, which provides a glimpse into early colonial life in New Netherland (later, New York state).

Notable Birthdays

1506 Birth of Francis Xavier, Spanish Jesuit missionary to the Orient, 1540s-50s. Known as the "Apostle of the Indies" and "of Japan," his work is remarkable for the extent of his journeys and the large number of his converts. He believed a missionary should adapt to the local customs. [d. 12/3/1552]

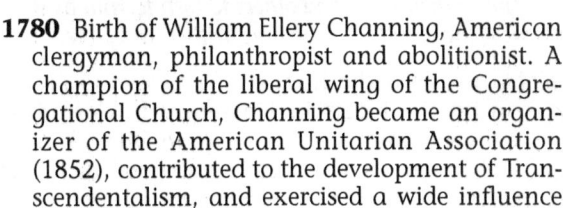

1780 Birth of William Ellery Channing, American clergyman, philanthropist and abolitionist. A champion of the liberal wing of the Congregational Church, Channing became an organizer of the American Unitarian Association (1852), contributed to the development of Transcendentalism, and exercised a wide influence on social and philanthropic issues. He pastored the Federal St. Church, Boston (1803-1842), and authored *The Perfect Life* (1873). [d. 10/2/1842]

1887 Birth of William H. F. Brothers, English-born religious leader. He was the founding bishop of the Old Catholic Church in America. Currently, the denomination is comprised of three parishes and four monastic communities. [d. 7/21/1979]

The Last Passage

1807 Death of Charles Pettigrew, 59. He was an organizer and bishop of the Episcopal Church in North Carolina, and also helped establish the University of North Carolina. (b. 3/20/1743)

1917 Death of James Hope Moulton, 53, English Greek and Iranian scholar. He is most widely remembered for his *Grammar of New Testament Greek: Vols. I-II* (1906-19), and (with George Milligan) *The Vocabulary of the Greek Testament, Parts I and II* (1914-15). (b. 10/11/1863)

1925 Death of Tikhon (born Vasili Belavin), 58, prelate of Moscow (1917-25). He became the first Patriarch of the Russian Church since 1700, following the restoration of Russian Orthodoxy. (b. 12/19/1866)

Words for the Soul

1763 Anglican evangelical Henry Venn objected in a letter: 'I hate opinions, and would not give a pin's point to have any one believe as I do, till the Scriptures, by the Spirit's teaching, open his understanding.'

1878 Scottish clergyman and children's novelist George MacDonald confessed in a letter: 'When I am well, I write prose – when ill, verse. But the verse is better than the prose.'

1968 In a letter penned in his 83rd and final year of life, Swiss Reformed theologian Karl Barth wrote: 'How one learns to be thankful for each day on which one can still do something.'

April 8

Highlights in History

1378 Bartolomeo Prignano was elected Pope Urban VI. His violent demeanor caused his electors to leave Rome and name a new pope (Clement VII), thus setting off the Great Western Schism.

1546 The Fourth Session of the Council of Trent officially declared Jerome's Latin Vulgate the authoritative Biblical text for Catholics, thereby also endorsing the 15 apocryphal books included in Jerome's translation.

1730 Shearith Israel, the first Jewish congregation organized in America, consecrated their synagogue in New York City. Theirs was the first permanent Jewish house of worship in America, and was completed on April 8, 1730.

1857 A small group of Dutch immigrants, meeting in Zeeland, Michigan, organized the Christian Reformed Church. The denomination's "Back to God Hour" radio program is broadcast on all the major continents.

1988 Television evangelist Jimmy Swaggert, 52, was defrocked by the Executive Presbytery of the Assemblies of God in Springfield, Missouri, following an exposure of his involvement with a prostitute. He had been ordered to stop preaching and stay off TV for a year, but returned after only 3 months, saying a year's absence would destroy his ministry. Swaggart afterward resigned from the Assemblies.

Notable Birthdays

1784 Birth of Gordon Hall, American Congregational missionary to India. He was the first American missionary to Bombay, where, joined by Samuel Newell, he spent his remaining 13 years, before dying of cholera while ministering to the stricken natives. [d. 3/20/1826]

1847 Birth of F[rederick] B. Meyer, English Baptist clergyman and devotional writer. Inspired by the preaching of Dwight Moody, Meyer became an exponent of the deeper Christian life, and was a popular speaker at the Northfield and Keswick conference centers. Many of his devotional writings are still in print. [d. 3/28/1929]

1947 Birth of Larry Norman, Christian singer and songwriter: "the Father of Christian Rock." Associated with the Jesus Movement of the late 1960s, Norman was known for the signature gesture: his index finger raised in the air to signify "One Way!" Norman's haunting ballad, "I Wish We'd All Been Ready," has since found its way into several church hymnals. [d. 2/24/2008]

The Last Passage

1943 Death of Mary Reed, 88, American Methodist missionary to the lepers in Chandag, India. She herself contracted the disease in 1890, and remained in Chandag the remainder of her life, leaving the area only a few times before her death. (b. 12/4/1854)

Words for the Soul

1743 Colonial American missionary to the New England Indians, David Brainerd confessed in his journal: *'Of late I have thought much of having the kingdom of God advanced in the world; but now I saw I had enough to do within myself.'*

1935 Anglican mystic Evelyn Underhill explained in a letter: *'The mystics always say [God] indwells... below the level of everyday consciousness, utterly distinct from and yet more present to us than we are to ourselves. Some find it easiest to withdraw and find Him in their souls and others to turn to Him as if He were the sun: both true and neither adequate.'*

1945 Before being hanged the following morning by the Nazis in Flossenburg, Germany, Lutheran pastor and theologian Dietrich Bonhoeffer spoke these last recorded words: *'This is the end–for me the beginning of life.'*

IN GOD'S WORD... OT: Deuteronomy 32:28-52 ~ NT: Luke 12:35-59 ~ Psalms 78:56-64 ~ Proverbs 12:24

April 9

Highlights in History

1816 The first African Methodist Episcopal Church convention opened in Philadelphia (held April 9-11), when 16 delegates from five independent churches met to form an African-American denomination based on the principles of Methodism. The following day, Richard Allen (1760-1831) was elected the new body's first bishop. A few years earlier, Allen and his colleagues had left the Methodist Episcopal Church when it exhibited racial discrimination, removing blacks from "white" seats during prayer.

1828 Baptist American missionary George Dana Boardman (Sr.) first arrived in Tavoy, Burma. A pioneer missionary to the Karen people, he made extensive jungle tours.

1906 The first group outbreak of charismatic gifts (in modern times) occurred in Los Angeles under the leadership of black evangelist William J. Seymour. Edward S. Lee, Jennie Evans Moore and five others on this night began speaking in tongues. Within a week, a building at 312 Azusa Street had been rented, and the three-year-long "Azusa Street" revival began. Ministers and laity both flocked to this old building in the downtown industrial area of L.A., and took away the Pentecostal experience with them across North America and overseas.

Notable Birthdays

1813 Birth of Jane Laurie Borthwick, Scottish philanthropist and hymnwriter: "Be Still, My Soul." [d. 9/7/1897]

1862 Birth of Charles Henry Brent, Canadian Episcopal prelate and ecumenical pioneer. He was consecrated the first missionary Protestant Episcopal bishop to the Philippine Islands (1901-18). He later served as chief of chaplains with the American forces in World War I, as Bishop of Western NY (1918-26), and as bishop in charge of Episcopal churches in Europe (1926-28). Brent was a principal force within the ecumenical movement to have the Episcopal Church sponsor the Faith and Order World Conference in Lausanne (1927), of which he served as conference president. [d. 3/27/1929]

The Last Passage

1761 Death of William Law, 75, English devotional writer. His most famous work, *A Serious Call to a Devout and Holy Life* (1728), had a decisive influence on a number of English Evangelicals, including John and Charles Wesley, George Whitefield, Henry Venn and William Wilberforce. (b. 1686)

1913 Death of William W. Borden ("Borden of Yale"), 26, American China Inland missionary to the Muslims. An heir to the Borden Dairy fortune, he came to a personal faith 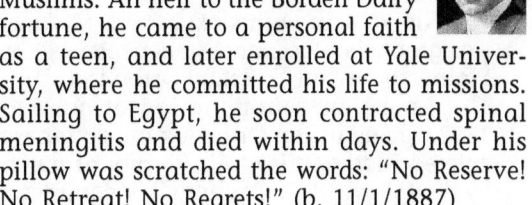 as a teen, and later enrolled at Yale University, where he committed his life to missions. Sailing to Egypt, he soon contracted spinal meningitis and died within days. Under his pillow was scratched the words: "No Reserve! No Retreat! No Regrets!" (b. 11/1/1887)

1945 Death of Dietrich Bonhoeffer, 39, German Lutheran pastor, theologian and Nazi martyr. His most popular writings were *The Cost of Discipleship, Ethics,* and *Letters and Papers from*  *Prison*. A member of the anti-Nazi resistance movement, Bonhoeffer was arrested by the Gestapo in April 1943, and hanged in a concentration camp two years later. (b. 2/4/1906)

Words for the Soul

1879 Scottish clergyman and children's novelist George MacDonald wrote in a letter: *'Oh how I hate forms and love St. Paul for the way he tells us to let no man burden us with them, even when he himself loved and kept those he had been used to from his childhood.'*

IN GOD'S WORD... OT: Deuteronomy 33:1-29 ~ NT: Luke 13:1-21 ~ Psalms 78:65-72 ~ Proverbs 12:25

April 10

Highlights in History

428 Nestorius was consecrated bishop of Constantinople. Soon attacking the "theotokos" (God-bearer) description of Mary, he suggested "christotokos" (Christbearer) instead, and was afterward branded a heretic. Nestorius, in fact, did not deny Jesus' nature as God, but believed "theotokos" challenged the reality of Christ's human nature, and modern theologians think "heretic" may have been too harsh a label.

1816 In Philadelphia, Richard Allen, 56, was elected the first bishop of the newly-created African Methodist Episcopal Church. It was the first black denomination established in the United States, and Allen's election also made him the first African-American bishop in the U.S.

1970 The Russian Orthodox Church in America was granted autocephaly (independence) by its Mother body, the Russian Orthodox Church. The American denomination originated in 1792, when Russian Orthodox missionaries first entered Alaska, prior to its territorial purchase by the U.S. in 1867. Currently headquartered in Syosset, NY, membership in the ROCA numbers approximately one million.

Notable Birthdays

1827 Birth of Lew[is] Wallace, American Civil War soldier, lawyer, diplomat and author of *Ben Hur: A Tale of the Christ* (1880). He conceived his famous novel (his second) while arguing on a train with Robert Ingersoll, a famous agnostic. Selling more than 300,000 copies in its first decade, Wallace was the best-selling religious author of his day – though he never officially joined a church. [d. 2/15/1905]

1829 Birth of William Booth, English denominational reformer. In 1865 he began a rescue mission in East London which, by 1878, had grown to become the Salvation Army. [d. 8/20/1912]

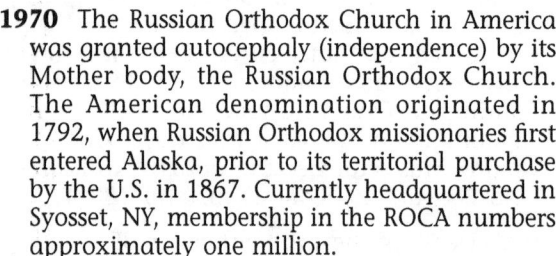

The Last Passage

1347 Death of William of Ockham (Occam), 67, medieval English Scholastic theologian and philosopher. From him originated the maxim known as "Ockham's Razor" ("Law of Parsimony"): *'It is futile to do with more elements what can be done with fewer.'* (b. ca. 1280)

1585 Death of Gregory XIII (Ugo Buoncompagni), 83, Italian-born pope from 1572-85. He reformed the Julian calendar by creating its replacement, the Gregorian calendar (first implemented in 1582). (b. 6/7[+var]/1502)

1899 Death of John R. Sweney, 61, American Presbyterian music teacher and choral director. He composed over 1,000 hymn tunes, including: SWENEY ("More About Jesus"); STORY OF JESUS ("Tell Me the Story of Jesus"); SUNSHINE ("Sunshine in My Soul"). (b. 12/31/1837)

1933 Death of Henry J. Van Dyke, 80, American Presbyterian clergyman, educator, poet, author and hymnwriter. He published a number of popular writings, including *The Story of the Other Wise Man* (1896). Van Dyke also created the popular hymn of praise, "Joyful, Joyful, We Adore Thee." (b. 11/10/1852)

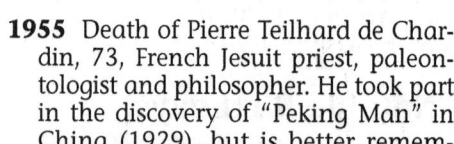

1955 Death of Pierre Teilhard de Chardin, 73, French Jesuit priest, paleontologist and philosopher. He took part in the discovery of "Peking Man" in China (1929), but is better remembered (and criticized) for his optimistic synthesis of Christianity and evolution. Comprising a unique amalgam of science, theology and poetry, Teilhard's *Phenomenon of Man* was published in 1955. (b. 5/1/1881)

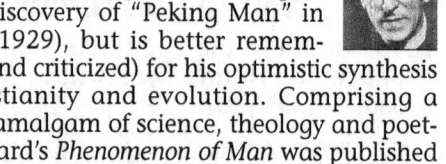

Words for the Soul

1886 Scottish clergyman, diarist and biographer Andrew Bonar, 75, noted in his journal: *'The Fountain of living water feels most satisfying when other waters fail.'*

IN GOD'S WORD... OT: Deuteronomy 34:1 – Joshua 2:24 ~ NT: Luke 13:22 – 14:6 ~ Psalms 79:1-13 ~ Proverbs 12:26

איר ALMANAC OF THE CHRISTIAN FAITH ניסן
IYYAR   NISAN

~ April 11 ~

Highlights in History

1506 Pope Julius II laid the foundation for construction of the new St. Peter's Basilica in Rome. Due to the immense size and cost, its completion was delayed until 1626. (Today, St. Peter's is known as the largest, most famous and most recognized church in the world.)

1680 Father Louis Hennepin was kidnapped by the Sioux Indians. Hennepin, a French Franciscan Recollect friar, came to Canada from Flanders in 1679, and traveled westward through Indiana as chaplain to Robert La Salle. During his captivity, the Indians starved and taunted him, but probably spared his life because they feared he could summon supernatural powers with his compass and chalice.

1836 George Mueller, 30, a leader of the Plymouth Brethren movement, opened his famous orphanage on Wilson Street in Bristol, England. By 1875, his ministry was providing care for over 2,000 children. As a preacher at Ebenezer Chapel, Mueller believed material needs could be supplied through prayer alone, so he abolished pew rents and refused a salary.

Notable Birthdays

1492 Birth of Margaret of Navarre, champion of the Reformed movement in France. The sister of Francis I of France, she married Henry d'Albret and thereafter lived and aided Protestants in Navarre. It was Marguerite's grandson Henry IV who signed the Edict of Nantes in 1598. [d. 12/21/1549]

1794 Birth of Edward Everett, American Unitarian clergyman and statesman, orator and author. At one time president of Harvard (1846-49), Everett was the major speaker on the day of the dedication of Gettysburg National Cemetery (Nov. 19, 1863). It was following Everett's two-hour oration that Abraham Lincoln delivered his brief "Gettysburg Address." [d. 1/15/1865]

1807 Birth of Samuel Hopkins, American Congregational clergyman and writer. He authored *The Puritans* (3 vols., 1859-1861), republished as *The Puritans and Queen Elizabeth* (3 vols., 1875). [d. 2/10/1887]

1836 Birth of William Porcher Du Bose, South Carolina-born Episcopal clergyman, theologian, educator and author: *High Priesthood and Sacrifice* (1908); *The Reason of Life* (1911). He served as founder and dean of the theology department, at the University of the South in Sewanee, Tennessee (1871-1918). Du Bose was one of greatest theological minds in Episcopal Church. [d. 8/18/1918]

The Last Passage

1079 Death of Stanislaus (Stanislaw), 49, Bishop of Cracow, Poland, and martyr. Whether or not he attempted to overthrow King Boleslaw II (called Boleslaw the Cruel) is debatable. But he certainly excommunicated the evil king, who deemed him a traitor and afterward had Stanislaus murdered. Today he is honored as the patron saint of Poland. (b. 1030)

1833 Death of Rowland Hill, 88, English clergyman. He was a Nonconformist, influenced by George Whitefield, and authored the hymn, "Cast Thy Burden on the Lord." (b. 8/23/1744)

Words for the Soul

1847 Scottish clergyman and children's novelist George MacDonald, 23, wrote in a letter to his father: *'I look forward to much increase of knowledge & power of thought in years to come, and I hope God will keep me from using his glorious gifts, without rendering him the homage, & devoting them to his service.'*

1941 American Trappist monk Thomas Merton affirmed in his *Secular Journal*: *'If we are willing to accept humiliation, tribulation can become, by God's grace, the mild yoke of Christ, His light burden.'*

IN GOD'S WORD... OT: Joshua 3:1–4:24 ~ NT: Luke 14:7-35 ~ Psalms 80:1-19 ~ Proverbs 12:27-28

April 12

Highlights in History

1204 The armies of the Fourth Crusade captured and pillaged Constantinople — an allied city! They established the Latin Empire, virtually destroying the Byzantine Empire and any hope of reunifying the rift between eastern and western Christianity.

1882 The Evangelical Reformed Church in Northwest Germany was created by royal decree when the king of Prussia ordered the 124 "reformed" congregations scattered throughout the area (then known as the Province of Han[n]over) to become incorporated as an independent territorial church.

1914 An 11-day constitutional convention in Hot Springs, Arkansas ended, during which the Assemblies of God denomination was founded. It would become the world's largest Pentecostal denomination.

Notable Birthdays

1500 Birth of Joachim Camerarius, German Reformer, classical scholar and Lutheran theologian. He mediated between Protestants and Catholics during the Reformation, and helped Philipp Melanchthon formulate the Augsburg Confession (1530). [d. 4/17/1574]

1867 Birth of Samuel M. Zwemer, American missionary to the Arab world. Born the 13th of 15 children, Samuel was influenced by the Student Volunteer Movement to become a missionary. In 1890 he was sent to Arabia under sponsorship of the Syrian Mission of the Presbyterian Church in the U.S.A. After 17 years in Cairo, Zwemer returned to the U.S. and taught at Princeton Seminary. [d. 4/2/1952]

The Last Passage

1443 Death of Henry Chichele, about 81, Archbishop of Canterbury (1414-43). As a diplomat, he served as an envoy to many countries. He was founder (1437) of two colleges at Oxford – St. Bernard's and All Souls. (Chichele is erroneously blamed in Shakespeare's "Henry V" for urging the conquest of France to divert Parliament from disendowment of the Church.) (b. ca. 1362)

1850 Pioneer American Baptist missionary Adoniram Judson, 61, died during a sea voyage. Serving as a missionary to India and Burma (1813-50), he translated the Bible into Burmese, and also authored the hymn, "Come, Holy Spirit, Dove Divine." Judson and his wife Ann were the foremost American missionary heroes of their day. (b. 8/9/1788)

1902 Death of T[homas] DeWitt Talmage, 70, American Presbyterian minister, lecturer and author. He was chaplain for the Union Army during American Civil War. His sermons were printed weekly in various papers for 30 years. (b. 1/7/1832)

Words for the Soul

1572 French-born Swiss reformer Theodore Beza (John Calvin's successor) exhorted Scottish reformer John Knox in a letter: 'They whose citizenship is in heaven ought to have their whole dependence on heaven.'

1939 English mystic Evelyn Underhill advised in a letter: 'Prayer should never be regarded as a science.... It is essentially a living and personal relationship, which tends to become more personal and also more simple, as one goes on.'

1968 American Presbyterian missionary Francis Schaeffer explained in a letter: 'The Bible says that God is not caught in the machine aspect of the universe which He has made, and that man is not caught in the machine either. Man is able by choice to interrupt the machine portion of the universe. Thus, from the biblical viewpoint, when I pray, God does hear and He can act into the cause and effect universe in answer to my prayer.'

IN GOD'S WORD... OT: Joshua 5:1–7:15 ~ NT: Luke 15:1-32 ~ Psalms 81:1-16 ~ Proverbs 13:1

April 13

Highlights in History

1598 The Edict of Nantes, promulgated by France's King Henry IV (of Navarre), granted to his Protestant subjects a large measure of religious freedom by establishing qualified religious toleration for French Huguenots. The Edict (which ended the French wars of religion) remained in effect until it was revoked by Louis XIV on Oct. 18, 1685, thereafter causing the regretted Huguenot exodus from France.

1742 George Frideric Handel's oratorio "Messiah" was first performed in Dublin. A German-born emigré to England, Handel is remembered today as one of the greatest of the Baroque composers, second only to Bach. (Note: "Messiah" was first performed as an oratorio for Lent (Easter), rather than for Advent (Christmas).

1819 The New York Port Society (org. May 1818) was officially chartered as the Society for Promoting the Gospel Among Seamen in the Port of New York. This nonsectarian organization finished construction of its first Mariners' church in June 1820. Rev. Ward Stafford, the first pastor, preached from 1818 to 1821.

1986 Pope John Paul II made an unprecedented visit to the central Jewish synagogue of Rome, marking the first such visit by a pope in recorded history. The pontiff explained that his visit was intended to contribute to good relations between Catholics and Jews.

Notable Birthdays

1519 Birth of Catherine de Medici, Italian consort. The daughter of Lorenzo de Medici, she married Henry II in 1533, and later became adviser to her son Charles IX (1560-1574). It was under her regency that the St. Bartholomew's Day massacre of the Huguenots took place, on August 23-24, 1572. [d. 1/5/1589]

1828 Birth of J[oseph] B. Lightfoot, Anglican prelate and biblical critic. He served as Bishop of Durham (1879-1889), but was better remembered for his analytical work on both the New Testament and the Apostolic Fathers. He also served on New Testament committee for the *English Revised Version* of the Bible (1881, 1885). [d. 12/21/1889]

The Last Passage

1886 Death of John Humphrey Noyes, 74, religious perfectionist and social reformer. He was founder of the Oneida Community, one of the most successful of the 19th century communes in America. (b. 9/6/1811)

1928 Death of Ernest A. Kilbourne, 63, American missionary to the Orient. In 1902 he went to Japan with Charles and Lettie Cowman, and in 1907 helped them organize the Oriental Missionary Society. (b. 9/6/1811)

Words for the Soul

1776 Anglican clergyman and hymnwriter John Newton concluded in a letter: *'When everything we receive from Him is received and prized as fruit and pledge of His covenant love, then His bounties, instead of being set up as rivals and idols to draw our heart from Him, awaken us to fresh exercises of gratitude and furnish us with fresh motives of cheerful obedience every hour.'*

1867 Scottish clergyman and biographer Andrew Bonar reflected in his journal: *'I sometimes feel as if there were two sides to my soul, the one looking earthward, the other heavenward. How the flesh shivers at times when missing its desired objects, and nothing relieves but getting heavenly and unseen objects to engage thought and feeling.'*

1776 Russian Orthodox liturgical scholar Alexander Schmemann noted in his journal: *'Eternal life is not what begins after temporal life; it is the eternal presence of the totality of life.'*

IN GOD'S WORD... OT: Joshua 7:16–9:2 ~ NT: Luke 16:1-18 ~ Psalms 82:1-8 ~ Proverbs 13:2-3

אייר ALMANAC OF THE CHRISTIAN FAITH ניסן
IYYAR   NISAN

~ April 14 ~

Highlights in History

1660 Charles II made the Declaration of Breda in Holland, immediately before the Restoration of the monarchy in England. The king expressed, among other things, his readiness to grant his subjects a "liberty to tender consciences" in matters of religion not affecting the peace of the kingdom in England. (An alternative date of April 4th is sometimes given for this event.)

1775 America's first society to abolish slavery was organized in Philadelphia. (Seven of the original ten members were Quakers.)

1813 The first privately operated hospital for insane patients was founded by the Religious Society of Friends (Quakers) in Philadelphia, PA, as The Asylum for the Relief of Persons Deprived of the Use of Their Reason. No manacles, handcuffs, iron grates, or bars were used. The name was changed in 1888 to the Friends Asylum for the Insane, and in 1914 to the Friends Hospital.

1883 The first edition of the "Journal of Christian Science" was published, consisting of 8 pages. Designed as a bimonthly, with a subscription price of $1 a year and 17 cents per copy, the periodical's stated mission was to be *'an independent Family paper to promote Health and Morals.'*

1906 The Azusa Street Revival began — the proto-mission out of which the modern world-wide Pentecostal movement was born. The Apostolic Faith Mission evangelistic services under the leadership of Elder William J. Seymour had moved into the building at 312 Azusa Street in Los Angeles, and the spiritual events which followed continued for up to seven years.

Notable Birthdays

1775 Birth of John Philip, Scottish missionary to South Africa. Sent in 1818 by the London Missionary Society, Philip stirred up controversy by defending the rights of the Africans against abuse by the European settlers. [d. 8/27/1851]

1866 Birth of Anne Sullivan Macy, American educator. Born "Joanna," she became (at age 21) Helen Keller's lifelong "miracle worker," until her own death at 70. [d. 10/20/1936]

The Last Passage

1682 Avvakum, 62, founder and archpriest of the Old Believer movement in the Russian Orthodox Church, was martyred. He had opposed patriarch Nikon's attempts to "reform" the church by making it more like the Greek Orthodox. Avvakum had previously been exiled to Siberia (1653), returned (1662), was tried and imprisoned (1666). Czar Theodore IV had Avvakum and his fellow prisoners locked in a log cabin and burned alive. (b. 12/5/1620)

1888 Death of William Fiske Sherwin, 62, sacred choralist and hymn composer: BREAD OF LIFE ("Break Thou the...") and CHAUTAUQUA ("Day is Dying in the West"). Trained under Lowell Mason, Sherwin possessed great ability to organize and direct amateur choirs. He served as the music director at Lake Chautauqua Assembly in New York. (b. 3/14/1826)

1975 Death of Charles Brandon Booth, 87, American social reformer. The grandson of Salvation Army founder William Booth, he served as head of the Volunteers of America, 1949-1958. (b. 12/26/1887)

Words for the Soul

1771 English founder of Methodism, John Wesley, commented in a letter: *'No part of Christian history is so profitable, as that which relates to great changes wrought in our souls: these therefore should be carefully noticed, and treasured up for the encouragement of our brethren.'*

1940 English Bible expositor Arthur W. Pink declared in a letter: *'Nothing is too great and nothing is too small to commit into the hands of the Lord.'*

IN GOD'S WORD... OT: Joshua 9:3–10:43 ~ NT: Luke 16:19–17:10 ~ Psalms 83:1-18 ~ Proverbs 13:4

ALMANAC OF THE CHRISTIAN FAITH

IYYAR · NISAN

~ April 15 ~

Highlights in History

1729 German composer Johann Sebastian Bach conducted the first and only performance of "The Passion According to St. Matthew" during his lifetime — at a Good Friday Vespers service at the St. Thomas Lutheran Church of Leipzig, Germany. Called by some *'the supreme cultural achievement of all Western civilization,'* even radical skeptic Friedrich Nietzsche admitted upon hearing the oratorio, *'One who has completely forgotten Christianity truly hears it here as gospel.'* From this work came one of Bach's most famous hymns: "O Sacred Head Now Wounded."

1914 In Belvedere (near Los Angeles), pioneer Pentecostal minister Frank Ewart preached his first public sermon on the "oneness" principle in Acts 2:38. On this same night he and evangelist, Glenn A. Cook baptized each other "in the name of Jesus," rather than invoking the traditional trinitarian formula. This act set in motion an issue that would afterward divide the Pentecostal movement between the Trinitarians and the "Jesus' Name," or Oneness, believers.

Notable Birthdays

1452 Birth of Leonardo da Vinci, Italian Renaissance artist, scientist, and inventor. Among his more memorable paintings was "The Last Supper" (1498) and the "Mona Lisa" (1503). [d. 5/2/1519]

1892 Birth of Corrie Ten Boom, Dutch evangelical and devotional author. She wrote of her experiences in a Nazi concentration camp, having been sent there for hiding Jews in her home during World War II. Her story was made into the 1971 film, "The Hiding Place." [d. 4/15/1983]

The Last Passage

1632 Death of George Calvert, about 52, the Lord Baltimore who planned the colony of Maryland as a refuge for English Roman Catholics. (b. ca. 1580)

1889 Death of Joseph de Veuster, 49, Belgian Catholic missionary priest to Hawaii. Known as Father Damien, he joined the Picpus Fathers at 20, and asked to be sent to minister to the lepers of Molokai Island. He contracted the disease in 1885, but continued to work there until he died. Father Damien's story was made famous by Robert Louis Stevenson. (b. 1/3/1840)

1910 Death of Henry Baker, 75, English civil engineer and hymnwriter. The son of an Anglican clergyman, Henry was encouraged by John B. Dykes to gain a musical education – as a result of which he composed QUEBEC ("Jesus, Thou Joy of Loving Hearts" and/or "'Take Up Your Cross,' the Savior Said"). (b. 1835)

Words for the Soul

1746 Colonial American missionary to the New England Indians David Brainerd cried out in his journal: *'My soul longed for more spirituality; and it was my burden that I could do no more for God. Oh, my barrenness in my daily affliction and heavy load! Oh, how precious is time, and how it pains me to see it slide away, while I do so little to any good purpose. Oh, that God would make me more fruitful and spiritual.'*

1851 Scottish children's novelist George MacDonald wrote in a letter to his father: *'I firmly believe people have hitherto been a great deal too much taken up about doctrine and far too little about practice. The word doctrine, as used in the Bible, means "teaching of duty" not "theory".... We are far too anxious to be definite, & have finished, well-polished, sharpedged systems.... I am neither Arminian nor Calvinist – to no system could I subscribe.'*

1958 In one of his *Letters to an American Lady*, British literary scholar and Christian apologist C. S. Lewis admitted: *'I had been a Christian for many years before I really believed in the forgiveness of sins, or more strictly, before my theoretical belief became a reality for me.'*

IN GOD'S WORD... OT: Joshua 11:1–12:24 ~ NT: Luke 17:11-37 ~ Psalms 84:1-12 ~ Proverbs 13:5-6

April 16

Highlights in History

556 Pelagius I was consecrated as pope, though originally named in 555. He served until 561, and rebuilt Rome after its war with the Ostrogoths under King Totila. Many Western bishops, especially in Gaul (France), opposed him.

1521 German Reformer Martin Luther first arrived at the Diet of Worms. This most celebrated of a long series of Imperial diets held in this German community convened from Jan. 27th through May 25th. It was here that Luther defended his doctrines before the Emperor Charles V, stating his final refusal to recant his doctrines at the session held on April 18th. Luther's teachings were afterward condemned by the Edict of Worms, issued May 25th.

1922 The first sermon preached from an airplane by radio was delivered by Belvin W. Maynard. Known as the "Flying Parson," Maynard was an ordained Baptist minister who broadcast his radio messages from a Fokker airplane. Listeners were asked to donate to the Veterans Mountain Camp, in Tupper Lake, NY.

1967 The "National Catholic Reporter," an independent American Catholic periodical, made public the formerly secret reports of the Papal Commission on Birth Control, revealing that a majority of the commission favored liberalization of the church's stand.

Notable Birthdays

1819 Birth of Edward A. Washburn, American Episcopal clergyman and writer. He was a member of the American branch of the Evangelical Alliance, and also served on the N. T. revision committee of the *English Revised Version* (EV/ERV). Among Washburn's published works: *Epochs in Church History* (1883). [d. 2/2/1881]

1851 Birth of William H. Hubbard, American Presbyterian clergyman and editor. He was pastor of First Presbyterian Church in Auburn, NY, and also edited and published two journals for the Presbyterian Church: "The Assembly Herald" (1894-1898) and "The Gospel Message" (1903-1905). [d. 1/31/1913]

1927 Birth of Bavarian (German) Catholic churchman Joseph Alois Ratzinger. He was ordained 1951, and made a cardinal by Paul VI in 1977. On April 19, 2005, following the death of John Paul II, Ratzinger was elected the 265th leader of the Roman Catholic Church, and took the name, "Pope Benedict XVI."

The Last Passage

1829 Death of Carl Gotthelf Gläser, 44, German composer. First trained in music by his father, he completed his musical studies in Leipzig. He afterward taught violin, voice, piano and choral music in Barmen, but is best remembered today for composing the hymn tune AZMON ("O For a Thousand Tongues to Sing") (b. 5/4/1784)

1879 Death of Bernadette Soubirous, 35, French Catholic visionary. As a 14-year-old, she experienced 18 visions of the Virgin Mary in a grotto (water-cave) at Lourdes (1858). Canonized in 1933, she was the subject of the 1943 Oscar-winning "Song of Bernadette." (b. 1/7/1844)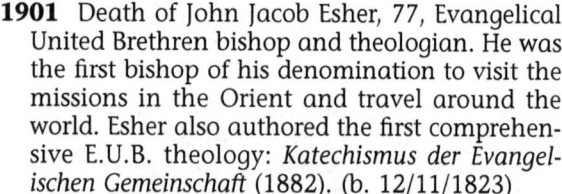

1901 Death of John Jacob Esher, 77, Evangelical United Brethren bishop and theologian. He was the first bishop of his denomination to visit the missions in the Orient and travel around the world. Esher also authored the first comprehensive E.U.B. theology: *Katechismus der Evangelischen Gemeinschaft* (1882). (b. 12/11/1823)

Words for the Soul

1772 Anglican clergyman John Newton testified in a letter: 'Though I rest and live upon the truths of the Gospel, they seldom impress me with warm and lively joy.... However, I think there is a scriptural distinction between faith and feeling, grace and comfort.... The degree of the one is not often the just measure of the other.'

IN GOD'S WORD... OT: Joshua 13:1–14:15 ~ NT: Luke 18:1-17 ~ Psalms 85:1-13 ~ Proverbs 13:7-8

April 17

Highlights in History

1492 Spain's King Ferdinand and Queen Isabella give Christopher Columbus a commission to seek a westward ocean passage to Asia. Though he was also interested in wealth, he saw himself as a new and true "christopher" (Christ-bearer) who would carry Christ across the ocean to people who had never heard the gospel.

1640 Reorus Torkillus, the first American Lutheran clergyman, arrived at Fort Christina (Wilmington), Delaware. He came over from Sweden on the *Kalmar Nyckel* with Governor Peter Hollander Ridder. Unfortunately, Torkillus died of the plague only three years later (1643).

Notable Birthdays

1772 Birth of American Presbyterian clergyman, theologian and educator Archibald Alexander. Appointed the first professor at Princeton Seminary, he remained there 40 years (1812-51), during which time he taught over 1,800 candidates for the ministry. [d. 10/22/1851]

1842 Birth of Charles Henry Parkhurst, American Presbyterian clergyman and social reformer. In addition to being pastor of the Madison Square Church (1880-1918), he also served as president of the Society for Prevention of Crime (1892), which helped defeat the Tammany Hall Democratic organization, and led to a reform in the administration of New York City. [d. 9/8/1933]

The Last Passage

1529 Death of Louis de Berquin, 39, French reformer and, because of his outspoken nature, the first Protestant martyr in France. (b. 6/1490)

1680 Death of St. Kateri (Catherine) Tekakwitha (Tegakwitha/Tegakouita), 24, Christianized Algonquian (Mohawk) Indian and Catholic religious. Known as the "Lily of the Mohawks," she was baptized in 1676 by Jesuit missionaries. She enrolled in 1678 in the Confraternity of the Holy Family, but took ill and died two years later. In 1932 she became the first North American Indian ever proposed for canonization as a saint. (b. ca. 1656)

1923 Death of Daniel S. Tuttle, 86, American Episcopal prelate. He served as missionary bishop of Montana (1869-86), and as Bishop of Missouri and presiding Episcopal bishop (1903-23). (b. 1/26/1837)

Words for the Soul

1646 Exiled Scottish clergyman Samuel Rutherford clarified in a letter:  'The saints are not Christ, there is no misjudging in him, there is much in us; and a doubt it is if we shall have fully one heart till we enjoy one heaven.'

1776 English founder of Methodism John Wesley assured in a letter: 'You have now such faith as is necessary for your living unto God. As yet you are not called to die. When you are, you shall have faith for this also. Today improve the faith you have, and trust God with tomorrow.'

1833 English statesman and historian Thomas B. Macaulay declared: 'The whole history of Christianity proves that she has little indeed to fear from persecution as a foe, but much to fear from persecution as an ally.'

1844 Scottish clergyman and biographer Andrew Bonar concluded in his journal: 'I have been coming to the conclusion for some time past that I have been of far less use in any manner than I used formerly to hope. I see now that there is nothing which another cannot carry on exactly as I have done, and probably with much more success.'

1960 Swedish Christian and Secretary General of the United Nations Dag Hammarskjöld penned in his *Markings*: 'Forgiveness breaks the chain of causality because he who "forgives" you – out of love – takes upon himself the consequences of what you have done. Forgiveness, therefore, always entails a sacrifice.'

IN GOD'S WORD... OT: Joshua 15:1-63 ~ NT: Luke 18:18-43 ~ Psalms 86:1-17 ~ Proverbs 13:9-10

ALMANAC OF THE CHRISTIAN FAITH

אייר IYYAR ניסן NISAN

~ April 18 ~

Highlights in History

1521 Two days after his arrival at the Diet of Worms — the most celebrated of the long series of Imperial diets held in this German community — Martin Luther defended his doctrines, ending with a refusal to recant his teachings: *"Hier stehe ich; ich kann nicht anders. Gott mir helfen. Amen."* (*"Here I stand, I can do no more...."*). When negotiations over the next few days failed to reach any compromise, Luther was condemned.

1874 The remains of David Livingstone were interred in London's Westminster Abbey. He had died a year earlier (May 1, 1873) in what is now northern Zambia. His body was afterward brought back to England, as his epitaph reads, "-by faithful hands over land and sea." Livingstone's tombstone adds: "For thirty years his life was spent in an unwearied effort to evangelize the native races, to explore the undiscovered secrets, and abolish the slave trade."

1909 In a ceremony held at St. Peter's in Rome, Joan of Arc (1412-1431) was beatified. Her efforts in France's military struggle against England had been driven by visions of Michael the Archangel and of the saints Catherine and Margaret.

Notable Birthdays

1829 Birth of Mother Mary Baptist Russell, Irish-born American Catholic religious. She entered the Sisters of Mercy convent in 1848, and in 1854 was named superior of eight sisters and novices and sent to establish the order in San Francisco. In 1857 she opened St. Mary's Hospital in San Francisco, the first Catholic hospital on the Pacific coast. [d. 8/6/1898]

1857 Birth of Clarence Darrow, American lawyer. Though an advocate for labor, Darrow's fame endures today as the defense attorney who opposed William Jennings Bryan in 1925 at the famous "Scopes Monkey Trial," in Dayton, Tennessee. [d. 3/13/1938]

1882 Birth of George Stark Schuler, hymn composer: SCHULER ("Out in the Highways and Byways of Life"). [d. 10/30/1973]

1916 Birth of Freda Schimpf, American missions pioneer. She was co-founder (along with her husband Gordon Lindsay) of Christ for the Nations, 1948.

The Last Passage

1743 Death of James Blair, 88, Scottish-born Episcopal clergyman and educator. He was founder and first president (1693-1743) of the College of William and Mary (VA). He was one of the few colonial commissaries to warmly welcome English revivalist George Whitefield. The pastor of Bruton Parish Church, Williamsburg (1710-43), Blair's most popular writing was a series of 117 discourses (5 vols.) on *Our Divine Saviour's Sermon on the Mount* (1722). (b. ca. 1655)

1928 Death of Walter H. R. Elliott, 86, Detroit-born Catholic priest, educator, editor and author. He was founder (1896) of "The Missionary," official organ of the Catholic Missionary Union. Elliott co-founded Apostolic Mission House in Washington, for training missionaries. He is also remembered for his *Life of Father Hecker* (1891). (b. 1/6/1842)

Words for the Soul

1862 Scottish clergyman and biographer Andrew Bonar remarked in his journal: *'Have been enjoying the thought that every drop in the well of life is given to us. O what a possession! Everything in the Mediator is something I can claim. O that I had a heart to take more every day!'*

1930 American linguistic pioneer Frank Laubach, while a Congregational missionary in the Philippines, declared in a letter: *'When I have tasted a thrill in fellowship with God, the thrill of filth repels me, for I know its power to drag me from God. And after an hour of close friendship with God, my soul feels clean as new fallen snow.'*

IN GOD'S WORD... OT: Joshua 16:1–18:28 ~ NT: Luke 19:1-27 ~ Psalms 87:1-7 ~ Proverbs 13:11

איר ALMANAC OF THE CHRISTIAN FAITH ניסן
IYYAR   NISAN

April 19

Highlights in History

526 Justinian I was crowned Roman Emperor in Constantinople's magnificent cathedral, the Santa Sophia. Attempting to restore political and religious unity in the eastern and western empires, he ruthlessly attacked paganism and heretics and created the Code of Justinian, which would be the basis of Italian legislation for nearly a millennium.

1529 At the Diet of Speyer (Germany), in a document addressed to Catholic Archduke Ferdinand, six princes and fourteen cities representing Lutheranism lodged a "protest" which defended freedom of conscience and the right of minorities: "In matters concerning God's honor and the salvation of souls each one must for himself stand before God and give account." Henceforward, German Lutherans were known as "Protestants."

1941 Robert F. Wagner, Sr. introduced a resolution in the U.S. Senate stating that U.S. policy favor the "restoration of the Jews in Palestine." The resolution was supported by 68 Senators.

Notable Birthdays

1823 Birth of Anna Laetitia Waring, a Welsh Quaker-turned-Anglican humanitarian who authored a number of hymns, including: "In Heavenly Love Abiding." [d. 5/10/1910]

1836 Birth of A[doniram] J[udson] Gordon, American Baptist clergyman, educator and hymn composer: GORDON ("My Jesus, I Love Thee"); CLARENDON ("In Tenderness He Sought Me"); "I Shall See the King in His Beauty." Gordon served Boston churches and was active in missionary work, founding the Boston Missionary Training School (now Gordon Divinity School). [d. 2/2/1895]

1870 Birth of Jay T. Stocking, American Congregational clergyman. Born in Lisbon, N.Y., he is remembered today as author of the hymn, "O Master Workman of the Race." [d. 1/27/1936]

The Last Passage

1560 Death of Philip Melanchthon (Philipp Schwarzerd), 63, German theologian and educator. An associate of Martin Luther, he composed theological treatises and creeds for the  emerging Lutheran Church, and originated the first systematic theology of the Protestant Reformation. As a peacemaker, he called for Lutherans and Zwinglians to put aside differences for the sake of the Reformation. (b. 2/16/1497)

1870 Death of William Henry Havergal, 77, Anglican clergyman. The father of Frances Ridley Havergal, he spent much of his active life writing and publishing church music. Havergal is remembered for improving the singing of psalms in his church, and for composing the hymn tunes EVAN ("Oh, For a Faith that Will Not Shrink") and WINCHESTER NEW ("Ride On, Ride On in Majesty"). (b. 1/18/1793)

Words for the Soul

1853 Scottish clergyman and biographer Andrew Bonar, 42, remarked in his journal: 'Very few need me or are benefited by me. But this is my comfort, "I will love Him." Christ  cares for me and will keep me to the end.'

1930 American Congregational missionary, Frank Laubach, explained in a letter: 'Fellowship with God is like a delicate little plant, for a long nurturing is the price of having it, while it vanishes in a second of time, as soon as we try to seat some other unworthy affection beside Him.'

1951 British literary scholar and Christian apologist C. S. Lewis reasoned in a letter: 'I think that if God forgives us we must forgive ourselves. Otherwise it is almost like setting up ourselves as a higher tribunal than Him.'

IN GOD'S WORD... OT: Joshua 19:1–20:9 ~ NT: Luke 19:28-48 ~ Psalms 88:1-18 ~ Proverbs 13:12-14

אייר IYYAR   ALMANAC OF THE CHRISTIAN FAITH   ניסן NISAN

April 20

Highlights in History

1441 During the Council of Florence (1438-45), Pope Eugenius IV issued the bull "Etsi non dubitemus," which asserted the superiority of the Pope over the Councils.

1785 The first statewide Methodist conference was held in Louisburg, NC with Superintendents Francis Asbury and Thomas Coke present. It was attended by 9,063 representatives from 31 pastoral circuits in Virginia and both Carolinas.

1855 St. John Nepomuk Church (the first Bohemian church in the United States) opened in St. Louis. Its first pastor, the Rev. Henry Lipowsky, was a former lieutenant in the Austrian Army.

1952 Three years after the 1949 revolution that established the People's Republic of China, evangelical Christian leader Watchman Nee, 48, was arrested by the Chinese government, and imprisoned for "corrupt business practices." Nee spent nearly all his last 20 years in prison, and died a martyr of the Communists.

1987 A two-week convention (4/20-5/3) opened in Columbus, OH, at which was organized the Evangelical Lutheran Church in America (ELCA), the largest Lutheran denomination in the U.S. It represented the merger of three former Lutheran bodies – the Lutheran Church in America (2.9 million members), the American Lutheran Church (2.3 million members) and the Association of Evangelical Lutheran Churches (110,000 members). The new denomination was officially born on January 1, 1988.

Notable Birthdays

1494 Birth of Johann Agricola, German religious reformer. A onetime disciple of Luther, he later became a proponent of Antinomianism, thus opposing Lutheranism. During his later years, Agricola was made general superintendent and court preacher for the Elector of Brandenburg (1540-1566). [d. 9/22/1566]

1594 Birth of Mattäus A. von Löwenstein, German hymn writer. Born in Silesia, his best known hymn was "Lord of Our Life and God of Our Salvation." [d. 4/11/1648]

1745 Birth of Nathanael Emmons, American Congregational clergyman and theologian. He pastored the Franklin (Massachusetts) Church for 52 years (1773-1825)! Though outwardly opposed to Arminianism, he nevertheless asserted that man's part in regeneration is active, not passive. He was one of the fathers of the Mass. Missionary Society. [d. 9/23/1840]

The Last Passage

1759 Death of George F. Handel, 74, German-born English composer. Of his religious compositions, the most famous are the oratorios. His best known, "Messiah," debuted in 1742. Handel also composed the hymn tunes CHRISTMAS ("While Shepherds Watched Their Flocks By Night"); ANTIOCH ("Joy to the World!"); and MACCABEUS ("Thine Be the Glory, Risen, Conquering Son"). (b. 2/23/1685)

1921 Death of George F. Wright, 83, American Congregational clergyman, educator and geologist. He taught theology at Oberlin Seminary (1881-92), and also edited "Bibliotheca Sacra" (1884-1921). Wright was devoted to establishing a harmony between geological discoveries and the Bible. (b. 1/22/1838)

Words for the Soul

1767 John Wesley, founder of Methodism, noted in a letter: 'Certainly the point we should always have in view is, what is best for eternity?'

1933 English mystic Evelyn Underhill reminded in a letter: 'When we receive absolution it is God Who enters our soul and frees us from the crippling fetters of sin and gives us a fresh start. It is for us to co-operate and use the fresh start.'

IN GOD'S WORD... OT: Joshua 21:1–22:20 ~ NT: Luke 20:1-26 ~ Psalms 89:1-13 ~ Proverbs 13:15-16

April 21

IYYAR — ALMANAC OF THE CHRISTIAN FAITH — NISAN

Highlights in History

1632 At a conference at Dordrecht, Holland, the Dutch Mennonites adopted a Confession of Faith. It consisted of eighteen articles, heavily weighted with Scriptural proof texts. The document afterward came to be known as the Dordrecht Confession of Faith.

1649 The Maryland Provincial Assembly adopted the "Act Concerning Religion." It was written by Lord Cecil Calvert, following the execution of England's Charles I. Designed to remove any suspicion by the British Commonwealth that the Maryland Colony was intolerant of Protestants, the document declared: *"noe person or persons whatsoever . . . professing to believe in Jesus Christ, shall from henceforth bee any waies troubled, Molested or discountenanced for or in any respect of his or her religion nor in the free exercise thereof."*

1782 In California, two missions were established by the Franciscan Order – one at San Buenaventura (founded by Father Junipero Serra), and one at Santa Barbara (sponsored by California Governor Felipe de Neve). Both missions were situated about halfway between San Diego to the south and San Francisco to the north.

Notable Birthdays

1783 Birth of Reginald Heber, Anglican prelate. He served as Bishop of Calcutta (1822-26), and authored the hymns, "Holy, Holy, Holy"; "From Greenland's Icy Mountains"; "The Son of God Goes Forth to War"; and "God That Madest Earth and Heaven." [d. 4/3/1826]

1783 Birth of Samuel J. Mills, American Congregational clergyman. During his brief life of 35 years, he was a prime mover in the founding of the first foreign mission societies in North America. He helped establish the American Board of Commissioners for Foreign Missions (ABCFM) in 1810, and the American Bible Society in 1816. [d. 6/16/1818]

The Last Passage

1109 Death of Italian-born St. Anselm, 76, Archbishop of Canterbury from 1093. Considered the first of the Scholastic philosophers and one of the most important thinkers between St. Augustine and Thomas Aquinas, Anselm originated the ontological argument for the existence of God — that faith is the precondition of knowledge (*"Credo ut intelligam"*) — and the "satisfaction theory" of the atonement: *"No one but one who is God-man can make the satisfaction by which man is saved."* His most important work was *Cur deus homo* (*Why God Became Man*). After Thomas Becket, Anselm is probably the most famous of all the Archbishops of Canterbury. (b. 1033)

1142 Death of Peter Abelard (Abailard), 63, French Scholastic philosopher, theologian and educator. Known by some because of his romance with the nun Heloise, as a theologian he used the method of logical analysis to arrive at religious realities. He also wrote the hymn "O What Their Joy and Their Glory Must Be." (b. 1079)

Words for the Soul

1777 English Methodist pastor John Fletcher encouraged in a letter: *'Absolute resignation to the Divine Will baffles a thousand temptations, and confidence in our Saviour carries us sweetly through a thousand trials. God fill us abundantly with both!'*

1828 English churchman John Henry Newman, reflecting on the death of his sister Mary, wrote to another sister, Harriett: *'It is so difficult to realize what one believes, and to make these trials, as they are intended, real blessings.'*

1867 Scottish clergyman Andrew Bonar confided in his journal: *'I have been asking calm faith, burning love, deep peace, bright hope, true compassion for souls, glowing zeal for God's glory.'*

IN GOD'S WORD... OT: Joshua 22:21–23:16 ~ NT: Luke 20:27-47 ~ Psalms 89:14-37 ~ Proverbs 13:17-19

April 22

Highlights in History

1418 The Council of Constance closed, ending the "Great Schism," during which time the Catholic Church had three popes! The Council deposed all three, Martin V was elected, and the Schism ended. The most inglorious moment of the Council was its hasty condemnation of Bohemian preacher (and forerunner of Protestantism), John Hus, which led to his being burned at the stake in 1415 for heresy.

1864 A bronze two-cent piece was imprinted with the words "In God We Trust," making it the first American coin  to carry the motto. The purpose of the motto served to remind the Union that the resolution of the American Civil War was in God's hands.

1960 In Minneapolis, the 3-day constitutional convention of The American Lutheran Church opened, representing a merger of 3 major Lutheran denominations – the Evangelical Lutheran Church (of Norwegian heritage), the American Lutheran Church (of German background) and the United Evangelical Lutheran Church (founded in 1896 by Danish immigrants). It gave the American Lutheran Church a resulting inclusive membership of 2.5 million.

Notable Birthdays

1711 Birth of Eleazar Wheelock, American Colonial Congregational clergyman and missionary to Native Americans. He later became the founder and first president of Dartmouth College, 1770-1779. [d. 4/29/1779]

1759 Birth of James Freeman, American Unitarian clergyman. He was the first minister in the U.S. to avow the name of Unitarian, and through his means the first Episcopal church established in New England (King's Chapel) became the first Unitarian church in the U.S. [d. 11/14/1835]

1801 Birth of Elijah C. Bridgman, Congregational missionary and Orientalist. He was the first American missionary to China, sent there in 1829 by ABCFM. He worked with David Abeel, and was active in Bible translation and revision. He also helped organize Society for the Diffusion of Useful Knowledge and the Medical Missionary Society. [d. 11/2/1861]

The Last Passage

1853 Death of William Freeman Lloyd, 61, English Sunday School worker and hymnwriter: "My Times are In Thy Hand." For many years he was a secretary of the British Sunday School Union. (b. 12/22/1791)

1986 Death of Mircea Eliade, 79, Romanian-born American theologian and religious historian. Noted for his research into symbolic religious language, Eliade taught at the University of Chicago,  and wrote several key works on comparative religion: *The Myth of the Eternal Return* (1954); *Patterns of Comparative Religion* (1958); and *A History of Religious Ideas* (1977-85). (b. 3/9/1907)

Words for the Soul

1776 English-born pioneer American Methodist bishop Francis Asbury confessed in his journal: *'I found Christ in me the hope of glory; but felt a pleasing, painful sensation of spiritual hunger and thirst for more of God.'*

1907 English mystic Evelyn Underhill explained in a letter: *'The material world, although an illusion in the form in which it appears to us, is an illusion which has strict relations to reality. It is the dim shadow of the thought of God. This... veil through which... we must see the Divine received its final sanction in the Incarnation of Christ.'*

1996 In his last year of life, Dutch Catholic diarist Henri Nouwen wrote in his "Sabbatical Journal": *'I realize how important it is not only to live well but also to remember well what we have lived.'*

IN GOD'S WORD... OT: Joshua 24:1-33 ~ NT: Luke 21:1-28 ~ Psalms 89:38-52 ~ Proverbs 13:20-23

April 23

IYYAR — NISAN

ALMANAC OF THE CHRISTIAN FAITH

Highlights in History

1619 At the Synod of Dort, five sets of articles were passed which asserted: (1) unconditional election; (2) a limited atonement; (3) the total depravity of man; (4) the irresistibility of grace; and (5) the final perseverance of the saints. With a bias against the Remonstrants (Arminians) from the start, this "TULIP" summary of Calvinist doctrine was primarily a foregone conclusion of the Synod.

1964 The Presbyterian Church in the United States opened its general assembly in Montreat, NC. At this assembly, the PCUS enacted a change in the Book of Church Order permitting the ordination of women as deacons, elders, and ministers.

1968 The Evangelical United Brethren Church officially joined with the much larger Methodist Church. The merger formed the United Methodist Church, the largest Methodist group in the world and America's second-largest Protestant denomination (after the Southern Baptist Convention).

Notable Birthdays

1586 Birth of Martin Rinkart, German Lutheran clergyman and hymn author. Born in Eilenberg, his best known hymns included "Now Thank We All Our God" and "Let All Men Praise the Lord." [d. 12/8/1649]

1720 Birth of Elijah ben Solomon. Lithuanian Hebrew scholar and religious writer. The author of over 70 treatises, he is called the greatest authority on classical Judaism in modern times. [d. 10/17/1797]

1828 Birth of F[enton] J. A. Hort, English New Testament scholar. He was professor of divinity at Cambridge (1878-91), and co-edited with B. F. Westcott a critical edition of the Greek New Testament. Their work, spanning 30 years, was first published in 1881. [d. 11/30/1892]

The Last Passage

1702 Death of Margaret Fell, 88, wife of Thomas Fell, vice-chancellor of the Duchy. She was converted to Quakerism by George Fox in 1652. Following her husband's death in 1658, she married Fox in 1669. Her estate, Swarthmore Hall, afterward became the center of Quaker activity. (b. 1614)

1888 Death of Edward Hopper, 72, American Presbyterian clergyman. In addition to his pastorates, Hopper also worked in New York City's harbor area, ministering to seamen from around the world. It is fitting, then, that Hopper left the Church with his moving hymn: "Jesus, Savior, Pilot Me." (b. 2/17/1816)

1982 Death of W. Cameron Townsend, 85, American missionary pioneer. He founded Wycliffe Bible Translators in 1935. The nonprofit group has since rendered the New Testament into more than 130 native languages. (b. 7/9/1896)

Words for the Soul

1623 Scottish pastor Samuel Rutherford wrote in a letter: *'The weightiest end of the cross of Christ, that is laid upon you, lieth upon your strong Saviour.'*

1779 Anglican clergyman and hymnwriter John Newton affirmed in a letter: *'"What Thou wilt, when Thou wilt, how Thou wilt." I had rather speak these three sentences from my heart in my mother tongue than be master of all the languages in Europe.'*

1840 Scottish clergyman and biographer Andrew Bonar remarked in his journal: *'There are many parts of work and duty for which I am quite unfit, and God therefore wisely uses other instruments: it also keeps me humble.'*

1951 Addressing Christian priorities, British literary scholar and Christian apologist C. S. Lewis advised in a letter: *'Put first things first and we get second things thrown in: put second things first and we lost both first and second things.'*

IN GOD'S WORD... OT: Judges 1:1–2:9 ~ NT: Luke 21:29–22:13 ~ Psalms 90:1–91:16 ~ Proverbs 13:24-25

ALMANAC OF THE CHRISTIAN FAITH

~ April 24 ~

Highlights in History

387 Abandoning a youth filled with profligacy, Augustine of Hippo (354-430) was baptized into the Christian faith. The 33-year-old had been a teacher of rhetoric and pagan philosophies at some of the Roman Empire's finest schools, but after being greatly influenced by his mother, Monica, and by the famous bishop Ambrose, Augustine turned to Christianity.

1870 The Vatican I Ecumenical Council issued the proclamation, "Dei filius," which decreed that God could be known by human thought and reason. Vatican I, presided over by Pius IX, was attended by 800 bishops worldwide.

1886 The Rev. Augustine Tolton became the first African-American priest assigned to work in the United States. He was ordained at the College of Propaganda in Rome, and later opened a mission in Quincy, Illinois, in the diocese of Springfield.

1922 The first Catholic nuns in a cloistered community were the Magdalen Sisters at the Convent of the Good Shepherd, founded on this date in Baltimore, Maryland.

1944 In deciding the legal case "United States v. Ballard," the U.S. Supreme Court upheld the general principle that "the truth of religious claims is not for secular authority to determine." The justices ruled that no governmental agency can determine "the truth or falsity of the beliefs or doctrines" of anyone — even if the beliefs "may seem incredible, if not preposterous, to most people."

Notable Birthdays

218 Birth of Mani, the Persian religious leader who once influenced St. Augustine. In AD 242 he founded Manichaeism — a dualistic religion which emphasized an eternal conflict between Light (goodness) and Darkness (evil). [d. 276]

1576 Birth of Vincent de Paul, Catholic clergyman and philanthropist. He devoted himself to the poor, and founded the missionary order of Lazarists (1625), and the Sisters of Charity (1632). Vincent helped to ransom over 1,000 Christian slaves in northern Africa. He was canonized in 1737 by Clement XII. [d. 9/27/1660]

The Last Passage

1866 Death of Hermann C. K. F. Hupfeld, 70, German Old Testament scholar. He was the first to distinguish between the two sources – the "P[riestly Editor]" and the "E[lohist]" – both of which utilize the same word "Elohim" for the divine name in Genesis. (b. 3/31/1796)

1875 Death of Samuel P. Tregelles, 62, English Presbyterian Bible text scholar. In 1838 he began assembling a new critical text of the Greek New Testament, to replace the older, less reliable "textus receptus" (on which the KJV was based). Tregelles' completed critical text of the entire Greek N.T. was published in 1870. (b. 1/30/1813)

1920 Death of Eliza E. Hewitt, 68, Philadelphia Presbyterian Sunday School teacher and author of a number of hymns, including: "More About Jesus I Would Know"; "There is Sunshine in My Soul Today"; and "Sing the Wondrous Love of Jesus." (b. 6/28/1851)

Words for the Soul

1739 English revivalist George Whitefield resolved in a letter: *'God grant I may behave so, that when I suffer, it may not be for my own imprudencies, but for righteousness sake, and then I am sure the Spirit of Christ and of glory will rest upon my soul.'*

1859 English Baptist clergyman Charles H. Spurgeon declared in a sermon: *'When Christ shall come he will make short work of that which is so long a labor to his church.... Tremble, sinner, for the advent of Christ must be thy destruction though it shall be the church's Joy and comfort.'*

IN GOD'S WORD... OT: Judges 2:10-3:31 ~ NT: Luke 22:14-34 ~ Psalms 92:1-93:5 ~ Proverbs 14:1-2

~ April 25 ~

Highlights in History

[ca. A.D. 30] This is the latest day in the spring on which Easter can fall. (Easter is determined by the Paschal full moon, and can occur as early as March 21st.) Easter has fallen on April 25th only three times during the last three centuries: 1734, 1886 and 1943. It will not be celebrated on this date again until the year 2038.

1940 In New York, the first Passover seder to be shown on television was held in the studio of the National Broadcasting Co., which had been set up as a dining room. Rabbi Saul Bezalel Applebaum of Central Synagogue, New York City, led seven participants in the seder, The program was produced with the cooperation of the United Jewish Layman's Committee.

1956 The Methodist General Conference opened in Minneapolis. During its sessions, the denomination granted full clergy rights to women.

1967 Janie McGaughey of the Presbyterian Church in the United States (PCUS) became the first woman in her denomination to be elected moderator of a presbytery (Atlanta).

Notable Birthdays

1214 Birth of King Louis IX of France (ruled 1226-70). The leader of two crusades, he was taken prisoner in 1250 and held four years during the Seventh Crusade. Known for his sanctity and humility, "St. Louis" planned another Crusade in 1267, embarked in 1270, but died of dysentery before reaching Tunis. [d. 8/25/1270]

1792 Birth of John Keble, Anglican clergyman and poet. A leader in the Oxford Movement (1833-45), which sought to purify Anglicanism, Keble was one of the Tractarians who did *not* ultimately convert to Roman Catholicism. Remembered today more for his poetry, it was Keble who penned the hymn, "Sun of My Soul, Thou Savior Dear." [d. 3/29/1866]

1819 Birth of Charles John Ellicott, Anglican prelate. He served as Bishop of Gloucester and Bristol (1863-1905). In addition to writing commentaries on both the Old and New Testaments, Ellicott was also chairman of the New Testament revision committee (1870-81), leading to the publication of the 1881 *English Revised Version* of the Bible. [d. 10/15/1905]

The Last Passage

1778 Death of James Relly, 56, English reformer. At one time a co-worker of George Whitefield, Relly broke away because of his belief in salvation for all, and preached Universalism in London. His convert, John Murray, formed the American Universalist Church. (b. ca. 1722)

1800 Death of William Cowper, 68, English poet. He suffered periods of great mental instability, and yet was able to produce numerous spiritual poems, including "Olney Hymns" (1779) with John Newton. In particular, he authored the hymns, "There Is a Fountain" and "Oh for a Closer Walk with God." (b. 11/26/1731)

Words for the Soul

1682 William Penn wrote in his famous "Frame of Government" for his new American colony of Pennsylvania: *'The origination and descent of all human power is from God... first, to terrify evil doers; secondly, to cherish those who do well.... Government seems to me to be a part of religion itself – a thing sacred in its institutions and ends....'*

1783 In the spirit of 1 Timothy 5:18, English founder of Methodism John Wesley reminded one of his congregations: *'To labour, and pay for our labour, is not right before God or man.'*

1879 Scottish clergyman and biographer Andrew Bonar remarked in his journal: *'When the Lord is with us in His fulness, it is the ocean sweeping away all that is unholy, and bringing in all that is pure. Every craving of the soul is met and filled.'*

IN GOD'S WORD...   OT: Judges 4:1–5:31 ~ NT: Luke 22:35-53 ~ Psalms 94:1-23 ~ Proverbs 14:3-4

April 26

Highlights in History

1655 In New Amsterdam (later New York), the Dutch West India Company ruled that Jews must be allowed to stay in the colony.

1832 A Conference in Independence, Missouri recognized Joseph Smith as president of the high priesthood of the Mormon Church.

1847 The Lutheran Church Missouri Synod met for the first time in Chicago.

1992 Worshipers celebrated the first Russian Orthodox Easter in Moscow in 74 years. (A Bolshevik decree of January 23, 1918, declaring a formal separation of church and state, was followed by the suppression and desecration of thousands of Russian Orthodox churches.)

Notable Birthdays

1806 Birth of Alexander Duff, Presbyterian missionary. He was the first member of the Church of Scotland to be sent to India. Duff helped establish several schools, including the University of Calcutta. He was also founder of the "Calcutta Review." [d. 2/12/1878]

1834 Birth of Horatio R. Palmer, American Baptist choralist and hymnwriter.  He settled in Chicago, following the Civil War, where he edited a monthly musical journal, "The Concordia," and conducted music festivals and conventions with great success. From 1877-1891 he was dean of the summer school of music at Chautauqua, NY. Palmer is probably best remembered today for penning the words and music to the hymn, "Yield Not to Temptation." [d. 11/15/1907]

1868 Birth of Walter Lowrie, American Episcopal clergyman and church history scholar. Teaching himself Danish at age 65, his researches contributed significantly to the discovery and influence of Kierkegaard among American theologians after World War II. [d. 8/13/1959]

1916 Birth of Morris L. West, Australian novelist. He is remembered for his best-selling *The Devil's Advocate* (1959) and *The Shoes of the Fisherman* (1963; later filmed in 1968). Both stories reflected West's Catholic background as a Christian Brother. [d. 10/9/1999]

The Last Passage

757 Death of Pope Stephen II. Following the death of Pope Zacharias in 752, another man named Stephen was in fact elected pope, but died three days later, before he could be enthroned (a singular event in all papal history!). Some label him Stephen II, which would make this, his successor, more aptly named Pope Stephen III.

865 Death of Paschasius Radbertus, ca. 80, French Benedictine theologian. His best-known work — a treatise for instructing Saxon monks — contained the first doctrinal treatment of the transubstantiation theory regarding the Eucharist. (b. ca. 785)

Words for the Soul

1518 German reformer Martin Luther stated in his disputation of Heidelberg: 'Grace is given to heal the spiritually sick, not to decorate spiritual heroes.'

1745 Colonial American missionary to the New England Indians, David Brainerd lamented in his journal: 'There are many with whom I can talk about religion; but alas! I find few with whom I can talk religion itself.'

1924 British Catholic essayist and critic G. K. Chesterton wrote in the "Illustrated London News": 'The  nineteenth century decided to have no religious authority. The twentieth century seems disposed to have any religious authority.'

1956 British literary scholar and Christian apologist C. S. Lewis wrote in one of his **Letters to An American Lady**: 'One of the many reasons for wishing to be a better Christian is that, if one were, one's prayers for others might be more effectual.'

IN GOD'S WORD... OT: Judges 6:1-40 ~ NT: Luke 22:54–23:12 ~ Psalms 95:1–96:13 ~ Proverbs 14:5-6

IYYAR ALMANAC OF THE CHRISTIAN FAITH NISAN

~ April 27 ~

Highlights in History

1537 The First Genevan Catechism was published, which imposed itself on the inhabitants of Geneva, Switzerland. Based on John Calvin's Institutes, the document was compiled either by Calvin himself or by fellow French Swiss Reformer, Guillaume Farel (1489-1565).

1667 Blind, bitter and poor, Puritan poet John Milton sold the copyright for "Paradise Lost" for 5 pounds (with the contingency of three further installments of the same sum, if additional editions were needed). Milton's work would eventually come to influence English thought and language nearly as much as the King James Bible and the plays of Shakespeare.

1875 Archbishop John McCloskey of New York, appointed to the Roman Curia by Pope Pius IX, was invested as the first American cardinal in St. Patrick's Cathedral, in New York City.

Notable Birthdays

1824 Birth of Anne Ross Cousin, Scottish musician and linguist. Raised in the Anglican Church, she later became a Presbyterian. A highly respected sacred poet, she was once called "a Scottish Christina Rossetti, with a more pronounced theology." "The Sands of Time are Sinking" is her most enduring hymn. [d. 12/6/1906]

1880 Birth of William Allen Harper, American educator. He taught religious education at Vanderbilt University (1932-42). Harper's writings include: *The New Church for the New Time* (1917); *Personal Religious Beliefs* (1937), and *The Minister of Education* (1939). [d. 5/11/1942]

The Last Passage

1124 Death of Alexander I, 46, King of Scotland. The fourth son of Malcolm Canmore, he succeeded his brother Edgar as king of Scotland in 1107. Alexander fought to free the Church in Scotland from subservience to Canterbury and York. He also endowed the abbeys of Scone and Incholm, and was notably charitable toward church institutions. (b. ca. 1078)

1775 Death of Peter Böhler, 62, the German Moravian missionary who introduced John Wesley to the joys of personal spiritual conversion and self-surrendering Christian faith. Sent by Count Zinzendorf to the American colonies in 1737, Böhler and Wesley's paths first crossed in London. Böhler's positive, assuring faith became a permanent mark upon Wesley's maturing theology, and it has characterized historic Methodism ever since. (b. 12/31/1712)

1859 Death of American Episcopal prelate George Washington Doane, 59. As Bishop of New Jersey (1832-59), he was a leader of the High Church party. Doane also penned several enduring hymns: "Softly Now the Light of Day," and "Fling Out the Banner! Let it Float." (b. 5/27/1799)

Words for the Soul

1740 English revivalist George Whitefield wrote in a letter: *'Oh that I had a thousand lives! My dear Lord Jesus should have them all. I long to be out of the body, that I may love and serve him as I would: but I must suffer before I can reign with him.'*

1784 Anglican-Methodist pastor John Fletcher resolved in a letter: *'To wait in deep resignation... and to leave to Him the times and the seasons, is what I am chiefly called to do. I take care in the meanwhile of falling into either ditch — I mean into speculation which is careless of action, or into the activity which is devoid of spirituality. I would not have a lamp without oil, and I could not have oil without a lamp.'*

1855 Scottish clergyman and biographer Andrew Bonar remarked in his journal: *'I lay at Christ's feet, trying to look up in His face and get from Him counsel, strength, knowledge of His will, all I need. I discover that very small distractions become very great temptations.'*

IN GOD'S WORD...   OT: Judges 7:1–8:17 ~ NT: Luke 23:13-43 ~ Psalms 97:1–98:9 ~ Proverbs 14:7-8

ALMANAC OF THE CHRISTIAN FAITH

IYYAR — NISAN

~ April 28 ~

Highlights in History

1552 The revolt of the princes against Charles V led to the suspension of the Council of Trent. Under the austere and violently anti-Protestant Pope Paul IV (1555-59), there was no hope of its reassembly, and it didn't meet again until ten years later, under Paul's more tolerant successor, Pius IV.

1829 In England, the Duke of Norfolk took his seat in the House of Lords, the first Catholic peer to be seated under the Emancipation Act. Earlier, the Roman Catholic Relief Bill had passed, allowing Roman Catholics to sit and vote in Parliament, giving them the right of suffrage and making them eligible for nearly all military, civil and corporate offices in England.

1840 The first meeting of the American Baptist Anti-Slavery Convention took place in NY City, with about 100 in attendance, and lasted two days. Its organization led to the acceleration of Baptist abolitionism in American history during the antebellum years.

1872 English devotional writer Frances Ridley Havergal (1836-1879) penned the words to the popular hymn, "Lord, Speak to Me That I May Speak." (The daughter of Anglican clergyman William Havergal, Frances's collected poems were first published in 1884.)

1930 In deciding the legal case "Cochran v. Board of Education," the U.S. Supreme Court upheld a Louisiana statute which provided textbooks at public expense for children attending public or parochial schools. The Court held that the children and the state were beneficiaries of the appropriations, with incidental secondary benefit going to the schools.

1960 Leaders of the 100th General Assembly of the Southern Presbyterian Church (PCUS) passed a resolution declaring that sexual relations within marriage, without intentions of procreation, were not sinful.

1968 The first Armenian Orthodox cathedral in America, the Cathedral of St. Vartan in New York City was consecrated by His Holiness Vasken I, Supreme Patriarch and Catholicos of All Armenians. The Most Reverend Torkom Manoogian became the first upon whom the Catholicos personally bestowed the rank of archbishop in the United States.

Notable Birthdays

1839 Birth of Vernon J. Charlesworth, English clergyman and hymnwriter. He was headmaster of Charles Spurgeon's Stockwell Orphanage, but is better remembered as author of the hymn: "A Shelter in the Time of Storm." [d. 1/5/1915]

1874 Birth of Susan Strachan, American missions pioneer. In 1921, along with her husband Harry, she co-founded the Latin America Mission (originally called the Latin America Evangelization Campaign). [d. 12/6/1950]

The Last Passage

1841 Death of St. Peter Chanel, 38, French missionary to the South Seas. Joining the Marist Fathers in 1831, he was sent as superior of their first Oceania mission. He won friends among the natives, but when a local chieftain's son asked to be baptized, Father Chanel was martyred, though the mission continued to flourish. Chanel was canonized in 1954 by Pius XII. (b. 7/12/1803)

1973 Death of Jacques Maritain, 90, French Thomist philosopher. He was a representative of liberal apologist school of Catholic thought. He also authored numerous influential works, including *Art and Scholasticism* and *True Humanism*. (b. 11/18/1882)

Words for the Soul

1521 German reformer Martin Luther remarked in a letter: 'The authority of Scripture is greater than the comprehension of the whole of man's reason.'

IN GOD'S WORD...   OT: Judges 8:18–9:21 ~ NT: Luke 23:44–24:12 ~ Psalms 99:1-9 ~ Proverbs 14:9-10

April 29

Highlights in History

1607 The first Anglican church in the American colonies was established at Cape Henry, near Jamestown, Virginia. It was started when Captain Gabriel Archer, Christopher Newport, George Percy, Bartholomew Gosnold, Edward Maria Wingfield, and 25 other English colonists set up a cross at Cape Henry. (The first Anglican parish was started at Jamestown on June 21.)

1920 Chinese college student Watchman Nee, 16, was converted to a personal Christian faith, under the influence of Dora Yu, a Chinese Methodist missionary from Shanghai. Born Nee Shu-zu, he was later called Duo-Sheng ("sound of bells") – hence, "Watchman." Embarking on a life of ministry and devotional writing, Nee founded the Little Flock Movement. He preached in China and abroad, reaching the height of his influence in 1948. Arrested in 1952, Nee died 20 years later, only a few months after his release from prison – a martyr of the Chinese communists.

1945 The Navigators trace their origin to this date when founder Dawson Trotman began teaching Bible memorization to American servicemen in San Pedro, CA. The interdenominational organization formally incorporated in 1943, and is headquartered today in Colorado Springs, CO.

Notable Birthdays

1751 Birth of John Rippon, English clergyman and sacred music publisher. Rippon was one of the most popular and influential of the dissenting (i.e., non-Anglican) ministers of his time. He is better remembered today, however, for his contributions to Christian hymnody, specifically, "How Firm a Foundation" and "All Hail the Power of Jesus' Name" (adapt.). [d. 12/17/1836]

1795 Birth of Lorrin Andrews, American Congregational missionary to Hawaii (1827-1840). Sent by ABCFM, Andrews did research into native folklore, and later translated a part of the Bible into Hawaiian. [d. 9/29/1868]

1834 Birth of Joseph H. Gilmore, American Baptist clergyman and educator. Ordained in 1862, he pastored for five years, then in 1868 began teaching Hebrew at the University of Rochester, NY, where he remained until his retirement in 1911. Today, Gilmore is remembered as author of the hymn, "He Leadeth Me, O Blessed Thought." [d. 7/23/1918]

The Last Passage

1380 Catherine of Siena (Caterina Benincasa), Dominican tertiary and greatest of the 14th century Italian mystics, died at 33. She had influenced Pope Gregory XI in 1376  to return the papacy to Rome from Avignon, France. Catherine died from illness brought on by her efforts to unite rival factions within her divided church. (b. 3/25/1347)

1749 Death of German-born clergyman John Philip Boehm, 63. He founded the German Reformed Church in Pennsylvania, and laid the basis for a strong Reformed Christian presence in the American middle colonies. (b. 11/1683)

1980 Death of Millar Burrows, 90, American clergyman, biblical and archaeological scholar. He taught Biblical theology at Yale Divinity School (1934-58), and was an authority on the Dead Sea Scrolls. Burrows published *Outline of Biblical Theology* (1946); *The Dead Sea Scrolls* (1955); and *More Light on the Dead Sea Scrolls* (1958). (b. 10/26/1889)

Words for the Soul

1853 Scottish clergyman and children's novelist George MacDonald, 29, wrote in a letter to his father: *'The Epistles are very different from the Apostles' preaching. The Gospels form the sum & substance of the apostles' teaching, and preaching. The Epistles are mostly written for a peculiar end and aim & are not intended as expositions of the central truth in general forms.'*

April 30

Highlights in History

418 Roman Emperor Honorius (395-423) issued an imperial decree denouncing the teachings of Pelagius. Pelagianism taught that human nature is able to take the initial and fundamental steps toward salvation by its own efforts, apart from empowerment by divine grace. Historically, this was an ascetic lay movement inspired by Pelagius who was born in Britain but taught in Rome in the late 4th and early 5th centuries. (Soon after Honorius's decree of condemnation, Pelagius disappeared from history, and his subsequent fate remains unknown.)

1794 The Rev. John Hurt resigned from his army chaplaincy. Holding the honor as the very first chaplain of the U.S. Army, he served during the American Revolution as chaplain of the 6th Virginia Infantry, beginning Oct. 1, 1776. He became brigade chaplain on Aug. 18, 1778, and served as such to the close of the war.

Notable Birthdays

1623 Birth of François Xavier Laval-Montmorency, French-born Jesuit prelate. Appointed bishop of Quebec, he thereby became the first Catholic Bishop of Canada (1674-88). Laval-Montmorency also founded Quebec Seminary, the first Canadian Catholic university. [d. 5/6/1708]

1771 Birth of Hosea Ballou, American Universalist clergyman and author. He was the founder and leader of New England Universalism, and wrote many Universalist hymns, including "When God Descends with Man to Dwell." He also authored *Treatise on the Atonement*. [d. 6/7/1852]

1816 Birth of George Bowen, American missionary to India. He was sent by ABCFM in 1847, and served the Methodist Church for 40 years (1848-88). Bowen became known as the "White Saint of India." [d. 2/5/1888]

1841 Birth of Orville J. Nave, the U.S. Armed Services chaplain who authored *Nave's Topical Bible* — a volume still in print! [d. 6/24/1917]

The Last Passage

1854 Death of James Montgomery, 82, Scottish editor and hymnwriter. When James was 12, his parents were sent as Moravian missionaries to the West Indies, where they both died. Montgomery authored over 400 hymns during his life, including "Angels From the Realms of Glory"; "Go to Dark Gethsemane"; "Prayer is the Soul's Sincere Desire"; and "Stand Up and Bless the Lord." (b. 11/4/1771)

1867 Death of Ithamar Conkey, 51, versatile and successful American Baptist (later Episcopal) musician. He served in CT and NY as a church organist, a choral director and a popular bass vocalist. Today he is still remembered for composing the hymn tune RATHBUN ("In the Cross of Christ I Glory"). (b. 5/5/1815)

Words for the Soul

1739 English revivalist George Whitefield noted in his journal: *'Our extremity is God's opportunity.'*

1771 English founder of Methodism John Wesley testified in a letter: *'Suffer all, and conquer all.'*

1944 English literary scholar J. R. R. Tolkien, in a letter to his son Christopher (a British soldier during WW II), declared: *'Evil labors with vast power and perpetual success – in vain: preparing always only the soil for unexpected good to sprout in. So it is in general, and so it is in our own lives.'*

1948 English Catholic psychiatrist Caryll Houselander explained in a letter: *'The ideal of our perfection that we set up, and often go through torture to achieve, may not be God's idea of how He wants us to be at all... and what seems like a failure to us may really be something bringing us closer to His plan.... Sooner or later we certainly will be just what He wants us to be.'*

IN GOD'S WORD... OT: Judges 11:1–12:15 ~ NT: John 1:1-28 ~ Psalms 101:1-8 ~ Proverbs 14:13-14

APRIL INDEX

A

ABBEYS
 Incholm (Scotland) 4/27
 Scone (Scotland) 4/27
ABCFM (American Board of Commissioners for Foreign Missions) 4/21, 4/22, 4/29, 4/30
Abeel, David 4/22
Abelard (Abailard), Peter
 (b. 1079) d. 4/21/1142
Abolition 4/4
AFRICAN-AMERICANS
 Abolition of Slavery 4/14, 4/28
 African Methodist Episcopal Church 4/9, 4/10
 Allen, Richard 4/9, 4/10
 American Baptist Anti-Slavery Convention 4/28
 King, Martin Luther, Jr. 4/3
 Seymour, William J. 4/9
 Slave Trade 4/18
 Tolton, Augustine 4/1, 4/24
Agricola, Johann
 b. 4/20/1494 [d. 9/22/1566]
Albret, Henry d' 4/11
Alexander, Archibald
 b. 4/17/1772 [d. 10/22/1851]
Alexander I, Scottish King (1107-24) 4/27
Allen, Richard 4/9, 4/10
Ambrose, St. 4/24
 (b. ca. 340) d. 4/4/397
American Baptist Anti-Slavery Convention 4/28
American Bible Society 4/21
American Board of Commissioners for Foreign Missions (ABCFM) 4/21
American Unitarian Association 4/7
Anacletus II, Antipope (1130-1138) 4/4
Andrews, Lorrin
 b. 4/29/1795 [d. 9/29/1868]
Anselm, St.
 (b. 1033) d. 4/21/1109
Antinomianism 4/20
ANTIPOPES
 Anacletus II (1130-38) 4/4
 Clement VII (1378-94) 4/8
 Felix V (1439-49) 4/7
Apocrypha 4/8

Apostolic Faith Mission 4/14
Apostolic Fathers 4/13
Apostolic Mission House 4/18
Applebaum, Saul Bezalel 4/25
Aquinas, Thomas 4/21
Archer, Gabriel 4/29
Arnold of Brescia 4/4
Asbury, Francis 4/20
 See also QUOTATIONS
Asylum for the Relief of Persons Deprived of the Use of their Reason 4/14
Augustine of Hippo, St. 4/4, 4/21, 4/24
Avignon Papacy 4/29
Avvakum
 (b. 12/15/1620) d. 4/14/1682
Azusa Street Revival 4/9, 4/14

B

Bach, Johann Sebastian 4/15
Baker, Henry
 (b. 1835) d. 4/15/1910
Balfour, (Lord) Arthur J. 4/1
Ballou, Hosea
 b. 4/30/1771 [d. 6/7/1852]
Barbarossa, German Emperor Frederick I (1152-90) 4/3
Barth, Karl 4/6
BATTLES, FAMOUS
 Battle of Kappel (1531) 4/2
Baxter, Richard 4/6
Becket, Thomas 4/21
Benedict X, Pope (1058-59) 4/3
Benedict XVI, Pope (2005-) 4/16
Benincasa, Caterina
 (b. 3/25/1347) d. 4/29/1380
Berquin, Louis de
 (b. 6/1490) d. 4/17/1529
Beza, Theodore.
 See QUOTATIONS
BIBLE VERSIONS
 Burmese 4/12
 English Revised Version (1885) 4/13, 4/16, 4/25
 Greek New Testament 4/23
 Hawaiian 4/29
 King James Bible (1611) 4/24, 4/27
 Latin Vulgate 4/8
 Marathi (India) 4/5
 Textus Receptus 4/24

Bird, Frederic Mayer
 (b. 6/28/1838) d. 4/2/1908
Blair, James
 (b. ca. 1655) d. 4/18/1743
Boardman, George Dana, Sr. 4/9
Boehm, John Philip
 (b. 11/1683) d. 4/29/1749
Böhler, Peter. See QUOTATIONS
 (b. 12/31/1712) d. 4/27/1775
Boleslaw II, Polish King 4/11
Bolshevism, Russian 4/26
Bonar, Andrew.
 See QUOTATIONS
Bonhoeffer, Dietrich.
 See also QUOTATIONS
 (b. 2/4/1906) d. 4/9/1945
BOOKS / PUBLICATIONS
 95 Theses (by Martin Luther) 4/4
 Art and Scholasticism and True Humanism 4/28
 Ben Hur (1880) 4/10
 Book of Common Prayer (American edition) 4/4
 Book of Common Prayer (BCP) 4/1
 Cur deus homo (Why God Became Man) 4/21
 David Brainerd's Diary 4/1
 Dictionary of Religion and Ethics (1921) 4/3
 Epochs in Church History (1883) 4/16
 Ethics 4/9
 Every-Day Religion (1886) 4/4
 Frame of Government (1682) 4/25
 Grammar of New Testament Greek: Vols. I-II (1906-1 4/7
 Greek New Testament 4/24
 High Priesthood and Sacrifice (1908) 4/11
 History of Religious Ideas, A (1977-85) 4/22
 History of the Puritans... (1732-38) 4/4
 Hymns and Sacred Poetry (1739) 4/3
 Hymns For Use of the Evangelical Lutheran Church (4/2
 Institutes, Calvin's 4/27
 Katechismus der Evangelischen Gemeinschaft (1882) 4/16
 Letters and Papers from Prison 4/9
 Letters to An American Lady 4/2, 4/26
 Letters to an American Lady 4/15
 Life of Father Hecker (1891) 4/18
 Life of Madame Guyon (1847) 4/2
 Markings 4/17
 More Light on the Dead Sea Scrolls (1958) 4/29

 Nave's Topical Bible 4/30
 Olney Hymns (1779) 4/25
 Orthodoxy: Its Truths and Errors (1866) 4/4
 Our Divine Saviour's Sermon on the Mount (1722) 4/18
 Outline of Biblical Theology (1946) 4/29
 Paradise Lost (1667) 4/27
 Patterns of Comparative Religion (1958) 4/22
 Personal Religious Beliefs (1937) 4/27
 Sabbatical Journal (1998) 4/22
 Secular Journal 4/11
 Sermons on the Lord's Prayer (1888) 4/4
 The Cost of Discipleship 4/9
 The Dead Sea Scrolls (1955) 4/29
 The Devil's Advocate (1959) 4/26
 The Divine Imperative (1932) 4/6
 The Man Without a Country (1863) 4/3
 The Mediator (1927) 4/6
 The Minister of Education (1939) 4/27
 The Myth of the Eternal Return (1954) 4/22
 The New Church for the New Time (1917) 4/27
 The Perfect Life (1873) 4/7
 The Phenomenon of Man (1955) 4/10
 The Puritans (1859-61) 4/11
 The Puritans and Queen Elizabeth (1875) 4/11
 The Reason of Life (1911) 4/11
 The Shoes of the Fisherman (1963) 4/26
 The Story of the Other Wise Man (1896) 4/10
 The Vocabulary of the Greek Testament, Parts I and 4/7
 Treatise on the Atonement 4/30
 When Bad Things Happen to Good People (1981) 4/3
Book of Church Order 4/23
Booth, Charles Brandon
 (b. 12/26/1887) d. 4/14/1975
Booth, William 4/14
 b. 4/10/1829 [d. 8/20/1912]
Borden, William Whiting
 (b. 1887) d. 4/9/1913
Borthwick, Jane Laurie
 b. 4/9/1813 [d. 9/7/1897]
Bourne, Hugh
 b. 4/3/1772 [d. 10/11/1852]
Bowen, George
 b. 4/30/1816 [d. 2/5/1888]
Brahms, Johannes
 (b. 5/7/1833) d. 4/3/1897

APRIL INDEX

Brainerd, David 4/1.
See also QUOTATIONS
Brandenburg, Elector of 4/20
Brent, Charles Henry
b. 4/9/1862 [d. 3/27/1929]
Bridgman, Elijah C.
b. 4/22/1801 [d. 11/2/1861]
British Sunday School Union 4/22
Brothers, William H. F.
b. 4/7/1887 [d. 7/21/1979]
Brunner, Heinrich Emil
(b. 12/23/1889) d. 4/6/1966
Bryan, William Jennings 4/18
Bucer, Martin 4/1
Burrows, Millar
(b. 10/26/1889) d. 4/29/1980
Byzantine Empire 4/12

C

CALENDARS
  Gregorian (New Style) 4/10
  Julian (Old Style) 4/10
Calvert, Cecil 4/21
Calvert, George
(b. ca. 1580) d. 4/15/1632
Calvin, John 4/12.
See QUOTATIONS
Camerarius, Joachim
b. 4/12/1500 [d. 4/17/1574]
Canmore, Malcolm 4/27
Cannon, Harriet Starr
(b. 5/7/1823) d. 4/5/1896
CANTERBURY ARCHBISHOPS
  Anselm (1093-1109)
  Becket, Thomas (1162-70) 4/21
  Chichele, Henry (1414-43) 4/12
Carey, William 4/1
Catherine, St. (d. ca. 305) 4/18
Catherine de Medici
b. 4/13/1519 [d. 1/5/1589]
Catherine of Siena
(b. 3/25/1347) d. 4/29/1380
Catholic Missionary Union 4/18
Chanel, Peter
(b. 7/12/1803) d. 4/28/1841
Channing, William Ellery
b. 4/7/1780 [d. 10/2/1842[
Chardin, Pierre Teilhard de
(b. 5/1/1881) d. 4/10/1955
Charismatic Healing Movement 4/1
Charlemagne (Charles the Great)
b. 4/2/742 [d. 1/28/814]
Charlesworth, Vernon J.
b. 4/28/1839 [d. 1/5/1915]

Charles I, English King (1600-49) 4/21
Charles II, English King (1649-85) 4/14
Charles IX, French King (1550-74) 4/13
Charles V, Holy Roman Emperor (1519-56) 4/16, 4/28
Chautauqua Assembly, Lake 4/14, 4/26
Chesterton, G. K.
See QUOTATIONS
Chichele, Henry
(b. ca. 1362) d. 4/12/1443
Christotokos (Christbearer) 4/10
CHURCHES
  American (Congregational) Church (Germany) 4/4
  Bruton Parish Church (VA) 4/18
  Cathedral of St. Vartan (NYC) 4/28
  Cathedral of the Holy Trinity (NYC) 4/1
  Ebenezer Chapel (Bristol, England) 4/11
  Federal Street Church (Boston) 4/7
  First Presbyterian Church (Auburn, NY) 4/16
  Franklin Church (MA) 4/20
  King's Chapel (Boston, MA) 4/22
  Madison Square Church (NYC) 4/17
  Santa Sophia (Constantinople) 4/19
  St. John Nepomuk Church (St. Louis) 4/20
  St. Patrick's Cathedral (NYC) 4/27
  St. Peter's-in-the-Fields (Oxford) 4/6
  St. Peter's Basilica (Rome) 4/11, 4/18
  St. Thomas Lutheran Church (Leipzig) 4/15
  Westminster Abbey (London) 4/18
  Zürich Cathedral (Switzerland) 4/2
Ciocchi del Monte, Giammaria.
See Julius III, Pope (1550-1555)
Clarke, James Freeman
b. 4/4/1810 [d. 6/8/1888]
Clement III, Pope (1187-91) 4/3
Clement VII, Antipope (1378-94) 4/8
Clement XII, Pope (1730-40) 4/24
Code of Justinian 4/19
Coke, Thomas 4/1, 4/20
COLLEGES / UNIVERSITIES
  All Souls (Oxford) 4/12
  Bowdoin College (ME) 4/2
  College of William and Mary (VA) 4/18
  Dartmouth College (NH) 4/22
  Harvard University (MA) 4/1, 4/11
  Hebrew University (Jerusalem) 4/1
  St. Bernard's (Oxford) 4/12

  University of Calcutta (India) 4/26
  University of Chicago 4/22
  University of North Carolina 4/7
  University of Rochester (NY) 4/29
  University of the South (TN) 4/11
  Vanderbilt University (TN) 4/27
College of Propaganda 4/24
Columbus, Christopher 4/17
Communism, Chinese 4/20, 4/29
Conkey, Ithamar
(b. 5/5/1815) d. 4/30/1867
CONVENTS
  Convent of the Good Shepherd (MD) 4/24
Cook, Glenn A. 4/15
COUNCILS, CHURCH
  Council of Constance (1414-18) 4/6, 4/22
  Council of Florence (1438-45) 4/20
  Council of Trent (1545-63) 4/8, 4/28
  Second Lateran Council (1139) 4/4
  Synod of Dort (1618-19) 4/23
  Vatican I (1869-70) 4/24
Cousin, Anne Ross
b. 4/27/1824 [d. 12/6/1906]
Cowman, Charles 4/13
Cowman, Lettie 4/13
Cowper, William
(b. 11/26/1731) d. 4/25/1800
Cranmer, Thomas 4/1
CREEDS / CONFESSIONS
  Augsburg Confession (1530) 4/12
  Dordrecht Confession of Faith (1632) 4/21
  Genevan Catechism, First (1537) 4/27
CRUSADES
  Fourth Crusade (1202-04) 4/12
  Seventh Crusade (1249) 4/6, 4/25
  Third Crusade (1189-92) 4/6

D

Damien, Father 4/15
Darrow, Clarence
b. 4/18/1857 [d. 3/13/1938]
Dead Sea Scrolls 4/29
Declaration of Breda 4/14
DECREES, CHURCH COUNCIL
  "Dei filius" (1870) 4/24
  "Haec sancta" (1415) 4/6
DENOMINATIONS, CHRISTIAN
  African Methodist Episcopal Church 4/9, 4/10
  American Lutheran Church 4/20, 4/22
  Anglicanism 4/4, 4/25
  Anglicanism, American 4/5
  Anglicanism, Scottish 4/27
  Armenian Orthodoxy 4/28

  Assemblies of God 4/2, 4/8, 4/12
  Association of Evangelical Lutheran Churches 4/20
  Baptists, American 4/12, 4/26, 4/30
  Calvinists, Hard-Shell 4/4
  Catholicism, American 4/1
  Christian Reformed Church 4/8
  Church of Scotland 4/26, 4/27
  Congregationalism 4/18
  Congregationalism, American 4/2, 4/4, 4/5, 4/7, 4/11, 4/19, 4/20, 4/21
  Congregationalism, American Colonial 4/22
  Dissenters, English 4/29
  Episcopalianism, American 4/16, 4/17, 4/26, 4/27
  Episcopalianism, Canadian 4/9
  Episcopal Church 4/2, 4/7, 4/11, 4/30
  Evangelical Lutheran Church 4/2, 4/22
  Evangelical Lutheran Church in America 4/20
  Evangelical Reformed Church, German 4/12
  Evangelical United Brethren 4/16, 4/23
  German Reformed Church 4/3, 4/29
  Greek Orthodoxy 4/1, 4/14
  Huguenots, French 4/13
  Independents, English 4/4
  Lutheranism, German 4/12, 4/19
  Lutheran Church in America 4/20
  Lutheran Church Missouri Synod 4/26
  Mennonites, Dutch 4/21
  Methodism 4/30
  Methodism, American 4/25
  Methodism, Chinese 4/29
  Methodist Church 4/22, 4/23, 4/27
  Methodist Episcopal Church 4/9
  Moravians 4/30
  Moravians, European 4/6
  Moravians, German 4/27
  Nonconformity, English 4/4, 4/11
  Old Catholic Church in America 4/7
  Pentecostalism 4/12, 4/14, 4/15
    "Oneness" 4/15
    Trinitarians 4/15
  Pentecostalism, American 4/9
  Plymouth Brethren 4/1, 4/11
  Presbyterianism, American 4/12, 4/16, 4/17, 4/23
  Presbyterianism, Scottish 4/27
  Presbyterians, English 4/24
  Presbyterian Church in the United States 4/23, 4/25
  Primitive Methodist Church 4/3
  Protestant Episcopal Church of America 4/4
  Puritanism, American 4/5
  Puritanism, English 4/4, 4/5
  Quakerism 4/14, 4/23

Quakerism, Welsh 4/19
Religious Society of Friends 4/14
Roman Catholicism 4/22, 4/25
Roman Catholicism, English 4/15
Russian Orthodoxy 4/2, 4/10, 4/14, 4/26
Russian Orthodox Church in America 4/10
Salvation Army 4/10, 4/14
Southern Baptist Convention 4/23
Southern Presbyterian Church 4/28
Swiss Reformed Church 4/7
Unitas Fratrum (Moravians) 4/6
United Evangelical Lutheran Church 4/22
United Methodist Church 4/23
Zwinglianism 4/19
Dialectical Theology 4/6
Diet of Speyer 4/19
Diet of Worms 4/16, 4/18
Disputation of Heidelberg 4/26
Doane, George Washington
(b. 5/27/1799) d. 4/27/1859
Doctors of the Early Church 4/4
Dow, Lorenzo 4/3
DRAMAS / PLAYS
"Henry V" 4/12
Duff, Alexander
b. 4/26/1806 [d. 2/12/1878]
Duo-Sheng 4/29
Dürer, Albrecht
(5/21/1471) d. 4/6/1528
Dutch West India Company 4/26
Du Bose, William Porcher
b. 4/11/1836 [d. 8/18/1918] 4/11
Dykes, John B. 4/15

E

"E[lohist]" 4/24
Easter 4/25
Edgar, King of Scotland (1097-1107) 4/27
Edict of Nantes (1598) 4/11, 4/13
Edict of Worms (1521) 4/16
Edwards, Jonathan 4/1
Eisenhower, Dwight D. 4/5
Eliade, Mircea
(b. 3/9/1907) d. 4/22/1986
Elijah ben Solomon
b. 4/23/1720 [d. 10/17/1797]
Ellicott, Charles John
b. 4/25/1819 [d. 10/15/1905]
Elliot, Jim.
See QUOTATIONS

Elliott, Walter H. R.
(b. 1/6/1842) d. 4/18/1928
Emmons, Nathanael
b. 4/20/1745 [d. 9/23/1840]
Esher, John Jacob
(b. 12/11/1823) d. 4/16/1901
Eucharist 4/26
Eugenius IV, Pope (1431-47) 4/20
Evangelical Alliance 4/16
Everett, Edward
b. 4/11/1794 [d. 1/15/1865]
Evolution 4/10
Ewart, Frank 4/15

F

Faith and Order World Conference (1927) 4/9
Farel, Guillaume 4/27
Father Damien 4/15
Felix V, Antipope (1439-49) 4/7
Fell, Margaret
(b. 1614) d. 4/23/1702
Fell, Thomas 4/23
Ferdinand, German Archduke 4/19
Ferdinand, Spanish King (1452-1516) 4/17
FILMS / MOVIES
Song of Bernadette (1943) 4/16
The Hiding Place (1971) 4/15
The Shoes of the Fisherman (1968) 4/26
FIRSTS
Abolitionist society 4/14
African-American bishop in the U.S. 4/10
African-American priest in the U.S. 4/24
African Methodist Episcopal Church convention 4/9
American Lutheran clergyman 4/17
American missionary to Bombay 4/8
Anglican bishop of New Zealand 4/5
Anglican church in the American colonies 4/29
Anglican missionary bishop of Melanesia (1861) 4/1
Anglican parish in the American colonies 4/29
Archbishop of New York 4/3
Armenian Orthodox cathedral in America 4/28
Bishop of the African Methodist Episcopal Church 4/10
Bishop of the AME Church 4/9
Black American to be ordained a Roman Catholic priest 4/1
Black denomination established in the U.S. 4/10

Bohemian church in the U.S. 4/20
Canadian Catholic university 4/30
Catholic archdiocese in the U.S. 4/6
Catholic Bishop of Canada 4/30
Catholic diocese in the U.S. 4/6
Catholic hospital on the Pacific coast 4/18
Catholic peer seated in English Parliament 4/28
Chaplain of the U.S. Army 4/30
Church of Scotland missionary to India 4/26
Doctrinal treatment of transubstantiation 4/26
Dutch Reformed minister to come to America 4/7
E.U.B. bishop to travel to missions around the world 4/16
Episcopal missionary bishop to the Philippine Isla 4/9
French pope 4/2
Governor of the Puritans in Massachusetts 4/5
Jewish congregation organized in America 4/8
North American Indian canonized 4/17
Official liturgy printed in the English language 4/1
Passover seder to be shown on TV 4/25
Patriarch of the Russian Church since 1700 4/7
Permanent Jewish house of worship in America 4/8
President of Dartmouth College 4/22
President of the College of William and Mary 4/18
Privately operated hospital for the insane 4/14
Professor at Princeton Seminary 4/17
Protestant martyr in France 4/17
Scholastic philosopher 4/21
Sermon preached from an airplane by radio 4/16
Statewide Methodist conference 4/20
Sunday School Union 4/5
Systematic theology of the Protestant Reformation 4/19
U.S. coins to carry "In God We Trust" 4/22
U.S. minister to claim to be Unitarian 4/22
Unitarian church in the U.S. 4/22
Woman moderator of a Presbytery 4/25
Woman superior of an Anglican monastic women's ord 4/5
Fletcher, John.
See QUOTATIONS
Fox, George 4/23
Francis I, French King (1515-47) 4/11

Frank, Anne.
See also QUOTATIONS
Frederick I (Barbarossa), German Emperor (1152-90) 4/3
Freeman, James
b. 4/22/1759 [d. 11/14/1835]
Friends Asylum for the Insane 4/14
Friends Hospital 4/14

G

Genevan Catechism, First (1537) 4/27
Gestapo, German 4/9
Gettysburg Address 4/11
Gettysburg National Cemetery 4/11
Gilmore, Joseph H.
b. 4/29/1834 [d. 7/23/1918]
Gläser, Carl Gotthelf
(b. 5/4/1784) d. 4/16/1829
Gordon, A[doniram] J[udson] 4/19/1836 [d. 2/2/1895]
Gosnold, Bartholomew 4/29
Graham, Billy 4/2
Great [Papal] Schism (1378-1417) 4/8, 4/22
Gregory XI, Pope (1370-78) 4/29
Gregory XIII, Pope (1572-85) (b/ca.7/1502) d. 4/10/1585
Guyon, Madame (Jean Marie Bouvier de la Mothe) 4/2

H

"House of Salvation" 4/5
Hale, Edward Everett
b. 4/3/1822 [d. 6/10/1909]
Hall, Gordon
b. 4/8/1784 [d. 3/20/1826]
Ham, Mordecai F[owler]
b. 4/2/1877 [d. 11/1/1961]
Hammarskjöld, Dag.
See QUOTATIONS
Handel, George Frideric 4/13
(b. 2/23/1685) d. 4/20/1759
Harper, William Allen
b. 4/27/1880 [d. 5/11/1942]
Hasseltine-Judson, Ann 4/12
Havergal, Frances Ridley 4/19, 4/28
Havergal, William Henry 4/28
(b. 1/18/1793) d. 4/19/1870
Heber, Reginald
b. 4/21/1783 [d. 4/3/1826]

APRIL INDEX

Hecker, Isaac 4/18
Heloise 4/21
Hennepin, Louis 4/11
Henry II, French King (1519-59) 4/13
Henry IV (of Navarre), French King (1589-1610) 4/11, 4/13
Herbert, George
   b. 4/3/1593 [d. 2/1632]
HERESIES, CHRISTIAN
   Antinomianism 4/20
   Nestorianism 4/10
   Pelagianism 4/30
HERETICS
   Nestorius 4/10
   Pelagius 4/30
Hewitt, Eliza E.
   (b. 6/28/1851) d. 4/24/1920
Hill, Rowland
   (b. 8/23/1744) d. 4/11/1833
Hitler, Adolf 4/1
Honorius, Roman Emperor (395-423) 4/30
Hopkins, Samuel
   b. 4/1/1807 [d. 2/10/1887]
Hopper, Edward
   (b. 2/17/1816) d. 4/23/1888
Hort, F[enton] J. A.
   b. 4/23/1828 [d. 11/30/1892]
Hubbard, William H.
   b. 4/16/1851 [d. 1/31/1913]
Hughes, John J. 4/3
Hunt, [William] Holman
   b. 4/2/1827 [d. 9/7/1910]
Hupfeld, C. K. F.
   (b. 3/31/1796) d. 4/24/1866
Hurt, John 4/30
Hus, John 4/22
Hutchinson, Anne 4/5
HYMNS
   "'Take Up Your Cross,' the Savior Said" 4/15
   "All Hail the Power of Jesus' Name" 4/29
   "Angels From the Realms of Glory" 4/30
   "A Shelter in the Time of Storm" 4/28
   "Be Still, My Soul" 4/9
   "Break Thou the Bread of Life" 4/14
   "Cast Thy Burden on the Lord" 4/11
   "Come, Holy Spirit, Dove Divine" 4/12
   "Day is Dying in the West" 4/14
   "Deus creator omnium" 4/4
   "Fling Out the Banner! Let it Float" 4/27
   "From Greenland's Icy Mountains" 4/21
   "God Calling Yet! Shall I Not Hear" 4/3
   "God Himself is With Us" 4/3
   "God That Madest Earth and Heaven" 4/21
   "Go to Dark Gethsemane" 4/30
   "He Leadeth Me, O Blessed Thought" 4/29
   "Holy, Holy, Holy" 4/21
   "How Firm a Foundation" 4/29
   "In Christ There Is No East Or West" 4/6
   "In Heavenly Love Abiding" 4/19
   "In Tenderness He Sought Me" 4/19
   "In the Cross of Christ I Glory" 4/30
   "It Came Upon the Midnight Clear" 4/6
   "I Shall See the King in His Beauty" 4/19
   "Jesus, Savior, Pilot Me" 4/23
   "Jesus, Thou Joy of Loving Hearts" 4/15
   "Joyful, Joyful, We Adore Thee" 4/10
   "Joy to the World!" 4/20
   "Lead on, O King Eternal" 4/4
   "Let All Men Praise the Lord" 4/23
   "Lord, Speak to Me That I May Speak" 4/28
   "Lord of Our Life and God of Our Salvation" 4/20
   "Make Me a Blessing" 4/3
   "More About Jesus" 4/10, 4/24
   "My Jesus, I Love Thee" 4/19
   "My Times are In Thy Hand" 4/22
   "Now Thank We All Our God" 4/23
   "Oh, For a Faith that Will Not Shrink" 4/19
   "Oh for a Closer Walk with God" 4/25
   "Out in the Highways and Byways of Life" 4/3, 4/18
   "O For a Thousand Tongues to Sing" 4/16
   "O Master Workman of the Race" 4/19
   "O Sacred Head Now Wounded" 4/15
   "O What Their Joy and Their Glory Must Be" 4/21
   "Prayer is the Soul's Sincere Desire" 4/30
   "Ride On, Ride On in Majesty" 4/19
   "Sing the Wondrous Love of Jesus" 4/24
   "Softly Now the Light of Day" 4/27
   "Stand Up and Bless the Lord" 4/30
   "Sunshine in My Soul" 4/10
   "Sun of My Soul, Thou Savior Dear" 4/25
   "Tell Me the Story of Jesus" 4/10
   "There Is a Fountain" 4/25
   "There is Sunshine in My Soul Today" 4/24
   "The Son of God Goes Forth to War" 4/21
   "Thine Be the Glory, Risen, Conquering Son" 4/20
   "Veni redemptor gentium" 4/4
   "When God Descends with Man to Dwell" 4/30
   "While Shepherds Watched Their Flocks By Night" 4/20
   "Years I Spent in Vanity and Pride" 4/1
   "Yield Not to Temptation" 4/26

HYMN TUNES
   ANTIOCH 4/20
   AZMON 4/16
   BREAD OF LIFE 4/14
   CHAUTAUQUA 4/14
   CHRISTMAS 4/20
   CLARENDON 4/19
   EVAN 4/19
   FILL ME NOW 4/10
   GORDON 4/19
   MACCABEUS 4/20
   QUEBEC 4/15
   RATHBUN 4/30
   SCHULER 4/18
   ST. PETER 4/6
   STORY OF JESUS 4/10
   SUNSHINE 4/10
   SWENEY 4/10
   WINCHESTER NEW 4/19

I

"In God We Trust" 4/5, 4/22
"I Wish We'd All Been Ready" 4/8
Iakovos, Greek Orthodox Archbishop (1959-1996) 4/1
INDIANS, AMERICAN
   Algonquian Indians 4/17
   MISSIONARIES TO
      Brainerd, David 4/8, 4/15, 4/26
      Hennepin, Louis 4/11
      Jesuit missionaries 4/17
   Mohawk Indians 4/17
   Native Americans of New Jersey 4/1
   New England Indians 4/15, 4/26
   Sioux Indians 4/11
   Tekakwitha (Tegakwitha/Tegakouita, Kateri (Catheri 4/17
Ingersoll, Robert 4/10
Innocent II, Pope (1130-43) 4/4
Irresistibility of Grace 4/23
Isabella, Spanish Queen (1451-1504) 4/17

J

Jerome, St. 4/8
Jesus Movement 4/8
Joan of Arc (1412-1431) 4/18
John Paul II, Pope (1978-2005) 4/13, 4/16
JUDAISM 4/26
   Anti-Semitic Day (Germany) 4/1
   Applebaum, Saul Bezalel 4/25
   Elijah ben Solomon 4/23
   Frank, Anne 4/4
   Greatest modern authority on classical Judaism 4/23
   Hiding Jews during WWII 4/15
   Jewish Holocaust 4/4
   Kushner, Harold S. 4/3
   Restoration of Jews in Palestine 4/19
   Shearith Israel 4/8
   United Jewish Layman's Committee 4/25
Judson, Adoniram
   (b. 8/9/1788) d. 4/12/1850
Julius II, Pope (1503-13) 4/11
Justinian I, Roman Emperor (526-565) 4/19

K

Keble, John
   b. 4/25/1792 [d. 3/29/1866]
Keller, Helen 4/14
Keswick Conference 4/8
Kierkegaard, Soren 4/26
Kilbourne, Ernest A.
   (b. 9/6/1811) d. 4/13/1928
King, Martin Luther, Jr.
   See QUOTATIONS
Knox, John 4/12
Kushner, Harold Samuel
   b. 4/3/1935

L

Latin Empire 4/12
Laubach, Frank.
   See QUOTATIONS
Laval-Montmorency, François Xavier
   b. 4/30/1623 [d. 5/6/1708]
Law of Parsimony 4/10
La Salle, Robert 4/11
Lee, Edward S. 4/9
LEGAL CASES, U.S.
   Cochran v. Board of Education (1930) 4/28
   United States v. Ballard (1944) 4/24
LEGISLATION
   Act Concerning Religion 4/21
   Conventicle Act 4/5
   Declaration of Breda 4/14
   Edict of Nantes 4/13
   Edict of Worms (1521) 4/16
   Emancipation Act 4/28
   Five Mile Act 4/5
   Roman Catholic Relief Bill 4/28
Leonardo da Vinci
   b. 4/15/1452 [d. 5/2/1519]
Leo III, Pope (795-816) 4/2

Lepers of Molokai Island 4/15
Lewis, C. S.
  See QUOTATIONS
Lightfoot, J[oseph] B.
  b. 4/13/1828 [d. 12/21/1889]
Limited Atonement 4/23
Lindsay, Freda (née Schimpf) 4/1
Lindsay, Gordon
  (b. 6/18/1906) d. 4/1/1973
Lipowsky, Henry 4/20
Livingstone, David 4/18
Lloyd, William Freeman
  (b. 12/22/1791) d. 4/22/1853
London Missionary Society 4/14
Lord Baltimore 4/15
Lorenzo de Medici 4/13
Louis IX, French King (1226-70) 4/6
  b. 4/25/1214 [d. 8/25/1270]
Louis XIV, French King (1638-1715) 4/13
Lourdes 4/16
Löwenstein, Mattäus A. von
  b. 4/20/1594 [d. 4/11/1648]
Lowrie, Walter
  b. 4/26/1868 [d. 8/13/1959]
Loyola, Ignatius 4/4
Luther, Martin 4/4, 4/6, 4/16, 4/18, 4/19, 4/20.
  See also QUOTATIONS

M

Macaulay, Thomas B.
  See QUOTATIONS
MacDonald, George.
  See QUOTATIONS
Macy, Anne Sullivan
  b. 4/14/1866 [d. 10/20/1936]
Mani
  b. 4/24/218 [d. 276]
Manichaeism 4/24
Manoogian, Torkom 4/28
Margaret, St. 4/18
Margaret of Navarre
  b. 4/11/1492 [d. 12/21/1549]
Maritain, Jacques
  (b. 11/18/1882) d. 4/28/1973
Martin V, Pope (1417-31) 4/22
Martyn, Henry 4/1.
  See QUOTATIONS
MARTYRS
  Avvakum 4/14
  Bonhoeffer, Dietrich 4/9
  Chanel, Peter 4/28
  Elliot, Jim 4/6
  Frank, Anne 4/4

Nee, Watchman 4/20
Patteson, John Coleridge 4/1
Stanislaus (Stanislaw) of Cracow 4/11
Maryland Provincial Assembly 4/21
Mason, Lowell 4/14
Massachusetts Bay Colony 4/5
Massachusetts Missionary Society 4/20
Mastai-Ferretti, Giovanni Maria.
  See Pius IX, Pope (1846-78)
Mathews, Shaler 4/3
Maynard, Belvin W. 4/16
McCheyne, Robert Murray.
  See QUOTATIONS
McCloskey, John 4/27
McGaughey, Janie 4/25
Medical Missionary Society 4/22
Melanchthon, Philip[p] 4/12
  (b. 2/16/1497) d. 4/19/1560
MENTAL PROBLEMS
  Cowper, William 4/25
Merton, Thomas.
  See QUOTATIONS
Meyer, Anna (née Reinhard) 4/2
Meyer, F[rederick] B.
  b. 4/8/1847 [d. 3/28/1929]
Michaelius, Jonas 4/7
Michael the Archangel 4/18
Milligan, George 4/7
Mills, Samuel J.
  b. 4/21/1783 [d. 6/16/1818]
Milton, John 4/27
MISSIONARIES
  Boardman, George Dana, Sr. 4/9
  Borden, William Whiting 4/9
  Bowen, George 4/30
  Brainerd, David 4/1, 4/8, 4/15, 4/26
  Brent, Charles Henry 4/9
  Bridgman, Elijah C. 4/22
  Chanel, Peter 4/28
  Duff, Alexander 4/26
  Elliot, Jim 4/6
  Hall, Gordon 4/8
  Judson, Adoniram 4/12
  Kilbourne, Ernest A. 4/13
  Laubach, Frank C. 4/18, 4/19
  Lindsay, Gordon 4/1
  Patteson, John Coleridge 4/1
  Philip, John 4/14
  Reed, Mary 4/8
  Russian Orthodox 4/10
  Schaeffer, Francis A. 4/12
  Townsend, W. Cameron 4/23
  Tuttle, Daniel Sylvester 4/17
  Veuster, Joseph de 4/15

Wheelock, Eleazar 4/22
Xavier, Francis 4/7
Zwemer, Samuel M. 4/12
MISSION AGENCIES
  ABCFM 4/22, 4/29, 4/30
  China Inland Mission 4/9
  Christ for the Nations 4/18
  Latin America Evangelization Campaign 4/28
  Latin America Mission 4/28
  London Missionary Society 4/14
  Massachusetts Missionary Society 4/20
  Oriental Missionary Society 4/13
  Student Volunteer Movement 4/12
  Syrian Mission of the Presbyterian Church in the U 4/12
  Wycliffe Bible Translators 4/23
Moltmann, Jürgen
  b. 4/8/1926
MONASTERIES
  St. Agnes Monastery 4/3
Monica 4/24
Montgomery, James
  (b. 11/4/1771) d. 4/30/1854
Moody, Dwight 4/8
Moore, Jennie Evans 4/9
Moulton, James Hope
  (b. 10/11/1863) d. 4/7/1917
MOVEMENTS, CHRISTIAN
  Arminianism 4/15, 4/20, 4/23
  Calvinism 4/15
  Fundamentalism 4/2
  Little Flock Movement 4/29
  Nonconformists, English 4/11
  Pentecostalism 4/2
  Pentecostal "Oneness" 4/15
  Perfectionism 4/13
  Protestantism 4/19
  Remonstrants 4/23
  Scholasticism 4/10
  Swiss reformers 4/2
Mueller, George 4/11
Mukti Sadan ("House of Salvation") 4/5
Murray, John 4/25
MUSIC, VOCAL
  "German Requiem" (1868) 4/3
  "Messiah, The" 4/13
  "Olney Hymns" (1779) 4/25
  "The Messiah" 4/20
  "The Passion According to St. Matthew," 4/15
MYSTICS
  Catherine of Siena 4/29
  Loyola, Ignatius 4/4
  Tersteegen, Gerhard 4/3
  Underhill, Evelyn 4/8, 4/12, 4/20, 4/22

N

National Broadcasting Co. 4/25
National Conference of Unitarian Churches 4/3
National Day of Prayer 4/5
National Prayer Breakfast 4/5
Nave, Orville J.
  b. 4/30/1841 [d. 6/24/1917]
Navigators 4/29
Nazism, German 4/8, 4/9, 4/15
Neal, Daniel
  (b. 12/14/1678) d. 4/4/1743
Nee, Watchman 4/20, 4/29
Nee Shu-zu 4/29
Neo-Orthodoxy 4/6
Nepomuk, John 4/20
Nepotism 4/2
Nestorius 4/10
Neve, Felipe de 4/21
Newell, Samuel 4/8
Newell, William Reed
  (b. 5/22/1868) d. 4/1/1956
Newport, Christopher 4/29
Newton, John 4/25
New England Universalism 4/30
New York Port Society 4/13
Newman, John Henry.
  See QUOTATIONS
Newton, John.
  See QUOTATIONS
Nicholas II, Pope (1447-55) 4/7
NICKNAMES / TITLES
  Apostle of Japan 4/7
  Apostle of the Indies 4/7
  A Scottish Christina Rossetti 4/27
  Boleslaw the Cruel 4/11
  Coeur-de-Lion 4/6
  Emperor of the Romans 4/2
  Father of Christian Rock 4/8
  Flying Parson 4/16
  Lily of the Mohawks 4/17
  Lionhearted 4/6
  Patron saint of Poland 4/11
  St. Louis 4/25
  White Saint of India 4/30
Nietzsche, Friedrich 4/15
Nikon, Russian Orthodox Patriarch 4/14
Northfield Conference 4/8
Newman, John Henry.
  See QUOTATIONS
Nouwen, Henri.
  See QUOTATIONS
Noyes, John Humphrey
  (b. 9/6/1811) d. 4/13/1886

APRIL INDEX

O

Ockham's Razor 4/10
Ockham (Occam), William of
   (b. ca. 1280) d. 4/10/1347
Oglethorpe, James 4/6
Oneida Community 4/13
Ontological argument for God 4/21
ORDINATION OF WOMEN
   Methodism, American 4/25
ORGANIZATIONS, CHRISTIAN
   New York Port Society 4/13
   Society for Promoting the Gospel Among Seamen 4/13
   Society for the Diffusion of Useful Knowledge 4/22
Oriental Missionary Society 4/13
Ostrogoths 4/16
Oxford Movement (1833-45) 4/25

P

"P[riestly Editor]" 4/24
PAINTINGS
   Mona Lisa (1503) 4/15
   The Last Supper (1498) 4/15
   The Light of the World (1854) 4/2
Palmer, Horatio Richmond
   b. 4/26/1834 [d. 11/15/1907]
Papal Commission on Birth Control 4/16
PAPAL DECREES
   "Etsi non dubitemus" 4/20
Parkhurst, Charles Henry
   b. 4/17/1842 [d. 9/8/1933]
Parliament, English 4/1
   House of Lords 4/28
Parliament, French 4/12
Patteson, John Coleridge
   b. 4/1/1827 [d. 9/20/1871]
Paul IV, Pope (1555-59) 4/28
Paul VI, Pope (1963-1978) 4/16
Pavonia, Ludovic
   (b. 1784) d. 4/1/1849
Peking Man 4/10
Pelagius 4/30
Pelagius I, Pope (556-561) 4/16
Penn, William.
   See QUOTATIONS
Percy, George 4/29
PERIODICALS
   "Bibliotheca Sacra" 4/20
   "Calcutta Review" 4/26
   "Illustrated London News" 4/26
   "Journal of Christian Science" 4/14
   "National Catholic Reporter" 4/16
   "The Assembly Herald" 4/16
   "The Concordia" 4/26
   "The Gospel Message" 4/16
   "The Missionary" 4/18
Perseverance of the Saints 4/23
Pettigrew, Charles
   (b. 3/20/1743) d. 4/7/1807
Philip, John
   b. 4/14/1775 [d. 8/27/1851]
Pink, Arthur W.
   See QUOTATIONS
Pius IV, Pope (1559-65) 4/28
Pius IX, Pope (1846-78) 4/6, 4/24, 4/27
Pius XII, Pope (1939-58) 4/28
POPES
   Benedict X (1058-59) 4/3
   Benedict XVI (2005-) 4/16
   Clement III (1187-91) 4/3
   Clement XII (1730-40) 4/24
   Eugenius IV (1431-47) 4/20
   Gregory XI (1370-78) 4/29
   Gregory XIII (1572-85)
   Innocent II (1130-43) 4/4
   John Paul II (1978-2005) 4/13, 4/16
   Julius II (1503-13) 4/11
   Leo III (795-816) 4/2
   Martin V (1417-31) 4/22
   Nicholas II (1447-55) 4/7
   Paul IV (1555-59) 4/28
   Paul VI (1963-1978) 4/16
   Pelagius I (556-561) 4/16
   Pius IV (1559-65) 4/28
   Pius IX (1846-78) 4/6, 4/24
   Pius XII (1939-58) 4/28
   Stephen II(?) (757) 4/26
   Stephen II/III (752-57)
   Sylvester II (999-1003) 4/2
   Urban VI (1378-89) 4/8
   Zacharias (741-52) 4/26
Pre-Raphaelite Brotherhood 4/2
Presidential Prayer Breakfast 4/5
PRESIDENTS, U.S.
   Eisenhower, Dwight D. (1953-61) 4/5
   Lincoln, Abraham (1861-65) 4/11
Prignano, Bartolomeo 4/8
Protestant Reformation 4/4

Q

QUOTATIONS
   Asbury, Francis 4/5, 4/22
   Beza, Theodore 4/12
   Bonar, Andrew 4/4, 4/10, 4/13, 4/17, 4/18, 4/19, 4/21, 4/23, 4/25, 4/27
   Bonhoeffer, Dietrich 4/8
   Brainerd, David 4/8, 4/15, 4/26
   Chesterton, G. K. 4/26
   Elliot, Jim 4/6
   Fletcher, John 4/6, 4/21, 4/27
   Frank, Anne 4/4
   Hammarskjöld, Dag 4/17
   Houselander, Caryll 4/30
   King, Martin Luther, Jr. 4/3
   Laubach, Frank C. 4/18
   Lewis, C. S. 4/2, 4/6, 4/15, 4/19, 4/23, 4/26
   Luther, Martin 4/2, 4/5, 4/26, 4/28
   Macaulay, Thomas B. 4/17
   MacDonald, George 4/1, 4/3, 4/7, 4/9, 4/11, 4/15, 4/29
   Merton, Thomas 4/11
   Newman, John Henry 4/21
   Newton, John 4/3, 4/13, 4/16, 4/23
   Nouwen, Henri 4/22
   Penn, William 4/25
   Pink, Arthur W. 4/14
   Rutherford, Samuel 4/1, 4/17, 4/23
   Schaeffer, Francis A. 4/12
   Schmemann, Alexander 4/2, 4/13
   Spurgeon, Charles H. 4/24
   Tolkien, J. R. R. 4/30
   Underhill, Evelyn 4/8, 4/20
   Venn, Henry 4/7
   Wesley, John 4/14, 4/17, 4/20, 4/25, 4/30
   Whitefield, George 4/24, 4/27, 4/30

R

Radbertus, Paschasius
   (b. ca. 785) d. 4/26/865
RADIO BROADCASTING
   "Back to God Hour" 4/8
Raikes, Robert
   (b. 9/14/1735) d. 4/5/1811
Ramabai, Pandita Sarasvati
   (b. 1858) d. 4/5/1922
Ratzinger, Joseph Alois
   b. 4/16/1927
Reed, Mary
   (b. 12/4/1854) d. 4/8/1943
Reformation, Protestant 4/4, 4/19
Reinagle, Alexander R.
   (b. 8/21/1799) d. 4/6/1877
RELIGIOUS ORDERS, ANGLICAN
   Community of St Mary 4/5
RELIGIOUS ORDERS, CATHOLIC
   Augustinians 4/4
   Benedictines 4/26
   Christian Brothers 4/26
   Claretian Missionaries 4/1
   Confraternity of the Holy Family 4/17
   Congregation of Sons of Mary Immaculate 4/1
   Dominican Tertiaries 4/29
   Franciscans 4/21
   Franciscan Recollect Friars 4/11
   Jesuits (Society of Jesus) 4/4, 4/7, 4/30
   Lazarists (est. 1625) 4/24
   Magdalen Sisters 4/24
   Marist Fathers 4/28
   Picpus Fathers 4/15
   Sisters of Charity (est. 1632) 4/24
   Sisters of Mercy 4/18
   Society of Priests at St.-Sulpice 4/2
   Trappists 4/11
Relly, James
   (b. ca. 1722) d. 4/25/1778
RENAISSANCE, THE
   German Renaissance 4/6
   Italian Renaissance 4/15
Richard I, English King (1189-99)
   (b. 9/8/1157) d. 4/6/1199
Ridder, Peter Hollander 4/17
Rinkart, Martin
   b. 4/23/1586 [d. 12/8/1797]
Rippon, John
   b. 4/29/1751 [d. 12/17/1836]
Roman Curia 4/27
Russell, Mary Baptist
   b. 4/18/1829 [d. 8/6/1898]
Russian Orthodox Easter 4/26
RUSSIAN ORTHODOX LEADERS
   Avvakum (1620-82) 4/14
   Nikon (1605-81) 4/14
Rutherford, Samuel.
   See QUOTATIONS

S

Sacred Congregation of the Propaganda 4/6
Schaeffer, Francis A..
   See QUOTATIONS
Schimpf, Freda
   b. 4/18/1914
Schmemann, Alexander.
   See QUOTATIONS
Schmucker, B. M. 4/2
Scholasticism, French 4/21
Schuler, George Stark
   b. 4/18/1882 [d. 10/30/1973]
Schwarzerd, Philipp. See also Melanchthon, Philipp
   (b. 2/16/1497) d. 4/19/1560
Scopes Monkey Trial 4/18

ALMANAC OF THE CHRISTIAN FAITH — APRIL INDEX

Sears, Edmund Hamilton
 b. 4/6/1810 [d. 1/14/1876]
SECTS, CHRISTIAN
 American Universalist Church 4/25
 Mormon Church 4/26
 Unitarianism, American 4/1, 4/3, 4/4, 4/11, 4/22
 Universalism, American 4/30
 Universalism, English 4/25
Selwyn, George Augustus
 b. 4/5/1809 [d. 4/11/1878]
SEMINARIES / BIBLE COLLEGES
 Andover Seminary (MA) 4/5
 Boston Missionary Training School (MA) 4/19
 Gordon Divinity School (MA) 4/19
 Harvard Divinity School (MA) 4/1, 4/5
 Oberlin Seminary (OH) 4/20
 Princeton Seminary (NJ) 4/12, 4/17
 Quebec Seminary (Canada) 4/30
 Yale Divinity School (CT) 4/29
Serra, Junipero 4/21
Seymour, William J. 4/9, 4/14
Shakespeare, William 4/12, 4/27
Sherwin, William Fiske
 (b. 3/14/1826) d. 4/14/1888
Shurtleff, Ernest W.
 b. 4/4/1862 [d. 8/29/1917]
Siefert, Anton 4/6
Simony 4/2
Smith, Gerald Birney 4/3
Smith, Joseph 4/26
Smith, William 4/4
Smoutius, Adrian 4/7
Society for Prevention of Crime 4/17
Society for Promoting the Gospel Among Seamen 4/13
Society for the Diffusion of Useful Knowledge 4/22
Soubirous, Bernadette
 (b. 1/7/1844) d. 4/16/1879
Spangenberg, Augustus G. 4/6
Sperry, William L.
 b. 4/5/1882 [d. 5/15/1954]
Spurgeon, Charles 4/28.
 See also QUOTATIONS
St. Bartholomew's Day Massacre 4/13
Stafford, Ward 4/13
Stanislaus (Stanislaw) of Cracow
 (b. 1030) d. 4/11/1079
Stephen II/III, Pope (752-57)
 (b. unk.) d. 4/26/757
Stevenson, Robert Louis 4/15
Stocking, Jay T.
 b. 4/19/1870 [d. 1/27/1936]

Stockwell Orphanage 4/28
Strachan, Harry 4/28
Strachan, Susan
 b. 4/28/1874 [d. 12/6/1950] 4/28
Sullivan Macy, Anne
 b. 4/14/1866 [d. 10/20/1936]
Sunday School Union 4/5
Supreme Court, U.S. 4/28
Swaggert, Jimmy 4/8
Swarthmore Hall 4/23
Sweney, John R.
 (b. 12/31/1837) d. 4/10/1899
Sylvester II, Pope (999-1003) 4/2
SYNAGOGUES
 Central Synagogue (NYC) 4/25
 Shearith Israel Synagogue (NY) 4/8
Synod of Dort 4/23

T

"TULIP" (Calvinist Doctrine) 4/23
Talmage, T[homas] DeWitt
 (b. 1/7/1832) d. 4/12/1902
Tammany Hall 4/17
Teilhard de Chardin, Pierre
 (b. 5/1/1881) d. 4/10/1955
Tekakwitha (Tegakwitha/Tegakouita), Kateri/Catherine
 (b. ca. 1656) d. 4/17/1680
TELEVISION BROADCASTING
 National Broadcasting Co. 4/25
Ten Boom, Corrie
 b. 4/15/1892 [d. 4/15/1983]
Tersteegen, Gerhard
 (b. 11/25/1697) d. 4/3/1769
Theodore IV, Russian Czar (1676-1682) 4/14
Theodosius I, Roman Emperor (379-95)
Theotokos (God-bearer) 4/10
Thomist philosophy 4/28
Tikhon, Russian Orthodox Patriarch (1917-25)
 (b. 12/19/1866) d. 4/7/1925
Tolkien, Christopher 4/30
Tolkien, J. R. R.
 See QUOTATIONS
Tolton, Augustine 4/24
 b. 4/1/1854 [d. 7/9/1897]
Toltschig, John 4/6
Torkillus, Reorus 4/17
Total Depravity 4/23
Totila, Ostrogoth King 4/16
Townsend, W. Cameron
 (b. 7/9/1896) d. 4/23/1982

Tractarians 4/25
Transcendentalism 4/7
Transubstantiation 4/26
TREATIES
 Edict of Nantes (1598) 4/11
 Peace of Strasbourg (1189) 4/3
Tregelles, Samuel P.
 (b. 1/30/1813) d. 4/24/1875
Trotman, Dawson 4/29
Tuttle, Daniel S.
 (b. 1/26/1837) d. 4/17/1923

U

Unconditional Election 4/23
Underhill, Evelyn 4/8, 4/12, 4/20, 4/22
 See also QUOTATIONS
Upham, Thomas Cogswell
 (b. 1/30/1799) d. 4/2/1872
Urban VI, Pope (1378-89) 4/8

V

Vanauken, Sheldon 4/6
Van Dyke, Henry J.
 (b. 11/10/1852) d. 4/10/1933
Vasken I, Patriarch 4/28
Venn, Henry.
 See QUOTATIONS
Verneuil, Jean-Jacques Olier de
 (b. 9/20/1608) d. 4/2/1657
Veterans Mountain Camp 4/16
Veuster, Joseph de
 (b. 1/3/1840) d. 4/15/1889
Vincent de Paul
 b. 4/24/1576 [d. 9/27/1660]
Virgin Mary, The 4/16
Volunteers of America 4/14

W

Wagner, Robert F., Sr. 4/19
Wallace, Lew[is]
 b. 4/10/1827 [d. 2/15/1905]
Ward, Seth
 b. 4/5/1617 [d. 1/6/1698]
Ware, Henry, Sr.
 b. 4/1/1764 [d. 7/12/1845]
Waring, Anna Laetitia
 b. 4/19/1823 [d. 5/10/1910]
WARS
 American Civil War (1861-65) 4/10, 4/12, 4/22, 4/26
 American Revolutionary War (1775-83) 4/30

World War II (1939-45) 4/15, 4/26, 4/30
World War I (1914-18) 4/9
Washburn, Edward A.
 b. 4/16/1819 [d. 2/2/1881]
Wesley, John.
 See QUOTATIONS
West, Morris L.
 b. 4/26/1916 [d. 10/9/1999]
Westcott, B. F. 4/23
Western Church 4/4
Wheelock, Eleazar
 b. 4/22/1711 [d. 4/29/1779]
White, William
 b. 4/4/1748 [d. 7/17/1836]
Whitefield, George 4/11, 4/18, 4/25.
 See also QUOTATIONS
William of Ockham (Occam)
 (b. ca. 1280) d. 4/10/1347
Wilson, Ira B.
 (b. 9/6/1880) d. 4/3/1950
Wingfield, Edward Maria 4/29
Winthrop, John
 (b. 1/22/1588) d. 4/5/1649
Wittenberg Castle 4/4
Wright, George F.
 (b. 1/22/1838) d. 4/20/1921
Wycliffe Bible Translators 4/23

X

Xavier, Francis 4/7
 b. 4/7/1506 [d. 12/3/1552]

Y

Yu, Dora 4/29

Z

Zacharias, Pope (741-52) 4/26
Zinzendorf, Nicholas von 4/27
Zwemer, Samuel M.
 b. 4/12/1867 [d. 4/2/1952]
Zwingli, Ulrich 4/2

MAY

SIVAN

ALMANAC OF THE CHRISTIAN FAITH

IYYAR

~ May 1 ~

Highlights in History

418 At the Council of Carthage, the African bishops issued a series of nine canons condemning the teachings of Pelagius and affirming in uncompromising terms the so-called "Augustinian" doctrine of the Fall and Original Sin.

1789 The United States House of Representatives elected Rev. William Lion, a Dutch Reformed minister in New York City, as its chaplain. (The Rt. Rev. Bishop Samuel Provost was elected chaplain of the Senate, and both the House and the Senate have since continued to regularly open every session with prayer.)

1886 In Method (a suburb of Raleigh), NC, the United Holy Church of America was founded. This predominantly African-American holiness denomination places great emphasis on sanctification as essential for the Christian life. Equal emphasis is placed on Spirit baptism which, like sanctification, is regarded as a work of grace subsequent to conversion. The greatest concentration of current membership lies along the East Coast, with the present headquarters located in Greensboro, NC.

Notable Birthdays

1816 Birth of Fidelia Fisk, American missionary to the Nestorians in Persia. She labored 15 years, much of the time as a teacher in a female seminary, and became the first principal of the seminary at Oroomiah. [d. 8/9/1864]

1858 Birth of A[nthony] J. Showalter, American Presbyterian hymnwriter. He was a highly respected conductor of singing schools throughout the Southeast, and also published 60 songbooks. But he is best remembered for composing the hymn tune SHOWALTER ("Leaning on the Everlasting Arms"). [d. 9/16/1924]

1881 Birth of Pierre Teilhard de Chardin, French Jesuit priest, paleontologist, philosopher and mystic. He helped discover the Peking Man, 1929. Teilhard's work belongs to an unique literary genre comprising an amalgam of science and theology. He is both remembered and criticized for his synthesis of Catholic Christianity and evolution in his 1955 publication, *The Phenomenon of Man*. [d. 4/10/1955]

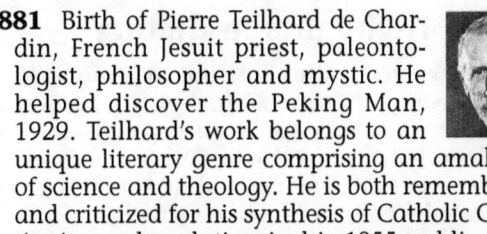

The Last Passage

1911 Death of Hannah Whitall Smith, 79, American Quaker holiness evangelist, reformer, philanthropist and devotional writer. She authored *The Christian's Secret of a Happy Life* (1875). (b. 2/7/1832)

1931 Death of Mary Elizabeth Wood, 69, American librarian and missionary. After visiting her missionary brother in China in 1899, in 1904 she herself was appointed a lay missionary by the American (Episcopal) Church. (b. 8/22/1861)

Words for the Soul

1740 English revivalist George Whitefield recorded this prayer in his journal: *'Lord, show that Thou dost love me, by humbling and keeping me humble as long as I live. The means I leave to Thee.'*

1871 American Quaker holiness author Hannah Whitall Smith, 49, wrote in a letter: *'Some old writer says that "God's will is a pillow to rest on, not a load to carry"; and this is so true to the soul that is entirely given up to Him.'*

1996 Dutch Catholic priest and diarist Henri Nouwen, 64, less than five months before his death, prayed in his journal: *'I do not know where you will lead me. I do not know the road ahead of me, but I know that you are with me to guide me and that, wherever you lead me, even where I would rather not go, you will bring me closer to my true home. Thank you, Lord, for my life, for my vocation, and for the hope that you have planted in my heart.'*

FROM GOD'S WORD...   OT: Judges 13:1–14:20 ~ NT: John 1:29–51 ~ Psalms 102:1–28 ~ Proverbs 14:15-16

סיון
SIVAN

ALMANAC OF THE CHRISTIAN FAITH

אייר
IYYAR

~ May 2 ~

Highlights in History

1507 Two years after entering the Augustinian monastery at Erfurt, Germany, young Martin Luther, 23, was consecrated a priest, and celebrated his first mass. Luther remained in the order for 13 years, until he was excommunicated from the Catholic Church in 1521.

1559 Having spent several years on the Continent studying and writing, John Knox, 54, returned to Scotland to help lead in the Scottish Reformation. It took hold the following year, when queen regent Mary of Guise died. Afterward, Knox and others drew up the Scots Confession, which Parliament approved in 1560.

1872 A lectureship was established at Yale University Divinity School in memory of Lyman Beecher, who graduated from Yale in 1797. It stipulated that the lectures cover topics on preaching and the work of the Christian ministry. Among the lecturers were Henry Ward Beecher (1872, 1873, 1874), Phillips Brooks (1877), Andrew M. Fairbairn (1892) and Harry E. Fosdick (1924).

Notable Birthdays

1821 Birth of William Taylor, American Methodist evangelist and missionary. He served during the Gold Rush in California (1849-56), and afterward became a missionary, traveling to various parts of the world. He belonged to the National Holiness Association, a group of Methodist pastors dedicated to holiness evangelism, and served as missionary Bishop of Africa (1884-96). Taylor University in Upland, Indiana, is named for him. [d. 5/18/1902]

1860 Birth of Theodor Herzl, Hungarian-born Austrian Jewish lawyer and journalist. In his signature work, *Der Judenstaat* (Eng. *The Jewish State*, 1896), Herzl advocated a Jewish state in Palestine. He became founder of modern political Zionism when, in 1897, he convened the first Zionist Congress in Basel. [d. 7/3/1904]

1870 Birth of William J. Seymour, African-American pioneer Pentecostal evangelist. It was under his preaching that the Azusa Street Revival broke out in 1906 — just nine days before the San Francisco earthquake! Jenny Evans Moore (b. 1844) – the first person there to speak in tongues – later married Seymour. [d. 9/28/1922]

The Last Passage

373 Death of St. Athanasius ("the Great"), 80, Bishop of Alexandria (328-373). Known as the "Father of Orthodoxy," Athanasius attended the Council of Nicea, and was exiled five times for his opposition to Arianism. He was the first Christian writer to list the 27 books of the New Testament as we know them today. (b. ca. 293)

1909 Death of Sheldon Jackson, 74, American educator and missionary. Known as the "Bishop of All Beyond," he served 50 years as superintendent of the missions of the Presbyterian Church in the American West. In all, Jackson oversaw the establishment of 886 churches. Standing just over five feet tall, someone once described him as "short, bewhiskered, and bespectacled, but a giant." (b. 5/18/1834)

Words for the Soul

1863 After losing an arm during the Civil War Battle of Chancellorsville, Confederate General Thomas "Stonewall" Jackson remarked: *'I am sure that my Heavenly Father designs this affliction for my good. I am perfectly satisfied, that either in this life, or in that which is to come, I shall discover that what is now regarded as a calamity, is a blessing.'*

1949 American missionary and Auca Indian martyr Jim Elliot recorded in his journal: *'The man who will not act until he knows all will never act at all.'*

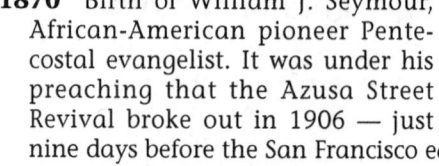

FROM GOD'S WORD...   OT: Judges 15:1–16:31 ~ NT: John 2:1-25 ~ Psalms 103:1-22 ~ Proverbs 14:17-19

ALMANAC OF THE CHRISTIAN FAITH

May 3

Highlights in History

1738 English revivalist George Whitefield, one of the most famous religious figures of the 1700s, arrived in America for his first of seven visits (staying until Aug. 28). During his lifetime, Whitefield preached at least 18,000 times to as many as 10 million hearers.

1845 At a called meeting of the South Carolina Baptist State Convention in Edgefield, Baptist leader W[illiam] B. Johnson proposed that a more centralized organizational structure embody Baptists in the Southern United States. Johnson was elected the first president of the new body, when the Southern Baptist Convention afterward came into being.

1861 The Southern Congress approved Bill 102, stating: *"There shall be appointed by the President chaplains to serve the armies of the Confederate States during the existing war."* (Chaplains were not previously common in the American military, but they became a permanent fixture during and after the Civil War.)

1987 In Columbus, Ohio, the Evangelical Lutheran Church in America was organized. The largest Lutheran denomination in the U.S., the ELCA resulted from the merger of three former Lutheran bodies (the Lutheran Church: 2.9 million members; the American Lutheran Church: 2.3 million members; and the Association of Evangelical Lutheran Churches: 110,000 members). The new denomination was officially born on Jan. 1, 1988.

Notable Birthdays

1650 Birth of Joachim Neander, German hymn author. As the author of 60 hymns, including "Praise to the Lord, the Almighty," Neander was the first important hymnwriter to come out of the German Reformed Church [d. 5/31/1680]

1781 Birth of Asa Shinn, American Methodist clergyman, theologian, and ecclesiastical reformer. He authored *An Essay on the Plan of Salvation* (1812); and *On the Benevolence and Rectitude of the Supreme Being* (1840), as well as a number of pamphlets. Throughout his lifetime Shinn suffered from bouts of insanity (1816, 1820, 1828), attributed to a skull fracture he suffered as a child. [d. 2/11/1853]

1868 Birth of Gerald Birney Smith, American Baptist linguistic scholar and theologian. He edited (with Shailer Mathews) the 513-page *Dictionary of Religion and Ethics* (1921). [d. 4/3/1929]

The Last Passage

1850 Death of John Herr, 67, Pennsylvania-born religious leader. He was founder (ca. 1812) of the Reformed Mennonite Church. The congregations of his denomination were established primarily in Western New York state and in Ontario. (b. 9/18/1782)

1878 Death of William Whiting, 52, English choir master. He was director of the Winchester College choristers for more than 35 years (1842-78). He also authored the single hymn: "Eternal Father, Strong to Save." (b. 11/1/1825)

Words for the Soul

1843 Scottish clergyman and biographer Andrew Bonar observed in his journal: *'I see that fasting and retirement [solitude], along with prayer, should go together. The effect upon the body and soul is somewhat like affliction. It brings down the tone of the spirit, subdues the flesh, draws off the soul from self-complacence, and makes the flesh unsatisfying. It discovers much to me that is humbling, it helps to remove my lightness of mind.'*

1941 English mystic Evelyn Underhill noted in a letter: *'Self-forgetfulness is the greatest of graces. The true relation between the soul and God is the perfectly simple one of a childlike dependence.*

FROM GOD'S WORD...   OT: Judges 17:1–18:31 ~ NT: John 3:1-21 ~ Psalms 104:1-23 ~ Proverbs 14:20-21

סיון
SIVAN

ALMANAC OF THE CHRISTIAN FAITH

אייר
IYYAR

~ May 4 ~

Highlights in History

1829 In Great Britain, the first English Catholic, the Earl of Surrey, was elected to Parliament. His election followed passage in April of the Roman Catholic Relief Bill, which first gave Catholics right of suffrage, eligibility for all military, civil and corporate offices, and permitted them to sit and vote in Parliament.

1988 Biloxi-born Catholic prelate Eugene A. Marino, S.S.J. (b. 1934), was installed as Archbishop of Atlanta. He served in this position for two years — the first African-American to be named an archbishop.

Notable Birthdays

1796 Birth of Horace Mann, American educator, statesman and humanitarian. By his offices, lectures and writings, he awakened a public interest in education that had never before been felt. An ardent abolitionist, Mann once said: "I consider no evil as great as slavery." He spent his last seven years as president of Antioch College in Ohio. [d. 8/2/1859]

1889 Birth of Francis Joseph Spellman, American Catholic prelate. He served as auxiliary bishop of Boston (1932-39); and Archbishop of New York (1939-67). He was elevated to the cardinalate, and in 1966 hosted the visit of Paul VI to the U.S. — the first visit of its kind by a reigning pontiff. A patron of literature, Cardinal Spellman authored a dozen books, and sponsored publication of the *Catholic Encyclopedia* (1915). [d. 12/2/1967]

The Last Passage

1038 Death of St. Gothard, Bishop (1022-38) of Hildesheim (in lower Saxony). He reformed many monasteries in Upper Germany. (b. 962)

1873 Death of William Holmes McGuffey, 72, American educator. He was noted for his development of the *Eclectic* ("*McGuffey's*") *Reader*, which became one of the most influential early textbook series in America. (b. 9/23/1800)

1903 Death of John Fletcher Hurst, 68, American Methodist prelate, educator and church historian. A former president (1873-80) of Drew Seminary, Hurst served as a bishop (1880-1903) in his denomination. He also authored *History of Methodism* (1902). (b. 8/17/1834)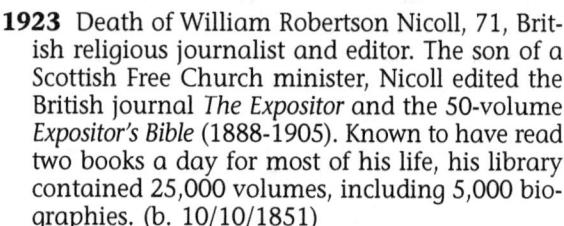

1923 Death of William Robertson Nicoll, 71, British religious journalist and editor. The son of a Scottish Free Church minister, Nicoll edited the British journal *The Expositor* and the 50-volume *Expositor's Bible* (1888-1905). Known to have read two books a day for most of his life, his library contained 25,000 volumes, including 5,000 biographies. (b. 10/10/1851)

Words for the Soul

1773 Anglican clergyman and hymnwriter John Newton observed in a letter: '*Unless the Lord shines, I cannot retain today the light I had yesterday; and though His presence makes a delightful difference, I have no more to boast of in myself at one time than another.*'

1962 British literary scholar and Christian apologist C. S. Lewis wrote in **Letters to An American Lady**: '*It is sometimes hard to obey St. Paul's "Rejoice." We must try to take life moment by moment. The actual present is usually pretty tolerable, if only we refrain from adding to its burden that of the past and the future.*'

1977 Russian Orthodox liturgical scholar Alexander Schmemann reflected in his journal: '*The fact that [seminary] students are "stuffed" for three years with scientific theology is, in my opinion, quite unfortunate for the Church. Some students are transformed into snobs, others into half-educated people; others into angry anti-intellectuals.*'

FROM GOD'S WORD...   OT: Judges 19:1–20:48 ~ NT: John 3:22–4:3 ~ Psalms 104:24-35 ~ Proverbs 14:22-24

סיון ALMANAC OF THE CHRISTIAN FAITH אייר
SIVAN   IYYAR

May 5

Highlights in History

1899 At Exeter Hall in London, the Religious Tract Society celebrated its 100th anniversary. Founded in 1799, during its first 100 years the organization published literature in 271 languages and dialects.

1901 The first Catholic mass for night workers was held at the Church of St. Andrew, in NY City. Father Luke J. Evers obtained special permission from the Pope to institute this service, as church law previously did not permit mass before sunrise.

1925 High school biology teacher John T. Scopes, 25, was arrested for teaching the theory of evolution in his Dayton, Tennessee biology classes. His subsequent trial resulted in a public mockery of extreme right-wing Christianity, and turned Fundamentalist Christians into a more insulative subculture.

Notable Birthdays

1813 Birth of Sören A. Kierkegaard, Danish philosopher and theologian.  Regarded as the "father of existentialism," he attacked organized religion, holding that an individual chooses truth on the basis of (ultimately subjective) faith. To Kierkegaard, faith is not a mental conviction about doctrine, nor a positive religious feeling, but a passionate spiritual commitment to God in the face of uncertainty. [d. 11/11/1855]

1815 Birth of Ithamar Conkey, American Baptist (later Episcopal) sacred choralist and hymnwriter. He was the organist and choir director in several New England churches and, from 1861, served as conductor of the quartet-choir of the Madison Avenue Baptist Church in New York City. Conkey is remembered today for composing the hymn tune RATHBUN ("In the Cross of Christ I Glory"). [d. 4/30/1867]

1852 Birth of Baron Friedrich von Hügel, Italian-born British Catholic religious philosopher. He was founder of the London Society for the Study of Religion, which became a center for modernist groups. Von Hügel also authored *The Mystical Element of Religion* (1908). [d. 1/27/1925]

1887 Birth of Geoffrey F. Fisher, Anglican prelate. He served as Archbishop of Canterbury from 1945-61, and initiated a revision of the English canons (last codified in 1603). In 1960 he traveled to meet the Orthodox Patriarchs of Jerusalem and of Constantinople. He also visited Pope John XXIII – making Fisher the first Archbishop of Canterbury to visit the Vatican since 1397. [d. 9/15/1972]

The Last Passage

1525 Death of Frederick III (the Wise), 62, Elector of Saxony from 1486. Growing increasingly sympathetic to the Reformation, this medieval prince protected Luther and, according to Philipp Melancthon, did more than any other to advance the Reformation. Frederick founded the University of Wittenberg in 1502. (b. 1/17/1463)

1875 Death of Heinrich Georg August von Ewald, 71, German Old Testament scholar and Orientalist. From 1862 he took active part in the Protestant reform in Germany. His *Hebrew Grammar* (1827) was a landmark in the history of Old Testament philology. (b. 11/16/1803)

Words for the Soul

1871 Scottish clergyman and biographer Andrew Bonar observed in his journal: *'Christ is at once the loftiest and the lowliest, so that He will often wait upon us and serve us.'*

1950 American missionary and Auca Indian martyr Jim Elliot recorded in his journal: *'The conflict of science and religion is fought between the errors of both camps.'*

FROM GOD'S WORD... OT: Judges 21:1–Ruth 1:22 ~ NT: John 4:4-42 ~ Psalms 105:1-15 ~ Proverbs 14:25

סיון SIVAN — ALMANAC OF THE CHRISTIAN FAITH — אייר IYYAR

May 6

Highlights in History

1210 The Cathedral in Reims, France was destroyed by a fire. A new cathedral was begun the following year.

1986 The Rev. Donald E. Pelotte, 41, was ordained in Gallup, New Mexico — the first American Indian to become a Roman Catholic Bishop.

Notable Birthdays

1702 Birth of Friedrich C. Oetinger, German Lutheran theosophist. A disciple, at different times, of both Jakob Boehme and Emanuel Swedenborg, Oetinger emphasized a oneness between the visible and invisible worlds, and believed in both communication with spirits and in the materialization of spirits. [d. 2/10/1782]

1809 Birth of William Walker, Southern American music teacher. Walker spent much of his life collecting traditional tunes of the Southern Appalachians. He also taught singing schools and was the inventor of the seven-shaped-note musical system. [d. 9/24/1875]

1831 Birth of Samuel I. J. Schereschewsky, Russian-born U.S. Episcopal missionary to China. He was stationed at Shanghai (1860-63), then Peking (1863-75), and translated the entire Bible into Mandarin Chinese. [d. 9/15/1906]

1867 Birth of George Washington Truett, American Southern Baptist clergyman and denominational leader. He pastored First Baptist Church, Dallas, from 1897 until his death 47 years later. [d. 7/7/1944]

The Last Passage

1638 Flemish Catholic ecclesiastic Cornelius Otto Jansen, 52, died of the plague. As Bishop of Ypres (1636), Jansen strongly opposed the semi-Pelagian doctrine of the Jesuits, and inspired a reform movement in the Catholic church. A book devoted to Augustine's doctrines – *Augustinus* (1640) – was published after his death, but was declared heretical because it taught predestination and that grace is reserved for only the elect. (b. 10/28/1585)

1746 Death of William Tennent, 73, Irish-born pioneer American Presbyterian minister and educator. He is remembered for his "Log College" (1735) in Pennsylvania, where he trained over 20 gifted men for the ministry. (b. 1673)

1877 Death of John Roberts, 54, Welsh Calvinistic Methodist clergyman and chorister. In 1874, Roberts published a Welsh translation of the Moody and Sankey hymnal, although he is better remembered today for composing the hymn tune LLANFAIR ("Hail the Day that Sees Him Rise") (arr.). (b. 12/22/1822)

Words for the Soul

1847 Scottish clergyman and biographer Andrew Bonar observed of God in his journal: *'Most wonderful to see how small disappointments in providence often lead to the very best results.'*

1955 Responding to a letter written him by a child, British scholar and Christian apologist C. S. Lewis advised: *'God knows quite well how hard we find it to love Him more than anyone or anything else, and He won't be angry with us as long as we are trying. And He will help us.'*

1996 Dutch Catholic diarist Henry Nouwen concluded in his journal: *'Without Pentecost the Christ-event... remains imprisoned in history as something to remember, think about, and reflect on. The Spirit of Jesus comes to dwell within us, so that we can become living Christs here and now. Pentecost lifts the whole mystery of salvation out of its particularities and makes it into something universal, embracing all peoples, all countries, all seasons, and all eras.'*

FROM GOD'S WORD...   OT: Ruth 2:1–4:22 ~ NT: John 4:43-54 ~ Psalms 105:16-36 ~ Proverbs 14:26-27

ALMANAC OF THE CHRISTIAN FAITH

May 7

Highlights in History

1787 In London, the New Jerusalem Church was formally established by five ex-Wesleyan preachers. Its theology, known popularly as Swedenborgianism, was based on the writings of Swedish scientist and mystic Emanuel Swedenborg (1688-1772). The first congregation in the U.S. was formed in Baltimore in 1792. Today, Swedenborgians claim a worldwide membership of about 50,000.

1951 "The Circuit Rider," a religious program sponsored by America for Christ, aired for the last time over ABC television. Having debuted two months earlier (on March 5), this series featured sacred music, special guests and dramatized biographies of great American frontier evangelists.

Notable Birthdays

1605 Birth of Nikon (Nikita Minin), Russian prelate. As Patriarch of Moscow (1652-66), he sought to reform the Russian liturgy. It was an unpopular enterprise because his pro-Greek stance offended many who looked on Moscow as the Third Rome. A schism subsequently erupted and Nikon was deposed and banished. Later, he was recalled to Moscow, but died on the return trip. [d. 1681]

1839 Birth of Elisha A. Hoffman, American Presbyterian clergyman and hymnwriter. After working 11 years with the Evangelical Association's denominational publishing house, his wife died, and he devoted the next 33 years pastoring Benton Harbor Presbyterian Church. His pastime was hymnwriting, and Hoffman penned the words and music to over 1,000 hymns, including: "I Must Tell Jesus" (& ORWIGSBURG); "Christ Hath for Sin Atonement Made" (& BENTON HARBOR); "Down at the Cross"; "Are You Washed in the Blood?" and "Leaning on the Everlasting Arms." [d. 11/25/1929]

1851 Birth of Adolf von Harnack, German Lutheran church historian and theologian. Arguably the most outstanding Patristic scholar of his generation, Harnack taught that much of the dogma of early Christianity was tainted with Greek thought, and should be scrutinized carefully for nonessentials. His *History of Dogma* (7 vols., 1894-99) is still a principal tool of historical theologians. [d. 6/10/1930]

1907 Birth of Kathryn Kuhlman, American itinerant evangelist and spiritual healer. She discovered her gift of healing while pastoring a small church in Pennsylvania, when people in her congregation began reporting unexpected healings during her services. Kuhlman's best-known book was her 1962 autobiography, *I Believe in Miracles*. [d. 2/20/1976]

The Last Passage

1508 Death of Nil Sorski, 75, Russian mystic. He was the first Orthodox believer to write about the contemplative life and asceticism. (b. 1433)

1887 Death of Carl F. W. Walther, 75, American Lutheran pioneer theologian and organizer. Born in Saxony, he came to America in 1839. He pastored the first Lutheran Church in St. Louis, and in 1847 organized the Lutheran Church Missouri Synod. (b. 10/25/1811)

Words for the Soul

1764 English founder of Methodism John Wesley assured in a letter: *'God is able and willing to give always what he gives once. And it is most certainly his design, that whatever he has given you should abide with you for ever.'*

1874 American Quaker holiness author Hannah Whitall Smith wrote in a letter: *'Oh, how he must love us, to take so much pains with each one of us in seeking to unite us to Himself!'*

FROM GOD'S WORD... OT: 1 Samuel 1:1–2:21 ~ NT: John 5:1-24 ~ Psalms 105:37-45 ~ Proverbs 14:28-29

סיון
SIVAN

ALMANAC OF THE CHRISTIAN FAITH

אייר
IYYAR

May 8

Highlights in History

1373 According to her own account, English mystic Julian of Norwich (ca.1342-ca.1413), while in a state of ecstasy lasting 5 hours, received a series of 15 revelations. Another vision followed the next day. Her *Sixteen Revelations of Divine Love,* was written 20 years later, comprising her meditations on the things she saw – chiefly, the sufferings of Christ and the Trinity. (Little else is known of her life except that she probably lived as an anchoress, near St. Julian's Church, in Norwich, England.)

1816 In the Dutch Reformed Church in New York City, delegates from 35 Bible societies met to establish the American Bible Society. Its formation stemmed, in part, from a late 18th century renewal of interest in world missions. This nonprofit society sought to promote a wider circulation of the Scriptures, unaccompanied by notes or comments. The first president, Elias Boudinot, served 1816 to 1821. In the first year, 6,140 Bibles were distributed.

1845 Nearly 300 Baptists from nine Southern states (primarily GA, SC, & VA) convened for a 3-day meeting at Augusta, GA, in response to a call issued by the Virginia Baptist Foreign Mission Society. It was at this gathering that the Southern Baptist Convention was founded. Dr. William Burrein Johnson of South Carolina was elected the first president of the convention.

Notable Birthdays

1829 Birth of Louis Moreau Gottschalk, American pianist and composer. He studied in Europe and later gave concerts in both North and South America. His more serious works included a symphony, an overture, a cantata and two operas. Today, Gottschalk is remembered for composing the hymn tune MERCY, to which is sung both "Softly Now the Light of Day" and "Holy Ghost, With Light Divine." [d. 12/18/1869]

1917 Birth of Kenneth N. Taylor, Bible translator and publisher. While Taylor was director of Moody Press (1947-63), a desire to communicate the faith to his own ten children led him to begin paraphrasing portions of the Bible in simple language, beginning with *Living Letters* (1962). In 1971, these combined paraphrases first appeared as *The Living Bible.* [d. 6/10/2005

The Last Passage

1655 Death of Edward Winslow, 60, English-born Puritan Separatist and Mayflower Pilgrim. He was a signer of the Mayflower Compact, and later became governor of Plymouth Colony (1633, 1636, 1644). Next to William Bradford, Winslow was the colony's most important chronicler. (b. 10/18/1595)

1920 Death of Handley C. G. Moule, 78, Anglican prelate and scholar. He pioneered the shape of evangelical ordination training at Cambridge through his teachings and writings. Later, he succeeded J. B. Lightfoot and B. F. Westcott as Bishop of Durham (1901-20). (b. 12/23/1841)

Words for the Soul

1883 Scottish clergyman Andrew Bonar, 72, reflected on his spiritual disposition in his journal: *'Still distressed at the fact that my fellowship with the Lord throughout the day is so broken instead of being constant and continuous.'*

1939 British literary scholar and Christian apologist C. S. Lewis wrote in a letter: *'The process of living seems to consist in coming to realize truths so ancient and simple that, if stated, they sound like barren platitudes. They cannot sound otherwise to those who have not had the relevant experience: that is why there is no real teaching of such truths possible and every generation starts from scratch.'*

FROM GOD'S WORD... OT: 1 Samuel 2:22–4:22 ~ NT: John 5:25-47 ~ Psalms 106:1-12 ~ Proverbs 14:30-31

סיון   ALMANAC OF THE CHRISTIAN FAITH   אייר

SIVAN   IYYAR

May 9

Highlights in History

1607 The first Episcopal church service in an English colony was held at Cape Henry, near Jamestown, VA. Rev. Robert Hunt celebrated the Eucharist. The founding of the Episcopal Church in America dates from the previous month when 30 English colonists first set up a cross at Cape Henry. The Episcopal Church originated as the Church of England (the Anglican Church).

1619 In the Dutch community of Dordrecht, the Synod of Dort closed. Convened by the Calvinist churches in November 1618, the Synod voted unanimously to condemn the Articles of the Remonstrance, which defended Arminianism and had been signed by 45 Calvinist ministers. In all, some 200 Arminian clergy were afterward deprived of their offices and banished.

1983 Pope John Paul II announced the reversal of the Catholic Church's 1633 condemnation of Galileo Galilei, the 17th century scientist who first espoused the Copernican (i.e., heliocentric, or sun-centered) theory of our solar system.

Notable Birthdays

1810 Birth of John Eadie, Scottish (Presbyterian) Secession clergyman and New Testament scholar. His works include *A Biblical Cyclopaedia* (1868), *A Condensed Concordance of the Holy Scriptures* (1875), and commentaries on Paul's shorter epistles. Eadie served on the English Committee for Revising the Authorized Version of the Bible, but died before the completion of its work. [d. 6/3/1876]

1869 In Damascus, Alexander III, Greek Orthodox patriarch of Antioch and All the East (1930-58), was born. [d. 1958]

1905 Birth of Merrill E. Dunlop, American sacred composer and Youth for Christ crusade evangelist. Associated with Moody Bible Institute, he penned "My Sins Are Blotted Out, I Know" and "Lonely Voices." [d. 6/15/2002]

The Last Passage

1760 Death of Nikolaus Ludwig, Count von Zinzendorf, 59, German Pietist reformer. He reorganized the Unitas Fratrum into the Moravian (Bohemian) Brethren. A pioneer in missions, by his death, the Moravians (numbering only in the hundreds) had sent out 226 missionaries around the world. (Zinzendorf's wife Anna survived him by only 13 days.) (b. 5/26/1700)

1911 Death of Catherine Hankey, 77, Anglican philanthropist. She belonged to the evangelical Clapham Sect associated with William Wilberforce. From a single book of hers, *The Old, Old Story and Other Verses* (1879), the Church gained the hymn: "I Love to Tell the Story." (b. 1834)

1918 Death of John B. Sumner, 80, American Methodist clergyman and singing school organizer. He also composed a number of hymn tunes, including BINGHAMTON ("My Father is Rich in Houses and Land"). (b. 3/25/1838)

Words for the Soul

1871 American Quaker holiness writer Hannah Whitall Smith wrote in a letter: *'I once suffered a great deal because I looked for joy as a thing by itself, and I never found it. And that discouraged me. But now I never think whether I have joy or not. I have Christ, and that is enough.'*

1892 Scottish clergyman and biographer Andrew Bonar, seven months before his death at age 82, reflected in his journal: *'My soul was in a state of pain today because of this discovery of my terrible shortcoming. It may be the Lord is preparing me for more usefulness. I know that I must "decrease."'*

1961 Regarding modern Bible versions, British literary scholar and Christian apologist C. S. Lewis advised in a letter: *'A modern translation is for most purposes far more useful than the Authorised [King James] Version.'*

FROM GOD'S WORD...   OT: 1 Samuel 5:1–7:17 ~ NT: John 6:1-21 ~ Psalms 106:13-31 ~ Proverbs 14:32-33

סיון ALMANAC OF THE CHRISTIAN FAITH אייר
SIVAN   IYYAR

~ May 10 ~

Highlights in History

1939 After 109 years of division, a Declaration of Union reunited the Methodist Church in the U.S. The Methodist Protestant Church had separated from its parent body, the Methodist Episcopal Church, in 1830. Then, in 1845, the Methodist Episcopal Church, South splintered off and created itself an independent religious organization. The recombined denomination comprised more than 8 million members.

1959 By a vote taken in both denominational bodies, the Unitarian Church and the Universalist Church — along with their fellowships, the American Unitarian Association and the Universalist Church of America — merged into a single body.

Notable Birthdays

1812 Birth of Frances Elizabeth Cox, Anglican translator. She was among the first to rediscover and translate German hymns, and is remembered today for the English hymn, "Sing Praise to God Who Reigns Above." [d. 9/23/1897]

1818 Birth of Arthur Cleveland Coxe, American Episcopal prelate, author, and poet. As Bishop of Western New York (1865-96), he also revised the first nine volumes of the American printing of the *Ante-Nicene Fathers* (1867-1885). Coxe also penned the hymn, "O, Where Are Kings and Empires Now?" [d. 7/20/1896]

1859 Birth of Wilhelm Wrede, German Lutheran New Testament scholar. He was named in Albert Schweitzer's title: *Quest for the Historical Jesus: From Reimarus to Wrede* (1909). [d. 11/23/1906]

1886 Birth of Karl Barth, the Swiss Reformed theologian who sought to restore belief in the fundamental dogmas of Christianity. Asked in 1962 (on his one visit to America) to summarize the essence of the millions of words he had published, he replied: *'Jesus loves me this I know, for the Bible tells me so.'* [d. 12/9/1968]

The Last Passage

1910 Death of Anna Laetitia Waring, 87, Welsh Quaker-turned-Anglican social reformer and hymn author. In 1850 she published *Hymns and Meditations*, a volume which contained nineteen of her own hymns, including "In Heavenly Love Abiding." (b. 4/19/1823)

1917 Death of Henry Barclay Swete, 82, Anglican Bible and Patristics scholar. He taught at Cambridge University for 25 years (1890-1915), and published numerous scholarly works. Perhaps his most important biblical publication was *The Old Testament in Greek According to the Septuagint*. (b. 3/14/1835)

Words for the Soul

1637 Exiled Scottish clergyman Samuel Rutherford lamented in a letter: *'O never-enough admired Godhead, how can clay get up to thee? How can creatures of yesterday be able to enjoy thee? O what pain is it, that time and sin should be as so many thousand miles betwixt a loved and longed-for Lord, and a pining and love-sick soul, who would rather than all the world have lodging with Christ!'*

1743 Colonial American missionary David Brainerd recorded in his journal: *'O the pride, selfishness, hypocrisy, ignorance, bitterness, party zeal, and the want of love... that have attended my attempts to promote... religion; and this, when I have reason to hope I had real assistance from above, and some sweet intercourse with heaven! But alas, what corrupt mixtures attended my best duties!'*

1938 English mystic Evelyn Underhill observed in a letter: *'[The Lord] comes to the soul when He wills and [when] that soul needs it, but never continuously in this life. We are always in His presence but He is not always in ours.'*

1986 Dutch Catholic priest and diarist Henri J. M. Nouwen penned in his journal: *'Being in the world without being of it involves very hard work. It requires a clear vision,... a deep desire, as well as a strong commitment to... the name of Jesus.'*

FROM GOD'S WORD...   OT: 1 Samuel 8:1–9:27 ~ NT: John 6:22-40 ~ Psalms 106:32-48 ~ Proverbs 14:34-35

ALMANAC OF THE CHRISTIAN FAITH

SIVAN — IYYAR

~ May 11 ~

Highlights in History

330 Constantine, the first Christian Roman emperor, inaugurated Constantinople as capital of the Eastern Roman Empire, on the site of the ancient Greek city of Byzantium. The pope in Rome and the patriarch of Constantinople afterward rivaled each other for 1,000 years, until the Great Schism of 1054 permanently divided Eastern and Western Christianity. (In 1453, Constantinople fell to the invading Turks.)

1825 The American Tract Society was organized in New York City. It was the first national tract society in America, and was formed by the merger of 50 smaller societies. As a nondenominational organization, it was publishing 30 million tracts a year by the time of its sesquicentennial celebration in 1975.

1949 General Assembly Resolution 273 formally admitted the newly reconstituted nation of Israel as a member of the United Nations.

Notable Birthdays

1851 Birth of James M. Gray, Bible teacher and clergyman. One of the editors of the *Scofield Bible* (1909), he also served as president of Moody Bible Institute, and in 1931 helped organize the Evangelical Teacher Training Association. Gray also penned the hymn, "Nor Silver Nor Gold Hath Obtained My Redemption." [d. 9/21/1935]

The Last Passage

1610 Matteo Ricci, 57, Italian Jesuit and the first Catholic missionary to China, died in Peking. After his arrival in Macao in 1582, Ricci soon adopted Chinese dress and customs. His adaptation of Christianity to the Chinese way of life led to eventual controversy and in the end the practice was censured by his Church. (b. 10/8/1552)

1621 Death of Johann Arndt, 65, German Lutheran theologian and mystic. He was a devoted follower of Philipp Melanchthon, and is best remembered for his *Four Books on True Christianity* (1606-10), which later became the inspiration of many Protestant and Catholic devotional books. (b. 12/27/1555)

1877 Death of Taylor Lewis, 75, American biblical and classical scholar. Acquainted with both the Greek and Latin classics, as well as Arabic, Syriac and the works of the Hebrew rabbis, Lewis was especially interested in the relationship between science and religion, particularly regarding creation. His best known works were *The Six Days of Creation* (1855), *The Bible and Science* (1856) and *The Divine Human in the Scriptures* (1860). (b. 3/27/1802)

1883 Death of Emily Sullivan Oakey, 53, American language teacher and hymnwriter. She was in frail health all her life. Nevertheless, inspired by the parables both of the sower and of the tares, Mrs. Oakey penned the hymn, "What Shall the Harvest Be?" (b. 10/8/1829)

Words for the Soul

1849 Scottish clergyman and children's novelist George MacDonald wrote in a letter to his future wife, Louisa Powell: *'Tell me, too, about the world within your own soul – that living world – without which the world without would be but a lifelessness. The beautiful things round about you are the expression of God's face, or, as in Faust, the garment whereby we see the deity.'*

1868 American Quaker holiness writer Hannah Whitall Smith, 36, penned in her journal: *'I was cherishing hard thoughts of Him because He did not bless me as I desired! I have passed a day of intense wretchedness. I seem to lose my hold of everything, and to be cut adrift upon a fearful sea.... So dreadful a thing is the slightest unbelief.'*

FROM GOD'S WORD... OT: 1 Samuel 10:1–11:15 ~ NT: John 6:41-71 ~ Psalms 107:1-43 ~ Proverbs 15:1-3

סיון
SIVAN

ALMANAC OF THE CHRISTIAN FAITH

אייר
IYYAR

~ May 12 ~

Highlights in History

1792 The English "Father of Modern Missions," William Carey published his highly influential (though deplorably titled) book on the importance of evangelism: *An Enquiry into the Obligations of Christians, to use means for the Conversion of the Heathens in which the Religious State of the Different Nations of the World, the Success of Former Undertakings, and the practicability of Further Undertakings, are Considered.* Despite its unwieldy title, this 87-page volume on the importance of foreign evangelism became a classic in Christian history, and led to the formation of a missionary society which in its turn sent Carey himself to India, thus launching the era of modern Protestant Christian missions.

1861 "The Battle Hymn of the Republic," written by Julia Ward Howe, was first performed at a flag-raising ceremony for Union recruits at Fort Warren (near Boston), during the American Civil War. The hymn had been published in the "Atlantic Monthly" three months earlier.

1985 Amy Eilberg, 30, became the first female Conservative rabbi when she was ordained (along with 18 male candidates) for the rabbinate during graduation ceremonies at Jewish Theological Seminary in New York City. Born (10/12/1954) in Philadelphia, Mrs. Eilberg lived in Bloomington, IN at the time of her ordination, where her husband served as a chaplain at Methodist Hospital in Indianapolis.

Notable Birthdays

1816 Birth of George L. Prentiss, American Presbyterian clergyman and educator. He was organizing pastor of the Church of the Covenant, in New York City (1862-73), and also taught pastoral theology at Union Theological Seminary (1873-97). Prentiss's wife Elizabeth was a popular writer, and penned the hymn, "More Love to Thee, O Christ." [d. 3/19/1903]

1865 Birth of Bernard Levinthal, Russian-born American rabbi. He served a Philadelphia congregation from 1891, and became founder and president of the Orthodox Rabbinical Association of America. [d. 9/23/1952]

The Last Passage

1858 Death of Johann G. B. Winer, 69, German Biblical scholar. His chief studies were in biblical linguistics, and his masterwork, *Grammar of the Idioms of the New Testament* (1825), demonstrated how the laws of linguistics also applied to the language and grammar of the Greek New Testament. (b. 4/13/1789)

1887 Death of Samuel A. W. Duffield, 43, American Presbyterian clergyman and hymnologist. The son of George Duffield, he compiled *English Hymns: Their Authors and History* (1886); *The Latin Hymn Writers and Their Hymns* (unfinished at Duffield's death, but completed by Robert E. Thompson, 1889). (b. 9/24/1843)

1945 Death of H[enry] Wheeler Robinson, 63, English Baptist theologian and biblical scholar. His most important work was in Hebrew psychology and Old Testament theology. Robinson also authored *The Religious Ideas of the Old Testament* (1913). (b. 2/7/1872)

Words for the Soul

1860 Scottish clergyman and biographer Andrew Bonar confessed in his diary: 'I feel the blessedness and the necessity too of getting far into the very presence of God and standing under His shadow.'

1907 English mystic Evelyn Underhill concluded in a letter: 'An entire willingness to live in the dark, in pain, anything — this is the real secret. I think no one really finds the Great Companion till their love is of that kind that they long only to give and not to get.'

FROM GOD'S WORD...   OT: 1 Samuel 12:1–13:22 ~ NT: John 7:1-29 ~ Psalms 108:1-13 ~ Proverbs 15:4

ALMANAC OF THE CHRISTIAN FAITH

סיון SIVAN   אייר IYYAR

May 13

Highlights in History

1871 The Italian Parliament passed the Law of Guarantees, which invested the pope with sovereignty, immunized him from arrest, permitted him a personal guard and communications, and granted him exclusive use of the Vatican and Lateran churches. This legislation thus regulated papal relations with the Italian government until the 1929 Lateran Treaty.

1917 Three shepherd children near Fatima, Portugal reported that the Virgin Mary had appeared to them. "Our Lady of Fatima" – the popular title given to the collective visions – regularly appeared to the three children on the 13th of each month between May and October. The last vision, seen by a crowd of 70,000, appeared as a spectacular display of the sun.

Notable Birthdays

1839 Birth of William P. Mackay, Scottish Presbyterian physician and clergyman. He published a number of hymns, of which perhaps the best-known is "We Praise Thee, O God! For the Son of Thy Love." [d. 8/22/1885]

1842 Birth of Arthur S. Sullivan, English composer and hymnwriter. Though better known for his operatic collaborations with William S. Gilbert, Sullivan also composed the hymn tunes ST. KEVIN ("Come, Ye Faithful, Raise the Strain") and ST. GERTRUDE ("Onward, Christian Soldiers"). [d. 11/22/1900]

1931 Birth of James Warren ("Jim") Jones, American sectarian religious leader. He founded the People's Temple in 1954. However, the congregation's increasing departure from standard Christian beliefs led, in 1978, to the mass suicide of Jones and over 900 of his followers in Guyana (located in northern South America), in the midst of a U.S. Congressional investigation. [d. 11/18/1978]

The Last Passage

1704 Death of Louis Bourdaloue, 71, French Jesuit theologian and court preacher. A favorite of Louis XIV, Bourdaloue was nicknamed "the king of orators and the orator of kings," and was considered the greatest court preacher of the 17th century. (b. 8/20/1632)

1963 Death of A[iden] W. Tozer, American Christian & Missionary Alliance clergyman and Christian writer. He spent 31 of his 44 years in the ministry as pastor of Chicago's Southside Alliance Church. Tozer's best-remembered writing is *The Pursuit of God* (1948). (b. 4/21/1897)

Words for the Soul

1742 Colonial American missionary to the American Indians, David Brainerd recorded in his journal: *'Saw so much of the wickedness of my heart that I longed to get away from myself. I never before thought that there was so much spiritual pride in my soul. I felt almost pressed to death with my own vileness.... O, the closest walk with God is the sweetest heaven that can be enjoyed on earth!'*

1855 English preacher Charles Spurgeon declared in a sermon: *'Men could be more content to die if they did not know it was a punishment.... [But] to the holiest Christian, death must appear to have a sting, because sin was its mother. O fatal offspring of sin, I only dread thee because of thy parentage!'*

1937 English mystic Evelyn Underhill advised in a letter: *'I think it is the quiet steady stuff that tells in the long run, not the startling sacrifices and acts of "reparation."'*

1996 Dutch priest and diarist Henri J. M. Nouwen concluded in his "Sabbatical Journal": *'The divine love of God reveals to us that fruitfulness is more important than success, that the love of God is more important than the praise of people, that community is more important than individualism, and compassion more important than competition.'*

FROM GOD'S WORD... OT: 1 Samuel 13:23–14:52 ~ NT: John 7:30-52 ~ Psalms 109:1-31 ~ Proverbs 15:5-7

סיון SIVAN — ALMANAC OF THE CHRISTIAN FAITH — אייר IYYAR

May 14

Highlights in History

1572 Gregory XIII was named pope, serving until 1585. His reign was marked by the replacement (beginning in 1582) of the ancient Julian (Old Style) calendar with the New Style (Gregorian) calendar.

1607 In Virginia, on the first Sunday after arrival of the 120 settlers comprising the Jamestown Expedition, Anglican priest Robert Hunt (c.1568-1608) presided over the first Anglican worship service held in the New World. As chaplain of the expedition, Hunt also became the first Anglican priest in America.

1935 In England, the Religious Tract Society (founded in 1799) merged with the Christian Literature Society for India and Africa (which originated in 1877), forming the United Society for Christian Literature.

1948 After nineteen centuries of enforced exile, the Jewish people once again gained their homeland in Palestine when the State of Israel was formally proclaimed in Tel Aviv.

Notable Birthdays

1752 Birth of Timothy Dwight, American colonial clergyman and educator. The grandson of Jonathan Edwards, he served as a chaplain in the Revolutionary War, a Congregational clergyman in CT, and at age 43 was elected president of Yale College. Little known to many biographers, Dwight suffered from an impaired eyesight which allowed him to read for only 15 minutes a day. [d. 1/11/1817]

1841 Birth of Alexander V. G. Allen, American Episcopal clergyman, theologian, biographer and educator. He taught church history at Episcopal Theological School in Cambridge from 1867 until his death. His 1900 publication, *Life and Letters of Phillips Brooks*, became the definitive biography of the man. [d. 7/1/1908]

The Last Passage

964 Death of John XII, pope from 955-964. Elevated at the mere age of 18, his addiction to pleasure and to vice generated great scandal. John XII died at the age of 27. (b. ca. 937)

1610 Henry IV of Navarre, 56, first Bourbon king of France (1589-1610) was assassinated by a religious fanatic. Raised a Protestant, Henry gave the Edict of Nantes to the Huguenots in 1598, which provided for them a large degree of religious freedom. (b. 12/13/1553)

1855 Death of Thomas Kelly, 85, Irish Anglican clergyman and hymn author: "Praise the Saviour, Ye Who Know Him!" (1806). Kelly authored 765 hymns in all. (b. 7/13/1769)

1932 Death of John Hughes, 59, Welsh hymn composer: CWM RHONDDA ("God of Grace and God of Glory" and "Guide Me, O Thou Great Jehovah"). (b. 1873)

Words for the Soul

1874 American "holiness" Quaker Hannah Whitall Smith described in a letter: *'The guidance of the Spirit is generally by gentle suggestions or drawings, and not in violent pushes; and it requires great childlikeness of heart to be faithful to it.'*

1950 American missionary and Auca Indian martyr Jim Elliot declared in his journal: *'To believe is to act as though a thing were so. Merely saying a thing is so is no proof of my believing it.'*

1996 Dutch priest and diarist Henri J. M. Nouwen reflected in his "Sabbatical Journal": *'A great part of me is not yet "abiding" in Jesus. My mind and heart keep running away from my true dwelling place, and they explore strange lands where I end up in anger, resentment, lust, fear, and anguish. I know that living a spiritual life means bringing every part of myself home to where it belongs.'*

FROM GOD'S WORD... OT: 1 Samuel 15:1–16:23 ~ NT: John 7:53–8:20 ~ Psalms 110:1-7 ~ Proverbs 15:8-10

סיון
SIVAN

ALMANAC OF THE CHRISTIAN FAITH

אייר
IYYAR

~ May 15 ~

Highlights in History

1532 The English Submission of the Clergy Act was passed, making the king supreme in all ecclesiastical causes. In 1534, this legislation was incorporated into an Act of Parliament (25 Henry VIII, c.19), which coupled it with restraint of appeals to Rome.

1785 John Marrant of New York became the first African-American missionary to the Native Americans, when he was ordained as a Methodist clergyman in London. Among his subsequent converts were the chief of the Cherokees and his daughter.

1889 A two-day conference closed in Cleveland, Ohio, during which the Epworth League of the Methodist Episcopal Church was organized. It became the forerunner of the youth ministry programs found within the local United Methodist Church today.

1902 The Christian Union Church (instituted in 1886) changed its name to the Holiness Church. After 1907, the denomination became officially known as the Church of God. Headquartered today in Cleveland, TN, the denomination is now one of the oldest and largest Pentecostal bodies in America.

Notable Birthdays

1265 Birth of Dante Alighieri, greatest of the early Italian poets. He was active in civic affairs until falsely charged with political intrigue and banished from his hometown of Florence in 1302 by Boniface VIII. He spent the rest of his life in exile. Dante's Christian epic, *The Divine Comedy* (1308-1321) is an extended allegory of the human journey toward salvation. [d. 9/13 or 14/1321]

1846 Birth of Philo M. Buck, American pioneer Methodist missionary to India (1870-1914). Born in Corning, NY, he became superintendent of the Meerut District (1893-1914). [d. 9/8/1924]

The Last Passage

1773 Death of Alban Butler, 62, English Catholic priest, historian and hagiographer. His research, begun in 1735, led to the publication (1756-59) of his best-known work, *Lives of the Principal Saints*. The volume contains some 1600 biographies and remains a classic. (b. 10/24/1710)

1883 Death of Josiah Henson, 96, African-American slave and American Methodist clergyman. Henson was said to be the biographical prototype of "Uncle Tom" in Harriet Beecher Stowe's 1849 best-seller, *Uncle Tom's Cabin*. (b. 6/15/1787)

1886 Death of Emily Elizabeth Dickinson, 55, reclusive American poet, known only posthumously. (Only 7 of her 1,775 poems were published before her death.) In spite of many religious themes treated within her poetry (God, eternity, death and the afterlife), Emily Dickinson rejected traditional Calvinism and the institutional church. (b. 12/1/1830)

1948 Death of Father Edward Joseph Flanagan, 61, the Irish-born parish priest who, in 1917, founded the Boys' Town orphanage near Omaha, Nebraska. Father Flanagan believed there was "no such thing as a bad boy." (b. 7/13/1886)

Words for the Soul

1553 French reformer John Calvin revealed in a letter: '*The time draws nigh when the earth shall disclose the blood which has been hid, and we, after having been disencumbered of these fading bodies, shall be completely restored.*'

1943 German Lutheran theologian and Nazi martyr Dietrich Bonhoeffer declared in a letter from prison: '*I read the Psalms every day, as I have done for years; I know them and love them more than any other book.*'

FROM GOD'S WORD... OT: 1 Samuel 17:1–18:4 ~ NT: John 8:21-30 ~ Psalms 111:1-10 ~ Proverbs 15:11

May 16

Highlights in History

1605 Paul V became pope, serving until 1621. He promoted church reforms set up by the Council of Trent, completed St. Peter's Basilica and enlarged the Vatican Library.

1805 Anglican missionary Henry Martyn first stepped ashore in Calcutta, India. He was met by William Carey, who soon influenced him into translation work. Martyn translated the Bible into three languages, including Hindustani, before his premature death seven years later.

Notable Birthdays

1905 Birth of Werner Georg Kümmel, German United Evangelical New Testament scholar. He taught at the universities of Marburg, Zurich and Mainz. Known for his basic textbooks, Kummel's best work, *Introduction to the New Testament* (19th edition, 1978), is one of the most popular New Testament introductions available in English. [d. 7/9/1995]

1929 Birth of Warren Wiersbe, American clergyman, Christian radio host and writer. He served as a pastor of Moody Bible Church and for ten years was the host of the Christian radio program, Back to the Bible Broadcast.

The Last Passage

1869 Death of Karl H. Graf, 54, German Protestant Orientalist and Old Testament text critic. He helped develop the theory, and lent his name to the Graf-Wellhausen (or JEDP) hypothesis — that the final form of the Pentateuch was shaped after 587 B.C. (b. 2/28/1815)

1931 Death of George Foote Moore, 79, American Presbyterian Old Testament scholar. He taught at Andover (1883-1902) and at Harvard (1904-21) seminaries, and is best remembered for his 3-volume *Judaism in the First Centuries of the Christian Era* (1927-30). (b. 10/15/1851)

1955 Death of Cyril A. Alington, 82, Anglican educator. The son of a clergyman, Alington was ordained into the Anglican priesthood in 1901. He taught at Shrewsbury and Eton (1908-33), and later served as Dean of Durham (1933-51). Today Alington is remembered as the author of the hymn, "Good Christian Men, Rejoice and Sing." (b. 10/22/1872)

Words for the Soul

1540 German reformer Martin Luther remarked: *'In the worst temptations nothing can help us but faith that God's Son has put on flesh, is bone, sits at the right hand of the Father, and prays for us. There is no mightier comfort.'*

1741 English revivalist George Whitefield wrote in a letter: *'The more perfect you are, the more you will see and bewail your imperfections in thought, word, and deed; the more you will be made to sing, "In the Lord alone, and not in myself, have I compleat righteousness and strength."'*

1851 Scottish clergyman Andrew Bonar prayed in his diary: *'Oh, Eternal Spirit, teach me more! for I am but a child, yet I am a minister, and ought to teach others by my life and by my words. Oh, Eternal Spirit! mould me to Christ's likeness.'*

1866 Founder of the Lutheran Church Missouri Synod, Carl F. W. Walther observed in a letter: *'God carries on His work through men with whom it sometimes seems as if one would go to the right and the other to the left and the third one would hold back, and yet the work progresses.'*

1871 American Quaker holiness author Hannah Whitall Smith observed in a letter: *'The Christian who wholly belongs to the Lord can afford to be natural. It is only the half-hearted Christians who have to walk on stilts. Like a child who is entirely obedient to its parents can go on at perfect ease and naturally until the parents tell it to change its course; so we may leave all responsibilities as to our course in the Lord's hands and go on at ease and naturally unless he... calls for a change of course.'*

FROM GOD'S WORD... OT: 1 Samuel 18:5–19:24 ~ NT: John 8:31-59 ~ Psalms 112:1-10 ~ Proverbs 15:12-14

ALMANAC OF THE CHRISTIAN FAITH

SIVAN | IYYAR

May 17

Highlights in History

1881 The New Testament of the *English Revised Version* (EV or ERV) was first published in England. It was the first modern English translation of the Scriptures published since 1611, and signaled 10 years of work by 54 biblical scholars from both sides of the Atlantic. (The ERV afterward provided the scholarly foundation for the 1901 and 1905 U.S. publication of the *American Standard Version* (ASV) of the Bible.

1907 The Northern Baptist Convention, a major Baptist denomination, was formed in Washington, D.C. In 1950 its name was changed to the American Baptist Convention.

1925 French Carmelite nun St. Thérèse of Lisieux (1873-97) was canonized. Entering the Carmelite convent in Lisieux at age 15, she was prevented in 1896 from joining the Carmelites in China by the first of a series of hemorrhages. She died of tuberculosis at the age of 24.

1969 Los Angeles pastor Thomas Kilgore, Jr. was elected the first African-American president of the predominantly white American Baptist Convention on this date at the denomination's annual convention in Boston.

Notable Birthdays

1831 Birth of Robert Machray, Scottish-born Anglican prelate. He was the first primate of the Church of England in Canada. [d. 1904]

1838 Birth of William H. Hare, American Episcopal prelate and "Apostle of the Sioux." He served as missionary Bishop of Niobrara (Nebraska and the Dakotas) for 37 years. [d. 10/23/1909]

1847 Birth of Charles C. Luther, American Baptist evangelist and hymnwriter. He compiled *Temple Chimes*, a book of hymns and gospel songs, but is best remembered for writing the hymn, "Must I Go, and Empty-Handed." [d. 11/4/1924]

The Last Passage

1575 Death of Matthew Parker, 70, second Anglican Archbishop of Canterbury (1559-75). He tried to set limits to reformers' doctrines – the beginnings of Puritanism, which he called "multinous individualism." He also prepared a new psalter and in 1572 published a revision of the Bishops' Bible. (b. 8/6/1504)

1945 Death of H[enry] E. Dana, 56, American Baptist clergyman and educator. He was president of Kansas City (KS) Baptist Theological Seminary (1938-). Dana's publications included: *New Testament Criticism* (1924); *Christ's Ecclesia* (1926); and *Jewish Christianity* (1937). (b. 6/21/1888)

1948 Death of David Evans, 74, Welsh hymn arranger: MADRID ("Come, Christians, Join to Sing") (arr.); NYLAND ("In Heavenly Love Abiding") (arr.); BUNESSAN ("Morning Has Broken") (arr.); and SLANE ("Be Thou My Vision"). (b. 2/6/1874)

Words for the Soul

1747 Colonial American missionary to the New England Indians, David Brainerd recorded in his journal: *'I saw that the grace of God in Christ is infinitely free toward sinners.... I also saw that God is the supreme good; that in his presence is life; and I began to long to die, that I might be with him, in a state of freedom from all sin.'* [Five months later, Brainerd, 29, died of tuberculosis, compounded by his prolonged outdoor exposure.]

1776 In a speech delivered at Princeton, Declaration of Independence signer John Witherspoon maintained: *'He is the best friend to American liberty, who is most sincere and active in promoting true and undefiled religion, and who sets himself with greatest firmness to bear down profanity and immorality of every kind. Whoever is an avowed enemy of God, I scruple not [do hot hesitate] to call him an enemy of his country.'*

FROM GOD'S WORD... OT: 1 Samuel 20:1–21:15 ~ NT: John 9:1-41 ~ Psalms 113:1–114:8 ~ Proverbs 15:15-17

סיון ALMANAC OF THE CHRISTIAN FAITH אייר
SIVAN   IYYAR

May 18

Highlights in History

1291 Acre – last-remaining of the Latin-held (Christian) possessions in Palestine – fell to invading Moslem armies. It brought an end to the return of Christian rule in the Near East. (Beginning in 1096, the movement known as the Crusades was a war-to-the-death between Christianity and the Moslem faith. In the end, Islam had conquered, and Palestine remained in the hands of the followers of Mohammed.)

1652 In the American colonies, Rhode Island enacted the first-ever law banning slavery. (Unfortunately, the law was never enforced.)

1766 The Church of the United Brethren in Christ was organized in Lancaster, PA, under leadership of Martin Boehm and Philip William Otterbein (who were later elected bishops in 1800). Originating among German Pietists, the denomination merged in 1946 with the Evangelical Church to form the Evangelical United Brethren. (Later, in 1968, the EUB merged with the Methodists to form the United Methodist Church.)

1843 Nearly half the member congregations of the National Church of Scotland seceded to form the Free Church of Scotland. Renowned clergymen associated with this reformed Presbyterian denomination included Thomas Chalmers (named first moderator), Horatius and Andrew Bonar and William Robertson Smith.

Notable Birthdays

1802 Birth of La (Le) Roy Sunderland, American Methodist abolitionist minister and one of the founders of the Wesleyan Methodist Church. [d. 5/15/1885]

1920 Birth of Karol Jozef Wojtyla, Polish Catholic cardinal. In 1978 he was elected the first non-Italian pope since Renaissance, taking the name of John Paul II. Known for his conservatism in doctrine, he became the most traveled of all the popes. [d. 4/2/2005]

The Last Passage

1864 Death of César H. A. Malan, 76, Swiss evangelist and hymnwriter. Ordained in 1810, he helped originate the hymn movement in the French Reformed Church. A friend of English hymnwriter Charlotte Elliott (author of "Just As I Am"), Malan himself is also remembered today as composer of the hymn tune HENDON ("Ask Ye What Great Thing I Know"). (b. 7/7/1787)

1902 Death of William Taylor, 81, American Methodist evangelist and missionary bishop. Taylor ministered to miners during the California Gold Rush (1849-56), and later became missionary Bishop of Africa (1884-96). Taylor University in Upland, Indiana, is named for him. (b. 5/2/1821)

1967 Death of John Wesley Work III, 65, American educator, musicologist and sacred composer. He spent over 30 years teaching music at Fisk University in Nashville. Work is especially remembered today for his arrangement of "Go, Tell It On the Mountain." (b. 6/15/1901)

Words for the Soul

1526 German reformer Martin Luther declared in a letter to Duke Frederick of Saxony: 'Serving God consists in serving our fellow man, as Christ and His apostles did; it does not consist of hiding away forever in the solitude of a monastery.'

1996 Colonial American missionary to the New England Indians, David Brainerd recorded in his journal: 'I live in the most lonesome wilderness.... most of my diet consists of boiled corn, hasty-pudding, etc. I lodge on a bundle of straw, my labor is hard and extremely difficult, and I have little appearance of success.... My circumstances are such that I have no comfort of any kind, but what I have in God.'

FROM GOD'S WORD...   OT: 1 Samuel 22:1–23:29 ~ NT: John 10:1-21 ~ Psalms 115:1-18 ~ Proverbs 15:18-19

סיון SIVAN — ALMANAC OF THE CHRISTIAN FAITH — אייר IYYAR

May 19

Highlights in History

715 Gregory II was elected pope, serving until 731. During his pontificate, he sent St. Boniface to preach in Germany, renovated many churches, and encouraged the monastic life.

1841 Unitarian clergyman Theodore Parker, 30, delivered his landmark sermon in South Boston, entitled "On the Transient and Permanent in Christianity."

1885 The *English Revised Version* (EV or ERV) of the Bible was first published in England. It was the first complete revision of the English Bible since the "authorized" 1611 translation. (In 1905, American scholars on the ERV committee, having waited a promised 20 years, published the *American Standard Version* — designed, in part, to remove unnecessary "anglicisms," or British forms of speech, from the ERV.)

1918 The *Codex Juris Canonici*, official collection of general Roman Catholic church law, became effective. (See the May 27, 1917 entry below.)

1971 "Godspell" first opened at the Cherry Lane Theater in New York City. This musical by Stephen Schwartz, based on the New Testament Gospel of Matthew, is still being produced by secular and religious theater groups today.

1976 Rev. Thelma D. Adair, a founder and elder of the Mt. Morris Church in New York City, was elected moderator of the United Presbyterian Church, making her the first African-American woman to hold this office in the PCUSA.

Notable Birthdays

1611 Birth of Innocent XI (Benedetto Odescalchi). During his pontificate (1676-89), he stressed moral reform. Today he is regarded as the finest pontiff of the 17th century. [d. 8/12/1689]

The Last Passage

804 Death of Alcuin of York, 69, medieval English Christian poet, educator, theologian, and the most prominent figure in the Carolingian Renaissance. He was preceptor (principal) of the palace school of Charlemagne (782-796), which kept learning alive during the Dark Ages. Alcuin made some important reforms in the liturgy, and also wrote 310 letters which reveal the history of the 8th century. (b. ca. 735)

1864 Death of Nathaniel Hawthorne, 59, New England novelist and author of *The Scarlet Letter* (1850). Hawthorne's writings represented the themes and atmosphere of Puritan New England, treating the ambiguities and complexities of a once predominantly Christian culture currently facing numerous changes. His fiction is marked by a preoccupation with evil and with the dark side of human nature. (b. 7/4/1804)

Words for the Soul

1643 The Constitution of the New England Confederation (framed by the colonists of New Plymouth, New Haven, Massachusetts and Connecticut) declared: *'We all came to these parts of America with the same end and aim, namely, to advance the kindgome of our Lord Jesus Christ, and to injoy the liberties of the Gospell thereof with purities and peace, and for preserving and propagating the truth and liberties of the gospell.'*

1775 Anglican clergyman and hymnwriter John Newton noted in a letter: *'I hope you will find the Lord present at all times, and in all places. When it is so, we are at home everywxhere; when it is otherwise, home is a prison, and abroad a wilderness.'*

1986 Dutch Catholic priest and diarist Henri J. M. Nouwen reflected in his journal: *'Listening together to Jesus is a very powerful way to grow closer to each other and reach a level of intimacy that no interpersonal exchange of words can bring about.'*

FROM GOD'S WORD... OT: 1 Samuel 24:1–25:44 ~ NT: John 10:22-42 ~ Psalms 116:1-19 ~ Proverbs 15:20-21

May 20

ALMANAC OF THE CHRISTIAN FAITH

SIVAN / IYYAR

Highlights in History

325 On the site of modern Ankara, Turkey, the Council of Nicaea convened. Counted as the first Ecumenical council of the Church, and attended by nearly 300 bishops, Nicaea met through July 25th. It was called by Emperor Constantine, who sought to establish peace and unity in the Christian Church. The council condemned Arius and all his writings, but the conflict remained unresolved, and Arianism continued to exist into the 700s.

1232 Anthony of Padua (1195-1231) was canonized by Pope Gregory IX. Born in Lisbon, Portugal, Anthony joined the newly instituted Franciscans about 1220. He was a brilliant orator and preacher, and became the most celebrated of the followers of St. Francis of Assisi.

1865 Union Theological Seminary, New York City, became the first college in America to sponsor an endowed lecture series, when it established the Morse Lectureship on the Relationship of the Bible to Any of the Sciences. The series was named in memory of the founder's father, Samuel Finley Breese Morse.

1978 The Museum of the Jewish Diaspora, Beth Hatefutsoth, opened on the campus of Tel Aviv University. Its holdings trace the history of the Jews over the centuries and within various countries.

Notable Birthdays

1470 Birth of Pietro Bembo, Italian Renaissance humanist. He codified the Italian alphabet, published one of the earliest Italian grammars and helped established the Italian literary language. Created a cardinal at age 69, Bembo devoted the rest of his life to the study of theology and classical history. [d. 1/18/1547]

1851 Birth of Rose Hawthorne Lathrop, American humanitarian and Catholic religious. The youngest daughter of Nathaniel Hawthorne, she converted to Catholicism in 1891, and from 1896 devoted her life to caring for victims of cancer. In 1899 she founded the Dominican Congregation of St. Rose of Lima, and adopted the name Sister (later Mother) Mary Alphonsa. [d. 7/9/1926]

The Last Passage

1690 Death of John Eliot, 85, English-born clergyman who became a Congregational missionary to colonial America and the "Apostle to the American Indians." He worked with the Pequot people in MA for 30 years. Eliot's Indian language catechism (1653) was the first book printed in English in America, and his translation of the Bible into Pequot (1661-63) became the first Bible published in America. (b. 8/5/1604)

1853 Death of Anthony N. Groves, 58, an independent English missionary to Baghdad and India (1828-48). He authored the influential book *Christian Devotedness* (1825), and helped influence the work of his brother-in-law George Mueller, and James Hudson Taylor. Groves was also a co-founder of the Plymouth Brethren. (b. 1795)

Words for the Soul

1530 German reformer Martin Luther affirmed in a letter: *'God's friendship is a bigger comfort than that of the whole world.'*

1940 During the early days of W.W. II, English mystic Evelyn Underhill resolved in a letter: *'There is nothing Pacifists can do but take their share of the agony and pray.... I must say it's not an easy creed to hold on to.... In fact, it can only be held for supernatural reasons and by a supernatural faith that love is the ultimate reality and must prevail.'*

FROM GOD'S WORD... OT: 1 Samuel 26:1–28:25 ~ NT: John 1:1-53 ~ Psalms 117:1-2 ~ Proverbs 15:22-23

סיון ALMANAC OF THE CHRISTIAN FAITH אייר
SIVAN   IYYAR

~ May 21 ~

Highlights in History

1536 The General Assembly of Geneva formally embraced the Protestant Reformation by adopting the evangelical faith of the Swiss reformers, and separating from its Roman Catholic diocese. John Calvin, who is forever associated with the Swiss city, arrived two months later.

1738 "Sweet singer of Methodism," Charles Wesley (1707-88) was converted on this date from a legalistic to an evangelical Christian faith. The 18th child of Samuel Wesley and younger brother of John Wesley, Charles entered the ministry the following year, and became the most gifted and indefatigable hymnwriter England has ever known. He penned over 5,500 hymns during the remainder of his life.

Notable Birthdays

1471 Birth of Albrecht Dürer, German Renaissance artist. His paintings, woodcuts and copperplate engravings rendered numerous biblical themes, and his works were frequently used to illustrate the Bibles of his day. Though he never renounced his Catholic faith, Dürer felt a sympathy for the Reformation, and enjoyed the friendship of several reformers of his time. He called Luther "the great Christian man who has helped me out of great anxieties." [d. 4/6/1528]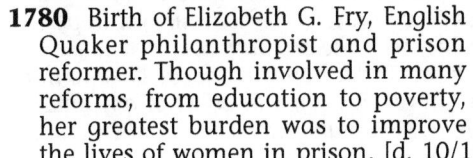

1780 Birth of Elizabeth G. Fry, English Quaker philanthropist and prison reformer. Though involved in many reforms, from education to poverty, her greatest burden was to improve the lives of women in prison. [d. 10/12/1845]

1813 Birth of Robert Murray McCheyne, Scottish Presbyterian clergyman. He was widely regarded as one of the most saintly young ministers of his day. Due to his fragile health, however, McCheyne was temporarily forced to retire from his parish. But the pastoral letters he penned to his congregation while away bore their own spiritual influence, especially in the years following his premature death at age 29. [d. 3/25/1843]

1841 Birth of Joseph Parry, Welsh sacred composer. Born in Merthyr, Wales, Parry penned a number of oratorios, cantatas, orchestral works, anthems and choruses. Today he is remembered as composer of the hymn tune ABERYSTWYTH ("Jesus, Lover of My Soul"). [d. 2/17/1903]

1922 Birth of Doris Akers, American Christian songwriter. She wrote her first gospel song at age 10. As an adult, she was affiliated with the Full Gospel Church in Columbus, Ohio, and served as its choir director. The author of over 300 gospel songs, she is perhaps best recognized today for creating the gospel refrain, "Sweet, Sweet Spirit" (1962). [d. 7/26/1995]

The Last Passage

1541 Death of Johannes Faber of Leutkirch, 63, German-born Catholic prelate. As Bishop of Vienna from 1530, Faber was a friend of Erasmus. He was also at one time a sympathizer with Zwingli and Melanchthon, but later became a vigorous opponent of Lutheranism. (b. 1478)

Words for the Soul

1540 German reformer Martin Luther declared in a Table Talk: *'The Spirit resists the proud. Even though some diligently study and for a while preach Christ in all purity, yet, if they become proud, God excludes them from the church.'*

1740 English revivalist George Whitefield summarized the purpose of Jesus' incarnation in a letter: *'He was God and man in one person, that God and man might be happy together again.'*

1944 German theologian Dietrich Bonhoeffer gave assurance in a letter from a Nazi prison: *'God alone protects; otherwise there is nothing.'*

FROM GOD'S WORD...   OT: 1 Samuel 29:1–31:13 ~ NT: 11:54–12:19 ~ Psalms 118:1-18 ~ Proverbs 15:24-26

סיון SIVAN — ALMANAC OF THE CHRISTIAN FAITH — אייר IYYAR

May 22

Highlights in History

452 Pope Leo I of Rome sent angry letters protesting the Council of Chalcedon's recent elevation of Constantinople to the preeminent see in Christendom. The two cities had been placed on equal footing by a 381 ecumenical council in Constantinople, but Chalcedon now declared that, since the imperial capital had moved to "New Rome" (Constantinople), the city should receive the benefits Rome once enjoyed. Leo's overreaction became one of several events leading to the East-West Schism of 1054.

1541 The 26-day-long Ratisbon Conference (in Regensburg, Germany) ended. It had sought to unite the ideas of 6 theologians – 3 Catholics (J. Eck, J. von Pflug, J. Gropper) and 3 Protestants (P. Melanchthon, M. Bucer, Pistorius). Doctrinal agreement was tentatively reached on most subjects, but subsequent hostilities by Martin Luther prevented any lasting reunion. After the failure of the Ratisbon Conference, the Protestant movement became permanent.

Notable Birthdays

1786 Birth of Arthur Tappan, American silk merchant, evangelical philanthropist and abolitionist. He was a founder of the American Missionary Association and, with his brother, Tappan helped establish both Oberlin and Kenyon Colleges in Ohio. [d. 7/23/1865]

1868 Birth of William R. Newell, American Plymouth Brethren pastor and Bible teacher. Associated with Moody Bible Institute in Chicago, Newell was a popular conference speaker, and is remembered today as author of the hymn, "Years I Spent in Vanity and Pride." [d. 4/1/1956]

The Last Passage

337 Death of Roman emperor Constantine I (the Great), about 49. He ruled 306-337 and was the first Roman emperor to become a Christian. Converted A.D. 312, Constantine later sought to unite the Early Church to the Roman state. He convened the Council of Nicea in 325, rejected Arianism, and increased the spiritual influence of the Bishop of Rome. (b. ca. 288)

1690 Death of Johann J. Schütz, 49, Lutheran-born German lawyer. A close friend of Philipp Spener, who founded the German Pietist movement, Schütz later left the Lutheran Church and became a Separatist. Today he is remembered as the author of the hymn, "Sing Praise to God Who Reigns Above" (b. 9/7/1640)

Words for the Soul

1537 German reformer Martin Luther declared in a sermon: 'Daily I must still work at the task of apprehending Christ.... For so many years I considered Him a Judge. This view has become an old, bad, rotten tree that has sunk its roots into me... a teaching that accords with reason: he who commits sin should render satisfaction for it. This is natural law.... But in this way I lose Christ, my Savior and Comforter, and turn Him into a taskmaster and a hangman of my soul.'

1740 English revivalist George Whitefield wrote in a letter: 'We must all have the spirit of martyrdom, though we may not all die martyrs.'

1847 Scottish clergyman and novelist George MacDonald remarked in a letter: 'The... smallest events are ordered for us, while yet in perfect consistency with the ordinary course of cause and effect in the world. I am strongly inclined to think that whatever has a moral effect of any kind on our minds, God manages for us – and even much more than this.'

1865 In the month following her husband's assassination, Mrs. Mary Todd Lincoln wrote in a letter to her pastor, Rev. Dr. Gurley: 'The recollection of your Christian kindness, extended to myself and family in our heavy bereavements, will ever be most gratefully cherished.'

FROM GOD'S WORD... OT: 2 Samuel 1:1–2:11 ~ NT: John 12:20-50 ~ Psalms 118:19-29 ~ Proverbs 15:27-28

ALMANAC OF THE CHRISTIAN FAITH

סיון SIVAN אייר IYYAR

May 23

Highlights in History

1430 French national peasant heroine Joan of Arc was captured by the Burgundians. Later turned over to the English, she was condemned on false charges of witchcraft and heresy and, at age 19 (1431), was burned at the stake in Rouen.

1633 By French edict, the country known then as New France (called "Canada" today) was closed to Huguenots as colonists. Only Roman Catholic settlers were permitted permanent residence, thus ending thirty years of attempted colonization by French Protestants.

1955 The General Assembly of the Presbyterian Church in the United States (PCUS) announced it would permit the ordination of women clergy.

1979 Members of the United Presbyterian Church in the U.S.A. (UPCUSA) and the Presbyterian Church in the United States (PCUS) took communion in a joint worship service, marking the first time the two churches came together to hold annual conventions since the denomination split over the Civil War issue of slavery.

Notable Birthdays

862 Birth of Hermann Gunkel, German Old Testament scholar. A pioneer of Form Criticism, he demonstrated how many formulas used in Hebrew poetry had taken shape in an earlier oral tradition. Gunkel's studies also cast new light on the Bible's inter-testamental period, and on Jewish apocalyptic. [d. 3/11/1932]

1873 Birth of Leo Baeck, German Reform rabbi and a foremost Jewish theologian of the 20th century. Baeck taught that Jesus was a profoundly Jewish figure, and that the Gospels belonged among the rabbinic literature. But he also argued that Judaism was the "classic" religion of reason, whereas Christianity comprised a romantic religion of irrational emotion. [d. 11/2/1956]

The Last Passage

1498 Italian Dominican reformer Girolamo Savonarola, 54, was burned at the stake, after being falsely accused of heresy. Savonarola had preached with zeal against worldliness in the clergy and against secular corruption. He led in the reformation of Florence, until his attacks on Pope Alexander VI brought about his excommunication and execution. (b. 9/21/1452)

1886 Death of German Lutheran historian Leopold Von Ranke, 90. He is regarded as the founder of the modern school of history writing, and is noted for his 3-volume *History of the Popes* (1834-39). Ranke's ultimate goal was to discover God in history. (b. 12/21/1795)

Words for the Soul

1534 Reformer Martin Luther declared in a letter: 'I, who have spent my former life sorrowing and looking sad, now seek and take joy wherever I can do so.'

1741 English revivalist George Whitefield cautioned in a letter: 'Before every increase of your work, you must expect some trials. Humblings are necessary for your spirit, and mine.'

1878 Scottish clergyman and biographer Andrew Bonar confided in his diary: 'The Lord has His own way of answering prayer.'

1974 Russian Orthodox liturgical scholar Alexander Schmemann reflected in his journal: 'The most important question is how does objective faith become subjective? How does it grow in the heart to become a personal faith? When do common words become one's own? The faith of the Church, the faith of the Fathers comes alive only when it is my own.'

FROM GOD'S WORD...   OT: 2 Samuel 2:12–3:39 ~ NT: John 13:1-30 ~ Psalms 119:1-16 ~ Proverbs 15:29-30

May 24

Highlights in History

1689 Britain's Parliament passed the Act of Toleration, designed to relieve the legal restrictions on Dissenters (non-Anglican Protestants). Catholics and nonbelievers were excluded from consideration by this legislation.

1738 In London, John Wesley, 34, underwent a personal and instantaneous spiritual experience while attending a Moravian meeting in Aldersgate Street. During the reading of Luther's *Preface to the Epistle to the Romans*, as Wesley later recorded in his journal: *'I felt my heart strangely warmed. I felt I did trust in Christ... for salvation; ...and an assurance was given me that He had taken away my sins....'*

1854 American Presbyterians founded the first (and still oldest) African-American college in the United States: Pennsylvania's Lincoln University. Located 4 miles east of Oxford and 45 miles SW of Philadelphia, Lincoln's current enrollment stands around 1,000.

1929 The general assemblies of the Church of Scotland and of the United Free Church of Edinburgh voted to reunite as a national body, the Church of Scotland.

1950 During its annual meeting in Boston, the Northern Baptist Convention formally changed its name to the American Baptist Convention. Twenty-two years later (1972), the denomination renamed itself the American Baptist Churches in the U.S.A.

Notable Birthdays

1824 Birth of John Gibson Paton, Scottish pioneer Presbyterian missionary to the New Hebrides. A member of the Reformed Presbyterian Church of Scotland, Paton worked on the Island of Tana; later, on Aneityum. [d. 1/28/1907]

The Last Passage

1089 Death of Lanfranc, 84, early scholastic theologian and Archbishop of Canterbury (1070-89). Best known for his development of the doctrine of transubstantiation (the eucharistic bread and wine becoming Christ's body and blood), Lanfranc also educated Anselm as well as future pope Alexander II. (b. ca. 1005)

1543 Death of Nicolas Copernicus (Niklas Kopernik), 70, the Polish Catholic astronomer who first proposed a formal heliocentric theory of the universe. Teaching that the sun, not the Earth, was at the center of the universe, the Copernican system eventually replaced the older Ptolemaic theory – that the sun and planets revolve around the Earth. (b. 2/19/1473)

1871 Death of Georges Darboy, 58, French Catholic prelate. As third Archbishop of Paris (1863-71), he consecrated the newly-restored Cathedral of Notre Dame. Darboy was shot as a prisoner during Franco-Prussian War, and died blessing his executioners. (b. 1/16/1813)

Words for the Soul

1740 English revivalist George Whitefield wrote in a letter: *'Those that have been most humbled, I find, always make the most solid, useful Christians.'*

1747 American colonial missionary to the New England Indians, David Brainerd wrote in his journal: *'I have often remarked to others, that much more of true religion consists in deep humility, brokenness of heart, and an abasing sense of barrenness and want of grace and holiness, than most who are called Christians imagine.'*

1930 Linguistic pioneer Frank C. Laubach, while serving as a Congregational missionary to the Philippines, commented in a letter: *'As one makes new discoveries about his friends by being with them, so one discovers the "individuality" of God if one entertains him continuously.'*

FROM GOD'S WORD...   OT: 2 Samuel 4:1–6:23 ~ NT: John 13:31–14:14 ~ Psalms 119:17–32 ~ Proverbs 15:31-32

May 25

Highlights in History

1793 In Baltimore, Bishop John Carroll consecrated Father Stephen Theodore Badin— making him the first Catholic priest to be ordained in the U.S. Badin later established Catholicism in Kentucky, Tennessee and Indiana. At his death, he donated the property where the University of Notre Dame is now located.

1824 The American Sunday School Union was established in Philadelphia. It pledged itself to *"plant a Sunday School wherever there was a population."* The Union held its position as the central agency of the Sunday School for the next 40 years. In 1970 its name was changed to the American Missionary Society.

1844 Baptists settling in Oregon and Washington state formed the West Union Baptist Church – the first Baptist church to be organized west of the Rocky Mountains.

1876 The Reformed Presbyterian Church of Scotland united with the Free Church of Scotland to form the new Free Church of Scotland. The Reformed Presbytery had been organized in 1743, and the Free Church in 1843, by splits from the Church of Scotland. (In 1929 the Free Church merged back with the Mother Church, retaining the name Church of Scotland.)

Notable Birthdays

1528 Birth of Jakob Andrea, Lutheran reformer, theologian and writer. Born near Stuttgart, he was an active promoter of the Lutheran Church in Germany, and one of the six authors of the "Formula of Concord," designed to end Lutheran discord. [d. 1/7/1590]

1865 Birth of John R. Mott, American Methodist lay evangelist, YMCA leader and pioneer of the 20th century ecumenical movement. He served as: general secretary of the YMCA (1915-31); head of the American YMCA Council, World Alliance (1926-37); a founder of the Foreign Missions Conference (1893); general secretary, World's Student Christian Federation (1892-1920), afterward chairman (1920-28); and chairman of the International Missionary Council (1921-42). Mott also played an important role in the founding of the World Council of Churches, for which he was awarded the 1946 Nobel Peace Prize. [d. 1/31/1955]

The Last Passage

1816 Death of Samuel Webbe, 76, English cabinet maker-turned-hymn composer. His most enduring sacred melody is CONSOLATION ("Come, Ye Disconsolate"). (b. 1740)

1868 Death of "Billy" Bray of Cornwall, 73, Welsh Methodist preacher. Formerly an alcoholic coal miner, he found the Lord at 29, and soon after joined the Methodists. Bray set out immediately to win others to Christ, and for 43 years he preached, built chapels and took orphans into his home. (b. 6/1 [or 11/4] /1794)

Words for the Soul

1544 Reformer Martin Luther declared in a sermon: *'After a man's body has decayed in the earth, it will rise in much greater beauty and glory. It will be the body of a human being, just as it was created, but the body will have a different appearance and use. It will not eat, drink, digest, procreate children, keep house, etc. It will need none of the things that pertain to this transient life and bodily sustenance.'*

1878 American Quaker holiness author Hannah Whitall Smith confessed in a letter: *'Our will carries along all the rest of our nature. If we control our will ourselves, then we live; if we surrender it to Christ and let Him control it, then He lives in us.... This is the point where faith comes in. It may seem to us that if we give up managing for ourselves, everything will fall apart; but... the Lord tells us to be careful for nothing, because He means to take care of everything we commit to Him, and all He wants is that we should really trust Him.'*

FROM GOD'S WORD...   OT: 2 Samuel 7:1–8:18 ~ NT: John 14:15-31 ~ Psalms 119:33-48 ~ Proverbs 15:33

ALMANAC OF THE CHRISTIAN FAITH

סיון SIVAN   אייר IYYAR

~ May 26 ~

Highlights in History

1521 Martin Luther's teachings were formally condemned by the Edict of Worms, and Luther himself was put under the ban of the Holy Roman Emperor. Luther was soon after "kidnapped" (by those who feared for his life) and carried off into hiding.

1808 The Fifth American General Conference of the Methodist Episcopal Church closed, in Baltimore. During this three-week gathering, William McKendree was ordained as the first American bishop of the Methodist Church.

1926 Aimee Semple McPherson, founder of the Church of the Foursquare Gospel, disappeared from a California beach. She was presumed drowned.  However, on June 23, McPherson reappeared in Arizona, saying she had been kidnapped. Rumors circulated that she had eloped for a romantic tryst, but while her support base remained strong, media coverage turned negative, and her image never fully recovered.

Notable Birthdays

1768 or 1773 Birth of Johann (Hans) Georg Nägeli, Swiss teacher and hymnwriter. A pioneer in music education, his music theories later influenced American hymnwriter  Lowell Mason. Nägeli is best remembered today as composer of the hymn tune DENNIS ("Blest Be the Tie That Binds"). [d. 12/26/1836]

1811 Birth of William Hunter, Irish-born American Methodist clergyman, Semitics scholar and hymnwriter. He pastored in the Pittsburgh conference, and afterward taught Hebrew at Allegheny College (1855-70). Hunter penned more than 100 hymns, including "The Great Physician Now is Near." [d. 10/18/1877]

The Last Passage

604 Death of Augustin of Canterbury, "Apostle to the English." His preaching converted Anglo-Saxon King Ethelbert in AD 597. Later, Augustin was made archbishop of the Anglo-Saxons (601-604), and Ethelbert gave him his own castle, thus establishing the archbishopric of Canterbury as the principal episcopal center of England.

735 Anglo-Saxon theologian Venerable Bede died at 62. Known as the monk of Jarrow, known also as the father of English history, Bede was the first great English scholar. He invented the  B.C./A.D. dating system, and his *Ecclesiastical History of the English People* (731) was crucial to England's conversion to Christianity. (b. ca. 673)

1927 Death of Francis E. Clark, 75, Canadian-born American Congregational clergyman and church youth reformer. Orphaned at age 7, Clark grew up to become a pioneer  in church youth ministry. In 1881 he founded Christian Endeavor, a prototype of the modern local church youth fellowships. (b. 9/12/1851)

Words for the Soul

1658 Scottish clergyman Samuel Rutherford declared in a letter to a bereaved mother: *'The temporal loss of creatures, dear to you here, may be the more easily endured, so that the gain of One who only hath immortality groweth.'*

1742 English revivalist George Whitefield noted in a letter: *'He hath continually fought my battles for me, and I am persuaded will do so till the end.'*

1956 British literary scholar and Christian apologist C. S. Lewis wrote in one of his **Letters to An American Lady**: *'One of the many reasons for wishing to be a better Christian is that, if one were, one's prayers for others might be more effectual.'*

FROM GOD'S WORD...   OT: 2 Samuel 9:1–11:27 ~ NT: John 15:1–27 ~ Psalms 119:49-64 ~ Proverbs 16:1-3

סיון ALMANAC OF THE CHRISTIAN FAITH אייר
SIVAN   IYYAR

~ May 27 ~

Highlights in History

1668 Thomas Gold, William Turner and John Farnum became the first Baptists exiled from an American colony when they were banished by the General Court of Massachusetts.

1917 Pope Benedict XV promulgated the "Codex Iuris Canonici" (CIC) by a papal bull. This comparatively small volume of canon law was divided into five books and 2,414 canons. It was the first redaction of the canon law to be made in the Catholic Church in modern times. The CIC came into force at Pentecost (May 19th) of the following year, 1918.

Notable Birthdays

1799 Birth of George W. Doane, American Episcopal prelate and hymnwriter. As Bishop of New Jersey (1832-59), Doane was a leader of the High Church party. He authored many hymns, including "Softly Now the Light of Day," "Thou Art the Way," "Father of Mercies, Hear" and "Fling Out the Banner! Let it Float." [d. 4/27/1859]

1819 Birth of Julia Ward Howe, American Unitarian abolitionist, social reformer, author and lecturer. At age 24 she married Dr. Samuel Gridley Howe of Boston, head of the Perkins Institute, the Mass. School for the Blind. Her most famous work was "The Battle Hymn of the Republic" (a.k.a. "Mine Eyes Have Seen the Glory"). [d. 10/17/1910]

1821 Birth of Henry W. Baker, English clergyman, editor and hymnwriter. He compiled *Hymns Ancient and Modern*, the most representative collection used by the Church of England. To this work Baker contributed 25 of his own hymns, including "The King of Love My Shepherd Is" and "Art Thou Weary, Art Thou Languid?" [d. 2/12/1877]

The Last Passage

1464 Death of Isidore of Kiev, 79, Metropolitan of the Russian Orthodox Church (1435-39). He was an architect of the reunion between the Catholic and Russian Orthodox churches (1439). Elevated to cardinal, he became a papal legate to Greece (1444-48) and Constantinople (1453-59), and was afterward titular Patriarch of Constantinople (1459-64). (b. ca. 1385)

1564 Death of John Calvin (Jean Chauvin), 54, French-born theologian and Swiss ecclesiastical reformer. Called "the organizer of Protestantism," Calvin built on the premise that the Bible is the only trustworthy source of knowledge, and thereby unified the scattered reform theologies of Europe. Much of the content of his classic, *Institutes of the Christian Religion*, was written out of pastoral concerns. (b. 7/10/1509)

Words for the Soul

1532 German reformer Martin Luther declared in a Table Talk: *'The devil wants to accuse and judge us and is himself worse than all human beings? What business of his is it that I have sinned? I have not sinned against him but against God. The devil has given me no Law. The Bible says: "Against Thee, Thee only, have I sinned."'*

1742 English revivalist George Whitefield noted in a letter: *'As a blind zeal often prompts us to speak too much, so tepidity and lukewarmness often cause us to speak too little.'*

1766 Revered English Methodist preacher John Fletcher concluded in a letter: *'If a sparrow falleth not to the ground, nor a hair from our head, without our heavenly Father's leave, it is certain that higher circumstances of our life are planned by the wise and gracious Governor of all things. This kind of faith I find of indispensable necessity to go calmly through life, and I think through death also.'*

FROM GOD'S WORD... OT: 2 Samuel 12:1-31 ~ NT: John 16:1-33 ~ Psalms 119:65-80 ~ Proverbs 16:4-5

May 28

Highlights in History

1577 The Formula of Concord was published — the last of the classical Lutheran confessions which were later assembled in the *Book of Concord* (1580). Being chiefly the work of Jakob Andrea and Martin Chemnitz, the 12 articles of the Formula steered a careful middle course between extremists on both sides, and reaffirmed the basic teaching of the Augsburg Confession of 1530.

1898 In Turin, Italy, city councillor Secundo Pia took the first modern photograph of the Shroud of Turin. The relic had previously rested undisturbed for 320 years in the Turin Cathedral. When Pia developed the negative, the image embedded in the Shroud was reversed, revealing a clearly detailed photographic positive!

1954 President Dwight Eisenhower signed into law the Congressional Act, Joint Resolution 243, which added the words "under God" to the *Pledge of Allegiance*. In a speech given soon after, Eisenhower declared, in support of the new bill: 'In this way we are reaffirming the transcendence of religious faith in America's heritage and future.'

1958 In Pittsburgh, the United Presbyterian Church of North America and the Presbyterian Church of the USA merged to form the United Presbyterian Church in the United States of America (UPCUSA).

1982 Pope John Paul II began a six-day itinerary to Great Britain, becoming the first pope in history to visit the U.K. During his visit, he had an audience with Queen Elizabeth.

Notable Birthdays

1779 Birth of Thomas Moore, Irish patriotic poet. He penned 32 hymns during his life. Among the greatest of these is "Come, Ye Disconsolate." During the last three years of Moore's life he suffered from senile dementia – probably Alzheimer's disease. [d. 2/25/1852]

The Last Passage

1884 Death of Samuel Fisk Green, 61, American medical missionary. He served in Ceylon under the American Board of Commissioners for Foreign Missions (ABCFM) for 26 years (1847-73), and wrote medical works in Tamil. (b. 10/10/1822)

1903 Death of John Henry W. Stuckenberg, 68, American Lutheran clergyman and sociologist. He wrote on problems of the state, international law and on the labor movement. His wife was a leader in the WCTU. (b. 1/6/1835)

Words for the Soul

1640 Scottish clergyman Samuel Rutherford wrote to a bereaving parent: 'Now the number of crosses lying in your way to glory are fewer by one than when I saw you; they must decrease.'

1725 English founder of Methodism, John Wesley asserted in a letter to his mother Susannah: "I can't think that when God sent us into the world He had irreversibly decreed that we should be perpetually miserable in it.'

1775 Anglican clergyman John Newton wondered in a letter: 'If a transient glance exceed all that the world can afford..., what must it be to dwell with Him? If a day in His courts be better than a thousand, what will eternity be in His presence?'

1831 On the eve of his 21st birthday, Andrew Bonar confided in his diary: 'Saturday evenings are often times of peculiar wandering and unhappy longings in my soul. But God by giving me joy in divine things, in the absence of all I wished from the earth, has shown me that there is better happiness.'

1892 Seven months before his death at 82, Scottish clergyman Andrew Bonar wrote in a letter to his son James: 'It was in the year 1830 that I found the Saviour, or rather that He found me and "laid me on His shoulders rejoicing," and I have never parted company with Him all these sixty-two years.'

FROM GOD'S WORD...   OT: 2 Samuel 13:1-39 ~ NT: John 17:1-26 ~ Psalms 119:81-96 ~ Proverbs 16:6-7

סיון ALMANAC OF THE CHRISTIAN FAITH אייר
SIVAN   IYYAR

May 29

Highlights in History

1453 Constantinople, capital of the Eastern Roman (Byzantine) Empire since 324, was besieged by the forces of Mohammed II and fell to the invading Turks of the Ottoman Empire. The Byzantine emperor was killed, the city was renamed Istanbul, and became the capital of the Turkish Empire. To many historical scholars, this event marked the end of the Middle Ages.

1788 In Philadelphia, the Westminster Larger and Shorter Catechisms were approved as part of the constitution of the Presbyterian Church.

1819 While visiting his father-in-law's church, Anglican bishop Reginald Heber first penned the poetic stanzas to the enduring hymn, "From Greenland's Icy Mountains."

1967 Pope Paul VI named 27 new members to the College of Cardinals. Among the appointees was the Archbishop of Krakow, Poland – Karol Wojtyla – who in 1978 became Pope John Paul II.

Notable Birthdays

1849 Birth of Joseph Samuel Exell, Anglican clergyman, and compiler of *The Pulpit Commentary* (1880), *The Homiletical Library* (1882), and *The Biblical Illustrator* (1887). [d. ca. 1909]

1874 Birth of G[ilbert] K[eith] Chesterton, English journalist, novelist, poet and apologist. He converted from Anglicanism to Catholicism in 1922. Called the "Prince of Paradox" for the  religious dogma underlying his light style, the 400-pound man was occasionally absent-minded, but brilliant. Chesterton was credited by poet T. S. Eliot with doing *'more than any man in his time... to maintain the existence of the [Christian] minority in the modern world.'* [d. 6/14/1936]

The Last Passage

1936 Death of Percy Dearmer, 69, Anglican scholar, teacher and author. He published scores of books, some titles running to twelve editions. He prepared at least 30 original hymns during his life. One which still endures is: "He Who Would Valiant Be." (b. 2/27/1867)

Words for the Soul

1742 English revivalist George Whitefield noted in a letter: *'Was not my Master's love like himself, infinite, I should have been cast off long before this time. But I find those whom he loves, he loves to the end.'*

1845 A few weeks before his death, former 7th U.S. President Andrew Jackson, 78, testified: *'I am in the hands of a merciful God. I have full confidence in his goodness and mercy.... The Bible is true. I have tried to conform to its spirit as near as possible. Upon that sacred volume I rest my hope for eternal salvation, through the merits and blood of our blessed Lord and Saviour, Jesus Christ.'*

1878 American Quaker holiness writer Hannah Whitall Smith confessed in a letter: *'I have often been compelled to say the blessed words, "Your will be done, Your will be done" over and over... before the sweetness has come. But at last, as surely as God is God, His will has encircled me and mine like the walls of an impregnable fortress, and my soul has sunk into complete repose!'*

1944 German Lutheran theologian and Nazi martyr Dietrich Bonhoeffer declared in a letter from prison: *'How wrong it is to use God as a stop-gap for the incompleteness of our knowledge. If in fact the frontiers of our knowledge are being pushed further and further back, then God is being pushed back with them, and is therefore continually in retreat. We are to find God in what we know, not in what we don't know; God wants us to realize His presence, not in unsolved problems, but in those that are solved.'*

FROM GOD'S WORD...   OT: 2 Samuel 14:1–15:22 ~ NT: John 18:1-24 ~ Psalms 119:97-112 ~ Proverbs 16:8-9

ALMANAC OF THE CHRISTIAN FAITH

May 30

Highlights in History

1812 In Lancaster County, PA, the Reformed Mennonite Church was organized under the leadership of John Herr. Reformed Mennonite clergy are not paid, and there is no Sunday School, the membership of the denomination believing that parents should teach their own children the main tenets of the Gospel.

1971 The Provincial Council of the Russian Orthodox Church, meeting in Zagorsk, elected Metropolitan Pimen to become Patriarch (1971-1990) of Moscow and All Russia.

Notable Birthdays

1838 Birth of English musician Charles William Fry. He was known as "the first bandmaster of the Salvation Army," and also authored the hymn, "Lily of the Valley." [d. 8/24/1882]

The Last Passage

340 Death of the "Father of Church History," Eusebius (Pamphili), 76. A Greek historian, he served as Bishop of Caesarea in Palestine (314-39), and authored the ten volume *Ecclesiastical History* (325), which treats the Early Church from the birth of Christ to A.D. 324. (b. 264)

1431 Death of Joan of Arc, 19, French peasant mystic and national heroine. At 13 she heard divine voices telling her to aid the Dauphin (Charles VII) by raising the English siege of Orléans (1428). With a small force, the "Maid of Orléans" forced the English to withdraw. Later, however, she was captured, tried for heresy, found guilty by the clergy and burned at the stake. In 1920 Joan was canonized. (b. 1/6/1412)

1976 Death of Mitsuo Fuchida, 73, the Japanese military commander who flew lead plane during the Japanese attack on Pearl Harbor. After WWII, Fuchida became disillusioned with his Buddhist beliefs and, after reading a tract published by the Pocket Testament League, was converted to Christianity in 1950. (b. 12/3/1902)

Words for the Soul

1518 Reformer Martin Luther declared in a letter: 'Without Christ's command not even a pope can speak, nor is the heart of a king in his own hand.'

1519 Dutch humanist Desiderius Erasmus wrote to German reformer Martin Luther in a letter: '[It] might be wiser of you to denounce those who misuse the Pope's authority than to censure the Pope himself.... Old institutions cannot be uprooted in an instant. Quiet argument may do more than wholesale condemnation. Keep cool. Do not get angry.'

1855 Scottish clergyman and biographer Andrew Bonar confided in his journal: 'If there is one thing for which I bless the Lord more than another, it is this, that He has so far opened my eyes to see that Christ pleases the Father to the full, and that this is the ground of acceptance. I look and look again at this sight... and in that sight I live.'

1871 American Quaker holiness writer Hannah Whitall Smith remarked in a letter: 'We Quakers are so thrifty that we do not like to live "from hand to mouth" as the expression is. We like a stock of goodness laid up ahead, and a stock of wisdom and of patience and of all the other graces. But... God's plan for us is different. God has laid it all up for us in Christ, and we have to draw it each moment as we need it.'

1907 English mystic Evelyn Underhill noted in a letter: 'Feeling must precede doing; but unless it finally results in doing, it is mere emotional satisfaction, of no value. The direction and constancy of the will is what really matters, and intellect and feeling are only important in so far as they contribute to that.'

FROM GOD'S WORD... OT: 2 Samuel 15:23-16:23 ~ NT: John 18:25-19:22 ~ Psalms 119:113-128 ~ Proverbs 16:10-11

סיון ALMANAC OF THE CHRISTIAN FAITH אייר
SIVAN   IYYAR

~ May 31 ~

Highlights in History

1578 Italian archaeologist Antonio Bosio (ca.1576-1629) accidentally discovered a burial chamber on the Via Salaria. Fifteen years later, on Dec. 10, 1593, he became the first man in modern times to descend into the catacombs of Rome. His extensive discoveries were published posthumously (1632, 1634) in his *Roma Sotterranea*, and remained the standard work until the researches of G. B. De Rossi, who afterward dubbed Bosio "the Columbus of the Catacombs."

1821 The Cathedral of the Assumption of the Blessed Virgin Mary – the first Catholic cathedral in the U.S. – was dedicated in Baltimore, MD, by Archbishop Ambrose Marechal. (The cornerstone having been laid in 1806, the structure was completed in 1851.) In 1936, the Baltimore Cathedral was raised to the rank of a minor basilica by Pope Pius XI.

Notable Birthdays

1684 Birth of Timothy Cutler, American Anglican leader and educator. Once Rector of Yale College in Boston (1720-22), he became best known in colonial New England as the central figure in the so-called Yale apostasy of 1722. At this time Cutler resigned to become Anglican rector of Christ Church, Boston (1723-65). Throughout his career, he was a domiant Anglican spokesman of his day and a leader of the anti-revival forces. [d. 8/17/1765]

1699 Birth of Alexander Cruden, Scottish bookseller and compiler. Prone to erratic behavior, he worked on compiling his concordance to the Scriptures between periods of mental breakdown and institutionalization. First published in 1737, *Cruden's Concordance* is still a standard reference for the King James Version of the Bible. [d. 11/1/1770]

1898 Birth of Norman Vincent Peale, Reformed Church of America clergyman and writer. He pastored Marble Collegiate Reformed Church, in New York City (1932-84). He was also co-founder (1937) of American Foundation for Religion and Psychiatry. Best known for his *Power of Positive Thinking* (1952), Peale combined psychology and Scripture in his messsage of "prayer and optimism." [d. 12/24/1993]

The Last Passage

1434 Death of Jagiello (aka Wladislaw), 83, king of Lithuania (1385-1434). Baptized into the Christian faith on February 15, 1386, Jagiello's conversion marked the ultimate fulfillment of the "Macedonian Vision" which led St. Paul to begin taking the Gospel to Europe. (b. 1351)

Words for the Soul

1769 Anglican hymnwriter John Newton declared in a letter: 'He fulfills his promise in making our strength equal to our day; and every new trial gives us a new proof how happy it is to be enabled to put our trust in Him.'

1769 Anglican clergyman and hymnwriter John Newton noted in a letter: 'It is an honour that he permits us to pray; and we shall surely find he is a prayer-hearing God.... And when our infirmities prevail, he does not bid us to be despondent, but reminds us that we have an Advocate with the Father, who is able to pity, to pardon and to save to the uttermost.'

1869 American Quaker holiness writer Hannah Whitall Smith confessed in her journal: 'Thank God it is the blood that cleanses, the precious blood of Christ! It is not discipline, nor effort, nor prayer, nor fasting that cleanse the heart and make it a fit dwelling place for the Father and the Son; it is the precious blood alone. And it can cleanse in a moment; yes, can make, even out of my heart, a holy temple for God to abide in!'

FROM GOD'S WORD...   OT: 2 Samuel 17:1-29 ~ NT: John 19:23-42 ~ Psalms 119:129-152 ~ Proverbs 16:12-13

MAY INDEX

A

Abolition of Slavery 5/18
Adair, Thelma D. 5/19
AFRICAN-AMERICANS
   Adair, Thelma D. 5/19
   Henson, Josiah 5/15
   Kilgore, Thomas 5/17
   Lincoln University (PA) 5/24
African-American Benchmarks 5/1, 5/2, 5/4, 5/15, 5/19, 5/24
Akers, Doris
   b. 5/21/1922
Alcuin of York
   (b. ca. 735) d. 5/19/804
Alexander II, Pope (1061-1073) 5/24
Alexander III, Greek Orthodox Patriarch
   b. 5/9/1869 [d. 1958]
Alexander VI, Pope (1492-1503) 5/23
Alington, Cyril Argentine
   (b. 10/22/1872) d. 5/16/1955
Allen, Alexander V. G.
   b. 5/14/1841 [d. 7/1/1908]
Alzheimer's Disease 5/28
American (Episcopal) Church Mission 5/1
American Board of Commissioners for Foreign Missions (ABCFM) 5/28
American Foundation for Religion and Psychiatry 5/31
American Missionary Association 5/22
American Missionary Society 5/25
American Sunday School Union 5/25
American Tract Society 5/11
Andrea, Jakob 5/28
   b. 5/25/1528 [d. 1/7/1590]
Anglicisms (British Forms of Speech) 5/19
Anthony of Padua 5/20
Arianism 5/2, 5/22
Arndt, Johann
   (b. 12/27/1555) d. 5/11/1621
Athanasius ("the Great")
   (b. ca. 293) d. 5/2/373
Augsburg Confession of 1530 5/28

Augustin[e] of Canterbury
   (b. ?) d. 5/26/604
Augustine of Hippo, St. 5/6
Azusa Street Revival 5/2

B

B.C./A.D. Dating System 5/26
Back to the Bible Broadcast 5/16
Badin, Stephen Theodore 5/25
Baeck, Leo
   5/23/1873 [d. 11/2/1956]
Baker, Henry W.
   b. 5/27/1821 [d. 2/12/1877]
Barth, Karl
   b. 5/10/1886 [d. 12/9/1968]
Bede, Venerable
   (b. ca. 673) d. 5/26/735
Beecher, Henry Ward 5/2
Beecher, Lyman 5/2
Bembo, Pietro
   b. 5/20/1470 [d. 1/18/1547]
Benedict XV, Pope (1914-1922) 5/27
BIBLE TRANSLATIONS
   American Standard Version (ASV) 5/17, 5/19
   Bishops' Bible (1568) 5/17
   English Revised Version (EV or ERV) 5/9, 5/17, 5/19
   Hindustani (by Henry Martyn) 5/16
   King James/"Authorized" (1611) 5/19, 5/25
   Mandarin Chinese 5/6
   Pequot (by John Eliot) 5/20
BIBLE VERSIONS
   Greek New Testament 5/12
   Living Letters (1962) 5/8
   The Living Bible (1971) 5/8
Boehm, Martin 5/18
Boehme, Jakob 5/6
Bonar, Andrew 5/18. See also QUOTATIONS
Bonar, Horatius 5/18
Bonhoeffer, Dietrich. See also QUOTATIONS
Boniface, St. 5/19
Boniface VIII, Pope (1294-1303) 5/15
BOOKS / PUBLICATIONS
   Ante-Nicene Fathers (1867-1885) 5/10

   An Enquiry into the Obligations of Christians, to use means for the Conversion of the Heathens in which the Religious State of the Different Nations of the World, the Success of Former Undertakings, and the practicability of Further Undertakings, are Considered 5/12
   An Essay on the Plan of Salvation (1812) 5/3
   Augustinus (1640) 5/6
   A Biblical Cyclopaedia (1868) 5/9
   A Condensed Concordance of the Holy Scriptures (1875) 5/9
   Book of Concord (1580) 5/28
   Catholic Encyclopedia (1915) 5/4
   Christ's Ecclesia (1926) 5/17
   Christian Devotedness (1825) 5/20
   Cruden's Concordance (1737) 5/31
   Der Judenstaat (1896) 5/2
   Dictionary of Religion and Ethics (1921) 5/3
   Ecclesiastical History (325) 5/30
   Ecclesiastical History of the English People (731) 5/26
   Eclectic ("McGuffey's) Reader 5/4
   English Hymns: Their Authors and History (1886) 5/12
   Expositor's Bible (1888-1905) 5/4
   Four Books on True Christianity (1606-10) 5/11
   Grammar of the Idioms of the New Testament (1825) 5/12
   Hebrew Grammar (1827) 5/5
   History of Dogma (7 vols., 1894-99) 5/7
   History of Methodism (1902) 5/4
   History of the Popes (1834-39) 5/23
   Hymns Ancient and Modern 5/27
   Hymns and Meditations (1850) 5/10
   Institutes of the Christian Religion (1559) 5/27
   Introduction to the New Testament (19th ed. 1978) 5/16
   I Believe in Miracles (1962) 5/7
   Jewish Christianity (1937) 5/17
   Judaism in the First Centuries of the Christian Era (1927-30) 5/16
   Letters to An American Lady (1967) 5/26
   Life and Letters of Phillips Brooks (1900) 5/14
   Lives of the Principal Saints (1756-1759) 5/15
   Living Letters (1962) 5/8

   Moody and Sankey Hymnal in Welsh (1874) 5/6
   New Testament Criticism (1924) 5/17
   On the Benevolence and Rectitude of the Supreme Being (1840) 5/3
   Power of Positive Thinking, The (1952) 5/31
   Preface to the Epistle to the Romans (1545) 5/24
   Quest for the Historical Jesus: From Reimarus to Wrede (1909) 5/10
   Roma Sotterranea (1634) 5/31
   Sabbatical Journal (1998) 5/13, 5/14
   Scofield Bible (1909) 5/11
   Sixteen Revelations of Divine Love (1393) 5/8
   Temple Chimes 5/17
   The Biblical Illustrator (1887) 5/29
   The Christian's Secret of a Happy Life (1875) 5/1
   The Divine Comedy (1308-1321) 5/15
   The Divine Human in the Scriptures (1860) 5/11
   The Jewish State (1896) 5/2
   The Latin Hymn Writers and Their Hymns (1889) 5/12
   The Mystical Element of Religion (1908) 5/5
   The Old, Old Story and Other Verses (1879) 5/9
   The Phenomenon of Man (1955) 5/1
   The Pulpit Commentary (1880) 5/29
   The Pursuit of God (1948) 5/13
   The Scarlet Letter (1850) 5/19
   The Six Days of Creation (1855) 5/11
   Uncle Tom's Cabin (1849) 5/15
Bosio, Antonio 5/31
Boudinot, Elias 5/8
Bourdaloue, Louis
   (b. 8/20/1632) d. 5/13/1704
Boys' Town Orphanage 5/15
Bradford, William 5/8
Brainerd, David 5/18. See also QUOTATIONS
Bray, Billy, of Cornwall
   (b. 6/1 or 11/4, 1794) d. 5/25/1868
Brooks, Phillips 5/2
Bucer, Martin 5/22
Buck, Philo M.
   b. 5/15/1846 [d. 9/8/1924]
Butler, Alban
   (b. 10/24/1710) d. 5/15/1773
Byzantium 5/11

C

CALENDARS
  Gregorian (New Style) 5/14
  Julian (Old Style) 5/14
California Gold Rush (1849-56) 5/2, 5/18
Calvin, John (Jean Chauvin) 5/21. See also QUOTATIONS
  (b. 7/10/1509) d. 5/27/1564
Calvinism 5/15
Canterbury, Archbishopric of 5/26
CANTERBURY, ARCHBISHOPS OF
  Anselm (1093-1109) 5/24
  Augustin[e] (601-604) 5/26
  Fisher, Geoffrey F. (1945-1961) 5/5
  Lanfranc (1070-1089) 5/24
  Parker, Matthew (1559-1575) 5/17
Carey, William 5/12, 5/16
Carolingian Renaissance 5/19
Carroll, John 5/25
Chalmers, Thomas 5/18
Chardin, Pierre Teilhard de
  b. 5/1/1881 [d. 4/10/1955]
Charlemagne 5/19
Charles VII, French King (1422-1461) 5/30
Chemnitz, Martin 5/28
Chesterton, G[ilbert] K[eith]
  b. 5/29/1874 [d. 6/14/1936]
CHURCHES
  Baltimore Cathedral (MD) 5/31
  Benton Harbor Presbyterian Church (MI) 5/7
  Cathedral of Notre Dame 5/24
  Cathedral of the Assumption of the Blessed Virgin 5/31
  Christ Church, Boston 5/31
  Church of the Covenant (NY City) 5/12
  First Baptist Church (Dallas, TX) 5/6
  Full Gospel Church (OH) 5/21
  Madison Avenue Baptist Church (NY City) 5/5
  Marble Collegiate Reformed Church (NY City) 5/31
  Moody Bible Church (Chicago) 5/16
  Moody Bible Church (IL) 5/16
  Mt. Morris Presbyterian Church (NY City) 5/19
  People's Temple 5/13
  Reims Cathedral (France) 5/6
  Southside Alliance (Chicago) 5/13
  St. Julian's Church (England) 5/8
  St. Peter's Basilica (Rome) 5/16

Ciocchi del Monte, Giammaria. See Julius III, Pope (1550-1555)
Civil War (American) 5/2, 5/3, 5/12
Clark, Francis E.
  (b. 9/12/1851) d. 5/26/1927
Codex Iuris / Juris Canonici 5/19, 5/27
COLLEGES / UNIVERSITIES
  Allegheny College (PA) 5/26
  Antioch College (OH) 5/4
  Cambridge University (England) 5/10
  Durham University (England) 5/16
  Eton College (England) 5/16
  Fisk University (Nashville) 5/18
  Kenyon College (OH) 5/22
  Lincoln University (PA) 5/24
  Log College (PA) 5/6
  Notre Dame University (IN) 5/25
  Oberlin College (OH) 5/22
  Princeton College (NJ) 5/17
  Shrewsbury School (England) 5/16
  Taylor University (IN) 5/2, 5/18
  Tel Aviv University (Israel) 5/20
  University of Wittenberg (Germany) 5/5
  Winchester College (England) 5/3
  Yale College (CT) 5/14
  Yale College (MA) 5/31
College of Cardinals 5/29
Conkey, Ithamar
  b. 5/5/1815 [d. 4/30/1867]
Constantine I, Roman Emperor (306-337) 5/11, 5/20
Constantine the Great
  (b. ca. 288) d. 5/22/337
Constantinople 5/5, 5/11, 5/22, 5/27, 5/29
Copernican Theory of the Universe 5/9
Copernicus, Nicolas (Niklas Kopernik)
  (b. 2/19/1473) d. 5/24/1543
COUNCILS OF THE CHURCH
  Carthage (418) 5/1
  Chalcedon (541) 5/22
  Nicea (325) 5/2, 5/20, 5/22
  Synod of Dort (1618-19) 5/9
  Trent (1545-63) 5/16
Cox, Frances Elizabeth
  b. 5/10/1812 [d. 9/23/1897]
Coxe, Arthur Cleveland
  b. 5/10/1818 [d. 7/20/1896]
Cruden, Alexander
  b. 5/31/1699 [d. 11/1/1770]

Crusades, The 5/18
Cutler, Timothy
  b. 5/31/1684 [d. 8/17/1765]

D

Dana, H[enry] E.
  (b. 6/21/1888) d. 5/17/1945
Darboy, Georges
  (b. 1/16/1813) d. 5/24/1871
Dark Ages, The 5/19
Dearmer, Percy
  (b. 2/27/1867) d. 5/29/1936
Declaration of Independence, American 5/17
Declaration of Union (1939) 5/10
DENOMINATIONS, CHRISTIAN
  American Baptists 5/3, 5/5
  American Baptist Churches in the U.S.A. 5/24
  American Baptist Convention 5/17, 5/24
  American Episcopal Church 5/10, 5/14, 5/17, 5/27
  American Lutheranism 5/3, 5/7, 5/28
  American Methodism 5/4, 5/9, 5/15
  American Presbyterianism 5/6, 5/7, 5/12, 5/16, 5/24
  Association of Evangelical Lutheran Churches (AELC) 5/3
  Catholicism 5/4
  Christian & Missionary Alliance 5/13
  Christian Union Church 5/15
  Church of England (Anglicanism) 5/8, 5/9, 5/14, 5/29
  Church of England in Canada 5/17
  Church of God 5/15
  Church of Scotland 5/24, 5/25
  Church of the Foursquare Gospel 5/26
  Congregationalism 5/24, 5/26
  Dutch Reformed Church 5/1, 5/8
  English Baptists 5/12
  English Catholicism 5/15
  English Congregationalism 5/20
  English Methodism 5/15
  Episcopal Church 5/6
  Episcopal Church in America 5/9
  Evangelical Church 5/18
  Evangelical Lutheran Church in America 5/3
  French Protestants 5/23
  French Reformed Church 5/18
  Full Gospel Church 5/21
  German Lutheranism 5/7, 5/10, 5/11, 5/23

  German Reformed Church 5/3
  Holiness Church 5/15
  Huguenots 5/23
  Irish Anglicanism 5/14
  Lutheranism 5/3, 5/21
  Lutheran Church in Germany 5/25
  Lutheran Church Missouri Synod 5/7, 5/16
  Methodism, American 5/3
  Methodist Episcopal Church 5/10, 5/15, 5/26
  Methodist Protestant Church 5/10
  Moravian (Bohemian) Brethren 5/9
  Moravian Church 5/24
  National Church of Scotland 5/18
  Northern Baptist Convention 5/17, 5/24
  Pentecostalism 5/2
  Plymouth Brethren 5/20, 5/22
  Polish Catholicism 5/24
  Presbyterian Church 5/2
  Presbyterian Church (PCUSA) 5/19, 5/28
  Presbyterian Church in the United States (PCUS) 5/23
  Quakerism (Society of Friends) 5/1, 5/16
  Reformed Church of America 5/31
  Reformed Mennonite Church 5/3, 5/30
  Reformed Presbyterian Church of Scotland 5/24, 5/25
  Roman Catholicism 5/6, 5/23
  Russian Orthodoxy 5/4, 5/7, 5/23
  Salvation Army 5/30
  Scottish (Presbyterian) Secession 5/9
  Scottish Free Church 5/4
  Scottish Presbyterianism 5/13, 5/21
  Society of Friends (Quakers) 5/1
  Southern Baptist Convention 5/3, 5/6, 5/8
  Unitas Fratrum 5/9
  United Brethren in Christ 5/18
  United Free Church of Scotland 5/24
  United Holy Church of America 5/1
  United Methodist Church 5/15, 5/18
  United Presbyterian Church in the U.S.A. (UPCUSA) 5/19, 5/23, 5/28
  United Presbyterian Church of North America 5/28
  Welsh Calvinism 5/6
  Welsh Methodism 5/25
  Wesleyan Methodist Church 5/18
DENOMINATIONS, CHRISTIAN SECTARIAN
  American Unitarian Association 5/10
  New Jerusalem Church 5/7

Swedenborgianism 5/7
Unitarian Church 5/10, 5/19, 5/27
Universalist Church of America 5/10
De Rossi, G. B. 5/31
Dickinson, Emily Elizabeth
(b. 12/1/1830) d. 5/15/1886
Dissenters (non-Anglican Protestants) 5/24
Doane, George Washington
b. 5/27/1799 [d. 4/27/1859]
Duffield, George 5/12
Duffield, Samuel A. W.
(b. 9/24/1843) d. 5/12/1887
Dunlop, Merrill E.
b. 5/9/1905 [d. unknown]
Dürer, Albrecht
b. 5/21/1471 [d. 4/6/1528]
Dwight, Timothy
b. 5/14/1752 [d. 1/11/1817]

E

Eadie, John
b. 5/9/1810 [d. 6/3/1876]
Earl of Surrey 5/4
Eastern Roman (Byzantine) Empire 5/29
Eastern Roman Empire 5/11
Eck, Johannes 5/22
Edict of Nantes (1598) 5/14
Edict of Worms 5/26
Edwards, Jonathan 5/14
Eilberg, Amy 5/12
Eisenhower, Dwight, President 5/28
Eliot, John
(b. 8/5/1604) d. 5/20/1690
Eliot, T. S. 5/29
Elliot, Jim. See QUOTATIONS
Elliott, Charlotte 5/18
Erasmus, Desiderius 5/21
Ethelbert, Anglo-Saxon King (560-616) 5/26
Eusebius (Pamphili)
(b. 264) d. 5/30/340
Evangelical United Brethren 5/18
Evans, David
(b. 2/6/1874) d. 5/17/1948
Evers, Luke J. 5/5
Evolution, Theory of 5/5
Ewald, Heinrich Georg August von
(b. 11/16/1803) d. 5/5/1875
Exell, Joseph Samuel
b. 5/29/1849 [d. ca. 1909]

F

Faber, Johannes (of Leutkirch)
(b. 1478) d. 5/21/1541
Fairbairn, Andrew M. 5/2
Fall and Original Sin, Doctrine of 5/1
Farnum, John 5/27
Feminine Benchmarks 5/12, 5/19
FIRSTS
African-American President of the American Baptist Convention 5/17
American Bishop of the Methodist Church 5/26
American College to Sponsor an Endowed Lecture Series 5/20
American Indian to Become a Roman Catholic Bishop 5/6
American Law Banning Slavery 5/18
Anglican Priest in America 5/14
Anglican Worship Service Held in the New World 5/14
Baptists Exiled from an American Colony 5/27
Bible Published in America 5/20
Book Printed in English in America 5/20
Catholic Cathedral in the U.S 5/31
Catholic Elected to Parliament 5/4
Catholic Mass for Night Workers 5/5
Catholic Missionary to China 5/11
Catholic Priest Ordained in the U.S. 5/25
Christian Writer to List the 27 Books of the New Testament 5/2
Complete Revision of the English Bible Since 1611 5/19
Episcopal Church Service in an English Colony 5/9
Lutheran Church in St. Louis 5/7
National Tract Society in America 5/11
Non-Italian Pope Since the Renaissance 5/18
Pope in History to Visit the U.K. 5/28
Primate of the Church of England in Canada 5/17
Principal of the seminary at Oroomiah in Persia 5/1
Redaction of Catholic Canon Law in Modern Times 5/27
Swedenborgian Congregation in the U.S. 5/7
Visit of a Reigning Pope to America 5/4
Zionist Congress (1897) 5/2
Fisher, Geoffrey F.
b. 5/5/1887 [d. 9/15/1972]

Fisk, Fidelia
b. 5/1/1816 [d. 8/9/1864]
Formula of Concord 5/25, 5/28
Form Criticism 5/23
Fosdick, Harry E. 5/2
Frederick III (the Wise)
(b. 1/17/1463) d. 5/5/1525
Free Church of Scotland 5/18, 5/25
Fry, Charles William
b. 5/30/1838 [d. 8/24/1882]
Fry, Elizabeth Gurney
b. 5/21/1780 [d. 10/12/1845]
Fuchida, Mitsuo
(b. 12/3/1902) d. 5/30/1976

G

Galileo Galilei 5/9
General Court of Massachusetts 5/27
Geneva (and the Reformation) 5/21
Gilbert, William S. 5/13
Gold, Thomas 5/27
Gothard, St.
(b. unknown) d. 5/4/1038
Gottschalk, Louis Moreau
b. 5/8/1829 [d. 12/18/1869]
Graf, Karl Heinrich
(b. 2/28/1815) d. 5/16/1869
Graf-Wellhausen Theory 5/16
Gray, James Martin
b. 5/11/1851 [d. 9/21/1935]
Green, Samuel Fisk
(b. 10/10/1822) d. 5/28/1884
Gregory II, Pope (715-731) 5/19
Gregory XIII, Pope (1572-1585) 5/14
Gropper, Johann 5/22
Groves, Anthony Norris
(b. 1795) d. 5/20/1853
Gunkel, Hermann
5/23/1862 [d. 3/11/1932]
Gurley, Rev. Dr. 5/22

H

Hankey, Arabella Catherine
(b. 1834) d. 5/9/1911
Hare, William H.
b. 5/17/1838 [d. 10/23/1909]
Harnack, Adolf von
b. 5/7/1851 [d. 6/10/1930]

Hawthorne, Nathaniel 5/20
(b. 7/4/1804) d. 5/19/1864
Heber, Reginald 5/29
Henry IV of Navarre, French King (1589-1610)
(b. 12/13/1553) d. 5/14/1610
Henson, Josiah
(b. 6/15/1787) d. 5/15/1883
HERESIES, CHRISTIAN
Arianism 5/2, 5/22
Nestorians 5/1
Semi-Pelagianism 5/6
HERETICS, CHRISTIAN
Arius 5/20
Pelagius 5/1
Herr, John 5/30
(b. 9/18/1782) d. 5/3/1850
Herzl, Theodor
b. 5/2/1860 [d. 7/3/1904]
Hoffman, Elisha A.
b. 5/7/1839 [d. 11/25/1929]
Howe, Julia Ward 5/12
b. 5/27/1819 [d. 10/17/1910]
Howe, Samuel Gridley 5/27
Hügel, Friedrich von
b. 5/5/1852 [d. 1/27/1925]
Hughes, John
(b. 1873) d. 5/14/1932
Hunt, Robert 5/9, 5/14
Hunter, William
b. 5/26/1811 [d. 10/18/1877]
Hurst, John Fletcher
(8/17/1834) d. 5/4/1903
HYMNS
"Are You Washed in the Blood?" 5/7
"Art Thou Weary, Art Thou Languid?" 5/27
"Ask Ye What Great Thing I Know" 5/18
"Battle Hymn of the Republic" 5/12
"Be Thou My Vision" 5/17
"Blest Be the Tie That Binds" 5/26
"Christ Hath for Sin Atonement Made" 5/7
"Come, Christians, Join to Sing" 5/17
"Come, Ye Disconsolate" 5/28
"Come, Ye Faithful, Raise the Strain" 5/13
"Down at the Cross" 5/7
"Eternal Father, Strong to Save" 5/3
"Father of Mercies, Hear" 5/27
"Fling Out the Banner! Let it Float" 5/27
"From Greenland's Icy Mountains" 5/29
"Go, Tell It On the Mountain" 5/18

"God of Grace and God of Glory" 5/14
"Good Christian Men, Rejoice and Sing." 5/16
"Guide Me, O Thou Great Jehovah" 5/14
"Hail the Day that Sees Him Rise" 5/6
"He Who Would Valiant Be" 5/29
"Holy Ghost, With Light Divine" 5/8
"In Heavenly Love Abiding" 5/10, 5/17
"In the Cross of Christ I Glory" 5/5
"I Love to Tell the Story" 5/9
"I Must Tell Jesus" 5/7
"Jesus, Lover of My Soul" 5/21
"Just As I Am" 5/18
"Leaning on the Everlasting Arms" 5/1, 5/7
"Lily of the Valley" 5/30
"Lonely Voices Crying in the City" 5/9
"Mine Eyes Have Seen the Glory" 5/27
"More Love to Thee, O Christ." 5/12
"Morning Has Broken" 5/17
"Must I Go, and Empty-Handed" 5/17
"My Father is Rich in Houses and Land" 5/9
"My Sins Are Blotted Out, I Know" 5/9
"Nor Silver Nor Gold Hath Obtained My Redemption" 5/11
"O, Where Are Kings and Empires Now?" 5/10
"Onward, Christian Soldiers" 5/13
"Praise the Saviour, Ye Who Know Him" 5/14
"Praise to the Lord, the Almighty," 5/3
"Sing Praise to God Who Reigns Above" 5/10, 5/22
"Softly Now the Light of Day" 5/27
"Sweet, Sweet Spirit" 5/21
"The Battle Hymn of the Republic" 5/27
"The Great Physician Now is Near" 5/26
"The King of Love My Shepherd Is" 5/27
"Thou Art the Way" 5/27
"We Praise Thee, O God! For the Son of Thy Love" 5/13
"What Shall the Harvest Be?" 5/11
"Years I Spent in Vanity and Pride" 5/22

HYMN TUNES
ABERYSTWYTH 5/21
BENTON HARBOR 5/7
BINGHAMTON 5/9
BUNESSAN 5/17
CONSOLATION 5/25
CWM RHONDDA 5/14
DENNIS 5/26
HENDON 5/18
LLANFAIR 5/6
MADRID 5/17
MERCY 5/8
NYLAND 5/17
RATHBUN 5/5
ST. GERTRUDE 5/13
ST. KEVIN 5/13
WIGSBURG 5/7

I

Innocent XI, Pope (1676-1689)
b. 5/19/1611 [d. 8/12/1689]
International Missionary Council 5/25
Isidore of Kiev, Russian Orthodox Metropolitan (1435-1439)
(b. ca. 1385) d. 5/27/1464
Islam 5/18

J

Jackson, Sheldon
(b. 5/18/1834) d. 5/2/1909
Jagiello, King of Lithuania (1385-1434)
(b. 1351) d. 5/31/1434
Jamestown Expedition 5/14
Jansen, Cornelius Otto
(b. 10/28/1585) d. 5/6/1638
Joan of Arc 5/23
(b. 1/6/1412) d. 5/30/1431
Johnson, W[illiam] B. 5/3
John Paul II, Pope (1978-2005) 5/9, 5/18, 5/28, 5/29
John XII, Pope (955-964)
(b. ca. 937) d. 5/14/964
John XXIII, Pope (1958-1963) 5/5
Jones, James Warren "Jim"
b. 5/13/1931 [d. 11/18/1978]
JUDAISM
Der Judenstaat (1896) 5/2
Eilberg, Amy 5/12
First Female Conservative Rabbi 5/12
Herzl, Theodor 5/2
Israel, Modern State of 5/11, 5/14
Israel a Member of the United Nations 5/11
Jewish Apocalyptic 5/23
Jewish Theological Seminary (NY City) 5/12
Levinthal, Bernard 5/12
Museum of the Jewish Diaspora 5/20
Orthodox Rabbinical Association of America 5/12
Reform Judaism 5/23
The Jewish State (1896) 5/2
Zionism 5/2
Julian of Norwich 5/8

K

Kelly, Thomas
(b. 7/13/1769) d. 5/14/1855
Kierkegaard, Sören A.
b. 5/5/1813 [d. 11/11/1855]
Kilgore, Thomas, Jr. 5/17
Knox, John 5/2
Kuhlman, Kathryn
b. 5/7/1907 [d. 2/20/1976]
Kümmel, Werner Georg
b. 5/16/1905 [d. 7/9/1995] 5/16

L

Lanfranc, Blessed
(b. ca. 1005) d. 5/24/1089
Lathrop, Rose Hawthorne
b. 5/20/1851 [d. 7/9/1926]
Laubach, Frank.
See QUOTATIONS
LECTURE SERIES
Lyman Beecher Lectures 5/2
Morse Lectureship on the Bible and Science 5/20
LEGISLATION
Edict of Nantes (1598) 5/14
Italy
Law of Guarantees (1871) 5/13
LEGISLATION, AMERICAN
Congressional Act, Joint Resolution 243 5/28
LEGISLATION, ENGLISH
Act of Parliament (25 Henry VIII, c.19) 5/15
Act of Toleration 5/24
Roman Catholic Relief Bill 5/4
Submission of the Clergy Act 5/15
Leo I, Pope (440-461) 5/22
Levinthal, Bernard
b. 5/12/1865 [d. 9/23/1952]
Lewis, C. S. 5/4. See also QUOTATIONS
Lewis, Taylor
(b. 3/27/1802) d. 5/11/1877
Lightfoot, J[oseph] B. 5/8
Lion, William 5/1
Louis XIV, French King (1643-1715) 5/13
Luther, Charles C.
b. 5/17/1847 [d. 11/4/1924]
Luther, Martin 5/2, 5/5, 5/18, 5/22, 5/26, 5/30

M

Macedonian Vision 5/31
Machray, Robert
b. 5/17/1831 [d. 1904]
Mackay, William Paton
b. 5/13/1839 [d. 8/22/1885]
Malan, César H. A.
(b. 7/7/1787) d. 5/18/1864
Mann, Horace
b. 5/4/1796 [d. 8/2/1859]
Marechal, Ambrose, Archbishop 5/31
Marino, Eugene A. 5/4
Marrant, John 5/15
Martyn, Henry 5/16
MARTYRS
Bonhoeffer, Dietrich 5/29
Elliot, Jim 5/2, 5/5, 5/14
Joan of Arc 5/30
Savonarola, Girolamo 5/23
Mary Alphonsa (Sister / Mother) 5/20
Mary of Guise 5/2
Mason, Lowell 5/26
Massachusetts School for the Blind 5/27
Mastai-Ferretti, Giovanni Maria. See Pius IX, Pope (1846-1878)
Mayflower Compact 5/8
Mayflower Pilgrims 5/8
McCheyne, Robert Murray
b. 5/21/1813 [d. 3/25/1843]
McGuffey, William Holmes
(b. 9/23/1800) d. 5/4/1873
McKendree, William 5/26
McPherson, Aimee Semple 5/26
Melanchthon, Philip[p] 5/5, 5/21, 5/22
MISSIONARIES
Brainerd, David 5/13, 5/17, 5/18, 5/24
Buck, Philo M. 5/15
Eliot, John 5/20
Elliot, Jim 5/2, 5/5, 5/14
Fiske, Fidelia 5/1
Green, Samuel Fisk 5/28
Groves, Anthony N. 5/20
Hare, William H. 5/17
Jackson, Sheldon 5/2
Laubach, Frank C. 5/24

ALMANAC OF THE CHRISTIAN FAITH — MAY INDEX

Marrant, John 5/15
Paton, John Gibson 5/24
Schere, Samuel I. J. 5/6
Taylor, William 5/18
Mohammed 5/18
Mohammed II 5/29
Moody Press 5/8
Moore, George Foote
  (b. 10/15/1851) d. 5/16/1931
Moore, Jenny Evans 5/2
Moore, Thomas
  b. 2/28/1779 [d. 2/25/1852]
Morse, Samuel Finley Breese 5/20
Mott, John R.
  b. 5/25/1865 [d. 1/31/1955]
Moule, Handley C. G.
  (b. 12/23/1841) d. 5/8/1920
MOVEMENTS, CHRISTIAN
  Arminianism 5/9
  Calvinist Churches 5/9
  Clapham Sect 5/9
  Fundamentalism 5/5
  German Pietism 5/9
  High Church Episcopalians 5/27
  New England Puritanism 5/19
  Pentecostalism 5/15
  Pietism, German 5/18, 5/22
  Protestant Reformation 5/21
  Puritanism 5/17
  Puritan Separatists 5/8
  Scottish Reformation 5/2
  Separatists 5/22
MOVEMENTS, CHRISTIAN SECTARIAN
  Theosophy 5/6
Mueller, George 5/20
MUSICALS
  Godspell 5/19
MYSTICS
  Joan of Arc 5/30
  Julian of Norwich 5/8
  Sorski, Nils 5/7
  Underhill, Evelyn 5/3, 5/10, 5/12, 5/13, 5/20, 5/30

N

Nägeli, Johann (Hans) Georg
  b. 5/26/1768 (or 1773) [d. 12/26/1836]
NATIVE AMERICANS
  Apostle to the American Indians 5/20
  Cherokees 5/15
Neander, Joachim Neumann
  b. 5/3/1650 [d. 5/31/1680]
Newell, William Reed
  b. 5/22/1868 [d. 4/1/1956]
New France (Canada) 5/23
NICKNAMES / TITLES
  Apostle of the Sioux 5/17
  Apostle to the American Indians 5/20
  Apostle to the English 5/26
  Bishop of All Beyond 5/2
  Columbus of the Catacombs 5/31
  Father of Church History 5/30
  Father of English History 5/26
  Father of existentialism 5/5
  Father of Orthodoxy 5/2
  First Bandmaster of the Salvation Army 5/30
  King of Orators and the Orator of Kings 5/13
  Maid of Orléans 5/30
  Monk of Jarrow 5/26
  New Rome (Constantinople) 5/22
  Prince of Paradox 5/29
  Sweet Singer of Methodism 5/21
Nicoll, William Robertson
  (b. 10/10/1851) d. 5/4/1923
Nikon, Patriarch of Moscow (1652-1666) 5/7
Nikita Minin
  b. 5/7/1605 [d. 1681]. See Nikon, Russian Orthodox Patriarch
Nobel Peace Prize 5/25

O

Oakey, Emily Sullivan
  (b. 10/8/1829) d. 5/11/1883
Odescalchi, Benedetto. See also Innocent XI, Pope
  b. 5/19/1611 [d. 8/12/1689] 5/19
Oetinger, Friedrich C.
  b. 5/6/1702 [d. 2/10/1782]
Ordination of Women 5/23
ORGANIZATIONS, CHRISTIAN
  American Bible Society 5/8
  American Tract Society 5/11
  America for Christ 5/7
  Christian Endeavor 5/26
  Christian Literature Society 5/14
  Epworth League 5/15
  Evangelical Association 5/7
  Evangelical Teacher Training Association 5/11
  London Society for the Study of Religion 5/5
  National Holiness Association 5/2
  Pocket Testament League 5/30
  Religious Tract Society 5/5, 5/14
  United Society for Christian Literature 5/14
  Virginia Baptist Foreign Mission Society 5/8
  YMCA, American 5/25
  Youth for Christ 5/9
ORTHODOXY, EASTERN
  Greek Orthodoxy 5/9
  Russian Orthodoxy 5/7, 5/27, 5/30
Otterbein, Philip William 5/18
Ottoman Empire 5/29
Our Lady of Fatima 5/13

P

Parker, Matthew
  (b. 8/6/1504) d. 5/17/1575
Parker, Theodore 5/19
Parliament, British 5/24
Parliament, Italian 5/13
Parry, Joseph
  b. 5/21/1841 [d. 2/17/1903]
Paton, John Gibson
  b. 5/24/1824 [d. 1/28/1907]
Patriarch of Constantinople 5/27
Paul V, Pope (1605-1621) 5/16
Paul VI, Pope (1963-1978) 5/4, 5/29
Peale, Norman Vincent
  b. 5/31/1898 [d. 12/24/1993]
Peking Man 5/1
Pelotte, Donald E. 5/6
PERIODICALS
  "Atlantic Monthly" 5/12
  "The Expositor" 5/4
Perkins Institute 5/27
Pflug, Julius von 5/22
Philip[p] Melanchthon 5/11
Pia, Secundo 5/28
Pimen, Patriarch of Moscow (1971-1990) 5/30
Pistorius, Johann 5/22
Pius XI, Pope (1922-1939) 5/31
Pledge of Allegiance 5/28
Plymouth Colony 5/8
POPES
  Alexander II (1061-1073) 5/24
  Alexander VI (1492-1503) 5/23
  Benedict XV (1914-1922) 5/27
  Boniface VIII (1294-1303) 5/15
  Gregory II (715-731) 5/19
  Gregory IX (1227-1241) 5/20
  Gregory XIII (1572-1585) 5/14
  Innocent XI (1676-1689) 5/19
  John Paul II (1978-2005) 5/9, 5/18, 5/28
  John XII (955-964) 5/14
  John XXIII (1958-1963) 5/5
  Leo I (440-461) 5/22
  Paul V (1605-1621) 5/16
  Paul VI (1963-1978) 5/4, 5/29
  Pius XI (1922-1939) 5/31
Predestination 5/6
Prentiss, Elizabeth 5/12
Prentiss, George L.
  b. 5/12/1816 [d. 3/19/1903]
PRESIDENTS, U.S.
  Eisenhower, Dwight (1953-1961) 5/28
  Jackson, Andrew (1829-1837) 5/29
Protestant Christian Missions, Modern 5/12
Protestant Reformation 5/21, 5/22
Provost, Samuel 5/1

Q

Quakerism 5/21, 5/30
Queen Elizabeth 5/28
QUOTATIONS
  Bonar, Andrew 5/3, 5/5, 5/6, 5/8, 5/9, 5/12, 5/23, 5/28, 5/30
  Bonhoeffer, Dietrich 5/15, 5/29
  Brainerd, David 5/10, 5/13, 5/17, 5/24
  Calvin, John 5/15
  Constitution of the New England Confederation 5/19
  Elliot, Jim 5/2, 5/5, 5/14
  Erasmus, Desiderius 5/30
  Fletcher, John 5/27
  Jackson, Andrew 5/29
  Jackson, Thomas "Stonewall" 5/2
  Laubach, Frank C. 5/24
  Lewis, C. S. 5/6, 5/8, 5/9, 5/26
  Lincoln, Mary Todd 5/22
  Luther, Martin 5/16, 5/20, 5/21, 5/22, 5/23, 5/25, 5/27, 5/30
  MacDonald, George 5/11, 5/22
  Newton, John 5/4, 5/19, 5/28, 5/31
  Nouwen, Henri J. M. 5/1, 5/6, 5/10, 5/13, 5/14, 5/19
  Rutherford, Samuel 5/10, 5/26, 5/28
  Schmemann, Alexander 5/4, 5/23
  Smith, Hannah Whitall 5/1, 5/7, 5/9, 5/11, 5/14, 5/16, 5/25, 5/29, 5/30, 5/31
  Spurgeon, Charles 5/13
  Underhill, Evelyn 5/3, 5/10, 5/12, 5/13, 5/20, 5/30
  Walther, C. F. W. 5/16
  Wesley, John 5/7, 5/28
  Whitefield, George 5/1, 5/16, 5/21, 5/22, 5/23, 5/24, 5/26, 5/27, 5/29
  Witherspoon, John 5/17

R

RADIO PROGRAMS
   Back to the Bible Broadcast 5/16
Ranke, Leopold Von
   (b. 12/21/1795) d. 5/23/1886
Ratisbon Conference 5/22
Reformation, The 5/5
RELIGIOUS ORDERS, CATHOLIC
   Dominican Congregation of St. Rose of Lima 5/20
   French Carmelites 5/17
   Order of Friars Minor (Franciscans) 5/20
   Order of Friars Preachers (Dominicans) 5/23
   Order of St. Augustine (Augustinians) 5/2
   Society of Jesus (Jesuits) 5/1, 5/6, 5/11, 5/13
Remonstrance, Articles of 5/9
RENAISSANCE, THE
   German Renaissance 5/21
   Italian Renaissance 5/20
Ricci, Matteo
   (b. 10/8/1552) d. 5/11/1610
Roberts, John
   (b. 12/22/1822) d. 5/6/1877
Robinson, H[enry] Wheeler
   (b. 2/7/1872) d. 5/12/1945
Rossi, G. B. De 5/31
Rutherford, Samuel. See QUOTATIONS

S

Savonarola, Girolamo
   (b. 9/21/1452) d. 5/23/1498
Schereschewsky, Samuel I. J.
   b. 5/6/1831 [d. 9/15/1906]
Schism of 1054 (East-West) 5/11, 5/22
Schmemann, Alexander. See QUOTATIONS
Schütz, Johann Jakob
   (b. 9/7/1640) d. 5/22/1690
Schwartz, Stephen 5/19
Schwarzerd, Philipp. See Melanchthon, Philip[p]
Schweitzer, Albert 5/10
Scopes, John T. 5/5
Scots Confession (1560) 5/2
SEMINARIES / BIBLE COLLEGES
   Drew Seminary (NJ) 5/4
   Episcopal Theological School (MA) 5/14
   Kansas City (KS) Baptist Theological Seminary 5/17
   Moody Bible Institute (Chicago) 5/9, 5/11, 5/22
   Oroomiah (Persia) 5/1
   Union Theological Seminary, New York City 5/20
   Union Theological Seminary (NY) 5/12
   Yale University Divinity School (CT) 5/2
SERMONS
   "On the Transient and Permanent in Christianity." 5/19
Seymour, William J.
   b. 5/2/1870 [d. 9/28/1922]
Shaped-note Musical System 5/6
Shinn, Asa
   b. 5/3/1781 [d. 2/11/1853]
Showalter, Anthony J.
   b. 5/1/1858 [d. 9/16/1924]
Shroud of Turin 5/28
Singing Schools 5/6
Slavery 5/23
Slavery Banned 5/18
Smith, Gerald Birney
   b. 5/3/1868 [d. 4/3/1929]
Smith, Hannah Whitall. See also QUOTATIONS
   (b. 2/7/1832) d. 5/1/1911
Smith, William Robertson 5/18
Sorski, Nil
   (b. 1433) d. 5/7/1508
Southern Congress, Confederate 5/3
South Carolina Baptist State Convention 5/3
Spellman, Francis Joseph
   b. 5/4/1889 [d. 12/2/1967]
Spener, Philipp 5/22
Spurgeon, Charles. See QUOTATIONS
St. Francis of Assisi 5/20
Stowe, Harriet Beecher 5/15
Stuckenberg, John Henry W.
   (b. 1/6/1835) d. 5/28/1903
Sullivan, Arthur S.
   b. 5/13/1842 [d. 11/22/1900]
Sumner, John B.
   (b. 3/25/1838) d. 5/9/1918
Sunderland, La (Le) Roy
   b. 5/18/1802 [d. 5/15/1885]
Swedenborg, Emanuel 5/6, 5/7
Swete, Henry Barclay
   (b. 3/14/1835) d. 5/10/1917

T

Tappan, Arthur
   b. 5/22/1786 [d. 7/23/1865]
Taylor, James Hudson 5/20
Taylor, Kenneth N.
   b. 5/8/1917
Taylor, William
   (b. 5/2/1821) d. 5/18/1902
   b. 5/2/1821 [d. 5/18/1902]
Teilhard de Chardin, Pierre
   b. 5/1/1881 [d. 4/10/1955]
TELEVISION PROGRAMS
   "The Circuit Rider," 5/7
Tennent, William
   (b. 1673) d. 5/6/1746
Thérèse of Lisieux 5/17
Thompson, Robert E. 5/12
Tozer, A. W.
   (b. 4/21/1897) d. 5/13/1963
Transubstantiation, Doctrine of 5/24
TREATIES
   Lateran Treaty (1929) 5/13
Truett, George Washington
   b. 5/6/1867 [d. 7/7/1944]
Turner, William 5/27

U

UNIVERSE, THEORY OF THE
   Copernican (Heliocentric) 5/24
   Ptolemaic (Earth-Centered) 5/9, 5/24

V

Vatican Library 5/16
Virgin Mary 5/13

W

Walker, William
   b. 5/6/1809 [d. 9/24/1875]
Walther, Carl F. W.
   (b. 10/25/1811) d. 5/7/1887
Waring, Anna Laetitia
   (b. 4/19/1823) d. 5/10/1910
WARS
   American Civil War (1861-1865) 5/23
   American Revolutionary War (1775-1783) 5/14
   Franco-Prussian War (1870-1871) 5/24
   World War II (1939-1945) 5/30
WCTU (Women's Christian Temperance Union) 5/28
Webbe, Samuel
   (b. 1740) d. 5/25/1816
Wesley, Charles 5/21
Wesley, John 5/21, 5/24. See also QUOTATIONS
Wesley, Samuel 5/21
Westcott, B[rooke] F. 5/8
Westminster Larger Catechism 5/29
Westminster Shorter Catechism 5/29
Whitefield, George 5/3. See also QUOTATIONS
Whiting, William
   (b. 11/1/1825) d. 5/4/1878
Wiersbe, Warren 5/16
Wilberforce, William 5/9
Winer, Johann G. B.
   (b. 4/13/1789) d. 5/12/1858
Winslow, Edward
   (b. 10/18/1595) d. 5/8/1655
Wladislaw, King of Lithuania (1385-1434)
   b. 1351 [d. 5/31/1434]
Wojtyla, Karol. See John Paul II, Pope
Wood, Mary Elizabeth
   d. 5/1/1931
Work, John Wesley III
   [b. 6/15/1901] d. 5/18/1967
World Council of Churches 5/25
World Student Christian Federation 5/25
Wrede, Wilhelm
   b. 5/10/1859 [d. 11/23/1906]

Y

Yale Apostasy of 1722 5/31

Z

Zinzendorf, Anna 5/9
Zinzendorf, Nikolaus Ludwig, Count von
   (b. 5/26/1700) d. 5/9/1760
Zwingli, Ulrich 5/21

תמוז
TAMMUZ

ALMANAC OF THE CHRISTIAN FAITH

סיון
SIVAN

~ June 1 ~

Highlights in History

1803 William Ellery Channing, 23, was ordained pastor of the Federal Street Congregational Church in Boston, serving there until his death in 1842. Channing is remembered today as the "apostle of Unitarianism."

1841 Scottish missionary David Livingstone, 28, having committed his life to Christian work, departed for Africa on this day to become a missionary explorer. Livingstone ultimately penetrated the deepest reaches of the continent, as he proclaimed the Good News.

1843 Black visionary Isabella Baumfree, 46, left New York, adopted the name "Sojourner Truth" and began a career as an activist for abolition and for women's rights. Her mission began in response to a vision from God telling her to *'travel up an' down the land showin' the people their sins and bein' a sign unto them.'*

Notable Birthdays

1618 Birth of German hymnwriter Johann Franck. A respected German lawyer, his fame today rests on a collection of 100 pietistic hymns, published in 1674. Franck introduced a mystical element into Lutheran hymnology, and his most enduring hymns include "Jesus, Priceless Treasure" and "Deck Thyself, My Soul, With Gladness." [d. 6/18/1677]

1793 Birth of Henry Francis Lyte, Scottish Anglican clergyman. Orphaned as a child, and never strong physically, Lyte wrote over 80 hymns, including "Abide with Me" and "Jesus, I My Cross Have Taken." [d. 11/20/1847]

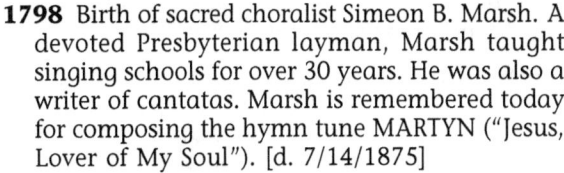

1798 Birth of sacred choralist Simeon B. Marsh. A devoted Presbyterian layman, Marsh taught singing schools for over 30 years. He was also a writer of cantatas. Marsh is remembered today for composing the hymn tune MARTYN ("Jesus, Lover of My Soul"). [d. 7/14/1875]

1849 Birth of American hymnwriter and music publisher James H. Fillmore. His Cincinnati music firm published church hymnals, anthems and sheet music. Of his own works, Fillmore is primarily remembered for composing the hymn tunes RESOLUTION ("I Am Resolved No Longer to Linger") and HANNAH ("I Know That My Redeemer Liveth"). [d. 2/8/1936]

The Last Passage

1854 Death of Emily Chubbock Judson, 36, American missionary to Burma (1846-47) and to Rangoon (1847). She was also fellow-missionary Adoniram Judson's third wife. (b. 8/22/1817)

1972 Death of Chinese pastor and devotional author Watchman Nee (Ni Shu-Tsu), 68. He adopted the teachings of the Plymouth Brethren on the victorious Christian life, and founded a congregation called "Little Flock." Nee was arrested by the Chinese and spent virtually the last 20 years of his life in prison — a martyr of the Communists. (b. 11/4/1903)

Words for the Soul

1760 English founder of Methodism John Wesley noted in a letter: *'It matters not how long we live, but how well.'*

1930 Missionary-linguist Frank C. Laubach wrote in a letter: *'I must talk about God, or I cannot keep Him in my mind. I must give Him away in order to have Him.'*

1952 English Catholic psychiatrist Caryll Houselander encouraged in a letter: *'If you sincerely wish to be well,... the first step towards it is absolutely to refuse to dwell on the past. What is past is past; it cannot be undone, it cannot be changed by self-torture. When it is sinful it can be and should be confessed once, and only once, and then forgotten; when it is just a mistake, confused or foolish thing, it should simply be left alone.'*

FROM GOD'S WORD...   OT: 2 Samuel 18:1–19:10 ~ NT: John 20:1-31 ~ Psalms 119:153-76 ~ Proverbs 16:14-15

תמוז
TAMMUZ

ALMANAC OF THE CHRISTIAN FAITH

סיון
SIVAN

~ June 2 ~

Highlights in History

553 The Second Council of Constantinople closed. Led by Eutychius, Patriarch of Constantinople, the council condemned the Nestorian writings of Theodore of Mopsuestia, Theodoret of Cyprus and Ibas of Edessa.

597 St. Augustine, missionary to England and first Archbishop of Canterbury, baptized Saxon king Ethelbert. Afterward, the Christian faith spread rapidly among the Angles and Saxons.

1875 In Maine, Father James Augustine Healy, 45, was consecrated bishop over the Diocese of Portland. Born a slave in Macon, GA, Healy grew to become a gifted administrator, and the first priest and bishop of African ancestry in the history of American Catholicism.

1930 Sarah F. Dickson of the Wauwatosa Presbyterian Church of Milwaukee, Wisconsin was elected the first female elder of the Presbyterian Church. Serving until January 1, 1934, Ms. Dickson's election was permitted by the church's General Assembly in its meeting at Cincinnati, on May 31, 1930.

Notable Birthdays

1794 Birth of William Allen Hallock, American inspirational writer and editor. In 1825 he took a prominent part in organizing the American Tract Society and became its first corresponding secretary, a position he kept for 45 years! He authored a number of tracts, among which "The Only Son" and "The Mother's Last Prayer" circulated over a million copies. [d. 10/2/1880]

1835 Birth of Italian cardinal Giuseppe Melchiorre Sarto, who from 1903-14 served as Pope Pius X. Widely venerated for his staunch opposition to Modernism, Pius also maintained a deep interest in social questions and in bettering the life of the poor. He was beatified in 1951, and canonized in 1954. [d. 8/20/1914]

1897 Birth of American Methodist bishop Reuben H. Mueller, who became a leader in the U.S. interfaith movement. In 1950 he founded the National Council of Churches, serving as its president from 1963-66. [d. 7/5/1982]

The Last Passage

829 Death of Nicephorus, 71, Greek Orthodox Patriarch of Constantinople (806-15). He attended the Second Council of Nicea in 787, after which he signed its mandate supporting the veneration of images. His *Historia Syntomos*, a history of Byzantium from 602-769, was popularly acclaimed for its objectivity. (b. ca. 758)

1754 Death of Ebenezer Erskine, 73, Scottish clergyman and a founder of the Scottish Secession Church (1740). He pastored at Portmoak from 1703-31, then at Stirling from 1731 until his death. (b. 6/22/1680)

1826 Death of Jean Frederic Oberlin, 85, German clergyman and educator. He spent 60 years working among the poverty-stricken in Alsace-Lorraine. His memory is preserved in America through the Ohio town and college which bear his name. (b. 8/31/1740)

Words for the Soul

1765 English Methodist preacher John Fletcher concluded in a letter: *'God's design in withholding... those gracious influences which work upon and melt the sensitive, affectionate part of the soul, is to put us more upon using the nobler powers — the understanding and the will. These are always more in the reach of a child of God.'*

1785 English founder of Methodism John Wesley explained to his brother Charles in a letter: *'I love ease... but I dare not take it while I believe there is another world.'*

1946 Catholic psychiatrist Caryll Houselander concluded in a letter: *'Time is [n]ever really lost; it is merely that sometimes it is used as God plans instead of as we do, and we consider it to be lost!'*

FROM GOD'S WORD...   OT: 2 Samuel 19:11–20:13 ~ NT: John 21:1-25 ~ Psalms 120:1-7 ~ Proverbs 16:16-17

June 3

Highlights in History

1162 English Catholic churchman Thomas à Becket, 43, was consecrated Archbishop of Canterbury. He served eight years, until increasing ideological conflicts with his king and former friend, Henry II, ended with Becket's martyrdom in Dec. 1170.

1647 Under control of the Puritans, British Parliament mandated Christmas and other Christian holidays should no longer be observed. This ancient religious festival had become so firmly established in Christian (Catholic) imagination, however, that even the Protestant Reformation could not dislodge it. So, in spite of the Puritan legislation (as well as the offensiveness of much modern holiday frivolity), the celebration of the birth of Christ continues to this day.

1972 In Cincinnati, Ohio, Sally J. Priesand, 25, became the first woman in Reform Judaism to be ordained a rabbi. She later (1972-78) became an associate to Rabbi Stephen Wise at the Free Synagogue in New York City.

Notable Birthdays

1726 Birth of Philip William Otterbein, a German Reformed pastor who in 1800 helped establish the Church of the United Brethren in Christ (an early branch of the modern United Methodist Church). [d. 11/17/1813]

1822 Birth of Episcopal clergyman Thomas Gallaudet. The son of Thomas Gallaudet (1787-1851), founder of the first U.S. school for the deaf, the younger Thomas also taught the deaf, and in 1859 founded St. Ann's Church for Deaf Mutes in New York City. [d. 1885]

1851 Birth of Theodore Baker, German-born American literary editor. In 1900 he published the bestseller, *Baker's Biographical Dictionary*, but is more popularly remembered today for his English translation of the hymn, "We Gather Together." [d. 10/13/1934]

1853 Birth of English Egyptologist Sir W. M. Flinders Petrie. He was founder of the British School of Archaeology, and established important synchronized timelines between Egyptian and Palestinian history. Petrie is regarded today as the greatest archaeological genius of his generation. [d. 7/28/1942]

The Last Passage

1879 English devotional writer Frances Ridley Havergal, 42, died of peritonitis. Writing poetry from age seven, she penned such enduring hymns as: "Take My Life and Let It Be," "Lord, Speak to Me That I May Speak," "Like a River Glorious" and "Who Is On The Lord's Side?" (b. 12/14/1836)

1905 Death of J[ames] Hudson Taylor, 73, pioneer English missionary. Converted at 17, he went to China at age 22, eventually adopting the native dress. In 1865 he founded the interdenominational China Inland Mission, which afterward established itself as the "shock troops" of Protestant advance. (b. 5/21/1832)

Words for the Soul

1855 Scottish writer George MacDonald noted in a letter to his father: *'None of us will live very long here, and then we shall go into the great unknown wondrous world, which so many of our dear friends know already, and where they are quietly awaiting our arrival.'*

1851 Following his spiritual conversion, Charles Spurgeon, 16, testified in a letter to his aunt: *'I have pursued Divinity with some ardour, and only wish that I could learn more of its wondrous mysteries.... In this course I find fresh and ever increasing delight.'*

1930 Missionary linguist Frank C. Laubach wrote in a letter: *'As we grow older all our paths diverge, and in all the world I suppose I could find nobody who could wholly understand me excepting God.'*

תמוז TAMMUZ

ALMANAC OF THE CHRISTIAN FAITH

סיון SIVAN

~ June 4 ~

Highlights in History

1939 During what came to be known as the "voyage of the damned," the SS St. Louis, carrying more than 900 Jewish refugees from Germany, was turned away from the Florida coast. Denied permission to dock in Cuba also, the ship eventually returned to Europe, and most of the refugees later died in Nazi concentration camps.

1948 In Manilla, radio FEBC – the first missionary radio station built in the Philippines by the Far East Broadcasting Company – first went on the air. Founded in 1945 by Robert H. Bowman and John Broger, today FEBC broadcasts to every country in Asia, in more than 150 languages.

1985 In the case of "Wallace v. Jaffree," the U.S. Supreme Court struck down an Alabama law which permitted one minute of prayer or meditation in the public schools.

Notable Birthdays

1820 Birth of Elvina Mable Reynolds Hall, American Methodist pastor's wife and poet. She was a member of the Monument Street Methodist Church in Baltimore for over forty years, and authored the hymn, "Jesus Paid It All" (a.k.a. "I Hear the Savior Say"). [d. 7/18/1889]

1836 Birth of Chauncey Goodrich, American Congregational missionary to Peking, China. Sent by the American Board of Commissioners for Foreign Missions, Goodrich helped create a Mandarin translation of the Bible in 1919, and his 10,000-character Chinese-English dictionary (1891) was a standard for years. [d. 1925]

1873 Birth of Charles Fox Parham, one of the chief founders of Pentecostalism. In 1898 he founded Bethel Bible College in Topeka, Kansas, where he and his students became convinced that an authentic baptism with the Holy Spirit was manifested by glossolalia (i.e., speaking in tongues). [d. 1929]

1878 Birth of Frank N. Buchman, American exponent of the social gospel. A lifelong bachelor, he founded the Oxford Group (1929) and the Moral Rearmament Movement (1938). He traveled widely to promote his ideas, but unfortunately none of his organizations survived after Buchman's death. [d. 8/7/1961]

1900 Birth of Nelson Glueck, American Jewish archaeologist and theologian. As director of the American School of Oriental Research in Jerusalem (1932-1947), and afterward president of Hebrew Union College (1947-71), he explored and dated over 1,000 ancient sites in Palestine and the Near East. [d. 2/12/1971]

The Last Passage

1663 Death of William Juxon, 81, Archbishop of Canterbury (1660-63). As Bishop of London (1633-49), Juxon attended Charles I at his trial, and on the scaffold. (b. 10/1582)

1826 Death of German composer Carl Maria von Weber, 39, from tuberculosis. Though he excelled most in the field of opera, Weber also bequeathed to the church the hymn tunes JEWETT ("My Jesus, As Thou Wilt") and SEYMOUR ("Softly Now the Light of Day"). (b. 11/18/1786)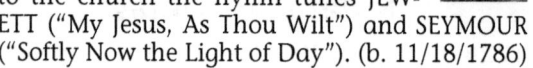

1929 Death of John Albert Jeffery, 73, English-born American sacred organist and choral director. His greatest contribution to sacred music was the hymn tune ANCIENT OF DAYS. (b. 10/26/1855)

1965 Death of Norwegian Old Testament scholar Sigmund O. P. Mowinckel, 80. He was best known for his work on the Psalms, and translated the greater part of the Old Testament into Norwegian. (b. 8/4/1884)

Words for the Soul

1848 Scottish clergyman and biographer Andrew Bonar reflected in his diary: *'It is praying much that makes preaching felt.'*

FROM GOD'S WORD... OT: 2 Samuel 22:21–23:23 ~ NT: Acts 2:1-47 ~ Psalms 122:1-9 ~ Proverbs 16:19-20

תמוז
TAMMUZ

ALMANAC OF THE CHRISTIAN FAITH

סיון
SIVAN

~ June 5 ~

Highlights in History

988 Kiev's Grand Prince Vladimir formally embraced the Gospel, ordering his people to be baptized into the Orthodox Christian faith. Considered the "apostle to the Russians," he became the first Christian ruler of that nation, and afterward erected numerous churches, promoted education and aided the poor.

1827 32-year-old Cynthia Farrar sailed for India. As the first unmarried American woman to become a foreign missionary, Farrar spent 34 years with the Marathi Mission, teaching young women who were previously prohibited by their Hindu fathers from receiving an education.

1967 The Arab-Israeli Six-Day War began, during which Israel took control of the Sinai Desert, the city of Jerusalem and the West Bank of the Jordan River. A cease-fire arranged by the U.N. ended the conflict on June 10th.

Notable Birthdays

1748 Birth of U.S. clergyman Charles H. Wharton. He helped prepare the constitution for the American Episcopal Church, and also helped Americanize the Anglican prayer book. [d. 1833]

1807 Birth of George Rawson, English lawyer and a prominent layman in the English Congregational Church. Rawson authored over 80 hymns, including "Holy Ghost, The Infinite" and "Cast Thy Burden on the Lord." [d. 3/25/1889]

1829 Birth of Polish-born American Orthodox Jewish leader, Marcus Jastrow. A rabbi, lexicographer and editor of the *Jewish Encyclopedia*, he compiled a *Dictionary of the Targumim* (1896-1903), and also helped form the Young Men's Hebrew Association (1875). [d. 1903]

1900 Birth of W[illiam] E. Sangster, English Methodist preacher. He was widely recognized for his saintly leadership, and published numerous devotional books, including *He Is*  *Able* (1936), *The Pure in Heart* (1954) and *The Secret of Radiant Life* (1957). [d. 5/24/1960]

The Last Passage

708 Death of Jacob of Edessa, ca. 75, most important of the ancient Syriac Christian writers. Known as a "man of three tongues," he was a theologian, historian and grammarian. In many respects Jacob was the Jerome of the Syrians, and is best known for his Syriac version of the Old Testament. (b. ca. 633)

754 English monk Boniface, missionary to Germany, was murdered in an attack by angry German pagans. Known for smashing pagan idols and for founding the important monastery at Fulda. Boniface, 74, is said to have died with a Bible clutched in his hand. (b. 680)

1625 Death of English sacred organist Orlando Gibbons, 41. He was an outstanding organist in his day, and composed 40 anthems and services, including the hymn tune CANTERBURY ("Depth of Mercy"). (bapt. 12/25/1583)

1965 Death of English writer Elizabeth Farjeon, 84. She published over 80 works (novels, plays, poems, music and children's books) and became a convert to Catholicism at age 70. It was Farjeon's 1931 hymn that modern singer Cat Stevens made popular in the early 1970's: "Morning Has Broken." (b. 2/13/1881)

Words for the Soul

1878 Scottish clergyman and novelist George MacDonald, wrote to a bereaving widow: 'Your dearest are nearly all out of sight now; but it is not visible proximity but love that is the bond, the oneness.... Age was drawing near him here, but he has escaped from it to the land of youth.'

1961 English apologist C.S. Lewis warned in a letter: 'Fixing the mind on old evils beyond what is absolutely necessary for repenting of our own sins and forgiving those of others is... usually bad for us.'

FROM GOD'S WORD...   OT: 2 Samuel 23:24–24:25 ~ NT: Acts 3:1-26 ~ Psalms 123:1-4 ~ Proverbs 16:21-23

June 6

Highlights in History

1622 Pope Gregory XV published "Inscrutabili divinae," the bull which created the Congregation of Propaganda. It mandated the Catholic Church's mission to the native populations in the recently discovered Americas.

1844 In London, young merchant George Williams, 23, and twelve co-workers founded the Young Men's Christian Association. Organized to combat unhealthy conditions arising from the Industrial Revolution, the original mission of the YMCA was to improve *'the spiritual condition of the young men engaged in the drapery and other trades.'*

1882 Within the walls of his Presbyterian manse in Innellan, blind Scottish clergyman George Matheson, 40, penned the words to a hymn which endures in popularity to this day: "O Love That Wilt Not Let Me Go."

1977 Joseph Lason was installed as Bishop of Biloxi, Mississippi, becoming the first African-American Roman Catholic bishop to be consecrated since the 19th century.

Notable Birthdays

1622 Birth of Claude Jean Allouez, French Jesuit missionary to the American Great Lakes. He began his work along the St. Lawrence River in 1658, and is said to have baptized 10,000 American Indians during his lifetime! He is called "founder of Catholicity in the West." [d. 1689]

1799 Birth of Russian Orthodox church musician Alexis F. Lvov (Lwoff). He directed the imperial court chapel at St. Petersburg, and edited a collection of music for the church year. Before deafness forced his retirement in 1867, Lvov composed the hymn tune RUSSIAN HYMN ("God, the Almighty One! Wisely Ordaining"). [d. 12/16(OS)/1870]

The Last Passage

1799 Death of American statesman Patrick Henry, 63. Born the second of nine children, he was a steadfast Anglican throughout his life – a warm friend of the Christian faith. (b. 5/29/1736)

1871 Death of Henry James Buckoll, 67, English hymn compiler, editor and translator. He is best remembered today for his English translation of Friedrich Canitz's German hymn, "Come, My Soul, Thou Must Be Waking." (b. 9/9/1803)

1915 Death of William H. Cummings, 83, English chorister and composer. He arranged the hymn tune MENDELSSOHN ("Hark! The Herald Angels Sing"). (b. 8/22/1831)

Words for the Soul

1535 German reformer Martin Luther explained in a sermon: *'A poor man does not go to heaven because he is poor, and a rich man does not go to hell because he is rich. On the contrary, the poor man is saved because he adapts himself aright to his poverty and uses it correctly, and the rich man is lost because he does not adapt himself aright to his wealth and uses it badly. . . . One must use these two economic conditions aright and must know how to adapt oneself correctly to them.'*

1868 American Quaker holiness author Hannah Whitall Smith, 36, wrote in her journal: *'This has been my great fear – that my faith might prove to be only an intellectual faith, and therefore would fail to actually grasp the promised blessings. But I have cast myself upon Jesus…and do trust Him to give me a real and living faith of His own power.'*

1947 English Catholic psychiatrist Caryll Houselander advised in a letter: *'If, apart from this work of being Christ in your own world, you have in fact some specific vocation to do some particular thing for Him, this will, in His own time, be made known to you, either by an irresistible inner compulsion or else by so obvious a chain of circumstances that they can only be regarded as a finger pointing clearly in one direction.'*

FROM GOD'S WORD...   OT: 1 Kings 1:1-53 ~ NT: Acts 4:1-37 ~ Psalms 124:1-8 ~ Proverbs 16:24

ALMANAC OF THE CHRISTIAN FAITH

תמוז TAMMUZ סיון SIVAN

~ June 7 ~

Highlights in History

1099 Fifteen thousand soldiers of the First Crusade reached the massive stone walls of Muslim-occupied Jerusalem. A five-week siege of the city soon followed, lasting until the city fell on July 15th.

1844 In Illinois, the first and only issue of "The Nauvoo Expositor" was published, attacking the local Mormon practice of polygamy. Three days later, on orders of Mormon leader Joseph Smith, the newspaper office was wrecked and burned.

1891 English clergyman Charles H. Spurgeon, 58, preached the last sermon of his 38-year-long ministry at London's Metropolitan Tabernacle. (He died the following January.) Spurgeon was a complex figure: he was a Calvinist by descent, a Methodist by conversion and a Baptist by profession. He is sometimes also called "the last of the Puritans."

1913 Ohio-born Methodist evangelist George Bennard, 40, introduced his new hymn, "The Old Rugged Cross," during a revival meeting he was conducting in Pokagon, Michigan.

1934 Wycliffe Bible Translators held its first study course in linguistics at Sulphur Springs, Arkansas. The training session lasted 3 months. Wycliffe (the world's largest Protestant overseas mission) is an agency devoted to the scientific study of linguistics and to translation of the Bible, particularly for those who lack the Scriptures in their own language. Over 5,000 members are now on staff worldwide, drawn from some 30 sending countries. To date, over 300 tribes now have the New Testament in their language as a result of the work of WBT.

Notable Birthdays

1502 Birth of Italian cardinal Ugo Buoncompagni — Pope Gregory XIII from 1572-85. He reformed the Julian (Old Style) calendar by correcting the formula for determining leap year. First implemented in Catholic countries in 1582, the Gregorian (or New Style) Calendar was not adopted by Great Britain and the American colonies until 1751. [d. 4/10/1585]

1804 Birth of Thomas S. Savage, the first American Episcopal missionary to Africa. He established a mission in Liberia (1836-46), and wrote a paper on the gorilla – an animal previously unknown to scientists. [d. 1880]

The Last Passage

1863 Death of Austrian church organist and composer Franz Gruber, 75. His sacred compositions number more than 90, but he is singularly remembered for the tune he composed the night of December 24, 1818 at the St. Nicholas Church in Oberndorf, Austria. It was set to a Nativity poem written by his pastor, Joseph Mohr: STILLE NACHT ("Silent Night"). (b. 11/25/1787)

1929 Death of Frederick L. Hosmer, 88, American hymnwriter and hymnologist. He co-authored "God, That Madest Earth and Heaven," also "Thy Kingdom Come, O Lord." (b. 10/16/1840)

Words for the Soul

1754 Converted English slaver John Newton encouraged his wife in a letter: 'In all the dangers and difficulties that may affect either of us, our God is ever present. May we learn to sanctify him in our hearts, and... we need fear nothing.'

1789 At age 86, English founder of Methodism John Wesley encouraged in a letter: 'Those that suffer all will surely conquer all.'

1959 English apologist C. S. Lewis wrote in a letter: 'If we really think that home is elsewhere and that this life is a "wandering to find home," why should we not look forward to the arrival?'

FROM GOD'S WORD...   OT: 1 Kings 2:1–3:2 ~ NT: Acts 5:1-42 ~ Psalms 125:1-5 ~ Proverbs 16:25

June 8

Highlights in History

1536 Ten "Articles of Religion" were published by the English clergy, in support of Henry VIII's Declaration of Supremacy. The Anglican Church thus began outlining its doctrinal distinctives, following its break with Rome.

1819 Dr. John Scudder, Sr., 25, of the Dutch Reformed Church, departed from New York for Ceylon under the American Board of Commissioners for Foreign Missions. His work in both Ceylon and India made Scudder the first foreign medical missionary sent from the U.S.

Notable Birthdays

1810 Birth of German composer Robert A. Schumann. Acclaimed in his time for his symphonies and chamber music, Schumann is better remembered today for his piano compositions, including the hymn tune CANONBURY ("Lord, Speak to Me That I May Speak"). [d. 7/29/1856]

1908 Birth of Nels F. S. Ferré, Swedish-born American clergyman and theologian. Teaching at Andover-Newton Theological School from 1939, Ferré emphasized love as the central interpretive principle of theology, and authored *Faith and Reason* (1946) and *The Christian Understanding of God* (1951). [d. 1971]

1915 Birth of Canadian Presbyterian hymnwriter Margaret E. Clarkson. She taught elementary school for 38 years in Toronto, and was active in Inter-Varsity Christian Fellowship. Her musical pen has bequeathed to the Church the probing missionary hymn, "So Send I You."

The Last Passage

632 Muslim prophet Mohammed died at age 62. He founded Islam in 622, and wrote the Koran. His teachings eventually converted all Arabia to the Muslim faith. Though not considered a central figure in Judeo-Christian history, Mohammed's last words are worth noting: 'O God, pardon my sins. Yes, I come.' (b. ca. 570)

1612 Death of Hans Leo Hassler, 47. The first Bavarian to study music in Italy, he afterward founded the German school of choral music using Italian methods of composition.  Hassler wrote masses, motets and litanies, but is better remembered today for creating the haunting hymn tune PASSION CHORALE ("O Sacred Head, Now Wounded"). (b. 10/25/1564)

1796 Death of Italian violinist Felice de Giardini, 80. An outstanding violin virtuoso in his day, he acquired a large income. Unfortunately, he was also a spendthrift and, in the end,  died penniless. The church remembers Giardini as composer of the hymn tune ITALIAN HYMN ("Come, Thou Almighty King"). (b. 4/12/1716)

1913 Death of Charles A. Briggs, 72, American Presbyterian-turned-Episcopalian clergyman and scholar. With Francis Brown and Samuel R. Driver he co-edited *A Hebrew and English Lexicon of the Old Testament* (1906) – affectionately known as *Brown, Driver & Briggs*, and still in print. (b. 1/15/1841)

Words for the Soul

1753 Anglican clergyman and hymnwriter John Newton wrote in a letter to his wife: *'He knows our passions and our weakness; and, unless we overrate the comforts he bestows, will never deprive us of them, but with a design of giving us something still better in their room.'*

1845 Just before his death at 78, Andrew Jackson called his family to his bedside and testified: *'I have suffered much bodily pain, but my sufferings are but as nothing compared with that which our blessed Redeemer endured upon the accursed Cross, that all might be saved who put their trust in Him.... I go but a short time before you, and ... I hope and trust to meet you all in Heaven.'*

תמוז ALMANAC OF THE CHRISTIAN FAITH סיון
TAMMUZ   SIVAN

~ June 9 ~

Highlights in History

1549 With Anglicanism having become the new national religion of England, Parliament passed the Act of Uniformity governing English worship and issued the first *Book of Common Prayer*.

1732 English philanthropist James Oglethorpe received a royal charter to form the American colony of Georgia. This *'land between the Altamah and Savannah rivers'* was first populated by imprisoned English debtors, the impoverished and the unemployed. However, the colony soon became a place of refuge for Protestant groups undergoing persecution in Europe.

1772 The first Protestant church west of the Alleghenies was built at Schoenbrunn, Ohio, by Moravian missionaries. The Reverend David Zeisberger served as the church's first preacher.

1784 In the first step toward formally organizing the Roman Catholic Church in the newly independent United States, Father John Carroll was appointed superior of the American missions.

Notable Birthdays

1775 Birth of Georg Friedrich Grotefend, the German archaeologist and linguistic scholar who, in 1802, made the first breakthrough in deciphering the ancient Persian cuneiform writing. [d. 12/15/1853]

1808 Birth of Frederick W. Evans, English-born American Shaker leader, reformer and author. He became a leading elder of the Shakers, following the death of founder Ann Lee. Under Evans' leadership, the movement reached its greatest prosperity and influence. [d. 3/6/1893]

1894 Birth of Wilbur M. Smith, American Fundamentalist Presbyterian educator. Ordained in 1922, Smith held no academic degrees, but he taught English Bible at Moody Bible Institute (1938-47), Fuller Theological Seminary (1938-47) and at Trinity Evangelical Divinity School (1963-71). [d. 1977]

The Last Passage

597 Death of St. Columba, 76, Irish-born pioneer missionary to Scotland. From the Isle of Iona, Columba evangelized the mainland of Scotland and Northumbria. (b. ca.521)

1717 Death of Madame Jeanne M. Guyon, 69, controversial French mystical leader. Her Quietism was defended by François Fenélon. As a poet, she authored the hymn, "O Lord, How Full of Sweet Content." (b. 4/13/1648)

1790 Death of Robert Robinson, 54, eccentric English clergyman and hymnwriter. At age 17 he was converted to a saving faith under the preaching of George Whitefield, and later authored the hymn, "Come, Thou Fount of Every Blessing." (b. 9/27/1735)

1834 English pioneer Baptist missionary William Carey died at 73. He translated portions of Scripture into as many as 25 Indian languages, including Bengali and Sanskrit, thereby making the Bible accessible to over 300 million souls. Carey is known today as the "father of modern missions." (b. 8/17/1761)

Words for the Soul

1752 English founder of Methodism John Wesley wrote in his journal: *'My lodging was not such as I should have chosen; but what Providence chooses is always good.'*

1832 Young Scottish clergyman Andrew A. Bonar reflected in his diary: *'Since I became alive to eternal things, all delight in earthly things of whatever kind seems to come only in order to depart.'*

1868 American Quaker holiness author Hannah Whitall Smith, 36, recorded in her journal: *'The more I examine the Scriptures on the subject, the more thoroughly am I convinced that the Holy Spirit is not an idea or an influence merely, but that He is a real and manifested presence in the soul – the witness to the soul of the divine reality of the things it [the soul] believes and trusts.'*

FROM GOD'S WORD...   OT: 1 Kings 5:1–6:38 ~ NT: John 7:1-29 ~ Psalms 127:1-5 ~ Proverbs 16:28-30

תמוז
TAMMUZ

ALMANAC OF THE CHRISTIAN FAITH

סיון
SIVAN

~ June 10 ~

Highlights in History

1850 The American Bible Union was formed, its policy being to circulate *'only such versions [of the Bible] as are conformed as nearly as possible to the original text.'* It grew out of the American and Foreign Bible Society (AFBS), which had been formed in 1836.

1925 Canada's largest Protestant denomination, the United Church of Canada was officially formed from the union of the Methodist Church, Canada; the Congregational Union of Canada; the Council of Local Union Churches; and about two-thirds of the Presbyterian Church of Canada. The denomination's government is presbyterian in form.

1935 New York stockbroker William G. Wilson, 40, and Ohio surgeon Dr. Robert H. Smith, 56, established Alcoholics Anonymous in Akron, Ohio. It was their bold experiment to aid themselves, and other alcoholics, heal their indulgence through self-help and mutual support. From its start, the AA program has had a deep social and (nonsectarian) spiritual basis.

1983 The Presbyterian Church in the U.S. (PCUS) reunited with the United Presbyterian Church (UPC) to form the Presbyterian Church of the U.S.A. (PCUSA). (The restored denomination had first divided in 1861 over the slavery issue.)

Notable Birthdays

1735 Birth of John Morgan, an American physician who in 1765 established the first medical school in the American colonies – the College of Philadelphia. (Its name was later changed to the University of Pennsylvania.) [d. 10/15/1789]

1773 Birth of American clergyman Finis Ewing, one of the three founders, in 1814, of the Cumberland Presbyterian Church. [d. 7/4/1841]

1844 Birth of John M. Wigner, English Baptist lay preacher and children's evangelist. He wrote the hymn, "Come to the Savior Now." [d. 3/31/1911]

The Last Passage

1579 Death of William Whittingham, 55, the Anglican Calvinist poet whose metrical version of Psalm 23 contributed to the 1650 Scottish Psalter, and gave the Church the hymn, "The Lord's My Shepherd, I'll Not Want." (b. 1524)

1692 Bridget Bishop became the first person hanged for witchcraft, during the ordeal known to history as the "Salem Witch Trials." In all, 20 people died before a sanity was restored in this isolated Puritan Massachusetts community.

1921 Death of Methodist songwriter, choral director and music editor Edwin O. Excel, 69. He composed the music for over 2,000 songs, and is remembered today for creating the hymn favorites: "Since I Have Been Redeemed" and "Count Your Blessings." (b. 12/13/1851)

1930 Death of Adolf von Harnack, 79, German Lutheran church historian and theologian. He was probably the most outstanding Patristic scholar of his generation, and his *History of Dogma* (1886) is still a major resource for historical theologians. (b. 5/7/1851)

Words for the Soul

1415 Following his arrest, Czech reformer Jan Hus wrote in a letter to his followers in Bohemia: *'What grace God hath shown me, and how he helps me in the midst of strange temptations, you will know when by his mercy we meet in joy in his presence.'* [Hus died 26 days later, burned at the stake in Constance, Germany.]

1637 Exiled Scottish clergyman Samuel Rutherford testified in a letter: *'If I had not sailed this sea-way to heaven, but had taken the land-way, as many do, I should not have known Christ's sweetness in such a measure. But the truth is,... I caused not Christ's wind to blow upon me: his love came upon a withered creature, whether I would or not; and yet by coming it procured from me a welcome.'*

FROM GOD'S WORD... OT: 1 Kings 7:1-51 ~ NT: Acts 7:30-50 ~ Psalms 128:1-6 ~ Proverbs 16:31-33

תמוז ALMANAC OF THE CHRISTIAN FAITH סיון
TAMMUZ   SIVAN

~ June 11 ~

Highlights in History

1509 England's young king, Henry VIII, 18, married his first wife, Catherine of Aragon, 24. (In 1533, Thomas Cranmer declared their marriage invalid and five days later pronounced Henry, now 42, to be lawfully married to Anne Boleyn, 26.)

1799 Church leader Richard Allen, 39, was ordained a deacon of the Methodist Episcopal Church in Philadelphia. Later, in 1816, Allen became founding bishop of the African Methodist Episcopal (AME) Church, making him the first African-American Protestant bishop in the U.S.

1918 Brazil's first Pentecostal church was established by missionaries Daniel Berg and Adolf Gunnar Vingren. The new body was registered as an Assembly of God congregation.

1932 The papal constitution "Christo pastorum principi" was published, making the Indian seaport city of Trivandrum a metropolitan see and officially constituting the Malankarese Church a part of the Roman Catholic communion.

1936 The Presbyterian Church of America (PCA) was organized in Philadelphia. (In 1938 the denomination changed its name to the Orthodox Presbyterian Church.)

Notable Birthdays

1850 Birth of David C. Cook, pioneer developer of Sunday School curriculum. Forced earlier to discontinue college studies due to ill health, in 1875, he founded the David C. Cook Publishing Co. — at one time the largest non-denominational publisher of S.S. literature in the world, and headquartered today in Elgin, IL. [d. 1927]

1872 Birth of Mennonite clergyman and hymnwriter Samuel F. Coffman. He served on the music committee of the Mennonite General Conference (1911-47), and also wrote a number of original hymns, including "We Bless the Name of Christ, The Lord." [d. 6/28/1954]

1881 Birth of Mordecai M. Kaplan, American rabbi and founder of the Jewish Reconstructionist movement. Reconstructionist Judaism adheres to the liturgical heritage of Conservative Judaism, but believes in shaping modern Jewish worship around contemporary issues rather than upon the "voice of God" in the Torah (i.e., Mosaic Covenant). [d. 11/8/1983]

The Last Passage

1860 Death of Friedrich W. K. Umbreit, 65, one of the founders of German mediating theology, which sought to find a meeting place between modern science and the dogmas of Christianity. Umbreit's works include commentaries on Job and the Old Testament prophets, and on Romans in the New Testament. (b. 4/11/1795)

1902 Henry G. Appenzeller, 44, died in an accident at sea. A Methodist from Pennsylvania, he went to Korea as a missionary in 1885. During his 17 years on the field, he edited the "Korean Christian Advocate" and helped translate the Bible into the Korean language. (b. 2/5/1858)

Words for the Soul

1638 Exiled Scottish clergyman Samuel Rutherford testified in a letter: *'I would wish such spiritual wisdom as to love the Bridegroom better than his gifts.'*

1739 English founder of Methodism John Wesley record in his journal: *'I look upon all the world as my parish.'*

1893 Scottish clergyman and novelist George MacDonald, 68, confessed in a letter: *'My memory plays me sad tricks now. It comes of the frosty invasion of old age – preparing me to go home, thank God. Till then I must work, and that is good.'* [NB: MacDonald died 12 years later, in 1905.]

FROM GOD'S WORD...   OT: 1 Kings 8:1-66 ~ NT: Acts 7:51–8:13 ~ Psalms 129:1-8 ~ Proverbs 17:1

תמוז
TAMMUZ

ALMANAC OF THE CHRISTIAN FAITH

סיון
SIVAN

~ June 12 ~

Highlights in History

1458 In England, the College of St. Mary Magdalen was founded at Oxford University. (The earliest colleges at Oxford – Merton, Balliol and University – date back to 1264.)

1744 David Brainerd, 26, was ordained a missionary to the Indians of Colonial New England by the Scottish Society for Propagating Christian Knowledge (SPCK). Unfortunately, his tuberculosis was aggravated by continued exposure to the elements, and Brainerd succumbed to the disease three years later. His *Journal*, published in 1749 by Jonathan Edwards, soon became a devotional classic and influenced hundreds to follow in Brainerd's footsteps.

1914 The first edition of A[rchibald] T. Robertson's monumental *Grammar of the Greek New Testament* was released. Its 1400+ pages make it the largest systematic analysis of the New Testament language ever published.

1972 The evangelical conference organized by Campus Crusade for Christ, "Expo '72" opened in the Dallas Cotton Bowl. In all, nearly 80,000 delegates (mostly young people) attended the five-day evangelistic gathering.

Notable Birthdays

1720 Birth of Isaac Pinto, translator of the first Jewish prayerbook published in America. A merchant and lay member of the Jewish community in New York City (Shearith Israel), he published a complete edition (1761) and a translation (1766) of the Sephardic liturgy for Sabbaths and festivals. Pinto's 1766 publication also represented the first translation of a Jewish prayer book into English. [d. 1791]

1804 Birth of David Abeel, American missionary to the Far East. In 1829 he sailed for China under the auspices of the Seaman's Friend Society, a year later placing himself under the American Board of Commissioners for Foreign Missions. Abeel ministered in Java, Singapore, Siam, Malacca, Borneo, and in parts of Asia. [d. 9/4/1846]

1909 Birth of Charles Feinberg, U.S. fundamentalist theologian. He taught at Dallas, BIOLA and Talbot Seminaries, and is remembered today as editor of *The Fundamentals* – a series of 12 volumes issued from 1910-15 which outlined what were considered the non-negotiable tenets of Fundamentalist Christian orthodoxy.

1929 Birth of Anne Frank, Jewish writer and Nazi martyr. Her diary depicted life as a Jewish teen in Amsterdam during WW II, and was penned during the two years she and her family hid from the Nazis. Betrayed to the Gestapo in August 1944, the family was arrested and Anne later died in the Bergen-Belsen concentration camp. [d. 3/12/1945]

The Last Passage

1800 Death of Ann Teresa Mathews, 68, American Catholic religious. She traveled to Belgium at 22 and joined the English order of Discalced Carmelites, taking the habit in 1755 as Sister Bernardina Teresa Xavier of St. Joseph. In 1790 she founded the first Catholic convent established in the newly-independent United States. (b. 1732)

1919 Death of John H. Sammis, 72, Presbyterian clergyman and educator. He was a faculty member of the Bible Institute of Los Angeles (BIOLA). In 1887 Sammis penned the hymn, "When We Walk With the Lord" (a.k.a. "Trust and Obey"). (b. 7/6/1846)

Words for the Soul

1776 Colonial statesman George Mason outlined in Article 16 of the Virginia Bill of Rights: *'Religion, or the duty which we owe to our Creator... can be directed only by reason and conviction, not by force or violence; and therefore all men are equally entitled to the free exercise of religion, according to the dictates of conscience....'*

1950 American missionary and martyr Jim Elliot wrote in his journal: *'Earthly blessing is no sign of heavenly favor. Behold how many wicked prosper.'*

FROM GOD'S WORD...   OT: 1 Kings 9:1–10:29 ~ NT: Acts 8:14-40 ~ Psalms 130:1-8 ~ Proverbs 17:2-3

תמוז
TAMMUZ

ALMANAC OF THE CHRISTIAN FAITH

סיון
SIVAN

~ June 13 ~

Highlights in History

449 Leo's Tome was published. It took the form of a letter sent by Pope Leo I to Flavian, the Patriarch of Constantinople. The document clarified Leo's position on certain Christological matters, and became the basis of the formulas set down in the A.D. 451 "Definition of Chalcedon."

1525 German Reformer Martin Luther, 42, married former nun Katherine von Bora, 26. Their 21-year marriage bore six children. Kate outlived her husband (who died 1546) by 6 years.

1541 French reformer John Calvin, 31, began organizing Geneva, Switzerland into a theocratic state. Geneva afterward became the flagship for Reformed theology throughout Europe.

1793 English missions pioneer William Carey, 31, first sailed for India. The previous year he had preached his famous sermon: "Expect Great Things from God; Attempt Great Things for God." Within five years he had translated nearly the entire Bible into Bengali. Today, Carey is acclaimed the "father of modern missions."

1876 The Presbyterian Church in England merged with the United Presbyterian Church of Scotland, in order to create a more uniform representation of the Reformed faith in the British Isles.

1903 The Church of God of Prophecy was inaugurated when founder A. J. Tomlinson, 37, joined the Holiness Church at Camp Creek, NC, and was chosen pastor of the fledgling congregation of 20.

1979 Delegates to the Reformed Church of America's 173rd Synod voted to amend the *Book of Church Order* to allow women to be ordained as ministers.

Notable Birthdays

1816 Birth of Edward F. Rimbault, the English sacred organist and music scholar who composed the hymn tunes HAPPY DAY ("O Happy Day, That Fixed My Choice") and RUTHERFORD ("The Sands of Time Are Sinking"). [d. 9/26/1876]

1893 Birth of Dorothy L. Sayers, English mystery writer and Christian apologist. Though better known for her "Father Brown" detective stories, Sayers spent the last twenty years of her life writing Christian dramas ("The Man Born to Be King," 1943) and scholarly translations of *The Song of Roland* and Dante's *Divine Comedy*. [d. 12/17/1957]

1897 Birth of Reuben E. Larson, U.S. Christian & Missionary Alliance missionary to Ecuador. In 1931, along with Clarence W. Jones, Larson founded radio HCJB in Quito – the first missionary radio station in Latin America. [d. 11/17/1981]

The Last Passage

1965 Death of Martin Buber, 87, Austrian Jewish philosopher, Bible translator and author. He was a Hasidic scholar whose religious philosophy of human encounter, or dialogue, was best represented in his short but popular book, *I and Thou* (1922). (b. 2/8/1878)

1976 Death of Earl B. Marlatt, 84, Methodist religious scholar and educator. He published several volumes of poetry, including four stanzas which later became the hymn, "'Are Ye Able?' Said the Master." (b. 5/24/1892)

Words for the Soul

1742 Founder of Methodism John Wesley wrote in his journal: *'Oh, let none think his labor is lost because the fruit does not immediately appear.'*

1951 British literary scholar and Christian apologist C. S. Lewis wrote in a letter: *'Continue seeking Him with seriousness. Unless He wanted you, you would not be wanting Him.'*

1972 American Presbyterian apologist Francis Schaeffer exhorted in a letter: *'As Christians we are called upon to exhibit the character of God, and this means the simultaneous exhibition of His holiness and His love.'*

FROM GOD'S WORD...   OT: 1 Kings 11:1–12:19 ~ NT: Acts 9:1-25 ~ Psalms 131:1-3 ~ Proverbs 17:4-5

June 14

Highlights in History

1940 Auschwitz, largest of the Nazi concentration camps, was first opened near Krakow, Poland. Before its liberation by the Allies in 1945, over three million Jews would be exterminated there.

1943 The U.S. Supreme Court ruled that, under the Bill of Rights, school children could not be compelled to salute the national flag if the ceremony conflicted with their religious beliefs. (The case had been brought before the courts by the Jehovah's Witnesses.)

1956 President Eisenhower signed a congressional resolution adding the words "under God" to the Pledge of Allegiance. The last phrase of this American credo now reads: '...one nation, under God, indivisible, with liberty and justice for all.'

1966 The Vatican announced that its *Index of Prohibited Books* had been abolished. First issued by the Inquisition under Pope Paul IV in 1557, the "Index Librorum Prohibitorum" comprised a list of books which members of the Catholic Church were forbidden to read or possess. In modern times, the "Index" declined both in prominence and importance, until it was formally abolished under Pope Paul VI.

Notable Birthdays

1682 Birth of Bartholomaeus Ziegenbalg, German Lutheran missionary. He joined Heinrich Plütschau in 1706 as one of the first Protestant missionaries from Denmark to India, and later translated the New Testament into the Tamil dialect. [d. 2/23/1719]

1811 Birth of American abolitionist and author Harriet Beecher Stowe. The daughter of Lyman Beecher (and sister of popular 19th century clergyman Henry Ward Beecher), in 1848 Harriet began writing her famous novel about slavery, *Uncle Tom's Cabin*. It was serialized in 1851, and published in complete book form the following year. [d. 7/1/1896]

1837 Birth of William C. Dix, English businessman. Though managing a marine insurance company in Glasgow, he also wrote a number of hymns, and versified several others from the Greek. Two of Dix's compositions remain popular today: "What Child Is This?" and "As With Gladness Men of Old." [d. 9/9/1898]
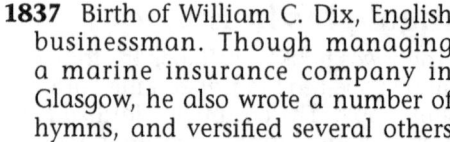

1938 Birth of Gloria Winter, better known as Sister Miriam Therese of the Medical Mission Sisters, a Catholic religious community in Philadelphia. She has authored over 140 Christian songs, the most popular of which include "Joy is Like the Rain" and "Spirit of God in the Clear Running Water."

The Last Passage

1901 Death of Ralph E. Hudson, 57, American Methodist preacher, evangelist and songwriter. He composed the hymn tunes: HUDSON ("Alas! and Did My Savior Bleed?") and SATISFIED ("All My Life Long I Had Panted"). (b. 7/9/1843)

Words for the Soul

1873 American Quaker holiness author Hannah Whitall Smith, 41, confided in her journal: 'Recently I have come to a new awareness of the suffering which His own sympathy for our suffering must cause Him.... To have all power both in Heaven and in earth, as He has, and yet not to use it for the relief of His poor suffering world, must be a bitter grief to our loving Saviour.'

1954 In a speech supporting the adding of the phrase "under God" to the American Pledge of Allegiance, President Dwight D. Eisenhower stated: 'In this way we are affirming the transcendence of religious faith in America's heritage and future; in this way we shall constantly strengthen those spiritual weapons which forever will be our country's most powerful resource in peace and war.'

FROM GOD'S WORD...   OT: Kings 12:20–13:34 ~ NT: John Acts 9:26-43 ~ Psalms 132:1-18 ~ Proverbs 17:6

June 15

Highlights in History

1215 Faced with a threatened revolt by his English subjects, King John Lackland yielded to the demands of the Church and of his baronial lords by signing the Magna Carta ("Great Charter") at Runnymeade (near Windsor).

1520 Pope Leo X issued "Exsurge domine," condemning German reformer Martin Luther as a heretic on 41 counts and giving him 60 days to recant and to burn all his writings. Instead, Luther burned the papal bull. Rome's response was to issue in January the following year the bull of excommunication, "Decet romanum pontificem."

1668 Jesuit missionary from Mexico, Padre Diego Luis de Sanvitores founded the first Roman Catholic mission on the island of Guam.

1686 In Boston, the King's Chapel was organized. It was the first Anglican church established in colonial New England.

1982 The (Southern) Presbyterian Church in the United States (PCUS) voted to rejoin the (Northern) United Presbyterian Church (UPC), following a 122-year schism dating back to the American Civil War. The merger was completed the following year.

Notable Birthdays

1787 Birth of Josiah Henson, freed American slave and African-American clergyman. He was said to be the biographical source and prototype of "Uncle Tom" in Harriet Beecher Stowe's *Uncle Tom's Cabin*. [d. 5/15/1883]

1807 Birth of William Nast, German religious leader and founder of German Methodism. He arrived in America in 1828, and afterward organized German settlers in the Midwest into Methodist congregations. Nast helped establish German Wallace College in Berea, Ohio (which later merged to become Baldwin-Wallace University). [d. 5/6/1899]

1919 Birth of John A. T. Robinson, the Anglican theologian best known for his explosive 1963 book, *Honest to God*. One critic summarized Robertson's theological impact: '*He showed that a highly intelligent British theologian, operating away from the world of worship and the Bible, was often more aware of the secular world's questions than of any convincing answers.*' [d. 12/5/1983]

The Last Passage

1649 The first trial for witchcraft in colonial America was held in Charlestown, Massachusetts. Margaret Jones was found guilty and executed.

1893 Death of John Ellerton, 66, Anglican clergyman and hymnologist. He penned 68 original hymns and translated many others, including: "Welcome, Happy Morning" (trans.); "Savior, Again to Thy Dear Name We Raise"; and "God, the Omnipotent" (alt.). (b. 12/16/1826)

1923 Death of Eudorus N. Bell, 56, American religious leader. A Southern Baptist pastor for 17 years, Bell afterward became one of the founders of the Assemblies of God. (b. 6/27/1866)

Words for the Soul

1637 Exiled Scottish clergyman Samuel Rutherford testified in a letter: '*My Lord in his sweet visits... makes me find that he will be a confined prisoner with me; when I sigh, he sigheth; when I weep, he suffereth with me; and I confess, here is the blessed issue of my suffering already begun, that my heart is filled with hunger and desire, to have him glorified in my sufferings.*'

1869 American Quaker holiness author Hannah Whitall Smith, 37, confided in her journal: '*I love His will now with a genuine love that makes a cross borne for His dear sake filled with an untold sweetness.*'

1950 American missionary martyr Jim Elliot wrote in his journal: '*A man without Christ has his roots only in his own times, and his fruits as well.*'

FROM GOD'S WORD...   OT: 1 Kings 14:1–15:24 ~ NT: Acts 10:1–23 ~ Psalms 133:1-3 ~ Proverbs 17:7-8

תמוז **TAMMUZ** ALMANAC OF THE CHRISTIAN FAITH סיון **SIVAN**

~ June 16 ~

Highlights in History

1654 After converting to Roman Catholicism, Queen Christina, 28, abdicated her Swedish (Lutheran) throne to devote the remainder of her life to religion and art.

1833 Anglican churchman John Henry Newman, 32, while traveling aboard ship from Italy to France, penned the words to the hymn, "Lead, Kindly Light, Amid the Encircling Gloom."

1846 Giovanni Maria Mastai-Ferretti, 54, was elected Pope Pius IX, and began his 32-year pontificate – the longest in Catholic history! During his reign, "Pio Nono" proclaimed the dogma of the Immaculate Conception (1860); convened the First Vatican Council (1869-70); promulgated the controversial doctrine of papal infallibility (1870); and lived to see the papacy both stripped of its temporal powers, and yet armed with vastly increased spiritual authority. When he died in 1878, Pius had effectively created the modern office of the papacy.

1974 The Rev. Dr. Lawrence W. Bottoms was elected moderator of the Presbyterian Church in the U.S. – the first black leader in the 113-year history of the Southern Presbyterian Church.

Notable Birthdays

1862 Birth of Alma Bridwell White, Kentucky-born founder (in 1901) of the Methodist Pentecostal Union Church. In 1917 the denomination changed its name to the Pillar of Fire Church. In 1918 Mrs. White was consecrated senior bishop of the Pillar of Fire – the first woman to attain the office of bishop of any Christian denomination. [d. 6/26/1946]

1871 Birth of Sergei Nikolaevich Bulgakov, expatriate Russian Orthodox priest and theologian. He headed the St. Sergius Theological Institute in Paris from 1925-44. Among his most important writings are *The Orthodox Church* (1935). [d. 7/12/1944]

The Last Passage

1361 Death of Johannes Tauler, 61, medieval German Dominican mystic. A disciple of Meister Eckhart, Tauler helped popularize mysticism during the Catholic Church's "Babylonian Captivity" (nickname for the 70-year-long removal of papal headquarters from Rome to Avignon in France). (b. ca.1300)

1752 Death of Joseph Butler, 60, Anglican bishop and theologian. His 1736 *Analogy of Religion* demonstrated strong probability for the existence of a caring God over against that of a disinterested Creator-Deity. (b. 5/18/1692)

1909 Erastus Johnson died at age 83. His life had spanned a wide range of careers. He was a Maine schoolteacher, a California rancher, a Washington farmer and a Pennsylvania oil worker. Through it all he remained a devoted Christian and a student of the Bible. In 1873 Johnson authored the hymn: "O Sometimes the Shadows Are Deep." (b. 4/20/1826]

1948 Death of Rufus M. Jones, 85, American Quaker scholar, educator, philosopher, humanitarian and mystic. He taught philosophy at Haverford College in Pennsylvania (1904-34), and was a founder of the American Friends Service Committee (1917). (b. 1/25/1863)

Words for the Soul

1539 German reformer Martin Luther declared: *'Faith justifies not as a work, nor as a quality, nor as knowledge, but as assent of the will and firm confidence in the mercy of God.'*

1637 Exiled Scottish clergyman Samuel Rutherford penned these words of comfort in a letter: *'All Christ's good bairns [children] go to heaven with a broken brow, and with a crooked leg.'*

1804 Anglican missionary to Persia, Henry Martyn confessed in his journal: *'My soul, alas, needs these uneasinesses in outward things, to be driven to take refuge in God.'*

FROM GOD'S WORD... OT: 1 Kings 15:25–17:24 ~ NT: Acts 10:24-48 ~ Psalms 134:1-3 ~ Proverbs 17:9-11

תמוז ALMANAC OF THE CHRISTIAN FAITH סיון
TAMMUZ   SIVAN

~ June 17 ~

Highlights in History

1207 English scholar and churchman Stephen Langton, 52, was consecrated Archbishop of Canterbury. It was Langton who, while still a teacher in Paris, became the first person to divide the books of the Bible into chapters.

1722 A band of religious fugitives from Moravia asked Count Ludwig von Zinzendorf if they might settle on his land. On his consent, the village of Herrnhut was founded, afterwards becoming a gathering place for persecuted Lutherans, Schwenkfelders, Separatist and Brethren believers. Herrnhut's missionaries later influenced John and Charles Wesley during the formative years of Methodism.

1821 In New York City, the first elders of the African Methodist Episcopal (AME) Zion Church were ordained. James Varick was elected the denomination's first bishop the following year. (The AMEZ church had its beginnings in 1796, when African-Americans, protesting discrimination in the Methodist Episcopal Church, organized their own denomination.)

1968 Meeting in Winona Lake, Indiana, the Pilgrim Holiness Church (org. 1897) voted to approve a proposed merger with the Wesleyan Methodist Church of America (org. 1843). (The merger was completed on June 26, 1968.)

Notable Birthdays

1703 [NS = 6/28] John (Benjamin) Wesley, English religious leader, was born the 15th of 19 children. He and his brother Charles founded Methodism at Oxford University in 1729, though John claimed for himself a "warmer" conversion only later, on May 24, 1738. ("Methodist" was originally a derisive nickname for Wesley's careful regimentation of Bible study and personal practice of his faith.) Methodists today number 30 million worldwide. [d. 3/3/1791]

1859 Birth of U.S. Presbyterian evangelist J. Wilbur Chapman. He was licensed to preach in 1881, but devoted himself to full-time evangelism after 1903. Chapman was first director of the Winona Lake Bible Conference Center (IN), and also penned the hymns: "One Day When Heaven Was Filled with His Praises" and "Jesus, What a Friend of Sinners!" [d. 12/25/1918]

1888 Birth of J. Roswell Flower, Assemblies of God clergyman and leader. He served his denomination in various executive capacities for 45 years, so that his name became synonymous with the Assemblies of God. [d. 1970]

The Last Passage

1719 Death of Joseph Addison, 47, English author and hymnwriter. His collected essays were published under the title, *Evidences of the Christian Religion*. Among Addison's several hymns, "The Spacious Firmament on High" is still sung. Addison's last words were: *'See in what peace a Christian can die.'* (b. 5/1/1672)

1887 Death of Mark Hopkins, 85, American educator and moral philosopher. For 30 years (1857-1887) he was president of the American Board of Commissioners for Foreign Missions. (b. 2/4/1802)

Words for the Soul

1843 In a speech delivered at the Bunker Hill monument in Charleston, MA, American statesman Daniel Webster declared: *'The Bible is a book of faith, and a book of doctrine, and a book of morals, and a book of religion, of special revelation from God; but it is also a book which teaches man his own individual responsibility, his own dignity, and his equality with his fellow-man.'*

1963 English apologist C. S. Lewis wrote in a letter: *'Has this world been so kind to you that you should leave it with regret? There are better things ahead than any we leave behind.'*

FROM GOD'S WORD...   OT: 1 Kings 18:1-46 ~ NT: Acts 11:1-30 ~ Psalms 135:1-21 ~ Proverbs 17:12-13

תמוז ALMANAC OF THE CHRISTIAN FAITH סיון
TAMMUZ   SIVAN

~ June 18 ~

Highlights in History

1464 Pope Pius II led a brief crusade into Italy, against the Turks. However, he became ill and died before the rest of his allies arrived. Soon after, the 300-year-old "crusades mentality" among European Christians came to an end.

1781 The first Baptist church established in Kentucky was organized at Elizabethtown.

1845 American religious Cornelia A.P. Connelly, 36, professed a solemn vow of chastity, after she and her husband converted from Episcopalianism to Catholicism, and he decided to enter the Catholic priesthood. In 1846, Cornelia founded the Society of the Holy Child Jesus, establishing its first convent in Derby, England.

Notable Birthdays

1804 Birth of American Congregationalist Peter Parker. Sent out by the American Board in 1834, he became the first Protestant medical missionary to go to China. [d. 1/10/1888]

1819 Birth of Samuel Longfellow, American Unitarian clergyman and hymnwriter. He gave the Church such hymn titles as: "Father, Give Thy Benediction" and "Holy Spirit, Truth Divine." [d. 10/3/1892]

1830 Birth of Elizabeth C. Clephane, an orphan who grew up in the Free Church of Scotland. She was a humanitarian and poet, and penned two of the most haunting hymns in the Church today: "Beneath the Cross of Jesus" and "The Ninety and Nine." [d. 2/19/1869]

1854 Birth of James M. Kirk, American hymnwriter. He joined the Christian and Missionary Alliance in 1887, soon after its founding by A.B. Simpson. Kirk traveled with a men's musical quartet and wrote numerous gospel song tunes, including BLESSED QUIETNESS. [d. 7/11/1945]

1906 Birth of Gordon Lindsay, U.S. leader in the charismatic healing movement and in missions. In 1948 Lindsay and his wife Freda began publishing "The Voice of Healing" magazine. They also founded Christ for the Nations, a non-denominational agency for supporting foreign missions. [d. 4/1/1973]

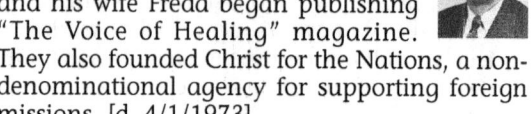

The Last Passage

373 Death of St. Ephraem, 67, a celebrated Syrian Christian biblical exegete and doctor of the Church. A prolific writer of biblical commentaries and homilies, Ephraem also composed over 70 hymns for the liturgy. (b. ca.315)

1849 Death of Congregational clergyman and evangelist William B. Tappan, 54. For many years he was a leader in the American Sunday School Union. He also published 10 volumes of poetry, one of which contained a hymn still sung in the Church: "'Tis Midnight, and on Olive's Brow." (b. 10/24/1794)

1956 Youth leader Dawson E. Trotman, 50, died of a heart attack while rescuing a swimmer at a summer conference in the Adirondacks. (Trotman, a Presbyterian-turned-Baptist, had chartered the Navigators — an evangelical discipleship ministry — in 1934.) (b. 3/25/1906)

Words for the Soul

1536 Spanish founder of the Jesuits, Ignatius of Loyola advised in a letter: 'The general procedure of the enemy with those who love God Our Lord and are beginning to serve him is to bring in hindrances and obstacles…. So we must take great care: if the enemy is raising us up, we ought to lower ourselves, listing our sins and wretchedness; and if he is casting us down and depressing us, we must raise ourselves up in true faith and hope in the Lord, counting the benefits we have received.'

1767 Founder of Methodism John Wesley promised in a letter: 'The more work the more blessing.'

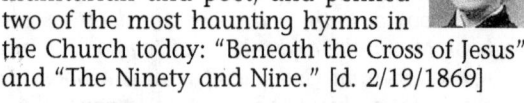

FROM GOD'S WORD...   OT: 1 Kings 19:1-21 ~ NT: Acts 12:1-23 ~ Psalms 136:1-26 ~ Proverbs 17:14-15

תמוז ALMANAC OF THE CHRISTIAN FAITH סיון
TAMMUZ   SIVAN

~ June 19 ~

Highlights in History

325 The Council of Nicea closed. The Church's first Ecumenical Council, it was called by Pope Sylvester I and Roman Emperor Constantine I. By the end of this month-long assembly, the 300 gathered bishops had formulated the Nicene Creed, condemned the Arian heresy (which had denied the deity of Christ) and established the method for calculating Easter.

1553 In England, Forty-Two Articles of Religion were published, and all clergy and schoolmasters were required to subscribe to them. Drafted mainly by Thomas Cranmer, they were never enforced, owing to the restoration of the Roman Catholic faith under Mary (1553-58). But they formed a basis for Anglicanism's later, more permanent Thirty-Nine Articles (1563).

1783 In England, followers of Swedish Lutheran scientist and mystic Emmanual Swedenborg (1688-1772) organized the Church of the New Jerusalem. Known as "The New Church" today, its doctrines are complex and the number of followers is small. Two great names in American history, however, who embraced Swedenborgianism were Jonathan Chapman (aka "Johnny Appleseed") and Helen Keller.

1910 In Spokane, WA, under sponsorship of the Spokane Ministerial Association and the YMCA, Father's Day was observed for the first time. Founder Louise Dodd had wanted to find a way to honor her own father who was left to raise six children when his wife died in childbirth.

1977 Paul VI canonized early United States prelate John Nepomucene Neumann (1811-1860), the first American-born male saint. As the fourth Bishop of the Philadelphia Diocese, Neumann is remembered for developing the parochial school system.

1987 The U.S. Supreme Court struck down a Louisiana law requiring public schools to teach creationism if they taught evolutionism. The court ruled the state law violated the First Amendment.

Notable Birthdays

1566 Birth of James VI, son of Mary Queen of Scots, and the King of Scotland (1567-1625). At the death of Queen Elizabeth I (1603), he also ascended the English throne (1603-25) as James I. Today he is best remembered for authorizing the translation known afterward as the King James Version (KJV) of the Bible. [d. 3/27/1625]

1623 Birth of Blaise Pascal, French mathematician, philosopher, theologian, inventor and mystic. Highly honored in scientific circles for inventing the barometer, the first digital calculator, the syringe and the hydraulic press, Pascal also left the religious community two famous writings: *Provinciales* and *Pensées*. [d. 8/19/1662]

1834 Birth of Charles Haddon Spurgeon, English Baptist preacher. He was one of the greatest public speakers of his day, whose London congregation grew to 6,000. A prolific writer as well, Spurgeon's sermons alone fill over 50 large volumes. [d. 1/31/1892]

The Last Passage

1954 Death of American Presbyterian clergyman William P. Merrill, 87. He pastored Brick Memorial Church (NYC) 1911-38, authored a number of books, and also many hymns, including "Rise Up, O Men of God." (b. 1/10/1867)

Words for the Soul

1771 Founder of Methodism John Wesley, at age 67, testified in a letter: *'When I was much younger than I am now, I thought myself almost infallible; but, I bless God, I know myself better now.'*

1849 Scottish Free Church clergyman Andrew A. Bonar recorded in his journal: *'The more I have been able to make God my chief joy the less do I feel in any way tormented with earthly desires, and I see myself surrounded with comforts.'*

FROM GOD'S WORD...   OT: 1 Kings 20:1–21:29 ~ NT: 12:24–13:12 ~ Psalms 137:1-9 ~ Proverbs 17:16

תמוז
TAMMUZ

ALMANAC OF THE CHRISTIAN FAITH

סיון
SIVAN

June 20

Highlights in History

1529 Caught in the struggle between Charles V and Francis I of France to dominate Italy, Clement VII signed the Peace of Barcelona with Charles V, and ended the attacks on Rome by Lutheran armies. Their reconciliation was sealed by Charles' coronation at Bologna on Feb. 24, 1530 – the last imperial coronation in history made by a pope.

1599 The Synod of Diamper reunited a native church in India with Rome. Discovered in 1498 by Portuguese explorers, this isolated pocket of worshipers traced their Christian origins back to the missionary efforts of the Apostle Thomas.

1667 Italian cardinal Giulio Rospigliosi, 67, was elected Clement IX. He negotiated a compromise over the issue of Jansenism in France, and was a strong opponent of nepotism. Unfortunately, Clement died only two years later.

1885 A band of Moravian missionaries landed on the shores of Alaska and founded the Bethel Mission. During their first year of mission work among the eskimos, winter temperatures fell to 50 degrees below zero!

1972 Judith Hurd was ordained as pastor of the Holy Cross Lutheran Church in Tom's River, New Jersey – the first female Lutheran pastor.

Notable Birthdays

1694 Birth of Hans A. Brorson, Danish Lutheran clergyman and hymnwriter. Seeking to promote personal piety among his people, he penned many powerful lyrics about God's creation and human redemption, including the hymns, "Thy Little Ones, Dear Lord, Are We" and "Behold a Host Arrayed in White." [d. 6/3/1764]

1779 Birth of Dorothy Ann Thrupp, English devotional writer. Many of her pieces were written for children, and most were left unsigned, or written under the pseudonym "Iota." Her greatest legacy today is the hymn, "Savior, Like a Shepherd Lead Us." [d. 12/14/1847]

1813 Birth of Charles T. Brooks, American Unitarian minister. He enjoyed a very long, and active ministry in Newport, RI (1837-83). With John S. Dwight, Brooks also co-wrote the hymn, "God Bless Our Native Land." [d. 6/14/1883]

The Last Passage

1904 Death of Joseph Augustus Seiss, 81, American Lutheran clergyman. Born of Moravian parentage, he founded the General Council of the Evangelical Lutheran Church in North America. Seiss also wrote many books on religion, and translated the fourth verse of the hymn, "Fairest Lord Jesus." (b. 3/18/1823)

1936 Death of Florence Crawford, 63, American Pentecostal leader. Born to atheist parents, she was converted after her marriage, and experienced a sanctification and healing at the 1906 Azusa Street Revival in Los Angeles. Crawford later founded the Apostolic Faith Church in Portland, Oregon, from which a broader Pentecostal movement afterward evolved. (b. 9/1/1872)

Words for the Soul

1764 To a church member going through severe trials, English founder of Methodism John Wesley explained in a letter: *'He has given you affliction upon affliction; he has used every possible means to unhinge your soul from things of earth, that it might fix on him alone.'*

1776 Anglican clergyman and hymnwriter John Newton wrote in a letter: *'A Christian is not of hasty growth... but rather like the oak, the progress of which is hardly perceptible, but in time becomes a deep-rooted tree.'*

1923 English mystical writer Evelyn Underhill clarified in a letter: *'We can never become unselfed on our own – it is God's work in us. We can only open the door and say, "Do what You like."'*

FROM GOD'S WORD...   OT: 1 Kings 22:1-53 ~ NT: Acts 13:13-41 ~ Psalms 138:1-8 ~ Proverbs 17:17-18

תמוז
TAMMUZ

ALMANAC OF THE CHRISTIAN FAITH

סיון
SIVAN

~ June 21 ~

Highlights in History

1054 Michael Cerularius, Patriarch of Constantinople (1043-58) and violently anti-Latin, sent the first of two anathemas against Rome, in response to a bull of excommunication issued by Pope Leo IX against the Easterns. It was during Cerularius's reign that the beginning of the Schism between Eastern and Western Christianity is conventionally dated.

1821 The African Methodist Episcopal Zion (AMEZ) Church was formally constituted in New York City. Nineteen clergymen were present, representing six African-American churches from New York City; Philadelphia; New Haven, CT; and Newark, NJ.

1963 Italian Cardinal Giovanni Battista Montini was elected Paul VI, the 261st pontiff of the Catholic Church. He became the first pope ever to visit the Holy Land, the first pope to travel to the United States and the first pope to meet with the Greek Orthodox patriarch in 500 years.

Notable Birthdays

1639 Birth of Increase Mather, leading American Colonial clergyman and theologian. The father of Cotton Mather, Increase published nearly 100 books, and is credited with helping end executions for witchcraft in the American colonies. [d. 8/23/1723]

1792 Birth of Ferdinand Christian Baur, German Protestant theologian. He was founder of the movement (called the "Tübingen School") which sought to apply historical "criticism" (i.e., analysis) to theology. [d. 12/2/1860]

1821 Birth of Henry W. Baker, English clergyman, musicologist and compiler of *Hymns Ancient and Modern* – regarded today as the unofficial Anglican church hymnal. Baker also authored a hymn based on Psalm 23: "The King of Love My Shepherd Is." [d. 2/12/1877]

1836 Birth of Sanford Fillmore Bennett, American physician and author. He published numerous works of prose and verse, including the popular hymn, "The Sweet Bye and Bye." [d. 6/12/1898]

1892 Birth of Reinhold Niebuhr, American clergyman, theologian and author. As Professor of Applied Christianity at Union Seminary in NYC (1928-60), Niebuhr pioneered the philosophy of "Christian realism," and his writings marked the beginning of the neo-orthodox movement in the U.S. His best-known work was *Nature and Destiny of Man* (1943). [d. 6/1/1971]

The Last Passage

1873 Death of Heinrich A. W. Meyer, 73, German Lutheran biblical scholar. Chiefly remembered for a N.T. commentary he initiated in 1829, and which was later named after him, Meyer was one of the first exegetes to apply a careful philological-historical method in determining the historical setting of the text. (b. 1/10/1800)

1897 Death of Clara H. Scott, 55, American music teacher and composer, who died when she was thrown from a buggy by a runaway horse. An innovater among women in music, she issued *The Royal Anthem Book* in 1882 – the first volume of anthems published by a woman. Today, Scott is better remembered as author and composer of the hymn, "Open My Eyes, That I May See" (& SCOTT). (b. 12/3/1841)

Words for the Soul

1754 Anglican John Newton wrote in a letter to his wife: *'That powerful love, which brought down the Most High to assume our nature, to suffer, and to die for us, will not permit those who depend on him to want [lack] what is really good for them.'*

1884 Scottish clergyman Andrew Bonar at age 74 lamented in his diary: *'I am not used in conversion work as I was in early days. ...Lord, use me yet! ...Give me souls still, before my sun has set.'*

FROM GOD'S WORD... OT: 2 Kings 1:1–2:25 ~ NT: Acts 13:42–14:7 ~ Psalms 139:1-24 ~ Proverbs 17:19-21

תמוז TAMMUZ — ALMANAC OF THE CHRISTIAN FAITH — סיון SIVAN

June 22

Highlights in History

431 The Council of Ephesus was opened in this ancient Asia Minor city by St. Cyril of Alexandria. It was this third ecumenical council of the Church at which Nestorius, bishop of Constantinople was deposed. His doctrines were also condemned and the Nicene Creed was reaffirmed. (Nestorianism held that Christ was two separate persons rather than one person with two natures.) In its rejection of Nestorianism, the council first gave formal approval to the title "Theotokos" ("God-bearer") for Mary.

1559 In England, Queen Elizabeth I's Prayer Book was issued. During her 45-year reign, Elizabeth rejected the Catholic faith, adopting instead the Thirty-Nine Articles of the Anglican Church.

1750 New England Congregational clergyman Jonathan Edwards was dismissed from his pulpit in Northampton, Massachusetts, after serving there 23 years. Maintaining an ultra-conservative theology, Edwards had grown to become too theologically and administratively inflexible for his congregation.

Notable Birthdays

1680 Birth of Ebenezer Erskine, founder of the Secession Church in Scotland. Ordained in 1703, Erskine was a synod moderator in 1731, and preached against assigning ministers by assembly legislation. In 1740 he and seven other clergymen were deposed from the Presbytery. Within five years the Seceders were ministering to over 40 congregations in Scotland. [d. 6/2/1754]

1759 Birth of William Bentley, American clergyman and diarist. In 1783 he was ordained pastor of the East Congregational Church at Salem, Mass., and served there his remaining 36 years. Book collecting was his life interest, and his valuable library was afterward bequeathed to the American Antiquarian Society. Bentley also kept a 35-year-long diary, which afterward became his most important contribution to American literature. [d. 12/19/1819]

The Last Passage

380 Death of Eusebius of Samosata. A champion of the Nicene faith, he strongly opposed Arianism. He was bishop of Samosata from 361.

1535 English Catholic Bishop of Rochester, John Fisher, 66, the was beheaded for denying that Henry VIII was supreme head of the Church of England, and for opposing the king's divorce from Catherine of Aragon. Fisher was canonized in 1935. (b. 1469)

1714 Death of Matthew Henry, 51, the English Nonconformist clergyman famed for his devotional Bible commentary, *Exposition of the Old and New Testaments* (1708-10). 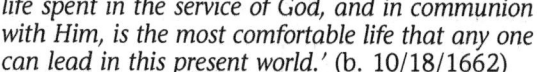 His last words: 'A life spent in the service of God, and in communion with Him, is the most comfortable life that any one can lead in this present world.' (b. 10/18/1662)

1850 Death of William Walford, 78, English Congregational clergyman and tutor in the classics. He wrote a popular book, *The Manner of Prayer* (1836), and also one of the beloved hymns of the Church: "Sweet Hour of Prayer." (b. 1772)

1874 Death of American Baptist devotional writer Lydia Baxter, 64. An invalid for many years, she authored inspirational poems and wrote her most enduring hymn at age 61: "Take the Name of Jesus With You." (b. 9/8/1809)

Words for the Soul

1745 Colonial missionary to New England Native Americans David Brainerd wrote in his journal: 'I am often weary of this world, and want to leave it on that account; but it is more desirable to be drawn, rather than driven out of it.'

1930 In a letter to his lifelong friend Arthur Greeves, British literary scholar and Christian apologist C.S. Lewis shared this discovery: 'It is terrible to find how little progress one's philosophy and charity have made when they are brought to the test of domestic life.'

FROM GOD'S WORD... OT: 2 Kings 3:1–4:17 ~ NT: Acts 14:8-28 ~ Psalms 140:1-13 ~ Proverbs 17:22

תמוז ALMANAC OF THE CHRISTIAN FAITH סיון
TAMMUZ   SIVAN

~ June 23 ~

Highlights in History

1683 English Quaker colonizer William Penn, 38, signed his famous treaty with the Indians of Pennsylvania. French skeptic Voltaire once remarked that it was *'the only treaty never sworn to, and never broken.'*

1863 Joseph E. Renan, 40, published his controversial biography, *Vie de Jésus*, in which he claimed that none of the supernatural elements in Jesus' scriptural biographies were true. The book set off a storm of controversy. Atheists charged that it did not go far enough in stripping veneration from the person of Jesus, and believers deplored its blasphemous denial of Christ's divinity.

1956 The General Council of the Congregational Christian Churches voted to unite with the Evangelical and Reformed Church. (The following year, the United Church of Christ was born.)

1967 Paul VI issued the encyclical "Sacerdotalis caelibatus," reaffirming the Catholic Church's requirement of celibacy within the priesthood.

1973 At its Ninth Biennial General Synod, Margaret A. Haywood was elected moderator of the United Church of Christ. An associate justice of the Superior Court in the District of Columbia, she became the first African-American woman to head a major U.S. denomination.

1986 The first conference held by Charismatic Bible Ministries opened in Tulsa. During the 3-day convention, Oral Roberts was elected chairman, Kenneth Copeland secretary and Paul Yonggi Cho honorary international chairman. CBM helps to make charismatic organizations more cooperative with one another.

Notable Birthdays

1738 Birth of Samuel Medley, English Baptist clergyman and author of the hymns, "O Could I Speak the Matchless Worth" and "I Know That My Redeemer Lives." [d. 7/17/1799]

1786 Birth of Nathaniel W. Taylor, American Congregational theologian. He led in the softening of Jonathan Edwards' Calvinism, stemming from the revivals of America's Great Awakening. Taylor believed both in predestination and in free agency, rescued God's nature from charges of tyranny, and made sin an act of moral failure. Sinners are punished by a just God because they freely choose evil, not because they were created with a depraved nature preventing any chance of virtue. [d. 3/10/1858]

The Last Passage

679 Death of Etheldreda, 49, daughter of a Christian king of the East Angles. She twice married, but refused both times to consummate the marriage and lose her virginity. Ultimately, she was permitted to become a nun (ca. 672). She founded the double monastery at Ely in 673, and served as its abbess until her death. (b. 630)

1942 Death of Emily D. Wilson, 77, a Philadelphia Conference Methodist preacher's wife. She contributed many gifts to the service of God and to the Church, including the hymn tune HEAVEN ("Sing the Wondrous Love"). (b. 5/24/1865)

Words for the Soul

1775 Anglican clergyman and hymnwriter John Newton wrote in a letter: *'True religion is not a science of the head so much as an inward and heartfelt perception.... Here the learned have no real advantage over the ignorant.'*

1788 Anglican Evangelical Henry Venn detailed in a letter: *'Now is the time of our warfare: we are to fight under Christ's banner – not once, or twice, but to our life's end – not against a single foe, or a feeble one, but against the world, the flesh, and the devil.'*

1889 Three years before his death, Scottish clergyman and biographer Andrew Bonar, 79, noted in his diary: *'The Lord is kinder to me than ever, the nearer I come to the end of my journey.'*

FROM GOD'S WORD...   OT: 2 Kings 4:18–5:27 ~ NT: Acts 15:1-35 ~ Psalms 141:1-10 ~ Proverbs 17:23

June 24

Highlights in History

64 The first state-sponsored terrorism against Christians in the Roman Empire came at the order of Nero, one of the most debased of all the early emperors. Thus began the first wave of Imperial persecutions against the Church.

1700 Massachusetts judge Samuel Sewall (who presided at the 1692 Salem Witch Trials) published a 3-page pamphlet entitled, "The Selling of Joseph." It was the first public appeal for the abolition of slavery to appear in America.

1844 Mormon leaders Joseph Smith and his brother Hyrum were arrested in Carthage, IL, for their part in a riot leading to the destruction of "The Nauvoo Expositor." (The paper had attacked the Mormon practice of polygamy.)

1941 The two-day Constitutional Assembly of the Nippon Kirisuto Kyodan opened, during which the United Church of Christ in Japan was formed. Today, the United Church membership contains one-third of all Japanese Protestants.

1967 Paul VI's encyclical, "Sacerdotalis caelibatus," was published, which reasserted an enforced celibacy among the clergy.

Notable Birthdays

1485 Birth of Johann Bugenhagen, German Protestant Reformer. He assisted Martin Luther in translating the Bible, and also introduced the Lutheran service and church discipline into many German cities. [d. 4/20/1558]

1519 Birth of Theodore Beza, French-born Swiss theological reformer. Beza became the acknowledged leader of the Swiss churches, following John Calvin's death in 1564. [d. 10/13/1605]

1542 Birth of St. John of the Cross, Spanish Carmelite monk, mystic and poet. A founder of the Discalced Carmelites, he authored the religious classic, *The Dark Night of the Soul*, and was canonized by Benedict XIII in 1726. [d. 12/14/1591]

1792 Birth of Pliny Fisk, American Congregational missionary to the Middle East. Before his premature death at 33, Fisk completed work on an Arabic-English dictionary. [d. 10/23/1825]

1803 Birth of George J. Webb, American church organist. He compiled several collections of sacred music during his lifetime, and composed the melody WEBB to which is sung, "Stand Up, Stand Up for Jesus." [d. 10/7/1887]

1813 Birth of Henry Ward Beecher, American Congregational clergyman, social reformer, and author. He was a forceful orator who spoke out on social and political issues, including slavery, the Civil War and Reconstruction. In his preaching, Beecher was graphic and picturesque, and as a writer imparted life to the dullest subjects. [d. 3/8/1887]

The Last Passage

1797 Death of Henry Venn, 72, Evangelical Anglican clergyman. He became a warm friend of George Whitefield, and was one of the founders of the Clapham Sect. (b. 3/2/1725)

1917 Death of Orville J. Nave, 76, U.S. Armed Services chaplain and compiler of the popular *Nave's Topical Bible* – still in print! (b. 4/30/1841)

1983 Death of Charles P. Taft, 85, American lawyer and religious leader. Son of U.S. president William H. Taft, Charles became a founder of the World Council of Churches. (b. 9/20/1897)

Words for the Soul

1846 Scottish clergyman Andrew A. Bonar wrote in his journal: *'O my God, never let me walk, even in the green pastures, without Thee!'*

1968 Romanian-born American comparative religions scholar Mircea Eliade observed in his journal: *'"The sacred" is an element of the structure of consciousness, and not a moment in the history of consciousness.'*

FROM GOD'S WORD... OT: 2 Kings 6:1–7:20 ~ NT: Acts 15:36–16:15 ~ Psalms 142:1-7 ~ Proverbs 17:24-25

June 25

Highlights in History

1115 French monk St. Bernard founded the monastery in Clairvaux, France. It became a popular center for the Cistercians, a religious order, famous throughout Europe, that flourished up until the Reformation. Bernard founded 70 monasteries in all, and was canonized in 1174.

1243 Italian cardinal Sinisbaldo Fieschi was elected Pope Innocent IV. He called the (failed) Seventh Crusade and, through his papal bull "Ad extirpenda" (1252), he permitted the use of torture during the Inquisition.

1530 The principal creed of Lutheranism, the Augsburg Confession was first presented to Emperor Charles V at the Diet of Augsburg. Prepared chiefly by Philip[p] Melanchthon (1497-1560), its Twenty-One articles later influenced Anglicanism's Thirty-Nine Articles, and John Wesley's Twenty-Three (Methodist) Articles.

1580 The German *Book of Concord* was published, containing all the official confessions of the Lutheran Church. It represented 30 years of efforts to heal divisions within the denomination following Luther's death in 1546. (A Latin version was prepared in 1584, but an English translation wasn't completed until 1851.)

1744 The first Methodist conference in history convened in London. This new society within Anglicanism imposed strict disciplines upon its members (earning them their nickname "Methodies"), but didn't formally separate from the English Church until 1795.

1865 English pioneer missionary J[ames] Hudson Taylor founded the China Inland Mission. Its headquarters moved to the U.S. in 1901, and in 1965 CIM changed its name to Overseas Missionary Fellowship (OMF) International.

1957 During a convention in Cleveland, Ohio, the United Church of Christ (UCC) was formed by a merger of the Congregational Christian and the Evangelical and Reformed denominations. Its constitution went into effect on July 4, 1961.

Notable Birthdays

1799 Birth of Philip E. Pusey, English scholar, author, and hymnwriter: "Lord of Our Life, and God of Our Salvation." [d. 7/9/1855]

1834 Birth of Henry C. Potter, American Episcopal clergyman and social reformer. He was Bishop of New York City (1887-1908), and in 1892 initiated the construction of the Cathedral of St. John the Divine. [d. 7/21/1908]

1842 Birth of Daniel S. Warner, American churchman and founder of the Church of God (headquartered in Anderson, Indiana). [d. 2/12/1925]

The Last Passage

1901 Death of Flavius J. Cook, 63, American Congregational author and lecturer. Though orthodox in his own thinking, his lectures explained Universalism, and his principal writings include: *Transcendentalism* (1877) and *Orthodoxy* (1877). (b. 1/26/1838)

Words for the Soul

1781 Anglican-Methodist preacher John Fletcher noted in a letter: *'It is often harder to keep in the way of faith and light than to get into it.... The work of sanctification... is hindered by holding out the being delivered from sin as the mark to be aimed at, instead of the being rooted in Christ and being filled with the fullness of God.'*

1858 Anglican-turned-Catholic poet, Frederick W. Faber noted in a letter: *'If it is sometimes a dread to us that God reads the heart, it is more often our best consolation.'*

1877 American Quaker writer Hannah Whitall Smith revealed in a letter: *'Of one thing I am convinced beyond a shadow of doubt,... that there is yet left in the church the gift of the Holy Ghost to be received definitely and consciously, and that all who do not receive it are but half-equipped.'*

FROM GOD'S WORD...   OT: 2 Kings 8:1–9:13 ~ NT: Acts 16:16-40 ~ Psalms 143:1-12 ~ Proverbs 17:26

June 26

Highlights in History

1097 The armies of the First Crusade (1096-99) occupied the ancient Byzantine city of Nicea. (In all, seven crusades were undertaken between 1096 and 1265, for the ostensible purpose of recovering the Holy Places and gaining a clear access to the Holy Land for Christian pilgrims.)

1934 In Cleveland, OH the Evangelical Synod of North America (organized in 1840 as the German Evangelical Church Society of the West) united with the Reformed Church in the United States to form the Evangelical and Reformed Church.

1968 The Wesleyan Church (a non-charismatic American holiness denomination) was formed through union of the Wesleyan Methodist Church and the Pilgrim Holiness Church. (Wesleyan Methodism was first organized in 1843 by abolitionist clergy of the Methodist Episcopal Church. The Pilgrim Holiness church began as the International Holiness Union and Prayer League, founded 1897 in Cincinnati, Ohio.)

Notable Birthdays

1702 Birth of English clergyman Philip Doddridge. The youngest of 20 children and orphaned at 13, he was trained in Nonconformist theology, became a man of great learning, and  authored many theological books, of which *The Rise and Progress of Religion in the Soul* (1745) was the most notable. He also authored 370 hymn-texts, including "O Happy Day That Fixed My Choice." [d. 10/26/1751]

1866 Birth of George E. S. Herbert, English Egyptologist and archaeologist. In 1922, he and Howard Carter discovered the tomb of the Egyptian pharaoh Tutankhamen. [d. 4/6/1923]

1877 Birth of William H. Foulkes, a 5th-generation U.S. Presbyterian clergyman and author of the hymn of submission, "Take Thou Our Minds, Dear Lord." [d. 12/9/1961]

1892 Birth of Pearl S. Buck (Mrs. Richard John Walsh), American educator and writer. The daughter of Presbyterian missionaries to China, she authored *The Good Earth* (1930), which won the Pulitzer Prize in 1932, and the Nobel Prize in 1938. [d. 3/6/1973]

The Last Passage

1691 Death of John Flavel, 61, English Presbyterian and Nonconformist clergyman. A prolific writer on practical religion, his many works include were collected in six volumes in the 19th century, and were later reprinted as *The Works of John Flavel* (1968). (b. ca.1630)

1893 Death of James Robinson Graves, 73, the U.S. Baptist preacher who helped lead formation of the Landmark Movement within his denomination. (Landmarkism believed the local congregation alone represents the true Church, and that there was an apostolic succession within any true Baptist church traceable all the way back to the first century.) (b. 4/10/1820)

1946 Death of Alma Bridwell White, 84, Kentucky-born religious leader. She founded the Methodist Pentecostal Union Church in 1901. In 1917 the church changed its name to the Pillar of Fire Church, and in 1918 she was consecrated senior bishop – the first female bishop of any Christian denomination. (b. 6/16/1862)

Words for the Soul

1837 Anglican poet-turned-Catholic Frederick W. Faber made observation in a letter: *'The world is truly impregnated with sacraments.'*

1839 Scottish clergyman and missionary Robert Murray McCheyne wrote in a letter: *'Joy is increased by spreading it to others.'*

1868 American Quaker holiness author Hannah Whitall Smith, 36, prayed in her journal: *'Oh my loving Saviour, I am in your hands. Do with me as you will. Glorify yourself in me! Lead me in darkness or in light – only keep me trusting you!'*

FROM GOD'S WORD... OT: 2 Kings 9:14–10:31 ~ NT: Acts 17:1-34 ~ Psalms 144:1-15 ~ Proverbs 17:27-28

תמוז ALMANAC OF THE CHRISTIAN FAITH סיון
TAMMUZ   SIVAN

June 27

Highlights in History

1299 In his encyclical "Scimus fili," Pope Boniface VIII claimed that Scotland owed allegiance to the Catholic Church.

1736 As a member of the Holy Club (to which John and Charles Wesley also belonged), future English revivalist George Whitefield, 21, preached his first sermon. (Whitefield went on to preach thousands more sermons, and became a force in colonial America's "Great Awakening.")

1519 The three-week Disputation of Leipzig opened. The debate was arranged as an attempt to discredit Martin Luther's theology and trick the reformer into espousing heresy. Here Luther first affirmed that church councils may not only err, but have in fact erred, and that the "power of the keys" (Matthew 16:19) had been given to faithful members of the Church rather than to the Pope. The outcome of the debate prepared the way for Luther's condemnation by the Diet of Worms the following year.

Notable Birthdays

1818 Birth of James L. Breck, American Episcopal missionary to the Wisconsin territory. Dedicating himself to missions at 16, he pursued the calling for 35 years. One of Breck's converts, Enmegahbowh, became the first Ojibway Indian to be ordained into Episcopal orders (1859). Breck was also a founder of Seabury Seminary (near St. Paul, MN). [d. 3/30/1876]

1819 Birth of Wolfgang F. Gess, German theologian. Solving the problem of how the Son of God actually "diminished" himself as the Son of Man became Gess's life-long literary obsession, and he was among the earliest kenotic theologians who studied the meaning of Christ's "emptying" ("kenosis") of himself as described in Philippians 2:5-11. [d. 6/1/1891]

1880 Birth of Helen Adams Keller, American author and lecturer. Deaf and blind from age 19 months, she began to overcome her handicaps from age 7 by learning to speak and write with the help of ("miracle worker") Anne Sullivan (1866-1936). [d. 6/1/1968]

1946 Sally Jane Priesand, the first American female (Reform Jewish) rabbi, was born in Cleveland, Ohio. Ordained in Cincinnati in 1972, following her graduation from Hebrew Union College, Rabbi Priesand later published *Judaism and The New Woman* (1975).

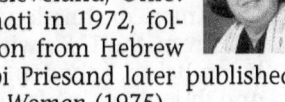

The Last Passage

1844 Mormon founder Joseph Smith and his brother Hyrum were shot and killed by a mob in Carthage, IL, in part due to the community's moral outrage at Smith's recent authorizing of polygamous Mormon marriages. (b. 12/23/1805)

1933 Death of James Mountain, 88, British Baptist revivalist. He authored a number of religious books, but is remembered today for composing the hymn tunes TRANQUILLITY ("Jesus, I am Resting, Resting"), WYE VALLEY ("Like a River Glorious") and EVERLASTING LOVE ("I Am His, and He is Mine"). (b. 7/16/1844)

1950 Death of Hugh T. Kerr, 78, U.S. Presbyterian clergyman. He pastored 1913-46 at Shadyside Presbyterian Church in Pittsburgh, while also pioneering in religious radio broadcasting. Kerr authored the hymn, "God of Our Life, Through All the Circling Years." (b. 2/11/1872)

Words for the Soul

1760 Founder of Methodism John Wesley wrote in a letter: *'Every one, though born of God in an instant, yet undoubtedly grows by slow degrees.'*

1781 Anglican Evangelical Henry Venn concluded in a letter: *'The victory pays for all. It is a glorious end to live for, that we may be like God in our temper, glorify Him for a few years on earth, and then dwell in His presence for ever.'*

FROM GOD'S WORD...   OT: 2 Kings 10:32–12:21 ~ NT: Acts 18:1-22 ~ Psalms 145:1-21 ~ Proverbs 18:1

June 28

Highlights in History

1629 The Peace of Alais was signed, ending the Huguenot Wars in France. By this treaty the French Protestants obtained a religious freedom of conscience, but lost a military advantage in their French homeland.

1890 American missionary Samuel Zwemer set sail from the U.S., with his final destination being Beirut, Lebanon. Zwemer lived, breathed and thought only of reaching the Muslim world for Christ. He set up presses, and authored numerous books about the need to share Christ with the Arabs. He noted that the concept of God as a tender father was unknown to Muslims.

1971 The U. S. Supreme Court declared that State funding of nonreligious instruction in parochial schools was unconstitutional.

Notable Birthdays

1476 Birth of Giovanni Pietro Caraffa, who served as Paul IV (1555-59) – the first of the Counter-Reformation popes. He published the *Index of Prohibited Books*, and also founded the Theatine Order. [d. 8/18/1559]

1491 Birth of Henry VIII (Tudor), the most colorful of the English kings (1509-47). In conflict with Catholicism over the issue of divorce, he married six times in an attempt to father a male heir to the throne. Henry finally established the Anglican (English Catholic) Church in 1534, severing all financial, judicial and administrative links with Rome. [d. 1/28/1547]

1577 Birth of Peter Paul Rubens, Flemish painter. His most famous canvases include "Erection of the Cross" (1610) and "Descent from the Cross" (1614). [d. 5/30/1640]

1814 Birth of Frederick W. Faber, English clergyman and hymnwriter. He was ordained in the Anglican Church in 1842, but in 1845 converted to Catholicism. Faber authored 150 hymns,  including "Faith of Our Fathers" and "There's a Wideness in God's Mercy." [d. 9/26/1863]

1851 Birth of Eliza E. Hewitt, American Presbyterian church worker and devotional author. Four of her hymns are still sung: "Will There Be Any Stars?", "More About Jesus Would I Know," "When We All Get to Heaven" and "Sunshine in the Soul." [d. 4/24/1920]

The Last Passage

1937 Death of Sir Edwyn C. Hoskyns, 52, Anglican clergyman and theologian. He argued that the "historical Jesus" of critical scholars was unhistorical and that the teaching behind the Synoptic Gospels was more complex than supposed by liberal theologians. (b. 8/9/1884)

1954 Death of Mennonite clergyman and hymnwriter Samuel F. Coffman, 82. He served on the music committee of the Mennonite General Conference 1911-47, and wrote a number of original hymns, including "We Bless the Name of Christ, The Lord." (b. 6/11/1872)

1984 Death of Yigael Yadin, 71, Israeli archaeologist. He organized digs at Masada and the Dead Sea caves, and also published many scholarly works. (Yadin was the son of Eliezer Sukenik, the scholar at Jerusalem's Hebrew Univ. who first received the Dead Sea Scrolls.) (b. 3/21/1917)

Words for the Soul

1868 Scottish clergyman and novelist George MacDonald exhorted in a letter: *'Let us work well while the evening closes in around us, and when we lie down at last God will give a glorious waking to all our dreams; all that was lovely in them we shall find true.'*

1943 English Catholic Christian psychiatrist Caryll Houselander observed in a letter: *'In each man's soul, one street and one house and a handful of people are his country.'*

FROM GOD'S WORD... OT: 2 Kings 13:1–14:29 ~ NT: Acts 18:23–19:12 ~ Psalms 146:1-10 ~ Proverbs 18:2-3

ALMANAC OF THE CHRISTIAN FAITH

TAMMUZ — SIVAN

~ June 29 ~

Highlights in History

1810 In Bradford, the first U.S. foreign missionary society was organized by the General Association of Massachusetts. It was named the American Board of Commissioners for Foreign Missions.

1875 The first "holiness" conference opened at Keswick, England. Keswick stressed a non-charismatic, "crisis" form of sanctification, in contrast to the older Calvinist view of sanctification as a lifelong "process," and opposing the post-1900 Pentecostal emphasis on speaking in tongues as outward evidence of sanctification.

1931 Unevangelized Fields Mission was founded in England. Headquartered today in Bala-Cynwyd, PA, UFM today sponsors over 300 missionaries who serve in over two dozen world nations – in Europe, Africa, Latin America, and the Caribbean and Pacific Islands.

1982 The United Presbyterian Church (UPC) voted to approve a merger with the Presbyterian Church in the United States (PCUS). The union (healing a division caused by the American Civil War) became official in 1983.

Notable Birthdays

1721 Birth of John Ettwein, German-born American Moravian clergyman and missionary. He founded the Society of the United Brethren for Propagating the Gospel Among the Heathen in 1787, to which Congress granted several Indian townships on the Tuscarawas River in Ohio. Ettwein was consecrated bishop of the Moravian Church in 1784. [d. 1/2/1802]

1908 Birth of Cyrus H. Gordon, American Jewish Ugaritic scholar. He taught Assyriology and Egyptology at Dropsie College (PA). His scholarly writings include the *Ugaritic Handbook* (1947). [d. 3/30/2001]

1933 Birth of Aubrey Lee Butler, American hymnwriter. Called "Pete" by his friends, Butler composed the hymn tune ADA ("Redeemed, How I Love to Proclaim It").

The Last Passage

62/67 According to tradition, the Apostle Paul was beheaded with a sword near Rome on this date. (The exact year varies among traditions.)

1894 Death of Frank Bottome, 61, English-born American Methodist Episcopal clergyman. He published two sacred songbooks, and penned a number of hymns, including "O Spread the Tidings 'Round" and "The Comforter Has Come." (b. 5/26/1823)

Words for the Soul

1757 Anglican clergyman and hymnwriter John Newton offered this encouragement in a letter: *'Whatever we may undertake with a sincere desire to promote His glory, we may comfortably pursue. Nothing is trivial that is done for Him.'*

1866 Two years before experiencing personal sanctification, Quaker Hannah Whitall Smith, 34, reasoned in her journal: *'It is not knowledge that I am lacking, but inward power, and I have to believe that there is a work of cleansing or sanctification which is mine because of the death of Jesus, but which I have never yet experienced.'*

1893 In a speech before the First International Convention of the Epworth League, Ohio governor William McKinley declared: *'Christian character is helpful in every avenue or emergency of life.... The demand of the time is the young [person] thoroughly grounded in Christianity and its Book.'*

1963 American Trappist Thomas Merton advised in a letter: *'It seems to me that the Bible is a much better source of light than the Jesus Prayer. But all sources fail, except God Himself. And He is after all the most accessible. We get tired of [religious] means once in a while, and that is perhaps because we are nearer to the end than we realize.'*

FROM GOD'S WORD...   OT: 2 Kings 15:1–16:20 ~ NT: Acts 19:13-41 ~ Psalms 147:1-20 ~ Proverbs 18:4-5

תמוז ALMANAC OF THE CHRISTIAN FAITH סיון
TAMMUZ   SIVAN

June 30

Highlights in History

1565 The first Christian "thanksgiving day" on what is now U.S. soil was celebrated by French Huguenots. Under leadership of Admiral Gaspard de Coligny, a contingent of French Calvinists had settled in Florida near the St. Johns River and named their town Fort Caroline.

1629 The settlers of Salem, Massachusetts appointed Samuel Skelton, 44, as their pastor. Their church covenant, composed by Skelton, established Salem as the first non-separating Congregational Puritan Church in New England.

1780 Benjamin Randall organized a fellowship of churches known as Free Will Baptists in New Hampshire. It became one of the early branches of the National Association of Free Will Baptists, which was formed in 1935 at Nashville, TN.

1870 The Committee for the *English Revised Version* (ERV) of the Bible began translation work on the Old Testament. (Discovery of numerous biblical manuscripts earlier in the 19th century had prompted this first revision of the English Bible in over 250 years.) The ERV was completed and first published in 1885.

1909 In Rome, the Catholic Pontifical Biblical Commission issued a decree interpreting the first 11 chapters of Genesis as history, and not myth.

1973 In Korea, the Far Eastern Broadcasting Co. began transmitting the Gospel from HLAZ, its first radio station in that country. (FBEC is active today through radio missions outreach, and focuses its work among the islands of Eastern Asia and the Pacific.)

Notable Birthdays

1818 Birth of Edward J. Hopkins, English sacred organist and composer. Regarded as "the greatest representative of the old school of English church organists," Hopkins composed the tune ELLERS ("Savior, Again to Thy Dear Name We Raise"). [d. 2/4/1901]

1872 Birth of Harry Strachan, American missions pioneer. In 1921, he and his wife Susan founded the Latin American Mission, afterward headquartered in San José, Costa Rica. [d. 3/28/1945]

The Last Passage

1315 Martyrdom of Raymond Lull, 83, a Spanish mystic who devoted his life as a missioner to the Islamic people. After years spent in preparing himself and others for ministry to the Muslims, Lull first traveled to North Africa in 1291. He was stoned to death outside Bougie. (b. ca.1233)

1523 Two Belgian Augustinian monks, Hendrik Voes and Johann Esch, were burned at the stake in Brussels for accepting the teachings of Martin Luther. It is said that they sang the famed evening song of the ancient Eastern Church, "Te Deum Laudamus" ("We Praise Thee, O God") antiphonally from their funeral pyres.

Words for the Soul

1629 The Salem Covenant (see above), composed by Samuel Skelton, reads: *'We Covenant with the Lord and one with an other; and doe bynd our selves in the presence of God, to walke together in all his waies, according as he is pleased to reveale himself unto us in his Blessed word of truth.'*

1871 American holiness writer Hannah Whitall Smith confessed in a letter: *'I only have to look at Him for the supply at the moment that the need comes and I will invariably get it. It is a sort of living from hand to mouth, which does not agree with the thrifty ways we [Quakers] are taught in other things, and therefore we are slow to learn it. But the Bible is just full of it.'*

1996 During the last year of his life, Dutch priest and mystic Henri Nouwen noted in his journal: *'I realize that finally human beings are very fickle in their judgments. God and only God knows us in our essence, loves us well, forgives us fully, and remembers us for who we truly are.'*

FROM GOD'S WORD...   OT: 2 Kings 17:1–18:12 ~ NT: Acts 20:1–38 ~ Psalms 148:1–14 ~ Proverbs 18:6-7

JUNE INDEX

A

Abeel, David
b. 6/11/1804 [d. 9/4/1846]
Abolition of slavery 6/1, 6/14, 6/24, 6/26
Addison, Joseph
(b. 5/1/1672) d. 6/17/1719
AFRICAN-AMERICANS 6/23
African Methodist Episcopal Zion Church 6/17
Allen, Richard 6/11
Baumfree, Isabella 6/1
Bottoms, Lawrence W. 6/16
Haywood, Margaret A. 6/23
Healey, James A. 6/2
Henson, Josiah 6/15
Lason, Joseph 6/6
Sojourner Truth 6/1
Varick, James 6/17
Alcoholics Anonymous 6/10
Allen, Richard 6/11
Allouez, Claude Jean
b. 6/6/1622 [d. 1689]
American and Foreign Bible Society 6/10
American Antiquarian Society 6/22
American Bible Union 6/10
American Board of Commissioners 6/4, 6/8, 6/12, 6/17, 6/18, 6/29
American Civil War 6/15, 6/24, 6/29
American Friends Service Committee 6/16
American Sunday School Union 6/18
American Tract Society 6/2
Apostolic Succession 6/26
Appenzeller, Henry G.
(b. 2/5/1858) d. 6/11/1902
Augsburg Confession 6/25
Augustine, St. (English) 6/2
Auschwitz Concentration Camp 6/14
Avignon, Papal Headquarters in 6/16
Azusa Street Revival 6/20

B

Babylonian Captivity 6/16
Baker, Henry W.
b. 6/21/1821 [d. 2/12/1877]
Baker, Theodore
b. 6/3/1851 [d. 10/13/1934]
Baptism with the Holy Spirit 6/4
Baumfree, Isabella 6/1
Baur, Ferdinand Christian
b. 6/21/1792 [d. 12/2/1860]
Baxter, Lydia
(b. 9/8/1809) d. 6/22/1874
Becket, Thomas à 6/3
Beecher, Henry Ward 6/14
b. 6/24/1813 [d. 3/8/1887]
Beecher, Lyman 6/14
Bell, Eudorus N.
(b. 6/27/1866) d. 6/15/1923
Benedict XIII, Pope (1724-1730) 6/24
Bennard, George 6/7
Bennett, Sanford Fillmore
b. 6/21/1836 [d. 6/12/1898]
Bentley, William
b. 6/22/1759 [d. 12/19/1819]
Berg, Daniel 6/11
Bergen-Belsen Concentration Camp 6/12
Bernard, St. 6/25
Bernardina Teresa Xavier of St. Joseph, Sister. See Mathews, Ann Teresa
Bethel Mission 6/20
Beza, Theodore
b. 6/24/1519 [d. 10/13/1605]
BIBLE VERSIONS
Bengali 6/9, 6/13
English Revised Version (1885) 6/30
King James Version (1611) 6/19
Korean language 6/11
Mandarin translation (1919) 6/4
Norwegian 6/4
Sanskrit 6/9
Syriac Old Testament 6/5
Tamil dialect 6/14
Bill of Rights 6/14
Bishop, Bridget
(b. unk.) d. 6/10/1692
Boleyn, Anne 6/11
Bonar, Andrew. See QUOTATIONS
Boniface, St.
(b. 680) d/ 6/5/754
Boniface VIII, Pope (1294-1303) 6/27
BOOKS / PUBLICATIONS
Analogy of Religion (1736) 6/16
Anglican Prayer Book 6/5
Arabic-English Dictionary (1825) 6/24
A Hebrew and English Lexicon of the Old Testament 6/8
Baker's Biographical Dictionary 6/3
Book of Church Order 6/13
Book of Common Prayer 6/9
Book of Concord (1580) 6/25
Brainerd's Journal 6/12
Brown, Driver & Briggs (1906) 6/8
Chinese-English Dictionary (1891) 6/4
Dante's Divine Comedy 6/13
Diary of Anne Frank 6/12
Dictionary of the Targumim (1896-1903) 6/5
Evidences of the Christian Religion 6/17
Exposition of the Old and New Testaments (1708-10) 6/22
Faith and Reason (1946) 6/8
"Father Brown" Detective Stories 6/13
Grammar of the Greek New Testament (1914) 6/12
He Is Able (1936) 6/5
Historia Syntomos 6/2
History of Dogma (1886) 6/10
Honest to God (1963) 6/15
Hymns Ancient and Modern 6/21
I and Thou (1922) 6/13
Jewish Encyclopedia 6/5
Judaism 6/27
Koran 6/8
Leo's Tome 6/13
Nature and Destiny of Man (1943) 6/21
Nave's Topical Bible 6/24
Orthodoxy (1877) 6/25
Pensées 6/19
Provinciales 6/19
Queen Elizabeth's Prayer Book 6/22
Rise and Progress of Religion in the Soul (1745) 6/26
Scottish Psalter 6/10
Sephardic liturgy for Sabbaths and festivals 6/12
The Christian Understanding of God (1951) 6/8
The Dark Night of the Soul 6/24
The Fundamentals (1910-15) 6/12
The Good Earth (1930) 6/26
The Manner of Prayer (1836) 6/22
The New Woman (1975) 6/27
The Orthodox Church (1935) 6/16
The Pure in Heart (1954) 6/5
The Royal Anthem Book 6/21
The Secret of Radiant Life (1957) 6/5
The Song of Roland 6/13
Trancendentalism (1877) 6/25
Ugaritic Handbook (1947) 6/29
Uncle Tom's Cabin (1851) 6/14, 6/15
Vie de Jésus (1863) 6/23
Works of John Flavel (1968) 6/26
Book of Concord
English Translation (1851) 6/25
German Translation (1580) 6/25
Latin Translation (1584) 6/25
Bora, Katherine von 6/13
Bottome, Frank
(b. 5/26/1823) d. 6/29/1894
Bottoms, Lawrence W. 6/16
Bowman, Robert H. 6/4
Brainerd, David 6/12. See also QUOTATIONS
Breck, James Lloyd
b. 6/10/1818 [d. 3/30/1876]
British Parliament 6/3
British School of Archaeology 6/3
Broger, John 6/4
Brooks, Charles T.
b. 6/20/1813 [d. 6/14/1883]
Brorson, Hans A.
b. 6/20/1694 [d. 6/3/1764]
Brown, Francis 6/8
Buber, Martin
(b. 2/8/1878) d. 6/13/1965
Buchman, Frank N.
b. 6/4/1878 [d. 8/7/1961]
Buck, Pearl S.
b. 6/26/1892 [d. 3/6/1973]
Buckoll, Henry James
(b. 9/9/1803) d. 6/6/1871
Bugenhagen, Johann
b. 6/24/1485 [d. 4/20/1558]
Bulgakov, Sergei Nikolaevich
b. 6/16/1871 [d. 7/12/1944]
Buoncompagni, Ugo. See Gregory XIII, Pope
Butler, Aubrey Lee
b. 6/29/1933
Butler, Joseph
(b. 5/18/1692) d. 6/16/1752
Byzantium 6/2

C

CALENDARS
Gregorian (New Style) 6/7
Julian (Old Style) 6/7
Calvin, John 6/13, 6/24
Campus Crusade for Christ 6/12

JUNE INDEX

Canitz, Friedrich 6/6
CANTERBURY ARCHBISHOPS
    Augustin[e] (597-ca.609) 6/2
    Becket, Thomas (1162-70) 6/3
    Juxon, William (1660-63)
    Langton, Stephen (1206-28) 6/17
Caraffa, Giovanni Pietro
    b. 6/28/1476 [d. 8/18/1559]
Carey, William 6/13
    (b. 8/17/1761) d. 6/9/1834
Carroll, John 6/9
Carter, Howard 6/26
Catherine of Aragon 6/11, 6/22
Celibacy of the Priesthood 6/23
Cerularius, Michael 6/21
Chalcedonian Definition (451) 6/13
Channing, William Ellery 6/1
Chapman, J. Wilbur
    b. 6/17/1859 [d. 12/25/1918]
Chapman, Jonathan 6/19
Charismatic Bible Ministries 6/23
Charles I, English King (1625-49) 6/4
Charles V, Holy Roman Emperor (1520-56) 6/20, 6/25
China Inland Mission 6/3
Cho, Paul Yonggi 6/23
Christian realism 6/21
Christina, Swedish Queen (1632-54) 6/16
Christ for the Nations 6/18
CHURCHES
    Apostolic Faith Church (OR) 6/20
    Brick Memorial Church (NYC) 6/19
    Cathedral of St. John the Divine 6/25
    East Congregational (Salem, MA) 6/22
    Federal Street Congregational (Boston) 6/1
    Holiness Church (NC) 6/13
    Holy Cross Lutheran Church (NJ) 6/20
    King's Chapel (Boston) 6/15
    London's Metropolitan Tabernacle 6/7
    Monument Street Methodist (Baltimore) 6/4
    Shadyside Presbyterian Church (PA) 6/27
    St. Ann's Church for Deaf Mutes (NY City) 6/3
    St. Nicholas Church (Austria) 6/7
    Wauwatosa Presbyterian Church (WI) 6/2
Church of God of Prophecy 6/13
Ciocchi del Monte, Giammaria.
    See Julius III, Pope (1550-1555)
Cistercians 6/25

Clapham Sect 6/24
Clarkson, Margaret E.
    b. 6/8/1915
Clement IX, Pope (1667-69) 6/20
Clement VII, Pope (1523-34) 6/20
Clephane, Elizabeth C.
    b. 6/18/1830 [d. 2/19/1869]
Coffman, Samuel F.
    (b. 6/11/1872) d. 6/28/1954
    b. 6/11/1872 [d. 6/28/1954]
Coligny, Gaspard de 6/30
COLLEGES / UNIVERSITIES
    American School of Oriental Research (Jerusalem) 6/4
    Baldwin-Wallace University (OH) 6/15
    Balliol College (Oxford) 6/12
    Bethel Bible College (KS) 6/4
    College of Philadelphia 6/10
    Dropsie College (PA) 6/29
    German Wallace College (OH) 6/15
    Haverford College (PA) 6/16
    Hebrew Union College (NY) 6/4
    Hebrew Union College (OH) 6/27
    Hebrew University (Israel) 6/28
    Merton College (Oxford) 6/12
    Oberlin College (OH) 6/2
    Oxford University 6/12, 6/17
    St. Mary Magdalen (Oxford) 6/12
    University College (Oxford) 6/12
    University of Pennsylvania 6/10
Columba, St.
    (b. ca.521) d. 6/9/597
Communism, Chinese 6/1
Congregation of Propaganda 6/6
Connelly, Cornelia A. P. 6/18
Conservative Judaism 6/11
Constantine I, Roman Emperor (312-37) 6/19
Cook, David C.
    b. 6/11/1850 [d. 1927]
Cook, Flavius J.
    (b. 1/26/1838) d. 6/25/1901
Copeland, Kenneth 6/23
COUNCILS, CHURCH
    Council of Ephesus (431) 6/22
    Council of Nicea (325) 6/19
    Diet of Augsburg 6/25
    Second Council of Constantinople (553) 6/2
    Second Council of Nicea (787) 6/2
    Synod of Diamper 6/20
Counter-Reformation 6/28
Cranmer, Thomas 6/11, 6/19
Crawford, Florence
    (b. 9/1/1872) d. 6/20/1936

CREEDS, CONFESSIONS
    Augsburg Confession (1530) 6/25
    Definition of Chalcedon (451) 6/13
    Nicene Creed (325) 6/19, 6/22
CRUSADES
    First Crusade (1096-99) 6/7, 6/26
    Seventh Crusade (1248-54) 6/25
Cummings, William H.
    (b. 8/22/1831) d. 6/6/1915
Cuneiform writing 6/9

D

David C. Cook Publishing Co. 6/11
Dead Sea Scrolls 6/28
Definition of Chalcedon 6/13
DENOMINATIONS, CHRISTIAN
    African Methodist Episcopal (AME) Church 6/11
    African Methodist Episcopal Zion (AMEZ) Church 6/17, 6/21
    American Congregationalism 6/23, 6/24, 6/25
    Anglicanism 6/6, 6/8, 6/9, 6/19, 6/20, 6/25, 6/27, 6/28
    Anglicanism, Scottish 6/1
    Anglican Calvinism 6/10
    Assemblies of God 6/11, 6/15, 6/17
    Baptists, American 6/22
    Baptists, English 6/10, 6/19
    Brethren 6/17
    Canadian Presbyterianism 6/8
    Catholicism, American 6/2
    Christian and Missionary Alliance 6/13, 6/18
    Church of God (Anderson, IN) 6/25
    Church of God of Prophecy 6/13
    Church of Scotland, Free 6/18
    Church of the United Brethren in Christ 6/3
    Colonial Puritanism 6/10
    Congregationalism, American 6/4, 6/18, 6/30
    Congregationalism, English 6/5, 6/22
    Congregational Christian Church 6/23, 6/25
    Congregational Union of Canada 6/10
    Council of Local Union Churches 6/10
    Cumberland Presbyterian Church 6/10
    Danish Lutheranism 6/20
    Dutch Reformed Church 6/8
    English Presbyterianism 6/26
    Episcopalianism 6/3, 6/18
    Episcopalianism, American 6/5, 6/7, 6/8, 6/27
    Evangelical and Reformed Church 6/23, 6/25, 6/26
    Evangelical Anglicanism 6/24

    Evangelical Lutheran Church in North America 6/20
    Evangelical Synod of North America 6/26
    Free Will Baptists 6/30
    French Calvinism 6/30
    French Huguenots 6/30
    French Protestants 6/28
    German Evangelical Church Society of the West 6/26
    Lutheranism, German 6/21
    German Protestantism 6/21
    German Reformed 6/3
    Landmark Baptists 6/26
    Lutheranism 6/17
    Lutheranism, American 6/20
    Lutheranism, German 6/1, 6/10, 6/25
    Lutheranism, Swedish 6/16
    Malankarese Church 6/11
    Mennonites 6/11, 6/28
    Methodism, American 6/2, 6/4, 6/11, 6/23
    Methodism, English 6/5, 6/17, 6/20
    Methodism, German 6/15
    Methodist Church, Canada 6/10
    Methodist Episcopal Church 6/11, 6/17, 6/26
    Methodist Pentecostal Union Church 6/16, 6/26
    Moravians 6/9, 6/17, 6/20, 6/29
    Nonconformity, English 6/22, 6/26
    Orthodoxy, Eastern 6/30
    Orthodoxy, Greek 6/21
    Orthodoxy, Russian 6/5, 6/6, 6/16
    Orthodox Presbyterian Church 6/11
    Pentecostalism 6/4, 6/20
    Pentecostal Church 6/11
    Pietism, German 6/1
    Pilgrim Holiness Church 6/17, 6/26
    Pillar of Fire Church 6/16, 6/26
    Plymouth Brethren 6/1
    Presbyterianism 6/1, 6/2, 6/12
    Presbyterianism, American 6/8, 6/19, 6/26, 6/27
    Presbyterianism, Scottish 6/6
    Presbyterian Church in England 6/13
    Presbyterian Church in the U.S. 6/10, 6/15, 6/16, 6/29
    Presbyterian Church of America 6/11
    Presbyterian Church of Canada 6/10
    Presbyterian Church of the U.S.A. 6/10
    Puritanism, English 6/3
    Puritanism, New England 6/30
    Quakers 6/9, 6/16, 6/25
    Reformed Church in the United States 6/26
    Reformed Church of America 6/13
    Roman Catholicism 6/9, 6/11, 6/16, 6/19

Schwenkfelders 6/17
Scottish Free Church 6/19
Scottish Secession Church 6/2, 6/22
Separatists 6/17
Shakers 6/9
Southern Baptists 6/15
Southern Presbyterian Church 6/16
Swedish Lutheranism 6/19
The New Church 6/19
U.S. Presbyterianism 6/17
Unitarianism 6/1, 6/18, 6/20
United Church of Canada 6/10
United Church of Christ 6/23, 6/25
United Church of Christ in Japan 6/24
United Methodist Church 6/3
United Presbyterian Church 6/10, 6/15, 6/29
United Presbyterian Church of Scotland 6/13
Universalism 6/25
Wesleyan Church 6/26
Wesleyan Methodist Church 6/17, 6/26

DENOMINATIONS, CHRISTIAN SECTARIAN
Church of the New Jerusalem 6/19
Swedenborgianism 6/19

Dickson, Sarah F. 6/2
Diet of Augsburg 6/25
Diet of Worms (1520) 6/27
Disputation of Leipzig (1519) 6/27
Dix, William C.
  b. 6/14/1837 [d. 9/9/1898]
Dodd, Louise 6/19
Doddridge, Philip
  b. 6/26/1702 [d. 10/26/1751]

DRAMAS
"The Man Born to Be King" (1943) 6/13

Driver, Samuel R. 6/8
Dwight, John S. 6/20

E

Easter 6/19
Edwards, Jonathan 6/12, 6/22, 6/23
Elizabeth I, English Queen (1558-1603) 6/19, 6/22
Ellerton, John
  (b. 12/16/1866) d. 6/15/1893
Elliot, Jim. See QUOTATIONS
Ely Monastery 6/23
Enmegahbowh 6/27
Ephraem, St.
  (b. ca.315) d. 6/18/373
Erskine, Ebenezer
  b. 6/22/1680 d. 6/2/1754

Ethelbert, Saxon King (ca.560-616) 6/2
Etheldreda
  (b. 630) d. 6/23/679
Ettwein, John
  b. 6/29/1721 [d. 1/2/1802]
Eusebius of Samosata
  (b. unk.) d. 6/22/380
Eutychius, Patriarch of Constantinople 6/2
Evans, Frederick W.
  b. 6/9/1808 [d. 3/6/1893]
Evolution 6/19
Ewing, Finis
  b. 6/10/1773 [d. 7/4/1841]
Excel, Edwin O.
  (b. 12/13/1851) d. 6/10/1921
Expo '72 6/12

F

Faber, Frederick W.
  b. 6/28/1814 [d. 9/26/1863]
Farjeon, Elizabeth
  (b. 2/13/1881) d. 6/5/1965
Farrar, Cynthia 6/5
Father's Day 6/19
Feinberg, Charles
  b. 6/12/1909
Fenélon, François 6/9
Ferré, Nels F. S.
  b. 6/8/1908 [d. 1971]
Fieschi, Sinisbaldo. See Innocent IV, Pope
Fillmore, James H.
  b. 6/1/1849 [d. 2/8/1936]

FIRSTS
"Holiness" conference 6/29
African-American bishop in the U.S. 6/11
African-American Catholic bishop since 19th centur 6/6
African-American moderator of the P.C.U.S. 6/16
African-American U.S. Catholic bishop 6/2
African-American woman to head a major U.S. denomination 6/23
American-born male saint 6/19
American female Reform Judaism rabbi 6/27
Anglican church established in colonial New Englan 6/15
Archbishop of Canterbury 6/2
Baptist church established in Kentucky 6/18
Book of anthems published by a woman 6/21
Catholic convent established in the U.S. 6/12

Christian ruler of Russia 6/5
Counter-Reformation pope 6/28
Digital calculator 6/19
Director of the Winona Lake Bible Conference Cente 6/17
Ecumenical Church Council 6/19
Female bishop of any Christian denomination 6/26
Female elder of the Presbyterian Church 6/2
Female Lutheran pastor 6/20
Female Reform Jewish rabbi 6/3
Foreign medical missionary sent from the U.S. 6/8
Jewish prayerbook published in America 6/12
Medical school in the American colonies 6/10
Methodist conference (England) 6/25
Missionary radio station in Latin America 6/13
Missionary radio station in the Philippines 6/4
Non-separating Congregational Puritan Church in Ne 6/30
Observation of Father's Day (1910) 6/19
Ojibway Indian ordained into Episcopal order 6/27
Pentecostal Church in Brazil 6/11
Person hanged for witchcraft at Salem Witch Trials 6/10
Person to divide the Bible into chapters 6/17
Pope to meet with the Greek Orthodox patriarch 6/21
Pope to travel to the United States 6/21
Pope to Visit the Holy Land 6/21
Protestant church west of the Alleghenies 6/9
Protestant medical missionary to China 6/18
Public appeal for the abolition of slavery 6/24
Revision of the English Bible in over 250 years 6/30
Roman Catholic mission on Guam 6/15
State-sponsored Roman persecution of Christians 6/24
Thanksgiving Day 6/30
Trial for witchcraft in colonial America 6/15
U.S. African-American Catholic priest 6/2
U.S. foreign missionary society 6/29
U.S. school for the deaf 6/3
Unmarried American female missionary 6/5
Woman bishop of any church denomination 6/16

First Amendment 6/19
Fisher, John
  (b. 1469) d. 6/22/1535
Fisk, Pliny
  b. 6/24/1792 [d. 10/23/1825]
Flavel, John
  (b. ca.1630) d. 6/26/1691
Flavian, Patriarch of Constantinople (446-49) 6/13
Fletcher, John. See QUOTATIONS
Flower, J. Roswell
  b. 6/17/1888 [d. 1970]
Foulkes, William H.
  b. 6/26/1877 [d. 12/9/1961]
Francis I, French King (1515-47) 6/20
Franck, Johann
  b. 6/1/1618 [d. 6/18/1677]
Frank, Anne
  b. 6/12/1929 [d. 3/12/1945]

G

Gallaudet, Thomas
  b. 6/3/1822 [d. 1885]
Gess, Wolfgang F.
  b. 6/10/1819 [d. 6/1/1891]
Giardini, Felice de
  (b. 4/12/1716) d. 6/8/1796
Gibbons, Orlando
  (bapt 12/25/1483) d. 6/5/1625
Giovanni Battista Montini. See Paul VI, Pope
Glossolalia 6/4
Glueck, Nelson
  b. 6/4/1900 [d. 2/12/1971]
Goodrich, Chauncey
  b. 6/4/1836 [d. 1925]
Gordon, Cyrus H.
  b. 6/29/1908
Graves, James Robinson
  (b. 4/10/1820) d. 6/26/1893
Great Awakening 6/23, 6/27
Greeves, Arthur 6/22
Gregory XIII, Pope (1572-1585)
  b. 6/7/1502 [d. 4/10/1585]
Gregory XV, Pope (1621-1623) 6/6
Grotefend, Georg Friedrich
  b. 6/9/1775 [d. 12/15/1853]
Gruber, Franz
  (b. 11/25/1787) d. 6/7/1863
Guyon, Jeanne M.
  (b. 4/13/1648) d. 6/9/1717

H

Hall, Elvina M.
  b. 6/4/1820 [d. 7/18/1889]
Hallock, William Allen
  b. 6/2/1794 [d. 10/2/1880]
Harnack, Adolf von
  (b. 5/7/1851) d. 6/10/1930
Hassler, Hans Leo
  (b. 10/25/1564) d. 6/8/1612
Havergal, Frances Ridley
  (b. 12/14/1836) d. 6/3/1879
Haywood, Margaret A. 6/23
Healey, James A. 6/2
Henry, Matthew
  (b. 10/18/1662) d. 6/22/1714
Henry, Patrick
  (b. 5/29/1736) d. 6/5/1799
Henry II, English King (1154-1589) 6/3
Henry VIII, English King (1509-1547) 6/8, 6/11, 6/22
  b. 6/28/1491 [d. 1/28/1547]
Henson, Josiah
  b. 6/15/1787 [d. 5/15/1883]
Herbert, George E. S.
  b. 6/26/1866 [d. 4/6/1923]
HERESIES, CHRISTIAN
  Arianism 6/19, 6/22
  Nestorianism 6/2, 6/22
HERETICS
  Nestorius 6/22
Herrnhut 6/17
Hewitt, Eliza E.
  b. 6/28/1851 [d. 4/24/1920]
Historical Criticism 6/21
Historical Jesus 6/28
Holiness (non-charismatic) 6/26
Holy Club 6/27
Hopkins, Edward J.
  b. 6/30/1818 [d. 2/4/1901]
Hopkins, Mark
  (b. 2/4/1802) d. 6/17/1887
Hoskyns, Edwyn C.
  (b. 8/9/1884) d. 6/28/1937
Hosmer, Frederick L.
  (b. 10/16/1840) d. 6/7/1929
Hudson, Ralph E.
  (b. 7/9/1843) d. 6/14/1901
Huguenot Wars 6/28
Hurd, Judith 6/20
HYMNS
  "'Are Ye Able?' Said the Master" 6/13
  "'Tis Midnight, and on Olive's Brow" 6/18
  "Abide with Me" 6/1
  "Alas! and Did My Savior Bleed?" 6/14
  "All My Life Long I Had Panted" 6/14
  "As With Gladness Men of Old" 6/14
  "Behold a Host Arrayed in White" 6/20
  "Beneath the Cross of Jesus" 6/18
  "Cast Thy Burden on the Lord" 6/5
  "Come, My Soul, Thou Must Be Waking" 6/6
  "Come, Thou Almighty King" 6/8
  "Come, Thou Fount of Every Blessing" 6/9
  "Come to the Savior Now" 6/10
  "Count Your Blessings" 6/10
  "Deck Thyself, My Soul, With Gladness" 6/1
  "Depth of Mercy" 6/5
  "Fairest Lord Jesus" 6/20
  "Faith of Our Fathers" 6/28
  "Father, Give Thy Benediction" 6/18
  "God, That Madest Earth and Heaven" 6/7
  "God, the Almighty One! Wisely Ordaining" 6/6
  "God, the Omnipotent" 6/15
  "God Bless Our Native Land" 6/20
  "God of Our Life, Through All the Circling Years" 6/27
  "Hark! The Herald Angels Sing" 6/6
  "Holy Ghost, The Infinite" 6/5
  "Holy Spirit, Truth Divine" 6/18
  "I Am His, and He is Mine" 6/27
  "I Am Resolved No Longer to Linger" 6/1
  "I Hear the Savior Say" 6/4
  "I Know That My Redeemer Lives" 6/23
  "I Know That My Redeemer Liveth" 6/1
  "Jesus, I am Resting, Resting" 6/27
  "Jesus, I My Cross Have Taken" 6/1
  "Jesus, Lover of My Soul" 6/1
  "Jesus, Priceless Treasure" 6/1
  "Jesus, What a Friend of Sinners!" 6/17
  "Jesus Paid It All" 6/4
  "Joy is Like the Rain" 6/14
  "Lead, Kindly Light" 6/16
  "Like a River Glorious" 6/3, 6/27
  "Lord, Speak to Me That I May Speak" 6/3, 6/8
  "Lord of Our Life, and God of Our Salvation" 6/25
  "More About Jesus Would I Know" 6/28
  "Morning Has Broken" 6/5
  "My Jesus, As Thou Wilt" 6/4
  "One Day When Heaven Was Filled with His Praises" 6/17
  "Open My Eyes, That I May See" 6/21
  "O Could I Speak the Matchless Worth" 6/23
  "O Happy Day, That Fixed My Choice" 6/13
  "O Happy Day That Fixed My Choice" 6/26
  "O Lord, How Full of Sweet Content" 6/9
  "O Love That Wilt Not Let Me Go" 6/6
  "O Sacred Head, Now Wounded" 6/8
  "O Sometimes the Shadows Are Deep" 6/16
  "O Spread the Tidings 'Round" 6/29
  "Redeemed, How I Love to Proclaim It" 6/29
  "Rise Up, O Men of God" 6/19
  "Savior, Again to Thy Dear Name We Raise" 6/15, 6/30
  "Savior, Like a Shepherd Lead Us" 6/20
  "Silent Night" 6/7
  "Since I Have Been Redeemed" 6/10
  "Sing the Wondrous Love" 6/23
  "Softly Now the Light of Day" 6/4
  "So Send I You" 6/8
  "Spirit of God in the Clear Running Water" 6/14
  "Stand Up, Stand Up for Jesus" 6/24
  "Sunshine in the Soul" 6/28
  "Sweet Hour of Prayer" 6/22
  "Take My Life and Let It Be" 6/3
  "Take the Name of Jesus With You" 6/22
  "Take Thou Our Minds, Dear Lord" 6/26
  "Te Deum Laudamus" 6/30
  "There's a Wideness in God's Mercy" 6/28
  "The Comforter Has Come" 6/29
  "The King of Love My Shepherd Is" 6/21
  "The Lord's My Shepherd, I'll Not Want" 6/10
  "The Ninety and Nine" 6/18
  "The Old Rugged Cross" 6/7
  "The Sands of Time Are Sinking" 6/13
  "The Spacious Firmament on High" 6/17
  "The Sweet Bye and Bye" 6/21
  "Thy Kingdom Come, O Lord" 6/7
  "Thy Little Ones, Dear Lord, Are We" 6/20
  "Trust and Obey" 6/12
  "Welcome, Happy Morning" 6/15
  "We Bless the Name of Christ, The Lord" 6/11, 6/28
  "We Gather Together" 6/3
  "We Praise Thee, O God" 6/30
  "What Child Is This?" 6/14
  "When We All Get to Heaven" 6/28
  "When We Walk With the Lord" 6/12
  "Who Is On The Lord's Side?" 6/3
  "Will There Be Any Stars?" 6/28

HYMN TUNES
  ADA 6/29
  ANCIENT OF DAYS 6/4
  CANONBURY 6/8
  CANTERBURY 6/5
  ELLERS 6/30
  EVERLASTING LOVE 6/27
  HANNAH 6/1
  HAPPY DAY 6/13
  HEAVEN 6/23
  HUDSON 6/14
  ITALIAN HYMN 6/8
  JEWETT 6/4
  MARTYN 6/1
  MENDELSSOHN 6/6
  PASSION CHORALE 6/8
  QUIETNESS 6/18
  RESOLUTION 6/1
  RUSSIAN HYMN 6/6
  RUTHERFORD 6/13
  SATISFIED 6/14
  SCOTT 6/21
  SEYMOUR 6/4
  STILLE NACHT 6/7
  TRANQUILLITY 6/27
  WEBB 6/24
  WYE VALLEY 6/27

I

Ibas of Edessa 6/2
Index of Prohibited Books 6/14, 6/28
INDIANS, AMERICAN 6/6
  Enmegahbowh 6/27
  Indians in Colonial New England 6/12
  Indians of Pennsylvania 6/23
  New England Native Americans 6/22
  Ohio Indians 6/29
  Ojibway Indians 6/27
Industrial Revolution 6/6
Inge, William R. 6/2
Innocent IV, Pope (1243-1254) 6/25
Inquisition, The 6/25
International Holiness Union and Prayer League 6/26
Islam 6/8, 6/28, 6/30

J

Jacob of Edessa
  (b. ca.633) d. 6/5/708
James I, English King (1603-25) 6/19
Jansenism 6/20
Jastrow, Marcus
  b. 6/5/1829 [d. 1903]

Jeffery, John Albert
(b. 10/26/1855) d. 6/4/1929
Jesus Prayer (Lord's Prayer) 6/29
Johnny Appleseed 6/19
John Lackland, English King (1199-1216) 6/15
John of the Cross, St.
b. 6/24/1542 [d. 12/14/1591]
Jones, Clarence W. 6/13
Jones, Margaret
(b. unk?) d. 6/15/1649
Jones, Rufus Matthew
(b. 1/25/1863) d. 6/16/1948
JUDAISM
"Voyage of the damned" 6/4
Conservative Judaism 6/11
Dead Sea Scrolls 6/28
Extermination at Auschwitz 6/14
First Jewish prayerbook published in America 6/12
Glueck, Nelson 6/4
Gordon, Cyrus H.
Hasidic scholarship 6/13
Jastrow, Marcus 6/5
Kaplan, Mordecai M. 6/11
Orthodox Judaism 6/5
Pinto, Isaac 6/12
Priesand, Sally Jane 6/27
Reconstructionist Judaism 6/11
Reform Judaism 6/3, 6/27
Sephardic 6/12
Sukenik, Eliezer 6/28
Torah 6/11
Wise, Rabbi Stephen 6/3
Young Men's Hebrew Association 6/5
Judson, Emily Chubbock
(b. 8/22/1817) d. 6/1/1854
Juxon, William
(b. 10/1582) d. 6/4/1663

K

Kaplan, Mordecai M.
b. 6/11/1881 [d. 11/8/1983]
Keller, Helen Adams 6/19
b. 6/10/1880 [d. 6/1/1968]
Kenosis / Kenotic Theory 6/27
Kerr, Hugh T.
(b. 2/11/1872) d. 6/10/1950
Keswick Holiness Conference 6/29
Kirk, James M.
b. 6/18/1854 [d. 7/11/1945]
Koran 6/8

L

Langton, Stephen 6/17

Larson, Reuben E.
b. 6/13/1897 [d. 11/17/1981]
Lason, Joseph 6/6
Laubach, Frank.
See QUOTATIONS
LECTURES / ADDRESSES
Bampton Lectures 6/2
Lee, Ann 6/9
LEGISLATION, RELIGIOUS
"Articles of Religion" (English) 6/8
Act of Uniformity (1549) 6/9
Forty-Two Articles of Religion 6/19
Salem Covenant 6/30
Thirty-Nine Articles (1563) 6/19, 6/25
Twenty-One (Lutheran) Articles 6/25
Twenty-Three (Methodist) Articles 6/25
Virginia Bill of Rights 6/12
Leo I, Pope (440-461) 6/13
Leo IX, Pope (1049-1054) 6/21
Leo X, Pope (1513-1521) 6/15
Lewis, C. S.. See QUOTATIONS
Lightfoot, Robert H. 6/2
Lindsay, Freda 6/18
Lindsay, Gordon
b. 6/18/1906 [d. 4/1/1973]
Little Flock 6/1
Livingstone, David 6/1
Longfellow, Samuel
b. 6/18/1819 [d. 10/3/1892]
Lull, Raymond
(b. ca.1233) d. 6/30/1315
Luther, Martin 6/13, 6/15, 6/24, 6/25, 6/27, 6/30
Lvov, Alexis F.
6/6/1799 [d. 12/16/1870]
Lyte, Henry Francis
b. 6/1/1793 [d. 11/20/1847]

M

Magna Carta 6/15
Marathi Mission 6/5
Marlatt, Earl B.
(b. 5/24/1892) d. 6/13/1976
Marsh, Simeon B.
b. 6/1/1798 [d. 7/14/1875]
MARTYRS
Becket, Thomas à 6/3
Boniface 6/5
Elliot, Jim 6/12, 6/15
Esch, Johann 6/30
Frank, Anne 6/12
Hus, Jan 6/10
Lull, Raymond 6/30
Smith, Hyrum 6/27
Smith, Joseph 6/27
Voes, Hendrik 6/30

Mary, English Queen (1553-1558) 6/19
Mary Queen of Scots 6/19
Masada 6/28
Mastai-Ferretti, Giovanni Maria 6/16. See Pius IX, Pope (1846-1878)
Mather, Cotton 6/21
Mather, Increase
b. 6/21/1639 [d. 8/23/1723]
Matheson, George 6/6
Mathews, Ann Teresa
(b. 1732) d. 6/12/1800
McCheyne, Robert Murray. See QUOTATIONS
Medical Mission Sisters 6/14
Medley, Samuel
b. 6/23/1738 [d. 7/17/1799]
Meister Eckhart 6/16
Melanchthon, Philip 6/25
Mennonite General Conference 6/11, 6/28
Merrill, William P.
(b. 1/10/1867) d. 6/19/1954
Meyer, Heinrich A. W.
(b. 1/10/1800) d. 6/21/1873
Miriam Therese, Sister 6/14
MISSIONARIES
Abeel, David 6/12
Allouez, Claude Jean 6/6
Appenzeller, Henry G. 6/11
Boniface 6/5
Brainerd, David 6/12, 6/22
Breck, James Lloyd 6/27
Buck, Pearl S. 6/26
Carey, William 6/9, 6/13
Columba, St. 6/9
Elliot, Jim 6/12, 6/15
Farrar, Cynthia 6/5
Fisk, Pliny 6/24
Goodrich, Chauncey 6/4
Jones, Clarence W. 6/13
Judson, Adoniram 6/1
Judson, Emily Chubbock 6/1
Larson, Reuben E. 6/13
Laubach, Frank C. 6/1, 6/3
Livingstone, David 6/1
Lull, Raymond 6/30
Martyn, Henry 6/16
McCheyne, Robert Murray 6/26
Moravian 6/20
Parker, Peter 6/18
Plütschau, Heinrich 6/14
Sanvitores, Padre Diego Luis de 6/15
Savage, Thomas S. 6/7
Scudder, Sr., John 6/8
Strachan, Harry 6/30
Strachan, Susan 6/30

Taylor, J. Hudson 6/3, 6/25
Thomas, The Apostle 6/20
Ziegenbalg, Bartholomaeus 6/14
Zwemer, Samuel 6/28
MISSION AGENCIES
American Board of Commissioners 6/12
China Inland Mission 6/3, 6/25
Christ for the Nations 6/18
Far East Broadcasting Company 6/4, 6/30
Latin American Mission 6/30
Overseas Missionary Fellowship (OMF) 6/25
Scottish Society for Propagating Christian Knowledge 6/12
Seaman's Friend Society 6/12
Society of the United Brethren for Propagating the Gospel 6/29
Unevangelized Fields Mission 6/29
Wycliffe Bible Translators 6/7
Modernism 6/2
Mohammed
(b. ca.570) d. 6/8/632
Mohr, Joseph 6/7
MONASTERIES
Clairvaux (France) 6/25
Ely (England) 6/23
Fulda (Germany) 6/5
Moral Rearmament Movement (1938) 6/4
Morgan, John
b. 6/10/1735 [d. 10/15/1789]
Mountain, James
(b. 7/16/1844) d. 6/10/1933
MOVEMENTS, CHRISTIAN
"Methodies" 6/25
Alcoholics Anonymous 6/10
American Friends Service Committee 6/16
Anglican Evangelicalism 6/23
Calvinism 6/23, 6/29
Clapham Sect 6/24
Fundamentalism 6/9, 6/12
German Mediating Theology 6/11
Inter-Varsity Christian Fellowship 6/8
Jansenism 6/20
Landmark Movement 6/26
Mysticism 6/9, 6/16
Neo-orthodoxy 6/21
Quietism 6/9
Reformed Faith in Britain 6/13
Reformed Theology 6/13
Syrian Christianity 6/18
Tübingen School 6/21
Mowinckel, Sigmund O. P.
(b. 8/4/1884) d. 6/4/1965
Mueller, Reuben H.
b. 6/2/1897 [d. 7/5/1982]

JUNE INDEX

N

Nast, William
  b. 6/15/1807 [d. 5/6/1899]
National Council of Churches 6/2
Nave, Orville J.
  (b. 4/30/1841) d. 6/24/1917
Naziism, German 6/4, 6/12, 6/14
Nee, Watchman
  (b. 11/4/1903) d. 6/1/1972
Nepotism 6/20
Nero, Roman Caesar (54-68) 6/24
Nestorianism 6/2, 6/22
Nestorius 6/22
Neumann, John Nepomucene 6/19
Newman, John Henry 6/16
NEWSPAPERS
  "The Nauvoo Expositor" (IL) 6/7, 6/24
New England Congregationalism 6/22
Nicea 6/26
Nicene Creed 6/19, 6/22
NICKNAMES / TITLES
  "Apostle of Unitarianism" 6/1
  "Apostle to the Russians" 6/5
  "Father of Modern Missions" 6/9, 6/13
  "Founder of Catholicity in the West" 6/6
  "Jerome of the Syrians" 6/5
  "Last of the Puritans" 6/7
  "Man of three tongues" 6/5
Niebuhr, Reinhold
  b. 6/21/1892 [d. 6/1/1971]
Nippon Kirisuto Kyodan 6/24
Nobel Prize 6/26

O

Oberlin, Jean Frederic
  (b. 8/31/1740) d. 6/2/1826
Odescalchi, Benedetto.
  See Innocent XI, Pope
Oglethorpe, James 6/9
ORGANIZATIONS
  Alcoholics Anonymous 6/10
  General Association of Massachusetts 6/29
  Young Men's Hebrew Association (1875) 6/5
ORGANIZATIONS, CHRISTIAN
  American and Foreign Bible Society 6/10
  American Bible Union 6/10
  American Sunday School Union 6/18
  Campus Crusade for Christ 6/12
  Charismatic Bible Ministries 6/23
  International Holiness Union and Prayer League 6/26
  Moral Rearmament Movement (1938) 6/4
  National Association of Free Will Baptists 6/30
  Navigators 6/18
  Oxford Group (1929) 6/4
  Seaman's Friend Society 6/12
  Young Men's Christian Association 6/6, 6/19
  World Council of Churches 6/24
Otterbein, Philip William
  b. 6/3/1726 [d. 11/17/1813]
Oxford Group (1929) 6/4

P

PAINTINGS
  "Descent from the Cross" (1614) 6/28
  "Erection of the Cross" (1610) 6/28
PAPAL DECREES
  "Ad extirpenda" (1252) 6/25
  "Christo pastorum principi" (1932) 6/11
  "Decet romanum pontificem" (1521) 6/15
  "Exsurge domine" (1520) 6/15
  "Index Librorum Prohibitorum" 6/14
  "Inscrutabili divinae" (1622) 6/6
  "Sacerdotalis caelibatus" (1967) 6/23, 6/24
  "Scimus filii" (1299) 6/27
  Immaculate Conception Dogma (1860) 6/16
  Index of Prohibited Books (1557) 6/14
Papal Infallibility 6/16
Parham, Charles Fox
  b. 6/4/1873 [d. 1926]
Parker, Peter
  b. 6/18/1804 [d. 1/10/1888]
Parochial School System 6/19
Pascal, Blaise
  b. 6/19/1623 [d. 8/19/1662]
Patriarch of Constantinople 6/21
Paul, Apostle
  (b. unk.) d. 6/29/62 or 67
Paul IV, Pope (1555-1559) 6/14, 6/28
Paul VI, Pope (1963-1978) 6/14, 6/19, 6/21, 6/23, 6/24
Peace of Alais 6/28
Peace of Barcelona 6/20
Penn, William 6/23
PERIODICALS
  "Korean Christian Advocate" 6/11
  "The Voice of Healing" 6/18
Petrie, Sir W. M. Flinders
  b. 6/3/1853 [d. 7/28/1942]
Pillar of Fire Church 6/16, 6/26
Pinto, Isaac
  b. 6/12/1720 [d. 1791]
Pius II, Pope (1458-64) 6/18
Pius IX, Pope (1846-78) 6/16
Pius X, Pope (1903-1914)
  b. 6/2/1835 [d. 8/20/1914]
Pledge of Allegiance 6/14
Plütschau, Heinrich 6/14
Polygamy 6/7, 6/24, 6/27
Pontifical Biblical Commission 6/30
POPES
  Benedict XIII (1724-1730) 6/24
  Boniface VIII (1294-1303) 6/27
  Clement IX (1667-1669) 6/20
  Clement VII (1523-1534) 6/20
  Gregory XIII (1572-1585) 6/7
  Gregory XV (1621-1623) 6/6
  Innocent IV (1243-1254) 6/25
  Leo IX (1049-1054) 6/21
  Leo I (440-461) 6/13
  Leo X (1513-1521) 6/15
  Paul IV (1555-1559) 6/14, 6/15
  Paul VI (1963-1978) 6/14, 6/19, 6/21, 6/23, 6/24
  Pius II (1458-1464) 6/18
  Pius IX (1846-1878) 6/16
  Pius X (1903-1914) 6/2
  Sylvester I (314-335) 6/19
Potter, Henry C.
  b. 6/25/1834 [d. 7/21/1908]
PRESIDENTS, U.S.
  Eisenhower, Dwight D. (1953-1961) 6/14
  Jackson, Andrew (1829-1837) 6/8
  McKinley, William (1897-1901) 6/29
  Taft, William H. (1909-1913) 6/24
Priesand, Sally Jane 6/3
  b. 6/10/1946
Protestant Reformation 6/3
Pulitzer Prize 6/26
Pusey, Philip E.
  b. 6/25/1799 [d. 7/9/1855]

Q

QUOTATIONS
  Bonar, Andrew 6/4, 6/9, 6/19, 6/21, 6/23, 6/24
  Brainerd, David 6/22
  Eisenhower, Dwight D. 6/14
  Eliade, Mircea 6/24
  Elliot, Jim 6/12, 6/15
  Fletcher, John 6/2, 6/25
  Faber, Frederick W. 6/25, 6/26
  Houselander, Caryll 6/1, 6/2, 6/6, 6/28
  Hus, Jan 6/10
  Ignatius of Loyola 6/18
  Jackson, Andrew 6/8
  Laubach, Frank C. 6/1, 6/3
  Lewis, C. S. 6/5, 6/7, 6/13, 6/17, 6/22
  Luther, Martin 6/6, 6/16
  MacDonald, George 6/3, 6/5, 6/11, 6/28
  Martyn, Henry 6/16
  Mason, George 6/12
  McCheyne, Robert Murray 6/26
  McKinley, William 6/29
  Merton, Thomas 6/29
  Newton, John 6/7, 6/8, 6/20, 6/21, 6/23, 6/29
  Nouwen, Henri 6/30
  Rutherford, Samuel 6/10, 6/11, 6/15, 6/16
  Schaeffer, Francis 6/13
  Skelton, Samuel 6/30
  Smith, Hannah Whitall 6/6, 6/9, 6/14, 6/15, 6/25, 6/26, 6/29, 6/30
  Spurgeon, Charles 6/3
  Underhill, Evelyn 6/20
  Venn, Henry 6/23, 6/27
  Webster, Daniel 6/17
  Wesley, Charles 6/2
  Wesley, John 6/1, 6/2, 6/7, 6/9, 6/11, 6/13, 6/18, 6/19, 6/20, 6/27

R

RADIO BROADCASTING 6/27
  FEBC (Korea) 6/30
  FEBC (Manilla, Philippines) 6/4
  HCJB (Quito, Ecuador) 6/13
  HLAZ (Korea) 6/30
Randall, Benjamin 6/30
Rawson, George
  b. 6/5/1807 [d. 3/25/1889]
Reconstruction 6/24
Reconstructionist Judaism 6/11
Reformation, The 6/25
RELIGIOUS ORDERS, CATHOLIC
  Augustinians 6/30
  Cistercians 6/25
  Discalced Carmelites 6/12, 6/24
  Dominicans 6/16
  Jesuits 6/6, 6/15, 6/18
  Medical Mission Sisters 6/14
  Society of the Holy Child Jesus 6/18
  Theatine Order 6/28
  Trappists 6/29
Renan, Joseph E. 6/23
Rimbault, Edward F.
  b. 6/13/1816 [d. 9/26/1876]
Roberts, Oral 6/23
Robertson, A[rchibald] T. 6/12

Robinson, John A. T.
  b. 6/15/1919 [d. 12/5/1983]
Robinson, Robert
  (b. 9/27/1735) d. 6/9/1790
Roman Empire 6/24
Rubens, Peter Paul
  b. 6/28/1577 [d. 5/30/1640]
Runnymeade 6/15
Rutherford, Samuel.
  See QUOTATIONS

S

Salem Covenant 6/30
Salem Witch Trials 6/10, 6/24
Sammis, John H.
  (b. 7/6/1846) d. 6/12/1919
Sanctification 6/29
Sangster, William E.
  b. 6/5/1900 [d. 5/24/1960]
Sanvitores, Diego Luis de 6/15
Sarto, Giuseppe Melchiorre.
  See Pius X, Pope
Savage, Thomas S.
  b. 6/7/1804 [d. 1880]
Sayers, Dorothy L.
  b. 6/13/1893 [d. 12/17/1957]
Schism between East and
  Western Church 6/21
Schumann, Robert A.
  b. 6/8/1810 [d. 7/29/1856]
Schwarzerd, Philipp.
  See Melanchthon, Philip[p]
Scott, Clara H.
  (b. 12/3/1841) d. 6/21/1897
Scudder, Sr., John 6/8
SECTS, CHRISTIAN
  Church of the New Jerusalem 6/19
  Jehovah's Witnesses 6/14
  Mormonism 6/7, 6/27
  Swedenborgianism 6/19
Seiss, Joseph Augustus
  (b. 3/18/1823) d. 6/20/1904
SEMINARIES / BIBLE
  COLLEGES
  Andover-Newton Theological School (MA) 6/8
  BIOLA (Bible Institute of Los Angeles) 6/12
  Dallas Theological Seminary (TX) 6/12
  Fuller Theological Seminary (CA) 6/9
  Moody Bible Institute (IL) 6/9
  Seabury Seminary (MN) 6/27
  St. Sergius Theological Institute (Paris) 6/16
  Talbot Seminary (CA) 6/12
  Trinity Evangelical Divinity School (IL) 6/9

  Union Seminary (NY City) 6/21
SERMONS
  "Expect Great Things from God; Attempt Great Things for God" 6/13
Seventh Crusade 6/25
Sewall, Samuel 6/24
Simpson, A. B. 6/18
Six-Day War, Arab-Israeli 6/5
Skelton, Samuel 6/30
Smith, Hyrum 6/24, 6/27
Smith, Joseph 6/7, 6/24
  (b. 12/23/1805) d. 6/10/1844
Smith, Robert H. 6/10
Smith, Wilbur M.
  b. 6/9/1894 [d. 1977]
Society of the United Brethren
  for Propagating the Gospel
  Among the Heathen 6/29
Spokane Ministerial Association 6/19
Spurgeon, Charles Haddon 6/7
  b. 6/19/1834 [d. 1/31/1892] See also QUOTATIONS
St. Cyril of Alexandria 6/22
Stevens, Cat 6/5
Stowe, Harriet Beecher 6/15
  b. 6/14/1811 [d. 7/1/1896]
Strachan, Harry
  b. 6/30/1872 [d. 3/28/1945]
Strachan, Susan 6/30
Sukenik, Eliezer 6/28
Sullivan, Anne 6/27
SUPREME COURT CASES, U.S.
  "Wallace v. Jaffree" (1985) 6/4
Swedenborg, Emmanual 6/19
Swedenborgianism 6/19
Sylvester I, Pope (314-335) 6/19
SYNAGOGUES
  Free Synagogue (NY City) 6/3
  Shearith Israel (NY City) 6/12
Synod of Diamper 6/20
Synoptic Gospels 6/28

T

"Theotokos" 6/22
Taft, Charles P.
  (b. 9/20/1897) d. 6/24/1983
Tappan, William B.
  (b. 10/24/1794) d. 6/18/1849
Tauler, Johannes
  (b. ca.1300) d. 6/16/1361
Taylor, J. Hudson 6/25
  (b. 5/21/1832) d. 6/3/1905
Taylor, Nathaniel W.
  b. 6/23/1786 [d. 3/10/1858]

Theodoret of Cyprus 6/2
Theodore of Mopsuestia 6/2
Thirty-Nine Articles (1563) 6/19, 6/22, 6/25
Thomas, the Apostle 6/20
Thrupp, Dorothy Ann
  b. 6/20/1779 [d. 12/14/1847]
Tomlinson, A. J. 6/13
Tongues, Speaking in 6/29
Torah 6/11
TRACTS / PAMPHLETS
  "The Mother's Last Prayer" 6/2
  "The Only Son" 6/2
  "The Selling of Joseph" 6/24
Trotman, Dawson E.
  (b. 3/25/1906) d. 6/18/1956
Truth, Sojourner 6/1
Tübingen School 6/21
Tutankhamen, Egyptian Pharaoh 6/26

U

U.S. Armed Services 6/24
U.S. Supreme Court 6/4, 6/14, 6/19, 6/28
Umbreit, Friedrich W. K.
  (b. 4/11/1795) d. 6/11/1860
Uncle Tom 6/15

V

"Voyage of the Damned" 6/4
Varick, James 6/17
Vatican, The 6/14
Vatican Council I (1869-70) 6/16
Venn, Henry
  (b. 3/2/1725) d. 6/24/1797
Vingren, Adolf Gunnar 6/11
Virginia Bill of Rights 6/12
Vladimir, Russian Prince (980-1015) 6/5
Voltaire 6/23

W

Walford, William
  (b. 1772) d. 6/22/1850
Walsh, Richard John 6/26
Warner, Daniel S.
  b. 6/25/1842 [d. 2/12/1925]
WARS
  American Civil War (1861-1865) 6/15, 6/24, 6/29
  Huguenot Wars (1562-1594) 6/28
  Six-Day War, Arab-Israeli (1967) 6/5
  World War II (1939-1945) 6/12
Webb, George J.
  b. 6/24/1803 [d. 10/7/1887]

Weber, Carl Maria von
  (b. 11/18/1786) d. 6/4/1826
Wesley, Charles 6/17, 6/27
Wesley, John 6/17, 6/25, 6/27.
  See also QUOTATIONS
Wharton, Charles H.
  b. 6/5/1748 [d. 1833]
White, Alma Bridwell
  b. 6/16/1862 d. 6/26/1946
Whitefield, George 6/9, 6/24, 6/27. See also QUOTATIONS
Whittingham, William
  (b. 1524) d. 6/10/1579
Wigner, John M.
  b. 6/10/1844 [d. 3/31/1911]
Williams, George 6/6
Wilson, Emily D.
  (b. 5/24/1865) d. 6/23/1942
Wilson, William G. 6/10
Winona Lake Bible Conference Center (IN) 6/17
Winter, Gloria
  b. 6/14/1938
Wise, Rabbi Stephen 6/3
Witchcraft in America 6/21
Wojtyla, Karol. See John Paul II, Pope
World Council of Churches 6/24
Wycliffe Bible Translators 6/7

Y

Yadin, Yigael
  (b. 3/21/1917) d. 6/28/1984
Young Men's Christian Association (YMCA) 6/6, 6/19
Young Men's Hebrew Association 6/5

Z

Zeisberger, David 6/9
Ziegenbalg, Bartholomaeus
  b. 6/14/1682 [d. 2/23/1719]
Zinzendorf, Ludwig von 6/17
Zwemer, Samuel 6/28

July 1

Highlights in History

1750 After 21 years as pastor of the Northampton (MA) Congregational Church, Jonathan Edwards, 46, delivered his final message. His sermons had influenced the Great Awakening, but the church let him go over differences on church admission. (Edwards had inflexibly refused to allow those not yet converted to take communion.)

1752 Philip W. Otterbein, founder of the Church of the United Brethren, arrived in New York with five others. He afterward established a congregation at Lancaster, Pennsylvania.

1769 Spanish Franciscan missionary, Father Junipero Serra founded Mission San Diego, the first of nine missions he eventually established in western California, and the first of 21 missions which ultimately stretched up the coast to San Francisco.

1899 In Boscobel, WI, the Christian Commercial Men's Association of America was formed by three traveling businessmen: John H. Nicholson, Samuel E. Hill and William J. Knights. Known today as the Gideons, the organization placed its first Bible at the Superior Hotel in Iron Mountain, Montana in 1908.

Notable Birthdays

1811 Birth of William J. Boone, the first American Protestant Episcopal missionary bishop to China. He first arrived in 1837, and eventually settled in Shanghai in 1845, where he remained until his death. Two of Boone's sons also went on to become missionaries. [d. 7/17/1864]

1825 Birth of William H. Walter, American Episcopal church organist and hymnwriter. He is best remembered for the hymn tune FESTAL SONG ("Rise Up, O Men of God"). [d. 1893]

1860 Birth of Williston Walker, American Congregational church historian. [d. 3/9/1922]

1899 Birth of Thomas A. Dorsey, African-American clergyman and the "father of black gospel music." He penned over 400 gospel songs, including "Peace in the Valley" — written for Mahalia Jackson in 1937. But Dorsey penned his most famous song, "Precious Lord, Take My Hand," in 1932, following the death of his wife in childbirth. [d. 1/23/1993]

The Last Passage

1878 Death of Catherine Winkworth, 50, English hymnwriter. She is regarded as the foremost English translator of German hymns, and rendered for the English church such favorites as: "Now Thank We All Our God"; "Praise to the Lord, the Almighty"; "If Thou But Suffer God to Guide Thee." (b. 9/13/1827)

1896 Death of Harriet Beecher Stowe, 85, American abolitionist and author. In 1851-52 she published in serial form her best-known work, *Uncle Tom's Cabin*, or *Life Among the Lowly*, which piqued anti-slavery sentiment prior to the American Civil War. She also wrote the hymn, "Still, Still With Thee." (b. 6/14/1811)

Words for the Soul

1539 German reformer Martin Luther remarked in a "Table Talk": *'As a young man I made myself familiar with the Bible; by reading it again and again I came to know my way about in it. Only then did I consult writers [commentaries].... It's better to see with one's own eyes than with another's.'*

1772 English founder of Methodism John Wesley advised in a letter: *'Entire resignation implies entire love. Give Him your will, and you give Him your heart.'*

1853 Scottish clergyman and biographer Andrew Bonar wrote in a letter: *'[Trials] help to make believers more thoroughly pilgrims, though it is faith and hope, not trial, that begins the pilgrimage.'*

FROM GOD'S WORD...   OT: 2 Kings 18:18–19:37 ~ NT: Acts 21:1-16 ~ Psalms 149:1-9 ~ Proverbs 18:8

July 2

Highlights in History

311 Miltiades was elected the 32nd pope of the Catholic Church. His 2-1/2-year pontificate was marked by the end of the early persecution of Christians, after Roman Emperor Constantine I was converted to the Christian faith.

1505 While returning from a visit to his parents, Martin Luther, 21, was overtaken by a thunderstorm and cried out, "Help, St. Anne, and I'll become a monk!" Two weeks later, he entered the Erfurt monastery of Augustinian Eremites.

1749 Mary Turpin of Illinois (b. 1731), having entered the Ursuline Convent in 1748, began her novitiate. Turpin made her profession of faith on January 31, 1752, making her the first Catholic nun born in the United States. (She died Nov. 20, 1761, at the age of 30.)

1865 In the East End of London, English Methodist revivalist William Booth presided over the first meeting of what would become the Salvation Army.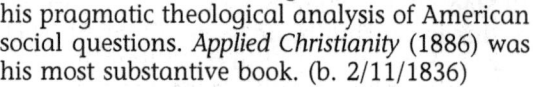

1973 The first female Navy chaplain, Lieutenant Florence Dianna Pohlman of La Jolla, California — a Presbyterian — was sworn in at Newport, Rhode Island. She was later assigned to the Naval Training Center in Orlando, Florida.

Notable Birthdays

1489 Thomas Cranmer, first Protestant Archbishop of Canterbury, was born. He nullified several of Henry VIII's marriages, maintained the divine right of kings, and promoted translation of the Bible into the vernacular. Cranmer was also the primary author of the 1549 *Book of Common Prayer*. On Mary's accession, however, he was condemned for treason and burned at the stake. [d. 3/21/1556]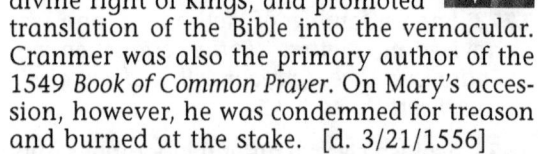

1813 Samuel Wolcott, American Congregational clergyman, was born. He wrote the hymn, "Christ for the World We Sing." [d. 2/24/1886]

1902 Birth of Everett F. Harrison, American Presbyterian clergyman and biblical scholar. Competent in Greek, Hebrew, Aramaic, German, Latin, and French, he was associated with Dallas Theological Seminary from 1928-47. Harrison served on two Bible translation committees – the NASV and the NIV – and was also editor of both the *Wycliffe Bible Commentary* and *Baker's Dictionary of Theology*.

The Last Passage

1899 Death of Rigdon M. McIntosh, 63, American Methodist sacred music educator, editor and hymn composer. He taught at Vanderbilt and Emory Universities, but is remembered for composing the hymn tune PROMISED LAND ("On Jordan's Stormy Banks"). (b. 4/3/1836)

1918 Death of Washington Gladden, 82, American Congregational clergyman and pioneer of the Christian social movement. His pastorates (1870-1918) served as the grounds for his pragmatic theological analysis of American social questions. *Applied Christianity* (1886) was his most substantive book. (b. 2/11/1836)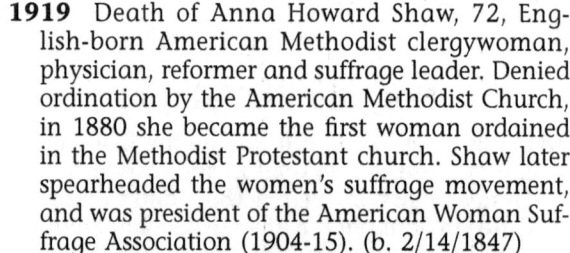

1919 Death of Anna Howard Shaw, 72, English-born American Methodist clergywoman, physician, reformer and suffrage leader. Denied ordination by the American Methodist Church, in 1880 she became the first woman ordained in the Methodist Protestant church. Shaw later spearheaded the women's suffrage movement, and was president of the American Woman Suffrage Association (1904-15). (b. 2/14/1847)

Words for the Soul

1930 Congregational missionary and literacy pioneer Frank C. Laubach disclosed in a letter: '[God said to me:] If I do not speak to you in words at times, it is because the reality all about you is greater than the imperfect symbols of things which you have in words.'

FROM GOD'S WORD... OT: 2 Kings 20:1–22:2 ~ NT: Acts 21:17-36 ~ Psalms 150:1-6 ~ Proverbs 18:9-10

July 3

Highlights in History

529 The Synod of Orange convened in southern France. Caesarius of Arles presided over the council of 13 bishops. The synod ended the struggle against semi-Pelagianism in Southern Gaul (as advocated by Faustus of Riez and John Cassian, who believed the human will and God's grace work together).

1721 Norwegian Lutheran missionary Hans Egede (1686-1758) landed on the western coast of Greenland with a party of 46 people. He soon began evangelizing the Inuit people, and is remembered today as "the Apostle of Greenland."

1878 Negro Lutheran Church was established in Little Rock, AR. Organized by LCMS missionaries J. Friedrich Doescher and Fredrick Berg, it was the first formal outreach to African-Americans made by Lutherans in the U.S.

1907 Pope Pius X published "Lamentabili," in which 65 propositions derived from the teachings of the "Modernist" intellectual movement of that time were condemned. In particular, the encyclical condemned those propositions which emphasized evolution.

Notable Birthdays

1836 Birth of George Batchelor, American Unitarian clergyman. He served as secretary of the American Unitarian Association (1893-98), and also editor of "The Christian Register" (1898-1911). [d. 1923]

1894 Birth of Don R. Falkenberg, founder of Bible Literature International. He incorporated this specialized ministry in 1923 in Columbus, Ohio, under the name Mid-West Businessmen's Council of the Pocket Testament League. In 1941 the name was changed to Bible Meditation League and in 1967 to Bible Literature International. [d. 12/13/1974]

The Last Passage

1897 Death of Augustine F. Hewitt, 76, co-founder of the Paulists. Born of Congregationalists in New England, he later became an Episcopalian, and in 1846 a Roman Catholic. In 1858 Hewitt and Isaac Hecker established the Paulists. As editor (1886-97) of "Catholic World," Hewitt became a major apologist of Catholicism in America during the second half of the 19th century. He also believed the Catholic Church needed to adapt itself to American institutions and methods of evangelization. (b. 11/27/1820)

1904 Death of Theodor Herzl, 44, Hungarian-born Austrian Jewish journalist and political writer. In 1895 he published "Der Judenstaat," a tract advocating the formation of a Jewish state in Palestine, and in 1897 founded the Congress of the Zionist Organizations. Herzl's efforts eventually culminated in the establishment of modern Israel in May 1948. (b. 5/2/1860)

1960 Death of Alfred H. Ackley, 73, American Presbyterian clergyman and hymnwriter. Ordained in 1914, he served churches in PA and CA, while becoming increasingly involved in the field of sacred music. Ackley penned about 1,500 songs, including the hymn tune HE LIVES ("I Serve a Risen Savior"). (b. 1/21/1887)

Words for the Soul

1756 English Methodism founder John Wesley allowed in a letter: *'One who lives and dies in error, or in dissent from our Church, may yet be saved, but one who lives and dies in sin, must perish.'*

1974 Dutch Catholic priest, educator and diarist Henri J. M. Nouwen reflected in his **Genesee Diary**: *'In times of doubt or unbelief, the community can "carry you along," so to speak; it can even offer on your behalf what you yourself overlook, and can be the context in which you may recognize the Lord again.'*

FROM GOD'S WORD... OT: 2 Kings 22:3–23:30 ~ NT: Acts 21:37–22:16 ~ Psalms 1:1-6 ~ Proverbs 18:11-12

July 4

Highlights in History

993 The first official Roman Catholic saint, Ulrich of Augsburg, was canonized. Before this time, saints were so named by popular consensus. After a period of time, the church began establishing rules of canonization.

1825 American missionaries Sarah Hall and George Dana Boardman were married. Later this same year they set sail to Calcutta, India, as missionaries to Burma. When Boardman died in 1831, Sarah chose to stay in Burma, and in 1834 she married another American missionary, Adoniram Judson. (Judson had lost his first wife, Ann, to illness in 1826.)

1836 Narcissa P. (Mrs. Marcus) Whitman, 26, and Eliza H. (Mrs. Henry) Spalding, 28, became the first white women to cross the Rockies into the Oregon Territory. They were the wives of a party of missionaries sent by the American Board of Commissioners for Foreign Missions to the Indians of the American Northwest.

Notable Birthdays

1804 Birth of New England novelist Nathaniel Hawthorne who authored *The Scarlet Letter*. Hawthorne's fiction was marked by a preoccupation with evil and the dark side of human nature. His writings, reflecting the themes and atmosphere of Puritan New England, represented the ambiguities and complexities of a once-predominantly Christian culture now facing changes. [d. 5/19/1864]

1840 Birth of James McGranahan, American sacred song writer and music pioneer. A song leader for the popular 19th-century evangelist Major D. W. Whittle, McGranahan also wrote numerous hymn tunes, including EL NATHAN ("I Know Not Why God's Wondrous Grace"), ("I Will Sing of...") MY REDEEMER, NEUMEISTER ("Christ Receiveth Sinful Men") and SHOWERS OF BLESSING. [d. 7/7/1907]

1870 Scottish theologian James Moffatt was born in Glasgow. He pastored in Scotland's Free Church (1894-1907), later teaching at Union Seminary in New York City (1927-1939). Moffatt is most widely remembered today for publishing *The Holy Bible* (1922-26), a translation of both the New (1913) and Old (1924) Testaments into modern colloquial English. [d. 6/27/1944]

The Last Passage

740 St. Andrew of Crete, regarded as one of the greatest hymn writers of the Orthodox Church, died at about 80. He is believed to have originated the Greek musical canon, and wrote a number of hymns, including "Christian, Dost Thou See Them?" (b. ca. 660)

1755 Death of John Cennick, 36, English clergyman and hymnwriter. Born of Quaker parents and raised in the Anglican Church, he first worked in the Methodist movement under John Wesley. Later he joined forces with George Whitefield. In 1845 he joined the Moravian Brethren. Cennick published several collections of hymns, including the table grace, "Be Present at Our Table, Lord." (b. 12/12/1718)

Words for the Soul

1964 American Trappist monk Thomas Merton warned in a letter: *'Wherever there is a special religious group there is danger of a ghetto spirit, of excessive self-concern, and as a result a kind of futile fighting with ourselves about ideals and intangibles.'*

1970 American Presbyterian missionary and apologist Francis Schaeffer observed in a letter: *'If standards are raised which are not really scriptural, and especially if these are put forth as the spiritual standard for which we should strive, it can only lead to sorrow. If we try to have a spirituality higher than the Bible sets forth, it will always turn out to be lower.'*

FROM GOD'S WORD... OT: 2 Kings 23:31–25:30 ~ NT: Acts 22:17–23:10 ~ Psalms 2:1-12 ~ Proverbs 18:13

ALMANAC OF THE CHRISTIAN FAITH

AV · TAMMUZ

~ July 5 ~

Highlights in History

649 Pope St. Martin I was consecrated. He was known for his fight against Monothelitism. The heresy taught Christ had two wills, the human and divine, but the divine was so dominant that it deprived the human of any ability to act.

1294 At age 79, Pietro di Murrone was elected to the papacy as Celestine V. His naiveté of procedure, however, turned his pontificate into a disaster, and he abdicated in December of this same year. His ambitious successor Boniface VIII afterward imprisoned Murrone in the castle of Fumone, where he died in 1296.

1865 In London, pioneer English revivalist William Booth, 35, held the first "rescue meeting" at his newly-founded Christian Mission. In 1878, Booth changed the name of his organization to the Salvation Army.

1963 Disposal of the dead by cremation was officially granted sanction by the Roman Catholic Church. (Belief in the resurrection of the dead had previously made cremation repugnant to Catholic Christians.)

Notable Birthdays

1775 Birth of William Crotch, English sacred organist and hymnwriter. He is best remembered for his setting of the hymn tune ST. MICHAEL ("Stand Up and Bless the Lord"). [d. 12/29/1847]

1908 Birth of Dana M. Greeley, American religious leader. He was first president of the Unitarian Universalist Association (1961-69), and co-founded the World Conference on Religion and Peace. [d. 6/13/1986]

The Last Passage

1663 Death of Samuel Newman, 61, English-born American clergyman. He was editor of the first Bible concordance printed in the English language. (b. 1602)

1806 Death of Richard Whatcoat, 70. Associated with the Wesleyan movement in England from age 22, in 1784 he and Thomas Vasey were sent as Methodist missionaries to America. In 1800 Whatcoat was elected a bishop of the American Methodist Church. (b. 2/23/1736)

1903 Death of William B. Pope, 81, English Methodist linguist and theologian. His greatest work, *Compendium of Christian Theology* (1875-76), set forth powerful arguments in support of the Wesleyan doctrine of Christian perfection — the "holiness doctrine of all Methodist systematic theology." (b. 2/19/1822)

1962 Death of H. Richard Niebuhr, 67, American Neo-orthodox theologian. Seen as more scholarly than his older brother Reinhold, Richard taught Christian ethics at Yale University for 30 years. In his best-known work, *Christ and Culture* (1951), Richard sought to determine the various relationships between one's Christian faith and their attitude toward civilization. (b. 9/3/1894)

Words for the Soul

1768 Methodism founder John Wesley declared in a letter: *'We are reasonable creatures, and undoubtedly reason is the candle of the Lord. By enlightening our reason to see the meaning of the Scriptures, the Holy Spirit makes our way plain before us.'*

1886 English Baptist preacher Charles H. Spurgeon encouraged in a letter: *'Go on to win other souls. It is the only thing worth living for. God is much glorified by conversions, and therefore this should be the great object of life.'*

1959 American Trappist monk Thomas Merton noted in his journal: *'A series of gestures and external acts [are] without much inner meaning and hardly able to produce any spiritual fruit excepting the satisfied sense of duty that warms the heart of a conformist—when he has conformed.'*

FROM GOD'S WORD... OT: 1 Chronicles 1:1–2:17 ~ NT: Acts 23:11-35 ~ Psalms 3:1-8 ~ Proverbs 18:14-15

ALMANAC OF THE CHRISTIAN FAITH

~ July 6 ~

Highlights in History

1054 The medieval Church suffered a permanent fracture when the four Eastern Patriarchates – Constantinople, Alexandria, Jerusalem and Antioch – broke fellowship with Rome, the single patriarchate in the West. It marked the beginning of a "Great Schism" between the Roman Catholic and the Eastern Orthodox churches.

1875 The first "holiness" conference at Keswick, England, ended. "Keswick" afterward became the byword for a movement within evangelical Christianity which stressed personal holiness through a "crisis" experience of sanctification. Holiness belief thus rejects the older traditional teaching that sanctification is a lifelong process which begins after one's religious conversion.

Notable Birthdays

1757 William McKendree, pioneer American Methodist prelate, was born in King William County, VA. Converted when nearly 30, he became a Methodist elder in 1791, and in 1808 was ordained the first American-born bishop of the Methodist Episcopal Church. [d. 3/5/1835]

1905 Birth of Harold J. Ockenga, American Congregational minister and evangelical leader. As first president of the National Association of Evangelicals (NAE) and co-founder of Fuller Theological Seminary (CA), Ockenga is credited with having helped shape the intellectual credibility of modern evangelicalism in America. [d. 1985]

The Last Passage

1415 Bohemian religious reformer Jan Hus[s], ca 43, was burned at the stake as a heretic, following his condemnation by the Council of Constance. Influenced by the writings of John Wycliffe, Hus was himself transitional between medieval thought and the Reformation. (b. ca. 1372)

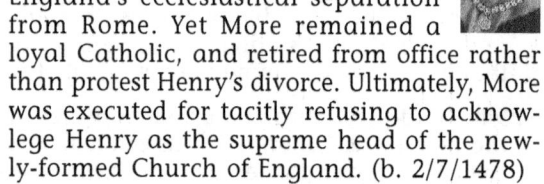

1535 English statesman Sir Thomas More was beheaded. He had served as Henry VIII's Lord Chancellor during England's ecclesiastical separation from Rome. Yet More remained a loyal Catholic, and retired from office rather than protest Henry's divorce. Ultimately, More was executed for tacitly refusing to acknowlege Henry as the supreme head of the newly-formed Church of England. (b. 2/7/1478)

1879 Death of English sacred organist Henry T. Smart, 65. Largely self-taught, he served in four prominent London churches starting in 1831. Smart's large output of compositions include the hymn tunes LANCASHIRE ("Lead On, O King Eternal") and REGENT SQUARE ("Angels from the Realms of Glory"). (b. 10/26/1813)

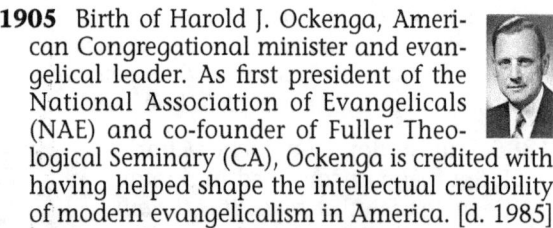

1888 Death of George Duffield, Jr., 69, American Presbyterian clergyman, and hymnwriter. Ordained in 1840, he served churches in NY, NJ, PA, IL and MI. Duffield also authored the hymn "Stand Up, Stand Up for Jesus" – inspired by the last words of a young Episcopal minister, Dudley Tyng, as he lay dying at 29 from a tragic farm accident. (b. 9/12/1818)

Words for the Soul

1636 Exiled Scottish clergyman Samuel Rutherford advised a fellow-sufferer in a letter: 'Slip yourself by faith under Christ's wings, till the storm be over.'

1941 English Bible expositor Arthur W. Pink observed in a letter: 'It is those who walk the closest with God who are most conscious of their sins.'

1961 Swiss Reformed theologian Karl Barth explained in a letter: 'Eternal life is not another and second life, beyond the present one. It is this life... in relation to what God has done for the whole world, and therefore for us too, in Jesus Christ.'

FROM GOD'S WORD...   OT: 1 Chronicles 2:18–4:4 ~ NT: Acts 24:1-27 ~ Psalms 4:1-8 ~ Proverbs 18:16-18

ALMANAC OF THE CHRISTIAN FAITH

אב AV

תמוז TAMMUZ

~ July 7 ~

Highlights in History

1870 The Vatican I Ecumenical Council held its last session. It first opened on Dec. 8, 1869 under Pius IX and was attended by 800 bishops. During its sessions, the popular Catholic belief in papal infallibility became an official dogma.

1946 Frances Xavier Cabrini (1850-1917) was canonized by Pius XII — the first American citizen to be made a saint in the Catholic Church. Born in Italy, she came to the U.S. in 1889 and was naturalized in 1909. Known as Mother Cabrini, she founded the Institute of the Missionary Sisters of the Sacred Heart and helped establish hospitals, schools and orphanages throughout the United States and in South America.

Notable Birthdays

1787 Birth of César H. A. Malan, French-born Swiss clergyman. Ordained to the Reformed Church ministry in 1810, he penned over 1000 hymns, including the words to "Take My Life and Let It Be" and the hymn tune HENDON ("Ask Ye What Great Thing I Know"). [d. 5/18/1864]

1851 Birth of Charles A. Tindley, African-American Methodist clergyman and hymnwriter. Orphaned at five, Tindley learned to read and write by age 17, and was ordained into the Methodist ministry in 1885. In 1902 he was called to pastor Philadelphia's Calvary Methodist Episcopal Church, where he preached for 30 years. Tindley also authored a number of hymns, including "Nothing Between," "By and By," and "Stand by Me." His best-known hymn, "I'll Overcome Some Day," later inspired the 1960s civil rights song, "We Shall Overcome." [d. 7/26/1933]

The Last Passage

1661 Death of George Fox, English founder of the Society of Friends (Quakers). He believed a true Christian must rely on the inward voice of the Holy Spirit ("inner light") for daily spiritual guidance. (b. 7/19/1624)

1912 Death of William H. Durham, 39, American Pentecostal leader. He was an exponent of the so-called "finished work of Calvary," and helped forge a non-Wesleyan view of sanctification as an option for Pentecostals. Today Durham's views are best represented by the Assemblies of God. (b. 1873)

1944 Death of George W. Truett, 77, American Southern Baptist clergyman. Ordained in 1890, Truett was called to the First Baptist Church of Dallas in 1897, and continued there until his death 47 years later. During his long pastorate, the membership in his church grew from 700 to 7,800. (b. 5/6/1867)

1972 Athenagoras I, Archbishop of Constantinople (1948-72), died in Istanbul at 86. Born Aristocles Spyrou, he was the spiritual leader of 150 million Orthodox Church members. (In 1964 Athenagoras met with Pope Paul VI in Jerusalem – the first such meeting between heads of the Eastern and Western churches since 1439!) (b. 3/25/1886)

Words for the Soul

1872 In a letter to a grieving widow, Scottish poet and children's novelist George MacDonald wrote: 'The sun shines, the wind blows soft, the summer is in the land; but your summer sun and your winter fire is gone, and the world is waste to you. So let it be. Your life is hid with Christ in God, at the heart of all summers — so "comfort thyself" that this world will look by and by a tearful dream fading away in the light of the morning.'

1959 English literary scholar and Christian apologist C.S. Lewis remarked in one of his **Letters To An American Lady**: 'I "believed" theoretically in the divine forgiveness for years before it really came home to me. It is a wonderful moment when it does.'

FROM GOD'S WORD... OT: 1 Chronicles 4:5–5:17 ~ NT: Acts 25:1-27 ~ Psalms 5:1-12 ~ Proverbs 18:19

July 8

Highlights in History

1654 Jacob Barsimon, the first known Jew to settle in North America, arrived in New York City. He was the first of 21 Jewish immigrants to American that year. The group eventually formed the Congregation Shearith Israel.

1741 Celebrated Colonial clergyman Jonathan Edwards delivered his famous sermon, "Sinners in the Hands of an Angry God," before a congregation at Enfield, CT. It was a rare word of exhortation, for Edwards was known for rarely preaching imprecatory sermons.

1835 The American Liberty Bell first cracked while tolling the death of Chief Justice John Marshall. The bell had been cast in England in 1752. Earlier, the Pennsylvania Provincial Assembly voted that it should bear an inscription: *"Proclaim liberty throughout all the land unto all the inhabitants thereof."* The text was from Leviticus 25:10.

Notable Birthdays

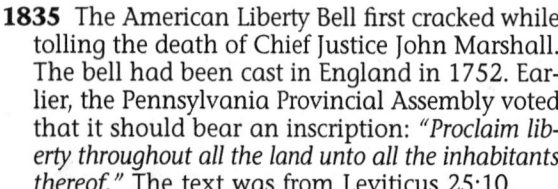

1621 French poet and fabulist Jean de La Fontaine was born. Known for his epigrammatic morals, it was de La Fontaine who coined the ever-popular (but also non-biblical!) proverb: *"Help yourself, and heaven will help you."* Today it is more commonly worded: *"God helps those who help themselves."* [d. 4/13/1695]

1792 Birth of Lowell Mason, American Presbyterian hymn composer. He gained early recognition for organizing church choirs and congregational singing. He published over 40 collections of music, and wrote or arranged over 1,000 hymn tunes, including DENNIS ("Blest Be the Tie That Binds"); OLIVET ("My Faith Looks Up to Thee"); HAMBURG ("When I Survey the Wondrous Cross"); BETHANY ("Nearer, My God, To Thee"); and UXBRIDGE ("Be Present At Our Table, Lord"). [d. 8/11/1872]

The Last Passage

1115 Peter the Hermit, the French preacher, died at 65. His 1093 report to Urban II of atrocities that Seljuk Turks were inflicting on Christian pilgrims to the Holy Land led to Urban's fiery pronouncement of the First Crusade at the Council of Clermont in 1095. (b. ca. 1050)

1623 Gregory XV, pope from 1621-23, died at 69. During his papacy Gregory reformed papal elections and canonized Ignatius Loyola, Francis Xavier and Philip de Neri. (b. 1/9/1554)

1884 Death of Johann Peter Lange, 82, German Reformed theologian and biblical scholar. He taught at the universities of Zurich and Bonn. A prolific writer, Lange's *Theologische-homiletisches Bibelwerk* was later translated by Philip Schaff into 25 English volumes entitled: *A Commentary on the Holy Scriptures*. (b. 4/10/1802)

1951 Death of Ida Reed Smith, 85, American hymnwriter. She was born, lived in relative poverty, and died in Philippi, WV. For years, though, she wrote spiritual verses for many tunes that were sent her, including the still-popular hymn: "I Belong to the King" (b. 11/30/1865)

Words for the Soul

1769 Anglican Evangelical Henry Venn expressed in a letter: *'May I rise with an active and steady purpose to be doing something for God, as the miser rises with the design to get more gain each day.'*

1940 During WW II, English mystic Evelyn Underhill suggested in a letter: *'Only apparently when everything is reeling do we begin to perceive the over-ruling presence of the Eternal Being. Don't you feel now that out of what at first was utter confusion bit by bit the Divine purifying purpose is beginning to emerge? Fear and bewilderment are giving place to a sort of hushed expectancy, as if people were beginning to realize the superhuman character of that which is taking place.'*

FROM GOD'S WORD... OT: 1 Chronicles 5:18–6:81 ~ NT: Acts 26:1-32 ~ Psalms 6:1-10 ~ Proverbs 18:20-21

July 9

Highlights in History

1572 After plundering a number of churches, rioters in Briel, the Netherlands, hanged nineteen secular priests and Franciscan friars for the crime of being Catholics. (Catholic Spain had previously treated Protestant Holland with such cruelty that ill-feeling against the Church was strong.) Known as the Gorcum martyrs, the 19 were canonized by Pius IX in 1867.

1962 Eighty-one countries sent 250 Protestant and Orthodox delegates to the third World Institute on Christian Education which opened in Belfast, Northern Ireland.

Notable Birthdays

381 Birth of Nestorius, first patriarch of Constantinople (428-431). He taught that in Jesus Christ a divine person and a human person were joined in perfect harmony of action but not in the unity of a single person. For this teaching — that Christ had two natures and two persons (rather than two natures in one person) — Nestorius was deposed for heresy by the Council of Ephesus in 431. [d. 451]

1838 Birth of Philip P. Bliss, American Baptist song evangelist. He penned numerous gospel favorites, including "Hold the Fort"; "'Man of Sorrows,' What a Name"; "Wonderful Words of Life"; "Let the Lower Lights Be Burning"; "The Light of the World is Jesus"; and "I Will Sing of My Redeemer." He also composed KENOSIS ("I Gave My Life for Thee") and VILLE DU HAVRE ("It Is Well with My Soul"). [d. 12/29/1876]

1896 Birth of W. Cameron Townsend, American missionary and linguistic pioneer. In 1917 he began working as a Bible salesman in Guatemala, Mexico and Peru. In 1935 Townsend founded the Wycliffe Bible Translators. Today, WBT's 4,500 members work with nearly 750 minority languages worldwide. [d. 4/23/1982]

The Last Passage

1228 Stephen Langton, Archbishop of Canterbury (1207-28), died at about 78. Arguably the greatest of the medieval archbishops of Canterbury, Langton was the first to create a division of the Bible into chapters. (b. ca. 1150)

1441 Death of Flemish painter Jan van Eyck, about 51. His intense emphasis on detail spiritualized his subjects so that the division between secular and religious art was virtually eliminated. Van Eyck's best-known religious work, the Ghent altarpiece (1432), dramatizes human redemption in twenty panels. (b. ca. 1390)

1766 Death of Jonathan Mayhew, 45, New England Congregational clergyman. He served West Church in Boston from 1747 until his death. Remembered for espousing American rights, his sermons and writings greatly influenced development of the movement for "Liberty and Independence." (b. 10/8/1720)

1926 Death of Mother Mary Alphonsa [née Rose Hawthorne] Lathrop, 75, Born the youngest child of novelist Nathaniel Hawthorne, she converted to the Catholic faith at age 40. Later, she founded a Dominican third order devoted to relief for patients with incurable cancer — the first American hospice for the care of the terminally ill (1900). (b. 5/20/1851)

Words for the Soul

1909 French scholar Albert Schweitzer, 30, wrote in an application to the Paris Mission Society: *'I have come to realize more and more clearly that the sole truth and the sole happiness consist in serving our Lord Jesus Christ wherever he needs us.'*

1974 Dutch priest and diarist Henri J. M. Nouwen reflected: *'We can develop a morbid destructive inner attitude toward our neighbor ... that ... leads us away from the road to God. As the most important way to deal with this passion: "He who prays for his enemies cannot be revengeful."'*

FROM GOD'S WORD...   OT: 1 Chronicles 7:1–8:40 ~ NT: Acts 27:1-20 ~ Psalms 7:1-17 ~ Proverbs 18:22

July 10

Highlights in History

1629 The first non-Separatist Congregational church in the American colonies was established in Salem, MA by Francis Higginson and Samuel Skelton, two newly-arrived ministers from England.

1858 In New York City, four Redemptorist priests, led by Isaac Thomas Hecker, founded the Missionary Society of St. Paul the Apostle (popularly known as the Paulist Fathers).

1925 The "Scopes Monkey Trial" opened in Dayton, TN, with popular opinion behind the Fundamentalist Christian prosecutor William Jennings Bryan. Clarence Darrow served as the lawyer defending John Scopes from charges of teaching evolution in his high school biology classroom, contrary to a Tennessee law which went into effect on March 13th of this year. At the trial's end (July 21), Scopes was found guilty of teaching evolution and fined $100. But Clarence Darrow's cross-examination was so masterful that it left Bryan a broken man, and he died on July 26th.

Notable Birthdays

1509 Reformer John Calvin was born Jean Chauvin in France. He sought to establish a political theocracy in Switzerland, but was driven out in 1538. Recalled in 1541, he succeeded in setting up a theocratic government in Geneva, which afterward served as a flagship of Reformed Protestantism throughout Europe. [d. 5/27/1564]

1888 Birth of Eduard Thurneysen, Swiss Protestant pastor. From 1913 he maintained a valuable correspondence with fellow pastor Karl Barth. Their written communications helped both elaborate the dynamics of dialectical theology. While Barth eventually went on to teach in the university, though, Thurneysen remained in the local church, treating dialectical theology at its pastoral level. [d. 1974]

The Last Passage

1863 Death of Clement C. Moore, 83, American Episcopal biblical language scholar, educator, lexicographer and poet. He established the General Theological (Episcopal) Seminary in 1819, and there taught Greek and Hebrew literature (1823-1850). Ironically, however, he is better remembered for authoring "A Visit from St. Nicholas" in 1823, making him the unwitting chief agent of the modern Santa Claus myth. (b. 7/15/1779)

1908 Phoebe Palmer Knapp, lay Methodist philanthropist and hymnwriter, died at 69. As the wife of the founder of the Metropolitan Life Insurance Co., she was active in Methodist ministries.  She also published more than 500 Gospel songs, including the hymn tune ASSURANCE ("Blessed Assurance, Jesus Is Mine"). (b. 3/9/1839)

Words for the Soul

1522 German reformer Martin Luther remarked in a sermon: *'Forbear entering upon questions concerning the saints in heaven and the deceased.... God decided not to let us know anything about His dealings with the deceased. Surely he is not committing sin who does not call upon any saint but only clings firmly to the one Mediator, Jesus Christ.'*

1746 Colonial missionary to the American Indians David Brainerd reflected in his journal: *'I saw plainly there was nothing in the world worthy of my affection — my heart was dead to all below; yet not through dejection... but from a view of a better inheritance.'*

1790 Irish barrister John Philpot declared in a speech: *'The condition upon which God hath given liberty to men is eternal vigilance.'*

1950 American missionary and Auca Indian martyr Jim Elliot revealed in his Journal: *'I am just trying to deliver familiar truth from the oblivion of general acceptance.'*

FROM GOD'S WORD... OT: 1 Chronicles 9:1-10:14 ~ NT: Acts 27:21-44 ~ Psalms 8:1-9 ~ Proverbs 18:23-24

ALMANAC OF THE CHRISTIAN FAITH

~ July 11 ~

Highlights in History

1533 In a papal bull, Clement VII excommunicated England's King Henry VIII for divorcing Catherine of Aragon, and afterward marrying Anne Boleyn. Within the next two years, England embarked on a complete break with Rome and established the Anglican communion as a national religion in its place.

1656 The first Quakers to arrive in America were two Englishwomen, Ann Austin and Mary Fisher, who landed at Boston. They were promptly arrested by Massachusetts authorities and deported back to England five weeks later.

1955 President Dwight D. Eisenhower signed into law a bill which required the inscription "In God We Trust" to be printed on all U.S. currency.

Notable Birthdays

1767 Birth of John Quincy Adams, Unitarian sixth president of the United States. He wrote an entire *Version of the Psalms*, seventeen of which (including five hymns) were inserted in the *Christian Psalmist* (1841). [d. 2/23/1848]

1918 Birth of John Dillenberger, American Evangelical and Reformed (United Church of Christ) clergyman, ecclesiastical scholar, educator and author. He taught at Drew University, and published: *God Hidden and Revealed* (1953); *Protestant Christianity Interpreted through Its Development* (with Claude Welch, 1954); *Protestant Thought and Natural Science* (1960). [d. 2/7/2008]

The Last Passage

1681 [OS=7/1] Oliver Plunkett, Archbishop of Armagh and primate of Ireland (1669-81), was martyred at 55. The last Catholic to die for his faith in England and the first Irish martyr to be beatified, Plunkett had been accused of involvement in the Popish plot and was found guilty of treason. (b. 11/1/1625)

1895 Death of Alexander Ewing, 65, hymn composer: EWING ("Jerusalem the Golden"). He spent 12 years as a Scottish soldier in the foreign service, enlisting in 1855 at the outbreak of the Crimean War. Before this time Ewing had studied law and music. (b. 1/3/1830)

1945 Death of James M. Kirk, 91, American hymnwriter. He arranged the hymn tune BLESSED QUIETNESS. (b. 6/18/1854)

1948 Death of Gerhard Kittel, 59, German biblical scholar. He gained fame as the editor of *Theologisches Wörterbuch zum Neuen Testament* (TWNT, 1933-79), which was afterward translated into English as the *Theological Dictionary of the New Testament* (TDNT) (b. 9/23/1888)

Words for the Soul

1939 In a letter Anglican mystic Evelyn Underhill pondered: *'Consider the Tractarian Revival. The Church of England before it happened was at the lowest possible ebb sacramentally and liturgically, and it must have seemed incredible that a handful of ardent souls could make any real difference. And then, when it had begun to get going, there was the crushing blow of the secession of Newman and his friends to Rome. That seemed like complete failure, and indeed many people did despair, yet in spite of it the movement struggled on and recovered itself and now there is hardly an English parish untouched by its influence; and the present real revival of the religious life is entirely due to it.'*

1952 American missionary and Auca Indian martyr Jim Elliot prayed in his Journal: *'Teach me, Lord Jesus,... not to be hungering for the "strange, rare, and peculiar" when the common, ordinary, and regular, rightly taken, will suffice to feed and satisfy the soul.'*

1955 American Presbyterian missionary and apologist Francis Schaeffer concluded in a letter: *'No price is too high to pay to have a free conscience before God.'*

FROM GOD'S WORD...   OT: 1 Chronicles 11:1–12:18 ~ NT: Acts 28:1-31 ~ Psalms 9:1-12 ~ Proverbs 19:1-3

ALMANAC OF THE CHRISTIAN FAITH

July 12

Highlights in History

1691 Italian cardinal Antonio Pignatelli, 76, was elected Pope Innocent XII. The highest moment of his nine-year reign was the papal bull he issued in 1692 – "Romanum decet pontificem" – which forbad nepotism for all time, and to which every future pope and cardinal had to swear to obey.

1739 David Brainerd, 21, underwent a personal conversion experience. He was later commissioned by the Society for the Propagation of Christian Knowledge as a missionary to the New England Indians. But Brainerd's health failed him after only three years in the field, and he died at the home of Jonathan Edwards on October 9, 1747. (Others, including William Carey and Henry Martyn, followed Brainerd's footsteps into the mission field.)

1843 Mormon founder Joseph Smith declared he had received a divine revelation sanctioning the practice of polygamy. The announcement stirred up bitterness within the community of Nauvoo, IL, where Smith and his followers were settled. The following June, Smith and his brother Hirum were killed by an angry mob in Carthage, IL — for practicing polygamy.

Notable Birthdays

1803 Birth of Thomas Guthrie, Free Church of Scotland minister, social reformer and philanthropist. He preached in Edinburgh (1837-64), and from 1847 was instrumental in establishing "Ragged Schools" (schools for destitute children) where the poor could be given a sound education on a Protestant basis. [d. 2/23/1873]

1906 Birth of Ernst Käsemann, German NT scholar and student of Rudolf Bultmann. His 1953 lectures on the historical Jesus sparked the "new quest" for the same. Käsemann's theology insisted on the primacy of Christology. [d. 1998]

The Last Passage

1536 Death of Dutch humanist and scholar Desiderius Erasmus, 66 or 69. Regarded as leader of the Renaissance in northern Europe, he was opposed to the fanaticism of the Reformation, choosing reform of the Church from within through scholarship and Christian instruction. His critical satire, *In Praise of Folly* (1509), demonstrated the need for reform. His *Greek New Testament* (1516) encouraged the church to go beyond its Latin (Vulgate) roots. (b. 10/28/1466 or 10/27/1469)

1845 Death of Henry Ware, Sr., 81, American clergyman and theologian. His courses at Harvard University (1805-40) led to the formation of the Harvard Divinity School in 1816. Today, Ware is considered one of the founders of American Unitarianism. (b. 4/1/1764)

1936 Death of Samuel P. Cadman, 71, American Congregational clergyman. He pastored churches in NY City (1895-1936). Later, as president and radio minister for the Federal Council of Churches of Christ in America (1928-36), Cadman thereby became the first American radio preacher. (b. 12/18/1864)

1944 Death of Sergei Nikolaevich Bulgakov, 73, Russian Orthodox philosopher, theologian, economist. (b. 6/16/1871)

Words for the Soul

1532 In a "Table Talk" Martin Luther pondered: *'How is God to arrange our life? Good days we cannot bear, evil days we cannot endure. If He gives us wealth, we strut about; if He gives us poverty, we despair.... We may well believe that our God will be gracious; otherwise we are utterly done for.'*

1963 Swiss Reformed theologian Karl Barth admonished in a letter: *'Do not stop testing and correcting your insights by holy scripture. Then, being sound in what really counts, you can live and represent a comforted life.'*

FROM GOD'S WORD... OT: 1 Chronicles 12:19–14:17 ~ NT: Romans 1:1-17 ~ Psalms 9:13-20 ~ Proverbs 19:4-5

July 13

Highlights in History

1587 Manteo became the first Native American baptized as a Protestant. This took place at Roanoke, Virginia where he was converted by members of Sir Walter Raleigh's expedition.

1727 Twenty-seven-year-old Count Nikolaus Zinzendorf organized the Bohemian Protestant refugees on his land into the Moravian community of Unitas Fratrum (United Brethren).

1813 Adoniram Judson and his wife Ann (née Hasseltine), first arrived in Burma. It would be five years before America's first foreign missionaries baptized their first convert. But before their deaths, over 7,000 Burmese would come to Christ — and today the Burmese church has grown to over two million Christians.

Notable Birthdays

1769 Thomas Kelly, Anglican clergyman and hymnwriter, was born in Ireland. Ordained in 1792, his fervent evangelicalism soon brought him into disfavor with the Archbishop of Dublin. Kelly then left the church, and devoted the rest of his life to working with the poor and establishing an independent ministry. He also authored 765 hymns, including "Praise the Savior, Ye Who Know Him!" [d. 5/14/1855]

1854 Birth of Edmund S. Lorenz, American United Brethren clergyman, college president and hymnwriter. He also founded the Lorenz and Co. music publishing house, and penned the hymns, "Tell It to Jesus" and "The Name of Jesus." [d. 7/10/1942]

1886 Edward Flanagan, Roman Catholic parish priest, was born in Ireland. He came to the U.S. in 1904 and was ordained in 1912. In 1917 he founded his Home for Homeless Boys outside Omaha, Nebraska, renaming it Boys' Town in 1922. Father Flanagan believed "There is no such thing as a bad boy." [d. 5/15/1948]

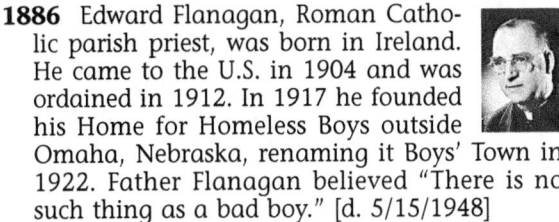

The Last Passage

1105 French Medieval scholar Rashi died at 65. The leading rabbinic commentator in his day, his Biblical and Talmudic commentaries became the basis for all later Jewish study. His life and work also made northern France one of the great centers of rabbinic scholarship during the eleventh and twelfth centuries. ("Rashi" is a Hebrew acrostic for Rabbi Sholomo ben Yitzhak.) (b. 1040)

1960 Death of Joy (née Davidman) Lewis, American-born Marxist poet and, during her last four years, the wife of British apologist C.S. Lewis. Davidman had earlier read the Lewis's apologetics, which influenced her conversion to Christianity. Her autobiographical essay, "The Longest Way Around" (1951), details her turning from communism to religious faith. (b. 4/18/1915)

Words for the Soul

1815 U.S. president John Adams wrote in a letter: 'The Hebrews have done more to civilize men than any other nation. If I were an atheist, and believed in blind eternal fate, I should still believe that fate had ordained the Jews to be the most essential instrument for civilizing the nations.'

1874 American Quaker holiness author Hannah Whitall Smith cautioned in a letter: 'It is not the place of everyone to reap the harvest; some must plant, and some must water, and all such services are equally necessary and acceptable. Often the reaping seems to me the least valuable of all.'

1974 Dutch Catholic priest and diarist Henri J. M. Nouwen reflected in his *Genesee Diary*: 'When we have given up the desire to be different and experience ourselves as sinners without any right to special attention, only then is there space to encounter our God who calls us by our own name and invites us into his intimacy.'

FROM GOD'S WORD... OT: 1 Chronicles 15:1–16:36 ~ NT: Romans 1:18-32 ~ Psalms 10:1-15 ~ Proverbs 19:6-7

ALMANAC OF THE CHRISTIAN FAITH

~ July 14 ~

Highlights in History

1773 The first annual conference of American Methodists convened in St. George's Church in Philadelphia. It was presided over by their first general superintendent, Francis Asbury.

1833 University don John Keble gave a sermon at Oxford in which he attacked the Whig plan to eliminate ten of the established bishoprics of the Church of Ireland as an act of "national apostasy." This sermon marked the start of the Oxford Movement, which sought a revival of sacramental piety within Anglicanism and a return to the theology of the 17th century High Church. Soon after, a series of "Tracts for the Times" were issued by Keble, John Henry Newman, R. H. Froude and Edward Pusey.

1892 The Baptist Young People's Union held its first annual national convention in Detroit, Michigan. Its organization the previous year was inspired by the founding in 1881 of the first formal organization for church youth, the Christian Endeavor Society.

Notable Birthdays

1716 Birth of Michael Schlatter, Swiss-born clergyman. Influenced by Swiss pietism, Schlatter became organizer (in 1747) of the German Reformed Church in early colonial America. [d. 10/31/1790]

1768 Birth of Scottish evangelist James A. Haldane, whose theological ideas were similar to those of the Plymouth Brethren. He founded the Society for the Propagation of the Gospel at Home in 1797. [d. 2/8/1851]

1800 Anglican poet and hymnwriter Matthew Bridges was born. He came under the influence of the Oxford Movement and, in 1848, followed John Henry Newman and others in joining the Roman Catholic Church. He spent the latter part of his life in Quebec, Canada. Bridges wrote several hymns, including "Crown Him with Many Crowns." [d. 10/6/1894]

The Last Passage

664 St. Deusdedit (birth name Frithonas) died. He was the first Anglo-Saxon Archbishop of Canterbury (655-664), though little is known of the events of his primacy.

1742 Death of Richard Bentley, 80, English divine, scholar, and Christian opponent to the Deists. He was the first to use philology as a test of literary authenticity. (b. 1/27/1662)

1875 Death of American Presbyterian chorister Simeon B. Marsh, 77. Gifted in music, Marsh taught his first singing school at age 19 and continued to teach in many churches of the Albany, NY Presbytery for over 30 years. Marsh also wrote the hymn tune MARTYN ("Jesus, Lover of My Soul"). (b. 6/1/1798)

Words for the Soul

1767 Anglican clergyman and hymnwriter John Newton explained in a letter: 'In his leadings there is usually a praying time and a waiting time. Yea, he often brings a seeming death upon our hopes and prospects just when he is going to accomplish them, and thereby we more clearly see and more thankfully acknowledge his interposition.'

1854 English Baptist preacher Charles Haddon Spurgeon warned in a letter: 'Harbour not that dark suggestion to forsake the house of God; remember you turn your back on Heaven, and your face to hell, the moment you do that.'

1855 In a letter to his wife, Scottish poet and children's novelist George MacDonald warned: 'Surely our hard time will wear over by degrees. It will, if it please God: that is, if we are ready to stand the harder trial of comfort – not to say prosperity.'

FROM GOD'S WORD... OT: 1 Chronicles 16:37–18:17 ~ NT: Romans 2:1-24 ~ Psalms 10:16-18 ~ Proverbs 19:8-9

ALMANAC OF THE CHRISTIAN FAITH

AV · TAMMUZ

~ July 15 ~

Highlights in History

1099 Jerusalem fell to the forces of the First Crusade, led by Godfrey of Bouillon. The Crusaders then set up a ruling government and the Holy Sepulchre was recovered — after most of the residents were massacred.

1549 Led by Francis Xavier, the Spanish Jesuits landed in Kagoshima, thereby becoming the first Christian missionaries to Japan. The years 1549-1639 afterward came to be known as "the Christian Century of Japan."

1662 The English Royal Society — the first scientific society in history — was chartered by Charles II. Inspired by active Christians with a deep interest in God's creation, the membership was overwhelmingly Puritan in makeup.

1801 Napoleon Bonaparte — recognizing that Catholicism was the faith of most Frenchmen — restored its authority in France in a concordat concluded with Pope Pius VII.

Notable Birthdays

1606 Rembrandt (Paul Harmens) van Rijn was born to a wealthy family in Leyden, Holland. Famous as a portrait artist by age 25, he moved to Amsterdam where his wife died in 1642. Subsequent financial difficulties led to bankruptcy, which appeared to deepen the spiritual dimensions of his art. Rembrandt's understanding of the passion of Christ led him to make it the theme of nearly 90 paintings and etchings. [d. 10/4/1669]

1704 German Moravian missionary leader August G. Spangenberg was born. Assistant to Nikolaus L. Zinzendorf and a bishop (1744-62) of the Unitas Fratrum, he founded the Moravian Church in North America. [d. 9/18/1792]

1850 Frances X. Cabrini was born in Italy. In 1880 she founded the Missionary Sisters of the Sacred Heart. She came to the U.S. in 1889 and became a naturalized citizen in 1909. Before her death, "Mother Cabrini" established hospitals, schools, and orphanages throughout the United States and South America. In 1946 she became the first American citizen to be canonized a saint in the Catholic Church. [d. 12/22/1917]

The Last Passage

1015 Death of St. Vladimir I (the Great), 59, grand prince and first Christian ruler of Russia. Known as the "Apostle of the Russians and Ruthenians," he and his grandmother Olga are honored today as the founders of Russian Christianity. (b. 956)

1274 During the Second Council of Lyons, Giovanni di Fidanza Bonaventura, 57, general of the Franciscan Order, died suddenly. Later known as the "Seraphic Doctor" and the "Prince of Mystics," St. Bonaventure's writings exude a spiritual passion. As a theologian, he taught that Christian illumination (special revelation) was superior to human reason (general revelation). (b. 1217)

1802 Scottish-born colonial printer Robert Aitken died at 68. In 1777 his presses had produced the first American edition of the King James Version of the New Testament, making it the first English Bible printed in America. (b. 1734)

Words for the Soul

1860 Scottish clergyman and biographer Andrew Bonar confessed in his diary: *'My heart ever feels the blessedness of prayer, and yet prays little.'*

1974 Dutch Catholic priest and educator Henri J. M. Nouwen reflected in his **Genesee Diary**: *'I should be happy to be part of the battle.... The battle is real, dangerous, and very crucial.... You will only know what victory is when you have been part of the battle.'*

FROM GOD'S WORD...   OT: 1 Chronicles 19:1–21:27 ~ NT: Romans 2:25–3:8 ~ Psalms 11:1-7 ~ Proverbs 19:10-12

ALMANAC OF THE CHRISTIAN FAITH

AV — TAMMUZ

~ July 16 ~

Highlights in History

1054 Negotiations broke down between the two major branches of Christendom when Pope Leo IX excommunicated Michael Cerularius, Patriarch of Constantinople. A "Great Schism" between the Western and Eastern churches persisted for 911 years! (In 1965, Pope Paul VI and Eastern Orthodox Patriarch Athenagoras I met to declare an official end to the schism.)

1769 Father Junipero Serra, a 55-year-old Spanish Franciscan friar, established the Mission San Diego de Alcala, the first permanent Spanish settlement on the West Coast of America. It also became the first of a chain of 21 Catholic missions that would be founded in modern-day California.

1937 In Eastern Germany near Weimar, the concentration camp at Buchenwald first opened. In the next eight years (before its liberation by American Allies in April 1945), nearly 57,000 prisoners would die in its gas chambers.

Notable Birthdays

1194 Clara Scefi was born in Assisi, Italy. Influenced by St. Francis to become a nun, she afterward became the founder and first abbess of the Order of Poor Clares. [d. 8/11/1253]

1821 Birth of Mary (née Morse) Baker Eddy, American sectarian religious leader. An invalid who sought healing, she founded the spiritual, metaphysical system called Christian Science in 1876. Mrs. Eddy was not a systematic theologian, but preached a divine self-healing power she believed to be inherent in human beings. [d. 12/3/1910]

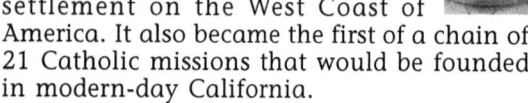

1844 Birth of James Mountain, English Baptist revivalist, author and hymnwriter. Influenced by Ira Sankey, Mountain penned WYE VALLEY ("Like a River Glorious") and TRANQUILLITY ("Jesus, I am Resting, Resting"). [d. 6/27/1933]

The Last Passage

1216 Innocent III (reigned 1198-1216) died. Born Lotario, Count of Segni, he was elevated to the papacy at age 37, became one of the greatest pontiffs of the Middle Ages, and was the first pope to use the title "Vicar of Christ." (b. 1160)

1915 Death of Ellen G. (née Harmon) White, 87, American sectarian religious leader. Born a Methodist, in 1860 she became co-founder of the Seventh-Day Adventist Church. She claimed to have had 2,000 visions. (b. 11/26/1827)

1931 Pioneer English missionary to China, India and Africa, C[harles] T. Studd died. Converted at 21, while a student at Cambridge, Studd was one of the group of young men known as the "Cambridge Seven" who offered themselves to missionary service. In 1913 he founded the Worldwide Evangelization Crusade (WEC). (b. 12/5/1862) (b. 12/2/1860)

Words for the Soul

1886 American Quaker holiness author Hannah Whitall Smith advised in a letter: 'If the Lord sets you to guard a lonely post in perfect stillness from all active work, you ought to be just as content as to be in the midst of the active warfare. It is no virtue to love the Master's work better than the Master's will.'

1944 German Lutheran theologian and Nazi martyr Dietrich Bonhoeffer observed in a letter from prison: 'One has to live for some time in a community to understand how Christ is "formed" in it (Gal 4:19).'

1962 In the spirit of Martin Buber's "I-It" and "I-Thou" categories, Swiss Reformed theologian Karl Barth explained in a letter: 'In no case is God a "what" that one may peep at close up or at a distance and value or disparage as one pleases. God is a "Who."'

FROM GOD'S WORD... OT: 1 Chronicles 21:28–23:32 ~ NT: Romans 3:9-31 ~ Psalms 12:1-8 ~ Proverbs 19:13-14

July 17

Highlights in History

431 The Council of Ephesus adjourned. Summoned by Theodosius II, it was chiefly noted for condemning Nestorianism, a heresy which denied the real unity of the divine and human natures in the Person of Christ.

1274 The Second Council of Lyons closed under Gregory X. Attended by approximately 500 bishops, its six sessions accomplished a temporary reunion of the separated Eastern churches with the Roman Church.

1505 In Germany, 21-year-old Martin Luther entered the Erfurt monastery of the Augustinian Eremites. Having survived a lightning strike, he had vowed to become a monk, took his vows in 1506, and was ordained a priest in 1507. Luther afterward began to study theology.

1794 The African Church of St. Thomas was dedicated, in Philadelphia. It was the first black church to be organized in New England, and began formal affiliation with the Protestant Episcopal Church the following month.

1942 Paul W. Fleming organized New Tribes Mission in Los Angeles. It has since become one of the largest interdenominational Christian missions in the world, dedicated especially to training Christian workers, translating the Bible and reaching tribes with the gospel.

Notable Birthdays

1674 Birth of Isaac Watts, English Nonconformist clergyman and pioneer hymnwriter. Regarded as the father of English hymnody, Watts penned over 750 titles, including: "When I Survey the Wondrous Cross"; "Come, We that Love the Lord"; "We're Marching to Zion"; "I Sing the Almighty Power of God"; "Joy to the World!"; "Alas! and Did My Savior Bleed"; and "My Shepherd Will Supply My Need." [d. 11/25/1748]

1768 Stephen T. Badin, the first Catholic priest ordained in the U.S. (1793), was born in Orleans, France. After his ordination by John Carroll, Badin helped establish Catholicism in KY, TN and IN. [d. 4/19/1853]

The Last Passage

1799 Death of Samuel Medley, 61, English Baptist preacher and hymn author: "Oh, Could I Speak the Matchless Worth" and "I Know That My Redeemer Lives." (b. 6/23/1738)

1836 Death of William White, 88, American prelate. Ordained for the Anglican priesthood (1772), White afterward sided with the colonies during the American Revolution. He helped create the Protestant Episcopal Church of America, and in 1786 was chosen first bishop of the new denomination. He remained in office for the next 50 years. (b. 4/4/1748).

1950 Death of Evangeline Cory Booth, 84, British-born American denominational reformer. The seventh child of William and Catherine Booth, she was promoted to head the American branch of the denomination in 1904 – the first woman Commander of the Salvation Army. (b. 12/25/1865)

Words for the Soul

1953 British literary scholar and Christian apologist C. S. Lewis cautioned in a letter: '"Give us this day our daily bread" (not an annuity for life) applies to spiritual gifts too; the little daily support for the daily trial. Life has to be taken day by day and hour by hour.'

1956 American Trappist monk Thomas Merton prayed: 'Whom I know and yet do not know. Whom I love but not enough.... Teach me to go to this country beyond words and beyond names. Teach me not to pray on this side of the frontier, here where the woods are. I need to be led by you.'

FROM GOD'S WORD... OT: 1 Chronicles 24:1–26:11 ~ NT: Romans 4:1-12 ~ Psalms 13:1-6 ~ Proverbs 19:15-16

ALMANAC OF THE CHRISTIAN FAITH

~ July 18 ~

Highlights in History

64 Roman emperor Nero blamed Christians for an extensive fire that destroyed most of the city of Rome. His accusation brought about the first great wave of persecutions on the Church.

954 Princess Olga of Kiev (grandmother of the man credited with Christianizing Russia) became regent for her son Svyatoslav upon the assassination of her husband, Igor I. Olga ruled for the next 20 years, implementing fiscal and other reforms. Possibly already a convert to Christianity, she visited Constantinople in 957 and was baptized.

1870 The Vatican I Council, after much debate, agreed on "papal infallibility" by promulgating the doctrinal constitution, "Pastor aeternus." Voting 533 to 2, the bishops asserted: *'The Roman Pontiff, when he speaks ex cathedra, ... by virtue of his supreme apostolic authority... is possessed of that infallibility with which the divine Redeemer willed that his church should be endowed.'*

1980 Rev. Marjorie S. Matthews, 64, became the first woman named to the ruling hierarchy of an American denomination when she was consecrated a bishop of the United Methodist Church.

Notable Birthdays

1504 Birth of Swiss reformer J. Heinrich Bullinger. After Zwingli's death in the Battle of Kappel (1531), Bullinger succeeded him as chief pastor of Zurich, remaining in that post for 40 years. He helped prepare two Helvetic confessions with John Calvin, and was a close associate of Cranmer, Melanchthon and Beza. [d. 9/17/1575]

1754 Birth of Lemuel Haynes, African-American clergyman. At age 27, Haynes was licensed to preach in the Congregational Church, which made him the first black minister to be certified by a predominantly white denomination. 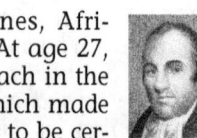 In 1785, Haynes was ordained and named pastor of a church in Torrington, CT, thereby also making him the first black minister to pastor a white church. [d. 9/28/1833]

1823 Birth of Archibald A. Hodge, American Presbyterian educator. He taught systematic theology at Western Theological Seminary (1864-77) and Princeton Seminary (1877-86). The son of Charles Hodge, Archibald was also a founder of the "Presbyterian Review." [d. 11/12/1886]

The Last Passage

1100 Death of Godfrey of Bouillon, about 42, French soldier. He led a German army during the First Crusade (1096-1099). After the capture of Jerusalem, Godfrey was elected its first Christian king, but died soon after. (b. ca. 1058)

1681 Death of Georg Neumark, 60, German educator, hymnist and composer. Twice during his life he lost everything he owned — once to robbers and later to fire. Those losses contributed much to the depth of his religious verse. It was Neumark who wrote the hymn, "If Thou but Suffer God to Guide Thee." (b. 3/16/1621)

Words for the Soul

1944 German Lutheran theologian and Nazi martyr Dietrich Bonhoeffer explained in a letter from prison: *'It is not the religious act that makes the Christian.... The religious act is always something partial; "faith" is something whole, involving the whole of one's life. Jesus calls men not to new religion but to life.'*

1974 Dutch Catholic priest, educator and diarist Henri J. M. Nouwen reflected in his ***Genesee Diary***: *'Prayer is the only real way to clean my heart and to create new space. I am discovering how important that inner space is. When it is there it seems that I can receive many concerns of others in it without becoming depressed. When I sense that inner quiet place, I can pray for many others and feel a very intimate relationship with them.'*

FROM GOD'S WORD... OT: 1 Chronicles 26:12–27:34 ~ NT: Romans 4:13–5:5 ~ Psalms 14:1-7 ~ Proverbs 19:17

ALMANAC OF THE CHRISTIAN FAITH

July 19

Highlights in History

1692 In the Massachusetts colony of Salem, five women were hanged for witchcraft. In all, 20 persons died this summer, many of whom were charged by 15 young girls in the community who claimed to have been bewitched by them.

1825 The American Unitarian Association was founded by members of the liberal wing of the Congregational churches in New England. The movement was inspired by a sermon preached in 1819 by William Ellery Channing in Boston. In 1961 the organization changed its name to the Unitarian Universalist Association after merging with the Universalists.

1913 The first Victorious Life Conference convened at Oxford, PA. Inspired by the Keswick Conferences held in England from 1875, and the Northfield Conferences held in the U.S. from 1880, these conventions promoted the belief that a Christian can gain immediate freedom from the whole power of every known sin.

Notable Birthdays

1624 English church founder George Fox was born. He left Anglicanism in 1647 to form "Friends of the Truth." Called "Quakers" by their enemies, they taught that spiritual truth could  be learned through the inner voice of God's Spirit, speaking to the soul. [d. 1/13/1691]

1757 Birth of Laban Ainsworth, American clergyman. A 1778 graduate of Dartmouth College, he was ordained pastor of the church at Jaffrey, NH in 1782. Ainsworth remained at this single pastorate until his death 76 years later, making it the longest-held American pastorate ever recorded. [d. 3/17/1858]

1759 Birth of Seraphim of Sarov, Russian Orthodox "staret" (spiritual teacher), contemplative and mystic. Seraphim was the original and most famous of the "startsi." Emphasizing  the need to be filled with the Holy Spirit, Seraphim revived monasticism among common believers in the Russian Orthodox Church. He was canonized in 1903. [d. 1/2/1833]

The Last Passage

1838 Death of Christmas Evans, 61, Welsh Baptist preacher. Evans grew up with little formal education, but possessed a gift for preaching and a great imagination. He was somewhat erratic 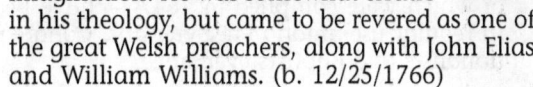 in his theology, but came to be revered as one of the great Welsh preachers, along with John Elias and William Williams. (b. 12/25/1766)

1938 Death of Paul Radar, 58. A former boxer-turned-evangelist, Radar pastored Moody Memorial Church in Chicago, served as president of the Christian and Missionary Alliance, and  pioneered in radio evangelism. (b. 8/24/1879)

2003 Bill Bright, founder of Campus Crusade for Christ, died at 81. He and his wife Vonette founded the student organization in 1951, and incorporated it in Los Angeles. (b. 10/19/1921)

Words for the Soul

1712 French mystical theologian and educator François Fenelon advised in a letter: *'No teaching is effectual without example: no authority is endurable except insofar as it is softened by example. Begin with acting, and let your words come after that. Action speaks and persuades.'*

1854 Writing to his father, young George MacDonald confessed: *'I want to do God's work and be God's servant. Who ever did this fully without more or less failing?'*

1961 Swedish U.N. General Dag Hammarskjöld prayed in his journal, **Markings**: *'Give us a pure heart, That we may see Thee, A humble heart, That we may hear Thee, A heart of Love, That we may serve Thee, A heart of faith, That we may live Thee, Thou, Whom I do not know, but Whose I am.'*

FROM GOD'S WORD... OT: 1 Chronicles 28:1–29:30 ~ NT: Romans 5:6-21 ~ Psalms 15:1-5 ~ Proverbs 19:18-19

ALMANAC OF THE CHRISTIAN FAITH

AV | TAMMUZ

July 20

Highlights in History

1539 Protestant reformer John Calvin arrived in Geneva, Switzerland, eventually developing the city as a flagship of the Reformed Church. William Farel assisted him in the work, and Geneva became a theocracy under Calvin's guidance.

1648 The Westminster Larger Catechism was adopted by the General Assembly of the Church of Scotland at Edinburgh. This document as well as the Westminster Shorter Catechism — both of which were compiled in 1647 — have been in regular use among Presbyterians, Congregationalists and Baptists ever since.

1726 Colonial American Puritan clergyman Jonathan Edwards, 23, married fellow Puritan Sarah Pierpont, age 16. Their marriage prospered through the next 32 years in a joint, active ministry, before his premature death from a smallpox vaccination in 1758. Barely outliving her husband, Sarah died of dysentery only six months later, at age 48.

1773 The first Protestant church west of the Alleghenies was built in 1772 at Schoenbrunn, Ohio by Moravian missionaries.

1956 By Joint Resolution, the Congress of the United States of America adopted the bill by Representative Charles E. Bennett (FL), providing that the official national motto of the United States of America be: 'In God We Trust.'

Notable Birthdays

1591 Anne Hutchinson, English-born American religious controversialist, was baptized. Charged with Antinomianism in 1637, she was banished from Massachusetts. Her family eventually moved to New York, where she and 15 others were murdered by Indians. (Some say Anne believed in a covenant of grace that opposed the Puritan covenant of works.) [d. 8/1643]

1886 Birth of Paul Tillich, German theologian. Ordained into the Lutheran ministry in 1912, he served as a chaplain during World War I. In 1933 his opposition to Hitler forced him to leave Germany, and he settled in the U.S. Tillich afterward taught at Union Seminary and Columbia University in New York, also at Harvard and at the University of Chicago. A prolific writer, *Systematic Theology* (1951-1963) was his best-known work. [d. 10/22/1965]

The Last Passage

1896 Death of Arthur Cleveland Coxe, 82, American Episcopal prelate, poet and hymnographer. He served as Bishop of Western New York (1865-96), and helped in the revision of the American printing of the *Ante-Nicene Fathers*. Coxe also penned the hymn, "O, Where Are Kings and Empires Now?" (b. 5/10/1818)

1922 Death of Belle Harris Bennett, 69, a missions leader and social reformer of the American Southern Methodist Church. She helped found Scarritt College for Christian Workers (now located in Nashville) in 1892. (b. 12/3/1852)

Words for the Soul

1545 Regarding Christian union, German reformer Martin Luther advised in a letter: *'If the heart and soul are one in the Lord, one person will readily bear the lack of uniformity in externals on the part of another. But if the striving of oneness of heart is not there, an external oneness will achieve little.'*

1933 Comparing faith vs. works, Anglican mystic and writer Evelyn Underhill noted in a letter: *'It is natural and right that the soul should desire Him in Himself and also to be used by Him. Both these phases are part of a full spiritual life.'*

1968 American Trappist Thomas Merton confided in a letter: *'We need a real solitude that will empty us out, help strip us of ourselves.... One needs periods of real silence, isolation, lostness, in order to be deeply convinced and aware that God is All.'*

FROM GOD'S WORD... OT: 2 Chronicles 1:1–3:17 ~ NT: Romans 6:1-23 ~ Psalms 16:1-11 ~ Proverbs 19:20-21

July 21

Highlights in History

1773 Pope Clement XIV issued the brief, "Dominus ac redemptor noster," which dissolved the Society of Jesus for the controversies in which they had been involved. The Jesuits had been founded during the Reformation era (1534), with Ignatius of Loyola serving as the society's first general when Pope Paul III approved it in 1540. Famed missionary, St. Francis Xavier, was also one of the original seven. Catholic historians today view this suppression as a moral defeat for the papacy, because it afterward left notable gaps in education and in foreign missions.

1886 The cardinal's hat was conferred upon Elzear Alexandre Taschereau, then archbishop of Quebec. It made him the first Canadian to be made a cardinal in the Catholic Church.

1900 Albert Schweitzer received his licentiate in theology. He later became famous as a musicologist, a physician and a missionary. Although a liberal in thinking, he clung tenaciously to the doctrine of Christ's resurrection.

Notable Birthdays

1515 Birth of St. Philip Neri, Italian religious. An outstanding figure of the Counter Reformation, he was known as the "second apostle of Rome." He founded the Institute of Oratory (1564) and the Confraternity of the Most Holy Trinity (1548) to care for pilgrims and convalescents. [d. 5/26/1595]

1829 Birth of Priscilla Jane Owens, American public school teacher and hymnwriter. She spent here entire life in Baltimore, where she taught for 49 years. A member of the Methodist Episcopal Church, she was active in the work of the Sunday school. Owens also published a number of articles and poems during her lifetime, including the hymn texts, "We Have an Anchor" and "Jesus Saves" (a.k.a. "We Have Heard the Joyful Sound"). [d. 12/5/1907]

1936 Birth of Bill McChesney, American missionary to the Belgian Congo (later Zaire) in Africa, under Worldwide Evangelization Crusade (WEC). While in the field, he was martyred by rebels at age 28. [d. 11/25/1964]

The Last Passage

1773 Death of Howell Harris, 59, Welsh lay evangelist. Called the "Welsh Boanerges," he was converted in 1735 and became a founder of Welsh Calvinistic Methodism. Harris was also the first lay preacher in the movement. (b. 1/14/1714)

1899 Death of Robert G. Ingersoll, 65, American trial lawyer, politician, and orator. Called "the great agnostic," he published influential religious lectures, and was a major advocate of scientific rationalism. (b. 8/11/1833)

1908 Death of Henry C. Potter, 74, American Episcopal prelate and social reformer. The son of Alonzo Potter, Henry served as Bishop of NYC (1887-1908), during which he initiated construction of the Cathedral of St. John the Divine in 1892. (b. 6/25/1834)

1979 Death of William H. F. Brothers, 92, English-born sect leader. He was the founding bishop of the Old Catholic Church in America. (b. 4/7/1887)

Words for the Soul

1843 Scottish clergyman and biographer Andrew Bonar concluded in his diary: *'I see plainly that fellowship with God is not means to an end, but is to be the end itself. I am not to use it as a preparation for study or for Sabbath labour: but as my chiefest end, the likest thing to heaven.'*

1958 English literary scholar and Christian apologist C.S. Lewis cautioned in one of his **Letters to an American Lady**: *'What the devil loves is that vague cloud of unspecified guilt or unspecified virtue by which he lures us into despair or presumption.'*

FROM GOD'S WORD... OT: 2 Chronicles 4:1–6:11 ~ NT: Romans 7:1-13 ~ Psalms 17:1-15 ~ Proverbs 19:22-23

July 22

Highlights in History

1620 A band of Separatist Puritans from England which had taken refuge in the Netherlands, along with its pastor, John Robinson, left Holland for England, to emigrate to America. This congregation became known as the Pilgrims.

1680 French Quietist and mystic Madame Guyon, 32, claimed to have achieved a union with Christ on this date. Her life and writings were marked by a fervent devotion to Jesus, but the publication of her spiritual experiences ultimately led to her arrest and imprisonment by the Catholic Church. Her mysticism nevertheless inspired Archbishop François Fenelon (1651-1715) to seek a deeper spirituality.

1972 A revised high holy days prayer book for Conservative Judaism was published in the United States. It sought to strike a balance between Orthodoxy's strict interpretation of Biblical themes and the liberal views of worship of Reformed Judaism.

Notable Birthdays

1647 Birth of St. Margaret Mary [Marguerite Marie] Alacoque, French Vistantine nun and mystic. She founded the modern practice of devotion to the Sacred Heart of Jesus, and was canonized in 1930. [d. 10/17/1690]

1822 Birth of Gregor J. Mendel, Augustinian monk, abbot and botanist. During the early 1860s he discovered the basic laws of biological inheritance through breeding experiments he conducted with peas in his monastery garden. But Mendel's work was ignored and almost forgotten before it was rediscovered by Dutch botanist Hugo M. DeVries in 1900. [d. 1/6/1884]

1849 Birth of Emma Lazarus, American Jewish poet and essayist. In 1883, at age 34, she authored the poem, "The New Colossus," which today is inscribed on the base of the Statue of Liberty. Emma died at age 38, after 4 years of declining health and intermittent depression. [d. 11/19/1887]

1865 Birth of Peter P. Bilhorn, American sacred composer. His father died in the American Civil War three months before his birth. Converted at age 18, Bilhorn began composing spiritual songs and eventually became a well-known publisher of sacred music. He produced more than 1,400 Gospel songs and is remembered today for composing "I Will Sing the Wondrous Story" and as author and composer of the hymn, "Sweet Peace, the Gift of God's Love." [d. 12/13/1936]

The Last Passage

1581 Death of Richard Cox, ca. 80, Bishop of Ely (1559-80). He was an active promoter of the Reformation in England, and helped compile the first English *Book of Common Prayer*. (b. ca. 1500)

1704 Death of Peregrine White, 83, the first white (male) child born in America. He was born on the "Mayflower" while it was anchored in Cape Cod Harbor. (b. 11/20/1620)

Words for the Soul

1746 Colonial American missionary to the Indians, David Brainerd wrote in his journal: *'I wanted to wear out life, and have it at an end; but had some desires of living to God, and wearing out life for him. Oh that I could indeed do so!'* (Brainerd achieved exactly that for which he prayed, for he died of tuberculosis, worsened by constant outdoor exposure, only 15 months later, on October 9, 1747.)

1772 Founder of Methodism John Wesley stated in a letter: *'It is easy to see the difference between those two things, sinfulness and helplessness. The former you need feel no more; the latter you will feel as long as you live. And indeed the nearer you draw to God, the more sensible of it you will be.'*

ALMANAC OF THE CHRISTIAN FAITH

July 23

Highlights in History

685 John V was consecrated as pope, serving until 686. Born a Syrian, he was the first of several pontiffs of Eastern origin.

1825 Kidnapped earlier by Muslim slave-traders from his Yoruba homeland in north-central Africa, Samuel Adjai Crowther, 17, was rescued by English missionaries and baptized into the church on this day. In 1864 Crowther was consecrated missionary bishop of the Niger Territory. He became an ardent opponent of slavery, human sacrifice, infanticide and other primitive African customs. He died in 1891.

Notable Birthdays

1823 Birth of Coventry Patmore, English Catholic poet and essayist. His best-remembered poetry, containing a mystical view of divine and married love is in *The Unknown Eros and Other Odes* (1877). [d. 11/26/1896]

1834 Birth of American Catholic prelate James Gibbons. He was archbishop of Baltimore from 1877-1921, and also founder and first chancellor of the Catholic University of America in Washington, D.C. (1877). [d. 3/24/1921]

The Last Passage

1373 Founder of the Brigittines (Order of our Saviour), and mother of St. Catherine of Sweden, St. Bridget of Sweden died at 70. A mystic, she published *Revelations*, a book of visions. (b. 1303)

1742 Death of Susannah Wesley, 73, a parson's daughter and a parson's wife. She was the youngest of 25 children, and the mother of 18. Her own children included John and Charles Wesley. Overcoming poverty and ill health, Susannah instilled a discipline in her family which no doubt influenced the later systematic character of English Methodism. (b. 1/20/1669)

1764 Death of Gilbert Tennent, 61, American Presbyterian clergyman and revivalist. Ordained in 1726, Tennent became chief spokesman for the Great Awakening, and pastored the Second Presbyterian Church of Philadelphia, composed largely of converts and followers of George Whitefield. (b. 2/5/1703)

1918 Death of Joseph Henry Gilmore, 84, American Baptist clergyman and scholar. Ordained in 1862, Gilmore is remembered today for a hymn he wrote when he was 28: "He Leadeth Me." (b. 4/29/1834)

1929 Death of Leila Naylor Morris, 67, American Methodist camp meeting hymnwriter who penned over 1,000 gospel melodies, including: "Near, Still Nearer" (& MORRIS); "Jesus is Coming to Earth Again" (& SECOND COMING). When her eyes began to fail in 1913, her son built a 28-foot blackboard with over-sized staff lines, so she could continue composing. (b. 4/15/1862)

Words for the Soul

1773 English founder of Methodism John Wesley advised in a letter: *'When you perceive nothing, it does not follow that the work of God stands still in your soul; especially while your desire is unto Him.... He does not leave you to yourself, though it may seem so to your apprehension.'*

1779 American Methodist circuit rider Francis Asbury recorded in his journal: *'Arose, as I commonly do, before five o'clock in the morning, to study the Bible. I find none like it; and find it of more consequence to a preacher to know his Bible well, than all the languages or books in the world.'*

1963 American Trappist monk Thomas Merton confided in a letter: *'I do not think that the American monasteries... have got out of this national obsession with productivity. It is one of the great delusions ... that wrecks monastic vocations, much more than the love of the pleasures of the world.'*

FROM GOD'S WORD...   OT: 2 Chronicles 8:11–10:19 ~ NT: Romans 8:9-21 ~ Psalms 18:16-36 ~ Proverbs 19:26

July 24

Highlights in History

1216 Cardinal Cencio Savelli was consecrated Pope Honorius III, and served until 1227. During his pontificate, he confirmed two well-known religious orders: the Dominicans (1216) and the Franciscans (1223). Personally gracious, Honorius died greatly beloved and respected.

1847 Having fled persecution in Nauvoo, Illinois, through violent clashes over polygamy, a band of Mormons (143 men, 3 women and 2 children) led by Brigham Young, 46, first reached the Great Salt Lake, in Utah.

1918 The cornerstone of Hebrew University was laid on Mt. Scopus in Jerusalem by Dr. Chaim Weizmann. (Construction of the campus was completed in 1925.)

Notable Birthdays

1725 Birth of John Newton, Anglican clergyman and hymnwriter. He was a slave shipmaster for 10 years, before his conversion in 1747. He later studied for Anglican ordination, and was appointed curate at Olney in 1764. There he became an intimate friend of poet William Cowper, and together they published *Olney Hymns* (1779), including such verses by Newton as: "Amazing Grace," "Glorious Things of Thee Are Spoken," and "How Sweet the Name of Jesus Sounds." [d. 12/21/1807]

1819 Birth of Josiah G. Holland, American novelist and hymnwriter. After a brief career in medicine, Holland became a newspaper editor, and later helped establish "Scribner's Magazine." Today Holland is remembered as author of the Christmas hymn, "There's a Song in the Air." [d. 10/12/1881]

1874 Birth of Oswald Chambers, Scottish Baptist evangelist and Bible teacher. Converted in his youth under Charles Spurgeon, Chambers studied art and archaeology before answering a call to the Christian ministry. He spent the last of his brief 42 years as chaplain to British troops stationed in Egypt, where he died of a ruptured appendix. His classic, *My Utmost for His Highest*, first published in 1923, has been in print ever since. [d. 11/15/1917]

The Last Passage

1921 Death of C[yrus] I. Scofield, American lawyer, clergyman and biblical lecturer. Converted at 36, Scofield was ordained into the Congregational ministry in 1882, and served the Moody Church in Northfield, MA. He also founded the Central American Mission in 1890. Theologically, Scofield held there were seven dispensations in Scripture – seven variants of God's relationship to humanity. His most popular and enduring publication was his *Scofield Reference Bible* (1909). (b. 8/19/1843)

1999 Death of Andrew Melendez, 96, Spanish-American Christian radio broadcaster. A native of Puerto Rico, he was associated with the LCMS Lutheran Church. For 31 years (1941-72) Melendez's voice brought the Gospel to the Spanish speaking world through "The Spanish Lutheran Hour." [b. 1903]

Words for the Soul

1766 Anglican clergyman and hymnwriter John Newton confessed in a letter: *'In our bright and lively frames, we learn what God can do for us; in our dark and dull hours, we feel how little we can do without him; and both are needful to perfect our experience and to establish our faith.'*

1960 French missionary/scholar Albert Schweitzer, 85, confided in a letter: *'I have resigned myself to the fact that once a heavy job is done, another equally heavy and equally urgent job pops up, and so on, in my life in Lambarene until my earthly pilgrimage reaches its end.'* [NB: Schweitzer died five years later, on 9/4/65.]

July 25

Highlights in History

325 The two-month-long Council of Nicea adjourned. The first of the ecumenical councils, Nicea was called by Roman Emperor Constantine, who sought to establish peace and unity in the Church and in the Empire.

1261 Byzantine emperor Michael VIII Palaeologus recovered Constantinople and overthrew the Latin Empire, which had been established by the Crusaders in 1204.

1968 Pope Paul VI published "Humanae Vitae," an encyclical condemning all forms of birth control except the "rhythm method." A widespread controversy followed its publication.

Notable Birthdays

1785 Birth of American missionary Samuel Newell. He was among the first five missionaries (along with Adoniram Judson, Gordon Hall, Samuel Nott, and Luther Rice) ordained by the American Board of Commissioners for Foreign Missions, on Feb. 6, 1812., Newell first sailed to India soon after. [d. 3/30/1821]

1825 Birth of Henry Blodget, American Congregational missionary to China, 1854-94. During his 40 years in the field he helped translate the New Testament into the colloquial Mandarin of Peking. [d. 5/23/1903]

1834 Birth of Frederick W. Grant, English-born sect leader. He was founder of one of the larger of the American branches of the Plymouth Brethren. Grant died on his 68th birthday. [d. 7/25/1902]

1848 Birth of Arthur J. Balfour, British statesman and philosopher. He was Britain's prime minister from 1902 to 1905, and later served as foreign secretary. He issued the Balfour Declaration in 1917, which favored the creation of *"a national home for the Jewish people"* in Palestine. [d. 3/19/1930]

1899 Birth of Stuart Wesley K. Hine, English Christian Brethren missionary to Poland and Czechoslovakia. In 1923, while among the people of Ukraine, he and his wife were introduced to a Russian version of the Swedish hymn, "O Store Gud." Later, while crossing the Carpathian Mountains into southern Russia, the surrounding beauty inspired them to write an English version to the song, which they afterward titled, "How Great Thou Art." [d. 1989]

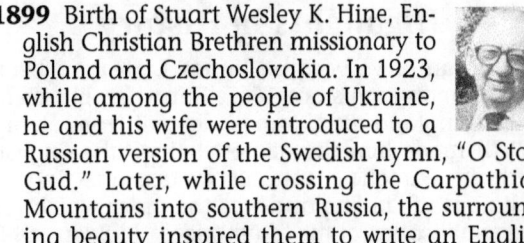

The Last Passage

1471 Death of Thomas à Kempis, about 91, German theologian, mystic, ascetical writer, and probable author of *The Imitation of Christ*, (ca. 1427). (b. ca. 1380)

1918 Death of Walter Rauschenbusch, 56, American Baptist clergyman and educator. As a pastor and later a seminary professor, Rauschenbusch held a lifelong interest in the social implications of the Gospel, and encouraged economic and political programs as ways of realizing God's Kingdom on earth. (b. 10/4/1861)

Words for the Soul

1741 English revivalist George Whitefield gave assurance in a letter: *'Your extremity shall be God's opportunity.'*

1767 Methodism founder John Wesley explained in a letter: *'The essential part of Christian holiness is giving the heart wholly to God.... Nevertheless, you will still be encompassed with numberless infirmities; for you live in a house of clay.'*

1996 Dutch priest and diarist Henry J. M. Nouwen inscribed in his last year's journal: *'When we make the effect of our work the criterion of our sense of self, we end up very vulnerable.... The final issue is not the result of our work but the obedience to God's will, as long as we realize that God's will is the expression of God's love.'*

FROM GOD'S WORD...   OT: 2 Chronicles 14:1–16:14 ~ NT: Romans 9:1-21 ~ Psalms 19:1-14 ~ Proverbs 20:1

ALMANAC OF THE CHRISTIAN FAITH

AV — TAMMUZ

July 26

Highlights in History

1603 James VI became James I. He had been Scotland's king since 1567. But when Elizabeth I of England died, James' descent from Henry VIII made him the nearest heir to the English throne. Among his numerous acts affecting religious life in England was the order which led to publication of the "Authorized" Bible in 1611.

1804 Russian hieromonk Manuel Gedeon began preaching among the Kodiak of Alaska. Father Gedeon translated the Lord's Prayer into the local Eskimo language, which afterward led them to become Russian Orthodox Christians.

1865 The constitution of Chile went into effect. It provided for freedom of worship for non-Catholic religions and permitted them to establish private schools.

1869 In Great Britain, the Disestablishment Bill was given royal assent, thereby dissolving the (Anglican) Church of Ireland. Founded as a missionary church by St. Patrick in the fourth century, the Irish Church early on exhibited an independence from Rome, growing more dependent on the English state. However, Irish Anglicanism in the early 19th century underwent a general spiritual decline, and became the faith of the well-to-do English landowners, not that of the common people. From this legislation we get the term "antidisestablishmentarianism," which was the organized opposition to the Disestablishment Bill.

1926 In Lackawanna, NY, the Sanctuary of Our Lady of Victory Church was dedicated as the first Roman Catholic basilica in the U.S.

Notable Birthdays

1030 Birth of St. Stanislaw (or Stanislaus), Bishop of Cracow (1071-79), and patron saint of Poland. He was murdered while celebrating mass by King Boleslaw II, for his denunciation of Boleslaw's excesses. Stanislaw later became the first Pole to be canonized. [d. 1079]

1856 Birth of William Rainey Harper, 50, American Baptist Hebrew scholar and educator. He taught Semitic languages at Baptist Union Theological Seminary, Chicago (1879-86), and at Yale (1886-91), before becoming founding president of the University of Chicago (1891-1906). Harper also wrote *Religion and the Higher Life* (1904), and published the ICC commentaries on Amos and Hosea (1905). [d. 1/10/1906]

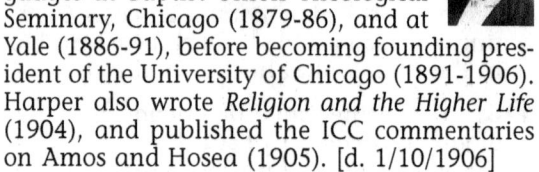

The Last Passage

1925 Death of William Jennings Bryan, American Presbyterian politician, orator, lawyer and three-time presidential candidate. Noted for his Christian fundamentalism, he served as prosecuting attorney in the famous 1925 Scopes Monkey Trial. Bryan was publicly ridiculed for his stance at the trial, however, and in spite of winning the judgment, died five days after the proceedings ended. (b. 3/19/1860)

1933 Death of Charles A. Tindley, 82, African-American clergyman and hymnwriter. Born of slave parents and orphaned at age 5, Tindley taught himself to read and write by age 17. He studied theology and in 1885 was ordained to the Methodist ministry. As a writer of Gospel songs, his most moving hymns include: "By and By," "Leave It There," "Nothing Between" and "Stand by Me." (b. 7/7/1851)

Words for the Soul

1700 French mystical writer François Fénelon encouraged noted in a letter: *'What you are now feeling is but the beginning. The most vivid and excited feelings are not the purest or deepest; but the keenness of newborn love sows the first seeds within the heart.'*

1774 Methodism founder John Wesley succinctly exhorted in a letter: *'Be zealous and humble, but never be still!'*

FROM GOD'S WORD... OT: 2 Chronicles 17:1–18:34 ~ NT: Romans 9:22–10:13 ~ Psalms 20:1-9 ~ Proverbs 20:2-3

July 27

Highlights in History

1516 Future reformer Martin Luther preached for the first time against indulgences. (It was Luther's posting of his "95 Theses" against indulgences and other church abuses in October 1517 which ultimately precipitated the Protestant Reformation.)

1649 An Act for Promoting and Propagating the Gospel in New England was ordered by England's House of Commons. It had been inspired by the mission work of John Eliot among the American Indians.

1681 During a bitter battle between Scottish Episcopalians and Presbyterians, five Scottish Presbyterian preachers (among them Donald Cargill) were martyred in Edinburgh. The Church of Scotland became Presbyterian permanently in 1690.

Notable Birthdays

1741 Birth of Francois H. Barthélémon, violinist and hymn composer. A member of the Swedenborgian church, he wrote five operas, six symphonies and one oratorio, as well as numerous concertos and violin sonatas. Ill health plagued him during his last years, and he died a paralytic. Two of his compositions, however, have since become hymn tunes: AUTUMN ("Hail, Thou Once Despised Jesus") and BALERMA ("Oh, for a Closer Walk with God"). [d. 7/23/1808]

1861 Birth of Cyrus S. Nusbaum, American Methodist clergyman. Ordained in 1886, he served six pastorates in Kansas, was appointed by President Woodrow Wilson to inspect the American Red Cross in France during World War I, and traveled through the Midwest as a conference evangelist. He wrote and composed several hymns, including "Would You Live for Jesus, and Be Always Pure and Good?" (a.k.a. "His Way with Thee"). [d. 12/27/1937]

1946 Sally Jane Priesand, the first American female (Reform Jewish) rabbi, was born in Cleveland, Ohio. Ordained in Cincinnati in 1972, following her graduation from Hebrew Union College, Rabbi Priesand later published *Judaism and The New Woman* (1975).

The Last Passage

1901 Death of B[rooke] F. Westcott, 76, English prelate and textual scholar. Ordained in 1851, Westcott became Regius Professor of Divinity at Cambridge in 1870. He was appointed Bishop of Durham in 1890, succeeding J. B. Lightfoot, and remained at this post until his death. In 1881 Westcott, along with his colleague F. J. A. Hort, published his most memorable work, a critical edition of the Greek New Testament — a work which has been foundational to almost all subsequent research in New Testament textual studies. (b. 1/12/1825)

1903 Death of Carolina ("Lina") V. Sandell Berg, 70, Swedish hymnwriter. She lost her father at sea when she was 26, and afterward wrote some of her most beautiful verse. Two of her hymns in English translation are "Day by Day, and With Each Passing Moment" and "Children of the Heavenly Father." (b. 10/3/1832)

Words for the Soul

1940 Russian Orthodox monk Father John [born Ivan Alekseyevich Alekseyev] advised in a letter: *'If we do not die today, we shall tomorrow, and there we face eternal life, and time stands still.'*

1950 French scholar and missionary physician Albert Schweitzer explained in a letter to the mother superior of a community of French nuns: *'St. Francis of Assisi made a deep impact on me.... When I came to formulate the idea of reverence for life as the fundamental idea of ethics, I felt I was enunciating ... something intrinsic to St. Francis but in a new revelation of his thinking.'*

FROM GOD'S WORD... OT: 2 Chronicles 19:1–20:37 ~ NT: Romans 10:14–11:12 ~ Psalms 21:1-13 ~ Proverbs 20:4-6

July 28

Highlights in History

1648 The Westminster Shorter Catechism was adopted by the General Assembly of the Church of Scotland at Edinburgh. This document, as well as the Westminster Larger Catechism — both compiled in the autumn of 1647 — have been in regular use among Presbyterians, Congregationalists and Baptists ever since.

1847 The Mormon community that followed Brigham Young across the American plains chose the site for their future temple on the Great Salt Lake in Utah. There the Mormon Tabernacle was constructed from 1853 to 1893.

1889 The first Divine Liturgy (worship service) of the Armenian Church in America was celebrated in Worcester, MA, by Rev. Hovsep Sarajian. Recently arrived from Constantinople, Sarajian was the first Armenian clergyman to come to America.

Notable Birthdays

1764 Birth of Samuel Marsden, Anglican chaplain to the convict colony of New South Wales. He also ministered to the Maoris of New Zealand for the Church of England. As "apostle to the Maoris," he made seven voyages in the course of his mission work. [d. 5/12/1838]

1881 Birth of J[ohn] Gresham Machen, American theologian and church reformer. Suspended from his Presbyterian ordination (1935) for attacking liberalism, Machen afterward co-founded the Orthodox Presbyterian Church (1936). Considered "Fundamentalism's most gifted theologian," Machen's *Christianity and Liberalism* (1923) is a severe critique of liberalism's solution to the relationship between Christianity and culture. Two of his other well-known writings are *New Testament Greek for Beginners* (1923) and *The Virgin Birth of Christ* (1930-1932) — both still in print. [d. 1/1/1937]

The Last Passage

1750 Death of Johann Sebastian Bach, 65, German composer and a master of keyboard compositions. Though largely unrecognized in his day and forgotten for years after his death, he is now considered one of history's unequaled musical masters. Nearly three-fourths of his 1000 compositions were written for use in worship. Between his musical genius, his devotion to Christ, and the affect of his music, Bach has come to be known in some circles as the "Fifth Evangelist." (b. 3/21/1685)

1942 Death of English Egyptologist Sir W[illiam] M. Flinders Petrie, 89. Ill health prevented his receiving a formal education, but his interest in archaeology as a boy spurred him to become the greatest archaeological genius of his generation. Petrie headed the British School of Archaeology in Egypt, directed its excavations between 1880 and 1937, and published over 100 books. (b. 6/3/1853)

Words for the Soul

1775 English founder of Methodism John Wesley exhorted in a letter: 'We have only to live today! God will take care of tomorrow.'

1960 American Trappist monk Thomas Merton confessed in a letter: 'I can depend less and less on my own power and sense of direction – as if I ever had any. But the Lord supports and guides me without my knowing how, more and more apart from my own action and even in contradiction to it. It is so strange to advance backwards and get to where you are going in a totally unexpected way.'

1974 Dutch Catholic priest and educator Henri J. M. Nouwen reflected in his **Genesee Diary**: 'In meditation we can come to the affirmation that we are not created by other people but by God, that we are not judged by how we compare with others but how we fulfill the will of God.'

FROM GOD'S WORD... OT: 2 Chronicles 21:1–23:21 ~ NT: Romans 11:13–36 ~ Psalms 22:1-18 ~ Proverbs 20:7

July 29

Highlights in History

1775 The Continental Army chaplaincy was established by the Continental Congress, thereby becoming the second oldest branch of that service in America, after the infantry.

1968 Pope Paul VI issued an encyclical on the birth control question, "Humanae vitae," which reasserted the church's prohibition against all artificial means of birth control.

1974 In Philadelphia, eleven woman were ordained Episcopal priests in the Church of the Advocate. The ordination was later ruled invalid by the House of Bishops, but on Oct. 17, the House approved in principle the ordination of women as priests. (The ordinations of the 11 women were finally approved Sept. 16, 1976.)

Notable Birthdays

1866 Birth of T[homas] O. Chisholm, American hymnwriter. He pursued careers as a grade school teacher, a newspaper editor, a farmer, a Methodist pastor and a life insurance salesman. But Chisholm also wrote more than 1,200 poems, several of which later became hymn texts, including "Great Is Thy Faithfulness" and "Living for Jesus." [d. 2/29/1960]

1905 Birth of Dag Hammarskjöld, Swedish statesman and Christian diarist. He served as Secretary-General of the U.N. from 1953-61, but especially endeared himself to Christians when his spiritual journal, *Markings*, was published in 1964, three years after his untimely death in a plane crash. [d. 9/18/1961]

1912 Birth of Clarence Jordan, founder of Koinonia Farm in Americus, GA. He published his *Cotton Patch Version* of the New Testament in four volumes (1968-1973), each of which paraphrased the New Testament in the Southern vernacular and setting. [d. 10/29/1969]

The Last Passage

1030 Death of Olaf II, Haraldsson, 35, king (1016-28) and patron saint of Norway. In 1022 he drew up Norway's first-ever set of church laws. Rivals forced him to flee in 1028, and he later died in the Battle of Stiklestad. As his legend grew, in time Olaf became one of the most well-known saints of medieval Christendom. (b. 995)

1644 Pope Urban VIII died at 76. He opened China and Japan to all religious orders and canonized Ignatius Loyola and Francis Xavier. Unfortunately, also under Urban, Italian astronomer Galileo was condemned (1633). (b. 4/5/1568)

1833 Death of William Wilberforce, 73, English humanitarian and abolitionist. As a leader of the "Clapham Sect" (a fellowship of evangelical Anglicans), Wilberforce was instrumental in having a bill against importation of slaves into British territory passed in 1807. He died a mere three days after England finally abolished slavery altogether. (b. 8/24/1759)

1919 Death of Frank E. Graeff, 58, American Methodist clergyman and hymnwriter. He authored over 200 hymns, including "Does Jesus Care?" (b. 12/19/1860)

Words for the Soul

1777 English founder of Methodism John Wesley explained in a letter: 'Rapturous joy, such as is frequently given in the beginning of justification, or of entire sanctification, is a great blessing; but it seldom continues long before it subsides into calm, peaceful love.'

1908 Regarding faith and works, Anglican mystic Evelyn Underhill wrote in a letter: 'The Church has always, of course, held up as the Christian ideal a mixture of the active and contemplative life — the one lit up by the other. Our Lord's human life was just that, wasn't it? Social intercourse regulated by nights spent in the mountain in prayer.'

FROM GOD'S WORD... OT: 2 Chronicles 24:1–25:28 ~ NT: Romans 12:1-21 ~ Psalms 22:19-31 ~ Proverbs 20:8-10

July 30

Highlights in History

1629 One month after arriving in America from England, the Puritan settlers of Salem, MA appointed Francis Higginson as their teacher and Samuel Skelton as pastor. The church covenant composed by the pair established in Salem the first non-separating Congregational Puritan church in New England.

1822 African-American clergyman James Varick was consecrated the first bishop of the African Methodist Episcopal Zion Church.

1956 President Eisenhower signed an act, passed by Congress, that made "In God We Trust" the official motto of the United States.

Notable Birthdays

1726 Birth of William Jones of Nayland, Anglican divine. Ordained in 1749, Jones sought to keep alive high church tradition among Anglicans who otherwise rejected the Oxford Movement.  In 1756 he published *The Catholic Doctrine of the Trinity*, in which he sought to prove from Scripture that the church's belief in the Trinity is not mere tradition. [d. 1/6/1800]

1890 Birth of Émile Mersch, Belgian Jesuit theologian. Fleeing Belgium during the Nazi invasion, he was killed in an air-raid attack in France while caring for the wounded. Mersch's writings helped articulate what came to be known as communion ecclesiology. [d. 5/23/1940]

The Last Passage

1718 Death of William Penn, 73, English Quaker statesman and colonizer. He was an advocate of religious toleration, and his *Frame of Government* for the American colony  of Pennsylvania (1682) was ultimately based on religious and political freedom. Penn's best-known writing was the ethically challenging *No Cross, No Crown* (1669). (b. 10/14/1644)

1286 Gregorius Bar-Hebraeus (Abú al-Faraj), Syrian scholar and primate of the Jacobite Church (1264-86), died at 60. (Jacobites were a Syrian Christian sect.) (b. 1226)

1898 Death of John Caird, 77, Church of Scotland clergyman, Hegelian theologian and educator. He was theology professor and principal of Glasgow University for 61 years (1837-98), and authored *An Introduction to the Philosophy of Religion*. (b. 12/15/1820)

1976 Death of Rudolf Bultmann, 91, German Lutheran theologian and biblical scholar. Associated primarily with the University of Marburg, his *History of the Synoptic Tradition* (1920)  was a pioneer study in modern form criticism. Bultmann also published *Kerygma and Myth* (1941), which stressed the need to "demythologize" (i.e., rework) obsolete metaphors in the New Testament, so that the central message of the Gospel (the *kerygma*) might be made more meaningful to modern readers. (b. 8/20/1884)

Words for the Soul

1701 To an over-scrupulous believer, French mystical theologian François Fénelon admonished in a letter: 'You deprive yourself of consolation of which God would not deprive you; and it is as wrong to take away what He does not take away, as to appropriate what He denies.'

1767 Anglican clergyman and hymnwriter John Newton affirmed in a letter: 'The Christian calling, like many others, is easy and clear in theory, but not without much care and difficulty to be reduced to practice. Things appear quite otherwise, when felt [through experience], to what they do when only read in a book.'

1946 French scholar and missionary physician Albert Schweitzer revealed in a letter: 'Bach is a spiritual educator through the spirit of the religious texts that he so movingly set to music.... Wherever his music has an impact on people, it influences them spiritually.'

FROM GOD'S WORD... OT: 2 Chronicles 26:1–28:27 ~ NT: Romans 13:1-14 ~ Psalms 23:1-6 ~ Proverbs 20:11

July 31

Highlights in History

1874 Patrick Francis Healy, S.J., was inaugurated president of Georgetown University, the oldest Catholic university in America. It made Healy the first African-American in U.S. history to head a predominantly white university.

1970 The complete *New American Standard Version* of the Bible was published. (The NASB New Testament had first appeared in 1963.)

Notable Birthdays

1892 Birth of Herbert W. Armstrong, American sectarian evangelist. The father of Garner Ted, Herbert founded the Worldwide Church of God in 1947, and hosted the radio show, "The World Tomorrow." [d. 1/16/1986]

The Last Passage

1556 Death of Ignatius Loyola, 64, Spanish reformer, mystic, founder of the Society of Jesus (Jesuits), and its first general (1541). His major contributions were the reform of the church through education, more frequent use of the sacraments, and preaching of the Gospel to the newly-discovered pagan world. He was canonized in 1622. (b. 12/24/1491)

1847 Death of Orange Scott, 47, American clergyman and ardent abolitionist. After withdrawing from his 21-year-long Methodist affiliation in 1842, Scott became a co-founder of the Wesleyan Methodist Church, a connection of antislavery churches from Maine to Michigan. (b. 2/13/1800)

1871 Death of Phoebe Cary, 46, American Universalist author, poet and hymnwriter. She collaborated with her sister Alice on numerous volumes of verse. One poem, which became a hymn, begins: "One Sweetly Solemn Thought" (a.k.a. "Nearer Home"). (b. 9/4/1824)

1886 Death of Franz Liszt, 74, Hungarian piano virtuoso and composer. Regarded by some as "perhaps the greatest pianist of all time," he advanced the methods of piano composition. Liszt's interest in religious music is not often noted, but he composed three large-scale settings of the Mass, two oratorios and a variety of other sacred works. In 1865 he joined the Franciscans. (b. 10/22/1811)

1889 Death of Horatius Bonar, Scottish Free Church clergyman hymnist and influential scholar. In theology Bonar was conservative and premillenarian. He authored numerous books, but is today remembered chiefly as a hymnwriter. (James Moffatt called him "the prince of Scottish hymnwriters.") Of the more than 600 hymns Bonar penned, 100 are still in use, including "Here, O My Lord, I See Thee Face to Face." (b. 12/19/1808)

1908 Death of Winfield Scott Weeden, 61, American sacred chorister. Weeden taught singing schools, spoke at Christian Endeavor and Epworth conventions and all the while composed numerous gospel songs. Today he is remembered for one hymn tune in particular: SURRENDER ("I Surrender All"). (b. 3/29/1847)

Words for the Soul

1773 Anglican hymnwriter John Newton declared in a letter: *'Duty is our part; the care is His.'*

1775 While recovering from an illness, John Wesley testified in a letter: *'My strength is gradually increasing.... I am now nearly as I was before my illness... more determined to sell all for the pearl.'*

1782 Anglican Evangelical Henry Venn entreated in a letter to his daughter: *'It is surely one of our sweetest pleasures, to copy the manner of those we love.... Keep your eye, therefore, my dear Catherine, fixed upon the Lord Jesus; and pray to Him that He would be your Counsellor, your Guide, and your most familiar Friend.'*

FROM GOD'S WORD... OT: 2 Chronicles 29:1-36 ~ NT: Romans 14:1-23 ~ Psalms 24:1-10 ~ Proverbs 20:12

JULY INDEX

A

Abolition (of Slavery) 7/1, 7/31
Abú al-Faraj. See Gregorius Bar-Hebraeus
Ackley, Alfred H.
  (b. 1/21/1887) d. 7/3/1960
Adams, John. See also PRESIDENTS, U.S. 7/13
Adams, John Quincy. See also Presidents, U.S.
  b. 7/11/1767 [d. 2/23/1848]
AFRICAN-AMERICANS
  Dorsey, Thomas A. 7/1
  Haynes, Lemuel 7/18
  Healey, Patrick Francis 7/31
  Jackson, Mahalia 7/1
  Tindley, Charles A. 7/7, 7/26
  Varick, James 7/30
Ainsworth, Laban
  b. 7/19/1757 [d. 3/17/1858] 7/19
Aitken, Robert
  (b. 1734) d. 7/5/1802
Alacoque, Margaret Mary [Marguerite Marie]
  b. 7/22/1647 [d. 10/17/1690]
Alekseyev, Ivan Alekseyevich. See Father John, Russian Orthodox Monk
American Board of Commissioners 7/4
American Board of Commissioners for Foreign Missions 7/25
American Red Cross 7/27
American Unitarian Association 7/3
American Woman Suffrage Association 7/2
Andrew of Crete
  (b. ca. 660) d. 7/4/740
Anne, St. 7/2
Antidisestablishmentarianism 7/26
Armstrong, Herbert W.
  b. 7/31/1892 [d. 1/16/1986]
Armstrong, Ted 7/31
Asbury, Francis 7/14
Athenagoras I, Patriarch (1948-1972) 7/16
  (b. 3/25/1886) d. 7/7/1972

Auca Indians 7/10, 7/11
Austin, Ann 7/11

B

Bach, Johann Sebastian
  (b. 3/21/1685) d. 7/28/1750
Badin, Stephen T.
  b. 7/17/1768 [d. 4/19/1853]
Balfour, Arthur J.
  b. 7/25/1848 [d. 3/19/1930] 7/25
Balfour Declaration (1917) 7/25
Barsimon, Jacob 7/8
Barth, Karl 7/10
Barthélémon, Francois H.
  b. 7/27/1741 [d. 7/23/1808]
Batchelor, George
  b. 7/3/1836 [d. 1923]
BATTLES
  Battle of Kappel (1531) 7/18
  Battle of Stiklestad (1030) 7/29
Bennett, Belle Harris
  (b. 12/3/1852) d. 7/20/1922 7/20
Bennett, Charles E. 7/20
Bentley, Richard
  (b. 1/27/1662) d. 7/14/1742
Berg, Carolina ("Lina") V. Sandell
  (b. 10/3/1832) d. 7/27/1903
Berg, Fredrick 7/3
Bernardina Teresa Xavier of St. Joseph, Sister. See Mathews, Ann Teresa
Beza, Theodore 7/18
BIBLE COLLEGES. See SEMINARIES / BIBLE COLLEGES
BIBLE VERSIONS
  "Authorized" Bible (1611) 7/26
  Latin (Vulgate) 7/12
  Mandarin of Peking (19th century) 7/25
  New American Standard Bible (1963, 1970) 7/2, 7/31
  New International Version 7/2
  The Holy Bible (1922-26) (Moffatt's) 7/4
Bilhorn, Peter P.
  b. 7/22/1865 [d. 12/13/1936]
Birth Control. See Paul VI, Pope
Bliss, Philip P.
  b. 7/9/1838 [d. 12/29/1876]

Blodget, Henry
  b. 7/25/1825 [d. 5/23/1903]
Boardman, George Dana 7/4
Boardman, Sarah Hall 7/4
Boleslaw II, Polish King (1076-1079) 7/26
Boleyn, Anne 7/11
Bonaparte, Napoleon 7/15
Bonar, Andrew. See QUOTATIONS
Bonar, Horatius
  (b. 12/19/1808) d. 7/31/1889
Bonaventura, Giovanni di Fidanza
  (b. 1217) d. 7/15/1274 7/15
Boniface VIII, Pope (1294-1303) 7/5
BOOKS / PUBLICATIONS
  Ante-Nicene Fathers (1885) 7/20
  An Introduction to the Philosophy of Religion 7/30
  Applied Christianity (1886) 7/2
  Baker's Dictionary of Theology 7/2
  Book of Common Prayer 7/22
  Book of Common Prayer (1549) 7/2
  Christianity and Liberalism (1923) 7/28
  Christian Psalmist (1841) 7/11
  Christ and Culture (1951) 7/5
  Commentary on the Holy Scriptures 7/8
  Compendium of Christian Theology (1875-76) 7/5
  Cotton Patch Version (of the New Testament) (1968-73) 7/29
  Frame of Government (1682) 7/30
  Genesee Diary (1976) 7/13, 7/15, 7/18, 7/28
  God Hidden and Revealed (1953) 7/11
  Greek New Testament (1516) 7/12
  History of the Synoptic Tradition (1920) 7/30
  ICC Commentary: Amos and Hosea (1905) 7/26
  In Praise of Folly (1509) 7/12
  Judaism 7/27
  Kerygma and Myth (1941) 7/30
  Letters to an American Lady (1967) 7/7, 7/21
  Life Among the Lowly 7/1
  Markings (1964) 7/19, 7/29
  Martin Luther's "95 Theses" 7/27

  My Utmost for His Highest (1923) 7/24
  New Testament Greek for Beginners (1923) 7/28
  No Cross, No Crown (1669) 7/30
  Olney Hymns (1779) 7/24
  Protestant Christianity Interpreted through Its Development (1954) 7/11
  Protestant Thought and Natural Science (1960) 7/11
  Religion and the Higher Life (1904) 7/26
  Revelations (14th century) 7/23
  Scofield Reference Bible (1909) 7/24
  Systematic Theology (1951-1963) 7/20
  Table Talk, Martin Luther's 7/12
  Theological Dictionary of the New Testament (TDNT) 7/11
  Theologische-homiletisches Bibelwerk 7/8
  Theologisches Wörterbuch zum Neuen Testament (TWNT, 1933-79) 7/11
  The Catholic Doctrine of the Trinity (1756) 7/30
  The Imitation of Christ, (ca. 1427) 7/25
  The Longest Way Around (1951) 7/13
  The New Woman (1975) 7/27
  The Scarlet Letter 7/4
  The Unknown Eros and Other Odes (1877) 7/23
  The Virgin Birth of Christ (1930-1932) 7/28
  Tracts for the Times (1833-45) 7/14
  Uncle Tom's Cabin 7/1
  Wycliffe Bible Commentary 7/2
Boone, William J.
  b. 7/1/1811 [d. 7/17/1864]
Booth, Catherine 7/17
Booth, Evangeline Cory
  (b. 12/25/1865) d. 7/17/1950 7/17
Booth, William 7/2, 7/5, 7/17
Brainerd, David 7/12. See also QUOTATIONS
Bridges, Matthew
  b. 7/14/1800 [d. 10/6/1894]
Bridget of Sweden, St.
  (b. 1302) d. 7/23/1373
Bright, Bill
  (b. 10/19/1921) d. 7/19/2003
Bright, Vonette 7/19. See also Bright, Bill

JULY INDEX

Brothers, William H. F.
  (b. 4/7/1887) d. 7/21/1979
Bryan, William Jennings 7/10
  (b. 3/19/1860) d. 7/26/1925
Buber, Martin 7/16
Buchenwald Concentration Camp 7/16
Bulgakov, Sergei Nikolaevich
  (b. 6/16/1871) d. 7/12/1944 7/12
Bullinger, J. Heinrich
  b. 7/18/1504 [d. 9/17/1575]
Bultmann, Rudolf 7/12
  (b. 8/20/1884) d. 7/30/1976
Buoncompagni, Ugo.
  See Gregory XIII, Pope

C

Cabrini, Frances Xavier 7/7
  b. 7/15/1850 [d. 12/22/1917]
Cadman, Samuel P.
  (b. 6/16/1871) d. 7/12/1936
Caesarius of Arles 7/3
Caird, John
  (b. 12/15/1820) d. 7/30/1898
Calvin, John 7/18, 7/20
  b. 7/10/1509 [d. 5/27/1564]
Canonization, Rules of 7/4
CANTERBURY ARCHBISHOPS
  Cranmer, Thomas (1533-1556) 7/2
  Deusdedit, St. (655-664) 7/14
  Langton, Stephen (1207-1228) 7/9
Carey, William 7/12
Cargill, Donald 7/27
Carroll, John 7/17
Cary, Alice 7/31
Cary, Phoebe
  (b. 9/4/1824) d. 7/31/1871
Cassian, John 7/3
Catherine of Aragon 7/11
Catherine of Sweden, St. 7/23
Celestine V, Pope (1294) 7/5
Cennick, John
  (b. 12/12/1718) d. 7/4/1755
Chambers, Oswald
  b. 7/24/1874 [d. 11/15/1917]
Channing, William Ellery 7/19
Charles II, English King (1660-1685) 7/15
Chauvin, Jean. See Calvin, John
Chisholm, T[homas] O.
  b. 7/29/1866 [d. 2/29/1960]
Christian Commercial Men's Association of America 7/1.
  See also Gideons
Christian Endeavor Society 7/14, 7/31
Christian perfection, Doctrine of 7/5
Christology 7/12
CHURCHES
  African Church of St. Thomas (PA) 7/17
  Calvary Methodist Episcopal (Phila.) 7/7
  Cathedral of St. John the Divine (NY) 7/21
  Church of the Advocate (PA) 7/29
  Mormon Tabernacle (UT) 7/28
  Negro Lutheran Church (AR) 7/3
  Northampton Congregational Church (MA) 7/1
  Sanctuary of Our Lady of Victory (NY) 7/26
  Second Presbyterian Church (Phila) 7/23
  St. George's Anglican Church (PA) 7/14
  West (Congregational) Church (MA) 7/9
Ciocchi del Monte, Giammaria.
  See Julius III, Pope
Clement VII, Pope (1523-1534) 7/11
Clement XIV, Pope (1769-1774) 7/21
COLLEGES / UNIVERSITIES
  Bonn University (Germany) 7/8
  British School of Archaeology (Egypt) 7/28
  Cambridge University (England) 7/16, 7/27
  Catholic University of America 7/23
  Columbia University (NY) 7/20
  Dartmouth College (NH) 7/19
  Drew University (NJ) 7/11
  Emory University (GA) 7/2
  Georgetown University (Washington, DC) 7/31
  Glasgow University (Scotland) 7/30
  Harvard University (MA) 7/12
  Hebrew Union College (OH) 7/27
  Hebrew University (Israel) 7/24
  Oxford University (England) 7/14
  Scarritt College for Christian Workers (TN) 7/20
  University of Chicago (IL) 7/20, 7/26
  University of Marburg (Germany) 7/30
  University of Zurich (Switzerland) 7/8
  Vanderbilt University (TN) 7/2
  Yale University (CT) 7/5, 7/26
Communion Ecclesiology 7/30
Congress of the United States of America 7/20
Constantine I, Roman Emperor (306-337) 7/2, 7/25
Constantinople 7/18
Continental Army, American 7/29
Continental Congress, American 7/29
COUNCILS, CHURCH
  Council of Clermont (1095) 7/8
  Council of Constance (1414-1417) 7/6
  Council of Ephesus (431) 7/9, 7/17
  Council of Nicea (325) 7/25
  Second Council of Lyons (1274) 7/15, 7/17
  Synod of Orange (529) 7/3
  Vatican I Council (1869-1870) 7/7, 7/18
Counter Reformation, The 7/21
Cowper, William 7/24
Cox, Richard
  (b. ca. 1500) d. 7/22/1581
Coxe, Arthur Cleveland
  (b. 5/10/1818) d. 7/20/1896
Cranmer, Thomas 7/18
  b. 7/2/1489 [d. 3/21/1556]
Cremation as Disposal of the Dead 7/5
Crotch, William
  b. 7/5/1775 [d. 12/29/1847]
Crowther, Samuel Adjai 7/23
CRUSADES, THE
  Crusaders, The 7/25
  First Crusade (1095-1099) 7/8, 7/15, 7/18

D

Darrow, Clarence 7/10
Davidman, Joy
  (b. 4/18/1915) d. 7/13/1960
DENOMINATIONS, CHRISTIAN
  American Baptists 7/25
  American Catholicism 7/23
  American Congregationalism 7/12, 7/25
  American Episcopalianism 7/10, 7/20, 7/21
  American Methodism 7/14, 7/23, 7/26, 7/27
  American Presbyterianism 7/14, 7/23, 7/26
  American Salvation Army 7/17
  Anglicanism 7/4, 7/11, 7/17, 7/30
  Armenian Church in America 7/28
  Assemblies of God 7/7
  Baptists 7/28
  Catholic Church 7/15, 7/22
  Christian and Missionary Alliance 7/19
  Church of England 7/6, 7/11
  Church of Ireland (Anglican) 7/14, 7/26
  Church of Scotland 7/20, 7/28
  Church of the United Brethren 7/1
  Congregationalism 7/1, 7/6, 7/18, 7/19, 7/24, 7/28
  Congregationalism, American 7/2, 7/3
  Congregationalism, New England 7/9
  Eastern Orthodoxy 7/6, 7/16, 7/17
  English Baptists 7/14, 7/16, 7/17
  English Christian Brethren 7/25
  English Methodism 7/2, 7/23
  English Quakerism 7/30
  Episcopalianism 7/3
  Evangelical and Reformed Church 7/11
  Free Church of Scotland 7/12
  German Lutheranism 7/16, 7/18
  German Reformed Church 7/8, 7/14
  Jacobite Church 7/30
  Lutheranism 7/20
  Lutheran Church Missouri Synod (LCMS) 7/24
  Methodism 7/10, 7/31
  Methodist Episcopal Church 7/6, 7/21
  Methodist Protestant church 7/2
  Moravians 7/13, 7/20
  Moravian Brethren 7/4, 7/15
  Moravian Church in North America 7/15
  Norwegian Lutheranism 7/3
  Old Catholic Church in America 7/21
  Orthodox Church 7/4, 7/7
  Orthodox Presbyterian Church 7/28
  Pentecostalism, American 7/7
  Plymouth Brethren 7/14, 7/25
  Presbyterianism 7/28
  Presbyterianism, American 7/2, 7/8
  Protestant Episcopal Church 7/1, 7/17
  Protestant Episcopal Church of America 7/17
  Quakerism 7/4, 7/11, 7/13, 7/16, 7/19
  Reformed Church 7/20
  Roman Catholicism 7/3, 7/5, 7/13, 7/14
  Russian Orthodoxy 7/12, 7/19, 7/26, 7/27
  Salvation Army 7/2, 7/5
  Scotland's Free Church 7/4
  Scottish Baptists 7/24

JULY INDEX

Scottish Episcopalians 7/27
Scottish Free Church 7/31
Scottish Presbyterians 7/27
Seventh-Day Adventists 7/16
Society of Friends (Quakers) 7/7
Southern Methodist Church, American 7/20
Swiss Protestantism 7/10
Swiss Reformed 7/6, 7/7, 7/12
Syrian Christianity 7/30
Unitas Fratrum (United Brethren) 7/13, 7/15
United Brethren 7/13
United Church of Christ 7/11
United Methodist Church 7/18
Welsh Baptists 7/19
Welsh Calvinistic Methodism 7/21
Wesleyan Methodist Church 7/31

DENOMINATIONS, CHRISTIAN SECTARIAN

Christian Science 7/16
Mormonism 7/12, 7/24, 7/28
Swedenborgian Church 7/27
Unitarianism 7/3, 7/11
Universalism 7/31
Worldwide Church of God 7/31

Deusdedit, St.
(b. unk.) d. 7/14/664
DeVries, Hugo M. 7/22
Dillenberger, John
b. 7/11/1918 [d. 2/7/2008]

DOCUMENTS, CHRISTIAN

Luther's "95 Theses" (1517) 7/27
Westminster Larger Catechism (1648) 7/20, 7/28
Westminster Shorter Catechism (1648) 7/20, 7/28

Doescher, J. Friedrich 7/3
Dorsey, Thomas A.
b. 7/1/1899 [d. 1/23/1993]
Duffield, George, Jr.
(b. 9/12/1818) [d. 7/7/1888]
Durham, William H.
(b. 1873) d. 7/7/1912

E

EASTERN PATRIARCHATES

Alexandria 7/6
Antioch 7/6
Constantinople 7/6
Jerusalem 7/6

Eddy, Mary Baker
b. 7/16/1821 [d. 12/3/1910]

Edwards, Jonathan 7/1, 7/8, 7/12, 7/20
Edwards, Sarah (née Pierpont). See Edwards, Jonathan
Egede, Hans 7/3
Eisenhower, Dwight D. 7/30. See also Presidents, U.S.
Elias, John 7/19
Eliot, John 7/27
Elizabeth I, English Queen (1558-1603) 7/26
Elliot, Jim. See QUOTATIONS
English Reformation 7/22
Erasmus, Desiderius
(b. 10/28/1466 or 10/27/1469) d. 7/12/1536
Erfurt Monastery (Germany) 7/2, 7/17
Evans, Christmas
(b. 12/25/1766) d. 7/19/1838
Ewing, Alexander
(b. 1/3/1830) d. 7/11/1895
Eyck, Jan van
(b. ca. 1390) d. 7/9/1441

F

Falkenberg, Don R.
b. 7/3/1894 [d. 12/13/1974]
Farel, William 7/20
Father John, Russian Orthodox Monk 7/27
Faustus of Riez 7/3
Federal Council of Churches of Christ in America 7/12
Fenelon, François 7/22
Fieschi, Sinisbaldo. See Innocent IV, Pope

FIRSTS

"Holiness" Conference at Keswick, England 7/6
Abbess of the Order of Poor Clares 7/16
African-American Lutheran Church in the U.S. 7/3
African-American to Head a White U.S. University 7/31
American-Born Bishop of the Methodist Episcopal Ch 7/6
American Edition of the King James Version New Testament 7/15
American Female Reform Judaism Rabbi 7/27
American Hospice 7/9
American Protestant Episcopal Missionary Bishop to 7/1
American Radio Preacher 7/12
American to Be Made a Catholic Saint 7/7
Anglo-Saxon Archbishop of Canterbury 7/14
Annual Conference of American Methodists 7/14
Armenian Clergyman to Come to America 7/28
Bible Concordance in the English Language 7/5
Bishop of the African Methodist Episcopal Zion Church 7/30
Black Church Organized in New England 7/17
Black Minister Certified by a Predominantly White Denomination 7/18
Black Minister to Pastor a White Church 7/18
Canadian to be Made a Catholic Cardinal 7/21
Catholic Mission Founded in Modern-day California 7/16
Catholic Nun Born in the U.S. 7/2
Catholic Pope of Eastern Origin 7/23
Catholic Priest Ordained in the U.S. 7/17
Chancellor of the Catholic University of America 7/23
Christian King of Jerusalem 7/18
Christian Missionaries to Japan 7/15
English Bible Printed in America 7/15
Female Navy Chaplain 7/2
Irish Martyr to be Beatified 7/11
Jew to Settle in North America 7/8
Native American Baptized as a Protestant 7/13
Non-Separating Congregational Puritan Church in New England 7/30
Non-Separatist Congregational Church in the American Colonies 7/10
Norway's Set of Church Laws 7/29
Official Roman Catholic saint 7/4
Patriarch of Constantinople 7/9
Permanent Spanish Settlement America's West Coast 7/16
Person To Divide the Bible into Chapters 7/9
Pole to be Canonized 7/26
Pope to Use the Title "Vicar of Christ" 7/16
President of National Association of Evangelicals 7/6
President of the Unitarian Universalist Associatio 7/5
Protestant Archbishop of Canterbury 7/2
Protestant Church West of the Alleghenies 7/20
Roman Catholic basilica in the U.S. 7/26
Scientific Society in History 7/15
State Persecutions of the Church 7/18
White Child Born in America 7/22
White Women to Cross the Rockies 7/4
Woman Commander of the Salvation Army 7/17
Woman Ordained in the Methodist Protestant Church 7/2
Woman Ruling the Hierarchy of an American Denomination 7/18

Fisher, Mary 7/11
Flanagan, Edward
b. 7/13/1886 [d. 5/15/1948]
Fleming, Paul W. 7/17
Form Criticism 7/30
Fox, George
b. 7/19/1624 d. 7/7/1661
Francis of Assisi, St. 7/16
Frithonas. See Deusdedit, St.
Froude, Richard Hurrell 7/14

G

Galilei, Galileo 7/29
Gedeon, Manuel 7/26
Ghent Altarpiece (1432) 7/9
Gibbons, James
b. 7/23/1834 [d. 3/24/1921]
Gideons, The 7/1
Gilmore, Joseph Henry
(b. 4/29/1834) d. 7/23/1918
Gladden, Washington
(b. 2/11/1836) d. 7/2/1918
Godfrey of Bouillon 7/15
(b. ca. 1058) d. 7/18/1100
Gorcum Martyrs 7/9
Graeff, Frank E.
(b. 12/19/1860) d. 7/29/1919
Grant, Frederick W.
b. 7/25/1834 [d. 7/23/1902]
Great Awakening, The 7/1, 7/23
Great Schism, The (1054) 7/6, 7/16
Greeley, Dana M.
b. 7/5/1908 [d. 6/13/1986]
Gregorius Bar-Hebraeus
(b. 1226) d. 7/30/1286
Gregory X, Pope (1271-1276) 7/17

Gregory XV, Pope (1621-1623) 7/8
Guthrie, Thomas
b. 7/12/1803 [d. 2/23/1873]
Guyon, Madame 7/22

H

Haldane, James A.
b. 7/14/1768 [d. 2/8/1851]
Hall, Gordon 7/25
Hall, Sarah 7/4. See also Boardman, Sarah Hall
Hammarskjöld, Dag
b. 7/29/1905 [d. 9/18/1961]
Harmens, Paul. See Rembrandt van Rijn
Harmon, Ellen. See White, Ellen G.
Harper, William Rainey
b. 7/26/1856 [d. 1/10/1906]
Harris, Howell
(b. 1/14/1714) d. 7/21/1773
Harrison, Everett F.
b. 7/2/1902
Hasseltine, Ann 7/4, 7/13. See also Judson, Ann Hasseltine
Hawthorne, Nathaniel 7/9
b. 7/4/1804 [d. 5/19/1864]
Hawthorne, Rose. See Lathrop, Mary Alphonsa
Haynes, Lemuel
b. 7/18/1754 [d. 9/28/1833]
Healy, Patrick Francis 7/31
Hecker, Isaac Thomas 7/10
Henry VIII, English King (1509-1547) 7/2, 7/6, 7/11, 7/26
HERESIES, CHRISTIAN
Antinomianism 7/20
Monothelitism 7/5
Nestorianism 7/17
Pelagianism 7/3
HERETICS, CHRISTIAN
Nestorius 7/9
Herzl, Theodor
(b. 5/2/1860) d. 7/3/1904
Hewitt, Augustine F.
(b. 11/27/1820) d. 7/3/1897
Higginson, Francis 7/10, 7/30
Hill, Samuel E. 7/1
Hine, Stuart Wesley K.
b. 7/25/1899 [d. 1989]
Hitler, Adolf 7/20

Hodge, Archibald A.
b. 7/18/1823 [d. 11/12/1886]
Hodge, Charles 7/18
Holiness Doctrine 7/6
Holiness Doctrine, Methodist 7/5
Holland, Josiah G.
b. 7/24/1819 [d. 10/12/1881]
Holy Land 7/8
Holy Sepulchre, The 7/15
Home for Homeless Boys. See Boys' Town
Honorius III, Pope (1216-1227) 7/24
Hort, F[enton] J. A. 7/27
House of Bishops, Episcopal 7/29
House of Commons, England's 7/27
Hus[s], Jan
(b. ca. 1372) d. 7/6/1415
Hutchinson, Anne
b. 7/20/1591 [d. 8/1643]
HYMNS
"'Man of Sorrows,' What a Name" 7/9
"Alas! and Did My Savior Bleed" 7/17
"Amazing Grace" 7/24
"Angels from the Realms of Glory" 7/6
"Ask Ye What Great Thing I Know" 7/7
"Be Present At Our Table, Lord" 7/4, 7/8
"Blessed Assurance, Jesus Is Mine" 7/10
"Blest Be the Tie That Binds" 7/8
"By and By" 7/7, 7/26
"Children of the Heavenly Father" 7/27
"Christians, Dost Thou See Them" 7/4
"Christ for the World We Sing" 7/2
"Christ Receiveth Sinful Men" 7/4
"Come, We that Love the Lord" 7/17
"Crown Him with Many Crowns" 7/14
"Day by Day, and With Each Passing Moment" 7/27
"Does Jesus Care?" 7/29
"Glorious Things of Thee Are Spoken" 7/24
"Great Is Thy Faithfulness" 7/29
"Hail, Thou Once Despised Jesus" 7/27
"Here, O My Lord, I See Thee Face to Face" 7/31
"He Leadeth Me" 7/23
"His Way with Thee" 7/27
"Hold the Fort" 7/9
"How Great Thou Art" 7/25

"How Sweet the Name of Jesus Sounds" 7/24
"I'll Overcome Some Day" 7/7
"If Thou But Suffer God to Guide Thee" 7/1, 7/18
"It Is Well with My Soul" 7/9
"I Belong to the King" 7/8
"I Gave My Life for Thee" 7/9
"I Know Not Why God's Wondrous Grace" 7/4
"I Know That My Redeemer Lives" 7/17
"I Serve a Risen Savior" 7/3
"I Sing the Almighty Power of God" 7/17
"I Surrender All" 7/31
"I Will Sing of My Redeemer" 7/4, 7/9
"I Will Sing the Wondrous Story" 7/22
"Jerusalem the Golden" 7/11
"Jesus, I am Resting, Resting" 7/16
"Jesus, Lover of My Soul" 7/14
"Jesus is Coming to Earth Again" 7/23
"Jesus Saves" (a.k.a. "We Have Heard the Joyful Sound") 7/21
"Joy to the World!" 7/17
"Lead On, O King Eternal" 7/6
"Leave It There" 7/26
"Let the Lower Lights Be Burning" 7/9
"Like a River Glorious" 7/16
"Living for Jesus" 7/29
"My Faith Looks Up to Thee" 7/8
"My Shepherd Will Supply My Need" 7/17
"Near, Still Nearer" 7/23
"Nearer, My God, To Thee" 7/8
"Nothing Between" 7/26
"Nothing Between [My Soul and the Savior]"" 7/7
"Now Thank We All Our God" 7/1
"O, Where Are Kings and Empires Now?" 7/20
"Oh, Could I Speak the Matchless Worth" 7/17
"Oh, for a Closer Walk with God" 7/27
"On Jordan's Stormy Banks" 7/2
"O Store Gud" 7/25
"Peace in the Valley" 7/1
"Praise the Savior, Ye Who Know Him!" 7/13
"Praise to the Lord, the Almighty" 7/1
"Precious Lord, Take My Hand" 7/1
"Rise Up, O Men of God" 7/1
"Stand by Me" 7/7, 7/26
"Stand Up, Stand Up for Jesus" 7/6
"Still, Still With Thee" 7/1

"Sweet Peace, the Gift of God's Love" 7/22
"Take My Life and Let It Be" 7/7
"Tell It to Jesus" 7/13
"There's a Song in the Air" 7/24
"The Light of the World is Jesus" 7/9
"The Name of Jesus" 7/13
"We're Marching to Zion" 7/17
"We Have an Anchor" 7/21
"We Shall Overcome" 7/7
"When I Survey the Wondrous Cross" 7/8, 7/17
"Wonderful Words of Life" 7/9
Stand Up and Bless the Lord 7/5
Would You Live for Jesus, and Be Always Pure and Good?" 7/27

HYMN TUNES
ASSURANCE 7/10
AUTUMN 7/27
BALERMA 7/27
BETHANY 7/8
BLESSED QUIETNESS 7/11
DENNIS 7/8
EL NATHAN 7/4
EWING 7/11
FESTAL SONG 7/1
HAMBURG 7/8
HENDON 7/7
HE LIVES 7/3
KENOSIS 7/9
LANCASHIRE 7/6
MARTYN 7/14
MORRIS 7/23
MY REDEEMER, NEUMEISTER 7/4
OLIVET 7/8
PROMISED LAND 7/2
REGENT SQUARE 7/6
SECOND COMING 7/23
SHOWERS OF BLESSING 7/4
ST. MICHAEL 7/5
SURRENDER 7/31
TRANQUILLITY 7/16
UXBRIDGE 7/8
VILLE DU HAVRE 7/9
WYE VALLEY 7/16

I

"I-Thou" and "I-It" 7/16
Ignatius [of] Loyola 7/21, 7/29
Igor I, Russian Ruler (912-945) 7/18
Indulgences 7/27

Ingersoll, Robert G.
  (b. 8/11/1833) d. 7/21/1899
Innocent III, Pope (1198-1216) 7/16
Innocent XII, Pope (1691-1700) 7/12
Inuit People (of Greenland) 7/3
Ireland, Primacy of 7/11

J

Jackson, Mahalia 7/1
James I, English King (1603-1625) 7/26
James VI, Scottish King. See James I, English King
Jesus, The Historical 7/12
John V, Pope (685-686) 7/23
Jones, William, of Nayland
  b. 7/30/1726 [d. 1/6/1800]
Jordan, Clarence
  b. 7/29/1912 [d. 10/29/1969]
JUDAISM
  "A National Home for the Jewish People" 7/25
  Barsimon, Jacob 7/8
  Buber, Martin 7/16
  Buchenwald Concentration Camp 7/16
  Congregation Shearith Israel 7/8
  Congress of the Zionist Organizations 7/3
  Conservative Judaism 7/22
  Hebrew University 7/24
  Herzl, Theodor 7/3
  Israel, Modern 7/3
  Lazarus, Emma 7/22
  Orthodox Judaism 7/22
  Priesand, Sally Jane 7/27
  Rashi (Rabbi Sholomo ben Yitzhak) 7/13
  Reform Judaism 7/22, 7/27
Judson, Adoniram 7/4, 7/13, 7/25
Judson, Ann (née Hasseltine) 7/13
Judson, Sarah (née Hall) Boardman 7/4

K

Käsemann, Ernst
  b. 7/12/1906 [d. 1998] 7/12
Keble, John 7/14

Kelly, Thomas
  b. 7/13/1769 [d. 5/14/1855]
Kempis, Thomas à
  (b. ca. 1380) d. 7/25/1471
Keswick Holiness Conferences 7/6, 7/19
Kirk, James M.
  (b. 6/18/1854) d. 7/11/1945
Kittel, Gerhard
  (b. 9/23/1888) d. 7/11/1948
Knapp, Phoebe Palmer
  (b. 3/9/1839) d. 7/10/1908
Knights, William J. 7/1
Koinonia Farm 7/29

L

Lange, Johann Peter
  (b. 4/10/1802) d. 7/8/1884
Langton, Stephen
  (b. ca. 1150) d. 7/9/1228
Lathrop, Mary Alphonsa
  (b. 5/20/1851) d. 7/9/1926
Laubach, Frank. See QUOTATIONS
Lazarus, Emma
  b. 7/22/1849 [d. 11/19/1887]
La Fontaine, Jean de
  (b. 7/8/1621) d. 4/13/1695]
LEGISLATION, ENGLISH
  Act for Promoting and Propagating the Gospel in New England (1649) 7/27
  Balfour Declaration (1917) 7/25
  Disestablishment Bill (1869) 7/26
Leo IX, Pope (1049-1054) 7/16
Lewis, C. S. 7/13. See QUOTATIONS
Lewis, Joy (née Davidman)
  (b. 4/18/1915) d. 7/13/1960
Liberty Bell, American 7/8
Lightfoot, J[oseph] B[arber] 7/27
Liszt, Franz
  (b. 10/22/1811) d. 7/31/1886
Lord's Prayer, The 7/26
Lorenz, Edmund S.
  b. 7/13/1854 [d. 7/10/1942]
Lotario, Count of Segni. See Innocent III, Pope
Loyola, Ignatius [of] 7/8, 7/29
  (b. 12/24/1491) d. 7/31/1556
Luther, Martin 7/2, 7/17, 7/27

M

Machen, J[ohn] Gresham
  b. 7/28/1881 [d. 1/1/1937]
Malan, César H. A.
  b. 7/7/1787 [d. 5/18/1864]
Manteo 7/13
Marsden, Samuel
  b. 7/28/1764 [d. 5/12/1838]
Marsh, Simeon B.
  (b. 6/1/1798) d. 7/14/1875
Marshall, John 7/8
Martin I, Pope (649-655) 7/5
Martyn, Henry 7/12
MARTYRS
  Bonhoeffer, Dietrich 7/16, 7/18
  Cargill, Donald 7/27
  Cranmer, Thomas 7/2
  Elliot, Jim 7/10, 7/11
  Hus[s], Jan 7/6
  McChesney, Bill 7/21
  Plunkett, Oliver 7/11
  Stanislaw (or Stanislaus), St. 7/26
Mary, English Queen 7/2
Mason, Lowell
  b. 7/8/1792 [d. 8/11/1872]
Mastai-Ferretti, Giovanni Maria. See Pius IX, Pope (1846-1878)
Matthews, Marjorie S. 7/18
Mayflower, The 7/22
Mayhew, Jonathan
  (b. 10/8/1720) d. 7/9/1766 7/9
McChesney, Bill
  b. 7/21/1936 [d. 11/25/1964]
McGranahan, James
  b. 7/4/18040 [d. 7/7/1907]
McIntosh, Rigdon M.
  (b. 4/3/1836) d. 7/2/1899
McKendree, William
  b. 7/6/1757 [d. 3/5/1835]
Medley, Samuel
  (b. 6/23/1738) d. 7/17/1799
Melanchthon, Philip[p] 7/18
Melendez, Andrew
  (b. 1903) d. 7/24/1999
Mendel, Gregor J.
  b. 7/22/1822 [d. 1/6/1884]
Mersch, Émile
  b. 7/30/1890 [d. 5/23/1940]
Metropolitan Life Insurance Co. 7/10
Michael Cerularius 7/16

Michael VIII Palaeologus, Byzantine Patriarch (1258-1282) 7/25
Mid-West Businessmen's Council. See Bible Literature International
Middle Ages 7/16
Miltiades, Pope (311-314) 7/2
MISSIONARIES
  Blodget, Henry 7/25
  Boardman, George Dana 7/4
  Boone, William J. 7/1
  Brainerd, David 7/10, 7/22
  Crowther, Samuel Adjai 7/23
  Egede, Hans 7/3
  Eliot, John 7/27
  Elliot, Jim 7/10, 7/11
  Gedeon, Hieromonk Manuel 7/26
  Hall, Gordon 7/25
  Hall, Sarah 7/4
  Hasseltine, Ann 7/13
  Hasseltine (Judson), Ann 7/4
  Hine, Stuart Wesley K. 7/25
  Judson, Adoniram 7/4, 7/13, 7/25
  Laubach, Frank C. 7/2
  Marsden, Samuel 7/28
  McChesney, Bill 7/21
  Moravians, The 7/20
  Newell, Samuel 7/25
  Nott, Samuel 7/25
  Rice, Luther 7/25
  Schaeffer, Francis 7/4, 7/11
  Schweitzer, Albert 7/21, 7/24, 7/27, 7/30
  Serra, Father Junipero 7/1
  Spalding, Eliza H. 7/4
  Spalding, Henry 7/4
  Studd, C[harles] T. 7/16
  Townsend, W. Cameron 7/9
  Vasey, Thomas 7/5
  Whatcoat, Richard 7/5
  Whitman, Marcus 7/4
  Whitman, Narcissa P. 7/4
MISSIONS, CHRISTIAN
  Bible Literature International 7/3
  Bible Meditation League 7/3
  Boys' Town 7/13
  Central American Mission 7/24
  New Tribes Mission 7/17
  Paris Mission Society 7/9
  Pocket Testament League 7/3
  Worldwide Evangelization Crusade (WEC) 7/16, 7/21
  Wycliffe Bible Translators 7/9

Mission San Diego de Alcala 7/16
Modernism 7/3
Moffatt, James 7/31
   b. 7/4/1870 [d. 6/27/1944]
Montini, Giovanni Battista. See Paul VI, Pope
Moore, Clement C.
   (b. 7/15/1779) d. 7/10/1863 7/10
More, Thomas
   (b. 2/7/1478) d. 7/6/1535
Morris, Leila Naylor
   (b. 4/15/1862) d. 7/23/1929
Morse, Mary. See Eddy, Mary Baker
MOTTOS
   "In God We Trust" 7/11, 7/20, 7/30
   "There is no such thing as a bad boy" 7/13
Mountain, James
   b. 7/16/1844 [d. 6/27/1933]
MOVEMENTS, CHRISTIAN
   American Puritanism 7/20
   Anglican Evangelicalism 7/8, 7/29, 7/31
   Bohemian Protestantism 7/13
   Fundamentalism, American 7/10
   Neo-Orthodoxy 7/5
   Oxford Movement (1833-45) 7/30
   Pietism, Swiss 7/14
   Puritanism 7/15
   Puritanism, New England 7/4
   Quietism, French 7/22
   Reformed Protestantism 7/10
   Russian Christianity 7/15
   Russian Monasticism 7/19
   Separatism, English 7/22
MOVEMENTS, CHRISTIAN SECTARIAN
   Deism 7/14
Murrone, Pietro di. See Celestine V, Pope
MYSTICS
   Alacoque, Margaret Mary 7/22
   Fénelon, François 7/26, 7/30
   Kempis, Thomas à 7/25
   Loyola, Ignatius 7/31
   Underhill, Evelyn 7/20, 7/29

N

National Association of Evangelicals (NAE) 7/6
NATIVE AMERICANS
   American Indians 7/27
   David Brainerd's Indians 7/22
   Indians of the American Northwest 7/4
   Manteo 7/13
   New England Indians 7/12
Nepotism 7/12
Neri, Philip
   b. 7/21/1515 [d. 5/26/1595]
Nero, Roman Emperor (54-68) 7/18
Neumark, Georg
   (b. 3/16/1621) d. 7/18/1681
Newell, Samuel
   b. 7/25/1785 [d. 3/30/1821]
Newman, John Henry 7/14
Newman, Samuel
   (b. 1602) d. 7/5/1663
Newton, John
   b. 7/24/1725 [d, 12/21/1807]
Nicholson, John H. 7/1
NICKNAMES / TITLES
   Apostle of Greenland 7/3
   Apostle of the Russians and Ruthenians 7/15
   Apostle to the Maoris 7/28
   Cambridge Seven 7/16
   Clapham Sect, The 7/29
   Father of Black Gospel Music 7/1
   Fifth Evangelist, The 7/28
   Friends of the Truth 7/19
   Fundamentalism's Most Gifted Theologian 7/28
   Perhaps the Greatest Pianist of all Time 7/31
   Prince of Mystics 7/15
   Prince of Scottish Hymnwriters 7/31
   Second Apostle of Rome 7/21
   Seraphic Doctor 7/15
   The Great Agnostic 7/21
   Vicar of Christ 7/16
   Welsh Boanerges, The 7/21
Niebuhr, H. Richard
   (b. 9/3/1894) d. 7/5/1962
Niebuhr, Reinhold 7/5
Nott, Samuel 7/25
Nusbaum, Cyrus S.
   b.7/27/1861 [d. 12/27/1937]

O

Ockenga, Harold J.
   b. 7/6/1905 [d. 1985]
Odescalchi, Benedetto. See Innocent XI, Pope
Olaf II, Haraldsson, Norwegian King (1016-1028)
   (b. 995) d. 7/29/1030
Olga of Kiev, Russian Princess (954-974) 7/18. See also Vladimir I (the Great)
Oregon Territory 7/4
ORGANIZATIONS
   English Royal Society 7/15
ORGANIZATIONS, CHRISTIAN
   Christian Commercial Men's Association of America 7/1
   Society for the Propagation of the Gospel at Home 7/14
ORGANIZATIONS, CHRISTIAN SECTARIAN
   American Unitarian Association 7/19
   Unitarian Universalist Association 7/5, 7/19
ORGANIZATIONS, CHRISTIAN YOUTH
   Baptist Young People's Union 7/14
   Campus Crusade for Christ 7/19
   Christian Endeavor Society 7/14, 7/31
Otterbein, Philip W. 7/1
Owens, Priscilla Jane
   b. 7/21/1829 [d. 12/5/1907]
Oxford Movement (1833-45) 7/14

P

PAPAL DECREES
   Dominus ac redemptor noster (1773) 7/21
   Humanae Vitae (1968) 7/25, 7/29
   Lamentabili (1907) 7/3
   Pastor aeternus (1870) 7/18
   Romanum decet pontificem (1692) 7/12
Papal Infallibility, Doctrine of 7/7, 7/18
Patmore, Coventry
   b. 7/23/1823 [d. 11/26/1896]
Patrick, St. 7/26
Paul III, Pope (1534-1549) 7/21
Paul VI, Pope (1963-1978) 7/7, 7/16, 7/25, 7/29
Penn, William
   (b. 10/14/1644) d. 7/30/1718
PERIODICALS / JOURNALS
   "Catholic World" 7/3
   "Presbyterian Review" 7/18
   "Scribner's Magazine" 7/24
   "The Christian Register" 7/3
Peter the Hermit 7/8
Petrie, W[illiam] M. Flinders
   (b. 6/3/1853) d. 7/29/1942
Philip de Neri 7/8
Pierpont, Sarah 7/20. See also Edwards, Jonathan
Pignatelli, Antonio. See Innocent XII, Pope
Pilgrims, The 7/22
Pius IX, Pope (1846-1878) 7/7, 7/9
Pius VII, Pope (1800-1823) 7/15
Pius X, Pope (1903-1914) 7/3
Plunkett, Oliver
   (b. 11/1/1625) d. 7/11[NS]/1681
POETRY
   "A Visit from St. Nicholas" 7/10
   "Nearer Home" 7/31
   "One Sweetly Solemn Thought" 7/31
   "The New Colossus" 7/22
Pohlman, Florence Dianna 7/2
Polygamy 7/12, 7/24
Pope, William B.
   (b. 2/19/1822) d. 7/5/1903
POPES
   Boniface VIII (1294-1303) 7/5
   Celestine V (1294) 7/5
   Clement VII (1523-1534) 7/11
   Clement XIV (1769-1774) 7/21
   Gregory XV (1621-1623) 7/8
   Gregory X (1271-1276) 7/17
   Honorius III (1216-1227) 7/24
   Innocent III (1198-1216) 7/16
   Innocent XII (1691-1700) 7/12
   John V (685-686) 7/23
   Leo IX (1049-1054) 7/16
   Martin I (649-655) 7/5
   Miltiades (311-314) 7/2
   Paul III (1534-1549) 7/21
   Paul VI (1963-1978) 7/7, 7/16, 7/25, 7/29
   Pius IX (1846-1878) 7/7, 7/9
   Pius VII (1800-1823) 7/15
   Pius X (1903-1914) 7/3
   Urban II (1088-1099) 7/8
   Urban VIII (1623-1644) 7/29
Popish Plot, The 7/11
Potter, Alonzo 7/21
Potter, Henry C.
   (b. 6/25/1834) d. 7/21/1908
PRESIDENTS, U.S.
   Adams, John (1797-1801) 7/13

Adams, John Quincy (1825-1829) 7/11
Eisenhower, Dwight D. (1953-1961) 7/11, 7/30
Wilson, Woodrow (1913-1921) 7/27
Priesand, Sally Jane
b. 6/10/1946
Protestant Reformation 7/27
Pusey, Edward 7/14

Q

QUOTATIONS
Adams, John 7/13
Asbury, Francis 7/23
Barth, Karl 7/6, 7/12, 7/16
Bonar, Andrew 7/1, 7/15, 7/21
Bonhoeffer, Dietrich 7/16, 7/18
Brainerd, David 7/10
Elliot, Jim 7/10, 7/11
Fénelon, François 7/19, 7/26, 7/30
Hammarskjöld, Dag 7/19
Laubach, Frank C. 7/2
Lewis, C. S. 7/7, 7/17, 7/21
Luther, Martin 7/1, 7/10, 7/12, 7/20
MacDonald, George 7/7, 7/14, 7/19
Merton, Thomas 7/4, 7/5, 7/17, 7/20, 7/23, 7/28
Newton, John 7/14, 7/24, 7/30, 7/31
Nouwen, Henri J. M. 7/3, 7/9, 7/13, 7/15, 7/18, 7/25, 7/28
Philpot, John 7/10
Pink, Arthur W. 7/6
Rutherford, Samuel 7/6
Schaeffer, Francis 7/4, 7/11
Schweitzer, Albert 7/9, 7/24, 7/27, 7/30
Smith, Hannah Whitall 7/13, 7/16
Spurgeon, Charles Haddon 7/5, 7/14
Underhill, Evelyn 7/8, 7/11, 7/20, 7/29
Venn, Henry 7/8, 7/31
Wesley, John 7/1, 7/3, 7/5, 7/22, 7/23, 7/25, 7/26, 7/28, 7/29, 7/31
Whitefield, George 7/25

R

Radar, Paul
(b. 8/24/1879) d. 7/19/1938
RADIO, CHRISTIAN
"The Spanish Lutheran Hour" 7/24
"The World Tomorrow" 7/31

RADIO EVANGELISM 7/19, 7/24
Ragged Schools 7/12
Raleigh, Sir Walter 7/13
Rashi (Rabbi Sholomo ben Yitzhak)
(b. 1040) d. 7/13/1105
Rauschenbusch, Walter
(b. 10/4/1861) d. 7/25/1918
Reformation, The 7/6, 7/12, 7/21
RELIGIOUS ORDERS, CATHOLIC
American Trappists 7/23
Augustinians 7/22
Augustinian Eremites 7/2, 7/17
Brigittines (Order of our Saviour) 7/23
Confraternity of the Most Holy Trinity 7/21
Dominicans 7/24
Dominicans (Third Order) 7/9
Franciscans 7/1, 7/9, 7/15, 7/16, 7/24, 7/31
Institute of Oratory 7/21
Institute of the Missionary Sisters of the Sacred Heart 7/7
Jesuits (Society of Jesus) 7/15, 7/21, 7/30, 7/31
Missionary Sisters of the Sacred Heart 7/15
Order of Poor Clares 7/16
Paulists 7/3
Paulist Fathers (Missionary Society of St. Paul the Apostle) 7/10
Redemptorists 7/10
Trappists 7/4, 7/17, 7/20, 7/28
Ursulines 7/2
Vistantines, French 7/22
Rembrandt van Rijn
b. 7/15/1606 [d. 10/4/1669]
Renaissance, The 7/12
Rice, Luther 7/25
Robinson, John 7/22
Rutherford, Samuel. See QUOTATIONS

S

Sacred Heart of Jesus 7/22
Salem Witch Trials 7/19
Sankey, Ira 7/16
Santa Claus Myth 7/10
Sarah Pierpont. See also Edwards, Jonathan

Sarajian, Hovsep 7/28
Sarto, Giuseppe Melchiorre. See Pius X, Pope
Savelli, Cencio. See Honorius III, Pope
Scefi, Clara
b. 7/16/1194 [d. 8/11/1253]
Schaff, Philip 7/8
Schlatter, Michael
b. 7/14/1716 [d. 10/31/1790]
Schmemann, Alexander. See QUOTATIONS
Schwarzerd, Philipp. See Melanchthon, Philip[p]
Schweitzer, Albert 7/21
Scientific Rationalism 7/21
Scofield, C[yrus] I.
(b. 8/19/1843) d. 7/24/1921
Scopes Monkey Trial (1925) 7/10, 7/26
Scott, Orange
(b. 2/13/1800) d. 7/31/1847
Seljuk Turks 7/8
SEMINARIES / BIBLE COLLEGES
Baptist Union Theological Seminary (IL) 7/26
Dallas Theological Seminary (TX) 7/2
Fuller Theological Seminary (CA) 7/6
General Theological Seminary (NY) 7/10
Princeton Seminary (CT) 7/18
Union Seminary (NY) 7/4, 7/20
Western Theological Seminary (MI) 7/18
Seraphim of Sarov
b. 7/19/1759 [d. 1/2/1833]
SERMONS
"Sinners in the Hands of an Angry God" (1741) 7/8
Serra, Junipero 7/1, 7/16
Shaw, Anna Howard
(b. 2/14/1847) d. 7/2/1919
Skelton, Samuel 7/10, 7/30
Slavery, English 7/29
Smart, Henry T.
(b. 10/26/1813) d. 7/7/1879
Smith, Hiram. See also Smith, Joseph
Smith, Hirum 7/12
Smith, Ida Reed
(b. 11/30/1865) d. 7/8/1951
Smith, Joseph 7/12
Society for the Propagation of Christian Knowledge (SPCK) 7/12

Spalding, Eliza H. 7/4
Spalding, Henry 7/4
Spangenberg, August G.
b. 7/15/1704 [d. 9/18/1792]
Spurgeon, Charles 7/24. See also QUOTATIONS
Spyrou, Aristocles. See Athenagoras I, Patriarch
Stanislaw (or Stanislaus), St. 7/26
Staret / Startsi 7/19
Statue of Liberty 7/22
Stowe, Harriet Beecher
(b. 6/14/1811) d. 7/1/1896
Studd, C[harles] T.
(b. 12/2/1860) d. 7/16/1931
Synod of Orange (529) 7/3

T

Taschereau, Elzear Alexandre 7/21
Tennent, Gilbert
(b. 2/5/1703) d. 7/23/1764
Theocracy 7/20
Theodosius II, Roman Emperor (408-450) 7/17
Thurneysen, Eduard
b. 7/10/1888 [d. 1974]
Tillich, Paul
b. 7/20/1886 [d. 10/22/1965]
Tindley, Charles A.
b. 7/7/1851 d. 7/26/1933
Townsend, W. Cameron
b. 7/9/1896 d. 4/23/1982]
Tractarian Revival. See Oxford Movement (1833-45)
TRACTS, RELIGIOUS
"Der Judenstaat" (1895) 7/3
Turpin, Mary 7/2
Tyng, Dudley 7/6

U

Ulrich of Augsburg 7/4
Unitarian Universalist Association 7/5
Unitas Fratrum (United Brethren) 7/13
UNIVERSITIES. See COLLEGES / UNIVERSITIES
Urban II, Pope (1088-1099) 7/8

Urban VIII, Pope (1623-1644)
(b. 4/5/1568) d. 7/29/1644

V

Varick, James 7/30
Vasey, Thomas 7/5
Victorious Life Conference 7/19
Vladimir I (the Great), Russian ruler (980-1015)
b. 956 [d. 7/15/1015]

W

Walker, Williston
b. 7/1/1860 [d. 3/9/1922]
Walter, William H.
b. 7/1/1825 [d. 1893]
Ware, Henry, Sr.
(b. 4/1/1764) d. 7/12/1845
WARS
American Civil War (1861-1865) 7/1, 7/22
American Revolution (1776-1781) 7/17
Crimean War (1853-1856) 7/11
World War I (1914-1918) 7/20, 7/27
Watts, Isaac
b. 7/17/1674 [d. 11/25/1748]
Weeden, Winfield Scott
(b. 3/29/1847) d. 7/31/1908
Weizmann, Chaim 7/24
Wesley, Charles 7/23
Wesley, John 7/4, 7/23. See also QUOTATIONS
Wesley, Susannah
(b. 1/20/1669) d. 7/23/1742
Westcott, B[rooke] F.
(b. 1/12/1825) d. 7/27/1901
Westminster Larger Catechism 7/20, 7/28
Westminster Shorter Catechism 7/20, 7/28
Whatcoat, Richard
(b. 2/23/1736) d. 7/5/1806
White, Ellen G.
(b. 11/26/1827) d. 7/16/1915
White, Peregrine
(b. 11/20/1620) d. 7/22/1704
White, William
(b. 4/4/1748) d. 7/17/1836
Whitefield, George 7/4, 7/23. See also QUOTATIONS
Whitman, Marcus 7/4
Whitman, Narcissa P. 7/4
Whittle, D. W. 7/4
Wilberforce, William
(b. 8/24/1759) d. 7/29/1833
Williams, William 7/19
Wilson, Woodrow 7/27. See also PRESIDENTS, U.S.
Winkworth, Catherine
(b. 9/13/1827) d. 7/1/1878
Wojtyla, Karol. See John Paul II, Pope
Wolcott, Samuel
b. 7/2/1813 [d. 2/24/1886]
World Conference on Religion and Peace 7/5
World Institute on Christian Education (1962) 7/9
Wycliffe, John 7/6

X

Xavier, Francis 7/8, 7/15, 7/21, 7/29

Y

Young, Brigham 7/24, 7/28
YOUTH ORGANIZATIONS. See ORGANIZATIONS, CHRISTIAN YOUTH

Z

Zinzendorf, Nikolaus L. 7/13, 7/15
Zwingli, Ulrich 7/18

August 1

Highlights in History

1652 Nikita M. Nikon, 47, was elected Patriarch of Moscow. Later, falling out of the czar's favor, this influential figure in Russian church history was deposed by the Council of Moscow in 1666, and banished. Nikon's theory that spiritual power superseded temporal might were factors in Peter the Great's decision to abolish the patriarchy.

1898 The first general council of the Fire-Baptized Holiness Church convened at Anderson, SC. With roots in Georgia, the group began as an "association" in 1890, after separating from the Pentecostal Fire-Baptized Holiness Church.

1979 Following her graduation from rabbinical college in Philadelphia, Linda Joy Holtzman was appointed spiritual leader of the Beth Israel congregation in Coatesville, PA. It made her the first female rabbi to head a Conservative Jewish congregation in America.

Notable Birthdays

1545 Birth of Andrew Melville, Scottish Presbyterian reformer. He gave the Scottish Church its Presbyterian character with a ruling passion to preserve church independence from Anglican control. Melville also helped draw up the Second Book of Discipline. He was later imprisoned in the Tower of London (1607-11) for preaching against popery. [d. 1622]

1843 Birth of William Sanday, Anglican New Testament scholar and theologian. Sanday was associated for 40 years with Oxford University, and authored or edited numerous scholarly publications, including Hastings' *Dictionary of the Bible* (5 vols., 1898-1906); *The Study of the New Testament* (1883); and *The New Testament Background* (1920). [d. 9/16/1920]

1890 Birth of Walther Eichrodt, German Reformed Old Testament scholar. He taught at the universities of Erlangen (1918-21) and Basel (1921-61). Among his many published works, Eichrodt is most highly regarded among Christian evangelicals today for his *Theology of the Old Testament* (1933-39; Eng. 1961). [d. 1978]

The Last Passage

1787 Death of Alphonsus Liguori, 90, Italian Catholic moral theologian and religious. In 1732 he founded the Congregation of the Most Holy Redeemer (Redemptorists). Liguori was canonized in 1839, and in 1950 was made a Doctor of the Church, and named patron of moralists and confessors. (b. 9/27/1696)

1834 Death of Robert Morrison, 52, first English Protestant missionary to reach China. Sent by the London Missionary Society in 1807, he concentrated his literary work in Canton. In 1823 Morrison completed a Chinese translation of the entire Bible in 23 volumes! (b. 1/5/1782)

Words for the Soul

1521 German reformer Martin Luther wrote in a letter: 'Be a sinner and sin boldly, but believe and rejoice in Christ even more boldly, for He is victorious over sin, death, and the world.'

1927 English writer and mystic Evelyn Underhill strongly advised in a letter: 'Develop and expand the wholesome, natural and intellectual interests of your life — don't allow yourself to concentrate on the religious side only. Remember all life comes to you from God, and is to be used for Him — so live in it all, and so get the necessary variety and refreshment without which religious intensity soon becomes stale and hard.'

1953 British literary scholar and Christian apologist C. S. Lewis wrote in a letter: 'How little people know who think that holiness is dull. When one meets the real thing, it is irresistible.'

FROM GOD'S WORD... OT: 2 Chronicles 30:1–31:21 ~ NT: Romans 15:1-22 ~ Psalms 25:1-15 ~ Proverbs 20:13-15

August 2

Highlights in History

1844 American religious Isaac Hecker joined the Catholic Church. Raised a Methodist, he later became a Mormon, then a Unitarian, before his conversion to Catholicism. Hecker joined the Redemptorists in 1845 and in 1856 founded the Society of Missionary Priests of Saint Paul the Apostle (the Paulists).

1907 The Vatican issued the decree "Ne temere," declaring that marriages of Catholics were valid only if celebrated before a duly qualified priest and at least two witnesses.

1955 Mrs. Sheldon (Betty) Robbins became the first female cantor in the history of Judaism.

Notable Birthdays

1788 Birth of Joseph J. Gurney, English banker and philanthropist. A descendant of Quaker theologian Robert Barclay and the brother of prison reformer Elizabeth Fry, Gurney was the leading evangelical Quaker theologian of the early 19th century. [d. 1/4/1847]

1819 Birth of Thomas Armitage, American Baptist clergyman. He was born in England, but came to America in 1838. In 1850 he helped found the American Bible Union. [d. 1/21/1896]

1863 Birth of American missionary Robert P. Wilder. The son of missionary parents in India, Wilder also became a missionary to India, where he ministered to students and was a chief founder and promoter of the Student Volunteer Movement. [d. 3/28/1938]

1875 Birth of William H. P. Hatch, American Episcopal clergyman, educator and editor. He taught New Testament at Episcopal Theological School, (MA), and published *The Greek Manuscripts of the New Testament at Mount Sinai* (1932); *The Greek Manuscripts of the New Testament in Jerusalem* (1934); *The Principal Uncial Manuscripts of the New Testament* (1939); *Album of Dated Syriac Manuscripts* (1947); and *Facsimiles and Descriptions of Minuscule Manuscripts of the New Testament* (1951). [d. 11/11/1972]

The Last Passage

1912 Death of Samuel Macauley Jackson, 61, American Presbyterian clergyman, church historian and educator. His most notable publication was the *New Schaff-Herzog Encyclopedia of Religious Knowledge* (12 vols., 1907-11), of which he was editor-in-chief. (b. 6/19/1851)

1977 Death of Makarios III, 63, Cypriot religious leader and politician. Born Michael C. Mouskos, he entered the monastic life at age 13. He served as Archbishop of the Cyprus Orthodox Church (1950-77), and later as the first president of Cyprus (1959-77). (b. 8/13/1913)

Words for the Soul

1776 English founder of Methodism John Wesley encouraged in a letter: *'Use all the ability which God gives, and He will give you more.'*

1946 Christian English scholar C. S. Lewis warned in a letter: *'Apologetic work is so dangerous to one's faith. A doctrine never seems dimmer to me than when I have just successfully defended it.'*

1948 American Plymouth Brethren missionary and martyr Jim Elliot prayed in his journal: *'Father, teach me the speed of eternity. Synchronize my movements with the speed of Thine Own heart – then, hasting or halting, I shall be in good time.'*

1974 Dutch educator and diarist Henri J. M. Nouwen observed in his GENESEE DIARY: *'The psalms... slowly become flesh in me; they become part of my night and lead me to a peaceful sleep.'*

1982 American Presbyterian apologist Francis Schaeffer wrote in a letter: *'There is the constant danger of slipping into the idea that if a person has sufficient faith, he will always be healed. This is clearly not what the Bible teaches.'*

~ August 3 ~

Highlights in History

1476 Pope Sixtus IV published the bull "Salvator noster," granting an indulgence to the church of Saintes, a town in western France. It was the first instance in history of a pope issuing an indulgence granting plenary (i.e., complete) remission of sins for the dead ("plenariam remissionem per modum suffragii").

1785 The first Episcopal ordination in the United States was held in Middleton, Connecticut, for the Rev. Ashbel Baldwin (3/7/1757 - 2/8/1846).

1845 With an enthusiasm for promoting missions around the world, Pope Gregory XVI signed a concordat between Russia's Czar Nicholas I and the Russian Latin rite. (Unfortunately, neither this concordat nor a later one, signed by Leo XIII in 1882, was carried out.)

Notable Birthdays

1797 Birth of William Ware, American Unitarian clergyman, writer and editor. As author of *Rome, and the Early Christians* (1851), this fictional narrative of the life of Christ was the first widely read American religious novel. Ware was also editor of *American Unitarian Biography* (2 vols., 1850-51). [d. 2/19/1852]

1802 Birth of Sarah P. Doremus, the founder and first president of the Woman's Union Missionary Society of America. She was inspired to her work by missionary David Abeel, a fellow member of the Reformed Church in America. [d. 1/29/1877]

1836 Birth of Augustus H. Strong, American Northern Baptist clergyman and educator. He pastored churches in MA and OH (1861-72), then became professor of biblical theology and president of Rochester Seminary (NY), until his retirement in 1912. Strong is best remembered for his monumental 3-volume work, *Systematic Theology* (1907-09). [d. 11/29/1921]

1858 Birth of Maltbie D. Babcock, American Presbyterian clergyman and hymnwriter. His pastoral work centered around Maryland and New York. Babcock is remembered today as the author of the hymn, "This is My Father's World." [d. 5/18/1901]

1902 Birth of Martin Noth, German Lutheran Old Testament scholar and archaeologist. His researches focused on the early history of Israel, as well as the 'history-of-traditions' approach to analyzing and understanding the Old Testament writings. [d. 5/30/1968]

The Last Passage

1874 Death of American Presbyterian missionary Henry H. Spalding, about 70. Assigned by the American Board of Commissioners to work among the Nez Perce Indians, Spalding labored in the American Northwest from 1836 until his death. (b. ca. 1803/04)

1897 Death of Emily E. S. Elliott, 61, editor and hymnwriter. The niece of hymnwriter Charlotte Elliott ("Just As I Am"), Emily edited "The Church Missionary Juvenile Instructor." Today her name endures as author of the hymn, "Thou Didst Leave Thy Throne." (b. 7/22/1836)

Words for the Soul

1739 English revivalist George Whitefield stated in a letter: *'I am no friend to sinless perfection. I believe the existence (though not the dominion) of sin remains in the hearts of the greatest believers.'*

1944 German Lutheran theologian and Nazi martyr Dietrich Bonhoeffer wrote in a letter from prison: *'The Church must not underestimate the importance of human example; it is not abstract argument, but example, that gives its word emphasis and power.'*

1959 British literary scholar and Christian apologist C. S. Lewis wrote in a letter: *'When we lose one blessing, another is often most unexpectedly given in its place.'*

FROM GOD'S WORD... OT: 2 Chronicles 33:14–34:33 ~ NT: Romans 16:8-27 ~ Psalms 26:1-12 ~ Proverbs 20:19

August 4

Highlights in History

1874 U.S. Methodist pastor John H. Vincent and manufacturer Lewis Miller established the Chautauqua Organization in Fair Point, New York. Beginning as a two-week summer retreat for training Sunday School teachers, the "Chautauqua Assembly" program grew to include additional lectures and entertainments addressing all branches of popular education.

1879 Pope Leo XIII issued the encyclical "Aeterni patris," which urged the study of 'true' philosophy, especially that of Thomas Aquinas. The injunction led to a great revival of both Thomist studies and scholastic philosophy.

1892 English physician and medical missionary Wilfred T. Grenfell, 26, first arrived in Labrador, Newfoundland. For 42 years he labored among the fisherfolk there, helping to build hospitals, churches and orphanages. He supported his missions with speaking tours and books, including *Vikings of To-Day* (1895) and *Adrift on an Ice-Pan* (1909).

Notable Birthdays

1792 Birth of Edward Irving, Scottish theologian, mystic and religious leader. He acquired fame as a preacher, but was compelled to resign from his church because of his acceptance of pentecostal phenomena (1832), and was condemned as a heretic. [d. 12/7/1834]

1841 Birth of James Chalmers, Scottish missionary to the South Sea Islands. Called the "Great Heart of New Guinea," he served in the Cook Islands from 1865, before going to New Guinea in 1877 – one of the first white men to set foot there – where he established a chain of mission stations along the coast. In 1901, Chalmers and several others landed on Goaribari Island, where they were all clubbed to death and cannibalized by the natives. [d. 4/8/1901]

1884 Birth of Sigmund O. P. Mowinckel, Norwegian Bible scholar and founder of the Scandinavian school of Old Testament studies. Associated with Oslo University from 1917-54, Mowinckel's most influential work was *The Psalms in Israel's Worship* (1951, Eng., 1963). [d. 6/4/1965]

The Last Passage

1910 Death of H[einrich] J. Holtzmann, 78, German Protestant theologian and NT scholar; he defended the Marcan hypothesis and later argued for a psychological development in the Lord's self-consciousness (b. 5/17/1832)

1947 Death of Rodney "Gipsy" Smith, 87, wandering English evangelist. Born of gypsy parents, he was converted in his mid-teens and served for a time with the Salvation Army, before turning to evangelism. He visited America several times, holding a succession of revivals in major cities on the East Coast. (b. 3/31/1860)

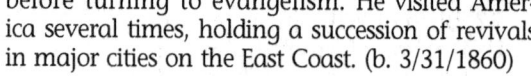

Words for the Soul

1636 Exiled Scottish clergyman Samuel Rutherford declared in a letter: 'When I look... beyond death, to the laughing side of the world, ...I am a faint, dead-hearted, cowardly man, often borne down, and hungry in waiting for the marriage-supper of the Lamb. Nevertheless I think it the Lord's wise love that feeds us with hunger, and makes us fat with wants and desertions.'

1743 Colonial American missionary to the New England Indians, David Brainerd wrote in his journal: 'Filling up our time with and for God, is the way to rise up and lie down in peace.'

1959 Swedish Christian diplomat and United Nations Secretary General Dag Hammarskjöld noted in his journal (*Markings*): 'We encounter a world where each man is a cosmos, of whose riches we can only catch glimpses.'

FROM GOD'S WORD... OT: 2 Chronicles 35:1–36:23 ~ NT: 1 Corinthians 1:1-17 ~ Psalms 27:1-6 ~ Proverbs 20:20-21

August 5

Highlights in History

1370 The Brigittine Order (Order of St. Saviour) was approved by Pope Urban V. The Brigittines were founded in 1346 by St. Bridget of Sweden, and became one of the most popular of the female religious orders, spreading to 14 countries until it was suppressed by the Reformation.

1570 Spanish Jesuits led by Fray Batista Segura arrived in the Chesapeake Bay area of Virginia, for the purpose of converting the American Indians to Christianity. (Six months later, the entire group was massacred by the same Indians they had come to evangelize.)

1656 Eight Quakers from England arrived in Boston and were immediately imprisoned by the local Puritan authorities. (The church-and-state mix of Puritanism regarded ritual-free Quakerism as politically subversive and theologically suspect).

Notable Birthdays

1540 Birth of Joseph Justus Scaliger, French Huguenot linguistic scholar. His mastery over a dozen ancient languages as well as his researches into the chronology of the world indirectly laid the foundations for modern biblical text criticism. [d. 1/21/1609]

1604 Baptism of John Eliot, English-born Congregational missionary who came to America in 1631. As the "Apostle to the Indians," he translated the Scriptures into the Pequot language of Massachusetts in 1663. Eliot also helped establish the Society for the Propagation of the Gospel in New England. [d. 5/21/1690]

1869 Birth of Grant Colfax Tullar, American Methodist evangelist and music publisher. Tullar is remembered today for composing, in 1898, the tune to the hymn, "Face to Face with Christ My Savior." [d. 5/20/1950]

1886 Birth of Bruce F. Barton, American journalist, advertising executive and popular author. In 1925 he published *The Man Nobody Knows*, a book that depicted Jesus as a prototype of the successful businessman. [d. 7/5/1967]

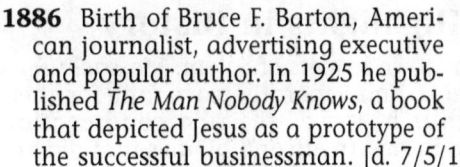

The Last Passage

642 Death of St. Oswald, 37, King of Northumbria. Exiled in Scotland in 616, following the death of his father Ethelfrith, Oswald was afterward converted by the monks of Columba at Iona. He then began establishing Christianity in England after his return in 634. (b. ca. 605)

1811 Death of Moses Hemmenway, 76, colonial American Calvinist clergyman. He spent over 50 years as pastor of First Church in Wells, ME. As a friend and correspondent of John Adams, Hemmenway was a strong voice that opposed Arian, Socinian and universalist tendencies in the New England churches of his day. (b. 1735)

1900 Death of James A. Healy, 70, American Catholic bishop. Born a slave to an Irish plantation owner near Macon, GA, Healy afterward joined the Catholic church, rose to become a priest (1854), and in 1875 was consecrated the first U.S.-born African-American bishop in U.S. Catholic history. (b. 4/6/1830)

Words for the Soul

1639 Exiled Scottish pastor Samuel Rutherford declared in a letter: *'If ye mind to walk to heaven, without a cramp or a crook, I fear you must go alone: he knoweth our dross and defects; and pitieth us, when weakness and deadness in our obedience is our cross, and not our darling.'*

1771 Anglican Evangelical Henry Venn reminded in a letter: *'Tribulation, of one kind or other, is our lot. In vain do we imagine we shall escape it.'*

FROM GOD'S WORD... OT: Ezra 1:1–2:70 ~ NT: 1 Corinthians 1:18–2:5 ~ Psalms 27:7-14 ~ Proverbs 20:22-23

August 6

Highlights in History

1629 The town leaders of Salem, Massachusetts framed a Non-Separatist covenant for their new church. It was the first congregation formed in the American Colonies that did not repudiate the Church of England.

1774 English religious leader Ann Lee (1736-84) and a small band of followers first arrived in America at New York City. Her sect established itself as the United Society of Believers in Christ's Second Coming, but the rest of the world came to know them as the 'Shakers.'

1801 The Great Religious Revival of the American West began during a week-long evangelical Presbyterian camp meeting held in Cane Ridge, KY. The meeting attracted some 25,000 people, and was afterward referred to as the greatest outpouring of the Holy Spirit since Pentecost.

1968 The Lambeth Conference of the Anglican Church unanimously reaffirmed its endorsement and sanction of contraceptive practices.

Notable Birthdays

1651 Birth of François Fénelon, French prelate and scholar. His controversial defense of the Quietism of Madame Guyon cost him his position on the French court. A mystical theologian and writer, Fénelon's *Christian Perfection* (1697) provided a reasoned defense of the mystical aspects of Christian spirituality. [d. 1/7/1715]

1821 Birth of Edward H. Plumptre, Anglican theologian. He served on the O.T. committee for the 1885 *English Revised Version* of the Bible. He also published several volumes of verse, and translated many hymns. Today, Plumptre is still remembered as author of the hymn, "Rejoice, Ye Pure in Heart." [d. 2/1/1891]

1854 Birth of Seth Cook Rees, pioneer Christian denominational leader. Born to devout Quaker parents, in 1883 he underwent a sanctification experience and afterward associated for a time with A. B. Simpson's Christian and Missionary Alliance. In 1917, after spending years in evangelism, Rees became a key organizer of the Pilgrim Holiness denomination (since 1968, a branch of the Wesleyan Church). [d. 5/22/1933]

1872 Birth of John Wesley Work, Jr., African American hymnwriter. Together with his brother Frederick J. Work, he wrote, collected, arranged, published and promoted several volumes of black spirituals, including one by his own hand: "Go, Tell It on the Mountain." [d. 9/7/1925]

The Last Passage

1221 Death of St. Dominic de Guzman, 51, Spanish founder in 1216 of the Order of Friars Preachers (Dominicans). The order combined the contemplative life of the monk and the active work of the evangelist. Dominic was canonized by Pope Gregory IX in 1234. (b. 1170)

1978 Pope Paul VI died of a heart attack at age 80. Born Giovanni Battista Montini, he was made a cardinal under John XXIII, succeeded him at his death in 1963, and spent most of his 15-year pontificate carrying through the reforms of the Vatican II Ecumenical Council (1962-65). (b. 9/26/1897)

Words for the Soul

1871 English Baptist clergyman and Bible expositor Charles Spurgeon declared in a sermon: *'There will be no more Lord's Suppers when Christ appears, because they will be needless.... But until he does come,... the cup will never be emptied till then.'*

1966 Swiss Reformed theologian Karl Barth affirmed in a letter: *'Since God does in fact address man in His Word, He obviously regards him as addressable in spite of the fact that man as a sinner closes his ears and heart to Him.'*

FROM GOD'S WORD... OT: Ezra 3:1–4:24 ~ NT: 1 Corinthians 2:6–3:4 ~ Psalms 28:1-9 ~ Proverbs 20:24-25

August 7

Highlights in History

1560 Ratification of the Scots Confession by the Scottish Parliament marked the triumph of the Reformation in Scotland, under the leadership of John Knox. (In 1647, the Scots Confession was superseded by the Westminster Confession.)

1814 With the publication of his bull, "Solicitudo omnium ecclesiarum," Pope Pius VII reinstituted the Society of Jesus to full legal status within the Catholic Church. (The Jesuits had been suppressed in 1773 by Clement XIV, after years of controversy regarding their interpretation of the doctrines of free will and grace.)

Notable Birthdays

1586 Birth of Johann Valentin Andreae, German Lutheran clergyman, theologian and alchemist. He is best remembered as the originator of the Rosicrucian legend. [d. 1/27/1654]

1831 Birth of Frederick W. Farrar, Dean of Canterbury. A "Broad Church Evangelical," he had great influence on the religious feeling and culture of the Victorian middle classes, especially through his *Life of Christ* (1874). [d. 3/22/1903]

1852 Birth of Franklin L. Sheppard, Presbyterian organist and hymnbook editor. He composed the hymn tune TERRA PATRIS, to which we sing "This is My Father's World." [d. 2/15/1930]

The Last Passage

117 Death of Marcus Trajan, 65, Roman emperor from AD 98-117. His attitude toward the Early Church gradually changed from toleration to persecution. It was during Trajan's rule that the Early Church Father Ignatius of Antioch was martyred. (b. 9/18/52)

1894 Death of James Strong, 71, American Methodist biblical scholar and editor. He was a member of the O.T. committee for the 1901-05 American Standard Version, but his chief contribution to scholarship was as editor of the *Cyclopaedia of Biblical, Theological, and Ecclesiastical Literature* (12 vols., 1867-87). Strong is also popularly remembered today as compiler of the *Exhaustive Concordance of the Bible*. (b. 8/14/1822)

1922 Death of William H. Jude, 70, English organist, musical editor and composer. He is remembered for creating the hymn tune GALILEE ("Jesus Calls Us O'er the Tumult"). (b. 9/1851)

1961 Death of Frank N. D. Buchman, 83, American religious leader. He was founder and director of the Oxford Group (1921) and Moral Rearmament (1938) – organizations which emphasized national and social morale rather than an individual Christian life. Buchman never married, and the movements he fostered declined after his death. (b. 6/4/1878)

Words for the Soul

1540 German reformer Martin Luther remarked in a conversation: *'Let all preachers see to it that they do not seek glory in the Holy Writings, or they will go to ruin. In Vergil and Cicero glory may be found. But Scripture calls for a humble and contrite spirit. This is the place where the Holy Spirit dwells.'*

1768 English clergyman Augustus Toplady exulted in his diary: *'I can never enough adore thy goodness, O thou God of all grace!'*

1878 Lutheran Church Missouri Synod founder Carl F. W. Walther exhorted in a letter: *'Do not deny the Word of God when it speaks to you.'*

1924 English writer and mystic Evelyn Underhill advised in a letter: *'A true contemplative vocation... involves... the development of a spiritual force by which you exercise not only spiritual adoration, but also mediatorship — a sort of redemptive and clarifying power working on other souls — a tiny cooperation in the work of Christ.'*

FROM GOD'S WORD... OT: Ezra 5:1–6:22 ~ NT: 1 Corinthians 3:5-23 ~ Psalms 29:1-11 ~ Proverbs 20:26-27

August 8

Highlights in History

1570 The Peace of St. Germain was signed, granting Protestants in France an amnesty from Catholic oppression, including a freedom of conscience and of worship. (Two years later, on Aug. 24, 1572, this treaty was nullified by the St. Bartholomew's Day Massacre, when thousands of Huguenots throughout France were murdered on orders of Catherine de Medici.)

1852 The roots of the Baptist General Conference were planted when Swedish immigrant pastor Gustaf Palmquist baptized his first three converts in the Mississippi River at Rock Island, IL. Today, the denomination numbers 140,000.

1910 The Vatican's Sacred Congregation ("Committee") of the Sacraments issued 'Quam singulari,' a decree which recommended children be permitted to receive Holy Communion as soon as they reach the 'age of discretion' (ca. age 7).

Notable Birthdays

1652 Birth of Jacques Basnage, French Reformed clergyman, patristic and Huguenot scholar. Exiled in Holland after revocation of the Edict of Nantes, he aided diplomatically in arranging the Triple Alliance at The Hague. [d. 12/22/1723]

1876 Birth of Metropolitan Leonty, Primate of the Russian Orthodox Eastern Church of America and Metropolitan of all America and Canada. Born in Kremenets, Russia, he was dean of the first Russian Orthodox theological seminary in the U.S. (located in Minneapolis; later moved to Tenafly, New Jersey), 1906-15. [d. 5/25/1965]

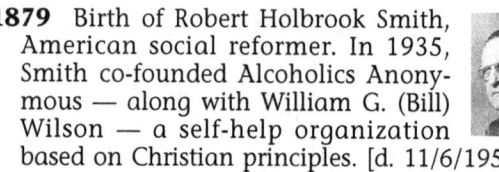

1877 Birth of Walter Bauer, German Lutheran theologian and lexicographer. His most enduring publication was the definitive *Greek-English Lexicon of the New Testament and Other Early Christian Literature*, whose 1979 English edition (affectionately known as *BAGD*) was translated and augmented by W. F. Arndt, F. W. Gingrich and (3rd ed.) F. W. Danker. [d. 1960]

1879 Birth of Robert Holbrook Smith, American social reformer. In 1935, Smith co-founded Alcoholics Anonymous — along with William G. (Bill) Wilson — a self-help organization based on Christian principles. [d. 11/6/1950]

The Last Passage

1796 Death of Peter Williams, 74, Welsh clergyman and hymn translator. Converted as a boy under the preaching of George Whitefield, he served for a time as an Anglican curate, later became a Calvinistic Methodist, and finally built his own independent chapel. Williams published a volume of Welsh hymns (1759), an annotated Welsh Bible and a concordance. His name endures as translator of the hymn, "Guide Me, O Thou Great Jehovah." (b. 1/7/1722)

1998 Death of Raymond E. Brown, 70, American Sulpician priest and biblical scholar. Associated with Union Seminary in NY (1971-90), Brown authored a number of books and articles, but is best known for his commentaries on the Gospel of John, as well as his studies on Jesus' Gospel birth and infancy narratives. (b. 5/22/1928)

Words for the Soul

1539 German reformer Martin Luther remarked in a sermon: 'Reason does not know that salvation must come down from above; we want to work up from below so that the satisfaction is rendered by us.'

1745 Describing his Native American listeners, colonial American missionary David Brainerd wrote: 'Those who had been awakened any considerable time complained more especially of the badness of their hearts; and those who were newly awakened, of the badness of their lives and actions; and all were afraid of the anger of God, and of everlasting misery as the desert of their sins.'

1773 John Wesley exhorted in a letter: 'Life is short! We need to improve every moment!'

FROM GOD'S WORD... OT: Ezra 7:1–8:20 ~ NT: 1 Corinthians 4:1-21 ~ Psalms 30:1-12 ~ Proverbs 20:28-30

August 9

Highlights in History

1471 Franciscan Cardinal Francesco della Rovere was elected Pope Sixtus IV, serving until 1484. He fostered the doctrine of the Immaculate Conception; condemned abuses of the Inquisition; built the Sistine Chapel; reorganized the Vatican Library and opened it to scholars.

1797 In England, six years after the death of founder John Wesley, the Methodist New Connection was formed at Leeds by Alexander Kilham and three other Methodist clergymen. (This branch denomination had favored complete separation from the Church of England.)

1973 In Asheville, NC, delegates from 200 congregations voted to sever ties with the Southern Presbyterian Church (PCUS), believing it had become too liberal. A new denomination was formed, and in 1974 adopted its current name: The Presbyterian Church in America (PCA).

Notable Birthdays

1779 Birth of Francis Scott Key, American lawyer and poet. During the War of 1812, the night of Sept. 14, 1814, he authored "The Bombing of Ft. McHenry," a poem which later became the U.S. National Anthem. [d. 1/11/1843]

1788 Birth of Adoniram Judson, pioneer American Baptist missionary. He first sailed to Burma in 1812, and spent nearly all his remaining 38 years in missionary and literacy work there.  Judson translated the Bible into Burmese by 1834. He also penned the hymn, "Come, Holy Spirit, Dove Divine." [d. 4/12/1850]

1884 Birth of Kenneth Scott Latourette, Baptist church historian. A lifelong bachelor, he taught at Yale (1921-53). Latourette's many works include  *History of the Expansion of Christianity* (7 vols., 1937-45) and his 5-volume *Christianity in a Revolutionary Age* (1958-62). [d. 12/26/1968]

The Last Passage

1864 Death of Fidelia Fisk, 58, American missionary and niece of missionary Pliny Fisk. Fidelia went to Persia in 1843, where she subsequently labored among the Nestorians for 15 years. Returning in broken health to the U.S. in 1858, Fisk had been the first single woman missionary to Persia. (b. 5/1/1816)

1883 Death of Robert Moffatt, 87, Scottish Congregationalist missionary to Africa. He established a major missionary center at Kuruman. The father-in-law of explorer David Livingstone, Moffatt completed a translation of the Bible into Bechuana in 1872. (b. 12/21/1795)

Words for the Soul

1765 English Methodist John Wesley wrote in a letter: 'You have but one Pattern; follow Him inwardly and outwardly. If other believers will go step for step with you, well; but if not, follow Him!'

1942 English Bible expositor Arthur W. Pink wrote in a letter: 'Waiting on the Lord (Isa. 40:31, etc.) describes an attitude of soul when we are engaged in true prayer, but waiting for the Lord is the exercise of patience while His answer tarries.'

1946 British literary scholar and Christian apologist C. S. Lewis warned in a letter: 'Apologetic work is so dangerous to one's own faith. A doctrine never seems dimmer to me than when I have just successfully defended it.'

1953 Russian monk Ivan Alekseyev outlined in a letter: 'When a person commits sin, he thinks he gets consolation from it, but after he has tasted sin, the result is the opposite: great sorrow... and the poor soul feels like a fish cast ashore.'

1996 Dutch priest and diarist Henri J. M. Nouwen admitted in his **Sabbatical Journey** journal: 'I was glad to have a quiet night alone. I prayed a little, read a little, and went early to bed.'

FROM GOD'S WORD... OT: Ezra 8:21–9:15 ~ NT: 1 Corinthians 5:1-13 ~ Psalms 31:1-8 ~ Proverbs 21:1-2

August 10

Highlights in History

1933 In Keswick, NJ, Wycliffe Bible Translators was first set in motion at the Day of Prayer for the tribes of Latin America. Founders W. Cameron Townsend and L[eonard] L. Legters incorporated WBT in 1942, and it has since grown into one of the largest interdenominational missionary agencies in the world.

1983 The sixth assembly of the World Council of Churches closed in Vancouver, Canada. It was the second assembly in North America, the first being at Evanston, IL, in 1952. This convention was attended by 4,500 participants, including 847 voting members from 301 member churches.

Notable Birthdays

1781 Birth of William Gibbons, American physician and polemic writer. In 1821 he published a series of letters in reply to attacks made by a Presbyterian clergyman against the Society of Friends. It became one of the clearest expositions of Quaker doctrine published in the nineteenth century. [d. 7/25/1845]

1794 Birth of Leopold Zunz, German rabbi and Jewish scholar. He was founder of the science of Judaism, wherein modern scholarly research methods are applied to the study of Jewish religion, history and ritual. [d. 3/18/1886]

1841 Birth of Mary A. Lathbury, American Sunday School leader, poet and artist. The daughter of a Methodist clergyman, two of Lathbury's published poems later became popular hymns: "Break Thou the Bread of Life" and "Day is Dying in the West." [d. 10/20/1913]

The Last Passage

1897 Death of William Walsham How, 74, Anglican prelate, philanthropist and hymnwriter. He was known as the "Poor Man's Bishop" for the humanitarian work he did in the slums of East London. He authored over 50 hymns, many of which are still in use, including "We Give Thee But Thine Own." (b. 12/13/1823)

1960 Death of Ralph S. Cushman, 80, American Methodist bishop, author and poet. His best-known verse begins: *"I met God in the morning / when my day was at its best, / And His Presence came like sunrise, / Like a glory in my breast...."* (b. 11/12/1879)

Words for the Soul

1742 English revivalist George Whitefield wrote in a letter: *'It is a very uncommon thing to be rooted and grounded in the love of Jesus. I find persons may have the idea, but are far from having the real substance.'*

1782 English clergyman and hymnwriter John Newton explained to his adopted daughter in a letter: *'The Lord's governing providence ... extends to the minutest concerns. He rules and manages all things, but in so secret a way that most people think he does nothing, when, in reality, he does all.'*

1856 English Baptist clergyman Charles Spurgeon declared in a sermon: *'It was the gospel which taught Paul how to say "brother." If he had not been a Christian, his Jewish dignity would never have condescended to call a Roman "brother"; for a Jew sneered at the Gentile, and called him "dog." But now in the breast of this "Hebrew of Hebrews," there is the holy recognition of Christian fraternity without reserve or hypocrisy.'*

1948 British literary scholar and Christian apologist C. S. Lewis concluded in a letter: *'We ought to give thanks for all fortune: if it is good, because it is good; if bad, because it works in us patience, humility, contempt of this world and the hope of our eternal country.'*

1961 Writing from his monastery, Italian religious Carlo Carretto advised in a letter to his sister Dolcidia: *'Life on this Earth is a roped-together climbing party and charity is its bond.'*

FROM GOD'S WORD... OT: Ezra 10:1-44 ~ NT: 1 Corinthians 6:1-20 ~ Psalms 31:9-18 ~ Proverbs 21:3

August 11

Highlights in History

1492 Italian Cardinal Rodrigo de Borgia became Pope Alexander VI, serving until 1503. Labeled by some as "history's worst pope," he initiated the censorship of books, practiced simony and condemned Savonarola. However, Alexander also issued the 1493 bull which demarcated the longitudinal line between Spanish and Portuguese land discoveries in the New World.

1760 Irish-born English minister Philip Embury, 32, arrived in New York, making him the first Methodist clergyman to come to America. In 1768 he founded Wesley Chapel. (Embury later joined a Lutheran church, apparently no longer interested in Methodism.)

Notable Birthdays

1869 Birth of Joseph Hillery King, American Pentecostal holiness leader. Converted on his 16th birthday in a Methodist holiness camp meeting in Georgia, King went on to become a founder and (in 1937) the first bishop of the Pentecostal Holiness Church. [d. 4/23/1946]

1914 Birth of Lee Shelley, missions pioneer. In 1957 he founded Christians in Action Missions in Huntington Park, CA – an interdenominational agency working overseas in evangelism, church planting and missionary training.

1933 Birth of Jerry Falwell, U.S. Baptist clergyman. Pastor of Thomas Road Baptist Church in Lynchburg, VA, he was an active political lobbyist and once headed the Liberty Federation (first called Moral Majority), a Christian lobby which Falwell founded in 1979. [d. 5/15/2007]

The Last Passage

1519 Death of Johann Tetzel, 54, the German Dominican priest who sold indulgences in 1516, prompting Martin Luther to post his "Ninety-Five Theses." Tetzel thus became the unwilling first public antagonist of Luther. (b. ca. 1465)

1778 Death of Augustus M. Toplady, 37, Anglican clergyman and hymnwriter. An ardent Calvinist and a bitter critic of John Wesley, his major publications include *Psalms and Hymns for Public and Private Worship* (1776). Today, Toplady is better known as the author of the hymn, "Rock of Ages." (b. 11/4/1740)

1872 Death of Lowell Mason, 80, American educator, composer and hymnwriter. He established the first public school music program in 1838. He also composed a number of enduring hymn tunes, including BETHANY ("Nearer, My God, To Thee"); HAMBURG ("When I Survey the Wondrous Cross"); OLIVET ("My Faith Looks Up to Thee"); MISSIONARY HYMN ("From Greenland's Icy Mountains"); and BOYLSTON ("A Charge to Keep I Have"). (b. 1/8/1792)

1890 Death of John Henry Cardinal Newman, British clergyman, theologian and writer. A co-founder of the Oxford Movement (which sought to return the Church of England to the high ideals of the latter 17th century), Newman explained his conversion to Catholicism in 1845 in his autobiographical masterpiece, *Apologia Pro Vita Sua* (1864). (b. 2/21/1801)

Words for the Soul

1537 German reformer Martin Luther pointed out in a sermon: *'That all do not accept it is not the fault of the Light.'*

1775 Anglican clergyman and hymnwriter John Newton explained in a letter: *'Scriptural faith is a very different thing from a rational assent to the Gospel. Christ is not only the object, but the Author and Finisher of faith.'*

1974 Dutch educator and diarist Henri J. M. Nouwen observed in his **Genesee Diary**: *'I am becoming more and more aware that solitude indeed makes you more sensitive to the good in people and even enables you to bring it to the foreground.'*

FROM GOD'S WORD... OT: Nehemiah 1:1–3:14 ~ NT: 1 Corinthians 7:1-24 ~ Psalms 31:19-24 ~ Proverbs 21:4

August 12

Highlights in History

1787 The first Anglican Bishop of Nova Scotia, Charles Inglis, was consecrated by the Archbishop of Canterbury at Lambeth. Inglis first arrived in Halifax on October 16th, 1787.

1908 Canadian Pentecostal Robert Semple, 27, married Aimee Kennedy, 18. Two years later, Robert died of malaria while the two were serving as missionaries in Hong Kong. Marrying Harold McPherson, 21, in 1911, Aimee Semple McPherson afterward went on to become the most successful and celebrated female evangelist of the early 20th century.

1950 Pope Pius XII issued the encyclical "Humani generis," which denounced certain "modernist" intellectual tendencies within Catholic theology. These included: (1) existentialism; (2) excessive emphasis on Scripture to the detraction of reason; (3) contempt for the authority of the Church; (4) distrust of scholastic philosophy (i.e., that of Thomas Aquinas); and (5) denial that Adam existed as a historical person.

Notable Birthdays

1591 Birth of St. Louise de Marillac, French Catholic religious. A co-founder (with St. Vincent de Paul) of the Daughters of Charity (a.k.a. the Sisters of Charity), she became its first superior, and was canonized in 1934. [d. 1660]

1805 Birth of Johann Jacob Herzog, Swiss-German Reformed theologian. He was a co-editor (with Philip Schaff) of the *Schaff-Herzog Encyclopedia of Religious Knowledge* (1853-68) — today known as "SHERK." [d. 9/30/1882]

1838 Birth of Joseph Barnby, English organist and choirmaster. He composed nearly 250 hymn tunes during his life. Among those still popular are LAUDES DOMINI ("When Morning Gilds the Skies"); LONGWOOD ("Spirit of God, Descend Upon My Heart"); and MERRIAL ("Now the Day is Over"). [d. 1/28/1896]

1859 Birth of Katharine Lee Bates, American English teacher. She published 20 books, but is better known today for authoring the hymn, "America, the Beautiful" (a.k.a. "O Beautiful for Spacious Skies"). [d. 3/28/1929]

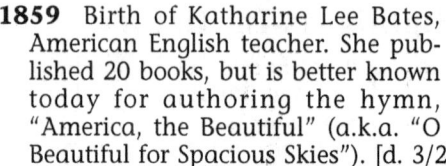

1905 Birth of Hans Urs von Balthasar, Swiss Catholic theologian and spiritual writer. Having been greatly influenced by Karl Barth, Balthasar's works emphasized the Christian implications of the Trinity and of the Incarnation. [d. 6/26/1988]

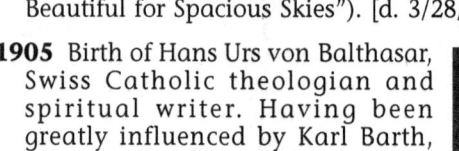

The Last Passage

1715 Death of Nahum Tate, 63, British poet and dramatist. Named poet laureate of England in 1692, Tate wrote primarily for the London stage. Today, he is remembered for his *New Version of the Psalms of David* (1696), and for authoring the popular Christmas carol, "While Shepherds Watched Their Flocks." (b. 1652)

1827 Death of William Blake, 69, English poet and artist. Noted for the mystical nature of his poetry, Blake authored *Songs of Innocence* (1789) and *Songs of Experience* (1794). His paintings also illustrated a famous edition of Milton's *Paradise Lost*. (b. 11/28/1757)

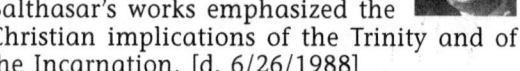

Words for the Soul

1940 English writer and mystic Evelyn Underhill advised in a letter: 'We each do what we can, mostly very badly. The point is that we do it with faith and love and offer it to God, who will take from it that act of will and love which alone really matters, and use it where and how He chooses.'

1952 American missionary and Auca Indian martyr Jim Elliot determined in his journal: 'I must come to be aware of Satan. He may never get me into hell, but he may cause God shame in defeating me. Preserve me from the lion, Lord. Let him not swallow me up.'

FROM GOD'S WORD... OT: Nehemiah 3:15–5:13 ~ NT: 1 Corinthians 7:25-40 ~ Psalms 32:1-11 ~ Proverbs 21:5-7

August 13

Highlights in History

1587 In Roanoke, Virginia, Manteo — the first American Indian converted to Protestantism — was baptized into the Church of England by members of Sir Walter Raleigh's expedition to the New World.

1682 The first Welsh immigrants to the American colonies arrived in Pennsylvania. They were Quakers who had bought land from William Penn, and settled near modern Philadelphia.

1727 In the German village of Herrnhut, religious reformer Nicolaus von Zinzendorf, 27, organized a group of Bohemian Protestant refugees into the first Moravian community of 'Unitas Fratrum' (United Brotherhood). Zinzendorf spent the following years in directing the spiritual nurture and administrative affairs of this pietist colony, many of whose members were descendants of the Bohemian Brethren of the 1400s.

Notable Birthdays

1821 Birth of Henry Martyn Dexter, American Congregational clergyman and editor. He served Pine St. Church, Boston (1849-67), and was editor-in-chief of "The Congregationalist" (1856-90). He is also remembered today as author of the English hymn translation, "Shepherd of Tender Youth." [d. 11/13/1890]

1834 Birth of Philip Phillips, American singing evangelist and hymnwriter: "I Have Heard the Savior's Love." A traveling associate with Dwight Moody, Phillips visited England in 1868, sang 200 nights for the Sunday School Union and prepared *The American Sacred Songster*, which sold over 1 million copies. [d. 1895]

1919 Birth of Rex Humbard, American pioneer radio and television evangelist. In 1958 he established the Cathedral of Tomorrow in Akron, Ohio, from which he afterward based his early television ministry.

The Last Passage

662 Death of St. Maximus the Confessor, 82, Byzantine monk, theologian and writer. A vigorous opponent of Monothelite doctrine, he was banished to Thrace and died a martyr. (b. ca. 580)

1772 Death of Charles C. Beatty, 57, Irish-born Presbyterian clergyman. In 1755 he became chaplain to the colonial troops of Pennsylvania. Beatty died of yellow fever soon after arriving in the West Indies to investigate the condition of Indian tribes at Duffield. (b. ca. 1715)

1878 Death of Elizabeth P. Prentiss, 60, American author. The evangelical spirit of her writings, many of which were thinly veiled autobiography, found a ready audience. Today she is also remembered as author of the hymn, "More Love To Thee, O Christ." (b. 10/26/1818)

1908 Death of Ira D. Sankey, 68, song evangelist for Dwight L. Moody from 1870. During their revival crusades, Sankey penned many hymn tunes, including HIDING IN THEE ("O Safe to the Rock That is Higher Than I") and SANKEY ("Faith is the Victory"). (b. 8/28/1840)

Words for the Soul

1775 On the brink of the American Revolution, English founder of Methodism John Wesley wrote to American Methodist Thomas Rankin: *'I am not sorry that brother [Francis] Asbury stays with you another year. In that time it will be seen what God will do with North America.'*

1776 Article XXXVI of the newly approved Constitution of the State of Maryland read, in part: *'All persons professing the Christian religion are equally entitled to protection in their religious liberty; wherefore no person ought by any law to be molested... on account of his religious practice; unless, under the color [pretense] of religion, any man shall disturb the good order, peace or safety of the State, or shall infringe the laws of morality....'*

FROM GOD'S WORD...   OT: Nehemiah 5:14–7:60 ~ NT: 1 Corinthians 8:1-13 ~ Psalms 33:1-11 ~ Proverbs 21:8-10

August 14

Highlights in History

1880 Exactly 632 years after rebuilding began, the Cologne Cathedral in Germany was completed (only to be damaged again during World War II). This largest Gothic style cathedral in Northern Europe was first built in 873 A.D., but was destroyed by fire in 1248. Rebuilding began on this day the same year (1248).

1814 While being held overnight in Baltimore as a British POW, and following the British shelling of Fort McHenry, American Revolutionary patriot Francis Scott Key penned the words to what later became the U.S. national anthem: "The Star-Spangled Banner."

Notable Birthdays

1742 Birth of Pius VII (Barnaba Chiaramonti), pope from 1800-23. He was imprisoned by Napoleon 1809-14, after which he re-established the Jesuit Order in 1814. [d. 8/20/1823]

1810 Birth of Samuel Sebastian Wesley, English organist and hymn composer. The grandson of Charles Wesley, Samuel composed over 130 original hymn tunes, of which perhaps the best remembered is AURELIA ("The Church's One Foundation"). [d. 4/19/1876]

1822 Birth of James Strong, American Methodist biblical scholar and editor. He served on the O.T. committee for the 1905 *American Standard Version* of the Bible. But his chief work was as editor of the monumental *Cyclopaedia of Biblical, Theological, and Ecclesiastical Literature* (12 vols., 1867-87). Today, Strong is remembered as author of the still-printed *Strong's Exhaustive Concordance of the Bible*. [d. 8/7/1894]

The Last Passage

1727 Death of William Croft, 48, English organist and hymn composer: ST. ANNE ("O God, Our Help in Ages Past"). (bapt. 12/30/1678)

1848 Death of English Unitarian devotional writer Sarah Flower Adams, 43. In 1845 she published *The Flock at the Fountain*, a catechism containing hymns for children. One of those hymns remains popular even to this day: "Nearer, My God, To Thee." (b. 2/22/1805)

1891 Death of John Henry Hopkins, 70, author and composer of the popular Christmas carol, "We Three Kings." (b. 10/28/1820)

1891 Death of Sarah Childress Polk, 87, American Presbyterian fundamentalist and wife of 11th US president James K. Polk. Sarah became the first "first lady" to institute strict Sabbath observance and ban dancing at presidential functions (b. 9/4/1803)

Words for the Soul

1739 English revivalist George Whitefield encouraged in a letter: *'Our extremity is God's opportunity.'*

1782 English founder of Methodism John Wesley advised in a letter: *'No one should wish or pray for persecution. On the contrary, we are to avoid it to the uttermost of our power. "When they persecute you in one city, flee unto another." Yet, when it does come, notwithstanding all our care to avoid it, God will extract good out of evil.'*

1809 English writer Hannah More appealed in a letter:  *'Pray for me, that I may be more detached from the world, more spiritually-minded, less engrossed by the things of time and sense.... What unspeakable consolation it is that I have a better righteousness than my own to trust to!'*

1944 German theologian and Nazi martyr Dietrich Bonhoeffer concluded in a letter from prison: *'God does not give us everything we want, but He does fulfill all His promises... leading us along the best and straightest paths to Himself.'*

FROM GOD'S WORD...   OT: Nehemiah 7:61–9:21 ~ NT: 1 Corinthians 9:1-18 ~ Psalms 33:12-22 ~ Proverbs 21:11-12

August 15

Highlights in History

1096 Armies of the First Crusade set out from Europe to deliver Jerusalem from the occupying Islamic Turks. Championed by Peter the Hermit in 1093, Pope Urban II had sanctioned the crusade at the Council of Clermont in 1095.

1456 Henry Cremer finished binding the first volume of the two-volume *Gutenberg Bible*. (The printing had occupied two years.) At its completion, the *Gutenberg Bible* became both the first full-length book to be printed in the West, and the first printed edition of the Scriptures.

1534 The Society of Jesus (Jesuits) was founded by Ignatius of Loyola, 43. Created to foster reform within Catholicism, this colorful religious order later elected to undertake education and missionary work, and was formally approved by Pope Paul III in 1540.

1790 Maryland-born former Jesuit missionary John Carroll, 55, was consecrated by Pius VI as the first Roman Catholic bishop (and in 1808 first archbishop) of the United States.

Notable Birthdays

1195 Birth of St. Anthony of Padua, French Catholic Biblical scholar. Born Ferdinand de Bulhoes, he was the first lector in theology of the Franciscan Order, and directed his sermons against avarice and usury. Anthony was canonized in 1232, and was named a Doctor of the Church in 1946. [d. 6/13/1231]

1613 Birth of Jeremy Taylor, English bishop, theologian and devotional writer. He was an important figure among the 17th Century Anglicans known as the "Caroline Divines." Two of Taylor's writings became classic expressions of Anglican spirituality: *The Rule and Exercise of Holy Living* (1650) and *The Rule and Exercise of Holy Dying* (1651). [d. 8/13/1667]

1752 Birth of Freeborn Garrettson, American clergyman and abolitionist. Influenced by the preaching of Francis Asbury, Garrettson began an evangelical ministry in 1775 which lasted more than 50 years. He married into a wealthy family and settled (1800) on the Hudson River. Garrettson's home afterward became a haven for traveling preachers, and a base for extending the message of Methodism into New York state. [d. 9/26/1827]

The Last Passage

1257 Death of St. Hyacinth (née Jacek Odrawaz), ca. 40, Dominican missionary to Poland and "Apostle of the North." He was founder of the Dominican houses in Cracow and Danzig, and was canonized in 1594. (b. 1185)

1666 Death of Johann A. Schall, 75, German astronomer and Jesuit missionary to China (1622-66). He revised the Chinese calendar, and translated many mathematical works into Chinese. (b. 1591)

1678 Death of René de Bréchant de Galinée, French Catholic missionary to North America. He was probably the first European to see Niagara Falls and to explore the northern shores of Lake Erie and Lake Huron. (b. 1600s)

Words for the Soul

1846 An Illinois newspaper carried the only public statement American statesman Abraham Lincoln ever made on his personal religious beliefs: *'That I am not a member of any Christian Church, is true; but I have never denied the truth of the Scripture; and I have never spoken with intentional disrespect of religion in general, of any denomination of Christians in particular.'*

1972 Benedictine monk Columba Cary-Elwes reasoned in a letter to English historian Arnold Toynbee: *'Faith is the basis of civilization, and with the collapse of religion comes the collapse of a decent way of life.'*

FROM GOD'S WORD...   OT: Nehemiah 9:22–10:39 ~ NT: 1 Corinthians 9:19–10:13 ~ Psalms 34:1-10 ~ Proverbs 21:13

August 16

Highlights in History

1773 The Jesuits were expelled from Rome by Pope Clement XIV. (They had been suppressed earlier this year by Clement's brief, "Dominus ac Redemptor Noster.")

1868 American Catholic prelate James Gibbons, 34, was consecrated titular bishop of Adramyttium, making him the youngest of the world's then-1200 Catholic bishops. Gibbons became Bishop of Richmond in 1872, and was later made Archbishop of Baltimore (1877-1921).

1972 African American Methodist clergyman from Dominica, West Indies, Philip A. Potter, 51, was named General Secretary of the World Council of Churches. Serving until 1984, Potter gave strong spiritual guidance to the WCC.

Notable Birthdays

1815 Birth of St. John Bosco, Italian Catholic educator. Poverty among the children in the city of Turin led him in 1859 to establish the Society of St. Francis of Sales (the Salesians). Bosco was canonized by Pius XI in 1934. [d. 1/31/1888]

1831 Birth of Hiram Bingham, Jr., American Congregational missionary to Micronesia (Gilbert Islands). He settled in Honolulu in 1868, prepared a New Testament translation into Gilbertese in 1873, and completed the entire Bible in 1890. As a translator and etymologist, Bingham's researches expanded the inadequate 4,000-word Gilbertese tongue into a language three times its original size. He also reduced the native language to writing. [d. 10/25/1908]

1852 Birth of Adolf von Schlatter, Swiss Protestant New Testament scholar. His *History of Christ* (1921) maintained that a valid systematic theology had to be based on a foundation of solid biblical exegesis. [d. 5/19/1938]

1877 Birth of John P. Scott, American hymn composer. Born in Norwich, NY, he wrote a number of popular hymns, including: "The Lord is My Shepherd," "The Old Road," "The Dearest Place" and "Come, Ye Blessed." [d. 1932]

1942 Birth of Don Wyrtzen, U.S. contemporary Christian songwriter. Among his most enduring compositions are "Yesterday, Today, and Tomorrow," "Worthy is the Lamb" and "Love Was When."

The Last Passage

1786 Death of English Catholic hymnwriter, John F. Wade, 76. He gave the Church ADESTE FIDELIS ("O Come, All Ye Faithful"). (b. ca. 1710).

1875 Death of American Presbyterian revivalist and educator Charles G. Finney, 82. Converted at 29, he led revivals for several years before affiliating with Oberlin College (OH), where he spent the remainder of his professional life teaching (1837-75), and later as president (1851-66). Finney authored *Lectures on Systematic Theology* (1847) and founded the "Oberlin Evangelist" (1839). (b. 8/29/1792)

Words for the Soul

1767 John Wesley noted in a letter: 'Everything is a blessing, a means of holiness, as long as you can clearly say, "Lord, do with me and mine what thou wilt, and when thou wilt, and how thou wilt."'

1951 Russian monk Ivan Alekseyev assured in a letter: 'If a person is chosen for some duty that he does not himself aspire to, it means that it is God's will and the Lord will help. But there is no place to which one can flee from annoyances; no matter where a person goes – they will go with him.'

1974 Dutch educator and diarist Henri J. M. Nouwen observed in his *Genesee Diary*: 'When I see God, I must pray. There is an inner must, an inner urge, or inner call that answers all those questions which are beyond explanation.'

August 17

Highlights in History

1635 English Puritan Richard Mather, 39, first arrived in Boston. A staunch defender of congregational church government, Mather is remembered today for founding the 'dynasty' to which was born his son Increase Mather in 1639, and his grandson Cotton Mather in 1663.

1643 The Solemn League and Covenant was formally accepted by the General Assembly of the Church of Scotland. Among its professed aims were the maintenance of the Presbyterian form of church polity in the Church of Scotland and the reformation of the Church of England.

1809 In Washington, PA, Thomas Campbell, 46, and his son Alexander, 20, formed the American Movement for Christian Unity, which later became the Disciples of Christ Church.

1837 The Auburn Convention opened in New York state. It resulted in a declaration that played an important part in dividing the Presbyterian Church – though later (1870) also forming the basis for its reunion.

Notable Birthdays

1761 Birth of William Carey, pioneer English missionary to India. He taught at Fort William College in Calcutta from 1801 until his death, and helped found the Serampore Press, which made the Bible accessible to over 300 million people. [d. 6/9/1834]

1780 Birth of George Croly, Irish churchman and author. During his life he published writings of biographical, historical and religious importance, but is primarily remembered today as author of the hymn, "Spirit of God, Descend Upon My Heart." [d. 11/24/1860]

1839 Birth of Hubert P. Main, American Methodist hymnologist. He is remembered today as composer of the hymn tune ELLESDIE ("Jesus, I My Cross Have Taken"). [d. 10/7/1925]

1851 Birth of Henry Drummond, Scottish evangelical writer and lecturer. He sought to reconcile evangelical Christianity with evolution, and authored *Natural Law in the Spiritual World*. Drummond is best remembered, however, for his famous 1887 address on First Corinthians 13, entitled "The Greatest Thing in the World." [d. 3/11/1897]

The Last Passage

1765 Death of American church leader and educator Timothy Cutler, 81. As Anglican rector of Christ Church, Boston (1723-65), Cutler was the central figure in the so-called Yale apostasy of 1722. He was also a dominant Anglican spokesman and a leader of the anti-revival forces of his time. (b. 5/31/1684)

1804 Barbara Heck, "Mother of American Methodism," died at 70. In 1766 she had encouraged her cousin Philip Embury to hold the first Methodist society meetings in America in his home in Troy, NY. The attendance grew, and in 1768 the John Street Methodist Church was organized – the first Methodist chapel built in America. British sympathies later compelled Barbara to emigrate to Canada during the American Revolution. (b. 1734)

Words for the Soul

1775 Anglican clergyman and hymnwriter John Newton encouraged in a letter: *'It is no great matter where we are, provided we see that the Lord has placed us there, and that He is with us.'*

1974 Dutch educator and diarist Henri J. M. Nouwen observed in his **Genesee Diary**: *'On this earth the experience of great beauty always remains mysteriously linked with the experience of great loneliness. This reminds me again that there still is a beauty I have not seen yet: the beauty that does not create loneliness but unity.'*

FROM GOD'S WORD... OT: Nehemiah 12:27–13:31 ~ NT: 1 Corinthians 11:2-16 ~ Psalms 35:1-16 ~ Proverbs 21:17-18

August 18

Highlights in History

1688 Puritan clergyman John Bunyan, 69, preached his last sermon, before dying 13 days later. In 1678 he had authored *Pilgrim's Progress*, an allegory describing the difficulties in a Christian's spiritual journey from this world to heaven.

1920 The Evangelization Society was founded by Charles Hamilton Pridgeon. Connected with the Pittsburgh Bible Institute, the mission agency originally worked in China. Today, its current outreach includes mission churches which have been established in Zaire, India and Taiwan.

1927 At age 20, Christian radio pioneer Theodore Epp was converted to a living faith. In 1939 he founded Back to the Bible Broadcast, an evangelistic radio program with outlets today on over 600 stations around the world.

1958 Through the leadership of the Manhattan Baptist Church in New York City, a mission of 44 persons was begun near Portsmouth, New Hampshire. On Feb. 22, 1960, the mission was constituted as the Screven Memorial Baptist Church, the first of its denomination established in the New England region.

Notable Birthdays

1856 Birth of Charles H. Gabriel, American sacred music artist. He edited a number of hymnbooks, and wrote several hymns, including "More Like the Master," "I Stand Amazed in the Presence" and "Send the Light." [d. 9/15/1932]

1888 Birth of Preston Bradley, American Unitarian clergyman and civic leader. In 1912 he founded the People's Church. Bradley's optimistic theism stressed human goodness, progress, openness to science, as well as interfaith and interracial understanding. He was also a pioneer in religious radio broadcasting, and authored *My Daily Strength* (1943) and *Happiness Through Creative Living* (1955). [d. 1983]

The Last Passage

1503 Death of Pope Alexander VI, 72. Born Rodrigo de Borgia, he is described by some as "history's worst pope." He also drew the famous Line of Demarcation between Spanish and Portuguese land discoveries in the New World (1493). Michelangelo also completed the Pietà under Alexander's reign in 1501. (b. 1/1/1431)

1922 Death of Marvin R. Vincent, 87, American Presbyterian biblical scholar. He authored *Word Studies in the New Testament* (1887-1900) and translated Johann Albrecht Bengel's 1742 *Gnomon Novi Testamenti*. (b. 9/11/1834)

1959 Death of Haldor Lillenas, 73, American hymnwriter. He founded Lillenas Music Company in 1924, and penned nearly 4,000 gospel texts and hymntunes, including "Wonderful Grace of Jesus" (WONDERFUL GRACE), and "Peace, Peace, Wonderful Peace." (b. 11/19/1885)

Words for the Soul

1532 German reformer Martin Luther declared in a "Table Talk": *'God is a Circle the center of which is everywhere and the circumference nowhere.'*

1930 English literary scholar C. S. Lewis wrote in a letter: *'One creeps home, tired and bruised, into a state of mind that is really restful, when all ambitions have been given up. Then one can really for the first time say, "Thy Kingdom come."'*

1963 Swiss theologian Karl Barth encouraged in a letter: *'Even if there is cause for great dissatisfaction with one's church, one should stay in it in the hope that new movements will come....'*

1974 Dutch priest, educator and diarist Henri J. M. Nouwen observed in his ***Genesee Diary***: *'The Bible is a realistic book and does not avoid any part of human reality.... God is not only where it is peaceful and quiet but also where there is persecution, struggle, division and conflict. God, indeed, did not promise us a rose garden.'*

FROM GOD'S WORD...   OT: Esther 1:1–3:15 ~ NT: 1 Corinthians 11:17-34 ~ Psalms 35:17-28 ~ Proverbs 21:19-20

ELUL

ALMANAC OF THE CHRISTIAN FAITH

AV

~ August 19 ~

Highlights in History

1099 The armies of the First Crusade defeated the Saracens at the Battle of Ascalon (a Palestinian city on the Mediterranean), one month after the Crusaders had captured Jerusalem.

1772 A revolution in Sweden, backed by France, re-established Gustavus III as monarch. He subsequently abolished torture, improved the code of laws and established religious tolerance.

1886 The Christian Union was founded by Baptist clergyman Richard G. Spurling in Tennessee. In 1923, this pentecostal denomination changed its name to the Church of God (HQ: Cleveland, TN). Current membership is nearly 500,000.

Notable Birthdays

1536 Birth of Kaspar Olevianus, early German reformer and theologian. Olevianus introduced the Calvinist Reformation into parts of Germany, and was a founder of the German Reformed Church. [d. 3/15/1587]

1813 Birth of Jemima T. Luke, Isle-of-Wight Congregational philanthropist and hymnwriter. She served as editor of the first missionary magazine in England for children, "The Missionary Repository." Today she is remembered as author of the hymn, "(I Think When I Read) That Sweet Story of Old." [d. 2/2/1906]

1831 Birth of William C. Langdon, an American Episcopal clergyman and a founder of the American branch of the Young Men's Christian Association (YMCA). [d. 1896]

1843 Birth of C[yrus] I. Scofield, American Congregational lawyer and biblical lecturer. He taught that there were seven dispensations in Scripture, in each of which God's relation to man was distinctly different. Scofield's most enduring contribution to Christian studies was his *Scofield Reference Bible* (1909). [d. 7/24/1921]

The Last Passage

1662 Death of Blaise Pascal, 39, French mathematician, philosopher, inventor, theologian and mystic. His name is honored in scientific circles for having invented the barometer, the first digital calculator, the syringe and the hydraulic press. Pascal also bequeathed the Church with two famous writings: *Provinciales* and *Pensées*. (b. 6/19/1623)
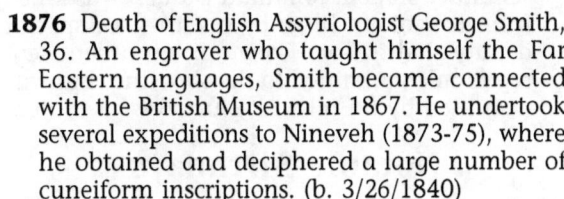

1876 Death of English Assyriologist George Smith, 36. An engraver who taught himself the Far Eastern languages, Smith became connected with the British Museum in 1867. He undertook several expeditions to Nineveh (1873-75), where he obtained and deciphered a large number of cuneiform inscriptions. (b. 3/26/1840)

1917 Death of Johannes Friedrich, 81, German church historian. Ordained to the Catholic priesthood in 1858, he attended the Vatican I Council, but refused to accept the dogma of papal infallibility. In 1871 Friedrich was excommunicated, but continued to publish and to teach church history at the universities of Munich and Bern. (b. 6/5/1836)

Words for the Soul

1759 John Wesley reasoned in a letter: 'All who expect to be sanctified at all, expect to be sanctified by faith. But, meantime, they know that faith will not be given but to them that obey. Remotely, therefore, the blessing depends on our works; although, immediately, on simple faith.'

1775 Anglican clergyman and hymnwriter John Newton assured in a letter: 'We are never more safe, never have more reason to expect the Lord's help, than when we are most sensible that we can do nothing without Him.'

1958 Writing from the monastery, Italian religious Carlo Carretto concluded in a letter to his sister Dolcidia: 'The world no longer concerns me except as an object of prayer.'

FROM GOD'S WORD...   OT: Esther 4:1–7:10 ~ NT: 1 Corinthians 12:1-26 ~ Psalms 36:1-12 ~ Proverbs 21:21-22

August 20

Highlights in History

1874 Theodore Tilton filed charges against renowned Congregational clergyman Henry Ward Beecher, for alleged adultery with Mrs. Tilton. A sensational trial ended after six months with a hung jury, and the Congregational Council exonerated Beecher (1876).

1965 During a civil rights march in Hayneville, Alabama, white New Hampshire Episcopal seminary student Jonathan Daniels was killed from a shotgun blast by a part-time special deputy sheriff. Tom Coleman, an ardent segregationist, admitted to the shooting, but was acquitted by an all-white jury 6 weeks later.

Notable Birthdays

1745 Birth of Francis Asbury, English Methodist missionary and circuit-riding bishop of the American colonies. During 42 years of labor, Asbury traveled 300,000 miles by horseback, ministering to congregations up and down the Eastern Seaboard. [d. 3/31/1816]

1884 Birth of Rudolf Bultmann, German New Testament scholar. He pioneered form criticism (analysis) with his *History of the Synoptic Tradition* (1921), whereby he sought to reinterpret Hebraic metaphors in order to make the Gospels more meaningful to moderns. [d. 7/30/1976]

1886 Birth of Paul Tillich, German philosophical theologian. Tillich advocated 'myth' as a signpost, participating in the reality to which it points. Evangelicals generally criticize Tillich today for exhibiting a pantheistic view of God. [d. 10/22/1965]

1908 Birth of Gerhard Friedrich, German Lutheran scholar. In 1948 he became editor of the encyclopedic Greek lexicon, *Theologisches Wörterbuch zum Neuen Testament* (TWNT), later translated into English as the (10-volume) *Theological Dictionary of the New Testament*.

The Last Passage

1384 Death of Gerhard de Groote, 44, Dutch mystic and religious reformer. Groote's preaching (and personal example) encouraged spiritual devotion within daily life rather than through ritual. He founded the Brethren of the Common Life religious order. Loved by the bishops, Groote was nevertheless attacked by the secular clergy for his censure of their luxury, simony and usury. (b. 10/1340)

1912 Death of William Booth, 83, English social reformer, founder and first general of the Salvation Army. On his death-bed, he turned to his son and successor Bramwell and said: *'I'm leaving you a bonnie handful.'* (b. 4/10/1829)

1953 Death of Clarence Tucker Craig, 58, American Methodist biblical scholar. He taught at Oberlin (1928-46) and Yale (1946-49), before becoming Dean at Drew Theological Seminary (NJ) in 1949. Craig participated extensively in the ecumenical movement through the Faith and Order work of the World Council of Churches. (b. 6/7/1895)

Words for the Soul

1553 Protestant reformer John Calvin concluded in a letter: *'Seeing that a Pilot steers the ship in which we sail, who will never allow us to perish even in the midst of shipwrecks, there is no reason why our minds should be overwhelmed with fear and overcome with weariness.'*

1768 John Wesley advised in a letter: *'When any trial comes, see that you do not look to the thing itself; but immediately look unto Jesus.... And, mean time, stay your whole soul upon Him who will never leave you nor forsake you. Tell Him simply all you fear, all you feel, all you want.'*

1878 Scottish clergyman and writer Andrew Bonar, 68, reflected in his diary: *'I see that faith is high just when our thoughts about our Lord Himself are high and great and satisfying.'*

FROM GOD'S WORD... OT: Esther 8:1–10:3 ~ NT: 1 Corinthians 12:27–13:13 ~ Psalms 37:1-11 ~ Proverbs 21:23-24

August 21

Highlights in History

1912 William Bramwell Booth, son of founder William Booth, became head of the American Salvation Army. He served until 1929.

1916 In New York City, the National Committee on Public Morals of the American Federation of Catholic Societies issued a report condemning "alien radicalism" in the form of socialism, claiming it could corrupt American youth. The report also underscored the related evils of divorce and motion pictures of doubtful morality, 'foisting upon our women and children... insidious attacks on Christianity.'

Notable Birthdays

12 Birth of Caius Caesar Germanicus Caligula, Roman emperor (AD 37-41). The great-grandson of Augustus Caesar, he followed Tiberius as emperor. A severe mental illness marked Caligula's reign and, assassinated in 41, he was succeeded by Claudius as emperor. [d. 1/24/41]

1567 Birth of St. Francis of Sales, French Catholic preacher, devotional writer, mystic and Counter-Reformation leader. In 1610 he founded the Order of the Visitation. His *Introduction to the Devout Life* (1609) became widely translated, as did his *Treatise on the Love of God* (1616). He was canonized in 1625, and declared a Doctor of the Church in 1877. [d. 12/28/1622]

1841 Birth of Frederick C. Atkinson, English sacred organist and choirmaster. He composed a number of Anglican anthems, instrumental pieces and hymn tunes, including MORECAMBE ("Spirit of God, Descend Upon My Heart"). [d. 11/30/1896]

1866 Birth of Nova Scotia pastor's wife and teacher Civilla D. Martin. In 1904 she penned the hymn, "Be Not Dismayed, Whate'er Betide" (a.k.a. "God Will Take Care of You"). [d. 3/9/1948]

The Last Passage

1160 Death of Italian scholastic theologian Peter Lombard, ca. 65. He studied at Bologna, Reims, and Paris, where he is said to have been a student of Peter Abelard. Later, as Bishop of Paris, he helped elaborate the doctrine of the Trinity. Lombard's "Libri quatuor sententiarum" (Eng., "The Sentences") became the standard textbook on theology in European universities for the next 400 years. (b. ca. 1095)

1245 English scholastic theologian Alexander of Hales (in Gloucestershire, England) died at 75. Alexander became a Franciscan in 1236, and is regarded as founder of the Franciscan school of theology. His unfinished *Summa Universae Theologiae* (begun in 1231) was the first attempt at a systematic outline of Catholic doctrine based on the scientific philosophy of Aristotle. (b. 1170)

Words for the Soul

1930 Pioneer linguistic educator Frank C. Laubach wrote in a letter: *'If this entire universe has a desperate need of love to incarnate itself, then "important duties" which keep us from helping little people are not duties but sins.'*

1930 English writer and mystic Evelyn Underhill advised in a letter: *'Emotional feeling is a pleasant stimulus but not the real foundation and there is always a risk at the beginning of mistaking fervour for faith.... God knows His job better than we do and will give you what you need at the right time.'*

1980 American Presbyterian missionary and apologist Francis Schaeffer noted in a letter: *'What a delicate balance it is not to see death as less than a present enemy, and yet not to be overcome by the sorrows of death when it comes to a very dear loved one. The balance is not easy, but is the only balance that makes sense in the midst of the world, broken and sorrowing as it is.'*

FROM GOD'S WORD...   OT: Job 1:1–3:26 ~ NT: 1 Corinthians 14:1-17 ~ Psalms 37:12-29 ~ Proverbs 21:25-26

August 22

Highlights in History

1244 The Egyptians and Khwarezmians recaptured Jerusalem from European Christian forces that had first wrested the city from Islam in 1096. Jerusalem never again fell in any of the subsequent Christian Crusades.

1654 Jacob Barsimon arrived in New Amsterdam (New York City) from Recife, Brazil, making him the first Jew to settle in America. Two weeks later, 23 Sephardic Jews followed him, arriving aboard the St. Charles, a French vessel. Previously, the Portuguese had seized control of Brazil from the Dutch, and had given the 5,000 Jews of Recife three months to leave.

1670 English-born colonial American missionary John Eliot, 66, established an Indian church in Martha's Vineyard, MA. Two educated Indians — Hiacoomes and Tackanash — were appointed pastor and teacher, respectively.

1968 Pope Paul VI arrived in Colombia, making it the first-ever papal visit to South America.

Notable Birthdays

1800 Birth of Edward B. Pusey, English biblical scholar and a leader of the Oxford Movement. A devoted churchman all his life, Pusey worked to establish religious orders in Anglicanism, and in 1845 founded the first Anglican sisterhood. [d. 9/16/1882]

1831 Birth of William H. Cummings, English musicologist. In 1855 he adapted a theme from Felix Mendelssohn's "Festgesang," to which we now sing the Christmas carol, "Hark! The Herald Angels Sing." [d. 6/6/1915]

1854 Birth of Charles Fillmore. In 1914, Charles and his wife Myrtle co-founded of the Unity School of Christianity. The movement is headquartered today at Lee's Summit, MO. [d. 7/5/1948]

The Last Passage

1885 Death of William P. Mackay, 46, Scottish Presbyterian clergyman, physician and hymn author. Educated at the University of Edinburgh, Mackay practiced medicine for a number of years. Feeling a call to the ministry, he was later ordained and became a Presbyterian pastor in Hull, Scotland. Mackay penned a number of hymns, among which we still sing, "We Praise Thee, O God, For the Son of Thy Love" (a.k.a. "Revive Us Again"). (b. 5/13/1839)

1952 Death of Lewis Sperry Chafer, 81, American Presbyterian clergyman and educator. While ministering at D. L. Moody's famous Northfield Training School, Chafer met Bible teacher C. I. Scofield. Under Scofield's influence, in 1924 Chafer founded (and became first president of) Dallas Theological Seminary – today a bastion of evangelical fundamentalism, premillennialism and dispensationalism. (b. 2/27/1871)

Words for the Soul

1787 At the American constitutional convention, Virginia plantation owner George Mason declared: *'As nations cannot be rewarded in the next world, they must be in this. By an inevitable chain of causes and effects, Providence punishes national sins by national calamities.'*

1889 English Baptist clergyman Charles Spurgeon declared in a sermon: *'It is poor Christianity that cannot bear the loss of all things. Now you may be poor yet, and you may be sore sick, but may you have such faith as that you may be able to say, "Though he slay me, yet will I trust him." It is no gold if it will not stand the fire, and it is no grace if it will not bear affliction.'*

1953 English psychiatrist Caryll Houselander confided in a letter to a friend: *'What a wonderful thing God's love is, always overflowing, always following you and, if one may say so, spoiling you.'*

FROM GOD'S WORD... OT: Job 4:1–7:21 ~ NT: 1 Corinthians 14:18-40 ~ Psalms 37:30-40 ~ Proverbs 21:27

August 23

Highlights in History

1572 In France, beginning late into this night, Catholic conspirators began massacring tens of thousands of Huguenots (Protestants), under orders of Catherine de Medici. The killing continued sporadically for six weeks, during which over 30,000 Huguenots lost their lives.

1823 Karl F. A. Gützlaff, 20, arrived in Bangkok — the first missionary ever to reach Thailand. Representing the Netherlands Missionary Society, Gützlaff and his wife later translated the complete Bible into Siamese, and portions of it into the Lao and Cambodian languages.

1879 The Church of Christ, Scientist, was chartered by Mary Baker Eddy in Lynn, MA. Its theology began in 1866, when a sudden recovery from severe back injuries convinced Eddy that reality is completely spiritual and that evil (e.g., sickness and death) is only an illusion.

1948 During its Amsterdam Assembly (Aug. 22 – Sept. 4), the World Council of Churches was established, with 144 member churches. It soon located its headquarters in Geneva, Switzerland.

Notable Birthdays

1744 Birth of Rowland Hill, English Nonconformist preacher and hymnwriter. He helped establish the London Missionary Society, and also authored the hymn, "Cast Thy Burden on the Lord." [d. 4/11/1833]

1761 Birth of Jedidiah Morse, American clergyman and controversialist. As pastor of the Charlestown, MA church (1789-1819), Morse upheld the faith of the New England Congregational Church, and launched a controversy which forced Unitarian believers out of the denomination. Morse also formed a coalition which led to the establishment of Andover Theological Seminary. [d. 6/9/1826]

The Last Passage

1723 Death of American colonial clergyman and theologian Increase Mather, 84. The son of Richard Mather and the father of Cotton Mather, Increase published nearly 100 books, and is credited with helping end executions for witchcraft in the American colonies. (b. 6/21/1639)

1882 Death of Charles W. Fry, 45, English Salvation Army worker. As the Army's first bandmaster, the power of Fry's brass band music warmed many restless crowds to the after-preaching of founder William Booth. Today Fry is remembered as author of the hymn, "Lily of the Valley" (a.k.a., "I Have Found a Friend in Jesus"). (b. 5/29/1837)

1952 Death of Frederick G. Kenyon, 89, British archaeologist and Near Eastern language scholar. Kenyon devoted his life to discovering biblical parallels in ancient Greek papyri, convincing critics that science does not disprove the Bible. The father of archaeologist Kathleen Kenyon, Frederick also published *Our Bible and the Ancient Manuscripts* (1895) and *The Bible and Archaeology* (1940). (b. 1/15/1863)

Words for the Soul

1763 John Wesley encouraged in a letter: *'You did well to write; this is one of the means which God generally uses to convey either light or comfort: Even while you are writing you will often find relief; frequently, while we propose a doubt, it is removed.'*

1783 English Methodist clergyman John Fletcher shared this concern in a letter: *'Let our faith and hope be in God, rooted and grounded in Him Who gives vital heat to our hearts, and Who fans there the spark of grace which His mercy has kindled.'*

1835 Young Scottish clergyman Andrew Bonar, 25, resolved in his diary: *'I must pray as much as if I were nothing, and labour as much as if I were to do all.'*

FROM GOD'S WORD... OT: Job 8:1–11:20 ~ NT: 1 Corinthians 15:1-28 ~ Psalms 38:1-22 ~ Proverbs 21:28-29

August 24

Highlights in History

410 Visigoth chief Alaric (ca. 370-410) entered Rome, becoming the city's first conqueror in Christian times. The Visigoths' conquest disillusioned many Christians who were trusting in God's favor and protection of this ecclesiastical center of the Early Church. Latin Church Father Augustine of Hippo later tackled this dilemma in his monumental work, *City of God*.

1456 In Mainz, Germany, Volume 2 of the famed *Gutenberg Bible* was bound, completing a two-year publishing project, and making it the first full-length book printed using movable type.

1854 The Evangelical Lutheran Synod of Iowa was organized by German Lutherans. In 1930 this synod merged with the synods of Ohio and Buffalo, forming the American Lutheran Church.

1906 Five Baptist congregations met at Jellico Creek, in Whitley County, KY to form the Church of God of the Mountain Assembly. Both pentecostal and holiness in its doctrine, the CGMA reports a current world membership of 7,000.

1964 In St. Louis, the Rev. Frederick McManus of Catholic University (in Washington, D.C.) led in the first full Roman Catholic mass to be celebrated in English in the United States.

1970 In Washington, D.C., editors and scholars at the Catholic University of America published the *New American Bible* (NAB). Its issue replaced the traditional 1610 Rheims-Douay version of the Scriptures — previously the authoritative Bible of the Roman Catholic Church.

Notable Birthdays

1707 Birth of Selina Hastings, Countess of Huntingdon. She was the founder of English Calvinistic Methodism. In 1739 she joined the Methodist movement, and in 1747 George Whitefield became one of her chaplains. [d. 6/17/1791]

1747 Birth of John A. Dickins, pioneer church leader. Born in London, he came to America before the American Revolution, and united with the Methodist movement. It was Dickins who first suggested the denominational name "Methodist Episcopal Church." [d. 9/27/1798]

The Last Passage

1883 Death of Stephen Return Riggs, 71, American ABCFM missionary to the Dakota Indians (1837-83). Reducing the Dakota language to writing, Riggs prepared a Dakota dictionary, translated nearly all of the Bible into Dakota, and also prepared a number of books for Dakota readers. (b. 3/23/1812)

1978 Death of Kathleen Kenyon, 72, the British archaeologist who supervised a major excavation of the ancient Biblical site of Jericho. She was the first to use radioactive carbon dating on artifacts from the site. (b. 1/5/1906)

Words for the Soul

1683 English Puritan John Owen, honored for his personal piety and literary achievements, died peacefully, having survived all his children. His last words were characteristic of Owen's faith: *'I am going to Him whom my soul loveth, or rather who has loved me with an everlasting love, which is the sole ground of all my consolation.'*

1771 John Wesley encouraged in a letter: *'Plead that promise, "The peace of God shall keep your hearts and minds through Christ Jesus." As the former word takes in all your passions, so does the latter all the workings of your reason and imagination.'*

1872 Scottish clergyman Andrew Bonar, 62, confided in his diary: *'Got about three hours for prayer this forenoon. Most truly did I join in Richard Baxter's cry, "Must I sit down with so low a measure of grace when I am almost there where faith is exchanged for sight; Lord, is no more to be expected here?"'*

August 25

Highlights in History

325 The Council of Nicea ended. This 3-month conclave — presided over by newly-converted Roman Emperor Constantine I — was the first ecumenical council in the history of the Church. Attended by 300 bishops, Nicea I condemned Arianism (which denied the co-eternal deity of Christ), created the Nicene Creed, and set down the formula for celebrating Easter.

1560 Protestantism was formally adopted at the First General Assembly of the Church of Scotland. Scottish Parliament had earlier voted to accept a Calvinist confession of faith, declaring the pope no longer had jurisdiction over Scotland.

1817 Joseph Mohr, 25, began serving as pastor of the St. Nicholas Church in Oberndorf, Austria.  (It was Christmas Eve of 1818 when Mohr and church organist Franz Gruber together created the enduring Christmas carol, "Silent Night."

1987 A federal appeals court overturned a lower court decision ordering Hawkins County, TN schools to excuse fundamentalist children from reading class because their parents found the books offensive to their religious beliefs.

Notable Birthdays

1744 Birth of Johann Gottfried von Herder, German Lutheran clergyman, theologian and critical scholar. Herder sought to preserve the purity of ancient texts, and his writings prepared the way for the modern sciences of comparative philology and comparative religion. [d. 12/18/1803]

1854 Birth of Wilbur F. Tillet, American Methodist theologian and hymnwriter. He began teaching at Vanderbilt in 1886, and soon became a leading theologian of the Methodist Episcopal Church, South. Serving on the hymnbook committees for both the Northern and Southern Methodist churches, Tillet also penned the hymn, "O Son of God Incarnate." [d. 1936]

1864 Birth of John Henry Jowett, English Congregational clergyman. In 1918, he succeeded G. Campbell Morgan as pastor of Westminster Chapel in London. Jowett preached his last sermon there on December 17, 1923, two days before his death at age 59. [d. 12/19/1923]

The Last Passage

1270 Death of Louis IX, 56, king of France from 1226-70. As a child, he exhibited great religious devotion. As king he was concerned for justice and the building of churches and hospitals. During the Sixth Crusade, Louis was taken prisoner (1250) and held for four years. He began another crusade in 1266, but died in Tunis of dysentery while en route. Louis was canonized in 1297. (b. 4/25/1214)

1828 Death of Jehudi Ashmun, 34, American Congregational missionary to Africa. In 1822 he sailed to Liberia as an agent of the American Colonization Society. Encouraging the demoralized inhabitants, he helped them repel incursions from neighboring savages, thus rebuilding morale of the newly founded colony. When he died six years later, Ashmun left a prosperous colony nearly 1,200 strong. (b. 4/1794)

Words for the Soul

1933 English writer and mystic Evelyn Underhill concluded in a letter: *'When the whole emphasis of religion is thrown on the transcendental and eschatological, the majority of people must have something to lay hold of, and if it isn't given them by the Incarnational and Sacramental path, uniting supernature with homeliness, they just vulgarize supernature, and claim familiarity with it.'*

1935 English Bible expositor Arthur W. Pink wrote in a letter: *'None but the Lord himself can afford us any help from the awful workings of unbelief, doubtings, carnal fears, murmurings. Thank God one day we will be done forever with "unbelief."'*

FROM GOD'S WORD...   OT: Job 16:1–19:29 ~ NT: 1 Corinthians 16:1-24 ~ Psalms 40:1-10 ~ Proverbs 22:1

August 26

Highlights in History

1498 Under Pope Alexander VI, Italian artist Michelangelo, 23, was commissioned to carve the Pietà, the marble sculpture of Mary lamenting over the dead body of Jesus, whom she holds across her lap. Completed in 1501, the work became one of the most poignant visual expressions of the emotional dimensions within both Christ and Mary.

1748 In Philadelphia, a meeting of ministers to consecrate St. Michael's Church ended with the formation of the first Lutheran synod in the American colonies. Six pastors, led by Henry Melchior Muhlenberg, agreed on a book of common worship and to the formation of a synodical organization.

1901 The New Testament of the *American Standard Version* (ASV) Bible was first published. This U.S. edition of the 1881 *English Revised Version* (ERV) comprised the first major American Bible translation since the Authorized Version of 1611.

1978 Italian Cardinal Albino Luciani, 65, was elevated to the papacy as John Paul I. His unexpected death only 34 days later left a profound sadness for millions of people who had been drawn to Luciani by his warm personality.

Notable Birthdays

1827 Birth of Beal M. Schmucker, American Lutheran liturgical scholar. The son of Samuel S. Schmucker, he collaborated with A. T. Geissenhainer in *A Liturgy for the Use of the Evangelical Lutheran Church*. [d. 10/18/1888]

1908 Birth of Cynthia Clark Wedel, American Ecumenical leader. Born in Dearborn, MI, she was the first woman to be elected president of the National Council of Churches (1969-72). Wedel later served as president of the World Council of Churches (1975-83). [d. 8/24/1986]

The Last Passage

1832 Death of Adam Clarke, 70, English Wesleyan preacher and theologian. Born in Ireland, Clarke became a Methodist in 1778, helped establish Methodism in the Shetland Islands, and served on the British and Foreign Bible Society. He authored many works, but Clarke's name endures primarily for his eight-volume commentary on the Bible (1810-26) — a popular work still reprinted today! (b. ca. 1762)

1948 Death of Maud Ballington (née Charlesworth) Booth, 82, American church leader. She came to the U.S. in 1887 with her husband Ballington (son of William Booth), and cofounded the American branch of the Salvation Army. In 1896 the couple broke their denominational ties and organized the Volunteers of America, closely patterned along their former denominational lines. (b. 9/13/1865)

Words for the Soul

1770 John Wesley exhorted in a letter: *'I hope you lose no opportunity of speaking a word for God, either to them that know Him, or them that do not. Why should you lose any time? Time is short.'*

1929 English mystic Evelyn Underhill advised in a letter: *'One has to make up one's mind to submit to... the drudgery of training; nor is one's spiritual state ever to be measured in terms of feeling.... This is where the corporate religious life comes in as such a support. You will find concentration difficult, and prayer and the things of the spirit will often seem unreal. Nevertheless, if persevered in, all those things will gradually train and expand your soul, as certainly as gymnastics train the body.'*

1956 Swedish Christian statesman Dag Hammarskjöld recorded in his devotional journal (*Markings*): *'Bless your uneasiness as a sign that there is still life in you.'*

FROM GOD'S WORD... OT: Job 20:1–22:30 ~ NT: 2 Corinthians 1:1-11 ~ Psalms 40:11-17 ~ Proverbs 22:2-4

August 27

Highlights in History

1640 Citizens of Providence, Rhode Island drew up a document in which they agreed, among other things, "to hould forth liberty of [religious] conscience."

1812 Colonial American missionary Adoniram Judson, who had embarked for India in February of this year, addressed a letter to William Carey, Joshua Marshman and William Ward, in Calcutta, stating his intentions of changing denominational views from Congregationalist to Baptist. Five days later (Sept. 1), Judson sent another letter to the Congregational Board, tendering his resignation from that denomination.

1865 Rhenish missionary L[udwig] I. Nommensen, 31, baptized four families of the Batak tribe in North Sumatra (Indonesia) – the first to be converted to the Christian faith. Nommensen later established a theological training school and in 1878 completed a translation of the New Testament into the Batak language.

1870 A group of professors, led by Johann J. I. Döllinger, met in Nuremberg to voice opposition to a decree of papal infallibility, giving rise to the creation of the Old Catholic Church.

1876 At age 13, future English clergyman G[eorge] Campbell Morgan delivered his first sermon. Morgan later grew to become one of the renowned expository preachers and writers of late 19th century England and America.

Notable Birthdays

1861 Birth of Arno C. Gaebelein, American Methodist clergyman, teacher and writer on prophecy. He authored *Studies in Prophecy* (1917) and *The Conflict of the Ages* (1933). Gaebelein was also editor of *The Annotated Bible* (9 vols., 1913-20). [d. 12/25/1945]

1877 Birth of Lloyd C. Douglas, American Lutheran clergyman and religious novelist. Many of his popular novels dramatized Christian faith and morals. He published his first best-seller, *Magnificent Obsession*, in 1929, followed by *The Robe* (1942) and *The Big Fisherman* (1948). [d. 2/13/1951]

1910 Birth of Albanian nun Agnes G. Bojaxhiu, who later became known as Mother Teresa of Calcutta. She joined the Sisters of Loreto in 1928, and from 1948 spent her life ministering to the poor of India. Her devotion to the dying earned her the Nobel Prize in 1979. [d. 9/5/1997]

The Last Passage

1737 Death of John Hutchinson, 63, English theologian. He wrote *Moses' Principia* and other works of religious symbolism. Hutchinson taught that the Bible contains a complete system of natural science and theology. (b. ca. 1674)

1869 Death of Rebecca Gratz, American Jewish philanthropist and humanitarian. A lifelong resident of Philadelphia, she grew up a celebrated beauty. In 1838 Miss Gratz founded the first Hebrew Sabbath School Society in America, and served as its president until 1864. (b. 3/4/1781)

Words for the Soul

1830 English churchman John Henry Cardinal Newman noted in a letter: *'It is our great relief that God is not extreme to mark what is done amiss, that He looks at the motives, and accepts and blesses in spite of incidental errors.'*

1965 Italian religious Carlo Carretto confessed in a letter to his sister: *'I always end up understanding that it is much better to abandon ourselves to the mysterious action of events, beneath which it is God who is acting.'*

FROM GOD'S WORD... OT: Job 23:1–27:23 ~ NT: 2 Corinthians 1:12–2:11 ~ Psalms 41:1-13 ~ Proverbs 22:5-6

August 28

Highlights in History

1565 The Spanish established the oldest permanent European settlement in North America at St. Augustine, Florida. Later, Spanish priests from St. Augustine established missions that at one point reached as far north as the Carolinas. (Other early Spanish missionary activity in North America during this period went on in the American Southwest, from today's Texas to California.)

1645 In Poland, King Vladislav IV convened the Conference of Thorn. Through it he sought to bring reunion among the 26 Catholic, 28 Lutheran and 24 Calvinist theologians in attendance. Discussions continued through November, but no satisfying agreement was achieved.

1953 Campus Crusade for Christ was incorporated in Los Angeles by founder Bill Bright. Today, CCC is an evangelical organization training Christian leaders in over 90 countries around the world.

Notable Birthdays

1774 Birth of Elizabeth Ann (née Bayley) Seton, American Catholic educator and religious leader. As founder and superior of the American Sisters of Charity (1809-21) — the first U.S. Catholic religious order — she laid the foundation for the U.S. parochial school system. She also founded the Society of Relief for Poor Widows with Small Children (1797), the first charitable organization in New York, and was a founder of St. Joseph's College, Emmittsburg, MD. Mrs. Seton was canonized in 1975 — the first American-born Catholic saint. [d. 1/4/1821]

1796 Birth of William H. Bathurst, English clergyman and hymnwriter. Born near Bristol, he published *Psalms and Hymns for Public and Private Use* (1831), and also penned more than 200 original hymns, including "O For a Faith That Will Not Shrink." [d. 11/25/1877]

1840 Birth of Ira D. Sankey, American singing evangelist associated with Dwight Moody. During their revival crusades (from 1870), Sankey penned a number of hymn tunes. Among the most enduring today are SANKEY ("Faith is the Victory") and HIDING IN THEE ("O Safe to the Rock That is Higher Than I"). [d. 8/13/1908]

The Last Passage

430 Death of Augustine of Hippo, 76, early Latin Church Father and one of the outstanding theological figures of the ages. It was St. Augustine who once wrote: *'Thou hast made us for thyself, O Lord, and our hearts are restless till they find their rest in thee.'* (b. 11/13/354)

1906 Death of George Matheson, 64, Scottish clergyman, author and hymnwriter. Though nearly blind by age 18, he was a popular pastor for over 30 years. He also published works on theology. Today Matheson is remembered for penning two of the Church's most haunting hymns: "Make Me a Captive, Lord" and "O Love That Wilt Not Let Me Go." (b. 3/27/1842)

Words for the Soul

1958 Writing from his monastery in Algeria, Italian religious Carlo Carretto advised in a letter: *'You tell me of the sense of impotence you feel about being what you would like to be. I think we've all got to go through this painful stage.... It's our pride which has to be destroyed in us, our feeling of self-sufficiency (even for good), the idea that it's up to us to achieve our holiness. Since God can do nothing else to bring the point home, he lets us do all we can by ourselves. Then we begin to understand that by ourselves we are nothing.'*

1974 Commenting on his dreams, Dutch priest and diarist Henri J. M. Nouwen observed in his *Genesee Diary*: *'While during the day I try to be in the world without being of it, during the night I am fully of it without really being in it.'*

FROM GOD'S WORD...   OT: Job 28:1–30:31 ~ NT: 2 Corinthians 2:12-17 ~ Psalms 42:1-11 ~ Proverbs 22:7

August 29

Highlights in History

1258 In central Italy, Conradin, the 16-year-old ruler of Germany, was defeated by Charles of Anjou (NW France). Conradin was afterward beheaded, under approval of Pope Clement IV, setting off waves of disapproval throughout Europe, and creating a long-lasting alienation between Germany and the Catholic Church.

1867 The Social Brethren were officially organized in Illinois. Today, there are about 1,000 total members of this small, evangelistic denomination, with most churches located in Illinois, Michigan and Indiana. Church doctrine is a blend of Methodist and Baptist polity.

Notable Birthdays

1769 Birth of Rose Philippine Duchesne, French-born pioneer missionary for the Society of the Sacred Heart. Arriving in America in 1818, she established the first free school west of the Mississippi River at St. Charles, MO. In 1841, at age 72, she began working among the Indians, and opened a school for Indian girls of the Potawatomi tribe in Sugar Creek, KS. Mother Duchesne lived in the seclusion of her St. Charles convent during her last ten years, and was beatified in 1940. [d. 11/18/1852]

1792 Birth of American revivalist and educator Charles G. Finney. Trained in law, Finney was converted to the Christian faith at 29, afterward becoming a Presbyterian evangelist. From 1835 until his death he developed a close affiliation with Oberlin College, serving as its president from 1851-66. [d. 8/16/1875]

1805 Birth of [John] F. D. Maurice, Anglican clergyman, theologian and educator. Of Unitarian parentage, Maurice ultimately turned to an evangelical theology, after which his literary output was remarkable. Among his many writings are *The Kingdom of Christ* (1837) and *The Lord's Prayer* (1848). [d. 4/1/1872]

1809 Birth of Oliver Wendell Holmes, Sr., American physician, author and poet. Remembered for his writings, Holmes authored the hymn, "Lord of All Being, Throned Afar." [d. 10/8/1894]

The Last Passage

1908 Death of Lewis H. Redner, 78, American Episcopal organist. Maintaining an interest in music all his life, Redner composed ST. LOUIS, the tune to which is commonly sung Phillips Brooks' Christmas hymn, "O Little Town of Bethlehem." (b. 12/15/1830)

1917 Death of Ernest W. Shurtleff, 55, American Congregational clergyman and author of the hymn, "Lead On, O King Eternal." Shurtleff died during World War I, while he and his wife were doing relief work. (b. 4/4/1862)

Words for the Soul

1768 English clergyman and hymn-writer Augustus Toplady noted in his diary: 'My meditation of him was sweet, and he gave me songs in the night season. I had sweet, melting views of his special goodness, and of my own utter unworthiness. The united sense of these two keeps the soul in an even balance.'

1908 English writer and mystic Evelyn Underhill wrote in a letter: 'Half an hour spent with Christ's poor is worth far more than half a million spent on them. It is necessary to a sane Christianity.'

1974 Dutch educator Henri J. M. Nouwen observed in his *Genesee Diary*: 'For me writing is a very powerful way of concentrating and of clarifying... many thoughts and feelings. Once I put my pen on paper and write for an hour or two, a real sense of peace and harmony comes to me.... After a day... filled with only reading and manual work, I often have a general feeling of mental constipation and go to bed with the sense that I did not do what I should have done that day.'

FROM GOD'S WORD... OT: Job 31:1–33:33 ~ NT: 2 Corinthians 3:1-18 ~ Psalms 43:1-5 ~ Proverbs 22:8-9

August 30

Highlights in History

1464 Italian Cardinal Pietro Barbo was elected Pope Paul II, serving until 1471. He was a patron of scholars, and is credited with bringing the first printing press to Rome.

1637 Colonial religious teacher Anne Hutchinson, 46, was charged with 'traducing (degrading) the ministry' and was banished from the Massachusetts Bay Colony. She moved to Rhode Island, and later to New York where, in 1643, Anne and her family were killed by Indians.

1856 Wilberforce University was established in Xenia, Ohio by the Methodist Episcopal Church. In 1863, its ownership was transferred to the African Methodist Episcopal (AME) Church.

1858 Reformed Presbyterian Church of Scotland missionary John G[ibson] Paton and his wife first arrived at Aneityum, to begin mission work in the New Hebrides. His wife died in childbirth the following year, but Paton remained in the work until 1881. His autobiography, published in 1889, did much to stimulate support for missions in the Pacific.

Notable Birthdays

1820 Birth of George F. Root, American composer and music editor. Root helped edit 75 musical collections, as well as composing several hundred of his own sacred melodies, including JEWELS ("When He Cometh") and QUAM DILECTA ("The Lord is in His Holy Temple"). [d. 8/6/1895]

1854 Birth of Swiss clergyman and hymnwriter Edmond L. Budry. He composed over 60 chorales, and was active in translating German, Latin and English hymns to the end of his life. Today Budry's name endures as author of the hymn "Thine Is the Glory, Risen, Conquering Son." [d. 11/12/1932]

1859 Birth of John Taylor Hamilton, British West Indies-born American Moravian bishop, educator and historian of the Moravian Church. Ordained at Herrnhut in 1905, Hamilton taught at Moravian College and Theological Seminary, Bethlehem, PA (1886-1903), and later served as its president (1918-28). [d. 1/29/1951]

1900 Birth of Franklin C. Fry, American Lutheran clergyman and ecumenist. Noted for his organizational and leadership skills, he served as president of the United Lutheran Church (1945-62); president of the American Lutheran Church (1962-68); president of the Lutheran World Federation (1957-63); and president of Lutheran World Relief, Inc. (1946-68). [d. 6/6/1968]

The Last Passage

410 Death of St. Pammachius, 70, Roman aristocrat, senator, and Christian. A friend of St. Jerome, he became a monk following the death of his wife and daughter, and spent his possessions on Christian ministries. Pammachius died during the Gothic invasion. (b. ca. 340)

1901 Death of James Walch, 64, English sacred organist and composer. He played in both Anglican and Nonconformist churches, and composed a variety of church music including the hymn tune TIDINGS ("O Zion, Haste, Your Mission High Fulfilling"). (b. 6/21/1837)

Words for the Soul

1770 Anglican clergyman and hymnwriter John Newton explained in a letter: 'The exercised and experienced Christian, by the knowledge he has gained of his own heart and the many difficulties he has had to struggle with, acquires a skill and compassion in dealing with others.'

1954 Russian Orthodox monk Ivan Alekseyev encouraged in a letter: 'Do not be surprised that you fall every day; do not give up, but stand your ground courageously. Assuredly the angel who guards you will honor your patience.... God is wonderful in his saints.'

FROM GOD'S WORD... OT: Job 34:1–36:33 ~ NT: 2 Corinthians 4:1-12 ~ Psalms 44:1-8 ~ Proverbs 22:10-12

August 31

Highlights in History

1954 The second assembly of the World Council of Churches closed in Evanston, IL. The theme of the 16-day convention was: "Christ — The Hope of the World." The 1,500 participants included 500 delegates from 163 Protestant and Orthodox churches. (Roman Catholics had been banned from attending the assembly in any capacity by Cardinal Samuel A. Stritch, Archbishop of Chicago.)

1989 Fundamentalist Baptist pastor Jerry Falwell, 56, officially dissolved Moral Majority, which he had founded in 1979 as a political-action agency for promoting conservative moral and political concerns. Falwell explained that Moral Majority had fulfilled its goal of establishing the Religious Right in the public arena.

Notable Birthdays

1820 Birth of Anna B. Warner, American hymnwriter. She never married, but lived with her sister in New York state. In 1860, a novel they co-authored contained a poem which became one of the most beloved of all children's hymns: "Jesus Loves Me, This I Know." [d. 1/23/1815]

1828 Birth of Lewis Hartsough, American Methodist clergyman. Hartsough pastored in New York state for 15 years. Then, for health reasons, he moved West and worked within the Methodist conferences in Utah, Wyoming, Iowa and the Dakotas. Hartsough penned a number of hymns during his life, including the hymn of commitment: "I am Coming, Lord" (a.k.a. "I Hear Thy Welcome Voice." [d. 1/1/1919]

1861 Birth of Jesse Brown Pounds, American hymnwriter. During her lifetime she published nine books, 50 cantatas and over 400 religious song texts. Three of her hymns remain popular today: "Anywhere With Jesus"; "I Know That My Redeemer Liveth"; and "The Way of the Cross Leads Home." [d. 3/3/1921]

1870 Birth of Maria Montessori, Italian physician and educator. She developed a theory of teaching which emphasized reinforcement of initiative and freedom of movement for the child. Today her theory of elementary education is called the Montessori Method. [d. 5/6/1952]

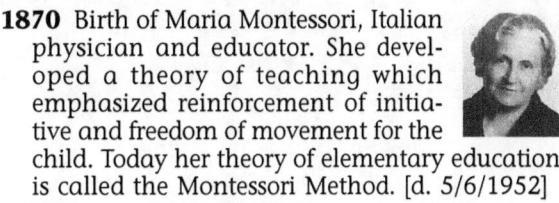

The Last Passage

651 Death of Aidan, Irish Celtic monk. A missionary of Iona (off the coast of Scotland), he evangelized Northumbria (Northern England), founding churches and monasteries. Renowned for his learning and charity, St. Aidan was the first bishop of Lindisfarne. (b. 600s)

1688 Death of English Separatist clergyman John Bunyan, 59. Imprisoned several times between 1660-72, Bunyan used these periods of isolation to pen his two literary masterpieces, *Grace Abounding to the Chief of Sinners* (1666) and *Pilgrim's Progress* (1678). (b. 11/30/1628)

Words for the Soul

1757 Anglican clergyman and hymnwriter John Newton concluded in a letter: *'I am persuaded that love and humility are the highest attainments in the school of Christ and the brightest evidences that He is indeed our Master.'*

1939 English psychiatrist Caryll Houselander confessed in a letter: *'I am confident now that the poetry, the beauty of life, which is nothing else but our divine Lord living in human souls, will go on, and that our lives, though they may seem to leave no visible trace, will not have been in vain.'*

1974 Dutch educator and diarist Henri J. M. Nouwen observed in his **Genesee Diary**: *'Maybe this is what makes the Jesus Prayer so good for me. Simply saying, "Lord Jesus Christ, have mercy on me" a hundred times, a thousand times, ten thousand times, as the Russian peasant did, might slowly clean my mind and give God a little chance.'*

FROM GOD'S WORD... OT: Job 37:1–39:30 ~ NT: 2 Corinthians 4:13–5:10 ~ Psalms 44:9-26 ~ Proverbs 22:13

ALMANAC OF THE CHRISTIAN FAITH

AUGUST INDEX

A

ABCFM (American Bd of Commissioners) 8/3, 8/24
Abeel, David 8/3
Abelard, Peter 8/21
Adams, John 8/5. See also PRESIDENTS, U.S.
Adams, Sarah Flower
  (b. 2/22/1805) d. 8/14/1848
AFRICAN-AMERICANS
  African Methodist Episcopal (AME) Church 8/30
  Healy, James A. 8/5
  Potter, Philip A. 8/16
  Wilberforce University 8/30
  Work, John Wesley, Jr. 8/6
Aidan, St.
  (b. 600s) d. 8/31/651
Alaric, Visigoth Chief (ca. 370-410) 8/24
Alekseyev, Ivan Alekseyevich. See Father John, Russian Orthodox Monk
Alexander of Hales
  (b. 1170) d. 8/21/1245
Alexander VI, Pope (1492-1503) 8/11, 8/18, 8/26
American Bible Union 8/2
American Colonization Society 8/25
American Federation of Catholic Societies 8/21
Amsterdam Assembly 8/23
Andreae, Johann Valentin
  b. 8/7/1586 [d. 1/27/1654]
Anthony of Padua, St.
  b. 8/15/05 [d. 6/13/1231]
Aquinas, Thomas 8/4, 8/12
Aristotle 8/21
Armitage, Thomas
  b. 8/2/1819 [d. 1/21/1896]
Arndt, William F. 8/8
Asbury, Francis 8/13
  b. 8/20/1745 [d. 3/31/1816]
Atkinson, Frederick C.
  b. 8/21/1841 [d. 11/30/1896]
Auburn Convention (1837) 8/17

Augustine of Hippo, St. 8/24
  (b. 11/13/354) d. 8/28/430
Augustus Caesar, Roman Emperor 8/21

B

Babcock, Maltbie D.
  b. 8/3/1858 [d. 5/18/1901]
Baldwin, Ashbel 8/3
Balthasar, Hans Urs von
  b. 8/12/1905 [d. 6/26/1988]
Baptist General Conference 8/8
Barbo, Pietro 8/30
Barclay, Robert 8/2
Barnby, Joseph
  b. 8/12/1838 [d. 1/28/1896]
Barsimon, Jacob 8/22
Barth, Karl 8/12
Barton, Bruce F.
  b. 8/5/1886 [d. 7/5/1967]
Basnage, Jacques
  b. 8/8/1652 [d. 12/22/1723]
Bates, Katharine Lee
  b. 8/12/1859 [d. 3/28/1929]
Bathurst, William H.
  b. 8/28/1796 [d. 11/25/1877]
Bauer, Walter
  b. 8/8/1877 [d. 1960]
Beatty, Charles C.
  (b. ca. 1715) d. 8/13/1772
Beecher, Henry Ward 8/20
Bengel, Albrecht 8/18
Bernardina Teresa Xavier of St. Joseph, Sister. See Mathews, Ann Teresa
BIBLE COLLEGES. See SEMINARIES / BIBLE COLLEGES
BIBLE VERSIONS
  American Standard Version (1905) 8/7, 8/14, 8/26
  Authorized Version (1611) 8/26
  Batak 8/27
  Bechuana (1872) 8/9
  Burmese Bible (1834) 8/9
  Cambodian 8/23
  Chinese (1823) 8/1

  English Revised Version (1885) 8/6, 8/26
  Gilbertese 8/16
  Gutenberg Bible 8/15, 8/24
  Lao 8/23
  New American Bible 8/24
  Rheims-Douay Version 8/24
  Scofield Reference Bible (1909) 8/19
  Siamese 8/23
  Welsh Bible 8/8
Bingham, Hiram, Jr.
  b. 8/16/1831 [d. 10/25/1908]
Birth Control. See Paul VI, Pope
Blake, William
  (b. 11/28/1757) d. 8/12/1827
Bojaxhiu, Agnes G.
  b. 8/27/1910 [d. 9/5/1997]
Bonaparte, Napoleon 8/14
Bonar, Andrew. See QUOTATIONS
BOOKS
  Adrift on an Ice-Pan (1909) 8/4
  Album of Dated Syriac Manuscripts (1947) 8/2
  American Unitarian Biography (1850-51) 8/3
  Apologia Pro Vita Sua (1864) 8/11
  A Liturgy for the Use of the Evangelical Lutheran 8/26
  Christianity in a Revolutionary Age (1958-62) 8/9
  Christian Perfection (1697) 8/6
  City of God 8/24
  Cyclopaedia of Biblical, Theological, and Ecclesia 8/7, 8/14
  Devout Life (1609) 8/21
  Facsimiles and Descriptions of Minuscule Manuscrip 8/2
  Genesee Diary (1976) 8/2, 8/11, 8/16, 8/17, 8/18, 8/28, 8/31
  Gnomon Novi Testamenti (1742) 8/18
  Grace Abounding to the Chief of Sinners (1666) 8/31
  Greek-English Lexicon of the New Testament 8/8
  Happiness Through Creative Living (1955) 8/18
  Hastings' Dictionary of the Bible (1898-1906) 8/1
  History of Christ (1921) 8/16

  History of the Expansion of Christianity (1937-45) 8/9
  History of the Synoptic Tradition (1921) 8/20
  Libri quatuor sententiarum (Eng., "The Sentences 8/21
  Life of Christ (1874) 8/7
  Magnificent Obsession (1929) 8/27
  Markings (1963) 8/4
  Moses' Principia 8/27
  My Daily Strength (1943) 8/18
  Natural Law in the Spiritual World 8/17
  New Schaff-Herzog Encyclopedia of Religious Knowle 8/2
  New Testament Background (1920) 8/1
  New Version of the Psalms of David (1696) 8/12
  Our Bible and the Ancient Manuscripts (1895) 8/23
  Paradise Lost (1667) 8/12
  Pensées, Pascal's (1670) 8/19
  Pilgrim's Progress (1678) 8/18, 8/31
  Provinciales 8/19
  Psalms and Hymns for.... (1831) 8/11, 8/28
  Psalms in Israel's Worship, The (1951) 8/4
  Rome, and the Early Christians (1851) 8/3
  Sabbatical Journey (1998) 8/9
  Schaff-Herzog Encyclopedia of Religious Knowledge 8/12
  Scofield Reference Bible (1909) 8/19
  Second Book of Discipline (Scottish) 8/1
  Strong's Exhaustive Concordance of the Bible 8/7, 8/14
  Studies in Prophecy (1917) 8/27
  Study of the New Testament (1883) 8/1
  Summa Universae Theologiae 8/21
  Systematic Theology (1907-09) 8/3
  Theological Dictionary of the New Testament 8/20
  Theologisches Wörterbuch zum Neuen Testament 8/20
  Theology of the Old Testament (1933-39) 8/1
  The American Sacred Songster 8/13
  The Annotated Bible (9 vols., 1913-20) 8/27

The Bible and Archaeology (1940) 8/23
The Big Fisherman (1948) 8/27
The Conflict of the Ages (1933) 8/27
The Flock at the Fountain (1845) 8/14
The Greek Manuscripts of the New Testament at Mount Sinai 8/2
The Greek Manuscripts of the New Testament in Jerusalem 8/2
The Kingdom of Christ (1837) 8/29
The Lord's Prayer (1848) 8/29
The Man Nobody Knows (1925) 8/5
The Principal Uncial Manuscripts of the New Testament 8/2
The Robe (1942) 8/27
The Rule and Exercise of Holy Dying (1651) 8/15
The Rule and Exercise of Holy Living (1650) 8/15
Treatise on the Love of God (1616) 8/21
Vikings of To-Day (1895) 8/4
Word Studies in the New Testament (1887-1900) 8/18

Booth, Ballington 8/26
Booth, Bramwell 8/20
Booth, Maud Ballington
  (b. 9/13/1865) d. 8/26/1948
Booth, William 8/21, 8/23, 8/26
  (b. 4/10/1829) d. 8/20/1912]
Booth, William Bramwell 8/21
Borgia, Rodrigo de 8/11
Bradley, Preston
  b. 8/18/1888 [d. 1983]
Brainerd, David. See also QUOTATIONS
Bréchant de Galinée, René de
  (b. 1600s) d. 8/15/1678
Bridget of Sweden, St. 8/5
Bright, Bill 8/28
Bright, Vonette. See also Bright, Bill
British Museum 8/19
Brooks, Phillips 8/29
Brown, Raymond E.
  (b. 5/22/1928) d. 8/8/1998
Buchman, Frank N. D.
  (b. 6/4/1878) d. 8/7/1961
Budry, Edmond L.
  b. 8/30/1854 [d. 11/12/1932]
Bulhoes, Ferdinand de 8/15
Bultmann, Rudolf
  b. 8/20/1884 [d. 7/30/1976]
Bunyan, John 8/18
  (b. 11/30/1628) d. 8/31/1688

Buonarotti, Michelangelo 8/18, 8/26

C

Caligula, Caius Caesar Germanicus
  b. 8/21/12 [d. 1/24/41]
Campbell, Alexander 8/17
Campbell, Thomas 8/17
Caretto, Dolcidia 8/10
Carey, William 8/27
  b. 8/17/1761 [d. 6/9/1834]
Carroll, John 8/15
Catherine de Medici 8/8
Chafer, Lewis Sperry
  (b. 2/27/1871) d. 8/22/1952
Chalmers, James
  b. 8/4/1841 [d. 4/8/1901]
Charles of Anjou 8/29
Chautauqua Assembly 8/4
Chautauqua Organization 8/4
Chauvin, Jean. See Calvin, John
Chiaramonti, Barnaba 8/14
CHURCHES
  Cathedral of Tomorrow (OH) 8/13
  Christ Church (MA) 8/17
  Cologne Cathedral (Germany) 8/14
  First Church in Wells (ME) 8/5
  John Street Methodist Church (NY) 8/17
  Manhattan Baptist Church (NY) 8/18
  Pine St. Church (MA) 8/13
  Screven Memorial Baptist Church (NH) 8/18
  St. Michael's Church (PA) 8/26
  St. Nicholas Church (Austria) 8/25
  Thomas Road Baptist Church (VA) 8/11
  Wesley Chapel (NY) 8/11
  Westminster Chapel (England) 8/25
Cicero 8/7
Clarke, Adam
  (b. ca. 1762) d. 8/26/1832
Claudius Caesar, Roman Emperor 8/21
Clement IV, Pope (1265-68) 8/29
Clement XIV, Pope (1769-74) 8/7, 8/16
Coleman, Tom 8/20
COLLEGES / UNIVERSITIES
  Basel (Switzerland) 8/1
  Catholic University of America (US) 8/24

Erlangen (Germany) 8/1
Fort William College (India) 8/17
Moravian College (PA) 8/30
Moravian Theological Seminary 8/30
Oberlin College (OH) 8/16, 8/20, 8/29
Oslo University 8/4
Oxford University (England) 8/1
St. Joseph's College (MD) 8/28
University of Edinburgh (Scotland) 8/22
Vanderbilt University (TN) 8/25
Wilberforce University (OH) 8/30
Yale University (CT) 8/9
Conradin, German ruler 8/29
Constantine I, Roman Emperor 8/25
Constitution of the State of Maryland 8/13
COUNCILS, CHURCH
  Council of Clermont (1095) 8/15
  Council of Moscow (1666) 8/1
  Council of Nicea I (325) 8/25
  Vatican II Council (1962-65) 8/6
  Vatican I Council (1869-70) 8/19
Counter-Reformation 8/21
Craig, Clarence Tucker
  (b. 6/7/1895) d. 8/20/1953 8/20
Cremer, Henry 8/15
Croft, William
  (bapt. 12/30/1678) d. 8/14/1727
Croly, George
  b. 8/17/1780 d. 11/24/1860]
CRUSADES, THE 8/22
  Battle of Ascalon (1099) 8/19
  First Crusade 8/15
  Sixth Crusade 8/25
Cummings, William H.
  b. 8/22/1831 [d. 6/6/1915]
Cushman, Ralph S.
  (b. 11/12/1879) d. 8/10/1960
Cutler, Timothy
  (b. 5/31/1684) d. 8/17/1765

D

Daniels, Jonathan 8/20
Danker, Frederick W. 8/8
DENOMINATIONS, CHRISTIAN
  African Methodist Episcopal (AME) Church 8/30
  American Baptists 8/9
  American Episcopal 8/29
  American Lutheranism 8/27, 8/30
  American Lutheran Church 8/24

American Moravianism 8/30
American Northern Baptists 8/3
American Presbyterianism 8/3
Anglicanism, American 8/17
Anglican Church 8/1, 8/6, 8/8, 8/15
Bohemian Brethren 8/13
Bohemian Protestants 8/13
Calvinism, American 8/5
Calvinistic Methodism 8/8
Christian and Missionary Alliance 8/6
Christian Union 8/19
Church of England 8/6, 8/9, 8/11, 8/13, 8/17
Church of God (HQ: TN) 8/19
Church of God of the Mountain Assembly 8/24
Church of Scotland 8/1, 8/17, 8/25
Congregationalism 8/5, 8/19, 8/20, 8/27, 8/29
Congregationalism, American 8/16
Congregationalism, New England 8/23
Cyprus Orthodox Church 8/2
Disciples of Christ 8/17
Eastern Churches
  Patriarch of Moscow 8/1
English Congregationalism 8/25
Episcopal, American 8/19
Episcopalianism, American 8/2
Evangelical Lutheran Church 8/26
Evangelical Lutheran Synod of Iowa 8/24
Fire-Baptized Holiness Church 8/1
French Catholicism 8/21
French Reformed 8/8
German Lutheranism 8/3, 8/7, 8/24
German Reformed 8/1, 8/19
Huguenots 8/5, 8/8, 8/23
Lutheranism 8/11
Lutheranism, German 8/14, 8/20
Lutheran Church Missouri Synod 8/7
Methodism 8/11
Methodism, American 8/5, 8/7
Methodist Episcopal Church 8/24, 8/30
Methodist Episcopal Church, South 8/25
Methodist New Connection 8/9
Moravians 8/13
Old Catholic Church 8/27
Pentecostal Fire-Baptized Holiness Church 8/1
Pentecostal Holiness Church 8/11
People's Church 8/18
Pilgrim Holiness 8/6
Plymouth Brethren 8/2

Presbyterianism 8/2, 8/10, 8/29
Presbyterianism, American 8/18
Presbyterian Church 8/17
Presbyterian Church in America (PCA) 8/9
Quakerism 8/2, 8/10, 8/13
Quakerism, English 8/5
Reformed Church in America 8/3
Reformed Presbyterian Church of Scotland 8/30
Russian Orthodoxy 8/1, 8/30
Russian Orthodox Eastern Church of America 8/8
Salvation Army 8/4, 8/20, 8/21, 8/23
Salvation Army, American 8/26
Shakers 8/6
Social Brethren 8/29
Society of Friends 8/10
Southern Presbyterian Church (PCUS) 8/9
Swiss Catholicism 8/12
Swiss Protestantism 8/16
Swiss Reformed 8/6
United Lutheran Church 8/30
United Society of Believers in Christ's Second Coming 8/6
Volunteers of America 8/26
Wesleyan Church 8/6
DENOMINATIONS, CHRISTIAN SECTARIAN
  Church of Christ, Scientist 8/23
  Mormonism 8/2
  Unitarianism 8/2, 8/18, 8/23, 8/29
  Unitarianism, American 8/3
  Universalism 8/5
Dexter, Henry Martyn
  b. 8/13/1821 [d. 11/13/1890]
Dickins, John A.
  b. 8/24/1747 [d. 9/27/1798]
Dispensations, Scriptural 8/19
Döllinger, Johann J. I. 8/27
Dominic de Guzman, St.
  (b. 1170) d. 8/6/1221
Doremus, Sarah P.
  b. 8/3/1802 [d. 1/29/1877]
Douglas, Lloyd C.
  b. 8/27/1877 [d. 2/13/1951]
Drummond, Henry
  b. 8/17/1851 [d. 3/11/1897]
Duchesne, Rose Philippine
  b. 8/29/1769 [d. 11/18/1852]

E

Eddy, Mary Baker 8/23
Edict of Nantes (1598) 8/8
Edwards, Sarah (née Pierpont). See Edwards, Jonathan
Eichrodt, Walther
  b. 8/1/1890 [d. 1978]
Eliot, John 8/22
  bapt. 8/5/1604 [d. 5/21/1690]
Elliot, Jim. See QUOTATIONS
Elliott, Charlotte 8/3
Elliott, Emily E. S.
  (b. 7/22/1836) d. 8/3/1897
Embury, Philip 8/11, 8/17
Epp, Theodore 8/18
Ethelfrith, King of Northumbria 8/5

F

Falwell, Jerry 8/31
  b. 8/11/1933
Farrar, Frederick W.
  b. 8/7/1831 [d. 3/22/1903]
Fénelon, François
  b. 8/6/1651 [d. 1/7/1715]
Fillmore, Charles 8/22
Finney, Charles G.
  b. 8/29/1792 d. 8/16/1875
FIRSTS
  American-born Catholic saint 8/28
  American Bible translation 8/26
  American Indian converted to Protestantism 8/13
  Anglican Bishop of Nova Scotia 8/12
  Anglican sisterhood 8/22
  Bishop of Lindisfarne 8/31
  Book printed in the West 8/15
  Catholic archbishop of the U.S. 8/15
  Catholic bishop of the U.S 8/15
  Catholic mass celebrated in English in the U 8/24
  English missionary magazine for children 8/19
  English Protestant missionary to reach China 8/1
  Episcopal ordination in the U.S. 8/3
  Female cantor in the history of Judaism 8/2
  Female rabbi to head a Conservative Jewish congreg 8/1
  Franciscan lector in theology 8/15
  Free school west of the Mississippi 8/29
  Hebrew Sabbath School Society in America 8/27
  Jew to settle in America 8/22
  Lutheran synod in the American colonies. 8/26
  Methodist chapel built in America 8/17
  Methodist clergyman to come to America 8/11
  Methodist society meetings in America 8/17
  Missionary to reach Thailand 8/23
  Permanent European settlement in North America 8/28
  Pope issuing an indulgence granting plenary (i.e., complete) forgiveness 8/3
  President of the Woman's Union Missionary Society 8/3
  Printed edition of the Scriptures 8/15
  Printing press in Rome 8/30
  Russian Orthodox theological seminary in the U.S. 8/8
  Single woman missionary to Persia 8/9
  U.S.-Born African-American Catholic Bishop 8/5
  Use of radioactive carbon dating 8/24
  Welsh immigrants to the American colonies 8/13
First Crusade 8/19
First General Assembly 8/25
Fisk, Fidelia
  (b. 5/1/1816) d. 8/9/1864
Fisk, Pliny 8/9
Form Criticism 8/20
Francis of Sales, St.
  b. 8/21/1567 [d. 12/28/1622]
Friedrich, Gerhard
  b. 8/20/1908
Friedrich, Johannes
  (b. 6/5/1836) d. 8/19/1917
Fry, Charles W.
  (b. 5/29/1837) d. 8/23/1882
Fry, Elizabeth 8/2
Fry, Franklin C.
  b. 8/30/1900 [d. 6/6/1968]

G

Gabriel, Charles H.
  b. 8/18/1856 [d. 9/15/1932]
Gaebelein, Arno C.
  b. 8/27/1861 [d. 12/25/1945]
Garrettson, Freeborn 8/15
Geissenhainer, A. T. 8/26
Gibbons, James 8/16
Gibbons, William
  b. 8/10/1781 [d. 7/25/1845]
Gingrich, F. W. 8/8
Gratz, Rebecca
  (b. 3/4/1781) d. 8/27/1869
Great Religious Revival of the American West 8/6
Gregory IX, Pope (1227-41) 8/6
Gregory XVI, Pope (1831-46) 8/3
Grenfell, Wilfred T. 8/4
Groote, Gerhard de
  (b. 10/1340) d. 8/20/1384
Gruber, Franz 8/25
Gurney, Joseph J.
  b. 8/2/1788 [d. 1/4/1847]
Gustavus III, Swedish King 8/19
Gützlaff, Karl F. A. 8/23
Guyon, Madame 8/6

H

Hall, Sarah. See also Boardman, Sarah Hall
Hamilton, John Taylor
  b. 8/30/1859 [d. 1/29/1951]
Harmens, Paul. See Rembrandt van Rijn
Hartsough, Lewis
  b. 8/31/1828 [d. 1/1/1919]
Hasseltine, Ann. See also Judson, Ann Hasseltine
Hastings, Selina
  b. 8/24/1707 [d. 6/17/1791]
Hatch, William H. P.
  b. 8/2/1875 [d. 11/11/1972]
Hawthorne, Rose. See Lathrop, Mary Alphonsa
Healy, James A.
  (b. 4/6/1830) d. 8/5/1900
Heck, Barbara
  (b. 1734) d. 8/17/1804
Hecker, Isaac 8/2
Hemmenway, Moses
  (b. 1735) d. 8/5/1811
Herder, Johann Gottfried von
  b. 8/25/1744 [d. 12/18/1803]
HERESIES, CHRISTIAN
  Arianism 8/5, 8/25
  Monothelitism 8/13
  Socinianism 8/5
Herrnhut 8/13, 8/30
Herzog, Johann Jacob
  b. 8/12/1805 [d. 9/30/1882]
Hill, Rowland
  b. 8/23/1744 [d. 4/11/1833]
History of Traditions, O.T. 8/3

AUGUST INDEX

Holmes, Oliver Wendell, Sr.
  b. 8/29/1809 [d. 10/8/1894]
Holtzman, Linda Joy 8/1
Holtzmann, H[einrich] J.
  (b. 5/17/1832] d. 8/4/1910
Home for Homeless Boys.
  See Boys' Town
Hopkins, John Henry
  (b. 10/28/1820] d. 8/14/1891
How, William Walsham
  (b. 12/13/1823] d. 8/10/1897
Humbard, Rex
  b. 8/13/1919
Hutchinson, Anne 8/30
Hutchinson, John
  (b. ca. 1674] d. 8/27/1737
Hyacinth, St.
  (b. 1185] d. 8/15/1257
HYMNS
  "America, the Beautiful" 8/12
  "Anywhere With Jesus" 8/31
  "A Charge to Keep I Have" 8/11
  "Be Not Dismayed, Whate'er Betide" 8/21
  "Break Thou the Bread of Life" 8/10
  "Cast Thy Burden on the Lord" 8/23
  "Come, Holy Spirit, Dove Divine" 8/9
  "Come, Ye Blessed" 8/16
  "Day is Dying in the West" 8/10
  "Face to Face with Christ My Savior" 8/5
  "Faith is the Victory" 8/13, 8/28
  "From Greenland's Icy Mountains" 8/11
  "Go, Tell It on the Mountain" 8/6
  "God Will Take Care of You" 8/21
  "Guide Me, O Thou Great Jehovah" 8/8
  "Hark! The Herald Angels Sing" 8/22
  "I am Coming, Lord" 8/31
  "I Have Found a Friend in Jesus" 8/23
  "I Have Heard the Savior's Love" 8/13
  "I Hear Thy Welcome Voice" 8/31
  "I Know That My Redeemer Liveth" 8/31
  "I Stand Amazed in the Presence" 8/18
  "Jesus, I My Cross Have Taken" 8/17
  "Jesus Calls Us O'er the Tumult" 8/7
  "Jesus Loves Me, This I Know" 8/31
  "Just As I Am" 8/3
  "Lead On, O King Eternal" 8/29
  "Lily of the Valley" 8/23
  "Lord of All Being, Throned Afar" 8/29
  "Love Was When" 8/16
  "Make Me a Captive, Lord" 8/28
  "More Like the Master" 8/18
  "More Love To Thee, O Christ" 8/13
  "My Faith Looks Up to Thee" 8/11
  "Nearer, My God, To Thee" 8/14
  "Now the Day is Over" 8/12
  "O Beautiful for Spacious Skies" 8/12
  "O Come, All Ye Faithful" 8/16
  "O For a Faith That Will Not Shrink" 8/28
  "O God, Our Help in Ages Past" 8/14
  "O Little Town of Bethlehem" 8/29
  "O Love That Wilt Not Let Me Go" 8/28
  "O Safe to the Rock That is Higher Than I" 8/13, 8/28
  "O Son of God Incarnate" 8/25
  "O Zion, Haste, Your Mission High Fulfilling" 8/30
  "Peace, Peace, Wonderful Peace" 8/18
  "Rejoice, Ye Pure in Heart" 8/6
  "Revive Us Again" 8/22
  "Rock of Ages" 8/11
  "Send the Light" 8/18
  "Shepherd of Tender Youth" 8/13
  "Silent Night" 8/25
  "Spirit of God, Descend Upon My Heart" 8/12, 8/17, 8/21
  "That Sweet Story of Old" 8/19
  "The Church's One Foundation" 8/14
  "The Dearest Place" 8/16
  "The Lord is in His Holy Temple" 8/30
  "The Old Road" 8/16
  "The Star-Spangled Banner" 8/14
  "The Way of the Cross Leads Home" 8/31
  "Thine Is the Glory, Risen, Conquering Son" 8/30
  "This is My Father's World" 8/3, 8/7
  "Thou Didst Leave Thy Throne" 8/3
  "We Give Thee But Thine Own" 8/10
  "We Praise Thee, O God, For the Son of Thy Love" 8/22
  "We Three Kings" 8/14
  "When He Cometh" 8/30
  "When I Survey the Wondrous Cross" 8/11
  "When Morning Gilds the Skies" 8/12
  "While Shepherds Watched Their Flocks" 8/12
  "Wonderful Grace of Jesus" 8/18
  "Worthy is the Lamb"
  "Yesterday, Today, and Tomorrow" 8/16
  The Lord is My Shepherd"
HYMN TUNES
  ADESTE FIDELIS 8/16
  AURELIA 8/14
  BETHANY 8/11
  BOYLSTON 8/11
  ELLESDIE 8/17
  FESTGESANG 8/22
  GALILEE 8/7
  HAMBURG 8/11
  HIDING IN THEE 8/13, 8/28
  JEWELS 8/30
  LAUDES DOMINI 8/12
  LONGWOOD 8/12
  MERRIAL 8/12
  MISSIONARY HYMN 8/11
  MORECAMBE 8/21
  OLIVET 8/11
  QUAM DILECTA 8/30
  SANKEY 8/13, 8/28
  ST. ANNE 8/14
  TERRA PATRIS 8/7
  TIDINGS 8/30
  WONDERFUL GRACE 8/18

I

Ignatius of Antioch 8/7
Immaculate Conception 8/9
INDIANS, AMERICAN 8/5
  Dakota Indians 8/24
  Hiacoomes 8/22
  Manteo 8/13
  Native Americans 8/8
  Pequots 8/5
  Potawatomi Tribe 8/29
  Tackanash 8/22
  West Indies 8/13
Inglis, Charles 8/12
Inquisition, The 8/9
Irving, Edward
  b. 8/4/1792 [d. 12/7/1834]
Islamic Turks 8/15

J

Jackson, Samuel Macauley
  (b. 6/19/1851] d. 8/2/1912
James VI, Scottish King.
  See James I, English King
Jehudi, Ashmun
  (b. 4/1794] d. 8/25/1828
Jerome, St. 8/30
John Bosco, St.
  b. 8/16/1815 [d. 1/31/1888]
John Paul I, Pope (1978) 8/26
John XXIII, Pope (1958-63) 8/6
Jowett, John Henry
  b. 8/25/1864 [d. 12/19/1923]
JUDAISM
  Barsimon, Jacob 8/22
  Conservative Judaism 8/1
  Gratz, Rebecca 8/27
  Hebrew Sabbath School 8/27
  Holtzman, Linda Joy 8/1
  Judaism, Science of 8/10
  Robbins, Betty (Mrs. Sheldon) 8/2
  Sephardic 8/22
  Zunz, Leopold 8/10
Jude, William H.
  (b. 9/1851] d. 8/7/1922
Judson, Adoniram 8/27
  b. 8/9/1788 [d. 4/12/1850]

K

Kennedy, Aimee. See
  also McPherson, Aimee Semple
Kenyon, Frederick G.
  (b. 1/15/1863] d. 8/23/1952
Kenyon, Kathleen 8/23
  (b. 1/6/1906] d. 8/24/1978
Key, Francis Scott 8/14
  b. 8/9/1779 [d. 1/11/1843]
Kilham, Alexander 8/9
King, Joseph Hillery
  b. 8/11/1869 [d. 4/23/1946]
Knox, John 8/7

L

Lambeth Conference 8/6
Langdon, William C.
  b. 8/19/1831 [d. 1896]
Lathbury, Mary A.
  b. 8/10/1841 [d. 10/20/1913]
Latourette, Kenneth Scott
  b. 8/9/1884 [d. 12/26/1968]
Laubach, Frank.
  See QUOTATIONS
LECTURES
  "The Greatest Thing in the World" 8/17
Lee, Ann 8/6
Legters, L[eonard] L. 8/10

Leonty, Russian Orthodox
  Metropolitan (1950-64)
  b. 8/8/1876 [d. 5/25/1965]
Leo XIII, Pope (1878-1903)
  8/3, 8/4
Lewis, C. S. See QUOTATIONS
Liberty Federation 8/11
Liguori, Alphonsus
  (b. 9/27/1696] d. 8/1/1787
Lillenas, Haldor
  (b. 11/19/1885] d. 8/18/1959
Lillenas Music Company 8/18
Line of Demarcation 8/11, 8/18
Livingstone, David 8/9
Lombard, Peter
  (b. ca. 1095] d. 8/21/1160
Louis IX, French King (1226-70)
  (b. 4/25/1214] d. 8/25/1270
Luciani, Albino. See also John
  Paul I, Pope 8/26
Luke, Jemima T.
  b. 8/19/1813 [d. 2/2/1906]
Luther, Martin 8/11
Lutheran World Federation 8/30

M

Mackay, William P.
  (b. 5/13/1839] d. 8/22/1885
Main, Hubert P.
  b. 8/17/1839 [d. 10/7/1925] 8/17
Makarios III (Michael C.
  Mouskos)
  (b. 8/13/1913] d. 8/2/1977
Marcan Hypothesis 8/4
Marillac, St. Louise de
  b. 8/12/1591 [d. 1660]
Marshman, Joshua 8/27
Martin, Civilla D.
  b. 8/21/1866 [d. 3/9/1948]
MARTYRS
  Bonhoeffer, Dietrich 8/3, 8/14
  Chalmers, James 8/4
  Elliot, Jim 8/2, 8/12
  Ignatius of Antioch 8/7
  Maximus the Confessor, St. 8/13
  Segura, Battista, Fray 8/5
Mason, Lowell
  (b. 1/8/1792] d. 8/11/1872
Massachusetts Bay Colony
  8/30
Mather, Cotton 8/17, 8/23
Mather, Increase 8/17
  (b. 6/21/1639] d. 8/23/1723

Mather, Richard 8/17, 8/23
Matheson, George
  (b. 3/27/1842] d. 8/28/1906
Maurice, [John] F. D.
  b. 8/29/1805 [d. 4/1/1872]
Maximus the Confessor, St.
  (b. ca. 580] d. 8/13/662
McManus, Frederick 8/24
McPherson, Aimee Semple
  8/12
McPherson, Harold 8/12
Medici, Catherine de 8/23
Melville, Andrew
  b. 8/1/1545 [d. 1622]
Mendelssohn, Felix 8/22
Milton, John 8/12
MISSIONARIES
  Abeel, David 8/3
  Aidan, St. 8/31
  Asbury, Francis 8/20
  Ashmun, Jehudi 8/25
  Batista Segura, Fray 8/5
  Bingham, Hiram, Jr. 8/16
  Brainerd, David 8/4, 8/8
  Bréchant de Galinée, René de 8/15
  Carey, William 8/17
  Carroll, John 8/15
  Chalmers, James 8/4
  Columba, St. 8/5
  Duchesne, Rose Philippine 8/29
  Elliot, Jim 8/2, 8/12
  Fisk, Fidelia 8/9
  Fisk, Pliny 8/9
  Grenfell, Wilfred T. 8/4
  Gützlaff, Karl F. A. 8/23
  Hyacinth, St. 8/15
  Judson, Adoniram 8/9, 8/27
  Legters, L[eonard] L. 8/10
  Livingstone, David 8/9
  Moffatt, Robert 8/9
  Morrison, Robert 8/1
  Nommensen, L[udwig] I. 8/27
  Paton, John G[ibson] 8/30
  Riggs, Stephen Return 8/24
  Schaeffer, Francis 8/21
  Schall, Johann A. 8/15
  Spalding, Henry H. 8/3
  Spanish missionary activity in North
    America 8/28
  Townsend, W. Cameron 8/10
  Wilder, Robert P. 8/2
MISSION AGENCIES
  American Board of Commissioners for
    Foreign Missions (ABCFM) 8/3

British and Foreign Bible Society 8/26
Campus Crusade for Christ 8/28
Christians in Action Missions 8/11
Evangelization Society 8/18
London Missionary Society 8/1, 8/23
Lutheran World Relief 8/30
Netherlands Missionary Society 8/23
Society for the Propagation of the
  Gospel in New England 8/5
Woman's Union Missionary Society of
  America 8/3
Wycliffe Bible Translators 8/10
Moffatt, Robert
  (b. 12/21/1795] d. 8/9/1883
Mohr, Joseph 8/25
Montessori, Maria
  b. 8/31/1870 [d. 5/6/1952]
Montessori Method 8/31
Montini, Giovanni Battista.
  See Paul VI, Pope
  (b. 9/26/1897] d. 8/6/1978
Moody, Dwight L. 8/13, 8/22,
  8/28
Moral Majority 8/11, 8/31
Morgan, G[eorge] Campbell
  8/25, 8/27
Morrison, Robert
  (b. 1/5/1782] d. 8/1/1834
Morse, Jedidiah
  b. 8/23/1761 [d. 6/9/1826]
Morse, Mary. See Eddy, Mary
  Baker
Mother Teresa of Calcutta 8/27
MOVEMENTS, CHRISTIAN
  American Movement for Christian
    Unity 8/17
  Broad Church Evangelicals 8/7
  Calvinism 8/11
  Caroline Divines 8/15
  Dispensationalism, Christian 8/22
  English Calvinistic Methodism 8/24
  English Puritanism 8/24
  English Separatism 8/31
  Evangelical Christianity 8/17
  Franciscan School of Theology 8/21
  Fundamentalism 8/22, 8/25, 8/31
  Moral Rearmament (1938) 8/7
  Non-Separatists 8/6
  Nonconformity, English 8/23, 8/30
  Oxford Group (1921) 8/7
  Oxford Movement 8/22
  Presbyterian Fundamentalists 8/14
  Puritanism, American 8/5
  Quietism 8/6
  Religious Right, The American 8/31

Scottish Reformation 8/7
Unity School of Christianity 8/22
Mowinckel, Sigmund O. P.
  b. 8/4/1884 [d. 6/4/1965]
Muhlenberg, Henry Melchior
  8/26
Murrone, Pietro di. See Celestine
  V, Pope
MYSTICS
  Blake, William 8/12
  Fénelon, François 8/6
  Francis of Sales, St. 8/21
  Groote, Gerhard de 8/20
  Irving, Edward 8/4
  Pascal, Blaise 8/19
  Underhill, Evelyn 8/1, 8/7, 8/12, 8/21,
    8/26, 8/29

N

"Ninety-Five Theses" 8/11
National Council of Churches
  8/26
NATIVE AMERICANS
  Nez Perce Indians 8/3
Newman, John Henry (Cardinal)
  (b. 2/21/1801] d. 8/11/1890
New World 8/13
Nez Perce Indians 8/3
Nicene Creed 8/25
Nicholas I, Russian Czar (1825-
  55) 8/3
NICKNAMES / TITLES
  "Apostle of the North" 8/15
  "Apostle to the Indians" 8/5
  "Caroline Divines" 8/15
  "Great Heart of New Guinea" 8/4
  "History's worst pope" 8/11
  "Mother of American Methodism" 8/17
  "Poor Man's Bishop" 8/10
Nikon, Nikita M. 8/1
Nobel Prize 8/27
Nommensen, L[udwig] I. 8/27
Northfield Training School 8/22
Noth, Martin
  b. 8/3/1902 [d. 5/30/1968]

O

Odescalchi, Benedetto.
  See Innocent XI, Pope
Odrawaz, Jacek 8/15
Olevianus, Kaspar
  b. 8/19/1536 [d. 3/15/1587]

Olga of Kiev, Russian Princess (954-974). See also Vladimir I (the Great)
ORGANIZATIONS, CHRISTIAN
   Alcoholics Anonymous 8/8
   Relief for Poor Widows with Small Children 8/28
   Young Men's Christian Association (YMCA) 8/19
Oswald, St., King of Northumbria (633-642)
   (b. ca. 605) d. 8/5/642
Oxford Movement 8/11, 8/22

P

Palmquist, Gustaf 8/8
Pammachius, St.
   (b. ca. 340) d. 8/30/410
PAPAL DECREES
   "Quam singulari" (1910) 8/8
   "Dominus ac Redemptor Noster" (1773) 8/16
   "Humani generis" (1950) 8/12
   "Ne temere" (1907) 8/2
   "Salvator noster" (1476) 8/3
   "Solicitudo omnium ecclesiarum" (1814) 8/7
Papal Infallibility 8/19
Pascal, Blaise
   (b. 6/19/1623) d. 8/19/1662
Paton, John G[ibson] 8/30
Patriarch of Moscow 8/1
Paul II, Pope (1464-71) 8/30
Paul III, Pope (1534-49) 8/15
Paul VI, Pope (1963-78) 8/6, 8/22
Peace of St. Germain (1570) 8/8
Pentecostal Holiness 8/11
PERIODICALS / JOURNALS
   "Oberlin Evangelist" 8/16
   "The Church Missionary Juvenile Instructor" 8/3
   "The Congregationalist" 8/13
   "The Missionary Repository" 8/19
Peter the Great, Russian Czar (1682-1725) 8/1
Peter the Hermit 8/15
Phillips, Philip
   b. 8/13/1834 [d. 1895]
Pierpont, Sarah. See also Edwards, Jonathan
Pius VI, Pope (1775-99) 8/15
Pius VII, Pope (1800-23) 8/7
   b. 8/14/1742 [d. 8/20/1823]
Pius XI, Pope (1922-39) 8/16
Pius XII, Pope (1939-58) 8/12
Plumptre, Edward H.
   b. 8/6/1821 [d. 2/1/1891]
POETRY
   "I met God in the morning" 8/10
   "The Bombing of Ft. McHenry" 8/9
   Songs of Experience (1794) 8/12
   Songs of Innocence (1789) 8/12
Poets Laureate of England
   Tate, Nahum (1692) 8/12
Polk, Sarah Childress
   (b. 9/4/1803) d. 8/14/1891
POPES
   Alexander VI (1492-1503) 8/11, 8/18, 8/26
   Clement IV (1265-68) 8/29
   Clement XIV (1769-74) 8/7, 8/16
   Gregory IX (1227-41) 8/6
   Gregory XVI (1831-46) 8/3
   John Paul I (1978) 8/26
   John XXIII (1958-63) 8/6
   Leo XIII (1878-1903) 8/3, 8/4
   Paul III (1534-49) 8/15
   Paul II (1464-71) 8/30
   Paul VI (1963-78) 8/6, 8/22
   Pius VII (1800-23) 8/7, 8/14
   Pius VI (1775-99) 8/15
   Pius XII (1939-58) 8/12
   Pius XI (1922-39) 8/16
   Sixtus IV (1471-84) 8/3, 8/9
   Urban V (1362-70) 8/5
Potter, Philip A. 8/16
Pounds, Jesse Brown
   b. 8/31/1861 [d. 3/3/1921]
Premillennialism, Christian 8/22
Prentiss, Elizabeth P.
   (b. 10/26/1818) d. 8/13/1878
PRESIDENTS, U.S.
   Adams, John (1797-1801) 8/5
   Lincoln, Abraham (1861-65) 8/15
   Polk, James K. (1845-49) 8/14
Pridgeon, Charles Hamilton 8/18
Pusey, Edward B.
   b. 8/22/1800 [d. 9/16/1882]

Q

QUOTATIONS
   Alekseyev, Ivan 8/9, 8/16, 8/30
   Barth, Karl 8/6, 8/18
   Bonar, Andrew 8/20, 8/23, 8/24
   Bonhoeffer, Dietrich 8/3, 8/14
   Brainerd, David 8/4, 8/8
   Calvin, John 8/20
   Carretto, Carlo 8/10, 8/19, 8/27, 8/28
   Cary-Elwes, Columba 8/15
   Elliot, Jim 8/2, 8/12
   Fletcher, John 8/23
   Hammarskjöld, Dag 8/4, 8/26
   Houselander, Caryll 8/22, 8/31
   Laubach, Frank C. 8/21
   Lewis, C. S. 8/1, 8/2, 8/3, 8/9, 8/10, 8/18
   Lincoln, Abraham 8/15
   Luther, Martin 8/1, 8/7, 8/8, 8/11, 8/18
   Mason, George 8/22
   More, Hannah 8/14
   Newman, John Henry 8/27
   Newton, John 8/10, 8/11, 8/17, 8/19, 8/30, 8/31
   Nouwen, Henri J. M. 8/2, 8/9, 8/11, 8/16, 8/17, 8/18, 8/28, 8/29, 8/31
   Owen, John 8/24
   Pink, Arthur W. 8/9, 8/25
   Rutherford, Samuel 8/4, 8/5
   Schaeffer, Francis 8/2, 8/21
   Spurgeon, Charles 8/6, 8/10, 8/22
   Toplady, Augustus 8/7, 8/29
   Underhill, Evelyn 8/1, 8/7, 8/12, 8/21, 8/25, 8/26, 8/29
   Venn, Henry 8/5
   Walther, Carl F. W. 8/7
   Wesley, John 8/2, 8/8, 8/9, 8/13, 8/14, 8/16, 8/19, 8/20, 8/23, 8/24, 8/26
   Whitefield, George 8/3, 8/10, 8/14

R

RADIO BROADCASTING
   Back to the Bible Broadcast 8/18
   Religious Radio 8/18
Raleigh, Sir Walter 8/13
Rankin, Thomas 8/13
Redner, Lewis H.
   (b. 12/15/1830) d. 8/29/1908
Rees, Seth Cook
   b. 8/6/1854 [d. 5/22/1933]
RELIGIOUS ORDERS, CATHOLIC
   American Sisters of Charity 8/28
   Benedictines 8/15
   Brethren of the Common Life 8/20
   Brigittines (Order of St. Saviour) 8/5
   Congregation of the Most Holy Redeemer 8/1
   Daughters of Charity 8/12
   Dominicans 8/6, 8/11, 8/15
   Franciscans 8/9, 8/15, 8/21
   Jesuits 8/5, 8/7, 8/14, 8/15, 8/16
   Missionary Priests of Saint Paul the Apostle 8/2
   Order of Friars Preachers 8/6
   Order of St. Saviour (Brigittines) 8/5
   Order of the Visitation 8/21
   Paulists 8/2
   Redemptorists 8/1, 8/2
   Salesians 8/16
   Sisters of Charity 8/12
   Sisters of Loreto 8/27
   Society of Jesus 8/7, 8/15
   Society of St. Francis of Sales 8/16
   Society of the Sacred Heart 8/29
   Sulpicians 8/8
Riggs, Stephen Return
   (b. 8/23/1812) d. 8/24/1883
Robbins, Betty (Mrs. Sheldon) 8/2
Root, George F.
   b. 8/30/1820 [d. 8/6/1895]
Rosicrucian legend 8/7
Russian Latin Rite 8/3
Rutherford, Samuel. See QUOTATIONS

S

Sanday, William
   b. 8/1/1843 [d. 9/16/1920]
Sankey, Ira D.
   (b. 8/28/1840) d. 8/13/1908
   b. 8/28/1840 [d. 8/13/1908]
Saracens 8/19
Scaliger, Joseph Justus
   b. 8/5/1540 [d. 1/21/1609]
Schaff, Philip 8/12
Schall, Johann A.
   (b. 1591) d. 8/15/1666
Schlatter, Adolf von
   b. 8/16/1852 [d. 5/19/1938]
Schmemann, Alexander. See QUOTATIONS
Schmucker, Beal M.
   b. 8/26/1827 [d. 10/18/1888]
Schmucker, Samuel S. 8/26
Scofield, C[yrus] I. 8/22
   b. 8/19/1843 [d. 7/24/1921]
Scots Confession 8/7
Scott, John P.
   b. 8/16/1877 [d. 1932]
Scottish Parliament 8/7

SCULPTURES
  Pietà (1501) 8/18, 8/26
Segura, Batista 8/5
SEMINARIES / BIBLE COLLEGES
  Andover Theological Seminary (MA) 8/23
  Dallas Theological Seminary (TX) 8/22
  Drew Theological Seminary (NJ) 8/20
  Episcopal Theological School, (MA) 8/2
  Pittsburgh Bible Institute 8/18
  Rochester Seminary (NY) 8/3
  Union Seminary (NY) 8/8
Semple, Robert 8/12
Serampore Press 8/17
Seton, Elizabeth Ann (Bayley)
  b. 8/28/1774 [d. 1/4/1821]
Shelley, Lee
  b. 8/11/1914
Sheppard, Franklin L.
  b. 8/7/1852 [d. 2/15/1930]
Shurtleff, Ernest W.
  (b. 4/4/1862] d. 8/29/1917
Simpson, A. B. 8/6
Sistine Chapel 8/9
Sixtus IV, Pope (1471-84) 8/3, 8/9
Smith, George
  (b. 3/26/1840] d. 8/19/1876
Smith, Robert Holbrook
  b. 8/8/1879 [d. 11/6/1950]
Smith, Rodney "Gipsy"
  (b. 3/31/1860] d. 8/4/1947
Solemn League and Covenent 8/17
Spalding, Henry H.
  (b. ca. 1803/04] d. 8/3/1874
Spurgeon, Charles. See also QUOTATIONS
Spurling, Richard G. 8/19

St. Bartholomew's Day Massacre 8/8
Stritch, Samuel A. 8/31
Strong, Augustus H.
  b. 8/3/1836 [d. 11/29/1921]
Strong, James
  (b. 8/14/1822] d. 8/7/1894
  b. 8/14/1822] [d. 8/7/1894]
Student Volunteer Movement 8/2
Sunday School Union 8/13
SYNAGOGUES, JEWISH
  Beth Israel (Coatesville, PA) 8/1

T

"Table Talk," Martin Luther's 8/18
Tate, Nahum
  (b. 1652] d. 8/12/1715
Taylor, Jeremy
  b. 8/15/1613 [d. 8/13/1667]
TELEVISION
  Television Ministry 8/13
Tetzel, Johann
  (b. ca. 1465] d. 8/11/1519
Textual Criticism, Biblical 8/5
Tiberius Caesar, Roman Emperor 8/21
Tillet, Wilbur F.
  b. 8/25/1854 [d. 1936]
Tillich, Paul
  b. 8/20/1886 [d. 10/22/1965]
Tilton, Theodore 8/20
Toplady, Augustus M.
  (b. 11/4/1740] d. 8/11/1778
Tower of London 8/1
Townsend, W. Cameron 8/10
Toynbee, Arnold 8/15
Tractarian Revival. See Oxford Movement (1833-45)

Trajan, Marcus, Emperor (98-117)
  (b. 9/18/52] d. 8/7/117
Triple Alliance at The Hague 8/8
Tullar, Grant Colfax
  b. 8/5/1869 [d. 5/20/1950]

U

'Unitas Fratrum' 8/13
U.S. National Anthem 8/9, 8/14
United Brotherhood 8/13
UNIVERSITIES. See COLLEGES / UNIVERSITIES
Urban V, Pope (1362-70) 8/5

V

Vatican Library 8/9
Vergil 8/7
Vincent, John H. 8/4
Vincent, Marvin R.
  (b. 9/11/1834] d. 8/18/1922
Vincent de Paul 8/12
Visigoths 8/24
Vladislav IV, Polish King (1632-48) 8/28

W

Wade, John F.
  (b. ca. 1710] d. 8/16/1786
Walch, James
  (b. 6/21/1837] d. 8/30/1901
Ward, William 8/27
Ware, William
  b. 8/3/1797 [d. 2/19/1852]
Warner, Anna B.
  b. 8/31/1820 [d. 1/23/1915]

WARS
  American Revolutionary War (1775-83) 8/13, 8/14, 8/17
  World War II (1939-45) 8/14
  World War I (1914-18) 8/29
Wedel, Cynthia Clark
  b. 8/26/1908 [d. 8/24/1986]
Wesley, Charles 8/14
Wesley, John 8/9, 8/11. See also QUOTATIONS
Wesley, Samuel Sebastian
  b. 8/14/1810 [d. 4/19/1876]
Westminster Confession 8/7
Whitefield, George 8/8, 8/24. See also QUOTATIONS
Wilder, Robert P.
  b. 8/2/1863 [d. 3/28/1938]
Williams, Peter
  (b. 1/7/1722] d. 8/8/1796
Wilson, William G. (Bill) 8/8
Work, Frederick J. 8/6
Work, John Wesley, Jr.
  b. 8/6/1872 [d. 9/7/1925]
World Council of Churches 8/10, 8/16, 8/20, 8/23, 8/26, 8/31
  Amsterdam Assembly (1948) 8/23
  Evanston Assembly (1954) 8/31
Wyrtzen, Don
  b. 8/16/1942

Y

Yale Apostasy of 1722 8/17

Z

Zinzendorf, Nicolaus von 8/13
Zunz, Leopold
  b. 8/10/1794 [d. 3/18/1886]

תשרי ALMANAC OF THE CHRISTIAN FAITH אלול
TISHRI   ELUL

~ September 1 ~

Highlights in History

451 The Council of Chalcedon first gathered at Nicea. Later, Marcian moved the venue to Chalcedon, where the council held 16 sessions between Oct. 8th and Nov. 1st of this year.

1192 In the Third Crusade, Richard I (the Lionhearted) of England and Moslem leader Saladin of Damascus signed a truce, allowing the Crusaders free access to the Holy Sepulchre.

1836 Missionaries Marcus Whitman and Henry H. Spalding, reached Fort Walla Walla on the Columbia River in the American Northwest, and established the first U.S. settlement in what was then called the Territory of Northern Oregon. Their wives (Narcissa Whitman and Eliza Spalding) also became the first white women to cross the American continent.

Notable Birthdays

1728 Birth of Philip Embury, the earliest known Methodist preacher in America. Born in Ireland, he converted under John Wesley, and in 1768 erected the first Methodist church in the American colonies. [d. 8/1775]

1785 Birth of pioneer circuit rider Peter Cartwright. Perhaps the best known of the early Methodist preachers along the [mid-]western American frontier, Cartwright later served in the Illinois state legislature, and  was defeated in an 1846 race for Congress by Abraham Lincoln. [d. 9/25/1872]

1866 Birth of Frederick R. Tennant, English philosophical theologian. Seeking to harmonize science and religion, Tennant's chief writing was *Philosophical Theology* (1930). [d. 9/9/1957]

1905 Birth of Norman Gerstenfeld, an English-born American leader of Reformed Judaism. He was rabbi of Washington Hebrew Congregation (1939-68). [d. 1968]

1925 Birth of John M. Moore, an English Baptist clergyman who wrote the words and music to "Burdens Are Lifted at Calvary."

The Last Passage

1159 Death of Adrian IV, about 44, who served as pope from December 1154. Born Nicholas Breakspear, he was the only Englishman ever elected to the papacy. Strong-willed and clear-sighted, Adrian renewed the treaty of Constance with German king Frederick I Barbarossa (1152-90). (b. ca. 1115)

1845 Death of Sarah Hall Boardman Judson, 41, American missionary to Burma. As the widow of missionary George Dana Boardman (1801-1831), she afterward became fellow-missionary Adoniram Judson's second wife. (b. 11/4/1803)

1936 Death of Lewis E. Jones, 71, American lifelong YMCA worker. He also wrote and composed a number of hymns, including POWER IN THE BLOOD ("Would You Be Free From Your Burden of Sin?"). (b. 2/8/1865)

Words for the Soul

1779 English slaver-turned-clergyman John Newton concluded in a letter: 'The weakest believer is born of God, and an heir of glory; the strongest and most advanced can be no more.'

1784 English spiritual reformer John Wesley recorded the following missionary resolve in his journal: 'Being now clear in my own mind, I took a step which I had long weighed... and appointed Mr. [Richard] Whatcoat and Mr. [Thomas] Vasey to go and serve the desolate sheep in America.'

1878 In a letter to an elderly widow, Scottish novelist and poet George MacDonald mused: 'How is your conscious world moving now, dear, lonely sister? You are now like the creature spinning its chrysalis. That is the use of the world to you. Have patience, and let your wings grow. There is no food for feathers like patience.'

IN GOD'S WORD... OT: Job 40:1–42:17 ~ NT: 2 Corinthians 5:11-21 ~ Psalms 45:1-17 ~ Proverbs 22:14

תשרי ALMANAC OF THE CHRISTIAN FAITH אלול
TISHRI   ELUL

~ September 2 ~

Highlights in History

1192 The Third Crusade ended with the signing of a treaty. The peace which followed lasted five years. While Jerusalem was not retaken in the Crusade, other Syrian territory was gained, which retained the presence of a Christian kingdom in the Palestinian area.

1636 French Jesuit missionary John Brebeuf baptized the first Iroquois ever to become a Christian. The man, a Seneca chief, was later tortured to death.

1784 English church founder John Wesley appointed Thomas Coke, 37, as superintendent (later called "bishop") of the American Methodist Church.

1895 The College of Notre Dame of Maryland, in Baltimore, opened its doors. Founded as a Catholic institution, it was the first college for women established in America.

1921 The first general synod of the African Orthodox Church convened in New York City. This branch of the Protestant Episcopal (not Eastern Orthodox!) Church was established in 1919 by founder George A. McGuire, who was also elected the denomination's first bishop.

Notable Birthdays

1838 Birth of Erastus Blakeslee, American Congregational clergyman. He organized the Bible Study Publishing Co. in Boston (1892), also the Bible Study Union. In all, Blakeslee published about 170 volumes of Bible lessons. [d. 7/12/1908]

1884 Birth of Frank C. Laubach, American missionary and linguist. While serving as a Congregational missionary to the Philippines (1915-36), he developed his famous "each one teach one" method of instilling literacy. The "Laubach Method" has since been copied by various mission boards around the world. [d. 6/11/1970]

The Last Passage

1969 Death of James A. Pike, 56, American Episcopal bishop, lawyer and author. He was ordained in 1944, and was elected bishop of California in 1958. But Pike's personal life was marked with tragedy: his son's suicide, a battle with alcoholism, an extramarital affair and two divorces. In 1966 he denounced his church and became a spiritualist, dying three years later, alone in the Judean desert. (b. 2/14/1913)

1973 Death of J[ohn] R. R. Tolkien, 81, English philologist and fantasy novelist. A devout Catholic, and a close friend of C. S. Lewis, Tolkien wrote *The Hobbit*, 1938 and *The Lord of the Rings (A Trilogy)*, 1954-55. (b. 1/3/1892)

Words for the Soul

1873 American Quaker Holiness author Hannah Whitall Smith wrote in a letter: *'In the lonely night hours, when sorrows and losses and anxieties are so sure to come and claim a hearing, I can only turn resolutely away and say over and over and over to myself and to God, "Thy will be done, Thy will be done!" until the sweet refrain lulls me to sleep when nothing else would. And so I have learned to make the sweet will of God literally my pillow....'*

1930 While a missionary in the Philippines, American literacy pioneer Frank Laubach wrote in a letter: *'God is always awaiting the chance to give us high days. We so seldom are in deep earnest about giving him his chance.'*

1949 English scholar and Christian apologist C. S. Lewis encouraged in a letter: *'God, who foresaw your tribulation, has specially armed you to go through it, not without pain but without stain.'*

1981 Dutch Catholic priest and diarist Henri J. M. Nouwen reflected in his *Road to Daybreak* journal: *'Time given to inner renewal is never wasted. God is not in a hurry.'*

IN GOD'S WORD... OT: Ecclesiastes 1:1–3:22 ~ NT: 2 Corinthians 6:1-13 ~ Psalms 46:1-11 ~ Proverbs 22:15

תשרי TISHRI — ALMANAC OF THE CHRISTIAN FAITH — אלול ELUL

September 3

Highlights in History

590 Gregory the Great was consecrated pope, serving to 604. Regarded as one of the greatest of the Early churchmen, he restored monastic discipline, enforced celibacy of the clergy, wrote several hymns, and is credited with having originated the Gregorian chants.

1752 This date became September 14th when Great Britain (including Scotland, Ireland, Wales and the American colonies) officially adopted the Gregorian Calendar — developed by Pope Gregory XIII in 1582 to replace the older, now-inaccurate Julian Calendar.

1934 Evangeline Cory Booth, 69, the seventh child of founders William and Catherine Booth, became the fourth elected commander and the first woman general of the Salvation Army, serving through 1939. She never married, but adopted and raised four children.

1965 Pope Paul VI issued the encyclical, "Mysterium fidei," restating the traditional Catholic eucharistic teaching which emphasizes the real presence of Christ through transubstantiation.

Notable Birthdays

1847 Birth of James Hannington, Anglican missionary and prelate. He went to Africa as an English missionary to Uganda. In 1884 he was named first Bishop of Eastern Equatorial Africa. In 1885 King Mwanga of Uganda took him prisoner, and he was beaten to death by soldiers in Mombasa. Hannington was reported to have died singing. [d. 10/29/1885]

1894 Birth of H[elmut] Richard Niebuhr, American Protestant Neo-orthodox theologian and professor of Christian ethics at Yale Divinity School (1938-62). The brother of Reinhold Niebuhr, Richard wrote in the area of ethics, and authored *Kingdom of God in America* (1937) and *Christ and Culture* (1951). [d. 7/5/1962]

The Last Passage

1815 Death of John Murray, 73, founder of American Universalism. Born in England, he came to America in 1770 preaching universal salvation, and later organized the Independent Church of Christ in Gloucester, MA, the first Universalist Church in the U.S. (b. 12/10/1741)

1857 Death of John McLoughlin, 72, American Catholic pioneer trader known as the "Father of Oregon." Born in Canada, McLoughlin used his influence for 22 years to keep the Indians in the U.S. Northwest in check, at the same time treating them with fairness. (b. 10/19/1784)

1958 Death of Bentley D. Ackley, 85, American song evangelist and hymnwriter. As editor of the Rodeheaver Music Co., Ackley penned over 3,000 hymn tunes, including SPRING HILL and JOY IN SERVING JESUS. (b. 9/27/1872)

1959 English-born American Catholic priest Tom Cunningham, 53, died in Point Barrow, Alaska. Known as the "parish priest of the Arctic," Father Tom Cunningham supervised 150,000 square miles north of the Arctic Circle. (b. 2/24/1906)

Words for the Soul

1776 Anglican clergyman and hymnwriter John Newton proclaimed in a letter: *'The love I bear Christ is but a faint and feeble spark, but it is an emanation from himself: He kindled it and he keeps it alive; and because it is His work, I trust many waters shall not quench it.'*

1876 Quaker Holiness author Hannah Whitall Smith confessed in a letter: *'While I do not for a moment think I have got hold of all truth, I dare not think He has permitted me to believe a direct lie, after all my special and earnest prayers on this very point.'*

1995 Dutch Catholic diarist Henri J. M. Nouwen confided in his journal: *'Prayer connects my mind with my heart, my will with my passions, my brain with my belly.... Prayer is the divine instrument of my wholeness, unity, and inner peace.'*

IN GOD'S WORD... OT: Ecclesiastes 4:1–6:12 ~ NT: 2 Corinthians 6:14–7:7 ~ Psalms 47:1-9 ~ Proverbs 22:16

תשרי
TISHRI

ALMANAC OF THE CHRISTIAN FAITH

אלול
ELUL

~ September 4 ~

Highlights in History

1645 The first Lutheran church building in America was dedicated by Rev. Johannes Campanius at Christina (Tinicum Island), near the present site of Essington, PA. Before the church was built, Campanius had conducted services in a small blockhouse at Fort Göteborg.

1813 The first religious weekly in the U.S., "The Religious Remembrancer" was founded by John W. Scott. (With successive mergers, the magazine later became "The Christian Observer.")

1847 Scottish Anglican clergyman Henry Francis Lyte (1793-1847) penned the words to his last (and best-known) hymn: "Abide With Me: Fast Falls the Eventide." Lyte died of frail health less than three months later, on November 20th.

Notable Birthdays

1802 Birth of Marcus Whitman, American Presbyterian ABCFM medical missionary to the American northwest. He and his wife Narcissa crossed the country by wagon train in 1836, arriving at Fort Walla Walla, where they set up an Indian mission in the Oregon Territory. In 1847 a measles epidemic broke out among the Cayuse. In retaliation, a band of Indians attacked and murdered Whitman, his wife and twelve others. [d. 11/29/1847]

1803 Birth of Sarah Childress Polk, American Presbyterian fundamentalist wife of 11th president James K. Polk. She was the first "first lady" to institute strict Sabbath observance, and banned dancing at presidential functions. [d. 8/14/1891]

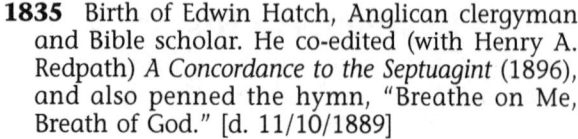

1824 Birth of Phoebe Cary, American Universalist author and poet. She collaborated with her sister Alice on several volumes of verse. One of Phoebe's poems became a hymn which begins: "One Sweetly Solemn Thought" (a.k.a. "Nearer Home"). [d. 7/31/1871]

1835 Birth of Edwin Hatch, Anglican clergyman and Bible scholar. He co-edited (with Henry A. Redpath) *A Concordance to the Septuagint* (1896), and also penned the hymn, "Breathe on Me, Breath of God." [d. 11/10/1889]

The Last Passage

1844 Death of Oliver Holden, 78, American Puritan clergyman, carpenter and composer of the hymn tune CORONATION ("All Hail the Power of Jesus' Name"). (b. 9/18/1765)

1846 Death of David Abeel, 42, American missionary. In 1829 he sailed for China under the auspices of the Seaman's Friend Society. A year later he placed himself under the American Board of Commissioners for Foreign Missions, and ministered in Java, Singapore, Siam, Malacca, Borneo and parts of Asia. (b. 6/12/1804)

1965 Death of Albert Schweitzer, 90, French theologian, musical scholar, physician and missionary. He founded Lambarene Hospital in French Equatorial Africa in 1913. As a religious scholar, Schweitzer's *Quest of the Historical Jesus* (1906) is considered a foundational work in theological studies. (b. 1/14/1875)

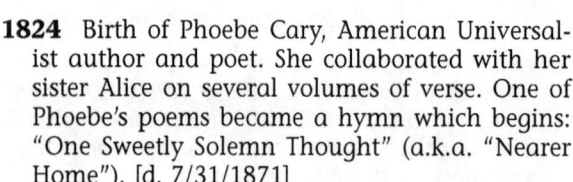

Words for the Soul

1778 English hymnwriter John Newton testified in a letter: *'I am prone to puzzle myself about twenty things, which are equally out of my power, and equally unnecessary, if the Lord be my Shepherd.'*

1864 President Abraham Lincoln wrote to Quaker Eliza P. Gurney: *'The purposes of the Almighty are perfect, and must prevail though we erring mortals may fail to accurately perceive them in advance.'*

1979 Russian Orthodox liturgical scholar Alexander Schmemann noted with concern in his diary: *'One gets the impression that the Church and Christianity are somehow busily bustling, but "without sails or wheels."'*

IN GOD'S WORD... OT: Ecclesiastes 7:1–9:18 ~ NT: 2 Corinthians 7:8-16 ~ Psalms 48:1-14 ~ Proverbs 22:17-19

תשרי TISHRI   ALMANAC OF THE CHRISTIAN FAITH   אלול ELUL

~ September 5 ~

Highlights in History

1692 At Harvard College in Cambridge, MA, colonial clergyman Increase Mather, 53, received the first Doctor of Sacred Theology (STD) degree awarded in America. Increase was the father of another famous colonial Puritan clergyman, Cotton Mather (1663-1728).

1810 The American Board of Commissioners for Foreign Missions (ABCFM) was formally organized by the Congregational churches of New England at Farmington, CT. It was the first foreign missions society established in America.

1888 American baseball player-turned evangelist Billy Sunday, 26, married Helen Thompson, 20. In later years Helen, affectionately known as "Ma Sunday," became Billy Sunday's evangelistic campaign advisor. She survived her husband (who died in 1935) by 22 years.

Notable Birthdays

1802 Birth of Frederick Oakeley, an Anglican clergyman who became a Catholic during the time of the Oxford Movement (1845). Oakeley authored several volumes of poetry, and his translation of the Latin "Adeste Fidelis" gave the Church the popular carol: "O Come, All Ye Faithful." [d. 1/29/1880]

1807 Birth of Richard Chenevix Trench, Irish Anglican prelate, poet and scholar. As Archbishop of Dublin (1864-84), he was a noted philologist who popularized the study of language. He authored and edited sacred poetical and theological works (*Notes on the Parables; Notes on the Miracles*). [d. 3/28/1886]

The Last Passage

1529 Death of Georg Blaurock, about 37, early Swiss Anabaptist evangelist. He helped plant the Anabaptist faith over much of central Europe before he was eventually arrested and burned for heresy. (b. ca. 1492)

1569 Death of infamous English prelate Edmund Bonner, about 69. The last Catholic bishop of London (1539-49), he was chaplain to Henry VIII (1532-40), and, at the ascendancy of Mary, became the principal agent in persecuting Protestant reformers. When Elizabeth I became queen, Bonner refused (1559) to take the oath under the Act of Supremacy, and spent the rest of his days in prison. (b. ca. 1500)

1914 Death of Charles Pierre Péguy, 41, a French Catholic writer and poet who reflected the spiritual conflict between the Catholic faith and socialism. His writings attacked the modern world and its belief in progress. Péguy lost his life in the Battle of the Marne. (b. 1/7/1873)

1997 Death of Mother Teresa of Calcutta, 86, Albanian-born Catholic missionary to India. Born Agnes Bojaxhiu, she took her first vows in 1931, and founded the Missionaries of Charity in 1950. Widely respected for her international humanitarian efforts for the poor, she was awarded the 1979 Nobel Peace Prize. (b. 8/27/1910)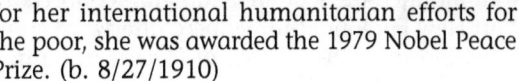

Words for the Soul

1516 Glarean, an influential Swiss humanist and philosopher of the early Reformation era, wrote in a letter to Dutch humanist Desiderius Erasmus: *'You taught me to know Christ.'*

1864 The "Washington Chronicle" reported that, having just been presented with an elegant Bible by the Committee of Colored People from Baltimore, President Abraham Lincoln declared: *'I believe the Bible is the best gift God has given to man. All the good Saviour gave to the world was communicated through this Book. But for this Book we could not know right from wrong. All things most desirable for man's welfare, here and hereafter, are to be found portrayed in it.'*

IN GOD'S WORD...   OT: Ecclesiastes 10:1–12:14 ~ NT: 2 Corinthians 8:1-15 ~ Psalms 49:1-20 ~ Proverbs 22:20-21

September 6

Highlights in History

1620 The Mayflower sailed from Plymouth, England for the New World. It was 90 feet long and 26 feet wide, and on board were 101 passengers. Two months and five days later, the ship landed near modern-day Cape Cod, MA.

1907 Pope Pius X issued the encyclical "Pascendi dominici gregis," in which he condemned the "Modernist" movement as evidenced within the branches of Christendom.

1938 "Boys Town" was released by MGM Studios. Starring Spencer Tracy, this award-winning film depicted the 1917 founding of the famous vocational institution in Nebraska by 31-year-old American Catholic parish priest, Father Edward J. Flanagan (1886-1948).

Notable Birthdays

1711 Birth of Lutheran religious leader Henry Melchior Mühlenberg. Arriving in America as a missionary from Germany in 1742, he organized and united the scattered Lutheran congregations in New England. Mühlenberg afterward came to be known as the "Father of American Lutheranism." [d. 10/7/1787]

1809 Birth of Bruno Bauer, German radical theologian. A lecturer on theology (1834-42), Bauer was one of the most negative theological critics of his day. He was eventually deprived of his license to teach as a result of his destructive criticism of the Bible. [d. 4/15/1882]

1880 Birth of Ira B. Wilson, sacred composer. As a music editor with the Lorenz Publishing Co. in Dayton, OH, Wilson penned a large number of choir cantatas, anthems and hymn arrangements under the pseudonym "Fred B. Holton." His most enduring hymn creation was "Make Me a Blessing" (a.k.a. "Out in the Highways and Byways of Life"). [d. 4/3/1950]

The Last Passage

1815 Death of Samuel Provoost, 73, the first Episcopal bishop of New York (1786-1801). Born in New York City, he was once chaplain of the U.S. Senate (1789-1801). (b. 3/11/1742)

1978 Death of Robert W. ("Bob") Pierce, 63, American evangelist and exponent of Christian social service. Pierce was the founder of World Vision International, an interdenominational humanitarian aid organization. (b. 10/8/1914)

1979 Death of Joachim Jeremias, 78, German Lutheran N.T. scholar. His positive conclusions through form criticism created a bridgehead to the English-speaking world for form critical analysis at a time when German skepticism was still widely distrusted. (b. 9/20/1900)

Words for the Soul

1768 English clergyman and hymnwriter John Newton testified in a letter: *'He has not promised to reveal new truths, but to enable us to understand what we read in the Bible: and if we venture beyond the pale of Scripture, we are upon enchanted ground, and exposed to all the illusions of imagination and enthusiasm.'*

1871 American Quaker author Hannah Whitall Smith wrote in a letter: *'God tells us that by nature our hearts are deceitful above all things and desperately wicked. If in another place He tells us they can be made pure, He must mean that all this deceit and wickedness is in some way gotten rid of and this is by the cleansing power of the blood of Christ. And this can only be appropriated... by faith. And if by faith, then it may be now!'*

1974 American Presbyterian missionary and apologist Francis Schaeffer wrote in a letter: *'Only the one who has been hurt can bring healing. The other person cannot. It is the one who has been hurt who has to be willing to be hurt again to show love, if there is to be hope that healing will come.'*

IN GOD'S WORD... OT: Song of Songs 1:1–4:16 ~ NT: 2 Corinthians 8:16-24 ~ Psalms 50:1-23 ~ Proverbs 22:22-23

תשרי TISHRI

ALMANAC OF THE CHRISTIAN FAITH

אלול ELUL

~ September 7 ~

Highlights in History

1724 In Germantown, PA, the first congregation of German Dunkards (a.k.a. Dunkers, Tunkers) was formed, led by Peter Becker. The group originated in Schwarzenau, Germany, in 1708. Their official name, Church of the Brethren, was adopted in 1908.

1774 In Philadelphia, the first Continental Congress assembly to open with prayer convened at Carpenters' Hall. Rev. Jacob Duché, rector of Christ Episcopal Church, based his invocation on the 35th Psalm, where David prays: *'Plead my cause, O Lord, with them that strive with me; fight against them that fight against me.'*

1785 The Sunday School Society was organized in London, under leadership of Robert Raikes and William Fox. Formally named the "Interdenominational Society for the Support and Encouragement of Sunday Schools in the Different Counties of England," it was the first group to promote Sunday Schools on a widespread level, and inspired a later formation of the American Sunday School Union (1824).

1807 Protestant missions first came to China when English missionary Robert Morrison, 25, arrived on this date. (Catholic missions had first penetrated China in the 16th century with the arrival of Jesuit Matteo Ricci and others.)

Notable Birthdays

1640 Birth of German lawyer Johann Jakob Schütz. He was a friend of Philip Spener, founder of Pietism within the German Lutheran Church. Schütz authored the hymn, "Sing Praise to God Who Reigns Above." [d. 5/22/1690]

1812 Birth of George N. Allen, American music educator. His work at Oberlin College in Ohio grew to become the famed Oberlin Conservatory of Music. Allen's best-known hymn composition is MAITLAND ("Must Jesus Bear the Cross Alone?"). [d. 12/9/1877]

The Last Passage

1559 Death of Robert Estienne (Latin: Stephanus), 56, French scholar and printer. He is credited with creating the first modern verse-divisions of the New Testament (1551). (b. 1503)

1643 Death of Reorus Torkillus, 44, the first Lutheran pastor of a parish in America. (b. 1599)

1892 Death of John Greenleaf Whittier, American Quaker poet. He used his pen to arouse the conscience of the North against slavery. He is also remembered for authoring the hymn, "Dear Lord and Father of Mankind."
It is said his last words before dying were: *'Give my love to the world.'* (b. 12/17/1807)

1897 Death of Jane L. Borthwick, 84, Scottish hymnwriter. Rated second only to Catherine Winkworth in her German-to-English hymn translations, two of Borthwick's more memorable hymns are: "My Jesus, As Thou Wilt" and "Be Still, My Soul." (b. 4/9/1813)

1910 Death of (William) Holman Hunt, 83, English painter of religious subjects. A founder of the pre-Raphaelite Brotherhood (1848), his most famous work, "The Light of the World" (1854), represents Christ knocking at the door of the soul. (b. 4/2/1827)

Words for the Soul

1774 Jacob Duché offered up the first prayer ever to open an American Congress: *'Be Thou present O God of Wisdom and direct the counsel of this Honorable Assembly; enable them to settle all things on the best and surest foundations . . . Truth and Justice, Religion and Piety. . . .'*

1853 Scottish poet and novelist George MacDonald honored his wife Louisa in a letter: *'Thank you dear love for your much precious love – the most precious thing I have – for I will not divide between the love of God directly to me and that which flows through you.'*

IN GOD'S WORD... OT: Song of Songs 5:1–8:14 ~ NT: 2 Corinthians 9:1-15 ~ Psalms 51:1-19 ~ Proverbs 22:24-25

ALMANAC OF THE CHRISTIAN FAITH

TISHRI · ELUL

September 8

Highlights in History

70 Following a six-month siege, Jerusalem surrendered to the 60,000 troops of Titus' Roman army. Over a million Jews had perished in the siege. Following the city's capture, another 97,000 were sold into slavery.

1565 The parish of St. Augustine, Florida, was founded by Father Don Martin Francisco Lopez de Mendozo Grajales, chaplain to the conquering Spanish forces. It became the first and oldest Roman Catholic parish established in America.

1892 The "Pledge of Allegiance," created by Baptist clergyman Francis Bellamy, first appeared in print in the "Youth's Companion" magazine. It was adopted by Congress in 1945 as a national affirmation of American values, and the words "under God" were added on June 14, 1954, by a Joint Resolution of Congress.

1974 At the Naval Air Station in Atlanta, GA, Lt. Vivian McFadden, a Methodist from John's Island, SC, was sworn in as the first female African-American chaplain of the U.S. Navy.

Notable Birthdays

1157 Birth of Richard I (Coeur-de-Lion / "the Lionhearted"), monarch of England from 1189. One of the three leaders of the Third Crusade (1189-92), Richard was kidnapped by Austrians in 1191, was ransomed and returned to England in 1194. Nevertheless, he negotiated a Christian access to Jerusalem. [d. 4/6/1199]

1809 Birth of American poet Lydia Baxter. Converted by a Baptist missionary, she afterward founded a church in her home town of Petersburg, New York. Lydia was an invalid for many years, but her home became a meeting place for many religious leaders. She herself penned a number of gospel songs, including "Take the Name of Jesus With You." [d. 6/22/1874]

1866 Birth of C[harles] H. Mason, African-American church founder. Raised in a Missionary Baptist home, in 1897 Mason co-founded the Church of God in Christ. Later experiencing a "baptism of the Holy Ghost" at the Azusa Street Revival in San Francisco in 1907, Mason soon after reorganized the denomination as the first Pentecostal General Assembly of the Church of God in Christ, headquartered now in Memphis, TN. Current membership is 8 million, and member churches are scattered throughout the world. [d. 11/17/1961]

The Last Passage

1644 Death of Francis Quarles, 52, English poet and secretary to Archbishop James Ussher. His last words before dying: 'O, sweet Saviour of the World, let Thy last words upon the Cross be my last words in this world – "Into Thy hands I commend my spirit."' (bapt. 5/8/1592)

1784 Death of Ann Lee, 48, English-born American religious leader. In 1776, "Mother" Ann established a spiritual colony in Watervliet, NY. She named her followers the United Society of Believers in Christ's Second Appearing. To the rest of the world, however, they came to be known as the Shakers. (b. 2/29/1736)

Words for the Soul

1811 Anglican missionary to Persia Henry Martyn reflected in a letter: 'It is my business... to make saints, where I cannot find them. I do use the means in a certain way, but frigid reasoning with men of perverse minds seldom brings men to Christ.... How powerless are the best-directed arguments, till the Holy Ghost renders them effectual!'

1830 Scottish clergyman and biographer Andrew Bonar noted in his diary: '[My brother] Horace came over. He told me a saying of Augustine's: "If we who are only seeking Thee have such delight, what shall they have who find Thee?"'

IN GOD'S WORD...   OT: Isaiah 1:1–2:22 ~ NT: 2 Corinthians 10:1-18 ~ Psalms 52:1-9 ~ Proverbs 22:26-27

תשרי TISHRI

ALMANAC OF THE CHRISTIAN FAITH

אלול ELUL

~ September 9 ~

Highlights in History

1530 The first cathedral in Mexico City was established by King Charles V and a bull of Pope Clement VII.

1833 In England, the first three "Tracts for the Times" were issued by Oxford Movement leader John Henry Newman. The essays, opposing religious liberalism and government interference, were first intended to revive and purify High Church Anglicanism. But Newman's Tract 90, appearing in 1841, provoked a storm that brought the series to an end, because it interpreted Anglicanism's "Thirty-Nine Articles" in too strongly a Roman Catholic direction.

1912 William W. Borden was ordained. Schooled at Yale (and thereafter called Borden of Yale), he was a millionaire at 21. However, Borden was spiritually precocious, and he offered himself for the China Inland Mission. Upon acceptance he sailed for Cairo, Egypt, proposing to study Arabic before going on to work among China's Muslims. While in Egypt, however, he contracted cerebrospinal meningitis and died in 1913, at age 26.

1982 The three largest Lutheran denominations in the United States – the Association of Evangelical Lutheran Churches (AELC), the American Lutheran Church (ALC), and the Lutheran Church of America (LCA) – gathered in simultaneous conventions, and separately voted to begin the process of a full merger.

Notable Birthdays

1747 Birth of Thomas Coke, the first Methodist missionary consecrated as a bishop to America. He served with Francis Asbury from 1784-97, afterward becoming president of the English Methodist Conference. He died at sea while sailing to do missionary work in India. [d. 5/3/1814]

1803 Birth of Henry J. Buckoll, an Anglican clergyman who translated many hymns from the original German, including the enduring stanzas by Friedrich R. L. Canitz: "Come, My Soul, Thou Must Be Waking." [d. 6/6/1871]

1828 [OS=8/28] Birth of Leo Nikolaevich Tolstoi, noted Russian novelist (*War and Peace, Anna Karenina*) and social reformer. He renounced his literary ambitions after 1876, and evolved a Christian faith whose central creed was non-resistance to evil. [d. 11/20/1910]

The Last Passage

1515 Death of St. Joseph of Volokolamsk, about 75, Russian Orthodox monastic reformer. He founded the celebrated monastery of Volokolamsk, near Moscow, which aimed at educating "learned monks" for high office in the church. Joseph was canonized 1578. (b. 1439/40)

1898 Death of William Chatterton Dix, 61, Scottish businessman and hymnwriter. He worked for a marine insurance company. In addition, he translated Greek and Ethiopian hymns into English, and also authored a number of original English hymns, including the majestic Christmas carol, "What Child Is This?" (b. 6/14/1837)

Words for the Soul

1848 Scottish clergyman and biographer Andrew Bonar noted in his diary: 'I notice that, in the first chapter of Joshua, courage is four times spoken of as necessary to his discharge of duty. How often would difficulties be moved out of the way did we but go forward!'

1979 Russian Orthodox scholar Alexander Schmemann noted in his diary: 'Christianity is not <u>about</u> culture, but it cannot avoid giving birth to culture, inasmuch as culture is a holistic vision of God, man and the world. By tearing itself away from culture, Christianity either becomes "clerical" (religion, not life) or betrays itself, "surrenders" to culture.'

IN GOD'S WORD... OT: Isaiah 3:1–5:30 ~ NT: 2 Corinthians 11:1-15 ~ Psalms 53:1-6 ~ Proverbs 22:28-29

September 10

Highlights in History

422 Celestine I was elected pope (serving until 432). He convoked the Council of Ephesus (431) to combat the Nestorian heresy (the belief that Christ had two natures and two persons), and also sent St. Patrick as a missionary to Ireland.

1832 English Moravian hymnwriter James Montgomery, 60, penned the words to "Holy, Holy, Holy Lord, God of Hosts." (Montgomery is also remembered for authoring "The Lord is My Shepherd," "Angels From the Realms of Glory," "Go to Dark Gethsemane" and "Prayer is the Soul's Sincere Desire.")

1862 Rabbi Jacob Frankel of Philadelphia was appointed the first Jewish U.S. Army chaplain, four months after Congress amended its earlier law of 1861 requiring chaplains to be Christians. Frankel served from 1863 through 1865 at the United States Hospital in Philadelphia.

Notable Birthdays

1487 Birth of Giovanni Maria Ciocchi del Monte, who served as Pope Julius III (1550-55). He re-opened the Council of Trent (1551); promoted the Jesuit Order; and, when Mary Tudor came to the throne (1553), welcomed the brief return of England to the Roman Church. An enthusiast for the arts, Julius made Michelangelo chief architect of St. Peters, and appointed the famed composer Giovanni Palestrina papal choirmaster. [d. 3/23/1555]

1819 Birth of Joseph M. Scriven, Irish-born poet. The accidental drowning of his fiancée the night before their wedding led to a life punctuated with periods of deep depression. A member of the Plymouth Brethren, Scriven moved to Canada in 1844, and afterward devoted much of his time to humanitarian service. It was Scriven who bequeathed to the Church the hymn of reassurance, "What a Friend We Have in Jesus." [d. 8/10/1886]

The Last Passage

1604 Death of William Morgan, about 59, Welsh prelate. He was Bishop of Llandaff (1595-1601), afterward of St. Asaph (1601-04). Morgan is credited with translating the Bible into Welsh in 1588, which afterward standardized the language of his country. (b. ca.1545)

1858 American Episcopal sacred organist Henry W. Greatorex, 44, died of yellow fever. Greatorex composed nearly 40 hymn tunes during his life, including the GLORIA PATRI ("Glory Be to the Father"). (b. 12/24/1813)

1898 Death of Alexander Crummell, 79, African-American Episcopal clergyman, scholar, and missionary to West Africa. Ordained in 1844, Crummell served as president of Liberia College for 20 years. (b. 3/3/1819)

1965 Death of Father Major Jealous Divine, 91, African-American religious leader. Born George Baker, he founded the International Peace Mission Movement, 1919 (which grew to about 200 centers in New York City and Philadelphia), and preached equality among races. (b. ca.1874)

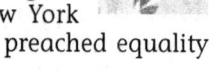

Words for the Soul

1946 English Catholic psychiatrist Caryll Houselander advised in a letter: *'Some people think it foolish to ask God for little things, but I do not think it matters at all what one asks for, so long as in asking for <u>anything</u> one recognizes one's own dependence on God, His Fatherhood and His longing to give <u>Himself</u>, no matter in what way.'*

1995 Dutch Catholic priest and diarist Henri J. M. Nouwen reflected in his Journal: *'There is much to enjoy in life, but unless it can be enjoyed as a foretaste of what we will see and hear in the house of God, our mortality will easily make all pleasure vain, transitory, and even empty.'*

IN GOD'S WORD... OT: Isaiah 6:1–7:25 ~ NT: 2 Corinthians 11:16-33 ~ Psalms 54:1-7 ~ Proverbs 23:1-3

תשרי ALMANAC OF THE CHRISTIAN FAITH אלול
TISHRI · ELUL

~ September 11 ~

Highlights in History

1672 American Congregational clergyman Solomon Stoddard (1643-1729) was ordained pastor of the church in Northampton, MA. In that pulpit he remained until his death 57 years later, assisted after 1727 by his grandson, Jonathan Edwards.

1892 Scarritt Bible and Training School in Nashville, TN, was dedicated, primarily as the result of the conception, urging and fund-raising of southern Methodist missions leader and social reformer, Belle Harris Bennett (1852-1922).

1958 A two-day convention opened in Winnepeg, Manitoba, at which assembly the Lutheran Church-Canada (LCC) was organized.

Notable Birthdays

1834 Birth of Marvin R. Vincent, American Presbyterian clergyman and biblical scholar. Associated after 1887 with Union Seminary in NY, Vincent is remembered for his four-volume *Greek Word Studies in the New Testament* (1887-1900). He also wrote commentaries on Philippians and Philemon for the *International Critical Commentary*. [d. 8/18/1922]

1880 Birth of Luther A. Weigle, American Lutheran Bible scholar and ecumenist. He taught and served as Dean at the Yale Divinity School and was chairman (1930-57) of the committee which produced the *Revised Standard Version* of the Bible. [d. 9/2/1976]

The Last Passage

1069 English prelate Aldred (Ealdred), Archbishop of York, died at about 69. He was the first English bishop to make a pilgrimage to Jerusalem. (b. ca. 1000)

1637 Death of Johannes [Jan] Bogermann, 61, Dutch theologian. A follower of strict Calvinism, he presided at the Synod of Dort (1618-19), also helped translate the Bible into Dutch. (b. 1576)

1940 Death of Melvin E[rnest] Trotter, 70, American evangelist and founder of urban rescue missions. An alcoholic who could not hold a job, Trotter hopped a freight car to Chicago on a bitterly cold night, intending to drown himself in Lake Michigan. But he heard the gospel preached at the Pacific Garden Mission, and found the spiritual strength to keep him from ever drinking again. Trotter afterward founded 67 rescue missions to help others as desperate as he himself once was. (b. 5/16/1870)

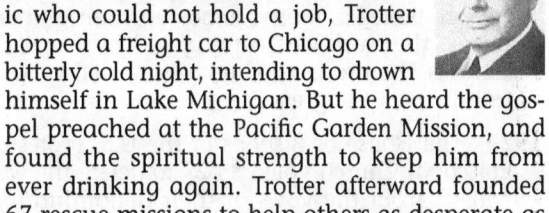

Words for the Soul

1834 In a letter to his son, President Andrew Jackson wrote: 'We ought all to rely with confidence on the promises of our dear Redeemer, and give Him our hearts. This is all he requires and all that we can do, and if we sincerely do this, we are sure of salvation through his atonement.'

1890 Two years before his death, Scottish clergyman/biographer Andrew Bonar, 80, reflected in his diary: 'I see distinctly that my Lord is teaching me to "glory in my infirmities," and to be willing to be set aside. My voice fails; some of my people, specially the younger part, going elsewhere; ...my influence with brethren manifestly declines – all this is saying, "He must increase, but I must decrease".... But... I know "He doeth all things well."'

1962 American Trappist monk Thomas Merton wrote in a letter: 'We have not tasted the things given to us in Christ. Instead, we have built around ourselves walls and cells, and buried ourselves in dust and documents, and now we wonder why we cannot see God, or leap to do his will.'

1974 Dutch priest and diarist Henri J. M. Nouwen reflected in his GENESEE DIARY: 'In the long run, some voluntary penance becomes necesssary to help us remember that we are not yet fulfilled. A good criticism, a frustrating day, an empty stomach, or tired eyes might help to re-awaken our expectation and deepen our prayer: Come, Lord Jesus.'

IN GOD'S WORD... OT: Isaiah 8:1–9:21 ~ NT: 2 Corinthians 12:1-10 ~ Psalms 55:1-23 ~ Proverbs 23:4-5

TISHRI — ALMANAC OF THE CHRISTIAN FAITH — ELUL

~ September 12 ~

Highlights in History

1808 The first Bible translated into English in America was published in Philadelphia, PA, by Jane Aitken. Issued in four volumes with unnumbered pages, the work was copyrighted by translator Charles Thomson, who had been secretary to the Continental Congress.

1922 The House of Bishops of the U.S. Protestant Episcopal Church voted 36-27 to delete the word "obey" from the vows of their denomination's official marriage service.

1928 The first international conference of the Pocket Testament League convened in Birmingham, England. (P.T.L. was first organized in Philadelphia, PA in 1908, by J. Wilbur Chapman and Charles M. Alexander.)

Notable Birthdays

1729 Birth of John William Fletcher (De La Flechiere), Vicar of Madeley and an early Methodist theologian. Born in Switzerland, he visited England in 1752, was influenced by the Methodist movement, and became a close friend of John and Charles Wesley. Fletcher authored a number of theological works, including a defense of his Arminian beliefs. [d. 8/14/1785]

1788 Birth of Alexander Campbell, Scotch-Irish Presbyterian who, along with his father Thomas Campbell, emigrated to America in 1809, and soon after founded the Disciples of Christ and the Churches of Christ in the U.S. Campbell sought to return to a "simple evangelical Christianity," founded on the Bible alone. He was also president (1840-66) of Bethany College, in West Virginia. (The Disciples of Christ give the New Testament higher authority than the Old, and currently claim over a million members and some 4,000 churches in the United States.) [d. 3/4/1866]

1818 Birth of George Duffield, Jr., American Presbyterian clergyman and hymn author. He helped build up small congregations in NY, NJ, PA, IL and MI. In 1858 he composed the hymn "Stand Up, Stand Up for Jesus." It was inspired by a friend, Dudley A. Tyng, a young Episcopal minister who died in a farm accident. In his last moments, Tyng had said: *'Tell my brethren of the ministry . . . to stand up for Jesus!'* [d. 7/6/1888]

1851 Birth of Francis E. Clark, the Canadian-born Congregational minister who founded the Christian Endeavor movement in 1881, while pastoring the Williston Church, in Portland, ME. (Christian Endeavor was the forerunner of today's church youth fellowships.) [d. 5/26/1927]

The Last Passage

1816 Death of Jesse Lee, 58, Virginia-born Methodist preacher. He was called "the Apostle of Methodism in New England." (b. 3/12/1758)

1830 Death of John Henry Hobart, 54, Episcopal bishop and controversialist. He led the revival of the Episcopal Church during the first decades after the American Revolution. In 1806 he established the Protestant Episcopal Theological Society, which went on to become the General Theological Seminary. (b. 9/14/1775)

Words for the Soul

1771 Pioneer Methodist bishop Francis Asbury, 26, on his maiden voyage to America, wrote in his journal: *'Whither am I going? To the New World. What to do? To gain honor? No, if I know my own heart. To get money? No, I am going to live to God, and to bring others to do so.'*

1981 Russian Orthodox scholar Alexander Schmemann reflected in his journal: *'Tomorrow I will be 60!... I am beginning to feel time – fragile, precious. Life becomes more tangible – as a gift. And of course death becomes tangible – my death, death as a question, an examination, as a kind of call.'*

IN GOD'S WORD... OT: Isaiah 10:1–11:16 ~ NT: 2 Corinthians 12:11-21 ~ Psalms 56:1-13 ~ Proverbs 23:6-8

תשרי ALMANAC OF THE CHRISTIAN FAITH אלול
TISHRI   ELUL

~ September 13 ~

Highlights in History

449 Leo's Tome was published. Originating as a letter sent by Pope Leo I to Flavian, the Patriarch of Constantinople, the document became the basis of the "Chalcedonian Creed" of 451.

1525 German Reformer Martin Luther, 42, married former nun Katherine von Bora, 26. Their 21-year marriage bore six children. Kate survived her husband (who died 1546) by 6 years.

1793 English missions pioneer William Carey, 31, first sailed for India. The previous year he had preached his famous sermon: "Expect Great Things from God; Attempt Great Things for God." Within five years he had translated nearly the entire Bible into Bengali. Today, Carey is acclaimed the "father of modern missions."

1903 The Church of God of Prophecy was inaugurated when founder A[mbrose] J. Tomlinson, 37, joined the Holiness Church at Camp Creek, NC, and was chosen pastor of the fledgling congregation of 20.

1979 Delegates to the Reformed Church of America's 173rd Synod voted to amend the *Book of Church Order* to allow women to be ordained as ministers.

Notable Birthdays

1827 Birth of Catherine Winkworth, English hymnwriter. An activist in the social issues of her day, she was a pioneer in the higher education of women. She also translated several German hymns into English, including "Praise Ye the Lord, the Almighty" and "If Thou But Suffer God to Guide Thee." [d. 7/1/1878]

1897 Birth of Reuben E. Larson, U.S. Christian & Missionary Alliance missionary to Ecuador. In 1931 Larson, along with Clarence W. Jones, founded HCJB in Quito – the first missionary radio station in Latin America. [d. 11/17/1981]

The Last Passage

1976 Death of Earl B. Marlatt, 84, Methodist religious scholar and educator. He published several volumes of poetry, including four stanzas which later became the hymn, "'Are Ye Able?' Said the Master." (b. 5/24/1892)

Words for the Soul

1771 English founder of Methodism John Wesley, in a letter to a young Christian, advised: *'It is right to pour out our whole soul before Him that careth for us. But it is good, likewise, to unbosom ourselves to a friend, in whom we can confide.'*

1874 Scottish clergyman and biographer Andrew Bonar prayed in his diary: *'Lord, before I finish my course, may I reach far further into the mystery of Godliness, and have more power with Thee to bring down blessing on earth.'*

1880 American Quaker Holiness author Hannah Whitall Smith wrote in a letter: *'The voice of God comes through our judgment [i.e., reasoned assurances], and not through our impressions [i.e., emotional impulses]. Our impressions may coincide with our judgments or they may not, but it is through the latter alone that God's voice comes. And when people go by impressions in opposition to their judgments, they are turning from the true voice of God, to follow the false voices of self, or of evil spirits, or of morbid consciences, or of some evil influence from other people.'*

1933 British literary scholar and Christian apologist C. S. Lewis wrote in a letter: *'The truth is that evil is not a real thing at all, like God. It is simply good spoiled. That is why I say there can be good without evil, but no evil without good. You know what the biologists mean by a parasite – an animal that lives on another animal. Evil is a parasite. It is there only because good is there for it to spoil and confuse.'*

1962 Swiss Reformed theologian Karl Barth wrote in a letter: *'God, according to 2 Cor. 5:19, reconciled the world to himself, not himself to the world.'*

IN GOD'S WORD... OT: Isaiah 12:1–14:32 ~ NT: 2 Corinthians 13:1-14 ~ Psalms 57:1-11 ~ Proverbs 23:9-11

תשרי TISHRI — ALMANAC OF THE CHRISTIAN FAITH — אלול ELUL

~ September 14 ~

Highlights in History

1741 English composer Georg[e] Friedrich Handel finished work on his great oratorio, "The Messiah," which he had begun composing only 24 days earlier. It is said Handel subsisted on coffee and prayer during the entire period.

1752 England officially implemented the Gregorian Calendar. The day preceding today's date, September 14th, was September 3rd. This effective loss of 11 days in the English calendar afterward created a notable public unrest.

1975 Mother Elizabeth Ann Bayley Seton, who lived 1774-1821, was canonized in Rome by Pope Paul VI, making her the first American-born Roman Catholic saint. The mother of five children, she converted to Roman Catholicism in 1805 and founded an order of nuns, the Sisters of Charity of St. Joseph.

Notable Birthdays

1543 Birth of Claudius Aquaviva, fifth general of the Jesuit order. He joined the Society in 1567, and rose quickly to become the Jesuits' youngest (some say greatest) general of the order, expanding their world missions role. [d. 1/31/1615]

1607 John Harvard was born in London. He became a Congregational clergyman in Massachusetts, and is remembered for donating his 300-book library and about £8,000 ($130,000) for the newly-founded college at Cambridge, MA. In turn, the founders of New Towne College renamed the school Harvard. [d. 9/14/1638]

1735 [OS=9/4] Robert Raikes was born in Gloucester, England. A newspaper editor, he was moved by the economic plight of the local children. As an experiment, he gathered them together on Sundays to teach them reading and religion. The changes which resulted in a short time led to the adoption of "Sunday schools" by churches worldwide. [d. 4/5/1811]

1883 Birth of Martin Dibelius, German New Testament scholar and theologian. A pupil of Harnack and Gunkel, he taught New Testament at Heidelberg, and became a pioneer of Form Criticism with his 1919 writing, *From Tradition to Gospel*. (Form criticism looks for speech patterns utilized in a story in order to make its hearing more memorable.). [d. 11/11/1947]

The Last Passage

407 Death of St. John Chrysostom, patriarch of Constantinople (398-404), famed for his preaching and charity. Considered one of the greatest Christian expositors, he was driven from his see and banished because his outspokenness offended the empress. Chrysostom died at Comana under a hot sun while on a forced march. (b. ca. 344/354)

1321 Death of Dante Alighieri, 56, Italian poet. As author of *The Divine Comedy* (1307-21), he has been styled the creator of the modern Italian language as a literary vehicle. Dante finished his epic poem just before his death, and it was almost immediately recognized as brilliant. (b. 5/ [15 or] 27/1265)

Words for the Soul

1772 English clergyman John Newton testified in a letter: 'Are these your desires? He that has wrought them in you is God; and he will not disappoint you. He would not say, Open your mouth wide, if he did not design to fill it. Oh, he gives bountifully; gives like a king. A little is too much for our deserts; but much is too little for his bounty.'

1856 American Quaker Holiness author Hannah Whitall Smith wrote the following prayer in her journal: 'If I have ever done anything right, it was You who did it in me and not I myself. Only my sins are my own doing; so the good in me is all yours. And the bad in me all my own.... My only comfort, my only hope is, that whether I love you or not, you love me and have sent your Son to save me.'

IN GOD'S WORD... OT: Isaiah 15:1–18:7 ~ NT: Galatians 1:1-24 ~ Psalms 58:1-11 ~ Proverbs 23:12

תשרי TISHRI ALMANAC OF THE CHRISTIAN FAITH אלול ELUL

~ September 15 ~

Highlights in History

1648 The "Larger" and "Shorter" Catechisms – prepared by the Westminster Assembly the previous year – were approved by the British Parliament. These two documents have been in regular use among Presbyterians, Congregationalists and Baptists ever since.

1853 Antoinette Louisa Brown began a pastorate at the First Congregational Church of Butler and Savannah, NY, making her the first woman in American history to be ordained a minister of a Protestant denomination. The following summer she resigned, married Samuel Charles Blackwell in 1856, and became a Unitarian, pastoring All Souls' Unitarian Church in Elizabeth, NJ, from 1908 till her death in 1921.

1877 The Pacific Garden Mission, an evangelical rescue work, first opened in Chicago. After WWII, it began making films, and produced radio broadcasts known today as "Unshackled."

1966 The American Bible Society published its *Good News for Modern Man* New Testament translation. Some evangelical readers were upset by certain uses of contemporary terminology, such as "happy" for "blessed."

Notable Birthdays

1855 Birth of Adam Geibel, German-born American composer: GEIBEL ("Stand Up, Stand Up for Jesus"). Like Fanny Crosby, Geibel lost his sight at a young age, through improper medical attention to an eye infection. Gifted in music, he worked for the Rodeheaver (sacred music) Company. [d. 8/3/1933]

1870 Birth of Agnes N. Ozman, U.S. Pentecostal evangelist. On January 1, 1901, as a student attending Charles Parham's Bethel Bible College in Topeka, KS, Miss Ozman became the first person in modern times to speak in tongues. In 1911 she married Pentecostal evangelist, Philemon LaBerge. [d. 11/29/1937]

The Last Passage

1906 Death of Samuel Isaac Joseph Schereschewsky, 75, Russian born U.S. Episcopal missionary to China. He translated the entire Bible into the Wen-li dialect. (b. 5/6/1831)

1926 Death of Daniel C. O. Opperman, 54, Oneness Pentecostal evangelist and educator. He was a founding member of the Assemblies of God and an executive presbyter. (b. 7/13/1872)

1932 Death of Charles H. Gabriel, 76, writer and composer of many enduring gospel hymns: "I Stand Amazed in the Presence" (& MY SAVIOR'S LOVE); "In Loving Kindness Jesus Came" (& HE LIFTED ME); "More Like the Master" (& HANFORD); "When All My Labors and Trials Are O'er" (& GLORY SONG); HIGHER GROUND ("I'm Pressing on the Upward Way"); GABRIEL ("Just When I Need Him Jesus is Near"); and WAY OF THE CROSS. (b. 8/18/1856)

Words for the Soul

1762 John Wesley, in a letter to a young disciple, explained: *'My judgment is, that... to overdo is to undo; and that to set perfection too high (so high as no man that we ever heard or read of attained) is the most effectual (because unsuspected) way of driving it out of the world.'*

1920 Benedict XV published the encyclical "Spiritus paraclitus," which restated the Catholic position on Scripture: *'The Bible, composed by men inspired of the Holy Ghost, has God himself as its principal author, the individual authors constituted as his live instruments. Their activity, however, ought not be described as automatic writing.'*

1995 In the last year of his life, Dutch Catholic priest and diarist Henri J. M. Nouwen reflected in his journal: *'My restless mind, anxious heart, and tired body easily lead me to experiences of loneliness and uselessness and tempt me to faithlessness.'*

IN GOD'S WORD...   OT: Isaiah 19:1–21:17 ~ NT: Galatians 2:1-16 ~ Psalms 59:1-17 ~ Proverbs 23:13-14

תשרי ALMANAC OF THE CHRISTIAN FAITH אלול
TISHRI   ELUL

~ September 16 ~

Highlights in History

681 The Third Council of Constantinople adjourned. Reckoned the Sixth General Council by Catholic theologians, sixteen sessions were held between Nov. 7, 680 and this date. During these sessions, The Monothelite controversy in the Eastern Church (which held there was only one will – the divine – in Christ) was condemned. The Council, in response, proclaimed there were two wills in Christ: the divine and the human.

1976 In Minneapolis, the Episcopal Church approved the ordination of women to the priesthood, specifically approving an action in which four bishops had ordained 11 women to the Episcopal priesthood on July 29, 1974 – at that time in defiance of church law.

Notable Birthdays

1796 Birth of William A. Mühlenberg, Protestant Episcopal clergyman, poet and great-grandson of Henry M. Mühlenberg. William was a founder (1858) of St. Luke's Hospital in Philadelphia, and also authored the hymn, "Shout the Glad Tidings." [d. 4/8/1877]

1803 Birth of Orestes A. Brownson, American clergyman and editor. A convert to the Catholic church (1844), he published *New Views of Christianity, Society and the Church* (1836). He also edited "Brownson's Quarterly Review," which became one of the nation's most influential journals of Catholic opinion. [d. 4/17/1876]

1906 Birth of J[ohn] B. Phillips, Anglican clergyman and writer. In the mid-1940s, he began updating the English of the King James Bible in order to help the youth of his church better understand the Scriptures. Encouraged by C. S. Lewis, Phillips continued the work, and in 1958 published the complete *Phillips Paraphrase of the New Testament*. It was one of the earliest successful modern translations of the Scriptures. [d. 1982]

The Last Passage

1498 Death of General Tomás de Torquemada, 78, the Spanish Dominican monk who, in 1483, organized the Spanish Inquisition, which sought to remove Jews and Muslims from Spain. The worst aspects of religious fanaticism and cruelty are still associated with him. (b. 1420)

1839 Death of Matthew Carey, 79, American Roman Catholic publisher and author. In 1790 he published the first edition of the Douay version of the Bible in America. (b. 1/28/1760)

1882 Death of E[dward] B. Pusey, 82, English clergyman, Hebrew scholar, and a leader of the Oxford Movement. As a contributor to "Tracts for the Times" (1834), he wrote on baptism and the Eucharist, and sought to unite the Anglican and Catholic churches, thus restoring the purity of the church. Pusey did not convert to Catholicism, as did some of the others. (b. 8/22/1800)

1924 Death of A[nthony] J. Showalter, 66, American Presbyterian hymnwriter. He conducted singing schools throughout the Southeast and published 60 songbooks. But he is best remembered today for composing the hymn tune SHOWALTER ("Leaning on the Everlasting Arms"). (b. 5/1/1858)

Words for the Soul

1974 Russian Orthodox liturgical scholar Father Alexander Schmemann reflected in his journal: *'When it considers life only as a preparation for death, Christianity makes... death meaningless as victory; it does not solve the neurosis of death.'*

1974 Dutch Catholic priest and diarist Henri J. M. Nouwen reflected in his *Genesee Diary*: *'We have always struggled to understand how God can be just as well as merciful. Indeed, the mystery of God is that he can be both to the highest degree. But we cannot. God's mercy does not make him less just. His justice does not make him less merciful. But we have to struggle to prevent mercy from becoming lack of justice, and justice lack of mercy.'*

IN GOD'S WORD...   OT: Isaiah 22:1–24:23 ~ NT: Galatians 2:17–3:9 ~ Psalms 60:1-12 ~ Proverbs 23:15-16

תשרי TISHRI — ALMANAC OF THE CHRISTIAN FAITH — אלול ELUL

~ September 17 ~

Highlights in History

284 Valerius Diocletianus (Diocletian), 38, became emperor of Rome. For a great part of his reign the Christians continued to enjoy a tranquility extending back to 260. In 303, however, Diocletian initiated a new persecution, demolishing churches, burning books and adding greatly to the martyrs. Ten years later, Constantine's "Edict of Milan" brought the Church into an official acceptance by the Roman Empire.

1792 The Rev. Thomas J. Claggett, founder of Trinity Episcopal Church, Upper Marlboro, MD, was consecrated at Trinity Church, New York City, by Bishops Seabury, White, Provoost, and Madison. It made him the first Episcopal bishop to be consecrated *in* the United States.

1929 The Apostolic Orthodox Catholic Church was established in North America as an English-speaking and non-ethnic autocephalous (independent) branch of the Russian Orthodox Church. (The AOCC's history began in 1794, when Russian missionaries established the first Orthodox Christian mission in present-day Alaska, while it still belonged to Russia.)

Notable Birthdays

1721 Birth of Samuel Hopkins, American Congregational clergyman and one of two most important disciples of Jonathan Edwards. His stern presentation of New England theology made him a leader in his denomination.  Hopkins wrote in favor of emancipation of African-Americans as early as 1776, and also published a systematic theology, *System of Doctrines Contained in Divine Revelation, Explained and Defended*. Hopkins opposed the inroads of a generalized Arminianism that legitimized human effort and the operation of free will in the conversion process. [d. 12/20/1803]

The Last Passage

1179 Death of Hildegard of Bingen, 81, German Benedictine abbess, mystic, and writer. Called the "Sibyl of the Rhine," she was a close friend of Bernard of Clairvaux. Hildegard was most renowned for her 26 mystical experiences, which were recorded in her book *Scivias* between 1141-50. (b. 1098)

1575 Death of Johann H. Bullinger, 71, Swiss religious reformer. He headed the Reformation in German Switzerland following Ulrich Zwingli's death in 1531, and drew up the Helvetic Confessions of 1536 and 1566. (b. 7/18/1504)

1683 Death of Johannes (John) Campanius, 82, pioneer Lutheran clergyman and missionary to the American Indians. Born in Stockholm, he accompanied the first Swedish settlers to America, settling at Ft. Christiana (now Wilmington), in Delaware (1642-48). There he became interested in the nearby Delaware Indians, learning their dialect and translating Luther's *Small Catechism* into their native tongue. (b. 8/15/1601)

Words for the Soul

1776 Anglican clergyman and hymnwriter John Newton wrote in a letter: *'Many good people are distressed and alternately elated by frames and feelings which perhaps are more constitutional than properly religious experiences. Our natural temperament and disposition have more influence upon our religious sensations than we are ordinarily aware.'*

1787 Ratified on this date, Article 6, Section 3 of the U.S. Constitution reads: *'No religious tests shall ever be required as a qualification to any office or public trust under the United States.'*

1952 English Catholic psychiatrist Caryll Houselander testified in a letter: *'I find that nowadays I cannot sleep much, but all the same when in bed I am too tired to write (as I used always to do at night). So this makes it possible for me to spend some hours every night praying for my friends.'*

IN GOD'S WORD... OT: Isaiah 25:1–28:13 ~ NT: Galatians 3:10-22 ~ Psalms 61:1-8 ~ Proverbs 23:17-18

תשרי TISHRI   ALMANAC OF THE CHRISTIAN FAITH   אלול ELUL

~ September 18 ~

Highlights in History

1634 Anne Hutchinson and her family arrived in the Massachusetts Bay Colony from England. The first female religious leader in America, Ann organized groups of women to discuss theological questions. She taught that one could attain understanding in matters of faith without obedience to church law. In 1637 Anne was charged with undermining the authority of the local clergy. Banished from the colony, she moved to Roger Williams' settlement (the future Providence, RI), along with 70 followers.

1924 The Old Testament of the *Moffatt Translation* of the Bible was completed by Scottish-born American scholar James Moffatt (1870-1944). (The work was revised and re-published in 1935.)

1979 The House of Deputies of the Episcopal Church concurred with an earlier action of the House of Bishops, declaring that homosexuals should be accepted into the church but not ordained if sexually active. (This ruling was superceded in 2003.)

Notable Birthdays

1643 Birth of Gilbert Burnet, Scottish prelate, theologian and historian. As Bishop of Salisbury (1689-1715), he sought ways to incorporate Nonconformists into the Church of England. Burnet also authored a *History of the English Reformation* (1734). [d. 3/17/1715]

1765 Birth of Oliver Holden, American carpenter and hymn composer. He built a Puritan church and became its pastor. Holden's love for music led him to publish several hymn books and to compose the hymn tune CORONATION ("All Hail the Power of Jesus' Name"). [d. 9/4/1844]

1877 Birth of J[ohn] Frank Norris, American fundamentalist clergyman. A flamboyant and controversial pastor of First Baptist Church of Fort Worth, TX, he was also founder of the World Baptist Fellowship. [d. 8/20/1952]

The Last Passage

1792 Death of Augustus G. Spangenberg, 88, German Moravian missionary and church administrator. In 1733 he became an assistant to Count Zinzendorf at Herrnhut. Consecrated a bishop in 1744, Spangenberg developed a conferential church government for the denomination following Zinzendorf's death. (b. 7/15/1704)

1905 Death of George MacDonald, 80, Scottish clergyman turned novelist and poet. He was at his best as a storyteller, and the cheerful goodness of MacDonald's writings later captured the imagination of C.S. Lewis, convincing him that true Christian righteousness is not dull. (b. 12/10/1824]

1961 Death of Dag Hammarskjöld, 56, Swedish statesman and Secretary-General of the United Nations (1953-61). Hammarskjöld's journal, *Markings* – released (1964) after his untimely death in a plane crash – revealed an inner spirituality which had guided the Swedish statesman throughout his life. (b. 7/29/1905)

Words for the Soul

1538 German reformer Martin Luther remarked in a Table Talk: *'Ah, what a calamity it is that man degenerates more in prosperity than in adversity!'*

1762 English clergyman and hymnwriter John Newton testified in a letter: *'I trust in his love, that, though I am sometimes faint, I shall not utterly fall; though I too often step aside, he will not suffer me to wander quite away.'*

1974 Dutch Catholic priest and diarist Henri J. M. Nouwen reflected in his GENESEE DIARY: *'When you stay with it and look back over a long period of prayer, you suddenly realize that something has happened. What is most close, most intimate, most present, often cannot be experienced directly but only with a certain distance.... Isn't this true of all really important events in life?'*

IN GOD'S WORD...   OT: Isaiah 28:14–30:11 ~ NT: Galatians 3:23–4:20 ~ Psalms 62:1-12 ~ Proverbs 23:19-21

תשרי ALMANAC OF THE CHRISTIAN FAITH אלול
TISHRI   ELUL

~ September 19 ~

Highlights in History

1914 In France during WWI, Reims Cathedral was badly damaged by German bombardment.

1938 The Carpatho-Russian Greek Catholic Diocese of the Eastern Rite of the U.S.A. was proclaimed a self-governing diocese in communion with the Ecumenical Patriarchate of Constantinople. Patriarch Benjamin I canonized the Diocese in the name of the Orthodox Church of Christ, and Father Orestes Chornock, bishop of Agathonikia, was made Metropolitan of the new diocese.

1772 Construction of the first Protestant church west of the Alleghenies was completed at Schoenbrunn, Ohio by Moravian missionaries. There the same missionaries built the first schoolhouse west of the Alleghenies, completing it in 1773. Rev. David Zeisberger became the church's first preacher and the school's first teacher.

Notable Birthdays

866 Birth of Leo VI, Byzantine Emperor. Educated under supervision of Photius, the patriarch of Constantinople, he succeeded his father Basil I as emperor in 866. Leo was regarded by later generations as a wise ruler. [d. 5/11/912]

1852 Birth of Charles J. Vincent, English sacred organist and composer. He wrote numerous anthems and cantatas, but is largely remembered today for arranging the hymn tune PAX TECUM ("Peace, Perfect Peace"). [d. 2/28/1934]

The Last Passage

1905 Death of Thomas J. Barnardo, 60, Irish evangelist and philanthropist. A convert to the Plymouth Brethren at 16, he went to London at 21. There being no public-sponsored child care provision in that day, in 1868 Barnardo opened a ministry to homeless children – the East End Juvenile Mission, which housed nearly 60,000 children during his lifetime. (b. 7/4/1845)

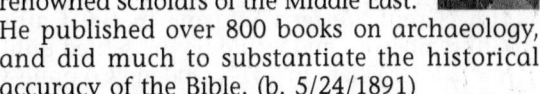

1971 Death of William Foxwell Albright, 80, American Orientalist and archaeologist. Noted for his excavations at Gibeah, Albright was one of the most renowned scholars of the Middle East. He published over 800 books on archaeology, and did much to substantiate the historical accuracy of the Bible. (b. 5/24/1891)

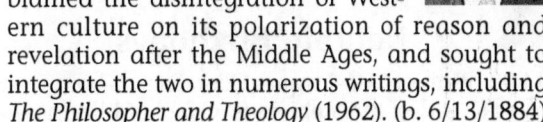

1978 Death of Étienne H. Gilson, 94, French Catholic Thomist philosopher, educator and historian of medieval philosophy. Believing that "revelation begets reason," Gilson blamed the disintegration of Western culture on its polarization of reason and revelation after the Middle Ages, and sought to integrate the two in numerous writings, including *The Philosopher and Theology* (1962). (b. 6/13/1884)

Words for the Soul

1740 During his second trip to America, English revivalist George Whitefield wrote in his journal: *'I saw regenerate souls among the Baptists, among the Presbyterians, among the Independents, and among the Church folks – all children of God, and yet all born again in a different way.'*

1974 Dutch Catholic priest Henri J. M. Nouwen reflected in his *Genesee Diary*: *'The experience of God's presence is not void of pain. But the pain is so deep that you do not want to miss it since it is in this pain that the joy of God's presence can be tasted. This seems close to nonsense except in the sense that it is beyond sense and, therefore, hard to capture within the limits of human understanding.'*

1981 Russian Orthodox liturgical scholar Father Alexander Schmemann reflected in his journal: *'The Church is a caricature of the world, with the difference that in the world, fights, institutions and so forth are real. In the Church, they are illusory because they are not related to anything. For salvation, this fussy activism is not needed; for joy and peace in the Holy Spirit – not needed either.'*

IN GOD'S WORD... OT: Isaiah 30:12–33:12 ~ NT: Galatians 4:21–5:12 ~ Psalms 63:1-11 ~ Proverbs 23:22

תשרי
TISHRI

ALMANAC OF THE CHRISTIAN FAITH

אלול
ELUL

~ September 20 ~

Highlights in History

1378 Robert of Geneva was elevated by the French cardinalate as Pope Clement VII. The only problem: Pope Urban VI was already in office! Thus the "Great Western Schism" in the Catholic Church began, and would not be settled until 40 years later when, in 1417, Oddone Colonna was elected Martin V.

1870 During the Franco-Prussian War (which began July 19th), Italian troops occupied Rome, thus effectively ending the Vatican I Ecumenical Council. (The council was officially suspended October 20th and never reopened.)

Notable Birthdays

1608 Birth of Jean-Jacques Olier, French-born founder (1641) of the Sulpicians. Cured of blindness, he was later converted during a pilgrimage to Italy. Today members of the order devote themselves to directing seminaries. [d. 4/2/1657]

1900 Birth of Visser 'T Hooft, Dutch Reformed ecumenical leader. He served as Secretary of the World Alliance of YMCA's, Switzerland (1924-31), and afterward became founding general secretary of the World Council of Churches (1948-66). [d. 7/4/1985]

1900 Birth of Joachim Jeremias, German Lutheran New Testament scholar. His positive use of form criticism created a bridgehead to the English-speaking world for the form critical approach at a time when German skepticism was still widely distrusted. [d. 9/6/1979]

The Last Passage

1852 Death of Philander Chase, 76, American Episcopal bishop and missionary. He served as bishop of Ohio (1819-31), bishop of Illinois (1835-52), and afterward became presiding bishop (1843-52). Chase also founded Kenyon College in Ohio (1824) and Jubilee College, a theological school in Illinois. (b. 12/14/1775)

1871 Death of John Coleridge Patteson, 44, the first Anglican missionary bishop of Melanesia. He left England for the South Seas in 1855. and was consecrated the first bishop of Melanesia in 1861. Patteson was martyred on the island of Nukapu – killed by tribesmen in retaliation for an earlier kidnapping of five of their youth. Patteson's death aroused new interest in England in missionary work. (b. 4/1/1827)

1921 Death of William J. Kirkpatrick, 83, American Methodist hymnwriter. He edited his first collection of sacred music at 21, and is still remembered today for creating such hymn tunes as: CRADLE SONG ("Away in a Manger"); DUNCANNON ("King of My Life, I Crown Thee Now"); LANDAS ("My Faith Has Found a Resting Place"); and GREENWELL ("I Am Not Skilled to Understand"). (b. 2/27/1838)

1957 Death of Jean Julius Christian Sibelius, 91, a pioneer composer of Finnish national music and creator of the hymn tune FINLANDIA ("Be Still, My Soul") in 1900. (b. 12/8/1865)

Words for the Soul

1974 Dutch Catholic diarist Henri J. M. Nouwen noted this spiritual insight once made by Abraham Heschel: *'The refusal to accept the harshness of God's ways in the name of his love was an authentic form of prayer. Indeed, the ancient Prophets of Israel... did not simply nod, saying "Thy will be done." They often challenged [God], as if to say, "Thy will be changed." They... countered and even annulled divine decrees.'*

1974 Russian liturgical scholar Alexander Schmemann reflected in his journal: *'Within religion I feel stifled, and I feel myself a radical "challenger." But among challengers I feel myself a conservative and traditionalist. I cannot identify with any complete system... or ideology. It seems to me that anything finished, complete and not open to another dimension is heavy and self-destructive.'*

IN GOD'S WORD... OT: Isaiah 33:13–35:10 ~ NT: Galatians 5:13-26 ~ Psalms 64:1-10 ~ Proverbs 23:23

תשרי ALMANAC OF THE CHRISTIAN FAITH אלול
TISHRI   ELUL

~ September 21 ~

Highlights in History

1522 Martin Luther's German New Testament was published. Based on Erasmus' Greek edition of 1516, it was the first vernacular translation from the original languages to avail itself of Gutenberg's technology. (Luther completed his translation of the entire Bible in 1534.)

1814 Francis Scott Key's "The Star Spangled Banner," penned during the War of 1812, was first published in the Baltimore "American." It became the U.S. national anthem in 1931.

1933 During the rise of Adolf Hitler, Martin Niemoeller and Friedrich Mueller sent letters to clergy throughout Germany in an effort to resist the Nazis. By January 15, 1934, one-third of the Protestant clergy had joined, and in May 1934 the Pastors' Emergency League gave birth to the famed Barmen (5/29-31/1934) Synod.

1944 A steady growth in religious radio programming (begun in 1921) led to the establishment of the National Religious Broadcasters. A daughter organization of the National Association of Evangelicals, the NRB today impacts nearly 1,400 religious radio stations in the U.S.

Notable Birthdays

1452 Birth of Italian Dominican reformer, Girolamo Savonarola. Preaching against licentiousness of the ruling class and the worldliness of the clergy, he led in the reformation of Florence, until his attacks on Pope Alexander VI brought about his excommunication and arrest. Savonarola was soon condemned, strangled and burned. [d. 5/23/1498]

1695 Birth of John Glass, Scottish independent Presbyterian clergyman and sectarian leader. Convinced that churches are gatherings of true believers rather than parochial congregations, he formed the Glassite church, a sect of Independent Presbyterians operating on the principle that he espoused. [d. 11/2/1773]

1874 Birth of Gustav Holst, English composer and music educator. He started his career as an Anglican church organist, and later began directing orchestras. Known for his interest in world religions, Holst composed such choral works as "The Hymn of Jesus." [d. 5/25/1934]

The Last Passage

1558 Death of Charles V, 58, Spanish king (1516) and Holy Roman Emperor (1519-56). A devout Catholic, Charles believed it his duty to defend Christendom from its enemies (e.g., the Turks), and the Church from schism. It was Charles who called the Diet of Worms in 1521, which had condemned Martin Luther. (b. 2/24/1500)

1935 Death of James M. Gray, 84, American clergyman, educator and author. He was president of Moody Bible Institute, one of the seven editors of the Scofield Bible, and was instrumental in organizing the Evangelical Teacher Training Association in 1931. Gray also wrote the hymn, "Nor Silver Nor Gold Hath Obtained My Redemption." (b. 5/11/1851)

1996 Death of Henri J. M. Nouwen, 64, Dutch Catholic priest and diarist. He spent most of his life in North America, searching for an ever deeper spirituality. He undertook various mission stays — in a Trappist monastery in NY, in impoverished communities of Bolivia and Peru, and finally in a Canadian institution for the severely disabled. Nouwen's published reflections on these experiences afterward became a source of spiritual help for many readers. (b. 1/24/1932)

Words for the Soul

1770 English clergyman and hymnwriter John Newton advised a newly-married couple: *'I need not tell you, that both the sphere of your comforts and your trials is now enlarged. Your opportunities for usefulness will be increased; so likewise will the snares and temptations in the path of duty.'*

IN GOD'S WORD... OT: Isaiah 36:1–37:38 ~ NT: Galatians 6:1-18 ~ Psalms 65:1-13 ~ Proverbs 23:24-25

~ September 22 ~

Highlights in History

1637 In New Towne, MA, the first church synod in America closed. Convened in August, the assembly met to judge the teachings of Anne Hutchinson – the first female religious leader in the American colonies. Eighty-two errors were condemned, and Hutchinson was afterward exiled from the Massachusetts Bay Colony.

1734 The first Moravian settlement in America began with the arrival of the Schwenkfelders, who landed at Philadelphia. Augustus Gottlieb Spangenberg became the first Moravian bishop in America in 1744. (Moravians are followers of Jan Hus, the 15th-century Bohemian religious reformer, and call themselves the Church of the Brethren, or Unitas Fratrum.)

1692 During the infamous Salem Witch Trials, the last eight of 20 condemned "witches" were hanged in Salem, MA. In all 13 women and seven men had been convicted of witchcraft.

Notable Birthdays

1791 Birth of Michael Faraday, English scientist. The son of an impoverished blacksmith, he went on to make great discoveries in electromagnetism and chemistry. Less well-known is Faraday's deep Christian faith, which led to his conversion at 29. Later elected an elder of his church, at age 48 Faraday became a preacher. [d. 8/25/1867]

1847 Birth of Alice (née Thompson) Meynell, English Catholic essayist and poet. She and her husband Wilfrid collaborated on numerous literary projects and were the first to publish such writers as Coventry Patmore and Francis Thompson. [d. 11/27/1922]

1865 Birth of A[mbrose] J. Tomlinson, Quaker-born pioneer American Pentecostal leader. Joining a Holiness group in NC in 1903, he soon began pastoring several affiliated churches. In 1907 those congregations adopted the denominational name Church of God. [d. 10/2/1943]

The Last Passage

1566 Death of Johann Agricola, 72, German reformer. Once an associate of Martin Luther, Agricola's friendship deteriorated over the issue of the authority of Mosaic Law in believers' and nonbelievers' lives. (b. 4/20/1494)

1662 Death of John Biddle, 47, father of modern English Unitarianism. He wrote *Twelve Arguments*, which denied the Trinity, and was imprisoned and later banished (1655) by Oliver Cromwell to the Scilly Islands to save his life. But Biddle returned and died of fever in a London prison. (bapt. 1/14/1615)

1871 Death of Charlotte Elliott, 82, Anglican hymnwriter. The granddaughter of Anglican evangelical Henry Venn, and influenced by Cesar Malan, she was converted to a Christian faith. Although an invalid 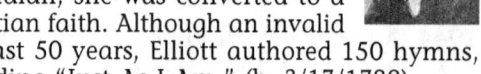 her last 50 years, Elliott authored 150 hymns, including "Just As I Am." (b. 3/17/1789)

1973 Death of C[harles] H. Dodd, 89, British Congregational minister and New Testament scholar. A Divinity professor at Cambridge and also an evangelical Christian, he was untiring in his defense of the importance of history in the Christian faith. Dodd served as director of the *New English Bible* New Testament translation committee, 1960-65. (b. 4/7/1884)

Words for the Soul

1764 English founder of Methodism John Wesley worried in a letter: 'When I have not heard from you for some time, I begin to be full of fears; I am afraid, either that your bodily weakness increases, or that your desires after God grow cold.'

1937 English mystic Evelyn Underhill remarked in a letter: 'No amount of solitary reading makes up for humble immersion in the life and worship of the Church. In fact the books are only addressed to those who are taking part in that life. The corporate and personal together make up the Christian ideal.'

IN GOD'S WORD... OT: Isaiah 38:1–41:16 ~ NT: Ephesians 1:1-23 ~ Psalms 66:1-20 ~ Proverbs 23:26-28

תשרי TISHRI ALMANAC OF THE CHRISTIAN FAITH אלול ELUL

~ September 23 ~

Highlights in History

1595 Led by Fray Juan de Silva, the Spanish began an intensive missionary campaign in the American Southeast. During the next two years, 1,500 Native Americans in the area of Florida, Georgia, and South Carolina were converted to the Christian faith.

1642 Harvard College held its first commencement exercises, conferring the B.A. degree on nine graduates. Established in 1636 in New Towne, MA and originally given the name Cambridge College, the school was renamed in 1638 in honor of the English clergyman, Rev. John Harvard, whose will bequeathed £800 and 300 books to the institution.

Notable Birthdays

1800 Birth of William Holmes McGuffey, pioneer American educator. As a clergyman and college president, McGuffey became an advocate for public education, and compiled a series of six *Eclectic Readers*. Owing to their strong moral tone, the "McGuffy Readers" became one of the most influential of the early textbooks in America. [d. 5/4/1873]

1843 Birth of George F. Pentecost, American Presbyterian clergyman and revivalist. Following a chaplaincy during the U.S. Civil War, he alternated between pastoring (1864-77, 1881-87, 1891-1902) and evangelistic work (1877-81, 1887-91, 1902-). He was also an active member of the American Board of Commissioners for Foreign Missions. [d. 1920]

1888 Birth of Gerhard Kittel, German New Testament scholar. The son of Rudolf Kittel, Gerhard became famous as the editor of *Theologisches Wörterbuch zum Neuen Testament*, completed by Gerhard Friedrich after Kittel's death. The ten-volume reference work was translated into English by Geoffrey Bromily as the *Theological Dictionary of the New Testament* (1964-76). [d. 7/11/1948]

The Last Passage

1840 Death of Nathanael Emmons, 95, American Congregational clergyman and theologian. He pastored the Franklin (MA) Church for 52 years (1773-1825). Though outwardly opposed to Arminianism, Universalism and Unitarianism, he nevertheless asserted that man's part in regeneration is active, not passive. Emmons was also one of the fathers of the Massachusetts Missionary Society. (b. 4/20/1745)

1907 Death of John S. Norris, 63, English-born, Canadian-American clergyman and evangelist. Ordained in the Methodist church, Norris later became a Congregationalist. He is chiefly remembered today for composing the hymns: NORRIS ("I Can Hear My Savior Calling") and "Where He Leads Me." (b. 12/4/1844)

Words for the Soul

1747 Two weeks before his early death from tuberculosis at age 29, colonial missionary to the American Indians David Brainerd penned in his journal: *'Felt uncommonly peaceful; it seemed as if I had now done all my work in this world, and stood ready for my call to a better. As long as I see any thing to be done for God, life is worth having; but O how vain and unworthy it is to live for any lower end!'*

1859 Scottish clergyman and biographer Andrew Bonar confessed in his diary: *'Envy is my hurt, and to-day I have been seeking grace to rejoice exceedingly over the usefulness of others, even where it casts me into the shade.'*

1947 English Catholic psychiatrist Caryll Houselander advised in a letter: *'It is very helpful to reflect that God loves those whom we love, far more than we do – infinitely more.'*

1960 Mourning the death of his wife Joy Davidman, British literary scholar and Christian apologist C. S. Lewis revealed in a letter: *'When I mourn Joy least I feel nearest to her. Passionate sorrow cuts us off from the dead.'*

IN GOD'S WORD... OT: Isaiah 41:17–43:13 ~ NT: Ephesians 2:1-22 ~ Psalms 67:1-7 ~ Proverbs 23:29-35

ALMANAC OF THE CHRISTIAN FAITH

תשרי TISHRI

אלול ELUL

September 24

Highlights in History

787 The Second Council of Nicea opened – seventh of the 21 ecumenical councils counted by the Catholic Church. (Eastern Orthodoxy considers this the last of the ecumenical councils.) Under Pope Adrian I, the council limited veneration of icons, but condemned iconoclasm.

1757 Noted colonial clergyman Jonathan Edwards, 53, became president of the College of New Jersey (i.e., Princeton). He served only a few months before his premature death from a smallpox vaccination.

1889 The Declaration of Utrecht was signed, and became the doctrinal basis of the Old Catholic Church. (Certain Continental churches had rejected papal authority and the Council of Trent decisions. Following the declaration of papal infallibility at Vatican I in 1870, other dioceses chose schism over submission.) Today, the Old Catholic liturgy is in the vernacular, and clerical celibacy has been abolished.

1988 In Boston, the Episcopal Diocese of Massachusetts elected the Rev. Barbara C. Harris as their new suffragen (assistant) bishop. Her consecration made Mrs. Harris, an African-American, the first female Bishop of the Worldwide Anglican Communion, breaking 454 years of Anglicanism's male-only tradition.

Notable Birthdays

1759 Birth of Charles Simeon, Anglican churchman. As a curate in Cambridge (1783-1836), he became an influential leader of the evangelical church movement, and left a mark on the religious life of Cambridge. [d. 11/13/1836]

1825 Birth of Frances Watkins Harper, African-American reformer. Orphaned at an early age, she later became an active spokesperson for the antislavery movement, and her home in Philadelphia became an important station in the underground railroad. [d. 2/22/1911]

The Last Passage

1868 Death of Henry Hart Milman, 77, Anglican historian and clergyman. He was dean of St. Paul's (1849-68), published several religious histories, and also wrote the hymn, "Ride On, Ride On in Majesty." (b. 2/10/1791)

1934 Death of A[rchibald] T. Robertson, 70, American New Testament Greek scholar. He taught at Southern Baptist Seminary in Louisville, KY for 46 years (1888-1934), and was a member of the revision committee for the 1901-05 *American Standard Version* Bible. But his monumental *Grammar of the Greek New Testament* (1914) established him as the foremost Greek scholar of his day. (b. 11/6/1863)

1939 Death of Juji Nakada, 68, Japanese Christian evangelist. He was responsible for bringing Charles and Lettie Cowman to Japan in 1901. Under their inspiration, the Wesleyan tradition Oriental Missionary Society (OMS) was established in 1910. (b. 10/29/1870)

Words for the Soul

1525 German reformer Martin Luther remarked in a sermon: 'Whoever wants to be saved should act as though all the comfort and promise of God found here and there in Scripture concerned him alone, and was written only for his sake.'

1753 Affirming belief in the person and work of God, English founder of Methodism John Wesley explained in a letter: 'Reason proves that this mystery is possible! Revelation assures us that it is true; Heaven alone can show us how it is.'

1995 Dutch Catholic priest and diarist Henri J. M. Nouwen concluded in his *Journal*: 'That's the loneliness of the mystic. Having seen and experienced what cannot be expressed in words and still must be communicated.... My own experience of priesthood... is a grace, it allows me to see a vision, and it is a call to let others know what I have seen; it is a long loneliness and an inexpressible joy.'

IN GOD'S WORD... OT: Isaiah 43:14–45:10 ~ NT: Ephesians 3:1-21 ~ Psalms 68:1-18 ~ Proverbs 24:1-2

תשרי ALMANAC OF THE CHRISTIAN FAITH אלול
TISHRI   ELUL

~ September 25 ~

Highlights in History

1789 The U.S. Congress voted on the final version of the first ten amendments to the Constitution, known today as the Bill of Rights. The establishment of religion on a national level was expressly prohibited by Congress with its adoption of the First Amendment. The opening words of the amendment read: *'Congress shall make no law respecting the establishment of religion, or prohibiting the free exercise thereof.'*

1794 A Russian Orthodox Christian mission arrived in the Aleutian Islands. Grigorii I. Shelekov, who founded a hunting settlement among the Kodiak Eskimos, had appealed to the Russian government for Orthodox churches to be established, and had promised to pay all expenses and provide transportation. As a result, eight monks and two ministers were sent. In eight months, they baptized 7,000.

1800 In the midst of the early American religious revival movement in Pennsylvania and Maryland, revival leaders Philip William Otterbein (1726-1813) and Martin Boehm (1725-1812) together established the Church of the United Brethren in Christ. Boehm was originally of Mennonite upbringing, and Otterbein was a pastor of the German Reformed Church.

Notable Birthdays

1866 Birth of Cleland B. McAfee, American Presbyterian clergyman, educator and hymnwriter. He taught Systematic Theology at McCormick Theological Seminary in Chicago (1912-30). But we remember him best for his hymn: "There Is a Place of Quiet Rest." [d. 2/4/1944]

1869 Birth of Rudolf Otto, German theologian and philosopher. As a Lutheran, he sought to deepen public and devotional worship, and wrote on the surpassing holiness of God. Otto's theology explores the "numinous" (i.e., non-rational) elements of awe, self-abasement, and religious fanaticism, which contributes to the religious consciousness. [d. 3/6/1937]

The Last Passage

1534 Death of Clement VII (Giuliode Medici), 56, pope from 1523-34. His reign was marked by intrigue. His delay on the request to annul Henry VIII's marriage to Catherine of Aragon led England to break with Rome. Similar action encouraged the spread of Lutheranism. (b. 5/26/1478)

1872 Death of Peter Cartwright, 87, American frontier evangelist and statesman. The most colorful of the Methodist circuit riders on the American western frontier, he later served in the Illinois state legislature, and was defeated in a race for Congress (1846) by Abraham Lincoln. (b. 9/1/1785)

1922 Death of Johnson Oatman, Jr., 66, business executive and poet. He penned over 5,000 sacred verses, set to music by John R. Sweney, William Kirkpatrick, Charles Gabriel and Edwin O. Excell. The resulting hymns include "No, Not One"; "Count Your Blessings"; and "Higher Ground." (b. 4/21/1856)

1924 Death of Charles E. Cowman, 60, American missions pioneer. He and his wife Lettie (née Burd) went to Japan as independent missionaries in 1901.  They soon organized the Oriental Missionary Society, which ultimately reached Korea and China with the gospel as well as Japan. (b. 3/13/1864)

Words for the Soul

1757 English founder of Methodism John Wesley testified in a letter: *'I love the poor; in many of them I find pure, genuine grace, unmixed with paint, folly, and affectation.'*

1891 The year before his death, Scottish clergyman and biographer Andrew Bonar, 81, confessed in his diary: *'It is very solemn to find myself near the threshold of Eternity, my ministry nearly done, and my long life coming to its close. Never was Christ to me more precious than He is now.'*

IN GOD'S WORD... OT: Isaiah 45:11–48:11 ~ NT: Ephesians 4:1-16 ~ Psalms 68:19-35 ~ Proverbs 24:3-4

תשרי TISHRI — ALMANAC OF THE CHRISTIAN FAITH — אלול ELUL

~ September 26 ~

Highlights in History

1814 The Flint River Association was organized, in Alabama. Comprised of over 1,000 initial members from 17 churches, it was the first official Baptist organization of its kind in the history of Alabama.

1835 The Suwanee Association was formed, in Florida. Comprised of eight member churches, it was the first official Baptist organization in Florida history.

1940 In Westville, NJ, the second Annual Session of the Eastern Conference of the Methodist Protestant Church began. During this convention, the denomination changed its name to the Bible Protestant Church. (In 1985, the BPC enlarged its membership and changed its name to the Fellowship of Fundamental Bible Churches.)

Notable Birthdays

1651 Birth of Francis Daniel Pastorius, German Lutheran emigration agent. He helped European Mennonites, Pietists and Quakers relocate in the American colony of Pennsylvania, and was a central figure in helping to establish Germantown, PA. [d. 9/27/1719]

1774 Birth of Jonathan Chapman (a.k.a. "Johnny Appleseed"), American pioneer ecological theologian. He traveled the American Midwestern frontier for fifty years, preaching a Swedenborgian "nature theology," and distributing apple seeds. He was later immortalized in poetry by Vachel Lindsay. [d. 3/11/1847]

1888 Birth of T[homas] S. Eliot, dramatist and poet. Raised in the U.S. as a Unitarian, he afterward emigrated to England, moved through agnosticism and on to High Church Anglicanism. As the most influential English writer in the twentieth century and a devout Christian, Eliot often wove his religious convictions into his literary work. [d. 1/4/1965]

The Last Passage

1626 Death of Lancelot Andrewes, 71, Anglican divine. A popular, learned preacher, he was one of the first scholars appointed by James I to prepare the (1611) *Authorized Version* of the Bible. Andrewes also exerted a marked influence on the development of Anglican theology and authored the spiritual classic, *Private Devotions*. (b. 1555)

1863 Death of Frederick W. Faber, 49, an Anglican clergyman and poet who, in 1845, followed John Henry Newman in converting to Roman Catholicism. Faber authored the popular hymns: "My God, How Wonderful Thou Art"; "Hark, Hark, My Soul"; "There's a Wideness in God's Mercy"; and "Faith of Our Fathers." (b. 6/28/1814)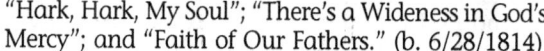

1876 Death of Edward F. Rimbault, 60, English sacred organist and composer of the hymn tunes: HAPPY DAY ("O Happy Day that Fixed My Choice"); and RUTHERFORD ("The Sands of Time Are Sinking") (arr.). (b. 6/13/1816)

1944 Death of Aimee Semple McPherson, 53, the colorful Canadian-born American evangelist who founded the International Church of the Foursquare Gospel in 1918. Her gospel of optimistic Fundamentalism was characterized by a dramatic preaching style. (b. 10/9/1890)

Words for the Soul

1853 Scottish clergyman and writer George MacDonald, while away from home, reminded his wife in a letter: *'It is a very good thing for us to be parted sometimes. It makes us think, both more truly about each other, and, because less interrupted, about our God.'*

1977 Russian liturgist Alexander Schmemann observed: *'The opposite of love is not hate, but fear.... Fear is, first of all, the absence of love, ... what grows like weeds where there is no love.... The fall of the world is its alienation from God, who is love – hence, darkness and shadows of death.'*

IN GOD'S WORD... OT: Isaiah 48:12–50:11 ~ NT: Ephesians 4:17-32 ~ Psalms 69:1-18 ~ Proverbs 24:5-6

תשרי TISHRI

ALMANAC OF THE CHRISTIAN FAITH

אלול ELUL

~ September 27 ~

Highlights in History

1540 Pope Paul III issued the bull, "Regimini militantis ecclesiae," which officially approved the Society of Jesus. This body of priests had organized six years earlier under Ignatius of Loyola and six companions. Today, its high schools and colleges make the Jesuit Society the largest teaching order in the U.S.

1785 Following the American Revolutionary War, American Anglicans met in Philadelphia to create a denomination independent from the Church of England. Today's date, therefore, marks the founding of the Protestant Episcopal Church in the U.S.A.

Notable Birthdays

1643 Birth of Solomon Stoddard, American Colonial Congregational clergyman. He pastored the church at Northampton, MA for over 50 years – the religious and political leader of Western Massachusetts in his time. Stoddard's grandson was Jonathan Edwards. [d. 2/11/1729]

1696 Birth of Alphonsus St. Maria dé Liguori, Italian Catholic moral theologian. In 1732 he founded the Congregation of the Most Holy Redeemer (Redemptorists), and was elected its superior general in 1749. [d. 8/1/1787]

1735 Birth of Robert Robinson, English Baptist clergyman and hymnwriter. Converted under George Whitefield in 1752, Robinson soon began preaching, even though he had no theological training. Today he is remembered for authoring the hymn, "Come Thou Fount of Every Blessing." [d. 6/9/1790]

1805 Birth of George Müller, pastor, philanthropist, and leader in the Christian Brethren movement. Born in Germany, he was converted from a profligate life in 1825 under the preaching of the Moravians. Müller afterward made Bristol, England his permanent home, and spent the next 66 years caring for over 10,000 orphan children, relying completely on prayer and private donations. [d. 3/10/1898]

1914 Birth of Catherine Marshall, American Presbyterian inspirational writer. The widow of U.S. Senate chaplain Peter Marshall, she authored *A Man Called Peter* (1951), following his premature death in 1949. In 1959, Catherine married Leonard E. LeSourd. [d. 3/18/1983]

The Last Passage

1660 Death of St. Vincent de Paul, 84, Catholic philanthropist and founder of the Lazarists. He established the first Confraternity of Charity in 1617, the Congregation of the Mission in 1625, and the Daughters of Charity in 1633 (the first non-monastic women's order completely given to care of the sick and poor). He was canonized in 1737, and was named patron saint of all charitable works in 1885. (b. 4/24/1576)

1899 Death of James Ellor, 80, English-born American hat maker, railroad construction worker and hymn composer: DIADEM ("All Hail the Power of Jesus' Name"). (b. 1819)

Words for the Soul

1536 German reformer Martin Luther wrote in a letter: *'One should not mix these two authorities, the temporal and the spiritual, the courthouse and the church. Otherwise the one devours the other and both perish, as happened under the papacy.'*

1704 English philosopher John Locke wrote in a letter: *'What is the best way to study religion?... The only way to attain a certain knowledge is the study of the Holy Scripture... because the Christian religion is a revelation from God Almighty, which is contained in the Bible, so all the knowledge we can have of it must be derived from thence.'*

1746 Missionary to the American Indians David Brainerd confided in his journal: *'O how blessed it is to be habitually prepared for death!'*

IN GOD'S WORD... OT: Isaiah 51:1–53:12 ~ NT: Ephesians 5:1-33 ~ Psalms 69:19-36 ~ Proverbs 24:7

תשרי   ALMANAC OF THE CHRISTIAN FAITH   אלול
TISHRI   ELUL

~ September 28 ~

Highlights in History

1832 Weary of the unsettled life of a revivalist, Charles G. Finney accepted the pulpit of the Chatham Street Church in New York. During the installation service he took ill with cholera, and it was actually months before Finney could take the pulpit on a regular basis, but he continued as pastor of the Chatham Street Church until 1837.

1895 At a meeting in Atlanta, three Baptist groups merged to form the National Baptist Convention. Today, it is the largest African-American church denomination in the world.

1931 C. S. Lewis underwent a spiritual conversion while riding to the zoo in his brother Warren's motorcycle sidecar: *'When we set out I did not believe that Jesus is the Son of God and when we reached the zoo I did.'* (Lewis's conversion followed a long conversation he had had the week before with two Christian friends: J. R. R. Tolkien and Hugo Dyson.)

Notable Birthdays

1839 Birth of Frances E. Willard, American Methodist temperance leader and reformer. While attending Northwestern Female College (IL), she underwent a strong religious conversion. Interested in the  temperance movement, she worked for a time with D. L. Moody. Later, as president of the National Women's Christian Temperance Union (WCTU), a forerunner of the Social Gospel Movement, Willard also helped press for women's rights and suffrage. [d. 2/18/1898]

1872 Birth of Shirley Jackson Case, American Baptist New Testament scholar and church historian. For 30 years Case was associated with the University of Chicago Divinity School (1908-38), and authored *The Historicity of Jesus* (1912); *Jesus Through the Centuries* (1931); *and Makers of Christianity* (1934). [d. 12/5/1947]

1927 Birth of Thomas J. J. Altizer, American theologian who helped lead the "God is dead" movement of the 1970s. As professor of theology at  Emory University, Altizer taught that while God, as known in history, no longer exists, *'Christ, the Incarnate Word, lives.'*

The Last Passage

929/935 Death of "good king" Wenceslas, 22 (or 28), Bohemian prince and martyr. During his brief reign (from ca. 922 until his brother Boleslav murdered him), Wenceslas sought to bring his people into closer connection with the Western world, and also showed particular concern for his country's poor. (b. ca. 907)

1908 Death of Calvin W. Mateer, 72, pioneer American Presbyterian missionary. Arriving in Tengchow in 1864 with his wife Julia (née Brown), they founded a boys' school which, by 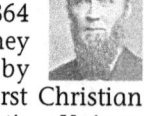 1898, had grown to become the first Christian college in China – Shantung Christian University. Mateer also translated much of the Bible into Mandarin Chinese (1907). (b. 1/9/1836)

Words for the Soul

1532 German reformer Martin Luther remarked in a Table Talk: *'To God this world is only a preparation and scaffolding for yonder world.... [In the next world] matters will for the first time really go according to the power and the will of God.'*

1745 English founder of Methodism John Wesley summarized in a letter: *'The Apostles used the expression, "salvation by faith" (importing inward holiness by the knowledge of God) in direct opposition to the then common persuasion of salvation by works; that is, going to heaven by outward works, without any inward holiness at all.'*

1774 Anglican clergyman and hymnwriter John Newton advised in a letter: *'We are always equally in danger in ourselves and always equally safe under the shadow of His wings.'*

IN GOD'S WORD...   OT: Isaiah 54:1–57:13 ~ NT: Ephesians 6:1-24 ~ Psalms 70:1-5 ~ Proverbs 24:8-9

תשרי TISHRI

ALMANAC OF THE CHRISTIAN FAITH

אלול ELUL

~ September 29 ~

Highlights in History

640 Leo I (the Great) was consecrated pope. He strengthened the authority of the church, suppressed the Manichean heresy, and wrote important letters, including one on the doctrine of the Incarnation.

1565 Nearly 500 Huguenot settlers in Florida – having fled persecution in their native France – were slaughtered by Spanish soldiers. It was the worst single case of religious persecution in the history of the North American continent.

1747 In Philadelphia, four ministers and 27 elders convened to organize the German Reformed Church.

1979 Pope John Paul II became the first Roman pontiff in history to visit Ireland, when he arrived there for a three-day visit. Over 2.5 million of the country's 3.5 million Catholics saw the pope during his tour which crisscrossed the country from Dublin to Drogheda to Galway to Knock to Maynooth to Limerick.

Notable Birthdays

1511 Birth of Michael (Miguel) Servetus, Spanish physician and theologian. The most outstanding anti-Trinitarian of the 16th century, he published "De Trinitatis Erroribus" in 1531, opposing the doctrine of Trinity. John Calvin afterward had Servetus arrested, and burned for his "crime." [d. 10/27/1553]

1636 Birth of Thomas Tenison, an English prelate who championed Protestantism during the reign of James II. He was Archbishop of Canterbury from 1695, and a founder of the Society for Propagation of the Gospel. [d. 12/14/1715]

1901 Birth of Frances Caryll Houselander, an English spiritual writer who converted to Catholicism at age 6. Though lacking formal theological training, her writings revealed deep psychological and religious insights. [d. 10/12/1954]

The Last Passage

1349 Death of Richard Rolle of Hampole, ca. 54, English mystic, hermit and teacher. (b. ca. 1295)

1642 Death of St. René Goupil, 35, American Roman Catholic martyr. A French Jesuit missionary to the Canadian Indians – and the first of seven North American Catholic martyrs – he was tortured, then tomahawked to death in Father Isaac Jogues's presence at an Iroquois village near Albany, NY. (b. 1607)

1868 Death of Lorrin Andrews, 73, American Congregational missionary to Hawaii. Sent by ABCFM in 1828, he severed his connection in 1842. Soon becoming one of the islands' most visible figures, Andrews translated the Bible into Hawaiian, published a Hawaiian dictionary and grammar, published its first newspaper and, at age 57, became the first associate justice of the Hawaiian Supreme Court. (b. 4/29/1795)

1978 Pope John Paul I (born Albino Luciani), 65, was found dead in his Vatican apartment a little over a month after his election to the office of pope in the Catholic Church. His ministry officially began on Sept. 3rd, in St. Peter's Square, but he returned to his Father's Home 26 days later. (b. 10/17/1912)

Words for the Soul

1770 The day before his early death at age 56, English revivalist George Whitefield prayed: *'Lord Jesus, I am weary in thy work, but not of it.'*

1773 In a letter, English founder of Methodism John Wesley outlined some of the changes which occur following a spiritual conversion: *'Grace in one sense will make all things new. And I have sometimes known this done to such a degree, that there has been no trace of the natural temper remaining. But generally the innocent natural temper does remain; only refined, softened, and cast into the mould of love.'*

IN GOD'S WORD... OT: Isaiah 57:14–59:21 ~ NT: Philippians 1:1-26 ~ Psalms 71:1-24 ~ Proverbs 24:10-11

תשרי ALMANAC OF THE CHRISTIAN FAITH אלול
TISHRI   ELUL

~ September 30 ~

Highlights in History

1751 Phillip Doddridge, clergyman and author of the influential book, *The Rise and Progress of Religion in the Soul*, sailed from Falmouth for a warmer climate in the hope of recovering from consumption. (He died a month later.)

1943 Pope Pius XII issued the encyclical "Divino afflante spiritu" ("On the Most Opportune Way to Promote Biblical Studies"), which urged a greater use of textual criticism among Roman Catholic scholars, and more emphasis on the historical background of Biblical passages.

Notable Birthdays

1709 Birth of Georg Schmidt, first German Moravian Brethren missionary to the Hottentots of South Africa. He was sent in 1737. [d. 8/2/1785]

1751 Birth of Elhanan Winchester, American Universalist minister and evangelist. He was arguably the most celebrated exponent of Universalism during the 19th century. [d. 4/18/1797]

1928 Birth of Elie[zer] Wiesel, American Jewish journalist and author. An Auschwitz concentration camp survivor, his books deal with the Holocaust. He won the Nobel Peace Prize in 1986.

The Last Passage

420 One of the most learned of the Latin Fathers, Jerome died at about 78. A Biblical scholar from Rome, he moved to Bethlehem, entered a monastery and devoted himself to translating the Bible into Latin (the Vulgate Bible). He also prepared numerous works of ecclesiastical history and biblical interpretation. (b. 345)

1770 Death of George Whitefield, English revivalist and religious reformer. He preached his last sermon the previous day, and on his death-bed, Whitefield uttered the prayer: *'Lord Jesus, I am weary in Thy work, but not of Thy work.'* (b.12/16 [NS=12/27] /1714)

1882 Death of Johann Jakob Herzog, 77, Swiss-German Reformed theologian. He co-edited in 1882-84 with Philip Schaff the *Schaff-Herzog Encyclopedia of Religious Knowledge* (13 vols., 1853-68). (b. 8/12/1805)

1897 Death of St. Thérèse of Lisieux, 24, French Carmelite nun and devotional writer. Known as the "Little Flower of Jesus," Thérèse was canonized in 1925, and has since became one of the most popular of the modern saints. (b. 1/2/1873)

Words for the Soul

1526 German reformer Martin Luther declared in a sermon: *'We should learn well how to please Christ... by dedicating our entire life... to the service of our neighbor.... Down, down, says Christ; you will find me in the poor; you are rising too high if you do not look for Me there.'*

1885 Scottish clergyman and writer George MacDonald assured a friend in a letter: *'I hope you and your visible soul are both in peace and hope. God lives, and our unbelief cannot kill him.'*

1935 English Catholic psychiatrist Caryll Houselander explained in a letter: *'Apprehending is an inner knowing; it is intimate and personal; it is like putting out your hand in the dark and finding someone else's hand stretched out to you, and somehow knowing this is the hand of one you love.'*

1961 Revealing of his morning habits, British literary scholar and Christian apologist C. S. Lewis wrote in a *Letter to an American Lady*: *'I am a barbarously early riser... I love the empty, silent, dewy, cobwebby hours.'*

1977 Russian Orthodox liturgical scholar Alexander Schmemann reflected in his journal: *'The fundamental error of the contemporary man is his belief that thanks to technology – (telephone, Xerox, etc.) — he can squeeze into a given time much more than before, whereas it's really impossible. Man becomes the slave of his always growing work. There is a need for rhythm, detachment, slowness.'*

IN GOD'S WORD... OT: Isaiah 60:1–62:5 ~ NT: Philippians 1:27–2:18 ~ Psalms 72:1-20 ~ Proverbs 24:12

SEPTEMBER INDEX

A

ABCFM (American Board of Commissioners) 9/4, 9/5, 9/23, 9/29
ABOLITION OF SLAVERY 9/17
Ackley, Bentley DeForest
 (b. 9/27/1872) d. 9/3/1958
Adrian I, Pope (772-95) 9/24
Adrian IV, Pope (1154-59) 9/1
AFRICAN-AMERICANS 9/2, 9/17, 9/24
 Abolition of Slavery 9/24
 Baker, George 9/10
 Committee of Colored People 9/5
 Crummell, Alexander 9/10
 Divine, Father Major Jealous 9/10
 Emancipation 9/17
 Harper, Frances Watkins 9/24
 Harris, Barbara C. 9/24
 Mason, C[harles] H. 9/8
 McFadden, Vivian 9/8
 National Baptist Convention 9/28
 Slavery 9/7
Agricola, Johann
 (b. 4/20/1494) d. 9/22/1566
Aitken, Jane 9/12
Albright, William Foxwell
 (b. 5/24/1891) d. 9/19/1971
Aldred (Ealdred)
 (b. ca. 1000) d. 9/11/1069
Alexander, Charles M. 9/12
Alexander VI, Pope (1492-1503) 9/21
Alighieri, Dante
 (b. 5/5 or 27/1265) d. 9/14/1321
Allen, George N.
 9/7/1812 [d. 12/9/1877]
Altizer, Thomas J. J.
 b. 9/28/1927
American Revolutionary War 9/12, 9/27
Andrewes, Lancelot
 (b. 1555) d. 9/26/1626
Andrews, Lorrin
 (b. 4/29/1795) d. 9/29/1868
Aquaviva, Claudius
 b. 9/14/1543 [d. 1/31/1615]
Arminianism 9/12, 9/17, 9/23
Asbury, Francis 9/9. See also QUOTATIONS
Auschwitz concentration camp 9/30
Azusa Street Revival 9/8

B

Baker, George 9/10. See also Divine, Father Major Jealous

Barnardo, Thomas John
 (b. 7/4/1845) d. 9/19/1905
Basil I, Byzantine Emperor (867-86) 9/19
BATTLES, FAMOUS
 Battle of the Marne (1914) 9/5
Bauer, Bruno
 b. 9/6/1809 [d. 4/15/1882]
Baxter, Lydia
 b. 9/8/1809 [d. 6/22/1874]
Becker, Peter 9/7
Bellamy, Francis 9/8
Benedict XV, Pope (1914-22) 9/15
Benjamin I, Orthodox Patriarch 9/19
Bennett, Belle Harris 9/11
Bernard of Clairvaux 9/17
Bible Study Publishing Co. 9/2
BIBLE VERSIONS
 American Standard Version (1905) 9/24
 Authorized (King James) Version (1611) 9/16, 9/26
 Bengali (1798) 9/13
 Douay Version (1610) 9/16
 Dutch 9/11
 Erasmus' Greek New Testament (1516) 9/21
 Good News for Modern Man (1966) 9/15
 Hawaiian 9/29
 Latin Vulgate 9/30
 Luther's German New Testament (1522) 9/21
 Mandarin Chinese (1907) 9/28
 Moffatt Translation (1924) 9/18
 New English Bible 9/22
 Phillips Paraphrase of the New Testament (1958) 9/16
 Revised Standard Version (1952) 9/11
 Welsh (1588) 9/10
 Wen-li (Chinese) dialect 9/15
Biddle, John
 (bapt. 1/14/1615) d. 9/22/1662
Bill of Rights
 First Amendment 9/25
Blackwell, Samuel Charles 9/15
Blakeslee, Erastus
 b. 9/2/1838 [d. 7/12/1908]
Blaurock, Georg
 (b. ca. 1492) d. 9/5/1529
Boardman, George Dana 9/1
Boehm, Martin 9/25
Bogermann, Johannes [Jan]
 (b. 1576) d. 9/11/1637
Bojaxhiu, Agnes See also Teresa of Calcutta
 (b. 8/27/1910) d. 9/5/1997
Boleslav 9/28
Bonner, Edmund
 (b. ca. 1500) d. 9/5/1569
BOOKS / PUBLICATIONS
 A Man Called Peter (1951) 9/27

Anna Karenina 9/9
Book of Church Order 9/13
Christ and Culture (1951) 9/3
Concordance to the Septuagint (1896) 9/4
"De Trinitatis Erroribus" (1531) 9/29
From Tradition to Gospel (1919) 9/14
Genesee Diary (1976) 9/11, 9/16, 9/18, 9/19
Grammar of the Greek New Testament (1914) 9/24
Greek Word Studies in the New Testament (1887-1900) 9/11
Helvetic Confession of 1536 9/17
Helvetic Confession of 1566 9/17
International Critical Commentary 9/11
Jesus Through the Centuries (1931) 9/28
Kingdom of God in America (1937) 9/3
Leo's Tome (449) 9/13
Lord of the Rings (1954-55) 9/2
Luther's Small Catechism 9/17
Makers of Christianity (1934) 9/28
Markings (1964) 9/18
New Views of Christianity, Society and the Church 9/16
Notes on the Miracles 9/5
Notes on the Parables 9/5
Philosophical Theology (1930) 9/1
Private Devotions 9/26
Quest of the Historical Jesus (1906) 9/4
"Religious Remembrancer" 9/4
Road to Daybreak (1988) 9/2
Schaff-Herzog Encyclopedia of Religious Knowledge 9/30
Scivias 9/17
System of Doctrines Contained in Divine Revelation 9/17
Table Talk, Luther's 9/18
The Divine Comedy (1307-21) 9/14
The Historicity of Jesus (1912) 9/28
The Hobbit (1938) 9/2
The Philosopher and Theology (1962) 9/19
The Rise and Progress of Religion in the Soul 9/30
Theological Dictionary of the N.T. (1964-76) 9/23
Theologisches Wörterbuch zum Neuen Testament 9/23
Tract 90 9/9
"Tracts for the Times" 9/9, 9/16
Twelve Arguments 9/22
War and Peace 9/9
Westminster "Larger" Catechism (1648) 9/15
Westminster "Shorter" Catechism (1648) 9/15
Booth, Catherine 9/3
Booth, Evangeline Cory 9/3
Booth, William 9/3
Bora, Katherine von 9/13
Borden, William W. 9/9
Borthwick, Jane L.
 (b. 4/9/1813) d. 9/7/1897
Brainerd, David. See QUOTATIONS
Breakspear, Nicholas (Pope Adrian IV)
 (b. ca. 1115) d. 9/1/1159

Brebeuf, John 9/2
Bromily, Geoffrey 9/23
Brown, Antoinette Louisa 9/15
Brownson, Orestes A.
 b. 9/16/1803 [d. 4/17/1876]
Buckoll, Henry J.
 b. 9/9/1803 [d. 6/6/1871]
Bullinger, Johann H.
 (b. 7/18/1504) d. 9/17/1575
Burnet, Gilbert
 b. 9/18/1643 [d. 3/17/1715]

C

CALENDARS
 Gregorian (New Style) 9/3, 9/14
 Julian (Old Style) 9/3
Calvin, John 9/29
Campanius, Johannes (John) 9/4
 (b. 8/15/1601) d. 9/17/1683
Campbell, Alexander
 b. 9/12/1788 [d. 3/4/1866]
Campbell, Thomas 9/12
Canitz, Friedrich R. L. 9/9
CANTERBURY ARCHBISHOPS
 Tenison, Thomas (1695-1715) 9/29
Carey, Matthew
 (b. 1/28/1760) d. 9/16/1839
Carey, William 9/13
Cartwright, Peter
 b. 9/1/1785 d. 9/25/1872
Cary, Alice 9/4
Cary, Phoebe
 b. 9/4/1824 [d. 7/31/1871]
Case, Shirley Jackson
 b. 9/28/1872 [d. 12/5/1947]
Catherine of Aragon 9/25
Celestine I, Pope (422-32) 9/10
Chapman, J. Wilbur 9/12
Chapman, Jonathan
 b. 9/26/1774 [d. 3/11/1847]
Charles V, Holy Roman Emperor (1519-56) 9/9
 (b. 2/24/1500) d. 9/21/1558
Chase, Philander
 (b. 12/14/1775) d. 9/20/1852
Chornock, Orestes 9/19
Chrysostom, John
 (b. ca. 344/354) d. 9/14/407
CHURCHES
 All Souls' Unitarian Church (NJ) 9/15
 Chatham Street Church (NY City) 9/28
 Christ Episcopal Church (Philadelphia) 9/7
 First Baptist Church (Fort Worth, TX) 9/18
 First Congregational Church (NY) 9/15
 Holiness Church (NC) 9/13
 Independent Church of Christ (MA) 9/3

SEPTEMBER INDEX

Reims Cathedral (France) 9/19
St. Peters (Rome) 9/10
St. Peter's Square (Vatican) 9/29
Trinity Church (NY City) 9/17
Trinity Episcopal Church (MD) 9/17
Ciocchi del Monte, Giovanni Maria 9/10. See also Julius III, Pope
Circuit riders 9/25
Claggett, Thomas J. 9/17
Clark, Francis E.
 b. 9/12/1851 [d. 5/26/1927]
Clement VII, Antipope (1378-94) 9/20
Clement VII, Pope (1523-34) 9/9
 (b. 5/26/1478) d. 9/25/1534
Coeur-de-Lion. See Richard I, English King
Coke, Thomas 9/2
 b. 9/9/1747 [d. 5/3/1814]
COLLEGES / UNIVERSITIES
 Bethany College (WV) 9/12
 Cambridge (England) 9/22, 9/24
 Cambridge College 9/23
 College of New Jersey 9/24
 Emory University (GA) 9/28
 Harvard College (MA) 9/5, 9/14, 9/23
 Heidelberg University (Germany) 9/14
 Jubilee College (IL) 9/20
 Kenyon College (OH) 9/20
 Liberia College (Africa) 9/10
 Northwestern Female College (IL) 9/28
 Notre Dame (IN) 9/2
 Oberlin College (OH) 9/7
 Oberlin Conservatory of Music (OH) 9/7
 Princeton College (NJ) 9/24
 Shantung Christian University 9/28
 Yale University 9/9
Colonna, Oddone 9/20. See also Martin V, Pope
Constance, Treaty of 9/1
Constitution, U.S. 9/25
Continental Congress 9/12
COUNCILS, CHURCH
 Barmen Synod (1934) 9/21
 Council of Chalcedon (451) 9/1
 Council of Ephesus (431) 9/10
 Council of Trent (1545-63) 9/10, 9/24
 Diet of Worms (1521) 9/21
 Second Council of Nicea (787) 9/24
 Synod of Dort (1618-19) 9/11
 Third Council of Constantinople (680-81) 9/16
 Vatican I (1869-70) 9/20, 9/24
Cowman, Charles E. 9/24
 (b. 3/13/1864) d. 9/25/1924
Cowman, Lettie 9/24, 9/25
CREEDS, CONFESSIONS
 Chalcedonian Creed (451) 9/13
Crosby, Fanny 9/15
Crummell, Alexander
 (b. 3/3/1819) d. 9/10/1898
CRUSADES
 Third Crusade (1189-92) 9/1, 9/2, 9/8

Cunningham, Tom
 (b. 2/24/1906) d. 9/3/1959

D

Dante Alighieri
 (b. 5/15 or 27/1265) d. 9/14/1321
Davidman, Joy 9/23
de Paul, St. Vincent
 (b. 4/24/1576) d. 9/27/1660
Declaration of Utrecht 9/24
DENOMINATIONS, CHRISTIAN
 African Orthodox Church 9/2
 American Lutheran Church 9/9
 Anabaptists, Swiss 9/5
 Anglicanism 9/3, 9/16
 Anglicanism, American 9/27
 Anglicanism, English 9/8, 9/20, 9/21, 9/24
 Anglicanism, High Church 9/26
 Anglicanism, Irish 9/5
 Apostolic Orthodox Catholic Church 9/17
 Assemblies of God 9/15
 Association of Evangelical Lutheran Churches 9/9
 Baptists, American 9/26, 9/28
 Baptists, English 9/27
 Bible Protestant Church 9/26
 Carpatho-Russian Greek Orthodoxy 9/19
 Catholicism 9/2
 Catholicism, American 9/3, 9/29
 Catholicism, Dutch 9/21, 9/24
 Catholicism, English 9/17
 Catholicism, French 9/19
 Catholicism, Roman 9/16
 Christian & Missionary Alliance 9/13
 Church of England 9/18, 9/27
 Church of God 9/22
 Church of God in Christ 9/8
 Church of God of Prophecy 9/13
 Church of the Brethren 9/7
 Church of the United Brethren in Christ 9/25
 Churches of Christ in the U.S. 9/12
 Congregationalism, American 9/2, 9/5, 9/14, 9/23, 9/27, 9/29
 Congregationalism, Canadian 9/23
 Disciples of Christ 9/12
 Eastern Orthodoxy 9/2, 9/16, 9/24
 Episcopal Church 9/20
 Episcopalianism, American 9/2, 9/12, 9/16
 Fellowship of Fundamental Bible Churches 9/26
 German Reformed Church 9/25, 9/29
 Huguenots, French 9/29
 International Church of the Foursquare Gospel 9/26
 Lutheran Church – Canada (LCC) 9/11
 Lutheran Church of America 9/9
 Lutheranism, American 9/17
 Lutheranism, European 9/25
 Lutheranism, German 9/6, 9/7, 9/20, 9/25
 Mennonites 9/25, 9/26
 Methodism, American 9/1, 9/2, 9/11, 9/25
 Methodism, Canadian 9/23
 Methodism, English 9/9, 9/12
 Methodist Protestant Church 9/26
 Missionary Baptists 9/8

 Moravian Brethren 9/30
 Moravians 9/19
 Moravians, English 9/10
 Nonconformity, English 9/18
 Old Catholic Church 9/24
 Oneness Pentecostalism 9/15
 Orthodox Church of Christ 9/19
 Pentecostalism, American 9/15
 Pietists 9/26
 Plymouth Brethren 9/10, 9/19
 Presbyterianism, American 9/4, 9/11, 9/23
 Presbyterianism, Scottish 9/21
 Protestant Episcopal Church 9/2
 Protestant Episcopal Church in the U.S.A. 9/27
 Puritanism, American 9/4, 9/18
 Quakerism, American 9/13
 Quakers 9/4, 9/6, 9/7, 9/26
 Reformed Church of America 9/13
 Russian Orthodoxy 9/4, 9/9, 9/16, 9/17, 9/19, 9/25, 9/30
 Salvation Army 9/3
 Shakers 9/8
 Swiss-German Reformed 9/30
 U.S. Protestant Episcopal Church 9/12
 United Society of Believers in Christ's Second Appearing 9/8
 Universalism, American 9/3
 Wesleyan tradition 9/24
Dibelius, Martin
 b. 9/14/1883 [d. 11/11/1947]
Diocletian, Roman Emperor Valerius 9/17
Divine, Father Major Jealous
 (b. ca. 1874) d. 9/10/1965
Dix, William Chatterton
 (b. 6/14/1837) d. 9/9/1898
Dodd, C[harles] H.
 (b. 4/7/1884) d. 9/22/1973
Doddridge, Phillip 9/30
Duché, Jacob 9/7
Duffield, Jr., George
 b. 9/12/1818 [d. 7/6/1888]
Dyson, Hugo 9/28

E

Edict of Milan 9/17
Edwards, Jonathan 9/11, 9/17, 9/24, 9/27
Eliot, T[homas] S.
 b. 9/26/1888 [d. 1/4/1965]
Elliott, Charlotte
 (b. 3/17/1789) d. 9/22/1871
Ellor, James
 (b. 1819) d. 9/27/1899
Embury, Philip
 b. 9/1/1728 [d. 8/1775]
Emmons, Nathanael
 (b. 4/20/1745) d. 9/23/1840
Episcopal Church
 House of Bishops 9/18
 House of Deputies 9/18

Erasmus, Desiderius 9/5, 9/21
Eskimos, Kodiak 9/25
Estienne, Robert See also Stephanus, Robert
 (b. 1503) d. 9/7/1559
Excell, Edwin O. 9/25

F

Faber, Frederick W.
 (b. 1555) d. 9/26/1626
Faraday, Michael
 b. 9/22/1791 [d. 8/25/1867]
FILMS / MOVIES
 "Boys Town" 9/6
Finney, Charles G. 9/28
FIRSTS
 American edition of the Douay Bible (1790) 9/16
 American woman ordained a Protestant minister 9/15
 American-born Roman Catholic saint 9/14
 Anglican Bishop of Eastern Equatorial Africa 9/3
 Anglican missionary bishop of Melanesia 9/20
 Associate justice of the Hawaiian Supreme Court 9/29
 Bible translated into English in America 9/12
 Bishop of Melanesia (1861) 9/20
 Bishop of the African Orthodox Church 9/2
 Cathedral in Mexico City 9/9
 Christian college in China 9/28
 College for women established in America 9/2
 Confraternity of Charity 9/27
 Continental Congress to open in prayer 9/7
 Doctor of Sacred Theology degree awarded in Americ 9/5
 English bishop to make a pilgrimage to Jerusalem 9/11
 Episcopal bishop consecrated in the United States 9/17
 Female African-American chaplain of the U.S. Navy 9/8
 Female Bishop of Worldwide Anglicanism 9/24
 Female religious leader in the American colonies 9/22
 "First lady" to institute strict Sabbath observanc 9/4
 Foreign missions society established in America 9/5
 German Dunkards in America 9/7
 German Moravian Brethren missionary to the Hottent 9/30
 Group to promote Sunday Schools 9/7
 Hawaiian newspaper 9/29
 International conference the Pocket Testament League 9/12
 Iroquois Indian to become a Christian 9/2
 Jewish U.S. Army chaplain 9/10
 Lutheran church building in America 9/4
 Lutheran pastor of an American parish 9/7
 Methodist church in the American colonies 9/1
 Methodist missionary bishop to America 9/9
 Missionary radio station in Latin America 9/13
 Moravian bishop in America 9/22
 Moravian settlement in America 9/22

Person in modern times to speak in tongues 9/15
Protestant church west of the Alleghenies 9/19
Religious weekly in the U.S. 9/4
Roman Catholic parish established in America 9/8
Roman pontiff in history to visit Ireland 9/29
Russian Orthodox Christian mission in Alaska 9/17
"Sabbath school" 9/4
Schoolhouse west of the Alleghenies 9/19
Swedish settlers to America 9/17
U.S. Settlement in Oregon 9/1
Universalist Church in the U.S. 9/3
White women to cross the American continent 9/1

Flanagan, Edward J. 9/6
Flavian, Patriarch of Constantinople (446-49) 9/13
Flechiere, De La 9/12. See also Fletcher, John William
Fletcher, John William
  b. 9/12/1729 [d. 8/14/1785]
Form Criticism 9/14, 9/20
Fort Walla Walla 9/1
Fox, William 9/7
Frankel, Rabbi Jacob 9/10
Frederick I Barbarossa, German King (1152-90) 9/1
Friedrich, Gerhard 9/23

G

Gabriel, Charles H. 9/25.
  (b. 8/18/1856) d. 9/15/1932
Geibel, Adam
  b. 9/15/1855 d. 8/3/1933
Gerstenfeld, Norman
  b. 9/1/1905 [d. 1968]
Gibeah 9/19
Gilson, Étienne H.
  (b. 6/13/1884) d. 9/19/1978
Glass, John
  b. 9/21/1695 [d. 11/2/1773]
Goupil, René
  (b. 1607) d. 9/29/1642
Grajales, Don Martin Francisco Lopez de Mendozo 9/8
Gray, James M.
  (b. 5/11/1851) d. 9/21/1935
Great Western Schism 9/20
Greatorex, Henry W.
  (b. 12/24/1813) d. 9/10/1858
Gregorian Calendar 9/3. See also CALENDARS
Gregorian chants 9/3
Gregory I (The Great), Pope (590-604) 9/3
Gregory XIII, Pope (1572-85) 9/3
Gunkel, Hermann 9/14
Gutenberg, Johannes 9/21

H

Hammarskjöld, Dag
  (b. 7/29/1905) d. 9/18/1961
Handel, Georg[e] F. 9/14
Hannington, James
  b. 9/3/1847 [d. 10/29/1885]
Harnack, Adolf 9/14
Harper, Frances Watkins
  b. 9/24/1825 [d. 2/22/1911]
Harris, Barbara C. 9/24
Harvard, John 9/23
  b. 9/1607 [d. 9/14/1638]
Hatch, Edwin
  b. 9/4/1835 [d. 11/10/1889]
Henry VIII, English King (1509-47) 9/25
HERESIES, CHRISTIAN
  Anti-Trinitarianism 9/29
  Manichaeism 9/29
  Nestorianism 9/10
Herrnhut 9/18
Herzog, Johann Jakob
  (b. 8/12/1805) d. 9/30/1882
Heschel, Abraham 9/20. See QUOTATIONS
Hildegard of Bingen
  (b. 1098) d. 11/17/1179
Hitler, Adolf 9/21
Hobart, John Henry
  (b. 9/14/1775) d. 9/12/1830
Holden, Oliver
  (b. 9/18/1765) d. 9/4/1844
  b. 9/18/1765 [d. 9/4/1844]
Holst, Gustav
  b. 9/21/1874 d. 5/25/1934
Holton, Fred B. See Wilson, Ira B.
Holy Sepulchre 9/1
Hooft, Visser 'T
  b. 9/20/1900 d. 7/4/1985
Hopkins, Samuel
  b. 9/17/1721 [d. 12/20/1803]
HOSPITALS
  St. Luke's (Philadelphia) 9/16
Hottentots 9/30
Houselander, Frances Caryll. See also QUOTATIONS
  b. 9/29/1901 [d. 10/12/1954]
Hunt, (William) Holman
  (b. 4/2/1827) d. 9/7/1910
Hus, Jan 9/22
Hutchinson, Anne 9/18, 9/22
HYMN TUNES
  CORONATION 9/4, 9/18
  CRADLE SONG 9/20
  DIADEM 9/27
  DUNCANNON 9/20
  FINLANDIA 9/20
  GABRIEL 9/15
  GEIBEL 9/15
  GLORIA PATRI 9/10
  GLORY SONG 9/15
  GREENWELL 9/20
  HANFORD 9/15
  HAPPY DAY 9/26
  HE LIFTED ME 9/15
  HIGHER GROUND 9/15
  JOY IN SERVING JESUS 9/3
  LANDAS 9/20
  MAITLAND 9/7
  MY SAVIOR'S LOVE 9/15
  NORRIS 9/23
  PAX TECUM 9/19
  POWER IN THE BLOOD 9/1
  RUTHERFORD 9/26
  SHOWALTER 9/16
  SPRING HILL 9/3
  WAY OF THE CROSS 9/15
HYMNS
  "Abide With Me: Fast Falls the Eventide" 9/4
  "Adeste Fidelis" 9/5
  "All Hail the Power of Jesus' Name" 9/4, 9/18, 9/27
  "Angels From the Realms of Glory" 9/10
  "'Are Ye Able?' Said the Master" 9/13
  "Away in a Manger" 9/20
  "Be Still, My Soul" 9/7, 9/20
  "Breathe on Me, Breath of God" 9/4
  "Burdens Are Lifted at Calvary" 9/1
  "Come, My Soul, Thou Must Be Waking" 9/9
  "Come Thou Fount of Every Blessing" 9/27
  "Count Your Blessings" 9/25
  "Dear Lord and Father of Mankind" 9/7
  "Faith of Our Fathers" 9/26
  "Glory Be to the Father" 9/10
  "Go to Dark Gethsemane" 9/10
  "Hark, Hark, My Soul" 9/26
  "Higher Ground" 9/25
  "Holy, Holy, Holy Lord, God of Hosts" 9/10
  "I Am Not Skilled to Understand" 9/20
  "I Can Hear My Savior Calling" 9/23
  "I Stand Amazed in the Presence" 9/15
  "I'm Pressing on the Upward Way" 9/15
  "In Loving Kindness Jesus Came" 9/15
  "Just As I Am" 9/22
  "Just When I Need Him Jesus is Near" 9/15
  "King of My Life, I Crown Thee Now" 9/20
  "Leaning on the Everlasting Arms" 9/16
  "Make Me a Blessing" 9/6
  "More Like the Master" 9/15
  "Must Jesus Bear the Cross Alone?" 9/7
  "My Faith Has Found a Resting Place" 9/20
  "My God, How Wonderful Thou Art" 9/26
  "My Jesus, As Thou Wilt" 9/7
  "Nearer Home" 9/4
  "No, Not One" 9/25
  "Nor Silver Nor Gold Hath Obtained My Redemption" 9/21
  "O Come, All Ye Faithful" 9/5
  "O Happy Day that Fixed My Choice" 9/26
  "One Sweetly Solemn Thought" 9/4
  "Out in the Highways and Byways of Life" 9/6
  "Peace, Perfect Peace" 9/19
  "Prayer is the Soul's Sincere Desire" 9/10
  "Ride On, Ride On in Majesty" 9/24
  "Shout the Glad Tidings" 9/16
  "Sing Praise to God Who Reigns Above" 9/7
  "Stand Up, Stand Up for Jesus" 9/12, 9/15
  "Take the Name of Jesus With You" 9/8
  "The Lord is My Shepherd" 9/10
  "The Sands of Time Are Sinking" 9/26
  "There Is a Place of Quiet Rest" 9/25
  "There's a Wideness in God's Mercy" 9/26
  "What a Friend We Have in Jesus" 9/10
  "What Child Is This?" 9/9
  "When All My Labors and Trials Are O'er" 9/15
  "Where He Leads Me" 9/23
  "Would You Be Free From Your Burden of Sin?" 9/1

I

Iconoclasm 9/24
INDIANS, AMERICAN 9/23, 9/27
  Canadian Indians 9/29
  Cayuse Indians 9/4
  Delaware Indians 9/17
  Iroquois 9/29
  Native Americans 9/23
  Seneca Indians 9/2
  U.S. Northwest Indians 9/3
Infallibility, Papal 9/24

J

Jackson, Andrew 9/11
James I, English King (1603-25) 9/26
Jeremias, Joachim
  b. 9/20/1900 d. 9/6/1979
Jerome, St.
  (b. 345) d. 9/30/420
Jogues, Isaac 9/29
John Paul I, Pope (1978) 9/29
John Paul II, Pope (1978-) 9/29
"Johnny Appleseed" 9/26
Jones, Clarence W.
Jones, Lewis E.
  (b. 2/8/1865) d. 9/1/1936
Joseph of Volokolamsk
  (b. 1439/40) d. 9/9/1515
JUDAISM
  Frankel, Rabbi Jacob 9/10
  Reformed Judaism 9/1
  Spanish Jews 9/16
  Wiesel, Elie[zer] 9/30
Judson, Adoniram 9/1
Judson, Sarah Hall Boardman
  (b. 11/4/1803) d. 9/1/1845
Julian Calendar 9/3. See also CALENDARS
Julius III, Pope (1550-55) 9/10

SEPTEMBER INDEX

K

Key, Francis Scott 9/21
Kirkpatrick, William J. 9/25
   (b. 2/27/1838] d. 9/20/1921
Kittel, Gerhard
   b. 9/23/1888 [d. 7/11/1948]
Kittel, Rudolf 9/23

L

LaBerge, Philemon 9/15
Lambarene Hospital 9/4
Larson, Reuben E.
   b. 9/13/1897 [d. 11/17/1981]
Latin Fathers 9/30
Laubach, Frank C. See also QUOTATIONS
   b. 9/2/1884 [d. 6/11/1970]
Laubach Method 9/2
Lee, Ann
   (b. 2/29/1736) d. 9/8/1784
Lee, Jesse
   (b. 3/12/1758) d. 9/12/1816
Leo I, Pope (640-61) 9/13, 9/29
Leo VI, Byzantine Emperor (886-912)
   b. 9/19/866 [d. 5/11/912]
Leo's Tome 9/13
LeSourd, Leonard E. 9/27
Lewis, C. S.
   9/2, 9/16, 9/18, 9/28. See also QUOTATIONS
Lewis, Warren 9/28
Liguori, Alphonsus St. Maria dé
   b. 9/27/1696 [d. 8/1/1787]
Lincoln, Abraham 9/1, 9/5, 9/25. See also QUOTATIONS
Lindsay, Vachel 9/26
Lionheart. See Richard I, English King
Lorenz Publishing Co. 9/6
Luciani, Albino 9/29. See also John Paul I, Pope
Luther, Martin 9/13, 9/21, 9/22. See also QUOTATIONS
Lyte, Henry Francis 9/4

M

MacDonald, George. See also QUOTATIONS
   (b. 12/10/1824) d. 9/18/1905
Madison, James 9/17
Malan, Cesar 9/22
Marcian, Eastern Emperor (450-57) 9/1
Marlatt, Earl B.
   (b. 5/24/1892) d. 9/13/1976
Marshall, Catherine
   b. 9/27/1914 [d. 3/18/1983]
Marshall, Peter 9/27

Martin V, Pope (1417-31) 9/20
MARTYRS
   Blaurock, Georg 9/5
   Chrysostom, St. John 9/14
   Goupil, René 9/29
   Hannington, James 9/3
   Jews of Jerusalem 9/8
   Jogues, Isaac 9/29
   Patteson, John Coleridge
   Savonarola, Girolamo 9/21
   Whitman, Marcus 9/4
   Whitman, Narcissa 9/4
   Zwingli, Ulrich 9/17
Mary Tudor, English Queen (1553-58) 9/10
Mason, C[harles] H.
   b. 9/8/1866 [d. 11/17/1961]
Massachusetts Bay Colony 9/18, 9/22
Mateer, Calvin W.
   (b. 1/9/1836) d. 9/28/1908
Mateer, Julia (née Brown) 9/28
Mather, Cotton 9/5
Mather, Increase 9/5
Mayflower 9/6
McAfee, Cleland B.
   b. 9/25/1866 [d. 2/4/1944]
McFadden, Vivian 9/8
McGuffey, William Holmes
   b. 9/23/1800 [d. 5/4/1873]
McGuire, George A. 9/2
McLoughlin, John
   (b. 10/19/1784) d. 9/3/1857
McPherson, Aimee Semple
   (b. 10/9/1890) d. 9/26/1944
Medici, Giulio de
   (b. 5/26/1478) d. 9/25/1534
Meynell, Alice
   b. 9/22/1847 [d. 11/27/1922]
Meynell, Wilfrid 9/22
Michelangelo 9/10
Middle Ages 9/19
Milman, Henry Hart
   (b. 2/10/1791) d. 9/24/1868
MISSION AGENCIES
   Catholic Missions 9/7
   China Inland Mission 9/9
   East End Juvenile Mission (1868) 9/19
   Pocket Testament League 9/12
   Rescue missions 9/11
MISSIONARIES
   Andrews, Lorrin 9/29
   Asbury, Francis 9/12
   Bennett, Belle Harris 9/11
   Boardman, George Dana 9/1
   Brainerd, David 9/23, 9/27
   Brebeuf, John 9/2
   Campanius, Johan (John)
   Carey, William 9/13
   Chase, Philander 9/20

   Coke, Thomas 9/9
   Cowman, Charles E. 9/24, 9/25
   Cowman, Lettie 9/24, 9/25
   Crummell, Alexander 9/10
   Goupil, René 9/29
   Hannington, James
   Judson, Adoniram 9/1
   Judson, Sarah Hall Boardman 9/1
   Larson, Reuben E.
   Laubach, Frank 9/2
   Laubach, Frank C. 9/2
   Martyn, Henry 9/8
   Mateer, Calvin W. 9/28
   Moravians, German 9/18
   Moravians in Ohio 9/19
   Morrison, Robert 9/7
   Mühlenberg, Henry Melchior 9/6
   Patrick, St. 9/10
   Patteson, John Coleridge 9/20
   Schaeffer, Francis 9/4
   Schereschewsky, Samuel Isaac Joseph
   Schmidt, Georg 9/30
   Schweitzer, Albert 9/4
   Silva, Juan de 9/23
   Spalding, Eliza 9/1
   Spalding, Henry H. 9/1
   Spangenberg, Augustus G.
   Teresa of Calcutta, Mother 9/5
   Vasey, Thomas 9/1
   Wesley, John 9/1
   Whatcoat, Richard 9/1
   Whitman, Marcus 9/1, 9/4
   Whitman, Narcissa 9/1, 9/4
MISSIONS, CHRISTIAN
   ABCFM (American Board of Commissioners) 9/5
   Oriental Missionary Society 9/25
   Pacific Garden Mission (Chicago) 9/11
   Society for Propagation of the Gospel 9/29
   World Vision International 9/6
Moffatt, James 9/18
MONASTERIES / CONVENTS
   Monastery of Volokolamsk 9/9
Monothelite Controversy 9/16
Montgomery, James 9/10
Moody, D. L. 9/28
Moore, John M.
   b. 9/1/1925
Morgan, William
   (b. ca. 1545) d. 9/10/1604
Morrison, Robert 9/7
MOVEMENTS, CHRISTIAN
   American revival movement 9/25
   Arminianism 9/12, 9/17, 9/23
   Calvinism, Dutch 9/11
   Fundamentalism 9/4, 9/18, 9/26
   "God is dead" movement 9/28
   Holiness 9/13, 9/14, 9/22
   International Peace Mission Movement (1919) 9/10
   Modernism 9/6
   Oneness Pentecostalism 9/15

   Oxford Movement 9/5, 9/9, 9/16
   Pietism, German 9/7
   Social Gospel Movement 9/28
   Sunday School movement 9/4
Mueller, Friedrich 9/21
Mühlenberg, Henry Melchior 9/16
   b. 9/6/1711 [d. 10/7/1787]
Mühlenberg, William A.
   b. 9/16/1796 [d. 4/8/1877]
Müller, George
   b. 9/27/1805 [d. 3/10/1898]
Murray, John
   (b. 12/10/1741) d. 9/3/1815
MUSIC, ORCHESTRAL
   "The Hymn of Jesus" 9/21
MUSIC, VOCAL
   "The Messiah" 9/14
   "The Star Spangled Banner" 9/21
Muslims 9/16
Mwanga, African King 9/3

N

Nakada, Juji
   (b. 10/29/1870) d. 9/24/1939
National Anthem, U.S. 9/21
National Association of Evangelicals 9/21
National Religious Broadcasters 9/21
Navy, U.S. 9/8
Nazijsm, German 9/21
New Towne College. See Harvard College
Newman, John Henry 9/9, 9/26
NEWSPAPERS
   "Baltimore American" 9/21
   "Washington Chronicle" 9/5
NICKNAMES / TITLES
   "Borden of Yale" 9/9
   "Creator of the modern Italian language" 9/14
   "Father of American Lutheranism" 9/6
   "Father of Modern Missions" 9/18
   "Father of Modern English Unitarianism" 9/22
   "Father of Oregon" 9/3
   "Johnny Appleseed" 9/26
   "Little Flower of Jesus" 9/30
   Patron saint of all charitable works 9/27
   "Sibyl of the Rhine" 9/17
Niebuhr, H[elmut] Richard
   b. 9/3/1894 [d. 7/5/1962]
Niebuhr, Reinhold 9/3
Niemoeller, Martin 9/21
Nobel Peace Prize 9/5
Norris, J[ohn] Frank
   b. 9/18/1877 [d. 8/20/1952]
Norris, John S.
   (b. 12/4/1844) d. 9/23/1907
Nouwen, Henri J. M. 9/10. See also QUOTATIONS
   (b. 1/24/1932) d. 9/21/1996
Numinous, The 9/25

O

Oakeley, Frederick
b. 9/5/1802 d. 1/29/1880]
Oatman, Johnson, Jr.
(b. 4/21/1856) d. 9/25/1922
Olier, Jean-Jacques
b. 9/20/1608 [d. 4/2/1657]
Oliver Cromwell 9/22
Opperman, Daniel C. O.
(b. 7/13/1872) d. 9/15/1926
Ordination of women 9/16
Oregon Territory 9/4
ORGANIZATIONS, CHRISTIAN
   American Bible Society 9/15
   American Sunday School Union (1824) 9/7
   Bible Study Union 9/2
   Evangelical Teacher Training Association 9/21
   Flint River Association 9/26
   Massachusetts Missionary Society 9/23
   National Association of Evangelicals 9/21
   National Baptist Convention 9/28
   National Religious Broadcasters 9/21
   Pacific Garden Mission (Chicago) 9/15
   Pre-Raphaelite Brotherhood (1848) 9/7
   Protestant Episcopal Theological Society (1806) 9/12
   Rodeheaver Publishing Co. 9/15
   Sunday School Society 9/7
   Suwanee Association 9/26
   Women's Christian Temperance Union (WCTU) 9/28
   World Baptist Fellowship 9/18
   World Council of Churches 9/20
   World's Alliance of Y.M.C.A.'s 9/20
   Y.M.C.A. 9/1, 9/20
Otterbein, Philip William 9/25
Otto, Rudolf
b. 9/25/1869 [d. 3/6/1937]
Ozman, Agnes N.
b. 9/15/1870 [d. 11/29/1937]

P

Pacific Garden Mission 9/15
PAINTINGS
   "The Light of the World" 9/7
Palestrina, Giovanni P. 9/10
PAPAL DECREES
   "Divino afflante spiritu" (1943) 9/30
   "Mysterium fidei" 9/3
   "On the Most Opportune Way to Promote Biblical Study 9/13
   "Pascendi dominici gregis" (1907) 9/6
   "Regimini militantis ecclesiae" (1540) 9/27
Parham, Charles 9/15
Pastorius, Francis Daniel
b. 9/26/1651 d. 9/27/1719]
Pastors' Emergency League 9/21
Patmore, Coventry 9/22
Patrick, St. 9/10

Patteson, John Coleridge
(b. 4/1/1827) d. 9/20/1871
Paul III, Pope (1534-49) 9/27
Paul VI, Pope (1963-78) 9/3, 9/14
Péguy, Charles Pierre
(b. 1/7/1873) d. 9/5/1914
Pentecost, George F.
b. 9/23/1843 [d. 1920]
PERIODICALS
   "Brownson's Quarterly Review 9/16
   "Youth's Companion" 9/8
Phillips, J[ohn] B.
b. 9/16/1906 [d. 1982]
Photius, Greek Patriarch (858-86) 9/19
Pierce, Robert W.
(b. 10/8/1914) d. 9/6/1978
Pike, James A.
(b. 2/14/1913) d. 9/2/1969
Pius X, Pope (1903-14) 9/6
Pius XII, Pope (1939-58) 9/30
"Pledge of Allegiance" 9/8
Polk, James K. 9/4
Polk, Sarah Childress
b. 9/4/1803 [d. 8/14/1891]
POPES
   Adrian I (772-95) 9/24
   Adrian IV (1154-59) 9/1
   Alexander VI (1492-1503) 9/1
   Celestine I (422-32) 9/10
   Clement VII (1523-34) 9/9, 9/25
   Clement VII, Antipope (1378-94) 9/20
   Gregory I (The Great) (590-604) 9/3
   Gregory XIII (1572-85) 9/3
   John Paul I (1978) 9/29
   John Paul II (1978-) 9/29
   Julius III (1550-55) 9/10
   Leo I (640-61) 9/13, 9/29
   Martin V (1417-31) 9/20
   Paul III (1534-49) 9/27
   Paul VI (1963-78) 9/3, 9/14
   Pius X (1903-14) 9/6
   Pius XII (1939-58) 9/30
   Urban VI (1378-89) 9/20
PRESIDENTS, U.S.
   Jackson, Andrew 9/11
   Lincoln, Abraham (1861-65) 9/1, 9/5, 9/25
Provoost, Samuel 9/17
(b. 3/11/1742) d. 9/6/1815
Pusey, E[dward] B.
(b. 8/22/1800) d. 9/16/1882

Q

Quarles, Francis
(bapt. 5/8/1592) d. 9/8/1866
QUOTATIONS
   Asbury, Francis 9/12
   Barth, Karl 9/13
   Benedict XV, Pope 9/15
   Bonar, Andrew 9/8, 9/9, 9/11, 9/13, 9/23, 9/25

   Brainerd, David 9/23, 9/27
   Duché, Jacob 9/7
   Glarean 9/5
   Gurney, Eliza P. 9/4
   Houselander, Caryll 9/10, 9/17, 9/23, 9/30
   Jackson, Andrew 9/11
   Laubach, Frank 9/2
   Lewis, C. S. 9/2, 9/13, 9/23, 9/30
   Lincoln, Abraham 9/4
   Locke, John 9/7
   Luther, Martin 9/18, 9/24, 9/27, 9/28, 9/30
   MacDonald, George 9/1, 9/7, 9/26, 9/30
   Martyn, Henry 9/8
   Merton, Thomas 9/11
   Newton, John 9/1, 9/3, 9/4, 9/6, 9/14, 9/17, 9/18, 9/21, 9/28
   Nouwen, Henri J. M. 9/2, 9/3, 9/10, 9/11, 9/15, 9/16, 9/18, 9/19, 9/20, 9/24
   Schaeffer, Francis 9/6
   Schmemann, Alexander 9/4, 9/9, 9/12, 9/16, 9/19, 9/20, 9/26, 9/30
   Smith, Hannah Whitall 9/2, 9/3, 9/6, 9/6, 9/13, 9/14
   U.S. Constitution 9/17
   Underhill, Evelyn 9/22
   Wesley, John 9/1, 9/13, 9/15, 9/22, 9/24, 9/25, 9/28, 9/29
   Whitefield, George 9/19, 9/29

R

RADIO BROADCASTING
   HCJB (Quito, Ecuador) 9/13
   "Unshackled" 9/15
Raikes, Robert 9/7
b. 9/14/1735 [d. 4/5/1811]
Redpath, Henry A. 9/4
RELIGIOUS ORDERS, CATHOLIC
   Benedictines 9/17
   Carmelite nuns 9/30
   Confraternity of Charity 9/27
   Congregation of the Mission 9/27
   Congregation of the Most Holy Redeemer 9/27
   Daughters of Charity 9/27
   Dominicans 9/16, 9/21
   Jesuits 9/2, 9/7, 9/10, 9/14, 9/29
   Lazarists 9/27
   Missionaries of Charity 9/5
   Redemptorists 9/27
   Sisters of Charity of St. Joseph 9/14
   Sulpicians 9/20
   Trappists 9/11, 9/21
Rescue missions 9/11
Ricci, Matteo 9/7
Richard I, English King (1189-99) 9/1
b. 9/8/1157 [d. 4/6/1199]
Rimbault, Edward F.
(b. 6/13/1816) d. 9/26/1876
Robert of Geneva 9/20
Robertson, A[rchibald] T.
(b. 11/6/1863) d. 9/24/1934

Robinson, Robert
b. 9/27/1735 [d. 6/9/1790]
Rodeheaver Music Co. 9/3
Rolle, Richard
(b. ca. 1295) d. 9/29/1349

S

Saladin of Damascus 9/1
Salem Witch Trials 9/22
Savonarola, Girolamo
b. 9/21/1452 [d. 5/23/1498]
Schaff, Philip 9/30
Schereschewsky, Samuel Isaac Joseph
(b. 5/6/1831) d. 9/15/1906
Schmidt, Georg
b. 9/30/1709 [d. 8/2/1785]
Schütz, Johann Jakob
b. 9/7/1640 [d. 5/22/1690]
Schweitzer, Albert
(b. 1/14/1875) d. 9/4/1965
Scott, John W. 9/4
Scriven, Joseph M.
b. 9/10/1819 [d. 8/10/1886]
Seabury, Samuel 9/17
SECTS, CHRISTIAN
   Glassite Church 9/21
   Swedenborgianism 9/26
   Unitarianism 9/15, 9/23, 9/26
   Universalism 9/4, 9/23, 9/30
SEMINARIES / BIBLE COLLEGES
   Bethel Bible College (KS) 9/15
   General Theological Seminary 9/12
   McCormick Theological Seminary (IL) 9/25
   Moody Bible Institute 9/21
   Scarritt Bible and Training School 9/11
   Southern Baptist Seminary (KY) 9/24
   Union Seminary (NY) 9/11
   University of Chicago Divinity School 9/28
   Yale Divinity School 9/3
SERMONS
   "Expect Great Things from God; Attempt Great Things for God" 9/13
Servetus, Michael
b. 9/29/1511 [d. 10/27/1553]
Seton, Elizabeth Ann Bayley 9/14
Shelekov, Grigorii I. 9/25
Showalter, A[nthony] J.
(b. 5/1/1858) d. 9/16/1924
Sibelius, Jean Julius Christian
(b. 12/8/1865) d. 9/20/1957
Silva, Juan de 9/23
Simeon, Charles
b. 9/24/1759 [d. 11/13/1836]
Society for Propagation of the Gospel 9/29
Spalding, Eliza 9/1
Spalding, Henry H. 9/1
Spangenberg, Augustus G. 9/22
(b. 7/15/1704) d. 9/18/1792

SEPTEMBER INDEX

Spanish Inquisition 9/16
Spener, Philip 9/7
Stephanus. See also Estienne, Robert
Stoddard, Solomon 9/11
   b. 9/27/1643 [d. 2/11/1729]
Sunday, Billy 9/5
Sunday, Ma 9/5. See also Thompson, Helen
Sunday Schools 9/14
Supreme Court, Hawaiian 9/29
Sweney, John R. 9/25
SYNAGOGUES
   Washington Hebrew Congregation 9/1

T

Tenison, Thomas
   b. 9/29/1636 [d. 12/14/1715]
Tennant, Frederick R.
   b. 9/1/1866 [d. 9/9/1957]
Teresa of Calcutta, Mother
   (b. 8/27/1910) d. 9/5/1997
Thérèse of Lisieux, St.
   (b. 1/2/1873) d. 9/30/1897
Thirty-Nine Articles 9/9
Thompson, Francis 9/22
Thompson, Helen 9/5. See also Sunday, Billy

Thomson, Charles 9/12
Titus, Roman General 9/8
Tolkien, J[ohn] R. R. 9/28
   (b. 1/3/1892) d. 9/2/1973
Tolstoi, Leo Nikolaevich
   b. 9/9/1828 [d. 11/20/1910]
Tomlinson, A[mbrose] J. 9/13
   b. 9/22/1865 [d. 10/2/1943]
Torkillus, Reorus
   (b. 1599) d. 9/7/1643
Torquemada, Tomás de
   (b. 1420) d. 9/16/1498
Tracy, Spencer 9/6
Trench, Richard Chenevix
   b. 9/5/1807 [d. 3/28/1886]
Trotter, Melvin E[rnest]
   (b. 5/16/1870) d. 9/11/1940
Tyng, Dudley A. 9/12

U

Underground Railroad 9/24
Unitarianism 9/23
United Nations 9/18
Universalism 9/23
Urban VI, Pope (1378-89) 9/20
Ussher, James 9/8

V

Vasey, Thomas 9/1
Vatican I Ecumenical Council 9/20
Venn, Henry 9/22
Vincent, Charles J.
   b. 9/19/1852 [d. 2/28/1934]
Vincent, Marvin R.
   b. 9/11/1834 [d. 8/18/1922]

W

WARS
   American Revolutionary War 9/12, 9/27
   Civil War, U.S. 9/23
   Franco-Prussian War 9/20
   War of 1812 (1812-15) 9/21
   World War I 9/19
   World War II (1939-45) 9/15
Weigle, Luther A.
   b. 9/11/1880 [d. 9/2/1976]
Wenceslas, Bohemian King
   (b. ca. 907) d. 9/28/929or935
Wesley, Charles 9/12
Wesley, John 9/1, 9/2, 9/12. See also QUOTATIONS
Whatcoat, Richard 9/1
White, William 9/17
Whitefield, George 9/27.

See also QUOTATIONS
   (b. 12/16/1714) d. 9/30/1770
Whitman, Marcus 9/1
   b. 9/4/1802 [d. 11/29/1847]
Whitman, Narcissa 9/1, 9/4
Whittier, John Greenleaf
   (b. 12/17/1807) d. 9/7/1892
Wiesel, Elie[zer]
   b. 9/30/1928
Willard, Frances E.
   b. 9/28/1839 [d. 2/18/1898]
Williams, Roger 9/18
Wilson, Ira B.
   b. 9/6/1880 [d. 4/3/1950]
Winchester, Elhanan
   b. 9/30/1751 [d. 4/18/1797]
Winkworth, Catherine 9/7
World Council of Churches 9/20
World Alliance of YMCA's 9/20

Y

YMCA 9/1, 9/20

Z

Zeisberger, David 9/19
Zinzendorf, Nicholas von 9/18
Zwingli, Ulrich 9/17

חשון HESHVAN — ALMANAC OF THE CHRISTIAN FAITH — תשרי TISHRI

~ October 1 ~

Highlights in History

366 Damasus I was elected pope. During his 18-year pontificate he helped bring about the final eclipse of Arianism, when it was condemned at the Second Council of Constantinople in 381. During his reign, Latin became the principal liturgical language in Rome, replacing Greek. Damasus also commissioned St. Jerome to compile the first authorized Latin text of the Bible (known after 382 as the Latin Vulgate).

1061 Alexander II, a student of the famed theologian Lanfranc of Bec, was elevated to the papacy. It made him the first pope to be elected by a college (i.e., committee) of cardinals.

1529 The three-day Colloquy of Marburg convened for the purpose of achieving unity between Luther, Zwingli, and other German and Swiss reformers. At this first council of Protestants, the reformers agreed on the doctrines of the Trinity, the person, death and resurrection of Christ, original sin, justification by faith, the Holy Spirit, and the sacraments. But they could not agree on the nature of the Eucharist. Whereas Luther believed Christ was spiritually present in the bread and wine, Zwingli believed the ceremony of Communion was only a symbolic memorial of Christ's death for us, and that Christ is not present in the elements — neither physically (like the Catholics taught) nor spiritually (as Lutheranism believed).

1878 The Regions Beyond Mission, an evangelical Baptist organization, opened Harley College in Ireland. The school has since trained hundreds of missionaries.

1883 In New York City, Presbyterian clergyman and religious pioneer Albert B. Simpson founded the Missionary Training College for Home and Foreign Missionaries and Evangelists. The first mission school in America, it formally opened with an enrollment of four students. In 1972 the school name was changed to Nyack College.

Notable Birthdays

1889 Birth of Ralph W. Sockman, American Methodist clergyman and poet. He was a popular New York City pastor (1916-61), and broadcast weekly sermons for 35 years. He also authored the poem which begins: *"I met God in the morning."* [d. 8/29/1970]

1904 Austin M. Farrer, Oxford biblical scholar and theologian, was born in London. He authored *Finite and Infinite* (1943) and *The Freedom of the Will* (1960). (d. 12/29/1968)

The Last Passage

1499 Death of Marsilio Ficino, 65, an Italian humanist who sought to relate Platonic thought to biblical revelation. (b. 10/19/1433)

1893 Death of Benjamin Jowett, 76, English classicist, theologian and educational reformer. A Broad Church Anglican, he became Master of Balliol College, Oxford, in 1870. Jowett's most important work was his translations of Plato and Aristotle. (b. 4/15/1817)

1915 Death of American hymnwriter Luther O. Emerson, 95. He compiled more than 70 collections of hymns, and created the harmony for the traditional Welsh melody AR HYD Y NOS ("All Through the Night"). (b. 9/29/1820)

Words for the Soul

1877 Scottish clergyman and children's novelist George MacDonald, 52, remarked in a letter: *'If all this world had grown a desert, there would only be the more stars in heaven.'*

1931 In a letter testifying to his recent religious conversion, 33-year-old British literary scholar C.S. Lewis wrote: *'I have just passed on from believing in God to definitely believing in Christ – in Christianity.'* [In 1929 Lewis had converted from agnosticism to theism.]

IN GOD'S WORD...   OT: Isaiah 62:6–65:25 ~ NT: Philippians 2:19–3:4a ~ Psalms 73:1-28 ~ Proverbs 24:13-14

ALMANAC OF THE CHRISTIAN FAITH

חשון HESHVAN

תשרי TISHRI

October 2

Highlights in History

1187 Jerusalem fell to the Moslems, led by Saladin of Damascus. This battle marked the end of the Second Crusade.

1786 The first Lutheran hymnbook in English was Johann Christoff Kunze's *A Hymn and Prayer Book for the Use of Such Lutheran Churches as Use the English Language*. Its 300 pages contained 240 hymns, 70 of which were of English origin. Kunze was the senior among the Lutheran clergy in New York State.

1792 Clergymen from twelve churches in Kettering, England met to form the Baptist Missionary Society for Spreading the Gospel Among the Heathen.  The Society was inspired by the preaching of William Carey (1761-1834), who afterward became England's first missionary to India. Individuals from the Society later also went to Ceylon, China, Palestine and Africa.

1929 The Church of Scotland and the United Free Church of Scotland reunited, ending an 86-year division. (The Free Church of Scotland was first formed in 1843 as a conservative Presbyterian splinter group which claimed historical and theological continuity with Scotland's National Church, first formed in 1560.)

1930 The International Lutheran Hour debuted on a network of 36 American radio stations, with Dr. Walter A. Maier as speaker.

Notable Birthdays

1538 St. Charles Borromeo, Archbishop of Milan (1560-84), was born in Arona, Italy. A nephew of Pope Pius IV, he was noted for his ecclesiastical reforms. Borromeo was a leader in the Counter Reformation who implemented the decisions of the Council of Trent. [d. 11/3/1584]

1805 William Cunningham, Scottish theologian, was born near Glasgow. He was one of the founders of the Free Church of Scotland, which was formed immediately following the Disruption (i.e., splintering) of the Scottish National Church (1843). [d. 12/14/1861]

1846 Samuel R. Driver, English Semitic language scholar, was born in Southampton. He was Regius Professor of Hebrew, Oxford, and co-edited the *Hebrew-English Lexicon of the Old Testament* (1891-1905) – a reference more affectionately known as *Brown-Driver-Briggs*. [d. 2/26/1914]

The Last Passage

1842 Death of William Ellery Channing, 62, American clergyman, philanthropist and abolitionist. He was the founder of American Unitarianism, and an organizer of the American Unitarian Association (1852). He exercised wide influence on social and philanthropic issues, contributed to the development of Transcendentalism and authored *The Perfect Life* (1873). (b. 4/7/1780)

1943 Death of A[mbrose] J. Tomlinson, 78, Quaker-born Pentecostal leader. A revivalist, he later founded the Church of God (now existing in several branches). (b. 9/22/1865)

Words for the Soul

1740 During one of his visits to America, English revivalist George Whitefield recorded in his journal: *'Rightly is Jesus called Immanuel: He is God not only in, but with us. Oh, that I may never provoke Him to depart from me.'*

1747 While suffering his final illness, colonial American missionary to the New England Indians David Brainerd recorded this last entry in his journal: *'My soul was this day, at turns, sweetly set on God: I longed to be with him, that I might behold his glory. I felt sweetly disposed to commit all to him... all my concerns for time and eternity.'* (Brainerd died of consumption seven days later, at the age of 29.)

IN GOD'S WORD... OT: Isaiah 66:1-24 ~ NT: Philippians 3:4b-21 ~ Psalms 74:1-23 ~ Proverbs 24:15-16

חשון ALMANAC OF THE CHRISTIAN FAITH תשרי
HESHVAN   TISHRI

~ October 3 ~

Highlights in History

1692 Colonial theologian Increase Mather published *Cases of Conscience Concerning Evil Spirits*, which soon brought an end to the executions resulting from the Salem Witch Trials this year. Subsequent published criticism of the trials included Cotton Mather's *Wonders of the Invisible World* (1692), Samuel Willard's *Miscellany Observances Respecting Witchcraft* (1693) and John Hale's *Nature of Witchcraft* (1698).

1852 In New York City, Rev. Thomas Gallaudet, an Episcopal priest, held the first church service for deaf worshipers in a small chapel at New York University. He held spoken worship services in the morning, and services using American Sign Language in the afternoon.

1875 Hebrew Union College was opened in Cincinnati, Ohio. It was the first (Reformed) Jewish college in the U.S. to train men for the rabbinate. Dr. Isaac Mayer Wise served as its first president (1875-1900).

Notable Birthdays

1802 Birth of George Ripley, American Unitarian clergyman and social reformer. A leading Transcendentalist, he founded "The Dial" (1840), helped organize the experimental Brook Farm community, and wrote as a literary critic for the "New York Tribune" (1849-80). [d. 7/4/1880]

1832 Birth of Carolina ("Lina") Sandell Berg, Swedish Lutheran hymnwriter. At age 12 she was miraculously healed of a childhood paralysis, and soon after began writing verses expressing her love and gratitude to God. She penned  over 650 hymns during her life, and came to be known as the "Fanny Crosby of Sweden." Two of her hymns still endure: "Day by Day, and With Each Passing Moment" and "Children of the Heavenly Father." [d. 7/27/1903]

The Last Passage

1226 Death of St. Francis of Assisi, about 44. Called the greatest of all Christian saints, he led a decadent early life. Recovering from a violent illness at age 25, he vowed to dedicate himself to the Church and lived the rest of his life in piety and poverty. He founded the Franciscan Order in 1209, and also wrote several hymns, including "All Creatures of Our God and King." (b. ca. 1182)

1690 Death of Robert Barclay, 41, Scottish theologian. Born near Aberdeen, he is considered the most weighty and remarkable of all early Quaker theologians. He published *An Apology for the True Christian's Divinity*, an important statement of Quaker doctrine. (b. 12/23/1648)

1919 Death of Daniel B. Towner, 69, American music teacher and hymn composer: TRUST AND OBEY ("When We Walk with the Lord"); MOODY ("Marvelous Grace of our Loving Lord"); PRICELESS ("Nor Silver Nor Gold 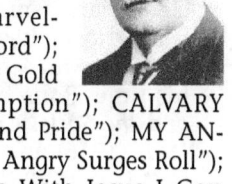 Hath Obtained My Redemption"); CALVARY ("Years I Spent in Vanity and Pride"); MY ANCHOR HOLDS ("Though the Angry Surges Roll"); and SECURITY ("Anywhere With Jesus I Can Safely Go"). (b. 3/5/1850)

Words for the Soul

1929 In a letter to an old friend, British literary scholar (and later, a Christian apologist) C. S. Lewis described a principle of education: *'So many things have now become interesting to me because at first I had to do them whether I liked them or not, and thus one is kicked into new countries where one is afterwards at home.'*

1985 Dutch Catholic mystic Henri J. M. Nouwen observed in his Road to Daybreak journal: *'When handicapped people pray for handicapped people, God comes very near.... Lord, give me a heart like these people have so that I may understand more fully the depth of your love.'*

IN GOD'S WORD...   OT: Jeremiah 1:1–2:30 ~ NT: Philippians 4:1-23 ~ Psalms 75:1-10 ~ Proverbs 24:17-20

חשון HESHVAN   ALMANAC OF THE CHRISTIAN FAITH   תשרי TISHRI

~ October 4 ~

Highlights in History

1535 The printing of the Coverdale Bible (an early English version of the Scriptures) was completed in London. (Lutheran preacher Miles Coverdale published little original material during his life, but he was a good translator.)

1867 In Southwest Africa, the Rhenish Missionary Church constituted itself as the Evangelical Lutheran Church in Southwest Africa.

1965 Paul VI arrived in New York City, making him the first pope in history to visit America. On this first day of his visit, he celebrated a mass in Yankee Stadium and addressed the United Nations on the need for world peace.

Notable Birthdays

1861 Birth of Walter Rauschenbusch, American Baptist clergyman and leader of the Social Gospel movement of the early 1900s. Considered a pioneer in applied Christianity and a shaper of American Christian thought of his time, Rauschenbusch authored *Christianity and the Social Crisis* (1907), *Social Principles of Jesus* (1916) and *A Theology for the Social Gospel* (1917). [d. 7/25/1918]

1880 Birth of Homer A. Rodeheaver, American song evangelist and hymnbook publisher. An associate of Billy Sunday's for 20 years, he composed many gospel choruses, and also established the Winona Lake Summer School of Music. [d. 12/18/1955]

1893 Birth of Walter A. Maier, American Lutheran clergyman and broadcaster. His life and ministries were diverse. During World War I, Maier served as a chaplain for German prisoners of war (1917-19). After the war, he taught Old Testament at Concordia Lutheran Seminary in St. Louis. Maier was perhaps best remembered as the dynamic speaker on the "Lutheran Hour" radio broadcast (1930-50). [d. 1/11/1950]

The Last Passage

1582 Death of Teresa of Avila, 67, Spanish Carmelite nun, reformer and mystic. She founded a reform movement which restored the original observance of austerity to the Carmelite order. Known during her life for her practicality and administrative skills, her legacy derives more from her mysticism, as evidenced in her writings: *Autobiography*, *Way of Perfection* and *Interior Castle*. (b. 3/28/1515)

1587 Death of John Foxe, 71, English Protestant clergyman, historian and martyrologist. His compilation of Christian persecutions (afterward popularly known as *Foxe's Book of Martyrs*) took eleven years to write, and was first published in English (1563) under the title, *History of the Actes and Monumentes of the Church*. Foxe's main object was to extol the heroism of the English Protestant martyrs during the reign of "Bloody" Queen Mary (1553-1558). (b. 1516)

1890 English social reformer Catherine (née Mumford) Booth, 61, died of cancer. The wife of William Booth, she played a leading role in the founding and developing of the Salvation Army. She designed the Salvation Army flag and the famous poke bonnet, and helped introduce the denomination into the U.S., Australia, Europe, India and Japan. Her dying words were: 'The waters are rising, but so am I. I am not going under but over. Do not be concerned about dying; go on living well, the dying will be right.' (b. 1/17/1829)

Words for the Soul

1530 German reformer Martin Luther declared: 'Next to theology no art is equal to music; for it is the only one, except theology, which is able to give a quiet and happy mind.... The prophets practiced music more than any art... intimately uniting theology and music, telling the truth in psalms and songs.... My love for music... has often refreshed me and set me free from great worries.'

IN GOD'S WORD...   OT: Jeremiah 2:31–4:18 ~ NT: Colossians 1:1-20 ~ Psalms 76:1-12 ~ Proverbs 24:21-22

ALMANAC OF THE CHRISTIAN FAITH

חשון HESHVAN　　תשרי TISHRI

~ October 5 ~

Highlights in History

869 The Fourth Constantinople Council opened, presided over by Pope Adrian II in the West and Emperor Basil I in the East. It was the last ecumenical council held in the East. During their six sessions, the 102 bishops in attendance condemned iconoclasm and argued over whether or not the Holy Spirit proceeded from the Son ("filioque") as well as from the Father.

1582 In Italy and several other Catholic countries, the new Gregorian Calendar went into effect, changing today's date from Oct. 5th to Oct. 15th! The decision to correct the Julian Calendar (created by Julius Caesar in 46 BC) was made by a papal commission of astronomers under Gregory XIII, who adopted a formula for providing a more accurate length of the year (i.e., 365.2422 days). It differed from the Julian calendar formula by 0.0078 of a day!

1744 David Brainerd, 26, expelled from Yale for criticizing a tutor and attending a forbidden revival meeting, began a missionary work with the Indians along New Jersey's Susquehanna River. (Brainerd would die of tuberculosis three years later, caused by the continued exposure required by his outdoor work with the Indians.)

Notable Birthdays

1703 Birth of Jonathan Edwards, considered by some the greatest theologian of American Puritanism. The fifth child and only son of eleven children, Edwards, curiously, exhibited few social graces. He was  absent-minded, deeply absorbed and introspective, and an extreme ascetic. Yet he became a leader during America's Great Awakening, and is most popularly remembered for his powerful Enfield, Connecticut sermon of 1741: "Sinners in the Hands of An Angry God." Edwards served briefly as president of the College of New Jersey (later Princeton) (1757-58). [d. 3/22/1758]

1833 Birth of William G. Tomer, American Methodist choral director. During his life he served as an American Civil War veteran, a U.S. government employee in Washington, DC (for 20 years), and as a schoolteacher during his last years. Today Tomer's name is remembered for composing the hymn tune FAREWELL ("God Be With You Till We Meet Again"). [d. 9/26/1896]

The Last Passage

1940 Death of Ballington Booth, 81, American church reformer. Born in England the second child of William Booth, he was placed in command of U.S. Salvation Army operations in 1887. Later, he became estranged from his father over the issue of the Army's authoritarian international hierarchy. In 1896 Ballington and his wife resigned from the denomination and founded the Volunteers of America, a denomination similar to the Salvation Army, but with a more democratic structure. (b. 7/28/1859)

1969 Death of Harry Emerson Fosdick, 91, American clergyman. As pastor of New York City's Riverside Baptist Church from 1926-46, he became a leading spokesman for modern liberal Protestantism, and authored several books, including *Dear Mr. Brown: Letters to a Person Perplexed about Religion* (1961). He also authored the hymn, "God of Grace and God of Glory." (b. 5/24/1878)

Words for the Soul

1544 Regarding the Sabbath, German reformer Martin Luther declared in a sermon: 'Now that our Lord has come and begun a new, eternal kingdom throughout the world, we Christians are no longer bound to such external, specific observance. On the contrary, we have the liberty to turn Monday or some other day of the week into Sunday.'

1741 English revivalist George Whitefield wrote in a letter: 'As to my own soul, it is very comfortable and composed; I feel the power of Jesus more, and the power of indwelling sin less.'

IN GOD'S WORD...　　OT: Jeremiah 4:19–6:15 ~ NT: Colossians 1:21–2:7 ~ Psalms 77:1-20 ~ Proverbs 24:23-25

October 6

HESHVAN / TISHRI — ALMANAC OF THE CHRISTIAN FAITH

Highlights in History

1520 German reformer Martin Luther published his famous writing, *Prelude on the Babylonian Captivity of the Church*, which attacked the entire sacramental system of the Catholic Church.

1683 The first Mennonites arrived in North America, at Philadelphia, on the ship "Concord." These thirteen German families founded a community they called Germantown. Their pastor, Francis Daniel Pastorious, was considered by many to be the most learned man in America at that time. They had been encouraged to come to America through the generosity of William Penn, who offered them 5,000 acres of land in Pennsylvania and freedom from religious persecution.

1979 While on a week-long American tour, John Paul II met with President Jimmy Carter in Washington, becoming the first pope ever to meet with an American president, or to visit the White House.

Notable Birthdays

1552 Birth of Matteo Ricci, Italian Jesuit missionary to China. He founded a mission in Peking. Though the number of his converts was relatively small, it included many influential Chinese scholars and families, who played key roles in the spread of Christianity in China. [d. 5/11/1610]

1816 Birth of William B. Bradbury, American music teacher, editor and publisher. He composed the music for several popular hymns, including "He Leadeth Me"; "Savior, Like a Shepherd Lead Us"; "My Hope is Built" and "Sweet Hour of Prayer." [d. 1/7/1868]

1818 Birth of Silas J. Vail, New England businessman and hymnwriter. Music was a hobby for Vail, yet he composed a number of hymn tunes during his lifetime, including CLOSE TO THEE ("Thou My Everlasting Portion"). [d. 5/20/1884]

The Last Passage

1536 Death of William Tyndale, 42, English scholar, Bible translator and reformer. His translation of the N.T. into English in 1525 became the basis for the King James Version. Tyndale was martyred in Flanders – strangled and burned at the stake for heresy. (b. ca. 1494)

1874 Death of John Ernest Bode, 58, Anglican clergyman and hymnwriter: "O Jesus, I Have Promised." (b. 2/23/1816)

1894 Death of Matthew Bridges, 94, English political and historical writer. As an Anglican-turned-Catholic, he afterward became a hymnwriter, and left to the Church: "Crown Him with Many Crowns." (b. 7/14/1800)

1945 Death of George C. Stebbins, 99, American hymn composer. He once worked closely with Dwight Moody and Ira Sankey in song ministry. He also composed many hymns, including HOLINESS ("Take Time To Be Holy"); FRIEND ("I've Found a Friend"); GREEN HILL ("There is a Green Hill Far Away"); JESUS, I COME ("Out of My Bondage, Sorrow and Night"); ADELAIDE ("Have Thine Own Way, Lord"); and "Take My Life and Let it Be." (b. 2/26/1846)

Words for the Soul

1537 German reformer Martin Luther declared in a sermon: 'The Law is a message directing me to life; and this teaching should and must be preserved. But the Law does not give me life. A hand that points out the way to me is a useful member of the body. But… the hand will not take me on the way, yet it correctly shows me the way. Just so the Law serves the purpose of indicating the will of God and of convincing us that we are unable to keep it.… The Law has been given us in order to reveal sin; but it cannot help us from sins, nor can it pull us out of them.… Then begins the cry: Oh, come, Lord Jesus Christ, help us, and grant us grace that we may be able to do what the Law requires of us.'

IN GOD'S WORD… OT: Jeremiah 6:16–8:7 ~ NT: Colossians 2:8-23 ~ Psalms 78:1-31 ~ Proverbs 24:26

ALMANAC OF THE CHRISTIAN FAITH

חשון HESHVAN   תשרי TISHRI

October 7

Highlights in History

1518 Martin Luther was interviewed by Cardinal Thomas Cajetan about his 95 theses. It soon widened into a discussion of the relation between faith and sacramental grace, and finally broke down when Cajetan dismissed Luther, telling him to cease his teachings or else recant unconditionally.

1857 Charles Spurgeon preached to his largest congregation ever, 23,654, at the Crystal Palace.

1873 Baptist missionary Lottie Moon arrived in China. This heroic woman was born into wealth, but when converted gave her whole life to missions and said, "If I had a thousand lives, I would give them all for the women of China."

Notable Birthdays

1573 William Laud, Archbishop of Canterbury (1633-45), was born. A strong opponent of Calvinism, Laud's violent measures led to the Bishops' War and the Long Parliament, which impeached him for high treason (1640), imprisoned him in the Tower of London (1641), and in the end beheaded him. [d. 1/10/1645]

1810 Birth of Henry Alford, Anglican clergyman and biblical philologist. He published a famous edition of the Greek New Testament (1849-61). Alford also penned the hymn, "Come, Ye Thankful People, Come." [d. 1/12/1871]

1832 Birth of Charles C. Converse, American hymnwriter: CONVERSE ("What a Friend We Have in Jesus"). [d. 10/18/1918]

1835 Birth of Folliott S. Pierpoint, English classical scholar and hymnwriter: "For the Beauty of the Earth." [d. 3/10/1917]

1931 Birth of Desmond M. Tutu, South African Anglican clergyman. He was the first black Anglican bishop of Johannesburg, South Africa, and was awarded the 1984 Nobel Peace Prize.

The Last Passage

1747 Death of Jonathan Dickinson, 59, Colonial American Presbyterian clergyman, theologian and educator. The author of at least 19 books, he was best known as a leader of the revivalist "New Light" Presbyterians and for his work in Christian education. In 1747, the College of New Jersey opened (in his home) to train "New Light" ministers, with Dickinson as its president. The college later changed its name to Princeton University. (b. 4/22/1688)

1772 Death of John Woolman, 52, American Quaker preacher and abolitionist. His simple and unaffected life and writings won great respect. He is best known for his *Journal*, first published in 1774. (b. 10/19/1720)

1787 Death of Henry Melchior Mühlenberg, 76, German-born religious pioneer. He organized the Lutheran Church in America, and is known today as the "Father of American Lutheranism." (b. 9/6/1711)

1925 Death of Hubert P. Main, 86, sacred music publisher and hymnologist. He continued the work of William Bradbury, as an owner/editor with the firm of Bigelow and Main. He wrote more than a thousand hymn compositions, and is still remembered for ELLESDIE ("Jesus, I My Cross Have Taken"). (b. 8/17/1839)

Words for the Soul

1877 Scottish clergyman and novelist George MacDonald remarked in a letter: 'If we can build castles of air, God can turn them into granite.'

1930 American Congregational missionary and pioneer linguist Frank C. Laubach wrote in a letter: 'Beside Jesus, the whole lot of us are so contemptible. I do not see how God stomachs us at all. But God is like Jesus, and like Jesus, He will not give up until we, too, are like Jesus.'

IN GOD'S WORD...   OT: Jeremiah 8:8–9:26 ~ NT: Colossians 3:1-7 ~ Psalms 78:32-55 ~ Proverbs 24:27

October 8

Highlights in History

451 The Council of Chalcedon opened in Asia Minor, near Istanbul (Byzantium), where over 500 bishops (the largest attendance of the early Councils) met until Nov. 1st. Convoked by the Eastern Emperor Marcian to deal with the Eutychian heresy, this fourth ecumenical council drew up a statement of faith (known afterward as the Chalcedonian Definition) and issued regulations for pastoral discipline.

1870 The Kingdom of Italy took over Rome from the pope, who was nevertheless guaranteed his sovereign powers as head of the church.

1924 In N.Y. City, the National Lutheran Conference banned the use of jazz in the local churches.

Notable Birthdays

1609 Birth of John Clarke, English-born American Baptist physician and clergyman. He obtained a royal charter for the colony of Rhode Island and, with Roger Williams, afterward took responsibility for maintaining the liberal democratic character of its institutions. [d. 4/20/1676]

1720 Birth of Jonathan Mayhew, clergyman, in Chilmark, Massachusetts. He pastored the West Church in Boston throughout his life (1747-66). Mayhew's liberalism helped foster the start of Unitarian Congregationalism. [d. 7/9/1766]

1882 Birth of Walter Russell Bowie, American Episcopal clergyman, theologian and author: *The Story of Jesus* (1938); *The Story of the Church* (1955); *The Living Story of the New Testament* (1959). Bowie taught at Union Theological Seminary (1939-50), and was an editor of "The Interpreter's Bible" project. [d. 4/23/1969]

1905 Birth of Günther Bornkamm, German biblical scholar. A student of Rudolf Bultmann, he pioneered the modern science of redaction criticism (analysis), especially of the Gospel of Matthew. Bornkamm later became a standard-bearer of the "new quest of the historical Jesus."

1927 Birth of Jim Elliot, American Plymouth Brethren missionary to Ecuador. During an attempt to make contact with the Aucas, Jim and four fellow missionaries (Nate Saint, Roger Youderian, Ed McCully and Pete Fleming) were killed by the Ecuadorean Indians they were attempting to evangelize. The story of the missionaries' deaths along the Curaray River was published the following year by Elliot's widow Elizabeth in *Through Gates of Splendor*. Elliot's most oft-quoted statement was: 'He is no fool who gives what he cannot keep to gain that which he cannot lose.' [d. 1/8/1956]

The Last Passage

1179 Death of Medieval abbess, musician and author Hildegard of Bingen, 81. Known as the "Sybil of the Rhine," her book of visions, *Scivias*, which took 10 years to complete, was a devotional masterpiece. Hildegard also pioneered a new approach to liturgical music that remains influential to this day. (b. 1098)

1772 Death of David Nitschmann, 75, the first bishop of the Renewed Moravian Church. An active pioneer missionary, Nitschmann made acquaintance with the Wesley brothers in 1735, while on a trip to America. (b. 12/27/1696)

1936 Death of Jonathan Goforth, 77, a Canadian Presbyterian who, with his wife, in 1888 became a missionary to Honan, China. He was noted for untiring evangelistic work, and for training native evangelists and preachers. (b. 2/10/1859)

Words for the Soul

1859 Scottish clergyman and biographer Andrew Bonar, 49, reflected in his journal: 'Felt this evening for a little as if speaking directly to the Holy Spirit... and asking Him to work among us. Somehow for the time I seemed nearer the Spirit than the Father and the Son, and yet I felt it was all through Jesus I had this audience.'

IN GOD'S WORD... OT: Jeremiah 10:1–11:23 ~ NT: Colossians 3:18–4:18 ~ Psalms 78:56-72 ~ Proverbs 24:28-29

October 9

Highlights in History

1596 In Poland and Lithuania, the Union of Brest-Litovsk was solemnly concluded, due in large measure to Jesuit missionaries who worked among the people and persuaded many Ruthenian bishops to seek communion with Rome. In 1595 Sigismund III, king of Poland, granted Ruthenian clergy the same rights as the Latin clergy, freed them of excommunication of the Orthodox patriarch of Constantinople, and allowed them to keep their property and Byzantine liturgy. The Union was later solemnized by Pope Clement VIII.

1845 Former Anglican John Henry Newman, a leader of the Oxford tractarian movement, left the Church of England, and was formally received into the Catholic Church.

1976 Delegates to the American Lutheran Church convention in Washington agreed to delete most references to gender in official church documents.

Notable Birthdays

1755 Birth of Richard Furman, considered by some the most important Baptist leader of the antebellum South. An aristocratic slave owner, in 1822 he wrote the classic Southern biblical defense of slavery. Furman University in Greenville, SC was named for him. [d. 8/25/1825]

1890 Birth of Aimee Semple McPherson, the colorful Canadian-born American evangelist who founded the International Church of the Foursquare Gospel (1918). Her ministry was characterized by a dramatic preaching style, and by an optimistic Fundamentalism. Aimee opened her flagship church, Angelus Temple in Los Angeles, in 1923. [d. 9/27/1944]

1909 (Frederick) Donald Coggan, English prelate, was born in London. As the Archbishop of Canterbury (1974-80), Coggan was a leading spokesman for the ecumenical movement in the Church of England. [d. 5/17/2000]

The Last Passage

1253 Death of Robert Grossteste, 85, English clergyman and theologian. Called a "harbinger of the Reformation," Grossteste was a reform-minded bishop who was a strong supporter of the Franciscans, and exerted an influence on John Wyclif. (b. ca. 1168)

1555 Death of Justus Jonas, 62, German Protestant Reformer and scholar. He translated the German works of Luther and Melanchthon into Latin, and their Latin works into German. (b. 6/5[or 6]/1493)

1747 Death of David Brainerd, 29, Presbyterian missionary (1743-47) to Native Americans along the Hudson Valley. Expelled from Yale for attending a revival meeting, Brainerd became famous only after his death, when his intended father-in-law Jonathan Edwards published *Brainerd's Journal*. The diary inspired countless others to become missionaries. (b. 4/20/1718)

1940 Death of Sir Wilfred Grenfell, 75, English-born medical missionary to Labrador, Newfoundland. He built hospitals and schools, and fitted out the first hospital ship to serve fishermen in the North Sea. Grenfell supported many of his labors with his writings. (b. 2/28/1865)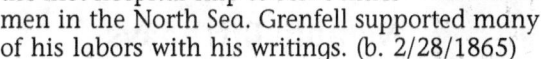

1974 Death of Czech-born German businessman Oskar Schindler, 66, who was credited with saving over 2,000 Jews during the Holocaust. Although a strong Catholic, at his own request Schindler was buried in Jerusalem. (b. 4/28/1908)

Words for the Soul

1740 English revivalist George Whitefield, during one of his early visits to America, recorded in his journal: *'Oh, how comfortable is sleep after working for Jesus! Lord, strengthen me yet a little longer, and then let me sleep in Thee, never to awake in this vain world again.'*

IN GOD'S WORD... OT: Jeremiah 12:1–14:10 ~ NT: 1 Thessalonians 1:1–2:8 ~ Psalms 79:1-13 ~ Proverbs 24:30-34

ALMANAC OF THE CHRISTIAN FAITH

חשון HESHVAN
תשרי TISHRI

~ October 10 ~

Highlights in History

732 Charles Martel met the Islamic invaders in France between Poiters and Tours, in a battle that lasted as many as seven days. The Arabs suffered heavy losses and their Muslim leader, Abd-ar-Rahman, was killed. Europe would remain Christian territory.

1802 The first Ashkenazic Jewish congregation in America, Rodeph Shalom ("Seeker of Peace") was established in Philadelphia. (Jews from Ashkenoz, the Hebrew word for Germany, are those whose families originated in Central and Eastern Europe. Sephardic Jews, whose name derives from Sfard, the Hebrew word for Spain, originated in Spain and Portugal.)

1821 Twenty-nine-year-old American law student Charles Finney was dramatically converted in the woods, near his home. He immediately abandoned his law career and went on to become one of America's great revivalists, credited with the conversion of 500,000 souls.

1863 In Baltimore, the building was purchased for the first Catholic parish church for African-Americans. Four months later, on Feb. 21, 1864, St. Francis Xavier's Church was dedicated.

Notable Birthdays

1560 Birth of Dutch Reformed clergyman James (Jacob) Arminius. As professor at Leiden (1603-09), he could not accept the strict Calvinist teaching on predestination, and instead developed a doctrine of universal redemption and conditional predestination. Arminian theology, named after him, is evident today in Methodist doctrine. [d. 10/19/1609]

1610 French Jesuit Gabriel Lalemant was born. While serving as a missionary to the Hurons in Canada, he was captured (along with St. Jean de Brebeuf) and killed by Iroquois Indians. Lalemant was canonized with six other North American martyrs in 1930. [d. 3/17/1649]

1793 Birth of Harriet ("Nancy") Atwood, pioneer Congregational missionary. The wife of Samuel Newell, she set sail for India with him, along with Adoniram Judson and his wife Ann, in Feb. 1812, making Harriet and Ann the first American women missionaries abroad. Harriet died later that same year at age 19, making her also the first American missionary to die in service on a foreign field. [d. 11/30/1812]

The Last Passage

1903 Death of Emma (née Revell) Moody, 61, Baptist wife of American Congregationalist evangelist Dwight L. Moody. Born in London of Huguenot stock, Emma's family emigrated to Chicago in 1849. She married Moody in 1862, when she was 20 and he 25. (b. 1842)

1958 Death of George Bennard, 85, American evangelist. Converted at 16, he married and served as a worker in the Salvation Army. Several years later he became a Methodist evangelist, preaching mostly in the North Central U.S. and Canada. Bennard is still remembered today for his hymns, "Sweet Songs of Salvation" and "Old Rugged Cross" (for years acknowledged to be America's favorite gospel song). (b. 2/4/1873)

Words for the Soul

1741 English revivalist George Whitefield, 26, clarified in a letter to John Wesley: *'Though I hold [i.e., believe in] particular election, yet I offer Jesus freely to every individual soul. You may carry sanctification to what degrees you will, only I cannot agree that the in-being of sin is to be destroyed in this life.'*

1960 In a letter to the National Conference of Christians and Jews, President John Kennedy wrote: *'Tolerance implies no lack of commitment to one's own beliefs. Rather it condemns the oppression or persecution of others.'*

IN GOD'S WORD... OT: Jeremiah 14:11–16:13 ~ NT: 1 Thessalonians 2:9–3:13 ~ Psalms 80:1-19 ~ Proverbs 25:1-5

חשון HESHVAN — ALMANAC OF THE CHRISTIAN FAITH — תשרי TISHRI

~ October 11 ~

Highlights in History

1521 Pope Leo X bestowed upon England's Henry VIII the title, "Fidei Defensor" (Defender of the Faith), in recognition of a work on the seven sacraments Henry had published against Martin Luther. (Thirteen years later Henry separated the Church of England from Rome, outraged because the pope would not annul his marriage to Catherine of Aragon.)

POPE LEO X

1962 Pope John XXIII opened the first session of the Vatican II Ecumenical Council. (The session lasted until Dec. 8th). Three more sessions followed during the next three years. These were led by John's successor Paul VI, with a total of 2,860 priests participating in the discussions.

1998 John Paul II decreed the first Jewish-born saint of the modern era, Edith Stein (b. 10/12/1891). A German Carmelite nun and spiritual writer, she was arrested by the Nazis because of her Jewish ancestry, and executed on Aug. 10, 1942 in the gas chambers of Auschwitz.

Notable Birthdays

1585 Birth of Johann Heermann, a Silesian clergyman who is regarded by some as the greatest hymnwriter between Martin Luther and Paul Gerhardt. He authored many sacred songs, including "Ah, Holy Jesus, How Hast Thou Offended." [d. 2/17/1647]

1792 Antoine Blanc, Catholic prelate, was born in France. He came to the U.S. in 1817, became Archbishop of New Orleans (1851-60), and founded the Sisters of the Holy Family, the first American black sisterhood. [d. 6/20/1860]

1863 Birth of James H. Moulton, English Methodist Greek and Iranian scholar. He is best remembered for his *Grammar of New Testament Greek* (1906-19), and (with George Milligan) *Vocabulary of the Greek Testament* (1914-15). [d. 4/7/1917]

The Last Passage

1424 Death of Bohemian general Jan Zizka, who fought to prevent Catholics from restoring their rule over his land. His army of Taborites fought using farm wagons mounted with movable cannon – an early conception of the tank. A victor in battle, Zizka succumbed to the plague.

1531 Death of Swiss Reformer Ulrich Zwingli, 47, the most important figure in the Swiss Reformation. He began preaching Biblical-centered Christianity in 1520. He was killed during the Battle of Kappel (fought between the Catholic and Protestant cantons of Switzerland), while serving as a chaplain for the Army of Zurich. His death brought a swift close to the Swiss religious wars. (Like Luther, Zwingli taught the authority of Scripture, but applied its principles more militantly.) (b. 1/1/1484)

1852 Death of Hugh Bourne, 80, English-born Methodist clergyman. He was co-founder in 1840 of the Primitive Methodist Church. (b. 4/3/1772)

Words for the Soul

1523 German reformer Martin Luther clarified in a letter written to a Christian congregation in Esslingen: *'This is the chief article and foundation of Christian doctrine: We are unable to atone for sin or to blot it out by our works; but we believe that Christ has atoned for it with His blood. This faith, without any works, blots out sin.'*

1746 American colonial missionary to the Indians David Brainerd recorded in his journal: *'O how precious is time! And how guilty it makes me feel, when I think that I have trifled away and misimproved or neglected to fill up each part of it with duty, to the utmost of my ability and capacity!'*

1954 American Presbyterian apologist Francis Schaeffer wrote in a letter: *'Doctrinal rightness and rightness of ecclesiastical position are important, but only as a starting point to go on into a living relationship – and not as ends in themselves.'*

IN GOD'S WORD... OT: Jeremiah 16:14–18:23 ~ NT: 1 Thessalonians 4:1–5:3 ~ Psalms 81:1-16 ~ Proverbs 25:6-7

חשון HESHVAN   ALMANAC OF THE CHRISTIAN FAITH   תשרי TISHRI

~ October 12 ~

Highlights in History

1762 The Association of Philadelphia Baptists voted to establish a college in Warren, Rhode Island. Incorporated in 1764 as Rhode Island College, the campus moved to Providence in 1770. In 1804 it became Brown University.

1971 "Jesus Christ, Superstar," by Andrew Lloyd Webber and Tim Rice, debuted on Broadway, starring Jeff Fenholt, Ben Vereen and Yvonne Elliman. The rock musical created an uproar because it implied that Christ was just a man.

Notable Birthdays

1883 Birth of Carl H. Lowden, American Evangelical and Reformed composer. He spent over 60 years working in various branches of sacred music, also serving 28 years as minister of music at the Linden Baptist Church  of Camden, NJ. His most enduring hymn tunes are GENEVA ("God, Who Touchest Earth with Beauty") and LIVING ("Living for Jesus A Life That is True"). [d. 2/27/1963]

1954 Birth of Amy Eilberg, who in 1985 became the first woman to be ordained a rabbi in Conservative Judaism. Born in Philadelphia, she was ordained during graduation ceremonies at Jewish Theological  Seminary in NY City. (Paula Ackerman was appointed 1/26/1951 as the first female rabbi in the Reform movement, to serve in place of her late husband as rabbi of Temple Beth Israel in Meridian, MS. The first woman to be ordained a Reform rabbi was Sally Jane Priesand, who was ordained on 6/3/1972 in the Isaac M. Wise Temple, in Cincinnati.)

The Last Passage

1864 Death of Roger B. Taney, 87, American lawyer and judge. He became the first Roman Catholic member of a presidential cabinet, when appointed Attorney General (1831-33) and Secretary to the Treasury (1833-34) by President Andrew Jackson. Taney was later appointed the first Catholic justice to the U.S. Supreme Court (1836-64). (b. 3/17/1777)

1881 Death of Josiah G. Holland, 62, American novelist and author of the Christmas carol, "There's a Song in the Air." Holland helped found "Scribner's Magazine" (1870), and served as its editor the rest of his life. (b. 7/24/1819)

1895 Death of Cecil Frances Alexander, Irish poet and hymnwriter. She was married to William Alexander, an Irish clergyman who became Primate of Ireland in 1893. During her life Mrs. Alexander published  several volumes of verse. Three of her poems later became popular hymns: "All Things Bright and Beautiful"; "Jesus Calls Us"; and "There is a Green Hill Far Away." (b. 1818/1823)

Words for the Soul

1534 German reformer Martin Luther coined the following analogy in a sermon: *'Where these two teachings, the Law and the Gospel, stay bright and clear... there the sun and the moon, the two great lights which God has created to rule the day and the night, send forth their rays.... Without the Gospel the Law is ugly and terrible. But when the sun shines on the moon, the moon has a bright, white light.... When these two lights are gone, nothing but night and blindness and darkness prevail.'*

1865 Twelve months after the illness and death of Isabella, his wife of 17 years, Scottish clergyman and biographer Andrew Bonar, 55, reflected in his diary: *'Saw my sorrow like a piece of a wreck upon the shore, and then came a glow of joy from the Lord, and I saw that He could make the tide rise and fill the shore so that fragments of the past might be absorbed in it.'*

1949 American missionary and martyr Jim Elliot noted in his journal: *'For my generation I must have the oracles of God in fresh terms.'*

IN GOD'S WORD...   OT: Jeremiah 19:1–21:14 ~ NT: 1 Thessalonians 5:4-28 ~ Psalms 82:1-8 ~ Proverbs 25:8-10

October 13

Highlights in History

539 BC The allied armies of Cyrus the Great of Persia captured Babylon, thereby gaining control of much of the Near East. (Babylon, under Nebuchadnezzar, was the former military power which had taken Judah (Israel) into exile, between 606 BC and 586 BC (cf. 2 Kings 25).

1534 Paul III was named pope, serving until 1549. A patron of the arts, he retained Michelangelo to work on the Vatican. Paul also excommunicated Henry VIII of England (1538); approved the Jesuit order (1540); called the Council of Trent (1545); reorganized the Curia and the Sacred College; and introduced the Inquisition into Italy.

POPE PAUL III

1670 In Virginia, slavery was banned for Negroes who arrived in the American colonies as Christians. (Unfortunately, the law was repealed twelve years later, in 1682.)

1877 English devotional poet Frances Ridley Havergal (1838-79) penned the words to the hymn, "Who Is On the Lord's Side?" She based her text on 1 Chronicles 12:1-8. The poem was first published in Havergal's *Loyal Responses* (1878).

1908 The Church of the Nazarene was organized in Pilot Point, Texas by the union of several small religious bodies, including the original Nazarene Church, the Association of Pentecostal Churches, and the Holiness Church of Christ.

1988 The Vatican officially announced that scientific carbon testing on the Shroud of Turin, revered for centuries as Jesus' burial cloth, indicated it was probably only about 728 years old, and dated back only to AD 1280, and not to the time of Jesus' crucifixion (AD 30-33).

Notable Birthdays

1821 Birth of Andrew R. Fausset, Anglican scholar. He was co-editor of the *Jamieson, Fausset, and Brown* Bible commentary. [d. 1910]

1873 Birth of Louis Berkhof, American Dutch Reformed theologian. Beginning in 1906, he spent three decades teaching systematic theology at Calvin Seminary in Grand Rapids, to nearly every Christian Reformed clergyman of his day. Berkhof was also an extensive writer, and some of his most popular works include *Reformed Dogmatics* (3 vols., 1932) and *The History of Christian Doctrine* (1937). [d. 5/19/1957]

The Last Passage

1605 Death of Theodore Beza, 86, John Calvin's successor in Geneva as the head of the Swiss Reformation. A Huguenot theologian, Beza's last words before dying were: *'Cover, Lord, what has been: govern what shall be. Oh, perfect that which Thou hast begun, that I suffer not shipwreck in the haven.'* (b. 6/24/1519)

1907 Death of George C. Hugg, 59, American Presbyterian sacred chorister. He composed and published many collections of songs for Sunday School, including his own enduring hymn tune, NO, NOT ONE ("There's Not a Friend Like the Lowly Jesus"). (b. 5/23/1848)

1934 Death of Theodore Baker, 83, German-born American musicologist and biographical scholar. In 1900 he published Baker's Biographical Dictionary. He also prepared the English translation of the German hymn, "We Gather Together to Ask the Lord's Blessing." (b. 6/3/1851)

Words for the Soul

1742 English revivalist George Whitefield wrote in a letter: *'My strength is daily renewed. Still I desire to cry, Grace! Grace!'*

1985 Dutch Catholic mystic Henri J. M. Nouwen observed in his Road to Daybreak journal: *'It struck me that selling what you own, leaving your family and friends, and following Jesus is not a once-in-a-lifetime event. You must do it many times and in many different ways. And it certainly does not become easier.'*

IN GOD'S WORD... OT: Jeremiah 22:1–23:22 ~ NT: 2 Thessalonians 1:1-12 ~ Psalms 83:1-18 ~ Proverbs 25:11-14

חשון **HESHVAN**   ALMANAC OF THE CHRISTIAN FAITH   תשרי **TISHRI**

~ October 14 ~

Highlights in History

1656 Massachusetts General Court passed the first punitive legislation against Quakers in the colony, imposing a 40-shilling fine on anyone harboring a Quaker. (New England Puritans, whose society was a virtually seamless amalgam of church and state, despised Quakers whose spiritual ideal was that of stripping away from Christianity all non-essential doctrines, ceremonies and statutes of the body politic.)

1735 John and Charles Wesley set sail for America, John to be a missionary to the Indians, Charles to become secretary to Georgia governor James Oglethorpe. The brothers soon discovered their own need for a genuine religious conversion. (On this day, also, John Wesley began keeping his famed journal, which he would maintain for the next 55 years, until 1790.)

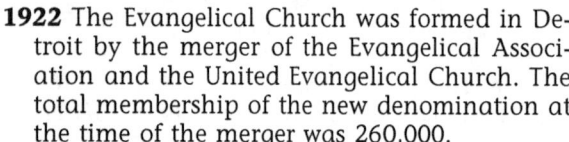
OGLETHORPE

1922 The Evangelical Church was formed in Detroit by the merger of the Evangelical Association and the United Evangelical Church. The total membership of the new denomination at the time of the merger was 260,000.

1983 The National Council of Churches issued *The Inclusive Language Lectionary*, a 3-volume translation of Scripture readings designed to omit or blur gender references. God was called either Father and Mother or the One; "man" was replaced by "humanity" or "humankind."

Notable Birthdays

1644 Birth of William Penn, English Quaker colonizer. Educated at Oxford, he converted to Quakerism and was afterward often jailed for his religious beliefs. Penn was later granted territory in North America in exchange for a debt owed to his father. Here in 1682 he founded the colony of Pennsylvania, based on religious and political freedom. [d. 7/30/1718]

1835 Birth of William G. Fischer, German-born American book binder, piano-maker and choral director. He also composed the hymn tunes HANKEY ("I Love to Tell the Story") and FISCHER ("Whiter Than Snow"). [d. 8/12/1912]

1876 Birth of Henry A. (Harry) Ironside, Canadian-born American clergyman, and Bible teacher. Called the "Archbishop of Fundamentalism," he pastored Chicago's Moody Memorial Church (1930-48). [d. 1/15/1951]

1893 English Methodist clergyman Leslie D. Weatherhead was born. He pastored London's City Temple (1936-50), and was president of the Methodist Conference (1955-56, 1966-67). [d. 1/3/1976]

The Last Passage

1552 Death of Oswald Myconius, 64, Swiss humanist, Reformed minister and theologian. A co-worker and first biographer of Swiss reformer Ulrich Zwingli, Myconius also helped draw up the first two Basel confessions. (b. 1488)

1897 Death of William A. Ogden, 56, American hymn author and composer: "He is Able to Deliver Thee." (b. 10/10/1841)

Words for the Soul

1871 Scottish clergyman and biographer Andrew Bonar, 61, reflected in his diary: 'My ambition now is very feeble compared with other days. To win souls and to know God more, and then to be in the kingdom is "all my desire."'

1974 While visiting a Trappist monastery in NY state, Dutch Catholic diarist Henri J. M. Nouwen wrote in his journal: 'Someone might read what I wrote and discover something there that I myself did not see, but which might be just as valid as my original thought. It seems important to allow this to happen.... After all, people will never follow anyone's ideas except their own; I mean, those which have developed within their inner self.'

IN GOD'S WORD...   OT: Jeremiah 23:23–25:38 ~ NT: 2 Thessalonians 2:1-17 ~ Psalms 84:1-12 ~ Proverbs 25:15

חשון ALMANAC OF THE CHRISTIAN FAITH תשרי
HESHVAN   TISHRI

~ October 15 ~

Highlights in History

1692 Colonial American theologian Cotton Mather published his *Wonders of the Invisible World*, which sought to explain the Salem Witch trials of the current year as part of New England's sins and God's retribution. Subsequent criticism of the trials included Samuel Willard's *Miscellany Observances respecting Witchcraft* (1693) and John Hale's *Nature of Witchcraft* (1698).

1790 Catholic religious Ann Teresa Mathews (aka Mother Bernardina) and Frances Dickinson founded a convent of Discalced Carmelites (a contemplative working order) in Port Tobacco, MD. Mathews afterward became its first prioress. It was the first Catholic convent founded in the U.S., and later moved to Baltimore (1830).

1840 The Evangelical Synod of North America was founded in Mehlville (near St. Louis). The denomination later merged with the Reformed Church (June 1943) to form the Evangelical and Reformed Church, which, in turn, merged with the Congregational Christian Church in 1957 to create the United Church of Christ.

1900 Pentecostal evangelist Charles Fox Parham opened Bethel Bible Institute in Topeka, KS. It was here where, on January 1, 1901, student Agnes Ozman became the first Christian in modern times to speak in tongues.

1932 Gladys Aylward, 30, sailed from Liverpool for Asia in a heroic effort to bring the gospel to China, after being told by mission boards that she couldn't go. (In 1958, her biography, *The Small Woman*, was made into the award-winning film, "Inn of the Sixth Happiness.")

Notable Birthdays

1784 Birth of Thomas Hastings, American Presbyterian hymnwriter. He composed the hymn tunes TOPLADY ("Rock of Ages") and ORTONVILLE ("Majestic Sweetness Sits Enthroned"). [d. 5/15/1872]

1851 Birth of George Foote Moore, American Presbyterian OT scholar. He taught religious history at Andover Theological Seminary (1883-1902), and at Harvard (1902-28). He also authored *History of Religions* (1913, 1919) and *Judaism* (2 vols., 1927). [d. 5/16/1931]

The Last Passage

1905 Death of Charles J. Ellicott, 86, Anglican prelate. As Bishop of Gloucester (1863-1905), he edited commentaries on both the NT (3 vols.) and the OT (5 vols.). Ellicott also served as chairman of the NT Committee for the *English Revised Version* of the Bible, 1870-81. (b. 4/25/1819)

1922 Death of James Hastings, 70, Scottish Presbyterian clergyman, biblical scholar and editor. In 1889 he founded "The Expository Times." He was also editor of both the *Dictionary of the Bible* (1898-1904) and *Encyclopaedia of Religion and Ethics* (12 vols., 1908-21). (b. 3/26/1852)

1972 Death of Athenagoras I, 78, exarch of the Greek Orthodox Church in western and central Europe. He had advocated reunion with the Roman Catholic Church. (b. 3/25/1886)

Words for the Soul

1640 Scottish clergyman Samuel Rutherford wrote in a letter: *'All that die for sin, die not in sin.'*

1886 On the 22nd anniversary of the death of Isabella, his wife of 17 years, Scottish clergyman and biographer Andrew Bonar, 76, reflected in his diary: *'I have learned... that the Lord can fill the soul with Himself, when He takes away what seemed indispensable to our happiness on earth.'*

1948 American missionary and martyr Jim Elliot noted in his journal: *'"They shall mount up with wings as eagles" (Isa. 40:31). These wings are not so typical of purity as they are of power – strength to live above snares and everything else. Grace to be alone as the eagle. Thanks for wings, Lord.'*

IN GOD'S WORD...   OT: Jeremiah 26:1–27:22 ~ NT: 2 Thessalonians 3:1-18 ~ Psalms 85:1-13 ~ Proverbs 25:16

ALMANAC OF THE CHRISTIAN FAITH

HESHVAN — TISHRI

~ October 16 ~

Highlights in History

1649 The independent government of the colony of Maine passed legislation granting religious freedom to all its citizens, provided that those of contrary religious persuasions behaved acceptably. (This tolerance lasted only three years, until Maine was annexed by Massachusetts.)

1701 In Saybrook, CT, Rev. John Pierpont gained a charter to establish the Collegiate School, under the auspices of Congregationalists who were dissatisfied with the growing liberalism at Harvard. (The school later changed its name to Yale University.)

1789 In Philadelphia, the second session of the second General Convention of the Protestant Episcopal Church closed. At this session, a church constitution was adopted, canons of the new denomination were ratified and a revised version of the *Book of Common Prayer* (for American Anglicans) was authorized.

1978 In the Vatican, 18 days after the death of John Paul I, the Roman Catholic College of Cardinals selected Polish Cardinal Karol Wojtyla as their new pope, John Paul II. He was the first non-Italian pope elected in 456 years.

Notable Birthdays

1840 Birth of Frederick L. Hosmer, Unitarian clergyman. He was a leader in liturgical renewal among Unitarians, and penned numerous hymns, including "God, That Madest Earth and Heaven"; "O Thou, in All Thy Might So Far"; "The Kingdom Comes on Bended Knee"; and "Thy Kingdom Come, O Lord." [d. 6/7/1929]

1847 Birth of Sam[uel] P. Jones, Alabama-born American Methodist evangelist and prohibitionist. Beginning his career in law, at 25 Jones underwent a Christian conversion. Known afterward as "the Moody of the South," he became one of the foremost evangelists of his day. [d. 10/15/1906]

The Last Passage

1553 Death of Lucas Cranach, 81, German artist. As court painter to Elector Frederick the Wise of Saxony, Cranach was known for his altarpieces, and for portraits of Martin Luther and of other friends among the reformers. (b. 10/4/1472)

1555 English bishop Nicholas Ridley, 55, and Protestant Reformer Hugh Latimer, 70, together were burned at the stake by Queen Mary I for heresy. Latimer's last words were: *'Be of good comfort, Master Ridley, and play the man. We shall this day light such a candle by God's grace in England, as I trust shall never be put out.'*

1812 Death of Henry Martyn, 29, Anglican missionary to Persia (India). During his brief ministry, Martyn translated the New Testament into Urdu and Persian. (b. 2/18/1781)

1888 Death of Horatio G. Spafford, 59, American lawyer and hymnwriter. In 1873 he planned a trip to Europe with his family, but last minute business caused him to delay his departure, so he sent his wife and four daughters ahead. On Nov. 22 their ship was struck by an English vessel and sank in only 12 minutes. The survivors landed at Cardiff, Wales, and Mrs. Spafford cabled her husband: "Saved alone." Spafford later crossed to meet his grieving wife, and his ship passed near the place where his four daughters had drowned. There he penned the hymn: "It Is Well with My Soul." (b. 10/20/1828)

Words for the Soul

1785 In a letter to his friend and fellow hymnwriter John Newton, Anglican poet William Cowper wrote: *'An escape from a life of suffering to a life of happiness and glory, is such a deliverance as leaves no room for the sorrow of survivors, unless they sorrow for themselves. We cannot, indeed, lose what we love without regretting it; but a Christian is in possession of such alleviations of that regret, as the world knows nothing of.'*

IN GOD'S WORD...   OT: Jeremiah 28:1–29:32 ~ NT: 1 Timothy 1:1–20 ~ Psalms 86:1–17 ~ Proverbs 25:17

October 17

Highlights in History

1483 Pope Sixtus IV officially launched the Spanish Inquisition, placing it under joint direction of the Church and state. The infamous Dominican Thomas de Torquemada, 63, was appointed Grand Inquisitor in charge of removing Jews and Muslims from Spain.

1855 The first conference of rabbis in the United States was held in the Medical College, Cleveland, with Rabbi Isidore Kalisch as chairman.

1979 Mother Teresa (born Agnes Bojaxhiu), the Albanian Catholic nun who founded the Society of the Missionaries of Charity, was awarded the 1979 Nobel Peace Prize.

1981 In Italy, Pope John Paul II met with Abuna Tekle Haimanot, Patriarch of the Ethiopian Orthodox Union Church (founded 328 AD). It was the first such meeting between leaders of these two churches in modern times.

Notable Birthdays

1582 Birth of Johann Gerhard, German Lutheran orthodox churchman and "Archtheologian of Lutheranism." He authored Lutheranism's most dogmatic exposition of strict orthodoxy, the 9-volume *Loci Theologici* (1622). Gerhard stressed the utter infallibility of Scripture and literal Biblical inspiration, including even the Hebrew vowel points. [d. 8/17/1637]

1792 Birth of John Bowring, English Unitarian linguist, traveler, diplomat and writer. He was the first editor of the "Westminster Review" (1825), and also wrote many hymns, including "God is Love, His Mercy Brightens"; "In the Cross of Christ I Glory"; and "Watchman, Tell Us of the Night." [d. 11/23/1872]

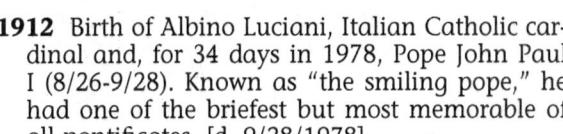

1912 Birth of Albino Luciani, Italian Catholic cardinal and, for 34 days in 1978, Pope John Paul I (8/26-9/28). Known as "the smiling pope," he had one of the briefest but most memorable of all pontificates. [d. 9/28/1978]

The Last Passage

107 Bishop Ignatius of Antioch, ca. 72, was eaten by lions in Rome. He had been brought there in chains by the emperor Trajan, who was eager to execute Christians as sport for spectators. Ignatius, one of the Apostolic Fathers, possessed a passionate devotion to Christ and, in his seven extant letters, he revealed a great desire to suffer martyrdom for his faith. [b. ca. 35]

1797 Death of Elijah ben Solomon, 77, Lithuanian Hebrew scholar and religious writer. He is called the greatest authority on classical Judaism in modern times, and authored over seventy treatises. (b. 4/23/1720)

1910 Death of Julia Ward Howe, 91, American Unitarian social reformer, author, lecturer and hymnwriter. At age 24 she married Dr. Samuel Gridley Howe of Boston, head of the Perkins Institute, the Massachusetts School for the Blind. The author of three volumes of verse, in 1861 she penned her greatest poem, the "Battle Hymn of the Republic." (b. 5/27/1819)

Words for the Soul

1740 British revivalist George Whitefield first met colonial American clergyman Jonathan Edwards on this date. Whitefield later wrote in his journal: 'Mr. Edwards is a solid, excellent Christian.... I think I have not seen his fellow [i.e., his equal] in all New England.'

1830 Scottish clergyman and biographer Andrew Bonar, at age 20, counted this date as the beginning of his spiritual "assurance." He testified in his diary: 'In reading [English Puritan William] Guthrie's **Saving Interest** I have been led to hope that I may be in Christ though I have never yet known it. All the marks of faith in a man which he gives are to be found in me, I think, although very feeble. This is the first beam of joy, perhaps, that I have yet found in regard to my state, and yet it is scarcely more than a hope.'

IN GOD'S WORD... OT: Jeremiah 30:1–31:26 ~ NT: 1 Timothy 2:1-15 ~ Psalms 87:1-7 ~ Proverbs 25:18-19

October 18

Highlights in History

1469 Isabella of Castille married Ferdinand II of Aragon, effectively uniting nearly all the Christian areas of Spain under one monarchy.

1685 The Edict of Fontainbleu, signed by French King Louis XIV, revoked all the concessions of religious freedom the 1598 Edict of Nantes had provided. (Strongly enforced from 1629-1665, the concessions of Nantes were gradually withdrawn as Catholic power within the French government solidified.) A mass exodus of over a half-million Huguenots followed.

1949 American country singer and songwriter Stuart Hamblin (b. 1908) was converted. Hamblen's star rose when his fast-paced song, "This Old House," topped the pop music charts in 1954. His more enduring Christian titles have included: "It Is No Secret What God Can Do"; "Open Up Your Heart and Let the Son Shine In"; "Known Only to Him"; and "How Big is God?"

1954 "The Week in Religion," a Sunday evening religious panel show, aired for the last time over Dumont television. First broadcast in March 1952, this ecumenical religious program telecast from 6:00-7:00 p.m. and was divided into 20-minute segments for Protestant, Catholic and Jewish news. The original hosts were Rabbi William S. Rosenbloom, Rev. Robbins Wolcott Barstow and Rev. Joseph N. Moody.

Notable Birthdays

1595 Birth of Edward Winslow, English-born Separatist and American Pilgrim leader. Winslow was a Mayflower passenger who later served as governor of the Plymouth Colony (1633, 1636, 1644). [d. 5/8/1655]

1662 Birth of Matthew Henry, English Nonconformist (Presbyterian) clergyman. His enduring reputation rests on his celebrated biblical commentary, *Exposition of the Old and New Testaments* (1708-10) – still in print! [d. 6/22/1714]

The Last Passage

1646 Death of French Jesuit missionary Isaac Jogues, 39. Born in Orleans, France, Jogues joined the Jesuits in 1624. He was ordained in 1636 and became a missionary to Canada, working with the Huron Indians in the Great Lakes area. In 1646 he sought to negotiate a treaty with the Iroquois in New Netherland (later New York), but was taken captive, blamed for a pestilence that had struck the tribe, and was tomahawked to death. (b. 1/10/1607)

1882 Robert F. Paine, the Methodist prelate who led in organizing the Methodist Episcopal Church South, and also became its first bishop (1846-82), died at 83. Paine had a lifelong interest in missions, and was president of LaGrange College in Alabama (1830-46). (b. 11/12/1799)

Words for the Soul

1765 Anglican poet William Cowper wrote in a letter: *'How happy it is to believe, with a steadfast assurance, that our petitions are heard even while we are making them; and how delightful to meet with a proof of it in the effectual and actual grant of them!'*

1931 In a letter to Arthur Greeves, British literary scholar and Christian apologist C. S. Lewis wrote regarding his recent conversion to the Christian faith: *'The "doctrines" [of the Christian faith]... are translations into our concepts and ideas of that which God has already expressed in language more adequate, namely, the actual incarnation, crucifixion, and resurrection.'*

1985 Dutch Catholic diarist Henri J. M. Nouwen observed in his *Road to Daybreak* journal: *'It is not so much the ability to think, to reflect, to plan, or to produce that makes us different from the rest of creation, but the ability to trust. It is the heart that makes us truly human.'*

IN GOD'S WORD... OT: Jeremiah 31:27–32:44 ~ NT: 1 Timothy 3:1-16 ~ Psalms 88:1-18 ~ Proverbs 25:20-22

October 19

HESHVAN / **TISHRI**

ALMANAC OF THE CHRISTIAN FAITH

Highlights in History

1656 Massachusetts passed a law prohibiting the further immigration of Quakers into the Puritan colony. This rejection indirectly led to a later establishment of the colony of Pennsylvania.

1779 English poet William Cowper collaborated with Anglican curate John Newton in publishing the *Olney Hymns* – a classic collection of Evangelical and Reformed hymns. (Cowper generally wrote about simple pleasures of country life and expressed a deep concern with human cruelty and suffering. Plagued by periods of acute depression, Cowper frequently composed poetry as a method toward recovery.)

Notable Birthdays

1433 Birth of Marsilio Ficino, a Florentine humanist who sought to relate Platonic thought to biblical revelation. [d. 10/1/1499]

1720 Birth of John Woolman, American Quaker preacher (1743-72), and abolitionist. His inspired appeal (1758) led the Philadelphia Yearly Meeting of Friends to abandon and condemn slave holdings. Woolman's *Journal* (first published in 1774) was recognized as one of the classics of the inner life. [d. 10/7/1772]

1921 Birth of Bill (William Rohl) Bright, American evangelist. Born in Oklahoma, Bright moved to California after college, began associating with Hollywood's First Presbyterian Church and was influenced by Christian educator Henrietta Mears to dedicate his life to Christ. He established Campus Crusade for Christ in 1951. [d. 7/19/2003]

The Last Passage

1609 Death of James (Jacob) Arminius, 49, Holland-born theologian. A minister of the Dutch Reformed Church, he could not accept strict Calvinist teachings on predestination, and subsequently developed a system of belief later named after him, and most evident today in Methodist theology. (b. 10/10/1560)

1873 Death of Robert S. Candlish, 67, leader of the Free Church of Scotland. As minister of St. George's Church in Edinburgh (1834-73), Candlish took a leading part in forming the independent denomination. He was also principal of New College, Edinburgh (1862-73). Following the death of Thomas Chalmers, Candlish became the ruling spirit of the Free Church of Scotland. (b. 3/23/1806)

1902 Death of William O. Cushing, 78, hymn author: "Hiding in Thee"; "Under His Wings I Am Safely Abiding"; "O Safe to the Rock that is Higher Than I." (b. 12/31/1823)

1952 Death of Ernest O. Sellers, 82, hymnwriter. He attended Moody Bible Institute, and later taught music at Baptist Bible Institute in New Orleans. Sellers is remembered today for composing the hymn tune EOLA ("Thy Word Is a Lamp to My Feet"). (b. 10/29/1869)

Words for the Soul

1516 The year before posting his 95 theses, German reformer Martin Luther wrote in a letter to Georg Spalatin: *'We are not, as Aristotle imagines, made righteous by doing what is righteous – except in appearance; but ... by becoming and being righteous we do what is right. The person must be changed before the deeds.'*

1746 During a time of illness, colonial American missionary to the Indians David Brainerd recorded in his journal: *'Was composed and comfortable, willing either to die or live; but found it hard to be reconciled to the thoughts of living useless. Oh that I might never live to be a burden to God's creation; but that I might be allowed to repair home, when my sojourning work is done!'*

1781 Anglican poet William Cowper wrote: *'Neither prose nor verse can reform the manners of a dissolute age, much less can they inspire a sense of religious obligation, unless assisted and made efficacious by the power who superintends the truth he has vouchsafed to impart.'*

IN GOD'S WORD... OT: Jeremiah 33:1–34:22 ~ NT: 1 Timothy 4:1-16 ~ Psalms 89:1-13 ~ Proverbs 25:23-24

חשון HESHVAN — ALMANAC OF THE CHRISTIAN FAITH — תשרי TISHRI

October 20

Highlights in History

1349 Self-flagellation was condemned by Pope Clement VI. The practice had arisen two hundred years earlier, initiated by the monk Peter Damien as a means to help himself suppress his lusts.

1629 John Winthrop was elected governor of Massachusetts Bay Colony. He is well-known for the journal he kept.

1870 In Rome, with the outbreak of the Franco-Prussian War, the Vatican I Ecumenical Council ended before all the business at hand could be completed. Italian troops took Rome, and the Council was suspended, but never formally brought to a close.

1949 On this evening the last of the Inklings' Thursday meetings was held. This group of British Christian intellectuals associated with Oxford included such notable thinkers as J. R. R. Tolkien, C. S. Lewis, and Owen Barfield.

Notable Birthdays

1632 Birth of Christopher Wren, English church architect and astronomer. He proposed the plan for rebuilding London after the Great Fire of 1666. In all, he designed over 50 London churches, including St Paul's Cathedral. [d. 2/25/1723]

1802 Birth of Ernst W. Hengstenberg, German Lutheran theologian and editor. He taught theology in Berlin (1828-69) and, for more than 40 years, edited a journal which opposed Bible criticism and rationalism, and championed Lutheran orthodoxy. He is best remembered for authoring *Christology of the Old Testament*. [d. 5/28/1869]

1828 Birth of Horatio G. Spafford, American lawyer and hymnwriter. In 1873 he planned a trip to Europe with his family, but last minute business caused him to delay his own departure, so he sent his wife and four daughters ahead. On Nov. 22 their ship was struck by an English vessel and sank in only 12 minutes. The survivors landed at Cardiff, Wales, and Mrs. Spafford cabled her husband: "Saved alone." Spafford later crossed to meet his grieving wife. As his ship passed near the place where his four daughters had drowned, there, in the midst of his sorrow, Spafford wrote the hymn of solace: "It Is Well with My Soul." [d. 10/16/1888]

The Last Passage

1893 Death of Philip Schaff, 74, Swiss-born American Reformed theologian, church historian and ecumenist. While teaching at Mercersburg (PA) Seminary (1844-63), he co-founded the "Mercersburg Theology." He later taught at Union Theological Seminary (1870-93). Schaff translated J.J. Herzog's religious encyclopedia into English (1882-84) and authored *History of the Christian Church* (1858-92) and *Creeds of Christendom* (1877). (b. 1/1/1819)

1913 Death of Mary Artemisia Lathbury, 72, American writer of children's books and sacred verse. She authored the hymns: "Day is Dying in the West"; "Break Thou the Bread of Life"; and "Rise and Shine." (b. 8/10/1841)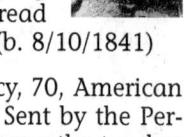

1936 Death of Anne Sullivan Macy, 70, American educator and "miracle worker." Sent by the Perkins Institute in 1887, Anne became the teacher and constant companion of Helen Keller until her own death. (b. 4/14/1866)

Words for the Soul

1532 German reformer Martin Luther declared: *'The Word is given not in order to achieve external or secular unity and peace but life eternal. Word and doctrine are to create unity of fellowship.'*

1957 English scholar and Christian apologist C. S. Lewis confessed in a letter: *'It'll be nice when we all wake up from this life, which has indeed something like a nightmare about it.'*

IN GOD'S WORD... OT: Jeremiah 35:1–36:32 ~ NT: 1 Timothy 5:1-25 ~ Psalms 89:14-37 ~ Proverbs 25:25-27

חשון **HESHVAN** — ALMANAC OF THE CHRISTIAN FAITH — תשרי **TISHRI**

~ October 21 ~

Highlights in History

1555 English Catholic Queen Mary Tudor began a series of fierce persecutions against Protestantism, in which more than 200 men, women and children were put to death for their faith. Mary was afterward startled to discover that the martyrdoms only intensified Protestant zeal.

1633 English-born colonial American religious leader Thomas Hooker (1586-1647) was named pastor of Newtown (CT) Congregational Church. Hooker also helped found Hartford (1636), and was active in framing the "Fundamental Orders," which long served as Connecticut's constitution.

1692 The English throne deposed Quaker statesman William Penn as Governor of Pennsylvania. (His overtures of thanksgiving to James II for permitting religious freedom for dissenters of the Church of England led William and Mary, upon taking the throne, to charge Penn with being a papist.) Penn was arrested and imprisoned, but later established his innocence, gained favor with the new monarchs, and was restored to his governorship in 1694.

Notable Birthdays

1672 Ludovico A. Muratori, Italian historian, was born near Florence. In 1740 he discovered the ancient treatise on the canon of the Bible known today as the Muratorian Fragment (1740). [d. 1/23/1750]

1749 Tadsusz Brzozowski was born in Malbork, Poland. He became the first general of the restored Society of Jesus (1814-20). [d. 1820]

1808 Birth of Samuel Francis Smith, American Baptist clergyman and poet. He served as editorial secretary of the American Baptist Missionary Union (1854-95). Smith also wrote the hymn, "The Morning Light is Breaking" and, in 1831, the lyrics for "America" (aka, "My Country, 'Tis of Thee"). [d. 11/16/1895]

1901 Birth of Gerhard von Rad, German Lutheran Old Testament scholar. He was professor at Göttingen from 1947, and from 1949 at Heidelberg, where he was the most important influence upon a whole generation of future pastors until his retirement in 1967. His classic work, *Die Theologie des Alten Testaments* (2 vols, 1957-60), was later translated into English. [d. 10/31/1971]

The Last Passage

1872 Death of Jean Henri Merle d'Aubigné, 78, Swiss-born historian of the Protestant Reformation. His principal writings were *Histoire de la Réformation du XVI siècle* (5 vols, 1835-53), and *Histoire de la Réformation en Europe au temps de Calvin* (8 vols, 1863-78). (b. 8/16/1794)

1970 Death of John T. Scopes, 70, American high school biology teacher. In 1925 he was tried and convicted for teaching the theory of evolution in his Dayton, Tennessee public school classroom. Scopes was defended by Clarence Darrow in the famous "Monkey Trial." (b. 8/3/1900)

Words for the Soul

1532 German reformer Martin Luther declared: *'For some years now I have read through the Bible twice every year. If you picture the Bible to be a mighty tree and every word a little branch, I have shaken every one of these branches because I wanted to know what it was and what it meant.'*

1856 Scottish clergyman and biographer Andrew Bonar, reflected in his diary: *'What health I have had here, what health to my children also!... Happy years have passed here, very happy; but we are pilgrims.'*

1981 Dutch Catholic priest and mystic Henri J. M. Nouwen noted in his ¡Gracias! Latin American journal: *'A true spirituality cannot be constructed, built, or put together; it has to be recognized in the daily life of people who search together to do God's will in the world.'*

IN GOD'S WORD... OT: Jeremiah 37:1–38:28 ~ NT: 1 Timothy 6:1-21 ~ Psalms 89:38-52 ~ Proverbs 25:28

חשון HESHVAN — ALMANAC OF THE CHRISTIAN FAITH — תשרי TISHRI

October 22

Highlights in History

451 During the Fifth Session of the Council of Chalcedon, the final form of the Chalcedonian Definition (or Creed) was drafted. It was immediately adopted and solemnly promulgated at the Sixth Session (convened on Oct. 25).

1746 In Elizabethtown, NJ, the College of New Jersey was founded by an evangelical group within the Presbyterian Church, afterward becoming a stronghold of conservatism during the denomination's conflicts with liberalism. The school moved to Princeton, NJ in 1752, and in 1896 changed its name to Princeton University.

1844 Across America, "The Great Disappointment" occurred when this last date for the return of Christ, set by lay preacher William Miller, passed without event. Vast numbers of followers soon lost all interest in "Adventism," and either returned to their former churches or abandoned their faith altogether.

WM. MILLER

Notable Birthdays

1697 Birth of Katharina von Schlegel, German Lutheran sacred poet. Little is known of her life. However, one of her poems was translated into English by Jane L. Borthwick 100 years after it was written, and became the hymn, "Be Still, My Soul." [d. ca. 1768]

1839 Birth of Louis A. Sabatier, French Protestant theologian. As a representative of liberalism in theology, he sought to reconcile faith and science, and thereby influenced the Modernist movement. [d. 4/12/1901]

The Last Passage

1575 In Königsberg, Germany lawyer John Luther died at age 49. He was the firstborn son of reformers Martin and Catherine (née von Bora) Luther, who had married June 13, 1525. Known affectionately as Hans or Hänschen, he was born June 7, 1526.

1808 Death of Benjamin Randall, 59, American denominational reformer. Influenced by the preaching of George Whitefield, Randall was converted in his 20s, and became an itinerant evangelist for the Baptists. But he differed from the common Baptist belief in predestination, and in 1780 formed the first Free Will Baptist Church in New Durham, NH. (b. 2/7/1749)

1882 Death of Oscar Ahnfelt, 69, Swedish hymn composer. Through the financial help of Jenny Lind, he published his musical settings of the words by Lina Sandell, including that of her most famous hymn tune: BLOTT EN DAG ("Day By Day, And With Each Passing Moment"). (b. 5/31/1813)

1903 Death of Susannah Spurgeon, 69, the widow of Charles Haddon Spurgeon. She was an invalid after 1868, though she outlived her husband by eleven years. (b. 1/15/1832)

1922 Death of Lyman Abbott, 86, American Congregational clergyman and editor. Though trained in law, Abbott was so impressed with Henry Ward Beecher that he entered the ministry, and succeeded Beecher at Brooklyn's Plymouth Congregational Church (1887-99). Greatly involved in religious journalism, Abbott was editor of "Illustrated Christian Weekly" (1870-76), "Christian Union" (1876-93) and "The Outlook" (1983-1922). Abbott was also a leading exponent of the social gospel, and interpreted Christianity as it applied to social and industrial problems. (b. 12/18/1835)

Words for the Soul

1892 Two months before his own death on Dec. 31, Scottish clergyman and biographer Andrew Bonar, 82, noted in his diary: *'Have been hearing how [Charles] Spurgeon frequently through the last days of his life spoke of not caring to fall asleep, because he had such fellowship with the Lord Jesus as he lay awake.'* [Spurgeon had died the previous January at age 57.]

IN GOD'S WORD... OT: Jeremiah 39:1–41:18 ~ NT: 2 Timothy 1:1-18 ~ Psalms 90:1–91:16 ~ Proverbs 26:1-2

חשון HESHVAN — ALMANAC OF THE CHRISTIAN FAITH — תשרי TISHRI

October 23

Highlights in History

4004 BC According to the Biblical chronology of Irish Archbishop James Ussher (1581-1656), "the heavens and the earth" were created on this date ... at 9:00 a.m. Greenwich Mean Time! (Ussher's *Chronology of the Old and New Testaments* was first published in 1650-54.)

1641 The notorious "Irish Massacre" occurred when Ulster Catholics massacred upwards of 40,000 Protestants. England's Charles I (ruled 1625-49), who married a Catholic wife and who secretly favored Rome, was accused of instigating the massacre.

1684 Massachusetts ended its law of church membership being a prerequisite for voting.

1819 Pioneer missionaries Hiram Bingham (1789-1869) and Asa Thurston (1787-1868) set sail — thereby becoming the first Protestant missionaries sent to the Sandwich Islands (Hawaii). They were sponsored by the American Board of Commissioners for Foreign Missions (ABCFM). (Bingham's good-natured persona was caricatured as Abner Hale in James Michener's novel *Hawaii*.)

1930 Under the influence of his mother, Taiwanese statesman Chiang Kai-Shek (1887-1975) converted to Christianity.

Notable Birthdays

1847 Birth of Henry Preserved Smith, American Presbyterian clergyman, Old Testament scholar, educator and author: *A Critical and Exegetical Commentary on the Books of Samuel* (1899); *The Religion of Israel* (1914); *The Heretic's Defense* (autobiography, 1926). [d. 2/26/1927]

1871 Birth of American New Testament scholar Edgar J. Goodspeed. He taught at the University of Chicago (1915-37), helped prepare the *Revised Standard Version* of the New Testament (1946), and also co-edited the renowned *Smith & Goodspeed* translation of the Bible. [d. 1/13/1962]

The Last Passage

524 Roman statesman Boethius, age ca. 44, was executed. This Christian philosopher, and author of *The Consolation of Philosophy*, also wrote in defense of the doctrine of the Trinity. His work was influential up to the Reformation. (b. ca. 480)

1825 Death of Pliny Fisk, 33, pioneer American Congregational missionary. Sent by the American Board (ABCFM) in 1819, he and Levi Parsons embarked on the first American-sponsored mission to the Near East, with the aim of converting the Jews of Palestine. Fisk nearly completed an Arab-English dictionary, before his early death. (b. 6/24/1792)

1842 Death of Heinrich F. W. Gesenius, 56, German Protestant theologian and Semitics scholar. A pioneer in Hebrew philology, he published the first edition of his groundbreaking Hebrew grammar in 1813 (expanded by E. Kautzsch, 1899+; Eng. trans. by A. E. Cowley, 1910). Today, the English edition of this work is more affectionately known as *Gesenius-Kautzsch-Cowley*. (b. 2/3/1786)

1926 Death of Olympia Brown, 91, American clergyperson and social reformer. She was the first woman to be ordained a minister by the full authority of her denomination. She served as president of the Wisconsin Women's Suffrage Association (1887-1917). In 1863 Olympia was ordained by the Northern Universalists at their association meeting in Malone, NY. (b. 1/5/1835)

Words for the Soul

1848 To his (future) wife, Louisa, Scottish clergyman George MacDonald, 23, wrote in a letter: *'I want to love you for ever — so that, though there is not marrying or giving in marriage in heaven, we may see each other there as the best beloved. Oh Louisa, is it not true that our life here is a growing unto life, and our death is being born – our true birth?'* [The couple married in 1851, and remained together almost 51 years, until Louisa's death in 1902.]

IN GOD'S WORD...   OT: Jeremiah 42:1–44:23 ~ NT: 2 Timothy 2:1-21 ~ Psalms 92:1–93:5 ~ Proverbs 26:3-5

October 24

HESHVAN — ALMANAC OF THE CHRISTIAN FAITH — **TISHRI**

Highlights in History

1260 In France, Chartres Cathedral, the purest example of Gothic architecture, was consecrated.

1648 The Peace of Westphalia was signed, ending the Thirty Years War in Central Europe. Extending equal political rights to Catholics and Protestants (including religious minorities), it effectively stripped the Holy Roman Empire of any real power.

1781 In Philadelphia, after the dispatch from General George Washington reporting his victory at Yorktown was read to Congress, the members adjourned to a nearby Dutch Lutheran Church to offer up prayers of thanksgiving.

1790 English founder of Methodism John Wesley (1703-91) made the last entry in his journal. (Begun 55 years earlier, on Oct. 14, 1735, the last words in Wesley's journal reads: *'I hope many even then resolved to choose the better part.'*)

1869 Scottish missionary John Paton observed the Lord's Supper with his first converts in the New Hebrides Islands (today's Vanuatu).

1956 In ceremonies held in Syracuse, NY, Margaret Ellen Towner became the first female clergyperson ordained in the Presbyterian Church.

Notable Birthdays

1710 Birth of Alban Butler, English hagiographer. He compiled *Lives of the Principal Saints* (1756-59), a work which remains a classic today. [d. 5/15/1773]

1794 Birth of William B. Tappan, American clergyman, poet and hymn author: "'Tis Midnight, and on Olive's Brow." [d. 6/18/1849]

1867 Birth of Charles M. Alexander, American singing evangelist with Reuben A. Torrey and J. Wilbur Chapman. In the words of George Stebbins, Alexander was "one of the most magnetic and successful leaders of Gospel song in the history of modern evangelism." [d. 1920]

The Last Passage

1669 William Prynne, English Puritan controversialist and pamphleteer, died at 69. His writings assailed Arminianism and ceremonialism, and attacked popular amusements. He served in Parliament (1648-50), but was expelled for his vehement opposition to Oliver Cromwell. He published valuable compilations of constitutional history. (b. 1600)

1821 Death of Elias Boudinot, 81, American Colonial philanthropist. He was president of the Continental Congress (1782), and later first president of the American Bible Society (1816-21). (b. 5/2/1740)

1826 Death of Ann (née Hasseltine) Judson, 36, American pioneer missionary. As Adoniram Judson's first wife, Ann, along with Harriet Newell, became one of the first two U.S. women commissioned to serve as overseas missionaries (1812). (b. 12/22/1789)

1958 Death of Martin F. Shaw, 83, English church organist and hymnwriter. He edited the *Oxford Book of Carols* (1928), but is better remembered for composing the hymn tune GENTLE JESUS ("Gentle Jesus, Meek and Mild"). (b. 3/9/1875)

Words for the Soul

1529 German reformer Martin Luther explained in a sermon: *'Moses does indeed teach and bid us do and observe what we should do and observe; but whence we are to get and take the power to do so the Gospel alone teaches, namely, from believing in Christ.'*

1746 During one of his frequent periods of illness, colonial American missionary to the New England Indians David Brainerd recorded in his journal: *'O how it pains me to see time pass away, when I can do nothing to any purpose!'*

IN GOD'S WORD...   OT: Jeremiah 44:24–47:7 ~ NT: 2 Timothy 2:22–3:17 ~ Psalms 94:1-23 ~ Proverbs 26:6-8

ALMANAC OF THE CHRISTIAN FAITH

חשון HESHVAN

תשרי TISHRI

~ October 25 ~

Highlights in History

431 The Council of Ephesus replaced Nestorius with a new patriarch of Constantinople. Nestorius was ousted for holding the belief that two separate persons indwelled the incarnate Christ.

1921 Franklin Small (1873-1961) and a group of dissatisfied members of the infant Pentecostal Assemblies of Canada obtained a Dominion charter as the Apostolic Church of Pentecost of Canada, with "oneness" as its central tenet. In 1953, this group merged with the Evangelical Churches of Pentecost, whose greatest concentration of local congregations today is in the Canadian prairie provinces.

1941 The first Youth For Christ rally was held at Bryant's Alliance Tabernacle on Manhattan Island in New York City. An international evangelical youth organization, YFC was founded by several influential personalities, probably the earliest being Lloyd Bryant. Later leaders within the movement included Jack Wyrtzen, Percy Crawford and Billy Graham.

1970 Pope Paul VI canonized forty English and Welsh Catholic martyrs of the 16th and 17th centuries. The "Forty Martyrs" were representative, selected from a total of 357 English and Welsh Roman Catholics who were put to death by the British State between 1535 and 1680.

Notable Birthdays

1564 Birth of Hans Leo Hassler, possibly the ablest German composer of the Renaissance. He is remembered today for creating the hymn harmony: PASSION CHORALE, to which is sung "O Sacred Head Now Wounded"). [d. 6/8/1612]

1800 Jacques P. Migne, French Catholic priest and publisher, was born near Marseilles. In his lifetime, he published *Patrology* (221 volumes in Latin, 166 volumes in Greek), a 171-volume theological encyclopedia, and a 100-volume collection of sacred orations. [d. 10/24/1875]

1811 Carl F. W. Walther, who organized the Lutheran Church Missouri Synod in the U.S., was born in Germany. He was also co-founder and president of Concordia Theological Seminary (1854-87), and authored *The Proper Distinction Between Law and Gospel*. [d. 5/7/1887]

The Last Passage

1180 Medieval philosopher and classical scholar John of Salisbury, Bishop of Chartres (1176-80) and a colleague of Thomas à Becket, died at 65. A prolific theological writer and biographer of St. Anselm and Becket, his letters shed important light on his time. (b. ca. 1115)

1514 William Elphinstone, Scottish bishop and educator, died at 83. He founded Aberdeen University (1494), and was partially responsible for the introduction of printing into Scotland (1507), when he had the Aberdeen Breviary printed. (b. 1431)

1908 Death of Hiram Bingham, Jr., 77, American Congregational missionary to Micronesia (Gilbert Islands). Son of Hawaiian missionary Hiram Bingham Sr., in 1856 he sailed from Boston for a tour of Micronesia and the Gilbert Islands, settling in Honolulu in 1868. Bingham translated the complete Bible by 1890, expanding the inadequate 4,000-word Gilbertese tongue into a language three times its original size. (b. 8/16/1831)

1931 Death of Harry Webb Farrington, 52, American Methodist religious education worker and poet. In all, he penned 29 hymns, including one that endures today: "I Know Not How That Bethlehem's Babe." (b. 7/14/1879)

Words for the Soul

1882 American Quaker holiness author Hannah Whitall Smith confided in a letter to her daughter Mary: *'There is no friendship so precious as that between a mother and daughter, as the daughter grows up into the mother's maturity. And I am filled with thankfulness for my daughter!'*

IN GOD'S WORD...   OT: Jeremiah 48:1–49:22 ~ NT: 2 Timothy 4:1-22 ~ Psalms 95:1–96:13 ~ Proverbs 26:9-12

ALMANAC OF THE CHRISTIAN FAITH

HESHVAN / TISHRI

~ October 26 ~

Highlights in History

312 Roman Emperor Constantine had a vision of the cross of Christ, two days before the Battle of Milvian Bridge. It ultimately turned him into a believer and a supporter of Christianity.

1948 The Pentecostal Fellowship of North America was organized during a three-day convention (Oct. 26-28) in Des Moines, IA. The association, comprised of a fellowship of 24 Pentecostal groups, meets annually to promote fellowship and to demonstrate unity among Pentecostals.

1950 Albanian-born Mother Teresa (born Agnes Bojaxhiu) founded her first Mission of Charity in Calcutta, India. Today this Catholic religious order has a presence in over 100 countries.

Notable Birthdays

1813 Birth of Henry T. Smart, English hymn composer: LANCASHIRE ("Lead On, O King Eternal"); REGENT SQUARE ("Angels from the Realms of Glory"). [d. 7/6/1879]

1818 Birth of American teacher, writer and Congregational clergyman's wife Elizabeth P. Prentiss. From age 16, she contributed numerous articles to the "Youth's Companion," published several books of verse, and authored the enduring hymn, "More Love to Thee, O Christ." [d. 8/13/1878]

1822 Birth of Richard F. Weymouth, English Baptist philologist and New Testament scholar. He published his best-known work, *The New Testament in Modern Speech*, in 1903. [d. 12/27/1902]

1888 Birth of Patrick J. Byrne, American Catholic missionary. He was the first priest to join the Maryknoll Fathers Society. He founded a mission in North Korea, and in 1929 was elected vicar-general of the Society. Arrested by the Communists when they invaded South Korea in 1950, Byrne died at Ha Chang Ri, Korea, while on an infamous "death march" to the Manchurian border with 700 other prisoners. [d. 11/25/1950]

The Last Passage

899 Death of Alfred the Great, 50, the Saxon king who saved England from conquest by the Danes, and unified the individual Saxon kingdoms under the supremacy of Wessex. Known for his ecclesiastical reforms and his desire to revive learning in his country, Alfred codified English law, founded monasteries, and translated Bede's *Ecclesiastical History*. (b. 849)

1751 Death of Philip Doddridge, 49, Nonconformist divine and hymn author: "O Happy Day, That Fixed My Choice"; "Awake, My Soul, Stretch Every Nerve." (b. 6/26/1702)

1928 Death of Reuben A. Torrey, 72, American Congregational clergyman, evangelist and educator. A successor to D. L. Moody, Torrey pastored Chicago's Moody Memorial Church and served as superintendent of the Moody Bible Institute (1889-1908). He was also one of the editors of *The Fundamentals*, a book series which welded conservative Christianity into a cohesive movement. (b. 1/28/1856)

1944 Death of William Temple, 63, Anglican theologian, philosopher and Archbishop of Canterbury from 1942-44. A Christian socialist, he actively promoted ecumenism. Temple's key teaching was that the loving purpose of God had been revealed in the event of Jesus Christ's life. (b. 10/15/1881)

Words for the Soul

1779 Anglican hymnwriter John Newton declared in a letter: 'The Lord is so rich that He easily can – so good that He certainly will – give His children more than He will ever take away.'

1963 In a letter penned to a child one month before his own death at 65, British literary scholar and Christian apologist C.S. Lewis wrote: 'If you continue to love Jesus, nothing much can go wrong with you, and I hope you may always do so.'

IN GOD'S WORD...   OT: Jeremiah 49:23–50:46 ~ NT: Titus 1:1-16 ~ Psalms 97:1–98:9 ~ Proverbs 26:13-16

חשון ALMANAC OF THE CHRISTIAN FAITH תשרי
HESHVAN   TISHRI

~ October 27 ~

Highlights in History

1746 Presbyterian pastor and theologian William Tennent chartered the College of New Jersey – later renamed Princeton University. He founded the school in 1726 as a seminary to train his sons and others for the ministry. (Critics derisively called it the "Log College.") Subsequent presidents of the institution included Jonathan Dickinson, Jonathan Edwards, Samuel Davies and John Witherspoon.

1771 Francis Asbury first landed in Philadelphia. He was sent from England by John Wesley to oversee America's few hundred Methodists. During his 45-year ministry in America, Asbury traveled an estimated 300,000 miles and delivered over 16,000 sermons. By the time of his death in 1816, there were over 200,000 Methodists in the U.S.

1889 St. Casimir's, the first Lithuanian church in America, was organized in Plymouth, PA.

1902 The Independent Catholic Church in the Philippine Islands was formed.

1978 The complete *New International Version* (NIV) of the Bible was first published by Zondervan Publishers of Grand Rapids, Michigan.

Notable Birthdays

1469 Birth of Desiderius Erasmus, Dutch Christian humanist, philosopher and scholar. Regarded as the leader of the Renaissance in northern Europe, Erasmus' writings paved the way for the Reformation, although his scholarly character prevented him from joining the more emotionally-driven militarism of the European Protestants. [d. 7/12/1536]

1814 Birth of John McClintock, Methodist clergyman and scholar. His chief literary work was the *Cyclopaedia of Biblical, Theological, and Ecclesiastical Literature* (12 vols.). Begun in 1853 in collaboration with James Strong, the first volume appeared in 1867. [d. 3/4/1870]

The Last Passage

1553 In Switzerland, Spanish physician Michael Servetus (b.1511) was convicted for his anti-Trinitarianism, condemned for heresy and blasphemy, and burned at the stake by order of the City of Geneva. (Denying the Trinity and the Incarnation was a capital crime in the Reformation, as it had been throughout the Middle Ages.) John Calvin has often been accused of issuing the order to burn Servetus, but he did not have that authority. It was the Geneva city council that implemented the sentence.

1659 Death of William Robinson, English Quaker martyr. He was one of the first two Quakers (along with Marmaduke Stevenson) to be hanged in Massachusetts, for defying a law which banished Quakers, and threatened returnees with capital punishment. (b. unk.)

Words for the Soul

1527 In a letter written to his friend Philipp Melanchthon, German reformer Martin Luther confessed: *'I am seeking and thirsting for nothing else than a gracious God. And He earnestly offers Himself as such and urges even those who spurn Him and are His enemies to accept Him as such.'*

1963 One month before his own death at age 65, British literary scholar and Christian apologist C. S. Lewis wrote in a letter on the subject of aging: *'Yes, autumn is really the best of the seasons; and I'm not sure that old age isn't the best part of life. But of course, like autumn, it doesn't last.'*

1974 While visiting a Trappist monastery in NY state, Dutch Catholic mystic Henri J. M. Nouwen wrote of the monks in his *Genesee Diary* journal: *'If the monastic life should lead them to a morbid introspection of their own sinfulness, it would lead them away from God for whom they came to the monastery. Therefore, the growing realization of one's sins and weaknesses must open the contemplative to a growing awareness of God's love and care.'*

IN GOD'S WORD...   OT: Jeremiah 51:1-53 ~ NT: Titus 2:1-15 ~ Psalms 99:1-9 ~ Proverbs 26:17

HESHVAN — ALMANAC OF THE CHRISTIAN FAITH — TISHRI

October 28

Highlights in History

312 The outnumbered forces of Roman Emperor Constantine (ca. 280-337) defeated the army of Maxentius at Milvian Bridge. Constantine afterward embraced Christianity as the state religion of Rome. (Before the battle, Constantine had seen the symbol of the cross in a vision, accompanied with the words 'By this sign conquer.')

1636 Harvard College was founded in New Towne (Cambridge), MA, with the Rev. Henry Dunster appointed its first president. (The college received its current name in 1639, after English Puritan cleric Rev. John Harvard endowed the school with his library and half of his personal estate.) Harvard was the first institution of higher education founded in North America, until the Anglicans established William & Mary (1694) in VA, and the conservative Congregationalists began Yale (1701) in CT.

1646 In Massachusetts, English missionary John Eliot preached the first Protestant worship service for Native Americans in their own language. (His accomplishment was no doubt in partial response to a call in 1644 by the Massachusetts General Court for pastors to learn Indian dialects in order to aid in conversions.)

1871 At Ujiji, in Africa, Henry Morton Stanley finally located "missing" British missionary and explorer, Dr. David Livingstone. Stanley's first words: "Dr. Livingstone, I presume?"

1958 Italian Cardinal Angelo Giuseppe Roncalli was elected Pope John XXIII (serving until 1963). He is best remembered for calling the Second Vatican Council, and for his encyclicals "Pacem in Terris" and "Mater et Magistra."

Notable Birthdays

1659 Birth of Nicholas Brady, Irish clergyman. He was chaplain to the English monarchs William and Mary, and to Queen Anne. With Nahum Tate, Brady prepared a metrical version of the book of Psalms. [d. 5/20/1726]

1752 Birth of Dimitri S. Bortniansky, Russian composer. Widely known for his operas, he also systematized modern Russian church music, and came to be known as "the Russian Palestrina." His most enduring hymn tune was ST. PETERSBURG ("I Sing the Praise of Love Unbounded"). [d. 9/28/1825]

1890 Thomas Tien, Archbishop of Peking, was born in Chang-tsui, China. In 1946 he became the first Oriental Catholic to be elevated to the office of cardinal. [d. 7/24/1967]

1892 Antonio Maria Barbieri, history's first Uruguayan Catholic cardinal (1958), was born in Montevideo. He founded the first major seminary in Uruguay, and in 1940 was appointed Archbishop of Uruguay. [d. 7/6/1979]

The Last Passage

1582 English Bible translator Gregory Martin died. A Jesuit from 1573, Martin was a leading member of the Catholic team which translated the Bible from the Latin Vulgate into English (the *Douay-Rheims Version*). (b. ca. 1540)

1966 Iakov I. Zhidkov, president of the All Soviet Union of Evangelical Christian Baptists, died in Moscow at about 82. (b. ca. 1884)

Words for the Soul

1777 Anglican hymnwriter John Newton pointed out in a letter: *'The Lord usually reserves dying strength for a dying hour.'*

1949 Jim Elliot, American missionary and Auca Indian martyr, recorded in his journal: *'He is no fool who gives what he cannot keep to gain that which he cannot lose.'* [This is arguably the most oft-cited quotation from Elliot's writings.]

1960 English literary scholar and Christian apologist C.S. Lewis wrote in *Letters to An American Lady*: *'I find FEAR a great help – the fear that my own unforgiveness will exclude me from all the promises. Fear tames wrath.'*

IN GOD'S WORD... OT: Jeremiah 51:54–52:34 ~ NT: Titus 3:1-15 ~ Psalms 100:1-5 ~ Proverbs 26:18-19

חשון **ALMANAC OF THE CHRISTIAN FAITH** תשרי
HESHVAN TISHRI

October 29

Highlights in History

1889 American missions-minded clergyman A[l-bert] B. Simpson (1843-1919) incorporated the Christian and Missionary Alliance, an ardent missions-centered denomination which merged two societies Simpson had earlier founded: the Missionary Union (1883) and the Christian Alliance (1887).

1919 The Apostolic Christian Association was incorporated in Atlanta, GA. Pentecostal evangelist and educator David Wesley Myland (1858-1943) served as the first chairman (1919-20). This association later merged with what is now the International Pentecostal Church of Christ (headquartered in London, OH).

1930 A three-day convention opened in Minneapolis, at which the American Lutheran Conference was organized. The American Lutheran Church, which was reconstituted in 1960, grew out of this federation, after it dissolved in 1954.

Notable Birthdays

1562 George Abbot, Archbishop of Canterbury (1611-27), was born in Guilford, England. A persistent advocate of Protestant causes in foreign policy, he encouraged Puritan elements in the House of Commons, and also became one of the translators of the King James Version of the New Testament. [d. 8/4/1633]

1792 Birth of William Sandys, English lawyer and hymnwriter. Sandys did pioneering work in reviving public interest in ancient Christmas hymns. He is best remembered today as the composer of the Christmas carol, THE FIRST NOEL. [d. 2/18/1874]

1870 Birth of Juji Nakada, the Japanese Christian evangelist responsible for bringing Charles and Lettie Cowman to Japan in 1901, after which they established the Oriental Missions Society (1910). [d. 9/24/1939]

The Last Passage

1216 Death of John (Lackland), 48, King of England (1199-1216). The son of Henry II and brother of Richard I, it was John whom the English barons forced to sign the Magna Carta in 1215. (b. 12/24/1167)

1885 Death of James Hannington, 38, Anglican missionary prelate. In 1884 he was appointed the first Bishop of Eastern Equatorial Africa. The following year Hannington was speared to death by natives in Mombasa, several days after he had already been savagely beaten. (b. 9/3/1847)

1919 Death of A[lbert] B. Simpson, 75, American Presbyterian clergyman, denominational founder and hymnwriter. He established the Christian and Missionary Alliance Church (1889), and also authored 175 hymns, including "Yesterday, Today, Forever," "Jesus Only" and "What Will You Do With Jesus?" (b. 12/15/1843)

1969 Death of Clarence Jordan, 57, founder of Koinonia Farm in Americus, GA. He published his *Cotton Patch Version* of the Bible in four volumes (1968-1973), which paraphrased the New Testament into the setting and vernacular of the American South. (b. 7/29/1912)

Words for the Soul

1866 American Quaker Hannah Whitall Smith, 34, while seeking the spiritual gift of "personal holiness," reflected in her journal: *'It seems to me that the early Friends must have known and experienced it, and that this accounts for their wonderful success. And isn't it the solution for all my difficulties and questions concerning the guidance of the Holy Spirit? At all events God cannot be displeased with me if I ask Him for it, and I believe this to be the very blessing of which the Methodists testify, calling it "entire sanctification," or "perfect love."'*

IN GOD'S WORD... OT: Lamentations 1:1–2:19 ~ NT: Philemon 1-25 ~ Psalms 101:-8 ~ Proverbs 26:20

ALMANAC OF THE CHRISTIAN FAITH

~ October 30 ~

Highlights in History

1536 Lutheranism became the official religion of Denmark, after reformers had carried the message to that land, and had converted many.

1650 In England, the popular name of "Quaker" was first conferred upon members of the Society of Friends by a local judge at a trial in Derby.

1768 In New York City, Wesley Chapel – the first Methodist church built in America and in the New World – was dedicated. Philip Embury, the pioneer Methodist carpenter and preacher who had also helped build the 42 x 60 ft. stone structure, delivered the dedicatory sermon. The church stood on the site of the present St. John Church.

PHILIP EMBURY

1902 Leo XIII published the apostolic letter "Vigilantiae," which established the Pontifical Commission of Biblical Studies. Originally a committee of cardinals, the Commission was created as an organ for the critical study of Scripture by the Catholic Church, in conformity with the requirements of modern scholarship, yet safeguarding the authority of the Bible against the attacks of exaggerated criticism.

1976 Dr. Joseph H. Evans was elected president of the United Church of Christ, thereby becoming the first African-American leader of a predominantly white denomination.

Notable Birthdays

1789 Birth of Hiram Bingham, Sr., pioneering American Congregational missionary to Hawaii. Twelve days after his marriage, he sailed (on Oct 23, 1819) for the Sandwich (Hawaiian) Islands, where he remained 21 years. Bingham reduced the Hawaiian language to writing, and helped translate the Bible into Hawaiian (1847). Returning to America in 1840 due in part to his wife's failing health, Bingham remained in the U.S. the remainder of his life, preaching and writing. [d. 11/11/1869]

1807 Birth of Christopher Wordsworth, English prelate. He was Bishop of Lincoln (1869-85), a scholar and a hymnwriter. The nephew of William Wordsworth, Christopher wrote 127 poems, including the hymns, "Gracious Spirit, Holy Ghost"; "O Day of Rest and Gladness"; and "O Lord of Heaven and Earth and Sea." [d. 3/20/1885]

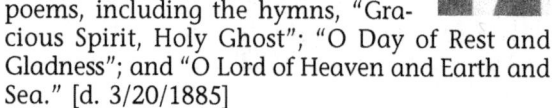

1820 Birth of John Freeman Young, American Episcopal bishop and hymn translator. It was Freeman who rendered the immortal German carol "Stille Nacht, Heilige Nacht" into the English: "Silent Night, Holy Night." [d. 11/15/1885]

1825 Adelaide A. Procter, English hymnwriter, was born in London. She penned numerous hymns, including "My God, I Thank Thee, Who Hast Made" and "The Shadows of the Evening Hour." [d. 2/2/1864]

The Last Passage

1934 Death of Andrew L. Skoog, 77, Swedish-born American hymnwriter. The editor-publisher of a popular Swedish language journal, Skoog also wrote many hymns and hymn tunes. It was he who rendered Lina Sandell's enduring Swedish verse into the enduring English hymn: "Day by Day, and With Each Passing Moment." (b. 12/17/1856)

1973 Death of George S. Schuler, 91. He was with the musical faculty of Moody Bible Institute 40 years. Schuler wrote many anthems, gospel songs and hymn tunes including SCHULER ("Out in the Highways and Byways of Life"). (b. 4/18/1882)

Words for the Soul

1738 English founder of Methodism John Wesley explained in a letter: *'By a "Christian" I mean one who so believes in Christ as that sin hath no more dominion over him.'*

IN GOD'S WORD... OT: Lamentations 2:20–3:66 ~ NT: Hebrews 1:1-14 ~ Psalms 102:1-28 ~ Proverbs 26:21-22

ALMANAC OF THE CHRISTIAN FAITH

חשון HESHVAN

תשרי TISHRI

~ October 31 ~

Highlights in History

1517 German reformer Martin Luther nailed *"Ninety-Five Theses... for the Purpose of Eliciting Truth"* to the door of the Wittenberg Palace Church, and touched off what would become the Protestant Reformation. By the beginning of 1522, Protestant public worship was being celebrated in Wittenberg for the first time.

1825 German-born Englishman George Müeller was converted at a Moravian mission. He went on to found orphanages that housed more than 10,000 orphans by the time of his death in 1898.

1909 The first baptismal service of the Sudan Interior Mission was held. Nearly a century later, Sudanese Christians make up about one-third of the country's population, despite terrible oppression by the Muslim majority.

1917 Tikhon (1865-1925), born Vasili Ivanovich Bolyavin, was named patriarch of the revived Church of Russia, the first patriarch since 1700. He had previously served as metropolitan of Moscow, and took took a determined stand against Bolsheviks, denouncing their cruelty, suppression of liberty, blasphemy, and sacrilege. Tikhon was subsequently imprisoned (1917-23), but released after worldwide protests, whereupon he retired to a monastery.

1992 Pope John Paul II formally admitted that the Roman Catholic Church had been wrong in condemning Italian astronomer Galileo Galilei in 1633 for teaching that the sun, and not the earth, was the center of the universe.

Notable Birthdays

1864 Birth of Cosmo Gordon Lang, Scottish-born Anglican prelate. As the Archbishop of Canterbury, 1928-42, Lang strongly opposed Edward VIII's abdication and marriage. He was also active in social work in industrial areas. [d. 12/5/1945]

1896 Birth of Ethel Waters, African-American singer and actress. She was active in Billy Graham's evangelistic crusades during the 1950's, and was known for singing "His Eye is On the Sparrow." [d. 9/1/1977]

1912 Birth of Frances Smith, American singer and film and television actress. Better known to the world as Dale Evans, she starred with husband Roy Rogers in "The Roy Rogers Show" TV series (1951-57), authored several books and wrote the songs: "Happy Trails" (1951) and "The Bible Tells Me So" (1955). [d. 2/7/2001]

The Last Passage

1879 Death of Jacob Abbott, 75, New England Congregational clergyman, educator and writer. The father of Lyman Abbott, he was one of the first Americans to attempt to write for children as human beings, and produced over 200 titles. (b. 11/14/1803)

1907 Death of Daniel C. Roberts, 65, Ohio-born American Civil War veteran, Episcopal clergyman and educator. For a number of years he was also president of the New Hampshire State Historical Society. Roberts is perhaps best remembered today as author of the hymn: "God of Our Fathers." (b. 11/5/1841)

1963 Death of Sam[uel] Shoemaker, 69, American Episcopal clergyman and writer. He pastored Calvary Protestant Episcopal Church in New York City (1925-52), and assisted the founders of Alcoholics Anonymous in formulating their "Twelve Steps." (b. 12/27/1893)

Words for the Soul

1806 Anglican missionary to Persia, Henry Martyn recorded in his journal: *'I saw it to be my part to pursue my way through the wilderness of this world, looking only to that redemption which daily draweth nigh.'*

IN GOD'S WORD... OT: Lamentations 4:1–5:22 ~ NT: Hebrews 2:1-18 ~ Psalms 103:1-22 ~ Proverbs 26:23

ALMANAC OF THE CHRISTIAN FAITH

OCTOBER INDEX

A

"Archtheologian of Lutheranism" 10/17
Abbot, George
 b. 10/29/1562 [d. 8/4/1633]
Abbott, Jacob
 (b. 11/14/1803) d. 10/31/1879
Abbott, Lyman 10/31
 (b. 12/18/1835) d. 10/22/1922
ABCFM
 American Board of Commissioners.... 10/23
Abd-ar-Rahman 10/10
Ackerman, Paula 10/12
AFRICAN-AMERICANS
 Evans, Joseph H. 10/30
 First American black sisterhood 10/11
 First Anglican bishop of Johannesburg, So. Africa 10/7
 First Black Leader of a White Denomination 10/30
 First Catholic parish church for.... 10/10
 Parham, Charles Fox 10/15
 Tutu, Desmond M. 10/7
 Waters, Ethel 10/31
Ahnfelt, Oscar
 (b. 5/31/1813) d. 10/22/1882
Alcoholics Anonymous 10/31
Alexander, Cecil Frances
 (b. 1818/1823) d. 10/12/1895
Alexander, Charles M.
 b. 10/24/1867 [d. 1920]
Alexander, William 10/12
Alexander II, Pope (1061-1073) 10/1
Alford, Henry
 b. 10/7/1810 [d. 1/12/1871]
Alfred the Great
 (b. 849) d. 10/26/899
All Soviet Union of Evangelical Christian Baptists 10/28
American Baptist Missionary Union 10/21
American Bible Society 10/24
American Civil War 10/5, 10/31
American Lutheran Church 10/9, 10/29
American Lutheran Conference 10/29
American Sign Language 10/3
American Unitarian Association 10/2
Anselm, St. 10/25
Anti-Trinitarianism 10/27
Apostolic Christian Association 10/29
Apostolic Church of Pentecost of Canada 10/25
Apostolic Fathers 10/17
Archbishop of Fundamentalism 10/14
Aristotle 10/1
Arminianism 10/10, 10/19, 10/24
Arminius, James (Jacob)
 b. 10/10/1560 d. 10/19/1609
Asbury, Francis 10/27
Ashkenazi Jews 10/10
Association of Pentecostal Churches 10/13
Association of Philadelphia Baptists 10/12
Athenagoras I, Greek Orthodox Exarch
 (b. 3/25/1886) d. 10/15/1972
Atwood (Newell), Harriet ("Nancy") 10/24
 b. 10/10/1793 [d. 11/30/1812]
Aubigné, Jean Henri Merle d'
 (b. 8/16/1794) d. 10/21/1872
Auca Indians of Ecuador 10/8, 10/12, 10/15, 10/28
Auschwitz Concentration Camp 10/11
Aylward, Gladys 10/15

B

Baker, Theodore
 (b. 6/3/1851) d. 10/13/1934
Baptist Missionary Society for Spreading the Gospel 10/2
Barbieri, Antonio Maria
 b. 10/28/1892 [d. 7/6/1979]
Barclay, Robert
 (b. 12/23/1648) d. 10/3/1690
Barfield, Owen 10/20
Barstow, Robbins Wolcott 10/18
Basil I, Greek Emperor 10/5
BATTLES, NOTABLE
 Battle of Kappel (1531) 10/11
 Irish Massacre (1641) 10/23
 Milvian Bridge (312) 10/26, 10/28
 Yorktown (1781) 10/24
Becket, Thomas à 10/25
Bede, Venerable 10/26
Beecher, Henry Ward 10/22
Bennard, George
 (b. 2/4/1873) d. 10/10/1958
Berg, Carolina ("Lina") Sandell 10/3, 10/22, 10/30
Berkhof, Louis
 b. 10/13/1873 [d. 5/19/1957]
Beza, Theodore
 (b. 6/24/1519) d. 10/13/1605
BIBLE TRANSLATIONS
 Cotton Patch Version (1968-1973) 10/29
 Coverdale Bible (1535) 10/4
 Douay-Rheims Version (1582, 1610) 10/28
 English Revised Version (1881, 1885) 10/15
 Gilbertese (by Hiram Bingham, Jr.) 10/25
 Hawaiian (by Hiram Bingham Sr.) (1847) 10/30
 King James Version (1611) 10/6, 10/29
 Latin Vulgate (382) 10/1, 10/28
 N.T. in Modern Speech (Weymouth, 1903) 10/26
 New International Version (1978) 10/27
 Persian (by Henry Martyn) 10/16
 Revised Standard Version (1946, 1952) 10/23
 Smith & Goodspeed Translation (1923) 10/23
 Tyndale New Testament (1535) 10/6
 Urdu (by Henry Martyn) 10/16
Biblical Chronology, Ussher's 10/23
Bingham, Hiram Jr.
 (b. 8/16/1831) d. 10/25/1908
Bingham, Hiram Sr. 10/23, 10/25, 10/30
 b. 10/30/1789 [d. 11/11/1869]
Bishops' War 10/7
Blanc, Antoine
 b. 10/11/1792 [d. 6/20/1860]
Bode, John Ernest
 (b. 2/23/1816) d. 10/6/1874
Boethius
 (b. unk.) d. 10/23/524
Bojaxhiu, Agnes 10/17, 10/26
Bolyavin, Vasili Ivanovich 10/31
Bonar, Andrew 10/8, 10/12, 10/14, 10/15, 10/17, 10/21, 10/22
Bonar, Isabella 10/12
Book of Common Prayer 10/16
Booth, Ballington
 (b. 7/28/1859) d. 10/5/1940
Booth, Catherine (née Mumford)
 (b. 1/17/1829) d. 10/4/1890
Booth, William 10/4, 10/5
Bornkamm, Günther 10/8
 b. 10/8/1905 [d. 1990]
Borromeo, St. Charles
 b. 10/2/1538 [d. 11/3/1584]
Borthwick, Jane L. 10/22
Bortniansky, Dimitri S.
 b. 10/28/1752 [d. 9/28/1825]
Boudinot, Elias 10/24
Bourne, Hugh
 (b. 4/3/1772) d. 10/11/1852
Bowie, Walter Russell
 b. 10/8/1882 [d. 4/23/1969]
Bowring, John
 b. 10/17/1792 [d. 11/23/1872]
Bradbury, William B. 10/7
 b. 10/6/1816 [d. 1/7/1868]
Brady, Nicholas
 b. 10/28/1659 [d. 5/20/1726]
Brainerd, David 10/2, 10/5, 10/11, 10/19, 10/24
 (b. 4/20/1718) d. 10/9/1747
Brebeuf, St. Jean de 10/10
Bridges, Matthew
 (b. 7/14/1800) d. 10/6/1894
Bright, Bill (William Rohl)
 b. 10/19/1921 [d. 7/19/2003]
Brook Farm Community 10/3
Brown, Olympia
 (b. 1/5/1835) d. 10/23/1926
Bryant, Lloyd 10/25
Brzozowski, Tadsusz
 b. 10/21/1749 [d. 1820]
Bultmann, Rudolf 10/8
Butler, Alban
 b. 10/24/1710 [d. 5/15/1773]
Byrne, Patrick J.
 10/26/1888 [d. 11/25/1950]

C

Caesar, Julius 10/5
Cajetan, Thomas 10/7
Calvin, John 10/13, 10/27
Calvinism 10/10, 10/19
Campus Crusade for Christ 10/19
Candlish, Robert S.
 (b. 3/23/1806) d. 10/19/1873
CANTERBURY, ARCHBISHOPS OF
 Abbot, George (1611-1627) 10/29
 Coggan, (Frederick) Donald (1974-1980) 10/9
 Lang, Cosmo Gordon (1928-1942) 10/31
 Laud, William (1633-45) 10/7
 Temple, William (1942-1944) 10/26
Carbon Dating 10/13
Carey, William 10/2
Carter, (President) Jimmy 10/6
Catherine of Aragon 10/11
CATHOLIC DENOMINATIONS
 Independent Catholic Church of the Philippines 10/27
 Ruthenian Church 10/9
CATHOLIC RELIGIOUS ORDERS
 Carmelite Nuns 10/4, 10/11
 Discalced Carmelites 10/15
 Franciscans (Order of Preachers) 10/3, 10/9
 Jesuits (Society of Jesus) 10/13, 10/18, 10/21
 Maryknoll Fathers Society 10/26
 Mission of Charity 10/26

OCTOBER INDEX

Sisters of the Holy Family 10/11
Society of the Missionaries of Charity 10/17
Chalcedonian Definition (Creed) 10/8, 10/22
Chalmers, Thomas 10/19
Channing, William Ellery
  (b. 4/7/1780) d. 10/2/1842
Chapman, J. Wilbur 10/24
Charles Martel 10/10
Chiang Kai-Shek 10/23
Christian Alliance 10/29
CHRISTIAN EDUCATORS
  Dickinson, Jonathan 10/7
  Farrington, Harry Webb 10/25
  Mears, Henrietta 10/19
CHRISTIAN RADIO BROADCASTERS
  Ironside, Harry 10/14
  Maier, Walter A. 10/2
  Sockman, Ralph W. 10/1
PROGRAMS
  Lutheran Hour 10/2, 10/4
CHURCHES, NOTABLE
  BALTIMORE (USA)
    St. Francis Xavier's Church 10/10
  BOSTON (USA)
    West Church 10/8
  BROOKLYN, NY (USA)
    Plymouth Congregational Church 10/22
  CHICAGO (USA)
    Moody Memorial Church 10/14, 10/26
  FRANCE
    Chartres Cathedral 10/24
  GERMANY
    Wittenberg Palace Church 10/31
  HOLLYWOOD (USA)
    First Presbyterian Church 10/19
  LONDON (England)
    London's City Temple 10/14
    St Paul's Cathedral 10/20
  LOS ANGELES (USA)
    Angelus Temple 10/9
  NEW YORK CITY (USA)
    Bryant's Alliance Tabernacle 10/25
    Calvary Protestant Episcopal Church 10/31
    Riverside Baptist Church 10/5
    Wesley Chapel 10/30
  SCOTLAND
    St. George's, Edinburgh 10/19
CHURCH COUNCILS
  Council of Chalcedon (451) 10/8, 10/22
  Council of Ephesus (431) 10/25
  Council of Trent (1545-1563) 10/2, 10/13
  Fourth Constantinople Council (869) 10/5
  Second Constantinople Council (381) 10/1
  Vatican I Council (1869-1870) 10/20
  Vatican II Council (1962-1965) 10/11
Church of England 10/9, 10/11
Church of God 10/2

Church of Scotland 10/2
Church of the Nazarene 10/13
Clarke, John
  b. 10/8/1609 [d. 4/20/1676]
Clement VI, Pope (1342-1352) 10/20
Clement VIII, Pope (1592-1605) 10/9
Coggan, (Frederick) Donald
  b. 10/9/1909 [d. 5/17/2000]
College of Cardinals 10/1
Colloquy of Marburg 10/1
Constantine I, Roman Emperor 10/26, 10/28
Continental Congress 10/24
Converse, Charles C.
  b. 10/7/1832 [d. 10/18/1918]
Council of Chalcedon (451) 10/8, 10/22
Council of Ephesus 10/25
Counter Reformation 10/2
Coverdale, Miles 10/4
Cowley, A. E. 10/23
Cowman, Charles 10/29
Cowman, Lettie 10/29
Cowper, William 10/16, 10/18, 10/19
Cranach, Lucas
  (b. 10/4/1472) d. 10/16/1553
Crawford, Percy 10/25
Cromwell, Oliver 10/24
Cunningham, William
  b. 10/2/1805 [d. 12/14/1861]
Cushing, William O.
  (b. 12/31/1823) d. 10/19/1902

D

Damasus I, Pope (366-384) 10/1
Darrow, Clarence 10/21
Davies, Samuel 10/27
Dickinson, Frances 10/15
Dickinson, Jonathan 10/27
  (b. 4/22/1688) d. 10/7/1747
Disruption, Scottish Church 10/2
Doddridge, Philip
  (b. 6/26/1702) d. 10/26/1751
Driver, Samuel R.
  b. 10/2/1846 [d. 2/26/1914]
Dunster, Henry 10/28

E

Edict of Fontainbleu (1685) 10/18
Edict of Nantes (1598) 10/18
Edwards, Jonathan 10/9, 10/27
  b. 10/5/1703 [d. 3/22/1758]
Eilberg, Amy 10/12
Elijah ben Solomon
  (b. 4/23/1720) d. 10/17/1797
Eliot, John 10/28

Ellicott, Charles J.
  (b. 4/25/1819) d. 10/15/1905
Elliman, Yvonne 10/12
Elliot, Elizabeth 10/8
Elliot, Jim 10/12, 10/15, 10/28
  b. 10/8/1927 [d. 1/8/1956]
Elphinstone, William
  (b. 1431) d. 10/25/1514
Embury, Philip 10/30
Emerson, Luther Orlando
  (b. 9/29/1820) d. 10/1/1915
Erasmus, Desiderius 10/27
Ethiopian Orthodox Union Church 10/17
Eutychian Heresy 10/8
Evangelical and Reformed Church 10/15
Evangelical Church, The 10/14
Evangelical Churches of Pentecost 10/25
Evangelical Lutheran Church in Southwest Africa 10/4
Evangelical Synod of North America 10/15
Evans, Dale
  b. 10/31/1912 [d. 2/7/2001]
Evans, Joseph H. 10/30
Evolution, Theory of 10/21

F

"Fidei Defensor" 10/11
Fanny Crosby of Sweden 10/3
Farrer, Austin M.
  b. 10/1/1889 [d. 12/29/1968]
Farrington, Harry Webb
  (b. 7/14/1879) d. 10/25/1931
Father of American Lutheranism 10/7
Fausset, Andrew R.
  b. 10/13/1821 [d. 1910]
Fenholt, Jeff 10/12
Ficino, Marsilio 10/19
  (b. 10/19/1433) d. 10/1/1499
Finney, Charles 10/10
Fischer, William G.
  b. 10/14/1835 [d. 8/12/1912]
Fisk, Pliny
  (b. 6/24/1792) d. 10/23/1825
Fleming, Pete 10/8
Forty Martyrs 10/25
Fosdick, Harry Emerson
  (b. 5/24/1878) d. 10/5/1969
Foxe, John
  (b. 1516) d. 10/4/1587
Francis of Assisi, St. 10/3
Franco-Prussian War 10/20
Frederick the Wise of Saxony, Elector 10/16
Free Church of Scotland 10/2
Free Will Baptist Church 10/22

Fundamentalism, Christian 10/9
Furman, Richard
  b. 10/9/1755 [d. 8/25/1825]

G

Galilei, Galileo 10/31
Gallaudet, Thomas 10/3
Gerhard, Johann
  b. 10/17/1582 [d. 8/17/1637]
Gerhardt, Paul 10/11
Gesenius, Heinrich F. W.
  (b. 2/3/1786) d. 10/23/1842
Goforth, Jonathan
  (b. 2/10/1859) d. 10/8/1936
Goodspeed, Edgar J.
  b. 10/23/1871 [d. 1/3/1962]
Graham, Billy 10/25, 10/31
Great Awakening 10/5
Great Disappointment, The 10/22
Great Fire of 1666 (London) 10/20
Greeves, Arthur 10/18
Gregorian Calendar 10/5
Gregory XIII, Pope (1572-1585) 10/5
Grenfell, Sir Wilfred
  (b. 2/28/1865) d. 10/9/1940
Grossteste, Robert
  (b. ca. 1168) d. 10/9/1253

H

Hale, John 10/3, 10/15
Hamblin, Stuart 10/18
Hannington, James
  (b. 9/3/1847) d. 10/29/1885
Harbinger of the Reformation 10/9
Harvard, John 10/28
Hassler, Hans Leo
  b. 10/25/1564 [d. 6/8/1612]
Hastings, James
  (b. 3/26/1852) d. 10/15/1922
Hastings, Thomas
  10/15/1784 [d. 5/15/1872]
Havergal, Frances Ridley 10/13
Hebrew-English Lexicon of the Old Testament 10/2
Heermann, Johann
  b. 10/11/1585 [d. 2/17/1647]
Hengstenberg, Ernst W.
  b. 10/20/1802 [d. 5/28/1869]
Henry, Matthew
  b. 10/18/1662 [d. 6/22/1714]
HERESIES, CHRISTIAN
  Anti-trinitarianism 10/27
  Arianism 10/1
  Eutychianism 10/8
  Nestorianism 10/25
Herzog, J. J. 10/20
Hildegard of Bingen
  (b. 1098) d. 10/8/1179

Holiness Church of Christ 10/13
Holland, Josiah G.
  (b. 7/24/1819) d. 10/12/1881
Holocaust, The 10/9
Holy Roman Empire 10/24
Hooker, Thomas 10/21
Hosmer, Frederick L.
  b. 10/16/1840 [d. 6/7/1929]
Howe, Julia Ward
  (b. 5/27/1819) d. 10/17/1910
Howe, Samuel Gridley 10/17
Hugg, George C.
  (b. 5/23/1848) d. 10/13/1907
Huron Indians of Canada 10/10
HYMNS
  "'Tis Midnight, and on Olive's Brow" 10/24
  "Ah, Holy Jesus, How Hast Thou Offended" 10/11
  "All Creatures of Our God and King" 10/3
  "All Things Bright and Beautiful" 10/12
  "All Through the Night" 10/1
  "America" 10/21
  "Angels from the Realms of Glory" 10/26
  "Anywhere With Jesus I Can Safely Go" 10/3
  "Awake, My Soul, Stretch Every Nerve" 10/26
  "Battle Hymn of the Republic" 10/17
  "Be Still, My Soul" 10/22
  "Break Thou the Bread of Life" 10/20
  "Children of the Heavenly Father" 10/3
  "Come, Ye Thankful People, Come" 10/7
  "Crown Him with Many Crowns" 10/6
  "Day By Day, and With Each Passing Moment" 10/22
  "Day by Day, and With Each Passing Moment" 10/3, 10/30
  "Day is Dying in the West" 10/20
  "For the Beauty of the Earth" 10/7
  "Gentle Jesus, Meek and Mild" 10/24
  "God, That Madest Earth and Heaven" 10/16
  "God, Who Touchest Earth with Beauty" 10/12
  "God Be With You Till We Meet Again" 10/5
  "God is Love, His Mercy Brightens" 10/17
  "God of Grace and God of Glory" 10/5
  "God of Our Fathers" 10/31
  "Gracious Spirit, Holy Ghost" 10/30
  "Happy Trails" 10/31
  "Have Thine Own Way, Lord" 10/6
  "He is Able to Deliver Thee" 10/14
  "He Leadeth Me" 10/6
  "Hiding in Thee" 10/19
  "His Eye is On the Sparrow" 10/31
  "How Big is God?" 10/18
  "I've Found a Friend" 10/6
  "In the Cross of Christ I Glory" 10/17
  "It Is No Secret What God Can Do" 10/18
  "It Is Well with My Soul" 10/16, 10/20
  "I Know Not How That Bethlehem's Babe" 10/25
  "I Love to Tell the Story" 10/14
  "I Sing the Praise of Love Unbounded" 10/28
  "Jesus, I My Cross Have Taken" 10/7
  "Jesus Calls Us" 10/12
  "Jesus Only" 10/29
  "Known Only to Him" 10/18
  "Living for Jesus A Life That is True" 10/12
  "Majestic Sweetness Sits Enthroned" 10/15
  "Marvelous Grace of our Loving Lord" 10/3
  "More Love to Thee, O Christ" 10/26
  "My Country, 'Tis of Thee" 10/21
  "My God, I Thank Thee, Who Hast Made" 10/30
  "My Hope is Built" 10/6
  "Nor Silver Nor Gold Hath Obtained My Redemption" 10/3
  "Old Rugged Cross" 10/10
  "Open Up Your Heart and Let the Son Shine In" 10/18
  "Out in the Highways and Byways of Life" 10/30
  "Out of My Bondage, Sorrow and Night" 10/6
  "O Day of Rest and Gladness" 10/30
  "O Happy Day, That Fixed My Choice" 10/26
  "O Jesus, I Have Promised" 10/6
  "O Lord of Heaven and Earth and Sea" 10/30
  "O Sacred Head Now Wounded" 10/25
  "O Safe to the Rock that is Higher Than I" 10/19
  "O Thou, in All Thy Might So Far" 10/16
  "Rise and Shine" 10/20
  "Rock of Ages" 10/15
  "Savior, Like a Shepherd Lead Us" 10/6
  "Silent Night, Holy Night" 10/30
  "Stille Nacht, Heilige Nacht" 10/30
  "Sweet Hour of Prayer" 10/6
  "Sweet Songs of Salvation" 10/10
  "Take My Life and Let it Be" 10/6
  "Take Time To Be Holy" 10/6
  "There's a Song in the Air" 10/12
  "There's Not a Friend Like the Lowly Jesus" 10/13
  "There is a Green Hill Far Away" 10/6, 10/12
  "The Bible Tells Me So" 10/31
  "The Kingdom Comes on Bended Knee" 10/16
  "The Morning Light is Breaking" 10/21
  "The Shadows of the Evening Hour" 10/30
  "This Old House" 10/18
  "Though the Angry Surges Roll" 10/3
  "Thou My Everlasting Portion" 10/6
  "Thy Kingdom Come, O Lord" 10/16
  "Thy Word Is a Lamp to My Feet" 10/19
  "Under His Wings I Am Safely Abiding" 10/19
  "Watchman, Tell Us of the Night" 10/17
  "We Gather Together to Ask the Lord's Blessing" 10/13
  "What a Friend We Have in Jesus" 10/7
  "What Will You Do With Jesus?" 10/29
  "When We Walk with the Lord" 10/3
  "Whiter Than Snow" 10/14
  "Who Is On the Lord's Side?" 10/13
  "Years I Spent in Vanity and Pride" 10/3
  "Yesterday, Today, Forever" 10/29
HYMN BOOKS
  A Hymn and Prayer Rook for the Use of Such Luthera 10/2

I

Iconoclasm 10/5
Ignatius of Antioch 10/17
Independent Catholic Church 10/27
Inklings, The 10/20
Inquisition, The 10/13, 10/17
Spanish Inquisition 10/17
International Church of the Foursquare Gospel 10/9
International Pentecostal Church of Christ 10/29
Interpreter's Bible, The 10/8
Irish Massacre 10/23
Ironside, Harry (Henry Allen)
  b. 10/14/1876 [d. 1/15/1951]

J

"Jesus Christ, Superstar" 10/12
Jackson, (President) Andrew 10/12
Jerome, St. 10/1
Jerusalem 10/2
Jogues, Isaac
  (b. 1/10/1607) d. 10/18/1646
John (Lackland)
  (b. 12/24/1167) d. 10/29/1216
John of Salisbury
  (b. ca. 1115) d. 10/25/1180
John Paul I, Pope (1978) 10/16, 10/17
John Paul II, Pope (1978-) 10/6, 10/11, 10/16, 10/17, 10/31
John XXIII, Pope (1958-1963) 10/11, 10/28
Jonas, Justus
  (b. 6/1 [or 6]/1493) d. 10/9/1555
Jones, Sam[uel Porter]
  b. 10/16/1847 [d. 10/15/1906]
Jordan, Clarence
  (b. 7/29/1912) d. 10/29/1969
Jowett, Benjamin
  (b. 4/15/1817) d. 10/1/1893

JUDAISM
  Ashkenazl Jews 10/10
  First Conference of Rabbis in the U.S. 10/17
  JEWISH DENOMINATIONS
    Conservative Judaism 10/12
    Judaism, Classical 10/17
    Reformed Judaism 10/3, 10/12
    Sephardic Jews 10/10
Judson, Adoniram 10/10, 10/24
Judson, Ann (née Hasseltine) 10/10
  (b. 12/22/1789) d. 10/24/1826
Julian Calendar 10/5

K

Kalisch, (Rabbi) Isidore 10/17
Kappel, Battle of 10/11
Kautzsch, E[mil] 10/23
Keller, Helen 10/20
Kennedy, (President) John 10/10
Koinonia Farm 10/29
Kunze, Johann Christoff 10/2

L

Lalemant, Gabriel 10/10
Lanfranc of Bec 10/1
Lang, Cosmo Gordon
  b. 10/31/1864 [d. 12/5/1945]
Lathbury, Mary Artemisia
  (b. 8/10/1841) d. 10/20/1913
Latimer, Hugh
  (b. ca. 1485-90) d. 10/16/1555
Latin Vulgate Bible 10/1, 10/28
Laubach, Frank C. 10/7
Laud, William
  b. 10/7/1573 [d. 1/10/1645]
Leo X, Pope (1513-1521) 10/11
Leo XIII, Pope (1878-1903) 10/30
Lewis, C. S. 10/3, 10/18, 10/20, 10/26, 10/27, 10/28
Lind, Jenny 10/22
Livingstone, David 10/28
Long Parliament 10/7
Lowden, Carl H.
  b. 10/12/1883 [d. 2/27/1963]
Luciani, Albino 10/17
Luther, Catherine (née von Bora) 10/22
Luther, John (Hans)
  (b. 6/7/1526) d. 10/22/1575 10/22
Luther, Martin 10/1, 10/4, 10/5, 10/6, 10/7, 10/9, 10/11, 10/12, 10/16, 10/19, 10/20, 10/21, 10/22, 10/24, 10/27, 10/31
Lutheran Church Missouri Synod 10/25

OCTOBER INDEX

M

"Moody of the South" 10/16
MacDonald, George 10/1, 10/7
Macy, Anne Sullivan
  (b. 4/14/1841) d. 10/20/1936
Magna Carta 10/29
Maier, Walter A. 10/2, 10/4
Main, Hubert P.
  (b. 8/17/1839) d. 10/7/1925
Marcian, Emperor 10/8
Martin, Gregory
  (b. ca. 1540) d. 10/28/1582
Martyn, Henry 10/16, 10/31
MARTYRS, CHRISTIAN
  Byrne, Patrick J. 10/26
  Elliot, Jim 10/15
  Forty Martyrs, The 10/25
  Hannington, James 10/29
  Ignatius of Antioch 10/17
  Jim Elliot 10/28
  Jogues, Isaac 10/18
  Latimer, Hugh 10/16
  Ridley, Nicholas 10/16
  Robinson, William 10/27
  Stein, Edith 10/11
  Tyndale, William 10/6
  Zwingli, Ulrich 10/11, 10/14
Maryknoll Fathers Society 10/26
Massachusetts General Court 10/14
Mather, Cotton 10/3, 10/15
Mather, Increase 10/3
Mathews, Ann Teresa 10/15
Mayflower, The 10/18
Mayhew, Jonathan
  b. 10/8/1720 [d. 7/9/1766]
McClintock, John
  b. 10/27/1814 [d. 3/4/1870]
McCully, Ed 10/8
McPherson, Aimee Semple
  b. 10/9/1890 [d. 9/27/1944]
Mears, Henrietta 10/19
Melanchthon, Philipp 10/9, 10/27
Mennonites 10/6
Methodist Episcopal Church South 10/18
Methodist theology 10/19
Michelangelo 10/13
Michener, James 10/23
Migne, Jacques P.
  b. 10/25/1800 [d. 10/24/1875]
Miller, William 10/22
Milligan, George 10/11
Milvian Bridge, Battle of 10/26, 10/28
MISSIONARIES
  Aylward, Gladys 10/15
  Bingham, Hiram Jr. 10/25
  Bingham, Hiram Sr. 10/23, 10/25
  Brainerd, David 10/5, 10/9, 10/11, 10/19, 10/24
  Brebeuf, Jean de 10/10
  Byrne, Patrick J. 10/26
  Carey, William 10/2
  Cowman, Charles 10/29
  Cowman, Lettie 10/29
  Eliot, John 10/28
  Elliot, Jim 10/8, 10/12, 10/15, 10/28
  Fisk, Pliny 10/23
  Goforth, Jonathan 10/8
  Grenfell, Wilfred 10/9
  Hannington, James 10/29
  Jogues, Isaac 10/18
  Judson, Adoniram 10/10, 10/24
  Judson, Ann (née Hasseltine) 10/10, 10/24
  Lalemant, Gabriel 10/10
  Laubach, Frank C. 10/7
  Livingstone, David 10/28
  Martyn, Henry 10/16, 10/31
  Moon, Charlotte (Lottie) 10/7
  Newell, Harriet 10/24
  Newell, Harriet (née Atwood) 10/10
  Newell, Samuel 10/10
  Nitschmann, David 10/8
  Parsons, Levi 10/23
  Paton, John 10/24
  Ricci, Matteo 10/6
  Thurston, Asa 10/23
  Wesley, John 10/14
Missionary Union 10/29
MISSIONS, FOREIGN
  MISSION FIELDS
    Africa 10/2
    Australia 10/4
    Ceylon 10/2
    China 10/2, 10/6, 10/8, 10/15
    Ecuador 10/8
    India 10/2, 10/4
    Japan 10/4, 10/29
    Korea 10/26
    Labrador, Newfoundland 10/9
    Micronesia (Gilbert Islands) 10/25
    New Hebrides 10/24
    Palestine 10/2, 10/23
    Persia 10/16
    Sandwich Islands (Hawaii) 10/23, 10/30
  ORGANIZATIONS
    American Baptist Missionary Union 10/21
    Baptist Missionary Society for Spreading the Gospel 10/2
    Oriental Missions Society 10/29
    Regions Beyond Mission 10/1
    Sudan Interior Mission 10/31
Monkey Trial, Scopes 10/21
Moody, Dwight L. 10/6, 10/10, 10/26
Moody, Emma (née Revell)
  (b. 1842) d. 10/10/1903
Moody, Joseph N. 10/18
Moody Bible Institute 10/26, 10/30
Moon, Charlotte (Lottie) 10/7
Moore, George Foote
  b. 10/15/1851 [d. 5/16/1931]
Mother Teresa (Agnes Bojaxhiu) 10/17, 10/26
Moulton, James H.
  b. 10/11/1863 [d. 4/7/1917]
MOVEMENTS, THEOLOGICAL
  "New Light" Presbyterians 10/7
  Adventism 10/22
  Arminianism 10/10, 10/19
  Calvinism 10/10, 10/19
  Fundamentalism, Christian 10/9
  Mercersburg Theology 10/20
  Modernist movement 10/22
  Oneness, Pentecostal 10/25
  Social Gospel 10/22
MOVIES
  "Inn of the Sixth Happiness" 10/15
Mueller, George 10/31
Mühlenberg, Henry Melchior
  (b. 9/6/1711) d. 10/7/1787
Muratori, Ludovico A.
  10/21/1672 [d. 1/23/1750]
Muratorian Fragment 10/21
MUSICALS
  "Jesus Christ, Superstar" 10/12
Myconius, Oswald
  (b. 1488) d. 10/14/1552
Myland, David Wesley 10/29

N

Nakada, Juji
  b. 10/29/1870 [d. 9/24/1939]
National Council of Churches 10/14
National Lutheran Conference 10/8
Naziism, German 10/11
Nebuchadnezzar 10/13
Nestorius 10/9
Newell, Harriet (née Atwood) 10/24
  b. 10/10/1793 [d. 11/30/1812]
Newell, Samuel 10/10
Newman, John Henry 10/9
Newton, John 10/19, 10/26, 10/28
NICKNAMES / TITLES
  "Archtheologian of Lutheranism" 10/17
  Archbishop of Fundamentalism 10/14
  Fanny Crosby of Sweden 10/3
  Father of American Lutheranism 10/7
  Harbinger of the Reformation 10/9
  "Moody of the South" 10/16
  "Smiling Pope, The" 10/17
  "Russian Palestrina, The" 10/28
Nitschmann, David
  (b. 12/27/1696) d. 10/8/1772
Nobel Peace Prize 10/7, 10/17
Nouwen, Henri J. M. 10/3, 10/13, 10/14, 10/18, 10/21

O

Ogden, William A.
  (b. 10/10/1841) d. 10/14/1897
Oglethorpe, James 10/14
Olney Hymns 10/19
ORGANIZATIONS, CHRISTIAN
  Campus Crusade for Christ 10/19
  Oriental Missions Society 10/29
  Youth For Christ 10/25
ORTHODOXY, CHRISTIAN
  Athenagoras I, Greek Orthodox Exarch 10/15
  Church of Russia, Revived 10/31
  Ethiopian Orthodoxy Union Church 10/17
  Greek Orthodoxy 10/9, 10/15
  Patriarch of Constantinople 10/9
Oxford Tractarian Movement 10/9
Ozman, Agnes 10/15

P

Paine, Robert F.
  (b. 11/12/1799) d. 10/18/1882
Parham, Charles Fox 10/15
Parsons, Levi 10/23
Pastorious, Francis Daniel 10/6
Paton, John 10/24
Paul III, Pope (1534-1549) 10/13
Paul VI, Pope (1963-1978) 10/4, 10/25
Peace of Westphalia 10/24
Penn, William 10/6, 10/21
  b. 10/14/1644 [d. 7/30/1718]
Pentecostal Assemblies of Canada 10/25
Pentecostal Fellowship of North America 10/26
PERIODICALS, RELIGIOUS
  "Christian Union" 10/22
  "Expository Times" 10/15
  "Illustrated Christian Weekly" 10/22
  "Outlook, The" 10/22
  "Westminster Review" 10/17
  "Youth's Companion" 10/26
Peter Damien 10/20
Pierpoint, Folliott S.
  b. 10/7/1835 [d. 3/10/1917]
Pierpont, John 10/16
Pius IV, Pope (1559-1565) 10/2
Plato 10/1, 10/19
Plymouth Colony 10/18
POEMS, NOTABLE
  "I met God in the morning..." 10/1
Pontifical Commission of Biblical Studies 10/30

POPES
  Alexander II (1061-1073) 10/1
  Clement VIII (1592-1605) 10/9
  Clement VI (1342-1352) 10/20
  Damasus I (366-384) 10/1
  Gregory XIII (1572-1585) 10/5
  John Paul II (1978-) 10/6, 10/11,
    10/16, 10/17, 10/31
  John Paul I (1978) 10/16, 10/17
  John XXIII (1958-1963) 10/11, 10/28
  Leo XIII (1878-1903) 10/30
  Leo X (1513-1521) 10/11
  Paul III (1534-1549) 10/13
  Paul VI (1963-1978) 10/4, 10/25
  Pius IV (1559-1565) 10/2
  Sixtus IV (1471-1484) 10/17
Powell, Louisa 10/23
Predestination 10/10, 10/19, 10/22
Prentiss, Elizabeth P.
  b. 10/26/1818 [d. 8/13/1878]
PRESIDENTS, U.S.
  Carter, Jimmy 10/6
  Jackson, Andrew 10/12
  Kennedy, John F. 10/10
  Washington, George 10/24
Priesand, Sally Jane 10/12
Primate of Ireland, Anglican 10/12,
  10/23
Primitive Methodist Church 10/11
Procter, Adelaide A.
  b. 10/30/1825 [d. 2/2/1864]
Protestant Reformation 10/21,
  10/27, 10/31
Prynne, William
  (b. 1600) d. 10/24/1669

Q

Quakers 10/2, 10/3, 10/14, 10/19,
  10/21, 10/27, 10/30
QUOTATIONS
  Bonar, Andrew 10/8, 10/12, 10/14,
    10/15, 10/17, 10/21, 10/22
  Brainerd, David 10/2, 10/11, 10/19,
    10/24
  Cowper, William 10/16, 10/18, 10/19
  Elliot, Jim 10/12, 10/15, 10/28
  Kennedy, (President) John 10/10
  Laubach, Frank C. 10/7
  Lewis, C. S. 10/3, 10/18, 10/20, 10/26,
    10/27, 10/28
  Luther, Martin 10/4, 10/5, 10/6, 10/11,
    10/12, 10/19, 10/20, 10/21, 10/24,
    10/27
  MacDonald, George 10/1, 10/7
  Martyn, Henry 10/16, 10/31
  Newton, John 10/26, 10/28
  Nouwen, Henri J. M. 10/3, 10/13,
    10/14, 10/18, 10/21, 10/27
  Rutherford, Samuel 10/15
  Schaeffer, Francis 10/11
  Smith, Hannah Whitall 10/25, 10/29

Wesley, John 10/30
Whitefield, George 10/2, 10/5, 10/9,
  10/10, 10/13, 10/17

R

"Russian Palestrina, The" 10/28
Rad, Gerhard von
  b. 10/21/1901 [d. 10/31/1971]
Randall, Benjamin
  (b. 2/7/1749) d. 10/22/1808
Rauschenbusch, Walter 10/4
Redaction Criticism 10/8
Reformation, Protestant 10/21,
  10/27
Reformed Church 10/15
Reformed Judaism 10/3
Regions Beyond Mission 10/1
Renaissance, The 10/25
REVIVALISTS / EVANGELISTS
  Bennard, George 10/10
  Bright, Bill 10/19
  Finney, Charles 10/10
  Jones, Sam[uel] Porter 10/16
  Moody, Dwight L. 10/10
  Nakada, Juji 10/29
  Randall, Benjamin 10/22
  Torrey Reuben A. 10/26
  Whitefield, George 10/10, 10/13,
    10/17, 10/22
Rhenish Missionary Church 10/4
Ricci, Matteo
  b. 10/6/1552 [d. 5/11/1610]
Rice, Tim 10/12
Ridley, Nicholas
  (b. ca. 1503) d. 10/16/1555
Ripley, George 10/3
Roberts, Daniel C.
  (b. 11/5/1841) d. 10/31/1907
Robinson, William
  (b. unk.) d. 10/27/1659
Rodeheaver, Homer A.
  b. 10/4/1880 [d. 12/18/1955]
Roncalli, Angelo Giuseppe 10/28
Rosenbloom, (Rabbi) William S.
  10/13
RULERS, ARAB/MUSLIM
  Abd-ar-Rahman 10/10
  Saladin of Damascus 10/2
RULERS, BYZANTINE
  Basil I 10/5
  Marcian, Emperor 10/8
RULERS, ENGLISH
  Anne (1702-1714) 10/28
  Charles I (1625-1649) 10/23
  Edward VIII (1936) 10/31
  Henry II (1154-1189) 10/29
  Henry VIII (1509-1547) 10/11, 10/13
  James II (1685-1688) 10/21
  John Lackland (1199-1216) 10/29

  Mary II (1689-1694) 10/21
  Mary I (Tudor) (1553-1558) 10/4,
    10/16, 10/21
  Richard I (1189-1199) 10/29
  William III (1689-1702) 10/21, 10/28
RULERS, FRENCH
  Louis XIV (1643-1715) 10/18
RULERS, PERSIAN
  Cyrus the Great (538-530 BC) 10/13
RULERS, POLISH
  Sigismund III, King 10/9
RULERS, ROMAN
  Constantine I (308-337) 10/26, 10/28
  Trajan (98-117) 10/17
RULERS, SPANISH
  Ferdinand II of Aragon 10/18
  Isabella of Castille 10/18
Ruthenian Church 10/9
Rutherford, Samuel 10/15

S

"Smiling Pope, The" 10/17
Sabatier, Louis A.
  b. 10/22/1839 [d. 4/12/1901]
Saint, Nate 10/8
Saladin of Damascus 10/2
Salem Witch Trials 10/3, 10/15
Salvation Army 10/4, 10/5, 10/10
Sandys, William
  b. 10/29/1792 [d. 2/18/1874]
Sankey, Ira 10/6
Schaeffer, Francis 10/11
Schaff, Philip 10/20
Schindler, Oskar
  (b. 4/28/1908) d. 10/9/1974
Schlegel, Katharina von
  b. 10/22/1697 [d. ca. 1768] 10/22
Schuler, George S.
  (b. 4/18/1882) d. 10/30/1973
Scopes, John T.
  (b. 8/3/1900) d. 10/21/1970
Scopes Monkey Trial 10/21
Scottish National Church 10/2
Second Crusade 10/2
Self-flagellation 10/20
Sellers, Ernest O.
  (b. 10/29/1869) d. 10/19/1952
SEMINARIES
  MASSACHUSETTS (USA)
    Andover Theological Seminary
      10/15
  MICHIGAN (USA)
    Calvin Seminary of Grand Rapids
      10/13
  MISSOURI (USA)
    Concordia Theological Seminary
      10/4, 10/25
  NEW YORK CITY (USA)
    Jewish Theological Seminary 10/12

    Union Theological Seminary 10/8,
      10/20
  PENNSYLVANIA (USA)
    Mercersburg Seminary 10/20
Sephardic Jews 10/10
SERMONS, NOTABLE
  "Sinners in the Hands of An Angry
    God" 10/5
Servetus, Michael 10/27
  (b. 1511) d. 10/27/1553
Shaw, Martin F.
  (b. 3/9/1875) d. 10/24/1958
Shoemaker, Sam[uel]
  (b. 12/27/1893) d. 10/31/1963
Shroud of Turin 10/13
Simpson, A[lbert] B. 10/1, 10/29
  (b. 12/15/1843) d. 10/29/1919
Sixtus IV, Pope (1471-1484) 10/17
Skoog, Andrew L.
  (b. 12/17/1856) d. 10/30/1934
SLAVERY & ABOLITION 10/2, 10/7,
  10/13, 10/19
Small, Franklin 10/25
Smart, Henry T.
  b. 10/26/1813 [d. 7/6/1879]
Smith, Hannah Whitall 10/25, 10/29
Smith, Henry Preserved
  b. 10/23/1847 [d. 2/26/1927]
Smith, Samuel Francis
  b. 10/21/1808 [d. 11/16/1895]
Social Gospel 10/4, 10/22
Society of the Missionaries of Charity
  10/17
Sockman, Ralph W.
  b. 10/1/1889 [d. 8/29/1970]
Spafford, Horatio G.
  b. 10/20/1828 d. 10/16/1888
Spalatin, Georg 10/19
Spurgeon, Charles H. 10/7, 10/22
Spurgeon, Susannah
  (b. 1/15/1832) d. 10/22/1903
Stanley, Henry M. 10/28
Stebbins, George C. 10/24
  (b. 2/26/1846) d. 10/6/1945
Stein, Edith 10/11
Stevenson, Marmaduke
  (b. unk.) d. 10/27/1659
Strong, James 10/27
Sudan Interior Mission 10/31
Sunday, Billy 10/4
Swiss Reformation 10/13
Sybil of the Rhine 10/8

T

Taborites 10/11
Taney, Roger B.
  (b. 3/17/1777) d. 10/12/1864

Tappan, William B.
  b. 10/24/1794 [d. 6/18/1849]
Tate, Nahum 10/28
TELEVISION PROGRAMS
  "The Roy Rogers Show" (1951-1957) 10/31
  "The Week in Religion" (1952-1954) 10/18
Temple, William
  (b. 10/15/1881) d. 10/26/1944
Tennent, William 10/27
Teresa, Mother (Agnes Bojaxhiu) 10/17, 10/26
Teresa of Avila, St. 10/4
Thirty Years War 10/24
Thurston, Asa 10/23
Tien, Thomas
  b. 10/28/1890 [d. 7/24/1967]
Tikhon, Russian Patriarch 10/31
Tolkien, J. R. R. 10/20
Tomer, William G.
  b. 10/5/1833 [d. 9/26/1896]
Tomlinson, A. J.
  (b. 9/22/1865) d. 10/2/1943
Torquemada, Thomas de 10/17
Torrey, Reuben A. 10/24
  (b. 1/28/1856) d. 10/26/1928
Towner, Margaret Ellen 10/24
Towner, Daniel B. 10/3
Transcendentalism 10/2, 10/3
Tutu, Desmond M.
  b. 10/7/1931
Tyndale, William
  (b. ca. 1494) d. 10/6/1536

U

Unitarian Congregationalism 10/8
United Church of Christ 10/15, 10/30
United Free Church of Scotland 10/2
Ussher, James 10/23

V

Vail, Silas J.
  b. 10/6/1818 [d. 5/20/1884]
Vatican II Ecumenical Council 10/11, 10/28
Vatican I Ecumenical Council 10/20
Vereen, Ben 10/12
Volunteers of America 10/5

W

Walther, Carl F. W.
  b. 10/25/1811 [d. 5/7/1887]
WARS, NOTABLE
  Bishops' War (1639-1640) 10/7
  Franco-Prussian War (1870) 10/20
  Korean Conflict (1950-53) 10/26
  Swiss Religious Wars 10/11
  Thirty Years War (1618-1648) 10/24
World War I (1914-1919) 10/4
Washington, (President) George 10/24
Waters, Ethel
  b. 10/31/1896 [d. 9/1/1977]
Weatherhead, Leslie D.
  b. 10/14/1893 [d. 1/3/1976]
Webber, Andrew Lloyd 10/12
Wesley, Charles 10/8, 10/14
Wesley, John 10/8, 10/14, 10/24, 10/27, 10/30
Weymouth, Richard F.
  b. 10/26/1822 [d. 12/27/1902]
Whitefield, George 10/2, 10/5, 10/9, 10/10, 10/13, 10/17, 10/22
Willard, Samuel 10/3, 10/15
Williams, Roger 10/8
Winona Lake Summer School of Music 10/4
Winslow, Edward
  b. 10/18/1595 [d. 5/8/1655]
Winthrop, John 10/20
Wisconsin Women's Suffrage Association 10/23
Wise, (Rabbi) Isaac Mayer 10/3
Witherspoon, John 10/27
Wojtyla, Karol 10/16
Woolman, John
  b. 10/19/1720 d. 10/7/1772
Wordsworth, Christopher
  b. 10/30/1807 [d. 3/20/1885]
Wordsworth, William 10/30
Wren, Christopher
  b. 10/20/1632 [d. 2/25/1723]
WRITINGS, NOTABLE
  "Fundamental Orders" 10/21
  "Mater et Magistra" (John XXIII) 10/28
  "Pacem in Terris" (John XXIII) 10/28
  "Vigilantiae" (Leo XIII) 10/30
  AA's Twelve Steps 10/31
  Aberdeen Breviary (Scottish) 10/25
  Baker's Biographical Dictionary (1900) 10/13
  Bede's Ecclesiastical History 10/26
  Book of Common Prayer (American, 1789) 10/16
  Brainerd's Journal 10/9
  Butler's Lives of the Saints (1756-59) 10/24
  Cyclopaedia of Biblical, Theological, and Ecclesia 10/27
  Encyclopaedia of Religion and Ethics 10/15
  Foxe's Book of Martyrs 10/4
  Fundamentals, The (1910-15) 10/26
  Gesenius-Kautzsch-Cowley Hebrew Grammar 10/23
  Hastings' Dictionary of the Bible 10/15
  Hengstenberg's Christology of the Old Testament 10/20
  Inclusive Language Lectionary (1983) 10/14
  Journal of John Woolman 10/7
  Luther's Ninety-Five Theses 10/31
  Matthew Henry's Exposition of the OT & NT 10/18
  Migne's Patrology 10/25
  Oxford Book of Carols (1928) 10/24
  Schaff's History of the Christian Church 10/20
  Schaff's Creeds of Christendom 10/20
  Ussher's Chronology of the OT & NT 10/23
  Woolman's Journal 10/19
Wyclif, John 10/9
Wyrtzen, Jack 10/25

Y

Youderian, Roger 10/8
Young, John Freeman
  b. 10/30/1807 [d. 3/20/1885]
Youth For Christ 10/25

Z

Zhidkov, Iakov I.
  (b. ca. 1884) d. 10/28/1966
Zizka, Jan
  (b. unk.) d. 10/11/1424
Zwingli, Ulrich 10/1, 10/14
  (b. 1/1/1484) d. 10/11/1531

KISLEV — ALMANAC OF THE CHRISTIAN FAITH — HESHVAN

November 1

Highlights In History

451 In the Roman province of Bithynia (modern Turkey), the Council of Chalcedon adjourned. Begun on Oct. 8th, the 17 sessions of this Fourth Ecumenical Council were attended by over 500 bishops – more than participated in any other ancient Church council.

1512 Italian Renaissance artist Michelangelo, 37, unveiled his 5,808-square-foot masterpiece – the ceiling of the Sistine Chapel in the Vatican. He had been commissioned in 1508 by Pope Julius II to do a work depicting the story of the Bible.

1950 Pope Pius XII proclaimed the dogma of the Assumption of the Blessed Virgin Mary. His Apostolic Constitution "Munificentissimus Deus" taught that at the end of her earthly life, Jesus' mother was taken, body and soul, into heaven to be united with the risen Christ.

Notable Birthdays

1757 Birth of George Rapp, German-born U.S. religious sectarian. He led a group of German Pietists to America and founded the successful societies of Harmony (in Indiana) and Economy (in Pennsylvania) — both of which were based on religious communal principles. Unfortunately, the rule of celibacy led to their eventual extinction.) [d. 8/7/1847]

1825 Birth of William Whiting, Anglican sacred chorister and hymnwriter. He was master of the Winchester College choristers from 1842-78, and is remembered as author of the hymn: "Eternal Father, Strong to Save." [d. 5/3/1878]

1873 Birth of Rudolph de Landas Berghes, aristocratic-born Austrian religious leader. During WWI, he came to America and in 1916 became the second person to introduce "Old Catholicism" into the United States. [d. 11/17/1920]

1880 Birth of Sholem Asch, Polish-born American Jewish author. Known for writing with biblical themes, his 1943 novel, *The Apostle*, based on the life of Paul, interpreted Christianity as a clear outgrowth of Judaism. [d. 7/10/1957]

1921 Birth of John W. Peterson, contemporary American sacred composer. He has written more than 1000 texts and tunes. His most familiar titles include: "So Send I You," "Heaven Came Down," "It Took a Miracle," "Surely Goodness and Mercy" and "Springs of Living Water." [d. 9/20/2006]

The Last Passage

1770 Death of Alexander Cruden, 71, Scottish bookseller and writer. His complete concordance of the Scripture (1737) is still a standard reference for the King James Version. Prone to erratic behavior, Cruden worked on his concordance between periods of mental breakdown. (b. 5/31/1699)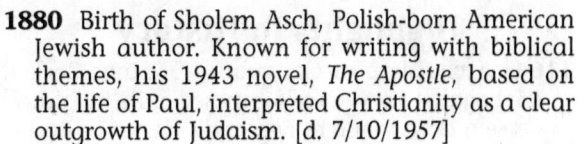

1918 American missionary and educator Howard A. Walter, 35, died in India during an influenza epidemic. Walter is remembered as author of the hymn, "I Would Be True." (b. 8/19/1883)

1966 Death of Albert S. Reitz, 87, American Baptist clergyman and hymnwriter. He published the words and music to over 100 hymns, including "Teach Me to Pray" (REITZ). (b. 1/20/1879)

Words For The Soul

1963 English linguistic scholar J.R.R. Tolkien summarized in a letter to his son: 'In the last resort, faith is an act of will, inspired by love.'

1974 Russian Orthodox liturgical scholar Father Alexander Schmemann reflected in his journal: 'One can love religion... for its own sake without relation to God.... Religion fascinates; it is entertaining. It has everything that is sought after:... esthetics, mystery, the sacred and a feeling of one's importance and exclusive depth, etc. That kind of religion is not necessarily faith.'

IN GOD'S WORD...   OT: Ezekiel 1:1–3:15 ~ NT: Hebrews 3:1-19 ~ Psalms 104:1-23 ~ Proverbs 26:24-26

כסלו KISLEV

ALMANAC OF THE CHRISTIAN FAITH

חשון HESHVAN

~ November 2 ~

Highlights In History

1164 Archbishop of Canterbury Thomas Becket, 45, began a six-year self-imposed exile in France. Once a close friend of England's Henry II, Becket had more recently become an outspoken opponent of the king's policies.

1789 During the chaos of the French Revolution, the property of the Church in France was confiscated by the leaders of the Revolution.

1830 In Baltimore, 114 Methodist Episcopal Church delegates met to establish the Methodist Protestant Church. These representatives were opposed to a bishop-led form of church government, and believed that any layman had a right to vote on any question at any church meeting.

1917 British foreign secretary Arthur J. Balfour, 69, issued the Balfour Declaration, calling for "establishment in Palestine of a national home for the Jewish people." This document planted a seed which in 1948 led to the founding of the modern state of Israel.

Notable Birthdays

1773 Birth of Stephen Grellet, French Quaker clergyman, missionary and philanthropist. Traveling through Europe and North America, Grellet reported on conditions in prisons and poorhouses, and introduced Elizabeth Fry to her life-work among prisoners. Grellet is remembered today for a single quote: 'I expect to pass through this world but once; any good thing therefore that I can do, or any kindness that I can show to any fellow-creature, let me do it now; let me not defer or neglect it, for I shall not pass this way again.' [d. 11/16/1855]

1827 Birth of Paul Anton de Lagarde, German Orientalist and theologian. He authored books on the Bible and on the church fathers. He also translated and edited many Greek, Chaldean, Arabic, Syriac and Coptic texts. [d. 12/22/1891]

1834 Birth of Harriett Eugenia Peck Buell, American Methodist poet. For 50 years she contributed her verses to the "Northern Christian Advocate." Today she is best remembered as the author of the hymn, "My Father is Rich in Houses and Lands." [d. 2/6/1910]

The Last Passage

1610 Death of Richard Bancroft, 66, Archbishop of Canterbury (1604-10). He was chief overseer of the committee which prepared the King James English translation of the Bible. Bancroft also helped establish the Anglican episcopacy in Scotland. (b. 1544)

1845 Death of Chrétien Urhan, 55, French violinist and concertmaster. Known for his religious asceticism, Urhan composed several melodies which were later adapted as hymn tunes, including RUTHERFORD ("The Sands of Time Are Sinking"). (b. 2/16/1790)

1915 Death of John T. Grape, 80, American Methodist businessman and sacred choral director. He composed a number of hymn tunes, including one melody which remains in common use today: ALL TO CHRIST ("I Heard the Savior Say"). (b. 5/6/1835)

Words For The Soul

1600 Anglican theologian Richard Hooker died at 46. His last words were: 'God hath my daily petitions, for I am at peace with all men, and He is at peace with me... and this witness makes the thoughts of death joyful.'

1918 Regarding the fulfillment of one's life dreams, young British literary scholar (and later Christian apologist) C. S. Lewis wrote in a letter to life-long friend Arthur Greeves: 'Once a dream has become a fact I suppose it loses something. This isn't affectation: we long & long for a thing and when it comes it turns out to be just a pleasant incident, very much like others.'

IN GOD'S WORD...   OT: Ezekiel 3:16–6:14 ~ NT: Hebrews 4:1-16 ~ Psalms 7104:24-35 ~ Proverbs 26:27

כסלו ALMANAC OF THE CHRISTIAN FAITH חשון
KISLEV   HESHVAN

~ November 3 ~

Highlights In History

1631 English-born clergyman John Eliot, 27, arrived in America, at Boston. He afterward became the first Protestant minister to devote himself to the evangelization of the native American, and began preaching to the Indians in 1646.

1784 English clergyman Thomas Coke, 37, arrived at New York City. Accompanied by Richard Whatcoat and Thomas Vasey, Coke was the first Methodist bishop to come to the New World to help organize the Methodist movement in the newly independent United States.

1818 Pliny Fisk, 26, set sail for Palestine. Ordained by the American Board of Commissioners for Foreign Missions, he was the first American missionary to travel to the Near East.

Notable Birthdays

1585 Birth of Cornelius O. Jansen, Dutch Catholic clergyman and father of Jansenism. This Catholic religious movement maintained that the teachings of St. Augustine on grace, free will and predestination opposed the teachings of the Jesuits of that day. (Jansenism was condemned by Pope Urban VIII in 1642.) [d. 5/6/1638]

1723 Birth of Samuel Davies, famed colonial American clergyman and a pioneer leader of Southern Presbyterianism. Davies founded the Hanover Presbytery (1755), the first in Virginia, and later served as president of Princeton College (1759-61). [d. 2/4/1761]

1794 Birth of William Cullen Bryant, American poet ("the American Wordsworth") and editor. His use of religious themes contributed in a subtle way to the influence of Unitarianism in 19th century America. Primarily a poet of nature, in 1811 (at age 17), Bryant produced his greatest verse: "Thanatopsis" ("A View of Death"). [d. 6/12/1878]

The Last Passage

753 Death of St. Pirminius, first abbot of the Benedictine monastery at Reichenau (in modern Germany). His name endures as the author of *Scarapsus* (or *Dicta Pirminii*)–the earliest known document to contain the Apostles' Creed in its present form. (b. 700's)

1584 Death of St. Charles Borromeo, 46, a leader of the Counter-Reformation. Appointed Archbishop of Milan in 1560 by his uncle, Pius IV, he set out to tighten the morals of his see, promoted education of the clergy, and took a personal interest in the sick and poor, notably during the plague of 1576. He was canonized in 1610. (b. 10/2/1538)

1600 Death of Richard Hooker, 46, Anglican clergyman and theologian. He was a staunch Anglican apologist of the Church of England, and is regarded as the greatest exponent of the Anglican Church's appeal to reason, Scripture and tradition. He authored *The Laws of Ecclesiastical Polity* (1594-97). (b. 3/1554)

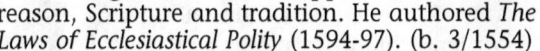

1759 Martin Luther's male lineage ended with the death of his great-great-grandson, Martin Gottlob Luther, a Dresden attorney descended through Paul, the Reformer's second youngest of six children. (Descendants of Margaret–Luther's 6th and youngest child–are still living.)

Words For The Soul

1537 German reformer Martin Luther declared in a sermon: 'Either sin is with you, lying on your shoulders, or it is lying on Christ, the Lamb of God. Now if it is lying on your back, you are lost; but if it is resting on Christ, you are free, and you will be saved. Now choose what you want.'

1976 Russian Orthodox liturgist Father Alexander Schmemann reflected in his journal: 'The feeling of property is the only way to safeguard people from the absolute, demonic power of money. Money, in the capitalistic system, is not property. People do not control money, but money controls them.'

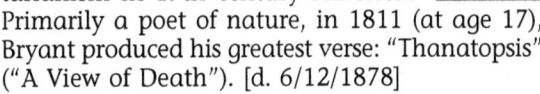

IN GOD'S WORD...   OT: Ezekiel 7:1–9:11 ~ NT: Hebrews 5:1-14 ~ Psalms 105:1-15 ~ Proverbs 26:28

ALMANAC OF THE CHRISTIAN FAITH

KISLEV — **HESHVAN**

~ November 4 ~

Highlights In History

1646 The Massachusetts Bay Colony passed a law making it a capital offense to deny that the Bible was the Word of God. A person convicted of the offense was liable to the death penalty.

1898 The first church to bear the Pentecostal Holiness name was organized at Goldsboro, NC, under the leadership of Methodist evangelist Ambrose Blackman Crumpler, 35.

1966 London's "Evening Standard" newspaper published John Lennon's controversial remark stating that the Beatles were *'more popular than Jesus.'* The quote touched off a storm of controversy and international protest, resulting in a worldwide boycott of Beatles music.

Notable Birthdays

1740 Birth of Augustus M. Toplady, English Calvinist clergyman and hymnwriter. A highly respected evangelical leader, Toplady was a bitter opponent both of John Wesley and of Methodist theology. Toplady's hymns promulgated his Calvinist beliefs, including the hymn "Rock of Ages," penned two years before his early death at 38 from tuberculosis. [d. 8/11/1778]

1771 Birth of James Montgomery, Scottish Moravian clergyman, editor and poet. The author of over 400 hymns, Montgomery's name endures today as author of "Angels From the Realms of Glory," "Prayer is the Soul's Sincere Desire" and "Go to Dark Gethsemane." [d. 4/30/1854]

1803 Birth of Sarah Hall, American missionary to Burma. She became the widow of missionary George Dana Boardman (1801-1831), and in 1834 married fellow-missionary Adoniram Judson (whose first wife, Ann Hasseltine, had died in 1826). [d. 9/1/1845]

1866 Birth of Joseph L. Hall, American sacred composer. He wrote music for a number of cantatas, oratorios, anthems and melodies for hundreds of gospel songs, including CLIFTON ("I Belong to the King") and MY SAVIOR CARES ("Does Jesus Care?"). [d. 11/29/1930]

1903 Birth of (Henry) Watchman Nee, Chinese spiritual leader. Converted in 1920, he adopted the Plymouth Brethren doctrine of the victorious life, and founded an Evangelical Christian group 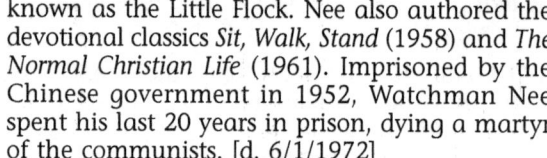 known as the Little Flock. Nee also authored the devotional classics *Sit, Walk, Stand* (1958) and *The Normal Christian Life* (1961). Imprisoned by the Chinese government in 1952, Watchman Nee spent his last 20 years in prison, dying a martyr of the communists. [d. 6/1/1972]

The Last Passage

1847 Death of Felix Mendelssohn (-Bartholdy), 38, German pianist and composer. The grandson of philosopher Moses Mendelssohn, Felix penned the hymn tune MENDELSSOHN ("Hark, The Herald Angels Sing"). (b. 2/3/1809)

1924 Death of Charles C. Luther, 77, American Baptist evangelist and clergyman. He penned about 25 hymn texts during his life, including "Must I Go, and Empty-Handed?" (b. 5/17/1847)

Words For The Soul

1745 Colonial missionary to the American Indians David Brainerd wrote in his journal: *'It is good to follow the path of duty, though in the midst of darkness and discouragement.'*

1852 In a letter to the American Bible Society, U.S. Supreme Court Justice John McLean (1785-1861) wrote: *'No one can estimate or describe the salutary influence of the Bible. What would the world be without it?... Life and immortality are brought to light by the Scriptures. Aside from Revelation... we begin our speculations as to our destiny in conjecture, and they end in uncertainty.'*

IN GOD'S WORD...   OT: Ezekiel 10:1–11:25 ~ NT: Hebrews 6:1-20 ~ Psalms 105:16-36 ~ Proverbs 27:1-2

November 5

Highlights In History

1414 The Council of Constance opened in Baden, Germany. It helped heal the "Great Schism" of the West by deposing three claimants to the papacy. On the downside, the gathered bishops condemned the teachings of English reformer John Wycliffe and burned Bohemian reformer Jan Hus. (The Council concluded in 1418.)

1917 In Moscow, following abdication of Russian Czar Nicholas II, the historic Orthodox Church Council of 1917-1918 restored the office of patriarch, suppressed by Peter the Great in 1700.

1935 In Nashville, the Cooperative General Association of Free Will Baptists (northern U.S.) and the General Conference of Free Will Baptists (southern U.S.) merged to form the National Association of Free Will Baptists.

Notable Birthdays

1727 American missionary to the American Indians, Gideon Hawley was born. He oversaw an Indian mission in Mashpee, Massachusetts for nearly 50 years (1758-1807). [d. 10/3/1807]

1841 Birth of Daniel C. Roberts, American clergyman and hymnwriter. Serving as a private in the U.S. Civil War, he was afterward ordained a Protestant Episcopal clergyman (1866), and served in New Hampshire for many years before his death. Roberts' name endures as author of the hymn, "God of Our Fathers, Whose Almighty Hand." [d. 10/31/1907]

1851 Birth of B[enjamin] B. Warfield, American Presbyterian scholar. A strict Fundamentalist, he taught an absolute Biblical inerrancy. His 20+ books principally comprised refutations of liberal theology. Warfield's influence dominated the General Assembly of his denomination from 1892-1910. [d. 2/17/1921]

1887 Birth of Donald M. Baillie, Church of Scotland theologian and ecumenist. His academic reputation and saintliness brought many foreign students to study at St. Andrews University. His best-known publications are *God Was in Christ* (1948) and *Theology of the Sacraments* (1957). Donald was the younger brother of John Baillie (1886-1960). [d. 10/31/1954]

The Last Passage

1921 Death of American clergywoman and feminist leader Antoinette L. (née Brown) Blackwell, 96. In 1853 she was ordained minister of the First Congregational Church of South Butler, NY, making her the first woman in the United States to be formally ordained to the pastorate. (b. 5/20/1825)

1960 Death of Donald Grey Barnhouse, 65, American Presbyterian minister and pioneer radio preacher. In 1927 Barnhouse began a 33-year-long pastorate at Tenth Presbyterian Church, Philadelphia. He was also founding editor of "Eternity" magazine. (b. 3/28/1895)

Words For The Soul

1891 Scottish clergyman and children's novelist George MacDonald wrote in a letter to his wife: 'This is your birthday, dearest. I hope you are full of hope in it. Though the outer decay, the inner, the thing that trusts in the perfect creative life, grows stronger – does it not? God will be better to us than we think, however expectant we be.'

1959 English literary scholar and Christian apologist C.S. Lewis wrote in a letter: 'All joy (as distinct from mere pleasure, still more amusement) emphasises our pilgrim status; always reminds, beckons, awakens desire. Our best havings are wantings.'

1970 American Presbyterian missionary and Christian apologist Francis Schaeffer wrote in a letter: 'The Bible does not minimize sexual sin, but neither does it make it different from any other sin.'

IN GOD'S WORD... OT: Ezekiel 12:1–14:11 ~ NT: Hebrews 7:1-17 ~ Psalms 105:37-45 ~ Proverbs 27:3

ALMANAC OF THE CHRISTIAN FAITH

KISLEV · HESHVAN

November 6

Highlights In History

1789 In Baltimore, following the American Revolutionary War, the first American Catholic diocese was created by Pope Pius VI in the newly independent United States of America. Father John Carroll, 54, was appointed the first American Roman Catholic bishop.

1853 The first Chinese Presbyterian Church in the U.S. was organized in San Francisco, California.

1977 In Toccoa Falls, GA, Barnes Lake Dam burst, following heavy rains. Resulting floods destroyed the Christian and Missionary Alliance campus of Toccoa Falls Bible Institute, and thirty-eight students and instructors were killed in the tragedy.

Notable Birthdays

1804 Birth of Benjamin Hall Kennedy, English educator and hymn translator. Devoting himself mainly to educational work, he served as professor of Greek at Cambridge and as Canon of Ely. Kennedy's name endures today as the English translator of the lyric German hymn, "Ask Ye What Great Thing I Know." [d. 4/6/1889]

1832 Birth of Mormon leader Joseph Smith, Jr. The son of Mormon church founder Joseph Smith, he became president of the Reorganized Church of Jesus Christ of Latter Day Saints – a non-polygamous offshoot of the original Mormon Church (1860-1914). [d. 12/10/1914]

1863 Birth of A[rchibald] T. Robertson, American Baptist biblical language scholar. He taught at Southern Baptist Seminary in Louisville for 46 years (1888-1934), and was a member of the translation committee for the 1905 *American Standard Version* (ASV) Bible. Robertson authored 45 books. Among these, his monumental, 1,454-page *Grammar of the Greek New Testament* (1914) remains the largest and most comprehensive biblical Greek grammar of its kind ever published. [d. 9/24/1934]

The Last Passage

1850 Death of Christoph Meineke, 68, German-born sacred composer. He came to America at 38, settling in Baltimore, where he afterward became organist at St. Paul's Episcopal Church, serving until his death. Meineke is remembered today for composing the hymn tune GLORIA PATRI ("Glory Be to the Father"). (b. 5/1/1782)

1905 Death of Sir George Williams, 84, British Congregational philanthropist and social reformer. In 1844, at age 23, he founded the Young Men's Christian Association (YMCA). A tireless businessman, evangelist and temperance advocate, Williams was knighted in 1894. (b. 10/11/1821)

1935 Death of 72-year-old American revivalist William Ashley ("Billy") Sunday. A professional baseball player from 1883-90, Sunday was ordained a Presbyterian minister in 1903. Until the advent of Billy Graham, no other American evangelist preached to as many nor counted as many conversions as did Billy Sunday. (b. 11/19/1862)

1950 Death of Robert Holbrook Smith, 71, American social reformer. In 1935, along with William G. Wilson, Smith became a co-founder of Alcoholics Anonymous, a self-help organization based on Christian principles. (b. 8/8/1879)

Words For The Soul

1777 Anglican hymnwriter John Newton wrote in a letter: *'God often takes a course for accomplishing His purposes directly contrary to what our narrow views would prescribe. He brings a death upon our feelings, wishes and prospects when He is about to give us the desire of our hearts.'*

1978 Russian Orthodox liturgical scholar Father Alexander Schmemann reflected in his journal: *'How wonderfully sickness purifies everything!'*

IN GOD'S WORD...   OT: Ezekiel 14:12–16:42 ~ NT: Hebrews 7:18-28 ~ Psalms 106:1-12 ~ Proverbs 27:4-6

כסלו KISLEV — ALMANAC OF THE CHRISTIAN FAITH — חשון HESHVAN

~ November 7 ~

Highlights In History

680 The Third Council of Constantinople opened under Pope St. Agatho. During its 16 sessions (held through Sept. 16, 681), monothelitism was condemned. (This heresy held that there was only one will – the divine – in Christ.)

1637 Controversial colonial American religious leader Anne Hutchinson, 46, was convicted of heresy and banished from the Massachusetts Bay Colony. Mrs. Hutchinson afterward relocated in Rhode Island with her family and friends.

1793 During the French Revolution, Christianity was abolished on this date. Reason was deified, and as many as 2,000 churches were destroyed throughout France.

Notable Birthdays

1531 German Protestant reformer Martin Luther, 48, and his wife Katie, 32, gave birth to their fourth child, Martin Jr. The couple bore six children altogether (3 boys and 3 girls): John, Elizabeth, Magdalene, Martin, Paul and Margaret. Elizabeth survived less than eight months (12/1527-8/1528), but Paul lived for 60 years (1533-1593). Martin Jr. lived to serve in private life, and died at age 33. [d. 3/3/1565]

1847 Birth of Will Lamartine Thompson, American songwriter. Known as "The Bard of Ohio," he penned both sacred and secular songs, as well as publishing many musical collections. Thompson's pen bequeathed to the Church two particularly enduring hymns: "Jesus is All the World to Me" and "Softly and Tenderly Jesus is Calling." [d. 9/20/1909]

1918 Birth of American Baptist evangelist Billy (William Franklin) Graham. Converted at 16 under revivalist Mordecai Ham, he began an evangelistic career in 1944 with Youth For Christ. In 1950 he founded the Billy Graham Evangelistic Association, and has since gone on to conduct evangelistic tours all over the world. Throughout his life, Graham has been characterized by a sterling integrity and a genuine humility, though he has preached the gospel to more people – nearly 100 million! — than any evangelist in the history of the church. During his meetings, over two million individuals have come forward to accept Christ.

The Last Passage

1837 Death of Elijah Parish Lovejoy, American Presbyterian abolitionist and newspaper publisher. Known as the "martyr abolitionist" because of his anti-slavery editorials, his presses were destroyed and he was killed by a mob, two days before his 35th birthday. Lovejoy's death helped to galvanize antislavery sentiment. (b. 11/9/1802)

1910 [NS=11/20] Death of Count Leo Tolstoy, 72, Russian novelist and social reformer. Known for authoring *War and Peace* (1860) and *Anna Karenina* (1877), Tolstoy underwent a mystical conversion in mid-life. He afterward identified with the poor. Rejecting Russian Orthodoxy, he evolved his own (somewhat incomplete!) form of the Christian faith. Tolstoy's thought often stressed the conflict between reason and the natural desire to live without the restraints of social convention. (b. 8/28/1828)

Words For The Soul

1537 German reformer Martin Luther clarified in a sermon: *'St. Paul does not teach Christians to forsake or throw away what they own; he tells them not to fasten their hearts to their possessions.'*

1985 Dutch Catholic priest and devotional diarist Henri J. M. Nouwen penned in his *Road to Daybreak* journal: *'When our love is rooted in God's love, we can carry the burden of life and discover it to be light.'*

IN GOD'S WORD...   OT: Ezekiel 16:43–17:24 ~ NT: Hebrews 8:1-13 ~ Psalms 106:13-31 ~ Proverbs 27:7-9

KISLEV כסלו ALMANAC OF THE CHRISTIAN FAITH חשון HESHVAN

~ November 8 ~

Highlights In History

1837 Mt. Holyoke Seminary first opened in Massachusetts. Founded by Mary Lyon, 39, it was the first college in the U.S. established specifically for the education of women.

1844 Knox College first opened in Toronto, Canada. It was founded as a theological seminary under the auspices of the Presbyterian Church.

1904 Emile Combs introduced a bill for the separation of Church and State in France. The bill passed in December 1905, thereby ending the Napoleonic Concordat of 1801 and allowing complete religious liberty of conscience.

Notable Birthdays

1889 Birth of Oswald J. Smith, Canadian clergyman. He was founder and, for 44 years, pastor of the People's Church of Toronto (1915-1959).  Smith also authored a multitude of books and composed more than 1,200 hymns, including "Deeper and Deeper," "The Song of the Soul Set Free," "Joy in Serving Jesus" and "God Understands." [d. 1/26/1986]

1897 Birth of Dorothy Day, American Catholic journalist and social reformer. In 1933 she co-founded the Catholic Workers Movement and "The Catholic Worker," a monthly newspaper which sought to unite workers and intellectuals in joint activities ranging from farming to educational discussions. [d. 11/29/1980]

1916 Birth of Alfred B. Smith, musical editor and hymnwriter. The founder of Singspiration, Inc., he served as president from 1941-62. Smith wrote approximately 500 sacred songs, including "Surely Goodness and Mercy" (a.k.a. "A Pilgrim Was I and A-Wandering"). [d. 8/9/2001]

The Last Passage

1308 Death of John Duns Scotus, 43, Scottish Franciscan scholastic. Known in the Catholic Church as "The Subtle Doctor," Duns Scotus was considered the greatest of the medieval British theologians and philosophers. He founded the system called Scotism, which later became the doctrinal basis for the theology of the Franciscan religious order. (b. 1266)

1517 Death of Francisco Ximenes de Cisneros, 81, Spanish cardinal and prelate. As archbishop of Toledo, he founded the University of Alcala (1500), and also edited the first critical edition of the Bible, the *Complutensian Polyglot*. Under him, Spain became the chief center of ecclesiastical reform. (b. 1436)

1674 Death of John Milton, 65, English poet and essayist. A master of English literature, Milton wrote in four languages. He is remembered today for his epic, *Paradise Lost* (1665-74) – written after losing his eyesight in 1652! (b. 12/9/1608)

1920 Death of Abraham Kuyper, 83, Dutch theologian and statesman. A major figure in the Netherlands during his latter years, Kuyper represented a consistent conservatism. He founded  the Free University of Amsterdam (1880), formed the Low Dutch Reformed Church (1892), created an alliance between Calvinist and Catholic political leaders, and served as Prime Minister of the Netherlands (1901-05). (b. 10/29/1837)

Words For The Soul

1931 Newly converted to the Christian faith, British literary scholar C. S. Lewis wrote in a letter: *'One needs the sweetness to start one on the spiritual life but, once started, one must learn to obey God for his own sake, not for the pleasure.'*

1951 As an American Presbyterian missionary to Switzerland, Francis Schaeffer wrote in a letter: *'The higher the mountains, the more understandable is the glory of Him who made them and who holds them in His hand.'*

IN GOD'S WORD... OT: Ezekiel 18:1–19:14 ~ NT: Hebrews 9:1-10 ~ Psalms 106:32-48 ~ Proverbs 27:10

ALMANAC OF THE CHRISTIAN FAITH

KISLEV / HESHVAN

November 9

Highlights In History

1732 In Scala, Italy, St. Alfonso Maria de Liguori founded the Congregation of the Most Holy Redeemer (Redemptorists). The religious order was officially approved in 1749.

1837 British philanthropist Moses Montefiore, 52, became the first Jew to be knighted in England. Montefiore was a banking executive who devoted his life to the political and civil emancipation of English Jews.

1938 The worst Jewish pogrom in peacetime Germany took place as Nazi thugs led a "spontaneous" campaign of terror. During the night 267 synagogues were plundered, 7,500 shops were wrecked, 91 Jews were killed and 20,000 others were arrested and sent to concentration camps. It became known as "Kristallnacht" ("Night of Broken Glass") because of the thousands of windows broken by the terrorists.

Notable Birthdays

1522 Birth of Martin Chemnitz, German theologian. He was one of the main influences in consolidating Lutheran doctrine and practice, following Martin Luther's death. [d. 4/8/1586]

1799 Birth of Asa Mahan, American educator and Congregational clergyman. As the first president of Oberlin College in Ohio (1835-1850), he was instrumental in establishing interracial education and in the granting of college degrees to women. [d. 4/4/1889]

1802 Birth of Elijah Parish Lovejoy, American Presbyterian newspaper editor and abolitionist. He was plagued by pro-slavery forces, and his presses were destroyed several times due to his unbending anti-slavery editorials. Ultimately, Lovejoy was killed by a mob during a midnight raid on his business. Known as the "martyr abolitionist," his death played a notable role in galvanizing antislavery sentiment. [d. 11/7/1837]

The Last Passage

1826 Death of Joseph Doddridge, 57, American frontier clergyman. Beginning as an itinerant Methodist circuit rider, Doddridge later transferred his allegiance to the Episcopal Church, studied medicine and worked as a missionary in West Virginia. (b. 10/14/1769)

1844 Death of Barton W. Stone, 71, American frontier evangelist. As leader of an early revivalist and restoration movement within Presbyterianism from 1804, in 1831 Stone's followers united with the "Disciples" of Alexander Campbell, to form the Christian (Disciples of Christ) Church. (b. 12/24/1772)

1952 Death of Chaim Weizmann, 77, Russian-born Jewish religious and political leader. Elected first president of the World Zionist Organization in 1923, Weizmann was later elected the first president of the modern state of Israel (1949-52). (b. 11/27/1874)

Words For The Soul

1538 German reformer Martin Luther declared: 'It would be a good thing if young people were wise and old people were strong, but God has arranged things better.'

1772 In a letter to his friend William Bradford, future U.S. president James Madison wrote: 'A watchful eye must be kept on ourselves lest while we are building ideal monuments of Renown and Bliss here we neglect to have our names enrolled in the Annals of Heaven....'

1931 Having recently become a convert to the Christian faith, British literary scholar (and later Christian apologist) C. S. Lewis wrote in a letter to Arthur Greeves: 'One needs the sweetness to start one on the spiritual life but, once started, one must learn to obey God for his own sake, not for the pleasure.'

IN GOD'S WORD... OT: Ezekiel 20:1-49 ~ NT: Hebrews 9:11-28 ~ Psalms 107:1-43 ~ Proverbs 27:11

ALMANAC OF THE CHRISTIAN FAITH

KISLEV   HESHVAN

~ November 10 ~

Highlights In History

432 Patrick, a young British monk who was once held as a captive by the Irish, returned to the land of his captivity and began a lifelong mission to the Irish people. Patrick preached to the pagan tribes in the Irish language he had learned while living there as a slave. Ministering for over 50 years, St. Patrick afterward came to be known as the "Apostle of Ireland."

1766 In New Brunswick, NJ, Queen's College was chartered under the Dutch Reformed Church, to provide education '...*especially in divinity, preparing [youth] for the ministry and other good offices.*' The present name for the school, Rutgers University, was adopted in 1924.

1871 Following a seven-month search expedition, American correspondent for the "New York Herald," Henry M. Stanley succeeded in locating "lost" Scottish missionary David Livingstone in Ujiji, Central Africa. Stanley prefaced his first encounter with the famed missionary-explorer with the words: '*Dr. Livingstone, I presume.*'

Notable Birthdays

1483 Birth of Martin Luther, German reformer. His "Ninety-Five Theses," posted on the door of the Wittenberg College Church door in 1517, was only intended to protest papal abuses and corruption in the Catholic Church, but they instead inaugurated the Protestant Reformation in Europe. Luther also translated the Bible into German and authored 37 hymns, including the still-popular "A Mighty Fortress." [d. 2/18/1546]

1835 Birth of James Langran, English sacred organist and hymnwriter. He received his Bachelor of Music degree from Oxford at age 49. Langran is best remembered today for composing the hymn tune LANGRAN, to which is sung the lyric hymn, "Here, O My Lord, I See Thee Face to Face." [d. 6/8/1909]

1852 Birth of Henry Van Dyke, American Presbyterian clergyman, educator, poet, author and hymnwriter. Van Dyke published many popular writings, including *The Story of the Other Wise Man* (1896). He also authored the hymn: "Joyful, Joyful, We Adore Thee." [d. 4/10/1933]

The Last Passage

1828 African-American Baptist clergyman and missionary Lott Cary, 48, died in an explosion in Liberia, Africa. In 1813 Cary organized the Richmond Baptist Missionary Society, and later helped establish the first Baptist church in Liberia (1821). In 1888, African-American Baptists named their foreign missionary organization after Cary. (b. ca.1780)

1889 Death of Edwin Hatch, 54, Anglican clergyman, educator and hymnwriter. He was widely acclaimed for his Bampton Lectures (1880) and his Hibbert Lectures (1888) on the history of the Church. Hatch also penned the enduring hymn, "Breathe on Me, Breath of God." (b. 9/4/1835)

Words For The Soul

1770 French philosopher (and self-confessed agnostic) François Voltaire, 75, uttered his famous observation: '*If God did not exist, it would be necessary to invent him.*'

1871 American Quaker holiness author Hannah Whitall Smith wrote in a letter: '*My heart yearns over the church. I feel the tenderest sympathy for every child of God whose feet are still wandering in the wilderness, and I long unspeakably to show them the way to the promised land and to help them over the Jordan that lies between.*'

1952 English literary scholar and Christian apologist C. S. Lewis wrote in a letter: '*I believe that, in the present divided state of Christendom, those who are at the heart of each division are all closer to one another than those who are at the fringes.*'

IN GOD'S WORD...   OT: Ezekiel 21:1–22:31 ~ NT: Hebrews 10:1-8 ~ Psalms 108:1-13 ~ Proverbs 27:12

כסלו KISLEV ALMANAC OF THE CHRISTIAN FAITH חשון HESHVAN

November 11

Highlights In History

1215 The Fourth Lateran Council was convened by Pope Innocent III. Meeting through Nov. 30th, it was the council which first defined "transubstantiation" – the Catholic belief that the bread and wine of the Eucharist changes into the literal body and blood of Christ.

1417 At the end of the three-day Council of Constance, Italian cardinal Oddone Colonna (1368-1431) was unanimously elected Pope Martin V. His election ended the Great Western Schism – a 40-year division during which there were as many as three rival popes within the Catholic Church.

1620 The Mayflower Compact was signed by the 41 Separatists among the 101 passengers of the *Mayflower*. The document served as the basis for organizing the Pilgrims "into a civil body politic." Democratic in form, the Compact comprised the first written American constitution, and remained in force until 1691.

1992 After years of debate regarding the biblical imperatives, the Church of England voted to ordain women as priests. In all, 92 women were ordained this first year – "92 in '92" – most of them within the Anglican Church of Australia.

Notable Birthdays

1491 Birth of Martin Bucer, German religious reformer. A Dominican-turned-Protestant who became known for his peacemaking efforts between conflicting reform groups, Bucer himself was a Zwinglian. [d. 2/28/1551]

1679 Birth of Firmin Abauzit, French Reformed scholar. Born of Huguenot parents, he was known for both his erudition as well as his modest nature. Abauzit is most often remembered today for translating the New Testament into French (1726). [d. 3/20/1767]

1789 Birth of William Meade, American Episcopal prelate. Entering the Episcopal ministry at the low point of its existence in 1811, he devoted his life to the revival of the church of his forefathers. Meade died while serving as presiding bishop of the denomination in the Confederate States of America. [d. 3/14/1862]

The Last Passage

1561 Death of Hans Tausen, 67, advocate of the Danish Reformation. Known as the "Danish Luther," Tausen served as Protestant bishop in Ribe (1542-61), and translated the Pentateuch into Danish. (b. 1494)

1778 Death of Anne Steele, 62, English Baptist poet. The first significant female hymnwriter to come out of England, she lost her fiance through his drowning the day before their wedding. She is remembered today for authoring the hymn, "Father of Mercies, In Thy Word." (b. 1716)

1921 Death of P[eter] T[aylor] Forsyth, 73, English Congregational clergyman and theologian. A liberal in his youth, he later developed a deepened respect for the atonement through the cross. Forsyth's writings anticipated the theology of Karl Barth. (b. 5/12/1848)

Words For The Soul

1760 English founder of Methodism John Wesley wrote in a letter: *'You cannot live on what He did yesterday. Therefore He comes today.'*

1894 Scottish clergyman and children's novelist George MacDonald, 70, wrote in a letter to an old friend: *'The shadows of the evening that precedes a lovelier morning are drawing down around us both. But our God is in the shadow as in the shine, and all is well and will be well.'*

1985 Dutch Catholic priest and devotional diarist Henri J. M. Nouwen penned in his *Road to Daybreak* journal: *'By not forgiving, I chain myself to a desire to get even, thereby losing my freedom. A forgiven person forgives. This is what we proclaim when we pray, "and forgive us our trespasses as we forgive those who have trespassed against us."'*

IN GOD'S WORD...   OT: Ezekiel 23:1-49 ~ NT: Hebrews 10:19-39 ~ Psalms 109:1-31 ~ Proverbs 27:13

November 12

KISLEV | ALMANAC OF THE CHRISTIAN FAITH | HESHVAN

Highlights In History

1701 The Carolina Assembly passed a Vestry Act making the Church of England the official religion of the Carolina Colony. (Strong opposition by Quakers and other resident Nonconformists forced the colony's proprietors to revoke the legislation two years later.)

1899 American evangelist Dwight L. Moody, 62, began his last evangelistic campaign in Kansas City, Missouri. Becoming ill during the last service, Moody was unable to complete his message, and died a few days later, on Dec. 22nd.

Notable Birthdays

1808 Birth of Ray Palmer, American Congregational clergyman and hymnwriter. Among his most abiding verses are his translations from the Latin: "My Faith Looks Up to Thee" and "Jesus, Thou Joy of Loving Hearts" are two of Palmer's hymns which endure today. [d. 3/29/1887]

1818 Birth of Henri Frederick Hemy, English Roman Catholic church organist and composer. His best known composition is the hymn tune ST. CATHERINE, to which today we commonly sing "Faith of Our Fathers." [d. 6/10/1888]

1879 Birth of Ralph S. Cushman, American Methodist prelate. He served as bishop of the Denver and St. Paul-Minneapolis conferences (1932-52). Cushman also penned 25 books of religious poetry and meditations on evangelism, stewardship and prayer. [d. 8/10/1960]

1914 Birth of Edward Schillebeeckx, Belgian-born Dutch Catholic theologian. He has contributed to a renewal and democratization within the Catholic Church. His writings include *An Experiment in Christology* (1979).

The Last Passage

1562 Death of Peter Martyr (Pietro Martire Vermigli), 62, Italian Biblical scholar and Protestant Reformer. As an Augustinian, he was sympathetic to the Reformers, and eventually fled to Switzerland. He later taught theology at Oxford, and helped work on the 1552 edition of the *Book of Common Prayer*. (b. 9/8/1500)

1886 Death of A[rchibald] A. Hodge, 53, American Presbyterian theologian. The son of theologian Charles Hodge, A.A. was a missionary to India, then pastored for 11 years, before following his father's footsteps at Princeton Theological Seminary. *Outlines of Theology* (1878) was Hodge's response to a naturalistic interpretation of Scripture. (b. 7/18/1823)

1956 Death of C[harles] C. Torrey, 92, American biblical and Semitics scholar. His expertise was in Aramaic, also in the Apocrypha and the Pseudepigrapha of the Old Testament. Torrey established — and was the first director in Jerusalem (1900-01) — of the American School of Oriental Research. (b. 12/20/1863)

Words For The Soul

1556 Dutch Anabaptist reformer Menno Simons wrote in a letter: *'I can neither teach nor live by the faith of others. I must live by my own faith as the Spirit of the Lord has taught me through His Word.'*

1704 English clergyman Matthew Henry, 42, began his famed Bible commentary. In his diary he wrote: *'This night, after many thoughts of heart and many prayers concerning it, I began my Notes on the Old Testament.... I go about it with fear and trembling, lest I exercise myself in things too high for me.... The Lord help me to set about it with great humility.'*

1954 American Presbyterian missionary Francis Schaeffer wrote in a letter: *'Loyalty to organizations and movements has always tended over time to take the place of loyalty to the person of Christ.'*

IN GOD'S WORD... OT: Ezekiel 24:1–26:21 ~ NT: Hebrews 11:1-16 ~ Psalms 110:1-7 ~ Proverbs 27:14

November 13

KISLEV / HESHVAN
ALMANAC OF THE CHRISTIAN FAITH

Highlights In History

1564 Pius IV ordered his bishops and scholars to subscribe to "Professio fidei," the Profession of the Tridentine Faith recently formulated at the Council of Trent (1545-63) as the new and final definition of the Roman Catholic faith.

1618 In the Dutch commune of Dordrecht, the Synod of Dort convened to discuss the Arminian controversy vexing the Reformed faith in Holland. Before the synod ended the following May (1619), doctrinal canons were framed which became the theological foundation for the Reformed Church of the Netherlands for the next 200 years.

1962 St. Joseph's name was added to the canon of the Roman Catholic mass. It constituted the first revision to this canon since the 7th century.

Notable Birthdays

354 Birth of St. Augustine of Hippo, Early Christian theologian and philosopher. He was the most distinguished among the Early Latin Fathers, and the greatest thinker in Christian antiquity. His autobiography *Confessions* describes the back story of his conversion to Christian faith. He also penned *The City of God*, written as a spiritual interpretation of the sacking of Rome by the Visigoths in 410. [d. 8/28/430]

1486 Birth of Johann M. Eck, German Catholic theologian. Formerly on good terms with Martin Luther, Eck opposed him in public debate at Leipzig in 1519, and afterward played a key role in securing Luther's excommunication by Leo X. [d. 2/10/1543]

1572 Birth of Cyril Lucar, Greek Orthodox theologian. He was Patriarch of Constantinople from 1620. [d. 6/27/1638]

1913 Birth of Alexander Scourby, American actor. His most memorable screen role was in "Giant," (1956), but he is better known for his resonant bass voice, which he lent to the some of the  first readings of the (King James) Bible on audio cassette. [d. 2/22/1985]

The Last Passage

1874 Death of Edward Mote, 77, English Baptist hymnwriter and poet. He began his career as a cabinet-maker, afterward becoming a Baptist pastor. Mote penned over 100 hymns, including "The Solid Rock" (a.k.a. "My Hope is Built On Nothing Less"). (b. 1/21/1797)

1907 Death of Francis Thompson, 47, English Roman Catholic essayist and poet. Known for his florid poetry on religious themes, Thompson's first volume, *Poems* (1893), contained his best known verse: "The Hound of Heaven." Thompson spent his last years recovering from a longterm opium addiction. (b. 12/18/1859)

1915 Death of Phineas F. Bresee, 76, American denominational leader. In October 1895 in Los Angeles, Bresee and Joseph P. Widney founded the Church of the Nazarene. In 1906, at Pilot Point, TX, their denomination merged with several other groups within the Holiness movement to form the Pentecostal Church of the Nazarene. (The word "Pentecostal" was dropped from the name in 1919.) (b. 12/31/1838)

Words For The Soul

1530 German reformer Martin Luther confessed in a sermon: 'I feel that I have been, and still am, a bad fellow. Nevertheless, I must say: All my sins have been forgiven me; for this word has been spoken over me, "Your sins are forgiven."'

1778 English founder of Methodism John Wesley wrote in a letter: 'There is frequently something very mysterious in the ways of divine Providence. A little of them we may understand; but much more is beyond our comprehension; and we must be content to say, "What thou doest I know not now; but I shall know hereafter."'

IN GOD'S WORD...   OT: Ezekiel 27:1–28:26 ~ NT: Hebrews 11:17-31 ~ Psalms 111:1-10 ~ Proverbs 27:15-16

KISLEV · ALMANAC OF THE CHRISTIAN FAITH · HESHVAN

~ November 14 ~

Highlights In History

1741 In Wales, English revivalist George Whitefield, 27, married widow Elizabeth Burnell, 36. (Whitefield apparently did not allow marriage to interrupt any evangelistic activities, since he was not home when their first child was born.)

1784 Samuel Seabury, 55, was consecrated Bishop of Connecticut and Rhode Island. He was the first bishop of the American Protestant Episcopal Church, and the first Anglican bishop in America.

1784 In the town of Frederica, at the first quarterly assembly of Methodists to convene in Delaware, Thomas Coke served communion to about 500 persons, making this also the first time communion was administered in North America by an authorized Methodist minister.

1918 The United Lutheran Church in America (ULCA) was organized. This successor to the first Lutheran synod, and the first Lutheran general body in America, was formed by a merger of three major branches of the denomination.

1941 Inter-Varsity Christian Fellowship was incorporated in Chicago. An interdenominational youth organization with chapters established at both colleges and schools of nursing, "IVCF" provides Christian fellowship, nurture and discipleship among Christian college students.

Notable Birthdays

1864 Birth of Helen H. Lemmel, English-born sacred vocalist and hymnwriter. She penned 500 hymns (many for children), including the still-popular "Turn Your Eyes Upon Jesus." [d. 11/1/1961]

1904 Birth of Arthur Michael Ramsey, Anglican prelate. Ordained in 1928, he was elevated to Archbishop of Canterbury in 1961. Ramsey also served as president of the World Council of Churches (1961-68). In 1966 he paid an official visit to Pope Paul VI. [d. 4/23/1988]

The Last Passage

565 Death of Justinian I, 82, Byzantine ruler (527-565). As the greatest of the Eastern Roman emperors, he made it his aim to restore the political and religious unity of the empire in the East and West. Justinian reconquered North Africa from the Vandals and Italy from the Goths. (b. 5/11/483)

1180 St. Lawrence O'Toole, first Irish Archbishop of Dublin (1161-80), died at age 58. Canonized in 1226, O'Toole was the first native citizen of Ireland to be made a Catholic saint. (b. 1122)

1633 Death of William Ames, 57, English Puritan, moral theologian and controversialist. He was a supporter of strict Calvinism, and his book *Medulla Theologiae* was the standard theological text used both at Harvard and at Yale until the mid-1700s. (b. 1576)

1835 Death of James Freeman, 76, American clergyman. He was the first minister in the U.S. to embrace the name of Unitarian. Through his influence the first established Episcopal church in New England – King's Chapel in Boston – afterward became (in 1785) the first Unitarian church in this country. (b. 4/22/1759)

1953 Death of Karl P. Harrington, 92, American educator, choralist and hymn composer. He taught Latin, served as a church organist, and founded several choral societies. Much of Harrington's work remains unpublished, but he is remembered for composing CHRISTMAS SONG ("There's a Song in the Air"). (b. 6/13/1861)

Words For The Soul

1558 Dutch Anabaptist reformer and founder of the Mennonites, Menno Simons wrote in a letter: *'We ought not to dread death so. It is but to cease from sin and to enter into a better life.'*

1739 English revivalist George Whitefield wrote in his journal: *'We can preach the Gospel of Christ no further than we have experienced the power of it in our own hearts.'*

IN GOD'S WORD... OT: Ezekiel 29:1–30:26 ~ NT: Hebrews 11:32–12:13 ~ Psalms 112:1-10 ~ Proverbs 27:17

כסלו
KISLEV

ALMANAC OF THE CHRISTIAN FAITH

חשון
HESHVAN

~ November 15 ~

Highlights In History

1626 The English Separatists known to history as the Mayflower Pilgrims, having lived in their American colony for six years, bought out their London investors for £1,800 – $300,000 today!

1905 In New York City, the seven-day-long Carnegie Hall Conference opened. Also known as the Interchurch Conference on Federation, this gathering led in 1908 to the establishment of the Federal Council of Churches of Christ in America. In 1950 the FCC merged with thirteen other interdenominational agencies to become the National Council of Churches.

1957 Patriarch Ignatius Yacoub III officially established the Archdiocese of the Syrian Orthodox Church in the U.S. and Canada. At the same time, Archbishop Mar Athanasius Yeshue Samuel, former Syrian Orthodox metropolitan of Jerusalem, was appointed primate of the new archdiocese, and soon after took up residence in Hackensack, New Jersey.

Notable Birthdays

1731 [NS=11/26] Birth of William Cowper, noted English poet and hymnwriter. Regarded by many as the leading English poet of his day, he suffered from poor mental health, including  fits of depression, throughout his life. Cowper collaborated with his Anglican pastor John Newton in compiling *Olney Hymns* (1779). The publication contained 67 of his own texts, including: "Oh For a Closer Walk with God," "There is a Fountain Filled With Blood," and "God Moves in Mysterious Ways." [d. 4/25/1800]

1769 Birth of Nicholas Snethen, American clergyman and denominational leader. Leaving the Methodist Episcopal Church, in 1828 Snethen helped found the Methodist Protestant Church. [d. 5/30/1845]

1877 Birth of H[enry] Orton Wiley, American Nazarene clergyman and theologian. A 1984 survey among evangelical Wesleyan theologians named Wiley as the author having the most impact on their academic work. [d. 1961]

The Last Passage

1280 Death of Albertus Magnus ("Albert the Great"), 87, German Dominican theologian and philosopher. He paraphrased Aristotle's works, and prepared the way for the modern conflict between theology and false science. He was also the teacher of Thomas Aquinas. Albertus once wrote that just as beauty in the universe consists in antithesis, so in music *'when rests are interposed in choral singing, it becomes sweeter than continuous sound.'* (b. ca. 1193)

1885 Death of John Freeman Young, 65, American Episcopal bishop, architect and hymnwriter. In his day, Young was responsible for designing many interesting church structures. Today he is immortalized for his English translation of the enduring German Christmas carol, "Silent Night, Holy Night." (b. 10/30/1820)

1917 Death of Oswald Chambers, Scottish Bible teacher and author. Converted under Charles Spurgeon, he trained for the Baptist ministry, after which he served briefly as a 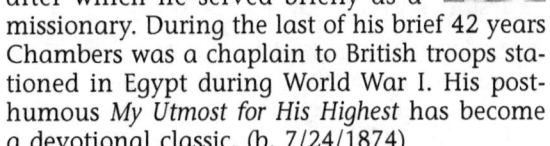 missionary. During the last of his brief 42 years Chambers was a chaplain to British troops stationed in Egypt during World War I. His posthumous *My Utmost for His Highest* has become a devotional classic. (b. 7/24/1874)

Words For The Soul

1804 Anglican missionary to Persia, Henry Martyn testified in his journal: *'Corruption always begins the day, but morning prayer never fails to set my mind in a right frame.'*

1839 Church of Scotland clergyman Robert Murray McCheyne wrote in a letter: *'I know well that when Christ is nearest, Satan also is busiest.'*

IN GOD'S WORD...   OT: Ezekiel 31:1–32:32 ~ NT: Hebrews 12:14–29 ~ Psalms 113:1–114:8 ~ Proverbs 27:18–20

November 16

Highlights In History

1621 The Papal Chancery adopted January 1st as the beginning of the calendar year. Previously, March had been the first month – which explains why our modern names for the 9th-12th months begin with Latin prefixes meaning "7" (sept-), "8" (oct-) "9" (nov-) and "10" (dec-).

1918 In New York City, the United Lutheran Church was organized by a merger of three general Lutheran bodies in the U.S. and Canada. (In 1962, the ULC became one of the branches of Lutheranism which joined to form the Lutheran Church in America.)

1946 The Evangelical United Brethren (EUB) Church was constituted at Johnstown, PA by a merger of the Church of the United Brethren in Christ and the Evangelical Church. The new denomination originated in the work of two German Reformed pastors, Philip W. Otterbein and Martin Boehm, who had ministered among Pennsylvania Germans two centuries earlier.

Notable Birthdays

1803 Birth of Georg H. A. von Ewald, German biblical scholar and Orientalist. His *Hebrew Grammar* (1827) set a benchmark in the history of Old Testament philology. [d. 5/4/1875]

1828 Birth of Timothy Dwight, American Congregational clergyman. The grandson of 19th century American clergyman also named Timothy Dwight (1752-1817), he was a renowned New Testament scholar and served on the revision committee of the *American Standard Version* of the Bible. (1886-98). [d. 5/26/1916]

1837 German New Testament scholar and church historian Franz C. Overbeck was born. He was a close friend of Friedrich Nietzsche, and an untiring critic of both orthodox and liberal theology. Overbeck is regarded today as the forerunner of dialectical theology. [d. 6/26/1905]

The Last Passage

1093 Death of Margaret, 48, Queen of Scotland. The wife of Malcolm III, Margaret did much to bring the Roman litanies into the Scottish Church. (b. ca.1045)

1200 Death of St. Hugh of Lincoln, 65, French-born English bishop and king's counselor. He fearlessly protected the rights of the underprivileged. It was St. Hugh who excommunicated England's King John in 1194. (b. 1135)

1853 Death of William Gardiner, 83, English manufacturer and musician. As a hymnwriter, he introduced the concept of adapting classic works for use as hymn tunes, including GERMANY ("Where Cross the Crowded Ways of Life") and LYONS ("O Worship the King, All Glorious Above"). (b. 3/15/1770)

1895 Death of Samuel Francis Smith, 87, American Baptist clergyman. Many of his 100 hymns were written for special occasions, such as ordinations and dedications. It was Smith who penned the famous patriotic hymn "America" (a.k.a. "My Country, 'Tis of Thee"), in 1831. (b. 10/21/1808)

1909 Death of Charles Nelson Crittenton, 76, American businessman and philanthropist. On NYC's Bleeker Street he opened a home for women that became the mother home of the Florence Crittenton missions (named after his daughter whose death had precipitated his conversion). The "Florence Homes" numbered over 70 by the time of his death. (b. 2/20/1833)

Words For The Soul

1853 Scottish clergyman and children's novelist George MacDonald wrote in a letter to his father: 'Real earnestness is scarcely to be attained in a high degree without doubts & inward questionings.... But increase of truth will always in greater or less degree look like error at first. But to suffer in this cause is only to be like the Master.'

IN GOD'S WORD...   OT: Ezekiel 33:1-34:31 ~ NT: Hebrews 13:1-25 ~ Psalms 115:1-18 ~ Proverbs 27:21-22

ALMANAC OF THE CHRISTIAN FAITH

כסלו KISLEV

חשון HESHVAN

November 17

Highlights In History

3 BC According to the reckoning of Christian theologian Clement of Alexandria (ca.155-ca.220 AD), Jesus Christ was born on this date.

1545 German reformer Martin Luther completed his lectures on Genesis, having begun them on June 3, 1535. This 10-year-long sermon series became Luther's "exegetical swansong," when he died the following February (1546).

1758 English churchman Philip Embury, 30, married Margaret Switzer. Afterward emigrating to America, Embury was soon after encouraged by his cousin Barbara Heck to found a Methodist society in New York City (1768). Embury thus became the first Methodist preacher in North America.

1876 English-born Rodney ("Gipsy") Smith, 16, was converted to a living faith. Smith later became an English Wesleyan singing evangelist, and made over 40 crusading trips abroad. His preaching emphasized the love of God.

1906 In Toronto, Ellen Hebden experienced a Pentecostal baptism, followed soon after by her husband James. Their East End Mission afterward became a source and focal point for establishing Pentecostal holiness throughout Canada.

Notable Birthdays

1790 Birth of Solyman Brown, American Congregational (later Swedenborgian) clergyman and writer. He is considered the founder of dentistry as an organized profession. [d. 2/13/1876]

1874 Birth of B[urnett] H. Streeter, Anglican theologian and New Testament scholar. His researches led to our better understanding of the origins of the Gospel. [d. 9/10/1937]

The Last Passage

594 Death of St. Gregory of Tours, 56. Gregory was the historian of the Franks, and a bishop from 573. (The Franks were a confederation of German barbarian tribes who occupied the right shore of the Rhine from Mainz to the sea.) (b. 11/30/538)

1808 Death of David Zeisberger, 87, Moravian missionary to the native American Indians. He established congregations of Christianized Indians in Pennsylvania, Ohio and Canada. (Unfortunately, the Indian churches he founded did not survive.) (b. 4/11/1721)

1813 Death of Philip William Otterbein, 87, German Reformed pastor. He came to America as a missionary in 1752, and in 1800 became co-founder (with Martin Boehm) of the Church of the United Brethren in Christ – an early branch of the United Methodist Church. (b. 6/3/1726)

1826 Death of C. Luise Reichardt, 47, German singer and voice teacher. She suffered misfortune in the death of her fiancé shortly before their wedding. Later in life, she also lost her voice. Miss Reichardt composed many songs, but is remembered today for the hymn tune ARMAGEDDON, to which is sung the hymn, "Who Is On the Lord's Side?" (b. 4/11/1779)

Words For The Soul

1532 German reformer Martin Luther declared in a sermon: 'He who is rich... ignores God's Word and treads it underfoot.... He who is poor does everything that pleases... the world in order to stave off poverty.... And so wealth to the right and poverty to the left are forever hindering God's Word and faith.'

1775 Anglican cleric John Newton wrote in a letter: 'Rational assent may be the act of our natural reason; faith is the effect of immediate almighty power.'

1975 Russian Orthodox liturgist Father Alexander Schmemann reflected in his journal: 'The soul seems to really be in a state where it receives no consolation, neither from heaven where it does not dwell yet, nor from earth where it does not dwell anymore and whence it does not want to receive any.'

IN GOD'S WORD...   OT: Ezekiel 35:1–36:38 ~ NT: James 1:1-18 ~ Psalms 116:1-19 ~ Proverbs 27:23-27

ALMANAC OF THE CHRISTIAN FAITH

KISLEV — HESHVAN

~ November 18 ~

Highlights In History

1095 Pope Urban II opened the Council of Clermont. Summoned to plan the First Crusade, it was attended by over 200 bishops. Among its official policies, the Council decreed that a pilgrimage to Jerusalem made every other penance superfluous.

1302 Boniface VIII published the papal decree "Unam Sanctam," declaring there was *'One Holy Catholic and Apostolic Church,'* outside of which there was *'neither salvation nor remission of sins.'* It was the first papal writing to decree that spiritual power took precedent over temporal power, and that subjection to the pope was necessary for spiritual redemption.

1626 In the Vatican at Rome, the newly completed St. Peter's Basilica was consecrated by Urban VIII. St. Peter's is presently the largest church in Christendom, with an overall length of 619 feet.

1866 English devotional writer Katherine Hankey, 32, penned the verses we sing today as the hymn, "I Love to Tell the Story."

1966 The National Conference of Catholic Bishops, in accordance with an earlier decree by Paul VI, issued "On Penance and Abstinence," declaring this to be the last meatless Friday ("under pain of sin") required for American Catholics.

Notable Birthdays

1647 Birth of Pierre Bayle, French Protestant philosopher. He authored *Dictionaire historique et critique*, and is regarded as the founder of 18th Century rationalism. [d. 12/28/1706]

1786 Birth of Carl Maria von Weber, German composer of symphonies, operas, masses, cantatas and chamber music. He is also remembered today for his hymn tunes JEWETT ("My Jesus, As Thou Wilt") and SEYMOUR ("Softly Now the Light of Day"). [d. 6/4/1826]

1800 Birth of J[ohn] N[elson] Darby, Irish-born English spiritual reformer. He was a gifted exponent of the early Plymouth Brethren movement, and following a schism in 1845-47, Darby became leader of the stricter Exclusive Brethren. (This denomination rejects all Church order and outward forms.) [d. 4/29/1883]

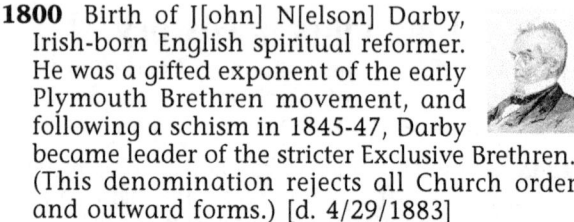

1849 Birth of Russell K. Carter, American Christian & Missionary Alliance entrepreneur and hymnwriter. During his life he was successively a professor, a sheep rancher, a clergyman, a physician and an author. Carter is remembered today as author and composer of the hymn, "Standing on the Promises." [d. 8/23/1928]

The Last Passage

1852 Death of Rose Philippine Duchesne, 83, French-born Catholic missionary and founder of the Society of the Sacred Heart. (b. 8/29/1769)

1978 In Guyana, South America, American cult leader Rev. Jim Jones, 47, ordered the mass suicide of over 900 followers, who swallowed a concoction of Kool-Aid and cyanide. Jones had founded the Peoples Temple in 1954 as a Disciples of Christ congregation. By 1965 it had devolved into an independent sect. (b. 5/13/1931)

Words For The Soul

1765 English founder of Methodism John Wesley wrote in a letter: *'Be temperate in speaking; never too loud, never too long: else Satan will befool you; and on pretence of being more useful, quite disable you from being useful at all.'*

1981 Dutch Catholic priest Henri J. M. Nouwen penned in his *¡Gracias!* Latin American journal: *'Without prayer I become irritable, tired, heavy of heart, and I lose the Spirit who directs my attention to the needs of others instead of my own. Without prayer, my attention moves to my own preoccupation. I become cranky and spiteful and often I experience resentment and a desire for revenge.'*

IN GOD'S WORD... OT: Ezekiel 37:1–38:23 ~ NT: James 1:19–2:17 ~ Psalms 117:1-2 ~ Proverbs 28:1

כסלו KISLEV — ALMANAC OF THE CHRISTIAN FAITH — חשון HESHVAN

~ November 19 ~

Highlights In History

1910 Swedish Pentecostal missionaries Daniel Berg, 26, and Adolf Vingren, 31, arrived in Brazil. In 1918 they established the first Pentecostal church there. From it grew Brazil's largest Protestant body, the Assemblies of God.

1961 The Third Assembly of the World Council of Churches convened at New Delhi, India. It was the first time the organization met in Asia. At this convention, the International Missionary Council and its work were integrated into the larger ecumenical organization.

Notable Birthdays

1770 Birth of Danish sculptor Albert B. Thorvaldsen. He was famous for his biblical figures decorating the cathedral Frue Kirke at Copenhagen. [d. 3/24/1844]

1834 Birth of Samuel F. Trevor, English merchant and Plymouth Brethren hymnwriter. He published many works of poetry, of which his most enduring verse became the haunting hymn of adoration: "O the Deep, Deep Love of Jesus." [d. 12/28/1925]

1862 Birth of Billy Sunday, American baseball player-turned-evangelist. He played outfield, 1883-90, then worked with evangelist J. Wilbur Chapman, and finally on his own. As a popular Fundamentalist, he is said to have made 98,624 converts. Before Billy Graham, no American evangelist had ever preached to as many people and counted as many conversions as did Billy Sunday. [d. 11/6/1935]

1885 Birth of Haldor Lillenas, Scandinavian-born American hymnwriter. As a Lutheran-turned-Nazarene evangelist, Lillenas penned nearly 4,000 Gospel texts and hymn tunes during his lifetime, including "It Is Glory Just to Walk With Him," "Wonderful Grace of Jesus" and "Peace, Peace, Wonderful Peace." [d. 8/18/1959]

The Last Passage

766 Death of Saxon ecclesiastic Egbert, a member of the royal house and Archbishop of York from ca. 732. A pupil of the Venerable Bede and later a teacher of Alcuin, Egbert was able to carry out numerous reforms after his brother ascended the Northumbrian throne. (b. 700s)

1887 Death of American Jewish poet Emma Lazarus, 38, following a period of declining health and intermittent bouts of depression. In 1883, she authored "The New Colossus," whose lines were afterward inscribed on the base of the Statue of Liberty. Sadly, Emma never lived to see the place where her words became a symbol of hope to many who came to America seeking freedom. (b. 7/22/1849)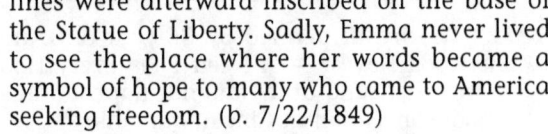

1900 Death of Samuel J. Stone, 61, Anglican clergyman and music editor. He was a member of the committee which prepared the 1909 edition of *Hymns Ancient and Modern*. Stone is remembered today for authoring the enduring hymn of hope, "The Church's One Foundation." (b. 4/25/1839)

Words For The Soul

1742 English revivalist George Whitefield exhorted in a letter: *'Plead His promises, be much in secret prayer, and never give God rest, till your soul is filled with all His fulness.'*

1672 Richard Baxter, considered the greatest preacher of his time, preached illegally in his own home after a ten year silence: *'I preached as never sure to preach again, and as a dying man to dying men.'*

1981 Dutch priest and devotional diarist Henri J. M. Nouwen penned in his *¡Gracias!* Latin American journal: *'Where the demon is, God is not far away; and where God shows his presence, the demon does not remain absent very long. There is always a choice to be made between the power of life and the power of death.'*

IN GOD'S WORD... OT: Ezekiel 39:1–40:27 ~ NT: James 2:18–3:18 ~ Psalms 118:1-18 ~ Proverbs 28:2

KISLEV — ALMANAC OF THE CHRISTIAN FAITH — HESHVAN

~ November 20 ~

Highlights In History

1541 In Switzerland, French reformer John Calvin, 32, established a theocratic government at Geneva, thereby creating a home base for emergent Reformed Protestantism throughout Europe.

1850 Frances ("Fanny") Crosby, blind from the age of six months, underwent a dramatic spiritual conversion at age 30. Fifteen years later, she began writing the first of over 8,000 devotional verses. Many of these remain popular today as hymns, including "Blessed Assurance," "All the Way My Savior Leads Me," "Rescue the Perishing," and "Jesus, Keep Me Near the Cross."

1872 The hymn penned by 36-year-old Annie Sherwood Hawks — "I Need Thee Every Hour" — was first sung at a National Baptist Sunday School convention in Cincinnati, Ohio.

1964 The Vatican II Ecumenical Council exonerated the Jews of any special guilt in the crucifixion of Christ.

Notable Birthdays

1620 Birth of Peregrine White, the first Pilgrim child born in America. His parents gave birth to him on the "Mayflower" while it was anchored in Cape Cod Harbor. [d. 7/22/1704]

1660 Birth of Daniel E. Jablonski, German Reformed theologian and Hebraist. He served as bishop of the Unitas Fratrum (Moravians) from 1699-1741, and worked for the union of Lutherans and Reformed Protestants. [d. 5/25/1741]

1741 Birth of Samuel Kirkland, American missionary to the Oneida Indians. He was influential in keeping the Six Nations neutral during the American Revolution. Kirkland was founder of the Hamilton Oneida Academy (1793), which later became Hamilton College. [d. 2/28/1808]

1867 Birth of Patrick Joseph Hayes, American Cardinal and Archbishop of New York (1919-38). Hayes overhauled the organizational apparatus of Catholic Charities, and stressed the need for professional training for Catholic social workers. He came to be called "the Cardinal of Charity." [d. 9/4/1938]

The Last Passage

1657 Jewish rabbi and scholar Manasseh Ben Israel, 53, died. Born in Holland, he went to England in 1655 to petition Oliver Cromwell and Parliament to abolish legislation forbidding Jews from immigrating to England. Today, he is considered the father of the modern Jewish community in England. (b. 1604)

1839 Death of John Williams, 43, English missionary to the South Pacific. This "apostle of Polynesia" first sailed to the Society Islands for the London Missionary Society in 1817, where he successfully opened chapels and translated portions of the Bible into the Raratongan language. At Dillon's Bay, Erromanga, however, he was killed and eaten by the natives, in retaliation for earlier cruelties inflicted on them by English sailors. (b. 6/29/1796)

1847 Death of Henry Francis Lyte, 56, Scottish-born Anglican clergyman and hymnwriter. He served as "perpetual curate" of the fishing village of Lower Brixham, Devonshire for 23 years. Lyte penned over 80 hymns, including "Abide With Me" and "Jesus, I My Cross Have Taken." (b. 6/1/1793)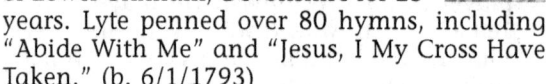

Words For The Soul

1767 English founder of Methodism John Wesley wrote in a letter: *'What is it God will not do if we can trust Him? Only cast your whole care upon Him, and He will do all things well: He will withhold from you no manner of thing that is good.'*

1798 In his last will and testament, American patriot Patrick Henry wrote: *'This is all the inheritance I give to my dear family. The religion of Christ will give them one which will make them rich indeed.'* [N.B. Henry died on 6/6/1799.]

IN GOD'S WORD... OT: Ezekiel 40:28–41:26 ~ NT: James 4:1-17 ~ Psalms 118:19-29 ~ Proverbs 28:3-5

ALMANAC OF THE CHRISTIAN FAITH

כסלו KISLEV חשון HESHVAN

November 21

Highlights In History

1638 A General Assembly at Glasgow abolished the episcopal form of church government, adopted the presbyterian form in its place, and gave final constitution to the Church of Scotland.

1852 Union Institute was chartered by the Methodists in Randolph County, NC. Renamed Trinity College in 1859, the campus moved to Durham in 1892. Tobacco magnate James B. Duke endowed the school with $40 million in 1924, upon which its name was changed to Duke University.

1948 The Sunday morning religious program "Lamp Unto My Feet" first aired over CBS television. It was one of TV's longest-running network shows, and aired through January 1979.

Notable Birthdays

1768 Birth of Friedrich D. E. Schleiermacher, German theologian and philosopher. Recognized as the most influential Protestant theologian between the Reformation and the 20th century, Schleiermacher emphasized the emotions as the organ of religion. He authored *On Religion* (1799) and *The Christian Faith* (1821-22). [d. 2/12/1834]

1854 Birth of Italian cardinal Giacomo della Chiesa, who served as Pope Benedict XV from 1914-22. His papacy urged peace and spurred missionary activity. A strict neutral during WWI, he refrained from condemning any actions of the belligerents. [d. 1/22/1922]

1907 Birth of James Alonzo ("Jim") Bishop, American journalist. A syndicated newspaper columnist for 27 years and later editor of "Catholic Digest," Bishop gave new life to great moments in history through his "day" books, including his 1957 chronicle: *The Day Christ Died*. [d. 7/26/1987]

The Last Passage

1136 Death of William of Corbeil, 76, Archbishop of Canterbury (1123-36). It was William who finished the construction of Canterbury Cathedral in 1130. He also crowned Stephen as King of England in 1135. (b. ca.1160)

1695 Death of Henry Purcell, 36, English composer of the early Baroque period. Known as the "father of Anglican Church Music," Purcell is remembered as a songwriter. Among the most elaborate of his compositions for the church was the anthem, "My Heart is Inditing," first performed in Westminster Abbey at the coronation of James II in 1685. (b. ca.1659)

Words For The Soul

1744 Colonial missionary to American Indians David Brainerd wrote in his journal: *'My soul loves the people of God, and especially the ministers of Jesus Christ who feel the same trials that I do.'*

1840 Scottish clergyman Andrew Bonar, 30, recalled in his diary: *'Coming home through the woods last night, I was refreshed and comforted in looking up to the stars. Ministers, like these stars, are set to give light through the night. We shine on, whether travellers will make use of our light or not.'*

1982 American theologian Norman K. Gottwald wrote in "Christian Century": *'Every method of knowing involves reduction of what is studied to regularities in phenomena and to abstractions about the relationship of the phenomena.... Historical criticism reduces events. Sociological criticism reduces social structures and processes. Theological criticism reduces religious beliefs and practices. Frankly, no discipline is more radical in its reductions than theology, which asserts how data drawn from many realms of experience and ways of knowing can be subsumed under the rubrics of God, humanity, sin, grace, faith, eschatology or whatever categories are favored.'*

IN GOD'S WORD...   OT: Ezekiel 42:1–43:27 ~ NT: James 5:1-20 ~ Psalms 119:1-16 ~ Proverbs 28:6-7

ALMANAC OF THE CHRISTIAN FAITH

KISLEV — HESHVAN

~ November 22 ~

Highlights In History

1220 Honorius III (pope from 1216) crowned Holy Roman Emperor Frederick in St. Peter's, on the promise that Frederick would uphold the rights of the Church, and promote a crusade.

1633 Irish Catholic Cecil Calvert, 27, sent two ships (the *Ark* and the *Dove*) from Ireland to establish a colony in America as a refuge for Catholics. His work earned Lord Calvert the nickname, "Colonizer of Maryland."

1987 Pope John Paul II beatified 85 English martyrs who were tortured and executed under the reign of Queen Elizabeth I (1558-1603). The number included 63 Catholic priests and 22 lay members of the Catholic Church.

Notable Birthdays

1786 Birth of Cyrus Kingsbury, American Congregational ABCFM missionary educator among the Midwestern Indians. Ordained in 1815, Kingsbury moved to the Cherokee and Choctaw reservations in Arkansas in 1836, and ministered among the Indians there until his death. [d. 6/27/1870]

1840 Birth of Daniel W. Whittle, American Civil War officer, evangelist, Bible teacher and hymnwriter. Influenced by Dwight L. Moody, Whittle became an evangelist following the Civil War, assisted by capable songleaders such as Philip P. Bliss, James McGranahan and George C. Stebbins. Whittle wrote many of his hymns later in life, including "Showers of Blessing," "Moment by Moment" and "I Know Whom I Have Believed." [d. 3/4/1901]

The Last Passage

1694 Death of John Tillotson, 64, English ecclesiastic. He was the first married Archbishop of Canterbury (1691-94) since Matthew Parker of the previous century. Tillotson was a member of the committee that revised the *Book of Common Prayer* (1689). (bapt. 10/10/1630)

1873 American lawyer Horatio G. Spafford's four daughters drowned when their passenger ship, while crossing the Atlantic, collided with another vessel and sank. The following month, as his own ship passed over the spot of the earlier tragedy, Spafford penned the words to the enduring hymn, "It is Well With My Soul."

1900 Death of Sir Arthur S. Sullivan, 58, English composer. Better known for his musical collaborations with William S. Gilbert, Sullivan also composed music for the church, including a number of anthems, oratorios, and also the hymn tunes ST. KEVIN ("Come, Ye Faithful, Raise the Strain") and ST. GERTRUDE ("Onward, Christian Soldiers"). (b. 5/13/1842)

1950 Death of Paul W. Fleming, 39, American missionary and founder (with Cecil Dye) of New Tribes Mission in 1942. Fleming died when his mission plane went down in the Grand Teton Mountains of Wyoming. (b. 1911)

1963 Death of C[live] S. Lewis, 65, English literary scholar, novelist, critic and Christian apologist. Well-known for *The Chronicles of Narnia* (1950-56), a children's series, Lewis also penned other Christian classics, including *The Screwtape Letters* (1940) and *The Great Divorce* (1946). (b. 11/29/1898)

Words For The Soul

1537 German reformer Martin Luther declared in a sermon: *'He remains eternally above and yet descends, without any change or mutation of the Godhead, to assume human sonship from His mother.... The Son of God... has two natures but is one Son, not two Christs or two Sons. How this takes place reason cannot comprehend.'*

1736 English founder of Methodism John Wesley wrote in a letter to his brother Samuel: *'All good men agree in judgment; they differ only in words, which all are in their own nature ambiguous.'*

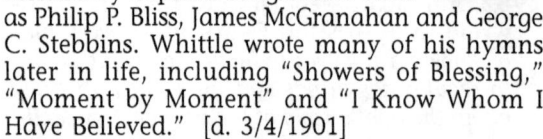

IN GOD'S WORD... OT: Ezekiel 44:1–45:12 ~ NT: 1 Peter 1:1-12 ~ Psalms 119:17-32 ~ Proverbs 28:8-10

ALMANAC OF THE CHRISTIAN FAITH

KISLEV — HESHVAN

~ November 23 ~

Highlights In History

1654 French mathematician Blaise Pascal, 31, underwent a profound religious conversion. He thereupon abandoned his study of science, having determined that *'the Christian religion obliges us to live only for God, and to have no other aim than him.'*

1729 German-born John Philip Boehm, 46, was formally ordained a pastor of the Dutch Reformed Church. Boehm had previously come to America in 1720, where he began organizing religious services among German Reformed immigrants in Pennsylvania.

1947 Eliezer L. Sukenik of Jerusalem's Hebrew University first received word of the existence of the Dead Sea Scrolls. The documents, dating between 200 BC and AD 70, had been discovered the previous winter (1946-47) by two Bedouin shepherds in the vicinity of Qumran.

Notable Birthdays

1712 Birth of Andrew Foulis, Scottish publisher and printer. He and his brother Robert were noted for their printed editions of Thomas Gray's poetry and John Milton's *Paradise Lost*. [d. 9/18/1775]

1726 Birth of Edward Bass, American prelate. He was the first Protestant Episcopal Bishop of Massachusetts, which then included the colonies of Rhode Island and New Hampshire (1797-1803). [d. 9/10/1803]

1803 Birth of Theodore D. Weld, American revivalist, abolitionist and temperance leader. A convert of Charles G. Finney's revivalism, his antislavery influence behind the scenes at the Presbyterian General Assembly of 1835 was a contributing factor in the Old School – New School division within this denomination two years later. [d. 2/3/1895]

1809/10 Birth of Henry Lyman, American ABCFM missionary to the Indian Archipelago (the Malay Archipelago; Malaysia; Indonesia). He and fellow ABCFM missionary Samuel Munson, mistaken for Muslim spies, were killed and eaten by Batak natives. [d. 6/28/1834]

The Last Passage

1585 Death of Thomas Tallis, 80, English organist and composer. He has been called the "father of English cathedral music," and was among the first to set English words to music for the Anglican liturgy. (b. ca.1505)

1872 Death of Sir John Bowring, 80, English linguist, traveler, diplomat and author. He was able to converse in 100 languages, and to read some 200. A poet, he wrote many hymns, including one which endures today: "In the Cross of Christ I Glory." (b. 10/17/1792)

1895 Death of Sylvanus D. Phelps, 79, American Baptist clergyman and hymn writer. He published several volumes of poetry and prose. Today, Phelps is remembered as author of the hymn, "Savior, Thy Dying Love." (b. 5/15/1816)

1906 Death of Wilhelm Wrede, 47, German Lutheran New Testament scholar. He was named in the title of Albert Schweitzer's classic Christological study: *The Quest for the Historical Jesus: From Reimarus to Wrede*. (b. 5/10/1859)

Words For The Soul

1742 English revivalist George Whitefield advised in a letter: *'Two things I would earnestly recommend to your constant study: the book of God, and your own heart. These two, well understood, will make you an able minister of the New Testament.'*

1981 Russian Orthodox liturgical scholar Father Alexander Schmemann, after a day spent away from home, reflected in his journal: *'How I love these times of falling out of life; even fleeting, but an immersion in something "other."'*

IN GOD'S WORD... OT: Ezekiel 45:13–46:24 ~ NT: 1 Peter 1:13–2:10 ~ Psalms 119:33-48 ~ Proverbs 28:8-11

כסלו KISLEV — ALMANAC OF THE CHRISTIAN FAITH — חשון HESHVAN

November 24

Highlights In History

1703 In Philadelphia, German-born pastor and hymnwriter Justus Falckner, 31, became the first Lutheran clergyman to be ordained in America.

1838 Canadian Sulpician missionary François Blanchet, 43, first arrived in the Oregon Territory. A native of Quebec, he spent 45 years planting churches in the American Northwest, and is remembered today as the "apostle of Oregon."

1880 In Montgomery, Alabama, more than 150 delegates from Baptist churches in 11 states met to form the Baptist Foreign Missions Convention of the United States. Liberian missionary William W. Colley was chief organizer. Rev. William H. McAlpine was elected first president.

Notable Birthdays

1713 Birth of Junipero Serra, Spanish-born Franciscan missionary to western North America. He first arrived in Mexico in 1749, extended his labors to upper California in 1769, and established 9 of the first 21 Franciscan missions founded along the Pacific coast, including San Francisco, Santa Barbara, Santa Clara and San Juan Capistrano. Serra has been aptly called the "Apostle of California." [d. 8/28/1784]

1800 Birth of Henry K. Oliver, American musician and hymnwriter. He composed the hymn tune FEDERAL STREET ("God Calling Yet! Shall I Not Hear?"). [d. 8/12/1885]

1865 Birth of Arthur Samuel Peake, English Nonconformist biblical scholar and writer. He was the first Rylands Professor of Biblical Criticism and Exegesis at Manchester University from 1904. [d. 8/19/1929]

The Last Passage

1531 Death of Johannes Oecolampadius, 49, German Reformer and a leader in the Swiss Reformation. He adopted Zwingli's theology in disputing Martin Luther and Philipp Melanchthon on the Lord's Supper. Oecolampadius also helped Erasmus edit his critical edition (1516) of the Greek New Testament. (b. 1482)

1572 Death of John Knox, 57 (or 67), Scottish Reformer. He fled on Mary Tudor's succession to the throne (1553), met John Calvin, and later returned to Scotland (1559), where he afterward published and preached against the Catholic priesthood, image worship, and mass. A chief leader of the Protestant Reformation, Knox was responsible for the creation of the Reformed Church of Scotland, which held its first general assembly in 1560. (b. 1505/1515)

1860 Death of George Croly, 80, Anglican clergyman, author and hymnwriter. After pastoring six years in Ireland, Croly moved to London, where he attained great literary success writing novels, historical and theological works, drama, poetry and satires. In 1854 he published *Psalms and Hymns for Public Worship*, which included one hymn still popular today: "Spirit of God, Descend Upon My Heart." (b. 8/17/1780)

Words For The Soul

1882 American Quaker holiness author Hannah Whitall Smith wrote in a letter: *'Somehow my two summers out in the wilds of nature, with no meetings and no religious influences, only God and His works, have been more helpful in my interior life than any other thing I have ever known. They have brought me face to face with God, and I have seen Him. Not in a vision, as so many think is the only way of seeing, but as one sees a truth.... And in the seeing I have found, what I never expected to find, more emotional joy than I have ever known before.'*

1941 American Trappist monk Thomas Merton wrote in his *Secular Journal*: *'Spiritual dryness is an acute experience of longing – therefore of love.'*

IN GOD'S WORD... OT: Ezekiel 47:1–48:35 ~ NT: 1 Peter 2:11–3:7 ~ Psalms 119:49-64 ~ Proverbs 28:12-13

November 25

Highlights In History

2348 BC According to the reckoning of Irish Archbishop James Ussher, the "Great Deluge" (i.e., Noah's flood) began on this date. Ussher's *Chronology of the Old and New Testaments* (published 1650-54) is the actual original source of the dates inserted in the margins of many editions of the King James Version of the Bible.

1742 In New York, David Brainerd, 24, was approved as a missionary to the New England Indians by the Scottish Society for the Propagating of Christian Knowledge (SPCK). Brainerd labored heroically for three years, before advancing tuberculosis forced him to relinquish his work (and from which he died in October 1747.)

1820 English poet and Oxford Movement leader John Keble, 28, penned the words to the hymn, "Sun of My Soul" (*'Sun of my soul, Thou Savior dear, It is not night if Thou be near....'*).

Notable Birthdays

1697 Birth of Gerhard Tersteegen, German Reformed clergyman, mystic, and hymnwriter. After years of depression, he renewed his faith (1724) and opened his home to all who needed spiritual counseling. The author of 111 hymns, Tersteegen is regarded as one of the important hymnwriters in the German Reformed Church. He is remembered today as author of "God Calling Yet! Shall I Not Hear?" [d. 4/3/1769]

1787 Birth of Franz Xaver Gruber, Austrian Catholic sacred organist and choral director. He served as organist for St. Nicholas, the parish church near Oberndorf, between 1807-29.  Gruber penned over 90 musical compositions during his life, yet is remembered today for a single hymn tune, using only three chords and written on Christmas Eve in 1818 for his pastor, Joseph Mohr: STILLE NACHT ("Silent Night"). [d. 6/7/1863]

1871 Birth of Mabel Johnston Camp, American professional singer and pianist. She was afflicted with physical problems, which caused her to be bedridden for months at a time, but she also wrote a number of hymns, including "That Beautiful Name." [d. 5/25/1937]

The Last Passage

1748 Death of Isaac Watts, 74, Anglican theologian and hymnwriter. Acclaimed "the father of English hymnody," he was the first to successfully challenge the long tradition of strict psalm-singing, and produced some 600 hymns.  The most enduring of these include: "When I Survey the Wondrous Cross," "O God, Our Help in Ages Past," "Come, We That Love the Lord," "I Sing the Mighty Power of God," "Joy to the World," "My Shepherd Will Supply My Need," "Jesus Shall Reign Where'er the Sun" and "Am I a Soldier of the Cross?" (b. 7/17/1674)

1899 Death of Robert Lowry, 73, American Baptist clergyman and hymnwriter. He collaborated with William H. Doane and others, and penned the melody and/or words to such hymns as  "Nothing But the Blood"; "Christ Arose"; "We're Marching to Zion"; "All the Way My Savior Leads Me" and "I Need Thee Every Hour." (b. 3/12/1826)

Words For The Soul

1807 Anglican missionary to Persia, Henry Martyn recorded in his journal: *'With thee, O my God, there is no disappointment; I shall never have to regret that I loved thee too well.'*

1864 British Jewish statesman Benjamin Disraeli declared in a speech: *'Man is a being born to believe, and if no church comes forward with all the title deeds of truth, he will find altars and idols in his own heart and his own imagination.'*

IN GOD'S WORD... OT: Daniel 1:1–2:23 ~ NT: 1 Peter 3:8–4:6 ~ Psalms 119:65-80 ~ Proverbs 28:14

KISLEV כסלו   ALMANAC OF THE CHRISTIAN FAITH   חשון HESHVAN

~ November 26 ~

Highlights In History

1539 In England, the monastery at the Fountains Abbey was surrendered to the crown. It was the richest of the Cistercian houses, prior to the time of the Dissolution of all monasteries in England, under the reign of Henry VIII.

1775 The American Navy began using chaplains within its regular service.

1789 President George Washington proclaimed this date (a Thursday) as the first national Thanksgiving Day holiday. (Days of national thanksgiving were periodically proclaimed by later presidents, until Abraham Lincoln inaugurated the practice, in 1863, of setting the fourth Thursday in November aside for an annual Thanksgiving Day.)

1970 During a 10-day visit to the Philippines, Pope Paul VI was attacked by a knife-wielding man in Manilla. The pontiff was unhurt and continued his journey.

Notable Birthdays

1607 English-born American Congregational clergyman John Harvard was baptized. When he died, he bequeathed his library of 300 volumes and half his estate of £8,000 (ca. $160,000 today!) to the newly organized college at New Towne, Mass. In 1639 the town's name was changed to Cambridge, and the college's name changed to Harvard. [d. 9/14/1638]

1609 Birth of Henry Dunster, American Congregational minister and educator. He was the first president of Harvard College. [d. 2/27/1659]

1827 Birth of Ellen G. White, American religious leader. Born and raised a Methodist, she later became co-founder and leader of the Seventh-Day Adventist Church (1860). During her lifetime, she was the most influential voice within her denomination, and claimed nearly 2,000 visions. [d. 7/16/1915]

1858 Birth of Katherine Drexel, American Catholic religious. Born into a wealthy family, she devoted her life to missions. She established the Sisters of the Blessed Sacrament for Indians and Colored People in 1891. In 1915 she founded Xavier University in New Orleans. [d. 3/3/1955]

1858 Birth of Israel Abrahams, English Judaic scholar. A leader of Judaism in Great Britain, Abrahams wrote a number of classics on Judaism and was co-editor of the "Jewish Quarterly Review" from 1889-1907. [d. 10/6/1925]

The Last Passage

1883 Death of Sojourner Truth (née Isabella Baumfree), 86, African-American abolitionist and orator. A freed slave, in 1843 Miss Baumfree changed her name and took up the cause of abolition. President Lincoln received her in the White House in 1864. (b. ca. 1797)

1901 Death of Joseph Henry Thayer, 73, American Congregational biblical lexicographer. Thayer's reputation was established by his scholarly translations of several critical German New Testament references, including Wilke's *Greek-English Lexicon of the New Testament* (1886). (b. 11/7/1828)

Words For The Soul

1962 English literary scholar and apologist C. S. Lewis wrote in a letter: 'No doubt [my body] has often led me astray: but not half so often, I suspect, as my soul has led IT astray. For the spiritual evils... arise more from the imagination than from the appetites.'

1973 Russian Orthodox liturgical scholar Father Alexander Schmemann reflected in his journal: '"Little children, keep yourselves from idols!" (1 John 5:21) Sometimes I see Orthodoxy in a thicket of idols. To be attached to the past always leads to idolatry, and I see many people living by the past, or rather, by many pasts. An Old Believer lies deeply buried in an Orthodox person.'

IN GOD'S WORD...   OT: Daniel 2:24–3:30 ~ NT: 1 Peter 4:7–5:14 ~ Psalms 119:81-96 ~ Proverbs 28:15-16

ALMANAC OF THE CHRISTIAN FAITH

כסלו KISLEV

חשון HESHVAN

~ November 27 ~

Highlights In History

1095 Pope Urban II solemnly proclaimed the First Crusade at the Council of Clermont, in France. Urban's twin-purpose was to relieve the pressure caused by the Seljuk Turks on the Eastern Roman Empire, and to secure free access by Christian pilgrims to the Holy Land.

1755 Land for the first Jewish settlement in America was purchased by Joseph Salvador, who bought 10,000 acres near Fort Ninety-Six, in the southern part of the Carolina Colony.

1921 The first church of the airwaves was established when services of the Radio Church of America were broadcast by Walter J. Garvey from his home in the Bronx, New York City. Hospitals, military installations and radio operators were alerted to the program.

1947 Eliezer L. Sukenik of Hebrew University in Jerusalem was shown four pieces of a Dead Sea Scroll – the first Westerner to recognize their value. (The documents, dating between 200 BC and AD 70, had been discovered the previous winter (1946-47) by two Bedouin shepherds in the vicinity of Qumran.)

Notable Birthdays

1654 Birth of Friedrich R. L. Canitz, German royal courtier and a hymnwriter. His 24 original hymns were all published anonymously. One of these – "Come, My Soul, Thou Must Be Waking" – is still sung today. [d. 8/11/1699]

1787 Birth of English Congregational clergyman, humanitarian and hymn author, Andrew Reed. He was instrumental in establishing orphanages, hospitals and homes for the insane. Reed penned the enduring hymn, "Holy Ghost, with Light Divine." [d. 2/25/1862]

1820 Birth of Nathaniel A. F. Hewit, American religious. Raised a Congregationalist, he later became a Roman Catholic. In 1858 Hewit and Isaac Hecker established the Congregation of the Missionary Priests of St. Paul (Paulist Fathers). Hewit served as superior of the order from 1888 until his death. [d. 7/3/1897]

1862 Birth of Adelaide Pollard, American Presbyterian hymnwriter. Plagued with frail health most of her years, she lived the life of a mystic. Of the several hymns she penned, "Have Thine Own Way, Lord" is still popular. [d. 12/20/1934]

1874 Birth of Chaim Weizmann, a successful Russian-born research chemist who became a Zionist leader in England. He was largely responsible for the Balfour Declaration, which helped establish Israel as a Jewish homeland. Weizmann was later elected the first president of Israel (1948-52). [d. 11/9/1952]

The Last Passage

1825 Death of Paul Henkel, 70, American Lutheran publisher. Converted under George Whitefield in 1776, he became an evangelist and printer. With his son Ambrose, Henkel operated a press in Virginia – for years the only Lutheran publishing house in the U.S. (b. 12/15/1754)

1922 Death of Alice Meynell, 75, English Catholic poet and essayist. She and her husband, British journalist Wilfred Meynell, befriended fellow-poet Francis Thompson during the latter years of his opium addiction. (b. 8/17/1847)

Words For The Soul

1950 American missionary and Auca Indian martyr Jim Elliot wrote in his journal: *'What gets me into the Kingdom, from Christ's own statement, is not saying "Lord, Lord," but acting "Lord, Lord."'*

1953 English Christian apologist C. S. Lewis wrote in a letter: *'Anxiety is not only a pain which we must ask God to assuage but also a weakness we must ask Him to pardon — for He's told us to take no care for the morrow.'*

IN GOD'S WORD... OT: Daniel 4:1-37 ~ NT: 2 Peter 1:1-21 ~ Psalms 119:97-112 ~ Proverbs 28:17-18

כסלו KISLEV — ALMANAC OF THE CHRISTIAN FAITH — חשון HESHVAN

November 28

Highlights In History

1863 Thanksgiving was first observed as a regular American holiday. Proclaimed by President Lincoln the previous month, it was declared the event would henceforth be observed annually, on the fourth Thursday in November.

1950 A constitutional convention (comprised of 14 Protestant, Anglican, and Eastern Orthodox denominations) met in Cleveland, Ohio, and brought into being the National Council of the Churches of Christ in the United States of America. Today, the NCCC serves to administer disaster relief, strengthen family life, provide leadership training, and promote world peace.

1972 The Anglican Church ordained its first two women priests.

1984 Pope John Paul II completed the last of 133 homilies in St. Peter's Square on the theme, "Theology of the Body." It was the first time in public catechesis that a pope made use of higher criticism of the Old Testament and freely cited a number of Protestant theologians.

Notable Birthdays

1757 Birth of William Blake, eccentric English poet and artist. Noted for the mystical nature of his poetry, he authored *Songs of Innocence* (1789) and *Songs of Experience* (1794). Blake's paintings also illustrated a famous edition of John Milton's *Paradise Lost*. [d. 8/12/1827]

1777 Birth of John H. Rice, American Presbyterian clergyman and educator. Rice was a founder of the American Bible Society (1816), and helped establish Union Theological Seminary in Richmond, Virginia, serving as its first president (1824-31). Rice directed many of his energies to Presbyterian missions, which led in part to the eventual forming of the Board of World Missions by his denomination. [d. 9/3/1831]

1918 Birth of Madeleine L'Engle, American author. She won the 1963 Newberry Prize for *A Wrinkle in Time*. Her writings have been censored by secular critics for being too religious, and by Christian reviewers for being too secular. L'Engle, who counts Shakespeare, C.S. Lewis and the Psalms among her own favorite writers, claims she is not so much a Christian writer but rather *'a writer who is struggling to be a Christian.'* [d. 9/7/2007]

The Last Passage

1859 Death of Carl J. P. Spitta, 59, German hymnwriter. An invalid from age 11, he was ordained to preach in 1828, and was regarded as a Pietist and mystic. Spitta wrote verse from childhood, and over 40 of his German hymns were translated into English, including "O Happy Home, Where Thou Art Loved." (b. 8/1/1801)

1904 Death of Jeremiah E. Rankin, 76, American Congregational clergyman, educator and hymnwriter. He penned a number of hymns, including "Tell It To Jesus" and "God Be With You Till We Meet Again." (b. 1/2/1828)

1922 Death of James M. Thoburn, 86, American Methodist missionary to India (1859-1908). He was co-founder of "The Indian Witness" magazine (1871), and helped to establish the Methodist Church in Burma (1879), Malaysia (1885), and the Philippines (1899). (b. 3/7/1836)

Words For The Soul

1739 English revivalist George Whitefield advised in a letter: *'Follow after, but do not run before the blessed Spirit; if you do, although you may benefit others, and God may overrule everything for your own good, yet you will certainly destroy the peace of your own soul.'*

1995 Dutch Catholic priest and writer Henri J. M. Nouwen noted in his journal: *'Our life is a seed that has to die to be dressed with immortality!'*

IN GOD'S WORD... OT: Daniel 5:1-31 ~ NT: 2 Peter 2:1-22 ~ Psalms 119:113-128 ~ Proverbs 28:19-20

ALMANAC OF THE CHRISTIAN FAITH

כסלו KISLEV

חשון HESHVAN

~ November 29 ~

Highlights In History

1223 Honorius III published "Regula bullata," formally authorizing the "Regula Prima," a settled rule of organization and administration for the Franciscan religious order.

1780 In Connecticut, Congregationalist Lemuel Haynes, 27, was licensed to preach, making him the first black minister to be certified by a predominantly white denomination. In 1785, Haynes was ordained pastor of a church in Torrington, Connecticut, also making him the first black clergyman to pastor a white church.

1964 Modifications in the U.S. Catholic liturgy, including the use of English in many of the prayers, first went into effect. The changes were a result of Vatican II directives. By 1970, the entire mass was in English (although some priests defied the Vatican and stuck to Latin).

1970 In Nagpur, India, six church bodies – the Anglicans, the United Church of Northern India, the Baptists, the Methodists, the Church of the Brethren and the Disciples of Christ – merged to form the Church of India.

Notable Birthdays

1898 Birth of C.S. Lewis, English Christian literary scholar. He penned numerous scholarly studies, works of science fiction (*Out of the Silent Planet*, 1938), children's fantasies (*Tales of Narnia*, 1950-56) and Christian apologetic works, including *Mere Christianity* (1943). [d. 11/22/1963].

The Last Passage

1530 English prelate Thomas Wolsey died at 55. As Henry VIII's lord chancellor (1515-29), he was the last great Catholic ecclesiastic to dominate the affairs of state. He fell from the king's grace after failing to get papal approval of Henry's divorce from Catherine of Aragon. Arrested on charges of high treason, Wolsey died en route to London. (b. 1475)

1577 Cuthbert Mayne, 34, was executed. He was the first seminary priest to die for Catholicism in England. Cuthbert was canonized in 1970 as one of the "Forty English martyrs." (b.1543)

1661 Death of Brian Walton, 60, Anglican biblical scholar and Bishop of Chester (1660-61). He edited the nine-language *London* (or Walton's) *Polyglot Bible* (1657). (b. ca.1601)

1847 American Presbyterian medical missionary to the American Northwest Indians, Marcus Whitman, 45, was murdered by a party of Cayuse Indians in (present-day) Washington State. Along with Whitman, his wife Narcissa (b. 3/14/1808), 39, and twelve others were also massacred. (b. 9/4/1802)

1937 Death of Agnes N. Ozman (married name: LaBerge), 67, American Pentecostal evangelist. She was a student at Charles Parham's Bethel Bible College in Topeka, KS when, on January 1, 1901 she became the first person in modern times to speak in tongues. (b. 9/15/1870)

Words For The Soul

1776 Anglican hymnwriter John Newton wrote in a letter: 'He knows our sorrows, not merely as He knows all things, but as one who has been in our situation, and who, though without sin himself, endured when upon earth inexpressibly more for us than He will ever lay upon us.'

1853 Scottish clergyman and children's novelist George MacDonald wrote in a letter to his wife: 'Every higher stage of Truth brings with it its own temptation like that in the Wilderness, and if one overcomes not in that, he overcomes not at all.'

1981 Dutch Catholic priest and diarist Henri J. M. Nouwen penned in his *¡Gracias!* Latin American journal: 'Why do we keep missing the most obvious signs of God's doing and allow our hearts to be filled with all those things that keep suggesting, not that the Lord is coming, but that nothing will happen unless we make it happen.'

IN GOD'S WORD... OT: Daniel 6:1-28 ~ NT: 2 Peter 3:1-18 ~ Psalms 119:129-152 ~ Proverbs 28:21-22

KISLEV — ALMANAC OF THE CHRISTIAN FAITH — HESHVAN

~ November 30 ~

Highlights In History

1215 The Fourth Lateran Council closed, under Innocent III. Summoned by Pope Innocent III, it was this council that made first official use of the term "transubstantiation," with reference to the Eucharist (Lord's Supper).

1554 Roman Catholicism was briefly restored to England, under Mary Tudor, the daughter of Henry VIII and Catherine of Aragon. During her reign, "Bloody Mary" had Thomas Cranmer, Hugh Latimer, Nicholas Ridley and nearly 300 other Protestant leaders burned at the stake.

1894 In Naperville, Illinois, seven groups of the Evangelical Association withdrew from the organization to form the United Evangelical Church. (In 1922 the two denominational groups reunited.)

Notable Birthdays

1628 English Nonconformist clergyman and writer John Bunyan was baptized. (His exact date-of-birth is unknown). Converted to the Christian faith by his wife (whose name, ironically, has been lost to the record), Bunyan afterward spent twelve years in Bedford Jail for preaching without a license. There, behind prison walls, where he did nearly all his writing, he penned his famed religious allegory, *Pilgrim's Progress* (1678). Bunyan was also a hymnwriter ("He Who Would Valiant Be"). [d. 8/31/1688]

1725 Birth of Martin Boehm, American church founder. Made a Mennonite bishop at 36, he was later excluded from that communion for associating with persons of other sects. Boehm then joined with German-born Philip Otterbein to help establish the United Brethren in Christ Church (1789), of which the two men were ultimately made bishops (1800). [d. 3/23/1812]

1729 Birth of Samuel Seabury, first bishop of the Episcopal Church (1784-96). Following the American Revolution, Seabury helped formulate the documents which constituted the American Protestant Episcopal Church as an independent religious denomination autonomous from the Church of England. [d. 2/25/1796]

1884 Birth of Daniel A. Poling, American Protestant radio evangelist, temperance leader and editor. He conducted a weekly radio program in the 1920s, and was editor of the "Christian Herald" for 40 years (1926-66). [d. 2/7/1968]

The Last Passage

1812 Death of Harriet Atwood Newell, 19, pioneer Congregational missionary. The wife of missionary Samuel Newell, whom she married in February 1812, the two set sail for India with the Adoniram Judsons that same month, thus making Harriet and Ann Judson the first American women commissioned for missionary work abroad. Harriet's death, nine months later, also made her the first American missionary to die in service on a foreign field. (b. 10/10/1793)

1892 Death of Fenton J. A. Hort, 64, English New Testament and linguistic scholar. He worked for nearly 30 years in close connection with Brooke Foss Westcott, identifying the exact text of the original Greek New Testament. The culmination of their work: *The New Testament in the Original Greek* (1881). (b. 4/23/1828)

Words For The Soul

1530 German reformer Martin Luther remarked: *'Whenever I happen to be prevented by the press of duties from observing my hour of prayer, the entire day is bad for me.'*

1770 English founder of Methodism John Wesley wrote in a letter: *'Let no study swallow up, or intrench upon, the hours of private prayer.'*

IN GOD'S WORD...   OT: Daniel 7:1-28 ~ NT: 1 John 1:1-10 ~ Psalms 119:153-176 ~ Proverbs 28:23-24

ALMANAC OF THE CHRISTIAN FAITH

NOVEMBER INDEX

A

Abauzit, Firmin
  b. 11/11/1679 [d. 3/20/1767]
Abolition 11/9, 11/26
Abrahams, Israel
  b. 11/26/1858 [d. 10/6/1925]
Agatho, Pope St. (678-81) 11/7
Alcoholics Anonymous 11/6
Alcuin 11/19
American Bible Society 11/4, 11/28
American Revolution 11/6, 11/20, 11/30
American School of Oriental Research 11/12
Ames, William
  (b. 1576) d. 11/14/1633
Apocrypha, O.T. 11/12
Apostles' Creed 11/3
Aristotle 11/15
Arminianism 11/13
Asch, Sholem
  b. 11/1/1880 [d. 7/10/1957]
Assumption of the Blessed Virgin Mary 11/1
Augustine of Hippo, St. 11/3
  b. 11/13/354 [d. 8/28/430]

B

Baillie, Donald M.
  b. 11/5/1887 [d. 10/31/1954]
Baillie, John 11/5
Balfour, Arthur J. 11/2
Balfour Declaration 11/2
Balfour Declaration (1917) 11/27
Bampton Lectures 11/10
Bancroft, Richard
  (b. 1544) d. 11/2/1610
Baptist Foreign Missions Convention 11/24
Barnhouse, Donald Grey
  (b. 3/28/1895) d. 11/5/1960
Barth, Karl 11/11
Bass, Edward
  b. 11/23/1726 [d. 9/10/1803]
Baumfree, Isabella (Sojourner Truth)
  (b. ca. 1797) d. 11/26/1883
Bayle, Pierre
  b. 11/18/1647 [d. 12/28/1706]
Beatles, The 11/4
Becket, Thomas 11/2
Bede, Venerable 11/19
Benedict XV, Pope (1914-22) 11/21
Berg, Daniel 11/19

BIBLE VERSIONS
  American Standard Version 11/6, 11/16
  Danish, Tausen's 11/11
  Erasmus' Greek New Testament (1516) 11/24
  French, Abauzit's (1726) 11/11
  German, Luther's 11/10
  Greek New Testament 11/30
  King James Version (1611) 11/1, 11/2, 11/25
  London Polyglot Bible (1657) 11/29
  Raratongan language 11/20
Billy Graham Evangelistic Association 11/7
Bishop, Jim (James Alonzo)
  b. 11/21/1907 [d. 7/26/1987]
Blackwell, Antoinette L.
  (b. 5/20/1825) d. 11/5/1921
Blake, William
  b. 11/28/1757 [d. 8/12/1827]
Blanchet, François 11/24
Blessed Virgin Mary, The 11/1
Bliss, Philip P. 11/22
Boardman, George Dana 11/4
Board of World Missions (Baptist) 11/28
Boehm, John Philip 11/23
Boehm, Martin 11/16, 11/17
  b. 11/30/1729 [d. 3/23/1812]
Boniface VIII, Pope (1294-1303) 11/18
Borromeo, St. Charles
  (b. 10/2/1538) d. 11/3/1584
Bowring, John
  (b. 10/17/1792) d. 11/23/1872
Bradford, William 11/9
Brainerd, David 11/25
Bresee, Phineas F.
  (b. 12/31/1838) d. 11/13/1915
Brown, Solyman
  b. 11/17/1790 [d. 2/13/1876]
Bryant, William Cullen
  b. 11/3/1794 [d. 6/12/1878]
Bucer, Martin
  b. 11/11/1491 [d. 2/28/1551]
Buell, Harriett Eugenia Peck
  b. 11/2/1834 [d. 2/6/1910]
Bunyan, John
  bapt. 11/30/1628 [d. 8/31/1688]
Burnell, Elizabeth 11/14

C

Calvert, Lord Cecil 11/22
Calvin, John 11/20, 11/24
Camp, Mabel Johnston
  b. 11/25/1871 [d. 5/25/1937]
Campbell, Alexander 11/9
Canitz, Friedrich R. L.
  b. 11/27/1654 [d. 8/11/1699]

CANTERBURY ARCHBISHOPS
  Bancroft, Richard (1604-10) 11/2
  Becket, Thomas (1162-70) 11/2
  Ramsey, Arthur Michael (1961-74) 11/14
  Tillotson, John (1691-94) 11/22
  William of Corbeil (1123-36) 11/21
Carnegie Hall Conference 11/15
Carolina Assembly 11/12
Carroll, John 11/6
Carter, Russell K.
  b. 11/18/1849 [d. 8/23/1928]
Cary, Lott
  (b. ca. 1780) d. 11/10/1828
Catherine of Aragon 11/29, 11/30
Catholic Charities 11/20
Chambers, Oswald
  (b. 7/24/1874) d. 11/15/1917
Chapman, J. Wilbur 11/19
Chemnitz, Martin
  b. 11/9/1522 [d. 4/8/1586]
Chiesa, Giacomo della 11/21
CHURCH COUNCILS
  Chalcedon (451) 11/1
  Constance (1417) 11/11
  Council of Clermont (1095) 11/18, 11/27
  Council of Constance (1414-18) 11/5
  Fourth Lateran (1215) 11/11, 11/30
  Third Council of Constantinople (680-81) 11/7
  Trent (1545-63) 11/13
  Vatican II (1962-65) 11/20, 11/29
Cisneros, Francisco Ximenes de
  (b. 1436) d. 11/8/1517
Civil War, American 11/22
Clement of Alexandria 11/17
Coke, Thomas 11/3, 11/14
Colley, William W. 11/24
Colonna, Oddone 11/11
Combs, Emile 11/8
Complutensian Polyglot 11/8
Confederate States of America 11/11
Congregation of the Most Holy Redeemer 11/9
Counter-Reformation 11/3
Cowper, William
  b. 11/15/1731 [d. 4/25/1800]
Cranmer, Thomas 11/30
Crittenton, Charles Nelson
  (b. 2/20/1833) d. 11/16/1909
Croly, George
  (b. 8/17/1780) d. 11/24/1860
Cromwell, Oliver 11/20
Crosby, Frances ("Fanny") 11/20
Cruden, Alexander
  (b. 5/31/1699) d. 11/1/1770
Crumpler, Ambrose Blackman 11/4
Crusade, First 11/18, 11/27

Cushman, Ralph S.
  b. 11/12/1879 [d. 8/10/1960]

D

Danish Reformation 11/11
Darby, J[ohn] N[elson]
  b. 11/18/1800 [d. 4/29/1883]
Davies, Samuel 11/3
Day, Dorothy
  b. 11/8/1897 [d. 11/29/1980]
Dead Sea Scrolls 11/23, 11/27
DENOMINATIONS, CHRISTIAN
  African-American Baptists 11/10
  American Lutheranism 11/27
  Anabaptists 11/12, 11/14
  Anglicanism 11/29
  Assemblies of God 11/19
  Calvinism, Strict 11/14
  Canadian Presbyterian Church 11/8
  Christian & Missionary Alliance 11/6, 11/18
  Church of England (Anglicanism) 11/3, 11/11, 11/12, 11/28, 11/30
  Church of India 11/29
  Church of Scotland 11/5, 11/15, 11/21
  Church of the Brethren 11/29
  Church of the Nazarene 11/13, 11/15, 11/19
  Congregationalism 11/5, 11/11, 11/12, 11/16, 11/26, 11/27, 11/29, 11/30
  Disciples of Christ 11/9, 11/18, 11/29
  Dutch Calvinism 11/8
  Dutch Reformed 11/10, 11/13, 11/23
  Eastern Orthodoxy 11/28
  English Nonconformity 11/30
  English Puritanism 11/14
  English Separatists 11/15
  English Wesleyanism 11/17
  Evangelical Church 11/16
  Evangelical United Brethren (EUB) 11/16
  Free Will Baptists 11/5
  French Reformed 11/11
  Fundamentalism 11/5, 11/19
  German Pietism 11/1, 11/28
  German Reformed Church 11/17, 11/20, 11/23, 11/25
  Greek Orthodoxy 11/13
  Holiness Movement 11/13
  Huguenot 11/11
  Low Dutch Reformed Church 11/8
  Lutheran Church in America 11/16
  Mennonites 11/30
  Methodist Episcopal Church 11/2, 11/3, 11/9, 11/15, 11/28
  Methodist Protestant Church 11/2, 11/15
  Moravian Church 11/4, 11/17
  Mormon Church 11/6
  New School (Presbyterianism) 11/23
  Nonconformity, English 11/12, 11/24

NOVEMBER INDEX

Old Catholicism 11/1
Old School (Presbyterianism) 11/23
Pentecostalism 11/29
Pentecostal Church of the Nazarene 11/13
Pentecostal Holiness 11/4, 11/17
Peoples Temple 11/18
Plymouth Brethren 11/4, 11/18, 11/19
Presbyterianism 11/9, 11/28
Protestant Episcopal 11/5, 11/9, 11/11, 11/14, 11/30
Quakerism 11/2, 11/12
Reformed Church of Scotland 11/24
Reformed Church of the Netherlands 11/13
Reformed Protestantism 11/20
Roman Catholicism 11/13
Russian Orthodoxy 11/3, 11/5, 11/6, 11/7, 11/17, 11/23, 11/26
Scottish Anglicanism 11/2
Separatists 11/11
Seventh-Day Adventist Church (1860) 11/26
Southern Presbyterianism 11/3
Swedenborgianism 11/17
Syrian Orthodox Church in the U.S. and Canada 11/15
Unitarianism 11/3
Unitas Fratrum (Moravians) 11/20
United Brethren in Christ 11/16, 11/17, 11/30
United Church of Northern India 11/29
United Evangelical Church 11/30
United Lutheran Church 11/16
United Lutheran Church in America (ULCA) 11/14
United Methodist Church 11/17
De Landas Berghes, Rudolph
 b. 11/1/1873 [d. 11/17/1920]
Dialectical Theology 11/16
Dicta Pirminii 11/3
Dissolution of English Monasteries 11/26
Doane, William H. 11/25
Doddridge, Joseph
 (b. 10/14/1769) d. 11/9/1826
Drexel, Katherine
 b. 11/26/1858 [d. 3/3/1955]
Duchesne, Rose Philippine
 (b. 8/29/1769) d. 11/18/1852
Duke, James B. 11/21
Dunster, Henry
 b. 11/26/1609 [d. 2/27/1659]
Dwight, Timothy
 b. 11/16/1828 [d. 5/26/1916]
Dwight, Timothy (1752-1817) 11/16
Dye, Cecil 11/22

E

Early Latin Fathers 11/13
Eastern Roman Empire 11/27
Eck, Johann M.
 b. 11/13/1486 [d. 2/10/1543]
Egbert
 (b. 700s) d. 11/19/766
Eliot, John 11/3
Elizabeth I, English Queen (1558-1603) 11/22
Embury, Philip 11/17
Erasmus 11/24
Eucharist (Lord's Supper) 11/11, 11/30
Evangelical Association 11/30
Ewald, Georg H. A. von
 b. 11/16/1803 [d. 5/4/1875]

F

Falckner, Justus 11/24
Federal Council of Churches of Christ in America 11/15
Finney, Charles G. 11/23
Fisk, Pliny 11/3
Fleming, Paul W.
 (b. 1911) d. 11/22/1950
Florence Crittenton Missions 11/16
Florence Homes 11/16
Forsyth, P[eter] T[aylor]
 (b. 5/12/1848) d. 11/11/1921
Forty English martyrs 11/29
Foulis, Andrew
 b. 11/23/1712 [d. 9/18/1775]
Fountains Abbey Monastery 11/26
Frederick, Holy Roman Emperor 11/22
Freeman, James
 b. 4/22/1759 [d. 11/14/1835]
Free Will Baptists (southern) 11/5
French Revolution 11/2, 11/7
Fry, Elizabeth 11/2

G

Gardiner, William
 (b. 3/15/1770) d. 11/16/1853
Garvey, Walter J. 11/27
Gilbert, William S. 11/22
Graham, Billy (William Franklin) 11/6, 11/19
 b. 11/7/1918
Grape, John T.
 (b. 5/6/1835) d. 11/2/1915
Gray, Thomas 11/23
Great Deluge 11/25
Great Schism 11/5
Greeves, Arthur 11/2, 11/9
Gregory of Tours, St.
 (b. 11/30/538) d. 11/17/594
Grellet, Stephen
 b. 11/2/1773 [d. 11/16/1855]
Gruber, Franz Xaver
 b. 11/25/1787 [d. 6/7/1863]

H

Hall, Joseph L.
 b. 11/4/1866 [d. 11/29/1930]
Hall, Sarah
 b. 11/4/1803 [d. 9/1/1845]
Ham, Mordecai 11/7
Hankey, Katherine 11/18
Harrington, Karl P.
 (b. 6/13/1861) d. 11/14/1953
Harvard, John 11/26
Hasseltine Judson, Ann 11/4
Hatch, Edwin
 b. 9/4/1835 [d. 11/10/1889]
Hawks, Annie Sherwood 11/20
Hawley, Gideon
 b. 11/5/1727 [d. 10/3/1807] 11/5
Hayes, Patrick Joseph
 b. 11/20/1867 [d. 9/4/1938]
Haynes, Lemuel 11/29
Hebden, Ellen 11/17
Hecker, Isaac 11/27
Hemy, Henri Frederick
 b. 11/12/1818 [d. 6/10/1888]
Henkel, Paul
 (b. 12/15/1754) d. 11/27/1825
Henry II, English King (1154-89) 11/2
Henry VIII, English King (1509-47) 11/26, 11/29, 11/30
Hewit, Nathaniel A. F.
 b. 11/27/1820 [d. 7/3/1897]
Hibbert Lectures 11/10
Higher criticism of the Old Testament 11/28
Hodge, A[rchibald] A[lexander]
 (b. 7/18/1823) d. 11/11/1886
Hodge, Charles 11/12
Honorius III, Pope (1216-27) 11/29
Hooker, Richard
 (b. 3/1554) d. 11/3/1600
Hort, Fenton J. A.
 (b. 4/23/1828) d. 11/30/1892
Hugh of Lincoln, St.
 (b. 1135) d. 11/16/1200
Hus, Jan 11/5
Hutchinson, Anne 11/7
HYMNS
 "Abide With Me" 11/20
 "All the Way My Savior Leads Me" 11/20, 11/25
 "America" 11/16
 "Am I a Soldier of the Cross?" 11/25
 "Angels From the Realms of Glory" 11/4
 "Ask Ye What Great Thing I Know" 11/6
 "A Mighty Fortress" 11/10
 "A Pilgrim Was I and A-Wandering" 11/8
 "Blessed Assurance" 11/20
 "Breathe on Me, Breath of God" 11/10
 "Christ Arose" 11/25
 "Come, My Soul, Thou Must Be Waking" 11/27
 "Come, We That Love the Lord" 11/25
 "Come, Ye Faithful, Raise the Strain" 11/22
 "Deeper and Deeper" 11/8
 "Does Jesus Care?" 11/4
 "Eternal Father, Strong to Save" 11/1
 "Faith of Our Fathers" 11/12
 "Father of Mercies, In Thy Word" 11/11
 "Glory Be to the Father" 11/6
 "God Be With You Till We Meet Again" 11/28
 "God Calling Yet! Shall I Not Hear?" 11/24, 11/25
 "God Moves in Mysterious Ways" 11/15
 "God of Our Fathers, Whose Almighty Hand" 11/5
 "God Understands" 11/8
 "Go to Dark Gethsemane" 11/4
 "Hark, The Herald Angels Sing" 11/4
 "Have Thine Own Way, Lord" 11/27
 "Heaven Came Down" 11/1
 "Here, O My Lord, I See Thee Face to Face" 11/10
 "He Who Would Valiant Be" 11/30
 "Holy Ghost, with Light Divine" 11/27
 "In the Cross of Christ I Glory" 11/23
 "It Is Glory Just to Walk With Him" 11/19
 "It is Well With My Soul" 11/22
 "It Took a Miracle" 11/1
 "I Belong to the King" 11/4
 "I Heard the Savior Say" 11/2
 "I Know Whom I Have Believed" 11/22
 "I Love to Tell the Story" 11/18
 "I Need Thee Every Hour" 11/20, 11/25
 "I Sing the Mighty Power of God" 11/25
 "I Would Be True" 11/1
 "Jesus, I My Cross Have Taken" 11/20
 "Jesus, Keep Me Near the Cross" 11/20
 "Jesus, Thou Joy of Loving Hearts" 11/12
 "Jesus is All the World to Me" 11/7
 "Jesus Shall Reign Where'er the Sun" 11/25
 "Joyful, Joyful, We Adore Thee" 11/10
 "Joy in Serving Jesus" 11/8
 "Joy to the World" 11/25
 "Moment by Moment" 11/22
 "Must I Go, and Empty-Handed?" 11/4
 "My Country, 'Tis of Thee" 11/16
 "My Faith Looks Up to Thee" 11/12
 "My Father is Rich in Houses and Lands" 11/2
 "My Heart is Inditing" 11/21

"My Hope is Built On Nothing Less" 11/13
"My Jesus, As Thou Wilt" 11/18
"My Shepherd Will Supply My Need" 11/25
"Nothing But the Blood" 11/25
"Onward, Christian Soldiers" 11/22
"O God, Our Help in Ages Past" 11/25
"O Happy Home, Where Thou Art Loved" 11/28
"O the Deep, Deep Love of Jesus" 11/19
"O Worship the King, All Glorious Above" 11/16
"Peace, Peace, Wonderful Peace" 11/19
"Rescue the Perishing" 11/20
"Rock of Ages" 11/4
"Savior, Thy Dying Love" 11/23
"Showers of Blessing" 11/22
"Silent Night, Holy Night" 11/15
"Silent Night" 11/25
"Softly and Tenderly Jesus is Calling" 11/7
"Softly Now the Light of Day" 11/18
"So Send I You" 11/1
"Spirit of God, Descend Upon My Heart" 11/24
"Springs of Living Water" 11/1
"Standing on the Promises" 11/18
"Sun of My Soul" 11/25
"Surely Goodness and Mercy" 11/1, 11/8
"Teach Me to Pray" 11/1
"Tell It To Jesus" 11/28
"That Beautiful Name" 11/25
"There's a Song in the Air" 11/14
"There is a Fountain Filled With Blood" 11/15
"The Church's One Foundation" 11/19
"The Sands of Time Are Sinking" 11/2
"The Solid Rock" 11/13
"The Song of the Soul Set Free" 11/8
"Turn Your Eyes Upon Jesus" 11/14
"We're Marching to Zion" 11/25
"When I Survey the Wondrous Cross" 11/25
"Where Cross the Crowded Ways of Life" 11/16
"Who Is On the Lord's Side?" 11/17
"Wonderful Grace of Jesus" 11/19
HYMN TUNES
ALL TO CHRIST 11/2
ARMAGEDDON 11/17
CHRISTMAS SONG 11/14
CLIFTON 11/4
FEDERAL STREET 11/24
GERMANY 11/16
GLORIA PATRI 11/6
JEWETT 11/18
KEVIN 11/22
LANGRAN 11/10
LYONS 11/16
MENDELSSOHN 11/4
MY SAVIOR CARES 11/4
REITZ 11/1
RUTHERFORD 11/2
SEYMOUR 11/18
ST. CATHERINE 11/12
ST. GERTRUDE 11/22
STILLE NACHT 11/25

I

INDIANS, AMERICAN 11/3, 11/4, 11/5, 11/21
American Northwest Indians 11/29
Cayuse 11/29
Cherokee 11/22
Choctaw 11/22
Christianized Indians 11/17
Oneida 11/20
Six Nations 11/20
Innocent III, Pope (1198-1216) 11/11, 11/30
Inter-Varsity Christian Fellowship 11/14
Interchurch Conference on Federation 11/15
International Missionary Council 11/19
Israel, Manasseh Ben
  (b. 1604) d. 11/20/1657
Israel, Modern 11/2

J

Jablonski, Daniel E.
  b. 11/20/1660 [d. 5/25/1741]
James II, English King (1685-88) 11/21
Jansen, Cornelius Otto
  b. 11/3/1585 [d. 5/6/1638]
Jansenism 11/3
Jesus Christ 11/17
JEWISH EVENTS
  "Kristallnacht" 11/9
  Balfour Declaration (1917) 11/2, 11/27
  Dead Sea Scrolls 11/27
  Exoneration from the crucifixion 11/20
JEWISH ORGANIZATIONS
World Zionist Organizatio 11/9
JEWISH PEOPLE
  Abrahams, Israel 11/26
  Asch, Sholem 11/1
  Disraeli, Benjamin 11/25
  Lazarus, Emma 11/19
  Manasseh Ben Israel 11/20
  Montefiore, Moses 11/9
  Salvador, Joseph 11/27
  Weizmann, Chaim 11/27
JEWISH WRITINGS
  "Jewish Quarterly Review" 11/26
John, English King (1199-1216) 11/16
John Paul II, Pope (1978-) 11/22, 11/28
Jones, Jim
  (b. 5/13/1931) d. 11/18/1978

Joseph, St. 11/13
Judson, Adoniram 11/4, 11/30
Judson, Ann 11/30
Julius II, Pope (1503-1513) 11/1
Justinian I, Byzantine Emperor (527-65) 11/14

K

Keble, John 11/25
Kennedy, Benjamin Hall
  b. 11/6/1804 [d. 4/6/1889]
Kingsbury, Cyrus
  b. 11/22/1786 [d. 6/27/1870]
Kirkland, Samuel
  b. 11/20/1741 [d. 2/28/1808]
Knox, John
  (b. 1505/1515) d. 11/24/1572
Kristallnacht 11/9
Kuyper, Abraham 11/8

L

L'Engle, Madeleine
  b. 11/28/1918 [d. 9/7/2007] 11/28
LaBerge, Agnes Ozman
  (b. 9/15/1870) d. 11/29/1937
Lagarde, Paul Anton de
  b. 11/2/1827 [d. 12/22/1891]
Langran, James
  b. 11/10/1835 [d. 6/8/1909]
Latimer, Hugh 11/30
Lazarus, Emma
  (b. 7/22/1849) d. 11/19/1887
Lemmel, Helen H.
  b. 11/14/1864 [d. 11/1/1961]
Lennon, John 11/4
Leo X, Pope (1513-21) 11/13
Lewis, C[live] S. 11/28
  b. 11/29/1898 d. 11/22/1963
Liguori, St. Alfonso Maria de 11/9
Lillenas, Haldor
  b. 11/19/1885 [d. 8/18/1959]
Lincoln, Abraham 11/26, 11/28
Little Flock 11/4
Livingstone, David 11/10
London Missionary Society 11/20
Lovejoy, Elijah Parish
  b. 11/9/1802 d. 11/7/1837
Lowry, Robert
  (b. 3/12/1826) d. 11/25/1899
Lucar, Cyril
  b. 11/13/1572 [d. 6/27/1638]
Luther, Charles C.
  (b. 5/17/1847) d. 11/4/1924
Luther, Elizabeth 11/7
Luther, John 11/7
Luther, Katie 11/7
Luther, Magdalene 11/7
Luther, Margaret 11/3, 11/7
Luther, Martin 11/3, 11/7, 11/9, 11/13, 11/17, 11/24
  b. 11/10/1483 [d. 2/18/1546]

Luther, Martin, Jr. 11/7
Luther, Martin Gottlob 11/3
Luther, Paul 11/3, 11/7
Lyman, Henry
  b. 11/23/1809/10 [d. 6/28/1834]
Lyon, Mary 11/8
Lyte, Henry Francis
  (b. 6/1/1793) d. 11/20/1847

M

Magnus, Albertus
  (b. ca. 1193) d. 11/15/1280
Mahan, Asa
  b. 11/9/1799 [d. 4/4/1889]
Malcolm III, Scottish King 11/16
Margaret, Queen of Scotland
  (b. 1045) d. 11/16/1093
Martin V, Pope (1417-31) 11/11
MARTYRS
  85 English martyrs 11/22
  Becket, Thomas 11/2
  Cary, Lott 11/10
  Elliot, Jim 11/27
  Forty English martyrs 11/29
  Lovejoy, Elijah Parish 11/7, 11/9
  Lyman, Henry 11/23
  Mayne, Cuthbert 11/29
  Munson, Samuel 11/23
  Nee, Watchman 11/4
  Smith, Joseph 11/6
  Whitman, Marcus 11/29
  Whitman, Narcissa 11/29
  Williams, John 11/20
Mary Tudor 11/24, 11/30
Massachusetts Bay Colony 11/4, 11/7
Mayflower, The 11/20
Mayflower Compact 11/11
Mayflower Pilgrims 11/15
Mayne, Cuthbert
  (b. 1543) d. 11/29/1577
McAlpine, William H. 11/24
McGranahan, James 11/22
Meade, William
  b. 11/11/1789 [d. 3/14/1862]
Meineke, Christoph
  (b. 5/1/1782) d. 11/6/1850
Melanchthon, Philipp 11/24
Mendelssohn, Moses 11/4
Mendelssohn (-Bartholdy), Felix
  (b. 2/3/1809) d. 11/4/1847
Meynell, Alice
  (b. 8/17/1847) d. 11/27/1922
Meynell, Wilfred 11/27
Michelangelo Buonarroti 11/1
Milton, John 11/23, 11/28
  (b. 12/9/1608) d. 11/8/1674
MISSIONARIES
  Berg, Daniel 11/19
  Blanchet, François 11/24
  Boardman, George Dana 11/4
  Brainerd, David 11/4, 11/21, 11/25
  Cary, Lott 11/10
  Chambers, Oswald 11/15

NOVEMBER INDEX

Colley, William W. 11/24
Doddridge, Joseph 11/9
Drexel, Katherine 11/26
Duchesne, Rose Philippine 11/18
Dye, Cecil 11/22
Elliot, Jim 11/27
Fisk, Pliny 11/3
Fleming, Paul W. 11/22
Grellet, Stephen 11/2
Hall, Sarah 11/4
Hasseltine, Ann 11/4
Hawley, Gideon 11/5
Henry Martyn 11/15
Hodge, A[rchibald] A[lexander] 11/12
Judson, Adoniram 11/4, 11/30
Judson, Ann 11/30
Kingsbury, Cyrus 11/22
Kirkland, Samuel 11/20
Livingstone, David 11/10
Lyman, Henry 11/23
Martyn, Henry 11/25
Munson, Samuel 11/23
Newell, Harriet Atwood 11/30
Newell, Samuel 11/30
Otterbein, Philip William 11/17
Patrick, St. 11/10
Schaeffer, Francis 11/5, 11/8, 11/12
Serra, Junipero 11/24
Thoburn, James M. 11/28
Vingren, Adolf 11/19
Walter, Howard A. 11/1
Whitman, Marcus 11/29
Whitman, Narcissa 11/29
William, John 11/20
Zeisberger, David 11/17
Mohr, Joseph 11/25
Montefiore, Moses 11/9
Montgomery, James 11/4
Moody, Dwight L. 11/12, 11/22
Mote, Edward
  b. 11/13/1874 [d. 1/21/1797]
MOVIES / FILMS
  "Giant" 11/13
Munson, Samuel 11/23

N

"Night of Broken Glass" 11/9
Napoleonic Concordat of 1801 11/8
National Association of Free Will Baptists 11/5
National Baptist Sunday School 11/20
National Council of Churches 11/15, 11/28
Nee, (Henry) Watchman
  b. 11/4/1903 [d. 6/1/1972]
Newberry Prize 11/28
Newell, Harriet Atwood
  (b. 10/10/1793) d. 11/30/1812
Newell, Samuel 11/30
Newton, John 11/15
New Tribes Mission 11/22
Nicholas II, Russian Czar 11/5
NICKNAMES / TITLES
  "Apostle of California" 11/24
  "Apostle of Ireland" 11/10
  "Apostle of Oregon" 11/24
  "Apostle of Polynesia" 11/20
  "Cardinal of Charity" 11/20
  "Colonizer of Maryland" 11/22
  "Danish Luther" 11/11
  "Father of Anglican Church Music" 11/21
  "Father of English cathedral music" 11/23
  "Father of English hymnody" 11/25
  "Martyr Abolitionist" 11/7, 11/9
  "The American Wordsworth" 11/3
  "The Bard of Ohio" 11/7
  "The Subtle Doctor" 11/8
Nietzsche, Friedrich 11/16

O

O'Toole, St. Lawrence
  (b. 1122) d. 11/14/1180
Oecolampadius, Johannes
  (b. 1482) d. 11/24/1531
Old Catholicism 11/1
Oliver, Henry K.
  b. 11/24/1800 [d. 8/12/1885]
Otterbein, Philip W. 11/16, 11/30
  (b. 6/3/1726) d. 11/17/1813
Overbeck, Franz C.
  b. 11/16/1837 [d. 6/26/1905]
Oxford Movement 11/25
Ozman, Agnes N.
  (b. 9/15/1870) d. 11/29/1937

P

Palmer, Ray
  b. 11/12/1808 [d. 3/29/1887]
Papal Chancery 11/16
PAPAL DECREES
  "Munificentissimus Deus" (1950) 11/1
  "Professio Fidei" 11/13
  "Regula bullata" (1223) 11/29
  "Unam Sanctam" 11/18
Parham, Charles 11/29
Parker, Matthew 11/22
Pascal, Blaise 11/23
Patrick, St. 11/10
Paul VI, Pope (1963-78) 11/14, 11/18, 11/26
Peake, Arthur Samuel
  b. 11/24/1865 [d. 8/19/1929]
Peterson, John W.
  b. 11/1/1921 [d. 9/20/2006]
Peter Martyr
  (b. 9/8/1500) d. 11/12/1562
Peter the Great 11/5
Phelps, Sylvanus Dryden
  (b. 5/15/1816) d. 11/23/1895
Pilgrims, The 11/11
Pirminius, St.
  (b. early 700s) d. 11/3/753
Pius IV, Pope (1559-65) 11/3, 11/13
Pius VI, Pope (1775-99) 11/6
Pius XII, Pope (1939-1958) 11/1
POETRY
  "Thanatopsis" (1811) 11/3
  "The Hound of Heaven" 11/13
  "The New Colossus" 11/19
Poling, Daniel A.
  b. 11/30/1884 [d. 2/7/1968]
Pollard, Adelaide
  b. 11/27/1862 [d. 12/20/1934]
POPES
  Agatho (678-81) 11/7
  Benedict XV (1914-22) 11/21
  Boniface VIII (1294-1303) 11/18
  Honorius III (1216-27) 11/29
  Innocent III (1198-1216) 11/11, 11/30
  John Paul II (1978-) 11/22, 11/28
  Julius II (1503-1513) 11/1
  Leo X (1513-21) 11/13
  Martin V (1417-31) 11/11
  Paul VI (1963-78) 11/14, 11/18, 11/26
  Pius IV (1559-65) 11/3, 11/13
  Pius VI (1775-99) 11/6
  Pius XII (1939-1958) 11/1
  Urban II (1088-99) 11/18, 11/27
  Urban VIII (1623-44) 11/3, 11/18
Protestant Reformation 11/10, 11/24
Pseudepigrapha, O.T. 11/12
PUBLICATIONS
  ¡Gracias! 11/18, 11/29
  "Catholic Digest" 11/21
  "Christian Century" 11/21
  "Christian Herald" 11/30
  "Eternity" magazine 11/5
  "Jewish Quarterly Review" 11/26
  "New York Herald" 11/10
  "Northern Christian Advocate" 11/2
  "Regula Prima" 11/29
  "The Catholic Worker" 11/8
  "The Indian Witness" 11/28
  Anna Karenina (1877) 11/7
  An Experiment in Christology 11/12
  A Wrinkle in Time 11/28
  Book of Common Prayer (1552) 11/12
  Book of Common Prayer (1689) 11/22
  Chronicles of Narnia (1950-56) 11/22
  Chronology of the Old and New Testaments (1650-54) 11/25
  Confessions 11/13
  Cruden's Concordance (1737) 11/1
  Dictionaire historique et critique 11/18
  God Was in Christ (1948) 11/5
  Grammar of the Greek N. T. (1914) 11/6
  Greek-English Lexicon of the New Testament (1886) 11/26
  Hebrew Grammar (1827) 11/16
  Hymns Ancient and Modern 11/19
  Laws of Ecclesiastical Polity (1594-97) 11/3
  London's "Evening Standard" 11/4
  Medulla Theologiae 11/14
  My Utmost for His Highest 11/15
  New Testament in the Original Greek (1881) 11/30
  Notes on the Old Testament 11/12
  Olney Hymns (1779) 11/15
  On Religion (1799) 11/21
  Paradise Lost (1665-74) 11/8, 11/23, 11/28
  Pilgrim's Progress (1678) 11/30
  Psalms and Hymns for Public Worship 11/24
  Quest for the Historical Jesus: From Reimarus to W 11/23
  Road to Daybreak 11/7, 11/11
  Screwtape Letters (1942) 11/29
  Screwtape Letters (1943) 11/22
  Secular Journal 11/24
  Sit, Walk, Stand (1958) 11/4
  Songs of Experience (1794) 11/28
  Songs of Innocence (1789) 11/28
  Theology of the Sacraments (1957) 11/5
  The Apostle (1943) 11/1
  The Christian Faith (1821-22) 11/21
  The City of God 11/13
  The Day Christ Died (1957) 11/21
  The Great Divorce (1946) 11/22
  The Normal Christian Life (1961) 11/4
  The Story of the Other Wise Man (1896) 11/10
  Walton's Polyglot Bible (1657) 11/29
  War and Peace (1860) 11/7
Purcell, Henry
  (b. ca. 1659) d. 11/21/1695

Q

Qumran 11/23, 11/27
QUOTATIONS
  Baxter, Richard 11/19
  Brainerd, David 11/4, 11/21
  Disraeli, Benjamin 11/25
  Elliot, Jim 11/27
  Gottwald, Norman K. 11/21
  Henry, Matthew 11/12
  Henry, Patrick 11/20
  Hooker, Richard 11/2
  Lewis, C. S. 11/2, 11/5, 11/8, 11/9, 11/10, 11/26, 11/27
  Luther, Martin 11/3, 11/7, 11/9, 11/13, 11/17, 11/22, 11/30
  MacDonald, George 11/5, 11/11, 11/16, 11/29
  Madison, James 11/9
  Martyn, Henry 11/15, 11/25
  McCheyne, Robert Murray 11/15
  McLean, John 11/4
  Merton, Thomas 11/24
  Newton, John 11/6, 11/17, 11/29
  Nouwen, Henri J. M. 11/7, 11/11, 11/18, 11/19, 11/28, 11/29
  Schaeffer, Francis 11/8, 11/12
  Schmemann, Alexander 11/1, 11/3, 11/6, 11/17, 11/23, 11/26
  Simons, Menno 11/12, 11/14
  Smith, Hannah Whitall 11/10, 11/24
  Tolkien, J. R. R. 11/1
  Voltaire, François 11/10

ALMANAC OF THE CHRISTIAN FAITH — NOVEMBER INDEX

Wesley, John 11/11, 11/13, 11/18, 11/20, 11/22, 11/30
Whitefield, George 11/14, 11/19, 11/23, 11/28

R

Radio Church of America 11/27
Ramsey, Arthur Michael
  b. 11/14/1904 [d. 4/23/1988]
Rankin, Jeremiah E.
  (b. 1/2/1828) d. 11/28/1904
Rapp, George
  b. 11/1/1757 [d. 8/7/1847]
Rationalism, 18th Century 11/18
Reed, Andrew
  b. 11/27/1787 [d. 2/25/1862]
Reichardt, C. Luise
  (b. 4/11/1779) d. 11/17/1826
Reitz, Albert S.
  (b. 1/20/1879) d. 11/1/1966
RELIGIOUS ORDERS, CATHOLIC
  Augustinians 11/12
  Cistercians 11/26
  Dominicans 11/11, 11/15
  Franciscans 11/8, 11/24, 11/29
  Jesuits 11/3
  Paulist Fathers 11/27
  Redemptorists 11/9
  Sisters of the Blessed Sacrament for Indians and C 11/26
  Society of the Sacred Heart 11/18
  Sulpicians 11/24
  Trappists 11/24
Reorganized Church of Jesus Christ of Latter Day S 11/6
Rice, John H.
  b. 11/28/1777 [d. 9/3/1831]
Ridley, Nicholas 11/30
Roberts, Daniel C.
  b. 11/5/1841 [d. 10/31/1907]
Robertson, A[rchibald] T.
  b. 11/6/1863 [d. 9/24/1934]

S

Sacking of Rome 11/13
Salvador, Joseph 11/27
Samuel, Mar Athanasius Yeshue 11/15
Scarapsus 11/3
Schaeffer, Francis 11/5
Schillebeeckx, Edward
  b. 11/12/1914
Schism, Great Western (papal) 11/11
Schleiermacher, F. D. E.
  b. 11/21/1768 [d. 2/12/1834]
Schweitzer, Albert 11/23
Scotism 11/8
Scotus, John Duns
  (b. 1266) d. 11/8/1308
Scourby, Alexander
  b. 11/13/1913 [d. 2/22/1985]
Seabury, Samuel 11/14
  b. 11/30/1729 [d. 2/25/1796]

Seljuk Turks 11/27
SEMINARIES / BIBLE COLLEGES
  Bethel Bible College (KS) 11/29
  Knox College (Canada) 11/8
  Mt. Holyoke Seminary 11/8
  Princeton Seminary 11/12
  Southern Baptist Seminary 11/6
  Toccoa Falls Bible Institute (GA) 11/6
  Union Theological Seminary (VA) 11/28
Serra, Junipero
  b. 11/24/1713 [d. 8/28/1784]
Six Nations 11/20
Smith, Alfred B.
  b. 11/8/1916 [d. 8/9/2001]
Smith, Joseph 11/6
Smith, Joseph, Jr.
  b. 11/6/1832 [d. 12/10/1914] 11/6
Smith, Oswald J.
  b. 11/8/1889 [d. 1/26/1986]
Smith, Robert Holbrook
  (b. 8/8/1879) d. 11/6/1950
Smith, Rodney ("Gipsy") 11/17
Smith, Samuel Francis
  (b. 10/21/1808) d. 11/16/1853
Snethen, Nicholas
  b. 11/15/1769 [d. 5/30/1845]
Society for the Propagating of Christian Knowledge 11/25
Society of the Sacred Heart 11/18
Sojourner Truth (Isabella Baumfree)
  (b. ca. 1797) d. 11/26/1883
Southern Presbyterianism 11/3
Spafford, Horatio G. 11/22
Spitta, Carl J. P.
  (b. 8/1/1801) d. 11/28/1859
Spurgeon, Charles 11/15
St. Peter's Square 11/28
Stanley, Henry M. 11/10
Statue of Liberty 11/19
Stebbins, George C. 11/22
Steele, Anne
  (b. 1716) d. 11/11/1778
Stephen, English King (1135-54) 11/21
Stone, Barton W.
  (b. 12/24/1772) d. 11/9/1844
Stone, Samuel J.
  (b. 4/25/1839) d. 11/19/1900
Streeter, Burnett H.
  b. 11/17/1874 [d. 9/10/1937]
Sukenik, Eliezer L. 11/23, 11/27
Sullivan, Sir Arthur S.
  (b. 5/13/1842) d. 11/22/1900
Sunday, Billy (William Ashley)
  b. 11/19/1862 d. 11/6/1935
Swiss Reformation 11/24
Switzer, Margaret 11/17
Synod of Dort 11/13

T

Tallis, Thomas
  (b. ca. 1505) d. 11/23/1585

Tausen, Hans
  (b. 1494) d. 11/11/1561
TELEVISION PROGRAMS
  "Lamp Unto My Feet" 11/21
Tersteegen, Gerhard 11/25
Thanksgiving Day holiday 11/26, 11/28
Thayer, Joseph Henry
  (b. 11/7/1828) d. 11/26/1901
Thoburn, James M.
  (b. 3/7/1836) d. 11/28/1922
Thomas Aquinas 11/15
Thompson, Francis 11/27
  (b. 12/18/1859) d. 11/13/1907
Thompson, Will Lamartine
  b. 11/7/1847 (d. 9/20/1909]
Thorvaldsen, Albert B.
  b. 11/19/1770 [d. 3/24/1844]
Tillotson, John
  (bapt. 10/10/1630) d. 11/22/1694
Tolstoy, Leo
  (b. 8/28/1828) d. 11/7/1910
Toplady, Augustus M.
  b. 11/4/1740 [d. 8/11/1778]
Torrey, C[harles] C.
  (b. 12/20/2863) d. 11/12/1956
Transubstantiation 11/11, 11/30
Trevor, Samuel F.
  b. 11/19/1834 [d. 12/28/1925]
Tridentine Faith 11/13

U

U.S. Civil War 11/5
Urban II, Pope (1088-99) 11/18, 11/27
Urban VIII, Pope (1623-44) 11/3, 11/18
Urhan, Chrétien
  (b. 2/16/1790) d. 11/2/1845
Ussher, James 11/25

V

Van Dyke, Henry
  b. 11/10/1852 [d. 4/10/1933]
Vasey, Thomas 11/3
Vatican 11/18
Vermigli, Pietro Martire
  (b. 9/8/1500) d. 11/12/1562
Vestry Act 11/12
Vingren, Adolf 11/19
Visigoths 11/13

W

Walter, Howard A.
  (b. 8/19/1883) d. 11/1/1918
Walton, Brian
  (b. ca. 1601) d. 11/29/1661
Warfield, B[enjamin] B.
  b. 11/5/1851 [d. 2/17/1921]
Washington, George 11/26
Watts, Isaac
  (b. 7/17/1674) d. 11/25/1748

Weber, Carl Maria von
  b. 11/18/1786 [d. 6/4/1826]
Weizmann, Chaim
  b. 11/27/1874 d. 11/9/1952
Weld, Theodore D.
  b. 11/23/1803 [d. 2/3/1895]
Wesley, John 11/4
Wesley, Samuel 11/22
Westcott, Brooke Foss 11/30
Whatcoat, Richard 11/3
White, Ellen G.
  b. 11/26/1827 [d. 7/16/1915]
White, Peregrine
  b. 11/20/1620 [d. 7/22/1704]
Whitefield, George 11/14, 11/27
Whiting, William
  b. 11/1/1825 [d. 5/3/1878]
Whitman, Marcus
  (b. 9/4/1802) d. 11/29/1847
Whitman, Narcissa 11/29
Whittle, Daniel W.
  b. 11/22/1840 [d. 3/4/1901]
Widney, Joseph P. 11/13
Wiley, H. Orton
  b. 11/15/1877 [d. 1961]
Williams, John
  (b. 6/29/1796) d. 11/20/1839
Williams, Sir George
  (b. 10/11/1821) d. 11/6/1905
William of Corbeil
  (b. ca. 1160) d. 11/21/1136
Wilson, William G. 11/6
Wolsey, Thomas
  (b. 1475) d. 11/29/1530
World Council of Churches 11/14, 11/19
World War I 11/15, 11/21
World Zionist Organization 11/9
Wrede, William
  (b. 5/10/1859) d. 11/23/1906
Wycliffe, John 11/5

Y

Yacoub III, Patriarch Ignatius 11/15
Young, John Freeman
  (b. 10/30/1820) d. 11/15/1885
Young Men's Christian Association (YMCA) 11/6
Youth For Christ 11/7

Z

Zeisberger, David
  (b. 4/11/1721) d. 11/17/1808
Zionism 11/27
Zwingli, Ulrich 11/11, 11/24

ALMANAC OF THE CHRISTIAN FAITH

TEVET — KISLEV

~ December 1 ~

Highlights in History

1742 Colonial Lutheran minister and patriarch of American Lutheranism Henry Melchior Muhlenberg (1711-87) first arrived in Philadelphia from Germany.

1891 Canadian Christian physical education teacher James Naismith, 30, invented the game of basketball when he instructed his students to toss soccer balls into one of two peach baskets that he had nailed to opposite ends of a gym. It was Naismith's desire to create an indoor sport for exercise in the winter.

1917 Edward J. Flanagan, 31, founded Boys Town — a home for orphaned or problem children — in Omaha, Nebraska. Father Flanagan believed there was no such thing as a boy beyond hope. The site later relocated, and girls began to be accepted, before Flanagan's death in 1948.

Notable Birthdays

1798 Birth of Albert Barnes, American Presbyterian clergyman and Bible commentator. While serving as a pastor in Philadelphia (1830-67), he penned eleven volumes of *Notes, Explanatory and Practical on the New Testament* (1832-53). One of his sermons, "The Way in Salvation," led to several heresy trials, and eventually triggered a schism in his denomination. [d. 12/24/1870]

1883 Birth of Henry Joel Cadbury, American Quaker New Testament scholar, educator and peace activist. In 1915 he organized a conference at Winona Lake, IN, that later developed into the American Friends Service Committee (AFSC). In biblical studies, Cadbury introduced German form criticism to American readers in *Style and Literary Method of Luke* (2 vols., 1919-20). Cadbury was also a key member of the RSV New Testament translation committee. [d. 10/7/1974]

The Last Passage

1581 After being tortured, Oxford humanist Edmund Campion, 41, and a number of other English Jesuits were hanged for sedition at Tyburn. (b. 1/25/1540)

1635 Death of Melchior Teschner, 51, German Lutheran clergyman and musician. He pastored a church at Oberprietschen, Silesia, where the congregation was served for several generations by him, his son, and a grandson. Teschner also composed the hymn tune ST. THEODULPH ("All Glory, Laud, and Honor"). (b. 4/29/1584)

1867 Death of Philaret (Vasily Mikhailovich Drozdov), 85, Russian prelate and writer. He was Metropolitan of Moscow (1825-1867), and composed a standard catechism (1829) which was adopted by the Holy Synod of the Church of Russia. (b. 12/26/1782)

1882 Death of Titus Coan, 81, American Presbyterian missionary to Hawaii. He first arrived in Honolulu in 1835, and remained there most of the rest of his life. Coan won 70% of the population of Hilo Island to the Christian faith within six years. (b. 2/1/1801)

1941 Death of Frederick J. Foakes-Jackson, 86, Anglican theologian and church historian. Born in England, he emigrated to America, and taught at Union Theological Seminary (1916-34). Jackson authored *The Beginnings of Christianity* (5 vols., 1919-32). (b. 8/10/1855)

Words for the Soul

1739 English revivalist George Whitefield confided in his journal: *'I always observe inward trials prepare me for, and are certain forerunners of fresh mercies.'*

1950 American missionary and Auca Indian martyr Jim Elliot recorded in his journal: *'Unwillingness to accept God's "way of escape" from temptation frightens me — what a rebel yet resides within.'*

IN GOD'S WORD... OT: Daniel 8:1-27 ~ NT: 1 John 2:1-17 ~ Psalms 120:1-7 ~ Proverbs 28:25-26

ALMANAC OF THE CHRISTIAN FAITH

טבת TEVET

כסלו KISLEV

~ December 2 ~

Highlights in History

1763 In Rhode Island, the Touro Synagogue opened. Twenty Sephardic families who made up the Congregation Jeshuat Israel in Newport had collected funds from other Sephardic Jews in Jamaica, Surinam, London and Amsterdam to cover the cost of building this first major center of Jewish culture in America.

1873 In New York City, former Episcopal assistant bishop of Kentucky, George David Cummins presided over a meeting of seven other clergymen and 20 lay leaders, who then organized the Reformed Episcopal Church (REC). Rev. Charles E. Cheney was elected its first bishop.

1950 A five-day constitutional convention ended, which brought into being the National Council of the Churches of Christ in the United States of America (NCCC). Comprised of 14 Protestant, Anglican, and Eastern Orthodox denominations, this ecumenical agency produces educational materials, administers disaster and relief funds, provides leadership training, and promotes world peace.

1960 The Archbishop of Canterbury, Geoffrey Fisher, met with Pope John XXIII in the Vatican. It was the first meeting between leaders of the Anglican and Roman Catholic faiths since the founding of the Church of England in 1534.

1966 The U.S. National Conference of Catholic Bishops, following the spirit of the Vatican II Ecumenical Council (1962-65), abolished the rule of abstinence from eating meat, except on Ash Wednesday and on Fridays during Lent.

Notable Birthdays

1831 Birth of Francis Nathan Peloubet, American Congregational clergyman. He authored numerous religious works, and was a Bible commentator and a writer of S.S. literature for 45 years (1875-1920). He published 44 annual volumes of *[Peloubet's] Select Notes on the International S.S. Lessons*. [d. 3/27/1920]

1841 Birth of William Newton Clarke, American Baptist clergyman, theologian and author. He published America's first systematic theology from a liberal perspective (*An Outline of Christian Theology*, 1898). Clarke was an influential professor at Colgate Seminary. [d. 1/14/1912]

The Last Passage

1381 Death of Flemish mystic Jan Van Ruysbroek, 88. He was called "the Ecstatic Doctor" because his religious teaching combined personal experience with metaphysical commentary on the Scriptures. Van Ruysbroek's life and work influenced the rise of German mysticism. (b. 1293)

1860 Death of Ferdinand C. Baur, 68, German theologian and educator. A skeptic who doubted the authenticity of most New Testament events, Baur founded the "Tübingen School" of German radical biblical criticism. (b. 6/21/1792)

1929 Death of William Henry Parker, 84, an English Baptist businessman and Sunday school advocate. He wrote a number of hymns for Sunday School anniversaries and similar special occasions, including "Tell Me the Stories of Jesus." (b. 3/4/1845)

Words for the Soul

1981 Dutch Catholic priest and educator Henri J. M. Nouwen reflected in his *Latin American Journal*: 'Somehow, I keep expecting loud and impressive events to convince me and others of God's saving power; but over and over again I am reminded that spectacles, power plays, and big events are the ways of the world.... [God's] promise is hidden in the shoot that sprouts from the stump, a shoot that hardly anyone notices.'

1981 Russian Orthodox liturgical scholar Alexander Schmemann reflected in his journal: '"Power over souls" is apparently an awesome and insatiable passion which devours the soul of whoever is possessed by it.'

IN GOD'S WORD... OT: Daniel 9:1-11:1 ~ NT: 1 John 2:18-3:3 ~ Psalms 121:1-8 ~ Proverbs 28:27-28

טבת TEVET — ALMANAC OF THE CHRISTIAN FAITH — כסלו KISLEV

December 3

Highlights in History

1557 In response to the preaching of Reformer John Knox, a group of important Protestant Scottish nobles signed their "First Covenant" at Edinburgh, uniting Presbyterians under the name "Congregation of the Lord." They solemnly swore to *"manteane, sett forward, and establish the most blessed word of God and His Congregatioun."*

1740 The first recorded modern papal encyclical, "Ubi primum" (which discussed episcopal duties) was issued by Benedict XIV (1740-58). (Historically, an encyclical was a circular letter from a Christian leader of recognized authority to the churches of a given area. In current usage, an encyclical is a formal pastoral letter sent by a pope or Anglican bishop on doctrinal, moral or disciplinary matters.)

1976 A two-day meeting opened in Chicago, during which the Association of Evangelical Lutheran Churches (AELC) was formally organized. The bulk of membership derived from former affiliates of the Lutheran Church Missouri Synod, as well as several other independent Lutheran congregations.

Notable Birthdays

1483 Birth of Nicholas von Amsdorf, German Reformer. He was one of Luther's most active supporters. His extensive correspondence with Luther includes the first literary mention of the hymn, "A Mighty Fortress." Amsdorf later supervised publication of the University of Jena edition of Luther's works. [d. 5/14/1565]

1850 Birth of Frank Mason North, American clergyman. He was the corresponding secretary of the New York City Society of Methodist Churches (1892-1912) and of the Methodist Board of Foreign Missions (1912-20). North is better remember today, however, as the author of the hymn: "Where Cross the Crowded Ways of Life." [d. 12/17/1935]

1902 Birth of Mitsuo Fuchida, the general who flew the lead plane in the Japanese attack on Pearl Harbor. Following World War II, he was converted from Buddhism to the Christian faith through representatives of the Pocket Testament League. [d. 5/30/1976]

1906 Birth of Allen P. Wikgren, American Baptist clergyman and editor of the United Bible Society's *Greek New Testament*, an acclaimed modern critical edition of the New Testament in its original language. [d. 5/7/1998]

The Last Passage

1552 Spanish Jesuit missionary Francis Xavier, the "father of modern Catholic missions," died of a fever at 46 while on a mission in China. He had previously preached in Goa (West India), Ceylon (Sri Lanka), and Japan, laying groundwork for Catholic evangelism of the Orient. (b. 4/7/1506)

1815 Death of John Carroll, 80, America's first Roman Catholic bishop, founder of Georgetown University (1791), and the main figure in establishing Catholicism in the newly independent United States. He served as Archbishop of Baltimore from 1808 until his death. (b. 1/8/1735)

1910 Death of Mary (née Morse) Baker Eddy, 89, American religious leader. She was the founder of the Christian Science Association (1876), and authored *Science and Health* (1875). 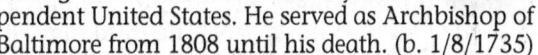 She later organized the First Church of Christ Scientist (1879) in Boston. (b. 7/16/1821)

Words for the Soul

1985 Dutch Catholic priest and diarist Henri J. M. Nouwen noted in his *Road to Daybreak* journal: *'I have to keep a careful eye on the difference between urgent things and important things. If I allow the urgent things to dominate my day, I will never do what is truly important and will always feel dissatisfied.'*

IN GOD'S WORD... OT: Daniel 11:2-35 ~ NT: 1 John 3:4-24 ~ Psalms 122:1-9 ~ Proverbs 29:1

טבת TEVET — ALMANAC OF THE CHRISTIAN FAITH — כסלו KISLEV

~ December 4 ~

Highlights in History

1093 Italian-born Anselm was consecrated Archbishop of Canterbury, serving until 1109. Deeply spiritual, he became the Father of Scholasticism by using logic to demonstrate a rationality for faith. It was Anselm who outlined the ontological argument for God's existence in his book, *Faith Seeking Understanding*.

1154 Nicholas Breakspear (ca.1100-1159) was unanimously elected Adrian IV. He thereby became the first (and so far the only!) Englishman in history to be named pope. A strong supporter of the clergy, Breakspear strove to establish universal domination for the papacy.

1861 At Augusta, GA, 75,000 members seceded from the Northern Assembly and adopted the name "Presbyterian Church in the Confederate States of America." The "United Synod of the South" joined them in 1865. The church later changed its name to "Presbyterian Church U.S.," and maintained an unflinching orthodoxy from that time forward. The PCUS reunited with the Northern Assembly in 1983.

1893 The first three missionaries of the Sudan Interior Mission arrived in Africa, in Nigeria. Of these three, Walter Gowans and Thomas Kent died of fever within a year. The third man, Rowland Bingham, returned home in broken health. Bingham nevertheless served as general director of SIM until his death in 1942.

Notable Birthdays

1847 Birth of Francis G. Peabody, American Unitarian clergyman, author and professor of theology at Harvard (1880-1913). He was one of the first clergymen to recognize that moral issues arising from social problems were a central factor in modern life. [d. 12/28/1936]

1854 Birth of Mary Reed, American Methodist missionary to the lepers at Chandag, India. Contracting leprosy in 1890, she remained in Chandag the rest of her life, leaving the area only five times before her death. [d. 4/8/1943]

The Last Passage

1848 Death of Joseph Mohr, 55, Austrian Catholic clergyman. While serving in Oberndorf, Austria, in 1818 he penned the words to the hymn "Stille Nacht" ("Silent Night"). (b. 12/11/1792)

1896 Death of American missions pioneer Peter Cameron Scott. A founder of the Africa Inland Mission, his first missionary party sailed in 1895 for East Africa. While in Kenya, he died of blackwater fever the following year. Scott was just twenty-nine. (b. 3/7/1867)

1968 Death of Homer A. Tomlinson, 76, Indiana-born sectarian religious leader. One of the most colorful individuals on the American religious scene in the 20th century, he became founder and bishop of one of the many branches of the Church of God. (b. 10/25/1892)

Words for the Soul

1786 Anglican poet and hymnwriter William Cowper wrote in a letter: *'Though my experience has long since taught me that this is a world of shadows, and that it is the more prudent as well as the more Christian course to possess the comforts that we find in it as if we possessed them not, it is no easy matter to reduce this doctrine into practice.'*

1882 American Quaker holiness author Hannah Whitall Smith, 50, wrote in a letter: *'It is God's plan to have us ask for what we want.... It is part of the family training, and brings us into communion with God, just as the child telling the parent what it wants makes a oneness of feeling and communion between them.'*

1966 Swiss Reformed theologian Karl Barth clarified in a letter: *'The good Lord, in spite of reports to the contrary, is not dead.'*

1985 Dutch Catholic priest, educator and mystic Henri J. M. Nouwen observed in his *Road to Daybreak* journal: *'The heart knows so much more than the mind.'*

IN GOD'S WORD... OT: Daniel 11:36–12:13 ~ NT: 1 John 4:1-21 ~ Psalms 123:1-4 ~ Proverbs 29:2-4

ALMANAC OF THE CHRISTIAN FAITH

טבת TEVET · כסלו KISLEV

~ December 5 ~

Highlights in History

633 Isidore of Seville presided over a Spanish church council that opened in Toledo. It forbad the compulsory conversion of Jews, declared baptism must plunge the person three times and approved hymn singing in the church.

1484 Innocent VIII issued "Summis desiderantes," in which he wrote: *'It has come to our ears that members of both sexes do not avoid to have intercourse with evil angels, incubi, and succubi'* The document ordered the Inquisition in Germany, initiating a systematic accusation, torture and execution of "witches" all over Europe.

1847 Brigham Young was elected to succeed Joseph Smith as head of the Mormon Church.

1948 The first televised church service in sign language was conducted by the Rev. Floyd F. Possehl, who read the Scriptures and preached from St. Matthew's Lutheran Church for the Deaf, in Jamaica, Queens, over NYC station WPIX-TV.

Notable Birthdays

1443 Birth of Julius II (Giuliano della Rovere), pope from 1503-13. The greatest art patron of all the popes. Julius commissioned Michelangelo's Sistine Chapel frescoes. But it was the issuance of Julius' indulgence for the rebuilding of St. Peter's Basilica that also occasioned Martin Luther's "95 Theses." [d. 2/21/1513]

1830 Birth of Christina G. Rossetti, British Anglican poet. She was noted chiefly for her sacred poetry, and authored the hymn, "Love Came Down at Christmas." [d. 12/29/1894]

1862 Birth of C[harles] T. Studd, pioneer Protestant English missionary. He served the China Inland Mission in China (1885-94), later in India and Central Africa. Studd inspired the formation of the Student Volunteer Movement, and in 1911 established the Worldwide Evangelization Crusade (WEC). [d. 7/16/1931]

1905 Birth of William Barclay, Scottish clergyman and theologian. The most evangelical preacher Bultmann ever claimed to have heard, all his writings aimed at confronting the individual with Christ. Barclay's most enduring publication was his *Daily Study Bible* series. [d. 1/24/1978]

1932 Birth of James Cleveland, African-American clergyman, vocalist and composer. With more than 400 songs to his credit, Cleveland's hits included "Peace Be Still" (1963). He became the first gospel singer immortalized with a gold star on Hollywood's Walk of Fame. [d. 2/9/1991]

The Last Passage

1902 Death of Henry Stephen Cutler, 78, sacred composer. He is said to have been the first church musician to introduce robed choirs to America. Today, Cutler is remembered for composing the hymn tune ALL SAINTS NEW ("The Son of God Goes Forth to War"). (b. 10/13/1824)

1907 Death of Priscilla Jane Owens, 78, an American Methodist school teacher and hymn writer. She spent her entire life in Baltimore, where she taught in the public schools for 49 years. Her best known songs are "Jesus Saves" and "We Have an Anchor." (b. 7/21/1829)

1983 Death of John A.T. Robinson, 64, Anglican theologian and Bishop of Woolwich (1959-69). His explosive 1963 publication, *Honest to God*, questioned such basic Christian assumptions as the Biblical view of God, the Incarnation and the Atonement. (b. 6/15/1919)

Words for the Soul

1951 American missionary and Auca Indian martyr Jim Elliot confessed in his journal: *'How sadly and how slowly I am learning that loud preaching and long preaching are not substitutes for inspired preaching.'*

IN GOD'S WORD... OT: Hosea 1:1–3:5 ~ NT: 1 John 5:1-21 ~ Psalms 124:1-8 ~ Proverbs 29:5-8

December 6

Highlights in History

1273 At age 48, while conducting Mass in the Chapel of St. Nicholas, a tremendous mystical experience broke over Thomas Aquinas. He never again wrote theology. 'I can do no more,' he told his servant. 'Such things have been revealed to me that all that I have written seems to me as so much straw. Now I await the end of my life.' (Thomas died three months later.)

1787 The first college in America founded as a Methodist institution, Cokesbury College opened in Abingdon, Maryland. It was named after Bishops Thomas Coke and Francis Asbury.

1950 The eighth All-American Synod of the Russian Orthodox Church unanimously elected New York Archbishop Leonty as the new metropolitan of the United States and Canada.

1983 In a London auction, a record £7.4 million ($14.6 million) was paid for a 12th century manuscript of the Gospels of Henry the Lion.

Notable Birthdays

1640 Birth of Claude Fleury, French church historian. Born in Paris, he is chiefly remembered for his 20-volume *Histoire ecclésiastique* (1691-1720), the first-ever large-scale history of the Church. [d. 7/14/1723]

1821 Birth of Dora Greenwell, English devotional author. Though fragile in health, she worked with retarded children. Publishing numerous volumes of mystical verse, her style was compared to Fénelon and Woolman. Greenwell is remembered today for authoring the hymn, "I Am Not Skilled to Understand." [d. 3/29/1882]

The Last Passage

1675 Death of John Lightfoot, 73, English Hebraist and biblical scholar. He assisted Brian Walton with the Polyglot Bible, and was the first Christian scholar to call attention to the importance of the Torah. (b. 3/29/1602)

1906 Death of Anne Ross Cousin, 82, Scottish linguist and hymnwriter. Called "a Scottish Christina Rossetti," Cousin penned the hymn, "The Sands of Time are Sinking." (b. 4/27/1824)

1925 Death of American Baptist clergyman and lecturer, Russell Conwell, 83. Popularly remembered for his inspirational lecture, "Acres of Diamonds," Conwell also helped establish Temple University in Philadelphia. (b. 2/15/1842)

1950 Death of Susan Strachan, 76. In 1921, along with her husband Harry, she founded the Latin America Evangelization Campaign (in 1938 renamed the Latin America Mission). Following Harry's death in 1945, Susan and their son Kenneth directed LAM. (b. 4/28/1874)

Words for the Soul

1930 American Congregational missionary and linguistic pioneer Frank C. Laubach noted in a letter: 'Sometimes one feels that there is a discord between the cross and beauty. But there really cannot be, for God is found best through these two doorways.... A man has not found his highest beauty until his brow is tinged with care for some cause he loves more than himself. The beauty of sacrifice is the final word in beauty.'

1955 British scholar and Christian apologist C. S. Lewis wrote in a letter: 'The state of having to depend solely on God is what we all dread most.... It is good of Him to force us; but dear me, how hard to feel that it is good at the time.'

1980 Russian liturgical scholar Alexander Schmemann reflected in his journal: 'In the West, theology, when it first became a science (i.e., since the appearance of scholasticism), became dependent on "this world" — on its categories, words, concepts, philosophies in the broad sense of this word. Hence a constant need of an adaptation, a verification... by this world and its "mutations."'

IN GOD'S WORD... OT: Hosea 4:1–5:15 ~ NT: 2 John 1-13 ~ Psalms 125:1-5 ~ Proverbs 29:9-11

טבת
TEVET

ALMANAC OF THE CHRISTIAN FAITH

KISLEV

~ December 7 ~

Highlights in History

430 Cyril of Alexandria delivered a formal sentence against Antiochene monk Nestorius, declaring as heresy his doctrine that there were two separate Persons in the Incarnate Christ (one divine, the other human). Nestorius was later banished to upper Egypt (436), where he died at an unknown date.

1941 The popular wartime phrase, "Praise the Lord and pass the ammunition!" was coined by naval chaplain Howell M. Forgy (1908-1983). He was on the U.S. cruiser New Orleans, which was among the ships attacked on this date during the Japanese air raid on Pearl Harbor.

1965 After meeting with Patriarch Athenagoras I, Pope Paul VI issued a joint declaration reversing the events of 1054, when Catholic Cardinal Humbert of Silva Candida and Eastern Orthodox Patriarch Michael Cerularius excommunicated each other, afterward dividing Eastern and Western Christianity.

Notable Birthdays

521 Birth of Columba, Irish Celtic priest and "Apostle to Scotland." In 563 he left his native land of Ireland, set up a monastery on the Scottish island of Iona, and from there sent missionaries out to modern-day Holland, France, Switzerland, Germany and Italy. Columba later made forays into Scotland where an entire tribe of pagans, the Picts, were won to the faith. [d. 6/9/597]

1827 Birth of George W. Kitchin, English hymnwriter: "Lift High the Cross." [d. 10/13/1912]

1847 Birth of Solomon Schechter, Romanian-born rabbi and editor of *The Jewish Encyclopedia*. A leader of Conservative Judaism, he discovered 50,000 manuscripts in a Cairo synagogue in 1896, donating them to Cambridge University. Schechter served as president of Jewish Theological Seminary (1902-15). [d. 11/19/1915]

The Last Passage

1683 Death of Algernon Sidney, 61, English writer and politician, 61. He was the first writer to coin the non-biblical phrase, *"God helps those who help themselves"* — quoted in his posthumously published *Discourses on Government* (1698). An English martyr for republican government, Sidney was charged with treason and executed for his part in a plot to assassinate Charles II. (b. 1/1623)

1874 Death of Lobegott Friedrich Konstantin von Tischendorf, 59, German Protestant theologian and textual critic. He is remembered for discovering and deciphering the "Codex Sinaiticus," an important fifth century Greek manuscript of the Pauline epistles. (b. 1/18/1815)

Words for the Soul

1773 Anglican evangelical Henry Venn wrote in a letter: 'Some most sweet hours indeed I find, when, walking in perfect stillness and solitude, I make mention by name of every one of my particular friends... thanking God for them, and begging the increase of His grace in their souls, and of usefulness in their lives.'

1785 Anglican poet and hymnwriter William Cowper wrote in a letter: 'See and observe how true it is that, by increasing the number of our conveniences, we multiply our wants in exactly the same proportion.'

1950 British literary scholar and Christian apologist C. S. Lewis wrote in a letter: 'The New Testament does not envisage solitary religion; some kind of regular assembly is everywhere taken for granted in the Epistles. So we must be regularly practising members of the Church... the Body of Christ.'

1981 Russian Orthodox liturgical scholar Alexander Schmemann reflected in his journal: 'Christianity is the overcoming of dead ends. The sin of our civilization is to deny the possibility of such an overcoming.'

IN GOD'S WORD... OT: Hosea 6:1–9:17 ~ NT: 3 John 1-15 ~ Psalms 126:1-6 ~ Proverbs 29:12-14

December 8

Highlights in History

1630 Roger Williams sailed for America to escape persecution in England for preaching against church-state unions. Persecuted also in the New World, he later fled to Narragansett Bay, where he purchased land from the Indians, and founded a settlement named Providence. There Williams established the colony of Rhode Island, and founded the first Baptist church in America.

1854 Pope Pius IX defined the dogma of the Immaculate Conception in the publication of his apostolic letter, "Ineffabilis Deus." The doctrine teaches that, from the beginning of her life, Mary was free from the original sin possessed by all of Adam's descendants. This doctrine remains a key issue over which Catholic and Protestant Christian bodies disagree today.

1869 The Vatican I Ecumenical Council opened with 803 present. Convened under Pope Pius IX, this 20th General Council of the Church lasted through September 1, 1870.

1907 In Wilmington, Delaware, Christmas seals were sold for the first time, raising funds to help care for victims of tuberculosis.

1952 The complete (Old and New Testament) edition of the *Revised Standard Version* (RSV) of the Bible was published. (The New Testament was completed earlier, and published in 1946).

1965 The fourth and last session of the Vatican II Ecumenical Council closed. (Decisions and documents of Vatican II with the most visible effects have been those treating the liturgy, ecumenism and the life and ministry of priests.)

Notable Birthdays

1865 Birth of Jean J. C. Sibelius, Finnish composer, and pioneer of Finnish national music. He is remembered today for composing the hymn tune FINLANDIA ("Be Still, My Soul") in 1900. [d. 9/20/1957]

1892 Birth of Jacob Tarshish, the American rabbi who was known on radio and through his books as "The Lamplighter." [d. 1960]

The Last Passage

1649 Death of Noël Chabanel, 36, French-born Jesuit missionary to the North American Indians. Killed by a Huron Indian in 1649, Chabanel was canonized 1930, along with six other Catholic missionaries martyred between 1646 and 1649 by American Indians. (b. 2/17/1613)

1691 Death of the English pastor and theologian, Richard Baxter, 76. Considered the greatest Puritan preacher of his day, Baxter's theology portrayed Christ's death as an act of universal redemption, penal and vicarious, though not strictly substitutionary. God thus made a new law offering amnesty to penitent breakers of the old law. Baxter's writings include *'The Saints' Everlasting Rest* (1650). (b. 11/12/1615)

1934 American Baptist missionaries to China, John and Betty (née Scott) Stam, 28, were martyred. Serving in Anwhei under sponsorship of the China Inland Mission, they were seized by Chinese Communists and beheaded. Miraculously, their infant daughter, Helen Priscilla, survived. (Betty b. 2/22/1906; John b. 1/18/1907)

Words for the Soul

1841 Scottish pastor Robert Murray McCheyne wrote in a letter to an unconverted friend: *'There is no believing, no repenting, no conversion in the grave — no minister will speak to you there. This is the time of conversion. We must either gain you now, or lose you for ever....'*

1985 Dutch Catholic priest, educator and diarist Henri J. M. Nouwen observed in his *Road to Daybreak* journal: *'Jesus always leads us to littleness. It is the place where misery and mercy meet. It is the place where we encounter God.'*

IN GOD'S WORD... OT: Hosea 10:1–14:9 ~ NT: Jude 1-25 ~ Psalms 127:1-5 ~ Proverbs 29:15-17

טבת
TEVET

ALMANAC OF THE CHRISTIAN FAITH

כסלו
KISLEV

~ December 9 ~

Highlights in History

1835 George Mueller first presented his plan for an orphanage at a public meeting in Bristol, England. Contributions soon began to come in, and Mueller rented the house at No. 6 Wilson Street. On April 11, 1836 the doors of the new orphanage opened, and 26 children were immediately taken in.

1905 The Act for Separation of Church and State was promulgated in France, abrogating Napoleon's Concordat of 1801-02. The new act guaranteed freedom of conscience, but put all religious groups on their own, with the state no longer offering financial support for religion.

1917 The Ottoman Empire surrendered Jerusalem to the British on this day, and 700 years of rule by the Moslem Turks came to an end. For the first time since the Crusades, Palestine was again governed by a Christian nation. It remained a protectorate of Great Britain until Israel became an independent nation in 1948.

Notable Birthdays

1608 Birth of John Milton, English Puritan poet and essayist, and one of the masters of English literature. He wrote in four languages, but is best-remembered today for his metrical epic masterpieces, *Paradise Lost* (1667) and *Paradise Regained* (1671) — both written after losing his eyesight in 1652. [d. 11/8/1674]

1667 Birth of William Whiston, English clergyman, church historian and a translator of Josephus. Whiston authored *Primitive Christianity Reviewed* (1711), began a revival of Arianism in the 18th century, and was afterward dismissed from Cambridge for his views. [d. 8/22/1752]

1865 Birth of Charles Price Jones, African-American clergyman and Pentecostal pioneer. Raised a Baptist in Georgia, Jones experienced sanctification in 1894. In 1909 he founded the Church of Christ (Holiness), U.S.A. [d. 1/19/1949]

1863 Birth of G[eorge] Campbell Morgan, English clergyman and Bible expositor. Though he had no formal academic training, he was ordained a Congregational minister in 1889. Pastoring Westminster Chapel for a total of 25 years, Morgan was credited with over 60 books, many of which were expositions of Scripture. [d. 5/16/1945]

The Last Passage

1877 Death of George Nelson Allen, 65, founder of the Oberlin Conservatory of Music, and composer of the hymn tune: MAITLAND ("Must Jesus Bear the Cross Alone?"). (b. 9/7/1812)

1893 Death of George J. Elvey, 77, English sacred organist. He served Queen Victoria 50 years as organist at St. George's Chapel, Windsor. Among his compositions are the two hymn tunes: ST. GEORGE'S, WINDSOR ("Come, Ye Thankful People, Come") and DIADEMATA, to which three hymns are sung: "Crown Him With Many Crowns"; "Make Me a Captive, Lord"; "Soldiers of Christ, Arise." (b. 3/27/1816)

1968 Death of Karl Barth, 82, Swiss Reformed theologian. He sought to restore belief in the fundamental dogmas of Christianity. When asked in 1962 (on his one visit to America) to summarize his theology, Barth replied: *'Jesus loves me, this I know, for the Bible tells me so.'* (b. 5/10/1886)

Words for the Soul

1739 English revivalist George Whitefield noted in his journal: *'Well might our Lord say, "The Kingdom of God is within you;" for they who are truly born of God carry Heaven in their hearts.'*

1981 Dutch Catholic priest Henri J. M. Nouwen wrote in his journal ¡Gracias!: *'The longer I live, the more I am aware of... faithlessness,... greed, lust, violence, and indignation roaring in my innermost self. Growing older has not made life with God easier.... Oh how much do I pray that he will let me know through all my senses that his love is more real than my sins.'*

IN GOD'S WORD... OT: Joel 1:1–3:21 ~ NT: Revelation 1:1-20 ~ Psalms 128:1-6 ~ Proverbs 29:18

טבת
TEVET

ALMANAC OF THE CHRISTIAN FAITH

כסלו
KISLEV

~ December 10 ~

Highlights in History

1520 With the words, *'Because you have corrupted God's truth, may God destroy you in this fire,'* German Reformer Martin Luther burned the papal bull "Exsurge, Domine," that Pope Leo X had issued in June of this year, condemning Luther as a heretic. In response to Luther's flagrant disobedience, Leo issued "Decet Romanum Pontificem" — the papal notice which officially excommunicated Luther from the Roman Catholic Church.

1593 Italian archaeologist Antonio Bosio (ca.1576-1629) first descended into the subterranean Christian burial places, located under the streets of Rome. Dubbed by later researchers as the "Columbus of the Catacombs," Bosio completed the writing of his extensive studies in 1620. His books remained the standard work until the researches of G. B. de Rossi.

1948 The United Nations General Assembly adopted a "Universal Declaration of Human Rights," which included the article: *'Everyone has the right to freedom of thought, conscience, and religion... and freedom... to manifest his religion or belief in teaching, practice, worship, and observance.'*

Notable Birthdays

1741 Birth of John Murray, British-born American religious leader. Known as the "Father of Universalism in America," Murray came to the U.S. in 1770 as an itinerant preacher. In 1779 he organized the Independent Church of Christ in Gloucester, MA — the first Universalist church in the U.S. Murray afterward pastored the Universalist Society in Boston (1793-1809). [d. 9/3/1815]

1824 Birth of George MacDonald, Scottish clergyman, novelist and poet. Trained for the Congregational ministry, he served only one church before leaving the pastorate, to become a lecturer and a writer of children's novels. MacDonald was best known as a mythmaker, and the cheerful goodness in his works later captured the imagination of English literary scholar C. S. Lewis, convincing him that real righteousness is not dull. [d. 9/18/1905]

The Last Passage

1561 Death of Kaspar Schwenkfeld, 72, German mystic and lay reformer. He taught the deification of Christ's humanity, and believed Luther's doctrine of justification by faith created serious moral dangers. A branch of his later disciples emigrated to Philadelphia in 1734. Today, small groups of followers in Pennsylvania continue to follow his teachings. (b. 1489)

1968 Death of Thomas Merton, 53, French-born American Trappist monk, mystic, poet and author. More than anyone else in the 20th century, Merton succeeded in interpreting to the Western mind the meaning of contemplation and the role of the monastic. He published his best-selling autobiography, *The Seven Storey Mountain*, in 1948. (b. 1/31/1915)

1979 Death of Fulton J. Sheen, 84, American Roman Catholic prelate and broadcasting personality. His "Catholic Hour" program ran on radio from 1930-52. Later, his "Life is Worth Living" television program made Sheen the most prominent American Catholic of broadcasting's golden era. (b. 5/8/1895)

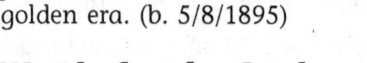

Words for the Soul

1739 English revivalist George Whitefield prayed: *'Lord, grant we may always keep between the two extremes of distrusting or tempting Thee.'*

1956 British scholar and Christian apologist C. S. Lewis reasoned in a letter: *'In so far as the things unseen are manifested by the things seen, one might from one point of view call the whole material universe an allegory.'*

IN GOD'S WORD...   OT: Amos 1:1–3:15 ~ NT: Revelation 2:1-17 ~ Psalms 129:1-8 ~ Proverbs 29:19-20

טבת
TEVET

ALMANAC OF THE CHRISTIAN FAITH

כסלו
KISLEV

~ December 11 ~

Highlights in History

1518 Swiss Reformer Ulrich Zwingli (1484-1531) was elected "people's priest" at Old Minster, the principal church in Zurich, where he remained for the remaining 13 years of his life.

1640 A London petition (modeled on Mal. 4:1) demanded *'that the said government (i.e., the episcopal system) with all its dependencies, roots, and branches, be abolished.'* Known afterward as the "Root and Branch" Petition, the legislation of 1641 embodied its demands and was itself known as the Root and Branch Bill.

Notable Birthdays

1475 Birth of Leo X (Giovanni de Medici), the second son of Lorenzo the Magnificent, and pope from 1513-21. He issued the bull in 1520 condemning Martin Luther's teaching on 41 counts. [d. 12/1/1521]

1792 Birth of Joseph Mohr, German Catholic priest, in Salzburg, Austria. Ordained in 1815, Mohr served as assistant priest at St. Nicholas Church in Oberndorf, Austria, from 1817-19. While at Oberndorf, Father Mohr penned the words to the Christmas poem, "Stille Nacht" ("Silent Night"), which was afterward set to music by the village schoolmaster and church organist, Franz Gruber. [d. 12/4/1848]

1822 Birth of George David Cummins, American Methodist (then Episcopal) clergyman, later the founder (1873) and first bishop (1876) of the Reformed Episcopal Church. [d. 6/25/1876]

1895 Birth of John R. Rice, flamboyant American Fundamentalist Baptist clergyman and controversialist. In 1934 he founded "The Sword of the Lord," an independent weekly paper. In 1959 he began the "Voice of Revival" radio program. Both media attacked modernism, Catholicism, communism, evolution, dancing, smoking, movies and alcohol. [d. 12/29/1980]

The Last Passage

384 Death of Damasus I, ca. 80, pope from 366. During his pontificate, the doctrine of the Trinity was finalized, and Arianism condemned. Damasus also commissioned Jerome to create a Latin (Vulgate) translation of the Bible. (b. ca. 304)

1893 Death of William Milligan, 72, Scottish clergyman and Bible scholar. He taught New Testament criticism at the University of Aberdeen from 1860, was a member of the New Testament committee for the *English Revised Version* (1881), and published numerous scholarly works, including commentaries on the Gospel of John and on Revelation. (b. 3/15/1821)

Words for the Soul

1532 German reformer Martin Luther declared in one of his Table Talks: *'My wife can persuade me to do whatever she pleases, for she has the entire household in her hand. And indeed I gladly grant her the complete control of domestic affairs, but despite this I intend to preserve my right [as head of the household] intact.'*

1887 Scottish clergyman and children's novelist George MacDonald, the day after his 63rd birthday, wrote in a letter to his sister: *'The days are growing very short, and the night is at hand. But, is it the night? At worst it will be a sweet twilight, full of hope. Or, even if I find that still I need the purification of loneliness and pain to free me from the phantom of life by me imagined, instead of accepting God's intention of my life, I will still yet be full of the hope of sunrise, and I will hope now in the Living One, by and in Whom I live.'*

1980 Russian Orthodox liturgical scholar Alexander Schmemann reflected in his journal: *'Truth... is at the same time simple and complex, so that while stating it, one has to fight an unnecessary complication as well as an unnecessary simplification (both are possible temptations). Truth about life is simple in its essence and complex in its application to concrete life.'*

IN GOD'S WORD... OT: Amos 4:1–6:14 ~ NT: Revelation 2:18–3:6 ~ Psalms 130:1-8 ~ Proverbs 29:21-22

December 12

TEVET / **KISLEV**

Highlights in History

1189 King ("Lion Hearted") Richard I departed England on the Third Crusade to retake Jerusalem from the Muslims. He negotiated a treaty allowing Christians access to the holy places.

1682 The Great Law of the colony of Pennsylvania was passed. Quaker founder William Penn had written into this law the principle of religious tolerance, no doubt as a result of the great persecution under which, in recent years, Penn and his fellow Quakers had suffered, both in England and in America.

1808 The first Bible society in America was organized in Philadelphia, with the Rev. William White as president. In 1840, it changed its name to the Pennsylvania Bible Society. Dues were $2 a year. Life membership was $50.

Notable Birthdays

1718 Birth of John Cennick, English Moravian clergyman and hymnwriter. He originally worked with John Wesley, later with George Whitefield. Today Cennick is remembered as author of the hymn, "Be Present At Our Table, Lord." [d. 7/4/1755]

1806 Birth of Isaac Leeser, Jewish clergyman, editor and author. As a Traditionalist rabbi, his most significant work was a translation of the Hebrew Bible into English in 1845, the result of 17 years' labor. Toward the end of his life, he founded Maimonides College, the first school for rabbinical training in America. [d. 2/1/1868]

1840 Birth of "Lottie" (Charlotte Diggs) Moon, American missionary. She was appointed by the Southern Baptist Mission Board to serve in P'ing-tu, China in 1887. Within two decades, P'ing-tu became the greatest Southern Baptist evangelistic center in all China. After many years of service, she suffered with her Chinese people in a terrible famine. Giving her food to others, she slowly starved herself, ultimately succumbing while aboard the ship taking her back to America. Today, Lottie Moon is regarded as the patron saint of Southern Baptist missions. [d. 12/24/1912]

1900 Birth of D[avid] Elton Trueblood, American Quaker theologian, educator and writer. Leaving a tenured position at Stanford in 1945 he moved to Indiana, where he helped establish the Earlham School of Religion in 1960. Trueblood spent much of his life lecturing and writing. As a young man he tended toward Unitarianism. Years later he became a spokesman for what he considered "rational evangelism." [d. 12/20/1994]

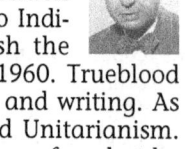

The Last Passage

1582 Death of the nefarious Spanish general, Alvarez de Toledo, the Duke of Alva, 74, who butchered thousands of Protestants in the Netherlands, during the Inquisition that was instituted in Holland under Phillip II of Spain. Alva eventually provoked a war of Independence among the Dutch that lasted 80 years. (b. 10/29/1507)

1895 Death of Daniel S. Warner, 53, American clergyman. Ordained in the Winebrennerian (German Reformed) Church, in 1880 he helped establish the Church of God (Anderson, IN), a denomination emphasizing entire sanctification as a second work of grace. (b. 6/25/1842)

Words for the Soul

1522 German reformer Martin Luther pleaded in a letter: *'To worship Christ in the Sacrament or not... should be a matter of personal liberty, for Christ... has commanded neither the one nor the other.... Therefore let each one do whatever he please... and make no sin or heresy of either the one of the other.'*

1739 English revivalist George Whitefield prayed in his journal: *'Lord, give us such a sense of Thy justice as to convince us that we cannot be saved if we continue in sin, and such a sense of Thy mercy as may keep us from despair.'*

IN GOD'S WORD... OT: Amos 7:1–9:15 ~ NT: Revelation 3:7-22 ~ Psalms 131:1-3 ~ Proverbs 29:23

טבת
TEVET

ALMANAC OF THE CHRISTIAN FAITH

כסלו
KISLEV

~ December 13 ~

Highlights in History

1545 The Council of Trent was opened by Pope Paul III, to deal with doctrinal issues raised by Protestants. Spread over several pontificates, the sessions were interrupted by long recesses, and finally ended in December 1563. Resulting reforms succeeded in restoring morale and pastoral efficiency to the Catholic Church.

1930 "Symphony of Psalms" — a work for chorus and orchestra by Igor Stravinsky — was first performed in Brussels. The piece is a setting of the Latin Vulgate translation of Psalms 39, 40 and 150. Stravinsky, who began each day with prayer, believed that *'the principal virtue of music is [as] a means of communication with God.'*

1959 Greek Orthodox primate of Cyprus (since 1950), Archbishop Makarios III was elected the first president of Cyprus, serving until 1977. The son of a shepherd, Makarios was formerly named Mihail Mouskos.

Notable Birthdays

1823 Birth of William Walsham How, Anglican bishop and the author of several enduring hymns, including "We Give Thee But Thine Own"; "For All the Saints Who From Their Labors Rest"; "O Word of God Incarnate"; and "O Jesus, Thou Art Standing." [d. 8/10/1897]

1835 Birth of Phillips Brooks, American Episcopal bishop. Considered one of the greatest preachers of his generation, Brooks preached the funeral sermon for Abraham Lincoln (1865) and in 1868 penned the Christmas hymn, "O Little Town of Bethlehem." [d. 1/23/1893]

1863 Birth of Johannes Weiss, German Protestant New Testament scholar. He stressed the eschatological element in the gospels, and laid the early foundations of form criticism. Weiss' major work, *The History of Primitive Christianity*, was unfinished at his death. [d. 8/24/1914]

The Last Passage

1204 Death of Spanish rabbi and scholar, Moses Maimonides, 69. A major intellectual of medieval Judaism, he attempted to reconcile his faith with Aristotelian philosophy. Maimonides condemned asceticism, believed in freedom of the will, and published *A Guide of the Perplexed* (1190), a title which had profound influence on Christian thought in the Middle Ages. (b. 3/30/1135)

1769 Death of Christian F. Gellert, 54, a German philosopher and poet whose hymns became popular with both Lutherans and Catholics. He died at Leipzig, where he had been professor of theology at the university. His last words were: *'Only repeat to me the name of Jesus. Whenever I hear it or pronounce it myself I feel refreshed with fresh joy.'* (b.7/4/1715)

1784 Death of Samuel Johnson, 75, English essayist and lexicographer. His level of Christian piety was rare in the 18th century Church of England, although he disliked Presbyterianism and Nonconformity. Johnson attributed the source of his conversion as a young man to the reading of William Law's *A Serious Call to a Devout and Holy Life*. (b. 9/18/1709)

Words for the Soul

1865 English religious reformer and founder of the Plymouth Brethren, John Nelson Darby reminded in a letter: *'Union is always good in itself, but faithfulness to Christ comes before even union.'*

1950 American missionary and Auca Indian martyr Jim Elliot pondered in his journal: *'I think God is to be glorified by asking the impossible of Him.'*

1985 Dutch Catholic priest, educator and mystic Henri J. M. Nouwen reflected in his *Road to Daybreak* journal: *'I must pray for the strength and courage to be truly obedient to Jesus, even if he calls me to go where I would rather not go.'*

IN GOD'S WORD... OT: Obadiah 1-21 ~ NT: Revelation 4:1-11 ~ Psalms 132:1-18 ~ Proverbs 29:24-25

טבת TEVET ALMANAC OF THE CHRISTIAN FAITH  KISLEV

~ December 14 ~

Highlights in History

1853 Illinois Institute opened under the Wesleyans. In 1860 the financially troubled trustees requested help from the wealthier Congregationalists. Jonathan Blanchard, a Presbyterian pastor and academic, was appointed president, and the school changed its name to Wheaton College.

1927 A newly revised edition of the Church of England prayer book (*Book of Common Prayer*, or BCP) was accepted by the House of Lords (241-88), but turned down by the House of Commons.

1981 Israel formally annexed the Golan Heights, captured from Syria during the 1967 Six-Day War. Rising to 1700 feet, Israel regarded the escarpment as having little military importance in the hands of a friendly neighbor. If controlled by a hostile force, however, the Golan could have become a strategic nightmare for Israel.

Notable Birthdays

1586 Birth of George Calixtus, German Lutheran theologian and early ecumenist. A theology professor at Helmstadt (1614-56), he developed a theological system known as syncretism, by which he attempted to reunite Lutherans, Calvinists and Catholics. [d. 3/19/1656]

1831 Birth of Griffith John, Welsh Congregational missionary. Sent by the London Missionary Society in 1855, he became the first Protestant missionary to penetrate Central China. A prolific writer and speaker, John is credited with having translated the New Testament into Mandarin Chinese. His career as a missionary spanned over 50 years. [d. 7/25/1912]

1836 Birth of Frances Ridley Havergal, English devotional poet. Though frail in health, she developed a great linguistic ability. An incessant writer, she also penned a number of enduring hymns,  including "Take My Life and Let It Be"; "Lord, Speak to Me That I May Speak" and "Who Is On the Lord's Side?" [d. 6/3/1879]

1891 Birth of Henry Barraclough, English-born sacred pianist and hymnwriter. He served over 40 years as an administrator of the General Assembly of the Presbyterian Church (1919-61). Barraclough also created 20 hymn texts and 120 tunes, including the words and music (MONTREAT) to "Ivory Palaces." [d. 8/1983]

The Last Passage

1417 Death of Lollard leader Sir John Oldcastle, 39. A follower of John Wycliffe, he served in Parliament, but was condemned for joining the Lollards, a dissident Christian sect. He was executed by hanging and was burned on the scaffold. Oldcastle was later portrayed by Shakespeare as the character Falstaff. (b. ca. 1378)

1591 Death of St. John of the Cross, 49, Spanish monk. He is regarded as Spain's greatest poet and among the Church's greatest mystics. His *Dark Night of the Soul* influenced both Catholic and Protestant thought. John once wrote: *'A Christian should always remember that the value of his good works is not based on their number and excellence, but on the love of God which prompts him to do these things.'* (b. 6/24/1542)

1715 Death of influential Anglican Thomas Tenison, 79, Archbishop of Canterbury (1695-1715) and one of the founders of the Society for the Propagation of the Gospel. (b. 9/29/1636)

Words for the Soul

1909 American Quaker holiness author Hannah Whitall Smith, 77, wrote to her daughter: *'Your "woes"... teach you the unalterable imperfection of all human things; and I believe in the end you will have to settle down to it, and consent to stop short of perfection. I long ago had to do this, and it has produced such a feeling of being only a stranger and a pilgrim here, with my real home beyond, that it has relieved me immensely.'*

IN GOD'S WORD... OT: Jonah 1:1–4:11 ~ NT: Revelation 5:1-14 ~ Psalms 133:1-3 ~ Proverbs 29:26-27

December 15

TEVET / **KISLEV**

ALMANAC OF THE CHRISTIAN FAITH

Highlights in History

1629 In England, proto-Baptist Roger Williams, 26, married Mary Barnard, the daughter of a Puritan clergyman. Two years later, he and his wife sailed from Bristol to the American colony of Massachusetts.

1791 The U.S. Bill of Rights was ratified. The First Amendment reads: 'Congress shall make no law respecting an establishment of religion, or prohibiting the free exercise thereof.'

1870 At a constituting conference held in Jackson, MS, African-American leader, Robert Payne organized the Colored Methodist Episcopal Church. The first two elected C.M.E. bishops were W. H. Miles and R. H. Vanderhorst. (In 1956, the denomination changed its name to the Christian Methodist Episcopal Church.)

Notable Birthdays

1727 Birth of Ezra Stiles, American Congregational clergyman and educator. As president of Yale College (1778-95), he was considered the most learned man in New England in his time. He taught that religious truth would benefit less from uniformity than from a free exchange of doctrinal opinions. [d. 5/12/1795]

1754 Birth of Paul Henkel, American Lutheran evangelist. His missionary endeavors spanned 40 years, taking him to the frontiers of VA, NC, TN, KY, OH and IN. From 1806 he distributed books produced by his son's print shop — the first and, for many years, the only Lutheran publishing house in the nation. [d. 11/27/1825]

1843 Birth of A[lbert] B. Simpson, Canadian-born American clergyman and hymnwriter. Ordained in the Presbyterian Church, Simpson later founded the Christian and Missionary Alliance (1897). With a passion for missions, Simpson established Nyack College in 1883, North America's earliest surviving Bible and missionary training college. He also authored 175 hymns, including "Jesus Only," "Yesterday, Today, Forever" and "What Will You Do With Jesus?" [d. 10/29/1919]

1900 Birth of Clarence W. Jones, pioneer missionary broadcaster. Graduating from Moody Bible Institute in 1921, he founded the Approved Workmen Are Not Ashamed (AWANA) youth program during the 1920s. In 1975 he became the first inductee into the NRB's Religious Broadcasting Hall of Fame. [d. 4/29/1986]

The Last Passage

1811 Death of Johannes Theodorus Van Der Kemp, 64, pioneer Dutch Reformed missionary to South Africa. The drowning of his wife and son in a boating accident in 1791 led to his conversion. Van Der Kemp first arrived in Cape Town in 1799, and soon after became an opponent of slavery and an advocate for the rights of the indigenous population. (b. 1747)

1853 Death of Georg Friedrich Grotefend, 78, the German archaeologist who successfully deciphered the cuneiform alphabet, first discovered in 1802. (b. 6/9/1775)

Words for the Soul

1558 Dutch Anabaptist Menno Simons asserted in a letter: 'Wherever there is a pulverized and penitent heart, there grace also is, and wherever there is a voluntary confession not gained by pressure, there love covereth a multitude of sins.'

1739 English revivalist George Whitefield pleaded in a letter: 'My brother, entreat the Lord that I may grow in grace, and pick up the fragments of my time, that not a moment of it may be lost.'

1957 British literary scholar and Christian apologist C.S. Lewis petitioned in a letter: 'May it please the Lord that... faith unimpaired may strengthen us, contrition soften us and peace make us joyful.'

IN GOD'S WORD... OT: Micah 1:1–4:13 ~ NT: Revelation 6:1-17 ~ Psalms 134:1-3 ~ Proverbs 30:1-4

טבת
TEVET

ALMANAC OF THE CHRISTIAN FAITH

כסלו
KISLEV

~ December 16 ~

Highlights in History

955 John XII was elected to the papacy, serving until 964. Sometimes called the "boy pope," he was only 17 at his ascension. Being originally named Octavian, John was the second pontiff to change his name upon ascending the throne. (The first was John II, pope from 533-35.)

1904 Future Indian mystic [Sadhu] Sundar Singh, 15, burned a Bible in his rage at the death of his mother. A few days later he was miraculously converted to the Christian faith, and went on to become an apostle to India and Tibet.

Notable Birthdays

1662 Birth of Samuel Wesley, Sr., English clergyman. As rector at Epworth (1695-1735), his chief fame rests on his role, as he put it, of being the "grandfather of Methodism" — i.e., the father of John and Charles Wesley. [d. 4/25/1735]

1714 [NS=12/27] Birth of George Whitefield, English revivalist. Associated with the Wesley brothers during his college years, Whitefield embarked on a lifelong calling as an evangelist. He sailed to America seven times during his ministry, dying in Newburyport, MA, while on his last visit. [d. 9/30/1770]

1770 Birth of Ludwig von Beethoven, German symphonic composer. By age 30 he was growing deaf, and by 50 could hear none of the music he wrote. Yet he composed some of his greatest works after deafness overtook him. Suffering much from ill health, Beethoven once declared: 'I owe it to myself, to mankind, and to the Almighty. I must write music to the glory of God.' Several of his musical pieces have been adapted to hymns, including ODE TO JOY ("Joyful, Joyful, We Adore Thee"). [d. 3/26/1827]

1786 Birth of Conrad Kocher, German composer. Among his several works were two operas, an oratorio, and the hymn tune DIX ("For the Beauty of the Earth"). [d. 3/12/1872]

1867 Birth of Amy Carmichael, Irish-born English missionary to India. Influenced by the Keswick Movement, in 1895 she was sent by the Anglican Zenana Missionary Society to South India, where she established a home for children rescued from temple prostitution. The Dohnavur Fellowship was formed in 1927 to sponsor her work, which had earlier become independent of the Church of England. [d. 1/18/1951]

1826 Birth of John Ellerton, Anglican clergyman and hymnwriter. Ellerton penned some 68 hymns during his lifetime, several of which he contributed to *Hymns Ancient and Modern*, including "Welcome, Happy Morning"; "Savior, Again to Thy Dear Name We Raise"; and "God the Omnipotent." [d. 6/15/1893]

The Last Passage

1935 Death of Walter S. Martin, 73, American holiness pastor. Ordained a Baptist, Martin later switched to the Disciples of Christ. From 1919 he held evangelistic meetings all over America. Today, Martin is better remembered for composing the hymn tune: GOD CARES ("God Will Take Care of You"). (b. 3/8/1862)

Words for the Soul

1536 In one of his "Table Talks" on a comparison of marriage versus celibacy, German reformer Martin Luther observed: 'Whether you marry or not, you will repent of what you have done.... We are so contaminated by original sin that there is not a walk of life which at times does not cause the person who has entered it to feel regretful.... It seems to me that the most delightful walk of life is to be found in a household of moderate means, to live there with an obliging spouse and to be satisfied with little.'

1977 Russian Orthodox liturgical scholar Alexander Schmemann reflected in his journal: 'Christianity requires, absolutely requires, simplicity.'

IN GOD'S WORD... OT: Micah 5:1–7:20 ~ NT: Revelation 7:1-17 ~ Psalms 135:1-21 ~ Proverbs 30:5-6

December 17

Highlights in History

1889 In Chicago, American revivalist Dwight L. Moody founded the Bible Institute for Home and Foreign Missions. Raised a Unitarian in Massachusetts, Moody was later converted to Evangelical Christianity, and in 1856 left his work as a shoe salesman in Boston to engage in "home missionary" work in Chicago.

1906 The first Jewish U.S. cabinet member, Oscar Solomon Straus of New York, was appointed Secretary of Commerce and Labor during President Theodore Roosevelt's second administration. Straus served until March 3, 1909.

1912 Chicago-born dairy industry heir William Borden became a missionary to the Muslims. A star athlete at Yale University, handsome, and worth $50 million, "Borden of Yale" (as he came to be called) sailed to Egypt. But a month after arriving, Borden contracted spinal meningitis and died. A final message stuffed under his pillow read: 'No Reserve! No Retreat! No Regrets!'

NOTABLE BIRTHDAYS

1534 Margaret Luther was born. She was the sixth and youngest child born to German reformer Martin Luther and his wife Katherine von Bora. Margaret died at age 36 as the wife of George von Kunheim. [d. 1570]

1807 Birth of John Greenleaf Whittier, American Quaker poet. He used his pen to raise the conscience of the North against slavery. "Ichabod" was among the best of his poems. He is also remembered for authoring the hymn, "Dear Lord and Father of Mankind." [d. 9/7/1892]

1834 Birth of Marianne Hearn, English Baptist newspaper editor and devotional writer. Her vast literary output, published in 20 volumes, included the hymn: "Just As I Am, Thine Own to Be." [d. 3/16/1909]

1856 Birth of Andrew L. Skoog, Swedish-born American music educator and choral director. He led sacred music in churches in both Chicago and Minneapolis. He also wrote many hymns, hymn tunes and anthems. Today Skoog is remembered for rendering Lina Sandell's hymn, "Day by Day [And With Each Passing Moment]," into English. [d. 10/30/1934]

1923 Birth of Jaroslav Pelikan, American clergyman and historian. He taught at Yale from 1962-96, and is one of the world's leading scholars in church history. Pelikan has authored over 30 books, including a five-volume history of *The Christian Tradition* (1971-89). [d. 5/13/2006]

The Last Passage

1187 Death of Gregory VIII, pope during the last two months of 1187. During his brief pontificate Saladin's Turks recaptured Jerusalem (first conquered in 1099 during the First Crusade).

1836 Death of John Rippon, 85, English Baptist clergyman, and collector and publisher of sacred music. He is remembered today for the hymns, "How Firm a Foundation" and "All Hail the Power of Jesus' Name." (b. 4/29/1751)

Words for the Soul

1874 American Quaker holiness author Hannah Whitall Smith wrote in a letter: 'It has cost me something to lay aside my old dependence upon my own judgment and good sense, and to let myself be helpless in the Lord's hands. But it is unspeakably sweet when it is done. And I believe it is to me the opening up of a life of conscious union with my Lord such as I have never known before.'

1943 German Lutheran theologian and Nazi martyr Dietrich Bonhoeffer confided in a letter from prison: 'The consciousness of being borne up by a spiritual tradition that goes back for centuries gives one a feeling of confidence and security in the face of all passing strains and stresses.'

IN GOD'S WORD... OT: Nahum 1:1–3:19 ~ NT: Revelation 8:1-13 ~ Psalms 136:1-26 ~ Proverbs 30:7-9

טבת
TEVET

ALMANAC OF THE CHRISTIAN FAITH

כסלו
KISLEV

~ December 18 ~

Highlights in History

1821 Future English reformer George Mueller, as a young man, spent his first night in jail on theft charges. After his release, the following year he became a Christian — and later one of the great prayer warriors of all time.

1836 In Oxford, GA, Emory College was chartered by the Georgia Methodist Conference. In 1914, the institution moved to Atlanta, and changed its name to Emory University.

1904 Indian mystic Sundar Singh, 15, was converted to Christianity. He afterward donned the robe of a Sadhu (i.e., holy man) in an endeavor to present Christianity in a Hindu form. Singh disappeared in April 1929, while undertaking a strenuous mission in Tibet.

Notable Birthdays

1707 [NS=12/29] English hymnwriter Charles Wesley, younger brother of John, was born the 18th child of Samuel and Susanna Wesley. As the "poet of Methodism," Charles penned 6,500 hymns, including "And Can It Be That I Should Gain"; "Jesus, Lover of My Soul"; "Hark! The Herald Angels Sing"; and "Love Divine, All Loves Excelling." [d. 3/29/1788]

1725 Birth of German Lutheran church historian and biblical scholar, Johann S. Semler. He taught at the University of Halle from 1752. Called the "father of German rationalism," Semler developed the early principles of textual criticism for the Bible. [d. 3/14/1791]

1819 Birth of Isaac T. Hecker, American Catholic priest, religious founder and journalist. He converted to the Catholic Church from Transcendentalism in 1844. Hecker afterward became a founder (and the first superior, 1858-88) of the Paulist Fathers, an order devoted to reaching Americans for Catholicism. [d. 12/22/1888]

1835 Birth of Lyman Abbott, American Congregational clergyman and editor. He succeeded Henry Ward Beecher at Brooklyn's Plymouth Congregational Church (1887-99). Abbott interpreted Christianity as it applied to social and industrial problems. [d. 10/22/1922]

1859 Birth of Francis Thompson, English Catholic essayist and poet. Best known for his religious themes, Thompson's first volume, *Poems*, 1893, contains his best known verse — "The Hound of Heaven" — which describes the crisis of a man pursued by God's love. Thompson spent the last 18 of his 48 years of life recovering from an opium addiction. [d. 11/13/1907]

The Last Passage

1789 Death of John Darwall, 58, Anglican clergyman and composer. He prepared music for all 150 of the Psalms. Of these, his most enduring hymn tune was DARWALL'S 148th ("Rejoice, The Lord is King"). (b. 1/13/1731)

1803 Death of Johann Gottfried von Herder, 59, German Lutheran clergyman and critical scholar. Using poetry as a mode of coming to terms with reality, Herder — a precursor of Schleiermacher — contributed several important ideas to the religio-historical school. (b. 8/25/1744)

Words for the Soul

1739 English revivalist George Whitefield gave testimony in his journal: *'I never feel the power of religion more than when under outward or inward trials. It is that alone which can enable any man to sustain with patience and thankfulness his bodily infirmities.'*

1846 Scottish clergyman and writer Andrew Bonar penned in his journal: *'I have often felt things in study so plainly given me, not at all like the products of my own skill, that this is the way in which I account for them. The Lord sends them because of people praying for me.'*

IN GOD'S WORD...   OT: Habakkuk 1:1–3:19 ~ NT: Revelation 9:1–21 ~ Psalms 137:1-9 ~ Proverbs 30:10

טבת ALMANAC OF THE CHRISTIAN FAITH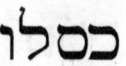
TEVET   KISLEV

~ December 19 ~

Highlights in History

1187 Cardinal Paolo Scolari was elected Pope Clement III, serving until 1191. He organized the Third Crusade, and gave papal protection to Jews and other persecuted people.

1562 With the Battle of Dreux, the French religious wars between the Huguenots and the Catholics began in earnest.

1790 An interdenominational meeting opened in Philadelphia to create the First Day Society to strengthen Sunday observance.

1861 English Baptist clergyman Charles Spurgeon erected an almshouse for the elderly. Later, in 1864, he established a school for the needy children of London. In 1866 he founded the Stockwell Orphanages, and in 1867, he established a private hospital. In explanation of this activity, Spurgeon said: *'God's intent in endowing any person with more substance than he needs is that he may have the pleasurable office, or rather the delightful privilege, of relieving want and woe.'*

1905 In France, the Church and State were completely separated by law, severing religious groups from any further economic support by the national government.

Notable Birthdays

1808 Birth of Horatius Bonar, Scottish clergyman and hymnist. Known as the greatest hymnwriter among the Scots, he prepared three series of *Hymns of Faith and Hope*, including such favorites as "Here, O My Lord, I See Thee Face to Face" and "I Heard the Voice of Jesus Say." [d. 7/31/1889]

1866 Birth of Tikhon (Vasili Belavin), Patriarch of Moscow (1917-25). Elected the Metropolitan of Moscow in 1917, he was soon after chosen the first Patriarch of Russia since 1700, following the restoration of the Russian Orthodox Church. Tikhon was later imprisoned and tortured for his faith. [d. 4/7/1925]

The Last Passage

1906 Death of Charles C. McCabe, 70, American Methodist prelate and home missionary. A prisoner during the American Civil War, "Chaplain McCabe's" subsequent enthusiasm, eloquent voice and rich baritone singing inspired both the public imagination and willing donations for his denomination as American Methodism moved West. (b. 10/11/1836)

1968 Death of Norman Matoon Thomas, 84, American Presbyterian clergyman and activist for social theology. He ran for the U.S. presidency six times on the Socialist Party ticket, declaring that America's capitalist system was "a gambler's economy." (b. 11/20/1884)

Words for the Soul

1534 In a sermon, Martin Luther discussed the relationship between "faith" and "works": *'Christ is not apprehended by works but by the faith of the heart.... Faith produces works while it justifies and blots out sins without works and before works. Faith does not exist because of works, but works are done because of faith.'*

1739 English revivalist George Whitefield testified in his journal: *'It often gives me unspeakable comfort, to see how wisely God overrules everything for the good of His Church.'*

1888 Scottish clergyman and children's novelist George MacDonald wrote in a letter to his sister: *'I... hope in God. I will not say believe, for that is a big word, and it means so much more than my low beginnings of confidence. But a little faith may wake a great big hope, and... the more we trust, the more reasonable we find it to trust.'*

1974 Dutch Catholic mystic Henri J. M. Nouwen reflected in his *Genesee Diary*: *'Just as a mother feels the child grow in her and is not surprised on the day of the birth but joyfully receives the one she learned to know during her waiting, so Jesus can be born in my life slowly and steadily and be received as the one I learned to know while waiting.'*

IN GOD'S WORD...   OT: Zephaniah 1:1–3:20 ~ NT: Revelation 10:1-11 ~ Psalms 138:1-8 ~ Proverbs 30:11-14

טבת
TEVET

ALMANAC OF THE CHRISTIAN FAITH

כסלו
KISLEV

~ December 20 ~

Highlights in History

1787 Under the guidance of their third leader, Rev. Joseph Meacham, the Shakers in America began experiencing a revival. Meacham had assumed leadership after the death of the Rev. Joseph Whittaker, who succeeded the English founder of the Shaker movement, Mother Ann Lee.

1856 Newberry College was chartered in South Carolina. With a current enrollment of 700, this 4-year liberal arts college is today privately controlled by the Lutheran Church in America.

1913 Howard Goss and Eudorus N. Bell called for a general council of Pentecostals (the Apostolic Faith Movement) because excesses, spiritual error, and lack of education were threatening to destroy the movement. Out of this gathering emerged the Assemblies of God.

Notable Birthdays

1490 Birth of Thomas Münzer, German religious reformer. In his disagreement with Luther, Münzer became increasingly radical in his socio-political ideas. Inaugurating the Peasants War against the nobility and clergy, Münzer was killed in the Battle of Frankenhausen. Many of his beliefs were rejected by later, nonviolent Anabaptists, but his rejection of infant baptism endured as a key teaching. [d. 5/27/1525]

1822 Birth of Samuel G. Green, English Baptist minister and Bible language writer. He was associated with London's Religious Tract Society from 1876-99. Among the most popular of his many works were his *Handbook to the Grammar of the Greek New Testament* (1870) and *Handbook of Old Testament Hebrew* (1901). [d. 9/15/1905]

1863 Birth of Charles C. Torrey, American linguist and Semitics scholar. He taught at Yale (1901-1932), specializing in the O.T. Apocrypha and Pseudepigrapha. Torrey held that, in the New Testament, the four Gospels and the book of Revelation were all translations into Greek from Aramaic originals. [d. 11/2/1956]

The Last Passage

1552 Death of Katherine von Bora, 53, the German Cistercian nun who married Martin Luther. At their wedding in 1525 she was 26 and he 42. All biographers agree their marriage was a happy one, and produced six children. Surviving her husband by only six years, Katie declared on her deathbed, 'I will stick to Christ like a burr.' (b. 1/29/1499)

1849 Death of William Miller, 67, American Baptist lay preacher and sectarian leader. He predicted the second coming of Christ in 1843, then in 1844. The doctrines of the Seventh Day Adventist Church, founded in 1860, were based on Miller's teachings. (b. 2/15/1782)

1930 Death of Harold Green, 59, English-born missionary to Pondoland in South Africa, and composer of the hymn tune QUIETUDE ("Speak, Lord, in the Stillness"). (b. 10/23/1871)

1934 Death of American Presbyterian hymn-writer Adelaide A. Pollard, 72. In poor health, she lived the life of a mystic and ascetic. She is remembered today for authoring the hymn, "Have Thine Own Way Lord." (b. 11/27/1862)

Words for the Soul

1886 Scottish clergyman and novelist George MacDonald wrote, after enclosing an original poem in a letter to his sister: 'I send you this new old song for Christmas Day. If the story were not true, nothing else would be worth being true.'

1961 Swiss Reformed theologian Karl Barth noted in a letter: 'What God chooses for us children of men is always the best.'

1979 Russian Orthodox liturgical scholar Alexander Schmemann reflected in his journal: '"A quiet and silent existence" is the summit of intelligence.... Humility stems from wisdom, from knowledge, from contact with life overabundant.'

IN GOD'S WORD...   OT: Haggai 1:1–2:23 ~ NT: Revelation 11:1-9 ~ Psalms 139:1-24 ~ Proverbs 30:15-16

טבת ALMANAC OF THE CHRISTIAN FAITH כסלו
TEVET   KISLEV

~ December 21 ~

Highlights in History

1620 The 103 passengers aboard the *Mayflower* anchored and disembarked at Plymouth Rock, in Massachusetts, following a three-month voyage from England to the New World.

1849 "Shepherd of Tender Youth," a hymn penned originally by Clement of Alexandria (ca.170-220), first appeared in print in English in "The Congregationalist," a denominational magazine edited by the poem's translator, Rev. Henry Martyn Dexter (1821-90). "Shepherd of Tender Youth" stands as the earliest known hymn in Christendom (outside the N.T.), and the earliest hymn whose exact authorship is known.

Notable Birthdays

1603 Birth of Roger Williams, English-born Puritan clergyman. He was first to advocate complete religious tolerance in America. He also founded the first Baptist church in the American colonies, in Providence, RI. [d. 1/27/1683]

1672 Birth of Benjamin Schmolck, German Lutheran poet. He was the most popular hymnwriter of his time, and authored, "My Jesus, As Thou Wilt." [d. 2/12/1737]

1672 Birth of Johann Christoph Schwedler, Silesian clergyman. He founded an orphanage, and wrote more than 500 hymns, including "Ask Ye What Great Thing I Know." [d. 1/12/1730]

1795 Birth of Robert Moffat, Scottish Congregational missionary to Africa. Sent by the London Missionary Society in 1816, Moffat spent 49 years in the field, where he translated the Bible and developed a major missionary community. In 1839 Moffat visited England and persuaded David Livingstone (who later became his son-in-law) to join him in Africa. [d. 8/9/1883]

1918 Birth of Robert P. Evans, American Naval chaplain and missions pioneer. He founded the European Bible Institute in 1949. Its name was changed to Greater Europe Mission in 1952.

The Last Passage

1549 Death of Margaret of Navarre, 57, monarch, poet, and champion of the Protestant reform movement in France. Her grandson, Henry IV, published the Edict of Nantes in 1598. (b. 4/11/1492)

1807 Death of John Newton, 82, the Anglican parson who had formerly been a slaver. He co-authored with poet William Cowper the *Olney Hymnbook* (1779), of which Newton composed over 300 hymn texts, including "Glorious Things of Thee Are Spoken," "How Sweet the Name of Jesus Sounds" and "Amazing Grace." (b. 7/24/1725)

1889 Death of Joseph B. Lightfoot, 61, Anglican Bishop of Durham (1879-89) and biblical critic. He was noted for his work on the New Testament and the Apostolic Fathers. (b. 4/13/1828)

1938 Death of James M. Black, 82, American Methodist singing school teacher, sacred music editor and gospel song composer: "When the Roll is Called Up Yonder." (b. 8/19/1856)

Words for the Soul

1516 German reformer Martin Luther explained in a sermon: *'Since God can make none righteous but those who are not righteous, He is obliged to operate with the strange work of making men sinners before He can get at His proper work of justifying them.'*

1776 Anglican clergyman and hymnwriter John Newton explained in a letter: *'It is necessary that our sharpest trials should sometimes spring from our dearest comforts, else we should be in danger of forgetting ourselves and setting up our rest here.... We shall often need something... to make us feel that our dependence... is upon the Lord alone.'*

1941 British literary scholar and Christian apologist C. S. Lewis wrote in a letter: *'Is any pleasure on earth as great as a circle of Christian friends by a good fire?'*

IN GOD'S WORD... OT: Zechariah 1:1-21 ~ NT: Revelation 12:1-17 ~ Psalms 140:1-13 ~ Proverbs 30:17

טבת
TEVET

ALMANAC OF THE CHRISTIAN FAITH

כסלו
KISLEV

~ December 22 ~

Highlights in History

401 Innocent I became pope, serving until 417 as head over both the Eastern and Western churches. He established anointing of the sick as a sacrament, and recommended clerical celibacy. During his pontificate, Rome was sacked in 410.

1216 Pope Honorius III formally approved the Dominican religious order (Order of Preachers). During the Middle Ages, many leaders of European thought were Dominicans. The popes also used them for preaching the Crusades and for staffing the Inquisition.

1838 John Hunt and his wife Hannah, both 26, arrived on the Fiji islands as English Methodist missionaries. At that time terrible cannibalism ravaged the islands of Rewa, Somosomo, Lakemba, and Viwa. John later translated the New Testament into Fijian. His evangelistic work was successful, and by the time of his death from dysentery in 1848, much of Fiji was transformed.

1922 The first sermon to be broadcast over English radio was delivered by Prebend J. A. Mayo, rector of St. Mary's Church in Whitechapel.

Notable Birthdays

1696 Birth of James E. Oglethorpe, Anglican philanthropist and colonizer. He was the founder and Governor of the Colony of Georgia (the last of the 13 American colonies to be established), 1733-43. Oglethorpe accompanied the first group of colonists in 1733, and later recruited John and Charles Wesley, founders of Methodism, to come to Georgia as missionaries in 1735. [d. 6/30/1785]

1770 Birth of Demetrius A. Gallitzin, Russian priest. Born in the Hague, he served as a missionary to the American Alleghenies, and was the first Catholic priest to receive his full theological training in the United States. Gallitzin, PA was named for him. [d. 5/6/1840]

1789 Birth of Ann Hasseltine Judson, American missionary. She was Adoniram Judson's first wife. Along with Harriet Newell, Ann became one of the first two U.S. women to serve as overseas missionaries (1812). [d. 10/24/1826]

The Last Passage

1668 Death of Stephen Daye, 74, English-born printer. In 1638 he established the first American colonial printing press in Cambridge, MA, and in 1640 published the *Bay Psalm Book*. (b. 1594)

1888 Death of Isaac T. Hecker, 69, American Catholic missionary priest. In 1858, Hecker became a founder (and first superior, 1858-88) of the Missionary Society of St. Paul the Apostle (the Paulist Fathers). (b. 12/18/1819)

1899 Death of Dwight L. Moody, 62, foremost American evangelist of the latter 19th century. He also founded the Northfield Seminary for girls, the Mt. Herman School for boys, and the Chicago (later Moody) Bible Institute. Speaking to 10,000 or 20,000 at a time, Moody presented his message, by voice or pen, to at least 100 million people. (b. 2/5/1837)

1917 Death of Frances X. Cabrini, 67, the first American citizen to be made a Catholic saint. She came to the U.S. from Italy in 1889. As "Mother Cabrini," she founded the Institute of the Missionary Sisters of the Sacred Heart. She was canonized in 1946 by Pius XII. (b. 7/15/1850)

Words for the Soul

1763 Founder of Methodism John Wesley penned in his journal: *'Lord, let me not live to be useless!'*

1974 Dutch Catholic mystic Henri J. M. Nouwen reflected in his *Genesee Diary*: *'The basis of community is not primarily our ideas, feelings, and emotions about each other but our common search for God. When we keep our minds and hearts directed toward God, we will come more fully "together."'*

IN GOD'S WORD... OT: Zechariah 2:1–3:10 ~ NT: Revelation 12:18–13:18 ~ Psalms 141:1-10 ~ Proverbs 30:18-20

טבת
TEVET

ALMANAC OF THE CHRISTIAN FAITH

כסלו
KISLEV

~ December 23 ~

Highlights in History

619 Boniface V became pope, serving until 625. He organized missions to England, established the see of Canterbury and was known for his love of the clergy and mild disposition.

1531 Swiss Reformer Heinrich Bullinger, 27, took the place of slain Ulrich Zwingli as pastor of the Grossmunster Church of Zurich. His wisdom and influence afterward spread across Europe. Bullinger continued Zwingli's practice of preaching through the Bible verse by verse.

1922 Pope Pius XI published the encyclical "Ubi arcano," which encouraged the creation of organizations within the Catholic Church which could serve in a social, educational or quasi-political capacity in European countries.

Notable Birthdays

1648 Birth of Robert Barclay, Scottish-born apologist. Considered the most notable of all Quaker theologians, Barclay published *An Apology for the True Christian's Divinity* (1675), a scholarly defense of Quaker doctrine. [d. 10/3/1690]

1790 Birth of Jean F. Champollion, French Egyptologist. A philologist who established the principles for translating Egyptian hieroglyphics, it was Champollion who first deciphered the trilingual Rosetta Stone, discovered in Egypt by French troops in 1799. [d. 3/4/1832]

1805 Birth of Joseph Smith, founder of the Mormon Church. He allegedly received a book on golden plates in 1827 which, after translation, became the *Book of Mormon*. Smith and his followers began a westward movement which ended in Utah, though Smith was murdered by a mob in Nauvoo, Illinois. [d. 6/27/1844]

1830 Birth of Charlotte A. Barnard, English pastor's wife. One of the most prolific ballad writers of the 19th century, she composed the hymn tune BARNARD ("Give of Your Best to the Master"). [d. 1/30/1869]

1862 Birth of Amos R. Wells, American educator and author. For 42 years he was editor of the "Christian Endeavor World," and from 1901-33 he edited *Peloubet's Notes on the Sunday School Lessons*. [d. 3/6/1933]

The Last Passage

1652 Death of John Cotton, 67, English-born American colonial clergyman. Called the "patriarch of New England" Cotton produced some of the clearest statements of Puritan theology. He was also responsible for the expulsion of Anne Hutchinson and Roger Williams from the Massachusetts Bay Colony, and helped publish the *Bay Psalm Book* (1640). (b. 12/4/1585)

1902 Death of Frederick Temple, 81, Anglican educational reformer and Archbishop of Canterbury from 1896. He was dedicated to both Christian higher education and church unity. (b. 11/30/1821)

1972 Death of Abraham J. Heschel, 65, Polish-born American theologian and the first Jewish faculty member at Union Theological Seminary. Heschel taught that much restlessness in modern man is due to a denial of transcendence. Heschel believed the God of the Bible was neither a philosophical abstraction nor a psychological projection. (b. 1907)

Words for the Soul

1843 Scottish clergyman and biographer Andrew Bonar noted in his journal: 'Finished my Memoir of Robert McCheyne *yesterday morning.... I am glad that the Lord has permitted me to finish this record of His beloved servant.*'

1855 Scottish clergyman Andrew Bonar noted in his journal: '*I feel tonight as if I and all the house were lying down to rest amid mercies on every side, as if the fragrance of the Lord's special kindness were spreading through every room in the house, quietly ascending back to the Giver.*'

IN GOD'S WORD... OT: Zechariah 4:1–5:11 ~ NT: Revelation 14:1-20 ~ Psalms 142:1-7 ~ Proverbs 30:21-23

תבת ALMANAC OF THE CHRISTIAN FAITH כסלו
TEVET   KISLEV

~ December 24 ~

Highlights in History

1652 The British Parliament, while under Quaker control, passed a law reminding the public that *'no observance shall be had on the five-and-twentieth of December, commonly called Christmas Day; nor any solemnity used or exercised in churches in respect thereof.'*

1784 The so-called "Christmas Conference" convened at Lovely Lane Chapel in Baltimore, MD, during which the Methodist Episcopal Church in the United States was established as a separate Protestant denomination.

1818 The first singing of "Silent Night" ("Stille Nacht") was heard. This timeless Christmas carol was written by Joseph Mohr, parish priest of Oberndorf, Austria. Its music was composed by church organist Franz Gruber.

Notable Birthdays

1491 Birth of Ignatius of Loyola, Spanish Catholic reformer. He was founder and first general of the Society of Jesus (1534). The Jesuit order — concerned with education and missionary work — was formally approved in 1540. St. Ignatius was canonized in 1622. [d. 7/31/1556]

1772 Birth of Barton W. Stone, American frontier Presbyterian evangelist. As leader of a wing of the early Restoration Movement, in 1830-31 he united with followers of Alexander Campbell to form a religious organization which, after 1832, came to be known as the Christian (or Disciples of Christ) Church. [d. 11/9/1844]

1866 Birth of Annie Johnson Flint, a crippled poet who penned the hymn, "He Giveth More Grace." She was a teacher in New Jersey, but had to leave the profession when severe arthritis made her unable to walk. She also wrote "Hands and Feet of Him": *'Christ has no hands but our hands / To do His work today; / He has no feet but our feet / To lead men in His way....'* [d. 9/8/1932]

The Last Passage

1870 Death of Albert Barnes, 72, the American Presbyterian clergyman who penned an exposition of The Bible: *Notes, Explanatory and Practical* (11 vols., 1832-53). As a pastor in Philadelphia (1830-67), one of his sermons, "The Way in Salvation," led to a schism within his denomination. (b. 12/1/1798)

1881 Death of American Congregational clergyman, editor and author, Leonard Bacon, 79. Sometimes called the "Congregational Pope," he pastored First Congregational Church in New Haven, CT for 56 years (1825-81)! Bacon also wrote the hymn, "O God, Beneath Thy Guiding Hand." (b. 2/19/1802)

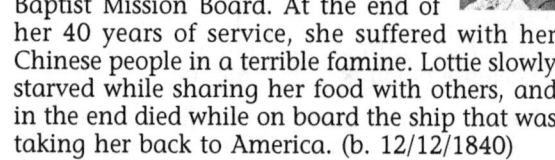

1912 Death of "Lottie" (Charlotte Diggs) Moon, 72, American Baptist missionary to China. At age 32 she was appointed to China by the Southern Baptist Mission Board. At the end of her 40 years of service, she suffered with her Chinese people in a terrible famine. Lottie slowly starved while sharing her food with others, and in the end died while on board the ship that was taking her back to America. (b. 12/12/1840)

1915 Death of William H. Doane, 83, American businessman and hymnwriter. He edited *Sabbath School Gems* (1862) and composed over 2,200 hymn tunes, including NEAR THE CROSS and MORE LOVE TO THEE. (b. 2/3/1832)

Words for the Soul

1943 German Lutheran theologian and Nazi martyr Dietrich Bonhoeffer observed in a letter: *'Gratitude changes the pangs of memory into a tranquil joy.'*

1985 Dutch Catholic priest, educator and diarist Henri J. M. Nouwen reflected in his *Road to Daybreak* journal: *'A life is like a day; it goes by so fast. If I am so careless with my days, how can I be careful with my life?'*

IN GOD'S WORD...   OT: Zechariah 6:1–7:14 ~ NT: Revelation 15:1-8 ~ Psalms 143:1-12 ~ Proverbs 30:24-28

טבת ALMANAC OF THE CHRISTIAN FAITH כסלו
TEVET   KISLEV

~ December 25 ~

Highlights in History

336 The earliest reference to observing Jesus' nativity on Dec. 25th is found in the Philocalian Calendar of A.D. 354, which dated the Roman origin of the practice to this year. (Commemorating Jesus' birth on Jan. 6th began in the Eastern Church, although by the 400s most of the Eastern churches had accepted the Roman date.)

496 Clovis, King of France, was baptized into the Christian faith, along with thousands of his followers. It was a momentous day in history, marking the first of the great mass conversions that turned Europe into a "Christian" continent.

1923 In Washington, D.C., during the presidential administration of Warren G. Harding, the first electrically-lit Christmas tree appeared in the White House.

Notable Birthdays

1766 Birth of Christmas Evans, Welsh revivalist. With little education, he grew up wild, but was converted under the preaching of another Welsh evangelist, David Davies. Evans afterward became famous for both his oratory and for his great imagination. He brought about a national revival, and has been called the "Bunyan of Wales." [d. 7/19/1838]

1821 Birth of Clar[iss]a Barton, American humanitarian, author, philanthropist and social reformer. During the American Civil War, she helped care for the wounded. In 1881 she became the founder and first president (–1904) of the American Red Cross. [d. 4/12/1912]

1835 Birth of Benjamin T. Tanner, African Methodist Episcopal clergyman and prelate. An advocate of black unity and self-help, Tanner sought to help secure an organic union between the Colored ME Church, the AME Zion Church and his own AME organization. [d. 1/15/1923]

1865 Birth of Evangeline Booth, commander of the Salvation Army in America. She was born in England the year her father, William Booth, left Methodism and founded the Salvation Army. In 1904 Evangeline came to the U.S. to begin a work which eventually spanned 30 years. In 1934 she was elected the fourth general and only woman, chosen to head up the international agency. She was also the last of the Booths to lead the Army. [d. 7/17/1950]

The Last Passage

795 Death of Pope Adrian I, who served from 772. He fought against the Adoptionist heresy, and worked closely with Charlemagne, symbolizing the medieval ideal of church and state working together in a united Christendom.

1907 Death of Sarah L. Borthwick Findlater, 84, Scottish hymnwriter. Along with her sister Jane Borthwick, she translated over 50 hymns from the German, including "O Happy Home, Where Thou Art Loved." (b. 11/26/1823)

1918 Death of J. Wilbur Chapman, 59, American Presbyterian pastor, evangelist and author of the hymns: "One Day When Heaven Was Filled With His Praises"; and "Jesus! What a Friend of Sinners." (b. 6/17/1859)

Words for the Soul

1413 In a letter composed 19 months before he was burned at the stake, Bohemian reformer Jan Hus exhorted: *'Rejoice, that the immortal God is born, so that mortal men may live in eternity.'*

1531 In a Christmas sermon, German reformer Martin Luther warned regarding the Church and State: *'To be able clearly to distinguish between these two kingdoms is a great art, for few people make the proper distinction.... The temporal lords want to rule the church, and, conversely, the theologians want to play the lord in the town hall. Under the papacy mixing the two was considered ruling well, and it is still so considered. But in reality this is ruling very badly.'*

IN GOD'S WORD... OT: Zechariah 8:1-23 ~ NT: Revelation 16:1-21 ~ Psalms 144:1-15 ~ Proverbs 30:29-31

ALMANAC OF THE CHRISTIAN FAITH

TEVET   KISLEV

~ December 26 ~

Highlights in History

1776 John Rosbrugh of Allen Township, PA, was commissioned chaplain of Northampton County. The following month, on Jan. 2, 1777, he was killed at the Battle of Assunpink (Second Battle of Trenton). It made Rosbrugh the first American Army chaplain to be killed in action.

1790 In Philadelphia, the First Day Society adopted a constitution whose purpose it was to instruct the rising generation from the Bible and *'from such other moral and religious books as the society might, from time to time, direct.'*

1948 Holy communion according to the rite of the Church of England was first broadcast in full over British television on this date.

Notable Birthdays

1716 Birth of Thomas Gray, English poet. His poems were concerned with melancholy and with love of nature. His best-known piece, "Elegy Written in a Country Churchyard" (1751), is the epitome of the Romantic period. [d. 7/30/1771]

1769 Birth of Ernst M. Arndt, German historian and poet. While teaching at Bonn, his fondest hope was for a union of Catholics and Protestants in a German national church. [d. 1/29/1860]

1830 Birth of William Caven, Scottish-born Canadian Presbyterian leader. He taught at Knox College in Toronto the last 39 years of his life. Though staunchly conservative, Caven was genuinely interested in social issues and thoroughly committed to Christian missions. He was also a promoter of the union of the Presbyterian churches in Canada. [d. 12/1/1904]

1887 Birth of Charles B. Booth, American social reformer. The grandson of Salvation Army founder William Booth, Charles was head of the Volunteers of America, 1949-58. [d. 4/14/1975]

The Last Passage

1800 Death of Anne Parrish, 40, American Quaker philanthropist. In 1795 she established the House of Industry to supply employment to poor women in Philadelphia — the first charitable organization for women founded in America. (b. 10/17/1760)

1836 Death of Johann (Hans) Georg Nägeli, 68 [or 63], Swiss pioneer music educator and publisher. In addition to publishing his theories of music education, he also composed the hymn tune DENNIS ("Blest Be the Tie That Binds"). (b. 5/26/1768 [or 1773])

1910 Death of Gustav Warneck, 76, German Lutheran clergyman and a pioneer of the science of missiology as an academic discipline. Warneck was an apprentice of the Rhenish Mission, although he never did actual mission work, nor visit an overseas mission field. (b. 3/6/1834)

1968 Death of the American Baptist clergyman and historian Kenneth Scott Latourette. As a scholar of the development of the Church, his *History of the Expansion of Christianity* (7 vols., 1937-48) remains among Latourette's most notable publications. (b. 8/9/1884)

Words for the Soul

1945 British literary scholar and Christian apologist C. S. Lewis affirmed in a letter: *'Something really new did happen at Bethlehem: not an interpretation but an event. God became man.'*

1970 American Presbyterian apologist Francis Schaeffer admitted in a letter: *'We can fail after we are truly Christians because becoming a Christian does not rob us of our true humanity.'*

1985 Dutch Catholic cleric, educator and diarist Henri J.M. Nouwen reflected in his *Road to Daybreak* journal: *'Speaking about spiritual things to spiritual people is quite easy. But speaking about... God's presence in our hearts, our families, and our daily lives to people for whom "God words" are often connected with hurtful memories seems nearly impossible.'*

IN GOD'S WORD...   OT: Zechariah 9:1-17 ~ NT: Revelation 17:1-18 ~ Psalms 145:1-21 ~ Proverbs 30:32

טבת
TEVET

ALMANAC OF THE CHRISTIAN FAITH

כסלו
KISLEV

~ December 27 ~

Highlights in History

1814 The gospel was preached to the Maori people of New Zealand for the first time by Samuel Marsden, 50, an Anglican missionary from Australia. Ordained in 1793, he was sent to serve as chaplain to a penal colony near Sydney. At his own expense, Marsden sailed with two associates from Australia to New Zealand, where he was greeted warmly by the Maoris. Marsden returned to New Zealand six times over the next 25 years.

1819 Three years after he first sailed to South Africa, English missionary Robert Moffat and Mary Smith (also of England) were married. They afterward labored side-by-side for 53 years, becoming one of the greatest husband-wife teams in missionary history.

1943 The film, "Song of Bernadette," was released by the Fox Film Corporation (later 20th Century Fox). It told the story of 14-year-old French Catholic peasant girl, Bernadette Soubirous, who in 1858 experienced 18 visions of the Virgin Mary at Lourdes.

Notable Birthdays

1525 Birth of Giovanni Palestrina, Italian composer. Among the great Renaissance composers, Palestrina wrote almost all of his music in service to the church. His most enduring hymn tune was VICTORY ("The Strife is O'er, The Battle Done"). [d. 2/2/1594]

1696 Birth of David Nitschmann, early Moravian leader in the New World. Consecrated the first bishop of the Renewed Unitas Fratrum in 1735, he traveled to America on the same voyage as John and Charles Wesley. [d. 10/8/1772]

1800 Birth of John Goss, English sacred organist and composer. With a reputation second only to that of Samuel S. Wesley, Goss taught at the Royal Academy of Music for 47 years. His most enduring hymn tune was ARMAGEDDON ("Who Is On the Lord's Side?"). [d. 5/10/1880]

1893 Birth of Samuel M. Shoemaker, American Episcopal clergyman. His work extended into missions, radio broadcasting and a ministry to university students. Shoemaker also assisted the founders of Alcoholics Anonymous in formulating their "Twelve Steps." [d. 10/31/1963]

The Last Passage

1656 Death of Andrew White, English Jesuit missionary and "Apostle of Maryland." He traveled to America in 1633 in answer to Cecelius Calvert's request for Jesuit assistance in his New World colony, "Terra Mariae." White returned to England in 1645. (b. 12/27/1579)

1826 Death of Thomas Vasey, ca. 80. Ordained by John Wesley in 1784, Vasey worked in the Thirteen Colonies as a circuit rider, helping to establish Methodism in America. (b. ca. 1746)

1902 Death of Richard F. Weymouth, 80, English Baptist biblical scholar. He produced a scholarly text-critical edition of the Greek New Testament in 1886, but will best be remembered for his more popular and enduring *New Testament in Modern Speech* (1903). (b. 10/26/1822)

1937 Death of Cyrus S. Nusbaum, 76, American Methodist clergyman, hymn author and composer: "Would You Live For Jesus, and Be Always Pure and Good?" (b. 7/27/1861)

Words for the Soul

1774 English founder of Methodism John Wesley explained in a letter: *'Although there is much advantage in long experience, and we may trust an old soldier more than a novice: yet God... gives to many, in a very short time, a closer and deeper communion with himself, than others attain in a long course of years.'*

1856 American soldier Robert E. Lee wrote in a letter: *'The doctrines and miracles of our Saviour have required nearly two thousand years to convert but a small part of the human race, and even among the Christian nations what gross errors still exist!'*

IN GOD'S WORD... OT: Zechariah 10:1–11:17 ~ NT: Revelation 18:1-24 ~ Psalms 146:1-10 ~ Proverbs 30:33

טבת
TEVET   ALMANAC OF THE CHRISTIAN FAITH   KISLEV

~ December 28 ~

Highlights in History

1384 English reformer John Wycliffe, "Morning Star of the Reformation," suffered a paralyzing stroke. He died three days later, on his 64th birthday. Wycliffe authored the first complete translation of the Bible into English. His life later influenced other reformers, including Jan Hus, Martin Luther and John Calvin.

1917 The insurgent Communist government of the Bolshevik Revolution confiscated all Russian church lands, decreed marriage a civil ordinance, and abolished all religious influence in the culture — imposing what Chairman Lenin called "a separation of church and state."

Notable Birthdays

1797 Birth of Charles Hodge, the leading American Presbyterian theologian of the 19th century. He taught at Princeton Seminary for nearly 60 years (1822-78), and was the major figure in the Reformed (Calvinistic) orthodoxy. Over 3,000 pastors prepared for ministry through his theology classes. Due to Hodge's influence, a spirit of conservatism remained within Princeton long after his passing. *Systematic Theology* (4 vols., 1872-73) was his most influential writing. [d. 6/19/1878]

1847 Birth of Samuel A. Ward, American Episcopal organist and merchant. He established a successful music store in his hometown of Newark, NJ. He also succeeded Henry S. Cutler as organist of Grace Episcopal Church in Newark. Today Ward is best remembered for composing the hymn tune MATERNA ("America The Beautiful"). [d. 9/28/1903]

The Last Passage

1622 Death of St. Francis of Sales, 55, French Catholic prelate, mystic, and leader of the Counter-Reformation. In 1610 he helped to found the Order of the Visitation. (b. 8/21/1567)

1870 [OS=12/16] Death of Alexis F. Lvov (Lwoff), 71, Russian violinist and composer. He served in the Russian army, and later followed his father as Director of the Russian Imperial Chapel. He edited and published chants of the Russian church, including the modern hymn tune RUSSIAN HYMN ("God the Omnipotent"). (b. 6/6/1799)

1925 Death of Samuel T. Francis, 91, English Plymouth Brethren poet and speaker. Among his collected verse, Francis's most enduring poem became the lyrics to the hymn: "O the Deep, Deep Love of Jesus." (b. 11/19/1834)

Words for the Soul

1531 In his "Table Talks," German reformer Martin Luther declared: *'The true God lets Himself be used and serves people. But mammon does not do this. He wants to lie still and let himself be served. This is the reason why the New Testament calls avarice idolatry, because it will be served.'*

1741 English revivalist George Whitefield advised in a letter: *'Go to bed seasonably, and rise early. Redeem your precious time... that not one moment of it may be lost. Be much in secret prayer. Converse less with man, and more with God.'*

1894 In a letter to his sister, Scottish novelist George MacDonald, 70, articulated the processes in dying: *'So many dear ones have gone through the straits before us, that we must not fear to follow them. Till then, like scholars too backward to be taught together, some of us are having much personal attention from the Master. Gradually we are shut in from the public, then the social relations are narrowed, then some, thank God, are shut up to their dear ones, and when, as so often is the case, there are no dear ones on this earth, then we are alone with the Living One, and have to take spoonfuls of life from his own hand; and there are some, doubtless, who call and think it only nasty medicine. Let us take it willingly and lovingly.'*

IN GOD'S WORD...   OT: Zechariah 12:1–13:9 ~ NT: Revelation 19:1-21 ~ Psalms 147:1-20 ~ Proverbs 31:1-7

טבת
TEVET

ALMANAC OF THE CHRISTIAN FAITH

כסלו
KISLEV

~ December 29 ~

Highlights in History

1851 The first American branch of the Young Men's Christian Association (YMCA) was organized in Boston. (The movement was founded in London in 1844 by English dry goods clerk George Williams, 23, who had been holding meetings for Bible study and prayer for fellow-workers.)

1901 In Denver, Methodist minister's wife Mrs. Alma White became founder (and first bishop) of the Pentecostal Union, a denomination emphasizing the holiness doctrine of crisis sanctification, and also speaking in tongues. In 1917 the organization changed its name to "Pillar of Fire."

Notable Birthdays

1832 Birth of Francis Pott, Anglican clergyman and hymnwriter. He served in parishes from 1856 until 1891, when he had to retire due to deafness. Afterward active in research and writing, Pott contributed to hymnody primarily through his translation of Latin hymns, including his English rendering of "The Strife Is O'er, The Battle Done." [d. 10/26/1909]

1865 Birth of William A. Brown, American Presbyterian scholar and social activist. He taught theology at Union Seminary (NY) for nearly 40 years (1892-1930). As a Christocentric liberal, he sought to bring together his denominational traditions with the secular standards of a scientific age. Brown taught that God was an ever-present Spirit who guided all that happened to a wise and holy end. As a social activist, Brown became the dean of American ecumenical leaders. [d. 12/15/1943]

1888 Birth of Josef Beran, Czech Catholic prelate. Born in Pilsen, Czechoslovakia, he was made Archbishop of Prague and primate of Czechoslovakia. In all, he spent some 17 years in Nazi and Communist prisons for his faith. Freed in 1965, Beran traveled to Rome, where he was elevated to cardinal. [d. 5/17/1969]

The Last Passage

1170 In England, Thomas à Becket, Archbishop of Canterbury (1162-70), was murdered by four of King Henry II's Norman knights. Though once a close friend with Henry II, as his archbishop Becket opposed the king over several critical tax and church issues. (T. S. Eliot's 1935 play, "Murder in the Cathedral," is based on this event.) (b. 12/21/1117)

1876 Death of Philip P. Bliss, 38, American Baptist song evangelist and hymnwriter. Returning from a family visit in PA, the train in which he was riding plunged into a ravine during a blinding snowstorm. Over 100 people perished in the wreck, including Bliss and his wife. His name, however, endures today as author of several hymns: "Wonderful Words of Life"; "The Light of the World is Jesus"; "I Will Sing of My Redeemer"; and "'Man of Sorrows,' What a Name." (b. 7/9/1838)

1980 Death of John R. Rice, 85, Fundamentalist American Baptist evangelist, editor, radio broadcaster and controversialist. (b. 12/11/1895)

Words for the Soul

1538 German reformer Martin Luther advised in a sermon: *'You parents cannot prepare a more dependable treasure for your children than an education in the liberal arts. House and home burn down and disappear, but an education is easy to carry off.'*

1870 Scottish clergyman and biographer Andrew Bonar, 60, confided in his diary: *'I see the only life worth living is to live for others.'*

1935 British literary scholar and Christian apologist C. S. Lewis wrote in a letter: *'Friendship is the greatest of worldly goods. Certainly to me it is the chief happiness of life. If I had to give a piece of advice to a young man about a place to live, I think I should say, "Sacrifice almost everything to live where you can be near your friends." I know I am very fortunate in that respect.'*

IN GOD'S WORD... OT: Zechariah 14:1-21 ~ NT: Revelation 20:1-15 ~ Psalms 148:1-14 ~ Proverbs 31:8-9

טבת
TEVET

ALMANAC OF THE CHRISTIAN FAITH

כסלו
KISLEV

~ December 30 ~

Highlights in History

1823 Charles G. Finney was licensed to preach. He afterward became one of 19th century America's most successful evangelists.

1852 Future statesman Rutherford B. Hayes, 30, married Lucy Webb, 21. Following his 1876 election as the 19th U.S. president, he and Lucy brought to the White House an open commitment to Jesus Christ. Official Washington was shocked by her banning of alcoholic beverages from the Executive Mansion, and the First Lady came to be known as "Lemonade Lucy."

1927 The International Church of the Foursquare Gospel was incorporated in Los Angeles, CA. Founded in 1923 by evangelist Aimee Semple McPherson, the denomination early on recognized and provided a significant outlet for women in ministry. Today, over 40% of its ministerial rolls consists of women.

Notable Birthdays

1637 Birth of William Cave, Anglican clergyman and church history scholar. His reputation was gained from an eminent knowledge of patristics. Cave authored *Apostolici* (1677), a book of the "Lives" of the apostles and fathers of the first three centuries of the Church. [d. 8/4/1713]

1678 Birth of William Croft, English organist. Early in life he wrote secular music. Later he became one of England's most significant composers of church music. Croft is remembered today for the hymn tune ST. ANNE ("O God, Our Help in Ages Past"). [d. 8/14/1727]

1794 American carpenter and religious leader Christian Metz was born in Germany. In 1842, he led 800 members of a Pietist group called the Community of True Inspiration to establish a settlement near Buffalo, NY, where they created the Amana Society. Their Christian commune grew to over 3,600 members, before declining in the late 19th century. [d. 7/27/1867]

1865 Birth of Rudyard Kipling, British novelist, short story writer and poet. Born in India, he lived for a brief time in England. Kipling's skill at versification also produced several Anglican hymns, including "God of Our Fathers, Known of Old" and "Father in Heaven, Who Lovest All." [d. 1/18/1936]

The Last Passage

1877 Death of William Keil, 65, German-born tailor and sect leader. Raised a Lutheran, he ultimately left the organized church. Keil's fundamental teaching, "Love one another," helped him to build two of the most successful communes in 19th century America: Bethel (in MO) and Aurora (in WA). (b. 3/6/1812)

1916 Death of Grigorii Rasputin, 47, the Russian monk and mystic who greatly influenced the royal Russian family of Czar Nicholas II. He represented himself as spiritual, but was perceived by friends of the Czar as dangerously evil, and so was assassinated. (b. 1/10/1869)

Words for the Soul

1741 English revivalist George Whitefield lamented in a letter: *'O how little do I for Jesus, who has done so much for me.'*

1835 Young Scottish clergyman and biographer Andrew Bonar, 25, noted in his diary: *'I was struck with the truth that our Christian undertakings generally flourish most at first, just because there is more simple faith while the thing is beginning, and resting on God for a blessing.'*

1985 Dutch Catholic priest, educator and diarist Henri J. M. Nouwen reflected in his *Road to Daybreak* journal: *'Knowing that the place where you live and the work you do is not simply your own choice but part of a mission makes all the difference. When difficulties arise, the knowledge of being sent will give me the strength not to run away, but to be faithful.'*

IN GOD'S WORD... OT: Malachi 1:1–2:17 ~ NT: Revelation 21:1-27 ~ Psalms 149:1-9 ~ Proverbs 31:10-24

טבת
TEVET

ALMANAC OF THE CHRISTIAN FAITH

כסלו
KISLEV

~ December 31 ~

Highlights in History

999 European Christians had expected the world to end after this night — the last day before 1000 A.D. (They were quite relieved when, on the next day, it didn't.)

1530 The German Protestant defense pact known as the Schmalkald League was formed to resist efforts by Holy Roman Emperor Charles V to eradicate Lutheranism from Germany.

1770 The first New Year's Eve "watchnight service" was held in Philadelphia, at the St. George's Methodist Church.

Notable Birthdays

1712 Birth of Peter Bohler, German Moravian missionary. His close association with the Wesley brothers introduced into Methodism the possibility of joy which can accompany one's spiritual conversion. Bohler also modelled a self-surrendering Christian faith. [d. 4/27/1775]

1823 Birth of William Orcutt Cushing, American Christian clergyman and author of over 300 hymns, including "Hiding in Thee"; "Under His Wings I Am Safely Abiding"; and "O Safe to the Rock that is Higher Than I." [d. 10/19/1902]

1837 Birth of John R. Sweney, American Presbyterian music professor, sacred choralist and composer. He wrote operettas, anthems, oratorios and hymn tunes, including: SWENEY ("More About Jesus"); STORY OF JESUS ("Tell Me the Story of Jesus"); and SUNSHINE ("There is Sunshine in My Soul Today"). [d. 4/10/1899]

1838 Birth of Phineas F. Bresee, American denominational leader. In 1895 Bresee and Joseph P. Widney founded the Church of the Nazarene. Several groups within the holiness movement joined in 1908 at Pilot Point, Texas to form the Pentecostal Church of the Nazarene. ("Pentecostal" was dropped in 1919.) [d. 11/13/1915]

The Last Passage

1384 English reformer John Wycliffe died of a stroke on his 64th birthday. In life, Wycliffe had been a leading Oxford scholar and a royal chaplain. He boldly spoke out against the pope, the medieval hierarchy of the Catholic church, and the corruption of the clergy. Under Wycliffe's direction the entire Bible was first translated into English. Wycliffe's work greatly influenced William Tyndale. (b. 12/31/1320)

1892 Death of Andrew Bonar, 82, Scottish clergyman and writer. He was an influential leader in the Scottish Free Church, visited Palestine in 1839 to inquire into the condition of Jews there, and authored the *Memoir of Robert Murray McCheyne* (1844). Bonar's *Diary and Letters* was published by his daughter Marjory (1893). (b. 5/29/1810)

Words for the Soul

1701 English Methodist Bible commentator Matthew Henry, 39, noted in his journal: *'Believing prayer to be an instituted way of communion with God, and fetching [i.e., attractive] in mercy and grace from him, I have comfort in it daily; my daily prayers are the sweetest of my daily comforts.'*

1816 Future U.S. president (1825-29) John Quincy Adams penned in his diary: *'My endeavors to quell the rebellion of the heart have been sincere, and have been assisted with the blessing from above. As I advance in life, its evils multiply, and the instances of mortality become more frequent and approach nearer to myself. The greater is the need for fortitude to encounter the woes that flesh is heir to, and of religion to support pains for which there is no other remedy.'*

1977 Russian Orthodox liturgical scholar Alexander Schmemann reflected in his journal: *'As the sacrament is impossible without bread, wine and water, so religion requires peace, true daily peace. Without it, religion becomes a neurosis, a self-deception, a delusion.'*

IN GOD'S WORD... OT: Malachi 3:1–4:6 ~ NT: Revelation 22:1-21 ~ Psalms 150:1-6 ~ Proverbs 31:25-31

DECEMBER INDEX

A

Abbott, Lyman
 b. 12/18/1835 [d. 10/22/1922]
Act for Separation of Church and State (1905) 12/9
Adoptionist Heresy 12/25
Adrian I, Pope (772-95)
 (b. unknown) d. 12/25/795
Adrian IV, Pope (1154-59) 12/4
Alcoholics Anonymous 12/27
Allen, George Nelson
 (b. 9/7/1812) d. 12/9/1877
Alvarez de Toledo
 (b. 10/29/1507) d. 12/12/1582
Amana Society 12/30
American Civil War 12/19
American Friends Service Committee 12/1
Amsdorf, Nicholas von
 b. 12/3/1483 [d. 5/14/1565]
Anselm of Canterbury, St. 12/4
Apocrypha 12/20
Aquinas, Thomas 12/6
Arianism 12/9, 12/11
Aristotelian philosophy 12/13
Arndt, Ernst Moritz
 b. 12/26/1769 [d. 1/29/1860]
Asbury, Francis 12/6
Association of Evangelical Lutheran Churches 12/3
Athenagoras I, Patriarch 12/7
Aurora Commune (WA) 12/30
AWANA (Approved Workmen Are Not Ashamed) 12/15

B

Bacon, Leonard
 (b. 2/19/1802) d. 12/24/1881
Baptism, Infant 12/20
Barclay, Robert
 b. 12/23/1648 [d. 10/3/1690]
Barclay, William
 b. 12/5/1905 [d. 1/24/1978]
Barnard, Charlotte A.
 b. 12/23/1830 [d. 1/30/1869]
Barnes, Albert
 b. 12/1/1798 d. 12/24/1870
Barraclough, Henry
 b. 12/14/1891 [d. 8/1983]
Barth, Karl
 (b. 5/10/1886) d. 12/9/1968
Barton, Clar[iss]a
 b. 12/25/1821 [d. 4/12/1912]
Battle of Assunpink 12/26
Battle of Dreux 12/19
Battle of Frankenhausen 12/20
Battle of Trenton, Second 12/26

Baur, Ferdinand Christian
 (b. 6/21/1792) d. 12/2/1860
Baxter, Richard
 (b. 11/12/1615) d. 12/8/1691
Becket, Thomas à
 (b. 12/21/1117) d. 12/29/1170
Beecher, Henry Ward 12/18
Beethoven, Ludwig von
 b. 12/16/1770 [d. 3/26/1827]
Bell, Eudorus N. 12/20
Benedict XIV, Pope (1740-58) 12/3
Beran, Josef 12/29
Bethel Commune (MO) 12/30
BIBLE VERSIONS
 Bay Psalm Book (1640) 12/22
 English Revised Version (1881, 1885) 12/11
 Fijian New Testament 12/22
 Latin Vulgate 12/11, 12/13
 Leeser's English Hebrew Bible (1845) 12/12
 Mandarin Chinese 12/14
 Polyglot Bible 12/6
 Revised Standard Version (1946, 1952) 12/1, 12/8
 Torah 12/6
Bingham, Rowland 12/4
Black, James M.
 (b. 8/19/1856) d. 12/21/1938
Blanchard, Jonathan 12/14
Bliss, Philip Paul
 (b. 7/9/1838) d. 12/29/1876
Bohler, Peter
 b. 12/31/1712 [d. 4/27/1775]
Bolshevik Revolution 12/28
Bonar, Andrew
 (b. 5/29/1810) d. 12/31/1892
Bonar, Horatius
 b. 12/19/1808 [d. 7/31/1889]
Bonar, Marjory 12/31
Boniface V, Pope (619-25) 12/23
BOOKS
 Apology for the True Christian's Divinity (1675) 12/23
 Apostolici 12/30
 Barnes Notes on the N.T. (1832-53) 12/1
 Bay Psalm Book (1640) 12/22 12/23
 Beginnings of Christianity (1919-32) 12/1
 Bible: Notes, Explanatory and Practical, The 12/24
 Bonar's Diary and Letters 12/31
 Book of Common Prayer (BCP) 12/14
 Book of Mormon 12/23
 Christian Tradition (1971-89) 12/17
 Dark Night of the Soul 12/14
 Discourses on Government (1698) 12/7
 Faith Seeking Understanding 12/4
 Greek New Testament (UBS) 12/3
 Guide of the Perplexed (1190) 12/13
 Handbook of Old Testament Hebrew (1901) 12/20

 Handbook to the Grammar of the Greek New Testament 12/20
 Histoire ecclésiastique (1691-1720) 12/6
 History of Primitive Christianity 12/13
 History of the Expansion of Christianity 12/26
 Honest to God (1963) 12/5
 Hymns Ancient and Modern 12/16
 Hymns of Faith and Hope 12/19
 Jewish Encyclopedia, The 12/7
 Latin American Journal 12/2
 Luther's Works (Univ. of Jena) 12/3
 Memoir of Robert Murray McCheyne (1844) 12/23, 12/31
 New Testament in Modern Speech (1903) 12/27
 Olney Hymnbook (1779) 12/21
 Outline of Christian Theology (1898) 12/2
 Paradise Lost (1667) 12/9
 Paradise Regained (1671) 12/9
 Peloubet's Notes on the Int'l. S.S. Lessons 12/2, 12/23
 Poems (1893) 12/18
 Primitive Christianity Reviewed (1711) 12/9
 Saints' Everlasting Rest, (1650) 12/8
 Serious Call to a Devout and Holy Life 12/13
 Seven Storey Mountain, The (1948) 12/10
 Style and Literary Method of Luke (1919-20) 12/1
 Systematic Theology 12/28
Booth, Charles B.
 b. 12/26/1887 [d. 4/14/1975]
Booth, Evangeline
 b. 12/25/1865 [d. 7/17/1950]
Booth, William 12/25, 12/26
Bora, Katherine von 12/17
 (b. 1/29/1499) d. 12/20/1552
Borden, William 12/17
Borthwick, Jane 12/25
Bosio, Antonio 12/10
Boys Town 12/1
Breakspear, Nicholas (Pope Adrian IV) 12/4
Bresee, Phineas F.
 b. 12/31/1838 [d. 11/13/1915]
Brooks, Phillips
 b. 12/13/1835 [d. 1/23/1893]
Brown, William A.
 b. 12/29/1865 [d. 12/15/1943]
Bullinger, Heinrich 12/23
Bultmann, Rudolf 12/5

C

Cabrini, Frances Xavier
 (b. 7/15/1850) d. 12/22/1917
Cadbury, Henry Joel
 b. 12/1/1883 [d. 10/7/1974]

Calixtus, George
 b. 12/14/1586 [d. 3/19/1656]
Calvert, Cecelius 12/27
Calvin, John 12/28
Campbell, Alexander 12/24
Campion, Edmund
 (b. 1/25/1540) d. 12/1/1581
CANTERBURY ARCHBISHOPS
 Anselm, St. (1093-1109) 12/4
 Becket, Thomas à (1162-1170) 12/29
 Fisher, Geoffrey (1945-1961) 12/2
 Temple, Frederick (1896-1902) 12/23
 Tenison, Thomas (1695-1715) 12/14
Carmichael, Amy
 b. 12/16/1867 [d. 1/18/1951]
Carroll, John
 (b. 1/8/1735) d. 12/3/1815
Cave, William
 b. 12/30/1678 [d. 8/4/1713]
Caven, William
 b. 12/26/1830 [d. 12/1/1904]
Celibacy, Clerical 12/22
Cennick, John
 b. 12/12/1718 [d. 7/4/1755]
Cerularius, Michael 12/7
Chabanel, Noël
 (b. 2/17/1613) d. 12/8/1649
Champollion, Jean F.
 b. 12/23/1790 [d. 3/4/1832]
CHAPLAINS
 Forgy, Howell M. 12/7
 McCabe, Charles C. 12/19
 Rosbrugh, John 12/26
 Wycliffe, John 12/31
Chapman, J. Wilbur
 (b. 6/17/1859) d. 12/25/1918
Charlemagne 12/25
Charles II, English King (1660-85) 12/7
Charles V, Holy Roman Emperor (1519-56) 12/31
Cheney, Charles E. 12/2
Christmas Day Celebration 12/24
Christmas Seals 12/8
Clarke, William Newton
 b. 12/2/1841 [d. 1/14/1912]
Clement III, Pope (1187-91) 12/19
Clement of Alexandria 12/21
Cleveland, James
 b. 12/5/1932 [d. 2/9/1991]
Clovis, French King (482-511) 12/25
Coan, Titus
 (b. 2/1/1801) d. 12/1/1882
Codex Sinaiticus 12/7
Coke, Thomas 12/6
COLLEGES / UNIVERSITIES
 Aberdeen (Scotland) 12/11
 Cambridge University (England) 12/7, 12/9

Cokesbury College (MD) 12/6
Emory College (GA) 12/18
Emory University (GA) 12/18
Georgetown University (MD) 12/3
Harvard (MA) 12/4
Helmstadt (Germany) 12/14
Illinois Institute (Wheaton College) 12/14
Knox College (Toronto, Ont.) 12/26
Maimonides College (PA) 12/12
Moody Bible Institute (IL) 12/15
Newberry College (SC) 12/20
Nyack College (NY) 12/15
Oxford University (England) 12/31
Stanford University (CA) 12/12
Temple University (PA) 12/6
Wheaton College (IL) 12/14
Yale College (CT) 12/15
Yale University (CT) 12/17, 12/20
Yale University (xx) 12/17
Columba, St.
  b. 12/7/521 [d. 6/9/597]
Community of True Inspiration 12/30
Conwell, Russell
  (b. 2/15/1842) d. 12/6/1925
Cotton, John
  (b. 12/4/1585) d. 12/23/1652
COUNCILS, CHURCH
  Council of Trent (1545-63) 12/13
  Vatican I (1869-70) 12/8
  Vatican II (1962-65) 12/2, 12/8
Counter-Reformation 12/28
Cousin, Anne Ross
  (b. 4/27/1824) d. 12/6/1906
Cowper, William 12/21
Croft, William
  b. 12/30/1678 [d. 8/14/1727]
CRUSADES 12/9, 12/22
  First Crusade (1096-99) 12/17
  Third Crusade (1189-91) 12/12, 12/19
Cummins, George David 12/2
  b. 12/11/1822 [d. 6/25/1876]
Cuneiform Alphabet 12/15
Cushing, William Orcutt
  b. 12/31/1832 [d. 10/19/1902]
Cutler, Henry Stephen 12/28
  (b. 10/13/1824) d. 12/5/1902
Cyril of Alexandria 12/7

D

Darwall, John
  (b. 1/13/1731) d. 12/18/1789
Davies, David 12/25
Daye, Stephen
  (b. 1594) d. 12/22/1668
DENOMINATIONS
  African Methodist Episcopal Church 12/25
  AME Zion Church 12/25
  Anabaptists 12/15, 12/20
  Anglicanism 12/1, 12/2, 12/5, 12/13, 12/14, 12/16, 12/26, 12/27
  Apostolic Faith Movement 12/20
  Assemblies of God 12/20
  Association of Evangelical Lutheran Churches 12/3
  Baptists 12/2, 12/6, 12/12, 12/15, 12/17, 12/24, 12/29
  Christian and Missionary Alliance 12/15
  Christian Church 12/24
  Christian Methodist Episcopal Church 12/15
  Church of God 12/4
  Church of God (Anderson, IN) 12/12
  Church of God in Christ Holiness, U.S.A. 12/9
  Church of the Nazarene 12/31
  Colored Methodist Episcopal Church 12/15, 12/25
  Congregationalism 12/2, 12/9, 12/14, 12/15, 12/18, 12/24
  Disciples of Christ 12/16, 12/24
  Dutch Reformed Church 12/15
  Eastern Church 12/25
  Episcopalianism 12/13, 12/28
  Fundamentalism, American 12/11, 12/29
  German Reformed Church 12/12
  Holiness 12/16
  Huguenots, French 12/19
  International Church of the Foursquare Gospel 12/30
  Lollards, English 12/14
  Lutheranism 12/18
  Lutheranism, American 12/1
  Lutheranism, German 12/1, 12/31
  Lutheran Church in America 12/20
  Lutheran Church Missouri Synod 12/3
  Methodism 12/5, 12/18, 12/19, 12/21, 12/22
  Methodism, American 12/24, 12/27
  Methodism, English 12/31
  Moravian Church 12/12, 12/31
  Mormon Church 12/5, 12/23
  Nonconformity 12/13
  Orthodoxy, Greek 12/13
  Orthodoxy, Russian 12/1, 12/2, 12/6, 12/7, 12/11, 12/16, 12/19, 12/20, 12/31
  Pentecostalism 12/9, 12/20
  Pentecostal Church of the Nazarene 12/31
  Pietism 12/30
  Pillar of Fire 12/29
  Plymouth Brethren 12/13, 12/28
  Presbyterianism 12/1, 12/13, 12/14, 12/15, 12/24
  Presbyterianism, American 12/19, 12/28, 12/29
  Presbyterianism, Canadian 12/26
  Presbyterian Church in the Confederate States of America 12/4
  Presbyterian Church U.S. 12/4
  Puritanism 12/21
  Puritanism, American 12/23
  Puritanism, English 12/9, 12/15
  Quakerism 12/1, 12/12, 12/17, 12/24
  Reformed Episcopal Church 12/11
  Renewed Unitas Fratrum 12/27
  Roman Catholicism 12/2, 12/4
  Salvation Army 12/25, 12/26
  Scottish Free Church 12/31
  Seventh Day Adventist 12/20
  Shakers, The 12/20
  Southern Baptist Church 12/24
  Unitarianism 12/4, 12/12
  Volunteers of America 12/26
  Winebrennerian (German Reformed) 12/12
Dexter, Henry Martyn 12/21
Doane, William H.
  (b. 2/3/1832) d. 12/24/1915
DOCUMENTS
  "Root and Branch" Petition 12/11
  "Twelve Steps" of A.A. 12/27
  "Universal Declaration of Human Rights" 12/10
  Edict of Nantes (1598) 12/21
  Gospels of Henry the Lion 12/6
  Great Law of the Colony of Pennsylvania 12/12
  Luther's "95 Theses" 12/5
  Root and Branch Bill 12/11
  U. S. Bill of Rights 12/15
Dohnavur Fellowship 12/16
DRAMA / DRAMATIC ARTS
  "Murder in the Cathedral" (1935) 12/29

E

Eastern Church 12/7, 12/22, 12/25
Ecstatic Doctor (Jan Van Ruysbroek) 12/2
Eddy, Mary Morse Baker
  (b. 7/16/1821) d. 12/3/1910
Eliot, T. S. 12/29
Ellerton, John 12/16
Elvey, George J.
  b. 3/27/1816 [d. 12/9/1893]
Evans, Christmas
  b. 12/24/1766 [d. 7/19/1838]
Evans, Robert P.
  b. 12/21/1818

F

Fénelon, François 12/6
FILMS / MOVIES
  "The Song of Bernadette" 12/27
Findlater, Sarah L. Borthwick
  (b. 11/26/1823) d. 12/25/1907
Finney, Charles G. 12/30
First Covenant, Scottish 12/3
First Day Society 12/19, 12/26
Fisher, Geoffrey 12/2
Fleury, Claude
  b. 12/6/1640 [d. 7/14/1723]
Flint, Annie Johnson 12/24
Form Criticism 12/1
Francis, Samuel T.
  (b. 11/19/1834) d. 12/28/1925
Fuchida, Mitsuo
  b. 12/3/1902 [d. 5/30/1976]

G

Gallitzin, Demetrius A.
  b. 12/22/1770 [d. 5/6/1840]
Gellert, Christian F.
  (b. 7/4/1715) d. 12/13/1769
Goss, Howard 12/20
Goss, John
  b. 12/27/1800 [d. 5/10/1880]
Gowans, Walter 12/4
Gray, Thomas
  b. 12/26/1716 [d. 7/30/1771]
Greater Europe Mission 12/21
Green, Harold
  (b. 10/23/1871) d. 12/20/1930
Green, Samuel G.
  b. 12/20/1822 [d. 9/15/1905]
Greenwell, Dora
  b. 12/6/1821 [d. 3/29/1882]
Gregory VIII, Pope (1187)
  (b. unk.) d. 12/17/1187
Grotefend, Georg Friedrich
  (b. 6/9/1775) d. 12/15/1853
Gruber, Franz 12/11, 12/24

H

Harding, Warren G. 12/25
Havergal, Frances Ridley
  b. 12/14/1836 [d. 6/3/1879]
Hayes, Rutherford B. 12/30
Hearn, Marianne
  b. 12/17/1834 [d. 3/16/1909]
Hecker, Isaac Thomas
  b. 12/18/1819 d. 12/22/1888
Henkel, Paul
  b. 12/15/1754 [d. 11/27/1825]
Henry II, English King (1154-89) 12/29
Henry IV, French King (1589-1610) 12/21
Herder, Johann Gottfried von
  (b. 8/25/1744) d. 12/18/1803
HERESIES
  Adoptionism 12/25
  Arianism 12/11
  Nestorianism 12/7
Heschel, Abraham J.
  (b. 1907) d. 12/23/1972
Hodge, Charles
  (b. 6/19/1878) d. 12/28/1797
Honorius III, Pope (1216-27) 12/22
How, William Walsham
  b. 12/13/1823 [d. 8/10/1897]
Humbert of Silva Candida 12/7
Hunt, Hanna 12/22
Hunt, John 12/22
Hus, Jan 12/25, 12/28
Hutchinson, Anne 12/23

ALMANAC OF THE CHRISTIAN FAITH — DECEMBER INDEX

HYMNS
"'Man of Sorrows,' What a Name" 12/29
"All Glory, Laud, and Honor" 12/1
"All Hail the Power of Jesus' Name" 12/17
"Amazing Grace" 12/21
"America The Beautiful" 12/28
"And Can It Be That I Should Gain" 12/18
"Ask Ye What Great Thing I Know" 12/21
"A Mighty Fortress" 12/3
"Be Present At Our Table, Lord" 12/12
"Be Still, My Soul" 12/8
"Blest Be the Tie That Binds" 12/26
"Come, Ye Thankful People, Come" 12/9
"Crown Him With Many Crowns" 12/9
"Day by Day" 12/17
"Dear Lord and Father of Mankind" 12/17
"Father in Heaven, Who Lovest All" 12/30
"For All the Saints Who From Their Labors Rest" 12/13
"For the Beauty of the Earth" 12/16
"Give of Your Best to the Master" 12/23
"Glorious Things of Thee Are Spoken" 12/21
"God of Our Fathers, Known of Old" 12/30
"God the Omnipotent" 12/16, 12/28
"God Will Take Care of You" 12/16
"Hark! The Herald Angels Sing" 12/18
"Have Thine Own Way Lord" 12/20
"Here, O My Lord, I See Thee Face to Face" 12/19
"He Giveth More Grace" 12/24
"Hiding in Thee" 12/31
"How Firm a Foundation" 12/17
"How Sweet the Name of Jesus Sounds" 12/21
"Ivory Palaces" 12/14
"I Am Not Skilled to Understand" 12/6
"I Heard the Voice of Jesus Say" 12/19
"I Will Sing of My Redeemer" 12/29
"Jesus! What a Friend for Sinners" 12/25
"Jesus, Lover of My Soul" 12/18
"Jesus Only" 12/15
"Jesus Saves" 12/5
"Joyful, Joyful, We Adore Thee" 12/16
"Just As I Am, Thine Own to Be" 12/17
"Lift High the Cross" 12/7
"Lord, Speak to Me That I May Speak" 12/14
"Love Came Down at Christmas" 12/5
"Love Divine, All Loves Excelling" 12/18
"Make Me a Captive, Lord" 12/9
"More About Jesus" 12/31
"Must Jesus Bear the Cross Alone?" 12/9
"My Jesus, As Thou Wilt" 12/21
"One Day When Heaven Was Filled With His Praises" 12/25
"O God, Beneath Thy Guiding Hand" 12/24
"O God, Our Help in Ages Past" 12/30
"O Happy Home, Where Thou Art Loved" 12/25
"O Jesus, Thou Art Standing" 12/13
"O Little Town of Bethlehem" 12/13
"O Safe to the Rock that is Higher Than I" 12/31
"O the Deep, Deep Love of Jesus" 12/28
"O Word of God Incarnate" 12/13
"Peace Be Still" 12/5
"Rejoice, The Lord is King" 12/18
"Savior, Again to Thy Dear Name We Raise" 12/16
"Shepherd of Tender Youth" 12/21
"Silent Night" 12/4, 12/11, 12/24
"Soldiers of Christ, Arise" 12/9
"Speak, Lord, in the Stillness" 12/20
"Stille Nacht" 12/4, 12/11, 12/24
"Take My Life and Let It Be" 12/14
"Tell Me the Stories of Jesus" 12/2
"Tell Me the Story of Jesus" 12/31
"There is Sunshine in My Soul Today" 12/31
"The Light of the World is Jesus" 12/29
"The Sands of Time are Sinking" 12/6
"The Son of God Goes Forth to War" 12/5
"The Strife Is O'er, The Battle Done" 12/29
"The Strife Is O'er, The Battle Done" 12/27
"Under His Wings I Am Safely Abiding" 12/31
"Welcome, Happy Morning" 12/16
"We Give Thee But Thine Own" 12/13
"We Have an Anchor" 12/5
"What Will You Do With Jesus?" 12/15
"When the Roll is Called Up Yonder" 12/21
"Where Cross the Crowded Ways of Life" 12/3
"Who Is On the Lord's Side?" 12/14, 12/27
"Wonderful Words of Life" 12/29
"Would You Live For Jesus, and Be Always Pure and 12/27
"Yesterday, Today, Forever" 12/15

HYMN TUNES
ALL SAINTS NEW 12/5
ARMAGEDDON 12/27
BARNARD 12/23
DARWALL'S 148th 12/18
DIADEMATA 12/9
DIX 12/16
FINLANDIA 12/8
GOD CARES 12/16
MAITLAND 12/9
MATERNA 12/28
MONTREAT 12/14
MORE LOVE TO THEE 12/24
NEAR THE CROSS 12/24
ODE TO JOY 12/16
QUIETUDE 12/20
RUSSIAN HYMN 12/28
ST. ANNE 12/30
ST. GEORGE'S, WINDSOR 12/9
ST. THEODULPH 12/1
STORY OF JESUS 12/31
SUNSHINE 12/31
SWENEY 12/31
VICTORY 12/27

I
Ignatius of Loyola
  b. 12/24/1491 [d. 7/31/1556]
Immaculate Conception 12/8
Innocent VIII, Pope (1484-92) 12/5
Inquisition, German 12/5
Inquisition, The 12/22
Isidore of Seville 12/5
Israel, Modern 12/14

J
Jackson, John Frederick Foakes-
  (b. 8/10/1855) d. 12/1/1941
Jerome, St. 12/11
JEWS
  Sephardic Jews 12/2
  Spanish Conversion of Jews 12/5
John, Griffith
  b. 12/14/1831 [d. 7/25/1912]
Johnson, Samuel
  (b. 9/18/1709) d. 12/13/1784
John of the Cross, St.
  (b. 6/24/1542) d. 12/14/1591
John XII, Pope (955-64) 12/16
John XXIII, Pope (1958-63) 12/2
Jones, Charles Price
  b. 12/9/1865 [d. 1/19/1949]
Jones, Clarence W.
  12/15/1900 [d. 4/29/1986]
Josephus 12/9
JUDAISM
  Conservative Judaism 12/7
  Jewish Encyclopedia, The 12/7
  Maimonides College 12/12
  Medieval Judaism 12/13
  Sephardic Jews 12/2
Judson, Adoniram 12/22
Judson, Ann Hasseltine
  b. 12/22/1789 [d. 10/24/1826]
Julius II, Pope (1503-13)
  b. 12/5/1443 [d. 2/21/1513]

K
Keil, William
  (b. 3/6/1812) d. 12/30/1877
Kent, Thomas 12/4
Keswick Movement 12/16
Kipling, Rudyard 12/30
Kitchin, George William
  b. 12/7/1827 [d. 10/13/1912]
Knox, John 12/3
Kocher, Conrad
  b. 12/16/1786 [d. 3/12/1872]
Kunheim, George von 12/17

L
Latourette, Kenneth Scott
  (b. 8/9/1884) d. 12/26/1968
Law, William 12/13
LECTURES
  "Acres of Diamonds" 12/6
Lee, Mother Ann 12/20
Leeser, Isaac
  b. 12/12/1806 [d. 2/1/1868]
Lenin, Nikolai 12/28
Leonty, Metropolitan of the U.S. 12/6
Leo X, Pope (1513-21) 12/10
  b. 12/11/1475 [d. 12/1/1521]
Lewis, C. S. 12/10
Lightfoot, John
  (b. 3/29/1602) d. 12/6/1675
Lightfoot, Joseph B.
  (b. 4/13/1828) d. 12/21/1889
Lincoln, Abraham 12/13
Livingstone, David 12/21
London's Religious Tract Society 12/20
London Missionary Society 12/14
Lorenzo the Magnificent 12/11
Luther, Margaret 12/17
Luther, Martin 12/5, 12/10, 12/17, 12/20, 12/28, 12/29
Lutheran Church Missouri Synod 12/3
Lvov, Alexis F.
  (b. 6/6/1799) d. 12/28/1870

M
MacDonald, George 12/28
  b. 12/10/1824 [d. 9/18/1905]
Maimonides, Moses
  (b. 3/30/1135) d. 12/13/1204
Makarios III, Orthodox Archbishop 12/13
Margaret of Navarre
  (b. 4/11/1492) d. 12/21/1549
Marsden, Samuel 12/27
Martin, Walter S.
  (b. 3/8/1862) d. 12/16/1935
MARTYRS
  Campion, Edmund 12/1
  Chabanel, Noël 12/8
  Elliot, Jim 12/1, 12/5, 12/13
  Oldcastle, Sir John 12/14
  Sidney, Algernon 12/7
  Stam, John and Betty 12/8
Massachusetts Bay Colony 12/23
Mayflower, The 12/21
Mayo, J. A. 12/22

McCabe, Charles C.
  (b. 10/11/1836) d. 12/19/1906
McPherson, Aimee Semple 12/30
Meacham, Joseph 12/20
Merton, Thomas
  (b. 1/31/1915) d. 12/10/1968
Methodist Board of Foreign
  Missions 12/3
Metz, Christian
  b. 12/30/1794 [d. 7/27/1867]
Michelangelo Buonarroti 12/5
Miles, W. H. 12/15
Miller, William
  (b. 2/15/1782) d. 12/20/1849
Milligan, William
  (b. 3/15/1821) d. 12/11/1893
Milton, John
  b. 12/9/1608 [d. 11/8/1674]
MISSIONARIES
  Bingham, Rowland 12/4
  Borden, William 12/17
  Carmichael, Amy 12/16
  Coan, Titus 12/1
  Columba, St. 12/7
  Gowans, Walter 12/4
  Green, Harold 12/20
  Hecker, Isaac T. 12/22
  Hunt, John and Hanna 12/22
  Judson, Adoniram 12/22
  Judson, Ann Hasseltine 12/22
  Kent, Thomas 12/4
  Marsden, Samuel 12/27
  McCabe, Charles C. 12/19
  Moffat, Robert and Mary 12/27
  Moody, Dwight L. 12/17
  Moon, Lottie 12/12, 12/24
  Newell, Harriet 12/22
  Reed, Mary 12/4
  Scott, Peter Cameron 12/4
  Van Der Kemp, Johannes Theodorus 12/15
  Wesley, Charles 12/22
  Wesley, John 12/22
  White, Andrew 12/27
  Xavier, Francis 12/3
MISSION AGENCIES
  Africa Inland Mission 12/4
  China Inland Mission 12/5
  Greater Europe Mission 12/21
  Latin America Evangelization
    Campaign 12/6
  Latin America Mission 12/6
  London Missionary Society 12/14, 12/21
  Methodist Board of Foreign Missions 12/3
  Pocket Testament League 12/3
  Rhenish Mission 12/26
  Society for the Propagation of the
    Gospel 12/14
  Southern Baptist Mission Board
    12/12
  Student Volunteer Movement 12/5
  Sudan Interior Mission 12/4
  Worldwide Evangelization Crusade
    12/5
  Zenana Missionary Society 12/16
Moffat, Robert 12/27
  b. 12/21/1795 [d. 8/9/1883]

Mohr, Joseph 12/24
  b. 12/11/1792 d. 12/4/1848
Moody, Dwight L. 12/17
  (b. 2/5/1837) d. 12/22/1899
Moon, Lottie (Charlotte Diggs)
  b. 12/12/1840 d. 12/24/1912
Morgan, G. Campbell
  b. 12/9/1863 [d. 5/16/1945]
Mueller, George 12/9, 12/18
Muhlenberg, Henry Melchior 12/1
Münzer, Thomas
  b. 12/20/ 1490 [d. 5/27/1525]
Murray, John
  b. 12/10/1741 [d. 9/3/1815]
MUSIC
  "Symphony of Psalms" 12/13
  Hymns Ancient and Modern 12/16
  Hymns of Faith and Hope 12/19
  Olney Hymnbook 12/21
Mysticism, German 12/2

N

Nägeli, Johann (Hans) Georg
  (b. 5/26/1768/73) d. 12/26/1836
Naismith, James 12/1
Napoleon's Concordat (1801-02)
  12/9
National Council of the Churches of
  Christ in the 12/2
Nestorius 12/7
Newell, Harriet 12/22
Newton, John
  (b. 7/24/1725) d. 12/21/1807
Nicholas II, Russian Czar (1894-
  1917) 12/30
NICKNAMES / TITLES
  "Apostle of Maryland" 12/27
  "Apostle to Scotland" 12/7
  "Borden of Yale" 12/17
  "Boy Pope" 12/16
  "Bunyan of Wales" 12/25
  "Columbus of the Catacombs" 12/10
  "Congregational Pope" 12/24
  "Ecstatic Doctor" 12/2
  "Father of German Rationalism,"
    12/18
  "Father of Modern Catholic Missions" 12/3
  "Father of Scholasticism" 12/4
  "Father of Universalism in America"
    12/10
  "Grandfather of Methodism" 12/16
  "Lamplighter, The" 12/8
  "Lemonade Lucy" 12/30
  "Morning Star of the Reformation"
    12/28
  "Mother Cabrini" 12/22
  "Patriarch of New England" 12/23
  "People's Priest" 12/11
  "Poet of Methodism" 12/18
  "Scottish Christina Rossetti" 12/6
  "Greatest Hymnwriter Among the
    Scots" 12/7
  "Patron Saint of Southern Baptist
    Missions" 12/12

Nitschmann, David 12/27
North, Frank Mason
  b. 12/3/1850 [d. 12/17/1935]
Nusbaum, Cyrus S.
  (b. 7/27/1861) d. 12/27/1937

O

Oberlin Conservatory of Music
  12/9
Oglethorpe, James E.
  b. 12/22/1696 [d. 6/30/1785]
Oldcastle, Sir John
  (b. ca. 1378) d. 12/14/1417
Ottoman Empire 12/9
Owens, Priscilla Jane
  (b. 7/21/1829) d. 12/5/1907

P

Palestrina, Giovanni
  b. 12/27/1525 [d. 2/2/1594]
PAPAL DECREES
  "Decet Romanum Pontificem" 12/10
  "Exsurge, Domine" 12/10
  "Ineffabilis Deus" (1854) 12/8
  "Summis desiderantes" 12/5
  "Ubi arcano" (1922) 12/23
  "Ubi primum" 12/3
Parker, William Henry
  (b. 3/4/1845) d. 12/2/1929
Parliament, British 12/24
Parrish, Anne
  (b. 10/17/1760) d. 12/26/1800
Paulists 12/18, 12/22
Paul III, Pope (1534-49) 12/13
Paul VI, Pope (1963-78) 12/7
Payne, Robert 12/15
Peabody, Francis G.
  b. 12/4/1847 [d. 12/28/1936]
Peasants War 12/20
Pelikan, Jaroslav
  b. 12/17/1923 [d. 5/13/2006]
Peloubet, Francis Nathan
  b. 12/2/1831 [d. 3/27/1920]
Penn, William 12/12
Pennsylvania Bible Society 12/12
Philaret, Metropolitan of Moscow
  (b. 12/26/1782) d. 12/1/1867
Philocalian Calendar (A.D. 354)
  12/25
Picts, The 12/7
Pilgrims, Mayflower 12/21
Pius IX, Pope (1846-78) 12/8
Pius XI, Pope (1922-39) 12/23
Pocket Testament League 12/3
POETRY
  "Elegy Written in a Country Church-
    yard" (1751) 12/26
  "Hands and Feet of Him" 12/24
  "Ichabod" 12/17
  "The Hound of Heaven" 12/18
Pollard, Adelaide A.
  (b. 11/27/1862) d. 12/20/1934

POPES
  Adrian I (772-95) 12/25
  Adrian IV (1154-59) 12/4
  Benedict XIV (1740-58) 12/3
  Boniface V (619-25) 12/23
  Clement III (1187-91) 12/19
  Gregory VIII (1187) 12/11, 12/17
  Honorius III (1216-27) 12/22
  John XII (955-64) 12/16
  John XXIII (1958-63) 12/2
  Julius II (1503-13) 12/5
  Leo X (1513-21) 12/10, 12/11
  Paul III (1534-49) 12/13
  Paul VI (1963-78) 12/7
  Pius IX (1846-78) 12/8
  Pius XI (1922-39) 12/23
Possehl, Floyd F. 12/5
Pott, Francis
  (b. 12/29/1832) d. 10/26/1909
Presbyterian Church in the
  Confederate States of A 12/4
Presbyterian Church U.S. 12/4
PRESIDENTS, U.S.
  Adams, John Quincy 12/31
  Harding, Warren G. 12/25
  Hayes, Rutherford B. 12/30
  Lincoln, Abraham 12/13
  Roosevelt, Theodore 12/17
Primate of Czechoslovakia 12/29
Pseudepigrapha 12/20
PUBLICATIONS
  Daily Study Bible 12/5
  "The Sword of the Lord" 12/11

Q

QUOTATIONS
  Adams, John Quincy 12/31
  Aquinas, Thomas 12/6
  Barth, Karl 12/4, 12/20
  Bonar, Andrew 12/18, 12/23, 12/29,
    12/30
  Bonhoeffer, Dietrich 12/17, 12/24
  Cowper, William 12/4, 12/7
  Darby, John Nelson 12/13
  Elliot, Jim 12/1, 12/5, 12/13
  Henry, Matthew 12/31
  Hus, Jan 12/25
  Laubach, Frank C. 12/6
  Lee, Robert E. 12/27
  Lewis, C. S. 12/6, 12/7, 12/10,
    12/15, 12/21, 12/26, 12/29
  Luther, Martin 12/11, 12/12, 12/16,
    12/19, 12/21, 12/25, 12/28
  MacDonald, George 12/11, 12/19,
    12/20
  McCheyne, Robert Murray 12/8
  Newton, John 12/21
  Nouwen, Henri J. M. 12/2, 12/3,
    12/4, 12/8, 12/9, 12/13, 12/19,
    12/22, 12/24, 12/26, 12/30
  Schaeffer, Francis 12/26
  Schmemann, Alexander 12/2, 12/6,
    12/7, 12/11, 12/16, 12/20, 12/31
  Simons, Menno 12/15
  Smith, Hannah Whitall 12/4, 12/14,
    12/17
  Venn, Henry 12/7

ALMANAC OF THE CHRISTIAN FAITH — DECEMBER INDEX

Wesley, John 12/22, 12/27
Whitefield, George 12/1, 12/9, 12/10, 12/12, 12/15, 12/18, 12/19, 12/30

QUOTATIONS, NOTABLE
"Jesus loves me this I know, for the Bible tells me so" 12/9
"No Reserve! No Retreat! No Regrets!" 12/17
"God helps those who help themselves" 12/7
"Praise the Lord and pass the ammunition!" 12/7

R

RABBIS, JEWISH
Leeser, Isaac 12/12
Maimonides, Moses 12/13
Schechter, Solomon 12/7
Tarshish, Jacob 12/8
Radical Biblical Criticism, German 12/2

RADIO PROGRAMS
"Catholic Hour" 12/10
"Voice of Revival" 12/11

RADIO STATIONS
WPIX-TV (NY City) 12/5
Rasputin, Grigorii
(b. 1/10/1869) d. 12/30/1916
Reed, Mary
b. 12/4/1854 [d. 4/8/1943]
Reformed (Calvinistic) Orthodoxy 12/28
Reformed Episcopal Church 12/2

RELIGIOUS ORDERS, CATHOLIC
Cistercians 12/20
Dominicans (Order of Preachers) 12/22
Missionary Sisters of the Sacred Heart 12/22
Missionary Society of St. Paul the Apostle (Paulists) 12/18, 12/22
Society of Jesus (Jesuits) 12/1, 12/24, 12/27
Rice, John R.
b. 12/11/1895 d. 12/29/1980
Richard I, English King (1189-99) 12/12
Rippon, John 12/17
Robinson, John A. T.
(b. 6/15/1919) d. 12/5/1983
Roosevelt, Theodore 12/17
Rosbrugh, John 12/26
Rosetta Stone 12/23
Rossetti, Christina G. 12/6
b. 12/5/1830 [d. 12/29/1894]
Rossi, G. B. de 12/10
Russian Imperial Chapel 12/28
Ruysbroek, Jan Van
(b. unk.) d. 12/2/1381

S

Saladin, Turkish Conqueror 12/17
Sales, St. Francis of
(b. 8/21/1567) d. 12/28/1622
Sanctification, Crisis 12/29

Sandell, Lina 12/17
Schechter, Solomon
b. 12/7/1847 [d. 11/19/1915]
Schleiermacher, F. D. E. 12/18
Schmalkald League 12/31
Schmolck, Benjamin
b. 12/21/1672 [d. 2/12/1737]
Schwedler, Johann Christoph
b. 12/21/1672 [d. 1/12/1730]
Schwenkfeld, Kaspar
(b. 1489) d. 12/10/1561
Scott, Peter Cameron
(b. 3/7/1867) d. 12/4/1896

SEMINARIES / BIBLE INSTITUTES
Bible Institute for Home and Foreign Missions (IL) 12/17
Colgate Seminary (NY) 12/2
Earlham School of Religion (IN) 12/12
European Bible Institute 12/21
Jewish Theological Seminary (NY) 12/7
Princeton Seminary (NJ) 12/28
Union Seminary (NY) 12/29
Union Theological Seminary (VA) 12/1, 12/23
Semler, Johann S.
b. 12/18/1725 [d. 3/14/1791]

SERMONS
"The Way in Salvation" 12/1, 12/24
Sheen, Fulton J.
(b. 5/8/1895) d. 12/10/1979
Shoemaker, Samuel M.
b. 10/27/1893 [d. 10/31/1963]
Sibelius, Jean
b. 12/8/1865 [d. 9/20/1957]
Sidney, Algernon
(b. 1/1623) d. 12/7/1683
Simpson, Albert B.
12/15/1843 [d. 10/29/1919]
Singh, Sundar 12/18
Six-Day War (1967) 12/14
Skoog, Andrew L.
b. 12/17/1856 [d. 10/30/1934]
Smith, Joseph 12/5
b. 12/23/1805 [d. 6/27/1844]
Society for the Propagation of the Gospel 12/14
Soubirous, Bernadette 12/27
Southern Baptist Mission Board 12/12
Spurgeon, Charles H. 12/19
Stam, Betty (Scott)
(b. 2/22/1906) d. 12/8/1934
Stam, John
(b. 1/18/1907) d. 12/8/1934
Stiles, Ezra
b. 12/15/1727 [d. 5/12/1795]
Stone, Barton W.
b. 12/24/1772 [d. 11/9/1844]
Strachan, Harry 12/6
Strachan, Kenneth 12/6
Strachan, Susan
(b. 4/28/1874) d. 12/6/1950
Straus, Oscar Solomon 12/17
Stravinsky, Igor 12/13

Studd, C[harles] T[homas]
b. 12/5/1862 [d. 7/16/1931]
Sudan Interior Mission 12/4
Sweney, John R.
b. 12/31/1837 [d. 4/10/1899]

T

"Twelve Steps" of A.A. 12/27
Tanner, Benjamin T.
b. 12/25/1835 [d. 1/15/1923]
Tarshish, Jacob
12/8/1892 [d. 1960]

TELEVISION PROGRAMS
"Life is Worth Living" 12/10
Temple, Frederick
(b. 11/30/1821) d. 12/23/1902
Tenison, Thomas
(b. 9/29/1636) d. 12/14/1715
Teschner, Melchior
(b. 4/29/1584) d. 12/1/1635
Textual Criticism 12/18
Thomas, Norman Matoon
(b. 11/20/1884) d. 12/19/1968
Thompson, Francis
b. 12/18/1859 [d. 11/13/1907]
Tikhon (Vasili Belavin), Patriarch of Moscow
b. 12/19/1866 [d. 4/7/1925]
Tischendorf, L. F. K. von
(b. 1/18/1815) d. 12/7/1874
Toledo, Alvarez de
(b. 10/29/1507) d. 12/12/1582
Tomlinson, Homer A.
(b. 10/25/1892) d. 12/4/1968
Torrey, Charles C.
b. 12/20/1863 [d. 11/2/1956]
Touro Synagogue 12/2
Transcendentalism 12/18
Trinity, Doctrine of the 12/11
Trueblood, David Elton
b. 12/12/1900 [d. 12/20/1994]
Tübingen School 12/2
Tyndale, William 12/31

U

U.S. Catholic Bishops Conference 12/2
United Bible Society 12/3
United Nations 12/10

V

Vanderhorst, R. H. 12/15
Van Der Kemp, Johannes Theodorus
(b. 1747) d. 12/15/1811
Vasey, Thomas
(b. ca. 1746) d. 12/27/1826
Victoria, (English) Queen 12/9

W

Walton, Brian 12/6
Ward, Samuel A.
b. 12/28/1847 [d. 9/28/1903]
Warneck, Gustav
(b. 3/6/1834) d. 12/26/1910
Warner, Daniel Sidney
(b. 6/25/1842) d. 12/12/1895
Weiss, Johannes
b. 12/13/1863 [d. 8/24/1914]
Wells, Amos R.
b. 12/23/1862 [d. 3/6/1933]
Wesley, Charles 12/16, 12/18, 12/22, 12/27, 12/31
Wesley, John 12/12, 12/16, 12/18, 12/22, 12/27, 12/31
Wesley, Samuel, Sr. 12/18
b. 12/16/1662 [d. 4/25/1735]
Wesley, Samuel S. 12/27
Wesley, Susanna 12/18
Western Church 12/7, 12/22
Weymouth, Richard F.
(b. 10/26/1822) d. 12/27/1902
Whiston, William
12/9/1667 [d. 8/22/1752]
White, Alma 12/29
White, Andrew
(b. 1579) d. 12/27/1656
White, William 12/12
Whitefield, George 12/12, 12/28
b. 12/16/1714 [d. 9/30/1770]
Whittaker, Joseph 12/20
Whittier, John Greenleaf
12/17/1807 [d. 9/7/1892]
Widney, Joseph P. 12/31
Wikgren, Allen P.
b. 12/3/1906 [d. 5/7/1998]
Williams, George 12/29
Williams, Roger 12/8, 12/23
b. 12/21/1603 [d. 1/27/1683]
Witches 12/5
Woolman, John 12/6
World War II 12/3
Wycliffe, John 12/14, 12/28
(b. 12/31/1320) d. 12/31/1384

X

Xavier, Francis
(b. 4/7/1506) d. 12/3/1552

Y

Young, Brigham 12/5
Young Men's Christian Association (YMCA) 12/29

Z

Zenana Missionary Society 12/16
Zwingli, Ulrich 12/11, 12/23

SELECT BIBLIOGRAPHY

Work on this project began over 35 years ago. Consequently, the number of contributing sources continues to grow, and now includes a collection of web sites which have been useful for providing many of the portraitures incorporated. The following bibliography, therefore, is given merely as an aid to further research on the part of the serious reader.

Addington, Raleigh, ed. *Faber: Poet and Priest: Selected Letters by Frederick William Faber, 1833-1863*. Glamorgan, Wales: D. Brown & Sons, 1974.

Anderson, Gerald H., ed. *Biographical Dictionary of Christian Missions*. Grand Rapids: William B. Eerdmans, 1998.

Backhouse, Halcyon, ed. [John Newton] *Collected Letters: Cardiphonia, or The Utterance of the Heart in the Course of a Real Correspondence*. London: Hodder and Stoughton, 1989.

Bähr, Hans Walter, ed. *Albert Schweitzer: Letters, 1905-1965*. Trans. Joachim Neugroschel. NY: Macmillan, 1992.

Baker, Robert A. *A Baptist Source Book: With Particular Reference to Southern Baptists*. Nashville: Broadman, 1966.

Bennett, Lerone, Jr. *Before the Mayflower: A History of Black America*. 5th ed. NY: Penguin Books, 1984.

Benson, Louis F. *Studies of Familiar Hymns*. Philadelphia: Westminster Press, 1921.

———. *Studies of Familiar Hymns*. Second Series. Philadelphia: Westminster Press, 1923.

Bethge, Eberhard, ed. *Dietrich Bonhoeffer: Letters and Papers from Prison*. NY: Macmillan, 1972.

Blaiklock, Edward M., and Harrison, R. K., eds. *The New International Dictionary of Biblical Archaeology*. Grand Rapids: Zondervan, 1983.

Bodensieck, Julius, ed. *Encyclopedia of the Lutheran Church*. 3 vols. Philadelphia: Fortress, Press, 1965.

Bochen, Christine M., ed. *Thomas Merton: Learning to Love: Exploring Solitude and Freedom*. Harper San Francisco: 1997.

Bonar, Andrew A. *Memoir and Remains of the Rev. Robert Murray McCheyne*. Grand Rapids: Baker Book House, 1978.

Bonar, Marjory, ed. *Andrew A. Bonar: Diary and Letters*. London: Hodder and Stoughton, 1893.

Bonner, Clint. *A Hymn Is Born*. Nashville: Broadman Press, 1959.

Bowden, Henry Warner. *Dictionary of American Religious Biography*. Westport, CT: Greenwood Press, 1977.

Bromily, Geoffrey W., trans. and ed. *A Late Friendship: The Letters of Karl Barth and Carl Zuckmayer*. Wm. B. Eerdmans, 1982.

———. Karl Barth: *Letters, 1961-1968*. Grand Rapids: Wm. B. Eerdmans, 1981.

Brooke, Stopford A., ed. *Life, Letters, Lectures, and Addresses of Fredk. W. Robertson, M.A., Incumbant of Trinity Chapel, Brighton, 1847-1853*. NY: Harper & Brothers, 1870.

Bunson, Matthew. *The Pope Encyclopedia: An A to Z of the Holy See*. New York: Crown Publishers, 1995.

Burgess, Stanley M. and McGee, Gary B. *Dictionary of Pentecostal and Charismatic Movements*. Grand Rapids: Zondervan, 1988.

Burke, W. J. and Howe, Will D., eds. Revised by Weiss, *Irving R. American Authors and Books: 1640 to the Present Day*. NY: Crown Publishers, 1962.

Burrage, Henry S. *Baptist Hymn Writers and Their Hymns*. Portland, ME: Brown, Thurston and Co. 1888.

Busch, Eberhard. *Karl Barth: His Life from Letters and Autobiographical Texts*. Trans. by John Bowden. Grand Rapids: Eerdmans, 1994.

Cameron, Nigel M. de S., ed. *Dictionary of Scottish Church History & Theology*. Downers Grove, IL: InterVarsity Press, 1993.

Carey, Patrick W. and Lienhard, Joseph T., eds. *Biographical Dictionary of Christian Theologians*. Peabody, MA: Hendrickson Publishers, 2002.

Carruth, Gorton, ed. *Encyclopedia of American Facts and Dates*. 8th ed. NY: Harper & Row, 1987.

Castle, Tony. *Lives of Famous Christians: A Biographical Dictionary*. Ann Arbor: Servant Books, 1988.

Castleden, Rodney. World History: *A Chronological Dictionary of Dates*. New York: Shooting Star Press, n.d. [ca. 1994]

Catholic Almanac, 1998 Our Sunday Visitor's. Foy, Felician A. and Avato, Rose M., eds. . Huntington, IN: Our Sunday Visitor, Inc., 1998.

Clark, Elmer T. et al., eds. *Journal and Letters of Francis Asbury*. 3 vols. Nashville: Abingdon Press, 1958.

Companion to the Hymnal: A Handbook to the 1964 Methodist Hymnal. Nashville, Abingdon, 1970.

Cook, Edward, ed. *Letters of John Fletcher*. Hampton, TN: Harvey Christian Publishers, 1999.

Cross, F. L. and Livingstone, E.A., eds. *The Oxford Dictionary of the Christian Church*. 3rd ed. NY: Oxford Univ. Press, 1997.

Curtis, A. Kenneth et al. *The 100 Most Important Events in Christian History*. Grand Rapids: Fleming H. Revell, 1991.

Darby, J. N. D. *Letters of J.N.D*. 3 vols. Sunbury, PA: Believers Bookshelf, 1971.

Delaney, John J., ed. *Dictionary of American Catholic Biography*. NY: Doubleday, 1984.

Dennis, Lane T., ed. *Letters of Francis A. Schaeffer: Spiritual Reality in the Personal Christian Life*. Westchester, IL: Crossway Books, 1985.

Diary and Selection of Hymns of Augustus Toplady. Gospel Standard Baptist Trust, Ltd., 1969.

Dieter, Melvin E., ed. *The Christian's Secret of a Holy Life: The Unpublished Personal Writings of Hannah Whitall Smith*. Grand Rapids: Zondervan, 1994.

Douglas, J. D., et al, eds. *New International Dictionary of the Christian Church*. 2nd ed. Grand Rapids, MI: Zondervan, 1978.

———. *Twentieth Century Dictionary of Christian Biography*. Grand Rapids: Baker Books, 1995.

Dunn, Richard S. and Yeandle, Laetitia, eds. *Journal of John Winthrop, 1630-1649*. Cambridge, MA: Belknap Press, 1996.

Dwight, Sereno Edwards. *Memoirs of the Rev. David Brainerd; Missionary to the Indians... Taken from His Own Diary, By Rev. Jonathan Edwards*. New Haven, CT: S. Converse, 1822. [Reprinted, St. Clair Shores, MI: Scholarly Press, 1970.]

Elliot, Elisabeth, ed. *The Journals of Jim Elliot*. Old Tappan, NJ: Fleming H. Revell Co.: Power Books, 1978.

Elwell, Walter A. *Evangelical Dictionary of Theology*. Grand Rapids: Baker Book House, 1984.

Epistles of Jacob Boehme, The. Montana: Kessinger Publishing Co., n.d. [1649].

Erickson, Hal. *Religious Radio and Television in the United States, 1921-1991: The Programs and Personalities*. Jefferson, NC: McFarland and Co., 1992.

Fangmeier, Jürgen and Stoevesandt, Hinrich, eds. *Karl Barth: Letters 1961-1968*. Grand Rapids: Eerdmans, 1981.

Federer, William J. *America's God and Country: Encyclopedia of Quotations*. Coppell, TX: FAME Publishing, 1994.

Fénelon, Francois. *Spiritual Letters to Women*. Trans. H. L. Sidney Lear. Grand Rapids: Zondervan, 1984.

Ferm, Vergilius, ed. *Encyclopedia of Religion*. Secaucus, NJ: Poplar Books, 1984.

Fiorelli, Lewis S., ed. *Sermons of St. Francis de Sales on Our Lady*. Vol. 2. Rockford, IL: Tan Books and Publishers, 1985.

SELECT BIBLIOGRAPHY

Frost, Maurice, ed. Historical *Companion to Hymns Ancient and Modern*. London: William Clowes and Sons, Ltd., 1962.

Gaustad, Edwin Scott. *A Religious History of America*. NY: Harper & Row, 1966.

Gentz, William H., ed. *Dictionary of Bible and Religion*. Nashville: Abingdon, 1986.

Gerhard Tersteegen: Life and Letters. Vol. 1. Yanceyville, NC: Harvey Christian Publishers, 1990.

Grant, George and Wilbur, Gregory. *The Christian Almanac: A Dictionary of Days Celebrating History's Most Significant People and Events*. Nashville: Cumberland House, 2000.

Greenspan, Karen. *Timetables of Women's History: A Chronology of the Most Important People and Events in Women's History*. New York: Simon & Schuster, 1994.

Gribetz, Judah et al., eds. *Timetables of Jewish History: A Chronology of the Most Important People and Events in Jewish History*. NY: Simon & Schuster, 1993.

Gross, Ernie. *This Day in Religion*. New York: Neal-Schuman Publishers, 1990.

Grun, Bernard. *The Timetables of History: A Horizontal Linkage of People and Events*. Rev. ed. NY: Simon and Schuster: Touchstone Books, 1979.

Haeussler, Armin, ed. *The Story of Our Hymns: The Handbook to the Hymnal of the Evangelical and Reformed Church*. St. Louis: Eden Publishing House, 1952.

Hall, J. H. *Biography of Gospel Song and Hymn Writers*. NY: Fleming H. Revell Co., 1914. [Reprinted, NY: AMS Press, Inc., 1971.]

Hammack, Mary L. *Dictionary of Women in Church History*. Moody Press, 1984.

Hanks, Geoffrey. *70 Great Christians: Changing the World*. Scotland: Christian Focus Publications, 1992.

———. *60 Great Founders*. Scotland: Christian Focus Publications, 1995.

Hart, Patrick. *Thomas Merton: Run to the Mountain: The Story of a Vocation*. Harper San Francisco: 1996.

Hart, Trevor A. et al., eds. *Dictionary of Historical Theology*. Grand Rapids: William B. Eerdmans, 2000.

Hattersley, Roy. Life of *John Wesley: A Brand from the Burning*. NY: Doubleday, 2003.

Henry, Matthew. *Complete Works of the Rev. Matthew Henry*. 2 vols. Grand Rapids: Baker Book House, 1978.

Hodgson, Irene B., trans. *Archbishop Oscar Romero: A Shepherd's Diary*. Cincinnati, OH: St. Anthony Messenger Press, 1986.

Houghton, Elsie. *Christian Hymn-Writers*. Bryntirion: Evangelical Press of Wales, 1982.

Hudson, Robert R. and Townsend-Hudson, Shelley. *Companions for the Soul: A yearlong journey of miracles, prayers and epiphanies*. Zondervan, 1995.

Hustad, Donald P. *Dictionary-Handbook to Hymns for the Living Church*. Carol Stream, IL: Hope Publishing, 1978.

Jaspert, Bernd and Bromily, Geoffrey W., eds. *Karl Barth – Rudolf Bultmann: Letters 1922-1966*. Grand Rapids: Eerdmans, 1981.

Johnson, Paul. *A History of Christianity*. NY: Simon & Schuster, 1976.

Journal of Charles Wesley. 2 vols. Grand Rapids: Baker Book House, 1980.

Julian, John, ed. *Dictionary of Hymnology: Setting Forth the Origin and History of Christian Hymns of all Ages and Nations*. Rev. ed. London: John Murray, 1907.

Kane, Joseph Nathan et al. *Famous First Facts: A Record of First Happenings, Discoveries, and Inventions in American History*. 5th ed. New York: H. W. Wilson Co., 1997.

Keller, Helen R. *Dictionary of Dates*. 2 vols. NY: Macmillan Co., 1934.

Kelly, J. N. D. *Oxford Dictionary of Popes*. Oxford: Oxford University Press, 1986.

Kerr, Hugh T., and Mulder, John M. *Conversions: The Christian Experience*. Grand Rapids: Wm. B. Eerdmans, 1983.

Kilby, Clyde S., ed. *C. S. Lewis: Letters to An American Lady*. Grand Rapids: Wm. B. Eerdmans, 1967.

Kuhner, Hans. *Encyclopedia of the Papacy*. Trans. Kenneth J. Northcott, from the original German, "Lexicon der Paepste." NY: Philosophical Library, 1958.

Lane, Hana Umlauf, ed. *The World Almanac Book of Who*. NY: World Almanac Publications, 1980.

Laubach, Frank C. *Letters by a Modern Mystic: Excerpts from Letters Written at Dansalan, Lake Lanao, Philippine Islands to His Father by Frank C. Laubach*. NY: Student Volunteer Movement, 1937.

Letters of Arthur W. Pink. Carlisle, PA: Banner of Truth Trust, 1978.

Letters of George Whitefield: For the Period 1734-1742. Carlisle, PA: Banner of Truth Trust, 1976.

Letters of John Calvin: Selected from the [1855-57] Bonnet Edition. Carlisle, PA: The Banner of Truth Trust, 1980.

Lewis, Jack P. *The English Bible: From KJV to NIV: A History and Evaluation*. Grand Rapids: Baker Book House, 1981.

Lewis, W. H., ed. *Letters of C. S. Lewis*. San Diego: Harcourt Brace Jovanovich, 1966.

Little, Charles E. *Cyclopedia of Classified Dates*. NY: Funk & Wagnalls, 1900.

Loane, Marcus L. *Makers of Puritan History*. Grand Rapids: Baker Book House, 1961.

Loetscher, Lefferts A., et al., eds. *Twentieth Century Encyclopedia of Religious Knowledge: An Extension of the New Schaff-Herzog Encyclopedia of Religious Knowledge*. Grand Rapids: Baker Book House, 1955.

Lehmann, Helmut T., ed. *Luther's Works*. Vols. 48, 49, 50: Letters I, II, III. Trans. by Gottfried G. Krodel. Philadelphia: Fortress Press, 1963, 1972, 1975.

Low, W. Augustus, and Clift, Virgil A., eds. *Encyclopedia of Black America*. NY: McGraw-Hill Book Company, 1981.

Lueker, Erwin L., ed. Lutheran *Cyclopedia: A Concise In-Home Reference for the Christian Family*. St. Louis: Concordia Publishing, 1975.

Marlin, George J. et al., eds. *More Quotable Chesterton: A Topical Compilation of the Wit, Wisdom and Satire of G.K. Chesterton*. San Francisco: Ignatius Press, 1988.

Martindale, Wayne and Root, Jerry, eds. *The Quotable [C.S.] Lewis*. Wheaton, IL: Tyndale House, 1989.

Mayer, F. E. *Religious Bodies of America*. St. Louis: Concordia Publishing, 1958.

McHenry, Robert, ed. *Famous American Women: A Biographical Dictionary from Colonial Times to the Present*. NY: Dover, 1980.

McNiel, Alex. *Total Television: A Comprehensive Guide to Programming from 1948 to the Present*. 2nd ed. Penguin Books, 1984.

Mead, Frank S., and Hill, Samuel S. *Handbook of Denominations in the United States*. 8th ed. Nashville: Abingdon, 1985.

Melton, J. Gordon. *Biographical Dictionary of American Cult and Sect Leaders*. NY: Garland Publishing, 1986.

Millard, Catherine. *The Rewriting of America's History*. Camp Hill, PA: Horizon House Publishers, 1991.

Mircea Eliade: Journal I, 1945-1955. Mac Linscott Ricketts, trans. Chicago: University of Chicago Press, 1990.

Mircea Eliade: No Souvenirs: Journal, 1957-1969. Fred Johnson, trans. San Francisco: Harper & Row, 1977.

Moreau, A. Scott et al., eds. *Evangelical Dictionary of World Missions*. Grand Rapids: Baker Books, 2000.

Morgan, Robert J. *On This Day: 365 Amazing and Inspiring Stories About Saints, Martyrs and Heroes*. Nashville: Thomas Nelson Publishers, 1997.

Mossman, Jennifer, ed. *Holidays and Anniversaries of the World*. 2nd ed. Detroit: Gale Research, Inc., 1990.

Moyer, Elgin, and Cairns, Earle E. *Wycliffe Biographical Dictionary of the Church*. Chicago: Moody Press, 1982.

Munitz, Joseph A. and Endean, Philip, trans. *St. Ignatius of Loyola: Personal Writings*. London: Penguin Books, 1996.

Murray, Iain H. *Letters of Charles Haddon Spurgeon: Selected with Notes*. Edinburgh: Banner of Truth Trust, 1992.

Newton, John. *Works of John Newton*. 6 vols. Edinburgh: Banner of Truth Trust, 1988.

Nouwen, Henri J. M. *Sabbatical: The Diary of His Final Year*. NY: Crossroad Publishing, 1998.

O'Brien, T. C., ed. *Corpus Dictionary of Western Churches*. Washington, DC: Corpus Publications, 1970.

O'Neill, Lois Decker, ed. *The Women's Book of World Records and Achievements*. Garden City, NY: Anchor Press, 1979.

Osbeck, Kenneth W. *101 Hymn Stories*. Grand Rapids: Kregel Publications, 1982.

———. *101 More Hymn Stories*. Grand Rapids: Kregel Publications, 1985.

Parise, Frank, ed. *The Book of Calendars*. NY: Facts on File, Inc., 1982.

Parker, Percy Livingstone, ed. *The Journal of John Wesley*. Chicago: Moody Press, n.d.

Peper, Christian B. *An Historian's Conscience: The Correspondence of Arnold J. Toynbee and Columba Cary-Elwes, Monk of Ampleforth*. Boston: Beacon Press, 1986.

Perry, Bliss. *The Heart of Emerson's Journals*. Boston: Houghton Mifflin, 1914.

Plass, Ewald M. *What Luther Says: A Practical In-Home Anthology for the Active Christian*. St. Louis: Condoria, 1959.

Price, Carl F. *One Hundred and One Hymn Stories*. NY: Abingdon Press, 1932.

Prichard, Robert W. *A History of the Episcopal Church*. Rev. ed. Harrisburg, PA: Morehouse Publishing, 1999.

Reid, Daniel G. et al., eds. *Dictionary of Christianity in America*. Downers Grove, IL: InterVarsity Press, 1990.

Reynolds, William Jensen. *Hymns of Our Faith: A Handbook for the Baptist Hymnal*. Rev. ed. Nashville: Broadman Press, 1967.

Rizk, Helen Salem. *Stories of the Christian Hymns*. Nashville: Abingdon, 1964.

Robertson, Patrick. *The Book of Firsts*. New York: Bramhall House, 1982.

Rossetti, William Michael, ed. *Family Letters of Christina Georgina Rossetti*. London: Brown, Langham & Co., Ltd: 1908.

Sadler, Glenn Edward, ed. *An Expression of Character: The Letters of George MacDonald*. Grand Rapids: Eerdmans, 1994.

Sargent, John. *The Life and Letters of Henry Martyn*. Edinburgh: Banner of Truth Trust, 1985.

Schlesinger, Arthur M., Jr., gen. ed. *The Almanac of American History*. NY: Putnam Publishing Group: Perigee Books: Bison Books, 1983.

Schmemann, Juliana, trans. *The Journals of Father Alexander Schmemann, 1973-1983*. Crestwood, NY: St. Vladimir's Seminary Press, 2000.

Selected Writings of C. F. W. Walther: Selected Letters. Trans. by Roy A. Suelflow. St. Louis: Concordia Publishing, 1981.

Shannon, William H., ed. *The Hidden Ground of Love: The Letters of Thomas Merton on Religious Experience and Social Concerns*. NY: Farrar, Straus, Giroux, 1985.

Smith, Logan Pearsall, ed. *Philadelphia Quaker: The Letters of Hannah Whitall Smith*. NY: Harcourt, Brace & Co., 1950.

Smith, Ronald Gregor, ed. and trans. *Soren Kierkegaard: The Last Years: Journals 1853-1855*. London: Collins, 1965.

Stambler, Irwin, and Landon, Grelun. *Encyclopedia of Folk, Country and Western Music*. NY: St. Martin's Press, 1969.

Steinberg, S. H. *Historical Tables: 58 B.C.-A.D. 1972*. NY: St. Martin's Press, 1973.

Stetler, Susan L. *Almanac of Famous People*. 4th ed. Detroit: Gale Research, 1989.

Storey, R. L., ed. *Chronology of the Medieval World: 800-1491*. NY: David McKay Co., 1973.

Suelflow, Roy A., trans. *Selected Writings of C.F.W. Walther: Selected Letters*. St. Louis: Concordia Publishing House, 1981.

Thomas, M. Halsey, ed. *The Diary of Samuel Sewall: 1674-1729*. 2 vols. NY: Farrar, Straus and Giroux, 1973.

Trager, James, ed. *The People's Chronology: A Year-by-Year Record of Human Events from Prehistory to the Present*. Revised and updated. NY: Holt, Rinehart and Winston, 1992.

———. *The Women's Chronology: A Year-by-Year Record, from Prehistory to the Present*. NY: Henry Holt and Co., 1994.

Urdang, Laurence, ed. *Timetables of American History*. NY: Simon & Schuster: Touchstone Books, 1981.

Vos, Howard F. *Archaeology in Bible Lands*. Chicago: Moody Press, 1977.

———. *Exploring Church History*. Nelson's Christian Cornerstone Series. Nashville: Thomas Nelson, 1994.

Walsh, John Evangelist, ed. *Letters of Francis Thompson*. NY: Hawthorn Books, 1969.

Walsh, Michael, ed. *Dictionary of Christian Biography*. Collegeville, MN: Liturgical Press, 2001.

Ward, Maisie, ed. *The Letters of Carryl Houselander*. NY: Sheed and Ward, 1965.

Ward, Wilfrid. *The Life of John Henry Cardinal Newman: Based on His Private Journals and Correspondence*. 2 vols. London: Longmans, Green, and Co., 1912.

Ware, Timothy. *The Orthodox Church*. Penguin Books, 1983.

Weinlick, John R. and Frank, Albert H. *The Moravian Church Through the Ages: The Story of a Worldwide, Pre-Reformation Protestant Church*. Revised. Bethelehem, PA: Moravian Church in America, 1996.

Wesley, John. *Works of Rev. John Wesley, A.M.* Vol. 12. London: Wesleyan Conference Office, 1872.

Whitefield, George. *George Whitefield's Journals*. Edinburgh: Banner of Truth Trust, 1985.

White's Conspectus of American Biography: A Tabulated Record of American History and Biography. 2 ed. NY: James T. White & Co., 1937.

Whitman, Narcissa. *Letters of Narcissa Whitman*. Fairfield, WA: Ye Galleon Press, 1986.

Williams, Charles, ed. *Letters of Evelyn Underhill*. London: Religious Book Club, 1945.

Williams, Neville. *Chronology of the Modern World: 1763 to the Present Time*. Rev. ed. NY: David McKay Co., Inc., 1968.

Wilson, Samuel, and Siewert, John, eds. *Twentieth Anniversary Mission Handbook: North American Protestant Ministries Overseas*. 13th ed. Monrovia, CA: Missions Advanced Research and Communication Center (MARC), 1986.

Young, Henry J. *Major Black Religious Leaders: 1755-1940*. Nashville: Abingdon Press, 1977.

www.ingramcontent.com/pod-product-compliance
Lightning Source LLC
Chambersburg PA
CBHW060227240426
43671CB00016B/2880